Organization Development and Change

EIGHTH EDITION

Thomas G. Cummings
University of Southern California

Christopher G. Worley
Pepperdine University

THOMSON
™
SOUTH-WESTERN

Australia · Canada · Mexico · Singapore · Spain · United Kingdom · United States

THOMSON

SOUTH-WESTERN

Organization Development and Change, 8e
Thomas G. Cummings & Christopher G. Worley

VP/Editorial Director:
Jack W. Calhoun

VP/Editor-in-Chief:
Michael P. Roche

Sr. Publisher:
Melissa S. Acuña

Acquisitions Editor:
Joe Sabatino

Developmental Editor:
Denise Simon

Marketing Manager:
Jacquelyn Carrillo

Sr. Production Editor:
Elizabeth A. Shipp

Technology Project Editor:
Kristen Meere

Media Editor:
Karen L. Schaffer

Manufacturing Coordinator:
Rhonda Utley

Production House:
Pre-Press Co., Inc.

Associate Designer:
Justin Klefeker

Internal and Cover Design:
Justin Klefeker

Cover Images:
© PhotoDisc and Digital Vision

Printer:
West

COPYRIGHT © 2005
by South-Western, part of the
Thomson Corporation. South-Western, Thomson, and the Thomson
logo are trademarks used herein
under license.

ISBNs-
Book: 0-324-22493-1
Book + InfoTrac: 0-324-26060-1
ISE: 0-324-22511-3
ISE + InfoTrac: 0-324-22510-5

Library of Congress Control
Number: 2003116385

ALL RIGHTS RESERVED.
No part of this work covered by the
copyright hereon may be reproduced or used in any form or by any
means-graphic, electronic, or mechanical, including photocopying,
recording, taping, Web distribution
or information storage and retrieval
systems-without the written permission of the publisher.

Printed in the United States of
America
4 5 07 06

For permission to use material from
this text or product, submit a
request online at http://www.
thomsonrights.com

Any additional questions about permissions can be submitted by email
to thomsonrights@thomson.com

For more information
contact South-Western,
5191 Natorp Boulevard,
Mason, Ohio, 45040.
Or you can visit our Internet site at:
http://www.swlearning.com

Dedication

To our big brothers and sisters:

Larry Greiner, Craig Lundberg, Warner Burke

Edie Seashore, Ed Schein, Tony Petrella

Brief Contents

Preface xvi

CHAPTER 1 General Introduction to Organization Development 1

Part 1
OVERVIEW OF ORGANIZATION DEVELOPMENT 21

CHAPTER 2 The Nature of Planned Change 22

CHAPTER 3 The Organization Development Practitioner 44

Part 2
THE PROCESS OF ORGANIZATION DEVELOPMENT 71

CHAPTER 4 Entering and Contracting 72

CHAPTER 5 Diagnosing Organizations 83

CHAPTER 6 Diagnosing Groups and Jobs 100

CHAPTER 7 Collecting and Analyzing Diagnostic Information 114

CHAPTER 8 Feeding Back Diagnostic Information 132

CHAPTER 9 Designing Interventions 143

CHAPTER 10 Leading and Managing Change 155

CHAPTER 11 Evaluating and Institutionalizing Organization Development Interventions 178

Part 3
HUMAN PROCESS INTERVENTIONS 215

CHAPTER 12 Individual, Interpersonal, and Group Process Approaches 216

CHAPTER 13 Organization Process Approaches 243

Part 4
TECHNOSTRUCTURAL INTERVENTIONS 273

CHAPTER 14 Restructuring Organization 274

CHAPTER 15 Employee Involvement 306

CHAPTER 16 Work Design 331

Part 5
HUMAN RESOURCES MANAGEMENT INTERVENTIONS 365

CHAPTER 17 Performance Management 366

CHAPTER 18 Developing and Assisting Members 396

Part 6
STRATEGIC CHANGE INTERVENTIONS 445

CHAPTER 19 Competitive and Collaborative Strategies 446

CHAPTER 20 Organization Transformation 479

Part 7
SPECIAL APPLICATIONS OF ORGANIZATION DEVELOPMENT 533

CHAPTER 21 Organization Development in Global Settings 534

CHAPTER 22 Organization Development in Nonindustrial Settings: Health Care, Family Businesses, School Systems, and the Public Sector 571

CHAPTER 23 Future Directions in Organization Development 611

Glossary 661
Name Index 671
Subject Index 677

Contents

Preface   xvi

CHAPTER 1   General Introduction to Organization Development   1

Organization Development Defined   1

The Growth and Relevance of Organization Development   4

A Short History of Organization Development   6

    Laboratory Training Background   7

    Action Research and Survey Feedback Background   8

    Normative Background   9

    Productivity and Quality-of-Work-Life Background   10

    Strategic Change Background   12

Evolution in Organization Development   12

Overview of the Book   14

Summary   17

Notes   17

Part 1
OVERVIEW OF ORGANIZATION DEVELOPMENT   21

CHAPTER 2   The Nature of Planned Change   22

Theories of Planned Change   22

    Lewin's Change Model   22

    Action Research Model   24

    The Positive Model   26

    Comparisons of Change Models   28

General Model of Planned Change   28

    Entering and Contracting   28

    Diagnosing   29

    Planning and Implementing Change   29

    Evaluating and Institutionalizing Change   30

Different Types of Planned Change   30

    Magnitude of Change   30

Application 2-1 Planned Change at the San Diego County Regional Airport Authority   31

    Degree of Organization   34

    Domestic vs. International Settings   35

Application 2-2 Planned Change in an Unorganized System   36

Critique of Planned Change   39

    Conceptualization of Planned Change   39

    Practice of Planned Change   40

Summary   41

Notes   41

CHAPTER 3   The Organization Development Practitioner   44

Who Is the Organization Development Practitioner?   44

Competencies of an Effective Organization Development Practitioner   46

The Professional Organization Development Practitioner   50

    Role of Organization Development Professionals   50

Application 3-1 Personal Views of the Internal and External Consulting Positions   53

    Careers of Organization Development Professionals   56

Professional Values   57

Professional Ethics   58

    Ethical Guidelines   58

    Ethical Dilemmas   58

Application 3-2 Kindred Todd and the Ethics of OD   62

Summary   63

Notes   64

Appendix   Ethical Guidelines for an Organization Development/Human Systems Development (OD/HSD) Professional   66

Part 2
THE PROCESS OF ORGANIZATION DEVELOPMENT   71

CHAPTER 4   Entering and Contracting   72

Entering into an OD Relationship   73

    Clarifying the Organizational Issue   73

    Determining the Relevant Client   73

    Selecting an OD Practitioner   74

Developing a Contract   76

    Mutual Expectations   76

    Time and Resources   76

Application 4-1 Entering American Healthways Corporation   77

    Ground Rules   78

Personal Process Issues in Entering and Contracting   78

Application 4-2 Contracting at American Healthways Corporation   79

Summary   81

Notes   82

CHAPTER 5   Diagnosing Organizations   83

What Is Diagnosis?   83

The Need for Diagnostic Models   84

Open-Systems Model   85

    Organizations as Open Systems   85

    Inputs, Transformations, and Outputs   86

    Boundaries   87

    Feedback   87

    Equifinality   87

    Alignment   88

    Diagnosing Organizational Systems   88

Organization-Level Diagnosis   89

    Inputs   90

    Design Components   91

    Outputs   93

    Alignment   93

    Analysis   93

Application 5-1 Steinway's Strategic Orientation   94

Summary   98

Notes   99

CHAPTER 6   Diagnosing Groups and Jobs   100

Group-Level Diagnosis   100

    Inputs   100

    Design Components   101

    Outputs   102

    Fits   103

    Analysis   103

Application 6-1 Top Management Team at Ortiv Glass Corporation   104

Individual-Level Diagnosis   106

    Inputs   106

    Design Components   107

    Fits   108

    Analysis   108

Application 6-2 Job Design at Pepperdine University   109

Summary   112

Notes   112

CHAPTER 7   Collecting and Analyzing Diagnostic Information   114

The Diagnostic Relationship   114

Methods for Collecting Data   116

    Questionnaires   117

    Interviews   119

    Observations   120

    Unobtrusive Measures   121

Sampling   122

Techniques for Analyzing Data   123

    Qualitative Tools   123

Application 7-1 Collecting and Analyzing Diagnostic Data at American Healthways   124

    Quantitative Tools   126

Summary   130

Notes   130

CHAPTER 8   Feeding Back Diagnostic Information   132

Determining the Content of the Feedback   132

Characteristics of the Feedback Process   134

Survey Feedback   135

    What Are the Steps?   135

Application 8-1 Training OD Practitioners in Data Feedback   136

    Survey Feedback and Organizational Dependencies   138

    Limitations of Survey Feedback   138

Application 8-2 Operations Review and Survey Feedback at Prudential Real Estate Affiliates   139

    Results of Survey Feedback   140

Summary   141

Notes   141

CHAPTER 9   Designing Interventions   143

What Are Effective Interventions?   143

How to Design Effective Interventions   144

    Contingencies Related to the Change Situation   144

    Contingencies Related to the Target of Change   145

Overview of Interventions   149

    Human Process Interventions   149

    Technostructural Interventions   150

    Human Resource Management Interventions   151

    Strategic Interventions   152

Summary   153

Notes   153

CHAPTER 10   Leading and Managing Change   155

Overview of Change Activities   155

Motivating Change   157

    Creating Readiness for Change   157

    Overcoming Resistance to Change   158

Application 10-1 Motivating Change at Johnsonville Sausage   160

Creating a Vision   160

    Describing the Core Ideology   161

    Constructing the Envisioned Future   162

Developing Political Support   163

Application 10-2 Creating a Vision at Premiere   164

    Assessing Change Agent Power   166

    Identifying Key Stakeholders   166

    Influencing Stakeholders   167

Managing the Transition   168

    Activity Planning   168

    Commitment Planning   168

Application 10-3 Using Social Networks to Implement Change in a Public Education Institution   169

    Change-Management Structures   169

Sustaining Momentum   170

    Providing Resources for Change   170

    Building a Support System for Change Agents   170

Application 10-4 Transition Management in the HP-Compaq Acquisition   171

    Developing New Competencies and Skills   172

    Reinforcing New Behaviors   172

    Staying the Course   173

Application 10-5 Sustaining Transformational Change at the Veterans Health Administration   174

Summary   173

Notes   175

CHAPTER 11   Evaluating and Institutionalizing Organization Development Interventions   178

Evaluating Organization Development Interventions 178

    Implementation and Evaluation Feedback   178

    Measurement   181

    Research Design   186

Institutionalizing Interventions   189

Application 11-1 Evaluating Change and Change Management at the World Bank   190

    Institutionalization Framework   192

Application 11-2 Institutionalizing Structural Change at Hewlett-Packard   197

Summary   198

Notes   199

SELECTED CASES   201

- It's Your Turn   201
- Sunflower Incorporated   203
- Evaluating the Change Agent Program at Siemens Nixdorf (A)   205
- Initiating Change in the Manufacturing and Distribution Division of PolyProd   209

Part 3
HUMAN PROCESS INTERVENTIONS 215

CHAPTER 12   Individual, Interpersonal, and Group Process Approaches   216

Coaching   216

    What Are the Goals?   217

    Application Stages   217

    The Results of Coaching   218

Training and Development   218

    What Are the Goals?   219

    Application Stages   219

    The Results of Training   220

Process Consultation   220

Application 12-1 Leading Your Business at Microsoft Corporation   221

    Group Process   222

    Basic Process Interventions   223

    Results of Process Consultation   225

Application 12-2 Process Consultation at Action Company   226

Third-Party Interventions   227

    An Episodic Model of Conflict   228

    Facilitating the Conflict Resolution Process   229

Team-Building   230

Application 12-3 Conflict Management at Balt Healthcare Systems   231

    Team-Building Activities   232

    Activities Relevant to One or More Individuals   232

    Activities Oriented to the Group's Operation and Behavior   235

Application 12-4 Building the Executive Team at Caesars Tahoe   236

    Activities Affecting the Group's Relationship with the Rest of the Organization   237

    The Manager's Role in Team Building   237

    The Results of Team Building   238

Summary   239

Notes   240

CHAPTER 13   Organization Process Approaches   243

Organization Confrontation Meeting   243

    Application Stages   244

    Results of Confrontation Meetings   244

Application 13-1 A Work-Out Meeting at General Electric Medical Systems Business   245

Intergroup Relations Intervention   246

 Microcosm Groups   246

 Resolving Intergroup Conflict   248

Application 13-2 Improving Intergroup Relationships in Johnson & Johnson's Drug Evaluation Department   251

Large-Group Interventions   252

 Application Stages   254

Application 13-3 The Seventh American Forest Congress   257

 Results of Large-Group Interventions   259

Application 13-4 Open-Space Meeting at a Consulting Firm   260

Summary   261

Notes   261

SELECTED CASES   264

• The Metric Division Case   264

• Gulf States Metals, Inc.   269

Part 4
TECHNOSTRUCTURAL INTERVENTIONS   273

CHAPTER 14   Restructuring Organization   274

Structural Design   274

 The Functional Structure   274

 The Divisional Structure   276

 The Matrix Structure   278

 The Process Structure   280

 The Network Structure   283

Application 14-1 American Healthways' Process Structure   284

Downsizing   287

Application 14-2 Amazon.com's Network Structure   288

 Application Stages   290

 Results of Downsizing   292

Application 14-3 Strategic Downsizing Process at Delta Air Lines   293

Reengineering   295

 Application Stages   297

 Results from Reengineering   300

Application 14-4 Honeywell IAC's Totalplant™ Reengineering Process   301

Summary   302

Notes   303

CHAPTER 15   Employee Involvement   306

Employee Involvement: What Is It?   306

 A Working Definition of Employee Involvement   306

 The Diffusion of Employee Involvement Practices   307

 How Employee Involvement Affects Productivity   308

Employee Involvement Applications   309

 Parallel Structures   310

Application 15-1 Union-Management Cooperation at GTE of California   313

 High-Involvement Organizations   315

 Total Quality Management   318

Application 15-2 Chrysler Corporation Moves Toward High Involvement   319

Application 15-3 Six-Sigma Success Story at GE Financial   325

Summary   328

Notes   328

CHAPTER 16   Work Design   331

The Engineering Approach   331

The Motivational Approach   332

 The Core Dimensions of Jobs   333

 Individual Differences   334

 Application Stages   335

 Barriers to Job Enrichment   337

Application 16-1 Job Enrichment at the Travelers Insurance Companies   338

 Results of Job Enrichment   339

The Sociotechnical Systems Approach   340

 Conceptual Background   340

 Self-Managed Work Teams   341

 Application Stages   345

 Results of Self-Managed Teams   347

Application 16-2 Moving to Self-Managed Teams at ABB   348

Designing Work for Technical and Personal Needs   351

 Technical Factors   352

 Personal-Need Factors   353

 Meeting Both Technical and Personal Needs   354

Summary   355

Notes   356

SELECTED CASES   359

• The Sullivan Hospital System   359

• City of Carlsbad, California
Restructuring the Public Works Department (A)   362

Part 5
HUMAN RESOURCES MANAGEMENT INTERVENTIONS   365

CHAPTER 17   Performance Management   366

A Model of Performance Management   367

Goal Setting   368

    Characteristics of Goal Setting   368

    Application Stages   370

    Management by Objectives   370

    Effects of Goal Setting and MBO   372

Performance Appraisal   372

Application 17-1 The Performance Enhancement Process at Monsanto   373

    The Performance Appraisal Process   374

    Application Stages   376

    Effects of Performance Appraisal   377

Reward Systems   377

Application 17-2 Changing the Appraisal Process in the Washington State Patrol   378

    Structural and Motivational Features of Reward Systems   379

    Skill-Based Pay Systems   382

    Performance-Based Pay Systems   383

    Gain Sharing Systems   385

    Promotion Systems   387

Application 17-3 Revising the Reward System at Lands End   388

    Reward-System Process Issues   390

Summary   391

Notes   392

CHAPTER 18   Developing and Assisting Members   396

Career Planning and Development Interventions   396

    Career Stages   397

    Career Planning   398

    Career Development   401

Application 18-1 Linking Career Planning, Human Resources Planning, and Strategy at Colgate-Palmolive   402

Workforce Diversity Interventions   410

    Age   411

    Gender   412

    Race/Ethnicity   413

    Sexual Orientation   414

    Disability   415

    Culture and Values   415

Application 18-2 Embracing Employee Diversity at Baxter Export   417

Employee Stress and Wellness Interventions   418

    Work Leaves   418

    Stress Management Programs   419

Application 18-3 Johnson & Johnson's Health and Wellness Program   427

Summary   428

Notes   429

SELECTED CASES   434

- Employee Benefits at HealthCo   434
- Sharpe BMW   438

Part 6
STRATEGIC CHANGE INTERVENTIONS   445

CHAPTER 19   Competitive and Collaborative Strategies   446

Environmental Framework   447

    Environmental Types   447

    Environmental Dimensions   448

Competitive Strategies   450

    Integrated Strategic Change   451

    Mergers and Acquisitions   454

Application 19-1 Managing Strategic Change at Microsoft Canada   455

Collaborative Strategies   461

Application 19-2 Lessons Learned from the Dow Chemical Company and Union Carbide Merger   462

    Collaboration Rationale   463

    Alliance Interventions   465

    Network Interventions   466

Application 19-3 Fragile and Robust—Network Change in Toyota Motor Corporation   473

Summary   475

Notes   475

CHAPTER 20   Organization Transformation   479

Characteristics of Transformational Change   480

    Change Is Triggered by Environmental and Internal Disruptions   480

    Change Is Systemic and Revolutionary   480

    Change Demands a New Organizing Paradigm   481

    Change Is Driven by Senior Executives and Line Management   481

    Continuous Learning and Change   482

Culture Change   482
  Concept of Organization Culture   483
  Organization Culture and Organization Effectiveness   484
  Diagnosing Organization Culture   486
  Application Stages   489
Application 20-1 Washington Mutual: Leveraging Culture as Competitive Advantage   492
Self-Designing Organizations   493
  The Demands of Transformational Change   493
  Application Stages   494
Application 20-2 Self-Design at American Healthways Corporation   496
Organization Learning and Knowledge Management   497
  Conceptual Framework   497
  Characteristics of a Learning Organization   499
  Organization Learning Processes   500
  Organization Knowledge   505
Application 20-3 Knowledge Management at BP Amoco   508
  Outcomes of OL and KM   508
Summary   509
Notes   510

SELECTED CASES   514

• Rondell Data Corporation   514
• Fourwinds Marina   523

Part 7
SPECIAL APPLICATIONS OF ORGANIZATION DEVELOPMENT 533

Chapter 21   Organization Development in Global Settings   534
Organization Development Outside the United States   535
  Cultural Context   536
  Economic Development   538
  How Cultural Context and Economic Development Affect OD Practice   539
Application 21-1 Modernizing China's Human Resource Development and Training Functions   544
Worldwide Organization Development   545
  Worldwide Strategic Orientations   546
  The International Strategic Orientation   548
  The Global Strategic Orientation   549
  The Multinational Strategic Orientation   551
  The Transnational Strategic Orientation   553
Application 21-2 Campbell Soup Company Moves to a Worldwide Strategic Orientation   554
Global Social Change   558
  Global Social Change Organizations   558
  Application Stages   560
  Change Agent Roles and Skills   563
Application 21-3 Social and Environmental Change at Floresta   564
Summary   566
Notes   566

CHAPTER 22   Organization Development in Non-industrial Settings: Health Care, Family Businesses, School Systems, and the Public Sector   571
Organization Development in Health Care   571
  Environmental Trends in Health Care   572
  Opportunities for Organization Development Practice   575
  Success Principles for OD in Health Care   576
Application 22-1 Work Redesign at Hamot Medical Center   577
  Conclusions   579
Organization Development in Family-Owned Businesses   579
  The Family Business System   580
  Critical Issues in Family Business   582
  OD Interventions in Family Business System   584
Application 22-2 OD in the Ross Family Business   588
Organization Development in School Systems   589
  Some Unique Characteristics of Schools   590
  Implications for OD in Schools   591
  High Involvement Management in Schools   592
  Total Quality Management   593
  School-based Management   594
  Classroom Interventions   594
  Conclusions   595
Organization Development in the Public Sector   596
  Comparing Public- and Private-Sector Organizations   597
  Recent Research and Innovations in Public Sector Organizational Development   602
  Conclusions   603
Application 22-3 Approaching Employee Orientation as a Cultural Experience   604
Summary   605
Notes   606

CHAPTER 23 Future Directions in Organization Development 611

Trends Within Organization Development 611

    Traditional 611

    Pragmatic 612

    Scholarly 613

    Implications for OD's Future 613

Trends in the Context of Organization Development 614

    The Economy 615

    The Workforce 617

    Organizations 619

    Implications for OD's Future 620

Summary 625

Notes 625

INTEGRATIVE CASES 629

- B.R. Richardson Timber Products 629
- Managing Strategy at Ceasars Tahoe 646
- Black & Decker International: Globalization of the Architectural Hardware Line 652

Glossary 661

Name Index 671

Subject Index 677

Preface

More and more, people are finding that the pace of change exceeds their physical and mental capacity to adapt. A burgeoning world population, arguably the root cause of so many social threats and opportunities, results in an ever increasing number of individuals, groups, start-ups, organizations, consortia, governments, countries, and economies pushing their technologies, products and services, economic agendas, social changes, innovations, ideologies and politics, and interventions. As these changes collide and interact, they accelerate the rate of perceived and real change. It's no wonder people feel overwhelmed. Sociologists call it *anomie*, a state of being characterized by the lack of social norms, or anchors of stable and shared values. We want more time with our families, but feel compelled to work longer hours, make more money, or satisfy short-term stock market expectations; we experience broadband, but are quickly frustrated at the slowness of 56k; we espouse diversity and environmental sustainability, but push other cultures to do it our way, argue that technology will eventually find an answer to the pollution problem, and put a Starbucks near Beijing's Forbidden City; we push for globalization, but only 10 percent of Americans have passports. Change, and the dilemmas it poses, is all around us.

In times like these, books on the subject of change—how to lead it, adapt to it, or manage it—should be best-sellers. On the one hand, that has never been more true. Bookstores are full of recommendations, advice, theories, and case studies relating to how the biggest organizations in the world have mastered change. For our part, this is the eighth edition of the market leading text about organization development (OD). OD is an applied field of change that uses behavioral science knowledge to increase the capacity for change, and to improve the functioning and performance of a human system. First, OD is more than change management. OD is not about change for change's sake. It is neither a way to implement the latest fad nor a pawn for doing management's bidding. It is about learning and improving in ways that make individuals, groups, organizations, and ultimately the world better off and more capable of managing change in the future. Second, OD is more than a set of values. It is not a front for the promulgation of humanistic and spiritual beliefs. It is a set of testable assertions and assumptions about how social and technical systems can coexist to produce individual satisfaction and sustainable organizational results. Finally, OD is more than a set of tools and techniques. It is not a bunch of "interventions" looking to be applied in whatever organization that comes along. It is an integrated theory and practice base aimed at increasing the effectiveness and efficiency of organizations.

On the other hand, today's reality is that OD is often misunderstood and its reputation questioned. OD is frequently seen through only one of the above lenses. OD is often used synonymously with change management; it is often defined and overly constrained by its association with a set of "touchy-feely" values; and it is often described as a hammer looking for a nail. As a result, OD's relevance has been challenged as not being up to the task of facilitating the changes taking place in the world. This is OD's challenge in the decade and century ahead. Can it implement change and teach the system to change itself at the same time? Will it cling to its humanistic traditions and focus on functioning or increase its relevance by integrating more performance-related values? How will it incorporate values related to globalization, cultural integration, the concentration of wealth, and environmental sustainability? Can it afford not to address the issues that threaten an organization's survival? These are heady questions for a field barely fifty years old.

The original edition of this text, authored by OD pioneer Edgar Huse in 1975, became a market leader because it recognized and dealt with the relevance issue. It took an objective, research perspective and placed OD practice on stronger theoretical footing. Ed showed that, in some cases, OD produced meaningful results but that additional work was still needed. Sadly, Ed passed away following publication of the second edition. His wife, Mary Huse, and West Publishing (now Thomson/South-Western) asked Tom Cummings to revise the book for subsequent editions. With the fifth edition, Tom asked Chris Worley to work with him in writing the text.

The most recent editions have had an important influence on the perception of OD. While maintaining the book's strengths of fair treatment and unbiased reporting, the newer editions made even larger strides in placing OD on a strong theoretical foundation. The third and fourth editions broadened the scope and increased the relevance of OD by including interventions that had a content component, such as work design, employee involvement, and organization structure. The fifth and sixth editions took another step toward relevance and suggested that OD had begun to incorporate a strategic perspective. This strategic orientation proposed that OD could be as concerned with performance issues as it was with human potential. Effective OD, from this newer perspective, relied as much on knowledge about organization theory and economics as it did on the behavioral sciences. It is our greatest hope that the current edition continues this tradition of rigor and relevance.

REVISIONS TO THE EIGHTH EDITION

Our goal in the eighth edition is to update the field once again. Although we have retained several features of the prior editions, we have made some important changes.

Individual Interventions

This edition takes new stances with respect to individually oriented interventions. This was not an easy decision, but we think it accurately reflects the current state of the field. First, the section on T-groups in Chapter 12 was eliminated. This venerable OD intervention's role in practice is and should be more focused on the development of OD practitioners than on being a method of organization change. In line with that clarified role, the history of OD in Chapter 1 continues to highlight the unquestioned impact and importance of T-groups, and Chapter 2 stresses their contribution to OD practitioner development. Second, several reviewers requested that training interventions be included in the text. In addition, a number of researchers have questioned why training, leadership development, and coaching have not appeared in prior editions. In this edition, we added sections on training and coaching because improvements in the definition of organization development now permit us to clarify when these are and are not OD interventions. Training and development processes have a long history within the human resources management field and are often an important element in large-scale organization change efforts. When educational interventions look to build organization capability and effectiveness, these efforts can rightly be called organization development. Coaching is one of the fastest growing human process interventions today. But it has had a fuzzy relationship to OD. Some want to distinguish it from OD and draw a boundary between them; others struggle with whether a distinction exists at all. OD practitioners are well-positioned to fulfill the coaching demand that exists and it can be an important aspect of organization development. The characteristics of effective coaching and training processes are described in Chapter 12.

Strategic Orientation of OD

For several editions now, we have tried to place OD within a strategic context, one that acknowledges that OD is not about change for change's sake but about the implementation of strategy and the alignment of organizational subsystems to promote member well-being and organization performance. The eighth edition of the text continues that tradition. First, the chapter on strategic change has been renamed and thoroughly revised. Chapter 19 in Part 6 is now called "Competitive and Collaborative Strategies." It reflects the latest thinking on the formulation and implementation of competitive strategies, including integrated strategic change and mergers and acquisitions. The second half of the chapter on collaborative strategies includes a new section on alliances and a thoroughly revised, renamed, and updated section on network development. Second, all of the chapters and sections on transformational change, including culture change, self-design, and organization learning and knowledge management, and on organization design, including organization structure, work design, and employee involvement, have been reviewed and updated.

Human Resources Interventions

The chapter on developing and assisting organization's members (Chapter 18) has been thoroughly revised and updated. Professor Karen Whelan-Berry of Utah Valley State College, based on her research in the field, graciously consented to reviewing and redrafting the chapter. It now places a variety of human resources interventions, including work-life balance, work leaves, diversity management, career planning and development, and stress management, into a more efficient framework. In combination with a revised section on reward systems in Chapter 17, Part 5, Human Resources Management Interventions, now presents a complete and current view of these interventions.

An Emphasis on OD in Different Settings

Reviewers of the textbook, as well as the varied audiences who use the text, have commented on the growing influence of OD in international and nonprofit settings. We continue to respond to these comments in several ways. First, the chapter on international OD continues to evolve and improve. We thoroughly revised the section on OD in organizations that operate on a worldwide basis, adding important conceptual frameworks and best-practice processes for implementing these strategic orientations. Second, as each intervention is discussed in the main body of the text, relevant international and nonprofit applications or research findings are referenced. Third, we revised the chapter about OD in nonprofit settings. A completely new section on family businesses has been added, and the sections on government and the public sector and OD health care have been updated.

The Future of OD

We have revised and expanded our thinking about the future. Chapter 23, on the future of OD, includes a new section examining the trends within the field of OD itself. This new section complements a revised discussion of the trends shaping the context of OD and their influence on OD practice. The interrelated changes in the economy, technology, the workforce, and organizations, as well as the trends within the OD field, provide an important crossroads for the content, process, and values of the field.

DISTINGUISHING PEDAGOGICAL FEATURES

The text is designed to facilitate the learning of organization development theory and interventions. We maintained the chapter sequence from the previous edition. Based on feedback from reviewers, this format closely matches the OD process. Professors can teach the process and then link OD practice to the interventions.

Organization

The eighth edition is organized into seven parts. Following an introductory chapter that describes the definition and history of OD, Part 1 provides an overview of organization development. It discusses the fundamental theories that underlie planned change (Chapter 2) and describes the people who practice it (Chapter 3). Part 2 is an eight-chapter description of the OD process. It describes how OD practitioners enter and contract with client systems (Chapter 4); diagnose organizations, groups, and jobs (Chapters 5 and 6); collect, analyze, and feed back diagnostic data (Chapters 7 and 8); design interventions (Chapter 9); lead and manage change (Chapter 10); and evaluate and institutionalize change (Chapter 11). In this manner, professors can focus on the OD process without distraction. Parts 3, 4, 5, and 6 then cover the major OD interventions used today, according to the same classification scheme used in previous editions of the text. Part 3 covers human process interventions; Part 4 describes technostructural approaches; Part 5 presents interventions in human resources management; and Part 6 addresses strategic change interventions. In the final section, Part 7, we cover special applications of OD, including international OD (Chapter 21); OD in health care, family businesses, schools, and the public sector (Chapter 22); and the future of OD (Chapter 23). We believe this ordering provides professors with more flexibility in teaching OD.

Applications

Within each chapter, we describe actual situations in which different OD techniques or interventions were used. These applications provide students with a chance to see how OD is actually practiced in organizations. In the eighth edition, more than 50 percent of the applications are new and many others have been updated to maintain the text's currency and relevance. In response to feedback from reviewers, almost all of the applications describe a real situation in a real organization (although sometimes we felt it necessary to use disguised names). In many cases, the organizations are large public companies that should be readily recognizable. We have endeavored to write applications based on our own OD practice or on cases that have appeared in the popular literature. In addition, we have asked several of our students to submit descriptions of their own practice, and these applications appear throughout the text. The time and effort to produce these vignettes of OD practice for others is gratefully acknowledged.

Cases

At the end of each major part in the book, we have included cases to permit a more in-depth discussion of the OD process. Six of the fifteen cases are new to the eighth edition. We have kept those cases that have been favorites over the years as well as several of the cases introduced in the last edition that received favorable feedback. Also in response to feedback from users of the text, we have endeavored to provide cases that vary in levels of detail, complexity, and sophistication to allow professors some flexibility in teaching the material to either undergraduate or graduate students.

Internet Resources

Throughout the book, we have tried to provide references to the World Wide Web and to sites related to the organizations discussed. Although these sites are often updated, moved, or altogether abandoned (which means we can't guarantee that the links will be maintained as cited), they provide students with an opportunity to explore the information available on the Internet.

Audience

This book can be used in a number of ways and by a variety of people. First, it serves as a primary textbook in organization development for students at both the graduate and undergraduate levels. Second, the book can also serve as an independent study guide for individuals wishing to learn more about how organization development can improve productivity and human satisfaction. Third, the book is intended to be of value to OD professionals, managers and administrators, specialists in such fields as personnel, training, occupational stress, and human resource management, and anyone interested in the complex process known as organization development.

EDUCATIONAL AIDS AND SUPPLEMENTS

Instructor's Manual with Test Bank (ISBN: 0-324-26061-X)

To assist instructors in the delivery of a course on organization development, an instructor's manual is available. The instructor's manual has been revised in response to feedback from users. The manual contains material that can improve the student's appreciation of OD and improve the professor's effectiveness in the classroom.

Chapter Objectives and Lecture Notes

Summary learning objectives provide a quick orientation to each chapter. The material in the chapter is then outlined and comments are made concerning important pedagogical points, such as crucial assumptions that should be noted for students, important aspects of practical application, and alternative points of view that might be used to enliven class discussion.

Exam Questions

A variety of multiple choice, true/false, and essay questions are suggested for each chapter. Instructors can use these questions directly or to suggest additional questions reflecting the professor's own style.

Case Notes

For each case in the text, teaching notes have been developed to assist instructors in preparing for case discussions. The notes provide an outline of the case, suggestions about where to place the case during the course, discussion questions to focus student attention, and an analysis of the case situation. In combination with the professor's own insights, the notes can help to enliven the case discussion or role plays.

Audiovisual Materials

Finally, a list is included of films, videos, and other materials that can be used to supplement different parts of the text, along with the addresses and phone numbers of vendors that supply the materials.

Instructor's Resource CD-ROM (0-324-26062-8)

Key instructor ancillaries (Instructor's Manual, Test Bank, ExamView and Power-Point slides) are provided on CD-ROM, giving instructors the ultimate tool for customizing lectures and presentations.

ExamView

Available on the Instructor's Resource CD-ROM, ExamView, contains all of the questions in the printed Test Bank. This program is an easy-to-use test creation software compatible with Microsoft Windows. Instructors can add or edit questions, instructions, and answers, and select questions (randomly or numerically) by previewing them on the screen. Instructors can also create and administer quizzes online, whether over the Internet, a local area network (LAN), or a wide area network (WAN).

PowerPoint Presentation Slides

Available on the Instructor's Resource CD-ROM and the Web site, the PowerPoint presentation package consists of tables and figures used in the book. These colorful slides can greatly aid the integration of text material during lectures and discussions.

Web Site

A rich Web site at (http://cummings.swlearning.com) complements the text, providing many extras for the student and instructor.

Videos (ISBN 0-324-26063-6)

A video library is available to users of the eighth edition to show how organizations and leaders apply organization development to the real world. The video examples examine a range of issues. Critical thinking questions appear at appropriate intervals in the ten- to fifteen-minute-long segments.

TextChoice: Management Exercises and Cases

TextChoice is the home of Thomson Learning's online digital content. TextChoice provides the fastest, easiest way for you to create your own learning materials. South-Western's Management Exercises and Cases database includes a variety of experiential exercises, classroom activities, management in film exercises, and cases to enhance any management course. Choose as many exercises as you like and even add your own material to create a supplement tailor-fitted to your course. Contact your South-Western/Thomson Learning sales representative for more information.

ACKNOWLEDGMENTS

People are always coming up to us and asking about "the text." "Why did you include that?" "Why didn't you include this?" "When are you going to revise it again?" "I have some suggestions that might improve this section." And so on. It is gratifying, after seven (and now eight) editions, that people find the book provocative, refer to it, use it to guide their practices, and assign it as required reading in their courses. Even though the text is revised every three years or so, it seems to be a common subject of conversation at any time we get together with our OD colleagues and students. When it does come time for revision, it provides us a chance to refresh, renew, and reestablish our relationship. "What have you heard about what's new in OD?" "How's your family?" "Do you think we should reorganize the book?" "What's next in your career?" "Did you see that article in [pick a journal or magazine]?" "What have you been reading lately?"

And then the research, reading, writing, editing, and proofing begins. Writing, debating, and editing occupy most of our time. "Can we say that better, more efficiently, and more clearly?" "Should we create a new section or revise the existing one?" "Do you really think people want to read that?" The permission requests go out and come in quickly . . . at least most of them. Follow-up faxes, reminder emails, and urgent phone calls are made. The search for new cases and applications is an ongoing activity. "Where can we find good descriptions of change?" "Would you be willing to write up that case?" Deadlines come . . . and go. The copyediting process is banter between two strangers. "No, no, no, I *meant* to say that." "Yes, that's a good idea, I hadn't thought of that." Six months into it, our wives start to ask, "When will it be done?" Then, because they have done this before, they ask, "No, I meant when will it be done, done?" When the final proofs arrive, things start to look finished. We get to see the artwork and the cover design, and a new set of problems emerges. "Where did *that* come from?" "No, this goes there, that goes here." Doesn't this sound fun?

So, yes, we continue to hope that our readers, colleagues, and friends ask us about "the text." We like talking about it, discussing it, and hearing about what we did right or wrong. But please don't ask us about *writing* "the text." We're very happy to be done (yes, done, done).

Finally, we'd like to thank those who supported us in this effort. We are thankful and grateful to our families: Nancy, Sarah, and Seth, and Debbie, Sarah, Hannah, and Samuel. We would also like to thank our students for their comments on the previous edition, for contributing many of the applications, and for helping us to try out new ideas and perspectives. A particular word of thanks goes to Gordon Brooks, Michael Gantman, and the master of science in organization development faculty (Ann Feyerherm, Miriam Lacey, Terri Egan, Scott Sherman, and David Hitchin) who withstood political inquisitions, absorbed a great deal of uncertainty, did extra work to help us prepare the manuscript, and protected us so we could write. Annette Flynn graciously performed the task of tracking down research articles, and Marjorie Walsleben patiently managed the permissions process. The following individuals reviewed the text and influenced our thinking with their honest and constructive feedback:

Sharon Crow, Marquette University

Jeanette Davy, Wright State University

Frank Hamilton, University of South Florida

Margaret Lohman, Florida State University

Susan Lynham, Texas A&M University

Barbara Mandell, Springfield College

George Mathison, University of South Florida

Daniel Svyantek, University of Akron

We also would like to express our appreciation to members of the staff at Thomson/South-Western for their aid and encouragement. Special thanks go to John Szilagyi, Joe Sabatino, Emma Guttler, and Denise Simon for their help and guidance throughout the development of this revision. Libby Shipp and Robin Gordon patiently took on the task of editing and producing this book.

Thomas G. Cummings   Christopher G. Worley

Palos Verdes Estates, California   San Juan Capistrano, California

December, 2003

General Introduction to Organization Development

This is a book about *organization development* (OD)—a process that applies behavioral science knowledge and practices to help organizations build the capacity to change and to achieve greater effectiveness, including increased financial performance and improved quality of work life. Organization development differs from other planned change efforts, such as technological innovation or new product development, because the focus is on building the organization's ability to assess its current functioning and to achieve its goals. Moreover, OD is oriented to improving the total system—the organization and its parts in the context of the larger environment that affects them.

This book reviews the broad background of OD and examines assumptions, strategies and models, intervention techniques, and other aspects of OD. This chapter provides an introduction to OD, describing first the concept of OD itself. Second, it explains why OD has expanded rapidly in the past 50 years, both in terms of people's needs to work with and through others in organizations and in terms of organizations' needs to adapt in a complex and changing world. Third, it reviews briefly the history of OD, and fourth, it describes the evolution of OD into its current state. This introduction to OD is followed by an overview of the rest of the book.

ORGANIZATION DEVELOPMENT DEFINED

Organization development is both a professional field of social action and an area of scientific inquiry. The practice of OD covers a wide spectrum of activities, with seemingly endless variations upon them. Team building with top corporate management, structural change in a municipality, and job enrichment in a manufacturing firm are all examples of OD. Similarly, the study of OD addresses a broad range of topics, including the effects of change, the methods of organizational change, and the factors influencing OD success.

A number of definitions of OD exist and are presented in Table 1.1. Each definition has a slightly different emphasis. For example, Burke's description focuses attention on culture as the target of change; French's definition is concerned with OD's long-term interest and the use of consultants; and Beckhard's and Beer's definitions address the process of OD. Worley and Feyerherm recently suggested that for a process to be called organization development, (1) it must focus on or result in the change of some aspect of the organizational system; (2) there must be learning or the transfer of knowledge or skill to the client system; and (3) there must be evidence or intention to improve the effectiveness of the client system.[1] The following definition incorporates most of these views and is used in this book: *Organization development is a systemwide application and transfer of behavioral science knowledge to the planned development, improvement, and reinforcement of the strategies, structures, and processes that lead to organization effectiveness.* This definition emphasizes several features that differentiate OD from other approaches to organizational change

Table 1•1	**Definitions of Organization Development**

- Organization development is a planned process of change in an organization's culture through the utilization of behavioral science technology, research, and theory. (Warner Burke)[2]
- Organization development refers to a long-range effort to improve an organization's problem-solving capabilities and its ability to cope with changes in its external environment with the help of external or internal behavioral-scientist consultants, or change agents, as they are sometimes called. (Wendell French)[3]
- Organization development is an effort (1) planned, (2) organization-wide, and (3) managed from the top, to (4) increase organization effectiveness and health through (5) planned interventions in the organization's "processes," using behavioral science knowledge. (Richard Beckhard)[4]
- Organization development is a systemwide process of data collection, diagnosis, action planning, intervention, and evaluation aimed at (1) enhancing congruence among organizational structure, process, strategy, people, and culture; (2) developing new and creative organizational solutions; and (3) developing the organization's self-renewing capacity. It occurs through the collaboration of organizational members working with a change agent using behavioral science theory, research, and technology. (Michael Beer)[5]

and improvement, such as management consulting, technological innovation, and operations management. The definition also helps to distinguish OD from two related subjects, *change management* and *organization change,* that also are addressed in this book.

First, OD applies to changes in the strategy, structure, and/or processes of an entire system, such as an organization, a single plant of a multiplant firm, a department or work group, or individual role or job. A change program aimed at modifying an organization's strategy, for example, might focus on how the organization relates to a wider environment and on how those relationships can be improved. It might include changes both in the grouping of people to perform tasks (structure) and in methods of communicating and solving problems (process) to support the changes in strategy. Similarly, an OD program directed at helping a top-management team become more effective might focus on interactions and problem-solving processes within the group. This focus might result in the improved ability of top management to solve company problems in strategy and structure. This contrasts with approaches focusing on one or only a few aspects of a system, such as technological innovation or operations management. In these approaches, attention is narrowed to improvement of particular products or processes, or to development of production or service delivery functions.

Second, OD is based on the application and transfer of behavioral science knowledge and practice, including microconcepts, such as leadership, group dynamics, and work design, and macroapproaches, such as strategy, organization design, and international relations. These subjects distinguish OD from such applications as management consulting, technological innovation, or operations management that emphasize the economic, financial, and technical aspects of organizations. These approaches tend to neglect the personal and social characteristics of a system. Moreover, OD is distinguished by its intent to transfer behavioral science knowledge and skill so that the system is more capable of carrying out planned change in the future.

Third, OD is concerned with managing planned change, but not in the formal sense typically associated with management consulting or technological innovation, which tend to be programmatic and expert-driven approaches to change. Rather, OD is more an adaptive process for planning and implementing change than a blueprint for how things should be done. It involves planning to diagnose and solve organizational problems, but such plans are flexible and often revised as new information is gathered about the progress of the change program. If, for example, there was concern about the performance of a set of international subsidiaries, a reorganization process might begin with plans to assess the current relationships between the international divisions and the corporate headquarters and to redesign them if necessary. These plans would be modified if the assessment discovered that most of the senior management teams were not given adequate cross-cultural training prior to their international assignments.

Fourth, OD involves both the creation and the subsequent reinforcement of change. It moves beyond the initial efforts to implement a change program to a longer-term concern for stabilizing and institutionalizing new activities within the organization. For example, implementing self-managed work teams might focus on ways in which supervisors could give workers more control over work methods. After workers had more control, attention would shift to ensuring that supervisors continued to provide that freedom. That assurance might include rewarding supervisors for managing in a participative style. This attention to reinforcement is similar to training and development approaches that address maintenance of new skills or behaviors, but it differs from other change perspectives that do not address how a change can be institutionalized.

Finally, OD is oriented to improving organizational effectiveness. This involves two major assumptions. First, an effective organization is able to solve its own problems and focus its attention and resources on achieving key goals. OD helps organization members gain the skills and knowledge necessary to conduct these activities by involving them in the change process. Second, an effective organization has both high performance, including financial returns, quality products and services, high productivity, and continuous improvement, and a high quality of work life. The organization's performance responds to the needs of external groups, such as stockholders, customers, suppliers, and government agencies, which provide the organization with resources and legitimacy. Moreover, it is able to attract and motivate effective employees, who then perform at high levels. Other forms of organization change clearly differ from OD in their focus. Management consulting, for example, primarily addresses financial performance, whereas operations management or industrial engineering focuses on productivity.

Organization development can be distinguished from change management and organization change. OD and change management both address the effective implementation of planned change. They are both concerned with the sequence of activities, processes, and leadership issues that produce organization improvements. They differ, however, in their underlying value orientation. OD's behavioral science foundation supports values of human potential, participation, and development in addition to performance and competitive advantage. Change management focuses more narrowly on values of cost, quality, and schedule.[6] As a result, OD's distinguishing feature is its concern with the transfer of knowledge and skill so that the system is more able to manage change in the future. Change management does not necessarily require the transfer of these skills. In short, all OD involves change management, but change management may not involve OD.

Similarly, organization change is a broader concept than OD. As discussed above, organization development can be applied to managing organizational change. However, it is primarily concerned with managing change in such a way that knowledge and skills are transferred to build the organization's capability to achieve goals and solve problems. It is intended to change the organization in a particular direction, toward improved problem solving, responsiveness, quality of work life, and effectiveness. Organization change, in contrast, is more broadly focused and can apply to any kind of change, including technical and managerial innovations, organization decline, or the evolution of a system over time. These changes may or may not be directed at making the organization more developed in the sense implied by OD.

The behavioral sciences have developed useful concepts and methods for helping organizations to deal with changing environments, competitor initiatives, technological innovation, globalization, or restructuring. They help managers and administrators to manage the change process. Many of these concepts and techniques are described in this book, particularly in relation to managing change.

THE GROWTH AND RELEVANCE OF ORGANIZATION DEVELOPMENT

In each of the previous editions of this book, we argued that organizations must adapt to increasingly complex and uncertain technological, economic, political, and cultural changes. We also argued that OD could help an organization to create effective responses to these changes and, in many cases, to proactively influence the strategic direction of the firm. The rapidly changing conditions of the past few years confirm our arguments and accentuate their relevance. According to several observers, organizations are in the midst of unprecedented uncertainty and chaos, and nothing short of a management revolution will save them.[7] Three major trends are shaping change in organizations: globalization, information technology, and managerial innovation.[8]

First, *globalization* is changing the markets and environments in which organizations operate as well as the way they function. New governments, new leadership, new markets, and new countries are emerging and creating a new global economy with both opportunities and threats.[9] The toppling of the Berlin Wall symbolized and energized the reunification of Germany; the European Union created a cohesive economic block that alters the face of global markets; entrepreneurs appeared in Russia, the Balkans, and Siberia to transform the former Soviet Union; terrorism has reached into every corner of economic and social life; and China is emerging as an open market and global economic influence. The rapid spread of Severe Acute Respiratory Syndrome (SARS) and its economic impact clearly demonstrated the interconnectedness among the social environment, organizations, and the global economy.

Second, *information technology* is redefining the traditional business model by changing how work is performed, how knowledge is used, and how the cost of doing business is calculated. The way an organization collects, stores, manipulates, uses, and transmits information can lower costs or increase the value and quality of products and services. Information technology, for example, is at the heart of emerging E-commerce strategies and organizations. Amazon.com, Yahoo, and eBay are among the survivors of a busted dot.com bubble, and the amount of business being conducted on the Internet is projected to grow at double-digit rates for well over 10 years. Moreover, the underlying rate of innovation is not expected to decline. Electronic data interchange—a state-of-the-art technology application a few years ago—is now considered routine business practice. The ability to move information easily and inexpensively throughout and among organizations has fueled the downsizing, delayering, and restructuring of firms. The Internet and the World Wide Web have enabled a new form of work known as telecommuting; organization members can work from their homes or cars without ever going to the office. Finally, information technology is changing how knowledge is used. Information that is widely shared reduces the concentration of power at the top of the organization. Organization members now share the same key information that senior managers once used to control decision making. Ultimately, information technology will generate new business models in which communication and information sharing is nearly free.

Third, *managerial innovation* has responded to the globalization and information technology trends and has accelerated their impact on organizations. New organizational forms, such as networks, strategic alliances, and virtual corporations, provide organizations with new ways of thinking about how to manufacture goods and deliver services. The strategic alliance, for example, has emerged as one of the indispensable tools in strategy implementation. No single organization, not even IBM, Mitsubishi, or General Electric, can control the environmental and market uncertainty it faces. Sun Microsystems' network is so complex that some products it sells are never touched by a Sun employee. In addition, new methods of change, such as downsizing or reengineering, have radically reduced the size of organizations and increased their flexibility; new large-group interventions, such as the search conference and open space, have increased the speed with which organizational change can take place; and organization learning interventions have acknowledged and leveraged knowledge as a critical organizational resource.[10] Managers, OD practitioners, and researchers argue that these forces not only are powerful in their own right but are interrelated. Their interaction makes for a highly uncertain and chaotic environment for all kinds of organizations, including manufacturing and service firms and those in the public and private sectors. There is no question that these forces are profoundly affecting organizations.

Fortunately, a growing number of organizations are undertaking the kinds of organizational changes needed to survive and prosper in today's environment. They are making themselves more streamlined and nimble, more responsive to external demands, and more ecologically sustainable. They are involving employees in key decisions and paying for performance rather than for time. They are taking the initiative in innovating and managing change, rather than simply responding to what has already happened.

Organization development is playing an increasingly key role in helping organizations change themselves. It is helping organizations assess themselves and their environments and revitalize and rebuild their strategies, structures, and processes. OD is helping organization members go beyond surface changes to transform the underlying assumptions and values governing their behaviors. The different concepts and methods discussed in this book increasingly are finding their way into government agencies, manufacturing firms, multinational corporations, service industries, educational institutions, and not-for-profit organizations. Perhaps at no other time has OD been more responsive and practically relevant to organizations' needs to operate effectively in a highly complex and changing world.

OD is obviously important to those who plan a professional career in the field, either as an internal consultant employed by an organization or as an external consultant practicing in many organizations. A career in OD can be highly rewarding, providing challenging and interesting assignments working with managers and employees to improve their organizations and their work lives. In today's environment, the demand for OD professionals is rising rapidly. For example, the large accounting firms not only have added significant "management consulting" practices; they also are moving aggressively to add "change management" to their service offerings. Career opportunities in OD should continue to expand in the United States and abroad.

Organization development also is important to those who have no aspirations to become professional practitioners. All managers and administrators are responsible for supervising and developing subordinates and for improving their departments' performance. Similarly, all staff specialists, such as accountants, financial analysts, engineers, information technologists, personnel specialists, or market researchers, are responsible for offering advice and counsel to managers and for introducing new methods and practices. Finally, OD is important to general managers and other senior executives because OD can help the whole organization be more flexible, adaptable, and effective.

Organization development can help managers and staff personnel perform their tasks more effectively. It can provide the skills and knowledge necessary for establishing effective interpersonal relationships. It can show personnel how to work effectively with others in diagnosing complex problems and in devising appropriate solutions. It can help others become committed to the solutions, thereby increasing chances for their successful implementation. In short, OD is highly relevant to anyone having to work with and through others in organizations.

A SHORT HISTORY OF ORGANIZATION DEVELOPMENT

A brief history of OD will help to clarify the evolution of the term as well as some of the problems and confusion that have surrounded it. As currently practiced, OD emerged from five major backgrounds or stems, as shown in Figure 1.1. The first was the growth of the National Training Laboratories (NTL) and the development of training groups, otherwise known as sensitivity training or T-groups. The second stem of OD was the classic work on action research conducted by social scientists interested in applying research to managing change. An important feature of action research was a technique known as survey feedback. Kurt Lewin, a prolific theorist, researcher, and practitioner in group dynamics and social change, was instrumental in the development of T-groups, survey feedback, and action research. His work led

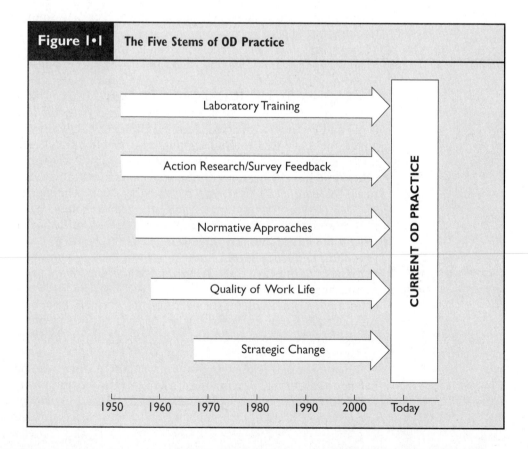

Figure 1•1   The Five Stems of OD Practice

Laboratory Training

Action Research/Survey Feedback

Normative Approaches

Quality of Work Life

Strategic Change

CURRENT OD PRACTICE

1950   1960   1970   1980   1990   2000   Today

to the creation of OD and still serves as a major source of its concepts and methods. The third stem reflects a normative view of OD. Rensis Likert's participative management framework and Blake and Mouton's Grid OD suggest a "one best way" to design and operate organizations. The fourth background is the approach focusing on productivity and the quality of work life. The fifth stem of OD, and the most recent influence on current practice, involves strategic change and organization transformation.

Laboratory Training Background

This stem of OD pioneered laboratory training, or the T-group—a small, unstructured group in which participants learn from their own interactions and evolving dynamics about such issues as interpersonal relations, personal growth, leadership, and group dynamics. Essentially, laboratory training began in the summer of 1946, when Kurt Lewin and his staff at the Research Center for Group Dynamics at the Massachusetts Institute of Technology (MIT) were asked by the Connecticut Interracial Commission and the Committee on Community Interrelations of the American Jewish Congress for help in research on training community leaders. A workshop was developed, and the community leaders were brought together to learn about leadership and to discuss problems. At the end of each day, the researchers discussed privately what behaviors and group dynamics they had observed. The community leaders asked permission to sit in on these feedback sessions. Reluctant at first, the researchers finally agreed. Thus, the first T-group was formed in which people reacted to data about their own behavior.[11] The researchers drew two conclusions about this first T-group experiment: (1) feedback about group interaction was a rich learning experience, and (2) the process of "group building" had potential for learning that could be transferred to "back-home" situations.[12]

As a result of this experience, the Office of Naval Research and the National Education Association provided financial backing to form the National Training Laboratories, and Gould Academy in Bethel, Maine, was selected as a site for further work (since then, Bethel has played an important part in NTL). The first Basic Skill Groups were offered in the summer of 1947. The program was so successful that the Carnegie Foundation provided support for programs in 1948 and 1949. This led to a permanent program for NTL within the National Education Association.

In the 1950s, three trends emerged: (1) the emergence of regional laboratories, (2) the expansion of summer program sessions to year-round sessions, and (3) the expansion of the T-group into business and industry, with NTL members becoming increasingly involved with industry programs. Notable among these industry efforts was the pioneering work of Douglas McGregor at Union Carbide, of Herbert Shepard and Robert Blake at Esso Standard Oil (now ExxonMobil), of McGregor and Richard Beckhard at General Mills, and of Bob Tannenbaum at TRW Space Systems.[13] Applications of T-group methods at these companies spawned the term "organization development" and, equally important, led corporate personnel and industrial relations specialists to expand their roles to offer internal consulting services to managers.[14]

Over time T-groups have declined as an OD intervention. They are closely associated with that side of OD's reputation as a "touchy-feely" process. NTL as well as UCLA and Stanford continue to offer T-groups to the public, a number of proprietary programs continue to thrive, and Pepperdine University and American University continue to utilize T-groups as part of Master's level OD practitioner education. The practical aspects of T-group techniques for organizations gradually became known as team building—a process for helping work groups become more effective in accomplishing tasks and satisfying member needs. Team building is one of the most common and institutionalized forms of OD today.

Action Research and Survey Feedback Background

Kurt Lewin also was involved in the second movement that led to OD's emergence as a practical field of social science. This second background refers to the processes of action research and survey feedback. The action research contribution began in the 1940s with studies conducted by social scientists John Collier, Kurt Lewin, and William Whyte. They discovered that research needed to be closely linked to action if organization members were to use it to manage change. A collaborative effort was initiated between organization members and social scientists to collect research data about an organization's functioning, to analyze it for causes of problems, and to devise and implement solutions. After implementation, further data were collected to assess the results, and the cycle of data collection and action often continued. The results of action research were twofold: Members of organizations were able to use research on themselves to guide action and change, and social scientists were able to study that process to derive new knowledge that could be used elsewhere.

Among the pioneering action research studies were the work of Lewin and his students at the Harwood Manufacturing Company[15] and the classic research by Lester Coch and John French on overcoming resistance to change.[16] The latter study led to the development of participative management as a means of getting employees involved in planning and managing change. Other notable action research contributions included Whyte and Edith Hamilton's famous study of Chicago's Tremont Hotel[17] and Collier's efforts to apply action research techniques to improving race relations when he was commissioner of Indian affairs from 1933 to 1945.[18] These studies did much to establish action research as integral to organization change. Today, it is the backbone of many OD applications.

A key component of most action research studies was the systematic collection of survey data that was fed back to the client organization. Following Lewin's death in 1947, his Research Center for Group Dynamics at MIT moved to Michigan and joined with the Survey Research Center as part of the Institute for Social Research. The Institute was headed by Rensis Likert, a pioneer in developing scientific approaches to attitude surveys. His doctoral dissertation at Columbia University developed the widely used 5-point "Likert Scale."[19]

In an early study by the Institute, Likert and Floyd Mann administered a companywide survey of management and employee attitudes at Detroit Edison.[20] The feedback process that evolved was an "interlocking chain of conferences." The major findings of the survey were first reported to the top management and then transmitted throughout the organization. The feedback sessions were conducted in task groups, with supervisors and their immediate subordinates discussing the data together. Although there was little substantial research evidence, the researchers intuitively felt that this was a powerful process for change.

In 1950, eight accounting departments asked for a repeat of the survey, thus generating a new cycle of feedback meetings. In four departments, feedback approaches were used, but the method varied, with two of the remaining departments receiving feedback only at the departmental level. Because of changes in key personnel, nothing was done in two departments.

A third follow-up study indicated that more significant and positive changes, such as job satisfaction, had occurred in the departments receiving feedback than in the two departments that did not participate. From those findings, Likert and Mann derived several conclusions about the effects of survey feedback on organization change. This led to extensive applications of survey-feedback methods in a variety of settings. The common pattern of data collection, data feedback, action planning, implementation, and follow-up data collection in both action research and survey feedback can be seen in these examples.

Normative Background

The intellectual and practical advances from the laboratory training stem and the action research/survey-feedback stem were followed closely by the belief that a human relations approach represented a "one best way" to manage organizations. This normative belief was exemplified in research that associated Likert's Participative Management (System 4, as outlined below) style and Blake and Mouton's Grid OD program with organizational effectiveness.[21]

Likert's Participative Management Program characterized organizations as having one of four types of management systems:[22]

- **Exploitive authoritative systems** (System 1) exhibit an autocratic, top-down approach to leadership. Employee motivation is based on punishment and occasional rewards. Communication is primarily downward, and there is little lateral interaction or teamwork. Decision making and control reside primarily at the top of the organization. System 1 results in mediocre performance.

- **Benevolent authoritative systems** (System 2) are similar to System 1, except that management is more paternalistic. Employees are allowed a little more interaction, communication, and decision making but within boundaries defined by management.

- **Consultative systems** (System 3) increase employee interaction, communication, and decision making. Although employees are consulted about problems and decisions, management still makes the final decisions. Productivity is good, and employees are moderately satisfied with the organization.

- **Participative group systems** (System 4) are almost the opposite of System 1. Designed around group methods of decision making and supervision, this system fosters high degrees of member involvement and participation. Work groups are highly involved in setting goals, making decisions, improving methods, and appraising results. Communication occurs both laterally and vertically, and decisions are linked throughout the organization by overlapping group membership. System 4 achieves high levels of productivity, quality, and member satisfaction.

Likert applied System 4 management to organizations using a survey-feedback process. The intervention generally started with organization members completing the *Profile of Organizational Characteristics*.[23] The survey asked members for their opinions about both the present and ideal conditions of six organizational features: leadership, motivation, communication, decisions, goals, and control. In the second stage, the data were fed back to different work groups within the organization. Group members examined the discrepancy between their present situation and their ideal, generally using System 4 as the ideal benchmark, and generated action plans to move the organization toward System 4 conditions.

Blake and Mouton's Grid® Organization Development originated from research about managerial and organizational effectiveness.[24] Data gathered on organizational excellence from 198 organizations located in the United States, Japan, and Great Britain found that the two foremost barriers to excellence were planning and communications.[25] Each of these barriers was researched further to understand its roots, and the research resulted in a normative model of leadership—the Managerial Grid.

According to the Managerial Grid, an individual's style can be described according to his or her concern for production and concern for people.[26] A concern for production covers a range of behaviors, such as accomplishing productive tasks, developing creative ideas, making quality policy decisions, establishing thorough and high-quality staff services, or creating efficient workload measurements. Concern for production is not limited to things but also may involve human accomplishment within the organization, regardless of the assigned tasks or activities. A concern for people encompasses a variety of issues, including concern for the individual's personal worth, good working conditions, a degree of involvement or commitment to completing the job, security, a fair salary structure and fringe benefits, and good social and other relationships. Each dimension is measured on a 9-point scale and results in 81 possible leadership styles.

For example, 1,9 managers have a low concern for production and a high concern for people: They view people's feelings, attitudes, and needs as valuable in their own right. This type of manager strives to provide subordinates with work conditions that provide ease, security, and comfort. On the other hand, 9,1 managers have a high concern for production but a low concern for people: They minimize the attitudes and feelings of subordinates and give little attention to individual creativity, conflict, and commitment. As a result, the focus is on the work organization.

Blake and Mouton proposed that the 9,9 managerial style is the most effective in overcoming the communications barrier to corporate excellence. The basic assumptions behind this managerial style differ qualitatively and quantitatively from those underlying the other managerial styles, which assume there is an inherent conflict between the needs of the organization and the needs of people. By showing a high concern for both people and production, managers allow employees to think and to influence the organization, thus promoting active support for organizational plans. Employee participation means that better communication is critical; therefore, necessary information is shared by all relevant parties. Moreover, better communication means self-direction and self-control, rather than unquestioning, blind obedience. Organizational commitment arises out of discussion, deliberation, and debate over major organizational issues.

One of the most structured interventions in OD, Blake and Mouton's Grid® Organization Development has two key objectives: to improve planning by developing a strategy for organizational excellence based on clear logic, and to help managers gain the necessary knowledge and skills to supervise effectively. It consists of six phases designed to analyze an entire business and to overcome the planning and communications barriers to corporate excellence. The first phase is the Grid Seminar, a 1-week program where participants analyze their personal style and learn methods of problem solving. Phase two consists of team development and Phase three involves intergroup development. In Phase four, an ideal model of organizational excellence is developed and in Phase five, the model is implemented. The final phase consists of an evaluation of the organization.

Despite some research support, the normative approach to change has given way to a contingency view that acknowledges the influence of the external environment, technology, and other forces in determining the appropriate organization design and management practices. Still, Likert's participative management and Blake and Mouton's Grid OD frameworks are both used in organizations today.

Productivity and Quality-of-Work-Life Background

The contribution of the productivity and quality-of-work-life (QWL) background to OD can be described in two phases. The first phase is described by the original projects developed in Europe in the 1950s and their emergence in the United States during the 1960s. Based on the research of Eric Trist and his colleagues at the Tavistock Institute of Human Relations in London, early practitioners in Great Britain, Ireland, Norway, and Sweden developed work designs aimed at better integrating technology and people.[27] These QWL programs generally involved joint participation by unions and management in the design of work and resulted in work designs giving employees high levels of discretion, task variety, and feedback about results. Perhaps the most distinguishing characteristic of these QWL programs was the discovery of self-managing work groups as a form of work design. These groups were composed of multiskilled workers who were given the necessary autonomy and information to design and manage their own task performances.

As these programs migrated to America, a variety of concepts and techniques were adopted and the approach tended to be more mixed than in European practice. For example, two definitions of QWL emerged during its initial development.[28] QWL was first defined in terms of people's reaction to work, particularly individual outcomes related to job satisfaction and mental health. Using this definition, QWL focused primarily on the personal consequences of the work experience and how to improve work to satisfy personal needs.

A second definition of QWL defined it as an approach or method.[29] People defined QWL in terms of specific techniques and approaches used for improving work.[30] It was viewed as synonymous with methods such as job enrichment, self-managed teams, and labor–management committees. This technique orientation derived mainly from the growing publicity surrounding QWL projects, such as the General Motors–United Auto Workers project at Tarrytown and the Gaines Pet Food plant project. These pioneering projects drew attention to specific approaches for improving work.

The excitement and popularity of this first phase of QWL in the United States lasted until the mid-1970s, when other more pressing issues, such as inflation and energy costs, diverted national attention. However, starting in 1979, a second phase of QWL activity emerged. A major factor contributing to the resurgence of QWL was growing international competition faced by the United States in markets at home and abroad. It became increasingly clear that the relatively low cost and high quality of foreign-made goods resulted partially from the management practices used abroad, especially in Japan. Books extolling the virtues of Japanese management, such as Ouchi's *Theory Z,*[31] made best-seller lists.

As a result, QWL programs expanded beyond their initial focus on work design to include other features of the workplace that can affect employee productivity and satisfaction, such as reward systems, work flows, management styles, and the physical work environment. This expanded focus resulted in larger-scale and longer-term projects than had the early job enrichment programs and shifted attention beyond the individual worker to work groups and the larger work context. Equally important, it added the critical dimension of organizational efficiency to what had been up to that time a primary concern for the human dimension.

At one point, the productivity and QWL approach became so popular that it was called an ideological movement. This was particularly evident in the spread of quality circles within many companies. Popularized in Japan, quality circles are groups of employees trained in problem-solving methods that meet regularly to resolve work-environment, productivity, and quality-control concerns and to develop more efficient ways of working. At the same time, many of the QWL programs started in the early 1970s were achieving success. Highly visible corporations, such as General Motors, Ford, and Honeywell, and unions, such as the United Automobile Workers, the Oil, Chemical, and Atomic Workers, the Communications Workers of America, and the Steelworkers, were more willing to publicize their QWL efforts. In 1980, for example, more than eighteen hundred people attended an international QWL conference in Toronto, Canada. Unlike previous conferences, which were dominated by academics, the presenters at Toronto were mainly managers, workers, and unionists from private and public corporations.

Today, this second phase of QWL activity continues primarily under the banner of "employee involvement" (EI) as well as total quality management and six-sigma programs, rather than of QWL. For many OD practitioners, the term EI signifies, more than the name QWL, the growing emphasis on how employees can contribute more to running the organization so it can be more flexible, productive, and competitive. Recently, the term "employee empowerment" has been used interchangeably with the term EI, the former suggesting the power inherent in moving decision making downward in the organization.[32] *Employee empowerment* may be too restrictive, however. Because it draws attention to the power aspects of these interventions, it may lead practitioners to neglect other important elements needed for success, such as information, skills, and rewards. Consequently, EI seems broader and less restrictive than does employee empowerment as a banner for these approaches to organizational improvement.

Strategic Change Background

The strategic change background is a recent influence on OD's evolution. As organizations and their technological, political, and social environments have become more complex and more uncertain, the scale and intricacies of organizational change have increased. This trend has produced the need for a strategic perspective from OD and encouraged planned change processes at the organization level.[33]

Strategic change involves improving the alignment among an organization's environment, strategy, and organization design.[34] Strategic change interventions include efforts to improve both the organization's relationship to its environment and the fit between its technical, political, and cultural systems.[35] The need for strategic change is usually triggered by some major disruption to the organization, such as the lifting of regulatory requirements, a technological breakthrough, or a new chief executive officer coming in from outside the organization.[36]

One of the first applications of strategic change was Richard Beckhard's use of open systems planning.[37] He proposed that an organization's environment and its strategy could be described and analyzed. Based on the organization's core mission, the differences between what the environment demanded and how the organization responded could be reduced and performance improved. Since then, change agents have proposed a variety of large-scale or strategic-change models;[38] each of these models recognizes that strategic change involves multiple levels of the organization and a change in its culture, is often driven from the top by powerful executives, and has important effects on performance. More recently, strategic approaches to OD have been extended into mergers and acquisitions, alliance formation, and network development.[39]

The strategic change background has significantly influenced OD practice. For example, implementing strategic change requires OD practitioners to be familiar with competitive strategy, finance, and marketing, as well as team building, action research, and survey feedback. Together, these skills have improved OD's relevance to organizations and their managers.

EVOLUTION IN ORGANIZATION DEVELOPMENT

Current practice in organization development is strongly influenced by those five backgrounds as well as by the trends shaping change in organizations. The laboratory training, action research and survey feedback, and normative roots of OD are evident in the strong value focus that underlies its practice. The more recent influences, the quality-of-work-life and strategic change backgrounds, have greatly improved the relevance and rigor of OD practice. They have added financial and economic indicators of effectiveness to OD's traditional measures of work satisfaction and personal growth. All of the backgrounds support the transfer of knowledge and skill to the client system and the building of capacity to better manage change in the future.

Today, the field is being influenced by the globalization and information technology trends described earlier. OD is being carried out in many more countries and in many more organizations operating on a worldwide basis. This is generating a whole new set of interventions as well as adaptations to traditional OD practice.[40] In addition, OD must adapt its methods to the technologies being used in organizations. As information technology continues to influence organization environments, strategies, and structures, OD will need to manage change processes in cyberspace as well as face-to-face. The diversity of this evolving discipline has led to tremendous growth in the number of professional practitioners, in the kinds of organizations involved with OD, and in the range of countries within which OD is practiced.

The expansion of the OD Network (http://www.odnetwork.org), which began in 1964, is one indication of this growth. It has grown from 200 members in 1970 to 2,800 in 1992 to 4,031 in 1999 to 4,118 in 2003. At the same time, Division 14 of the American Psychological Association, formerly known as the Division of Industrial Psychology, has changed its title to the Society for Industrial and Organizational Psychology (http://www.siop.org). In 1968, the American Society for Training & Development (http://www.astd.org) set up an OD division, which currently has more than 2,000 members. In 1971, the Academy of Management established a Division of Organization Development and Change (http://www.aom.pace.edu/odc), which currently has more than 2,400 members. Pepperdine University (http://bschool.pepperdine.edu/programs/msod), Bowling Green State University (http://www.bgsu.edu), and Case Western Reserve University (http://www.cwru.edu) offered the first master's degree programs in OD in 1975, and Case Western Reserve University began the first doctoral program in OD. Organization development now is being taught at the graduate and undergraduate levels in a large number of universities.[41]

In addition to the growth of professional societies and educational programs in OD, the field continues to develop new theorists, researchers, and practitioners who are building on the work of the early pioneers and extending it to contemporary issues and conditions. The first generation of contributors included Chris Argyris, who developed a learning and action-science approach to OD;[42] Warren Bennis, who tied executive leadership to strategic change;[43] Edie Seashore, who keeps diversity in the forefront of practice; Edgar Schein, who developed process approaches to OD, including the key role of organizational culture in change management;[44] Richard Beckhard, who focused attention on the importance of managing transitions;[45] and Robert Tannenbaum, who sensitized OD to the personal dimension of participants' lives.[46]

Among the second generation of contributors are Warner Burke, whose work has done much to make OD a professional field;[47] Larry Greiner, who has brought the ideas of power and evolution into the mainstream of OD;[48] Edward Lawler III, who has extended OD to reward systems and employee involvement;[49] Anthony Raia and Newton Margulies, who together have kept our attention on the values underlying OD and what those mean for contemporary practice;[50] and Peter Vaill and Craig Lundberg, who continue to develop OD as a practical science.[51]

Included among the newest generation of OD contributors are Dave Brown, whose work on action research and developmental organizations has extended OD into community and societal change;[52] Thomas Cummings, whose work on sociotechnical systems, self-designing organizations, and transorganizational development has led OD beyond the boundaries of single organizations to groups of organizations and their environments;[53] Max Elden, whose international work in industrial democracy draws attention to the political aspects of OD;[54] Richard Woodman, William Pasmore, and Jerry Porras, who have done much to put OD on a sound research and conceptual base;[55] and Peter Block, who has focused attention on consulting skills, empowerment processes, and reclaiming our individuality.[56] Others making important contributions to the field include Ken Murrell, who has focused attention on the internationalization of OD;[57] Sue Mohrman and Gerry Ledford, who have focused on team-based organizations and compensation;[58] and David Cooperrider, who has turned our attention toward the positive aspects of organizations.[59] These academic contributors are joined by a large number of internal OD practitioners and external consultants who lead organizational change.

Many different organizations have undertaken a wide variety of OD efforts. In many cases, organizations have been at the forefront of innovating new change techniques and methods as well as new organizational forms. Larger corporations that have engaged in organization development include General Electric, Boeing, Texas Instruments, American Airlines, DuPont, Intel, Hewlett-Packard, Microsoft, GTE, John Hancock Mutual Life Insurance, Polaroid, Ralston Purina, General Foods, Procter & Gamble, IBM, TRW Systems, Bank of America, and Cummins Engine. Traditionally, much of the work was considered confidential and was not publicized. Today, however, organizations increasingly have gone public with their OD efforts, sharing the lessons with others.

OD work also is being done in schools, communities, and local, state, and federal governments. A recent review of OD projects is directed primarily at OD in public administration.[60] Extensive OD work was done in the armed services, including the army, navy, air force, and coast guard, although OD activity and research have declined with the reduction in the size of the military. Public schools began using both group training and survey feedback relatively early in the history of OD.[61] Usually, the projects took place in suburban middle-class schools, where stresses and strains of an urban environment were not prominent and ethnic and socioeconomic differences between consultants and clients were not high. In more recent years, OD methods have been extended to urban schools and to colleges and universities.

Organization development is increasingly international. It has been applied in Canada, Sweden, Norway, Germany, Japan, Australia, Israel, South Africa, Mexico, Venezuela, the Philippines, China, Hong Kong, Russia, New Zealand, and The Netherlands. These efforts have involved such organizations as Saab (Sweden), Imperial Chemical Industries (England), Shell Oil Company, Orrefors (Sweden), Akzo-Nobel (The Netherlands), Neusoft Corporation (China), Air New Zealand, and Vitro (Mexico).

Although it is evident that OD has expanded vastly in recent years, relatively few of the total number of organizations in the United States are actively involved in formal OD programs. However, many organizations are applying OD approaches and techniques without knowing that such a term exists.

OVERVIEW OF THE BOOK

This book presents the process and practice of organization development in a logical flow, as shown in Figure 1.2. Part 1 provides an overview of OD that describes the process of planned change and those who perform the work. It consists of two chapters. Chapter 2 discusses the nature of planned change and presents some models describing the change process. Planned change is viewed as an ongoing cycle of four activities: entering and contracting, diagnosing, planning and implementing, and evaluating and institutionalizing. Chapter 3 describes the OD practitioner and provides insight into the knowledge and skills needed to practice OD and the kinds of career issues that can be expected.

Part 2 is composed of eight chapters that describe the process of organization development. Chapter 4 characterizes the first activity in this process: entering an or-

Figure 1•2   Overview of the Book

Part 1: Overview of Organization Development

The Nature of Planned Change
(Chapter 2)

The Organization Development Practitioner
(Chapter 3)

Part 2: The Process of Organization Development

Entering and
Contracting
(Chapter 4)

Diagnosing
Organizations
(Chapter 5)

Diagnosing
Groups and
Jobs
(Chapter 6)

Collecting and
Analyzing
Diagnostic
Information
(Chapter 7)

Feeding Back
Diagnostic
Information
(Chapter 8)

Designing
Interventions
(Chapter 9)

Leading and
Managing Change
(Chapter 10)

Evaluating and
Institutionalizing
Interventions
(Chapter 11)

**Part 3:
Human Process
Interventions**

Individual,
Interpersonal, and
Group Process
Approaches
(Chapter 12)

Organization
Process Approaches
(Chapter 13)

**Part 4:
Technostructural
Interventions**

Restructuring
Organizations
(Chapter 14)

Employee
Involvement
(Chapter 15)

Work Design
(Chapter 16)

**Part 5:
Human Resources
Management
Interventions**

Performance
Management
(Chapter 17)

Developing and
Assisting Members
(Chapter 18)

**Part 6:
Strategic
Interventions**

Competitive
and
Collaborative
Strategies
(Chapter 19)

Organization
Transformation
(Chapter 20)

Part 7: Special Applications of Organization Development

Organization Development
in Global Settings
(Chapter 21)

OD in Health Care, Family-
Owned Businesses, School
Systems, and the Public Sector
(Chapter 22)

Future Directions
in Organization
Development
(Chapter 23)

ganizational system and contracting with it for organization development work. Chapters 5, 6, 7, and 8 present the steps associated with the next major activity of the OD process: diagnosing. This involves helping the organization understand its current functioning and discover areas for improvement. Chapters 5 and 6 present an open-systems model to guide diagnosis at three levels of analysis: the total organization, the group or department, and the individual job or position. Chapters 7 and 8 review methods for collecting, analyzing, and feeding back diagnostic data. Chapters 9 and 10 address issues concerned with the third activity: planning and implementing change. Chapter 9 presents an overview of the intervention design process. Major kinds of interventions are identified, and the specific approaches that make up the next four parts of the book are introduced. Chapter 10 discusses the process of managing change and identifies key factors contributing to the successful implementation of change programs. Chapter 11 describes the final activity of the planned change process: evaluating OD interventions and stabilizing or institutionalizing them as a permanent part of organizational functioning.

Parts 3 through 6 present the major interventions used in OD today. Part 3 (Chapters 12 and 13) is concerned with human process interventions aimed at the social processes occurring within organizations. These are the oldest and most traditional interventions in OD. Chapter 12 describes individual, interpersonal, and group process approaches, such as coaching, training and development, process consultation, third-party interventions, and team building. Chapter 13 presents more systemwide process approaches, such as organizational confrontation meetings, intergroup relations, and large-group interventions.

Part 4 (Chapters 14, 15, and 16) reviews technostructural interventions that are aimed at organization structure and at better integrating people and technology. Chapter 14 is about restructuring organizations; it describes the alternative methods of organizing work activities as well as processes for downsizing and reengineering the organization. Chapter 15 presents interventions for improving employee involvement. These change programs increase employee knowledge, power, information, and rewards through parallel structures, high-involvement organizations, and total quality management. Chapter 16 describes change programs directed at work design, both of individual jobs and of work groups, for greater employee satisfaction and productivity.

Part 5 (Chapters 17 and 18) presents human resource management interventions that are directed at integrating people into the organization. These interventions are associated traditionally with the personnel function in the organization and increasingly have become a part of OD activities. Chapter 17 concerns the process of performance management. This is a cycle of activities that helps groups and individuals to set goals, appraise work, and reward performance. Chapter 18 discusses three interventions—career planning and development, workforce diversity, and employee wellness—that develop and assist organization members.

Part 6 (Chapters 19 and 20) concerns strategic interventions that focus on organizing the firm's resources to gain a competitive advantage in the environment. These change programs generally are managed from the top of the organization and take considerable time, effort, and resources. Chapter 19 presents four interventions having to do with strategies of competition, including integrated strategic change and mergers and acquisitions, and strategies of collaboration, including alliances and networks. Chapter 20 describes three interventions for radically transforming organizations: culture change, self-designing organizations, and organization learning and knowledge management.

Part 7 (Chapters 21, 22, and 23) is concerned with special topics in OD. Chapter 21 describes the practice of OD in international settings. OD in organizations operating outside of the United States requires modification of the interventions to fit the country's cultural context. Organization development in worldwide organizations is aimed at improving the internal alignment of strategy, structure, and process to achieve global objectives. Furthermore, the practice of OD in global social change organizations promotes sustainable development and improving human potential in emerging countries. Chapter 22 presents broad applications of OD in different kinds of organizations, including educational, government, family-owned, and health care agencies. Finally, Chapter 23 examines the future of organization development, including the trends affecting the field and the prospects for its influence on organization effectiveness.

SUMMARY

This chapter introduced OD as a planned change discipline concerned with applying behavioral science knowledge and practice to help organizations achieve greater effectiveness. Managers and staff specialists must work with and through people to perform their jobs, and OD can help them form effective relationships with others. Organizations are faced with rapidly accelerating change, and OD can help them cope with the consequences of change. The concept of OD has multiple meanings. The definition provided here resolved some of the problems with earlier definitions. The history of OD reveals its five roots: laboratory training, action research and survey feedback, normative approaches, productivity and quality of work life, and strategic change. The current practice of OD goes far beyond its humanistic origins by incorporating concepts from organization strategy and structure that complement the early emphasis on social processes. The continued growth in the number and diversity of OD approaches, practitioners, and involved organizations attests to the health of the discipline and offers a favorable prospect for the future.

NOTES

1. C. Worley and A. Feyerherm, "Reflections on the Future of OD," *Journal of Applied Behavioral Science* 39 (2003): 97–115.

2. W. Burke, *Organization Development: Principles and Practices* (Boston: Little, Brown, 1982).

3. W. French, "Organization Development: Objectives, Assumptions, and Strategies," *California Management Review* 12, 2 (1969): 23–34.

4. R. Beckhard, *Organization Development: Strategies and Models* (Reading, Mass.: Addison-Wesley, 1969).

5. M. Beer, *Organization Change and Development: A Systems View* (Santa Monica, Calif.: Goodyear Publishing, 1980).

6. R. Marshak, "Reclaiming the Heart of OD: Putting People Back into Organizations," (keynote address to the National OD Network Conference, Orlando, Fl., 6 October 1996); N. Worren, K. Ruddle, and K. Moore, "From Organization Development to Change Management: The Emergence of a New Profession," *Journal of Applied Behavioral Science* 35 (1999): 273–86; M. Davis, "OD and Change Management Consultants: An Empirical Examination and Comparison of Their Values and Interventions" (working paper, Shenandoah University, 2001).

7. W. Burke, *Organization Change* (Newbury Park, Calif.: Sage Publications, 2002); D. Watts, *Six Degrees* (New York: W. W. Norton, 2003); J. Kotter, *Leading Change* (Boston: Harvard Business School Press, 1996); S. Brown and K. Eisenhardt, *Competing on the Edge* (Boston: Harvard Business School Press, 1998); M. Wheatley, *Leadership and the*

New Science (San Francisco: Berrett-Koehler, 1999); W. Joyce, *Megachange* (New York: Free Press, 1999); S. Chowdhury, ed., *Organization 21C* (Upper Saddle River, N.J.: Financial Times Prentice Hall, 2002).

8. T. Stewart, "Welcome to the Revolution," *Fortune* (13 December 1993) 66–80; M. Hitt, R. Ireland, R. Hoskisson, *Strategic Management* (Cincinnati: Southwestern College Publishing, 1999).

9. International Forum on Globalization, *Alternatives to Economic Globalization* (San Francisco: Berrett-Koehler, 2002).

10. M. Anderson, ed., *Fast Cycle Organization Development* (Cincinnati: South-Western College Publishing, 2000); M. Hammer and J. Champy, *Reengineering the Corporation* (New York: HarperCollins, 1993); P. Senge, *The Fifth Discipline* (New York: Doubleday, 1990).

11. A. Kleiner, *The Age of Heretics* (New York: Doubleday, 1996); A. Freedman, "The History of Organization Development and the NTL Institute: What We have Learned, Forgotten, and Rewritten," *The Psychologist-Manager Journal* 3 (1999): 125–41.

12. L. Bradford, "Biography of an Institution," *Journal of Applied Behavioral Science* 3 (1967): 127; A. Marrow, "Events Leading to the Establishment of the National Training Laboratories," *Journal of Applied Behavioral Science* 3 (1967): 145–50.

13. Kleiner, *Age of Heretics*; M. Mortara, "Organization Development and Change at TRW Space Technology

Laboratories," (unpublished master's thesis, Pepperdine University, 2003).

14. W. French, "The Emergence and Early History of Organization Development with Reference to Influences upon and Interactions among Some of the Key Actors," in *Contemporary Organization Development: Current Thinking and Applications*, ed. D. Warrick (Glenview, Ill.: Scott, Foresman, 1985): 12–27.

15. A. Marrow, D. Bowers, and S. Seashore, *Management by Participation* (New York: Harper & Row, 1967).

16. L. Coch and J. French, "Overcoming Resistance to Change," *Human Relations* 1 (1948): 512–32.

17. W. Whyte and E. Hamilton, *Action Research for Management* (Homewood, Ill.: Irwin-Dorsey, 1964).

18. J. Collier, "United States Indian Administration as a Laboratory of Ethnic Relations," *Social Research* 12 (May 1945): 275–76.

19. French, "Emergence and Early History," 19–20.

20. F. Mann, "Studying and Creating Change," in *The Planning of Change: Readings in the Applied Behavioral Sciences*, eds. W. Bennis, K. Benne, and R. Chin (New York: Holt, Rinehart, & Winston, 1962), 605–15.

21. R. Likert, *The Human Organization* (New York: McGraw-Hill, 1967); S. Seashore and D. Bowers, "Durability of Organizational Change," *American Psychologist* 25 (1970): 227–33; D. Mosley, "System Four Revisited: Some New Insights," *Organization Development Journal* 5 (Spring 1987): 19–24; R. Blake and J. Mouton, *The Managerial Grid* (Houston: Gulf, 1964); R. Blake, J. Mouton, L. Barnes, and L. Greiner, "Breakthrough in Organization Development," *Harvard Business Review* 42 (1964): 133–55; R. Blake and J. Mouton, *Corporate Excellence Through Grid Organization Development: A Systems Approach* (Houston: Gulf, 1968); R. Blake and J. Mouton, *Building a Dynamic Corporation Through Grid Organization Development* (Reading, Mass.: Addison-Wesley, 1969).

22. Likert, *Human Organization*.

23. Ibid.

24. Blake and Mouton, *The Managerial Grid*; R. Blake, J. Mouton, L. Barnes, and L. Greiner, "Breakthrough in Organization Development," 133–55; Blake and Mouton, *Corporate Excellence*; Blake and Mouton, *Building a Dynamic Corporation*; R. Blake and A. McCanse, *Leadership Dilemmas—Grid Solutions* (Houston: Gulf, 1991).

25. Blake and Mouton, *Corporate Excellence*.

26. Blake and Mouton, *Managerial Grid*.

27. A. Rice, *Productivity and Social Organization: The Ahmedabad Experiment* (London: Tavistock Publications, 1958); E. Trist and K. Bamforth, "Some Social and Psychological Consequences of the Longwall Method of Coal-Getting," *Human Relations* 4 (January 1951): 1–38; P. Gyllenhamer, *People at Work* (Reading, Mass.: Addison-Wesley, 1977); E. Thorsrud, B. Sorensen, and B. Gustavsen, "Sociotechnical Approach to Industrial Democracy in Norway," in *Handbook of Work Organization and Society*, ed. R. Dubin (Chicago: Rand McNally, 1976): 648–87; *Work in America: Report of a Special Task Force to the Secretary of Health, Education, and Welfare* (Cambridge: MIT Press, 1973); L. Davis and A. Cherns, eds., *The Quality of Working Life*, 2 vols. (New York: Free Press, 1975).

28. D. Nadler and E. Lawler III, "Quality of Work Life: Perspectives and Directions" (working paper, Center for Effective Organizations, University of Southern California, Los Angeles, 1982); L. Davis, "Enhancing the Quality of Work Life: Developments in the United States," *International Labour Review* 116 (July-August 1977): 53–65; L. Davis, "Job Design and Productivity: A New Approach," *Personnel* 33 (1957): 418–30.

29. Ibid.

30. R. Ford, "Job Enrichment Lessons from AT&T," *Harvard Business Review* 51 (January-February 1973): 96–106; J. Taylor, J. Landy, M. Levine, and D. Kamath, *Quality of Working Life: An Annotated Bibliography, 1957–1972* (Center for Organizational Studies, Graduate School of Management, University of California at Los Angeles, 1972); J. Taylor, "Experiments in Work System Design: Economic and Human Results," *Personnel Review* 6 (1977): 28–37; J. Taylor, "Job Satisfaction and Quality of Working Life: A Reassessment," *Journal of Occupational Psychology* 50 (December 1977): 243–52.

31. W. Ouchi, *Theory Z* (Reading, Mass.: Addison-Wesley, 1981).

32. J. Vogt and K. Murrell, *Empowerment in Organizations* (San Diego: University Associates, 1990).

33. M. Jelinek and J. Litterer, "Why OD Must Become Strategic," in *Research in Organizational Change and Development*, vol. 2, eds. W. Pasmore and R. Woodman (Greenwich, Conn.: JAI Press, 1988), 135–62; P. Buller, "For Successful Strategic Change: Blend OD Practices with Strategic Management," *Organizational Dynamics* (Winter 1988): 42–55; C. Worley, D. Hitchin, and W. Ross, *Integrated Strategic Change* (Reading, Mass.: Addison-Wesley, 1996).

34. Worley, Hitchin, and Ross, *Integrated Strategic Change*; N. Rajagopalan and G. Spreitzer, "Toward a Theory of Strategic Change: A Multi-Lens Perspective and Integrative Framework," *Academy of Management Review* 22 (1997): 48–79.

35. R. Beckhard and R. Harris, *Organizational Transitions: Managing Complex Change*, 2d ed. (Reading, Mass.: Addison-Wesley, 1987); N. Tichy, *Managing Strategic*

Change (New York: John Wiley & Sons, 1983); E. Schein, *Organizational Culture and Leadership* (San Francisco: Jossey-Bass, 1985); C. Lundberg, "Working with Culture," *Journal of Organization Change Management* 1 (1988): 38–47.

36. D. Miller and P. Freisen, "Momentum and Revolution in Organization Adaptation," *Academy of Management Journal* 23 (1980): 591–614; M. Tushman and E. Romanelli, "Organizational Evolution: A Metamorphosis Model of Convergence and Reorientation," in *Research in Organizational Behavior,* vol. 7, eds. L. Cummings and B. Staw (Greenwich, Conn.: JAI Press, 1985), 171–222.

37. Beckhard and Harris, *Organizational Transitions.*

38. T. Covin and R. Kilmann, "Critical Issues in Large-Scale Organization Change," *Journal of Organization Change Management* 1 (1988): 59–72; A. Mohrman, S. Mohrman, G. Ledford Jr., T. Cummings, and E. Lawler, eds., *Large-Scale Organization Change* (San Francisco: Jossey-Bass, 1989); W. Torbert, "Leading Organizational Transformation," in *Research in Organizational Change and Development,* vol. 3, eds. R. Woodman and W. Pasmore (Greenwich, Conn.: JAI Press, 1989), 83–116; J. Bartunek and M. Louis, "The Interplay of Organization Development and Organization Transformation," in *Research in Organizational Change and Development,* vol. 2, eds. W. Pasmore and R. Woodman (Greenwich, Conn.: JAI Press, 1988), 97–134; A. Levy and U. Merry, *Organizational Transformation: Approaches, Strategies, Theories* (New York: Praeger, 1986).

39. M. Marks and P. Mirvis, *Joining Forces* (San Francisco: Jossey-Bass, 1998).

40. A. Jaeger, "Organization Development and National Culture: Where's the Fit?" *Academy of Management Review* 11 (1986): 178; G. Hofstede, *Culture's Consequences: International Differences in Work-Related Values* (London: Sage, 1980); P. Sorensen Jr., T. Head, N. Mathys, J. Preston, and D. Cooperrider, *Global and International Organization Development* (Champaign, Ill.: Stipes, 1995); A. Chin (with C. Chin), *Internationalizing OD: Cross-Cultural Experiences of NTL Members* (Alexandria, Va.: NTL Institute, 1997).

41. G. Varney and A. Darrow, "Market Position of Master-Level Graduate Programs in OD," *OD Practitioner* 27 (1995): 39–43; OD Institute, *International Registry of O.D. Professionals and O.D. Handbook* (Cleveland: OD Institute, 1995); G. Varney and A. Darrow, "Name Recognition of Master's Level Graduate Programs in Organization Development and Change," *OD Practitioner* 30 (1998).

42. C. Argyris and D. Schon, *Organizational Learning II* (Reading, Mass.: Addison-Wesley, 1996); C. Argyris, R. Putnam, and D. Smith, *Action Science* (San Francisco: Jossey-Bass, 1985).

43. W. Bennis, *Managing People Is Like Herding Cats: Warren Bennis on Leadership* (New York: Executive Excellence, 1997); W. Bennis and B. Nanus, *Leaders* (New York: Harper & Row, 1985).

44. E. Schein, *Process Consultation Revisited: Creating the Helping Relationship* (Reading, Mass.: Addison-Wesley, 1999); E. Schein, *Process Consultation: Its Role in Organization Development* (Reading, Mass.: Addison-Wesley, 1969); E. Schein, *Process Consultation Volume II: Lessons for Managers and Consultants* (Reading, Mass.: Addison-Wesley, 1987); E. Schein, *Organizational Culture and Leadership,* 2d ed. (San Francisco: Jossey-Bass, 1997).

45. Beckhard and Harris, *Organizational Transitions;* R. Beckhard and W. Pritchard, *Changing the Essence* (San Francisco: Jossey-Bass, 1992); R. Beckhard, *Agent of Change* (San Francisco: Jossey-Bass, 1997).

46. R. Tannenbaum and R. Hanna, "Holding On, Letting Go, and Moving On: Understanding a Neglected Perspective on Change," in *Human Systems Development,* eds. R. Tannenbaum, N. Margulies, and F. Massarik (San Francisco: Jossey-Bass, 1985), 95–121.

47. W. Burke, *Organization Development: Principles and Practices* (Boston: Little, Brown, 1982); W. Burke, *Organization Development: A Normative View* (Reading, Mass.: Addison-Wesley, 1987); W. Burke, "Organization Development: Then, Now, and Tomorrow," *OD Practitioner* 27 (1995): 5–13.

48. L. Greiner, "Evolution and Revolution as Organizations Grow," *Harvard Business Review* 50 (July-August, 1972): 37–46; L. Greiner and V. Schein, *Power and Organizational Development: Mobilizing Power to Implement Change* (Reading, Mass.: Addison-Wesley, 1988).

49. E. Lawler III, *Pay and Organization Development* (Reading, Mass.: Addison-Wesley, 1981); E. Lawler III, *High-Involvement Management* (San Francisco: Jossey-Bass, 1986); E. Lawler III, *From the Ground Up* (San Francisco: Jossey-Bass, 1996); E. Lawler III, *Rewarding Excellence* (San Francisco: Jossey-Bass, 2000).

50. A. Raia and N. Margulies, "Organization Development: Issues, Trends, and Prospects," in *Human Systems Development,* eds. R. Tannenbaum, N. Margulies, and F. Massarik (San Francisco: Jossey-Bass, 1985), 246–72; N. Margulies and A. Raia, "Some Reflections on the Values of Organizational Development," *Academy of Management OD Newsletter* (Winter 1988): 1, 9–11.

51. P. Vaill, "OD as a Scientific Revolution," in *Contemporary Organization Development: Current Thinking and Applications* (Glenview, Ill.: Scott, Foresman, 1985), 28–41; C. Lundberg, "On Organization Development Interventions: A General Systems-Cybernetic Perspective," in *Systems Theory for Organizational Development,* ed. T.

Cummings (Chichester, England: John Wiley & Sons, 1980), 247–71; P. Frost, L. Moore, M. Louis, C. Lundberg, *Reframing Organizational Culture* (Newbury Park, Calif.: Sage Publications, 1991).

52. L. D. Brown and J. Covey, "Development Organizations and Organization Development: Toward an Expanded Paradigm for Organization Development," in *Research in Organizational Change and Development,* vol. 1, eds. R. Woodman and W. Pasmore (Greenwich, Conn.: JAI Press, 1987), 59–87.

53. T. Cummings and S. Srivastva, *Management of Work: A Socio-Technical Systems Approach* (San Diego: University Associates, 1977); T. Cummings, "Transorganizational Development," in *Research in Organizational Behavior,* vol. 6, eds. B. Staw and L. Cummings (Greenwich, Conn.: JAI Press, 1984), 367–422; T. Cummings and S. Mohrman, "Self-Designing Organizations: Towards Implementing Quality-of-Work-Life Innovations," in *Research in Organizational Change and Development,* vol. 1, eds. R. Woodman and W. Pasmore (Greenwich, Conn.: JAI Press, 1987), 275–310.

54. M. Elden, "Sociotechnical Systems Ideas as Public Policy in Norway: Empowering Participation through Worker-Managed Change," *Journal of Applied Behavioral Science* 22 (1986): 239–55.

55. R. Woodman and W. Pasmore, *Research in Organizational Change and Development,* vols. 1–14. (Oxford: Elsevier, 1987–2003); W. Pasmore, C. Haldeman, and A. Shani, "Sociotechnical Systems: A North American Reflection on Empirical Studies in North America," *Human Relations* 32 (1982): 1179–1204; W. Pasmore and J. Sherwood, *Sociotechnical Systems: A Source Book* (San Diego: University Associates, 1978); J. Porras, *Stream Analysis: A Powerful Way to Diagnose and Manage Organizational Change* (Reading, Mass.: Addison-Wesley, 1987); J. Porras, P. Robertson, and L. Goldman, "Organization Development: Theory, Practice, and Research," in *Handbook of Industrial and Organizational Psychology,* 2d ed., ed. M. Dunnette (Chicago: Rand McNally, 1990); J. Collins and J. Porras, *Built to Last: Successful Habits of Visionary Companies* (New York: Harper Business, 1997).

56. P. Block, *Flawless Consulting* (Austin, Tex.: Learning Concepts, 1981); P. Block, *The Empowered Manager: Positive Political Skills at Work* (San Francisco: Jossey-Bass, 1987); P. Block, *Stewardship* (San Francisco: Berrett-Koehler, 1994); P. Block, *The Answer to How Is Yes* (San Francisco: Berrett-Koehler, 2002).

57. K. Murrell, "Organization Development Experiences and Lessons in the United Nations Development Program," *Organization Development Journal* 12 (1994): 1–16; J. Vogt and K. Murrell, *Empowerment in Organizations* (San Diego: Pfeiffer, 1990); J. Preston and L. DuToit, "Endemic Violence in South Africa: An OD Solution Applied to Two Educational Settings," *International Journal of Public Administration* 16 (1993): 1767–91; J. Preston, L. DuToit, and I. Barber, "A Potential Model of Transformational Change Applied to South Africa," in *Research in Organizational Change and Development,* vol. 9 (Greenwich, Conn.: JAI Press, 1998).

58. S. Mohrman, S. Cohen, and A. Mohrman, *Designing Team-Based Organizations* (San Francisco: Jossey-Bass, 1995); S. Cohen and G. Ledford Jr., "The Effectiveness of Self-Managing Teams: A Quasi-Experiment," *Human Relations* 47 (1994): 13–43; G. Ledford and E. Lawler, "Research on Employee Participation: Beating a Dead Horse?" *Academy of Management Review* 19 (1994): 633–36; G. Ledford, E. Lawler, and S. Mohrman, "The Quality Circle and Its Variations," in *Productivity in Organizations: New Perspectives from Industrial and Organizational Psychology,* eds. J. Campbell, R. Campbell, and Associates (San Francisco: Jossey-Bass, 1988); Mohrman, Ledford, Mohrman, et al., *Large-Scale Organization Change.*

59. D. Cooperrider and T. Thachankary, "Building the Global Civic Culture: Making Our Lives Count," in *Global and International Organization Development,* eds. Sorensen, Head, Mathys, et al., 282–306; D. Cooperrider, "Positive Image, Positive Action: The Affirmative Basis for Organizing," in *Appreciative Management and Leadership,* eds. S. Srivastva, D. Cooperrider, and Associates (San Francisco: Jossey-Bass, 1990); D. Cooperrider and S. Srivastva, "Appreciative Inquiry in Organizational Life," in *Organizational Change and Development,* vol. 1, eds. R. Woodman and W. Pasmore (Greenwich, Conn.: JAI Press, 1987), 129–70.

60. R. Golembiewski, C. Proehl, and D. Sink, "Success of OD Applications in the Public Sector, Toting Up the Score for a Decade, More or Less," *Public Administration Review* 41 (1981): 679–82; R. Golembiewski, *Humanizing Public Organizations* (Mt. Airy, Md.: Lomond, 1985); P. Robertson and S. Seneviratne, "Outcomes of Planned Organization Change in the Public Sector: A Meta-Analytic Comparison to the Private," *Public Administration Review* 55 (1995): 547–61.

61. R. Shmuck and M. Miles, *Organizational Development in Schools* (Palo Alto, Calif.: National Press Books, 1971); R. Havelock, *The Change Agent's Guide to Innovation in Education* (Englewood Cliffs, N.J.: Educational Technology, 1973); R. Schmuck and P. Runkel, "Organization Development in Schools," *Consultation* 4 (Fall 1985): 236–57; S. Mohrman and E. Lawler, "Motivation for School Reform" (working paper, Center for Effective Organizations, University of Southern California, Los Angeles, 1995).

PART 1

Overview of Organization Development

Chapter 2   The Nature of Planned Change

Chapter 3   The Organization Development
Practitioner

2

The Nature of Planned Change

The pace of global, economic, and technological development makes change an inevitable feature of organizational life. However, change that happens to an organization can be distinguished from change that is planned by its members. In this book, the term *change* will refer to planned change. Organization development is directed at bringing about planned change to increase an organization's effectiveness and capability to change itself. It is generally initiated and implemented by managers, often with the help of an OD practitioner from either inside or outside of the organization. Organizations can use planned change to solve problems, to learn from experience, to reframe shared perceptions, to adapt to external environmental changes, to improve performance, and to influence future changes.

All approaches to OD rely on some theory about planned change. The theories describe the different stages through which planned change may be effected in organizations and explain the temporal process of applying OD methods to help organization members manage change. In this chapter, we first describe and compare three major theories of organization change that have received considerable attention in the field: Lewin's change model, the action research model, and the positive model. Next we present a general model of planned change that integrates the earlier models and incorporates recent conceptual advances in OD. The general model has broad applicability to many types of planned change efforts and serves to organize the chapters in this book. We then discuss different types of change and how the process can vary depending on the change situation. Finally, we present several critiques of planned change.

THEORIES OF PLANNED CHANGE

Conceptions of planned change have tended to focus on how change can be implemented in organizations.[1] Called "theories of changing," these frameworks describe the activities that must take place to initiate and carry out successful organizational change. In this section, we describe and compare three theories of changing: Lewin's change model, the action research model, and the positive model. These frameworks have received widespread attention in OD and serve as the primary basis for a general model of planned change.

Lewin's Change Model

One of the early fundamental models of planned change was provided by Kurt Lewin.[2] He conceived of change as modification of those forces keeping a system's behavior stable. Specifically, a particular set of behaviors at any moment in time is the result of two groups of forces: those striving to maintain the status quo and those pushing for change. When both sets of forces are about equal, current behaviors are maintained in what Lewin termed a state of "quasi-stationary equilibrium." To change that state, one can increase those forces pushing for change, decrease those forces maintaining the current state, or apply some combination of both. For example, the level of performance of a work group might be stable because group norms maintaining that level are equivalent to the supervisor's pressures for change to higher levels. This level can be increased either by changing the group norms to support higher levels of performance or by increasing supervisor pressures to produce at higher levels. Lewin suggested that modifying those forces maintaining the status quo produces less tension and resistance than increasing forces for change and consequently is a more effective change strategy.

Lewin viewed this change process as consisting of the following three steps, which are shown in Figure 2.1(A):

1. **Unfreezing.** This step usually involves reducing those forces maintaining the organization's behavior at its present level. Unfreezing is sometimes

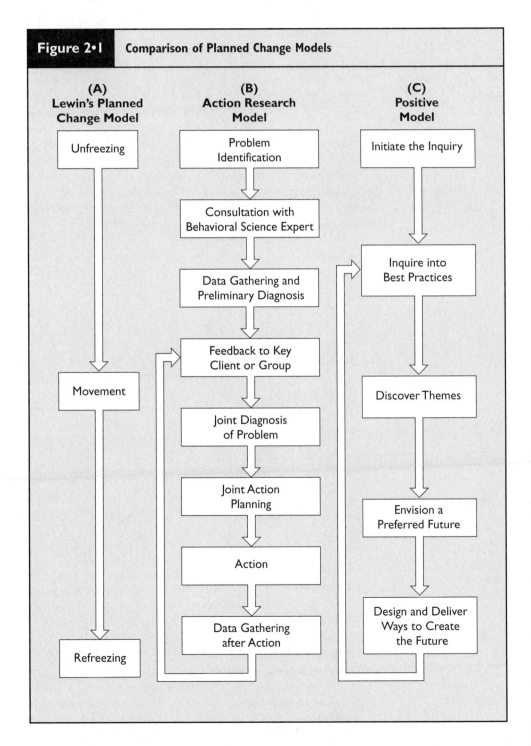

Figure 2•1   Comparison of Planned Change Models

(A) Lewin's Planned Change Model	(B) Action Research Model	(C) Positive Model
Unfreezing	Problem Identification	Initiate the Inquiry
Movement	Consultation with Behavioral Science Expert	Inquire into Best Practices
	Data Gathering and Preliminary Diagnosis	Discover Themes
	Feedback to Key Client or Group	Envision a Preferred Future
	Joint Diagnosis of Problem	Design and Deliver Ways to Create the Future
	Joint Action Planning	
Refreezing	Action	
	Data Gathering after Action	

accomplished through a process of "psychological disconfirmation." By introducing information that shows discrepancies between behaviors desired by organization members and those behaviors currently exhibited, members can be motivated to engage in change activities.[3]

2. **Moving.** This step shifts the behavior of the organization, department, or individual to a new level. It involves intervening in the system to develop new behaviors, values, and attitudes through changes in organizational structures and processes.

3. **Refreezing.** This step stabilizes the organization at a new state of equilibrium. It is frequently accomplished through the use of supporting mechanisms that reinforce the new organizational state, such as organizational culture, norms, policies, and structures.

Lewin's model provides a general framework for understanding organizational change. Because the three steps of change are relatively broad, considerable effort has gone into elaborating them. For example, the planning model developed by Lippitt, Watson, and Westley arranges Lewin's model into seven steps: scouting, entry, diagnosis (unfreezing), planning, action (movement), stabilization and evaluation, and termination (refreezing).[4] Lewin's model remains closely identified with the field of OD, however, and is used to illustrate how other types of change can be implemented. For example, Lewin's three-step model has been used to explain how information technologies can be implemented more effectively.[5]

Action Research Model

The classic action research model focuses on planned change as a cyclical process in which initial research about the organization provides information to guide subsequent action. Then the results of the action are assessed to provide further information to guide further action, and so on. This iterative cycle of research and action involves considerable collaboration among organization members and OD practitioners. It places heavy emphasis on data gathering and diagnosis prior to action planning and implementation, as well as careful evaluation of results after action is taken.

Action research is traditionally aimed both at helping specific organizations implement planned change and at developing more general knowledge that can be applied to other settings.[6] Although action research was originally developed to have this dual focus on change and knowledge generation, it has been adapted to OD efforts in which the major emphasis is on planned change.[7] Figure 2.1(B) shows the cyclical phases of planned change as defined by the original action research model. There are eight main steps.

1. **Problem identification.** This stage usually begins when a key executive in the organization or someone with power and influence senses that the organization has one or more problems that might be solved with the help of an OD practitioner.

2. **Consultation with a behavioral science expert.** During the initial contact, the OD practitioner and the client carefully assess each other. The practitioner has his or her own normative, developmental theory or frame of reference and must be conscious of those assumptions and values.[8] Sharing them with the client from the beginning establishes an open and collaborative atmosphere.

3. **Data gathering and preliminary diagnosis.** This step is usually completed by the OD practitioner, often in conjunction with organization members. It involves gathering appropriate information and analyzing it to determine the underlying causes of organizational problems. The four basic methods of gathering

data are interviews, process observation, questionnaires, and organizational performance data (unfortunately, often overlooked). One approach to diagnosis begins with observation, proceeds to a semistructured interview, and concludes with a questionnaire to measure precisely the problems identified by the earlier steps.[9] When gathering diagnostic information, OD practitioners may influence members from whom they are collecting data. In OD, any action by the OD practitioner can be viewed as an intervention that will have some effect on the organization.[10]

4. **Feedback to a key client or group.** Because action research is a collaborative activity, the diagnostic data are fed back to the client, usually in a group or work-team meeting. The feedback step, in which members are given the information gathered by the OD practitioner, helps them determine the strengths and weaknesses of the organization or unit under study. The consultant provides the client with all relevant and useful data. Obviously, the practitioner will protect confidential sources of information and, at times, may even withhold data. Defining what is relevant and useful involves consideration of privacy and ethics as well as judgment about whether the group is ready for the information or if the information would make the client overly defensive.

5. **Joint diagnosis of the problem.** At this point, members discuss the feedback and explore with the OD practitioner whether they want to work on identified problems. A close interrelationship exists among data gathering, feedback, and diagnosis because the consultant summarizes the basic data from the client members and presents the data to them for validation and further diagnosis. An important point to remember, as Schein suggests, is that the action research process is very different from the doctor–patient model, in which the consultant comes in, makes a diagnosis, and prescribes a solution. Schein notes that the failure to establish a common frame of reference in the client–consultant relationship may lead to a faulty diagnosis or to a communications gap whereby the client is sometimes "unwilling to believe the diagnosis or accept the prescription." He believes "most companies have drawers full of reports by consultants, each loaded with diagnoses and recommendations which are either not understood or not accepted by the 'patient.'"[11]

6. **Joint action planning.** Next, the OD practitioner and the client members jointly agree on further actions to be taken. This is the beginning of the moving process (described in Lewin's change model), as the organization decides how best to reach a different quasistationary equilibrium. At this stage, the specific action to be taken depends on the culture, technology, and environment of the organization; the diagnosis of the problem; and the time and expense of the intervention.

7. **Action.** This stage involves the actual change from one organizational state to another. It may include installing new methods and procedures, reorganizing structures and work designs, and reinforcing new behaviors. Such actions typically cannot be implemented immediately but require a transition period as the organization moves from the present to a desired future state.[12]

8. **Data gathering after action.** Because action research is a cyclical process, data must also be gathered after the action has been taken to measure and determine the effects of the action and to feed the results back to the organization. This, in turn, may lead to rediagnosis and new action.

The action research model underlies most current approaches to planned change and is often considered synonymous with OD. Recently, it has been refined and extended to new settings and applications, and consequently researchers and practitioners have made requisite adaptations of its basic framework.[13]

Trends in the application of action research include movement from smaller sub-units of organizations to total systems and communities.[14] In these larger contexts, action research is more complex and political than in smaller settings. Therefore, the action research cycle is coordinated across multiple change processes and includes a diversity of stakeholders who have an interest in the organization. (We describe these applications more thoroughly in Chapters 19 and 20.) Action research also is applied increasingly in international settings, particularly in developing nations in the southern hemisphere.[15] Embedded within the action research model, however, are "northern-hemisphere" assumptions about change. For example, action research traditionally views change more linearly than do Asian cultures, and it treats the change process more collaboratively than do Latin American and African countries.[16] To achieve success in those settings, action research is tailored to fit cultural assumptions. (See "Different Types of Planned Change" below and Chapter 21.) Finally, action research is applied increasingly to promote social change and innovation,[17] as demonstrated most clearly in community development and global social change projects.[18] Those applications are heavily value laden and seek to redress imbalances in power and resource allocations across different groups. Action researchers tend to play an activist role in the change process, which is often chaotic and conflictual. (Chapter 21 reviews global social change processes.)

In light of these general trends, contemporary applications of action research have substantially increased the degree of member involvement in the change process. This contrasts with traditional approaches to planned change, whereby consultants carried out most of the change activities, with the agreement and collaboration of management.[19] Although consultant-dominated change still persists in OD, there is a growing tendency to involve organization members in learning about their organization and how to change it. Referred to as "participatory action research,"[20] "action learning,"[21] "action science,"[22] or "self-design,"[23] this approach to planned change emphasizes the need for organization members to learn firsthand about planned change if they are to gain the knowledge and skills needed to change the organization. In today's complex and changing environment, some argue that OD must go beyond solving particular problems to helping members gain the competence needed to change and improve the organization continually.[24]

In this modification of action research, the role of OD consultants is to work with members to facilitate the learning process. Both parties are "co-learners" in diagnosing the organization, designing changes, and implementing and assessing them.[25] Neither party dominates the change process. Rather, each participant brings unique information and expertise to the situation, and they combine their resources to learn how to change the organization. Consultants, for example, know how to design diagnostic instruments and OD interventions, and organization members have "local knowledge" about the organization and how it functions. Each participant learns from the change process. Organization members learn how to change their organization and how to refine and improve it. OD consultants learn how to facilitate complex organizational change and learning.

The action research model will continue to be the dominant methodological basis for planned change in the near future. But the basic philosophy of science on which traditional action research operates is also evolving and is described below.

The Positive Model

The third model of change, the positive model, represents a significant departure from Lewin's model and the action research process. Those models are primarily deficit based; they focus on the organization's problems and how they can be solved so it functions better. The positive model focuses on what the organization is doing right. It helps members understand their organization when it is working at its best and builds off of those capabilities to achieve even better results. This positive approach to change is consistent with a growing movement in the social sciences called "positive organizational scholarship," which focuses on positive dynamics in organizations that give rise to extraordinary outcomes.[26] Considerable research on expectation effects also supports this model of planned change.[27] It shows that people tend to act in ways that make their expectations occur. Thus, positive expectations about the organization can create an anticipation that energizes and directs behavior toward making those beliefs happen.

The positive model has been applied to planned change primarily through a process called *appreciative inquiry* (AI).[28] As a "reformist and rebellious" form of social constructionism, AI explicitly infuses a positive value orientation into analyzing and changing organizations.[29] Social constructionism assumes that organization members' shared experiences and interactions influence how they perceive the organization and behave in it.[30] Because such shared meaning can determine how members approach planned change, AI encourages a positive orientation to how change is conceived and managed. It promotes broad member involvement in creating a shared vision about the organization's positive potential. That shared appreciation provides a powerful and guiding image of what the organization could be.

Drawing heavily on appreciative inquiry, the positive model of planned change involves five phases that are depicted in Figure 2.1(C).

1. **Initiate the Inquiry.** This first phase determines the subject of change. It emphasizes member involvement to identify the organizational issue they have the most energy to address. For example, members can choose to look for successful male–female collaboration (as opposed to sexual discrimination), instances of customer satisfaction (as opposed to customer dissatisfaction), particularly effective work teams, or product development processes that brought new ideas to market especially fast. If the focus of inquiry is real and vital to organization members, the change process itself will take on these positive attributes.

2. **Inquire into Best Practices.** This phase involves gathering information about the "best of what is" in the organization. If the topic is organizational innovation, then members help to develop an interview protocol that collects stories of new ideas that were developed and implemented in the organization. The interviews are conducted by organization members; they interview each other and tell stories of innovation in which they have personally been involved. These stories are pulled together to create a pool of information describing the organization as an innovative system.

3. **Discover the Themes.** In this third phase, members examine the stories, both large and small, to identify a set of themes representing the common dimensions of people's experiences. For example, the stories of innovation may contain themes about how managers gave people the freedom to explore a new idea, the support organization members received from their co-workers, or how the exposure to customers sparked creative thinking. No theme is too small to be represented; it is important that all of the underlying mechanisms that helped to generate and support the themes be described. The themes represent the basis for moving from "what is" to "what could be."

4. **Envision a Preferred Future.** Members then examine the identified themes, challenge the status quo, and describe a compelling future. Based on the organization's successful past, members collectively visualize the organization's future and develop "possibility propositions"—statements that bridge the organization's current best practices with ideal possibilities for future organizing.[31]

These propositions should present a truly exciting, provocative, and possible picture of the future. Based on these possibilities, members identify the relevant stakeholders and critical organization processes that must be aligned to support the emergence of the envisioned future. The vision becomes a statement of "what should be."

5. **Design and Deliver.** The final phase involves the design and delivery of ways to create the future. It describes the activities and creates the plans necessary to bring about the vision. It proceeds to action and assessment phases similar to those of action research described previously. Members make changes, assess the results, make necessary adjustments, and so on as they move the organization toward the vision and sustain "what will be." The process is continued by renewing the conversations about the best of what is.

Comparisons of Change Models

All three models—Lewin's change model, the action research model, and the positive model—describe the phases by which planned change occurs in organizations. As shown in Figure 2.1, the models overlap in that their emphasis on action to implement organizational change is preceded by a preliminary stage (unfreezing, diagnosis, or initiate the inquiry) and is followed by a closing stage (refreezing or evaluation). Moreover, all three approaches emphasize the application of behavioral science knowledge, involve organization members in the change process to varying degrees, and recognize that any interaction between a consultant and an organization constitutes an intervention that may affect the organization. However, Lewin's change model differs from the other two in that it focuses on the general process of planned change, rather than on specific OD activities.

Lewin's model and the action research model differ from the positive approach in terms of the level of involvement of the participants and the focus of change. Lewin's model and traditional action research emphasize the role of the consultant with relatively limited member involvement in the change process. Contemporary applications of action research and the positive model, on the other hand, treat both consultants and participants as co-learners who are heavily involved in planned change. In addition, Lewin's model and action research are more concerned with fixing problems than with focusing on what the organization does well and leveraging those strengths.

GENERAL MODEL OF PLANNED CHANGE

The three models of planned change suggest a general framework for planned change as shown in Figure 2.2. The framework describes the four basic activities that practitioners and organization members jointly carry out in organization development. The arrows connecting the different activities in the model show the typical sequence of events, from entering and contracting, to diagnosing, to planning and implementing change, to evaluating and institutionalizing change. The lines connecting the activities emphasize that organizational change is not a straightforward, linear process but involves considerable overlap and feedback among the activities. Because the model serves to organize the remaining parts of this book, Figure 2.2 also shows which specific chapters apply to the four major change activities.

Entering and Contracting

The first set of activities in planned change concerns entering and contracting (described in Chapter 4). Those events help managers decide whether they want to engage further in a planned change program and to commit resources to such a

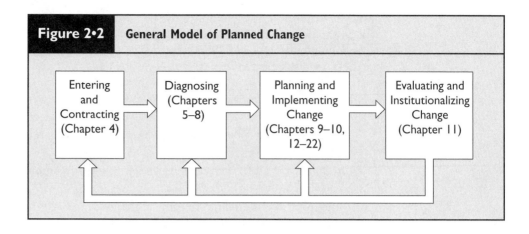

Figure 2•2   General Model of Planned Change

Entering and Contracting (Chapter 4) → Diagnosing (Chapters 5–8) → Planning and Implementing Change (Chapters 9–10, 12–22) → Evaluating and Institutionalizing Change (Chapter 11)

process. Entering an organization involves gathering initial data to understand the problems facing the organization or to determine the positive areas for inquiry. Once this information is collected, the problems or opportunities are discussed with managers and other organization members to develop a contract or agreement to engage in planned change. The contract spells out future change activities, the resources that will be committed to the process, and how OD practitioners and organization members will be involved. In many cases, organizations do not get beyond this early stage of planned change because one or more situations arise: Disagreements about the need for change surface, resource constraints are encountered, or other methods for change appear more feasible. When OD is used in nontraditional and international settings, the entering and contracting process must be sensitive to the context in which the change is taking place.

Diagnosing

In this stage of planned change, the client system is carefully studied. Diagnosis can focus on understanding organizational problems, including their causes and consequences, or on collecting stories about the organization's positive attributes. The diagnostic process is one of the most important activities in OD. It includes choosing an appropriate model for understanding the organization and gathering, analyzing, and feeding back information to managers and organization members about the problems or opportunities that exist.

Diagnostic models for analyzing problems (described in Chapters 5 and 6) explore three levels of activities. Organization issues represent the most complex level of analysis and involve the total system. Group-level issues are associated with department and group effectiveness. Individual-level issues involve the way jobs are designed and performed.

Gathering, analyzing, and feeding back data are the central change activities in diagnosis. Chapter 7 describes how data can be gathered through interviews, observations, survey instruments, or such archival sources as meeting minutes and organization charts. It also explains how data can be reviewed and analyzed. In Chapter 8, we describe the process of feeding back diagnostic data. Organization members, often in collaboration with an OD practitioner, jointly discuss the data and their implications for change.

Planning and Implementing Change

In this stage, organization members and practitioners jointly plan and implement OD interventions. They design interventions to achieve the organization's vision or goals and make action plans to implement them. There are several criteria for designing interventions, including the organization's readiness for change, its current change capability, its culture and power distributions, and the change agent's skills and abilities (discussed in Chapter 9). Depending on the outcomes of diagnosis, there are four major types of interventions in OD:

1. Human process interventions at the individual, group, and total system levels (Chapters 12 and 13)
2. Interventions that modify an organization's structure and technology (Chapters 14, 15, and 16)
3. Human resource interventions that seek to improve member performance and wellness (Chapters 17 and 18)
4. Strategic interventions that involve managing the organization's relationship to its external environment and the internal structure and process necessary to support a business strategy (Chapters 19 and 20).

Chapters 21 and 22 present specialized information for carrying out OD in international settings and in such nontraditional organizations as schools, health care institutions, family-owned businesses, and the public sector.

Implementing interventions is concerned with leading and managing the change process. As discussed in Chapter 10, it includes motivating change, creating a desired future vision of the organization, developing political support, managing the transition toward the vision, and sustaining momentum for change.

Evaluating and Institutionalizing Change

The final stage in planned change involves evaluating the effects of the intervention and managing the institutionalization of successful change programs so they persist. (Those two activities are described in Chapter 11.) Feedback to organization members about the intervention's results provides information about whether the changes should be continued, modified, or suspended. Institutionalizing successful changes involves reinforcing them through feedback, rewards, and training.

Application 2.1 describes the initiation of a planned change process in a government organization. It provides especially rich detail on the planning and implementing phase of change, and on how people can be involved in the process.[32]

DIFFERENT TYPES OF PLANNED CHANGE

The general model of planned change describes how the OD process typically unfolds in organizations. In actual practice, the different phases are not nearly as orderly as the model implies. OD practitioners tend to modify or adjust the stages to fit the needs of the situation. Steps in planned change may be implemented in a variety of ways, depending on the client's needs and goals, the change agent's skills and values, and the organization's context. Thus, planned change can vary enormously from one situation to another.

To understand the differences better, planned change can be contrasted across situations on three key dimensions: the magnitude of organizational change, the degree to which the client system is organized, and whether the setting is domestic or international.

Magnitude of Change

Planned change efforts can be characterized as falling along a continuum ranging from incremental changes that involve fine-tuning the organization to quantum changes that entail fundamentally altering how it operates.[33] Incremental changes tend to involve limited dimensions and levels of the organization, such as the

PLANNED CHANGE AT THE SAN DIEGO COUNTY REGIONAL AIRPORT AUTHORITY

APPLICATION 2•1

The San Diego County Regional Airport Authority (SD-CRAA) was created by a California state law in October 2001; this gave it the responsibility to establish and operate airports within San Diego County. Most importantly, from Thella Bowens's perspective, the law required the San Diego Unified Port District (Port of San Diego) to transfer operation of San Diego's international airport to the SDCRAA by January 2003. Bowens was the current senior director of the Aviation Division within the Port of San Diego that was responsible for operating the San Diego International Airport. When the law was passed, she was named Interim Executive Director of the SDCRAA, and assigned an interim advisory board to help manage the transition.

Bowens's tenure with the organization gave her an important understanding of the organization's operations and its history. For example, the San Diego International Airport accounted for about $4.3 billion or roughly 4% of San Diego's regional economy. Forecasts called for air travel to more than double to 35 million passengers by 2030, and contribute up to $8 billion to the regional economy. In addition, Bowens had participated in the Aviation Division's strategic planning process in 2001. She was well positioned to lead this effort.

As she thought about managing the start-up of the SDCRAA, two broad but interdependent categories of initial activity emerged: developing the transition plan and managing the legal and regulatory issues.

Developing the Transition Plan

In April 2002, Bowens took the senior team from the old Aviation Division to an off-site workshop to discuss the creation and management of an effective transition process. This group understood the importance of SDCRAA quickly becoming a stand-alone agency and the need to be seen differently in the marketplace. The group recommended revising the existing strategic plan, to hire staff to research, discuss, and create a transition plan, and to conduct retreats with employees from multiple organizational levels. In response, Bowens chartered the Airport Transition Team to ensure the smooth and seamless transfer of operations and public services provided by the airport without regard to which agency was responsible for their provision.

In May 2002, seven employees were handpicked from the Aviation Division to become members of the Airport Transition Team and relieved of their day-to-day job responsibilities so they could focus on the transition. The selection criteria included the ability to work within a process yet think outside of the box, to communicate well with others in a team, and to influence directors and managers without having formal authority. A one-and-a-half-day kick-off meeting was held

to set expectations, to communicate goals and responsibilities, and to initiate the team. A "war room" was established for the team to keep records, hold meetings, and serve as a communication hub. The team named themselves the "Metamorphs."

Many Metamorph members came from different parts of the organization and, having never worked together, needed to rely on each other to effectively design the transition process. Senior team member Angela Shafer-Payne, then director of airport business and administration, worked closely with the Metamorphs and led formal team-building activities throughout the year. Through their work together, the Metamorphs discovered how large and daunting the organizational change was and yet appreciated the unique, once-in-a-lifetime opportunity to make an impact. As one member put it, "How many times in your life can you say that you helped put together a brand-new organization?"

The Metamorphs decided that to meet their charter, any transition plan had to be designed specifically to minimize disruption to customers and service, minimize airport and non-airport financial impacts, and properly address and resolve all legal and regulatory matters. These criteria guided the creation of 12 functional teams (which expanded later to 19). Responsibility for the teams was divided among the transition team members, and each team was composed of employees from the old Aviation Division and other Port of San Diego departments. Their mission was to collect data, establish new or parallel functions for the SDCRAA, and highlight any issues related to the start-up of that particular function. Once the teams were in place, they were given tools to use and questions that needed to be addressed. Each team set aside time to review all of the records in each functional area. For example, the human resources functional team consisted of Aviation Division employees, HR professionals from the Port of San Diego, and Port attorneys; it was charged with developing the actual transition mechanism, HR operations, and HR organizational structure. Another team focused on the environmental issues involved in the transition. They examined over 100 different environmental permits held by the Port of San Diego to understand if SDCRAA needed a similar permit, needed to be a co-permittee with the Port of San Diego, or if the SDCRAA could stand alone. If it were a stand-alone situation, then documentation was prepared to transfer the permit.

To ensure that no issues fell through the cracks, three distinct peer reviews were held in the summer and fall of 2002. The peer review panels were staffed by professionals within the aviation industry, people who had experienced a transition of some type within an organization, or those who were integral to the start-up of the organization. The first peer review panel examined the transition plan and offered advice on whether to add any other critical and/or missing components. The second peer review panel, consisting of mostly human resource professionals, examined the proposed organizational structure. The final peer review panel focused on the IT systems portion of the transition plan because of technology's critical role in the overall success of many of the internal processes.

Dealing with the Legal and Regulatory Issues

By January 2002, the SDCRAA was not yet a full agency and had only one employee, Thella Bowens. Despite all the work of the Metamorphs and the functional teams, and sometimes because of it, Bowens also had to interface with the California legislature. The original legislation (California Senate Bill AB93 [2001–2002]) provided a framework for setting up the new agency but left many unanswered questions, including issues relating to property transfer (SDCRAA would lease land from the Port on a 66-year lease) and the transitioning of employees from one public agency to another. To provide clarity and another layer of understanding, "clean-up" legislation (SB 1896) was passed in mid-2002. Together with the original bill, the legislation protected employees to ensure no loss of jobs or benefits. This gave the Metamorphs additional information and guidance to deal with employee contract issues. For example, in the middle of the transition planning process, the Port District had to renegotiate its union contract. The Metamorphs had to work closely with the airport's external counsel, the Port of San Diego counsel, and state senators to ensure a smooth negotiation.

Finally, Bowens and the Metamorphs had to address changes to federal security regulations outlined in the Aviation & Transportation Security Act that resulted from the September 11, 2001, attacks. Those events caused a number of disruptions for many stakeholders in the air transportation industry. They required the transition plan to include a component that focused on keeping costs contained to enable aviation partners, the airlines, the gate gourmets, and tenants, to weather the storm.

Implementation and Evaluation

The final transition plan was presented to the interim board and then to the Board of Port Commissioners for approval in October 2002. The approved plan was comprised of several components, including an IT conversion plan and the process for formally transferring responsibility to the SDCRAA, but the key elements were human resource and communication plans.

The human resource plan specified the transition of 145 budgeted Aviation Division employees to 52 vacancies plus the 90 other positions identified by the Metamorphs to make the organization whole. The plan called for all of the posi-

tions to be filled by mid-2005. The human resources plan also provided for the purchase of services, like the Harbor Police, from the Port of San Diego until mid-2005.

The communication plan was critical to the implementation phase. The Metamorphs regularly carried information about their progress to co-workers in their respective departments. In addition, communication meetings with the entire organization, called "all hands meetings," were held to provide information about the transition. The Airport Transition Plan contained a special emphasis on the needs of the employee. Bowens understood the sociotechnical nature of change and did not want the human factor to be forgotten in the midst of all the legal, technical, and other transitions. She included a number of change management education sessions for all employees. The change management education sessions were developed to reassure employees; to encourage genuine, candid, frequent, high-quality communications; and to neutralize anxiety and fears.

During the sessions, employees were: (1) updated on the progress of the transition, (2) introduced to change theories, models, and concepts, and (3) encouraged to share their issues, fears, anxieties, concerns, and creative ideas. Employee input was organized into themes, then documented and communicated to Bowens and her direct reports. The leadership team was committed to answering questions and addressing concerns that emerged from the change management sessions. Airport managers met regularly to select and answer questions for publication in the organization newsletter or live communication at "all hands meetings." In addition, the employee satisfaction survey was updated with questions to learn about transition concerns.

Thella Bowens was named President and CEO of the SDCRAA on January 1, 2003. By June 2003, the SDCRAA had received awards based on superb customer service and outstanding levels of performance. The SDCRAA, based on all available metrics, is successfully operating San Diego's international airport and serving over 15.2 million passengers on 620 daily flights in and out of the airport. Part of the success is due to the way the transition plan was developed. Because of the broad participation in its creation, many employees understood the plan. When issues arose, identifying the personnel to become part of an ad hoc problem-solving group already familiar with the topic was easy.

"Ms. Bowens accomplished the extraordinary job of leading a successful transition of the airport from the Unified Port of San Diego to the Authority," said Joseph W. Craver, Authority (SDCRAA) Chairman; "She is highly regarded and respected for both her breadth of knowledge of aviation management issues and her visionary leadership." Thella Bowens added, "Fortunately, we've been supported by very dedicated professional employees who have exhibited great resolve and sheer hard work through the transition process, and continue to do so as we create a 'world-class' organization."

decision-making processes of work groups. They occur within the context of the organization's existing business strategy, structure, and culture and are aimed at improving the status quo. Quantum changes, on the other hand, are directed at significantly altering how the organization operates. They tend to involve several organizational dimensions, including structure, culture, reward systems, information processes, and work design. They also involve changing multiple levels of the organization, from top-level management through departments and work groups to individual jobs.

Planned change traditionally has been applied in situations involving incremental change. Organizations in the 1960s and 1970s were concerned mainly with fine-tuning their bureaucratic structures by resolving many of the social problems that emerged with increasing size and complexity. In those situations, planned change involves a relatively bounded set of problem-solving activities. OD practitioners are typically contracted by managers to help solve specific problems in particular organizational systems, such as poor communication among members of a work team or low customer satisfaction scores in a department store. Diagnostic and change activities tend to be limited to the defined issues, although additional problems may be uncovered and may need to be addressed. Similarly, the change process tends to focus on those organizational systems having specific problems, and it generally terminates when the problems are resolved. Of course, the change agent may contract to help solve additional problems.

In recent years, OD has been increasingly concerned with quantum change. As described in Chapter 1, the greater competitiveness and uncertainty of today's environment have led a growing number of organizations to alter drastically the way in which they operate. In such situations, planned change is more complex, extensive, and long term than when applied to incremental change.[34] Because quantum change involves most features and levels of the organization, it is typically driven from the top, where corporate strategy and values are set. Change agents help senior executives create a vision of a desired future organization and energize movement in that direction. They also help them develop structures for managing the transition from the present to the future organization and may include, for example, a variety of overlapping steering committees and redesign teams. Staff experts also may redesign many features of the firm, such as performance measures, rewards, planning processes, work designs, and information systems.

Because of the complexity and extensiveness of quantum change, OD professionals often work in teams comprising members with different yet complementary areas of expertise. The consulting relationship persists over relatively long time periods and includes a great deal of renegotiation and experimentation among consultants and managers. The boundaries of the change effort are more uncertain and diffuse than those in incremental change, thus making diagnosis and change seem more like discovery than like problem solving. (We describe complex strategic and transformational types of change in more detail in Chapters 19 and 20.)

It is important to emphasize that quantum change may or may not be developmental in nature. Organizations may drastically alter their strategic direction and way of operating without significantly developing their capacity to solve problems and to achieve both high performance and quality of work life. For example, firms may simply change their marketing mix, dropping or adding products, services, or customers; they may drastically downsize by cutting out marginal businesses and laying off managers and workers; or they may tighten managerial and financial controls and attempt to squeeze more out of the labor force. On the other hand, organizations may undertake quantum change from a developmental perspective. They may seek to make themselves more competitive by developing their human resources; by getting managers and employees more involved in problem solving and innovation; and by promoting flexibility and direct, open communication. The OD approach to quantum change is particularly relevant in today's rapidly changing and competitive environment. To succeed in this setting, firms such as General Electric, Kimberly-Clark, ABB, Hewlett-Packard, and Motorola are transforming themselves from control-oriented bureaucracies to high-involvement organizations capable of changing and improving themselves continually.

Degree of Organization

Planned change efforts also can vary depending on the degree to which the organization or client system is organized. In overorganized situations, such as in highly mechanistic, bureaucratic organizations, various dimensions such as leadership styles, job designs, organization structure, and policies and procedures are too rigid and overly defined for effective task performance. Communication between management and employees is typically suppressed, conflicts are avoided, and employees are apathetic. In underorganized organizations, on the other hand, there is too little constraint or regulation for effective task performance. Leadership, structure, job design, and policy are poorly defined and fail to direct task behaviors effectively. Communication is fragmented, job responsibilities are ambiguous, and employees' energies are dissipated because they lack direction. Underorganized situations are typically found in such areas as product development, project management, and community development, where relationships among diverse groups and participants must be coordinated around complex, uncertain tasks.

In overorganized situations, where much of OD practice has historically taken place, planned change is generally aimed at loosening constraints on behavior. Changes in leadership, job design, structure, and other features are designed to liberate suppressed energy, to increase the flow of relevant information between employees and managers, and to promote effective conflict resolution. The typical steps of planned change—entry, diagnosis, intervention, and evaluation—are intended to penetrate a relatively closed organization or department and make it increasingly open to self-diagnosis and revitalization. The relationship between the OD practitioner and the management team attempts to model this loosening process. The consultant shares leadership of the change process with management, encourages open communications and confrontation of conflict, and maintains flexibility in relating to the organization.

When applied to organizations facing problems in being underorganized, planned change is aimed at increasing organization by clarifying leadership roles, structuring communication between managers and employees, and specifying job and departmental responsibilities. These activities require a modification of the traditional phases of planned change and include the following four steps:[35]

1. **Identification.** This step identifies the relevant people or groups who need to be involved in the change program. In many underorganized situations, people and departments can be so disconnected that there is ambiguity about who should be included in the problem-solving process. For example, when managers of different departments have only limited interaction with each other, they may disagree or be confused about which departments should be involved in developing a new product or service.

2. **Convention.** In this step, the relevant people or departments in the company are brought together to begin organizing for task performance. For example, department managers might be asked to attend a series of organizing meetings to discuss the division of labor and the coordination required to introduce a new product.

3. **Organization.** Different organizing mechanisms are created to structure the newly required interactions among people and departments. This might include

creating new leadership positions, establishing communication channels, and specifying appropriate plans and policies.

4. **Evaluation.** In this final step, the outcomes of the organization step are assessed. The evaluation might signal the need for adjustments in the organizing process or for further identification, convention, and organization activities.

In carrying out these four steps of planned change in underorganized situations, the relationship between the OD practitioner and the client system attempts to reinforce the organizing process. The consultant develops a well-defined leadership role, which might be autocratic during the early stages of the change program. Similarly, the consulting relationship is clearly defined and tightly specified. In effect, the interaction between the consultant and the client system supports the larger process of bringing order to the situation.

Application 2.2 is an example of planned change in an underorganized situation. In this case, the change agent is a person from industry who identifies a multifaceted problem: University research that should be helpful to manufacturing organizations is not being shaped, coordinated, or transferred. In response, he forms an organization to tighten up the relationships between the two parties.[36]

Domestic vs. International Settings

Planned change efforts have traditionally been applied in North American and European settings, but they are increasingly used outside of these cultures. Developed in Western societies, OD reflects the underlying values and assumptions of these cultural settings, including equality, involvement, and short-term time horizons. Under these conditions, it works quite well. In other societies, a different set of cultural values and assumptions can be operating and make the application of OD problematic. In contrast to Western societies, for example, the cultures of most Asian countries are more hierarchical and status conscious, less open to discussing personal issues, more concerned with "saving face," and have a longer time horizon for results. These cultural differences can make OD more difficult to implement, especially for North American or European practitioners; they may simply be unaware of the cultural norms and values that permeate the society.

The cultural values that guide OD practice in the United States, for example, include a tolerance for ambiguity, equality among people, individuality, and achievement motives. An OD process that encourages openness among individuals, high levels of participation, and actions that promote increased effectiveness are viewed favorably. The OD practitioner is also assumed to hold these values and to model them in the conduct of planned change. Most reported cases of OD involve Western-based organizations using practitioners trained in the traditional model and raised and experienced in Western society.

When OD is applied outside of North America or Europe (and sometimes even within these settings), the action research process must be adapted to fit the cultural context. For example, the diagnostic phase, which is aimed at understanding the current drivers of organization effectiveness, can be modified in a variety of ways. Diagnosis can involve many organization members or include only senior executives; be directed from the top, conducted by an outside consultant, or performed by internal consultants; or involve face-to-face interviews or organizational documents. Each step in the general model of planned change must be carefully mapped against the cultural context.

Conducting OD in international settings can be highly stressful on OD practitioners. To be successful, they must develop a keen awareness of their own cultural biases, be open to seeing a variety of issues from another perspective, be fluent in the values and assumptions of the host country, and understand the economic and

APPLICATION 2•2

PLANNED CHANGE IN AN UNDERORGANIZED SYSTEM

The Institute for Manufacturing and Automation Research (IMAR) was founded in 1987 in Los Angeles by a group of manufacturing industry members. In its earliest stages of development, one person who had a clear picture of the obstacles to manufacturing excellence was Dale Hartman, IMAR's executive director and former director for manufacturing at Hughes Aircraft Company. He and several other industry associates pinpointed the predominant reasons for flagging competitiveness: needless duplication of effort among manufacturing innovators; difficulties in transferring technological breakthroughs from university to industry; frequent irrelevance of university research to the needs of industry; and the inability of individual industry members to commit the time and funds to research projects needed for continued technological advances.

Hartman and his colleagues determined that organizations should create a pool of funds for research and concluded that the research would most efficiently be carried out in existing university facilities. They worked through at least several plans before they arrived at the idea of the IMAR consortium. The U.S. Navy had been interested in joint efforts for innovations in artificial intelligence, but its constraints and interests were judged to be too narrow to address the problems that Hartman and the others identified.

Networking with other industry members—TRW, Hughes, Northrop, and Rockwell—and two universities with which Hughes had been engaging in ongoing research—the University of Southern California (USC) and University of California, Los Angeles (UCLA)—this original group formed a steering committee to investigate the viability of a joint research and development consortium. Each of the six early planners contributed $5,000 as seed money for basic expenses. The steering committee, based on experience in cooperative research, determined that a full-time person was needed to assume leadership of the consortium. Members of the committee persuaded Dale Hartman to retire early from Hughes and take on IMAR's leadership full time. Hartman brought with him a wealth of knowledge about barriers to innovation and technology transfer, and a solid reputation in both industry and academia that was crucial for the success of multiple-sector partnerships. As a former Hughes networker, he knew how to lobby state and federal government sources for funds and legislation that promoted industry innovation. He also knew a host of talented people in southern California whom he would persuade to become IMAR members.

In his 30 years in manufacturing, Hartman found that university-driven research had not produced a respectable yield of usable information. University research was frequently irrelevant to industry needs and seldom provided for transfer of usable innovation to the plant floor. Industry was only tangentially involved in what the university was doing and Hartman saw little opportunity for the two sectors to benefit from a partnership. Therefore, it was determined that IMAR would be user-driven. Industry would set the agenda by choosing projects from among university proposals that promised to be of generic use to industry members, and it would benefit by influencing the direction of research and receiving early information about research results.

In the next several months, the steering committee and Hartman met regularly to define common research needs and locate funding sources. They sought industry sponsors from high-technology companies with an understanding of the problems in manufacturing research and a desire to do more than merely supply money. They wanted members who would be willing to get involved in IMAR's programs. Furthermore, they wanted all members to be able to use the results of IMAR's generic research while not competing directly with each other. Finally, they decided that they wanted a relatively small membership. If the membership grew too large, it might become unwieldy and thus obstruct efforts to get things done.

IMAR's industrial advisory board was formed with six industrial organizations represented—Xerox, Hughes, TRW, Northrup, IBM, and Rockwell—in addition to USC and UCLA. Members were to pay $100,000 each and make a 3-year commitment to IMAR. With initial objectives in place and a committed membership, Hartman was already searching for additional funding sources. He was successful in getting a bill introduced in California's state legislature, later signed by the governor, that authorized the state department of commerce to fund IMAR $200,000. Moreover, IMAR was able to tie into the Industry–University Cooperative Research Center Program (IUCRCP) of the National Science Foundation (NSF) by forming an industry–university consortium called the Center for Manufacturing and Automation Research (CMAR). NSF funded CMAR with a $2 million grant and a 5-year commitment. NSF funding in particular was sought because of the instant credibility that NSF sponsorship gives to such an institute.

NSF requested that several more universities be added to the consortium. In addition, an NSF evaluator was to be present at all IMAR meetings and conduct ongoing evaluation of CMAR's progress. IMAR already had UCLA and USC among its members and now added four university affiliates to work on research projects: the University of California, Irvine; University of California, Santa Barbara; Caltech; and Arizona State University. The IMAR steering committee then voted to fund research projects at an affiliated university only if it involved cooperation with either USC or UCLA. Each of the four university affiliates was paired with either USC or UCLA. Each affiliate university was selected because it provided expertise in an area of interest to IMAR's industrial membership. Arizona State, for example, had expertise in knowledge-based simulation systems in industrial engineering, a field of special concern to IMAR's membership. IMAR funded a number of projects, including projects between the affiliated universities, between joint investigators at USC and UCLA, and independent projects at USC and UCLA. Figure 2.3 shows IMAR's structure.

CMAR operated under the auspices of IMAR with the same board of directors serving both consortia. There are two co-directors of CMAR: Dr. George Bekey, chairman of the Computer Science Department at USC, and Dr. Michel Melkanoff, director of UCLA's Center for Integrated Manufacturing. As co-directors they had an indirect reporting relationship to Dale Hartman. Their responsibilities included distributing the research funds and serving as the focal point on their respective campuses. Questions from project team members are directed to one or the other co-director,

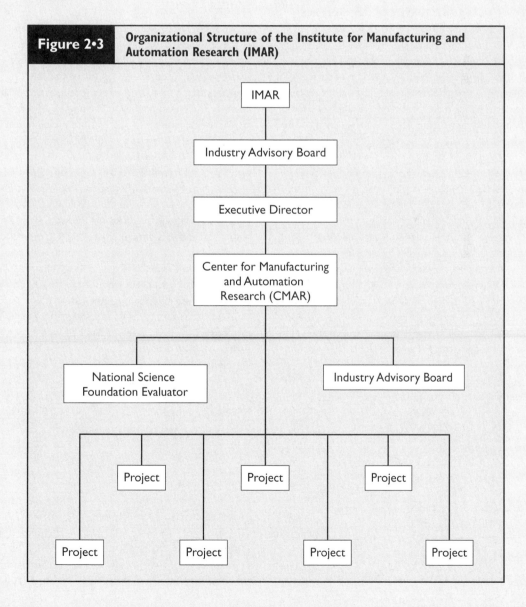

Figure 2•3 **Organizational Structure of the Institute for Manufacturing and Automation Research (IMAR)**

depending on the project. Each of the co-directors takes responsibility for managing project team members and providing rewards, such as reduced course loads, to research professors wherever possible.

The co-directors further work to encourage informal ties with industry members. For example, Dr. Bekey initiated efforts to have IMAR representatives regularly visit others' facilities to encourage them to cooperate and share ideas. That practice further deepens each industrial member's commitment to IMAR because the representatives were associating with one another and other colleagues in the workplace. In the event that an industry or university representative left, an associate was more likely to be there to take his or her place. Further, Bekey noted that the association between industry and university helped industry to overcome its short-term orientation and helped university people appreciate applied problems and manufacturing needs.

IMAR's board of directors set the research agenda at annual reviews in which it made recommendations for topics to be funded. IMAR took these recommendations and translated them into "requests for proposals" that were circulated among the participating university members. CMAR's co-directors then solicited proposals from the university membership. Researchers' proposals were evaluated and ranked by industry representatives and then passed back to the industry advisory board, which made final determinations on which projects would be funded.

Not only did IMAR engage in research projects such as microelectronics, digital computers, lasers, and fiber optics; it worked to resolve critical problems for manufacturing innovation research. One area of study was technology transfer. IMAR established a pilot production facility that Hartman called "a halfway house for manufacturing." The facility permitted basic research to be brought to maturity and was capable of producing deliverable parts. The facility also engaged in systems-level research in such areas as management and systems software, and provided an excellent training ground for students.

Another strength of IMAR was its affiliation with an NSF evaluator who was appointed to follow the progress of the industry–university cooperative research center. Dr. Ann Marczak was IMAR's initial NSF evaluator. NSF conducted regular audits of the 39 IUCRCPs it sponsored and made information available about survey results, others' reports of what works, and so forth. Dr. Marczak served a valuable function to IMAR as an objective source of feedback. After her first evaluation, for example, Marczak recommended that a project team be formed to conduct ongoing progress assessment for each of the research projects IMAR sponsored. The evaluator's findings also served as NSF's means of determining how well each of the funded centers was performing. A center was judged successful if after 5 years it could exist without NSF funds. NSF also evaluated each center in terms of how much industry money its projects generated, how much additional money the center generated in research projects, the number of patents granted, products produced, and the satisfaction of faculty and industry participants.

After two years of operation, IMAR had dealt with many of the problems that so frequently plague collaborative research and development efforts among organizations. It had a well-defined purpose that was strongly supported by its members. It was well structured and had a good balance of resources and needs among its membership. Formal and informal communication networks were established. It had strong leadership. Members of IMAR respected Hartman for his technological expertise and skills as a networker. Hartman had a strong sense of IMAR's mission. After a discussion with him, one got the sense that there was not an obstacle he would not overcome. His vision continued to inspire commitment among the IMAR membership. As one member put it, "You end up wanting to see what you can do for the cause."

Not only did IMAR have the commitment of a full-time leader and strong feedback from its NSF evaluator, it involved user-driven research. Although the research was basic, it was chosen by the users themselves to benefit all members of the consortium. If the research had been applied, it would have been more difficult for members to find projects yielding information that all of them could use. The involvement of multiple universities further provided the talent of top researchers in diverse areas of technological expertise. Finally, NSF was furnishing a large proportion of the funding for the first 5 years as well as regular evaluations.

political context of business in the host country. Most OD practitioners are not able to meet all of those criteria and partner with a "cultural guide," often a member of the client organization, to help navigate the cultural, operational, and political nuances of change in that society.

CRITIQUE OF PLANNED CHANGE

Despite their continued refinement, the models and practice of planned change are still in a formative stage of development, and there is considerable room for improvement. Critics of OD have pointed out several problems with the way planned change has been conceptualized and practiced.

Conceptualization of Planned Change

Planned change has typically been characterized as involving a series of activities for carrying out effective organization development. Although current models outline a general set of steps to be followed, considerably more information is needed to guide how those steps should be performed in specific situations. In an extensive review and critique of planned change theory, Porras and Robertson argued that planned change activities should be guided by information about (1) the organizational features that can be changed, (2) the intended outcomes from making those changes, (3) the causal mechanisms by which those outcomes are achieved, and (4) the contingencies upon which successful change depends.[37] In particular, they noted that the key to organizational change is change in the behavior of each member and that the information available about the causal mechanisms that produce individual change is lacking. Overall, Porras and Robertson concluded that the necessary information to guide change is only partially available and that a good deal more research and thinking are needed to fill the gaps. Chapters 12 through 20 on OD interventions review what is currently known about change features, outcomes, causal mechanisms, and contingencies.

A related area where current thinking about planned change is deficient is knowledge about how the stages of planned change differ across situations. Most models specify a general set of steps that are intended to be applicable to most change efforts. However, the previous section of this chapter showed how change activities can vary depending on such factors as the magnitude of change, the degree to which the client system is organized, and whether change is being conducted in a domestic or an international setting. Considerably more effort needs to be expended identifying situational factors that may require modifying the general stages of planned change. That would likely lead to a rich array of planned change models, each geared to a specific set of situational conditions. Such contingency thinking is greatly needed in planned change.

Planned change also tends to be described as a rationally controlled, orderly process. Critics have argued that although this view may be comforting, it is seriously misleading.[38] They point out that planned change has a more chaotic quality, often involving shifting goals, discontinuous activities, surprising events, and unexpected combinations of changes. For example, executives often initiate changes without plans that clarify their strategies and goals. As change unfolds, new stakeholders may emerge and demand modifications reflecting previously unknown or unvoiced needs. Those emergent conditions make planned change a far more disorderly and dynamic process than is customarily portrayed, and conceptions need to capture that reality.

Finally, the relationship between planned change and organizational performance and effectiveness is not well understood. OD traditionally has had problems assessing whether interventions are producing observed results. The complexity of the change situation, the lack of sophisticated analyses, and the long time periods for producing results have contributed to weak evaluation of OD efforts. Moreover, managers have often accounted for OD efforts with post hoc testimonials, reports of possible future benefits, and calls to support OD as the right thing to do. In the absence of rigorous assessment and measurement, it is difficult to make resource allocation decisions about change programs and to know which interventions are most effective in certain situations.

Practice of Planned Change

Critics have suggested several problems with the way planned change is carried out.[39] Their concerns are not with the planned change model itself but with how change takes place and with the qualifications and activities of OD practitioners.

A growing number of OD practitioners have acquired skills in a specific technique, such as team building, total quality management, appreciative inquiry, large-group interventions, or gain sharing, and have chosen to specialize in that method. Although such specialization may be necessary, it can lead to a certain myopia given the complex array of techniques that define OD. Some OD practitioners favor particular techniques and ignore other strategies that might be more appropriate, tending to interpret organizational problems as requiring the favored technique. Thus, for example, it is not unusual to see consultants pushing such methods as diversity training, reengineering, organization learning, or self-managing work teams as solutions to most organizational problems.

Effective change depends on a careful diagnosis of how the organization is functioning. Diagnosis identifies the underlying causes of organizational problems, such as poor product quality and employee dissatisfaction, or determines the positive opportunities that need to be promoted. It requires both time and money, and some organizations are not willing to make the necessary investment. Rather, they rely on preconceptions about what the problem is and hire consultants with skills appropriate to solve that problem. Managers may think, for example, that work design is the problem, so they hire an expert in job enrichment to implement a change program. The problem may be caused by other factors such as poor reward practices, however, and job enrichment would be inappropriate. Careful diagnosis can help to avoid such mistakes.

In situations requiring complex organizational changes, planned change is a long-term process involving considerable innovation and learning on-site. It requires a good deal of time and commitment and a willingness to modify and refine changes as the circumstances require. Some organizations demand more rapid solutions to their problems and seek quick fixes from experts. Unfortunately, some OD consultants are more than willing to provide quick solutions.[40] They sell prepackaged programs for organizations to adopt. Those programs appeal to managers because they typically include an explicit recipe to be followed, standard training materials, and clear time and cost boundaries. The quick fixes have trouble gaining wide organizational support and commitment, however, and seldom produce the positive results that have been advertised.

Other organizations have not recognized the systemic nature of change. Too often they believe that intervention into one aspect or subpart of the organization will be sufficient to ameliorate the problems, and they are unprepared for the other changes that may be necessary to support a particular intervention. For example, at Verizon, the positive benefits of an employee involvement program did not begin to appear until after the organization redesigned its reward system to support the cross-functional collaboration necessary to solve highly complex problems. Changing any one part or feature of an organization often requires adjustments in the other parts to maintain an appropriate alignment. Thus, although quick fixes and change programs that focus on only one part or aspect of the organization may resolve some specific problems, they generally do not lead to complex organizational change or increase members' capacity to carry out change.[41]

SUMMARY

Theories of planned change describe the activities necessary to modify strategies, structures, and processes to increase an organization's effectiveness. Lewin's change model, the action research model, and the positive model offer different views of the phases through which planned change occurs in organizations. Lewin's change model views planned change as a three-step process of unfreezing, movement, and refreezing. It provides a general description of the process of planned change. The action research model focuses on planned change as a cyclical process involving joint activities between organization members and OD practitioners. It involves eight sequential steps that overlap and interact in practice: problem identification, consultation with a behavioral science expert, data gathering and preliminary diagnosis, feedback to a key client or group, joint diagnosis of the problem, joint action planning, action, and data gathering after action. The action research model places heavy emphasis on data gathering and diagnosis prior to action planning and implementation, and on assessment of results after action is taken. In addition, change strategies often are modified on the basis of continued diagnosis, and termination of one OD program may lead to further work in other areas of the firm. The positive model is oriented to what the organization is doing right. It seeks to build on positive opportunities that can lead to extraordinary performance.

Planned change theories can be integrated into a general model. Four sets of activities—entering and contracting, diagnosing, planning and implementing, and evaluating and institutionalizing—can be used to describe how change is accomplished in organizations. These four sets of activities also describe the general structure of the chapters in this book. The general model has broad applicability to planned change. It identifies the steps an organization typically moves through to implement change and specifies the OD activities needed to effect change. Although the planned change models describe general stages of how the OD process unfolds, there are different types of change depending on the situation. Planned change efforts can vary in terms of the magnitude of the change and the degree to which the client system is organized. When situations differ on those dimensions, planned change can vary greatly. Critics of OD have pointed out several problems with the way planned change has been conceptualized and practiced, and specific areas where planned change can be improved.

NOTES

1. W. Bennis, *Changing Organizations* (New York: McGraw-Hill, 1966); J. Porras and P. Robertson, "Organization Development Theory: A Typology and Evaluation," in *Research in Organizational Change and Development*, vol. 1, eds. R. Woodman and W. Pasmore (Greenwich, Conn.: JAI Press, 1987), 1–57.

2. K. Lewin, *Field Theory in Social Science* (New York: Harper & Row, 1951).

3. E. Schein, *Process Consultation*, vols. 1 and 2 (Reading, Mass.: Addison-Wesley, 1987).

4. R. Lippitt, J. Watson, and B. Westley, *The Dynamics of Planned Change* (New York: Harcourt, Brace and World, 1958).

5. R. Benjamin and E. Levinson, "A Framework for Managing IT-Enabled Change," *Sloan Management Review* (Summer 1993): 23–33.

6. A. Shani and G. Bushe, "Visionary Action Research: A Consultation Process Perspective," *Consultation* 6 (Spring 1987): 3–19; G. Sussman and R. Evered, "An Assessment of the Scientific Merit of Action Research," *Administrative Science Quarterly* 12 (1978): 582–603.

7. W. French, "Organization Development: Objectives, Assumptions, and Strategies," *California Management Review* 12 (1969): 23–34; A. Frohman, M. Sashkin, and M. Kavanagh, "Action Research as Applied to Organization Development," *Organization and Administrative Sciences* 7

(1976): 129–42; E. Schein, *Organizational Psychology,* 3d ed. (Englewood Cliffs, N.J.: Prentice Hall, 1980).

8. N. Tichy, "Agents of Planned Change: Congruence of Values, Cognitions, and Actions," *Administrative Science Quarterly* 19 (1974): 163–82.

9. M. Beer, "The Technology of Organization Development," in *Handbook of Industrial and Organizational Psychology,* ed. M. Dunnette (Chicago: Rand McNally, 1976), 945.

10. E. Schein, *Process Consultation Revisited: Building the Helping Relationship* (Reading, Mass.: Addison-Wesley, 1998).

11. E. Schein, *Process Consultation: Its Role in Organization Development* (Reading, Mass.: Addison-Wesley, 1969), 6.

12. R. Beckhard and R. Harris, *Organizational Transitions,* 2d ed. (Reading, Mass.: Addison-Wesley, 1987).

13. P. Reason and H. Bradbury (eds.), *Handbook of Action Research: Participative Inquiry and Practice* (Thousand Oaks, Calif.: Sage Publications, 2001); M. Elden and R. Chisholm, "Emerging Varieties of Action Research: Introduction to the Special Issue," *Human Relations* 46, 2 (1993): 121–42.

14. A. Martin, "Large-Group Processes as Action Research," in *Handbook of Action Research,* eds. P. Reason and H. Bradbury (Thousand Oaks, Calif.: Sage Publications, 2001); P. Senge and O. Scharmer, "Community Action Research: Learning as a Community of Practitioners, Consultants and Researchers," in *Handbook of Action Research,* eds. P. Reason and H. Bradbury (Thousand Oaks, Calif.: Sage Publications, 2001); B. B. Bunker and B. Alban, "The Large Group Intervention—A New Social Innovation?" *Journal of Applied Behavioral Science* 28, 4 (1992): 473–80.

15. M. Swantz, E. Ndedya, and M. Saiddy Masaiganah, "Participatory Action Research in Southern Tanzania, with Special Reference to Women," in *Handbook of Action Research,* eds. P. Reason and H. Bradbury (Thousand Oaks, Calif.: Sage Publications, 2001); K. Murrell, "Evaluation as Action Research: The Case of the Management Development Institute in Gambia, West Africa," *International Journal of Public Administration* 16, 3 (1993): 341–56; J. Preston and L. DuToit, "Endemic Violence in South Africa: An OD Solution Applied to Two Educational Settings," *International Journal of Public Administration* 16 (1993): 1767–91.

16. D. Brown, "Participatory Action Research for Social Change: Collective Reflections with Asian Nongovernmental Development Organizations," *Human Relations* 46, 2 (1993): 208–27.

17. D. Cooperrider and S. Srivastva, "Appreciative Inquiry in Organizational Life," in *Research in Organizational Change and Development,* vol. 1, eds. R. Woodman and W. Pasmore (Greenwich, Conn.: JAI Press, 1987), 129–70; D. Cooperrider and J. Dutton (eds.), *Organizational Dimensions of Global Change: No Limits to Cooperation* (Newbury Park, Calif.: Corwin Press, 1999).

18. D. Cooperrider and W. Pasmore, "Global Social Change: A New Agenda for Social Science?" *Human Relations* 44, 10 (1991): 1037–55.

19. W. Burke, *Organization Development: A Normative View* (Reading, Mass.: Addison-Wesley, 1987); J. Heron and P. Reason, "The Practice of Co-operative Inquiry: Research 'with' Rather than 'on' People," in *Handbook of Action Research,* eds. P. Reason and H. Bradbury (Thousand Oaks, Calif.: Sage Publications, 2001).

20. D. Greenwood, W. Whyte, and I. Harkavy, "Participatory Action Research as Process and as Goal," *Human Relations* 46, 2 (1993): 175–92.

21. G. Morgan and R. Ramirez, "Action Learning: A Holographic Metaphor for Guiding Social Change," *Human Relations* 37 (1984): 1–28.

22. C. Argyris, R. Putnam, and D. Smith, *Action Science* (San Francisco: Jossey-Bass, 1985).

23. S. Mohrman and T. Cummings, *Self-Designing Organizations: Learning How to Create High Performance* (Reading, Mass.: Addison-Wesley, 1989).

24. P. Senge, *The Fifth Discipline* (New York: Doubleday, 1990).

25. M. Weisbord, *Productive Workplaces* (San Francisco: Jossey-Bass, 1987).

26. K. Cameron, J. Dutton, and R. Quinn, eds., *Positive Organizational Scholarship: Foundations of a New Discipline* (New York: Berrett-Kohler, 2003).

27. D. Eden, "Creating Expectation Effects in OD: Applying Self-Fulfilling Prophecy," in *Research in Organizational Change and Development,* vol. 2, eds. W. Pasmore and R. Woodman (Greenwich, Conn.: JAI Press, 1988); D. Eden, "OD and Self-Fulfilling Prophecy: Boosting Productivity by Raising Expectations," *Journal of Applied Behavioral Science* 22 (1986): 1–13; D. Cooperrider, "Positive Image, Positive Action: The Affirmative Basis for Organizing," in *Appreciative Management and Leadership,* eds. S. Srivastva, D. Cooperrider, and Associates (San Francisco: Jossey-Bass, 1990).

28. D. Cooperrider and D. Whitney, "A Positive Revolution in Change: Appreciative Inquiry," in *Appreciative Inquiry: Rethinking Human Organization Toward a Positive Theory of Change,* eds, D. Cooperrider, P. Sorensen, D. Whitney, and T. Yaeger. (Champaign, Ill.: Stipes Publishing, 2000), 3–28; J. Watkins and B. Mohr, *Appreciative Inquiry* (San Francisco: Jossey-Bass, 2001).

29. I. Hacking, *The Social Construction of What?* (Cambridge: Harvard University Press, 1999).

30. P. Berger and T. Luckman, *The Social Construction of Reality* (New York: Anchor Books, 1967); K. Gergen, "The Social Constructionist Movement in Modern Psychology," *American Psychologist* 40 (1985): 266–75; V. Burr, *An Introduction to Social Constructionism* (London: Routledge, 1995).

31. Gergen, "Social Constructionist Movement"; D. Cooperrider, F. Barrett, and S. Srivastva, "Social Construction and Appreciative Inquiry: A Journey in Organization Theory," in *Management and Organization: Relational Alternatives to Individualism*, eds. D. Hosking, P. Dachler, and K. Gergen (Aldershot, England: Avebury Press, 1995).

32. This application was submitted by Dr. Evelyn D. Robertson, who participated in the airport's transition. The following documents were used in developing the case: *Air Transportation and the Future of the San Diego Region: The Impact of Constrained Air Transportation Capacity on the San Diego Regional Economy. Airport Economic Analysis* (Fall 2000), Port of San Diego, San Diego Association of Governments (pp. 2–3), http://www.san.org/sdcraa/documents/sandag/publicationid_374_507.pdf; *The Impacts of Constrained Air Transportation Capacity on the San Diego Regional Economy, Final Report*, January 5, 2000, Hamilton, Rabinovitz & Alschuler, Inc. (p. 1), http://www.san.org/sdcraa/documents/sandag/publicationid_227_546.pdf; San Diego International Airport Web site, Planning http://www.san.org/sdcraa/planning.asp ; California Senate Bill AB93, California State Session 2000–2001, Introduced by Assembly Member Wayne (Coauthors: Assembly Members Kehoe and Vargas) (Principal coauthor: Senator Peace) (Coauthor: Senator Alpert) http://gillespiepilots.org/ab93.htm; San Diego Port District, Internal Document, COMPASS, 2002; San Diego County Regional Airport Authority, live interview teleconference, Angela Shafer-Payne, Vice President, Strategic Planning.

33. D. Nadler, "Organizational Frame-Bending: Types of Change in the Complex Organization," in *Corporate Transformation*, eds. R. Kilmann and T. Covin (San Francisco: Jossey-Bass, 1988), 66–83; P. Watzlawick, J. Weakland, and R. Fisch, *Change* (New York: W. W. Norton, 1974); R. Golembiewski, K. Billingsley, and S. Yea-

ger, "Measuring Change and Persistence in Human Affairs: Types of Change Generated by OD Designs," *Journal of Applied Behavioral Science* 12 (1975): 133–57; A. Meyer, G. Brooks, and J. Goes, "Environmental Jolts and Industry Revolutions: Organizational Responses to Discontinuous Change," *Strategic Management Journal* 11 (1990): 93–110.

34. A. Mohrman, G. Ledford Jr., S. Mohrman, E. Lawler III, and T. Cummings, *Large-Scale Organization Change* (San Francisco: Jossey-Bass, 1989).

35. L. D. Brown, "Planned Change in Underorganized Systems," in *Systems Theory for Organization Development*, ed. T. Cummings (Chichester, England: John Wiley & Sons, 1980), 181–203.

36. T. Cummings and M. Nathan, "Fostering New University–Industry Relationships" in *Making Organizations Competitive*, ed. R. Kilman (San Francisco: Jossey-Bass, 1991).

37. Porras and Robertson, "Organization Development Theory"; J. Porras and P. Robertson, "Organization Development: Theory, Practice, and Research," in *Handbook of Industrial and Organizational Psychology*, 2d ed., vol. 3, eds. M. Dunnette and M. Hough (Palo Alto, Calif: Consulting Psychologists Press, 1992).

38. T. Cummings, S. Mohrman, A. Mohrman, and G. Ledford, "Organization Design for the Future: A Collaborative Research Approach," in *Doing Research That Is Useful for Theory and Practice*, eds. E. Lawler III, A. Mohrman, S. Mohrman, G. Ledford, and T. Cummings (San Francisco: Jossey-Bass, 1985), 275–305.

39. Frohman, Sashkin, and Kavanagh, "Action Research"; Mohrman and Cummings, *Self-Designing Organizations*; M. Beer, R. Eisenstat, and B. Spector, "Why Change Programs Don't Produce Change," *Harvard Business Review* 6 (November-December 1990): 158–66.

40. C. Worley and R. Patchett, "Myth and Hope Meet Reality: The Fallacy of and Opportunities for Reducing Cycle Time in Strategic Change," in *Fast Cycle Organization Development*, ed. M. Anderson (Cincinnati: South-Western College Publishing, 2000).

41. Beer, Eisenstat, and Spector, "Change Programs."

3

The Organization Development Practitioner

Chapters 1 and 2 provided an overview of the field of organization development and a description of the nature of planned change. This chapter extends that introduction by examining the people who perform OD. A closer look at OD practitioners can provide a more personal perspective on the field and can help us understand how and why OD relies so heavily on personal relationships between practitioners and organization members.

Much of the literature about OD practitioners views them as internal or external consultants providing professional services—diagnosing systems, developing interventions, and helping to implement them. More recent perspectives expand the practice scope to include professionals in related disciplines, such as industrial psychology and strategic management, as well as line managers who have learned how to carry out OD to change and develop their organizations.

A great deal of opinion and some research studies have focused on the necessary skills and knowledge of an effective OD practitioner. Studies of the profession provide a comprehensive list of basic skills and knowledge that all effective OD practitioners must possess.

Most of the relevant literature focuses on people specializing in OD as a profession and addresses their roles and careers. The OD role can be described in relation to the position of practitioners: internal to the organization, external to it, or in a team comprising both internal and external consultants. The OD role also can be examined in terms of its marginality in organizations, of the emotional demands made on the practitioner, and of where it fits along a continuum from client-centered to consultant-centered functioning. Finally, organization development is an emerging profession providing alternative opportunities for gaining competence and developing a career. The stressful nature of helping professions, however, suggests that OD practitioners must cope with the possibility of professional burnout.

As in other helping professions, such as medicine and law, values and ethics play an important role in guiding OD practice and in minimizing the chances that clients will be neglected or abused.

WHO IS THE ORGANIZATION DEVELOPMENT PRACTITIONER?

Throughout this text, the term *organization development practitioner* refers to at least three sets of people. The most obvious group of OD practitioners are those people specializing in OD as a profession. They may be internal or external consultants who offer professional services to organization clients, including top managers, functional department heads, and staff groups. OD professionals traditionally have shared a common set of humanistic values promoting open communications, employee involvement, and personal growth and development. They tend to have common training, skills, and experience in the social processes of organizations (for example, group dynamics, decision making, and communications). In recent years, OD professionals have expanded those traditional values and skill sets to include more concern for organizational effectiveness, competitiveness, and bottom-line results, and greater attention to the technical, structural, and strategic parts of organizations. That expansion, mainly in response to the highly competitive demands facing modern organizations, has resulted in a more diverse set of OD professionals geared to helping organizations cope with those pressures.[1]

Second, the term OD practitioner applies to people specializing in fields related to OD, such as reward systems, organization design, total quality, information technology, and business strategy. These content-oriented fields increasingly are becoming integrated with OD's process orientation, particularly as OD projects have become more comprehensive, involving multiple features and varying parts of organizations. The integrated strategic change intervention described in Chapter 19, for example, is the result of marrying OD with business strategy.[2] A growing number of professionals in these related fields are gaining experience and competence in OD, mainly through working with OD professionals on large-scale projects and through attending OD training sessions. For example, most of the large accounting firms have diversified into management consulting and change management.[3] In most cases, professionals in these related fields do not subscribe fully to traditional OD values, nor do they have extensive OD training and experience. Rather, they have formal training and experience in their respective specialties, such as industrial relations, management consulting, information systems, health care, and work design. They are OD practitioners in the sense that they apply their special competence within an OD-like process, typically by engaging OD professionals and managers to design and implement change programs. They also practice OD when they apply their OD competence to their own specialties, thus spreading an OD perspective into such areas as compensation practices, work design, labor relations, and planning and strategy.

Third, the term OD practitioner applies to the increasing number of managers and administrators who have gained competence in OD and who apply it to their own work areas. Studies and recent articles argue that OD increasingly is applied by managers rather than by OD professionals.[4] Such studies suggest that the faster pace of change affecting organizations today is highlighting the centrality of the manager in managing change. Consequently, OD must become a general management skill. Along those lines, Kanter studied a growing number of firms, such as General Electric, Hewlett-Packard, and 3M, where managers and employees have become "change masters."[5] They have gained the expertise to introduce change and innovation into the organization.

Managers tend to gain competence in OD through interacting with OD professionals in actual change programs. This on-the-job training frequently is supplemented with more formal OD training, such as the variety of workshops offered by the National Training Laboratories (NTL), the Center for Creative Leadership, the Gestalt Institute, UCLA's Extension Service, and others. Line managers increasingly are attending such external programs. Moreover, a growing number of organizations, including Motorola, Disney, and General Electric, have instituted in-house training programs for managers to learn how to develop and change their work units. As managers gain OD competence, they become its most basic practitioners.

In practice, the distinctions among the three sets of OD practitioners are blurring. A growing number of managers have transferred, either temporarily or permanently, into the OD profession. For example, companies such as Procter & Gamble have trained and rotated managers into full-time OD roles so that they can gain skills and experience needed for higher-level management positions. Also, it is increasingly common to find managers using their experience in OD to become external consultants. More OD practitioners are gaining professional competence in related specialties, such as business process reengineering, reward systems, and organization design. Conversely, many specialists in those related areas are achieving professional competence in OD. Cross-training and integration are producing a more comprehensive and complex kind of OD practitioner—one with a greater diversity of values, skills, and experience than a traditional practitioner.

COMPETENCIES OF AN EFFECTIVE ORGANIZATION DEVELOPMENT PRACTITIONER

The literature about OD competencies reveals a mixture of personality traits, experiences, knowledge, and skills presumed to lead to effective practice. For example, research on the characteristics of successful change practitioners yields the following list of attributes and abilities: diagnostic ability, basic knowledge of behavioral science techniques, empathy, knowledge of the theories and methods within the consultant's own discipline, goal-setting ability, problem-solving ability, ability to perform self-assessment, ability to see things objectively, imagination, flexibility, honesty, consistency, and trust.[6] Although these qualities and skills are laudable, there has been relatively little consensus about their importance to effective OD practice.

Two ongoing projects are attempting to define and categorize the skills and knowledge required of OD practitioners. In the first effort, a broad and growing list of well-known practitioners and researchers annually update a list of professional competencies. The most recent list has grown to 187 statements in nine areas of OD practice, including entry, start-up, assessment and feedback, action planning, intervention, evaluation, adoption, separation, and general competencies.[7] The statements range from "staying centered in the present, focusing on the ongoing process" and "understanding and explaining how diversity will affect the diagnosis of the culture" to "basing change on business strategy and business needs" and "being comfortable with quantum leaps, radical shifts, and paradigm changes." The discussion is currently considering additional items related to international OD, large-group interventions, and transorganization skills.

The second project, sponsored by the Organization Development and Change Division of the Academy of Management,[8] seeks to develop a list of competencies to guide curriculum development in graduate OD programs. So far, more than 40 OD practitioners and researchers have worked to develop the two competency lists shown in Table 3.1. First, foundation competencies are oriented toward descriptions of an existing system. They include knowledge from organization behavior, psychology, group dynamics, management and organization theory, research methods, and business practices. Second, core competencies are aimed at how systems change over time. They include knowledge of organization design, organization research, system dynamics, OD history, and theories and models for change; they also involve the skills needed to manage the consulting process, to analyze and diagnose systems, to design and choose interventions, to facilitate processes, to develop clients' capability to manage their own change, and to evaluate organization change.

The information in Table 3.1 applies primarily to people specializing in OD as a profession. For them, possessing the listed knowledge and skills seems reasonable, especially in light of the growing diversity and complexity of interventions in OD. Gaining competence in those areas may take considerable time and effort, and it is questionable whether the other two types of OD practitioners—managers and specialists in related fields—also need that full range of skills and knowledge. It seems more reasonable to suggest that some subset of the items listed in Table 3.1 should apply to all OD practitioners, whether they are OD professionals, managers, or related specialists. Those items would constitute the practitioner's basic skills and knowledge. Beyond that background, the three types of OD practitioners likely would differ in areas of concentration. OD professionals would extend their breadth of skills across the remaining categories in Table 3.1; managers would focus on the functional knowledge of business areas; and related specialists would concentrate on skills in their respective areas.

Based on the data in Table 3.1 and the other studies available, all OD practitioners should have the following basic skills and knowledge to be effective.[9]

Intrapersonal skills or "self-management" competence. Despite the growing knowledge base and sophistication of the field, organization development is still a human craft. As the primary instrument of diagnosis and change, practitioners often must process complex, ambiguous information and make informed judgments about its relevance to organizational issues.

The core competency of analysis and diagnosis listed in Table 3.1 includes the ability to inquire into one's self, and it remains one of the cornerstone skills in OD.[10] Practitioners must have the personal centering to know their own values, feelings, and purposes as well as the integrity to behave responsibly in a helping relationship with others. Bob Tannenbaum, one of the founders of OD, argued that self-knowledge is the most central ingredient in OD practice and suggested that practitioners are becoming too enamored with skills and techniques.[11] There are data to support his view. A study of 416 OD practitioners found that 47% agreed with the statement, "Many of the new entrants into the field have little understanding of or appreciation for the history or values underlying the field."[12] Because OD is a highly uncertain process requiring constant adjustment and innovation, practitioners must have active learning skills and a reasonable balance between their rational and emotional sides. Finally, OD practice can be highly stressful and can lead to early burnout, so practitioners need to know how to manage their own stress.

Interpersonal skills. Practitioners must create and maintain effective relationships with individuals and groups within the organization and help them gain the competence necessary to solve their own problems. Table 3.1 identifies group dynamics, comparative cultural perspectives, and business functions as foundation knowledge, and managing the consulting process and facilitation as core skills. All of these interpersonal competencies promote effective helping relationships. Such relationships start with a grasp of the organization's perspective and require listening to members' perceptions and feelings to understand how they see themselves and the organization. This understanding provides a starting point for joint diagnosis and problem solving. Practitioners must establish trust and rapport with organization members so that they can share pertinent information and work effectively together. This requires being able to converse in members' own language and to give and receive feedback about how the relationship is progressing.

To help members learn new skills and behaviors, practitioners must serve as role models of what is expected. They must act in ways that are credible to organization members and provide them with the counseling and coaching necessary to develop and change. Because the helping relationship is jointly determined, practitioners need to be able to negotiate an acceptable role and to manage changing expectations and demands.

General consultation skills. Table 3.1 identifies the ability to manage the consulting process and the ability to design interventions as core competencies that all OD practitioners should possess. OD starts with diagnosing an organization or department to understand its current functioning and to discover areas for further development. OD practitioners need to know how to carry out an effective diagnosis, at least at a rudimentary level. They should know how to engage organization members in diagnosis, how to help them ask the right questions, and how to collect and analyze information. A manager, for example, should be able to work with subordinates to determine jointly the organization's or department's strengths or problems. The manager should know basic diagnostic questions (see Chapters 5 and 6),

Table 3•1	Knowledge and Skill Requirements of OD Practitioners

	FOUNDATION COMPETENCIES	**CORE COMPETENCIES**

Knowledge	1. Organization behavior
	  A. Organization culture
	  B. Work design
	  C. Interpersonal relations
	  D. Power and politics
	  E. Leadership
	  F. Goal setting
	  G. Conflict
	  H. Ethics
	
	2. Individual psychology
	  A. Learning theory
	  B. Motivation theory
	  C. Perception theory
	
	3. Group dynamics
	  A. Roles
	  B. Communication processes
	  C. Decision-making process
	  D. Stages of group development
	  E. Leadership
	
	4. Management and organization theory
	  A. Planning, organizing, leading, and controlling
	  B. Problem solving and decision making
	  C. Systems theory
	  D. Contingency theory
	  E. Organization structure
	  F. Characteristics of environment and technology
	  G. Models of organization and system
	
	5. Research methods/statistics
	  A. Measures of central tendency
	  B. Measures of dispersion
	  C. Basic sampling theory
	  D. Basic experimental design
	  E. Sample inferential statistics
	
	6. Comparative cultural perspectives
	  A. Dimensions of natural culture
	  B. Dimensions of industry culture
	  C. Systems implications
	
	7. Functional knowledge of business
	  A. Interpersonal communication (listening, feedback, and articulation)
	  B. Collaboration/working together
	  C. Problem solving
	  D. Using new technology
	  E. Conceptualizing
	  F. Project management
	  G. Present/education/coach
		1. Organization design: the decision process associated with formulating and aligning the elements of an organizational system, including but not limited to structural systems, human resource systems, information systems, reward systems, work design, political systems, and organization culture
		  A. The concept of fit and alignment
		  B. Diagnostic and design model for various sub-systems that make up an organization at any level of analysis, including the structure of work, human resources, information systems, reward systems, work design, political systems, and so on
		  C. Key thought leaders in organization design
		
		2. Organization research: field research methods; interviewing; content analysis; design of questionnaires and interview protocol; designing change evaluation processes; longitudinal data collection and analysis; understanding and detecting alpha, beta, and gamma change; and a host of quantitative and qualitative methods
		
		3. System dynamics: the description and understanding of how systems evolve and develop over time, how systems respond to exogenous and endogenous disruption as well as planned interventions (e.g., evolution and revolution, punctuated equilibrium theory, chaos theory, catastrophe theory, incremental vs. quantum change, transformation theory and so on)
		
		4. History of organization development and change: an understanding of the social, political, economic, and personal forces that led to the emergence and development of organization development and change, including the key thought leaders, the values underlying their writings and actions, the key events and writings, and related documentation
		  A. Human relations movement
		  B. NTL/T-groups/sensitivity training
		  C. Survey research
		  D. Quality of work life
		  E. Tavistock Institute
		  F. Key thought leaders
		  G. Humanistic values
		  H. Statement of ethics
		
		5. Theories and models for change: the basic action research model, participatory action research model, planning model, change typologies (e.g., fast, slow, incremental, quantum, revolutionary), Lewin's model, transition models, and so on

Table 3•1	Knowledge and Skill Requirements of OD Practitioners, *continued*

FOUNDATION COMPETENCIES	CORE COMPETENCIES
Skills	1. Managing the consulting process: the ability to enter, contract, diagnose, design appropriate interventions, implement those interventions, manage unprogrammed events, and evaluate change process
	2. Analysis/diagnosis: the abilities to conduct an inquiry into a system's effectiveness, to see the root cause(s) of a system's current level of effectiveness; the core skill is interpreted to include all systems—individual, group, organization, and multiorganization—as well as the ability to understand and inquire into one's self
	3. Designing/choosing appropriate, relevant interventions: understanding how to select, modify, or design effective interventions that will move the organization from its current state to its desired future state
	4. Facilitation and process consultation: the ability to assist an individual or group toward a goal; the ability to conduct an inquiry into individual and group processes such that the client system maintains ownership of the issue, increases its capacity for reflection on the consequences of its behaviors and actions, and develops a sense of increased control and ability
	5. Developing client capability: the ability to conduct a change process in such a way that the client is better able to plan and implement a successful change process in the future, using technologies of planned change in a values-based and ethical manner
	6. Evaluating organization change: the ability to design and implement a process to evaluate the impact and effects of change intervention, including control of alternative explanations and interpretation of performance outcomes

some methods for gathering information, such as interviews or surveys, and some techniques for analyzing it, such as force-field analysis or statistical means and distributions (see Chapters 7 and 8).

In addition to diagnosis, OD practitioners should know how to design and execute an intervention. They need to be able to define an action plan and to gain commitment to the program. They also need to know how to tailor the intervention to the situation, using information about how the change is progressing to guide implementation (see Chapter 11). For example, managers should be able to develop action steps for an intervention with subordinates. They should be able to gain their commitment to the program (usually through participation), sit down with them and assess how it is progressing, and make modifications if necessary.

Organization development theory. The last basic tool OD practitioners should have is a general knowledge of organization development, such as is presented in this book. They should have some appreciation for planned change, the action research model, and the positive approaches to managing change. They should be familiar with the range of available interventions and the need for evaluating and institutionalizing change programs. Perhaps most important is that OD practitioners should understand their own role in the emerging field of organization development, whether it is as an OD professional, a manager, or a specialist in a related area.

THE PROFESSIONAL ORGANIZATION DEVELOPMENT PRACTITIONER

Most of the literature about OD practitioners has focused on people specializing in OD as a profession. In this section, we discuss the role and typical career paths of OD professionals.

Role of Organization Development Professionals

Position

Organization development professionals have positions that are either internal or external to the organization. Internal consultants are members of the organization and may be located in the human resources department or report directly to a line manager. They may perform the OD role exclusively, or they may combine it with other tasks, such as compensation practices, training, or employee relations.[13] Many large organizations, such as Intel, Merck, Microsoft, Philip Morris, Levi Strauss, Procter & Gamble, Weyerhaeuser, GTE, and Citigroup, have created specialized OD consulting groups. These internal consultants typically have a variety of clients within the organization, serving both line and staff departments.

External consultants are not members of the client organization; they typically work for a consulting firm, a university, or themselves. Organizations generally hire external consultants to provide a particular expertise that is unavailable internally, to bring a different and potentially more objective perspective into the organization development process, or to signal shifts in power.[14]

Table 3.2 describes the differences between these two roles at each stage of the action research process.[15]

During the entry process, internal consultants have clear advantages. They have ready access to and relationships with clients, know the language of the organization, and have insights about the root cause of many of its problems. This allows internal consultants to save time in identifying the organization's culture, informal practices, and sources of power. They have access to a variety of information, including rumors, company reports, and direct observations. In addition, entry is more efficient and congenial, and their pay is not at risk. External consultants, however, have the advantage of being able to select the clients they want to work with according to their own criteria. The contracting phase is less formal for internal consultants and there is less worry about expenses, but there is less choice about whether to complete the assignment. Both types of consultants must address issues of confidentiality, risk project termination (and other negative consequences) by the client, and fill a third-party role.

During the diagnosis process, internal consultants already know most organization members and enjoy a basic level of rapport and trust. But external consultants often have higher status than internal consultants, which allows them to probe difficult issues and assess the organization more objectively. In the intervention phase, both types of consultants must rely on valid information, free and informed choice, and internal commitment for their success.[16] However, an internal consultant's strong ties to the organization may make him or her overly cautious, particularly

Table 3•2	The Differences Between External and Internal Consulting	
STAGE OF CHANGE	**EXTERNAL CONSULTANTS**	**INTERNAL CONSULTANTS**
Entering	• Source clients • Build relationships • Learn company jargon • "Presenting problem" challenge • Time consuming • Stressful phase • Select project/client according to own criteria • Unpredictable outcome	• Ready access to clients • Ready relationships • Knows company jargon • Understands root causes • Time efficient • Congenial phase • Obligated to work with everyone • Steady pay
Contracting	• Formal documents • Can terminate project at will • Guard against out-of-pocket expenses • Information confidential • Loss of contract at stake • Maintain third-party role	• Informal agreements • Must complete projects assigned • No out-of-pocket expenses • Information can be open or confidential • Risk of client retaliation and loss of job at stake • Acts as third party, driver (on behalf of client), or pair of hands
Diagnosing	• Meet most organization members for the first time • Prestige from being external • Build trust quickly • Confidential data can increase political sensitivities	• Has relationships with many organization members • Prestige determined by job rank and client stature • Sustain reputation as trustworthy over time • Data openly shared can reduce political intrigue
Intervening	• Insist on valid information, free and informed choice, and internal commitment • Confine activities within boundaries of client organization	• Insist on valid information, free and informed choice, and internal commitment • Run interference for client across organizational lines to align support
Evaluating	• Rely on repeat business and customer referral as key measures of project success • Seldom see long-term results	• Rely on repeat business, pay raise, and promotion as key measures of success • Can see change become institutionalized • Little recognition for job well done

SOURCE: M. Lacey, "Internal Consulting: Perspectives on the Process of Planned Change," *Journal of Organizational Change Management* 8 (1995): 76, ©1995. Reprinted with permission of the publisher. All rights reserved.

when powerful others can affect a career. Internal consultants also may lack certain skills and experience in facilitating organizational change. Insiders may have some small advantages in being able to move around the system and cross key organizational boundaries. Finally, the measures of success and reward differ from those of the external practitioner in the evaluation process.

A promising approach to having the advantages of both internal and external OD consultants is to include them both as members of an internal–external consulting team.[17] External consultants can combine their special expertise and objectivity with the inside knowledge and acceptance of internal consultants. The two parties can use complementary consulting skills while sharing the workload and possibly accomplishing more than either would by operating alone. Internal consultants, for example, can provide almost continuous contact with the client, and their external counterparts can provide specialized services periodically, such as 2 or 3 days each month. External consultants also can help train their organization partners, thus transferring OD skills and knowledge to the organization.

Although little has been written on internal–external consulting teams, studies suggest that the effectiveness of such teams depends on members developing strong, supportive, collegial relationships. They need to take time to develop the consulting team, confronting individual differences and establishing appropriate roles and exchanges. Members need to provide each other with continuous feedback and make a commitment to learning from each other. In the absence of these team-building and learning activities, internal–external consulting teams can be more troublesome and less effective than consultants working alone.

Application 3.1 provides a personal account of the internal and external consulting positions as well as interactions between them.[18]

Marginality

A promising line of research on the professional OD role centers on the issue of marginality.[19] The marginal person is one who successfully straddles the boundary between two or more groups with differing goals, value systems, and behavior patterns. Whereas in the past the marginal role always was seen as dysfunctional, marginality now is seen in a more positive light. There are many examples of marginal roles in organizations: the salesperson, the buyer, the first-line supervisor, the integrator, and the project manager.

Evidence is mounting that some people are better at taking marginal roles than are others. Those who are good at it seem to have personal qualities of low dogmatism, neutrality, open-mindedness, objectivity, flexibility, and adaptable information-processing ability. Rather than being upset by conflict, ambiguity, and stress, they thrive on it. Individuals with marginal orientations are more likely than others to develop integrative decisions that bring together and reconcile viewpoints among opposing organizational groups and are more likely to remain neutral in controversial situations. Thus, the research suggests that the marginal role can have positive effects when it is filled by a person with a marginal orientation. Such a person can be more objective and better able to perform successfully in linking, integrative, or conflict-laden roles.[20]

A study of 89 external OD practitioners and 246 internal ones (response rates of 59% and 54%, respectively) showed that external professionals were more comfortable with the marginal role than were internal professionals. Internal consultants with more years of experience were more marginally oriented than were those with less experience.[21] These findings, combined with other research on marginal roles, suggest the importance of maintaining the OD practitioner's marginality, with its flexibility, independence, and boundary-spanning characteristics.

Emotional Demands

The OD practitioner role is emotionally demanding. Research and practice support the importance of understanding emotions and their impact on the practitioner's effectiveness.[22] The research on emotional intelligence in organizations suggests a set of abilities that can aid OD practitioners in conducting successful change efforts.[23] Emotional intelligence refers to the ability to recognize and express emotions appropriately, to use emotions in thought and decisions, and to regulate emotion in one's self and in others.[24] It is, therefore, a different kind of intelligence from problem-solving ability, engineering aptitude, or the knowledge of concepts. In tandem with traditional knowledge and skill, emotional intelligence affects and supplements rational thought; emotions help prioritize thinking by directing attention to important information not addressed in models and theories. In that sense,

PERSONAL VIEWS OF THE INTERNAL AND EXTERNAL CONSULTING POSITIONS

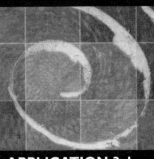

The Internal Consultant's View

I am an agent of change. I am also a member of this organization. I was hired for my OD skills, but also for the fact that I was seen as a "cultural fit." Sometimes I struggle between my dual roles of "team member" and "free radical." After all, it is my job to disrupt the status quo around here, helping leaders to find ways to make the organization more effective.

I have the great advantage of knowing and understanding how my organization works—its processes, policies, norms, and areas of resistance. I can usually anticipate how difficult a given change will be for members of the organization, and where the resistance will come from. Because I believe in the mission of my organization, I am able to cope with the inevitable challenges of the change process. Still, I am frequently a magnet for resistance and a receptacle of institutional anxiety. While I understand how people can be frustrated and frightened by change, it can still be difficult for me to bear the disruption I help to create.

To keep myself sharp and healthy, I breathe, run, meditate, and read. I take every learning opportunity that comes my way, and work diligently to create and maintain a network of colleagues who can support me through the rough patches. I find that my best support comes not from friends, but from people who know and understand the hard work of planned change.

As an internal consultant, I have exposure to many of the same people over time—executives, managers, and employees get to know who I am and what I do. I get to know who they are and what they do. I have the opportunity to leverage my executive relationships from project to project; over time the executives here have come to understand my work and trust my skills as a consultant. This understanding and trust saves us time and energy each time we work together. Of course, I realize that if I fail one of my executive clients, my life in this organization could become less pleasant. That can stress me out when I'm working on a messy or unpopular project. After all, my performance review is affected by client feedback, and my compensation is tied to people's perceptions of my performance. This can make it difficult to press forward with risky interventions. I am proud of my reputation around here—proud of the fact that I have built solid relationships at the executive level, that managers respect my work, and that employees value having me in the organization. Still, I am ever aware that I must walk the fine line between "respected insider" and "paid agitator."

Sometimes I'm lonely—often I'm the only OD person working in an organization; sometimes there are two or more of us, but we're always spread so thin that connecting is difficult and truly supporting one another is virtually impossible. I may work with other staff people—HR for instance—but they don't always understand my role and can't really relate to my challenges. Sometimes they can be resentful of my relationship with the client, which makes me feel alienated. I enjoy my client groups, but I must be careful not to over-identify with them; the greatest value I bring to my clients is a clean "outsider" perspective. I can't do hard change efforts with them if I'm worried about them liking me. Being a lone ranger can be thrilling, but being an outsider can get tiring.

Occasionally I bring in an external consultant to work on a specific project or problem in my organization. This can be both challenging and rewarding for me. It is time consuming to bring an outsider up to speed on my organization's business, processes, and politics. I seek external consultants who will fit in our culture, while helping us see our issues more clearly and realistically. I enjoy the process of partnering with people who have exposure to other organizations, who possess different skills and strengths from mine, and who understand the inherent discomfort of the change process. Still, this can be risky, because my reputation will be affected by this person's work and the outcomes we are able to achieve. When it works best, my partnership with the external consultant leads to improved effectiveness for my organization while affording me a valued learning opportunity and professional support.

The best thing to me about being an internal consultant is knowing that I am contributing to the mission of my organization with every client I work with, every day.

The External Consultant's View

I am an agent of change. I work for many different organizations of varying sizes with different missions and goals. I spend most of my time helping managers, HR people, and internal consultants initiate and manage change—both planned and unplanned. I enjoy the variety in my work and the learning that comes from seeing the way change happens in different organizations and contexts.

But it is hard being an "outsider." I must work quickly to understand each new organization I work with. As an outsider it can be frustrating to navigate the inner workings of the organization—its politics, pecking order, and culture—and to root out what's important and what's not. In my role,

I'm not around while the unglamorous, time-consuming, and important work of nurturing a change along is being done. So, although I experience the risk and excitement of some part of the change, I do not always get to experience the whole change process from start to finish. I rarely get to see the project bear fruit and the organization become more effective as a result of the work I've done. Sometimes the process feels incomplete, and I almost always wonder how much I've actually helped.

Being an external consultant is both rewarding and risky work. On the one hand, I am seen as an expert. I am appreciated for my assistance, applauded for my knowledge, and liked for my interpersonal skills. I have the benefit of many revenue sources, so I'm never overly dependent on one client. I am often rewarded handsomely for my time and effort, although most people mistake "daily fee" as actual income and forget about self-employment taxes and the health benefits I have to pay myself. The other truth is that I am always at risk—economic crises, budget cuts, personnel changes, executive shake ups, organizational politics, and the occasional hostile HR person are but a few of the land mines an external consultant faces. For the most part, I feel pleased and rewarded for my work as a consultant. But I always know that my situation is dependent on my client's situation, and I can never afford to get too comfortable.

When I'm hired by an executive or manager, sometimes the HR person or internal consultant may be resistant, feeling threatened by my presence. When this happens, I have to find ways to address their concern, partner with them, and still do the important work of organizational change. Sometimes just creating space for the conversation by using simple probes—"You seem very concerned about this situation," or "You must feel pretty unsupported right now"—help me uncover their discomfort so we can move forward. Sometimes these relationships are difficult throughout the engagement. It's the downside of being brought in as an "expert."

I am asked by clients to perform a wide variety of tasks ranging from content expert to process expert to personal coach. Regardless of the request, however, I am frequently aware of an unspoken need on the part of the client—manager, HR person, or internal consultant—to have me support his or her project, position, or person. When the request is to support a project, it is usually clear. When the request is to support a position, it is less clear but typically surfaces during the course of our work together. However, when the request is to support the individual personally, the request is almost never overt. This is where my self-as-instrument work serves me best, helping me to understand the unspoken— the question behind the question. While my goal is always to help my client organizations become more effective, I never forget that change can happen many different ways and at multiple levels of the system. It is my work to be aware of opportunities to intervene, and to have the skill and courage to do so as an outsider.

some researchers argue that emotional intelligence is as important as cognitive intelligence.[25]

Reports from OD practitioners support the importance of emotional intelligence in practice. From the client's perspective, OD practitioners must understand emotions well enough to relate to and help organization members address resistance, commitment, and ambiguity at each stage of planned change. Despite the predominant focus on rationality and efficiency, almost any change process must address important and difficult issues that raise emotions such as the fear of failure, rejection, anxiety, and anger.[26] OD practitioners can provide psychological support, model appropriate emotional expression, reframe client perspectives, and provide resources.[27] OD practitioners must also understand their own emotions. Ambiguity, unfamiliarity, or denial of emotions can lead to inaccurate and untimely interventions. For example, a practitioner who is uncomfortable with conflict may intervene to defuse an argument between two managers because of the discomfort he or she feels, not because the conflict is destructive. In such a case, the practitioner is acting to address a personal need rather than intervening to improve the system's effectiveness.

Evidence suggests that emotional intelligence increases with age and experience.[28] The research also supports the conclusion that competence with emotions can be developed through personal growth processes such as sensitivity training, counseling, and therapy. It seems reasonable to suggest that professional OD practitioners dedicate themselves to a long-term regimen of development that includes acquiring both cognitive learning and emotional intelligence.

Use of Knowledge and Experience

The professional OD role has been described in terms of a continuum ranging from client-centered (using the client's knowledge and experience) to consultant-centered (using the consultant's knowledge and experience), as shown in Figure 3.1. Traditionally, OD consultants have worked at the client-centered end of the continuum. Organization development professionals, relying mainly on sensitivity training, process consultation, and team building (see Chapter 12), have been expected to remain neutral, refusing to offer expert advice on organizational problems. Rather than contracting to solve specific problems, the consultant has tended to work with organization members to identify problems and potential solutions, to help them study what they are doing now and consider alternative behaviors and solutions, and to help them discover whether, in fact, the consultant and they can learn to do things better. In doing that, the OD professional has generally listened and reflected upon members' perceptions and ideas and helped clarify and interpret their communications and behaviors.

The recent proliferation of OD interventions in the structural, human resource management, and strategy areas has expanded that limited definition of the professional OD role to include the consultant-centered end of the continuum. In many of the newer approaches, the consultant may have to take on a modified role of expert, with the consent and collaboration of organization members. For example, managers trying to bring about a major structural redesign (see Chapter 14) may not have the appropriate knowledge and expertise to create and manage the change and need the help of an OD practitioner with experience in this area. The consultant's role might be to present the basic concepts and ideas and then to struggle jointly with the managers to select an approach that might be useful to the organization and to decide how it might best be implemented. In this situation, the OD professional recommends or prescribes particular changes and is active in planning how to implement them. This expertise, however, is always shared rather than imposed.

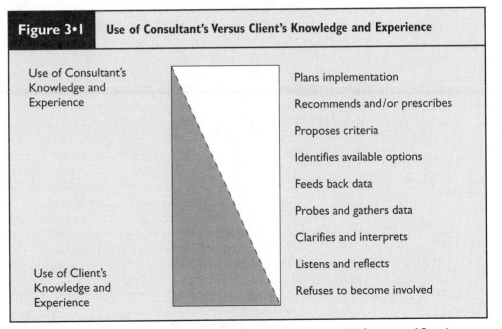

| Figure 3•1 | Use of Consultant's Versus Client's Knowledge and Experience |

Use of Consultant's Knowledge and Experience

Plans implementation

Recommends and/or prescribes

Proposes criteria

Identifies available options

Feeds back data

Probes and gathers data

Clarifies and interprets

Listens and reflects

Use of Client's Knowledge and Experience

Refuses to become involved

SOURCE: Adapted by permission of the authors from W. Schmidt and A. Johnson, "A Continuum of Consultancy Styles" (unpublished manuscript, July 1970), p. 1.

With the development of new and varied intervention approaches, the OD professional's role needs to be seen as falling along the entire continuum from client-centered to consultant centered. At times, the consultant will rely mainly on organization members' knowledge and experiences to identify and solve problems. At other times, it will be more appropriate to take on the role of expert, withdrawing from that role as managers gain more knowledge and experience.

Careers of Organization Development Professionals

In contrast to such long-standing occupations as medicine and law, organization development is an emerging practice, still developing the characteristics of an established profession: a common body of knowledge, educational requirements, a recognized code of ethics, and rules and methods for governing conduct. People enter professional OD careers from a variety of educational and work backgrounds. Because they do not have to follow an established career path, they have some choice about when to enter or leave an OD career and whether to be an internal or external consultant.[29]

Despite the looseness or flexibility of the field, most professionals have had specific training in OD. That training can include relatively short courses (1 day to 2 weeks), programs, and workshops conducted within organizations or at outside institutions (such as NTL, University Associates, Columbia University, the University of Michigan, Stanford University, and UCLA). OD training also can be more formal and lengthy, including master's programs (for example, at American University, Benedictine University, Bowling Green State University, Case Western Reserve University, Loyola University, the Fielding Institute, and Pepperdine University) and doctoral training (for example, at Benedictine University, Case Western Reserve University, Columbia University Teachers College, the Fielding Institute, George Washington University, UCLA, Pepperdine University, and Stanford University).

As might be expected, career choices widen as people gain training and experience in OD. Those with rudimentary training tend to be internal consultants, often taking on OD roles as temporary assignments on the way to higher managerial or staff positions. Holders of master's degrees generally are evenly split between internal and external consultants. Those with doctorates may join a university faculty and do consulting part-time, join a consulting firm, or seek a position as a relatively high-level internal consultant.

External consultants tend to be older, to have more managerial experience, and to spend more of their time in OD than do internal practitioners. However, one study suggested there were no differences between internal and external consultants in pay or years of consulting experience.[30] Perhaps the most common career path is to begin as an internal consultant, gain experience and visibility through successful interventions or publishing, and then become an external consultant. A field study found that internal consultants acquired greater competence by working with external consultants who purposely helped develop them. This development took place through a tutorial arrangement of joint diagnosis and intervention in the organization, which gave the internal consultants a chance to observe and learn from the model furnished by the external consultants.[31]

There is increasing evidence that an OD career can be stressful, sometimes leading to burnout.[32] Burnout comes from taking on too many jobs, becoming overcommitted, and generally working too hard. The number-one complaint of OD practitioners is constant traveling.[33] OD work often requires 6-day work weeks, with some days running as long as 15 hours. Consultants may spend a week working with one organization or department and then spend the weekend preparing for the next client. They may spend 50–75% of their time on the road, living in planes, cars, hotels, meetings, and restaurants. Indeed, one practitioner has suggested that the majority of OD consultants would repeat the phrase "quality of work life for consultants" this way: "Quality of work life? For consultants?"[34]

OD professionals increasingly are taking steps to cope with burnout. They may shift jobs, moving from external to internal roles to gain more predictable hours or avoid travel. They may learn to pace themselves better and to avoid taking on too much work. Many are engaging in fitness and health programs and are using stress-management techniques, such as those described in Chapter 18.

PROFESSIONAL VALUES

Values have played an important role in organization development from its beginning. Traditionally, OD professionals have promoted a set of values under a humanistic framework, including a concern for inquiry and science, democracy, and being helpful.[35] They have sought to build trust and collaboration; to create an open, problem-solving climate; and to increase the self-control of organization members. More recently, OD practitioners have extended those humanistic values to include a concern for improving organizational effectiveness (for example, to increase productivity or to reduce turnover) and performance (for example, to increase profitability). They have shown an increasing desire to optimize both human benefits and production objectives.[36]

The joint values of humanizing organizations and improving their effectiveness have received widespread support in the OD profession as well as increasing encouragement from managers, employees, labor leaders, and government officials. Indeed, it would be difficult not to support those joint concerns. But in practice OD professionals face serious challenges in simultaneously pursuing greater humanism and organizational effectiveness.[37] More practitioners are experiencing situations in which there is conflict between employees' needs for greater meaning and the organization's need for more effective and efficient use of its resources. For example, expensive capital equipment may run most efficiently if it is highly programmed and routinized, but people may not derive satisfaction from working with such technology. Should efficiency be maximized at the expense of people's satisfaction? Can technology be changed to make it more humanly satisfying while remaining efficient? What compromises are possible? How do these trade-offs shift when they are applied in different social cultures? These are the value dilemmas often faced when we try to optimize both human benefits and organizational effectiveness.

In addition to value issues within organizations, OD practitioners are dealing more and more with value conflicts with powerful outside groups. Organizations are open systems and exist within increasingly turbulent environments. For example, hospitals are facing complex and changing task environments. This has led to a proliferation of external stakeholders with interests in the organization's functioning, including patients, suppliers, medical groups, insurance companies, employers, the government, stockholders, unions, the press, and various interest groups. Those external groups often have different and competing values for judging the organization's effectiveness. For example, stockholders may judge the firm in terms of earnings per share, the government in terms of compliance with equal employment opportunity legislation, patients in terms of quality of care, and ecology groups in terms of hazardous waste disposal. Because organizations must rely on these external groups for resources and legitimacy, they cannot simply ignore these competing values. They must somehow respond to them and try to reconcile the different interests.

Recent attempts to help firms manage external relationships suggest the need for new interventions and competence in OD.[38] Practitioners must have not only social skills like those proposed in Table 3.1 but also political skills. They must understand the distribution of power, conflicts of interest, and value dilemmas inherent in managing external relationships and be able to manage their own role and values with respect to those dynamics. Research suggests this is especially true in interorganizational and international applications of OD.[39] Interventions promoting collaboration and system maintenance may be ineffective in this larger arena, especially when there are power and dominance relationships among organizations and competition for scarce resources. Under those conditions, OD practitioners may need more power-oriented interventions, such as bargaining, coalition forming, and pressure tactics.

For example, organizations are coming under increasing pressure to align their practices with ecologically sound design principles. Popular and scientific concerns over global warming, toxic waste, natural resource depletion, and sustainability each have formidable nonprofit groups, citizen action committees, and professional lobbyists representing them. In addition, an increasing number of consulting firms are marketing products and processes to help organizations achieve a more sustainable relationship with the environment. In response, firms have "gone green," announced contributions to environmental funds, and created alliances with environmental nongovernmental groups. Many argue that these changes are more window dressing than real, more political than operational, and more public relations than substantive. To be fair, a number of organizations have made important changes in their philosophies, strategies, and resource allocations. As a result, the relationships between organizations and environmental groups range from benign to hostile to collaborative. People practicing OD in such settings may need to help organizations manage these relationships and implement strategies to manage their constituencies effectively. That effort will require political skills and greater attention to how the OD practitioner's own values fit with those of the organization.

PROFESSIONAL ETHICS

Ethical issues in OD are concerned with how practitioners perform their helping relationship with organization members. Inherent in any helping relationship is the potential for misconduct and client abuse. OD practitioners can let personal values stand in the way of good practice or use the power inherent in their professional role to abuse (often unintentionally) organization members.

Ethical Guidelines

To its credit, the field of OD always has shown concern for the ethical conduct of its practitioners. There have been several articles and symposia about ethics in OD.[40] In addition, statements of ethics governing OD practice have been sponsored by the Organization Development Institute (http://members.aol.com/ODInst),[41] the American Society for Training & Development (http://www.astd.org),[42] and a consortium of professional associations in OD. The consortium has jointly sponsored an ethical code derived from a large-scale project conducted at the Center for the Study of Ethics in the Professions at the Illinois Institute of Technology. The project's purposes included preparing critical incidents describing ethical dilemmas and using that material for preprofessional and continuing education in OD, providing an empirical basis for a statement of values and ethics for OD professionals, and initiating a process for making the ethics of OD practice explicit on a continuing basis.[43] The ethical guidelines from that project appear in the appendix to this chapter.

Ethical Dilemmas

Although adherence to statements of ethics helps prevent the occurrence of ethical problems, OD practitioners still encounter ethical dilemmas. Figure 3.2 is a process

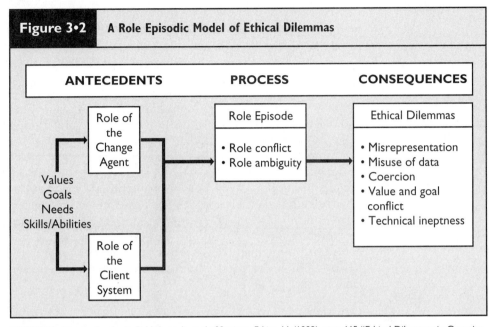

Figure 3•2   **A Role Episodic Model of Ethical Dilemmas**

SOURCE: Kluwer Academic Publishers, *Journal of Business Ethics*, 11 (1992), page 665, "Ethical Dilemmas in Organization Development: A Cross-Cultural Analysis," L. White and M. Rhodeback, Figure 1. © 1992, Kluwer. With kind permission of Kluwer Academic Publishers.

model that explains how ethical dilemmas can occur in OD. The antecedent conditions include an OD practitioner and a client system with different goals, values, needs, skills, and abilities. The entry and contracting phase of planned change is intended to address and clarify these differences. As a practical matter, however, it is unreasonable to assume that all of the differences will be identified and resolved. Under such circumstances, the subsequent intervention process or role episode is almost certainly subject to role conflict and role ambiguity. Neither the client nor the OD practitioner is clear about respective responsibilities. Each party is pursuing different goals, and each is using different skills and values to achieve those goals. The role conflict and ambiguity may produce five types of ethical dilemmas: misrepresentation, misuse of data, coercion, value and goal conflict, and technical ineptness.

Misrepresentation

Misrepresentation occurs when OD practitioners claim that an intervention will produce results that are unreasonable for the change program or the situation. The client can contribute to the problem by portraying inaccurate goals and needs. In either case, one or both parties is operating under false pretenses and an ethical dilemma exists. For example, in an infamous case called "The Undercover Change Agent," an attempt was made to use laboratory training in an organization whose top management did not understand it and was not ready for it. The OD consultant sold T-groups as the intervention that would solve the problems facing the organization. After the president of the firm made a surprise visit to the site where the training was being held, the consultant was fired because the nature and style of the T-group was in direct contradiction to the president's concepts about leadership.[44] Misrepresentation is likely to occur in the entering and contracting phases of planned change when the initial consulting relationship is being established. To prevent misrepresentation, OD practitioners need to gain clarity about the goals of the change effort, and to explore openly with the client its expected effects, its relevance to the client system, and the practitioner's competence in executing the intervention.

Misuse of Data

Misuse of data occurs when information gathered during the OD process is used punitively. Large amounts of information are invariably obtained during the entry and diagnostic phases of OD. Although most OD practitioners value openness and trust, it is important that they be aware of how such data are going to be used. It is a human tendency to use data to enhance a power position. Openness is one thing, but leaking inappropriate information can be harmful to individuals and to the organization. It is easy for a consultant, under the guise of obtaining information, to gather data about whether a particular manager is good or bad. When, how, or if this information can be used is an ethical dilemma not easily resolved. To minimize misuse of data, practitioners should reach agreement up front with organization members about how data collected during the change process will be used. This agreement should be reviewed periodically in light of changing circumstances.

Coercion

Coercion occurs when organization members are forced to participate in an OD intervention. People should have the freedom to choose whether to participate in a change program if they are to gain self-reliance to solve their own problems. In team building, for example, team members should have the option of deciding not to become involved in the intervention. Management should not decide unilaterally that team building is good for members. However, freedom to make a choice requires knowledge about OD. Many organization members have little information about OD interventions, what they involve, and the nature and consequences of becoming involved with them. This makes it imperative for OD practitioners to educate clients about interventions before choices are made for implementing them.

Coercion also can pose ethical dilemmas for the helping relationship between OD practitioners and organization members. Inherent in any helping relationship are possibilities for excessive manipulation and dependency, two facets of coercion. Kelman pointed out that behavior change "inevitably involves some degree of manipulation and control, and at least an implicit imposition of the change agent's values on the client or the person he [or she] is influencing."[45] This places the practitioner on two horns of a dilemma: (1) Any attempt to change is in itself a change and thereby a manipulation, no matter how slight, and (2) there exists no formula or method to structure a change situation so that such manipulation can be totally absent. To attack the first aspect of the dilemma, Kelman stressed freedom of choice, seeing any action that limits freedom of choice as being ethically ambiguous or worse. To address the second aspect, Kelman argued that the OD practitioner must remain keenly aware of her or his own value system and alert to the possibility that those values are being imposed on a client. In other words, an effective way to resolve this dilemma is to make the change effort as open as possible, with the free consent and knowledge of the individuals involved.

The second facet of coercion that can pose ethical dilemmas for the helping relationship involves dependency. Helping relationships invariably create dependency between those who need help and who provide it.[46] A major goal in OD is to lessen clients' dependency on consultants by helping clients gain the knowledge and skills to address organizational problems and manage change themselves. In some cases, however, achieving independence from OD practitioners can result in clients being either counterdependent or overdependent, especially in the early stages of the relationship. To resolve dependency issues, consultants can openly and explicitly discuss with the client how to handle the dependency problem, especially what the client and consultant expect of one another. Another approach is to focus on problem finding. Usually, the client is looking for a solution to a perceived problem. The consultant can redirect the energy to improved joint diagnosis so that both are working on problem identification and problem solving. Such action moves the energy of the client away from dependency. Finally, dependency can be reduced by changing the client's expectation from being helped or controlled by the practitioner to a greater focus on the need to manage the problem. Such a refocusing can reinforce the understanding that the consultant is working for the client and offering assistance that is at the client's discretion.

Value and Goal Conflict

This ethical conflict occurs when the purpose of the change effort is not clear or when the client and the practitioner disagree over how to achieve the goals. The important practical issue for OD consultants is whether it is justifiable to withhold services unilaterally from an organization that does not agree with their values or methods. OD pioneer Gordon Lippitt suggested that the real question is the following: Assuming that some kind of change is going to occur anyway, doesn't the consultant have a responsibility to try to guide the change in the most constructive fashion possible?[47] That question may be of greater importance and relevance to an internal consultant or to a consultant who already has an ongoing relationship with the client.

Argyris takes an even stronger stand, maintaining that the responsibilities of professional OD practitioners to clients are comparable to those of lawyers or physicians, who, in principle, may not refuse to perform their services. He suggests that the very least the consultant can do is to provide "first aid" to the organization, as long as the assistance does not compromise the consultant's values. Argyris suggests that if the Ku Klux Klan asked for assistance and the consultant could at least determine whether the KKK was genuinely interested in assessing itself and willing to commit itself to all that a valid assessment would entail concerning both itself and other groups, the consultant should be willing to help. If later the Klan's objectives proved to be less than honestly stated, the consultant would be free to withdraw without being compromised.[48]

Technical Ineptness

This final ethical dilemma occurs when OD practitioners try to implement interventions for which they are not skilled or when the client attempts a change for which it is not ready. Critical to the success of any OD program is the selection of an appropriate intervention, which depends, in turn, on careful diagnosis of the organization. Selecting an intervention is closely related to the practitioner's own values, skills, and abilities. In solving organizational problems, many OD consultants emphasize a favorite intervention or technique, such as team building, total quality management, or self-managed teams. They let their own values and beliefs dictate the change method.[49] Technical ineptness dilemmas also can occur when interventions do not align with the ability of the organization to implement them. Again, careful diagnosis can reveal the extent to which the organization is ready to make a change and possesses the skills and knowledge to implement it.

Application 3.2 presents an ethical dilemma that arises frequently in OD consulting.[50] What points in the process represent practical opportunities to intervene? Do you agree with Todd's resolution to the problem? What other options did she have?

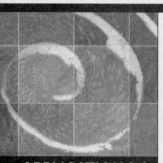

KINDRED TODD AND THE ETHICS OF OD

Kindred Todd had just finished her master's degree in organization development and had landed her first consulting position with a small consulting company in Edmonton, Alberta, Canada. The president, Larry Stepchuck, convinced Todd that his growing organization offered her a great opportunity to learn the business. He had a large number of contacts, an impressive executive career, and several years of consulting experience behind him.

In fact, the firm was growing; adding new clients and projects as fast as its president could hire consultants. A few weeks after Todd was hired, Stepchuck assigned her to a new client, a small oil and gas company. "I've met with the client for several hours," he told her. "They are an important and potentially large opportunity for our firm. They're looking to us to help them address some long-range planning issues. From the way they talk, they could also use some continuous quality improvement work as well."

As Todd prepared for her initial meeting with the client, she reviewed financial data from the firm's annual report, examined trends in the client's industry, and thought about the issues that young firms face. Stepchuck indicated that Todd would first meet with the president of the firm to discuss initial issues and next steps.

When Todd walked into the president's office, she was greeted by the firm's entire senior management team. Team members expressed eagerness to get to work on the important issues of how to improve the organization's key business processes. They believed that an expert in continuous quality improvement (CQI), such as Todd, was exactly the kind of help they needed to increase efficiency and cut costs in the core business. Members began to ask direct questions about technical details of CQI, the likely timeframe within which they might expect results, how to map key processes, and how to form quality improvement teams to identify and implement process improvements.

Todd was stunned and overwhelmed. Nothing that Stepchuck said about the issues facing this company was being discussed and, worse, it was clear that he had sold her to the client as an "expert" in CQI. Her immediate response was to suggest that all of their questions were good ones, but that they needed to be answered in the context of the long-range goals and strategies of the firm. Todd proposed that the best way to begin was for team members to provide her with some history about the organization. In doing so,

she was able to avert disaster and embarrassment for herself and her company, and to appear to be doing all the things necessary to begin a CQI project. The meeting ended with Todd and the management team agreeing to meet again the following week.

Immediately the next day, Todd sought out the president of her firm. She reported on the results of the meeting and her surprise at being sold to this client as an expert on CQI. Todd suggested that her own competencies did not fit the needs of the client and requested that another consultant—one with expertise in CQI—be assigned to the project.

Larry Stepchuck responded to Todd's concerns: "I've known these people for over 10 years. They don't know exactly what they need. CQI is an important buzzword. It's the flavor of the month and if that's what they want, that's what we'll give them." He also told her that there were no other consultants available for this project. "Besides," he said, "the president of the client firm just called to say how much he enjoyed meeting with you and was looking forward to getting started on the project right away."

Kindred Todd felt that Stepchuck's response to her concerns included a strong, inferred ultimatum: If you want to stay with this company, you had better take this job. "I knew I had to sink or swim with this job and this client," she later reported.

As Todd reflected on her options, she pondered the following questions:

- How can I be honest with this client and thus not jeopardize my values of openness and honesty?
- How can I be helpful to this client?
- How much do I know about quality improvement processes?
- How do I satisfy the requirements of my employer?
- What obligations do I have?
- Who's going to know if I do or don't have the credentials to perform this work?
- What if I fail?

After thinking about those issues, Todd summarized her position in terms of three dilemmas: a dilemma of self (who is Kindred Todd?), a dilemma of competence (what can I do?), and a dilemma of confidence (do I like who I work for?). Based on the issues, Todd made the following tactical decisions. She spent 2 days at the library reading about and studying total quality management and continuous improvement. She also contacted several of her friends and former classmates who had experience with quality improvement efforts. Eventually, she contracted with one of them to be her "shadow" consultant—to work with her behind the scenes on formulating and implementing an intervention for the client.

Based on her preparation in the library and the discussions with her shadow consultant, Kindred Todd was able to facilitate an appropriate and effective intervention for the client. Shortly after her assignment was completed, she resigned from the consulting organization.

■ SUMMARY

This chapter has examined the role of the organization development practitioner. That term applies to three sets of people: individuals specializing in OD as a profession, people from related fields who have gained some competence in OD, and managers having the OD skills necessary to change and develop their organizations or departments. Comprehensive lists enumerate core and advanced skills and knowledge that an effective OD specialist should possess, but a smaller set of basic skills and knowledge is applicable for all practitioners at all levels. These include four kinds of background: intrapersonal skills, interpersonal skills, general consultation skills, and knowledge of OD theory.

The professional OD role can apply to internal consultants who belong to the organization undergoing change, to external consultants who are members of universities and consulting firms or are self-employed, and to members of internal–external consulting teams. The OD role may be described aptly in terms of marginality and emotional demands. People with a tolerance for marginal roles seem especially suited for OD practice because they are able to maintain neutrality and objectivity and to develop integrative solutions that reconcile viewpoints among opposing organizational departments. Similarly, the OD practitioner's emotional intelligence and awareness are keys to implementing the role successfully. Whereas in the past the OD role has been described as standing at the client end of the continuum from client-centered to consultant-centered functioning, the development of new and varied interventions has shifted the role of the OD professional to cover the entire range of that continuum.

Although OD is still an emerging field, most practitioners have specific training that ranges from short courses and workshops to graduate and doctoral education. No single career path exists, but internal consulting is often a stepping-stone to becoming an external consultant. Because of the hectic pace of OD practice, specialists should be prepared to cope with high levels of stress and the possibility of career burnout.

Values have played a key role in OD, and traditional values promoting trust, collaboration, and openness have been supplemented recently with concerns for improving organizational effectiveness and productivity. OD specialists may face value dilemmas in trying to jointly optimize human benefits and organization performance. They also may encounter value conflicts when dealing with powerful external stakeholders, such as the government, stockholders, and customers. Dealing with those outside groups may take political skills, as well as the more traditional social skills.

Ethical issues in OD involve how practitioners perform their helping role with clients. As a profession, OD always has shown a concern for the ethical conduct of its practitioners, and several ethical codes for OD practice have been developed by various professional associations. Ethical dilemmas in OD arise around misrepresentation, misuse of data, coercion, value and goal conflict, and technical ineptness.

NOTES

1. A. Church and W. Burke, "Practitioner Attitudes about the Field of Organization Development," in *Research in Organizational Change and Development,* eds. W. Pasmore and R. Woodman (Greenwich, Conn.: JAI Press, 1995).

2. C. Worley, D. Hitchin, and W. Ross, *Integrated Strategic Change* (Reading, Mass.: Addison-Wesley, 1996).

3. R. Henkoff, "Inside Anderson's Army of Advice," *Fortune* (4 October 1993); N. Worren, K. Ruddle, and K. Moore, "From Organization Development to Change Management: The Emergence of a New Profession," *Journal of Applied Behavioral Science* 35 (1999): 273–86.

4. M. Beer and E. Walton, "Organization Change and Development," *Annual Review of Psychology* 38 (1987): 229–72; S. Sherman, "Wanted: Company Change Agents," *Fortune* (11 December 1999): 197–98.

5. R. Kanter, *The Change Masters* (New York: Simon & Schuster, 1983).

6. B. Glickman, "Qualities of Change Agents" (unpublished manuscript, May 1974); R. Havelock, *The Change Agent's Guide to Innovation in Education* (Englewood Cliffs, N.J.: Educational Technology, 1973); R. Lippitt, "Dimensions of the Consultant's Job," in *The Planning of Change,* eds. W. Bennis, K. Benne, and R. Chin (New York: Holt, Rinehart, & Winston, 1961), 156–61; C. Rogers, *On Becoming a Person* (Boston: Houghton Mifflin, 1971); N. Paris, "Some Thoughts on the Qualifications for a Consultant" (unpublished manuscript, 1973); "OD Experts Reflect on the Major Skills Needed by Consultants: With Comments from Edgar Schein," *Academy of Management OD Newsletter* (Spring 1979): 1–4; K. Shepard and A. Raia, "The OD Training Challenge," *Training & Development Journal* 35 (April 1981): 90–96; J. Esper, "Core Competencies in Organization Development" (independent study conducted as partial fulfillment of the M.B.A. degree, Graduate School of Business Administration, University of Southern California, June 1987); E. Neilsen, *Becoming an OD Practitioner* (Englewood Cliffs, N.J.: Prentice Hall, 1984); S. Eisen, H. Steele, and J. Cherbeneau, "Developing OD Competence for the Future," in *Practicing Organization Development,* eds. W. Rothwell, R. Sullivan, and G. McLean (San Diego: Pfeiffer, 1995); A. Church, "The Professionalization of Organization Development," in *Research in Organization Change and Development,* eds. R. Woodman and W. Pasmore (Oxford: JAI Press, 2001).

7. R. Sullivan and K. Quade, "Essential Competencies for Internal and External OD Consultants," in *Practicing Organization Development,* eds. Rothwell, Sullivan, and McLean.

8. C. Worley and G. Varney, "A Search for a Common Body of Knowledge for Master's Level Organization Development and Change Programs—An Invitation to Join the Discussion," *Academy of Management ODC Newsletter* (Winter 1998): 1–4.

9. A. Freedman and R. Zackrison, *Finding Your Way in the Consulting Jungle* (San Francisco: Jossey-Bass, 2001).

10. C. Worley and A. Feyerherm, "Reflections on the Future of Organization Development," *Journal of Applied Behavioral Science* 39 (2003): 97–115.

11. B. Tannenbaum, "Letter to the Editor," Consulting Practice Communique, Academy of Management Managerial Consultation Division 21, 3 (1993): 16–17; B. Tannenbaum, "Self-Awareness: An Essential Element Underlying Consultant Effectiveness," *Journal of Organizational Change Management* 8, 3 (1995): 85–86.

12. A. Church and W. Burke, "Practitioner Attitudes about the Field of Organization Development," in *Research in Organizational Change and Development,* eds. Pasmore and Woodman.

13. M. Lacey, "Internal Consulting: Perspectives on the Process of Planned Change," *Journal of Organizational Change Management* 8, 3 (1995): 75–84.

14. M. Kaarst-Brown, "Five Symbolic Roles of the External Consultant–Integrating Change, Power, and Symbolism," *Journal of Organizational Change Management* 12 (1999): 540–61.

15. Lacey, "Internal Consulting."

16. C. Argyris, *Intervention Theory and Method* (Reading, Mass.: Addison-Wesley, 1973).

17. E. Kirkhart and T. Isgar, "Quality of Work Life for Consultants: The Internal–External Relationship," *Consultation* 5 (Spring 1986): 5–23; J. Thacker and N. Kulick, "The Use of Consultants in Joint Union/Management Quality of Work Life Efforts," *Consultation* 5 (Summer 1986): 116–26.

18. This application was developed by Kimberly McKenna based on her experiences as both an external and internal OD practitioner and on Kirkhart and Isgar, "Quality of Work Life for Consultants."

19. R. Ziller, *The Social Self* (Elmsford, N.Y.: Pergamon, 1973).

20. R. Ziller, B. Stark, and H. Pruden, "Marginality and Integrative Management Positions," *Academy of Management Journal* 12 (December 1969): 487–95; H. Pruden and B. Stark, "Marginality Associated with Interorganizational Linking Process, Productivity and Satisfaction," *Academy of Management Journal* 14 (March 1971): 145–48; W. Lid-

dell, "Marginality and Integrative Decisions," *Academy of Management Journal* 16 (March 1973): 154–56; P. Brown and C. Cotton, "Marginality, A Force for the OD Practitioner," *Training & Development Journal* 29 (April 1975): 14–18; H. Aldrich and D. Gerker, "Boundary Spanning Roles and Organizational Structure," *Academy of Management Review* 2 (April 1977): 217–30; C. Cotton, "Marginality—A Neglected Dimension in the Design of Work," *Academy of Management Review* 2 (January 1977): 133–38; N. Margulies, "Perspectives on the Marginality of the Consultant's Role," in *The Cutting Edge,* ed. W. Burke (La Jolla, Calif.: University Associates, 1978), 60–79.

21. P. Brown, C. Cotton, and R. Golembiewski, "Marginality and the OD Practitioner," *Journal of Applied Behavioral Science* 13 (1977): 493–506.

22. C. Lundberg and C. Young, "A Note on Emotions and Consultancy," *Journal of Organizational Change Management* 14 (2001): 530–38; A. Carr, "Understanding Emotion and Emotionality in a Process of Change," *Journal of Organizational Change Management* 14 (2001): 421–36.

23. D. Goleman, *Emotional Intelligence* (New York: Bantam Books, 1995); R. Cooper and A. Sawaf, *Executive EQ: Emotional Intelligence in Leadership and Organizations* (New York: Grosset/Putnum, 1997); P. Salovey and D. Sluyter, eds., *Emotional Development and Emotional Intelligence* (New York: Basic Books, 1997).

24. J. Mayer and P. Salovey, "What Is Emotional Intelligence?" in Salovey and Sluyter, *Emotional Development.*

25. Goleman, *Emotional Intelligence.*

26. J. Sanford, *Fritz Kunkel: Selected Writings* (Mahwah, N.J.: Paulist Press, 1984); Lundberg and Young, "Note on Emotions"; Carr, "Understanding Emotion."

27. Lundberg and Young, "Note on Emotions."

28. J. Ciarrochi, J. Forgas, and J. Mayer, *Emotional Intelligence in Everyday Life: A Scientific Inquiry* (New York: Psychology Press, 2001).

29. D. Kegan, "Organization Development as OD Network Members See It," *Group and Organization Studies* 7 (March 1982): 5–11.

30. D. Griffin and P. Griffin, "The Consulting Survey," *Consulting Today,* Special Issue (Fall 1998): 1–11 (http://www.consultingtoday.com).

31. J. Lewis III, "Growth of Internal Change Agents in Organizations" (Ph.D. Diss., Case Western Reserve University, 1970).

32. G. Edelwich and A. Brodsky, *Burn-Out Stages of Disillusionment in the Helping Professions* (New York: Human Science, 1980); M. Weisbord, "The Wizard of OD: Or, What Have Magic Slippers to Do with Burnout, Evaluation, Resistance, Planned Change, and Action Research?"

OD Practitioner 10 (Summer 1978): 1–14; M. Mitchell, "Consultant Burnout," in *The 1977 Annual Handbook for Group Facilitators,* eds. J. Jones and W. Pfeiffer (La Jolla, Calif: University Associates, 1977), 145–56.

33. Griffin and Griffin, "Consulting Survey."

34. T. Isgar, "Quality of Work Life of Consultants," *Academy of Management OD Newsletter* (Winter 1983): 2–4.

35. P. Hanson and B. Lubin, *Answers to Questions Most Frequently Asked about Organization Development* (Newbury Park, Calif.: Sage Publications, 1995).

36. Church and Burke, "Practitioner Attitudes."

37. M. Wheatley, R. Tannenbaum, P. Griffin, and K Quade, *Organization Development at Work* (San Francisco: Pfeiffer, 2003).

38. Church, "Professionalization of Organization Development"; S. Guastello, *Chaos, Catastrophe, and Human Affairs* (Mahwah, N.J.: LEA Publishers, 1995); R. Stacey, D. Griffin, and P. Shaw, *Complexity and Management* (London: Routledge, 2000); R. Garud, A. Kumaraswamy, and R. Langlois, *Managing in the Modular Age* (Malden, Mass.: Blackwell Publishing, 2003); A. Shani and P. Docherty, *Learning by Design* (Malden, Mass.: Blackwell Publishing, 2003).

39. R. Saner and L.Yiu, "Porous Boundary and Power Politics: Contextual Constraints of Organization Development Change Projects in the United Nations Organizations," *Gestalt Review* 6 (2002): 84–94.

40. D. Warrick and H. Kelman, "Ethical Issues in Social Intervention," in *Processes and Phenomena of Social Change,* ed. G. Zaltman (New York: John Wiley & Sons, 1973), 377–449; R. Walton, "Ethical Issues in the Practice of Organization Development," working paper no. 1840, Harvard University Graduate School of Business Administration, Boston 1973; D. Bowen, "Value Dilemmas in Organization Development," *Journal of Applied Behavioral Science* 13 (1977): 545–55; L. Greiner and R. Metzger, *Consulting to Management* (Englewood Cliffs, N.J.: Prentice Hall, 1983), 311–25; L. White and K. Wooten, "Ethical Dilemmas in Various Stages of Organization Development," *Academy of Management Review* 8 (1963): 690–97; K. Scalzo, "When Ethics and Consulting Collide" (unpublished master's thesis, Pepperdine University, Graziadio School of Business and Management, Culver City, Calif., 1994); L. White and M. Rhodeback, "Ethical Dilemmas in Organization Development: A Cross-Cultural Analysis," *Journal of Business Ethics* 11, 9 (1992): 663–70; S. DeVogel, R. Sullivan, G. McLean, and W. Rothwell, "Ethics in OD," in *Practicing Organization Development,* eds. Rothwell, Sullivan, and McLean.

41. OD Institute, *International Registry of O.D. Professionals and O.D. Handbook* (Cleveland: OD Institute, 1992).

42. *Who's Who in Training and Development* (Alexandria, Va: American Society for Training & Development, 1992).

43. W. Gellerman, M. Frankel, and R. Ladenson, *Values and Ethics in Organization and Human System Development: Responding to Dilemmas in Professional Life* (San Francisco: Jossey-Bass, 1990).

44. W. Bennis, *Organization Development: Its Nature, Origins, and Prospects* (Reading, Mass.: Addison-Wesley, 1969).

45. H. Kelman, "Manipulation of Human Behavior: An Ethical Dilemma for the Social Scientist," in *The Planning of Change*, 2d ed., eds. W. Bennis, K. Benne, and R. Chin (New York: Holt, Rinehart, & Winston, 1969), 584.

46. E. Schein, *Process Consultation Revisited* (Reading, Mass.: Addison-Wesley, 1999); R. Beckhard, "The De-pendency Dilemma," *Consultants' Communique* 6 (July-September 1978): 1–3.

47. G. Lippitt, *Organization Renewal* (Englewood Cliffs, N.J.: Prentice Hall, 1969).

48. C. Argyris, "Explorations in Consulting–Client Relationships," *Human Organizations* 20 (Fall 1961): 121–33.

49. J. Slocum Jr., "Does Cognitive Style Affect Diagnosis and Intervention Strategies?" *Group and Organization Studies* 3 (June 1978): 199–210.

50. This application was submitted by Kathy Scalzo and is based on an actual case from her interviews with OD consultants on how they resolve ethical dilemmas. The names and places have been changed to preserve anonymity.

▄ APPENDIX

Ethical Guidelines for an Organization Development/Human Systems Development (OD/HSD) Professional

Sponsored by the Human Systems Development Consortium (HSDC), a significant integrative effort by Bill Gellermann has been under way to develop "A Statement of Values and Ethics for Professionals in Organization and Human System Development." HSDC is an informal collection of the leaders of most of the professional associations related to the application of the behavioral and social sciences. A series of drafts based on extensive contributions, comments, and discussions involving many professionals and organizations has led to the following version of this statement.

As an OD/HSD Professional, I commit to supporting and acting in accordance with the following guidelines:

I. Responsibility for Professional Development and Competence

A. Accept responsibility for the consequences of my acts and make every effort to ensure that my services are properly used.

B. Recognize the limits of my competence, culture, and experience in providing services and using techniques; neither seek nor accept assignments outside those limits without clear understanding by the client when exploration at the edge of my competence is reasonable; refer client to other professionals when appropriate.

C. Strive to attain and maintain a professional level of competence in the field, including

1. broad knowledge of theory and practice in
   a. applied behavioral science generally.
   b. management, administration, organizational behavior, and system behavior specifically.
   c. multicultural issues including issues of color and gender.
   d. other relevant fields of knowledge and practice.
2. ability to
   a. relate effectively with individuals and groups.
   b. relate effectively to the dynamics of large, complex systems.
   c. provide consultation using theory and methods of the applied behavioral sciences.

    d. articulate theory and direct its application, including creation of learning experiences for individuals, small and large groups, and for whole systems.

D. Strive continually for self-knowledge and personal growth; be aware that "what is in me" (my perceptions of myself in my world) and "what is outside me" (the realities that exist apart from me) are not the same; be aware that my values, beliefs, and aspirations can both limit and empower me and that they are primary determinants of my perceptions, my behavior, and my personal and professional effectiveness.

E. Recognize my own personal needs and desires and deal with them responsibly in the performance of my professional roles.

F. Obtain consultation from OD/HSD professionals who are native to and aware of the specific cultures within which I work when those cultures are different from my own.

II. Responsibility to Clients and Significant Others

A. Serve the short- and long-term welfare, interests, and development of the client system and all its stakeholders; maintain balance in the timing, pace, and magnitude of planned change so as to support a mutually beneficial relationship between the system and its environment.

B. Discuss candidly and fully goals, costs, risks, limitations, and anticipated outcomes of any program or other professional relationship under consideration; seek to avoid automatic confirmation of predetermined conclusions, either the client's or my own; seek optimum involvement by client system members in every step of the process, including managers and workers' representatives; fully inform client system members about my role, contribution, and strategy in working with them.

C. Fully inform participants in any activity or procedure as to its sponsorship, nature, purpose, implications, and any significant risk associated with it so that they can freely choose their participation in any activity initiated by me; acknowledge that their choice may be limited with activity initiated by recognized authorities; be particularly sensitive to implications and risks when I work with people from cultures other than my own.

D. Be aware of my own personal values, my values as an OD/HSD professional, the values of my native culture, the values of the people with whom I am working, and the values of their cultures; involve the client system in making relevant cultural differences explicit and exploring the possible implications of any OD/HSD intervention for all the stakeholders involved; be prepared to make explicit my assumptions, values, and standards as an OD/HSD professional.

E. Help all stakeholders while developing OD/HSD approaches, programs, and the like, if they wish such help; for example, this could include workers' representatives as well as managers in the case of work with a business organization.

F. Work collaboratively with other internal and external consultants serving the same client system and resolve conflicts in terms of the balanced best interests of the client system and all its stakeholders; make appropriate arrangements with other internal and external consultants about how responsibilities will be shared.

G. Encourage and enable my clients to provide for themselves the services I provide rather than foster continued reliance on me; encourage, foster, and support self-education and self-development by individuals, groups, and all other human systems.

H. Cease work with a client when it is clear that the client is not benefiting or the contract has been completed; do not accept an assignment if its scope is so limited that the client will not benefit or it would involve serious conflict with the values and ethics outlined in this statement.

I. Avoid conflicts of interest.

1. Fully inform the client of my opinion about serving similar or competing organizations; be clear with myself, my clients, and other concerned stakeholders about my loyalties and responsibilities when conflicts of interest arise; keep parties informed of these conflicts; cease work with the client if the conflicts cannot be adequately resolved.

2. Seek to act impartially when involved in conflicts between parties in the client system; help them resolve their conflicts themselves, without taking sides; if necessary to change my role from serving as impartial consultant, do so explicitly; cease work with the client, if necessary.

3. Identify and respond to any major differences in professionally relevant values or ethics between myself and my clients with the understanding that conditions may require ceasing work with the client.

4. Accept differences in the expectations and interests of different stakeholders and realize that those differences cannot be reconciled all the time.

J. Seek consultation and feedback from neutral third parties in case of conflict between myself and my client.

K. Define and protect the confidentiality of my client–professional relationships.

1. Make limits of confidentiality clear to clients/participants.

2. Reveal information accepted in confidence only to appropriate or agreed-upon recipients or authorities.

3. Use information obtained during professional work in writings, lectures, or other public forums only with prior consent or when disguised so that it is impossible from my presentations alone to identify the individuals or systems with whom I have worked.

4. Make adequate provisions for maintaining confidentiality in the storage and disposal of records; make provisions for responsibly preserving records in the event of my retirement or disability.

L. Establish mutual agreement on a contract covering services and remuneration.

1. Ensure a clear understanding of and mutual agreement on the services to be performed; do not shift from that agreement without both a clearly defined professional rationale for making the shift and the informed consent of the clients/participants; withdraw from the agreement if circumstances beyond my control prevent proper fulfillment.

2. Ensure mutual understanding and agreement by putting the contract in writing to the extent feasible, yet recognize that

a. the spirit of professional responsibility encompasses more than the letter of the contract.

b. some contracts are necessarily incomplete because complete information is not available at the outset.

c. putting the contract in writing may be neither necessary nor desirable.

3. Safeguard the best interests of the client, the profession, and the public by making sure that financial arrangements are fair and in keeping with appropriate statutes, regulations, and professional standards.

M. Provide for my own accountability by evaluating and assessing the effects of my work.

1. Make all reasonable efforts to determine if my activities have accomplished the agreed-upon goals and have not had other undesirable consequences; seek to undo any undesirable consequences, and do not attempt to cover up these situations.

    2. Actively solicit and respond with an open mind to feedback regarding my work and seek to improve.

    3. Develop, publish, and use assessment techniques that promote the welfare and best interests of clients/participants; guard against the misuse of assessment results.

N. Make public statements of all kinds accurately, including promotion and advertising, and give service as advertised.

    1. Base public statements providing professional opinions or information on scientifically acceptable findings and techniques as much as possible, with full recognition of the limits and uncertainties of such evidence.

    2. Seek to help people make informed choices when making statements as part of promotion or advertising.

    3. Deliver services as advertised and do not shift without a clear professional rationale and the informed consent of the participants/clients.

III. Responsibility to the Profession

A. Act with due regard for the needs, special competencies and obligations of my colleagues in OD/HSD and other professions; respect the prerogatives and obligations of the institutions or organizations with which these other colleagues are associated.

B. Be aware of the possible impact of my public behavior upon the ability of colleagues to perform their professional work; perform professional activity in a way that will bring credit to the profession.

C. Work actively for ethical practice by individuals and organizations engaged in OD/HSD activities and, in case of questionable practice, use appropriate channels for confronting it, including

    1. direct discussion when feasible.

    2. joint consultation and feedback, using other professionals as third parties.

    3. enforcement procedures of existing professional organizations.

    4. public confrontation.

D. Contribute to continuing professional development by

    1. supporting the development of other professionals, including mentoring with less experienced professionals.

    2. contributing ideas, methods, findings, and other useful information to the body of OD/HSD knowledge and skill.

E. Promote the sharing of OD/HSD knowledge and skill by various means including

    1. granting use of my copyrighted material as freely as possible, subject to a minimum of conditions, including a reasonable price defined on the basis of professional as well as commercial values.

    2. giving credit for the ideas and products of others.

IV. Social Responsibility

A. Strive for the preservation and protection of fundamental human rights and the promotion of social justice.

B. Be aware that I bear a heavy social responsibility because my recommendations and professional actions may alter the lives and well-being of individuals within my client systems, the systems themselves, and the larger systems of which they are subsystems.

C. Contribute knowledge, skill, and other resources in support of organizations, programs, and activities that seek to improve human welfare; be prepared to accept clients who do not have sufficient resources to pay my full fees at reduced fees or no charge.

D. Respect the cultures of the organization, community, country, or other human system within which I work (including the cultures' traditions, values, and moral and ethical expectations and their implications), yet recognize and constructively confront the counterproductive aspects of those cultures whenever feasible; be sensitive to cross-cultural differences and their implications; be aware of the cultural filters which bias my view of the world.

E. Recognize that accepting this statement as a guide for my behavior involves holding myself to a standard that may be more exacting than the laws of any country in which I practice.

F. Contribute to the quality of life in human society at large; work toward and support a culture based on mutual respect for each other's rights as human beings; encourage the development of love, trust, openness, mutual responsibility, authentic and harmonious relationships, empowerment, participation, and involvement in a spirit of freedom and self-discipline as elements of this culture.

G. Engage in self-generated or collaborative endeavor to develop means for helping across cultures.

H. Serve the welfare of all the people of Earth, all living things, and their environment.

The Process of Organization Development

Chapter 4   Entering and Contracting

Chapter 5   Diagnosing Organizations

Chapter 6   Diagnosing Groups and Jobs

Chapter 7   Collecting and Analyzing
                     Diagnostic Information

Chapter 8   Feeding Back Diagnostic Information

Chapter 9   Designing Interventions

Chapter 10   Leading and Managing Change

Chapter 11   Evaluating and Institutionalizing
                     Organization Development
                     Interventions

Selected Cases   It's Your Turn
                     Sunflower Incorporated
                     Evaluating the Change Agent
                        Program at Siemens
                        Nixdorf (A)
                     Initiating Change in the
                        Manufacturing and
                        Distribution Division of
                        PolyProd

4

Entering and Contracting

The planned change process described in Chapter 2 generally starts when one or more key managers or administrators somehow sense a new vision or opportunity for their organization, department, or group or that the unit could be improved through organization development. The organization might be successful yet have room for improvement. It might be facing impending environmental conditions that necessitate a change in how it operates. The organization could be experiencing particular problems, such as poor product quality, high rates of absenteeism, or dysfunctional conflicts among departments. Conversely, the problems might appear more diffuse and consist simply of feelings that the organization should be "more innovative," "more competitive," or "more effective."

Entering and contracting are the initial steps in the OD process. They involve defining in a preliminary manner the organization's problems or opportunities for development and establishing a collaborative relationship between the OD practitioner and members of the client system about how to work on those issues. Entering and contracting set the initial parameters for carrying out the subsequent phases of OD: diagnosing the organization, planning and implementing changes, and evaluating and institutionalizing them. They help to define what issues will be addressed by those activities, who will carry them out, and how they will be accomplished.

Entering and contracting can vary in complexity and formality depending on the situation. In those cases where the manager of a work group or department serves as his or her own OD practitioner, entering and contracting typically involve the manager and group members meeting to discuss what issues to work on and how they will jointly meet the goals they set. Here, entering and contracting are relatively simple and informal. They involve all relevant members directly in the process—with a minimum of formal procedures. In situations where managers and administrators are considering the use of professional OD practitioners, either from inside or from outside the organization, entering and contracting tend to be more complex and formal.[1] OD practitioners may need to collect preliminary information to help define the problematic or development issues. They may need to meet with representatives of the client organization rather than with the total membership; they may need to formalize their respective roles and how the change process will unfold. In cases where the anticipated changes are strategic and large in scale, formal proposals from multiple consulting firms are requested and legal contracts are drawn up.

This chapter first discusses the activities and content-oriented issues involved in entering into and contracting for an OD initiative. Major attention here will be directed at complex processes involving OD professionals and client organizations. Similar entering and contracting issues, however, need to be addressed in even the simplest OD efforts, where managers serve as OD practitioners for their own work units. Unless there is clarity and agreement about what issues to work on, who will address them and how that will be accomplished, and what timetable will be followed, subsequent stages of the OD process are likely to be confusing and ineffective. The chapter concludes with a discussion of the interpersonal process issues involved in entering and contracting for OD work.

ENTERING INTO AN OD RELATIONSHIP

An OD process generally starts when a member of an organization or unit contacts an OD practitioner about potential help in addressing an organizational issue.[2] The organization member may be a manager, staff specialist, or some other key participant; the practitioner may be an OD professional from inside or outside of the organization. Determining whether the two parties should enter into an OD relationship typically involves clarifying the nature of the organization's current functioning and the issue(s) to be addressed, the relevant client system for that issue, and the appropriateness of the particular OD practitioner.[3] In helping assess these issues, the OD practitioner may need to collect preliminary data about the organization. Similarly, the organization may need to gather information about the practitioner's competence and experience.[4] This knowledge will help both parties determine whether they should proceed to develop a contract for working together.

This section describes the activities involved in entering an OD relationship: clarifying the organizational issue, determining the relevant client, and selecting the appropriate OD practitioner.

Clarifying the Organizational Issue

When seeking help from OD practitioners, organizations typically start with a presenting problem—the issue that has caused them to consider an OD process. It may be specific (decreased market share, increased absenteeism) or general ("we're growing too fast," "we need to prepare for rapid changes"). The presenting problem often has an implied or stated solution. For example, managers may believe that because members of their teams are in conflict, team building is the obvious answer. They may even state the presenting problem in the form of a solution: "We need some team building."

In many cases, however, the presenting problem is only a symptom of an underlying problem. For example, conflict among members of a team may result from several deeper causes, including ineffective reward systems, personality differences, inappropriate structures, and poor leadership. The issue facing the organization or department must be clarified early in the OD process so that subsequent diagnostic and intervention activities are focused correctly.[5]

Gaining a clearer perspective on the organizational issue may require collecting preliminary data.[6] OD practitioners often examine company records and interview a few key members to gain an introductory understanding of the organization, its context, and the nature of the presenting problem. Those data are gathered in a relatively short period of time—typically over a few hours to 1 or 2 days. They are intended to provide enough rudimentary knowledge of the organizational issue to enable the two parties to make informed choices about proceeding with the contracting process.

The diagnostic phase of OD involves a far more extensive assessment of the problematic or development issue than occurs during the entering and contracting stage. The diagnosis also might discover other issues that need to be addressed, or it might lead to redefining the initial issue that was identified during the entering and contracting stage. This is a prime example of the emergent nature of the OD process: Things may change as new information is gathered and new events occur.

Determining the Relevant Client

A second activity in entering an OD relationship is defining the relevant client for addressing the organizational issue.[7] Generally, the relevant client includes those organization members who can directly impact the change issue, whether it is solving a particular problem or improving an already successful organization or department. Unless these members are identified and included in the entering and contracting process, they may withhold their support for and commitment to the OD process. In trying to improve the productivity of a unionized manufacturing plant, for example, the relevant client may need to include union officials as well as managers and staff personnel. It is not unusual for an OD project to fail because the relevant client was inappropriately defined.

Determining the relevant client can vary in complexity depending on the situation. In those cases where the organizational issue can be addressed in a specific organization unit, client definition is relatively straightforward. Members of that unit constitute the relevant client. They or their representatives must be included in the entering and contracting process. For example, if a manager asked for help in improving the decision-making process of his or her team, the manager and team members would be the relevant client. Unless they are actively involved in choosing an OD practitioner and defining the subsequent change process, there is little likelihood that OD will improve team decision making.

Determining the relevant client is more complex when the organizational issue cannot readily be addressed in a single unit. Here, it may be necessary to expand the definition of the client to include members from multiple units, from different hierarchical levels, and even from outside of the organization. For example, the manager of a production department may seek help in resolving conflicts between his or her unit and other departments in the organization. The relevant client would extend beyond the boundaries of the production department because that department alone cannot resolve the issue. The client might include members from all departments involved in the conflict as well as the executive to whom all of the departments report. If that interdepartmental conflict also involved key suppliers and customers from outside of the firm, the relevant client might include members of those groups.

In such complex situations, OD practitioners need to gather additional information about the organization to determine the relevant client, generally as part of the preliminary data collection that typically occurs when clarifying the issue to be addressed. When examining company records or interviewing personnel, practitioners can seek to identify the key members and organizational units that need to be involved. For example, they can ask organization members such questions as: Who can directly impact the organizational issue? Who has a vested interest in it? Who has the power to approve or reject the OD effort? Answers to those questions can help determine who is the relevant client for the entering and contracting stage, although the client may change during the later stages of the OD process as new data are gathered and changes occur. If so, participants may have to return to and modify this initial stage of the OD effort.

Selecting an OD Practitioner

The last activity involved in entering an OD relationship is selecting an OD practitioner who has the expertise and experience to work with members on the organizational issue. Unfortunately, little systematic advice is available on how to choose a competent OD professional, whether from inside or outside of the organization.[8] To help lower the uncertainty of choosing from among external OD practitioners, organizations may request that proposals be submitted. In these cases, the OD practitioner must take all of the information gathered in the prior steps and create an outline of how the process might unfold. Table 4.1 provides one view of the key elements of such a proposal. It suggests that a written proposal include project goals, outlines of action plans, a list of roles and responsibilities, recommended interventions, and proposed fees and expenses.

For less formal and structured selection processes, the late Gordon Lippitt, a pioneering practitioner in the field, suggested several criteria for selecting, evaluating, and developing OD practitioners.[9] Lippitt listed areas that managers should consider

Table 4•1	Elements of an Effective Proposal
CONTENT	**DESCRIPTION**
Goals of proposed effort	Provide descriptive, clear, and concise goals including measurable results to be achieved.
Recommended action or implementation plan	Provide integrated action steps. These include (1) an organizational diagnosis, (2) a process to be used to convert data into useful information, (3) a data feedback process, and (4) an action-planning process.
Specification of responsibilities	Provide specific responsibilities for which various leaders, including the OD practitioner and other parties, will be held accountable.
Strategy for achieving the desired state	Provide recommended change strategies, including education/training, political influence, redesigning the structure, and confrontation of resistant individuals.
Fees, terms, and conditions	Provide an outline of the fees and expenses associated with project.

SOURCE: A. Freedman and R. Zackrison, *Finding Your Way in the Consulting Jungle*, 141-47. (San Francisco: Jossey-Bass/Pfeiffer. Copyright © 2001. This material is used by permission of John Wiley & Sons, Inc.

before selecting a practitioner—including their ability to form sound interpersonal relationships, the degree of focus on the problem, the skills of the practitioner relative to the problem, the extent that the consultant clearly informs the client as to his or her role and contribution, and whether the practitioner belongs to a professional association. References from other clients are highly important. A client may not like the consultant's work, but it is critical to know the reasons for both pleasure and displeasure. One important consideration is whether the consultant approaches the organization with openness and an insistence on diagnosis or whether the practitioner appears to have a fixed program that is applicable to almost any organization.

Certainly, OD consulting is as much a person specialization as it is a task specialization. The OD professional needs not only a repertoire of technical skills but also the personality and interpersonal competence to use himself or herself as an instrument of change. Regardless of technical training, the consultant must be able to maintain a boundary position, coordinating among various units and departments and mixing disciplines, theories, technology, and research findings in an organic rather than a mechanical way. The practitioner is potentially the most important OD technology available.

Thus, in selecting an OD practitioner, perhaps the most important issue is the fundamental question, "How effective has the person been in the past, with what kinds of organizations, using what kinds of techniques?" In other words, references must be checked. Interpersonal relationships are tremendously important, but even con artists have excellent interpersonal relationships and skills.

The burden of choosing an effective OD practitioner should not rest entirely with the client organization.[10] Consultants also bear a heavy responsibility for seeking an appropriate match between their skills and knowledge and what the organization or department needs. Few managers are sophisticated enough to detect or to understand subtle differences in expertise among OD professionals, and they often do not understand the difference between intervention specialties. Thus, practitioners should help educate potential clients, being explicit about their strengths and weaknesses and their range of competence. If OD professionals realize that a good match does not exist, they should inform managers and help them find more suitable help.

Application 4.1 describes the entering process at American Healthways and high-lights the importance of collecting preliminary data and identifying the relevant client. This is the first in a series of applications used throughout the text to provide a more detailed picture of a large-scale OD intervention.

DEVELOPING A CONTRACT

The activities of entering an OD relationship are a necessary prelude to developing an OD contract. They define the major focus for contracting, including the relevant parties. Contracting is a natural extension of the entering process and clarifies how the OD process will proceed. It typically establishes the expectations of the parties, the time and resources that will be expended, and the ground rules under which the parties will operate.

The goal of contracting is to make a good decision about how to carry out the OD process.[11] It can be relatively informal and involve only a verbal agreement between the client and OD practitioner. A team leader with OD skills, for example, may voice his or her concerns to members about how the team is functioning. After some discussion, they might agree to devote 1 hour of future meeting time to diagnosing the team with the help of the leader. Here, entering and contracting are done together, informally. In other cases, contracting can be more protracted and result in a formal document. That typically occurs when organizations employ outside OD practition-ers. Government agencies, for example, generally have procurement regulations that apply to contracting with outside consultants.[12]

Regardless of the level of formality, all OD processes require some form of explicit contracting that results in either a verbal or a written agreement. Such contracting clarifies the client's and the practitioner's expectations about how the OD process will take place. Unless there is mutual understanding and agreement about the process, there is considerable risk that someone's expectations will be unfulfilled.[13] That can lead to reduced commitment and support, to misplaced action, or to pre-mature termination of the process.

The contracting step in OD generally addresses three key areas:[14] setting mu-tual expectations or what each party expects to gain from the OD process; the time and resources that will be devoted to it; and the ground rules for working together.

Mutual Expectations

This part of the contracting process focuses on the expectations of the client and the OD practitioner. The client states the services and outcomes to be provided by the OD practitioner and describes what the organization expects from the process and the consultant. Clients usually can describe the desired outcomes, such as de-creased turnover or higher job satisfaction. Encouraging them to state their wants in the form of outcomes, working relationships, and personal accomplishments can facilitate the development of a good contract.[15]

The OD practitioner also should state what he or she expects to gain from the OD process. This can include opportunities to try new interventions, report the results to other potential clients, and receive appropriate compensation or recognition.

Time and Resources

To accomplish change, the organization and the OD practitioner must commit time and resources to the effort. Each must be clear about how much energy and how many resources will be dedicated to the change process. Failure to make explicit the necessary requirements of a change process can quickly ruin an OD effort. For ex-ample, a client may clearly state that the assignment involves diagnosing the causes

ENTERING AMERICAN HEALTHWAYS CORPORATION

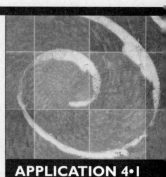

APPLICATION 4•1

American Healthways Corporation (AMHC)(http://www. americanhealthways.com) is a provider of specialized disease management services to health plans and hospitals. In fiscal year 2002, AMHC had revenues of $122 million. The company, founded in 1981 as American Healthcorp, originally owned and managed hospitals. In 1984 it offered its first disease management service focused on diabetes. Under the name Diabetes Treatment Centers of America, it worked with hospitals to create "centers of excellence" to improve hospital volumes and lower costs. After going public in 1991, it offered in 1993, its first diabetes management program to health plans—an entirely new customer segment. This shift in customer base was a key event in the company's history, and two new disease management programs for cardiac and respiratory diseases were offered in 1998 and 1999. By 2000, hospital revenues, once 100% of the company's mix, had dropped to 38% as the health plan business grew.

One day in mid-2001, a university-based OD practitioner got a call from one of his former students, now the Director of Training and OD at AMHC. After some time as an external consultant, he had taken an internal position at AMHC. He described the company and some of the challenges it was facing, how exciting it was to be working at a growing organization, and that he was looking for some consulting help with organization design and structure. He wondered whether the professor was interested in such a challenge. The professor and the Director had a few conversations over a period of a couple of months, and several suggestions for other practitioners were made. The professor was willing to help with advice, feedback, and coaching for one of his old alums, but the demands of teaching, research, and administration, as well as another client, was filling up his time. After a couple of additional phone calls, however, the Director convinced the professor to meet.

Prior to the visit, the professor accessed the company's 10k reports through AMHC's Web site. The company's revenue growth had indeed been phenomenal, and profits from the health plan business had more than doubled from 1998 to 2000. In addition, the Director provided the following information on the company. First, the COO, described as brilliant and charismatic, led the health plan business (but not the hospital business) and was likely to become the corporation's next CEO. Second, an external OD consultant had worked with the organization for a long time on various projects related to culture, executive coaching, and team building. Third, the company had a long tradition of very conservative personnel practices; the culture was described as "nice" and nobody was ever fired. Fourth, growth was the overriding issue in the organization: Many people needed to be hired quickly, every person and every office were frantically trying to keep up, and consequently, there was no "bandwidth" to attend to key issues facing the company. Finally, the organization was also engaged in several other "initiatives" including a culture and values group and a strategy group.

In mid-December, 2001, the professor visited the Nashville, Tennessee headquarters of AMHC and met with the COO, the Senior VP of Human Resources, the long-time external OD consultant, and the Director. The meeting consisted of the COO providing additional background on the company, especially its organization structure. The current structure was more divisional than functional, and reflected the senior leadership team's view that the health plan business was different from the hospital business. Such a structure also allowed the organization to signal the importance of the health plan business to the future of the company. For example, the human resources group and the CFO were assigned to the COO of the health plan business rather than the CEO. The COO also described how he and the CEO saw the health plan business as an important opportunity and misunderstood threat to the company. The business's revenue potential had clearly attracted Wall Street's attention, but there was little appreciation for how the current structure limited the organization's ability to expand. By mid-2001, they were in strong agreement that the structure which had supported $75 million in sales in fiscal year 2001 would not support the revenue growth they envisioned over the next 5 to 10 years. In collaboration with the Senior VP of Human Resources and the Director of Training and OD, they began to look for consulting assistance.

The COO asked several questions of the professor, including experience with other organizations, experience with similar projects, and what options did the organization have with respect to organization structure. The OD professor responded with examples of former clients and experiences as well as a listing and description of alternative structures that were being implemented at different companies. The COO pressed for more information about the newer structural ideas, such as networks and team-based organizations. There was considerable discussion about these alternatives and their applicability to AMHC.

The meeting ended with promises to stay in touch.

of poor productivity in a work group. However, the client may expect the practitioner to complete the assignment without talking to the workers. Typically, clients want to know how much time will be necessary to complete the assignment, who needs to be involved, how much it will cost, and so on.

Block has suggested that resources can be divided into two parts.[16] Essential requirements are things that are absolutely necessary if the change process is to be successful. From the practitioner's perspective, they can include access to key people or information, enough time to do the job, and commitment from certain people. The organization's essential requirements might include a speedy diagnosis or assurances that the project will be conducted at the lowest price. Being clear about the constraints on carrying out the assignment will facilitate the contracting process and improve the chances for success. Desirable requirements are those things that would be nice to have but are not absolutely necessary, such as access to special resources or written rather than verbal reports.

Ground Rules

The final part of the contracting process involves specifying how the client and the OD practitioner will work together. The parameters established may include such issues as confidentiality, if and how the OD practitioner will become involved in personal or interpersonal issues, how to terminate the relationship, and whether the practitioner is supposed to make expert recommendations or help the manager make decisions. For internal consultants, organizational politics make it especially important to clarify issues of how to handle sensitive information and how to deliver "bad news."[17] Such process issues are as important as the needed substantive changes. Failure to address the concerns may mean that the client or the practitioner has inappropriate assumptions about how the process will unfold.

Application 4.2 describes the contracting meeting for the structural change project at American Healthways.

PERSONAL PROCESS ISSUES IN ENTERING AND CONTRACTING

The prior discussion on entering and contracting addressed the activities and content-oriented issues associated with beginning an OD project. In this final section, we discuss the interpersonal issues an OD practitioner must be aware of to produce a successful agreement. In most cases, the client's expectations, resources, and working relationship requirements will not fit perfectly with the OD practitioner's essential and desirable requirements. Negotiating the differences to improve the likelihood of success can be intra- and interpersonally challenging.

Entering and contracting are the first exchanges between a client and an OD practitioner. Establishing a healthy relationship at the outset makes it more likely that the client's desired outcomes will be achieved and that the OD practitioner will be able to improve the organization's capacity to manage change in the future. In this initial stage, both parties are facing a considerable amount of uncertainty and ambiguity. On the one hand, the client is likely to feel exposed, inadequate, or vulnerable. The organization's current effectiveness and the request for help may seem to the client like an admission that they are incapable of solving the problem or providing the leadership necessary to achieve a set of results. Moreover, they are entering into a relationship where they may feel unable to control the activities of the OD practitioner. As a result, they feel vulnerable because of their dependency on the practitioner to provide assistance. Consciously or unconsciously, feelings of exposure, inadequacy, or vulnerability may lead the client to resist coming to closure on the contract. The OD practitioner must be alert to the signs of resistance, such as asking for extraordinary amounts of detail, and be able to address them skillfully.

CONTRACTING AT AMERICAN HEALTHWAYS CORPORATION

The meeting with the COO and the other members of the organization had gone well. The COO, in discussion with the Senior VP of HR, the Director of Training and OD, and others, believed that the OD professor was qualified to facilitate the effort and had the requisite knowledge about organization design to provide AMHC with both traditional and innovative structural options. In line with the Director of Training and OD's description of the culture as driven and fast-paced, the COO wanted to move quickly and asked for a detailed proposal.

The OD practitioner/professor was reluctant to prepare such a document; the effort to make a thorough, week-by-week estimate of how many meetings there would be, the deliverables to be committed to, and how other events might go was really a waste of time. The professor explained that in large-scale changes such as this, any written proposal would likely be thrown out after the first few meetings or initial workshop. It was just too complex a change to be predicted accurately. What was more important, the professor argued, was that a good decision be made about whether he was the right person for the job or not. If he was, then time would be better spent getting agreement on how the parties would work together and toward what end. The COO and the Director countered that some kind of contract was necessary. The professor understood the need for some documentation, and agreed to draft a short letter outlining the goals, proposed process, and other key elements of a working relationship once some additional conversations about the working relationship occurred.

As the contracting moved forward, the COO and the OD professor had two hour-long phone calls about their emerging relationship. Importantly, they discussed how the two of them should go about disagreeing with each other. The professor asked a hypothetical question about being in a meeting and the COO wanting to go in one direction, but the professor, based on experience or research, believing that the direction was inappropriate. The COO indicated that while he wanted to understand the sources of the disagreement, the final decision was his to make. The professor appreciated his frankness and understood his answer. Moreover, he agreed with the idea that the COO had ultimate responsibility for the success of the project. The OD professor then confirmed that his role was as advisor to the COO and the organization on the process of change and as a source of knowledge and experience about organization design. The OD professor then asked, "Can I push this idea out a little further? What if I or others think the process isn't moving forward appropriately and the reason, in my judgment, is that your behavior is getting in the way? How do we handle that?" The COO re-

sponded, "I expect to be confronted, appropriately, with that information." The professor indicated his agreement.

The COO had his own set of questions. He wanted to know, for example, how long

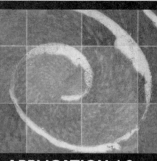

the project would take. The OD professor responded that there was some good news and bad news. The good news was that a decision about which structure to implement could be arrived at within a 3-to-6-month time frame. The bad news was that implementation of a large-scale change like this would probably take years, not months. The COO appreciated the difference between choosing and implementing and talked about how the organization's culture and the growth expectations would push things along. The conversation then turned to how to make the structural decision. The OD professor shared his biases about participation, the transfer of knowledge, and learning. The COO responded, "Professor, I understand your preference to 'go slow to go fast' and that people will support decisions they've participated in. I also understand you would like to build capacity in my organization. But the pressures for growth and the speed with which this organization moves will resist such an approach." The professor acknowledged those concerns, and the COO followed up with questions about whether the process could be speeded up. The COO and the professor began a dialogue about the importance of a process that often results in feelings that things are going too slowly at first, but has the advantage of helping things move more quickly later on. The biases of the two were explored in the context of learning, speed, and the culture of the organization. The COO and OD professor discussed these values and agreed that the professor would propose an initial process that would move the decision about the new structure forward quickly, but that discussions and decisions about how to implement the chosen structure would be outlined in broad terms.

The OD professor asked one other set of questions during their conversations. He asked the COO, "What's your experience with these kinds of changes? Have you led big restructurings before? Do you know what you are getting into? The hassles, upset people, delays, arguments, and politics? Are you sure you are ready to do this?" The COO was very clear in his answer. He said, "Absolutely. I was able to engineer the last structural change here. But the scope and scale of that was clearly different from this one. I need your knowledge about the pros and cons of different structures. But on the leadership side, I'm good and ready."

Based on these conversations, the OD professor and COO agreed to work together, and the OD professor produced a letter of understanding that represented their first contract. The letter is shown below. (To read more about this case, go to Application 7.1.)

January, 2002
EVP and Chief Operating Officer
American Healthways, Inc.
Nashville, TN

Dear COO:
Thanks for making time in your schedule to talk about the structure and design of American Healthways, the challenges of managing rapid growth, and the elements of our working together. I promised to put together some ideas about how we might proceed.

What I heard:

- You believe the current organization structure and design (successfully implemented in response to an earlier period of growth) is no longer able to sustain the expected growth in the company.

- You would like an organization structure that not only will support the next phase of growth but is flexible enough to serve the organization for several years.

- You would like a 3-to-5-year plan, with milestones and indicators, to guide the transition from the current structure to the future structure.

- Speed is of the essence ... the existing symptoms are acute.

This proposal begins with my recommendations for the process of crafting a new structure and developing a plan for its implementation. It then abstracts from this process a timetable and cost proposal.

Process Proposal

The process I propose below provides the best balance of quality, education, speed, and implementation ease. The key steps include selecting a design team; learning, visioning, and diagnosing; designing an action plan; initiating the implementation; and monitoring, adapting, and evaluating the implementation.

Design Team Selection. The process begins with the **selection of a design team.** The team should consist of about seven to nine individuals—including the owner of the structural design process (nominally, the COO), representatives from key areas in the company (e.g., IT, call centers, sales and marketing, HR, etc.), and key influencers and implementers (e.g., opinion leaders, informal champions of change, etc.). Care should be taken to design the team for both (a) repre-sentation and (b) energy. It should also be seen as a potential developmental opportunity for key employees.

Learning, Visioning, and Diagnosing. Once the team is selected, there should be a period of **education** where the group becomes "collectively smart" about organization structure and design issues. Typically this involves some reading, benchmarking, and other activities to ensure that the team makes appropriate decisions about the new organization structure. In addition, the group engages in some **visioning** activities that focus attention on the end state. In this process, we will imagine American Healthways 5 to 10 years in the future, as a larger and more powerful organization in the health care industry. From that visioning process, related aspects of the design of the organization can be induced and articulated. Finally, the group will engage in a **diagnosis** of the current organization structure. This may include a categorization of the current structure's strengths and weaknesses, the organization's key processes, the building of an "assumption pool," an inventory of the current human resources, an understanding of the cultural values the organization wishes to retain, other systems (e.g., reward/recognition, performance management, communication), and so on.

Action Planning. The first key output of the team will be a **3-to-5-year action plan** that identifies the recommended organization structure the organization should move to (and its justification), the key activities and milestones that need to be implemented, assigned responsibilities/accountabilities for those activities, and contingencies/assumptions that need to be monitored.

Initial Implementation Steps. The new structure and action plan need to be communicated to the organization. The design team will conduct its initial activities in such a way that this should be a relatively easy matter.

Implementation Monitoring, Correction, and Evaluation. As the plan is implemented, new information, changes in the environment, and other issues always arise that require **adaptation and adjustment.** In this phase, the design team is charged with monitoring implementation by collecting "implementation feedback" to find out if the plan is on track. In light of the data collected, medications to the plan can be discussed, designed, and implemented. In addition, and at appropriate times over the 3-to-5-year implementation horizon, the design team will engage in more formal **evaluation processes and discuss their learnings** about structure, organization design, and change.

Contracting Issues

As with proposals, I like to keep things simple. I will provide consulting services up to and including the development of the action plan for $xx,xxx plus direct expenses (airfare, hotel, taxis, parking, and so on). Additional consulting time beyond that point can be contracted.

In addition, we should be clear about the expectations of our relationship. Because of my association with a university, I'm not a "typical" consultant. Some of those expectations are outlined below:

- Relatively free access. You should expect to have your phone calls/email messages answered promptly and vice versa. If either of us wants to schedule a phone conference or face-to-face conversation, we should respect each other's schedules and demands and make every effort to accommodate each other's requests.

- I expect that you will take into account that I have duties as a professor that may need to take priority over my consulting tasks. In addition, I have a prior consulting commitment and this, too, may hinder my flexibility, especially in the short run as we begin the project.

- I will need access to potentially sensitive data. Since you are a public company, I expect to sign or at least be bound by a "nondisclosure agreement." However, I would also like permission to use this experience in the classroom as a teaching case subject to the limitations of the nondisclosure agreement.

I'll be in touch with you in the next week or two to begin the design team selection process.

Sincerely,
John Doe
President

On the other hand, the OD practitioner may have feelings of empathy, unworthiness, and dependency. The practitioner may overidentify with the client's issues and want to be so helpful that he or she agrees to unreasonable deadlines or inadequate resources. The practitioner's desire to be seen as competent and worthy may lead to an agreement on a project for which the practitioner has few skills or experience. Finally, in response to reasonable client requests, the practitioner may challenge the client's motivation and become defensive. Schein notes that OD practitioners too often underestimate or ignore the power and impact of entry and contracting as an intervention in their own right.[18] With even the simplest request for help, there are a myriad of things the OD practitioner, entering a system for the first time, does not know. Establishing a relationship with a client must be approached carefully; the initial contacts and conversations must represent a model of how the OD process will be conducted. As a result, actually coming to agreement during the contracting phase can be difficult and intense. A number of complex emotional and psychological issues are in play, and OD practitioners must be mindful of their own as well as the client's perspectives. Attending to those issues as well as to the content of the contract will help increase the likelihood of success.

■ SUMMARY

Entering and contracting constitute the initial activities of the OD process. They set the parameters for the phases of planned change that follow: diagnosing, planning and implementing change, and evaluating and institutionalizing it. Organizational entry involves clarifying the organizational issue or presenting problem, determining the relevant client, and selecting an OD practitioner. Developing an OD contract focuses on making a good decision about whether to proceed and allows both the client and the OD practitioner to clarify expectations about how the change process will unfold. Contracting involves setting mutual expectations, negotiating time and resources, and developing ground rules for working together.

NOTES

1. M. Lacey, "Internal Consulting: Perspectives on the Process of Planned Change," *Journal of Organization Change Management* 8, 3 (1995): 75–84; J. Geirland and M. Maniker-Leiter, "Five Lessons for Internal Organization Development Consultants," *OD Practitioner* 27 (1995): 44–48; A. Freedman and R. Zackrison, *Finding Your Way in the Consulting Jungle* (San Francisco: Jossey-Bass/Pfeiffer, 2001).

2. P. Block, *Flawless Consulting: A Guide to Getting Your Expertise Used,* 2d ed. (San Francisco: Jossey-Bass, 1999); C. Margerison, "Consulting Activities in Organizational Change," *Journal of Organizational Change Management* 1 (1988): 60–67; R. Harrison, "Choosing the Depth of Organizational Intervention," *Journal of Applied Behavioral Science* 6 (1970): 182–202.

3. M. Beer, *Organization Change and Development: A Systems View* (Santa Monica, Calif.: Goodyear, 1980); G. Lippitt and R. Lippitt, *The Consulting Process in Action,* 2d ed. (San Diego: University Associates, 1986).

4. L. Greiner and R. Metzger, *Consulting to Management* (Englewood Cliffs, N.J.: Prentice Hall, 1983): 251–58; Beer, *Organization Change and Development,* 81–83.

5. Block, *Flawless Consulting.*

6. D. Jamieson, "Start-up," in *Practicing Organization Development,* eds. W. Rothwell, R. Sullivan, and G. McLean (San Diego: Pfeiffer, 1995); J. Fordyce and R. Weil, *Managing WITH People,* 2d ed. (Reading, Mass.: Addison-Wesley, 1979).

7. Beer, *Organization Change and Development;* Fordyce and Weil, *Managing WITH People.*

8. L. Forcella, "Marketing Competency and Consulting Competency for External OD Practitioners," (unpublished master's thesis, Pepperdine University, Malibu, Calif., 2003).

9. G. Lippitt, "Criteria for Selecting, Evaluating, and Developing Consultants," *Training and Development Journal* 28 (August 1972): 10–15.

10. Greiner and Metzger, *Consulting to Management.*

11. Block, *Flawless Consulting;* Beer, *Organization Change and Development.*

12. T. Cody, *Management Consulting: A Game Without Chips* (Fitzwilliam, N.H.: Kennedy and Kennedy, 1986): 108–16; H. Holtz, *How to Succeed as an Independent Consultant,* 2d ed. (New York: John Wiley & Sons, 1988): 145–61.

13. G. Bellman, *The Consultant's Calling* (San Francisco: Jossey-Bass, 1990).

14. M. Weisbord, "The Organization Development Contract," *Organization Development Practitioner* 5 (1973): 1–4; M. Weisbord, "The Organization Contract Revisited," *Consultation* 4 (Winter 1985): 305–15; D. Nadler, *Feedback and Organization Development: Using Data-Based Methods* (Reading, Mass.: Addison-Wesley, 1977): 110–14.

15. Block, *Flawless Consulting.*

16. Ibid.

17. Lacey, "Internal Consulting."

18. E. Schein, "Taking Culture Seriously in Organization Development: A New Role for OD," working paper no. 4287–03, MIT Sloan School of Management, Cambridge, Mass. 2003.

Diagnosing Organizations

5

Diagnosing organizations is the second major phase in the model of planned change described in Chapter 2 (Figure 2.2). It follows the entering and contracting stage (Chapter 4) and precedes the planning and implementation phase. When it is done well, diagnosis clearly points the organization and the OD practitioner toward a set of appropriate intervention activities that will improve organization effectiveness.

Diagnosis is the process of understanding a system's current functioning. It involves collecting pertinent information about current operations, analyzing those data, and drawing conclusions for potential change and improvement. Effective diagnosis provides the systematic knowledge of the organization needed to design appropriate interventions. Thus, OD interventions derive from diagnosis and include specific actions intended to improve organizational functioning. (Chapters 12 through 20 present the major interventions used in OD today.)

This chapter is the first of four chapters that describe different aspects of the diagnostic process. This chapter presents a general definition of diagnosis and discusses the need for diagnostic models in guiding the process. Diagnostic models derive from conceptions about how organizations function, and they tell OD practitioners what to look for in diagnosing organizations, departments, groups, or jobs. They represent a road map for discovering current functioning. A general, comprehensive diagnostic model is presented based on open-systems theory. The chapter concludes with a description and application of an organization-level diagnostic model. Chapter 6 describes and applies diagnostic models at the group and job levels. Chapters 7 and 8 complete the diagnostic phase by discussing processes of data collection, analysis, and feedback.

WHAT IS DIAGNOSIS?

Diagnosis is the process of understanding how the organization is currently functioning, and it provides the information necessary to design change interventions. It generally follows from successful entry and contracting, which set the stage for successful diagnosis. Those processes help OD practitioners and client members jointly determine organizational issues to focus on, how to collect and analyze data to understand them, and how to work together to develop action steps from the diagnosis.

Unfortunately, the term diagnosis can be misleading when applied to organizations. It suggests a model of organization change analogous to medicine: An organization (patient) experiencing problems seeks help from an OD practitioner (doctor); the practitioner examines the organization, finds the causes of the problems, and prescribes a solution. Diagnosis in organization development, however, is much more collaborative than such a medical perspective implies and does not accept the implicit assumption that something is wrong with the organization.

First, the values and ethical beliefs that underlie OD suggest that both organization members and change agents should be involved in discovering the determinants of current organizational effectiveness. Similarly, both should be involved actively in developing appropriate interventions and implementing them. For example, a manager might seek OD help to reduce absenteeism in his or her department. The manager and an OD consultant jointly might decide to diagnose the cause of the problem by examining company absenteeism records and by interviewing selected employees about possible reasons for absenteeism. Alternatively, they might examine employee loyalty and discover the organizational elements that encourage people to stay. Analysis of those data could uncover determinants of absenteeism or loyalty in the department, thus helping the manager and the practitioner to develop an appropriate intervention to address the issue. The choice about how to approach the issue of absenteeism and the decisions about how to address it are made jointly by the OD practitioner and the manager.

Second, the medical model of diagnosis also implies that something is wrong with the patient and that one needs to uncover the cause of the illness. In those cases where organizations do have specific problems, diagnosis can be problem oriented, seeking reasons for the problems. On the other hand, as suggested by the absenteeism example above, the practitioner and the client may choose one of the newer views of organization change and frame the issue positively. Additionally, the client and OD practitioner may be looking for ways to enhance the organization's existing functioning. Many managers involved with OD are not experiencing specific organizational problems. Here, diagnosis is development oriented. It assesses the current functioning of the organization to discover areas for future development. For example, a manager might be interested in using OD to improve a department that already seems to be functioning well. Diagnosis might include an overall assessment of both the task-performance capabilities of the department and the impact of the department on its individual members. This process seeks to uncover specific areas for future development of the department's effectiveness.

In organization development, diagnosis is used more broadly than a medical definition would suggest. It is a collaborative process between organization members and the OD consultant to collect pertinent information, analyze it, and draw conclusions for action planning and intervention. Diagnosis may be aimed at uncovering the causes of specific problems, focused on understanding effective processes, or directed at assessing the overall functioning of the organization or department to discover areas for future development. Diagnosis provides a systematic understanding of organizations so that appropriate interventions may be developed for solving problems and enhancing effectiveness.

THE NEED FOR DIAGNOSTIC MODELS

Entry and contracting processes can result in a need to understand either a whole system or some part, process, or feature of the organization. To diagnose an organization, OD practitioners and organization members need to have an idea about what information to collect and analyze. Choices about what to look for invariably depend on how organizations are perceived. Such perceptions can vary from intuitive hunches to scientific explanations of how organizations function. Conceptual frameworks that people use to understand organizations are referred to as diagnostic models.[1] They describe the relationships among different features of the organization, as well as its context and its effectiveness. As a result, diagnostic models point out what areas to examine and what questions to ask in assessing how an organization is functioning.

However, all models represent simplifications of reality and therefore choose certain features as critical. As discussed in Chapter 2, the Positive Model of change supports the conclusion that focusing attention on those features, often to the exclusion of others, can result in a biased diagnosis. For example, a diagnostic model that relates team effectiveness to the handling of interpersonal conflict would lead an OD practitioner to ask questions about relationships among members, decision-making processes, and conflict resolution methods. Although relevant, those questions ignore other group issues such as the composition of skills and knowledge, the complexity of the tasks performed by the group, and member interdependencies. Thus, diagnostic models and processes must be chosen carefully to address the organization's presenting problems as well as to ensure comprehensiveness.

Potential diagnostic models are everywhere. Any collection of concepts and relationships that attempts to represent a system or explain its effectiveness can potentially qualify as a diagnostic model. Major sources of diagnostic models in OD are the thousands of articles and books that discuss, describe, and analyze how organizations function. They provide information about how and why certain organizational systems, processes, or functions are effective. The studies often concern a specific facet of organizational behavior, such as employee stress, leadership, motivation, problem solving, group dynamics, job design, and career development. They also can involve the larger organization and its context, including the environment, strategy, structure, and culture. Diagnostic models can be derived from that information by noting the dimensions or variables that are associated with organizational effectiveness.

Another source of diagnostic models is OD practitioners' experience in organizations. That field knowledge is a wealth of practical information about how organizations operate. Unfortunately, only a small part of that vast experience has been translated into diagnostic models that represent the professional judgments of people with years of experience in organizational diagnosis. The models generally link diagnosis with specific organizational processes, such as group problem solving, employee motivation, or communication between managers and employees. The models list specific questions for diagnosing such processes.

This chapter presents a general framework for diagnosing organizations rather than trying to cover the range of OD diagnostic models. The framework describes the systems perspective prevalent in OD today and integrates several of the more popular diagnostic models. The systems model provides a useful starting point for diagnosing organizations or departments. (Additional diagnostic models that are linked to specific OD interventions are presented in Chapters 12 through 20.)

OPEN-SYSTEMS MODEL

This section introduces systems theory, a set of concepts and relationships describing the properties and behaviors of things called systems—organizations, groups, and people, for example. Systems are viewed as unitary wholes composed of parts or subsystems; the system serves to integrate the parts into a functioning unit. For example, organization systems are composed of departments such as sales, operations, and finance. The organization serves to coordinate behaviors of its departments so that they function together in service of a goal or strategy. The general diagnostic model based on systems theory that underlies most of OD is called the open-systems model.

Organizations as Open Systems

Systems can vary in how open they are to their outside environments. Open systems, such as organizations and people, exchange information and resources with their environments. They cannot completely control their own behavior and are influenced in part by external forces. Organizations, for example, are affected by such environmental conditions as the availability of raw material, customer demands, competition, and government regulations. Understanding how these external forces affect the organization can help explain some of its internal behavior.

Open systems display a hierarchical ordering. Each higher level of system comprises lower-level systems: Systems at the level of society comprise organizations; organizations comprise groups (departments); and groups comprise individuals. Although systems at different levels vary in many ways—in size and complexity, for example—they have a number of common characteristics by virtue of being open systems, and those properties can be applied to systems at any level. The following key properties of open systems are described below: inputs, transformations, and outputs; boundaries; feedback; equifinality; and alignment.

Inputs, Transformations, and Outputs

Any organizational system is composed of three related parts: inputs, transformations, and outputs, as shown in Figure 5.1. Inputs consist of human or other resources, such as information, energy, and materials, coming into the system. Inputs are acquired from the system's external environment. For example, a manufacturing organization acquires raw materials from an outside supplier. Similarly, a hospital nursing unit acquires information concerning a patient's condition from the attending physician. In each case, the system (organization or nursing unit) obtains resources (raw materials or information) from its external environment.

Transformations are the processes of converting inputs into outputs. In organizations, a production or operations function composed of both social and technological components generally carries out transformations. The social component consists of people and their work relationships, whereas the technological component involves tools, techniques, and methods of production or service delivery. Organizations have developed elaborate mechanisms for transforming incoming resources into goods and services. Banks, for example, transform deposits into mortgage loans and interest income. Schools attempt to transform students into more educated people. Transformation processes also can take place at the group and individual levels. For example, research and development departments can transform the latest scientific advances into new product ideas, and bank tellers can transform customer requests into valued services.

Outputs are the results of what is transformed by the system and sent to the environment. Thus, inputs that have been transformed represent outputs ready to leave the system. Group health insurance companies receive premiums, healthy and unhealthy individuals, and medical bills; transform them through physician visits and record keeping; and export treated patients and payments to hospitals and physicians.

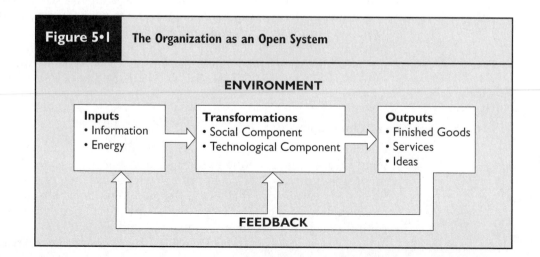

Figure 5•1   The Organization as an Open System

ENVIRONMENT

Inputs
• Information
• Energy

Transformations
• Social Component
• Technological Component

Outputs
• Finished Goods
• Services
• Ideas

FEEDBACK

Boundaries

The idea of boundaries helps to distinguish between systems and environments. Closed systems have relatively rigid and impenetrable boundaries, whereas open systems have far more permeable borders. Boundaries—the borders, or limits, of the system—are easily seen in many biological and mechanical systems. Defining the boundaries of social systems is more difficult because there is a continuous inflow and outflow through them. For example, where are the organizational boundaries in the following case? An individual customer installing a wireless home network gets a message that the software is conflicting with another piece of software from the Internet service provider (ISP). The customer calls the network software provider who talks to the ISP technical support people and provides technical support and suggestions that resolve the conflict. The customer feels completely supported by the process and never knew that the network software technical support person she was talking to was in India. The continued development of the Internet will continue to challenge the notion of boundaries in open systems.

The definition of a boundary is somewhat arbitrary because a social system has multiple subsystems and the boundary line for one subsystem may not be the same as that for a different subsystem. As with the system itself, arbitrary boundaries may have to be assigned to any social organization, depending on the variable to be stressed. The boundaries used for studying or analyzing leadership, for instance, may be quite different from those used to study intergroup dynamics.

Just as systems can be considered relatively open or closed, the permeability of boundaries also varies from fixed to diffuse. The boundaries of a community's police force are probably far more rigid and sharply defined than those of the community's political parties. Conflict over boundaries is always a potential problem within an organization, just as it is in the world outside the organization.

Feedback

As shown in Figure 5.1, feedback is information regarding the actual performance or the output results of the system. Not all such information is feedback, however. Only information used to control the future functioning of the system is considered feedback. Feedback can be used to maintain the system in a steady state (for example, keeping an assembly line running at a certain speed) or to help the organization adapt to changing circumstances. McDonald's, for example, has strict feedback processes to ensure that a meal in one outlet is as similar as possible to a meal in any other outlet. On the other hand, a salesperson in the field may report that sales are not going well and may insist on some organizational change to improve sales. A market research study may lead the marketing department to recommend a change to the organization's advertising campaign.

Equifinality

In closed systems, a direct cause-and-effect relationship exists between the initial condition and the final state of the system: When a computer's "on" switch is pushed, the system powers up. Biological and social systems, however, operate quite differently. The idea of equifinality suggests that similar results may be achieved with different initial conditions and in many different ways. This concept suggests that a manager can use varying degrees of inputs into the organization and can transform them in a variety of ways to obtain satisfactory outputs. Thus, the function of management is not to seek a single rigid solution but rather to develop a variety of satisfactory options. Systems and contingency theories suggest that there is no universal best way to design an organization. Organizations and departments providing routine services, such as Earthlink's, AOL's, or Microsoft's Internet services could be designed quite differently and still achieve the same result. Similarly, customer service functions at major retailers, software manufacturers, or airlines could be designed according to similar principles.

Alignment

A system's overall effectiveness is partly determined by the extent to which the different subsystems are aligned with each other. This alignment or fit concerns the relationships between inputs and transformations, between transformations and outputs, and among the subsystems of the transformation process. Diagnosticians who view the relationships among the various parts of a system as a whole are taking what is referred to as a systemic perspective.

Alignment refers to a characteristic of the relationship between two or more parts. It represents the extent to which the features, operations, and characteristics of one system support the effectiveness of another system. Just as the teeth in two wheels of a watch must mesh perfectly for the watch to keep time, so do the parts of an organization need to mesh for it to be effective. For example, General Electric attempts to achieve its goals through a strategy of diversification, and a divisional structure is used to support that strategy. A functional structure would not be a good fit with the strategy because it is more efficient for one division to focus on one product line than for one manufacturing department to try to make many different products. The systemic perspective suggests that diagnosis is the search for misfits among the various parts and subsystems of an organization.

Diagnosing Organizational Systems

When viewed as open systems, organizations can be diagnosed at three levels. The highest level is the overall organization and includes the design of the company's strategy, structure, and processes. Large organization units, such as divisions, subsidiaries, or strategic business units, also can be diagnosed at that level. The next-lowest level is the group or department, which includes group design and devices for structuring interactions among members, such as norms and work schedules. The lowest level is the individual position or job. This includes ways in which jobs are designed to elicit required task behaviors.

Diagnosis can occur at all three organizational levels, or it may be limited to issues occurring at a particular level. The key to effective diagnosis is knowing what to look for at each level as well as how the levels affect each other.[2] For example, diagnosing a work group requires knowledge of the variables important for group functioning and how the larger organization design affects the group. In fact, a basic understanding of organization-level issues is important in almost any diagnosis because they serve as critical inputs to understanding groups and individuals.

Figure 5.2 presents a comprehensive model for diagnosing these different organizational systems. For each level, it shows: (1) the inputs that the system has to work with, (2) the key design components of the transformation subsystem, and (3) the system's outputs.

The relationships shown in Figure 5.2 illustrate how each organization level affects the lower levels. The larger environment is an input to organization design. Organization design is an input to group design, which in turn serves as an input to job design. These cross-level relationships emphasize that organizational levels must fit with each other if the organization is to operate effectively. For example, organization structure must fit with and support group task design, which in turn must fit with individual job design.

The following discussion on organization-level diagnosis and the discussion in Chapter 6 on group- and job-level diagnosis provide a general overview of the dimensions (and their relationships) that need to be understood at each level. It is beyond the scope of this book to describe in detail the many variables and relation-

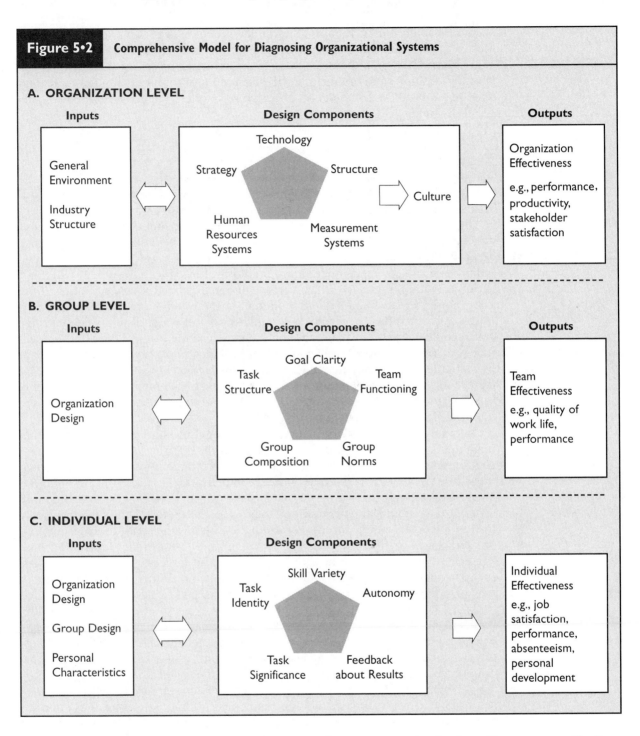

Figure 5•2   Comprehensive Model for Diagnosing Organizational Systems

A. ORGANIZATION LEVEL

Inputs

General Environment

Industry Structure

Design Components

Technology

Strategy   Structure

Human Resources Systems   Measurement Systems

Culture

Outputs

Organization Effectiveness

e.g., performance, productivity, stakeholder satisfaction

B. GROUP LEVEL

Inputs

Organization Design

Design Components

Goal Clarity

Task Structure   Team Functioning

Group Composition   Group Norms

Outputs

Team Effectiveness

e.g., quality of work life, performance

C. INDIVIDUAL LEVEL

Inputs

Organization Design

Group Design

Personal Characteristics

Design Components

Skill Variety

Task Identity   Autonomy

Task Significance   Feedback about Results

Individual Effectiveness

e.g., job satisfaction, performance, absenteeism, personal development

ships reported in the extensive literature on organizations. However, specific diagnostic questions are identified and concrete examples are included as an introduction to this phase of the planned change process.

ORGANIZATION-LEVEL DIAGNOSIS

The organization level of analysis is the broadest systems perspective typically taken in diagnostic activities. The model shown in Figure 5.2(A) is similar to other popular organization-level diagnostic models. These include Weisbord's six-box model,[3] Nadler and Tushman's congruency model,[4] Galbraith's star model,[5] and Kotter's organization dynamics model.[6] Figure 5.2(A) proposes that an organization's transformation processes, or design components, represent the way the organization positions and organizes itself within an environment (inputs) to achieve specific outputs. The combination of design component elements is called a strategic orientation.[7]

Inputs

To understand how a total organization functions, it is necessary to examine particular inputs, design components, and the alignment of the two sets of dimensions. Figure 5.2 shows that two key inputs affect the way an organization designs its strategic orientation: the general environment and industry structure.

The general environment represents the external elements and forces that can affect the attainment of organization objectives.[8] It can be described in terms of the amount of uncertainty present in social, technological, economic, ecological, and political forces. The more uncertainty there is in how the environment will affect the organization, the more difficult it is to design an effective strategic orientation. For example, the technological environment in the watch industry has been highly uncertain over time. The Swiss, who build precision watches with highly skilled craftspeople, were caught off guard by the mass production and distribution technology of Timex in the 1960s. Similarly, many watch manufacturers were surprised by and failed to take advantage of digital technology. On the other hand, the increased incidence of AIDS in the workplace (social environment) and the passage of the Americans with Disabilities Act (political environment) have forced changes in the strategic orientations of organizations.

An organization's industry structure or task environment is another important input into strategic orientation. As defined by Michael Porter, an organization's task environment consists of five forces: supplier power, buyer power, threats of substitutes, threats of entry, and rivalry among competitors.[9] First, strategic orientations must be sensitive to powerful suppliers who can increase prices (and therefore lower profits) or force the organization to pay more attention to the supplier's needs than to the organization's needs. For example, unions represent powerful suppliers of labor that can affect the costs of any organization within an industry. Second, strategic orientations must be sensitive to powerful buyers. Airplane purchasers, such as American Airlines or country governments, can force Airbus Industrie or Boeing to lower prices or appoint the planes in particular ways. Third, strategic orientations must be sensitive to the threat of new firms entering into competition. Profits in the restaurant business tend to be low because of the ease of starting a new restaurant. Fourth, strategic orientations must be sensitive to the threat of new products or services that can replace existing offerings. Ice cream producers must carefully monitor their costs and prices because it is easy for a consumer to purchase frozen yogurt or other types of desserts instead. Finally, strategic orientations must be sensitive to rivalry among existing competitors. If many organizations are competing for the same customers, for example, then the strategic orientation must monitor product offerings, costs, and structures carefully if the organization is to survive and prosper. Together, these forces play an important role in determining the success of an organization, whether it is a manufacturing or service firm, a nonprofit organization, or a government agency.

General environments and industry structures describe the input content. In addition to understanding what inputs are available, the inputs must be understood for their rate of change and complexity.[10] An organization's general environment or industry structure can be characterized along a dynamic–static continuum. Dynamic environments change rapidly and unpredictably and suggest that the organization adopt a flexible strategic orientation. Dynamic environments are relatively high in uncertainty. The complexity of the environment refers to the number of important elements in the general environment and industry structure. For example, software development organizations face dynamic and complex environments. Not only do technologies, regulations, customers, and suppliers change rapidly, but all of them are important to the firm's survival. On the other hand, manufacturers of glass jars face more stable and less complex environments.

Design Components

Figure 5.2(A) shows that a strategic orientation is composed of five major design components—strategy, technology, structure, measurement systems, and human resources systems—and an intermediate output—culture. Effective organizations align their design components to each other and to the environment.

A strategy represents the way an organization uses its resources (human, economic, or technical) to achieve its goals and gain a competitive advantage.[11] It can be described by the organization's mission, goals and objectives, strategic intent, and functional policies. A mission statement describes the long-term purpose of the organization, the range of products or services offered, the markets to be served, and the social needs served by the organization's existence. Goals and objectives are statements that provide explicit direction, set organization priorities, provide guidelines for management decisions, and serve as the cornerstone for organizing activities, designing jobs, and setting standards of achievement. Goals and objectives should set a target of achievement (such as 50% gross margins, an average employee satisfaction score of 4 on a 5-point scale, or some level of productivity); provide a means or system for measuring achievement; and provide a deadline or time frame for accomplishment.[12] A strategic intent is a succinct label or metaphor that describes how the organization intends to achieve its goals and objectives. For example, an organization can achieve goals through differentiation of its product or service, by achieving the lowest costs in the industry, or by growth. Finally, functional policies are the methods, procedures, rules, or administrative practices that guide decision making and convert plans into actions. In the semiconductor business, for example, Intel has a policy of allocating about 30% of revenues to research and development to maintain its lead in microprocessors production.[13]

Technology is concerned with the way an organization converts inputs into products and services. It represents the core of the transformation function and includes production methods, work flow, and equipment. Automobile companies have traditionally used an assembly line technology to build cars and trucks. Two features of the technological core have been shown to influence other design components: interdependence and uncertainty.[14] Technical interdependence involves ways in which the different parts of a technological system are related. High interdependence requires considerable coordination among tasks, such as might occur when departments must work together to bring out a new product. Technical uncertainty refers to the amount of information processing and decision making required during task performance. Generally, when tasks require high amounts of information processing and decision making, they are difficult to plan and routinize. The technology of car manufacturing is relatively certain and moderately interdependent. As a result, automobile manufacturers can specify in advance the behaviors workers should perform and how their work should be coordinated.

The structural system describes how attention and resources are focused on task accomplishment. It represents the basic organizing mode chosen to (1) divide the overall work of an organization into subunits that can assign tasks to individuals or groups and (2) coordinate these subunits for completion of the overall work.[15] Structure, therefore, needs to be closely aligned with the organization's technology.

Two ways of determining how an organization divides work are to examine its formal structure or to examine its level of differentiation and integration. Formal structures divide work by function (accounting, sales, or production), by product or service (Chevrolet, Buick, or Pontiac), or by some combination of both (a matrix composed of functional departments and product groupings). These are described in more detail in Chapter 14. The second way to describe how work is divided is to specify the amount of differentiation and integration there is in a structure. Applied to the total organization, differentiation refers to the degree of similarity or difference in the design of two or more subunits or departments.[16] In a highly differentiated organization, there are major differences in design among the departments. Some departments are highly formalized with many rules and regulations, others have few rules and regulations, and still others are moderately formal or flexible.

The way an organization coordinates the work across subunits is called integration. Integration can be achieved in a variety of ways—for example, by using plans and schedules; using budgets; assigning special roles, such as project managers, liaison positions, or integrators; or creating cross-departmental task forces and teams. The amount of integration required in a structure is a function of (1) the amount of uncertainty in the environment, (2) the level of differentiation in the structure, and (3) the amount of interdependence among departments. As uncertainty, differentiation, and interdependence increase, more sophisticated integration devices are required.

Measurement systems are methods of gathering, assessing, and disseminating information on the activities of groups and individuals in organizations. Such data tell how well the organization is performing and are used to detect and control deviations from goals. Closely related to structural integration, measurement systems monitor organizational operations and feed data about work activities to managers and members so that they can better understand current performance and coordinate work. Effective information and control systems clearly are linked to strategic objectives; provide accurate, understandable, and timely information; are accepted as legitimate by organization members; and produce benefits in excess of their cost.

Human resources systems include mechanisms for selecting, developing, appraising, and rewarding organization members. These influence the mix of skills, personalities, and behaviors of organization members. The strategy and technology provide important information about the skills and knowledge required if the organization is to be successful. Appraisal processes identify whether those skills and knowledge are being applied to the work, and reward systems complete the cycle by recognizing performance that contributes to goal achievement. Reward systems may be tied to measurement systems so that rewards are allocated on the basis of measured results. (Specific human resources systems, such as rewards and career development, are discussed in Chapters 15 and 16.)

Organization culture is the final design component. It represents the basic assumptions, values, and norms shared by organization members.[17] Those cultural elements are generally taken for granted and serve to guide members' perceptions, thoughts, and actions. For example, McDonald's culture emphasizes efficiency, speed, and consistency. It orients employees to company goals and suggests the kinds of behaviors necessary for success. In Figure 5.2(A), culture is shown as an intermediate output from the five other design components because it represents both an outcome and a constraint. It is an outcome of the organization's history and environment[18] as well as of prior choices made about the strategy, technology, structure, measurement systems, and human resources systems. It is also a constraint in that it is more difficult to change than the other components. In that sense it can either hinder or facilitate change. In diagnosis, the interest is in understanding the current culture well enough to determine its alignment with the other design factors. Such information may partly explain current outcomes, such as performance or effectiveness. (Culture is discussed in more detail in Chapter 18.)

Outputs

The outputs of a strategic orientation can be classified into three components. First, organization performance refers to financial outputs such as sales, profits, return on investment, and earnings per share. For nonprofit and government agencies, performance often refers to the extent to which costs were lowered or budgets met. Second, productivity concerns internal measurements of efficiency such as sales per employee, waste, error rates, quality, or units produced per hour. Third, stakeholder satisfaction reflects how well the organization has met the expectations of different groups. Customer satisfaction can be measured in terms of market share or focus-group data; employee satisfaction can be measured in terms of an opinion survey; investor satisfaction can be measured in terms of stock price.

Alignment

The effectiveness of an organization's current strategic orientation requires knowledge of the above information to determine the alignment among the different elements.

1. Does the organization's strategic orientation fit with the inputs?
2. Do the design components fit with each other?

For example, if the elements of the external environment (inputs) are fairly similar in their degree of certainty, then an effective organization structure (design factor) should have a low degree of differentiation. Its departments should be designed similarly because each faces similar environmental demands. On the other hand, if the environment is complex and each element presents different amounts of uncertainty, a more differentiated structure is warranted. Chevron Oil Company's regulatory, ecological, technological, and social environments differ greatly in their amount of uncertainty. The regulatory environment is relatively slow paced and detail oriented. Accordingly, the regulatory affairs function within Chevron is formal and bound by protocol. In the technological environment, on the other hand, new methods for discovering, refining, and distributing oil and oil products are changing at a rapid pace. Those departments are much more flexible and adaptive, very different from the regulatory affairs function.

Analysis

Application 5.1 describes the Steinway organization and provides an opportunity to perform the following organization-level analysis.[19] A useful starting point is to ask how well the organization is currently functioning. Steinway has excellent market shares in the high-quality segment of the grand piano market, a string of improving financial measures, and strong customer loyalty. However, the data on employee satisfaction is mixed (there are both long-tenured people and an indication that workers are leaving for other jobs), and the financial improvements appear modest when contrasted with the industry averages. Understanding the underlying causes of these effectiveness issues begins with an assessment of the inputs and strategic orientation and then proceeds to an evaluation of the alignments among the different parts. In diagnosing the inputs, two questions are important.

1. **What is the company's general environment?** Steinway's external environment is only moderately uncertain and not very complex. Socially, Steinway is an important part of a country's artistic culture and the fine arts. It must be

STEINWAY'S STRATEGIC ORIENTATION

Steinway & Sons, which turned 150 years old in April 2003, is generally regarded as the finest piano maker in the world. Founded in 1853 by the Steinway family, the firm was sold to CBS in 1972, taken private in 1985 by John and Robert Birmingham, and sold again in 1995 to Dana Messina and Kyle Kirkland, who took it public in 1996. Steinway & Sons is the piano division of the Steinway Musical Instruments Company that also owns Selmer Instruments and other manufacturers of band instruments (http://www.steinwaymusic.com). Piano sales in 2002 were $169 million, down 7.6% from the prior year and mirroring the general economic downturn. Since going public, Steinway's corporate revenues have grown a compounded 6%–7% a year, while earnings per share have advanced, on average, a compounded 11%. The financial performance for the overall company in 2002 was slightly below industry averages.

The Steinway brand remains one of the company's most valuable assets. The company's president notes that despite only 2% of all keyboard unit sales in the United States, they have 25% of the sales dollars and 35% of the profits. Their market share in the high-end grand piano segment is consistently over 80%. For example, 98% of the piano soloists at 30 of the world's major symphony orchestras chose a Steinway grand during the 2000/2001 concert season. Over 1,300 of the world's top pianists, all of whom own Steinways and perform solely on Steinways, endorse the brand without financial compensation.

Workers at Steinway & Sons manufacturing plants in New York and Germany have been with the company for an average of 15 years, often over 20 or 30 years. Many of Steinway's employees are descendants of parents and grandparents who worked for the company.

The External Environment

The piano market is typically segmented into grand pianos and upright pianos with the former being a smaller but higher-priced segment. In 1995, about 550,000 upright and 50,000 grand pianos were sold. Piano customers can also be segmented into professional artists, amateur pianists, and institutions such as concert halls, universities, and music schools. The private (home) market accounts for about 90% of the upright and 80% of the grand piano sales with the balance being sold to institutional customers. New markets in Asia represent important new growth opportunities.

The piano industry has experienced several important and dramatic changes for such a traditional product. Industry

sales, for example, dropped 40% between 1980 and 1995. Whether the decline was the result of increased electronic keyboard sales, a real decline in the total market, or some temporary decline was a matter of debate in the industry. Since then, sales growth has tended to reflect the ups and downs of the global economy.

Competition in the piano industry has also changed. In the United States, several hundred piano makers at the turn of the century had consolidated to eight by 1992. The Baldwin Piano and Organ Company is Steinway's primary U.S. competitor. It offers a full line of pianos under the Baldwin and Wurlitzer brand names through a network of over 700 dealers. In addition to relatively inexpensive upright pianos produced in high-volume plants, Baldwin also makes handcrafted grand pianos that are well respected and endorsed by such artists as Dave Brubeck and Stephen Sondheim, and by the Boston, Chicago, and Philadelphia orchestras. Annual sales are in the $100 million range; Baldwin was recently sold to the Gibson Guitar Company. The European story is similar. Only Bösendorfer of Austria and Fazioli of Italy remain as legitimate Steinway competitors.

Several Asian companies have emerged as important competitors. Yamaha, Kawai, Young Chang, and Samick collectively held about 35% of the vertical piano market and 80% of the grand piano market in terms of units and 75% of global sales in 1995. Yamaha is the world's largest piano manufacturer with sales of over $1 billion and a global market share of about 35%. Yamaha's strategy has been to produce consistent piano quality through continuous improvement. A separate handcrafted concert grand piano operation has also tried to use continuous improvement methods to create consistently high-quality instruments. More than any other high-quality piano manufacturer, Yamaha has been able to emulate and compete with Steinway.

The Steinway Organization

Steinway & Sons offers several different pianos, including two brands (Steinway and the less expensive Boston brand) and both upright and grand piano models. The company hand crafts its grand pianos in New York and Germany, and sells them through more than 200 independent dealers. About half of the dealers are in North and South America and approximately 85% of all Steinway pianos are sold through this network. The company also owns seven retail outlets in New York, New Jersey, London, Munich, Hamburg, and Berlin.

The dealer network is an important part of Steinway's strategy because of its role in the "concert bank" program. Once artists achieve a certain status, they are invited to become part of this elite group. The performer can go to any local dealer, try out different pianos, and pick the one they want to use at a performance for only the cost of bringing the piano to the concert hall. The concert bank contains over 300 pianos in more than 160 cities. In return for the service, Steinway is given exclusive use of the performer's name for publicity purposes.

Creating a Steinway concert grand piano is an art, an intricate and timeless operation (although alternate methods have been created and improved, the basic process hasn't changed much). It requires more than 12,000 mostly hand-crafted parts and more than a little magic. The tone, touch, and sound of each instrument is unique, and 120 technical patents and innovations contribute to the Steinway sound. Two years are required to make a Steinway grand as opposed to a mass-produced piano that takes only about 20 days. There are three major steps in the production process: wood drying (which takes about a year), parts making, and piano making.

Wood-drying operations convert moisture-rich lumber into useable raw material through air drying and computer-controlled kilns. Time is a critical element in this process because slow and natural drying is necessary to ensure the best sound-producing qualities of the wood. Even after all the care of the drying process, the workers reject approximately 50% of the lumber.

After drying, the parts-making operations begin. The first of these operations involves bending of the piano rim (the curved side giving a grand piano its familiar shape). These rims are formed of multiple layers of specially selected maple that are manually forced into a unified shape, held in presses for several hours, and then seasoned for 10 weeks before being joined to other wooden parts. During this time, the sounding board (a specially tapered Alaska Sitka spruce panel placed inside the rim to amplify the sound) and many other case parts are made. The final critical operation with parts making involves the fabrication of the 88 individual piano action sets that exist inside a piano. Piano "actions" are the intricate mechanical assemblies—made almost completely of wood and some felt, metal, and leather—that transmit finger pressure on the piano keys into the force that propels the hammers that strike the strings. The action is a particularly important part of a piano because this mechanical linkage gives Steinways their distinctive feel. In the action department, each operator was responsible for inspecting his or her own work, with all assembled actions further subject to 100% inspection.

Piano-making operations include "bellying," finishing, and tone regulating. The bellying process involves the precise and careful fitting of the soundboard, iron piano plate, and rim to each other. It requires workers to lean their stomachs against the rim of the piano to complete this task. Because of individual variations in material and the high degree of precision required, bellying takes considerable skill and requires several hours per piano. After the bellying operations, pianos are strung and moved to the finishing department. During finishing, actions and keyboards are individually fit to each instrument to accommodate differences in materials and tolerances to produce a working instrument. The final piano-making step involves tone regulating. Here, the pianos are "voiced" for Steinway sound. Unlike tuning, which involves the loosening and tightening of strings, voicing requires careful adjustments to the felt surrounding the hammers that strike the strings. This operation is extremely delicate and is performed by only a small handful of tone regulators. The tone regulators at Steinway are widely considered to be among the most skilled artisans in the factory. Their voicing of a concert grand can take as much as 20 to 30 hours. All tone regulators at Steinway have worked for the company in various other positions before reaching their present posts, and several have more than 20 years with the firm. Finally, after tone regulation, all pianos are polished, cleaned, and inspected one last time before packing and shipment.

Steinway produced more than 3,500 pianos in 2002 at its New York and Hamburg, Germany, plants. Almost 430 people work in the New York plant and all but about 100 of them work in production. They are represented by the United Furniture Worker's union. Seventy-five percent of the workers are paid on a straight-time basis; the remainder, primarily artisans, are paid on piece rates. Keeping workers has proved increasingly difficult as well-trained Steinway craftspeople are coveted by other manufacturers, and many of the workers could easily set up their own shop to repair or rebuild older Steinway pianos. Excess inventories due to weak sales both pre– and post–September 11 forced Steinway to adjust its production schedule; workers in its New York plant reported to work every other week rather than lay off the highly skilled workers needed to build its pianos.

aware of fickle trends in music and display an appropriate sensitivity to them. Politically, the organization operates on a global basis and so must be attuned to different governmental and country requirements in its distribution and sales networks. The manufacturing plant in Hamburg, Germany, suggests an important political dependency that must be monitored. Technologically, Steinway appears reasonably concerned about the latest breakthroughs in piano design, materials, and construction. They are aware of alternative technologies, such as the assembly line process at Yamaha, but prefer the classic methods they have always used. Ecologically, Steinway must be mindful. Their product requires lumber and they are very picky (some would say wasteful) about the choices, rejecting many pieces. It's likely that environmentalists would express concern over how Steinway uses this natural resource. Together, these environmental forces paint a relatively moderate level of uncertainty. Most of these issues are knowable and can be forecast with some confidence. In addition, while there are several environmental elements that need to be addressed, not all of them are vitally important. The environment is not very complex.

2. **What is the company's industry structure?** Steinway's industry is moderately competitive and profit pressures can be mapped by looking at five key forces. First, the threat of entry is fairly low. There are some important barriers to cross if an organization wanted to get into the piano business. For example, Steinway, Yamaha, and Baldwin have very strong brands and dealer networks. Any new entrant would need to overcome these strong images to get people to buy their product. Second, the threat of substitute products is moderate. On the one hand, electronic keyboards have made important advances and represent an inexpensive alternative to grand and upright pianos. On the other hand, the sophisticated nature of many of the artists and audiences suggests that there aren't many substitutes for a concert grand piano. Third, the bargaining power of suppliers, such as providers of labor and raw materials, is high. The labor union has effective control over the much-sought-after craftsworkers who manufacture and assemble grand pianos. Given the relatively difficult time that most high-end piano manufacturers have in holding onto these highly trained employees, the organization must expend considerable resources to retain them. Similarly, given the critical nature of wood to the final product, lumber suppliers can probably exert significant influence. Fourth, the bargaining power of buyers varies by segment. In the high-end segment, the number of buyers is relatively small and sophisticated, and the small number of high-quality pianos means that customers can put pressure on prices although they are clearly willing and able to pay more for quality. In the middle and lower segments, the number of buyers is much larger and fragmented. It is unlikely that they could collectively exert influence over price. Finally, the rivalry among firms is severe. A number of well-known and well-funded domestic and international competitors exist. Almost all of them have adopted marketing and manufacturing tactics similar to Steinway's in the high-end segment, and they are competing for the same customers. The extensive resources available to Yamaha as a member of their *keiretsu*, for example, suggests that it is a strong and long-term competitor that will work hard to unseat Steinway from its position. Thus, powerful buyers and suppliers as well as keen competition make the piano industry only moderately attractive and represent the key sources of uncertainty.

The following questions are important in assessing Steinway's strategic orientation:

1. **What is the company's strategy?** Steinway's primary strategy is a sophisticated niche and differentiation strategy. They attempt to meet their financial and other objectives by offering a unique and high-quality product to sophisticated artists. However, its product line does blur the strategy's focus. With both Boston and Steinway brands and both upright and grand models, a question about Steinway's commitment to the niche strategy could be raised. No formal mission or goals are mentioned in the case and this makes it somewhat difficult to judge the effectiveness of the strategy. But it seems reasonable to assume a clear intent

to maintain its dominance in the high-end segment. However, with new owners in 1995, it is also reasonable to question whether goals of profitability or revenue growth, implying very different tactics, have been sorted out.

2. **What are the company's technology, structure, measurement systems, and human resources systems?** First, Steinway's core technology is highly uncertain and moderately interdependent. The manufacturing process is craft based and dependent on the nature of the materials. Each piano is built and adjusted with the specific characteristics of the wood in mind. So much so that each piano has a different sound that is produced as a result of the manufacturing process. The technology is moderately interdependent because the major steps in the process are not linked in time. Making the "action sets" is independent of the "bellying" process, for example. Similarly, the key marketing program, the concert bank, is independent of manufacturing. Second, the corporate organization is divisional (pianos and band instruments), while the piano subsidiary appears to have a functional structure. The key functions are manufacturing, distribution, and sales. A procurement, finance, and human resources group is also reasonable to assume. Third, formal measurement systems within the production process are clearly present. There are specific mentions of inspections by both the worker and the organization. For example, 100% inspection (as opposed to statistical sampling) costs time and manpower and no doubt is seen as critical to quality. In addition, there must be some system of keeping track of work-in-progress, finished goods, and concert bank system inventories. Fourth, the human resource system is highly developed. The reward system includes both hourly and piece rate processes; the union relationships; worker retention programs; and global hiring, compensation, benefits, and training programs.

3. **What is Steinway's culture?** While there is little specific information, Steinway's culture can be inferred. The dominant focus on the high-end segment, the craft nature of the production process, the importance of the concert bank program, and the long history of family influence all point to culture of quality, craftsmanship, and responsiveness. These values are manifest in the way the organization chooses its raw materials, the way it caters to its prized customers, the care in the production process, and the image it works to retain.

Now that the organization inputs, design components, and outputs have been assessed, it is time to ask the crucial question about how well they fit together. The first concern is the fit between the environmental inputs and the strategic orientation. The moderate complexity and uncertainty in the general environment argue for a strategy that is flexible enough to address the few critical dependencies but formal enough to control. Its focus on the high-end segment of the industry and the moderate breadth in its product line support this flexibility. On the one hand, the flexible and responsive manufacturing process supports and defends its preeminence as the top grand piano in the world. This also mitigates the powerful buyer forces in this segment. Its moderate product line breadth gives it some flexibility and efficiency as well. It can achieve some production efficiencies in the upright and medium-market grand piano segments, and its brand image helps in marketing these products. The alignment between its strategic orientation and its environment appears sound.

The second concern is the alignment of the design components. With respect to strategy, the individual elements of Steinway's strategy are mostly aligned. Steinway clearly intends to differentiate its product by serving the high-end segment with unique high-quality pianos. But a broad product line (both uprights and grands as well as two brand names) could dilute the focus. The market for higher-priced and more specialized concert grands is much smaller than the market for moderately priced uprights and limits the growth potential of sales unless Steinway wants to compete vigorously in the emerging Asian markets where the Asian companies have a proximity advantage. That hypothesis is supported by the lack of clear goals in general and policies that support neither growth nor profitability. However, there appears to be a good fit between strategy and the other design components. The differentiated strategic intent requires technologies, structures, and systems that focus on creating sophisticated and unique products, specialized marketing and distribution, and the concert bank program. The flexible structure, formal inspection systems, and responsive culture would seem well suited for that purpose.

The technology appears well supported and aligned with the structure. The production process is craft based and deliberately ambiguous. The functional structure promotes specialization and professionalization of skills and knowledge. Specific tasks that require flexibility and adaptability from the organization are given a wide berth. Although a divisional structure overlays Steinway's corporate activities, the piano division's structure is functional but not rigid, and there appears to be a cultural willingness to be responsive to the craft and the artists they serve. In addition, the concert bank program is important for two reasons. First, it builds loyalty into the customer and ensures future demand. Second, it is a natural source of feedback on the instruments themselves, keeping the organization close to the artist's demands and emerging trends in sound preferences. Finally, the well-developed human resources system supports the responsive production and marketing functions as well as the global nature of the enterprise.

Steinway's culture of quality and responsiveness promotes coordination among the production tasks, serves as a method for socializing and developing people, and establishes methods for moving information around the organization. Clearly, any change effort at Steinway will have to acknowledge this role and design an intervention accordingly. The strong culture will either sabotage or facilitate change depending on how the change process aligns with the culture's impact on individual behavior.

Based on this diagnosis of the Steinway organization, at least two intervention possibilities are suggested. First, in collaboration with the client, the OD practitioner could suggest increasing Steinway's clarity about its strategy. In this intervention, the practitioner would want to talk about formalizing—rather than changing—Steinway's strategy because the culture would resist such an attempt. However, there are some clear advantages to be gained from a clearer sense of Steinway's future goals, its businesses, and the relationships among them. Second, Steinway could focus on increasing the integration and coordination of its structure, measurement systems, and human resources systems. The difficulty of retaining key production personnel warrants continuously improved retention systems as well as efforts to codify and retain key production knowledge in case workers do leave. This would apply to the marketing and distribution functions as well since they control an important interface with the customer.

■ SUMMARY

This chapter presented background information for diagnosing organizations, groups, and individual jobs. Diagnosis is a collaborative process, involving both managers and consultants in collecting pertinent data, analyzing them, and drawing conclusions for action planning and intervention. Diagnosis may be aimed at discovering the causes of specific problems, or it may be directed at assessing the organization or department to find areas for future development. Diagnosis provides the necessary practical understanding to devise interventions for solving problems and improving organization effectiveness.

Diagnosis is based on conceptual frameworks about how organizations function. Such diagnostic models serve as road maps by identifying areas to examine and questions to ask in determining how an organization or department is operating.

The comprehensive model presented here views organizations as open systems. The organization serves to coordinate the behaviors of its departments. It is open to exchanges with the larger environment and is influenced by external forces. As open systems, organizations are hierarchically ordered; that is, they are composed of groups, which in turn are composed of individual jobs. Organizations also display five key systems properties: inputs, transformations, and outputs; boundaries; feedback; equifinality; and alignment.

An organization-level diagnostic model was described and applied. It consists of environmental inputs; a set of design components called a strategic orientation; and a variety of outputs, such as performance, productivity, and stakeholder satisfaction. Diagnosis involves understanding each of the parts in the model and then assessing how the elements of the strategic orientation align with each other and with the inputs. Organization effectiveness is likely to be high when there is good alignment.

▪ NOTES

1. D. Nadler, "Role of Models in Organizational Assessment," in *Organizational Assessment,* eds. E. Lawler III, D. Nadler, and C. Cammann (New York: John Wiley & Sons, 1980): 119–31; M. Harrison, *Diagnosing Organizations,* 2d ed. (Thousand Oaks, Calif.: Sage Publications, 1994); R. Burton, B. Obel, H. Starling, M. Sondergaard, and D. Dojbak, *Strategic Organizational Diagnosis and Design: Developing Theory for Application,* 2d ed. (Dordrecht, The Netherlands: Kluwer Academic Publishers, 2001).

2. D. Coghlan, "Organization Development through Interlevel Dynamics," *International Journal of Organizational Analysis* 2 (1994): 264–79.

3. M. Weisbord, "Organizational Diagnosis: Six Places to Look for Trouble with or without a Theory," *Group and Organizational Studies* 1 (1976): 430–37.

4. D. Nadler and M. Tushman, *Competing by Design: The Power of Organizational Architecture* (New York: Oxford University Press, 1997).

5. J. Galbraith, *Competing with Flexible Lateral Organizations,* 2d ed. (Reading, Mass.: Addison-Wesley, 1994).

6. J. Kotter, *Organizational Dynamics: Diagnosis and Intervention* (Reading, Mass.: Addison-Wesley, 1978).

7. M. Tushman and E. Romanelli, "Organization Evolution: A Metamorphosis Model of Convergence and Reorientation," in *Research in Organizational Behavior,* vol. 7, eds. L. Cummings and B. Staw (Greenwich, Conn.: JAI Press, 1985); C. Worley, D. Hitchin, and W. Ross, *Integrated Strategic Change: How OD Builds Competitive Advantage* (Reading, Mass.: Addison-Wesley, 1996).

8. F. Emery and E. Trist, "The Causal Texture of Organizational Environments," *Human Relations* 18 (1965): 21–32; H. Aldrich, *Organizations and Environments* (Englewood Cliffs, N.J.: Prentice Hall, 1979).

9. M. Porter, *Competitive Strategy* (New York: Free Press, 1980).

10. Emery and Trist, "Causal Texture"; Aldrich, *Organizations and Environments.*

11. M. Porter, *Competitive Advantage* (New York: Free Press, 1985); M. Hitt, R. D. Ireland, and R. Hoskisson, *Strategic Management: Competitiveness and Globalization* (Cincinnati: South-Western College Publishing, 2003).

12. C. Hofer and D. Schendel, *Strategy Formulation: Analytical Concepts* (St. Paul, Minn.: West Publishing, 1978).

13. R. Hoff, "Inside Intel," *Business Week* (1 June 1992): 86–94.

14. J. Thompson, *Organizations in Action* (New York: McGraw-Hill, 1967); D. Gerwin, "Relationships between Structure and Technology," in *Handbook of Organizational Design,* vol. 2, eds. P. Nystrom and W. Starbuck (Oxford: Oxford University Press, 1981): 3–38.

15. J. Galbraith, *Designing Organizations* (San Francisco: Jossey-Bass, 2002); R. Daft, *Organization Theory and Design* (Cincinnati: South-Western College Publishing, 2003).

16. P. Lawrence and J. Lorsch, *Organization and Environment* (Cambridge: Harvard University Press, 1967).

17. J. Martin, *Organizational Culture: Mapping the Terrain* (Newbury Park, Calif.: Sage Publishing, 2002); E. Schein, *Organizational Culture and Leadership,* 2d ed. (San Francisco: Jossey-Bass, 1990).

18. E. Abrahamson and C. Fombrun, "Macrocultures: Determinants and Consequences," *Academy of Management Review* 19 (1994): 728–56.

19. Adapted from material in R. Brammer, "Sizing Up Small Caps: Stay Tuned," *Barrons* (19 April 2002); A. Serwer, "Happy Birthday, Steinway," *Fortune* (17 March 2003), 96–98; D. Garvin, "Steinway & Sons," *Harvard Business School Case 628-025* (Boston: Harvard Business School, 1981); J. Gourville and J. Lassiter, *Steinway & Sons: Buying a Legend* (Boston: Harvard Business School, 1999).

6

Diagnosing Groups and Jobs

Chapter 5 introduced diagnosis as the second major phase in the model of planned change. Based on open-systems theory, a comprehensive diagnostic framework for organization-, group-, and job-level systems was described. The organization-level diagnostic model was elaborated and applied. After the organization level, the next two levels of diagnosis are the group and job. Many large organizations have groups or departments that are themselves relatively large, like the operating divisions at Viacom, Akzo-Nobel, or General Motors. Diagnosis of large groups can follow the dimensions and relational fits applicable to organization-level diagnosis. In essence, large groups or departments operate much like organizations, and their functioning can be assessed by diagnosing them as organizations.

Small departments and groups, however, can behave differently from large organizations; they need their own diagnostic models to reflect those differences. In the first section of this chapter, we discuss the diagnosis of work groups. Such groups generally consist of a relatively small number of people working face-to-face on a shared task. Work groups are prevalent in all sizes of organizations. They can be relatively permanent and perform an ongoing function, or they can be temporary and exist only to perform a certain task or to make a specific decision.

Finally, we describe and apply a diagnostic model of an individual job—the smallest unit of analysis in organizations. An individual job is constructed to perform a specific task or set of tasks. How jobs are designed can affect individual and organizational effectiveness.

GROUP-LEVEL DIAGNOSIS

Figure 6.1 replicates the comprehensive model introduced in Chapter 5 but highlights the group- and individual-level models. It shows the inputs, design components, outputs, and relational fits for group-level diagnosis.[1] The model is similar to other popular group-level diagnostic models such as Hackman and Morris's task group design model,[2] McCaskey's framework for analyzing groups,[3] and Ledford, Lawler, and Mohrman's participation group design model.[4]

Inputs

Organization design is clearly the major input to group design. It consists of the design components characterizing the larger organization within which the group is embedded: technology, structure, measurement systems, and human resources systems, as well as organization culture. Technology can determine the characteristics of the group's task; structural systems can specify the level of coordination required among groups. The human resources and measurement systems, such as performance appraisal and reward systems, play an important role in determining team functioning.[5] For example, individually based performance appraisal and reward systems tend to interfere with team functioning because members may be concerned with maximizing their individual performance to the detriment of team performance. Collecting information about the group's organization design context can greatly improve the accuracy of diagnosis.

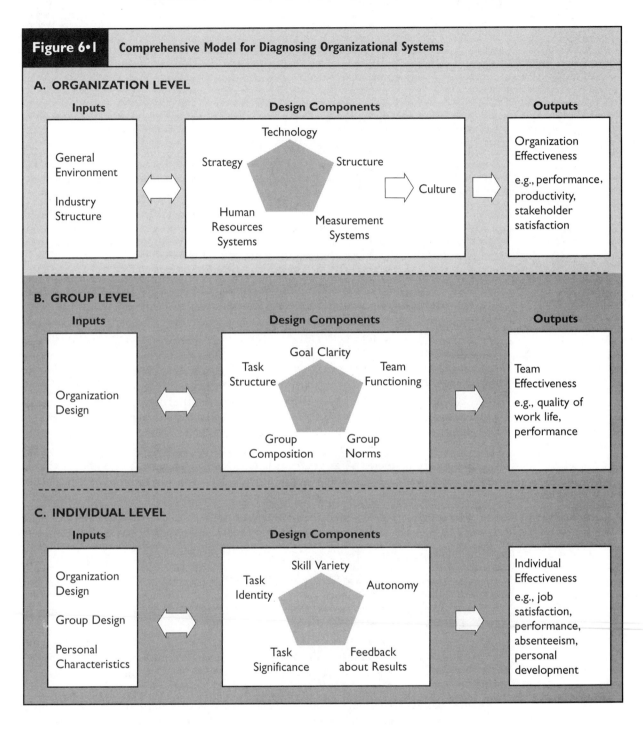

Figure 6•1   Comprehensive Model for Diagnosing Organizational Systems

Design Components

Figure 6.1(B) shows that groups have five major components: goal clarity, task structure, group composition, team functioning, and performance norms.

Goal clarity involves how well the group understands its objectives. In general, goals should be moderately challenging; there should be a method for measuring, monitoring, and feeding back information about goal achievement; and the goals should be clearly understood by all members.

Task structure is concerned with how the group's work is designed. Task structures can vary along two key dimensions: coordination of members' efforts and regulation of their task behaviors.[6] The coordination dimension involves the degree to which group tasks are structured to promote effective interaction among group members. Coordination is important in groups performing interdependent tasks, such as surgical teams and problem-solving groups. It is relatively unimportant, however, in groups composed of members who perform independent tasks, such as a group of telephone operators or salespeople. The regulation dimension involves the degree to which members can control their own task behaviors and be relatively free from external controls such as supervision, plans, and programs. Self-regulation generally occurs when members can decide on such issues as task assignments, work methods, production goals, and membership. (Interventions for designing group task structure are discussed in Chapter 16.)

Composition concerns the membership of groups. Members can differ on a number of dimensions having relevance to group behavior. Demographic variables, such as age, education, experience, and skills and abilities, can affect how people behave and relate to each other in groups. Demographics can determine whether the group is composed of people having task-relevant skills and knowledge, including interpersonal skills. People's internal needs also can influence group behaviors. Individual differences in social needs can determine whether group membership is likely to be satisfying or stressful.[7]

Group functioning is the underlying basis of group life. How members relate to each other is important in work groups because the quality of relationships can affect task performance. In some groups, for example, interpersonal competition and conflict among members result in their providing little support and help for each other. Conversely, groups may become too concerned about sharing good feelings and support and spend too little time on task performance. In organization development, considerable effort has been invested to help work group members develop healthy interpersonal relations, including an ability and a willingness to share feelings and perceptions about members' behaviors so that interpersonal problems and task difficulties can be worked through and resolved.[8] Group functioning therefore involves task-related activities, such as advocacy and inquiry; coordinating and evaluating activities; and the group-maintenance function, which is directed toward holding the group together as a cohesive team and includes encouraging, harmonizing, compromising, setting standards, and observing.[9] (Interpersonal interventions are discussed in Chapter 12.)

Performance norms are member beliefs about how the group should perform its task and include acceptable levels of performance.[10] Norms derive from interactions among members and serve as guides to group behavior. Once members agree on performance norms, either implicitly or explicitly, then members routinely perform tasks according to those norms. For example, members of problem-solving groups often decide early in the life of the group that decisions will be made through voting; voting then becomes a routine part of group task behavior. (Interventions aimed at helping groups to develop appropriate performance norms are discussed in Chapter 12.)

Outputs

Group effectiveness has two dimensions: performance and quality of work life. Performance is measured in terms of the group's ability to control or reduce costs, increase productivity, or improve quality. This is a "hard" measure of effectiveness. In addition, effectiveness is indicated by the group member's quality of work life. It concerns work satisfaction, team cohesion, and organizational commitment.

Fits

The diagnostic model in Figure 6.1(B) shows that group design components must fit inputs if groups are to be effective in terms of performance and the quality of work life. Research suggests the following fits between the inputs and design dimensions:

1. Group design should be congruent with the larger organization design. Organization structures with low differentiation and high integration should have work groups that are composed of highly skilled and experienced members performing highly interdependent tasks. Organizations with differentiated structures and formalized human resources and information systems should spawn groups that have clear, quantitative goals and that support standardized behaviors. Although there is little direct research on these fits, the underlying rationale is that congruence between organization and group designs supports overall integration within the company. When group designs are not compatible with organization designs, groups often conflict with the organization.[11] They may develop norms that run counter to organizational effectiveness, such as occurs in groups supportive of horseplay, goldbricking, and other counterproductive behaviors.

2. When the organization's technology results in interdependent tasks, coordination among members should be promoted by task structures, composition, performance norms, and group functioning. Conversely, when technology permits independent tasks, the design components should promote individual task performance.[12] For example, when coordination is needed, task structure might physically locate related tasks together; composition might include members with similar interpersonal skills and social needs; performance norms would support task-relevant interactions; and healthy interpersonal relationships would be developed.

3. When the technology is relatively uncertain and requires high amounts of information processing and decision making, then group task structure, composition, performance norms, and group functioning should promote self-regulation. Members should have the necessary freedom, information, and skills to assign members to tasks, to decide on production methods, and to set performance goals.[13] When technology is relatively certain, group designs should promote standardization of behavior, and groups should be externally controlled by supervisors, schedules, and plans.[14] For example, when self-regulation is needed, task structure might be relatively flexible and allow the interchange of members across group tasks; composition might include members with multiple skills, interpersonal competencies, and social needs; performance norms would support complex problem solving; and efforts would be made to develop healthy interpersonal relations.

Analysis

Application 6.1 presents an example of applying group-level diagnosis to a top-management team engaged in problem solving.

The group is having a series of ineffective problem-solving meetings. Members report a backlog of unresolved issues, poor use of meeting time, lack of follow-through and decision implementation, and a general dissatisfaction with the team meetings. Examining group inputs and design components and seeing how the two fit can help explain the causes of those group problems.

The key issue in diagnosing group inputs is the design of the larger organization within which the group is embedded. The Ortiv Glass Corporation's design is

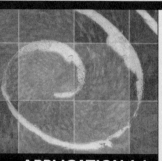

APPLICATION 6•1

TOP-MANAGEMENT TEAM AT ORTIV GLASS CORPORATION

The Ortiv Glass Corporation produces and markets plate glass for use primarily in the construction and automotive industries. The multiplant company has been involved in OD for several years and actively supports participative management practices and employee-involvement programs. Ortiv's organization design is relatively organic, and the manufacturing plants are given freedom and encouragement to develop their own organization designs and approaches to participative management. It recently put together a problem-solving group made up of the top-management team at its newest plant.

The team consisted of the plant manager and the managers of the five functional departments reporting to him: engineering (maintenance), administration, human resources, production, and quality control. In recruiting managers for the new plant, the company selected people with good technical skills and experience in their respective functions. It also chose people with some managerial experience and a desire to solve problems collaboratively, a hallmark of participative management. The team was relatively new, and members had been working together for only about 5 months.

The team met formally for 2 hours each week to share pertinent information and to deal with plantwide issues affecting all of the departments, such as safety procedures, interdepartmental relations, and personnel practices. Members described these meetings as informative but often chaotic in terms of decision making. The meetings typically started late as members straggled in at different times. The latecomers generally offered excuses about more pressing problems oc-

curring elsewhere in the plant. Once started, the meetings were often interrupted by "urgent" phone messages for various members, including the plant manager, and in most cases the recipient would leave the meeting hurriedly to respond to the call.

The group had problems arriving at clear decisions on particular issues. Discussions often rambled from topic to topic, and members tended to postpone the resolution of problems to future meetings. This led to a backlog of unresolved issues, and meetings often lasted far beyond the 2-hour limit. When group decisions were made, members often reported problems in their implementation. Members typically failed to follow through on agreements, and there was often confusion about what had actually been agreed upon. Everyone expressed dissatisfaction with the team meetings and their results.

Relationships among team members were cordial yet somewhat strained, especially when the team was dealing with complex issues in which members had varying opinions and interests. Although the plant manager publicly stated that he wanted to hear all sides of the issues, he often interrupted the discussion or attempted to change the topic when members openly disagreed in their views of the problem. This interruption was typically followed by an awkward silence in the group. In many instances when a solution to a pressing problem did not appear forthcoming, members either moved on to another issue or they informally voted on proposed options, letting majority rule decide the outcome. Members rarely discussed the need to move on or vote; rather, these behaviors emerged informally over time and became acceptable ways of dealing with difficult issues.

relatively differentiated. Each plant is allowed to set up its own organization design. Similarly, although no specific data are given, the company's technology, structure, measurement systems, human resources systems, and culture appear to promote flexible and innovative behaviors at the plant level. Indeed, freedom to innovate in the manufacturing plants is probably an outgrowth of the firm's OD activities and participative culture.

In the case of decision-making groups such as this one, organization design also affects the nature of the issues that are worked on. The team meetings appear to be devoted to problems affecting all of the functional departments. This suggests that the problems entail high interdependence among the functions; consequently, high coordination among members is needed to resolve them. The team meetings also seem to include many issues that are complex and not easily solved, so there is probably a relatively high amount of uncertainty in the technology or work process.

The causes of the problems or acceptable solutions are not readily discernible. Members must process considerable information during problem solving, especially when there are different perceptions and opinions about the issues.

Diagnosis of the team's design components answers the following questions:

1. **How clear are the group's goals?** The team's goals seem relatively clear: They are to solve problems. There appears to be no clear agreement, however, on the specific problems to be addressed. As a result, members come late because they have "more pressing" problems needing attention.

2. **What is the group's task structure?** The team's task structure includes face-to-face interaction during the weekly meetings. That structure allows members from different functional departments to come together physically to share information and to solve problems mutually affecting them. It facilitates coordination of problem solving among the departments in the plant. The structure also seems to provide team members with the freedom necessary to regulate their task behaviors in the meetings. They can adjust their behaviors and interactions to suit the flow of the discussion and problem-solving process.

3. **What is the composition of the group?** The team is composed of the plant manager and managers of five functional departments. All members appear to have task-relevant skills and experience, both in their respective functions and in their managerial roles. They also seem to be interested in solving problems collaboratively. That shared interest suggests that members have job-related social needs and should feel relatively comfortable in group problem-solving situations.

4. **What are the group's performance norms?** Group norms cannot be observed directly but must be inferred from group behaviors. The norms involve member beliefs about how the group should perform its task, including acceptable levels of performance. A useful way to describe norms is to list specific behaviors that complete the sentences "A good group member should . . ." and "It's okay to. . . ." Examination of the team's problem-solving behaviors suggests the following performance norms are operating in the example:
   - "It's okay to come late to team meetings."
   - "It's okay to interrupt meetings with phone messages."
   - "It's okay to leave meetings to respond to phone messages."
   - "It's okay to hold meetings longer than 2 hours."
   - "A good group member should not openly disagree with others' views."
   - "It's okay to vote on decisions."
   - "A good group member should be cordial to other members."
   - "It's okay to postpone solutions to immediate problems."
   - "It's okay not to follow through on previous agreements."

5. **What is the nature of team functioning in the group?** The case strongly suggests that interpersonal relations are not healthy on the management team. Members do not seem to confront differences openly. Indeed, the plant manager purposely intervenes when conflicts emerge. Members feel dissatisfied with the meetings, but they spend little time talking about those feelings. Relationships are strained, but members fail to examine the underlying causes.

The problems facing the team can now be explained by assessing how well the group design fits the inputs. The larger organization design of Ortiv is relatively differentiated and promotes flexibility and innovation in its manufacturing plants. The firm supports participative management, and the team meetings can be seen as an attempt to implement that approach at the new plant. Although it is too early to tell whether the team will succeed, there does not appear to be significant incongruity between the larger organization design and what the team is trying to do. Of course, team problem solving may continue to be ineffective, and the team might revert to a more autocratic approach to decision making. In such a case, a serious mismatch between the plant management team and the larger company would exist, and conflict between the two would likely result.

The team's issues are highly interdependent and often uncertain, and meetings are intended to resolve plantwide problems affecting the various functional departments. Those problems are generally complex and require the members to process a great deal of information and create innovative solutions. The team's task structure and composition appear to fit the nature of team issues. The face-to-face meetings help to coordinate problem solving among the department managers, and except for the interpersonal skills, members seem to have the necessary task-relevant skills and experience to drive the problem-solving process. There appears, however, to be a conflict in the priority between the problems to be solved by the team and the problems faced by individual managers.

More important, the key difficulty seems to be a mismatch between the team's performance norms and interpersonal relations and the demands of the problem-solving task. Complex, interdependent problems require performance norms that support sharing of diverse and often conflicting kinds of information. The norms must encourage members to generate novel solutions and to assess the relevance of problem-solving strategies in light of new issues. Members need to address explicitly how they are using their knowledge and skills and how they are weighing and combining members' individual contributions.

In our example, the team's performance norms fail to support complex problem solving; rather, they promote a problem-solving method that is often superficial, haphazard, and subject to external disruptions. Members' interpersonal relationships reinforce adherence to the ineffective norms. Members do not confront personal differences or dissatisfactions with the group process. They fail to examine the very norms contributing to their problems. In this case, diagnosis suggests the need for group interventions aimed at improving performance norms and developing healthy interpersonal relations.

INDIVIDUAL-LEVEL DIAGNOSIS

The final level of organizational diagnosis is the individual job or position. An organization consists of numerous groups; a group, in turn, is composed of several individual jobs. This section discusses the inputs, design components, and relational fits needed for diagnosing jobs. The model shown in Figure 6.1(C) is similar to other popular job diagnostic frameworks, such as Hackman and Oldham's job diagnostic survey and Herzberg's job enrichment model.[15]

Inputs

Three major inputs affect job design: organization design, group design, and the personal characteristics of jobholders.

Organization design is concerned with the larger organization within which the individual job is the smallest unit. Organization design is a key part of the larger context surrounding jobs. Technology, structure, measurement systems, human resources systems, and culture can have a powerful impact on the way jobs are designed and on people's experiences in jobs. For example, company reward systems can orient employees to particular job behaviors and influence whether people see job performance as fairly rewarded. In general, technology characterized by relatively uncertain tasks and low interdependency is likely to support job designs allowing employees flexibility and discretion in performing tasks. Conversely, low-uncertainty work systems are likely to promote standardized job designs requiring routinized task behaviors.[16]

Group design concerns the larger group or department containing the individual job. Like organization design, group design is an essential part of the job context. Group task structure, goal clarity, composition, performance norms, and group functioning serve as inputs to job design. They typically have a more immediate impact on jobs than do the larger, organization design components. For example, group task structure can determine how individual jobs are grouped together—as in groups requiring coordination among jobs or in ones comprising collections of independent jobs. Group composition can influence the kinds of people who are available to fill jobs. Group performance norms can affect the kinds of job designs that are considered acceptable, including the level of jobholders' performances. Goal clarity helps members to prioritize work, and group functioning can affect how powerfully the group influences job behaviors. When members maintain close relationships and the group is cohesive, group norms are more likely to be enforced and followed.[17]

Personal characteristics of individuals occupying jobs include their age, education, experience, and skills and abilities. All of these can affect job performance as well as how people react to job designs. Individual needs and expectations can also affect employee job responses. For example, individual differences in growth need—the need for self-direction, learning, and personal accomplishment—can determine how much people are motivated and satisfied by jobs with high levels of skill variety, autonomy, and feedback about results.[18] Similarly, work motivation can be influenced by people's expectations that they can perform a job well and that good job performance will result in valued outcomes.[19]

Design Components

Figure 6.1(C) shows that individual jobs have five key dimensions: skill variety, task identity, task significance, autonomy, and feedback about results.[20]

Skill variety identifies the degree to which a job requires a range of activities and abilities to perform the work. Assembly line jobs, for example, generally have limited skill variety because employees perform a small number of repetitive activities. Most professional jobs, on the other hand, include a great deal of skill variety because people engage in diverse activities and employ several different skills in performing their work.

Task identity measures the degree to which a job requires the completion of a relatively whole, identifiable piece of work. Skilled craftspeople, such as tool-and-die makers and carpenters, generally have jobs with high levels of task identity. They are able to see a job through from beginning to end. Assembly line jobs involve only a limited piece of work and score low on task identity.

Task significance identifies the degree to which a job has a significant impact on other people's lives. Custodial jobs in a hospital are likely to have more task significance than similar jobs in a toy factory because hospital custodians are likely to see their jobs as affecting someone else's health and welfare.

Autonomy indicates the degree to which a job provides freedom and discretion in scheduling the work and determining work methods. Assembly line jobs generally have little autonomy: The work pace is scheduled, and people perform preprogrammed tasks. College teaching positions have more autonomy: Professors usually can determine how a course is taught, even though they may have limited say over class scheduling.

Feedback about results involves the degree to which a job provides employees with direct and clear information about the effectiveness of task performance. Assembly line jobs often provide high levels of feedback about results, whereas college professors must often contend with indirect and ambiguous feedback about how they are performing in the classroom.

Those five job dimensions can be combined into an overall measure of job enrichment. Enriched jobs have high levels of skill variety, task identity, task significance, autonomy, and feedback about results. They provide opportunities for self-direction, learning, and personal accomplishment at work. Many people find enriched jobs internally motivating and satisfying. (Job enrichment is discussed more fully in Chapter 16.)

Fits

The diagnostic model in Figure 6.1(C) suggests that job design must fit job inputs to produce effective job outputs, such as high quality and quantity of individual performance, low absenteeism, and high job satisfaction. Research reveals the following fits between job inputs and job design:

1. Job design should be congruent with the larger organization and group designs within which the job is embedded.[21] Both the organization and the group serve as a powerful context for individual jobs or positions. They tend to support and reinforce particular job designs. Highly differentiated and integrated organizations and groups that permit members to self-regulate their behavior fit enriched jobs. These larger organizations and groups promote autonomy, flexibility, and innovation at the individual job level. Conversely, bureaucratic organizations and groups relying on external controls are congruent with job designs scoring low on the five key dimensions. Both organizations and groups reinforce standardized, routine jobs. As suggested earlier, congruence across different levels of organization design promotes integration of the organization, group, and job levels. Whenever the levels do not fit each other, conflict is likely to emerge.

2. Job design should fit the personal characteristics of the jobholders if they are to perform effectively and derive satisfaction from work. Generally, enriched jobs fit people with strong growth needs.[22] These people derive satisfaction and accomplishment from performing jobs involving skill variety, autonomy, and feedback about results. Enriched jobs also fit people possessing moderate to high levels of task-relevant skills, abilities, and knowledge. Enriched jobs generally require complex information processing and decision making; people must have comparable skills and abilities to perform effectively. Jobs scoring low on the five job dimensions generally fit people with rudimentary skills and abilities and with low growth needs. Simpler, more routinized jobs requiring limited skills and experience fit better with people who place a low value on opportunities for self-direction and learning. In addition, because people can grow through education, training, and experience, job design must be monitored and adjusted from time to time.

Analysis

Application 6.2 presents an example of applying individual-level diagnosis to job design. The university is considering a change in the job design of a program administrator. The application provides information about the current job and asks whether or not the proposed change makes sense. Examination of the inputs and job design features and how the two fit can help to make predictions about the advisability of the change.

JOB DESIGN AT PEPPERDINE UNIVERSITY

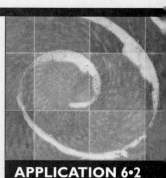

The Graziadio School of Business and Management (GSBM) at Pepperdine University is one of the largest business schools in the country and has the third largest part-time MBA program. The school also provides graduate education aimed at different markets including an executive MBA (EMBA), a presidential/key executive MBA (PKE), and a specialized master's degree in organization development (MSOD). The MSOD program's curriculum consists of 10 four-unit classes over 22 months. Eight of the classes are conducted off-site during 8-day sessions at both domestic and international locations. The MSOD program office consists of a faculty director, a program administrator, and an administrative assistant. In response to cost-cutting initiatives at the university level, a proposal was being considered to alter the job designs of the MSOD program staff.

The MSOD Program Administrator, the focus of this application, was responsible for marketing and recruiting new students, managing the delivery logistics of the off-site program, managing the students' registration and financial relationships with the university, and maintaining relationships with the MSOD alumni. The marketing and recruiting duties involved working with the Program Director and the Director of Marketing for GSBM to develop marketing tactics including advertisements, brochures, conference marketing and support, and other market development activities. The recruiting process involved explaining the curriculum to prospective applicants, overseeing the application process for each applicant, working with the faculty to have qualified applicants interviewed, and managing the admissions process. This too had to be coordinated with the director and the administrative assistant. Once a class was admitted, the Program Administrator worked with various off-site facilities to establish room and board rates and catering services; managed the faculty's travel and teaching requirements; managed various intersession activities including the final exam; managed the students' enrollment and graduation processes including their interface with the university's registrar and finance office and the school's financial aid office; and coached students through the program. After graduation, the Program Administrator served as an unofficial placement service, hooking up eligible graduates with prospective employers who called looking for MSOD talent, provided career guidance, and worked with the program's alumni organization to sponsor conferences and other alumni activities.

Each of the above activities was somewhat programmable in that they occurred at specific times of the year and could be scheduled. However, because each applicant, student, class, or graduate was somewhat unique, the specific tasks or actions could not always be specified in advance and there were a number of exceptions and unique situations that arose during each day, month, or year.

The MSOD Program Administrator has worked with the MSOD program for over 15 years and was a fixture in both the MSOD and the general OD communities. Year over year, the Program Administrator delivered qualified applicants in excess of available space although that task had become increasingly difficult in the face of tuition increases, increasingly restrictive corporate policies on tuition reimbursement, and the ups and downs of the economy. He has handled both routine and nonroutine administrative details professionally, displays and reports a high level of job satisfaction and commitment to the program, and has been complimented formally and informally by the students in the program. In fact, each cohort develops its own relationship with the administrator and he becomes a de facto member of almost every class. The alumni considered the Program Administrator a key and integral part of the MSOD program. The set of duties described above has evolved considerably over the Program Administrator's tenure. In particular, he has become more involved and responsible for marketing and recruiting activities, and the alumni relations duties have been added in response to alumni requests that cannot be filled by traditional university departments.

In an effort to improve efficiencies, and in recognition of the MSOD Program Administrator's outstanding productivity, a proposal was being considered by GSBM administration to change the design of his job. The proposal suggested that the MSOD Program Administrator continue to perform all of the current duties of the position, and, in addition, provide administrative support to two PKE classes from their initial class to graduation. The duties of administrating the PKE program would be similar in nature to the delivery aspects of the MSOD program, including working with faculty to support their teaching efforts, managing textbook ordering processes, and providing different facilities logistics activities. It would not include marketing, recruiting, and alumni development activities. He would receive additional compensation for the increased responsibilities and a title change. The new position would share, with the EMBA program administrator, the supervision of an assistant program administrator, who would in turn supervise a pool of administrative assistants. The assistant program administrator would also report to the EMBA Program Administrator. The MSOD/PKE program administrator would be shared between the MSOD program director and a director of EMBA/PKE programs.

Diagnosis of individual-level inputs answers the following questions:

1. **What is the design of the larger organization within which the individual jobs are embedded?** Although the example says little about the organization's design, a number of inferences are possible. The school's administration was attempting to reward the Program Administrator with a more enriched job. This suggests that the culture of the organization was supportive of employee involvement. The proposed change was also being considered, however, as part of an efficiency drive. The school is large in size, hosting the third-largest part-time MBA program. This helps to explain, at the organization level, why a specialized master's degree has been paired with two executive MBA programs. To the extent the OD program has different students or different marketing, delivery, and alumni relations processes, there may be difficult points of integration.

2. **What is the design of the group containing the individual jobs?** Three individual jobs were grouped together according to the type of program. In this case, a faculty director, program administrator, and administrative assistant comprise the program office, but the office is clearly dependent on other university and school functions, such as the registrar's office and financial aid, as well as with the teaching faculty. Each of the three roles has specific duties but there is a clear sense that all three roles are highly interdependent. The Program Administrator must coordinate with the director on marketing, admissions, and curriculum decisions and with the administrative assistant on recruiting, program delivery, and routine administrative processes. Interaction during task performance is thus intense and although partly scheduled, the work also must deal with a high number of exceptions.

3. **What are the personal characteristics of jobholders?** The application provides some clues about the Program Administrator's personal characteristics. First, he has stayed in the position for more than 15 years; this speaks to a loyalty or commitment trait. Second, his role has evolved considerably and suggests at least a moderate amount of growth need strength.

Diagnosis of individual jobs involves the following job dimensions:

1. **How much skill variety is included in the job?** The Program Administrator's role involves a wide variety of tasks, including recruiting students; advising prospective and current students on career opportunities; making input into marketing strategies and tactics; handling routine and nonroutine administrative matters such as registration, grade changes, and graduation processes; supervision of an administrative assistant; coordination with other functions and departments within the school and university; traveling to several sessions and handling logistics details; negotiating with a variety of resort properties on rooming costs, menus, meal costs, and room setup; working with alumni; and a variety of other tasks.

2. **How much task identity does the job contain?** The Program Administrator's job is "all of a piece." He sees and follows individuals through an entire process, as applicants, students, and alumni. He sees them as individuals, as professionals, and as members of a family or other community.

3. **How much task significance is involved in the job?** The Program Administrator's task significance is very high. As a result of his work, he brings potential students into a well-respected program, works with them during their matriculation, advises them on their experiences in the program, and takes great pride in having an important hand in their personal and professional

development. The opportunity to be integrally involved in a transformational educational process results in high task significance.

4. **How much autonomy is included in the job?** There is a moderate-to-high amount of autonomy and it has evolved and increased over the years of experience in the job. The Program Administrator's long tenure suggests that he is able to handle, without much supervision, almost every aspect of his job.

5. **How much feedback about results does the job contain?** Assuming a traditional performance management process, the Program Administrator probably receives feedback on his performance and his strengths and weaknesses as a supervisor; from program evaluations, he receives feedback on how the program office is perceived in terms of its service quality; and from the students, he receives feedback on his willingness and ability to provide support and guidance. In short, the Program Administrator receives a lot of feedback about his work.

When the job characteristics are examined together, the program administrator job appears to contain high levels of enrichment. Task variety, task identity, task significance, autonomy, and feedback about results are all high. Over time, the level of enrichment appears to have increased because skill variety and autonomy have increased.

The hypothesis that the job is currently well designed can be tested by assessing how well the job design fits the inputs. The fit between the job and the organization context is not clear. As a specialized master's degree that is different from an executive MBA program, the MSOD program office and the administrator's job in particular have evolved to be somewhat independent of the other programs. There doesn't appear to be much sharing of tasks despite obvious opportunities such as student registration, graduation, book ordering, and others. Either the program is sufficiently different from the MBA programs that it warrants such independence or there are some important opportunities for improved efficiencies from the proposed change. The program administrator job is well fit to the other roles in the program office and to the worker's personal characteristics. For example, the technology of recruiting and educating students and managing the alumni is at least moderately if not highly uncertain and very interdependent. Tasks that are uncertain require considerable information processing and decision making. Organic and enriched jobs fit such tasks, and the program administrator job has gradually evolved to fit the high levels of uncertainty and interdependence.

In this context, the proposed change to the program administrator job needs to be addressed. Will the changes likely improve productivity, enhance quality, or increase job satisfaction? In general, the answer appears to be "no." For example, the proposed change argues that adding new responsibilities will increase task variety, task identity, and task significance. However, the addition of the PKE classes does not increase the skill variety of the incumbent. There are, in fact, no new skills required to administer the PKE classes and adding these responsibilities may actually unbalance the existing skill mix. That is, under the new job, the program delivery component of the job will increase dramatically with respect to the other skills and more or less dominate the mix. This could actually result in a decreased perception of task variety.

The proposed change also argues that task significance will increase since the Program Administrator would be able to affect the lives of MSOD program participants as well as the lives of PKE participants. There is some merit to this idea, but it must be tempered with knowledge from the change in task identity. The MSOD Program Administrator's task identity, as described in the application, is high while the task identity for the PKE program is relatively low. In the PKE program, the Program Administrator would interact with the students only during the program; he has no involvement in the recruiting process and no involvement with them as alumni. Thus, any increase in the number of people his job affects (task significance) is likely to be offset by the reduced involvement he has with about half of these people (task identity).

Finally, the proposed change argues that the incumbent is being given more responsibility, which is true, but he will have less autonomy. The new MSOD/PKE program administrator position will have two bosses: the MSOD program director and the EMBA/PKE director. Thus, the Program Administrator will probably have more, not less, supervision as the MSOD program director ensures that the MSOD program objectives are addressed and the EMBA/PKE program director ensures that his or her program objectives are being addressed.

Examining the proposed changes against the dimensions of job enrichment suggests an intervention dilemma in this case. Should the school's administration continue with the proposed change? The hoped-for efficiencies may or may not materialize. The skills and knowledge of the Program Administrator may in fact be applied to improve productivity but will it do so at the cost to the Program Administrator's work satisfaction? Over time, such a solution may not be sustainable. If the change is implemented, interventions probably should be aimed at mitigating the negative implications in task identity, task significance, and autonomy. The MSOD director and the EMBA/PKE director need to clearly work out expectations of the Program Administrator and figure out methods to allow the Program Administrator to perform certain tasks that he finds more rewarding. (Interventions for matching people, technology, and job design are discussed in Chapter 16.) If the proposed changes are not implemented, alternative structural arrangements within the executive programs organization will have to be examined.

SUMMARY

In this chapter, diagnostic models associated with groups and individuals were described and applied. Each of the models derive from the open-systems view of organizations developed in Chapter 5. Diagnostic models include the input, design component (transformation processes), and output dimensions needed to understand groups and individual jobs.

Group diagnostic models take the organization's design as the primary input; examine goal clarity, task structure, group composition, performance norms, and group functioning as the key design components; and list group performance and member quality of work life as the outputs. As with any open-systems model, the alignment of these parts is the key to understanding effectiveness.

At the individual job level, organization design, group design, and characteristics of each job are the salient inputs. Task variety, task significance, task identity, autonomy, and feedback work together to produce outputs of work satisfaction and work quality.

NOTES

1. S. Cohen, "Designing Effective Self-Managing Work Teams," in *Advances in Interdisciplinary Studies of Work Teams*, vol. 1, ed. M. Beyerlein (Greenwich, Conn.: JAI Press, 1995); M. Turner, ed., *Groups at Work* (Mahwah, N.J.: LEA Publishers, 2001).

2. J. Hackman and C. Morris, "Group Tasks, Group Interaction Process, and Group Performance Effectiveness: A Review and Proposed Integration," in *Advances*

in Experimental Social Psychology, vol. 9, ed. L. Berkowitz (New York: Academic Press, 1975): 45–99; J. Hackman, ed., *Groups That Work (and Those That Don't): Creating Conditions for Effective Teamwork* (San Francisco: Jossey-Bass, 1989).

3. M. McCaskey, "Framework for Analyzing Work Groups," *Harvard Business School Case 9-480-009* (Boston: Harvard Business School, 1997).

4. G. Ledford, E. Lawler, and S. Mohrman, "The Quality Circle and Its Variations," in *Productivity in Organizations: New Perspectives from Industrial and Organizational Psychology,* eds. J. Campbell, R. Campbell, and Associates (San Francisco: Jossey-Bass, 1988): 255–94.

5. D. Ancona and D. Caldwell, "Bridging the Boundary: External Activity and Performance in Organizational Teams," *Administrative Science Quarterly* 37 (1992): 634–65; Cohen, "Self-Managing Work Teams"; S. Mohrman, S. Cohen, and A. Mohrman, *Designing Team-Based Organizations* (San Francisco: Jossey-Bass, 1995).

6. G. Susman, *Autonomy at Work* (New York: Praeger, 1976); T. Cummings, "Self-Regulating Work Groups: A Socio-Technical Synthesis," *Academy of Management Review* 3 (1978): 625–34; J. Slocum and H. Sims, "A Typology for Integrating Technology, Organization, and Job Design," *Human Relations* 33 (1980): 193–212.

7. J. R. Hackman and G. Oldham, *Work Redesign* (Reading, Mass.: Addison-Wesley, 1980).

8. E. Schein, *Process Consultation,* vols. I–II (Reading, Mass.: Addison-Wesley, 1987).

9. W. Dyer, *Team Building,* 3d ed. (Reading, Mass.: Addison-Wesley, 1994).

10. Hackman and Morris, "Group Tasks"; T. Cummings, "Designing Effective Work Groups," in *Handbook of Organizational Design,* vol. 2, eds. P. Nystrom and W. Starbuck (Oxford: Oxford University Press, 1981): 250–71.

11. Cummings, "Designing Effective Work Groups."

12. Susman, *Autonomy at Work*; Cummings, "Self-Regulating Work Groups"; Slocum and Sims, "Typology."

13. Cummings, "Self-Regulating Work Groups"; Slocum and Sims, "Typology."

14. Ibid.

15. Hackman and Oldham, *Work Redesign*; F. Herzberg, "One More Time: How Do You Motivate Employees?" *Harvard Business Review* 46 (1968): 53–62.

16. J. Pierce, R. Dunham, and R. Blackburn, "Social Systems Structure, Job Design, and Growth Need Strength: A Test of a Congruence Model," *Academy of Management Journal* 22 (1979): 223–40.

17. Susman, *Autonomy at Work*; Cummings, "Self-Regulating Work Groups"; Slocum and Sims, "Typology."

18. Hackman and Oldham, *Work Redesign*; Pierce, Dunham, and Blackburn, "Social Systems Structure."

19. E. Lawler III, *Motivation in Work Organizations* (Monterey, Calif.: Brooks/Cole, 1973).

20. Hackman and Oldham, *Work Redesign.*

21. Pierce, Dunham, and Blackburn, "Social Systems Structure"; Susman, *Autonomy at Work*; Cummings, "Self-Regulating Work Groups"; Slocum and Sims, "Typology."

22. Hackman and Oldham, *Work Redesign*; Pierce, Dunham, and Blackburn, "Social Systems Structure."

7

Collecting and Analyzing Diagnostic Information

Organization development is vitally dependent on *organization diagnosis:* the process of collecting information that will be shared with the client in jointly assessing how the organization is functioning and determining the best change intervention. The quality of the information gathered, therefore, is a critical part of the OD process. In this chapter, we discuss several key issues associated with collecting and analyzing diagnostic data on how an organization or department functions.

Data collection involves gathering information on specific organizational features, such as the inputs, design components, and outputs presented in Chapters 5 and 6. The process begins by establishing an effective relationship between the OD practitioner and those from whom data will be collected and then choosing data-collection techniques. Four methods can be used to collect data: questionnaires, interviews, observations, and unobtrusive measures. Data analysis organizes and examines the information to make clear the underlying causes of an organizational problem or to identify areas for future development. The next step in the cyclical OD process is the feedback of data to the client system, an important process described in Chapter 8. The overall process of data collection, analysis, and feedback is shown in Figure 7.1.

THE DIAGNOSTIC RELATIONSHIP

In most cases of planned change, OD practitioners play an active role in gathering data from organization members for diagnostic purposes. For example, they might interview members of a work team about causes of conflict among members; they might survey employees at a large industrial plant about factors contributing to poor product quality. Before collecting diagnostic information, practitioners need to establish a relationship with those who will provide and subsequently use it. Because the nature of that relationship affects the quality and usefulness of the data collected, it is vital that OD practitioners clarify for organization members who they are, why the data are being collected, what the data gathering will involve, and how the data will be used.[1] That information can help allay people's natural fears that the data might be used against them and gain members' participation and support, which are essential to developing successful interventions.

Establishing the diagnostic relationship between the consultant and relevant organization members is similar to forming a contract. It is meant to clarify expectations and to specify the conditions of the relationship. In those cases where members have been directly involved in the entering and contracting process described in Chapter 4, the diagnostic contract will typically be part of the initial contracting step. In situations where data will be collected from members who have not been directly involved in entering and contracting, however, OD practitioners will need to establish a diagnostic contract as a prelude to diagnosis. The answers to the following questions provide the substance of the diagnostic contract:[2]

1. **Who am I?** The answer to this question introduces the OD practitioner to the organization, particularly to those members who do not know the consultant and yet will be asked to provide diagnostic data.

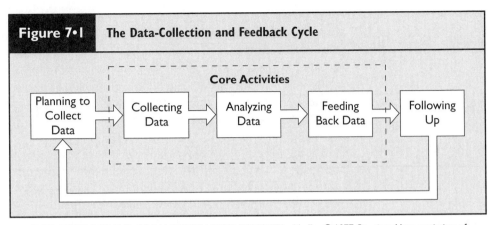

SOURCE: FEEDBACK AND ORGANIZATON DEVELOPMENT by Nadler, © 1977. Reprinted by permission of Pearson Education, Inc., Upper Saddle River, NJ.

2. **Why am I here, and what am I doing?** These answers are aimed at defining the goals of the diagnosis and data-gathering activities. The consultant needs to present the objectives of the action research process and to describe how the diagnostic activities fit into the overall developmental strategy.

3. **Who do I work for?** This answer clarifies who has hired the consultant, whether it be a manager, a group of managers, or a group of employees and managers. One way to build trust and support for the diagnosis is to have those people directly involved in establishing the diagnostic contract. Thus, for example, if the consultant works for a joint labor–management committee, representatives from both sides of that group could help the consultant build the proper relationship with those from whom data will be gathered.

4. **What do I want from you, and why?** Here, the consultant needs to specify how much time and effort people will need to give to provide valid data and subsequently to work with these data in solving problems. Because some people may not want to participate in the diagnosis, it is important to specify that such involvement is voluntary.

5. **How will I protect your confidentiality?** This answer addresses member concerns about who will see their responses and in what form. This is especially critical when employees are asked to provide information about their attitudes or perceptions. OD practitioners can either ensure confidentiality or state that full participation in the change process requires open information sharing. In the first case, employees are frequently concerned about privacy and the possibility of being punished for their responses. To alleviate concern and to increase the likelihood of obtaining honest responses, the consultant may need to assure employees of the confidentiality of their information, perhaps through explicit guarantees of response anonymity. In the second case, full involvement of the participants in their own diagnosis may be a vital ingredient of the change process. If sensitive issues arise, assurances of confidentiality can co-opt the OD practitioner and thwart meaningful diagnosis. The consultant is bound to keep confidential the issues that are most critical for the group or organization to understand.[3] OD practitioners must think carefully about how they want to handle confidentiality issues.

6. **Who will have access to the data?** Respondents typically want to know whether they will have access to their data and who else in the organization will have similar access. The OD practitioner needs to clarify access issues and, in most cases, should agree to provide respondents with their own results.

Indeed, the collaborative nature of diagnosis means that organization members will work with their own data to discover causes of problems and to devise relevant interventions.

7. **What's in it for you?** This answer is aimed at providing organization members with a clear delineation of the benefits they can expect from the diagnosis. This usually entails describing the feedback process and how they can use the data to improve the organization.

8. **Can I be trusted?** The diagnostic relationship ultimately rests on the trust established between the consultant and those providing the data. An open and honest exchange of information depends on such trust, and the practitioner should provide ample time and face-to-face contact during the contracting process to build this trust. This requires the consultant to listen actively and discuss openly all questions raised by participants.

Careful attention to establishing the diagnostic relationship helps to promote the three goals of data collection.[4] The first and most immediate objective is to obtain valid information about organizational functioning. Building a data collection contract can ensure that organization members provide honest, reliable, and complete information.

Data collection also can rally energy for constructive organizational change. A good diagnostic relationship helps organization members start thinking about issues that concern them, and it creates expectations that change is possible. When members trust the consultant, they are likely to participate in the diagnostic process and to generate energy and commitment for organizational change.

Finally, data collection helps to develop the collaborative relationship necessary for effecting organizational change. The diagnostic stage of action research is probably the first time that most organization members meet the OD practitioner, and it can be the basis for building a longer-term relationship. The data collection contract and subsequent data-gathering and feedback activities provide members with opportunities for seeing the consultant in action and for knowing her or him personally. If the consultant can show employees that he or she is trustworthy, is willing to work with them, and is able to help improve the organization, then the data collection process will contribute to the longer-term collaborative relationship so necessary for carrying out organizational changes.

METHODS FOR COLLECTING DATA

The four major techniques for gathering diagnostic data are questionnaires, interviews, observations, and unobtrusive measures. Table 7.1 briefly compares the methods and lists their major advantages and problems. No single method can fully measure the kinds of variables important to OD because each has certain strengths and weaknesses.[5] For example, perceptual measures, such as questionnaires and surveys, are open to self-report biases, such as respondents' tendency to give socially desirable answers rather than honest opinions. Observations, on the other hand, are susceptible to observer biases, such as seeing what one wants to see rather than what is really there. Because of the biases inherent in any data collection method, more than one method should be used when collecting diagnostic data. If data from the different methods are compared and found to be consistent, it is likely that the variables are being measured validly. For example, questionnaire measures of job discretion could be supplemented with observations of the number and kinds of decisions employees are making. If the two kinds of data support one another, job discretion is probably being assessed accurately. If the two kinds of data conflict, then the validity of the measures should be examined further—perhaps by using a third method, such as interviews.

Table 7•1	A Comparison of Different Methods of Data Collection	
METHOD	**MAJOR ADVANTAGES**	**MAJOR POTENTIAL PROBLEMS**
Questionnaires	1. Responses can be quantified and easily summarized 2. Easy to use with large samples 3. Relatively inexpensive 4. Can obtain large volume of data	1. Nonempathy 2. Predetermined questions/missing issues 3. Overinterpretation of data 4. Response bias
Interviews	1. Adaptive—allows data collection on a range of possible subjects 2. Source of "rich" data 3. Empathic 4. Process of interviewing can build rapport	1. Expense 2. Bias in interviewer responses 3. Coding and interpretation difficulties 4. Self-report bias
Observations	1. Collects data on behavior, rather than reports of behavior 2. Real time, not retrospective 3. Adaptive	1. Coding and interpretation difficulties 2. Sampling inconsistencies 3. Observer bias and questionable reliability 4. Expense
Unobtrusive measures	1. Nonreactive—no response bias 2. High face validity 3. Easily quantified	1. Access and retrieval difficulties 2. Validity concerns 3. Coding and interpretation difficulties

SOURCE: FEEDBACK AND ORGANIZATON DEVELOPMENT by Nadler, © 1977. Reprinted by permission of Pearson Education, Inc., Upper Saddle River, NJ.

Questionnaires

One of the most efficient ways to collect data is through questionnaires. Because they typically contain fixed-response queries about various features of an organization, these paper-and-pencil measures can be administered to large numbers of people simultaneously. Also, they can be analyzed quickly, especially with the use of computers, thus permitting quantitative comparison and evaluation. As a result, data can easily be fed back to employees. Numerous basic resource books on survey methodology and questionnaire development are available.[6]

Questionnaires can vary in scope, some measuring selected aspects of organizations and others assessing more comprehensive organizational characteristics. They also can vary in the extent to which they are either standardized or tailored to a specific organization. Standardized instruments generally are based on an explicit model of organization, group, or individual effectiveness and contain a predetermined set of questions that have been developed and refined over time. For example, Table 7.2 (on page 118) presents a standardized questionnaire for measuring the job-design dimensions identified in Chapter 6: skill variety, task identity, task significance, autonomy, and feedback about results. The questionnaire includes three items or questions for each dimension, and a total score for each job dimension is computed simply by adding the responses for the three relevant items and arriving at a total score from 3 (low) to 21 (high). The questionnaire has wide applicability. It has been used in a variety of organizations with employees in both blue-collar and white-collar jobs.

Several research organizations have been highly instrumental in developing and refining surveys. The Institute for Social Research at the University of Michigan (http://www.isr.umich.edu) and the Center for Effective Organizations at the

Table 7•2 Job Design Questionnaire

Here are some statements about your job. How much do you agree or disagree with each?

MY JOB:	STRONGLY DISAGREE	DISAGREE	SLIGHTLY DISAGREE	UNDECIDED	SLIGHTLY AGREE	AGREE	STRONGLY AGREE
1. provides much variety	[1]	[2]	[3]	[4]	[5]	[6]	[7]
2. permits me to be left on my own to do my own work	[1]	[2]	[3]	[4]	[5]	[6]	[7]
3. is arranged so that I often have the opportunity to see jobs or projects through to completion	[1]	[2]	[3]	[4]	[5]	[6]	[7]
4. provides feedback on how well I am doing as I am working	[1]	[2]	[3]	[4]	[5]	[6]	[7]
5. is relatively significant in our organization	[1]	[2]	[3]	[4]	[5]	[6]	[7]
6. gives me considerable opportunity for independence and freedom in how I do my work	[1]	[2]	[3]	[4]	[5]	[6]	[7]
7. gives me the opportunity to do a number of different things	[1]	[2]	[3]	[4]	[5]	[6]	[7]
8. provides me an opportunity to find out how well I am doing	[1]	[2]	[3]	[4]	[5]	[6]	[7]
9. is very significant or important in the broader scheme of things	[1]	[2]	[3]	[4]	[5]	[6]	[7]
10. provides an opportunity for independent thought and action ...	[1]	[2]	[3]	[4]	[5]	[6]	[7]
11. provides me with a great deal of variety at work	[1]	[2]	[3]	[4]	[5]	[6]	[7]
12. is arranged so that I have the opportunity to complete the work I start	[1]	[2]	[3]	[4]	[5]	[6]	[7]
13. provides me with the feeling that I know whether I am performing well or poorly	[1]	[2]	[3]	[4]	[5]	[6]	[7]
14. is arranged so that I have the chance to do a job from the beginning to the end (i.e., a chance to do the whole job)	[1]	[2]	[3]	[4]	[5]	[6]	[7]
15. is one where a lot of other people can be affected by how well the work gets done	[1]	[2]	[3]	[4]	[5]	[6]	[7]

Scoring:
Skill variety .... questions 1, 7, 11
Task identity .... questions 3, 12, 14
Task significance .... questions 5, 9, 15
Autonomy .... questions 2, 6, 10
Feedback about results .... questions 4, 8, 13

SOURCE: Reproduced by permission of E. Lawler, S. Mohrman, and T. Cummings, Center for Effective Organizations, University of Southern California.

University of Southern California (http://www.marshall.usc.edu/web/ceo.cfm?doc_id-611) are two prominent examples. Two of the Institute's most popular measures of organizational dimensions are the *Survey of Organizations and the Michigan Organizational Assessment Questionnaire.* Few other instruments are supported by such substantial reliability and validity data.[7] Other examples of packaged instruments include Weisbord's *Organizational Diagnostic Questionnaire,* Dyer's *Team Development Survey,* Cameron and Quinn's *Organizational Culture Assessment Instrument,* and Hackman and Oldham's *Job Diagnostic Survey.*[8] In fact, so many questionnaires are available that rarely would an organization have to create a totally new one. However, because every organization has unique problems and special jargon for referring to them, almost any standardized instrument will need to have organization-specific additions, modifications, or omissions.

Customized questionnaires, on the other hand, are tailored to the needs of a particular client. Typically, they include questions composed by consultants or organization members, receive limited use, and do not undergo longer-term development. They can be combined with standardized instruments to provide valid and reliable data focused toward the particular issues facing an organization.

Questionnaires, however, have a number of drawbacks that need to be taken into account in choosing whether to employ them for data collection. First, responses are limited to the questions asked in the instrument. They provide little opportunity to probe for additional data or to ask for points of clarification. Second, questionnaires tend to be impersonal, and employees may not be willing to provide honest answers. Third, questionnaires often elicit response biases, such as the tendency to answer questions in a socially acceptable manner. This makes it difficult to draw valid conclusions from employees' self-reports.

Interviews

A second important measurement technique is the *individual* or *group interview.* Interviews are probably the most widely used technique for collecting data in OD. They permit the interviewer to ask the respondent direct questions. Further probing and clarification is, therefore, possible as the interview proceeds. This flexibility is invaluable for gaining private views and feelings about the organization and for exploring new issues that emerge during the interview.

Interviews may be highly structured—resembling questionnaires—or highly unstructured—starting with general questions that allow the respondent to lead the way. Structured interviews typically derive from a conceptual model of organization functioning; the model guides the types of questions that are asked. For example, a structured interview based on the organization-level design components identified in Chapter 5 would ask managers specific questions about organization structure, measurement systems, human resources systems, and organization culture.

Unstructured interviews are more general and include broad questions about organizational functioning, such as:

- What are the major goals or objectives of the organization or department?
- How does the organization currently perform with respect to these purposes?
- What are the strengths and weaknesses of the organization or department?
- What barriers stand in the way of good performance?

Although interviewing typically involves one-to-one interaction between an OD practitioner and an employee, it can be carried out in a group context. Group interviews save time and allow people to build on others' responses. A major drawback, however, is that group settings may inhibit some people from responding freely.

A popular type of group interview is the *focus group* or *sensing meeting.*[9] These are unstructured meetings conducted by a manager or a consultant. A small group of 10 to 15 employees is selected to represent a cross section of functional areas and hierarchical levels or a homogenous grouping, such as minorities or engineers. Group discussion is frequently started by asking general questions about organizational features and functioning, an intervention's progress, or current performance. Group members are then encouraged to discuss their answers more fully. Consequently, focus groups and sensing meetings are an economical way to obtain interview data and are especially effective in understanding particular issues in greater depth. The richness and validity of the information gathered will depend on the extent to which the manager or consultant develops a trust relationship with the group and listens to member opinions.

Another popular unstructured group interview involves assessing the current state of an intact work group. The manager or consultant generally directs a question to the group, calling its attention to some part of group functioning. For example, group members may be asked how they feel the group is progressing on its stated task. The group might respond and then come up with its own series of questions about barriers to task performance. This unstructured interview is a fast, simple way to collect data about group behavior. It allows members to discuss issues of immediate concern and to engage actively in the questioning and answering process. This technique is limited, however, to relatively small groups and to settings where there is trust among employees and managers and a commitment to assessing group processes.

Interviews are an effective method for collecting data in OD. They are adaptive, allowing the interviewer to modify questions and to probe emergent issues during the interview process. They also permit the interviewer to develop an empathetic relationship with employees, frequently resulting in frank disclosure of pertinent information.

A major drawback of interviews is the amount of time required to conduct and analyze them. Interviews can consume a great deal of time, especially if interviewers take full advantage of the opportunity to hear respondents out and change their questions accordingly. Personal biases also can distort the data. Like questionnaires, interviews are subject to the self-report biases of respondents and, perhaps more important, to the biases of the interviewer. For example, the nature of the questions and the interactions between the interviewer and the respondent may discourage or encourage certain kinds of responses. These problems suggest that interviewing takes considerable skill to gather valid data. Interviewers must be able to understand their own biases, to listen and establish empathy with respondents, and to change questions to pursue issues that develop during the course of the interview.

Observations

One of the more direct ways of collecting data is simply to *observe* organizational behaviors in their functional settings. The OD practitioner may do this by walking casually through a work area and looking around or by simply counting the occurrences of specific kinds of behaviors (for example, the number of times a phone call is answered after three rings in a service department). Observation can range from complete participant observation, in which the OD practitioner becomes a member of the group under study, to more detached observation, in which the observer is clearly not part of the group or situation itself and may use film, videotape, and other methods to record behaviors.

Observations have a number of advantages. They are free of the biases inherent in self-report data. They put the practitioner directly in touch with the behaviors in question, without having to rely on others' perceptions. Observations also involve real-time data, describing behavior occurring in the present rather than the past. This avoids the distortions that invariably arise when people are asked to recollect their behaviors. Finally, observations are adaptive in that the consultant can modify what he or she chooses to observe, depending on the circumstances.

Among the problems with observations are difficulties interpreting the meaning underlying the observations. Practitioners may need to devise a coding scheme to make sense out of observations, and this can be expensive, take time, and introduce biases into the data. Because the observer is the data collection instrument, personal bias and subjectivity can distort the data unless the observer is trained and skilled in knowing what to look for; how, where, and when to observe; and how to record data systematically. Another problem concerns sampling: Observers not only must decide which people to observe; they also must choose the time periods, territory, and events in which to make those observations. Failure to attend to these sampling issues can result in highly biased samples of observational data.

When used correctly, observations provide insightful data about organization and group functioning, intervention success, and performance. For example, observations are particularly helpful in diagnosing the interpersonal relations of members of work groups. As discussed in Chapter 6, interpersonal relationships are a key component of work groups; observing member interactions in a group setting can provide direct information about the nature of those relationships.

Unobtrusive Measures

Unobtrusive data are not collected directly from respondents but from secondary sources, such as company records and archives. These data are generally available in organizations and include records of absenteeism or tardiness; grievances; quantity and quality of production or service; financial performance; meeting minutes; and correspondence with key customers, suppliers, or governmental agencies.

Unobtrusive measures are especially helpful in diagnosing the organization, group, and individual outputs presented in Chapters 5 and 6. At the organization level, for example, market share and return on investment usually can be obtained from company reports. Similarly, organizations typically measure the quantity and quality of the outputs of work groups and individual employees. Unobtrusive measures also can help to diagnose organization-level design components—structure, work systems, control systems, and human resources systems. A company's organization chart, for example, can provide useful information about organization structure. Information about control systems usually can be obtained by examining the firm's management information system, operating procedures, and accounting practices. Data about human resources systems often are included in a company's personnel manual.

Unobtrusive measures provide a relatively objective view of organizational functioning. They are free from respondent and consultant biases and are perceived as being "real" by many organization members. Moreover, unobtrusive measures tend to be quantified and reported at periodic intervals, permitting statistical analysis of behaviors occurring over time. Examining monthly absenteeism rates, for example, might reveal trends in employee withdrawal behavior.

The major problems with unobtrusive measures occur in collecting such information and drawing valid conclusions from it. Company records may not include data in a form that is usable by the consultant. If, for example, individual performance data are needed, the consultant may find that many firms only record production information at the group or departmental level. Unobtrusive data also may have their own built-in biases. Changes in accounting procedures and in methods of recording data are common in organizations, and such changes can affect company records independently of what is actually happening in the organization. For example, observed changes in productivity over time might be caused by modifications in methods of recording production rather than by actual changes in organizational functioning.

Despite these drawbacks, unobtrusive data serve as a valuable adjunct to other diagnostic measures, such as interviews and questionnaires. Archival data can be used in preliminary diagnosis, identifying those organizational units with absenteeism, grievance, or production problems. Then, interviews might be conducted or observations made in those units to discover the underlying causes of the problems. Conversely, unobtrusive data can be used to cross-check other forms of information. For example, if questionnaires reveal that employees in a department are dissatisfied with their jobs, company records might show whether that discontent is manifested in heightened withdrawal behaviors, in lowered quality work, or in similar counterproductive behaviors.

SAMPLING

Before discussing how to analyze data, the issue of *sampling* needs to be emphasized. Application of the different data collection techniques invariably raises the following questions: "How many people should be interviewed and who should they be?" "What events should be observed and how many?" "How many records should be inspected and which ones?"[10]

Sampling is not an issue in many OD cases. Because practitioners collect interview or questionnaire data from all members of the organization or department in question, they do not have to worry about whether the information is representative of the organization or unit.

Sampling becomes an issue in OD, however, when data are collected from selected members, behaviors, or records. This is often the case when diagnosing organization-level issues or large systems. In these cases, it may be important to ensure that the sample of people, behaviors, or records adequately represents the characteristics of the total population. For example, a sample of 50 employees might be used to assess the perceptions of all 300 members of a department. A sample of production data might be used to evaluate the total production of a work group. OD practitioners often find that it is more economical and quicker to gather a sampling of diagnostic data than to collect all possible information. If done correctly, the sample can provide useful and valid information about the entire organization or unit.

Sampling design involves considerable technical detail, and consultants may need to become familiar with basic references in this area or to obtain professional help.[11] The first issue to address is *sample size,* or how many people, events, or records are needed to carry out the diagnosis or evaluation. This question has no simple answer: The necessary sample size is a function of population size, the confidence desired in the quality of the data, and the resources (money and time) available for data collection.

First, the larger the population (for example, number of organization members or total number of work outcomes) or the more complex the client system (for example, the number of salary levels that must be sampled or the number of different functions), the more difficult it is to establish a "right" sample size. As the population increases in size and complexity, the less meaning one can attach to simple measures, such as an overall average score on a questionnaire item. Because the population comprises such different types of people or events, more data are needed to ensure an accurate representation of the potentially different subgroups. Second, the larger the proportion of the population that is selected, the more confidence one can have about the quality of the sample. If the diagnosis concerns an issue of great importance to the organization, then extreme confidence may be needed, indicative of a very large sample size. Third, limited resources constrain sample size. If resources are limited but the required confidence is high, then questionnaires will be preferred over interviews because more information can be collected per member per dollar.

The second issue to address is *sample selection.* Probably the most common approach to sampling diagnostic data in OD is a simple *random sample,* in which each member, behavior, or record has an equal chance of being selected. For example, assume that an OD practitioner would like to select 50 people randomly out of the 300 employees at a manufacturing plant. Using a complete list of all 300 employees, the consultant can generate a random sample in one of two ways. The first method is to use a random number table printed in the back of almost any statistics text; the consultant would pick out the employees corresponding to the first 50 numbers under 300 beginning anywhere in the table. The second method is to pick every sixth name (300/50 = 6) starting anywhere in the list.

If the population is complex, or many subgroups need to be represented in the sample, a *stratified sample* may be more appropriate than a random one. In a stratified sample, the population of members, events, or records is segregated into a number of mutually exclusive subpopulations and a random sample is taken from each subpopulation. For example, members of an organization might be divided into three groups (managers, white-collar workers, and blue-collar workers), and a random sample of members, behaviors, or records could be selected from each grouping to reach diagnostic conclusions about each of the groups.

Adequate sampling is critical to gathering valid diagnostic data, and the OD literature has paid little attention to this issue. OD practitioners should gain rudimentary knowledge in this area and use professional help if necessary.

TECHNIQUES FOR ANALYZING DATA

Data analysis techniques fall into two broad classes: qualitative and quantitative. Qualitative techniques generally are easier to use because they do not rely on numerical data. That fact also makes them easier to understand and interpret. Quantitative techniques, on the other hand, can provide more accurate readings of the organizational problem.

Qualitative Tools

Of the several methods for summarizing diagnostic data in qualitative terms, two of the most important are content analysis and force-field analysis.

Content Analysis

A popular technique for assessing qualitative data, especially interview data, is *content analysis,* which attempts to summarize comments into meaningful categories. When done well, a content analysis can reduce hundreds of interview comments into a few themes that effectively summarize the issues or attitudes of a group of respondents. The process of content analysis can be quite formal, and specialized references describe this technique in detail.[12] In general, however, the process can be broken down into three major steps. First, responses to a particular question are read to gain familiarity with the range of comments made and to determine whether some answers are occurring over and over again. Second, based on this sampling of comments, themes are generated that capture recurring comments. Themes consolidate different responses that say essentially the same thing. For example, in answering the question "What do you like most about your job?" different respondents might list their coworkers, their supervisors, the new machinery, and a good supply of tools. The first two answers concern the social aspects of work, and the second two address the resources available for doing the work. Third, the respondents' answers to a question are then placed into one of the categories. The categories with the most responses represent those themes that are most often mentioned.

Application 7.1 describes another installment in the change process at American Healthways. (The introduction of this longitudinal case began in Chapter 4.) In this application, the initial task force performs two diagnostic processes: The first one is

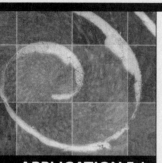

COLLECTING AND ANALYZING DIAGNOSTIC DATA AT AMERICAN HEALTHWAYS

APPLICATION 7•1

Two Applications in Chapter 4 introduced you to the American Healthways (AMHC) organization. In anticipation of future growth, especially in their "health plan" business, AMHC wanted to explore the fitness of their current structure, determine an appropriate structure to support growth and a larger organization in the future, and implement the change. The OD professor, the COO, the senior VP of human resources, and the Director of Training and OD named a task force to begin the process.

The task force's first meeting introduced members to the process and provided some history to the project. They agreed to call themselves the Organization Development and Design (ODD) team. The ODD team consisted of the COO, the human resources senior VP, the Director of Training and OD, a physician, the senior VP of information technology, an outside IT consultant, an account manager, the senior VP for operations, a regional VP from the hospital business, and a finance manager. The agenda for the first meeting included creating a team charter, including mission, goals, and list of deliverables; a quick environmental scan; and an initial diagnosis of the current organization design from this group's point of view. Using categories similar to the ones listed in Chapter 5, the group brainstormed responses to the strengths and weaknesses of the current structure as well as characteristics of the reward/recognition systems, the information/measurement systems, the work as designed, and the culture of the organization.

Based on these initial beliefs, opinions, and understandings, a subgroup was tasked with creating a more formal diagnostic survey. After debating the pros and cons of different survey forms, the group proposed a survey consisting of 17 open-ended questions. The subgroup believed that data "richness" was more important than "quantification." They wanted to be sure that they understood why people believed certain things about the current organization. As a result, the first four questions asked for opinions about the organization's BHAG (big, hairy, audacious goal). The BHAG had been drafted and discussed by the ODD team as part of their organization design efforts and presented to AMHC's senior managers. The diagnostic effort provided a good opportunity to test the attractiveness of this vision. The next 13 questions concerned the organization's current structure. It included generic questions: "What words and phrases would you use to describe the current structure of the organization?" and "What do you see as the key strengths/weaknesses of the organization?" More specific questions about

certain features of the structure were also included, such as "Where and how are important decisions made in the current design?" "Is the information you need delivered in a timely and accurate way?" and "How would you describe the level of teamwork at AMHC?" Finally, the survey concluded with a vision question, "If you were granted a magic wand and could make any change at all, what two things would you wish for?"

The survey was used in one-on-one interviews with key managers in the organization as well as focus groups of organization members. Employees from both the health plan and the hospital business were included. In all, 40 interviews with managers in leadership positions were conducted, and 20 focus groups of 3–5 members were conducted. Employees were randomly selected from different job classes to insure both representation and fairness.

Once all the data were collected, the ODD team members met to summarize and analyze the data. Prior to the meeting, all of the answers from the interviews and focus groups were transcribed and sorted by question and business. For example, the responses to the four BHAG questions were pooled together for each question and divided by whether the answers were from health plan members and managers or hospital members and managers. These transcribed pages were then assigned to two-person groups in the ODD team. For example, the BHAG questions were given to one two-person group, the final "wish" question was given to another two-person group, questions about decision making were given to a third two-person group, and so on.

Each group read through the transcribed answers and performed a "content analysis" of the data. The process consisted of reading through all of the answers and then generating buckets or themes thought to represent most of the answers. The group then went back through the data and sorted the answers according to these themes. For example, some questions, such as "How much influence would you say you have over decisions that affect you?", lent themselves to high/medium/low categorization. Within each category, the reasons could then be sorted to provide a sense about why individuals felt they did or did not have influence. Other questions, such as the one about words and phrases used to describe the organization, were more difficult and required some coaching from the OD professor.

After a day of intense work, each group made a presentation summarizing the answers to their question(s). The ODD team discussed both the summaries themselves and the implications of each summary on the emerging patterns in the other summaries. In this way, the group began to get a deeper understanding of the current organization. Some of the key patterns that became clear to the group included:

- The BHAG was seen as ambitious and visionary; it would change the face of health care and provided opportunities for personal and professional growth.

- Teamwork was an issue: People within functions or groups saw themselves as performing well, but did not always get along with people from other groups or organizations.

- Colleagues did not feel empowered: Timely and accurate information was not available, roles and responsibilities were not clear, there was little trust in the system, and most decisions were made at the top of the organization.

- Organization members wanted more opportunity for professional development.

- There was a disconnect in the way people delivered valued services: The pace and quantity of work, the resources to get work done, and relationships between operations and sales were not in alignment.

- The sample clearly believed that the organization had the right people, product, and pay, and that growth was leading to opportunity.

The group then discussed the implications of the data on their task. What did the data suggest about the characteristics of the future structure for AMHC? The group agreed, for example, that the organization's design needed to facilitate communication across functions; it needed to address people's fear that a new structure won't be less flexible, adaptable, or growth oriented; it had to increase people's clarity about how value was added by the organization; and it needed to leverage the things people liked and admired in the organization.

In Application 14.1, the ODD team's recommendation for AMHC's new organization structure is presented.

informal, and the second one uses surveys and content analysis to understand the organization's current structure and design. What do you see as the strengths and weaknesses of this diagnostic process?

Force-Field Analysis

A second method for analyzing qualitative data in OD derives from Kurt Lewin's three-step model of change. Called *force-field analysis,* this method organizes information pertaining to organizational change into two major categories: forces for change and forces for maintaining the status quo or resisting change.[13] Using data collected through interviews, observation, or unobtrusive measures, the first step in conducting a force-field analysis is to develop a list of all the forces promoting change and all those resisting it. Then, based either on the OD practitioner's personal belief or perhaps on input from several members of the client organization, a determination is made of which of the positive and which of the negative forces are most powerful. One can either rank the order or rate the strength of the different forces.

Figure 7.2 (on page 126) illustrates a force-field analysis of the performance of a work group. The arrows represent the forces, and the length of the arrows corresponds to the strength of the forces. The information could have been collected in a group interview in which members were asked to list those factors maintaining the current level of group performance and those factors pushing for a higher level. Members also could have been asked to judge the strength of each force, with the average judgment shown by the length of the arrows.

This analysis reveals two strong forces pushing for higher performance: pressures from the supervisor of the group and competition from other work groups performing similar work. These forces for change are offset by two strong forces for maintaining the status quo: group norms supporting present levels of performance and well-learned skills that are resistant to change. According to Lewin, efforts to change to a higher level of group performance, shown by the darker band in Figure 7.2, should focus on reducing the forces maintaining the status quo. This might entail changing the group's performance norms and helping members to learn

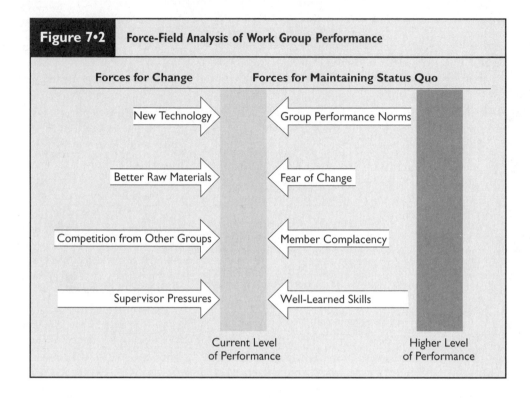

Figure 7•2   Force-Field Analysis of Work Group Performance

Forces for Change   Forces for Maintaining Status Quo

New Technology   Group Performance Norms

Better Raw Materials   Fear of Change

Competition from Other Groups   Member Complacency

Supervisor Pressures   Well-Learned Skills

Current Level   Higher Level
of Performance   of Performance

new skills. The reduction of forces maintaining the status quo is likely to result in organizational change with little of the tension or conflict typically accompanying change caused by increasing the forces for change.

Quantitative Tools

Methods for analyzing quantitative data range from simple descriptive statistics of items or scales from standard instruments to more sophisticated, multivariate analysis of the underlying instrument properties and relationships among measured variables.[14] The most common quantitative tools are means, standard deviations, frequency distributions, scattergrams, correlation coefficients, and difference tests. These measures are routinely produced by most statistical computer software packages. Therefore, mathematical calculations are not discussed here.

Means, Standard Deviations, and Frequency Distributions

One of the most economical and straightforward ways to summarize quantitative data is to compute a *mean* and *standard deviation* for each item or variable measured. These represent the respondents' average score and the spread or variability of the responses, respectively. These two numbers easily can be compared across different measures or subgroups. For example, Table 7.3 shows the means and standard deviations for six questions asked of 100 employees concerning the value of different kinds of organizational rewards. Based on the 5-point scale ranging from 1 (very low value) to 5 (very high value), the data suggest that challenging work and respect from peers are the two most highly valued rewards. Monetary rewards, such as pay and fringe benefits, are not as highly valued.

But the mean can be a misleading statistic. It only describes the average value and thus provides no information on the distribution of the responses. Different patterns of responses can produce the same mean score. Therefore, it is important to use the standard deviation along with the frequency distribution to gain a clearer

Table 7•3	Descriptive Statistics of Value of Organizational Rewards	
ORGANIZATIONAL REWARDS	**MEAN**	**STANDARD DEVIATION**
Challenging work	4.6	0.76
Respect from peers	4.4	0.81
Pay	4.0	0.71
Praise from supervisor	4.0	1.55
Promotion	3.3	0.95
Fringe benefits	2.7	1.14

Number of respondents = 100
1 = very low value; 5 = very high value

understanding of the data. The *frequency distribution* is a graphical method for displaying data that shows the number of times a particular response was given. For example, the data in Table 7.3 suggest that both pay and praise from the supervisor are equally valued with a mean of 4.0. However, the standard deviations for these two measures are very different at 0.71 and 1.55, respectively. Table 7.4 shows the frequency distributions of the responses to the questions about pay and praise from the supervisor. Employees' responses to the value of pay are distributed toward the higher end of the scale, with no one rating it of low or very low value. In contrast, responses about the value of praise from the supervisor fall into two distinct groupings: Twenty-five employees felt that supervisor praise has a low or very low value, whereas 75 people rated it high or very high. Although both rewards have the same mean value, their standard deviations and frequency distributions suggest different

Table 7•4	Frequency Distributions of Responses to "Pay" and "Praise from Supervisor" Items	
Pay (Mean = 4.0)		
RESPONSE	**NUMBER CHECKING EACH RESPONSE**	**GRAPH***
(1) Very low value	0	
(2) Low value	0	
(3) Moderate value	25	XXXXX
(4) High value	50	XXXXXXXXXX
(5) Very high value	25	XXXXX
Praise from Supervisor (Mean = 4.0)		
RESPONSE	**NUMBER CHECKING EACH RESPONSE**	**GRAPH***
(1) Very low value	15	XXX
(2) Low value	10	XX
(3) Moderate value	0	
(4) High value	10	XX
(5) Very high value	65	XXXXXXXXXXXXX

*Each X = five people checking the response.

interpretations of the data.

In general, when the standard deviation for a set of data is high, there is considerable disagreement over the issue posed by the question. If the standard deviation is small, the data are similar on a particular measure. In the example described above, there is disagreement over the value of supervisory praise (some people think it is important but others do not), but there is fairly good agreement that pay is a reward with high value.

Scattergrams and Correlation Coefficients

In addition to describing data, quantitative techniques also permit OD consultants to make inferences about the relationships between variables. Scattergrams and correlation coefficients are measures of the strength of a relationship between two variables. For example, suppose the problem being faced by an organization is increased conflict between the manufacturing department and the engineering design department. During the data collection phase, information about the number of conflicts and change orders per month over the past year is collected. The data are shown in Table 7.5 and plotted in a scattergram in Figure 7.3.

A *scattergram* is a diagram that visually displays the relationship between two variables. It is constructed by locating each case (person or event) at the intersection of its value for each of the two variables being compared. For example, in the month of August, there were eight change orders and three conflicts, whose intersection is shown on Figure 7.3 as an X.

Three basic patterns can emerge from a scattergram, as shown in Figure 7.4. The first pattern is called a positive relationship because as the values of x increase, so do the values of y. The second pattern is called a negative relationship because as the values of x increase, the values of y decrease. Finally, there is the "shotgun" pattern wherein no relationship between the two variables is apparent. In the example shown in Figure 7.3, an apparently strong positive relationship exists between the number of change orders and the number of conflicts between the engineering design department and the manufacturing department. This suggests that change orders may contribute to the observed conflict between the two departments.

The *correlation coefficient* is simply a number that summarizes data in a scattergram. Its value ranges between +1.0 and −1.0. A correlation coefficient of +1.0 means that

Table 7·5	Relationship between Change Orders and Conflicts	
MONTH	**NUMBER OF CHANGE ORDERS**	**NUMBER OF CONFLICTS**
April	5	2
May	12	4
June	14	3
July	6	2
August	8	3
September	20	5
October	10	2
November	2	1
December	15	4
January	8	3
February	18	4
March	10	5

there is a perfect, positive relationship between two variables, whereas a correlation of –1.0 signifies a perfectly negative relationship. A correlation of 0 implies a "shotgun" scattergram where there is no relationship between two variables.

Difference Tests

The final technique for analyzing quantitative data is the *difference test*. It can be used to compare a sample group against some standard or norm to determine whether the group is above or below that standard. It also can be used to determine whether two samples are significantly different from each other. In the first case, such com-

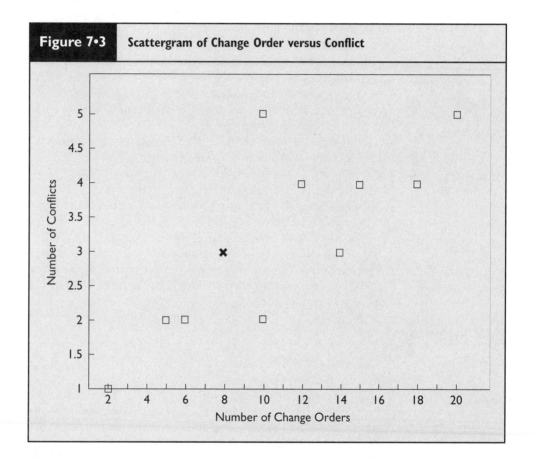

Figure 7•3   **Scattergram of Change Order versus Conflict**

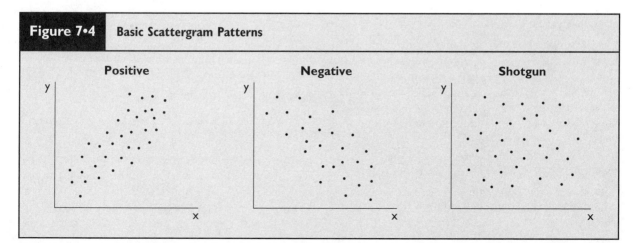

Figure 7•4   **Basic Scattergram Patterns**

parisons provide a broader context for understanding the meaning of diagnostic data. They serve as a "basis for determining 'how good is good or how bad is bad.'"[15] Many standardized questionnaires have standardized scores based on the responses of large groups of people. It is critical, however, to choose a comparison group that is similar to the organization being diagnosed. For example, if 100 engineers take a standardized attitude survey, it makes little sense to compare their scores against standard scores representing married males from across the country. On the other hand, if industry-specific data are available, a comparison of sales per employee (as a measure of productivity) against the industry average would be valid and useful.

The second use of difference tests involves assessing whether two (or more) groups differ from one another on a particular variable, such as job satisfaction or absenteeism. For example, job satisfaction differences between an accounting department and a sales department can be determined with this tool. Given that each group took the same questionnaire, their means and standard deviations can be used to compute a difference score (t-score or z-score) indicating whether the two groups are statistically different. The larger the difference score relative to the sample size and standard deviation for each group, the more likely that one group is more satisfied than the other.

Difference tests also can be used to determine whether a group has changed its score on job satisfaction or some other variable over time. The same questionnaire can be given to the same group at two points in time. Based on the group's means and standard deviations at each point in time, a difference score can be calculated. The larger the score, the more likely that the group actually changed its job satisfaction level.

The calculation of difference scores can be very helpful for diagnosis but requires the OD practitioner to make certain assumptions about how the data were collected. These assumptions are discussed in most standard statistical texts, and OD practitioners should consult them before calculating difference scores for purposes of diagnosis or evaluation.[16]

■ SUMMARY

This chapter described several different methods for collecting and analyzing diagnostic data. Because diagnosis is an important step that occurs frequently in the planned change process, a working familiarity with these techniques is essential. Methods of data collection include questionnaires, interviews, observation, and unobtrusive measures. Methods of analysis include qualitative techniques, such as content and force-field analysis, and quantitative techniques, such as the determination of mean, standard deviation, correlation coefficient, as well as difference tests.

■ NOTES

1. S. Mohrman, T. Cummings, and E. Lawler III, "Creating Useful Knowledge with Organizations: Relationship and Process Issues," in *Producing Useful Knowledge for Organizations,* eds. R. Kilmann and K. Thomas (New York: Praeger, 1983): 613–24; C. Argyris, R. Putnam, and D. Smith, eds., *Action Science* (San Francisco: Jossey-Bass, 1985); E. Lawler III, A. Mohrman, S. Mohrman, G. Ledford Jr., and T. Cummings, *Doing Research That is Useful for Theory and Practice* (San Francisco: Jossey-Bass, 1985).

2. D. Nadler, *Feedback and Organization Development: Using Data-Based Methods* (Reading, Mass.: Addison-Wesley, 1977): 110–14.

3. W. Nielsen, N. Nykodym, and D. Brown, "Ethics and Organizational Change," *Asia Pacific Journal of Human Resources* 29 (1991).

4. Nadler, *Feedback,* 105–7.

5. W. Wymer and J. Carsten, "Alternative Ways to Gather Opinion," *HR Magazine* (April 1992): 71–78.

6. Examples of basic resource books on survey methodology include: L. Rea, R. Parker, and A. Shrader, *Designing and Conducting Survey Research: A Comprehensive Guide* (San Francisco: Jossey Bass, 1997); S. Seashore, E. Lawler III, P. Mirvis, and C. Cammann, *Assessing Organizational Change*

(New York: Wiley Interscience, 1983); J. Van Mannen and J. Dabbs, *Varieties of Qualitative Research* (Beverly Hills, Calif.: Sage Publications, 1983); E. Lawler III, D. Nadler, and C. Cammann, *Organizational Assessment: Perspectives on the Measurement of Organizational Behavior and the Quality of Worklife* (New York: Wiley-Interscience, 1980); Nadler, *Feedback;* S. Sudman and N. Bradburn, *Asking Questions* (San Francisco: Jossey-Bass, 1983).

7. J. Taylor and D. Bowers, *Survey of Organizations: A Machine Scored Standardized Questionnaire Instrument* (Ann Arbor: Institute for Social Research, University of Michigan, 1972); C. Cammann, M. Fichman, G. Jenkins, and J. Klesh, "Assessing the Attitudes and Perceptions of Organizational Members," in *Assessing Organizational Change: A Guide to Methods, Measures, and Practices,* eds. S. Seashore, E. Lawler III, P. Mirvis, and C. Cammann (New York: Wiley Interscience, 1983): 71–138.

8. M. Weisbord, "Organizational Diagnosis: Six Places to Look for Trouble with or without a Theory," *Group and Organization Studies* 1 (1976): 430–37; R. Preziosi, "Organizational Diagnosis Questionnaire," in *The 1980 Handbook for Group Facilitators,* ed. J. Pfeiffer (San Diego: University Associates, 1980); W. Dyer, *Team Building: Issues and Alternatives* (Reading, Mass.: Addison-Wesley, 1977); J. Hackman and G. Oldham, *Work Redesign* (Reading, Mass.: Addison-Wesley, 1980); K. Cameron and R. Quinn, *Diagnosing and Changing Organizational Culture* (Reading, Mass.: Addison-Wesley, 1999).

9. J. Fordyce and R. Weil, *Managing WITH People,* 2d ed. (Reading, Mass.: Addison-Wesley, 1979); W. Wells, "Group Interviewing," in *Handbook of Marketing Research,* ed. R. Ferder (New York: McGraw-Hill, 1977); R. Krueger, *Focus Groups: A Practical Guide for Applied Research,* 2d ed. (Thousand Oaks, Calif.: Sage Publications, 1994).

10. C. Emory, *Business Research Methods* (Homewood, Ill.: Richard D. Irwin, 1980), 146.

11. W. Deming, *Sampling Design* (New York: John Wiley & Sons, 1960); L. Kish, *Survey Sampling* (New York: John Wiley & Sons, 1995).

12. B. Berelson, "Content Analysis," *Handbook of Social Psychology,* ed. G. Lindzey (Reading, Mass.: Addison-Wesley, 1954); K. Krippendorf, *Content Analysis: An Introduction to Its Methodology* (Thousand Oaks, Calif.: Sage Publications, 1980); W. Weber, *Basic Content Analysis* (Thousand Oaks, Calif.: Sage Publications, 1990).

13. K. Lewin, *Field Theory in Social Science* (New York: Harper & Row, 1951).

14. A simple explanation on quantitative issues in OD can be found in: S. Wagner, N. Martin, and C. Hammond, "A Brief Primer on Quantitative Measurement for the OD Professional," *OD Practitioner* 34 (2002): 53–57. More sophisticated methods of quantitative analysis are found in the following sources: W. Hays, *Statistics* (New York: Holt, Rinehart, & Winston, 1963); J. Nunnally and I. Bernstein, *Psychometric Theory,* 3d ed. (New York: McGraw-Hill, 1994); F. Kerlinger, *Foundations of Behavioral Research,* 2d ed. (New York: Holt, Rinehart, & Winston, 1973); J. Cohen and P. Cohen, *Applied Multiple Regression/Correlation Analysis for the Behavioral Sciences,* 2d ed. (Hillsdale, N.J.: Lawrence Erlbaum Associates, 1983); E. Pedhazur, *Multiple Regression in Behavioral Research* (New York: Harcourt Brace, 1997).

15. A. Armenakis and H. Field, "The Development of Organizational Diagnostic Norms: An Application of Client Involvement," *Consultation* 6 (Spring 1987): 20–31.

16. Cohen and Cohen, *Applied Multiple Regression.*

8

Feeding Back Diagnostic Information

Perhaps the most important step in the diagnostic process is feeding back diagnostic information to the client organization. Although the data may have been collected with the client's help, the OD practitioner often organizes and presents them to the client. Properly analyzed and meaningful data can have an impact on organizational change only if organization members can use the information to devise appropriate action plans. A key objective of the feedback process is to be sure that the client has ownership of the data.

As shown in Figure 8.1, the success of data feedback depends largely on its ability to arouse organizational action and to direct energy toward organizational problem solving. Whether feedback helps to energize the organization depends on the content of the feedback data and on the process by which they are fed back to organization members.

In this chapter, we discuss criteria for developing both the content of feedback information and the processes for feeding it back. If these criteria are overlooked, the client is not apt to feel ownership of the problems facing the organization. A flexible and potentially powerful technique for data feedback that has arisen out of the wide use of questionnaires in OD work is known as survey feedback. Its central role in many large-scale OD efforts warrants a special look.

DETERMINING THE CONTENT OF THE FEEDBACK

In the course of diagnosing the organization, a large amount of data is collected. In fact, there is often more information than the client needs or can interpret in a realistic period of time. If too many data are fed back, the client may decide that changing is impossible. Therefore, OD practitioners need to summarize the data in ways that enable clients to understand the information and draw action implications from it. The techniques for data analysis described in Chapter 7 can inform this task. Additional criteria for determining the content of diagnostic feedback are described below.

Several characteristics of effective feedback data have been described in the literature.[1] They include the following nine properties:

1. **Relevant.** Organization members are likely to use feedback data for problem solving when they find the information meaningful. Including managers and employees in the initial data collection activities can increase the relevance of the data.

2. **Understandable.** Data must be presented to organization members in a form that is readily interpreted. Statistical data, for example, can be made understandable through the use of graphs and charts.

3. **Descriptive.** Feedback data need to be linked to real organizational behaviors if they are to arouse and direct energy. The use of examples and detailed illustrations can help employees gain a better feel for the data.

4. **Verifiable.** Feedback data should be valid and accurate if they are to guide action. Thus, the information should allow organization members to verify

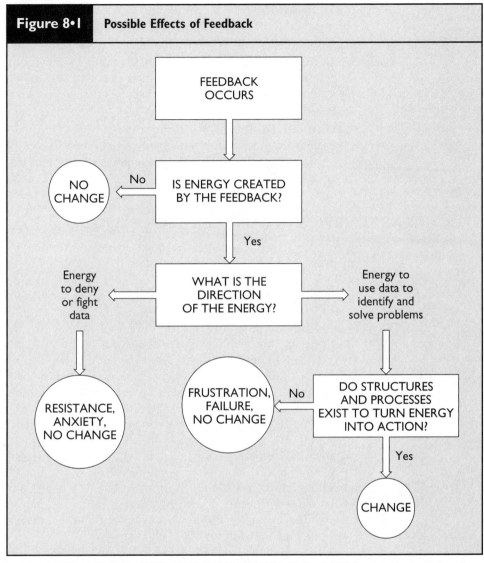

| Figure 8•1 | Possible Effects of Feedback |

SOURCE: FEEDBACK AND ORGANIZATON DEVELOPMENT by Nadler, © 1977. Reprinted by permission of Pearson Education, Inc., Upper Saddle River, NJ.

whether the findings really describe the organization. For example, questionnaire data might include information about the sample of respondents as well as frequency distributions for each item or measure. Such information can help members verify whether the feedback data accurately represent organizational events or attitudes.

5. **Timely.** Data should be fed back to members as quickly as possible after being collected and analyzed. This will help ensure that the information is still valid and is linked to members' motivations to examine it.

6. **Limited.** Because people can easily become overloaded with too much information, feedback data should be limited to what employees can realistically process at one time.

7. **Significant.** Feedback should be limited to those problems that organization members can do something about because it will energize them and help direct their efforts toward realistic changes.

8. **Comparative.** Feedback data can be ambiguous without some benchmark as a reference. Whenever possible, data from comparative groups should be provided to give organization members a better idea of how their group fits into a broader context.

9. **Unfinalized.** Feedback is primarily a stimulus for action and thus should spur further diagnosis and problem solving. Members should be encouraged, for example, to use the data as a starting point for more in-depth discussion of organizational issues.

CHARACTERISTICS OF THE FEEDBACK PROCESS

In addition to providing effective feedback data, it is equally important to attend to the process by which that information is fed back to people. Typically, data are provided to organization members in a meeting or series of meetings. Feedback meetings provide a forum for discussing the data, drawing relevant conclusions, and devising preliminary action plans. Because the data might include sensitive material and evaluations about organization members' behaviors, people may come to the meeting with considerable anxiety and fear about receiving the feedback. This anxiety can result in defensive behaviors aimed at denying the information or providing rationales. More positively, people can be stimulated by the feedback and the hope that desired changes will result from the feedback meeting. Because people are likely to come to feedback meetings with anxiety, fear, and hope, OD practitioners need to manage the feedback process so that constructive discussion and problem solving occur. The most important objective of the feedback process is to ensure that organization members own the data. Ownership is the opposite of resistance to change and refers to people's willingness to take responsibility for the data, their meaning, and the consequences of using them to devise a change strategy.[2] If the feedback session results in organization members rejecting the data as invalid or useless, then the motivation to change is lost and members will have difficulty engaging in a meaningful process of change.

Ownership of the feedback data is facilitated by the following five features of successful feedback processes:[3]

1. **Motivation to work with the data.** People need to feel that working with the feedback data will have beneficial outcomes. This may require explicit sanction and support from powerful groups so that people feel free to raise issues and to identify concerns during the feedback sessions. If people have little motivation to work with the data or feel that there is little chance to use the data for change, then the information will not be owned by the client system.

2. **Structure for the meeting.** Feedback meetings need some structure or they may degenerate into chaos or aimless discussion. An agenda or outline and a discussion leader can usually provide the necessary direction. If the meeting is not kept on track, especially when the data are negative, ownership can be lost in conversations that become too general. When this happens, the energy gained from dealing directly with the problem is lost.

3. **Appropriate attendance.** Generally, people who have common problems and can benefit from working together should be included in the feedback meeting. This may involve a fully intact work team or groups comprising members from different functional areas or hierarchical levels. Without proper representation

in the meeting, ownership of the data is lost because participants cannot address the problem(s) suggested by the feedback.

4. **Appropriate power.** It is important to clarify the power possessed by the group. Members need to know on which issues they can make necessary changes, on which they can only recommend changes, and over which they have no control. Unless there are clear boundaries, members are likely to have some hesitation about using the feedback data for generating action plans. Moreover, if the group has no power to make changes, the feedback meeting will become an empty exercise rather than a real problem-solving session. Without the power to address change, there will be little ownership of the data.

5. **Process help.** People in feedback meetings require assistance in working together as a group. When the data are negative, there is a natural tendency to resist the implications, deflect the conversation onto safer subjects, and the like. An OD practitioner with group process skills can help members stay focused on the subject and improve feedback discussion, problem solving, and ownership.

When combined with effective feedback data, these features of successful feedback meetings enhance member ownership of the data. They help to ensure that organization members fully discuss the implications of the diagnostic information and that their conclusions are directed toward relevant and feasible organizational changes.

Application 8.1 presents excerpts from some training materials that were delivered to a group of internal facilitators at a Fortune 100 telecommunications company.[4] It describes how the facilitators were trained to deliver the results of a survey concerning problem solving, team functioning, and perceived effectiveness.

SURVEY FEEDBACK

Survey feedback is a process of collecting and feeding back data from an organization or department through the use of a questionnaire or survey. The data are analyzed, fed back to organization members, and used by them to diagnose the organization and to develop interventions to improve it. Because questionnaires often are used in organization diagnosis, particularly in OD efforts involving large numbers of participants, and because it is a powerful intervention in its own right, survey feedback is discussed here as a special case of data feedback.

As discussed in Chapter 1, survey feedback is a major technique in the history and development of OD. Originally, this intervention included only data from questionnaires about members' attitudes. However, attitudinal data can be supplemented with interview data and more objective measures, such as productivity, turnover, and absenteeism.[5] Another trend has been to combine survey feedback with other OD interventions, including work design, structural change, large-group interventions, and intergroup relations. These change methods are the outcome of the planning and implementation phase following from survey feedback and are described fully in Chapters 12 through 20.

What Are the Steps?

Survey feedback generally involves the following five steps:[6]

1. **Members of the organization, including those at the top, are involved in preliminary planning of the survey.** In this step, all parties must be clear about the level of analysis (organization, department, or small group) and the objectives of the survey. Because most surveys derive from a model about organizational or group functioning, organization members must, in effect, approve

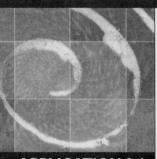

TRAINING OD PRACTITIONERS IN DATA FEEDBACK

Following deregulation of the telecommunications industry, GTE of California initiated a large-scale organization change to adapt to a rapidly changing environment. A key feature of the change was the implementation of an employee involvement (EI) process by management and the Communications Workers of America union. EI had as its stated goals the improvement of productivity and quality of work life. As part of that effort, the Center for Effective Organizations at the University of Southern California assisted the organization in collecting and feeding back implementation data on the EI intervention.

The data collected included observation of various work processes and problem-solving meetings; unobtrusive measures such as minutes from all meetings, quarterly income statements, operational reports, and communications; and questionnaire and interview data. A 3-page questionnaire was administered every 3 months and asked participants on EI problem-solving teams for their perceptions of team functioning and performance. Internal EI facilitators were appointed from both management and union employees, and part of their work required them to feed back the results of the quarterly surveys.

To provide timely feedback to the problem-solving teams, the EI facilitators were trained to deliver survey feedback. Some of the material developed for that training is summarized below.

I. Planning for a Survey-Feedback Session

The success of a survey-feedback meeting often has more to do with the level of preparation for the meeting than with anything else. There are several things to do in preparing for a survey-feedback meeting.

A. *Distribute copies of the feedback report in advance.* This enables people to devote more time at the meeting to problem solving and less to just digesting the data. This is especially important when a large quantity of data is being presented.

B. *Think about substantive issues in advance.* Formulate your own view of what the data suggest about the strengths and weaknesses of the group. Does the general picture appear to be positive or problematic? Do the data fit the experience of the group as you know it? What issues do the data suggest need group attention? Is the group likely to avoid any of these issues? If so, how will you help the group confront the difficult issues?

C. *Make sure you can answer likely technical questions about the data.* Survey data have particular strengths and weaknesses. Be able to acknowledge that the data are not perfect, but that a lot of effort has gone into ensuring that they are reliable and valid.

D. *Plan your introduction to the survey-feedback portion of the meeting.* Make the introduction brief and to the point. Remind the group of why it is considering the data, set the stage for problem solving by pointing out that many groups find such data helpful in tracking their progress, and be prepared to run through an example that shows how to understand the feedback data.

II. Problem Solving with Survey-Feedback Data

A. *Chunk the feedback.* If a lot of data are being fed back, use your knowledge of the group and the data to present small portions of data. Stop periodically to see if there are questions or comments about each section or "chunk" of data.

B. *Stimulate discussion on the data.* What follows are various ways to help get the discussion going.

1. Help clarify the meaning of the data by asking
   • What questions do you have about what the data mean?
   • What does [a specific number] mean?
   • Does anything in the data surprise you?
   • What do the data tell you about how we're doing as a group?

2. Help develop a shared diagnosis about the meaning of the data by commenting
   • What I hear people saying is ... Does everyone agree with that?
   • Several people are saying that ... is a problem. Do we agree that this is something the group needs to address?
   • Some people seem to be saying ... while other comments suggest ... Can you help me understand how the group sees this?
   • The group has really been struggling with [specific issue that the facilitator is familiar with], but the data say that we are strong on this. Can someone explain this?

3. Help generate action alternatives by asking
   • What are some of the things we can do to resolve ...?
   • Do we want to brainstorm some action steps to deal with ...?

C. *Focus the group on its own data.* The major benefit of survey feedback for EI teams will be in learning about the group's own behavior and outcomes. Often, however, groups will avoid dealing with issues concerning their own group in favor of broader and less helpful discussions about what other groups are doing right and wrong. Comments you might use to help get the group on track include:
   - What do the data say about how we are doing as a group?
   - There isn't a lot we can do about what other groups are doing. What can we do about the things that are under our control?
   - The problem you are mentioning sounds like one this group also is facing [explain]. Is that so?

D. *Be prepared for problem-solving discussions that are only loosely connected to the data.* It is more important for the group to use the data to understand itself better and to solve problems than it is to follow any particular steps in analyzing the data. Groups often are not very systematic in how they analyze survey-feedback data. They may ignore issues that seem obvious to them and instead focus on one or two issues that have meaning for them.

E. *Hot issues and how to deal with them.* Survey data can be particularly helpful in addressing some hot issues within the group that might otherwise be overlooked. For example, a group often will prefer to portray itself as very effective when group members privately acknowledge that such is not the case. If the data show problems that are not being addressed, you can raise this issue as a point for discussion. If someone denies that group members feel there is a problem, you can point out that the data come from the group and that group members reported such-and-such on the survey. Be careful not to use a parental tone; if you sound like you're wagging your finger at or lecturing the group, you're likely to get a negative reaction. Use the data to raise issues for discussion in a less emotional way.

Ultimately, the group must take responsibility for its own use of the data. There will be times when you see the issues differently from the way group members see them or times when it appears certain to you that the group has a serious problem that it refuses to acknowledge. A facilitator cannot push a group to do something it's not ready to do, but he or she can poke the group at times to find out if it is ready to deal with tough issues. "A little irritation is what makes a pearl in the oyster."

that diagnostic framework. This is an important initial step in gaining ownership of the data and in ensuring that the right problems and issues are addressed by the survey.

Once the objectives are determined, the organization can use one of the standardized questionnaires described in Chapter 7, or it can develop its own survey instrument. If the survey is developed internally, pretesting the questionnaire is essential to ensure that it has been constructed properly. In either case, the survey items need to reflect the objectives established for the survey and the diagnostic issues being addressed.

2. **The survey instrument is administered to all members of the organization or department.** That breadth of data collection is ideal, but it may be necessary to administer the instrument to a sample of members because of cost or time constraints. If so, the size of the sample should be as large as possible to improve the motivational basis for participation in the feedback sessions.

3. **The OD consultant usually analyzes the survey data, tabulates the results, suggests approaches to diagnosis, and trains client members to lead the feedback process.**

4. **Data feedback usually begins at the top of the organization and cascades downward to groups reporting to managers at successively lower levels.** This waterfall approach ensures that all groups at all organizational levels involved in the survey receive appropriate feedback. Most often, members of each organization group at each level discuss and deal with only that portion of the data involving their particular group. They, in turn, prepare to introduce data to groups at the next lower organizational level if appropriate.

Data feedback also can occur in a "bottom-up" approach. Initially, the data for specific work groups or departments are fed back and action items proposed. At this point, the group addresses problems and issues within its control. The group notes any issues that are beyond its authority and suggests actions. That information is combined with information from groups reporting to the same manager, and the combined data are fed back to the managers who review the data and the recommended actions. Problems that can be solved at this level are addressed. In turn, their analyses and suggestions regarding problems of a broader nature are combined, and feedback and action sessions proceed up the hierarchy. In such a way, the people who most likely will carry out recommended action get the first chance to propose suggestions.

5. **Feedback meetings provide an opportunity to work with the data.** At each meeting, members discuss and interpret their data, diagnose problem areas, and develop action plans. OD practitioners can play an important role during these meetings,[7] facilitating group discussion to produce accurate understanding, focusing the group on its strengths and weaknesses, and helping to develop effective action plans.

Although the preceding steps can have a number of variations, they generally reflect the most common survey-feedback design.[8] Application 8.2 presents a contemporary example of how the survey-feedback methodology can be adapted to serve strategic purposes. The application describes how Prudential Real Estate Affiliates combines attitudinal surveys with hard measures to increase change ownership in real estate sales offices.[9]

Survey Feedback and Organizational Dependencies

Traditionally, the steps of survey feedback have been applied to work groups and organizational units with little attention to dependencies among them. Research suggests, however, that the design of survey feedback should vary depending on how closely the participating units are linked with one another.[10] When the units are relatively independent and have little need to interact, survey feedback can focus on the dynamics occurring within each group and can be applied to the groups separately. When there is greater dependency among units and they need to coordinate their efforts, survey feedback must take into account relationships among the units, paying particular attention to the possibility of intergroup conflict. In these situations, the survey-feedback process needs to be coordinated across the interdependent groups. The process will typically be managed by special committees and task forces representing the groups. They will facilitate the intergroup confrontation and conflict resolution generally needed when relations across groups are diagnosed.

Limitations of Survey Feedback

Although the use of survey feedback is widespread in contemporary organizations, the following limits and risks have been identified:[11]

1. **Ambiguity of purpose.** Managers and staff groups responsible for the survey-feedback process may have difficulty reaching sufficient consensus about the purposes of the survey, its content, and how it will be fed back to participants. Such confusion can lead to considerable disagreement over the data collected and paralysis about doing anything with them.

2. **Distrust.** High levels of distrust in the organization can render the survey feedback ineffective. Employees need to trust that their responses will remain anonymous and that management is serious about sharing the data and solving problems jointly.

OPERATIONS REVIEW AND SURVEY FEEDBACK AT PRUDENTIAL REAL ESTATE AFFILIATES

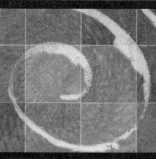

APPLICATION 8•2

Prudential Real Estate Affiliates, Inc. (PREA) is a subsidiary of the Prudential Insurance Company of America. Throughout the United States, it franchises the Prudential name to independently owned and operated real estate offices that help people buy and sell homes and commercial real estate. PREA works with approximately 1,200 of these offices. Although some real estate firms are large, multioffice organizations, many are small independent offices with an owner/manager and several sales associates. PREA's primary work is to help the offices do their job better by offering a range of support services, including technical support, sales training, advertising, and business assistance.

PREA has adapted successfully the survey-feedback technology to assist their customers in improving profitability, productivity, and sales associate work satisfaction. The survey-feedback methodology is called an "operations review." It is a voluntary service annually provided free of charge to any office. PREA describes the operations review as an "interactive process." Each office manager is required to gather internal information about its operations and to send the data to PREA. In addition, each sales associate completes a confidential 43-item opinion survey that is returned directly to PREA for analysis.

These data are entered into a database, and a four-color report is produced. The report is then fed back to the owner/manager of a single office or to the management team in the larger offices. In the best cases, all or part of the data is then shared with the sales associates at a sales meeting. The data are discussed, areas of improvement are identified, and action plans are developed. "When there are discrepancies, especially on the sales force attitudes, it is a great opportunity for discussion," says Skip Newberg, one of the process designers.

The data are presented in three major areas: financial performance, including income, expense, and profit ratios; productivity, including units sold or revenues per full-time sales associate; and management practices, including office climate, service orientation, and sales associates' attitudes. The data for each question are presented in colorful graphs that compare the office's productivity with that of similar offices (in terms of size or structure) and with the productivity of the top-performing sales office in the country. "Presenting the data in this simple way has an impact. Reams of computer printouts with numbers are not interesting. . . . Graphs and colors grab a manager's attention," says Newberg.

Although the financial and productivity data are important, it is the management practices data that get the most attention in the feedback process. Newberg believes that

"the power is not in the printed book; the power is in the skill of the people who sit down with the sales office people and help them interpret it. A skilled person can show an office their strengths and weaknesses in such a way that they can use the data to make improvements." The "management practices" section examines three areas that are related to sales office performance: climate, service orientation, and fundamental attitudes. *Climate* refers to the associates' perceptions of the extent and degree to which their work and well-being are promoted by management and other associates. It also indicates the degrees to which associates have a sense of pride in their office. Items in the survey, such as "This real estate office is considered to be a leader by others in the market" and "We get a lot of customers in this office based on customer referrals," tap that dimension. *Service orientation* refers to an office's emphasis on service quality and customer satisfaction. To assess this dimension, the survey asks sales associates to agree or disagree with statements such as "Our office places so much emphasis on selling to customers that it is difficult to serve customers properly" and "Our advertising is consistent with the service we deliver." Finally, *fundamental attitudes* of sales associates and their perceptions of management's attitudes can range from optimistic to pessimistic. The survey taps these attitudes with statements such as "Clients have no loyalty regardless of how you treat them" and "Giving customers truly excellent custom service takes too much; it's just not worth it."

Including sales office performance next to sales associates' opinions and attitudes provides an important motivational aspect to the feedback process. Newberg believes that "there isn't a manager alive who doesn't want to know how they compare to their peers. The profit and productivity information gets the office's attention and makes it easier to get the message across." The message he refers to is the results of research conducted by PREA. It has produced some remarkable evidence of relationships between sales office performance and the attitudes and opinions of the sales associates. For example, PREA's research has provided strong evidence of a positive relationship between the fundamental attitudes of sales associates and sales office profitability.

Invariably during the feedback session, owner/managers or senior managers say, "OK, that's great—sales associate attitudes and office performance are related. But how can I improve sales associate attitudes?" Glenn Sigmund, a PREA manager who has worked extensively with the operations review, says, "If we can get managers to this point, we have their interest, motivation, and most importantly, commitment to address change." Additional research by PREA found certain key behaviors, practices, and policies that were directly related to positive scores on fundamental attitudes, service orientation, and office climate. These practices and policies give the sales office something tangible to work with and implement.

Response to the system has been favorable. More than 20,000 sales associates have taken the survey, and many of-

fices are back for the third year of feedback. One CEO from a large multioffice firm said, "This is one of the most valuable services PREA offers. Our managers see it as a great tool and one of the best mechanisms for feedback from our sales associates to check how we're really doing." Another manager in a smaller office reported that "the operations review has had a definite impact. It helps us focus on carrying out our business plan and increase profits. We also use it to help our sales associates plan how to improve their own effectiveness."

3. **Unacceptable topics.** Most organizations have certain topics that they do not want examined. This can severely constrain the scope of the survey process, particularly if the neglected topics are important to employees.

4. **Organizational disturbance.** The survey-feedback process can unduly disturb organizational functioning. Data collection and feedback typically infringe on employee work time. Moreover, administration of a survey can call attention to issues with which management is unwilling to deal, and can create unrealistic expectations about organizational improvement.

Results of Survey Feedback

Survey feedback has been used widely in business organizations, schools, hospitals, federal and state governments, and the military. The navy has used survey feedback in more than 500 navy commands. More than 150,000 individual surveys were given, and a large bank of computerized research data was generated. Promising results were noted between survey indices and nonjudicial punishment rates, incidence of drug abuse reports, and performance of ships undergoing refresher training (a postoverhaul training and evaluation period).[12] Positive results have been reported in such diverse areas as an industrial organization in Sweden and the Israeli Army.[13]

One of the most important studies of survey feedback was done by Bowers, who conducted a 5-year longitudinal study (the Intercompany Longitudinal Study) of 23 organizations in 15 companies involving more than 14,000 people in both white-collar and blue-collar positions.[14] In each of the 23 organizations studied, repeat measurements were taken. The study compared survey feedback with three other OD interventions: interpersonal process consultation, task process consultation, and laboratory training. The study reported that survey feedback was the most effective of the four treatments and the only one "associated with large across-the-board positive changes in organization climate."[15] Although these findings have been questioned on a number of methodological grounds,[16] the original conclusion that survey feedback is effective in achieving organizational change was supported. The study suggested that any conclusions to be drawn from action research and survey-feedback studies should be based, at least in part, on objective operating data.

Comprehensive reviews of the literature reveal differing perspectives on the effects of survey feedback. In one review, survey feedback's biggest impact was on attitudes and perceptions of the work situation. The study suggested that survey feedback might best be viewed as a bridge between the diagnosis of organizational problems and the implementation of problem-solving methods because little evidence suggests that survey feedback alone will result in changes in individual behavior or organizational output.[17] This view is supported by research suggesting that the more the data were used to solve problems between initial surveys and later surveys, the more the data improved.[18] Another study suggested that survey feedback has positive effects on both outcome variables (for example, productivity, costs, and absenteeism) and process variables (for example, employee openness, decision making, and motivation) in 53% and 48%, respectively, of the studies measuring those variables. When compared with other OD approaches, survey feedback was only bettered by interventions using several approaches together—for example, change programs involving a combination of survey feedback, process consultation, and team building.[19] On the other hand, another review found that, in contrast to laboratory training and team building, survey feedback was least effective, with only 33% of the studies that measured hard outcomes reporting success. The success rate increased to 45%, however, when survey feedback was combined with team building.[20] Finally, a meta-analysis of OD process interventions and individual attitudes suggested that survey feedback was not significantly associated with overall satisfaction or attitudes about co-workers, the job, or the organization. Survey feedback was able to account for only about 11% of the variance in satisfaction and other attitudes.[21]

Studies of specific survey-feedback interventions identify conditions that improve the success of this technique. One study in an urban school district reported difficulties with survey feedback and suggested that its effectiveness depends partly on the quality of those leading the change effort, members' understanding of the process, the extent to which the survey focuses on issues important to participants, and the degree to which the values expressed by the survey are congruent with those of the respondents.[22] Another study in the military concluded that survey feedback works best when supervisors play an active role in feeding back data to employees and helping them to work with the data.[23] Similarly, a field study of funeral cooperative societies concluded that the use and dissemination of survey results increased when organization members were closely involved in developing and carrying out the project and when the consultant provided technical assistance in the form of data analysis and interpretation.[24] Finally, a long-term study of survey feedback in an underground mining operation suggested that continued, periodic use of survey feedback can produce significant changes in organizations.[25]

SUMMARY

This chapter described the process of feeding back data to a client system. It concerned identifying the content of the data to be fed back and designing a feedback process that ensures ownership of the data. Feeding back data is a central activity in almost any OD program. If members own the data, they will be motivated to solve organizational problems. A special application of the data collection and feedback process is called survey feedback. It is one of the most accepted processes in organization development, enabling practitioners to collect diagnostic data from a large number of organization members and to feed back that information for purposes of problem solving. Survey feedback highlights the importance of contracting appropriately with the client system, establishing relevant categories for data collection, and feeding back the data as necessary steps for diagnosing organizational problems and developing interventions for resolving them.

NOTES

1. S. Mohrman, T. Cummings, and E. Lawler III, "Creating Useful Knowledge with Organizations: Relationship and Process Issues," in *Producing Useful Knowledge for Organizations*, eds. R. Kilmann and K. Thomas (New York: Praeger, 1983), 613–24.

2. C. Argyris, *Intervention Theory and Method: A Behavioral Science View* (Reading, Mass.: Addison-Wesley, 1970); P. Block, *Flawless Consulting: A Guide to Getting Your Expertise Used*, 2d ed. (San Francisco: Jossey-Bass, 1999).

3. D. Nadler, *Feedback and Organization Development: Using Data-Based Methods* (Reading, Mass.: Addison-Wesley, 1977): 156–8.

4. G. Ledford and C. Worley, "Some Guidelines for Effective Survey Feedback," working paper, Center for Effective Organizations, University of Southern California, Los Angeles, 1987.

5. D. Nadler, P. Mirvis, and C. Cammann, "The Ongoing Feedback System: Experimenting with a New Managerial Tool," *Organizational Dynamics* 4 (Spring 1976): 63–80.

6. F. Mann, "Studying and Creating Change," in *The Planning of Change*, eds. W. Bennis, K. Benne, and R. Chin (New York: Holt, Rinehart, & Winston, 1964), 605–15; Nadler, *Feedback*; J. Wiley, "Making the Most of Survey Feedback as a Strategy for Organization Development," *OD Practitioner* 23 (1991): 1–5; A. Church, A. Margiloff, and C. Coruzzi, "Using Surveys for Change: An Applied Example in a Pharmaceuticals Organization," *Leadership and Organization Development Journal* 16 (1995): 3–12; J. Folkman and J. Zenger, *Employee Surveys That Make a Difference: Using Customized Feedback Tools to Transform Your Organization* (New York: Executive Excellence, 1999).

7. Ledford and Worley, "Effective Survey Feedback."

8. N. Margulies and J. Wallace, *Organizational Change* (Glenville, Ill.: Scott, Foresman, 1973).

9. This application was contributed by S. Newberg and G. Sigmund of Prudential Real Estate Affiliates, Inc.

10. M. Sashkin and R. Cooke, "Organizational Structure as a Moderator of the Effects of Data-Based Change Programs" (paper delivered at the thirty-sixth annual meeting of the Academy of Management, Kansas City, 1976); D. Nadler, "Alternative Data-Feedback Designs for Organizational Intervention," *The 1979 Annual Handbook for Group Facilitators*, eds. J. Jones and J. Pfeiffer (La Jolla, Calif.: University Associates, 1979), 78–92.

11. S. Seashore, "Surveys in Organizations," in *Handbook of Organizational Behavior*, ed. J. Lorsch (Englewood Cliffs, N.J.: Prentice Hall, 1987), 142.

12. R. Forbes, "Quo Vadis: The Navy and Organization Development" (paper delivered at the Fifth Psychology in the Air Force Symposium, United States Air Force Academy, Colorado Springs, Colo., April 8, 1976).

13. S. Rubenowitz, Gottenburg, Sweden: Göteborg Universitet, personal communication, 1988; D. Eden and S. Shlomo, "Survey-Based OD in the Israel Defense Forces: A Field Experiment" (undated manuscript, Tel Aviv University).

14. D. Bowers, "OD Techniques and Their Result in 23 Organizations: The Michigan ICL Study," *Journal of Applied Behavioral Science* 9 (January-March 1973): 21–43.

15. Ibid., p. 42.

16. W. Pasmore, "Backfeed, The Michigan ICL Study Revisited: An Alternative Explanation of the Results," *Journal of Applied Behavioral Science* 12 (April-June 1976): 245–51; W. Pasmore and D. King, "The Michigan ICL Study Revisited: A Critical Review," working paper no. 548, Krannert Graduate School of Industrial Administration, West Lafayette, Ind., 1976.

17. F. Friedlander and L. Brown, "Organization Development," in *Annual Review of Psychology*, eds. M. Rosenzweig and L. Porter (Palo Alto, Calif.: Annual Reviews, 1974).

18. D. Born and J. Mathieu, "Differential Effects of Survey-Guided Feedback: The Rich Get Richer and the Poor Get Poorer," *Group and Organization Management* 21 (1996): 388–404.

19. J. Porras and P. O. Berg, "The Impact of Organization Development," *Academy of Management Review* 3 (April 1978): 249–66.

20. J. Nicholas, "The Comparative Impact of Organization Development Interventions on Hard Criteria Measures," *Academy of Management Review* 7 (October 1982): 531–42.

21. G. Neuman, J. Edwards, and N. Raju, "Organizational Development Interventions: A Meta-Analysis of Their Effects on Satisfaction and Other Attitudes," *Personnel Psychology* 42 (1989): 461–83.

22. S. Mohrman, A. Mohrman, R. Cooke, and R. Duncan, "Survey Feedback and Problem-Solving Intervention in a School District: 'We'll Take the Survey But You Can Keep the Feedback,'" in *Failures in Organization Development and Change*, eds. P. Mirvis and D. Berg (New York: John Wiley & Sons, 1977), 149–90.

23. F. Conlon and L. Short, "An Empirical Examination of Survey Feedback as an Organizational Change Device," *Academy of Management Proceedings* (1983): 225–9.

24. R. Sommer, "An Experimental Investigation of the Action Research Approach," *Journal of Applied Behavioral Science* 23 (1987): 185–99.

25. J. Gavin, "Observation from a Long-Term Survey-Guided Consultation with a Mining Company," *Journal of Applied Behavioral Science* 21 (1985): 201–20.

Designing Interventions

An organization development intervention is a sequence of activities, actions, and events intended to help an organization improve its performance and effectiveness. Intervention design, or action planning, derives from careful diagnosis and is meant to resolve specific problems and to improve particular areas of organizational functioning identified in the diagnosis. OD interventions vary from standardized programs that have been developed and used in many organizations to relatively unique programs tailored to a specific organization or department.

This chapter serves as an overview of the intervention design process: It describes criteria that define effective OD interventions and identifies contingencies that guide successful intervention design. Finally, the various types of OD interventions presented in this book are introduced. Parts 3 through 6 of this book describe fully the major interventions used in OD today.

WHAT ARE EFFECTIVE INTERVENTIONS?

The term *intervention* refers to a set of sequenced planned actions or events intended to help an organization increase its effectiveness. Interventions purposely disrupt the status quo; they are deliberate attempts to change an organization or subunit toward a different and more effective state. In OD, three major criteria define an effective intervention: (1) the extent to which it fits the needs of the organization; (2) the degree to which it is based on causal knowledge of intended outcomes; and (3) the extent to which it transfers change-management competence to organization members.

The first criterion concerns the extent to which the intervention is relevant to the organization and its members. Effective interventions are based on valid information about the organization's functioning; they provide organization members with opportunities to make free and informed choices; and they gain members' internal commitment to those choices.[1]

Valid information is the result of an accurate diagnosis of the organization's functioning. It must reflect fairly what organization members perceive and feel about their primary concerns and issues. *Free and informed choice* suggests that members are actively involved in making decisions about the changes that will affect them. (It also means that they can choose not to participate and that interventions will not be imposed on them.) *Internal commitment* means that organization members accept ownership of the intervention and take responsibility for implementing it. If interventions are to result in meaningful changes, management, staff, and other relevant members must be committed to carrying them out.

The second criterion of an effective intervention involves knowledge of outcomes. Because interventions are intended to produce specific results, they must be based on valid knowledge that those outcomes actually can be produced. Otherwise there is no scientific basis for designing an effective OD intervention. Unfortunately—and in contrast to other applied disciplines, such as medicine and engineering—knowledge of intervention effects is in a rudimentary stage of development in OD. Much of the evaluation research lacks sufficient rigor to make strong causal inferences about the success or failure of change programs. (Chapter 11 discusses how to evaluate OD programs rigorously.) Moreover, few attempts have been made to examine the comparative effects of different OD techniques. All of these factors make it difficult to know whether one method is more effective than another.

Despite these problems, more attempts are being made to assess systematically the strengths and weaknesses of OD interventions and to compare the impact of different techniques on organization effectiveness.[2] Many of the OD interventions that will be discussed briefly here and in more depth in Parts 3 through 6 have been subjected to evaluative research; chapters on the various change programs explore the research appropriate to them.

The third criterion of an effective intervention involves the extent to which it enhances the organization's capacity to manage change. The values underlying OD suggest that following an intervention, organization members should be better able to carry out planned change activities on their own. From active participation in designing and implementing the intervention they should gain knowledge and skill in managing change. Competence in change management is essential in today's environment, where technological, social, economic, and political changes are rapid and persistent.

HOW TO DESIGN EFFECTIVE INTERVENTIONS

Designing OD interventions requires paying careful attention to the needs and dynamics of the change situation and crafting a change program that will be consistent with the previously described criteria of effective interventions. Current knowledge of OD interventions provides only general prescriptions for change. There is scant precise information or research about how to design interventions or how they can be expected to interact with organizational conditions to achieve specific results.[3] Moreover, because the ability to implement most OD interventions is highly dependent on the skills and knowledge of the change agent, the design of an intervention will depend to some extent on the expertise of the practitioner.

Two major sets of contingencies that can affect intervention success have been discussed in the OD literature: those having to do with the change situation (including the practitioner) and those related to the target of change. Both kinds of contingencies need to be considered in designing interventions.

Contingencies Related to the Change Situation

Researchers have identified a number of contingencies present in the change situation that can affect intervention success. These include individual differences among organization members (for example, needs for autonomy), organizational factors (for example, management style and technical uncertainty), and dimensions of the change process itself (for example, degree of top-management support). Unless these factors are taken into account, designing an intervention will have little impact on organizational functioning or, worse, it may produce negative results. For example, to resolve motivational problems among blue-collar workers in an oil refinery, it is important to know whether interventions intended to improve motivation (for example, job enrichment) will succeed with the kinds of people who work there. In many cases, knowledge of these contingencies results in modifying or adjusting the change program to fit the setting. In applying a reward-system intervention to an organization, the changes might have to be modified depending on whether the firm wants to reinforce individual or team performance.

Although knowledge of contingencies is still at a rudimentary stage of development in OD, researchers have discovered several situational factors that can affect intervention success.[4] These factors include contingencies for many of the interventions reviewed in this book, and they will be discussed in respective chapters describing the change programs. The more generic contingencies that apply to all OD interventions are presented below. They include situational factors that must be considered in designing any intervention: the organization's readiness for change, its change capability, its cultural context, and the change agent's skills and abilities.

Readiness for Change

Intervention success depends heavily on the organization being ready for planned change. Indicators of readiness for change include sensitivity to pressures for change, dissatisfaction with the status quo, availability of resources to support change, and commitment of significant management time. When such conditions are present, interventions can be designed to address the organizational issues uncovered during diagnosis. When readiness for change is low, however, interventions need to focus first on increasing the organization's willingness to change.[5]

Capability to Change

Managing planned change requires particular knowledge and skills (as outlined in Chapter 10), including the ability to motivate change, to lead change, to develop political support, to manage the transition, and to sustain momentum. If organization members do not have these capabilities, then a preliminary training intervention may be needed before members can engage meaningfully in intervention design.

Cultural Context

The national culture within which the organization is embedded can exert a powerful influence on members' reactions to change, so intervention design must account for the cultural values and assumptions held by organization members. Interventions may have to be modified to fit the local culture, particularly when OD practices developed in one culture are applied to organizations in another culture.[6] For example, a team-building intervention designed for top managers at an American firm may need to be modified when applied to the company's foreign subsidiaries. (Chapter 21 will describe the cultural values of different countries and show how interventions can be modified to fit different cultural contexts.)

Capabilities of the Change Agent

Many failures in OD result when change agents apply interventions beyond their competence. In designing interventions, OD practitioners should assess their experience and expertise against the requirements needed to implement the intervention effectively. When a mismatch is discovered, practitioners can explore whether the intervention can be modified to fit their talents better, whether another intervention more suited to their skills can satisfy the organization's needs, or whether they should enlist the assistance of another change agent who can guide the process more effectively. The ethical guidelines under which OD practitioners operate require full disclosure of the applicability of their knowledge and expertise to the client situation. Practitioners are expected to intervene within their capabilities or to recommend someone more suited to the client's needs.

Contingencies Related to the Target of Change

OD interventions seek to change specific features or parts of organizations. These targets of change are the main focus of interventions, and researchers have identified two key contingencies related to change targets that can affect intervention success: the organizational issues that the intervention is intended to resolve and the level of organizational system at which the intervention is expected to have a primary impact.

Organizational Issues

Organizations need to address certain issues to operate effectively. Figure 9.1 lists these issues along with the OD interventions that are intended to resolve them. (The parts and chapters of this book that describe the specific interventions are also identified in the figure.) It shows the following four interrelated issues that are key targets of OD interventions:

1. **Strategic issues.** Organizations need to decide what products or services they will provide and the markets in which they will compete, as well as how to relate to their environments and how to transform themselves to keep pace with changing conditions. These strategic issues are among the most critical facing organizations in today's changing and highly competitive environments. OD methods aimed at these issues are called strategic interventions. The methods are among the most recent additions to OD and include integrated strategic change, mergers and acquisitions, alliance and network development, and organization learning.

2. **Technology and structure issues.** Organizations must decide how to divide work into departments and then how to coordinate among those departments to support strategic directions. They also must make decisions about how to deliver products or services and how to link people to tasks. OD methods for dealing with these structural and technological issues are called technostructural interventions and include OD activities relating to organization design, employee involvement, and work design.

3. **Human resources issues.** These issues are concerned with attracting competent people to the organization, setting goals for them, appraising and rewarding their performance, and ensuring that they develop their careers and manage stress. OD techniques aimed at these issues are called human resources management interventions.

4. **Human process issues.** These issues have to do with social processes occurring among organization members, such as communication, decision making, leadership, and group dynamics. OD methods focusing on these kinds of issues are called human process interventions; included among them are some of the most common OD techniques, such as conflict resolution and team-building.

Consistent with system theory as described in Chapter 5, these organizational issues are interrelated and need to be integrated with each other. The double-headed arrows connecting the different issues in Figure 9.1 represent the fits or linkages among them. Organizations need to match answers to one set of questions with answers to other sets of questions to achieve high levels of effectiveness. For example, decisions about gaining competitive advantage need to fit with choices about organization structure, setting goals for and rewarding people, communication, and problem solving.

The interventions presented in this book are intended to resolve these different concerns. As shown in Figure 9.1, particular OD interventions apply to specific issues. Thus, intervention design must create change methods appropriate to the organizational issues identified in diagnosis. Moreover, because the organizational issues are themselves linked together, OD interventions similarly need to be integrated with one another. For example, a goal-setting intervention that tries to establish motivating goals may need to be integrated with supporting interventions, such as a reward system that links pay to goal achievement. The key point is to think systemically. Interventions aimed at one kind of organizational issue will invariably have repercussions on other kinds of issues. Careful thinking about how OD interventions affect the different kinds of issues and how different change

Figure 9•1   Types of OD Interventions and Organizational Issues

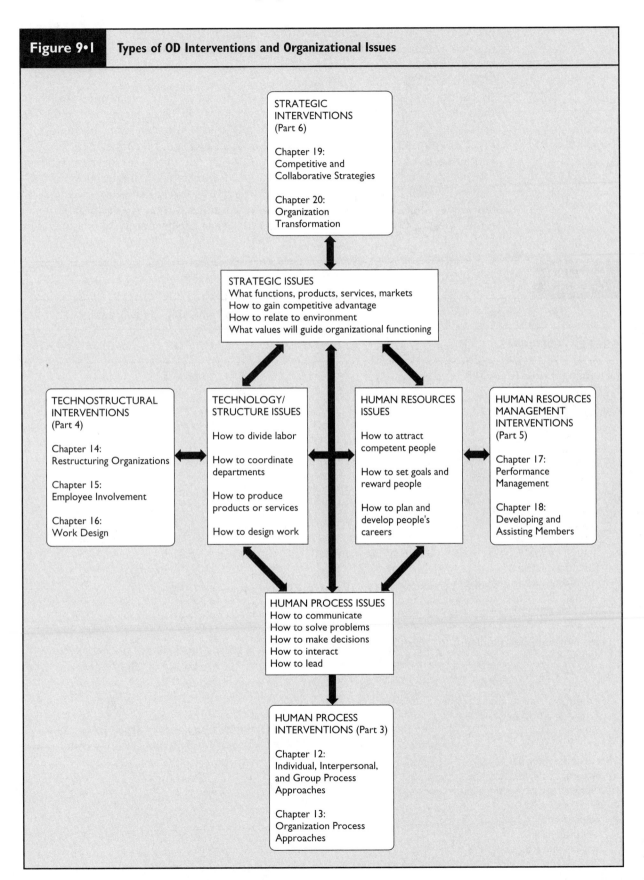

programs might be integrated to bring about a broader and more coherent impact on organizational functioning are critical to effective intervention.

Organizational Levels

In addition to facing interrelated issues, organizations function at different levels: individual, group, organization, and transorganization. Thus, organizational levels are targets of change in OD. Table 9.1 lists OD interventions in terms of the level of organization that they primarily affect. For example, some technostructural interventions affect mainly individuals and groups (for example, work design), whereas others impact primarily the total organization (for example, structural design).

It is important to emphasize that only the primary level affected by the intervention is identified in Table 9.1. Many OD interventions also have a secondary impact on the other levels. For example, structural design affects mainly the organization

Table 9·1	Types of Interventions and Organizational Levels		
	Primary Organizational Level Affected		
INTERVENTIONS	**INDIVIDUAL**	**GROUP**	**ORGANIZATION**
Human process (Part 3)			
Coaching and training	X		
Process consultation		X	
Third-party intervention	X	X	
Team-building		X	
Organization confrontation meeting		X	X
Intergroup relations		X	X
Large-group interventions			X
Technostructural (Part 4)			
Structural design			X
Downsizing			X
Reengineering		X	X
Parallel structures		X	X
High-involvement organizations	X	X	X
Total quality management		X	X
Work design	X	X	
Human resources management (Part 5)			
Goal setting	X	X	
Performance appraisal	X	X	
Reward systems	X	X	X
Career planning and development	X		
Managing workforce diversity	X	X	
Employee wellness	X		
Strategic (Part 6)			
Integrated strategic change			X
Mergers and acquisitions integration			X
Alliances			X
Networks			X
Culture change			X
Self-designing organizations		X	X
Organization learning and knowledge management		X	X

level, but it can have an indirect effect on groups and individuals because it sets the broad parameters for designing work groups and individual jobs. Again, practitioners need to think systemically. They must design interventions to apply to specific organizational levels, address the possibility of cross-level effects, and perhaps integrate interventions affecting different levels to achieve overall success.[7] For example, an intervention to create self-managed work teams may need to be linked to organization-level changes in measurement and reward systems to promote team-based work.

OVERVIEW OF INTERVENTIONS

The OD interventions discussed in Parts 3 through 6 of this book are briefly described below. They represent the major organizational change methods used in OD today.

Human Process Interventions

Part 3 of the book presents interventions focusing on people within organizations and the processes through which they accomplish organizational goals. These processes include communication, problem solving, group decision making, and leadership. This type of intervention is deeply rooted in the history of OD. It represents the earliest change programs characterizing OD, including process consultation and the organizational confrontation meeting. Human process interventions derive mainly from the disciplines of psychology and social psychology and the applied fields of group dynamics and human relations. Practitioners applying these interventions generally value human fulfillment and expect that organizational effectiveness follows from improved functioning of people and organizational processes.[8]

Chapter 12 discusses human process interventions related to individual competencies, interpersonal relationships, and group dynamics. These include the following four interventions:

1. **Coaching.** This intervention helps managers and executives to clarify their goals, deal with potential stumbling blocks, and improve their performance. It often involves a one-on-one relationship between the OD practitioner and the client and focuses on personal learning that gets transferred into organizational results and more effective leadership skills.

2. **Training and development.** Among the oldest strategies for organizational change, training and development interventions increase organization members' skills and knowledge. The focus of training is on the competencies needed to perform work and includes traditional classroom lectures as well as simulations, action learning, computer-based or on-line training, and case studies.

3. **Process consultation.** This intervention focuses on interpersonal relations and social dynamics occurring in work groups. Typically, a process consultant helps group members diagnose group functioning and devise appropriate solutions to process problems, such as dysfunctional conflict, poor communication, and ineffective norms. The aim is to help members gain the skills and understanding necessary to identify and solve problems themselves.

4. **Third-party intervention.** This change method is a form of process consultation aimed at dysfunctional interpersonal relations in organizations. Interpersonal conflict may derive from substantive issues, such as disputes over work methods, or from interpersonal issues, such as miscommunication. The third-party intervener helps people resolve conflicts through such methods as problem solving, bargaining, and conciliation.

5. **Team building.** This intervention helps work groups become more effective in accomplishing tasks. Like process consultation, team building helps members diagnose group processes and devise solutions to problems. It goes beyond group processes, however, to include examination of the group's task, member roles, and strategies for performing tasks. The consultant also may function as a resource person offering expertise related to the group's task.

Chapter 13 presents human process interventions that are more systemwide than those described in Chapter 12. They typically focus on the total organization or an entire department, as well as on relations between groups. These include the following three change programs:

1. **Organization confrontation meeting.** This change method mobilizes organization members to identify problems, set action targets, and begin working on problems. It is usually applied when organizations are experiencing stress and when management needs to organize resources for immediate problem solving. The intervention generally includes various groupings of employees in identifying and solving problems.

2. **Intergroup relations.** These interventions are designed to improve interactions among different groups or departments in organizations. The microcosm group intervention involves a small group of people whose backgrounds closely match the organizational problems being addressed. This group addresses the problem and develops means to solve it. The intergroup conflict model typically involves a consultant helping two groups understand the causes of their conflict and choose appropriate solutions.

3. **Large-group interventions.** These interventions involve getting a broad variety of stakeholders into a large meeting to clarify important values, to develop new ways of working, to articulate a new vision for the organization, or to solve pressing organizational problems. Such meetings are powerful tools for creating awareness of organizational problems and opportunities and for specifying valued directions for future action.

Technostructural Interventions

Part 4 of the book presents interventions focusing on an organization's technology (for example, task methods and job design) and structure (for example, division of labor and hierarchy). These change methods are receiving increasing attention in OD, especially in light of current concerns about productivity and organizational effectiveness. They include approaches to employee involvement, as well as methods for designing organizations, groups, and jobs. Technostructural interventions are rooted in the disciplines of engineering, sociology, and psychology and in the applied fields of sociotechnical systems and organization design. Practitioners generally stress both productivity and human fulfillment and expect that organization effectiveness will result from appropriate work designs and organization structures.[9]

In Chapter 14, we discuss the following three technostructural interventions concerned with restructuring organizations:

1. **Structural design.** This change process concerns the organization's division of labor—how to specialize task performances. Interventions aimed at structural design include moving from more traditional ways of dividing the organization's overall work (such as functional, self-contained–unit, and matrix structures) to more integrative and flexible forms (such as process-based and network-based structures). Diagnostic guidelines exist to determine which structure is appropriate for particular organizational environments, technologies, and conditions.

2. **Downsizing.** This intervention reduces costs and bureaucracy by decreasing the size of the organization through personnel layoffs, organization redesign, and outsourcing. Each of these downsizing methods must be planned with a clear understanding of the organization's strategy.

3. **Reengineering.** This recent intervention radically redesigns the organization's core work processes to create tighter linkage and coordination among the different tasks. This work flow integration results in faster, more responsive task performance. Reengineering is often accomplished with new information technology that permits employees to control and coordinate work processes more effectively. Reengineering often fails if it ignores basic principles and processes of OD.

Chapter 15 is concerned with *employee involvement* (EI). This broad category of interventions is aimed at improving employee well-being and organizational effectiveness. It generally attempts to move knowledge, power, information, and rewards downward in the organization. EI includes parallel structures (such as cooperative union–management projects and quality circles), high-involvement plants, and total quality management.

Chapter 16 discusses *work design*. These change programs are concerned with designing work for work groups and individual jobs. The intervention includes engineering, motivational, and sociotechnical systems approaches that produce traditionally designed jobs and work groups; enriched jobs that provide employees with greater task variety, autonomy, and feedback about results; and self-managing teams that can govern their own task behaviors with limited external control.

Human Resources Management Interventions

Part 5 of the book focuses on personnel practices used to integrate people into organizations. These practices include career planning, reward systems, goal setting, and performance appraisal—change methods that traditionally have been associated with the personnel function in organizations. In recent years, interest has grown in integrating human resources management with OD. Human resources management interventions are rooted in the disciplines of economics and labor relations and in the applied personnel practices of wages and compensation, employee selection and placement, performance appraisal, and career development. Practitioners in this area typically focus on the people in organizations, believing that organizational effectiveness results from improved practices for integrating employees into organizations.

Chapter 17 deals with interventions concerning performance management, including the following change programs:

1. **Goal setting.** This change program involves setting clear and challenging goals. It attempts to improve organization effectiveness by establishing a better fit between personal and organizational objectives. Managers and subordinates periodically meet to plan work, review accomplishments, and solve problems in achieving goals.

2. **Performance appraisal.** This intervention is a systematic process of jointly assessing work-related achievements, strengths, and weaknesses. It is the primary human resources management intervention for providing performance feedback to individuals and work groups. Performance appraisal represents an important link between goal setting and reward systems.

3. **Reward systems.** This intervention involves the design of organizational rewards to improve employee satisfaction and performance. It includes innovative approaches to pay, promotions, and fringe benefits.

Chapter 18 focuses on these three change methods associated with developing and assisting organization members:

1. **Career planning and development.** This intervention helps people choose organizations and career paths and attain career objectives. It generally focuses on managers and professional staff and is seen as a way of improving the quality of their work life.

2. **Managing workforce diversity.** This change program makes human resources practices more responsive to a variety of individual needs. Important trends, such as the increasing number of women, ethnic minorities, and physically and mentally challenged people in the workforce, require a more flexible set of policies and practices.

3. **Employee stress and wellness.** These interventions include employee assistance programs (EAPs) and stress management. EAPs are counseling programs that help employees deal with substance abuse and mental health, marital, and financial problems that often are associated with poor work performance. Stress management programs help workers cope with the negative consequences of stress at work. They help managers reduce specific sources of stress, such as role conflict and ambiguity, and provide methods for reducing such stress symptoms as hypertension and anxiety.

Strategic Interventions

Part 6 of the book considers interventions that link the internal functioning of the organization to the larger environment and transform the organization to keep pace with changing conditions. These change programs are among the newest additions to OD. They are implemented organizationwide and bring about a fit between business strategy, structure, culture, and the larger environment. The interventions derive from the disciplines of strategic management, organization theory, open-systems theory, and economics.

In Chapter 19, we discuss interventions that shape the competitive and collaborative strategies of organizations:

1. **Integrated strategic change.** This comprehensive OD intervention describes how planned change can make a value-added contribution to strategic management. It argues that business strategies and organizational systems must be changed together in response to external and internal disruptions. A strategic change plan helps members manage the transition between a current strategy and organization design and the desired future strategic orientation.

2. **Mergers and acquisitions.** This intervention describes how OD practitioners can assist two or more organizations to form a new entity. Addressing key strategic, leadership, and cultural issues prior to the legal and financial transaction helps to smooth operational integration.

3. **Alliances.** This collaborative intervention helps two organizations pursue a set of private and common goals through the sharing of resources, including intellectual property, people, capital, technology, capabilities, or physical assets. Effective alliance development generally follows a process of strategy formulation, partner selection, alliance structuring and start-up, and alliance operation and adjustment.

4. **Networks.** This intervention helps organizations develop relationships with three or more organizations to perform tasks or solve problems that are too complex for single organizations to resolve. It helps organizations recognize the need for partnerships and develop appropriate structures for implementing them. It also addresses how to manage change within existing networks.

Chapter 20 addresses three major interventions for transforming organizations:

1. **Culture change.** This intervention helps organizations develop cultures (behaviors, values, beliefs, and norms) appropriate to their strategies and environments. It focuses on developing a strong organization culture to keep organization members pulling in the same direction.

2. **Self-designing organizations.** This change program helps organizations gain the capacity to alter themselves fundamentally. It is a highly participative process involving multiple stakeholders in setting strategic directions and designing and implementing appropriate structures and processes. Organizations learn how to design and implement their own strategic changes.

3. **Organization learning and knowledge management.** This intervention describes two interrelated change processes: organization learning (OL), which seeks to enhance an organization's capability to acquire and develop new knowledge, and knowledge management (KM), which focuses on how that knowledge can be organized and used to improve organization performance. These interventions move the organization beyond solving existing problems so as to become capable of continuous improvement.

SUMMARY

This chapter presented an overview of interventions currently used in OD. An intervention is a set of planned activities intended to help an organization improve its performance and effectiveness. Effective interventions are designed to fit the needs of the organization, are based on causal knowledge of intended outcomes, and transfer competence to manage change to organization members.

Intervention design involves understanding situational contingencies such as individual differences among organization members and dimensions of the change process itself. Four key organizational factors—readiness for change, capability to change, cultural context, and the capabilities of the change agent—affect the design and implementation of almost any intervention.

Furthermore, OD interventions seek to change specific features or parts of organizations. These targets of change can be classified based on the organizational issues that the intervention is intended to resolve and the level of organizational system at which the intervention is expected to have a primary impact. Four types of OD interventions are addressed in this book: (1) human process programs aimed at people within organizations and their interaction processes; (2) technostructural methods directed at organization technology and structures for linking people and technology; (3) human resources management interventions focused at integrating people into the organization successfully; and (4) strategic programs targeted at how the organization uses its resources to gain a competitive advantage in the larger environment. For each type of intervention, specific change programs at different organization levels are discussed in Parts 3 through 6 of this book.

NOTES

1. C. Argyris, *Intervention Theory and Method: A Behavioral Science View* (Reading, Mass.: Addison-Wesley, 1970).

2. T. Cummings, E. Molloy, and R. Glen, "A Methodological Critique of 58 Selected Work Experiments," *Human Relations* 30 (1977): 675–708; J. Porras and P. O. Berg, "The Impact of Organization Development," *Academy of Management Review* 3 (1978): 249–66; J. Nicholas, "The Comparative Impact of Organization Development Interventions on Hard Criteria Measures," *Academy of Management Review* 7 (1982): 531–42; R. Golembiewski, C. Proehl, and D. Sink, "Estimating the Success of OD Applications," *Training and Development Journal* 72 (April 1982): 86–95; D. Russ-Eft and H. Preskill, *Evaluation in Organizations: A Systematic Approach to Enhancing Learning,*

Performance, and Change (Cambridge: Perseus Books, 2001).

3. D. Warrick, "Action Planning," in *Practicing Organization Development,* eds. W. Rothwell, R. Sullivan, and G. McClean (San Diego: Pfeiffer, 1995).

4. Nicholas, "Comparative Impact"; J. Porras and P. Robertson, "Organization Development Theory: A Typology and Evaluation," in *Research in Organizational Change and Development,* vol. 1, eds. R. Woodman and W. Pasmore (Greenwich, Conn.: JAI Press, 1987), 1–57.

5. T. Stewart, "Rate Your Readiness for Change," *Fortune* (7 February 1994): 106–10; C. Cunningham, C. Woodward, H. Shannon, J. MacIntosh, et al., "Readiness for Organizational Change: A Longitudinal Study of Workplace, Psychological, and Behavioural Correlates," *Journal of Occupational and Organizational Psychology* 75 (2002): 377–93.

6. G. Hofstede, *Culture's Consequences* (Beverly Hills, Calif.: Sage Publications, 1980); K. Johnson, "Estimating National Culture and O.D. Values," in *Global and International Organization Development,* 3d ed., eds. P. Sorensen Jr., T. Head, T. Yaeger, and D. Cooperrider (Champaign, Ill.: Stipes, 2001), 329–44.

7. D. Coghlan, "Rediscovering Organizational Levels for OD Interventions," *Organization Development Journal* 13 (1995): 19–27.

8. F. Friedlander and L. D. Brown, "Organization Development," *Annual Review of Psychology* 25 (1974): 313–41.

9. E. Lawler III, *The Ultimate Advantage* (San Francisco: Jossey-Bass, 1992).

Leading and Managing Change

After diagnosis reveals the causes of problems or identifies opportunities for development, organization members begin planning and subsequently leading and implementing the changes necessary to improve organization effectiveness and performance. A large part of OD is concerned with interventions for improving organizations. The previous chapter discussed the design of interventions and introduced the major ones currently used in OD. Chapters 12 through 20 describe those interventions in detail. This chapter addresses the key activities associated with successfully leading and managing organizational changes.

Change can vary in complexity from the introduction of relatively simple processes into a small work group to transforming the strategies and design features of the whole organization. Although change management differs across situations, in this chapter we discuss tasks that must be performed in managing any kind of organizational change. (Tasks applicable to specific kinds of changes are examined in the intervention chapters in Parts 3 through 6.)

OVERVIEW OF CHANGE ACTIVITIES

The OD literature has directed considerable attention at leading and managing change. Much of the material is highly prescriptive, advising managers about how to plan and implement organizational changes. For example, one study suggested that successful managers in continuously changing organizations should (1) provide clear responsibility and priorities with extensive communication and freedom to improvise; (2) explore the future by experimenting with a wide variety of low-cost probes; and (3) link current projects to the future with predictable (time-paced rather than event-paced) intervals and choreographed transition procedures.[1] Traditionally, change management has focused on identifying sources of resistance to change and offering ways to overcome them.[2] More recent contributions have challenged the focus on resistance and have been aimed at creating visions and desired futures, gaining political support for them, and managing the transition of the organization toward them.[3]

The diversity of practical advice for managing change can be organized into five major activities, as shown in Figure 10.1. The activities contribute to effective change management and are listed roughly in the order in which they typically are performed. Each activity represents a key element in change leadership.[4] The first activity involves *motivating change* and includes creating a readiness for change among organization members and helping them address resistance to change. Leadership must create an environment in which people accept the need for change and commit physical and psychological energy to it. Motivation is a critical issue in starting change because ample evidence indicates that people and organizations seek to preserve the status quo and are willing to change only when there are compelling reasons to do so. The second activity is concerned with *creating a vision* and is closely aligned with leadership activities. The vision provides a purpose and reason for change and describes the desired future state. Together, they provide the "why" and "what" of planned change. The third activity involves *developing political support for change*. Organizations are composed of powerful individuals and groups that can

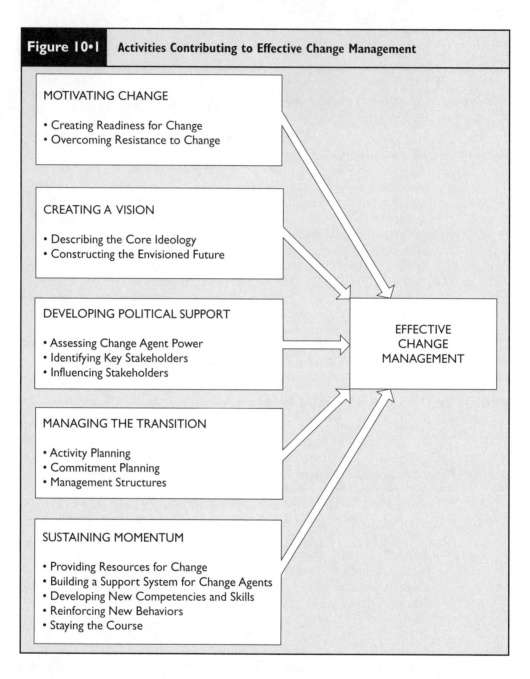

Figure 10•1   Activities Contributing to Effective Change Management

MOTIVATING CHANGE

• Creating Readiness for Change
• Overcoming Resistance to Change

CREATING A VISION

• Describing the Core Ideology
• Constructing the Envisioned Future

DEVELOPING POLITICAL SUPPORT

• Assessing Change Agent Power
• Identifying Key Stakeholders
• Influencing Stakeholders

MANAGING THE TRANSITION

• Activity Planning
• Commitment Planning
• Management Structures

SUSTAINING MOMENTUM

• Providing Resources for Change
• Building a Support System for Change Agents
• Developing New Competencies and Skills
• Reinforcing New Behaviors
• Staying the Course

EFFECTIVE
CHANGE
MANAGEMENT

either block or promote change, and leaders and change agents need to gain their support to implement changes. The fourth activity is concerned with *managing the transition* from the current state to the desired future state. It involves creating a plan for managing the change activities as well as planning special management structures for operating the organization during the transition. The fifth activity involves *sustaining momentum* for change so that it will be carried to completion. This includes providing resources for implementing the changes, building a support system for change agents, developing new competencies and skills, and reinforcing the new behaviors needed to implement the changes.

Each of the activities shown in Figure 10.1 is important for managing change. Although little research has been conducted on their relative contributions, organizational leaders must give careful attention to each activity when planning and implementing organizational change. Unless individuals are motivated and committed to change, unfreezing the status quo will be extremely difficult. In the absence of vision, change is likely to be disorganized and diffuse. Without the support of powerful individuals and groups, change may be blocked and possibly sabotaged. Unless the transition process is managed carefully, the organization will have difficulty functioning while it moves from the current state to the future state. Without efforts to sustain momentum for change, the organization will have problems carrying the changes through to completion. Thus, all five activities must be managed effectively to realize success.

In the following sections of this chapter, we discuss more fully each of these change activities, directing attention to how the activities contribute to planning and implementing organizational change.

MOTIVATING CHANGE

Organizational change involves moving from the known to the unknown. Because the future is uncertain and may adversely affect people's competencies, worth, and coping abilities, organization members generally do not support change unless compelling reasons convince them to do so. Similarly, organizations tend to be heavily invested in the status quo, and they resist changing it in the face of uncertain future benefits. Consequently, a key issue in planning for action is how to motivate commitment to organizational change. As shown in Figure 10.1, this requires attention to two related tasks: creating readiness for change and overcoming resistance to change.

Creating Readiness for Change

One of the more fundamental axioms of OD is that people's readiness for change depends on creating a felt need for change. This involves making people so dissatisfied with the status quo that they are motivated to try new work processes, technologies, or ways of behaving. Creating such dissatisfaction can be difficult, as anyone knows who has tried to lose weight, stop smoking, or change some other habitual behavior. Generally, people and organizations need to experience deep levels of hurt before they will seriously undertake meaningful change. For example, IBM, GM, and Sears experienced threats to their very survival before they undertook significant change programs. The following three methods can help generate sufficient dissatisfaction to produce change:

1. **Sensitize organizations to pressures for change.** Innumerable pressures for change operate both externally and internally to organizations. As described in Chapter 1, modern organizations face unprecedented environmental pressures to change themselves, including heavy foreign competition, rapidly changing technology, and the draw of global markets. Internal pressures to change include new leadership, poor product quality, high production costs, and excessive employee absenteeism and turnover. Before these pressures can serve as triggers for change, however, organizations must be sensitive to them. The pressures must pass beyond an organization's threshold of awareness if managers are to respond to them. Many organizations, such as Kodak, Apple, Polaroid, and Jenny Craig, set their thresholds of awareness too high and neglected pressures for change until those pressures reached disastrous levels.[5] Organizations can make themselves more sensitive to pressures for change by encouraging leaders to surround themselves with devil's advocates;[6] by cultivating external

networks that comprise people or organizations with different perspectives and views; by visiting other organizations to gain exposure to new ideas and methods; and by using external standards of performance, such as competitors' progress or benchmarks,[7] rather than the organization's own past standards of performance. At Wesley Long Community Hospital, in Greensboro, North Carolina, for example, managers visited the Ritz-Carlton Hotel, Marconi Commerce Systems' high-involvement plant, and other hospitals known for high quality to gain insights about revitalizing their own organization.

2. **Reveal discrepancies between current and desired states.** In this approach to generating a felt need for change, information about the organization's current functioning is gathered and compared with desired states of operation. (See "Creating a Vision," page 160, for more information about desired future states.) These desired states may include organizational goals and standards, as well as a general vision of a more desirable future state.[8] Significant discrepancies between actual and ideal states can motivate organization members to initiate corrective changes, particularly when members are committed to achieving those ideals. A major goal of diagnosis, as described in Chapters 5 and 6, is to provide members with feedback about current organizational functioning so that the information can be compared with goals or with desired future states. Such feedback can energize action to improve the organization. At Waste Management, Sunbeam, and Banker's Trust, for example, financial statements had reached the point at which it was painfully obvious that drastic renewal was needed.[9]

3. **Convey credible positive expectations for the change.** Organization members invariably have expectations about the results of organizational changes. The positive approaches to planned change described in Chapter 2 suggest that these expectations can play an important role in generating motivation for change.[10] Expectations can serve as a self-fulfilling prophecy, leading members to invest energy in change programs that they expect will succeed. When members expect success, they are likely to develop greater commitment to the change process and to direct more energy into the constructive behaviors needed to implement it.[11] The key to achieving these positive effects is to communicate realistic, positive expectations about the organizational changes. Research suggests that information about why the change is occurring, how it will benefit the organization, and how people will be involved in the design and implementation of the change were most helpful.[12] Organization members also can be taught about the benefits of positive expectations and be encouraged to set credible positive expectations for the change program.

Overcoming Resistance to Change

Change can generate deep resistance in people and in organizations, thus making it difficult, if not impossible, to implement organizational improvements.[13] At a personal level, change can arouse considerable anxiety about letting go of the known and moving to an uncertain future.[14] People may be unsure whether their existing skills and contributions will be valued in the future, or have significant questions about whether they can learn to function effectively and to achieve benefits in the new situation. At the organization level, resistance to change can come from three sources.[15] *Technical resistance* comes from the habit of following common procedures and the consideration of sunk costs invested in the status quo. *Political resistance* can arise when organizational changes threaten powerful stakeholders, such as top executive or staff personnel, or call into question the past decisions of leaders.[16] Organization change often implies a different allocation of already scarce resources, such as capital, training budgets, and good people. Finally, *cultural resistance* takes the form of systems and procedures that reinforce the status quo, promoting conformity to existing values, norms, and assumptions about how things should operate.

There are at least three major strategies for dealing with resistance to change:[17]

1. **Empathy and support.** A first step in overcoming resistance is learning how people are experiencing change. This strategy can identify people who are having trouble accepting the changes, the nature of their resistance, and possible ways to overcome it, but it requires a great deal of empathy and support. It demands a willingness to suspend judgment and to see the situation from another's perspective, a process called *active listening.* When people feel that those people who are responsible for managing change are genuinely interested in their feelings and perceptions, they are likely to be less defensive and more willing to share their concerns and fears. This more open relationship not only provides useful information about resistance but also helps establish the basis for the kind of joint problem solving needed to overcome barriers to change.

2. **Communication.** People resist change when they are uncertain about its consequences. Lack of adequate information fuels rumors and gossip and adds to the anxiety generally associated with change. Effective communication about changes and their likely results can reduce this speculation and allay unfounded fears. It can help members realistically prepare for change. However, communication is also one of the most frustrating aspects of managing change. Organization members constantly receive data about current operations and future plans as well as informal rumors about people, changes, and politics. Managers and OD practitioners must think seriously about how to break through this stream of information. One strategy is to make change information more salient by communicating through a new or different channel. If most information is delivered through memos and emails, then change information can be sent through meetings and presentations. Another method that can be effective during large-scale change is to substitute change information for normal operating information deliberately. This sends a message that changing one's activities is a critical part of a member's job.

3. **Participation and involvement.** One of the oldest and most effective strategies for overcoming resistance is to involve organization members directly in planning and implementing change. Participation can lead both to designing high-quality changes and to overcoming resistance to implementing them.[18] Members can provide a diversity of information and ideas, which can contribute to making the innovations effective and appropriate to the situation. They also can identify pitfalls and barriers to implementation. Involvement in planning the changes increases the likelihood that members' interests and needs will be accounted for during the intervention. Consequently, participants will be committed to implementing the changes because doing so will suit their interests and meet their needs. Moreover, for people having strong needs for involvement, the act of participation itself can be motivating, leading to greater effort to make the changes work.[19]

Application 10.1 describes how Ralph Stayer struggled to motivate change in Johnsonville Sausage.[20] The CEO clearly understood the need for change, and he had to find ways to get his employees involved. After several ill-fated attempts, he achieved the motivation he was looking for by finding the areas where his interests intersected with the interests of his workforce.

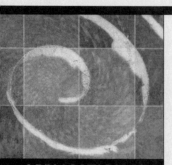

MOTIVATING CHANGE AT JOHNSONVILLE SAUSAGE

APPLICATION 10•1

In the early 1980s, Johnsonville Sausage was a successful Wisconsin manufacturer. It was growing at an annual rate of 20% and steadily increasing market shares in neighboring states. The quality of its products was high, and the organization was a respected member of the community. But CEO Ralph Stayer was worried. As a medium-size organization, Johnsonville Sausage was neither large enough to promote and advertise its products on the same scale as large producers nor small enough to provide superior customer service as a local producer.

Of more concern was that the organization's members did not seem to be aware of the problem and did not care. Every day, Stayer observed people bored by their jobs and making thoughtless mistakes. They mislabeled products, used the wrong ingredients in a batch of sausage and, in an extreme case, drove the prongs of a forklift through a new wall. Although no one was deliberately wasting money, it was obvious to Stayer that people were not taking responsibility for their work. How could the organization survive a competitive challenge when no one cared about the organization and its success?

Over time, Stayer tried many tactics to get his workforce to change. Strategic planning exercises resulted in carefully drawn organization charts and reports that described who was responsible for what and who would report to whom. The discussions were thoughtful and detailed, but nothing happened. In the mid-1980s, after much soul searching and an employee survey that confirmed his fears about the state of the workforce, Stayer decided that the best way to improve the company was to increase the workers' involvement. He announced, "From now on, you are all responsible for making your own decisions." The problem was that no one had asked for more responsibility. Despite the workers' best efforts, the organization floundered. People had become accustomed to Stayer making all of the decisions, and he became frustrated when they didn't make the decisions he wanted. Not only was the organization resisting change, but Stayer

himself was contributing to the problem. "I didn't really want them to make independent decisions. I wanted them to make the decisions I would have made. Deep down, I was still in love with my own control; I was just making people guess what I wanted instead of telling them."

Ordering change and watching it go nowhere helped Stayer learn that he didn't control people directly but that he could control and manage the context within which people worked. He began by helping people to see the issues that needed changing and by overcoming resistance through participation and involvement. For example, he began sending customer letters directly to the line workers who, coming face-to-face with customer complaints, began to understand how their work affected others. Similarly, when complaints about working on weekends surfaced, managers encouraged the workers to look at the problem. Through the workers' initiatives, it became clear that overtime and customer complaints were the result of worker tardiness and absenteeism, sloppy maintenance, slow shift start-ups, and other behaviors entirely under their control. Once the employees began to see themselves as part of the problem, change came fairly quickly.

How the quality-control process was changed provides another example of motivating change through participation. In the company's sausage-making process, the package-ready sausage was inspected for taste, flavor, color, and texture by the quality department. Stayer reasoned that by checking the product after it was made, management had assumed responsibility for quality. Instead, the people who made the sausage were given the responsibility for tasting the product. Teams of workers began tasting the sausage every morning and discussing how to improve it. They asked for information about costs and customer reactions, and they used that to improve processes. Eventually, work design, compensation systems, and performance-appraisal systems also were changed. Johnsonville Sausage became a benchmark of self-management, highlighted by author Tom Peters and declared one of *Business Week*'s Management Meccas. All of this because Ralph Stayer figured out how to motivate his workforce to change.

CREATING A VISION

The second activity in leading and managing change involves creating a vision of what members want the organization to look like or become. It is one of the most popular yet least understood practices in management.[21] Generally, a vision describes the core values and purpose that guide the organization as well as an envisioned future toward which change is directed. It provides a valued direction for designing, implementing, and assessing organizational changes. The vision also can energize commitment to change by providing members with a common goal and a compelling rationale for why change is necessary and worth the effort. However, if the vision is seen as impossible or promotes changes that the organization cannot implement, it actually can depress member motivation. For example, George Bush's unfulfilled "thousand points of light" vision was emotionally appealing, but it was too vague and contained little inherent benefit. In contrast, John Kennedy's vision of "putting a man on the moon and returning him safely to the earth" was just beyond engineering and technical feasibility. In the context of the 1960s, it was bold, alluring, and vivid; it provided not only a purpose but a valued direction as well.[22] Recent research suggests that corporations with carefully crafted visions can significantly outperform the stock market over long periods of time.[23]

Creating a vision is considered a key element in most leadership frameworks.[24] Organization or subunit leaders are responsible for effectiveness, and they must take an active role in describing a desired future and energizing commitment to it. In many cases, leaders encourage participation in developing the vision to gain wider input and support. For example, they involve subordinates and others who have a stake in the changes. The popular media frequently offer accounts of executives who have helped to mobilize and direct organizational change, including Nobuhiko Kawamoto of Honda and Jack Welch at General Electric. Describing a desired future is no less important for people leading change in small departments and work groups than for senior executives. At lower organizational levels, there are ample opportunities to involve employees directly in the visioning process.

Developing a vision is heavily driven by people's values and preferences for what the organization should look like and how it should function. The envisioned future represents people's ideals, fantasies, or dreams of what they would like the organization to look like or become. Unfortunately, dreaming about the future is discouraged in most organizations[25] because it requires creative and intuitive thought processes that tend to conflict with the rational, analytical methods prevalent there. Consequently, leaders may need to create special conditions in which to describe a desired future, such as off-site workshops or exercises that stimulate creative thinking.

Research by Collins and Porras suggests that compelling visions are composed of two parts: (1) a relatively stable core ideology that describes the organization's core values and purpose, and (2) an envisioned future with bold goals and a vivid description of the desired future state that reflects the specific change under consideration.[26]

Describing the Core Ideology

The fundamental basis of a vision for change is the organization's core ideology. It describes the organization's core values and purpose and is relatively stable over time. *Core values* typically include three to five basic principles or beliefs that have stood the test of time and best represent what the organization stands for. Although the vision ultimately describes a desired future, it must acknowledge the organization's historical roots—the intrinsically meaningful core values and principles that have guided and will guide the organization over time. Core values are not "espoused values"; they are the "values in use" that actually inform members what is important in the organization. The retailer Nordstrom, for example, has clear values around the importance of customer service; toymaker Lego has distinct values around the importance of families; and the Disney companies have explicit values around wholesomeness and imagination. These values define the true nature of these firms and cannot be separated from them. Thus, core values are not determined or designed; they are discovered and described through a process of inquiry.

Members can spend considerable time and energy discovering their organization's core values through long discussions about organizational history, key events, founder's beliefs, the work people actually do, and the "glue" that holds the organization together.[27] In many cases, organizations want the core values to be something they are not. For example, many U.S. firms want "teamwork" to be a core value despite strong cultural norms and organizational practices that reward individuality.

The organization's *core purpose* is its reason for being, the idealistic motivation that brings people to work each day. A core purpose is not a strategy. Purpose describes why the organization exists; strategy describes how an objective will be achieved. Organizations often create a slogan or metaphor that captures the real reason they are in business. For example, part of Disneyland's return to prominence in the late 1980s and 1990s was guided by the essential purpose of "creating a place where people can feel like kids again." Similarly, Apple's original vision of "changing the way people do their work" described well the benefits the organization was providing to its customers and society at large. Many Apple employees previously had experienced the drudgery of a boring job, an uninspired boss, or an alienating workplace, and it was alluring to be part of a company that was changing work into something more challenging, creative, or satisfying.

The real power of an organization's core ideology is its stability over time and the way it can help the organization change itself. Core values and purpose provide guidelines for the strategic choices that will work and can be implemented versus those that will not work because they contradict the real nature of the organization's identity. An envisioned future can be compelling and emotionally powerful to members only if it aligns with and supports the organization's core values and purpose.

Constructing the Envisioned Future

The core ideology provides the context for the envisioned future. Unlike core values and purpose, which are stable aspects of the organization and must be discovered, the envisioned future is specific to the change project at hand and must be created. The envisioned future varies in complexity and scope depending on the changes being considered. A relatively simple upgrading of a work group's word-processing software requires a less complex envisioned future than the transformation of a government bureaucracy.

The envisioned future typically includes the following elements that can be communicated to organization members:[28]

1. **Bold and valued outcomes.** Descriptions of envisioned futures often include specific performance and human outcomes that the organization or unit would like to achieve. These valued outcomes can serve as goals for the change process and standards for assessing progress. For example, BHAGs (Big, Hairy, Audacious Goals) are clear, tangible, energizing targets that serve as rallying points for organization action. They can challenge members to meet clear target levels of sales growth or customer satisfaction, to overcome key competitors, to achieve role-model status in the industry, or to transform the organization in some meaningful way. For example, in 1990 Wal-Mart Stores made a statement of intent "to become a $125 billion company by the year 2000." (Net sales in 1999 exceeded $137.6 billion.) Following the downsizing of the U.S. military

budget, Rockwell proposed the following bold outcome for its change efforts: "Transform this company from a defense contractor into the best diversified high-technology company in the world."

2. **Desired future state.** This element of the envisioned future specifies, in vivid detail, what the organization should look like to achieve bold and valued outcomes. It is a passionate and engaging statement intended to draw organization members into the future. The organizational features described in the statement help define a desired future state toward which change activities should move. This aspect of the visioning process is exciting and compelling. It seeks to create a word picture that is emotionally powerful to members and motivates them to change.

Application 10.2 describes how Premier recognized the need for change and built a vision of the future for their organization.[29]

DEVELOPING POLITICAL SUPPORT

From a political perspective, organizations can be seen as loosely structured coalitions of individuals and groups having different preferences and interests.[30] For example, shop-floor workers may want secure, high-paying jobs, and top executives may be interested in diversifying the organization into new businesses. The marketing department might be interested in developing new products and markets, and the production department may want to manufacture standard products in the most efficient ways. These different groups or coalitions compete with one another for scarce resources and influence. They act to preserve or enhance their self-interests while managing to arrive at a sufficient balance of power to sustain commitment to the organization and achieve overall effectiveness.

Given this political view, attempts to change the organization may threaten the balance of power among groups, thus resulting in political conflicts and struggles.[31] Individuals and groups will be concerned with how the changes affect their own power and influence, and they will act accordingly. Some groups will become less powerful; others will gain influence. Those whose power is threatened by the change will act defensively and seek to preserve the status quo. For example, they may try to present compelling evidence that change is unnecessary or that only minor modifications are needed. On the other hand, those participants who will gain power from the changes will push heavily for them, perhaps bringing in seemingly impartial consultants to legitimize the need for change. Consequently, significant organizational changes are frequently accompanied by conflicting interests, distorted information, and political turmoil.

Methods for managing the political dynamics of organizational change are relatively recent additions to OD. Traditionally, OD has neglected political issues mainly because its humanistic roots promoted collaboration and power sharing among individuals and groups.[32] Today, change agents are paying increased attention to power and political activity, particularly as they engage in strategic change involving most parts and features of organizations. Some practitioners are concerned, however, about whether power and OD are compatible. A growing number of advocates suggest that OD practitioners can use power in positive ways.[33] They can build their own power base to gain access to other power holders within the organization. Without such access, those who influence or make decisions may not have the advantage of an OD perspective. OD practitioners can use power strategies that are open and aboveboard to get those in power to consider OD applications. They

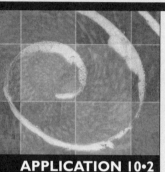

CREATING A VISION AT PREMIER

Premier (http://www.premierinc.com) is a leading health care alliance collectively owned by more than 200 independent hospitals and health care systems in the United States. Together, the owners operate or are affiliated with nearly 1,500 hospitals and other health care sites. Premier resulted from the 1995 merger of Chicago-based Premier Health Alliance, San Diego-based American Healthcare Systems, and The SunHealth Alliance of Charlotte, North Carolina. Premier offers a comprehensive array of services and products through its companies and business units, including group purchasing, consulting services, technology management services, insurance services, benchmarking and market intelligence services, and legislative advocacy.

Two and a half years after the organization's formation, a comprehensive organizational assessment suggested that Premier had not been successful in establishing a common organizational culture. Many of its services and employees continued to operate in a fractured or isolated fashion relating largely to their prior organization and its geographic location. As a result, Premier's strategy and business model were poorly understood, and more importantly, not well implemented. The assessment pointed to a growing lack of trust in the organization. Premier executives conceded that the organization was culturally adrift and without a well-understood or widely accepted sense of direction.

Another key finding of the assessment concerned the organization's vision. Shortly after the merger, a new set of values, mission, and vision statements had been developed. The statements themselves were clear and compelling; however, they had been developed by a relatively small group of executives. At best, most employees did not feel much ownership of the values; at worst, they saw the failure of top management to behave consistently with the values as evidence that they were not trusted, supported, or important.

In the fall of 1997, Premier hired Richard Norling as COO. Norling had been a chief executive at one of the health care systems that owned Premier, and his arrival signaled the potential for change and new possibilities. At his former organization, Norling had initiated and sustained a comprehensive OD effort, based on identifying core organizational values and the behaviors that supported them. The experience of that health care system had demonstrated that core values shaped and accepted by an organization's employees could build a deep sense of community in the organi-

zation, lead to greater levels of trust and commitment, and be harnessed to enhance organization performance and effectiveness. Given Premier's emerging problem, a similar approach made sense.

In the spring of 1998, Premier executives determined to address these issues by building on the values and mission statements that had been developed. Their intent was to involve a large number of employees in validating Premier's values, specifying the behaviors that supported them, and identifying ways in which the values could be integrated into the routines and processes of the organization—all of which would (they hoped) infect the organization with a renewed sense of identity and enthusiasm.

The first step in Premier's change process was planning and conducting a 3-day 200-employee values conference. The conference was designed by a team of employees representing a diagonal slice of the organization and assisted by an OD practitioner. At the conference, employees examined Premier's business model and their organizational culture; developed and recommended a set of core organizational values for the organization; crafted an envisioned future; and identified and proposed strategies for employee involvement, integration, and organization transformation companywide.

Following the conference, the team of Premier employees who had planned the meeting was asked to become a permanent committee, charged with refining and implementing plans and recommendations that the conference participants had generated.

Ultimately, input was obtained from over 60% of the workforce and 16 actions were recommended and approved by senior management. Some of those actions included:

- Incorporating the values into Premier's performance management/performance appraisal system

- Incorporating the values into the recruitment and selection process by developing sample interview questions for use by hiring managers aimed at helping them learn whether prospective employees would be a good match to Premier's organizational culture

- Instituting an annual meeting of approximately 200 employees from all parts of Premier modeled after the 1998 values conference. The agenda should be focused on business issues, strategy, and organizational culture and values. Rotate those invited so that every Premier employee has an opportunity to attend every 3 to 5 years.

The outcome of the vision and values effort follows:

PREMIER
FOUNDATION STATEMENTS

CORE IDEOLOGY

Core Values

- Integrity of the individual and the enterprise
- A passion for performance and a bias for action, creating real value for all stakeholders, and leading the pace
- Innovation: seeking breakthrough opportunities, taking risks, and initiating meaningful change
- Focus on people: showing concern and respect for all with whom we work, building collaborative relationships with the community, our customers, co-workers, and business associates

Core Purpose

To improve the health of communities

Core Roles of the Enterprise

- Improve quality, reduce costs
- Improve financial health
- Create value for owners
- Improve organizational health
- Facilitate knowledge transfer
- Grow the enterprise

ENVISIONED FUTURE

10–30 Year Goal

Premier's owners will be the leading health care systems in their markets, and, with them, Premier will be the major influence in reshaping health care

Vivid Description

By the year 2020, we will have changed the world's view of U.S. health care to "the best and most cost-effective" at sustaining the good health of populations. In the United States, the health care industry will be considered the best managed and most innovative of all the economic sectors.

Across the nation, our owners, physicians, and other allies will lead the local transformations that are the building blocks of a reshaped health care system. These transformations will begin to make *public health and health services* indistinguishable, engaging citizens and civic resources in endeavors that attack the causes of illness and injury. Through efforts that go far beyond providing treatment, people will have a sense of responsibility for their own personal health *and* the health of their communities.

Together in Premier, we will invent new and superior models of delivering health services, and we will leverage the size, linkages, and resources of Premier to deliver those services to more people, at a lower cost and higher quality, than any

others. Our owners will operate at costs in the lowest quarter among all similar organizations at quality levels in the highest quarter. We will research and use the most effective and seamless clinical approaches to achieve superior health outcomes and increased values. Our competitive edge will be the unmatched ability to transfer and act on our collective experience and innovation.

Our owners will earn recognition as the most valued community resource for health. As a result of their efforts, "Premier" will be viewed as the hallmark of quality and value that all others seek to emulate. When people see our emblem, they will associate it with health care improvement and advances in health status.

Demonstrating a better way and supported by our constituencies, we will build consensus for national policy directions that stimulate and reward health and healthy communities.

We will indeed be *premier*.

can facilitate processes for examining the uses of power in organizations and help power holders devise more creative and positive strategies than political bargaining, deceit, and the like. They can help power holders confront the need for change and can help ensure that the interests and concerns of those with less power are considered. Although OD professionals can use power constructively in organizations, they probably will continue to be ambivalent and tense about whether such uses

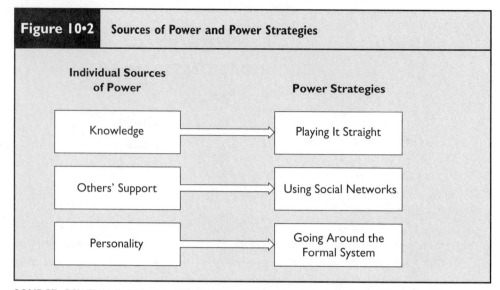

Figure 10•2   Sources of Power and Power Strategies

SOURCE: POWER AND ORGANIZATIONAL DEVELOPMENT by Greiner/Schein, © 1988. Reprinted by permission of Pearson Education, Inc., Upper Saddle River, NJ.

promote OD values and ethics or whether they represent the destructive, negative side of power. That tension seems healthy, and we hope that it will guide the wise use of power in OD.

As implied in Figure 10.2, managing the political dynamics of change includes the following activities: assessing the change agent's power, identifying key stakeholders, and influencing stakeholders.

Assessing Change Agent Power

The first task is to evaluate the change agent's own sources of power. This agent may be the leader of the organization or department undergoing change, or he or she may be the OD consultant if professional help is being used. By assessing their own power base, change agents can determine how to use it to influence others to support changes. They also can identify areas in which they need to enhance their sources of power.

Greiner and Schein, in the first OD book written entirely from a power perspective, identified three key sources of personal power in organizations (in addition to one's formal position): knowledge, personality, and others' support.[34] Knowledge bases of power include having expertise that is valued by others and controlling important information. OD professionals typically gain power through their expertise in organizational change. Personality sources of power can derive from change agents' charisma, reputation, and professional credibility. Charismatic leaders can inspire devotion and enthusiasm for change from subordinates. OD consultants with strong reputations and professional credibility can wield considerable power during organizational change. Others' support can contribute to individual power by providing access to information and resource networks. Others also may use their power on behalf of the change agent. For example, leaders in organizational units undergoing change can call on their informal networks for resources and support, and encourage subordinates to exercise power in support of the change.

Identifying Key Stakeholders

Having assessed their own power bases, change agents can identify powerful individuals and groups with an interest in the changes, such as staff groups, unions, departmental managers, and top-level executives. These key stakeholders can thwart or support change, and it is important to gain broad-based support to minimize the risk that a single interest group will block the changes. Identifying key stakeholders can start with the simple question "Who stands to gain or to lose from the changes?" Once stakeholders are identified, creating a map of their influence may be useful.[35] The map could show relationships among the stakeholders in terms of who influences whom and what the stakes are for each party. This would provide change agents with information about which people and groups need to be influenced to accept and support the changes.

Influencing Stakeholders

This activity involves gaining the support of key stakeholders to motivate a critical mass for change. There are at least three major strategies for using power to influence others in OD: playing it straight, using social networks, and going around the formal system.[36] Figure 10.2 links these strategies to the individual sources of power discussed above.

The strategy of playing it straight is very consistent with an OD perspective, and thus it is the most widely used power strategy in OD. It involves determining the needs of particular stakeholders and presenting information about how the changes can benefit them. This relatively straightforward approach is based on the premise that information and knowledge can persuade people about the need and direction for change. The success of this strategy relies heavily on the change agent's knowledge base. He or she must have the expertise and information to persuade stakeholders that the changes are a logical way to meet their needs. For example, a change agent might present diagnostic data, such as company reports on productivity and absenteeism or surveys of members' perceptions of problems, to generate a felt need for change among specific stakeholders. Other persuasive evidence might include educational material and expert testimony, such as case studies and research reports, demonstrating how organizational changes can address pertinent issues.

The second power strategy, using social networks, is more foreign to OD and includes forming alliances and coalitions with other powerful individuals and groups, dealing directly with key decision makers, and using formal and informal contacts to gain information. In this strategy, change agents attempt to use their social relationships to gain support for changes. As shown in Figure 10.2, they use the individual power base of others' support to gain the resources, commitment, and political momentum needed to implement change. This social networking might include, for example, meeting with other powerful groups and forming alliances to support specific changes. This would likely involve ensuring that the interests of the different parties—labor and management, for example—are considered in the change process. Many union and management quality-of-work-life efforts involve forming such alliances. This strategy also might include using informal contacts to discover key roadblocks to change and to gain access to major decision makers who need to sanction the changes.

The power strategy of going around the formal system is probably least used in OD and involves purposely circumventing organizational structures and procedures to get the changes made. Existing organizational arrangements can be roadblocks to change, and working around the barriers may be more expedient and effective than taking the time and energy to remove them. As shown in Figure 10.2, this strategy relies on a strong personality base of power. The change agent's charisma, reputation, or professional credibility lend legitimacy to going around the system and can reduce the likelihood of negative reprisals. For example, managers with reputations as winners often can bend the rules to implement organizational changes. Their judgment is trusted by those whose support they need to enact the changes. This power strategy is relatively easy to abuse, however, and OD practitioners should consider carefully the ethical issues and possible unintended consequences of circumventing formal policies and practices.

Application 10.3 shows how one manager used the personal power bases of expertise and reputation to form social networks with key stakeholders and gained support for a statewide change in the public schools.[37]

MANAGING THE TRANSITION

Implementing organizational change involves moving from the existing organization state to the desired future state. Such movement does not occur immediately but, as shown in Figure 10.3, instead requires a transition state during which the organization learns how to implement the conditions needed to reach the desired future. Beckhard and Harris pointed out that the transition state may be quite different from the present state of the organization and consequently may require special management structures and activities.[38] They identified three major activities and structures to facilitate organizational transition: activity planning, commitment planning, and change-management structures.

Activity Planning

Activity planning involves making a road map for change, citing specific activities and events that must occur if the transition is to be successful. It should clearly identify, temporally orient, and integrate discrete change tasks, and it should explicitly link these tasks to the organization's change goals and priorities. Activity planning also should gain top-management approval, be cost effective, and remain adaptable as feedback is received during the change process.

An important feature of activity planning is that visions and desired future states can be quite general when compared with the realities of implementing change. As a result, it may be necessary to supplement them with midpoint goals as part of the activity plan.[39] Such goals represent desirable organizational conditions between the current state and the desired future state. For example, if the organization is implementing continuous improvement processes, an important midpoint goal can be the establishment of a certain number of improvement teams focused on understanding and controlling key work processes. Midpoint goals are clearer and more detailed than desired future states, and thus they provide more concrete and manageable steps and benchmarks for change. Activity plans can use midpoint goals to provide members with the direction and security they need to work toward the desired future.

Commitment Planning

This activity involves identifying key people and groups whose commitment is needed for change to occur and formulating a strategy for gaining their support. Although commitment planning is generally a part of developing political support, discussed above, specific plans for identifying key stakeholders and obtaining their commitment to change need to be made early in the change process.

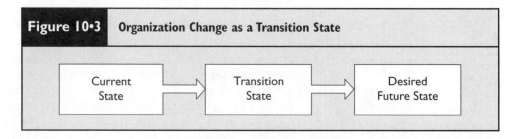

| Figure 10•3 | Organization Change as a Transition State |

Current State → Transition State → Desired Future State

USING SOCIAL NETWORKS TO IMPLEMENT CHANGE IN A PUBLIC EDUCATION INSTITUTION

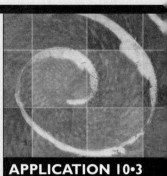

APPLICATION 10•3

Tom Forcella, the chief administrative officer for a California county office of education, had learned through his 7-year tenure that implementing a technology infrastructure in the public school system was not an easy or smooth process. Many districts and school offices, each with its own county offices of education, had to be coordinated. It was nearly impossible to control at a statewide level and no efforts were being made to streamline an already overly bureaucratic oversight process. To make matters worse, money was being expended on a variety of projects that rarely related to other projects and seldom required an evaluation process upon exhaustion of funding.

In 1998, however, Forcella was asked to oversee a statewide initiative to provide technical connectivity to disadvantaged school systems. Children in schools where the parents' average income was lower did not have as many opportunities to work with computers and the Internet. As part of the initiative, he identified a process for implementing the change. Over the years, Forcella had developed relationships with high-technology companies from Silicon Valley to deliver technology-based solutions for his local county jurisdiction. He thought about how he might use those relationships to bring Internet connections, hardware, and software to the schools that needed it most.

With the help of schools that chose to apply for aid, Forcella and his staff developed partnerships with network engineering and design firms, hardware manufacturers, software developers, Internet service providers (ISPs), application service providers (ASPs), and learning service providers (LSPs). Working together, the parties designed hardware and software packages that bundled quality products and services specifically created for school systems. Through Forcella's leadership, a coordination team that specialized in technology tools for schools was launched to offer consulting services to those who wanted to learn how best to move technology into the curriculum.

The technology companies provided products and services to school systems within 44 of the 58 counties in the state. They learned about educational processes and procedures that were later used to improve the design of their own hardware and software systems. In addition, those companies learned how to serve the specific needs of the public education system market. At the same time, schools began benefiting in financial and practical ways from services designed to meet their needs. In 1999, Forcella resigned from his position within the county office of education and became president of a nonprofit organization working to enact the change on a statewide basis.

Change-Management Structures

Because organizational transitions tend to be ambiguous and to need direction, special structures for managing the change process need to be created. These management structures should include people who have the power to mobilize resources to promote change, the respect of the existing leadership and change advocates, and the interpersonal and political skills to guide the change process. Alternative management structures include the following:[40]

- The chief executive or head person manages the change effort.
- A project manager temporarily is assigned to coordinate the transition.
- The formal organization manages the change effort in addition to supervising normal operations.
- Representatives of the major constituencies involved in the change jointly manage the project.
- Natural leaders who have the confidence and trust of large numbers of affected employees are selected to manage the transition.

- A cross section of people representing different organizational functions and levels manages the change.
- A "kitchen cabinet" representing people whom the chief executive consults with and confides in manages the change effort.

Application 10.4 shows how Hewlett-Packard and Compaq used all of these techniques to manage the integration activities associated with this acquisition. Despite research on the high proportion of failed acquisition processes, the extraordinary detail used in this process, and the bank of institutionalized knowledge (see Application 11.2), the HP–Compaq integration process is receiving very positive reviews.[41]

SUSTAINING MOMENTUM

Once organizational changes are under way, explicit attention must be directed to sustaining energy and commitment for implementing them. The initial excitement and activity of changing often dissipate in the face of practical problems of trying to learn new ways of operating. A strong tendency exists among organization members to return to what is learned and well known unless they receive sustained support and reinforcement for carrying the changes through to completion. In this section, we present approaches for sustaining momentum for change. The subsequent tasks of assessing and stabilizing changes are discussed in Chapter 11. The following five activities can help to sustain momentum for carrying change through to completion: providing resources for change, building a support system for change agents, developing new competencies and skills, reinforcing new behaviors, and staying the course.

Providing Resources for Change

Implementing organization change generally requires additional financial and human resources, particularly if the organization continues day-to-day operations while trying to change itself. These extra resources are needed for such change activities as training, consultation, data collection and feedback, and special meetings. Extra resources also are helpful to provide a buffer as performance drops during the transition period. Organizations can underestimate seriously the need for special resources devoted to the change process. Significant organizational change invariably requires considerable management time and energy, as well as the help of consultants. A separate "change budget" that exists along with capital and operating budgets can earmark the resources needed for training members in how to behave differently and for assessing progress and making necessary modifications in the change program.[42] Unless these extra resources are planned for and provided, meaningful change is less likely to occur.

Building a Support System for Change Agents

Organization change can be difficult and filled with tension, not only for participants but for change agents as well.[43] They often must give members emotional support, but they may receive little support themselves. They often must maintain "psychological distance" from others to gain the perspective needed to lead the change process. This separation can produce considerable tension and isolation, and change agents may need to create their own support system to help them cope with such problems. A support system typically consists of a network of people with whom the change agent has close personal relationships—people who can give emotional support, serve as a sounding board for ideas and problems, and challenge untested assumptions. For example, OD professionals often use trusted colleagues as "shadow consultants" to help them think through difficult issues with clients and

TRANSITION MANAGEMENT IN THE HP–COMPAQ ACQUISITION

In the Fall of 2001, Carly Fiorina announced HP's intent to acquire Compaq Corporation. Over the next 9 months, a proxy fight ensued as many shareholders and employees challenged the wisdom of the proposed change. Wall Street analysts and organization researchers too debated whether or not the acquisition made sense, especially given the size of the change and the rather dismal history of performance in acquisition cases. Scott McNealy, chief executive of rival Sun Microsystems Inc., predicted "a slow-motion collision of two garbage trucks."

Within days of the initial announcement, however, Fiorina and Michael Capellas, then CEO of Compaq, met with Webb McKinney, a 19-year HP veteran, and Jeff Clarke, Compaq's CFO and survivor of Compaq's acquisition of Digital Equipment Corporation. These two men were named to lead the transition process, one that would involve redeploying a combined 145,000 workers in 160 countries including more than 15,000 layoffs, untangling 163 overlapping product lines, and producing $2.5 billion dollars in promised cost reductions.

It was no accident that McKinney and Clarke were asked to lead the integration team. Both were senior managers with substantial followings and excellent reputations. Days after their initial meeting, they began recruiting managers in equal numbers; Clarke rounded up Compaq talent and McKinney lined up their HP matches. Within weeks of the merger's announcement, the integration group, called the "clean team," had 500 members; by March 2002, more than 900. Even after the merger closed in May 2002, it kept growing, peaking at more than 1,000 full-time employees. By establishing such a huge body of outstanding managers and reassuring them that their jobs would be safe even if the merger failed, Clarke and McKinney were able to coax them to share in confidence everything they knew. It also kept most of them motivated to stay—another critical benchmark.

In addition to getting the right people on board, McKinney and Clarke set up an assembly line for decision making. Their research on successful and unsuccessful acquisitions, and Clarke's experience with the Digital acquisition, convinced them that slow decision making and the lack of a clear decision-making process was like a cancer in the transition process. In response, they created the "adopt and go" strategy: Get cross-company pairs of managers to meet daily to determine the best choice or best course of action on any particular issue. Weekly meetings kept the pace fast. If any issues couldn't be resolved by the teams, McKinney and Clarke would jump in. If those two couldn't resolve the impasse, they'd pass it to a committee chaired by Fiorina.

APPLICATION 10•4

In addition to getting the right people on board and setting up a decision process built for speed, the transition team organized to create activity plans for the key issues facing the integration, including people, products, culture, day-one activities, and day-to-day operations. Excerpts and examples from some of those plans are overviewed below.

- The "adopt and go" process was used to decide which products to keep and which to discontinue. At weekly presentations with McKinney and Clarke, managers had to offer up one for elimination. In contrast to Compaq's merger with Digital, HP executives made quick product decisions and every week pored over progress charts with red, green, and yellow markers to review how each product exit was proceeding. Red and yellow markers indicated a task was troubled; green signaled a task going well. In 4 months, a road map for product lines emerged and helped to close redundant warehouses and factories, ultimately saving $500 million in procurement costs. In the end, while many Compaq products beat out HP's, such as Compaq's iPac over HP's Jornada, the HP brand survived.

- The "adopt and go" process also helped HP make the hard decisions about personnel appointments. HP appointed its top three tiers of executives before the acquisition was finalized and made new levels of appointments every few weeks. While not perfect—rumors that Compaq people were favored in the sales organization—Clarke contends that all decisions were made "by the book."

- HP created a team to deal specifically with melding the corporate cultures and hired consultants to document the differences. To address perceptions that Compaq employees were "shoot from the hip cowboys" and that HP staff were "bureaucrats," the team created a series of cultural workshops. They were designed to identify the various cultures and subcultures, and then integrate them. For example, key sales managers and about two dozen salespeople from both HP and Compaq held a workshop designed to address sales integration and transition issues. Many attendees first looked at each other suspiciously. Following some icebreaker exercises, however, an HP representative talked about how they had been working with key customer SBC, the telecommunications company. That was followed by a Compaq rep discussing how they sold to SBC. Then the big group drew up a 100-day work plan for selling to SBC in the future, including a weekly conference call for the team every Friday. The progress from these sessions was tracked by a team of 650 part-time internal "cultural consultants," who also continued in their normal jobs at the company.

The cultural workshops delivered in the first quarter after the deal was signed set the stage for a further cultural integration. The workshops welcomed everyone to the new team, described the HP business, HP's values and operating models, the roles and objectives of different groups, and how people were expected to work together. All of this material was pushed out into the HP market before the launch, inviting a few thousand of the top HP managers to an orientation and education session on what to do, how to communicate, and the details of the new HP and their roles in it.

- The clean team also made extensive "day one" plans. Day one readiness included plans to address customers, issues of leadership and structure, and internal administrative issues. The new HP was launched with everyone on the same email, not a paycheck missed,

and every sign changed the morning of launch day. Customers participated heavily in the transition process. Customer councils, interviews, research, information sessions, education, and other data were included in the knowledge transfer to groups that faced the customer. The go-to-market plans were detailed, with playbooks given to each group manager who touched the customers, so that on launch day they knew what to do, what to say to a customer, where to get information. Each customer was given a buddy from the other company at the same level so that he or she could contact that person and get whatever information the customer needed. There was an enormous amount of detail, down to the script of what to say, what answers to give to specific questions, where to get further information, and how to transition an inquiry to the right person.

By most measures, the work has paid off: HP has met the integration goals that Chairman and Chief Executive Carleton S. Fiorina set for the merged company. The biggest of these is cost-savings, which have surpassed expectations. By mid-2003, HP said it saved $734 million—14% more than projected—from payroll cuts and better terms with its suppliers.

to offer conceptual and emotional support. Similarly, a growing number of companies, such as Intel, Procter & Gamble, BP, TRW, and Texas Instruments, are forming internal networks of change agents to provide mutual learning and support.

Developing New Competencies and Skills

Organizational changes frequently demand new knowledge, skills, and behaviors from organization members. In many cases, the changes cannot be implemented unless members gain new competencies. For example, employee-involvement programs often require managers to learn new leadership styles and new approaches to problem solving. Change agents must ensure that such learning occurs. They need to provide multiple learning opportunities, such as traditional training programs, on-the-job counseling and coaching, and experiential simulations, covering both technical and social skills. Because it is easy to overlook the social component, change agents may need to devote special time and resources to helping members gain the social skills required to implement changes. As part of McKesson's commitment to quality, the corporation identifies specially selected high performers to become six-sigma black belts and then promotes them accordingly to signal the importance of these skills and knowledge in career planning. In addition, senior managers in all of the divisions are required to attend training that builds new problem-solving skills, team behaviors, and a commitment to the quality philosophy.[44]

Reinforcing New Behaviors

In organizations, people generally do those things that bring them rewards. Consequently, one of the most effective ways to sustain momentum for change is to reinforce the kinds of behaviors needed to implement the changes. This can be accomplished by linking formal rewards directly to the desired behaviors. For example, Integra Financial encouraged more teamwork by designing a rewards and recognition program in which the best team players got both financial rewards and management attention, and a variety of behaviors aimed at promoting self-interest were directly discouraged.[45] (Chapter 17 discusses several reward-system interventions.) In addition, desired behaviors can be reinforced more frequently through informal recognition, encouragement, and praise. Perhaps equally important are the intrinsic rewards that people can experience through early success in the change effort. Achieving identifiable early successes can make participants feel good about themselves and their behaviors, and thus reinforce the drive to change.

Staying the Course

Change requires time, and many of the expected financial and organizational benefits from change lag behind its implementation. If the organization changes again too quickly or abandons the change before it is fully implemented, the desired results may never materialize. There are two primary reasons that managers do not keep a steady focus on change implementation. First, many managers fail to anticipate the decline in performance, productivity, or satisfaction as change is implemented. Organization members need time to practice, develop, and learn new behaviors; they do not abandon old ways of doing things and adopt a new set of behaviors overnight. Moreover, change activities, such as training, extra meetings, and consulting assistance, are extra expenses added onto current operating expenditures. There should be little surprise, therefore, that effectiveness declines before it gets better. However, perfectly good change projects often are abandoned when questions are raised about short-term performance declines. Patience and trust in the diagnosis and intervention design work are necessary.

Second, many managers do not keep focused on a change because they want to implement the next big idea that comes along. When organizations change before they have to, in response to the latest management fad, a "flavor-of-the-month" cynicism can develop. As a result, organization members provide only token support to a change under the (accurate) notion that the current change won't last. Successful organizational change requires persistent leadership that does not waver unnecessarily.

Application 10.5 describes the transformation at the Veteran's Hospital Administration and how the leadership team sustained momentum for change by instituting a performance management system and utilizing evaluation feedback to modify the change process.[46]

■ SUMMARY

In this chapter, we described five kinds of activities that change agents must carry out when planning and implementing changes. The first activity is motivating change, which involves creating a readiness for change among organization members and overcoming their resistance. The second activity concerns creating a vision that builds on an organization's core ideology. It describes an envisioned future that includes a bold and valued outcome and a vividly described desired future state. The core ideology and envisioned future articulate a compelling reason for implementing change. The third task for change agents is developing political support for the changes. Change agents first must assess their own sources of power, then identify key stakeholders whose support is needed for change and devise strategies for gaining their support. The fourth activity concerns managing the transition of the organization from its current state to the desired future state. This requires planning a

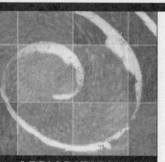

SUSTAINING TRANSFORMATIONAL CHANGE AT THE VETERANS HEALTH ADMINISTRATION

The Veterans Health Administration (VHA) is a federally funded and centrally administered health care system for veterans. It is one of the country's largest health care delivery systems with 172 hospitals, 132 nursing homes, 73 home health care programs, 40 residential care programs, and more than 600 outpatient clinics. The VHA's 1999 budget of over $17 million covered a workforce of approximately 180,000 individuals.

In the mid-1990s, a number of pressures threatened the organization's existence and its ability to change, including an overreliance on outmoded and unprofitable in-patient services; a series of health care reforms that threatened to place the VHA in direct competition with more efficient, for-profit, managed care organizations; a Congressional budgeting process that threatened to freeze the organization's budget; and a primary customer base that was aging and dwindling. In addition, the agency's management systems and culture were deeply rooted in a command-and-control, military-style mind-set. Decision making was highly centralized and bureaucratic. Politically, the VHA had multiple stakeholders with different and sometimes conflicting interests regarding agency priorities and activities. Finally, the VHA operated within a framework of extensive rules and regulations that constrained the agency's ability to adapt, limited the agency's ability to treat patients on an outpatient basis, or contract for services with private-sector organizations.

In response to these conditions, Congress appointed Dr. Kenneth Kizer, an organizational outsider, to transform the VHA. Dr. Kizer pulled together a leadership team composed mostly of respected insiders and developed a vision for change and related documents that provided a comprehensive statement of purpose and goals for the transformation. The documents made clear that the "transformation would fundamentally change the way veterans health care is provided" and that this would include "increasing ambulatory care access points and a marked emphasis on providing primary care, decentralizing decision making, and integrating the delivery assets to provide a seamless continuum of care." The vision documents also established high standards for the transformation. The VHA was to provide care at a level that "must be demonstratively equal to, or better than, what is available in the local community."

In cooperation with Congress, important reforms were initiated, including patient eligibility requirements that provided the agency with more flexibility to shift patient care to outpatient settings, expanded authority to contract with private-sector organizations, and the ability to market its services to veterans who lacked priority status under the traditional eligibility requirements. Congress formalized these reforms in the Veterans Eligibility Reform Act of 1996 and allowed the VHA to make important shifts in its product and service mix.

As these initial changes in strategy were being implemented, the VHA's senior leadership team reorganized the VHA's operating units into 22 networks known as Veterans Integrated Service Networks. Within this structure, the networks replaced hospitals as the primary planning and budgeting units within the VHA. In addition, much of the authority for operational decision making was effectively transferred from headquarters to the networks. The role of the VHA headquarters, which as part of the transformation had its staff cut by more than one-third, was to set overall policy and to provide technical support to network managers.

The new structure stimulated experimentation and entrepreneurial activity. For example, in an effort to save money and streamline care, network directors consolidated hospitals in more than 45 locations where two or more facilities operated in close proximity to each other. Network directors also implemented many innovative organizational arrangements to coordinate patient care across operating units within the same network. Other arrangements often featured managed care principles related to primary care and preventive services.

With the transformation under way, Dr. Kizer and the leadership team began to implement changes intended to maintain the momentum. These included commitment to a performance management system and an evaluation process that helped the leadership team understand how the change could be adapted.

The most important reinforcement for change was the creation and implementation of an accountability system for network directors. Each director was required to sign a performance contract that stipulated a set of outcomes to which he or she would be held accountable. The contracts provided directors with financial incentives in the form of a bonus for achieving performance goals. The goals were to change each year to reflect different agency priorities, such as implementing new programs or functions, achieving quantitatively measurable improvements in key efficiency and quality indicators for their network (e.g., patient satisfaction), or core competencies in such areas as interpersonal effectiveness. To monitor performance, the senior leadership team used existing data and measurement systems and also created new ones. Routinely generated and disseminated were reports that provided feedback on each network's relative performance on key measures for the transformation.

The VHA's senior leadership team's ability to stay the course was tested when the accountability system was challenged by upper-level managers. The new accountability system entailed the development of new performance measures, and managers complained about the adequacy of the data, the reliability of the measures, and the potential to "game" the system. They also objected to the number and attainability of performance goals.

Many of the complaints were valid and the leadership team took the opportunity to improve the databases and measures. However, the leadership team also believed the value of the new accountability system exceeded its short-term, technical limitations. The new accountability system's emphasis on performance data had a symbolic significance. In fact, managers at lower levels of the agency began measuring the performance of their own units or departments in ways that supported the transformation agenda. These new performance systems often came to be known by such clinically oriented nicknames as "pulse points" and "vital signs." The result was a substantial shift in focus among VHA managers—a shift away from inputs, such as how large is my budget and how many staff do I have, to that of outputs as defined by the goals in network directors' performance contracts. Moreover, the focus of the senior leadership team was reportedly not on whether network directors precisely met each and every goal stipulated in their contracts but rather whether they met the spirit of their contracts in the sense that performance was moving in a direction that promoted the transformation agenda.

In addition to the new accountability system, an evaluation process pointed out two important areas for the leadership to focus on in sustaining the transformation's momentum. First, the evaluation pointed to the need for an improved communications process. To inform employees about the transformation, the senior leadership team distributed written notices and videotapes, held town meetings, and conducted video-conferences. Employee surveys and focus group interviews suggested that frontline employees, including physicians in nonsupervisory positions, had substantially less understanding of the purpose and nature of the transformation than did those to whom they reported. As a result, the leadership team revised communication channels and the data and information that was communicated to VHA members.

Second, the evaluation pointed out that training and education programs had been forgotten and represented an important opportunity to institutionalize the structural changes. That is, although the new structure helped achieve credibility for the transformation and helped stimulate innovations, it also placed managers in situations they were ill-prepared to handle. Many managers struggled in their efforts to adapt to a structure that now called for them to make innovative and strategic decisions in a turbulent environment. Such decision making was not the common experience of most VHA managers, who had spent much of their careers carrying out directives from agency headquarters. As a result, the planned training and education programs were initiated to provide managers with the skills to conduct sophisticated analyses for strategic and marketing plans, capital investment decisions, and contract negotiations with private-sector organizations.

road map for the change activities, as well as planning how to gain commitment for the changes. It also may involve creating special change-management structures. The fifth change task is sustaining momentum for the changes so that they are carried to completion. This includes providing resources for the change program, creating a support system for change agents, developing new competencies and skills, reinforcing the new behaviors required to implement the changes, and staying the course.

◼ NOTES

1. K. Brown and M. Eisenhardt, "The Art of Continuous Change: Linking Complexity Theory and Time-Paced Evolution in Relentlessly Shifting Organizations," *Administrative Science Quarterly* 42 (1997): 1–34.

2. J. Kotter and L. Schlesinger, "Choosing Strategies for Change," *Harvard Business Review* 57 (1979): 106–14; R. Ricardo, "Overcoming Resistance to Change," *National*

Productivity Review 14 (1995): 28–39; A. Armenakis, S. Harris, and K. Mossholder, "Creating Readiness for Organizational Change," *Human Relations* 46 (1993): 681–704.

3. E. Dent and S. Goldberg, "Challenging 'Resistance to Change,'" *Journal of Applied Behavioral Science* 35 (March 1999): 25; M. Weisbord, *Productive Workplaces* (San Francisco: Jossey-Bass, 1987); R. Beckhard and R. Harris,

Organizational Transitions: Managing Complex Change, 2d ed. (Reading, Mass.: Addison-Wesley, 1987); R. Beckhard and W. Pritchard, *Changing the Essence* (San Francisco: Jossey-Bass, 1991); J. Collins and J. Porras, *Built to Last* (New York: Harper Business, 1994); J. Conger, G. Spreitzer, and E. Lawler, *The Leader's Change Handbook* (San Francisco: Jossey-Bass, 1999).

4. Conger, Spreitzer, and Lawler, *Change Handbook*.

5. N. Tichy and M. Devanna, *The Transformational Leader* (New York: John Wiley & Sons, 1986); Armenakis, Harris, and Mossholder, "Creating Readiness."

6. R. Cosier and C. Schwenk, "Agreement and Thinking Alike: Ingredients for Poor Decisions," *Academy of Management Executive* 4 (1990): 69–74.

7. S. Walleck, D. O'Halloran, and C. Leader, "Benchmarking World-Class Performance," *McKinsey Quarterly* 1 (1991).

8. W. Burke, *Organization Development: A Normative View* (Reading, Mass.: Addison-Wesley, 1987); Collins and Porras, *Built to Last*.

9. R. Charan and G. Colvin, "Why CEOs Fail," *Fortune* (21 June 1999): 69–78.

10. D. Eden, "OD and Self-Fulfilling Prophecy: Boosting Productivity by Raising Expectations," *Journal of Applied Behavioral Science* 22 (1986): 1–13; D. Cooperrider, "Positive Image, Positive Action: The Affirmative Basis of Organizing," in *Appreciative Management and Leadership: The Power of Positive Thought and Actions in Organizations*, eds., S. Srivastva, D. Cooperrider, and associates (San Francisco: Jossey-Bass, 1990).

11. Eden, "OD and Self-Fulfilling Prophecy," 8.

12. L. Szamosi and L. Duxbury, "Development of a Measure to Assess Organizational Change," *Journal of Organizational Change* 15 (2002): 184–201.

13. Kotter and Schlesinger, "Choosing Strategies"; P. Block, *Flawless Consulting: A Guide to Getting Your Expertise Used* (Austin, Tex.: Learning Concepts, 1981); P. Strebel, "Why Do Employees Resist Change?" *Harvard Business Review* (May-June 1996): 86–93; S. Piderit, "Rethinking Resistance and Recognizing Ambivalence: A Multidimensional View of Attitudes Toward an Organizational Change," *Academy of Management Review* (2000): 783–95; K. Trader-Leigh, "Case Study: Identifying Resistance in Managing Change," *Journal of Organizational Change Management* 15 (2002): 138–56.

14. C. Neck, "Thought Self-leadership: A Self-regulatory Approach Towards Overcoming Resistance to Organizational Change," *The International Journal of Organizational Analysis*, 4 (1996): 202–16; J. Wolfram Cox, "Manufacturing the Past: Loss and Absence in Organizational Change," *Organization Studies* 18 (1996): 623–54.

15. N. Tichy, "Revolutionize Your Company," *Fortune* (13 December 1993): 114–18.

16. D. Macri, M. Tagliaventi, and F. Bertolotti, "A Grounded Theory for Resistance to Change in a Small Organization," *Journal of Organizational Change Management* 15 (2002): 292–311.

17. D. Kirkpatrick, ed., *How to Manage Change Effectively* (San Francisco: Jossey-Bass, 1985).

18. V. Vroom and P. Yetton, *Leadership and Decision Making* (Pittsburgh: University of Pittsburgh Press, 1973).

19. T. Cummings and E. Molloy, *Improving Productivity and the Quality of Work Life* (New York: Praeger, 1977).

20. R. Stayer, "How I Learned to Let My Workers Lead," *Harvard Business Review* (Nov.-Dec. 1990): 66–83; J. Byrne, "Management Meccas," *Business Week* (18 September 1995).

21. Collins and Porras, *Built to Last*; T. Stewart, "A Refreshing Change: Vision Statements That Make Sense," *Fortune* (30 September 1996): 195–96; T. Stewart, "Why Value Statements Don't Work," *Fortune* (10 June 1996): 137–38.

22. P. Senge, *The Fifth Discipline* (New York: Doubleday, 1990).

23. Collins and Porras, *Built to Last*.

24. J. Kotter, *Leading Change* (Boston: Harvard Business School Press, 1994); W. Bennis and B. Nanus, *Leadership* (New York: Harper & Row, 1985); J. O'Toole, *Leading Change: Overcoming the Ideology of Comfort and the Tyranny of Custom* (San Francisco: Jossey-Bass, 1995); F. Hesselbein, M. Goldsmith, and R. Beckhard, eds., *The Leader of the Future* (San Francisco: Jossey-Bass, 1995).

25. Tichy and Devanna, *Transformational Leader*.

26. Collins and Porras, *Built to Last*.

27. T. Stewart, "Company Values That Add Value," *Fortune* (8 July 1996): 145–47; J. Pearce II and F. David, "Corporate Mission Statements: The Bottom Line," *Academy of Management Executive* 1 (1987): 109–15.

28. Collins and Porras, *Built to Last*.

29. This application was adapted from R. Barnett and J. Scott, "Partnership in Organizational Culture Transformation," a paper presented to the 14th annual conference of the Society for Industrial and Organizational Psychology, Atlanta, Ga., May, 1999.

30. J. Pfeffer, *Power in Organizations* (New York: Pitman, 1982).

31. D. Nadler, "The Effective Management of Change," in *Handbook of Organizational Behavior*, ed. J. Lorsch (Englewood Cliffs, N.J.: Prentice Hall, 1987), 358–69.

32. C. Alderfer, "Organization Development," *Annual Review of Psychology* 28 (1977): 197–223.

33. T. Bateman, "Organizational Change and the Politics of Success," *Group and Organization Studies* 5 (June 1980): 198–209; A. Cobb and N. Margulies, "Organization Development: A Political Perspective," *Academy of Management Review* 6 (1981): 49–59; A. Cobb, "Political Diagnosis: Applications in Organization Development," *Academy of Management Review* 11 (1986): 482–96; L. Greiner and V. Schein, *Power and Organization Development: Mobilizing Power to Implement Change* (Reading, Mass.: Addison-Wesley, 1988); D. Buchanan and R. Badham, "Politics and Organizational Change: The Lived Experience," *Human Relations* 52 (1999): 609–11.

34. Greiner and Schein, *Power and Organization Development.*

35. Nadler, "Effective Management"; Beckhard and Pritchard, *Changing the Essence.*

36. Greiner and Schein, *Power and Organization Development.*

37. Christine Mattos wrote and contributed this application.

38. Beckhard and Harris, *Organizational Transitions.*

39. Ibid.

40. Ibid.

41. This application was derived from the following articles: B. Caulfield, "Saving $3 Billion the HP Way," *Business 2.0,* 4 (2003): 52–57; P. Tam, "Elaborate Planning Helps Keep HP Union on Target," *Wall Street Journal* (23 April 2003): A1; L. Segil, "Why the HP/Compaq Merger Will Go Down in History as the Best Ever," *Wall Street Journal* (28 April 2003); D. Takahashi and T. Poletti, "Combined Company Is Faring Better Than Some Rivals," *San Jose Mercury News* (12 April 2003): 1F. The kind assistance of Emily Horn and Jenny Galitz from Hill and Knowlton, and Sarah Peterson and Cathy Fitzgerald from HP is gratefully acknowledged.

42. C. Worley, D. Hitchin, and W. Ross, *Integrated Strategic Change: How OD Helps to Build Competitive Advantage* (Reading, Mass.: Addison-Wesley, 1996).

43. M. Beer, *Organization Change and Development: A Systems View* (Santa Monica, Calif.: Goodyear, 1980).

44. S. Gale, "Building Frameworks for Six Sigma Success," *Workforce* 82 (2003): 64–69.

45. A. Fisher, "Making Change Stick," *Fortune* (17 April 1995): 121–31.

46. This application was adapted from G. Young, "Managing Organizational Transformations: Lessons from The Veterans Health Administration." *California Management Review* 43 (2000): 66–82.

11 Evaluating and Institutionalizing Organization Development Interventions

This chapter focuses on the final stage of the organization development cycle—evaluation and institutionalization. *Evaluation* is concerned with providing feedback to practitioners and organization members about the progress and impact of interventions. Such information may suggest the need for further diagnosis and modification of the change program, or it may show that the intervention is successful. *Institutionalization* involves making a particular change a permanent part of the organization's normal functioning. It ensures that the results of successful change programs persist over time.

Evaluation processes consider both the implementation success of the intended intervention and the long-term results it produces. Two key aspects of effective evaluation are measurement and research design. The institutionalization or long-term persistence of intervention effects is examined in a framework showing the organization characteristics, intervention dimensions, and processes contributing to institutionalization of OD interventions in organizations.

EVALUATING ORGANIZATION DEVELOPMENT INTERVENTIONS

Assessing organization development interventions involves judgments about whether an intervention has been implemented as intended and, if so, whether it is having desired results. Managers investing resources in OD efforts increasingly are being held accountable for results—being asked to justify the expenditures in terms of hard, bottom-line outcomes. More and more, managers are asking for rigorous assessment of OD interventions and are using the results to make important resource allocation decisions about OD, such as whether to continue to support the change program, to modify or alter it, or to terminate it and try something else.

Traditionally, OD evaluation has been discussed as something that occurs after the intervention. Chapters 12 through 20, for example, present evaluative research about the interventions after discussions of the respective change programs. That view can be misleading, however. Decisions about the measurement of relevant variables and the design of the evaluation process should be made early in the OD cycle so that evaluation choices can be integrated with intervention decisions.

There are two distinct types of OD evaluation: one intended to guide the implementation of interventions and another to assess their overall impact. The key issues in evaluation are measurement and research design.

Implementation and Evaluation Feedback

Most discussions and applications of OD evaluation imply that evaluation is something done after intervention. It is typically argued that once the intervention is implemented, it should be evaluated to discover whether it is producing intended effects. For example, it might be expected that a job enrichment program would lead to higher employee satisfaction and performance. After implementing job enrichment, evaluation would involve assessing whether these positive results indeed did occur. This after-implementation view of evaluation is only partially correct. It assumes that interventions have been implemented as intended and that the key purpose of evaluation is to assess their effects. However, in many, if not most, organization development programs, implementing interventions cannot be taken for granted.[1] Most OD interventions require significant changes in people's behaviors and ways of thinking about organizations, but they typically offer only broad prescriptions for how such changes are to occur. For example, job enrichment (see Chapter 16) calls for adding discretion, variety, and meaningful feedback to people's jobs. Implementing such changes requires considerable learning and experimentation as employees and managers discover how to translate these general prescriptions into specific behaviors and procedures. This learning process involves much trial and error and needs to be guided by information about whether behaviors and procedures are being changed as intended.[2] Consequently, we should expand our view of evaluation to include both *during-implementation* assessment of whether interventions are actually being implemented and *after-implementation* evaluation of whether they are producing expected results.

Both kinds of evaluation provide organization members with feedback about interventions. Evaluation aimed at guiding implementation may be called *implementation feedback,* and assessment intended to discover intervention outcomes may be called *evaluation feedback.*[3] Figure 11.1 shows how the two kinds of feedback fit with the diagnostic and intervention stages of OD. The application of OD to a particular organization starts with a thorough diagnosis of the situation (Chapters 5 through 8), which helps identify particular organizational problems or areas for improvement, as well as likely causes underlying them. Next, from an array of possible interventions (Chapters 12 through 20), one or some set is chosen as a means of improving the organization. The choice is based on knowledge linking interventions to diagnosis (Chapter 9) and change management (Chapter 10).

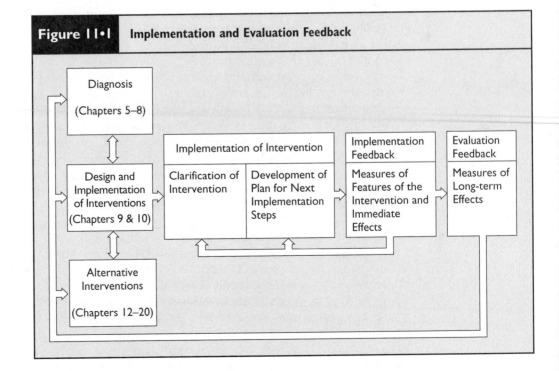

Figure 11•1   Implementation and Evaluation Feedback

In most cases, the chosen intervention provides only general guidelines for organizational change, leaving managers and employees with the task of translating those guidelines into specific behaviors and procedures. Implementation feedback informs this process by supplying data about the different features of the intervention itself and data about the immediate effects of the intervention. These data, collected repeatedly and at short intervals, provide a series of snapshots about how the intervention is progressing. Organization members can use this information, first, to gain a clearer understanding of the intervention (the kinds of behaviors and procedures required to implement it) and, second, to plan for the next implementation steps. This feedback cycle might proceed for several rounds, with each round providing members with knowledge about the intervention and ideas for the next stage of implementation.

Once implementation feedback informs organization members that the intervention is sufficiently in place, evaluation feedback begins. In contrast to implementation feedback, it is concerned with the overall impact of the intervention and with whether resources should continue to be allocated to it or to other possible interventions. Evaluation feedback takes longer to gather and interpret than does implementation feedback. It typically includes a broad array of outcome measures, such as performance, job satisfaction, absenteeism, and turnover. Negative results on these measures tell members either that the initial diagnosis was seriously flawed or that the wrong intervention was chosen. Such feedback might prompt additional diagnosis and a search for a more effective intervention. Positive results, on the other hand, tell members that the intervention produced expected outcomes and might prompt a search for ways to institutionalize the changes, making them a permanent part of the organization's normal functioning.

An example of a job enrichment intervention helps to clarify the OD stages and feedback linkages shown in Figure 11.1. Suppose the initial diagnosis reveals that employee performance and satisfaction are low and that jobs being overly structured and routinized are an underlying cause of this problem. An inspection of alternative interventions to improve productivity and satisfaction suggests that job enrichment might be applicable for this situation. Existing job enrichment theory proposes that increasing employee discretion, task variety, and feedback can lead to improvements in work quality and attitudes and that this job design and outcome linkage is especially strong for employees who have growth needs—needs for challenge, autonomy, and development. Initial diagnosis suggests that most of the employees have high growth needs and that the existing job designs prevent the fulfillment of these needs. Therefore, job enrichment seems particularly suited to this situation.

Managers and employees now start to translate the general prescriptions offered by job enrichment theory into specific behaviors and procedures. At this stage, the intervention is relatively broad and must be tailored to fit the specific situation. To implement the intervention, employees might decide on the following organizational changes: job discretion can be increased through more participatory styles of supervision; task variety can be enhanced by allowing employees to inspect their job outputs; and feedback can be made more meaningful by providing employees with quicker and more specific information about their performances.

After 3 months of trying to implement these changes, the members use implementation feedback to see how the intervention is progressing. Questionnaires and interviews (similar to those used in diagnosis) are administered to measure the different features of job enrichment (discretion, variety, and feedback) and to assess employees' reactions to the changes. Company records are analyzed to show the short-term effects on productivity of the intervention. The data reveal that productivity and satisfaction have changed very little since the initial diagnosis. Employee perceptions of job discretion and feedback also have shown negligible change, but perceptions of task variety have shown significant improvement. In-depth discussion and analysis of this first round of implementation feedback help supervisors gain a better feel for the kinds of behaviors needed to move toward a participatory leadership style. This greater clarification of one feature of the intervention leads to a decision to involve the supervisors in leadership training to develop the skills and knowledge needed to lead participatively. A decision also is made to make job feedback more meaningful by translating such data into simple bar graphs, rather than continuing to provide voluminous statistical reports.

After these modifications have been in effect for about 3 months, members institute a second round of implementation feedback to see how the intervention is progressing. The data now show that productivity and satisfaction have moved moderately higher than in the first round of feedback and that employee perceptions of task variety and feedback are both high. Employee perceptions of discretion, however, remain relatively low. Members conclude that the variety and feedback dimensions of job enrichment are sufficiently implemented but that the discretion component needs improvement. They decide to put more effort into supervisory training and to ask OD practitioners to provide on-line counseling and coaching to supervisors about their leadership styles.

After 4 more months, a third round of implementation feedback occurs. The data now show that satisfaction and performance are significantly higher than in the first round of feedback and moderately higher than in the second round. The data also show that discretion, variety, and feedback are all high, suggesting that the job enrichment intervention has been successfully implemented. Now evaluation feedback is used to assess the overall effectiveness of the program.

The evaluation feedback includes all the data from the satisfaction and performance measures used in the implementation feedback. Because both the immediate and broader effects of the intervention are being evaluated, additional outcomes are examined, such as employee absenteeism, maintenance costs, and reactions of other organizational units not included in job enrichment. The full array of evaluation data might suggest that after 1 year from the start of implementation, the job enrichment program is having expected effects and thus should be continued and made more permanent.

Measurement

Providing useful implementation and evaluation feedback involves two activities: selecting the appropriate variables and designing good measures.

Selecting Variables

Ideally, the variables measured in OD evaluation should derive from the theory or conceptual model underlying the intervention. The model should incorporate the key features of the intervention as well as its expected results. The general diagnostic models described in Chapters 5 and 6 meet this criteria, as do the more specific models introduced in Chapters 12 through 20. For example, the job-level diagnostic model described in Chapter 6 proposes several major features of work: task variety, feedback, and autonomy. The theory argues that high levels of these elements can be expected to result in high levels of work quality and satisfaction. In addition, as we shall see in Chapter 16, the strength of this relationship varies with the degree of employee growth need: the higher the need, the more that job enrichment produces positive results.

The job-level diagnostic model suggests a number of measurement variables for implementation and evaluation feedback. Whether the intervention is being implemented could be assessed by determining how many job descriptions have been rewritten to include more responsibility or how many organization members have received cross-training in other job skills. Evaluation of the immediate and long-term impact of job enrichment would include measures of employee performance and satisfaction over time. Again, these measures would likely be included in the initial diagnosis, when the company's problems or areas for improvement are discovered.

Measuring both intervention and outcome variables is necessary for implementation and evaluation feedback. Unfortunately, there has been a tendency in OD to measure only outcome variables while neglecting intervention variables altogether.[4] It generally is assumed that the intervention has been implemented, and attention, therefore, is directed to its impact on such organizational outcomes as performance, absenteeism, and satisfaction. As argued earlier, implementing OD interventions generally takes considerable time and learning. It must be empirically determined that the intervention has been implemented; it cannot simply be assumed. Implementation feedback serves this purpose, guiding the implementation process and helping to interpret outcome data. Outcome measures are ambiguous without knowledge of how well the intervention has been implemented. For example, a negligible change in measures of performance and satisfaction could mean that the wrong intervention has been chosen, that the correct intervention has not been implemented effectively, or that the wrong variables have been measured. Measurement of the intervention variables helps determine the correct interpretation of outcome measures.

As suggested above, the selection of intervention variables to be measured should derive from the conceptual framework underlying the OD intervention. OD research and theory increasingly have come to identify specific organizational changes needed to implement particular interventions (much of that information is discussed in Chapters 12 through 20). These variables should guide not only implementation of the intervention but also choices about what change variables to measure for evaluative purposes. Additional sources of knowledge about intervention variables can be found in the numerous references at the end of each of the intervention chapters in this book and in several of the books in the Wiley Series on Organizational Assessment and Change.[5]

The choice of what outcome variables to measure also should be dictated by intervention theory, which specifies the kinds of results that can be expected from particular change programs. Again, the material in this book and elsewhere identifies numerous outcome measures, such as job satisfaction, intrinsic motivation, organizational commitment, absenteeism, turnover, and productivity.

Historically, OD assessment has focused on attitudinal outcomes, such as job satisfaction, while neglecting hard measures, such as performance. Increasingly, however, managers and researchers are calling for development of behavioral measures of OD outcomes. Managers are interested primarily in applying OD to change work-related behaviors that involve joining, remaining, and producing at work, and are assessing OD more frequently in terms of such bottom-line results. Macy and Mirvis have done extensive research to develop a standardized set of behavioral outcomes for assessing and comparing intervention results.[6] Table 11.1 lists 11 outcomes, including their behavioral definitions and recording categories. The outcomes are in two broad categories: participation-membership, including absenteeism, tardiness, turnover, internal employment stability, and strikes and work stoppages; and performance on the job, including productivity, quality, grievances, accidents, unscheduled machine downtime and repair, material and supply overuse, and inventory shrinkage. All of the outcomes should be important to most managers, and they represent generic descriptions that can be adapted to both industrial and service organizations.

Designing Good Measures

Each of the measurement methods described in Chapter 7 has advantages and disadvantages. Many of these characteristics are linked to the extent to which a measurement is operationally defined, reliable, and valid. These assessment characteristics are discussed below.

Table 11•1	Behavioral Outcomes for Measuring OD Interventions: Definitions and Recording Categories

BEHAVIORAL DEFINITIONS	RECORDING CATEGORIES
Absenteeism: each absence or illness over 4 hours	*Voluntary:* short-term illness (less than 3 consecutive days), personal business, family illness *Involuntary:* long-term illness (more than 3 consecutive days), funerals, out-of-plant accidents, lack of work (temporary layoff), presanctioned days off *Leaves:* medical, personal, maternity, military, and other (e.g., jury duty)
Tardiness: each absence or illness under 4 hours	*Voluntary:* same as absenteeism *Involuntary:* same as absenteeism
Turnover: each movement beyond the organizational boundary	*Voluntary:* resignation *Involuntary:* termination, disqualification, requested resignation, permanent layoff, retirement, disability, death
Internal employment stability: each movement within the organizational boundary	*Internal movement:* transfer, promotion, promotion with transfer *Internal stability:* new hires, layoffs, rehires
Strikes and work stoppages: each day lost as a result of strike or work stoppage	*Sanctioned:* union-authorized strike, company-authorized lockout *Unsanctioned:* work slowdown, walkout, sitdown
Accidents and work-related illness: each recordable injury, illness, or death from a work-related accident or from exposure to the work environment	*Major:* OSHA accident, illness, or death which results in medical treatment by a physician or registered professional person under standing orders from a physician *Minor:* non-OSHA accident or illness which results in one-time treatment and subsequent observation not requiring professional care *Revisits:* OSHA and non-OSHA accident or illness which requires subsequent treatment and observation
Grievances: written grievance in accordance with labor–management contract	*Stage:* recorded by step (first through arbitration)
Productivity:* resources used in production of acceptable outputs (comparison of inputs with outputs)	*Output:* product or service quantity (units or $) *Input:* direct and/or indirect (labor in hours or $)
Production quality: resources used in production of unacceptable outputs	*Resource utilized:* scrap (unacceptable in-plant products in units or $); customer returns (unacceptable out-of-plant products in units or $); recoveries (salvageable products in units or $); rework (additional direct and/or indirect labor in hours or $)
Downtime: unscheduled breakdown of machinery	*Downtime:* duration of breakdown (hours or $) *Machine repair:* nonpreventive maintenance ($)
Inventory, material, and supply variance: unscheduled resource utilization	*Variance:* over- or underutilization of supplies, materials, inventory (resulting from theft, inefficiency, and so on)

*Reports only labor inputs.

SOURCE: B. Macy and P. Mirvis, "Organizational Change Efforts: Methodologies for Assessing Organizational Effectiveness and Program Costs Versus Benefits," *Evaluation Review* 6, pp. 306–10. Copyright © 1982 by Sage Publications, Inc. Reprinted by permission of Sage Publications, Inc.

Operational definition. A good measure is operationally defined; that is, it specifies the empirical data needed, how they will be collected and, most important, how they will be converted from data to information. For example, Macy and Mirvis developed operational definitions for the behavioral outcomes listed in Table 11.1 (see Table 11.2).[7] They consist of specific computational rules that can be used to construct measures for each of the behaviors. Most of the behaviors are reported as rates adjusted for the number of employees in the organization and for the possible incidents of behavior. These adjustments make it possible to compare the measures across different situations and time periods. These operational definitions should have wide applicability across both industrial and service organizations, although some modifications, deletions, and additions may be necessary for a particular application.

Operational definitions are extremely important in measurement because they provide precise guidelines about what characteristics of the situation are to be observed and how they are to be used. They tell OD practitioners and the client system exactly how diagnostic, intervention, and outcome variables will be measured.

Reliability. Reliability concerns the extent to which a measure represents the "true" value of a variable—that is, how accurately the operational definition translates data into information. For example, there is little doubt about the accuracy of the number of cars leaving an assembly line as a measure of plant productivity; although it is possible to miscount, there can be a high degree of confidence in the measurement. On the other hand, when people are asked to rate their level of job satisfaction on a scale of 1 to 5, there is considerable room for variation in their response. They may just have had an argument with their supervisor, suffered an accident on the job, been rewarded for high levels of productivity, or been given new responsibilities. Each of these events can sway the response to the question on any given day. The individuals' "true" satisfaction score is difficult to discern from this one question, and the measure lacks reliability.[8]

OD practitioners can improve the reliability of their measures in four ways. First, rigorously and operationally define the chosen variables. Clearly specified operational definitions contribute to reliability by explicitly describing how collected data will be converted into information about a variable. An explicit description helps to allay the client's concerns about how the information was collected and coded.

Second, use multiple methods to measure a particular variable. As discussed in Chapter 7, the use of questionnaires, interviews, observations, and unobtrusive measures can improve reliability and result in more comprehensive understanding of the organization. Because each method contains inherent biases, several different methods can be used to triangulate on dimensions of organizational problems. If the independent measures converge or show consistent results, the dimensions or problems likely have been diagnosed accurately.[9]

Third, use multiple items to measure the same variable on a questionnaire. For example, in Hackman and Oldham's Job Diagnostic Survey for measuring job characteristics (Chapter 16), the intervention variable "autonomy" has the following operational definition: the average of respondents' answers to the following three questions (measured on a 7-point scale):[10]

1. The job permits me to decide *on my own* how to go about doing the work.
2. The job denies me any chance to use my personal initiative or judgment in carrying out the work. (reverse scored)
3. The job gives me considerable opportunity for independence and freedom in how I do the work.

By asking more than one question about "autonomy," the survey increases the accuracy of its measurement of this variable. Statistical analyses (called *psychometric*

Table 11•2	Behavioral Outcomes for Measuring OD Interventions: Measures and Computational Formulae

BEHAVIORAL MEASURE*	COMPUTATIONAL FORMULA
Absenteeism rate** (monthly)	$\dfrac{\Sigma \text{ Absence days}}{\text{Average workforce size} \times \text{Working days}}$
Tardiness rate** (monthly)	$\dfrac{\Sigma \text{ Tardiness incidents}}{\text{Average workforce size} \times \text{Working days}}$
Turnover rate (monthly)	$\dfrac{\Sigma \text{ Turnover incidents}}{\text{Average workforce size}}$
Internal stability rate (monthly)	$\dfrac{\Sigma \text{ Internal movement incidents}}{\text{Average workforce size}}$
Strike rate (yearly)	$\dfrac{\Sigma \text{ Striking Workers} \times \text{Strike days}}{\text{Average workforce size} \times \text{Working days}}$
Accident rate (yearly)	$\dfrac{\Sigma \text{ of Accidents, illnesses}}{\text{Total yearly hours worked}} \times 200{,}000$***
Grievance rate (yearly)	Plant: $\dfrac{\Sigma \text{ Grievance incidents}}{\text{Average workforce size}}$ Individual: $\dfrac{\Sigma \text{ Aggrieved individuals}}{\text{Average workforce size}}$
Productivity:**** Total	$\dfrac{\text{Output of goods or services (units or \$)}}{\text{Direct and/or indirect labor (hours or \$)}}$

Below standard
   Below budget
   Variance
   Per employee
	Actual versus engineered standard
	 Actual versus budgeted standard
	 Actual versus budgeted variance
	 Output/average workforce size

Quality:****
   Total
	Scrap + Customer returns + Rework
	    − Recoveries (\$, units, or hours)

Below standard
   Below budget
   Variance
   Per employee
	Actual versus engineered standard
	 Actual versus budgeted standard
	 Actual versus budgeted variance
	 Total/average workforce size

Downtime	Labor (\$) + Repair costs or dollar value of replaced equipment (\$)
Inventory, supply, and material usage	Variance (actual versus standard utilization) (\$)

*All measures reflect the number of incidents divided by an exposure factor that represents the number of employees in the organization and the possible incidents of behavior (e.g., for absenteeism, the average workforce size × the number of working days). Mean monthly rates (i.e., absences per workday) are computed and averaged for absenteeism, leaves, and tardiness for a yearly figure and summed for turnover, grievances, and internal employment stability for a yearly figure. The term *rate* refers to the number of incidents per unit of employee exposure to the risk of such incidences during the analysis interval.

**Sometimes combined as number of hours missing/average workforce size × working days.

***Base for 100 full-time equivalent workers (40 hours × 50 weeks).

****Monetary valuations can be expressed in labor dollars, actual dollar costs, sales dollars; overtime dollar valuations can be adjusted to base year dollars to control for salary, raw material, and price increases.

SOURCE: B. Macy and P. Mirvis, "Organizational Change Efforts: Methodologies for Assessing Organizational Effectiveness and Program Costs Versus Benefits," *Evaluation Review* 6, pp. 306–10. Copyright © 1982 by Sage Publications, Inc. Reprinted by permission of Sage Publications, Inc.

tests) are readily available for assessing the reliability of perceptual measures, and OD practitioners should apply these methods or seek assistance from those who can apply them.[11] Similarly, there are methods for analyzing the content of interview and observational data, and OD evaluators can use these methods to categorize such information so that it can be understood and replicated.[12]

Fourth, use standardized instruments. A growing number of standardized questionnaires are available for measuring OD intervention and outcome variables. For example, the Center for Effective Organizations at the University of Southern California (http://www.marshall.usc.edu/web/ceo.cfm?doc_id-611) and the Institute for Social Research at the University of Michigan (http://www.isr.umich.edu) have developed comprehensive survey instruments to measure the features of many of the OD interventions described in this book, as well as their attitudinal outcomes.[13] Considerable research and testing have gone into establishing measures that are reliable and valid. These survey instruments can be used for initial diagnosis, for guiding implementation of interventions, and for evaluating immediate and long-term outcomes.

Validity.   Validity concerns the extent to which a measure actually reflects the variable it is intended to reflect. For example, the number of cars leaving an assembly line might be a reliable measure of plant productivity, but it may not be a valid measure. The number of cars is only one aspect of productivity; they may have been produced at an unacceptably high cost. Because the number of cars does not account for cost, it is not a completely valid measure of plant productivity.

OD practitioners can increase the validity of their measures in several ways. First, ask colleagues and clients if a proposed measure actually represents a particular variable. This is called *face validity* or *content validity*. If experts and clients agree that the measure reflects the variable of interest, then there is increased confidence in the measure's validity. Second, use multiple measures of the same variable, as described in the section about reliability, to make preliminary assessments of the measure's *criterion* or *convergent validity*. That is, if several different measures of the same variable correlate highly with each other, especially if one or more of the other measures has been validated in prior research, then there is increased confidence in the measure's validity. A special case of criterion validity, called *discriminant validity*, exists when the proposed measure does not correlate with measures that it is not supposed to correlate with. For example, there is no good reason for daily measures of assembly line productivity to correlate with daily air temperature. The lack of a correlation would be one indicator that the number of cars is measuring productivity and not some other variable. Finally, *predictive validity* is demonstrated when the variable of interest accurately forecasts another variable over time. For example, a measure of team cohesion can be said to be valid if it accurately predicts improvements in team performance in the future.

It is difficult, however, to establish the validity of a measure until it has been used. To address this concern, OD practitioners should make heavy use of content validity processes and use measures that already have been validated. For example, presenting proposed measures to colleagues and clients for evaluation prior to measurement has several positive effects: It builds ownership and commitment to the data collection process and improves the likelihood that the client system will find the data meaningful. Using measures that have been validated through prior research improves confidence in the results and provides a standard that can be used to validate any new measures used in collecting the data.

Research Design

In addition to measurement, OD practitioners must make choices about how to design the evaluation to achieve valid results. The key issue is how to design the assessment to show whether the intervention did in fact produce the observed results.

This is called *internal validity*. The secondary question of whether the intervention would work similarly in other situations is referred to as *external validity*. External validity is irrelevant without first establishing an intervention's primary effectiveness, so internal validity is the essential minimum requirement for assessing OD interventions. Unless managers can have confidence that the outcomes are the result of the intervention, they have no rational basis for making decisions about accountability and resource allocation.

Assessing the internal validity of an intervention is, in effect, testing a hypothesis—namely, that specific organizational changes lead to certain outcomes. Moreover, testing the validity of an intervention hypothesis means that alternative hypotheses or explanations of the results must be rejected. That is, to claim that an intervention is successful, it is necessary to demonstrate that other explanations—in the form of rival hypotheses—do not account for the observed results. For example, if a job enrichment program appears to increase employee performance, such other possible explanations as new technology, improved raw materials, or new employees must be eliminated.

Accounting for rival explanations is not a precise, controlled, experimental process such as might be found in a research laboratory.[14] OD interventions often have a number of features that make determining whether they produced observed results difficult. They are complex and often involve several interrelated changes that obscure whether individual features or combinations of features are accounting for the results. Many OD interventions are long-term projects and take considerable time to produce desired outcomes. The longer the time period of the change program, the greater are the chances that other factors, such as technology improvements, will emerge to affect the results. Finally, OD interventions almost always are applied to existing work units rather than to randomized groups of organization members. Ruling out alternative explanations associated with randomly selected intervention and comparison groups is, therefore, difficult.

Given the problems inherent in assessing OD interventions, practitioners have turned to *quasi-experimental research designs*.[15] These designs are not as rigorous and controlled as are randomized experimental designs, but they allow evaluators to rule out many rival explanations for OD results other than the intervention itself. Although several quasi-experimental designs are available, those with the following three features[16] are particularly powerful for assessing changes:

1. **Longitudinal measurement.** This involves measuring results repeatedly over relatively long time periods. Ideally, the data collection should start before the change program is implemented and continue for a period considered reasonable for producing expected results.

2. **Comparison unit.** It is always desirable to compare results in the intervention situation with those in another situation where no such change has taken place. Although it is never possible to get a matching group identical to the intervention group, most organizations include a number of similar work units that can be used for comparison purposes.

3. **Statistical analysis.** Whenever possible, statistical methods should be used to rule out the possibility that the results are caused by random error or chance. Various statistical techniques are applicable to quasi-experimental designs, and OD practitioners should apply these methods or seek help from those who can apply them.[17]

Table 11.3 (on page 188) provides an example of a quasi-experimental design having these three features. The intervention is intended to reduce employee absenteeism. Measures of absenteeism are taken from company monthly records for both

Table 11•3	Quasi-Experimental Research Design								
	Monthly Absenteeism (%)								
	SEPT.	**OCT.**	**NOV.**	**DEC.**		**JAN.**	**FEB.**	**MAR.**	**APR.**
Intervention group	5.1	5.3	5.0	5.1	Start of intervention	4.6	4.0	3.9	3.5
Comparison group	2.5	2.6	2.4	2.5		2.6	2.4	2.5	2.5

the intervention and comparison groups. The two groups are similar yet geographically separate subsidiaries of a multiplant company. Table 11.3 shows each plant's monthly absenteeism rate for 4 consecutive months both before and after the start of the intervention. The plant receiving the intervention shows a marked decrease in absenteeism in the months following the intervention, whereas the control plant shows comparable levels of absenteeism in both time periods. Statistical analyses of these data suggest that the abrupt downward shift in absenteeism following the intervention was not attributable to chance variation. This research design and the data provide relatively strong evidence that the intervention was successful.

Quasi-experimental research designs using longitudinal data, comparison groups, and statistical analysis permit reasonable assessments of intervention effectiveness. Repeated measures often can be collected from company records without directly involving members of the experimental and comparison groups. These unobtrusive measures are especially useful in OD assessment because they do not interact with the intervention and affect the results. More obtrusive measures, such as questionnaires and interviews, are reactive and can sensitize people to the intervention. When this happens, it is difficult to know whether the observed findings are the result of the intervention, the measuring methods, or some combination of both.

Multiple measures of intervention and outcome variables should be applied to minimize measurement and intervention interactions. For example, obtrusive measures such as questionnaires could be used sparingly, perhaps once before and once after the intervention. Unobtrusive measures, such as the behavioral outcomes shown in Tables 11.1 and 11.2, could be used repeatedly, thus providing a more extensive time series than the questionnaires. When used together, the two kinds of measures should produce accurate and nonreactive evaluations of the intervention.

The use of multiple measures also is important in assessing perceptual changes resulting from interventions. Considerable research has identified three types of change—alpha, beta, and gamma—that occur when using self-report, perceptual measures.[18]

Alpha change refers to movement along a measure that reflects stable dimensions of reality. For example, comparative measures of perceived employee discretion might show an increase after a job enrichment program. If this increase represents alpha change, it can be assumed that the job enrichment program actually increased employee perceptions of discretion.

Beta change involves the recalibration of the intervals along some constant measure of reality. For example, before-and-after measures of perceived employee discretion can decrease after a job enrichment program. If beta change is involved, it can explain this apparent failure of the intervention to increase discretion. The first measure of discretion may accurately reflect the individual's belief about the ability to move around and talk to fellow workers in the immediate work area. During implementation of the job enrichment intervention, however, the employee may learn that the ability to move around is not limited to the immediate work area. At a second measurement of discretion, the employee, using this new and recalibrated understanding, may rate the current level of discretion as lower than before.

Gamma change involves fundamentally redefining the measure as a result of an OD intervention. In essence, the framework within which a phenomenon is viewed changes. For example, the presence of gamma change would make it difficult to compare measures of employee discretion taken before and after a job enrichment program. The measure taken after the intervention might use the same words, but they represent an entirely different concept. As described above, the term "discretion" may originally refer to the ability to move about the department and interact with other workers. After the intervention, discretion might be defined in terms of the ability to make decisions about work rules, work schedules, and productivity levels. In sum, the job enrichment intervention changed the way discretion is perceived and how it is evaluated.

These three types of change apply to perceptual measures. When other than alpha changes occur, interpreting measurement changes becomes far more difficult. Potent OD interventions may produce both beta and gamma changes, and this severely complicates interpretations of findings reporting change or no change. Further, the distinctions among the three different types of change suggest that the heavy reliance on questionnaires, so often cited in the literature, should be balanced by using other measures, such as interviews and unobtrusive records. Analytical methods have been developed to assess the three kinds of change, and OD practitioners should gain familiarity with these recent techniques.[19]

Application 11.1 describes the evaluation of a large-scale change at the World Bank, specifically the way the change was managed.[20] It is a good example of how multiple types of data can be collected and used to validate the evaluation data. The material presented so far in this chapter can be used to assess the evaluation's effectiveness. What are the strengths and weaknesses of the assessment? How could it have been improved? How much confidence do you have in the lessons learned for this organization?

INSTITUTIONALIZING INTERVENTIONS

Once it is determined that a change has been implemented and is effective, attention is directed at institutionalizing the changes—making them a permanent part of the organization's normal functioning. Lewin described change as occurring in three stages: unfreezing, moving, and refreezing. Institutionalizing an OD intervention concerns refreezing. It involves the long-term persistence of organizational changes: To the extent that changes persist, they can be said to be institutionalized. Such changes are not dependent on any one person but exist as a part of the culture of an organization. This means that numerous others share norms about the appropriateness of the changes.

How planned changes become institutionalized has not received much attention in the OD literature. Rapidly changing environments have led to admonitions from consultants and practitioners to "change constantly," to "change before you have to," and "if it's not broke, fix it anyway." Such a context has challenged the utility of the institutionalization concept. Why endeavor to make any change permanent given that it may require changing again soon? However, the admonitions also have resulted in institutionalization concepts being applied in new ways. Change itself has become the focus of institutionalization. Total quality management, organization

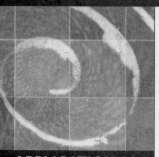

EVALUATING CHANGE AND CHANGE MANAGEMENT AT THE WORLD BANK

In the mid-'90s the World Bank (http://www.worldbank.org/), an international agency with a mission to help reduce poverty worldwide, was facing criticism and declining support from many of its key constituencies. The concerns included arrogance, insularity, slowness, cost, and a lack of client focus. Moreover, stakeholders believed the quality and relevance of funded projects and the advice the Bank provided were deteriorating.

To stem its slide toward irrelevance, the Bank undertook a massive change program affecting every dimension of the organization and every principle behind its way of doing business. The culmination of this effort was reached in 1997 with the conclusion—shortly after the arrival of a new president at the Bank—of a Strategic Compact between the Bank and its shareholders. In exchange for a one-time injection of $250 million, the Bank committed to delivering a substantially transformed institution within 3 years.

The Compact was ambitious in both its timetable and scope and focused on the implementation of four priority change programs:

- **Refueling the Current Business Activity.** This program committed the Bank to revitalize existing lines of business by enhancing quality, improving client responsiveness and operational efficiency, and shifting resources to the front line.

- **Refocusing the Development Agenda.** This program responded to the changes in the development landscape by targeting resources to high-priority sectoral and thematic initiatives, such as the social dimensions of sustainable development, financial-sector development, building capacity in Africa, and anticorruption efforts; investing in the development of new products and services; and enhancing partnerships.

- **Retooling the Knowledge Base.** This program identified three broad thrusts for action: building a world-class knowledge management program; expanding and strengthening the World Bank Institute (which transfers knowledge to developing countries); and producing a *World Development Report* to advance the understanding of knowledge as an enabler of development.

- **Revamping Institutional Capabilities.** This program was intended to create the institutional enablers (structure, culture, people, decentralization, etc.) of a substantially more effective, client-focused, agile, and cost-efficient Bank.

A large number of task forces and other parallel structures were deployed to implement the resulting agenda, with senior management assuming an active role.

In early 2001, an evaluation of the Compact's transformation effort and a report to the Board were begun. An evaluation team, assembled to look at each change program, was expected to address both the content and effectiveness of the change and also how the change was managed. This application focuses on the evaluation of the change management process.

The subteam responsible for evaluating change management settled early on an evaluation framework and on a variety of methodologies to collect, integrate, and validate evaluation data. The framework was based on Kotter's "Eight Steps to Transforming Your Organization," a widely recognized set of best practices that were well known within the Bank, and expanded to include classic change management principles advocated by Richard Beckhard.[20] The headings of the framework are shown below:

1. Establish a Sense of Urgency
2. Form a Powerful Guiding Coalition
3. Create a Vision
4. Communicate the Vision
5. Manage the Transition
6. Build Change Capacity/Readiness
7. Empower Others to Act on the Vision
8. Plan for and Create Short-term Wins
9. Consolidate Improvements, Sustain Momentum, Produce More Change
10. Institutionalize New Approaches

Multiple sources of data were used:

- *Written materials* were collected documenting statements and events associated with the Compact.

- *Numeric data,* such as surveys or organizational data, were collected to supplement and validate other data.

- *Interviews* were conducted with key change actors to generate data about what happened, and to gather perspectives on how to interpret data and events.

- *Focus groups* gathered additional data and diverse perspectives to validate, compare, and confront different assessments. Six focus groups were organized consisting of staff (3), change managers (1), human resource managers (1), and leadership and change advisors (1).

- *A time line* was constructed of significant events affecting the change process. The timeline was then validated and upgraded by those participating in interviews and focus groups and used to refresh memories and to provide useful context to their recollections.

- *The Assessment team's* own perspectives from researching each main element of the Compact.

The reliability and the completeness of the data were ensured in several ways. First, focus group questions were
framed to elicit positive evidence before eliciting critical assessments, so as to counteract well-documented natural ten-
dencies to be overly negative toward the past. Thus a typical
group session might include a series of questions such as
"Cite examples in which the Compact was effectively communicated across the Bank" and follow with an exercise in
which the group is asked to rate change communications
within the framework (in this instance the element Communicating the Vision) on a scale of 1 to 6, and then to comment
on their ratings. Second, discordant data were surfaced with
the interviewees or the groups to ensure any discordance
was understood and reconciled wherever possible. Third, the
process was carried to the point where further interviews
and focus groups were deemed not to be necessary as the
later ones added little new data or perspectives to the data
produced earlier, thus suggesting the data were reasonably
complete. Finally, the resulting assessments were submitted
to all interviewees and focus group participants for validation
purposes.

Overall, the Compact process was seen as quite successful from a change management perspective. In many ways, the
Bank emerged from the Compact a changed institution. It
had made considerable progress in a relatively short time.
The Bank had also put in place the foundations for future
change. For example, the touchstone of any change management effort is culture. Based on focus group findings, the
evaluation found that the Bank's culture had shifted. The
most pronounced change was a movement from being in-
ward-looking to being client focused. Against this solid
record of achievement, the evaluation concluded with the
following six lessons learned.

1. **Trust is central.** "[...] Staff need to feel that managers are partners with them on the journey, and can
give clear direction and example. Without trust there
can be compliance but not commitment."
2. **The Bank needs to find a better balance between the hardware of change (strategy, structure, process, systems) and the software
(culture, behaviors, mindsets, management,
leadership).** [...] many of the transformation's limitations result from a tension between the mindsets
and behaviors required by change designs and vision,
and the existing culture. This is especially true of managers: They have three demanding if overlapping
change roles, including modeling new behaviors, communicating change to their staff, and coaching their
staff to help them develop the new behaviors themselves. Few managers come fully equipped for these
tasks, and little was done [...] to help them develop
these competencies.
3. **The Bank needs to rethink the way change is
communicated.** [...] the main issue appears to be
qualitative. Information is not getting through to many
staff because it is perceived as "selling," insufficiently
candid, and out of touch with staff reality. Communication is too often seen as a one-way information flow,
and not also as a process of engagement and consultation. And there is little communication on how the
changes experienced by staff all come together, where
they lead and what they mean.
4. **There is still a gap between design and implementation.** [...] Change resources were cut off after
the launch phase; change communications declined
in the early stages of implementation; problems in
the matrix were left to accumulate before they were
addressed in a meaningful way; and implementation-
intensive issues, such as culture change, were not sufficiently attended to.
5. **There is a need for a more integrated change vision.** Staff need to understand how their individual experience of change fits into the larger scheme, how the
numerous initiatives build purposefully toward implementing strategy [...] and have consistent expectations
about the overall pace, depth, and sequencing of change.
6. **The Bank needs to focus on how to build its
capacity for ongoing change.** There is still mixed
acceptance by staff that change is inevitable and continuous. How to engage all managers and staff as active
change partners, who are confident to both initiate
needed changes themselves and embrace those initiated by others, is a key challenge.

learning, integrated strategic change, and self-design interventions all are aimed at
enhancing the organization's capability for change.[21] In this vein, processes of institutionalization take on increased utility. This section presents a framework for identifying factors and processes that contribute to the institutionalization of OD
interventions, including the process of change itself.

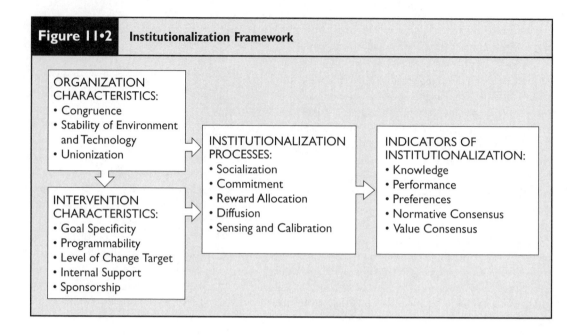

Figure 11·2   Institutionalization Framework

Institutionalization Framework

Figure 11.2 presents a framework that identifies organization and intervention characteristics and institutionalization processes affecting the degree to which change programs are institutionalized.[22] The model shows that two key antecedents—organization and intervention characteristics—affect different institutionalization processes operating in organizations. These processes, in turn, affect various indicators of institutionalization. The model also shows that organization characteristics can influence intervention characteristics. For example, organizations having powerful unions may have trouble gaining internal support for OD interventions.

Organization Characteristics

Figure 11.2 shows that the following three key dimensions of an organization can affect intervention characteristics and institutionalization processes:

1. **Congruence.** This is the degree to which an intervention is perceived as being in harmony with the organization's managerial philosophy, strategy, and structure; its current environment; and other changes taking place.[23] When an intervention is congruent with these dimensions, the probability is improved that it will be institutionalized. Congruence can facilitate persistence by making it easier to gain member commitment to the intervention and to diffuse it to wider segments of the organization. The converse also is true: Many OD interventions promote employee participation and growth. When applied in highly bureaucratic organizations with formalized structures and autocratic managerial styles, participative interventions are not perceived as congruent with the organization's managerial philosophy.

2. **Stability of environment and technology.** This involves the degree to which the organization's environment and technology are changing. Unless the change target is buffered from these changes or unless the changes are dealt with directly by the change program, it may be difficult to achieve long-term intervention stability.[24] For example, decreased demand for the firm's products or services can lead to reductions in personnel that may change the composition

of the groups involved in the intervention. Conversely, increased product demand can curtail institutionalization by bringing new members on board at a rate faster than they can be socialized effectively.

3. **Unionization.** Diffusion of interventions may be more difficult in unionized settings, especially if the changes affect union contract issues, such as salary and fringe benefits, job design, and employee flexibility. For example, a rigid union contract can make it difficult to merge several job classifications into one, as might be required to increase task variety in a job enrichment program. It is important to emphasize, however, that unions can be a powerful force for promoting change, particularly when a good relationship exists between union and management.

Intervention Characteristics

Figure 11.2 shows that the following five major features of OD interventions can affect institutionalization processes:

1. **Goal specificity.** This involves the extent to which intervention goals are specific rather than broad. Specificity of goals helps direct socializing activities (for example, training and orienting new members) to particular behaviors required to implement the intervention. It also helps operationalize the new behaviors so that rewards can be linked clearly to them. For example, an intervention aimed only at increasing product quality is likely to be more focused and readily put into operation than a change program intended to improve quality, quantity, safety, absenteeism, and employee development.

2. **Programmability.** This involves the degree to which the changes can be programmed or the extent to which the different intervention characteristics can be specified clearly in advance to enable socialization, commitment, and reward allocation.[25] For example, job enrichment specifies three targets of change: employee discretion, task variety, and feedback. The change program can be planned and designed to promote those specific features.

3. **Level of change target.** This concerns the extent to which the change target is the total organization, rather than a department or small work group. Each level of organization has facilitators and inhibitors of persistence. Departmental and group change are susceptible to countervailing forces from others in the organization. These can reduce the diffusion of the intervention and lower its ability to impact organization effectiveness. However, this does not preclude institutionalizing the change within a department that successfully insulates itself from the rest of the organization. Such insulation often manifests itself as a subculture within the organization.[26]

   Targeting the intervention to wider segments of the organization, on the other hand, also can help or hinder change persistence. A shared belief about the intervention's value can be a powerful incentive to maintain the change, and promoting a consensus across organizational departments exposed to the change can facilitate institutionalization. But targeting the larger system also can inhibit institutionalization. The intervention can become mired in political resistance because of the "not invented here" syndrome or because powerful constituencies oppose it.

4. **Internal support.** This refers to the degree to which there is an internal support system to guide the change process. Internal support, typically provided by an internal consultant, can gain commitment for the changes and help organization members implement them. External consultants also can provide support,

especially on a temporary basis during the early stages of implementation. For example, in many interventions aimed at implementing high-involvement organizations (see Chapter 15), both external and internal consultants provide change support. The external consultant typically brings expertise on organizational design and trains members to implement the design. The internal consultant generally helps members relate to other organizational units, resolve conflicts, and legitimize the change activities within the organization.

5. **Sponsorship.** This concerns the presence of a powerful sponsor who can initiate, allocate, and legitimize resources for the intervention. Sponsors must come from levels in the organization high enough to control appropriate resources, and they must have the visibility and power to nurture the intervention and see that it remains viable. There are many examples of OD interventions that persisted for several years and then collapsed abruptly when the sponsor, usually a top administrator, left the organization. There also are numerous examples of middle managers withdrawing support for interventions because top management did not include them in the change program.

Institutionalization Processes

The framework depicted in Figure 11.2 shows the following five institutionalization processes that can directly affect the degree to which OD interventions are institutionalized:

1. **Socialization.** This concerns the transmission of information about beliefs, preferences, norms, and values with respect to the intervention. Because implementation of OD interventions generally involves considerable learning and experimentation, a continual process of socialization is necessary to promote persistence of the change program. Organization members must focus attention on the evolving nature of the intervention and its ongoing meaning. They must communicate this information to other employees, especially new members. Transmission of information about the intervention helps bring new members onboard and allows participants to reaffirm the beliefs, norms, and values underlying the intervention.[27] For example, employee involvement programs often include initial transmission of information about the intervention, as well as retraining of existing participants and training of new members. Such processes are intended to promote persistence of the program as new behaviors are learned and new members introduced.

2. **Commitment.** This binds people to behaviors associated with the intervention. It includes initial commitment to the program, as well as recommitment over time. Opportunities for commitment should allow people to select the necessary behaviors freely, explicitly, and publicly. These conditions favor high commitment and can promote stability of the new behaviors. Commitment should derive from several organizational levels, including the employees directly involved and the middle and upper managers who can support or thwart the intervention. In many early employee involvement programs, for example, attention was directed at gaining workers' commitment to such programs. Unfortunately, middle managers were often ignored and considerable management resistance to the interventions resulted.

3. **Reward allocation.** This involves linking rewards to the new behaviors required by an intervention. Organizational rewards can enhance the persistence of interventions in at least two ways. First, a combination of intrinsic and extrinsic rewards can reinforce new behaviors. Intrinsic rewards are internal and derive from the opportunities for challenge, development, and accomplishment found in the work. When interventions provide these opportunities, motivation

to perform should persist. This behavior can be further reinforced by providing extrinsic rewards, such as money, for increased contributions. Because the value of extrinsic rewards tends to diminish over time, it may be necessary to revise the reward system to maintain high levels of desired behaviors.

Second, new behaviors will persist to the extent that rewards are perceived as equitable by employees. When new behaviors are fairly compensated, people are likely to develop preferences for those behaviors. Over time, those preferences should lead to normative and value consensus about the appropriateness of the intervention. For example, many employee involvement programs fail to persist because employees feel that their increased contributions to organizational improvements are unfairly rewarded. This is especially true for interventions relying exclusively on intrinsic rewards. People argue that an intervention that provides opportunities for intrinsic rewards also should provide greater pay or extrinsic rewards for higher levels of contribution to the organization.

4. **Diffusion.** This refers to the process of transferring interventions from one system to another. Diffusion facilitates institutionalization by providing a wider organizational base to support the new behaviors. Many interventions fail to persist because they run counter to the values and norms of the larger organization. Rather than support the intervention, the larger organization rejects the changes and often puts pressure on the change target to revert to old behaviors. Diffusion of the intervention to other organizational units reduces this counter-implementation force. It tends to lock in behaviors by providing normative consensus from other parts of the organization. Moreover, the act of transmitting institutionalized behaviors to other systems reinforces commitment to the changes.

5. **Sensing and calibration.** This involves detecting deviations from desired intervention behaviors and taking corrective action. Institutionalized behaviors invariably encounter destabilizing forces, such as changes in the environment, new technologies, and pressures from other departments to nullify changes. These factors cause some variation in performances, preferences, norms, and values. To detect this variation and take corrective actions, organizations must have some sensing mechanism. Sensing mechanisms, such as implementation feedback, provide information about the occurrence of deviations. This knowledge can then initiate corrective actions to ensure that behaviors are more in line with the intervention. For example, if a high level of job discretion associated with a job enrichment intervention does not persist, information about this problem might initiate corrective actions, such as renewed attempts to socialize people or to gain commitment to the intervention.

Indicators of Institutionalization

Institutionalization is not an all-or-nothing concept but reflects degrees of persistence of an intervention. Figure 11.2 shows five indicators of the extent of an intervention's persistence. The extent to which the following factors are present or absent indicates the degree of institutionalization:

1. **Knowledge.** This involves the extent to which organization members have knowledge of the behaviors associated with an intervention. It is concerned with whether members know enough to perform the behaviors and to recognize the consequences of that performance. For example, job enrichment includes a number of new behaviors, such as performing a greater variety of tasks, analyzing information about task performance, and making decisions about work methods and plans.

2. **Performance.** This is concerned with the degree to which intervention behaviors are actually performed. It may be measured by counting the proportion of relevant people performing the behaviors. For example, 60% of the employees in a particular work unit might be performing the job enrichment behaviors described above. Another measure of performance is the frequency with which the new behaviors are performed. In assessing frequency, it is important to account for different variations of the same essential behavior, as well as highly institutionalized behaviors that need to be performed only infrequently.

3. **Preferences.** This involves the degree to which organization members privately accept the organizational changes. This contrasts with acceptance based primarily on organizational sanctions or group pressures. Private acceptance usually is reflected in people's positive attitudes toward the changes and can be measured by the direction and intensity of those attitudes across the members of the work unit receiving the intervention. For example, a questionnaire assessing members' perceptions of a job enrichment program might show that most employees have a strong positive attitude toward making decisions, analyzing feedback, and performing a variety of tasks.

4. **Normative consensus.** This focuses on the extent to which people agree about the appropriateness of the organizational changes. This indicator of institutionalization reflects how fully changes have become part of the normative structure of the organization. Changes persist to the degree members feel that they should support them. For example, a job enrichment program would become institutionalized to the extent that employees support it and see it as appropriate to organizational functioning.

5. **Value consensus.** This is concerned with social consensus on values relevant to the organizational changes. Values are beliefs about how people ought or ought not to behave. They are abstractions from more specific norms. Job enrichment, for example, is based on values promoting employee self-control and responsibility. Different behaviors associated with job enrichment, such as making decisions and performing a variety of tasks, would persist to the extent that employees widely share values of self-control and responsibility.

These five indicators can be used to assess the level of institutionalization of an OD intervention. The more the indicators are present in a situation, the higher will be the degree of institutionalization. Further, these factors seem to follow a specific development order: knowledge, performance, preferences, norms, and values. People must first understand new behaviors or changes before they can perform them effectively. Such performance generates rewards and punishments, which in time affect people's preferences. As many individuals come to prefer the changes, normative consensus about their appropriateness develops. Finally, if there is normative agreement about the changes reflecting a particular set of values, over time there should be some consensus on those values among organization members.

Given this developmental view of institutionalization, it is implicit that whenever one of the last indicators is present, all the previous ones are automatically included as well. For example, if employees normatively agree with the behaviors associated with job enrichment, then they also have knowledge about the behaviors, can perform them effectively, and prefer them. An OD intervention is fully institutionalized only when all five factors are present.

Application 11.2 describes Hewlett-Packard's successful history of institutionalizing a new set of behaviors through structural change. It describes how culture and reward systems can play a strong role in both supporting and constraining change.[28]

INSTITUTIONALIZING STRUCTURAL CHANGE AT HEWLETT-PACKARD

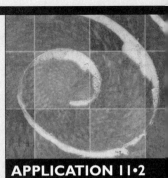

APPLICATION 11•2

In May 2002, the hotly contested acquisition of Compaq by Hewlett-Packard (http://www.hp.com) was finalized. Unlike the major organization changes before it, the acquisition challenged the abilities of this perennial "most admired company" to execute a complex structural change. The success of the integration process described in Application 10.5 is partly due to a store of institutionalized knowledge and capability within the HP organization. This application describes a number of large-scale structural changes at HP. Its repeated ability to carry out such change speaks to the institutionalized capability to manage change.

Since its founding in 1939, HP has implemented successfully no fewer than a dozen major organizational changes, including the transition from a high-tech entrepreneurial start-up to a professionally managed company; from a small instruments business to a leading computer company; from a company oriented around complex-instruction-set computing technology to reduced-instruction-set computing technology; from a technology/engineering-based company to a market/brand-driven company; and, since the appointment of Carly Fiorina as CEO, from a "pure products" company to a services company.

HP's electronics and computer business was characterized by highly volatile technological and market change. It had to quickly adopt, innovate, and implement a variety of technological and organizational changes just to survive. HP's traditional and current strategies were built on innovation, differentiation, and high quality. Another important feature of HP, and one of its more enduring characteristics, is the "HP Way"—a cultural artifact that supports a participative management style and emphasizes commonness of purpose and teamwork on one hand and individual freedom and initiative on the other. Over time, however, the HP Way has been both a constraint to and a facilitator of change.

For example, the HP Way has been at the root of the company's difficulties in institutionalizing structural and behavioral changes to bring about more cooperation among the computer divisions. The initial structural change occurred in 1982 when HP transformed itself from a producer of high-quality electronic measuring instruments into a computer company. At the time, computers and computer-related equipment accounted for only about one-third of revenues and HP was structured into more than 50 highly autonomous and decentralized product divisions focused on specialized niche markets. Individual engineers came up with innovative ideas and "bootstrapped" new products any way they could. Organization members were encouraged to work with other engineers in other departments within the same division, but there was little incentive to coordinate the development of technologies across divisions. This focus on the individual was supported by a performance management system that measured and rewarded "sustained contributions;" the key to success for an individual was working with many people in the division. HP prospered by maximizing each of its parts.

Former CEO John Young's decision to focus on computers fundamentally shifted the keys to success. Computer production required a coordinated effort among the different component divisions and market shares large enough to encourage software vendors to write programs for their machines. In a culture that supported individual contributions over divisional cooperation, Young placed all the instruments divisions into one group and all the computer divisions into another group, a basic design that persisted until the spin-off of the instruments business in 1999. In addition, he centralized research, marketing, and manufacturing, which had previously been assigned to the divisions. Problems quickly arose. In one case, the company's new and highly touted graphics printer would not work with its HP3000 minicomputer. The operating software, made by a third HP division, would not allow the two pieces of hardware to interface.

In response, the computer group formed committees to figure out what new technologies to pursue, which to ignore, which of HP's products should be saved, and which would be shelved. As the committees came up with recommendations, the committees themselves kept multiplying. The company's entrenched culture, built around the HP Way's philosophy of egalitarianism and mutual respect, promoted consensus: Everyone had to have a hand in making a decision.

By 1988, the organization chart still showed a predominantly decentralized divisional structure. What it didn't show was the overwhelming number of committees that slowed decision making and product development. In one case, it took 7 months and nearly a hundred people on nine committees to name the company's new software product. This web of committees, originally designed to foster communication among HP's operating divisions, had pushed up costs and slowed development. In the rapidly changing world of software, personal computers, minicomputers, and printers, the HP Way was hamstringing the organization's success. The ethic of individual freedom balanced by teamwork had produced an unwieldy bureaucracy.

After a series of delays of important new products, John Young reorganized the computer group. In late 1990, he eliminated most of the committees and removed layers of management by dividing the computer business into two groups: one to handle personal computers and peripherals sold through dealers, and the other to handle sales of workstations and minicomputers to big customers. To match the organization structure, the previously centralized corporate salesforce was split and assigned to particular divisions. This change focused HP's computer systems on the market and restored much of the autonomy to the divisions. The balance between individuality and common purpose that characterized the original HP Way was unleashed, leading to several years of strong revenue and profit growth.

In 1993, and before he was officially installed as the new CEO, Lewis Platt announced that HP would pursue the convergence of several base technologies, such as wireless communication, printing, and measurement, to create whole new products for the converging computer, communication, and consumer electronics markets. Implementing such a strategy again depended on strong coordination among HP's product divisions. To ensure that the gains in cooperation were not lost as HP embarked on its new strategy, CEO Platt tied division managers' incentive compensation to working cooperatively with other divisions to create new products that used multiple-division technologies.

The new structure was also a big success. Growth in the printer and PC markets drove revenues from $13.2 billion in 1990 to $38.4 billion in 1996, with profits growing in the same proportions. In 1996, they were the fifth-most-admired company in the United States. In the Internet world, however, their success was short-lived, and critics argued that Platt's subsequent attention to "soft" issues such as work/life balance and promoting diversity, rather than launching an Internet strategy, resulted in stalled growth. For 1997 and 1998, and aided by the Asian financial crisis, growth rates slipped to single digits. In the summer of 1998, Platt believed that HP had simply become too big and complex. In March 1999, he announced and implemented the spin-off of HP's $7.6 billion instruments division, the business on which the company had been founded.

Shortly after being named HP's fourth CEO in 1999, and the first to come from outside the company, Carly Fiorina laid out her agenda: create a compelling vision for HP, implement a structure to support the vision, and launch a marketing campaign to build the HP brand. The vision called for a shift from a stand-alone products company to a services company. The structural change involved merging the four major product divisions into a group focused on computing and a group focused on printing. This structure for the first time united HP's laser and inkjet printing divisions and furthered the opportunities for computer products to coordinate their activities. Fiorina also announced a major marketing campaign focused on the HP Way's value of innovation. Then, in the fall of 2001, Fiorina announced the intended acquisition of Compaq computers.

The lessons of history have not been lost on the CEO. The acquisition process pulled knowledge from the experiences of other mergers and other changes within HP; it acknowledged the strengths and weaknesses of the HP Way; and structural changes have been backed up with changes in the compensation system. Few organizations have implemented as many major changes and still maintained both strong financial performance and corporate reputation. HP's history of seeing the need for, implementing, and reaping the benefits of structural change is a testament to its ability to institutionalize change, as these examples demonstrate.

■ SUMMARY

We discussed in this chapter the final two stages of planned change—evaluating interventions and institutionalizing them. Evaluation was discussed in terms of two kinds of necessary feedback: implementation feedback, concerned with whether the intervention is being implemented as intended, and evaluation feedback, indicating whether the intervention is producing expected results. The former comprises collected data about features of the intervention and its immediate effects, which are fed back repeatedly and at short intervals. The latter comprises data about the long-term effects of the intervention, which are fed back at long intervals.

Evaluation of interventions also involves decisions about measurement and research design. Measurement issues focus on selecting variables and designing good measures. Ideally, measurement decisions should derive from the theory underlying the intervention and should include measures of the features of the intervention and its immediate and long-term consequences. Further, these measures should be operationally defined, reliable, and valid and should involve multiple methods, such as a combination of questionnaires, interviews, and company records.

Research design focuses on setting up the conditions for making valid assessments of an intervention's effects. This involves ruling out explanations for the observed results other than the intervention. Although randomized experimental designs are rarely feasible in OD, quasi-experimental designs exist for eliminating alternative explanations.

OD interventions are institutionalized when the change program persists and becomes part of the organization's normal functioning. A framework for understanding and improving the institutionalization of interventions identified organization characteristics (congruence, stability of environment and technology, and unionization) and intervention characteristics (goal specificity, programmability, level of change target, internal support, and sponsorship) that affect institutionalization processes. The framework also described specific institutionalization processes (socialization, commitment, reward allocation, diffusion, and sensing and calibration) that directly affect indicators of intervention persistence (knowledge, performance, preferences, normative consensus, and value consensus).

■ NOTES

1. T. Cummings and E. Molloy, *Strategies for Improving Productivity and the Quality of Work Life* (New York: Praeger, 1977); J. Whitfield, W. Anthony, and K. Kacmar, "Evaluation of Team-Based Management: A Case Study," *Journal of Organizational Change Management* 8, 2 (1995): 17–28.

2. S. Mohrman and T. Cummings, "Implementing Quality-of-Work-Life Programs by Managers," in *The NTL Manager's Handbook,* eds. R. Ritvo and A. Sargent (Arlington, Va.: NTL Institute, 1983), 320–28; T. Cummings and S. Mohrman, "Self-Designing Organizations: Towards Implementing Quality-of-Work-Life Innovations," in *Research in Organizational Change and Development,* vol. 1, eds. R. Woodman and W. Pasmore (Greenwich, Conn.: JAI Press, 1987), 275–310.

3. T. Cummings, "Institutionalizing Quality-of-Work-Life Programs: The Case for Self-Design" (paper delivered at the annual meeting of the Academy of Management, Dallas, Tex., August 1983).

4. Cummings and Molloy, *Strategies.*

5. P. Goodman, *Assessing Organizational Change: The Rushton Quality of Work Experiment* (New York: John Wiley & Sons, 1979); A. Van de Ven and D. Ferry, eds., *Measuring and Assessing Organizations* (New York: John Wiley & Sons, 1985); E. Lawler III, D. Nadler, and C. Cammann, eds., *Organizational Assessment: Perspectives on the Measurement of Organizational Behavior and Quality of Work Life* (New York: John Wiley & Sons, 1980); A. Van de Ven and W. Joyce, eds., *Perspectives on Organizational Design and Behavior* (New York: John Wiley & Sons, 1981); S. Seashore, E. Lawler III, P. Mirvis, and C. Cammann, eds., *Assessing Organizational Change: A Guide to Methods, Measures, and Practices* (New York: Wiley-Interscience, 1983).

6. B. Macy and P. Mirvis, "Organizational Change Efforts: Methodologies for Assessing Organizational Effectiveness and Program Costs Versus Benefits," *Evaluation Review* 6 (1982): 301–72.

7. Macy and Mirvis, "Organizational Change Efforts."

8. J. Nunnally, *Psychometric Theory,* 2d ed. (New York: McGraw-Hill, 1978); J. Kirk and M. Miller, *Reliability and Validity in Qualitative Research* (Beverly Hills, Calif.: Sage Publications, 1985).

9. D. Miller, *Handbook of Research Design and Social Measurement* (Thousand Oaks, Calif.: Sage Publications, 1991); N. Denzin and Y. Lincoln, eds., *Handbook of Qualitative Research* (Thousand Oaks, Calif.: Sage Publications, 1994).

10. R. Hackman and G. Oldham, *Work Redesign* (Reading, Mass.: Addison-Wesley, 1980), 275–306.

11. Nunnally, *Psychometric Theory.*

12. M. Huberman and M. Miles, *Qualitative Data Analysis: An Expanded Sourcebook,* 2d ed. (Newbury Park, Calif.: Sage Publications, 1994).

13. J. Taylor and D. Bowers, *Survey of Organizations: A Machine-Scored Standardized Questionnaire Instrument* (Ann Arbor: Institute for Social Research, University of Michigan, 1972); *Comprehensive Quality-of-Work-Life Survey* (Los Angeles: Center for Effective Organizations, University of Southern California, 1981); C. Cammann, M. Fichman, G. D. Jenkins, and J. Klesh, "Assessing the Attitudes and Perceptions of Organizational Members," in *Assessing Organizational Change: A Guide to Methods, Measures, and Practices,* eds. S. Seashore, E. Lawler III, P. Mirvis, and C. Cammann (New York: Wiley-Interscience, 1983), 71–119.

14. R. Bullock and D. Svyantek, "The Impossibility of Using Random Strategies to Study the Organization Development Process," *Journal of Applied Behavioral Science* 23 (1987): 255–62.

15. D. Campbell and J. Stanley, *Experimental and Quasi-Experimental Design for Research* (Chicago: Rand McNally, 1966); T. Cook and D. Campbell, *Quasi-Experimentation: Design and Analysis Issues for Field Settings* (Chicago: Rand McNally, 1979).

16. E. Lawler III, D. Nadler, and P. Mirvis, "Organizational Change and the Conduct of Assessment Research," in *Assessing Organizational Change: A Guide to Methods, Measures and Practices*, eds. S. Seashore, E. Lawler III, P. Mirvis, and C. Cammann (New York: Wiley-Interscience, 1983), 19–47.

17. Cook and Campbell, *Quasi-Experimentation.*

18. R. Golembiewski and R. Munzenrider, "Measuring Change by OD Designs," *Journal of Applied Behavioral Science* 12 (April-June 1976): 133–57.

19. W. Randolph and R. Edwards, "Assessment of Alpha, Beta and Gamma Changes in a University-Setting OD Intervention," *Academy of Management Proceedings* (1978): 313–17; J. Terborg, G. Howard, and S. Maxwell, "Evaluating Planned Organizational Change: A Method for Assessing Alpha, Beta, and Gamma Change," *Academy of Management Review* 7 (1982): 292–95; R. Millsap and S. Hartog, "Alpha, Beta, and Gamma Change in Evaluation Research: A Structural Equation Approach," *Journal of Applied Psychology* 73 (1988): 574–84; R. Thompson and J. Hunt, "Inside the Black Box of Alpha, Beta, and Gamma Change: Using a Cognitive-processing Model to Assess Attitude Structure," *Academy of Management Review* 21 (1996): 655–91.

20. This application was written and contributed by Louis DeMerode. The references in the application are to J. Kotter, *Leading Change.* (Cambridge: Harvard Business School Press, 1996) and R. Beckhard and R. Harris, *Organization Transitions: Managing Complex Change*, 2nd ed. (Reading, Mass.: Addison Wesley, 1987).

21. D. Ciampa, *Total Quality: A User's Guide for Implementation* (Reading, Mass.: Addison-Wesley, 1992); P. Senge, *The Fifth Discipline* (New York: Doubleday, 1990); Cummings and Mohrman, "Self-Designing Organizations"; C. Worley, D. Hitchin, and W. Ross, *Integrated Strategic Change* (Reading, Mass.: Addison-Wesley, 1996).

22. This section is based on the work of P. Goodman and J. Dean, "Creating Long-Term Organizational Change," in *Change in Organizations*, ed. P. Goodman (San Francisco: Jossey-Bass, 1982), 226–79. To date, the framework is largely untested and unchallenged. Ledford's process model of persistence (see note 22) is the only other model proposed to explain institutionalization. The empirical support for either model, however, is nil.

23. G. Ledford, "The Persistence of Planned Organizational Change: A Process Theory Perspective" (Ph.D. diss., University of Michigan, 1984).

24. L. Zucker, "Normal Change or Risky Business: Institutional Effects on the 'Hazard' of Change in Hospital Organizations, 1959–1979," *Journal of Management Studies* 24 (1987): 671–700.

25. S. Mohrman and T. Cummings, *Self-Designing Organizations: Learning How to Create High Performance* (Reading, Mass.: Addison-Wesley, 1989).

26. J. Martin and C. Siehl, "Organizational Cultures and Counterculture: An Uneasy Symbiosis," *Organizational Dynamics* (1983): 52–64; D. Meyerson and J. Martin, "Cultural Change: An Integration of Three Different Views," *Journal of Management Studies* 24 (1987): 623–47.

27. L. Zucker, "The Role of Institutionalization in Cultural Persistence," *American Sociological Review* 42 (1977): 726–43; R. Jacobs, "Institutionalizing Organization Change Through Cascade Training," *Journal of European Industrial Training* 26 (2002): 177–83.

28. R. Von Werssowetz and M. Beer, "Human Resources at Hewlett-Packard," *Harvard Business School Case 9-482-125* (Boston: Harvard Business School, 1982); B. Buell and R. Hof, "Hewlett-Packard Rethinks Itself," *Business Week* (1 April 1991): 76–79; R. Hof, "Suddenly, Hewlett-Packard Is Doing Everything Right," *Business Week* (23 March 1992): 88–89; "Can John Young Redesign Hewlett-Packard," *Business Week* (6 December 1982): 72–78; J. Levine, "Mild-Mannered Hewlett-Packard Is Making Like Superman," *Business Week* (7 March 1988): 110–14; R. Hof, "Hewlett-Packard Digs Deep for a Digital Future," *Business Week* (18 October 1993): 72–75; A. Fisher, "America's Most Admired Corporations," *Fortune* (4 March 1996): 90–98; P. Burrows with P. Elstrom, "The Boss," *Business Week* (2 August 1999): 76–83; D. Hamilton, "H-P to Relaunch Its Brand, Adopt New Logo," *Wall Street Journal* (16 November 1999): B6; D. Hamilton and S. Thurm, "H-P to Spin Off Its Measurement Operations," *Wall Street Journal* (3 March 1999): A3; E. Nee, "Lew Platt: Why I Dismembered HP," *Fortune* (29 March 1999): 167–69.

It's Your Turn

To: STEVE@xyz.com
From: TOM@university.edu

Dear Steve,

I enjoyed seeing you at the OD Network conference. I've been trying to reach you by phone, but no luck, so I thought I would drop you an e-mail. Your secretary said you were on a job out of state. I have been working with several clients and my teaching load is getting pretty hectic. Are you interested in working together again? I've been contacted by Newfangled Software to discuss some management training, possibly OD. It seems like you worked for them several years ago. Is this correct or have I got my organizations mixed up?

Hope to hear from you soon and maybe we can work something out at Newfangled.

Tom

To: TOM@university.edu
From: STEVE@xyz.com

Dear Tom,

Sorry to have missed your calls, but I was in Oklahoma City doing some work with the State Department. Thanks for the e-mail, although it triggered some old memories. Excuse my rambling in what I will share with you about Newfangled Software. Please keep this confidential. Yes, you were right about me working with them. I looked in my records and it was nine years ago. I have been indirectly keeping in touch with how things are going there through some of my old contacts.

Their president, David Dyer, has been under severe pressure from three of their five board members. I can't say he doesn't deserve at least some of the blame for their current problems, though I suspect the board members have their own political agendas. I was contacted by a guy named Irwin from their training department to go on their annual retreat with the middle and top managers. Irwin is OK, and if he has a fault, it's his taking his work too seriously given the current culture at Newfangled. I was to initially do

some management development training on a very superficial level. David Dyer had only been there for several months. Irwin and I decided it would be prudent to go easy at first until David got the lay of the land. Irwin, not David, was my contact person because Irwin was responsible for all of the management and technical training.

Anyway, the three-day retreat was "weird" but, reflecting back on things, not at all unusual. The retreat started when we were all loaded up in a bus. None of the participants was told where they were going, so it was to be a big surprise. We traveled about three hours to a dude ranch in the local mountains. I was supposed to provide the training for one afternoon and the following morning. Irwin helped out. We did a few icebreaker exercises, followed by some kind of nonthreatening team exercise. This was followed by reports from the teams on what they thought were effective supervision skills. It was really low-key stuff. I arranged the teams to be composed of managers from both middle and top levels.

You know, I can remember what happened as if it were yesterday. David remained real aloof. I had previously arranged for him, like everyone else, to be in a team. He joked around with several other men for about thirty minutes before joining his team. Meanwhile, his team went to work without him. He finally joined them but did not say much. After a few minutes he got up and went over to another team and talked with them about the tennis game they had the previous day. I did not confront him at the time, which, reflecting on things, may have been a mistake on my part. But I rationalized that he was new and wanted to get to know his people on a social basis. Besides, don't us OD types say we should take our clients "where they're at"?

Well, that was the afternoon session. Not exactly a roaring success, but a number of the participants were really getting into the exercises. The next morning went about the same. David played the part of the social butterfly. His behavior was a bit obvious to others. Reflecting back on things, I think he was intimidated. This was his first president position. We had a team-building exercise followed by a discussion on how departments in general could work better together—nothing specific. I remember one fellow got real annoyed at some of the other teams for joking around. He said something to the effect that this was why it took so long for new products to get out the door. Several others agreed, but then David said what we were doing in the teams was just a fun game and did not mean anything. The morning session ended OK, for the most part, though David and several others left early.

Nothing more happened with me and the company. Irwin called me to say his budget had been cut, and they were not able to do any more training for a while. I read between the lines and politely wished him well. Several years ago, I heard from a friend, Patricia Kingsley, who I have worked with on other jobs. She said she had been recruited to conduct training at Newfangled's annual retreat. They flew over a thousand miles to a retreat at Cape Cod. Big bucks on this trip. It was for five days, and she was to provide training for four half-day sessions. Halfway through the first session, David recruited three of his top administrators and they went for a canoe ride. Patricia said you could hear them out on the lake laughing and carrying on while the rest of the team was working. At each of the other three sessions, participation dropped off dramatically until she ended up with less than a quarter of the people in the last session. She said she had never seen anything like it.

Their training sessions occur every May, so it looks like it is your turn. No consultant seems to get past the annual retreat. I would like to work with you again, but I think it would be in everyone's best interest that I pass on this one. The pay is good and maybe you will get a good vacation out of it. On the other hand, don't take your lack of success personally. You may have a different experience because the board may have made some changes. Stay in touch and give me a call.

Sincerely,

Steve

Questions

1. Assume that you are going to meet with Irwin to discuss the training session for the next management retreat. What contracting issues are most important for you?

2. How will you address the issue of David's past behavior?

Source: *Reprinted and adapted with permission from a case titled "The OD Letters" that appeared in D. Harvey and D. Brown,* An Experiential Approach to Organization Development *(Upper Saddle River, N.J.: Prentice Hall, 1996).*

Sunflower Incorporated

Sunflower Incorporated is a large distribution company with over 5,000 employees and gross sales of over $700 million (1991). The company purchases and distributes salty snack foods and liquor to independent retail stores throughout the United States and Canada. Salty snack foods include corn chips, potato chips, cheese curls, tortilla chips, and peanuts. The United States and Canada are divided into 22 regions, each with its own central warehouse, salespeople, finance department, and purchasing department. The company distributes national as well as local brands and packages some items under private labels. The head office encourages each region to be autonomous because of local tastes and practices. The northeast United States, for example, consumes a greater percentage of Canadian whisky and American bourbon, while the West consumes more light liquors, such as vodka, gin, and rum. Snack foods in the Southwest are often seasoned to reflect Mexican tastes.

Early in 1989, Sunflower began using a financial reporting system that compared sales, costs, and profits across regions. Management was surprised to learn that profits varied widely. By 1990, the differences were so great that management decided some standardization was necessary. They believed that highly profitable regions were sometimes using lower-quality items, even seconds, to boost profit margins. This practice could hurt Sunflower's image. Other regions were facing intense price competition in order to hold market share. National distributors were pushing hard to increase their market share. Frito-lay, Bordens, Nabisco, Procter & Gamble (Pringles), and Standard Brands (Planter's peanuts) were pushing hard to increase market share by cutting prices and launching new products.

As these problems accumulated, Mr. Steelman, president of Sunflower, decided to create a new position to monitor pricing and purchasing practices. Agnes Albanese was hired from the finance department of a competing organization. Her new title was director of pricing and purchasing, and she reported to the vice president of finance, Mr. Mobley. Steelman and Mobley gave Albanese great latitude in organizing her job and encouraged her to establish whatever rules and procedures were necessary. She was also encouraged to gather information from each region. Each region was notified of her appointment by an official memo sent to the regional managers. A copy of the memo was posted on each warehouse bulletin board. The announcement was also made in the company newspaper.

After 3 weeks on the job, Albanese decided that pricing and purchasing decisions should be standardized across regions. As a first step, she wanted the financial executive in each region to notify her of any change in local prices of more than 3%. She also decided that all new contracts for local purchases of more than $5,000 should be cleared through her office. (Approximately 60% of items distributed in the regions was purchased in large quantities and supplied from the home office. The other 40% was purchased and distributed within the region.) Albanese believed that the only way to standardize operations was for each region to notify the home office in advance of any change in prices or purchases. Albanese discussed the proposed policy with Mobley. He agreed, so they submitted a formal proposal to the president and board of directors, who approved the plan. Sunflower was moving into the peak holiday season, so Albanese wanted to implement the new procedures right away. She decided to send an email to the financial and purchasing executives in each region notifying them of the new procedures. The change would be inserted in all policy and procedure manuals throughout Sunflower within 4 months.

Albanese showed a draft of the email to Mobley and invited his comments. Mobley said the Internet was an excellent idea but wondered if it was sufficient. The regions handle hundreds of items and were used to decentralized decision making. Mobley suggested that Albanese ought to visit the regions and discuss purchasing and pricing policies with the executives. Albanese refused, saying that the trips would be expensive and time-consuming. She had so many things to do at headquarters that a trip was impossible. Mobley also suggested waiting to implement the procedures until after the annual company meeting in 3 months. Albanese said this would take too long because the procedures would not take effect until after the peak sales season. She believed the procedures were needed now. The email went out the next day.

During the next few days, replies came in from most of the regions. The executives were in agreement with the email and said they would be happy to cooperate.

Eight weeks later, Albanese had not received notices from any regions about local price or purchase changes. Other executives who had visited regional warehouses indicated to her that the regions were busy as usual. Regional executives seemed to be following usual procedures for that time of year.

Questions

1. How well did Albanese manage the pricing and purchasing changes at Sunflower? Were the changes implemented successfully? How would you find this out?

2. What might Albanese have done differently? What should she do now?

Source: Adapted from R. Daft, Organization Theory and Design *(St. Paul: West, 1983), pp. 334–36.*

Evaluating the Change Agent Program at Siemens Nixdorf (A)

Siemens Nixdorf Informationssysteme (SNI) was the largest European-owned computer manufacturer and information technology vendor in 1994. The company was created by a 1990 merger between Nixdorf Computer, an entrepreneurial minicomputer firm, and the mainframe computer division of Siemens AG, the German electronics giant. The company offered a broad range of computer products, from personal computers and mainframes to software and support services. In 1994, the company posted $8 billion in revenues and employed 39,000 people worldwide. Despite its size and a strong market presence in Europe, SNI had not posted a profitable quarter since the merger. The company lost over $350 million in fiscal 1994. Over 65% of its products were sold in Germany, and the company had a weak base in the growing Asian and North American markets. While the organization had a strong technological focus, SNI was slow to respond to market changes requiring more customer responsiveness and market shifts away from large mainframe systems. In addition, SNI's efforts to trim high labor costs were hampered by strong union pressure and strict German layoff regulations. Industry analysts observed that the company was constrained by a rigid corporate culture established during the merger. The organizational structure was considered too bureaucratic in its approach to decision making for the rapidly evolving market.

In mid-1994, in the search for profitability, a decision was made by the Chairman of Siemens AG (the 100% shareholder of SNI) to bring in a new CEO for Siemens Nixdorf. Gerhard Schulmeyer, President and CEO of the American division of Asea Brown Boveri (ABB), a Swedish-Swiss engineering company, was chosen. Schulmeyer wanted SNI to become more customer driven and responsive to the market, and he was convinced that the major adjustments necessary to recreate SNI could only occur alongside a radical change in the corporate culture. He wanted to create an SNI culture that enhanced entrepreneurial thinking and team building. He aimed to replace top-down procedures with innovative leadership that rewarded decision making and risk taking.

To accomplish these goals, Schulmeyer initiated a companywide culture change program that had three major objectives:

1. To change the behavior of managers and employees with a view to achieving dramatic improvement in performance and results
2. To change work systems to foster a culture of operational excellence
3. To change processes to emphasize the customer and to ensure the primacy of customer service

He believed that SNI's radical change requirements could only be met holistically, addressing structure, systems, behavior, and strategic philosophy together, underpinned by a continuous learning process for both individuals and the organization itself. A road map (Figure 1) was created and published, and execution was set in motion in October 1994. Of particular importance in creating a foundation for change at SNI were the behavioral and learning components of the road map. On the behavioral side, a set of mutually reinforcing initiatives was introduced to encourage new ways of acting and to support the development of new capabilities. These initiatives included the Culture Change and Friday Forum Programs (described below), a fine-tuning of the organization's matrix structure, a reengineering and profit improvement program, the introduction of a new management information system (MIS), and corporate and business strategy initiatives. On the learning side, the organization committed to a Change Agent Program (described below). Two additional educational programs, the Entrepreneurial Development Program and the Management Development Program, supported the learning objectives of the change agent program.

THE CULTURE CHANGE PROGRAM

The process started with the scheduling of four major change events in Hanover, Germany. The first, Hanover I, held in December 1994, was a gathering of selected SNI employees with the theme of "Giving Employees a Voice in Defining

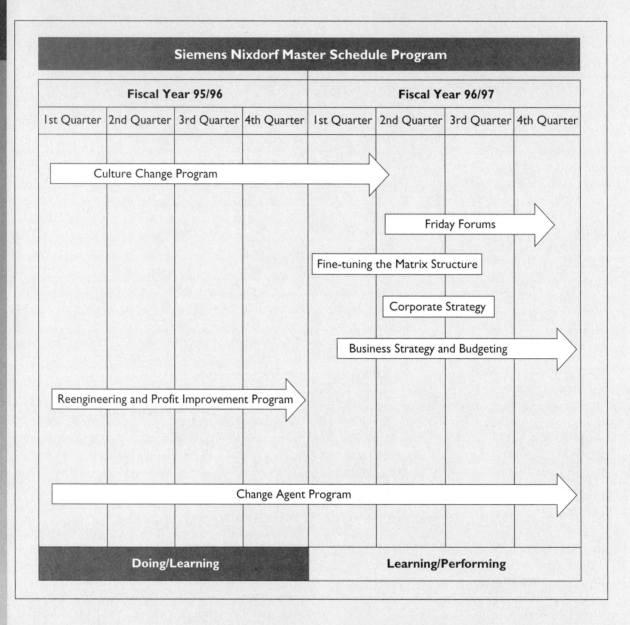

Siemens Nixdorf Master Schedule Program

	Fiscal Year 95/96				Fiscal Year 96/97			
	1st Quarter	2nd Quarter	3rd Quarter	4th Quarter	1st Quarter	2nd Quarter	3rd Quarter	4th Quarter

Culture Change Program

Friday Forums

Fine-tuning the Matrix Structure

Corporate Strategy

Business Strategy and Budgeting

Reengineering and Profit Improvement Program

Change Agent Program

Doing/Learning | **Learning/Performing**

the New Culture." Over 300 employees, called Opinion Leaders, met with 75 managers, known as Business Leaders, to agree on changes that were worth striving for at the company. Nineteen topics were identified (e.g., "Establishing an Environment of Creativity"), followed by brainstorming to translate ideas for change into actions. The discussions led to the establishment of 60 action teams with agendas that required tangible results within 90 days. A Results Fair was held in Munich in May 1995, where 12,000 employees were shown what had been accomplished so far on the action items and what would happen in the future.

Hanover II, in June 1995, followed the theme of "Giving Customers a Voice in Defining the New Culture." A new set of 300 SNI Opinion Leaders and 75 SNI managers teamed up with 54 customer representatives to develop change ideas and recommendations. An additional 18 action initiatives were generated, such as "How to Hear the Voice of the Internal Customer." As with Hanover I, a Results Fair in January 1996 presented the status of the work on the actions identified and assigned during Hanover II.

Hanover III, in December 1995, had the theme of "Giving Partners a Voice in Defining the New Culture." During this meeting, SNI worked on strengthening its partner relationships. In attendance were 350 employees and 40 SNI partners, who looked for new ways to reinforce and expand the areas in which they worked together.

Hanover IV took place in October 1996, with a presentation by Schulmeyer on the need to develop a new matrix organization. This final event involved decentralizing the organization's businesses and associated responsibilities and delegating them to some 250 "entrepreneurs" (Unit Managers) out in the field with full profit-and-loss responsibility.

The Hanover meetings were designed to help people learn new patterns of behavior. Instead of the typical hierarchical distinctions, first names were the rule, and everyone was free to intervene in the discussions. This atmosphere deeply affected participants, who returned to their day-to-day activities motivated and fired up with a new sense of mission.

To disseminate change information from the Hanover conferences and to stimulate change ideas from throughout the company, a series of Friday Forums was introduced. Whereas the Hanover meetings were large and one-off public events, Friday Forums were small-group discussions that attempted to build a frank and open communication environment within the fabric of the organization. Any topic could be brought to the meetings, from day-to-day problems to "hot potatoes," and involved employees from all levels of the company. Information exchanged in the forums was broadcast more widely throughout the organization via electronic mail twice a month. In addition to sharing information, employees were encouraged to form small groups to act on issues raised in the meetings.

THE CHANGE AGENT PROGRAM

During Hanover I, Schulmeyer introduced the Change Agent Program (CAP) that sent 20 employees to the United States to participate in a 13-week training event administered by a well-known management consulting firm known for business reengineering. The goal of the CAP was to build an understanding of business fundamentals and business change along three dimensions: customer, competitiveness, and culture.

The high-potential participants were selected from the original 300 "opinion leaders" invited to the Hanover I conference. A key element of the CAP was that each participant, or change agent

(CA), was sponsored by two members of management: (1) a "Business Leader," who was typically a senior manager in the division in which the CA worked, and who funded the CA's participation in the program and (2) an "Executive Sponsor," one of 14 Executive Board members, who was responsible for the entire division in which the CA worked.

The 13-week program was held at MIT and Stanford, with site visits arranged to high-technology companies in the Boston and Silicon Valley areas. In addition to classroom learning, each participant performed an analysis of a project drawn from a previously defined list of the most important challenges facing the company. The projects spanned a variety of topics from improving innovation at SNI to exploring international markets for the company. The CAs discussed and defined their projects in cooperation with their sponsors. The program expected the sponsors to provide leadership, guidance, and support to the CAs, and to help them implement their project and other goals upon return to SNI. Much of the CAP instruction, including case studies, company visits, and coaching was intended to help CAs find innovative ways to approach and implement their projects. The project findings were to be implemented on the employee's return to SNI. A further post-program task for the employee was to act as a catalyst and multiplier of change to ensure that the culture change initiative would be spread across the company.

Over the course of 6 years and 142 participants, several changes were made to the Change Agent Program. Although the broad "catalyst for change" goal remained constant, the operational dynamics shifted over the tenure of the program. For example, although the first program comprised 13 continuous weeks of study, subsequent programs broke down into 2-to-3-week modules to avoid long periods away from home. The projects continued to receive heavy emphasis as did the retention of a high level of stress among participants. In years 2 and 3 of the program, the management consulting firm administrating the program also changed. Internally, questions were raised about whether the consulting firm or Siemens Nixdorf was in control of the program. Towards the end of the third program, the participants' level of discontent grew to a point where they decided to take over design of the final module. There was a sense that the project was too dominant with a resultant lack of concern in the program design for individual development.

In 1998, substantial changes were made to the program. An internal design team was formed that included three CAs from the previous year's program. Supporting the culture change process within SNI continued as an important goal, but the development of leadership, business, and project management skills grew in significance. The projects shifted from being the driving force in the program to being an important but not dominant way for participants to apply their new skills. An original intent for a "10X" return—the cost of instruction was estimated to be about $100,000 and the projects were expected to produce $1 million in revenue increases or cost decreases—was dropped. It was replaced by a stretch goal agreed on by the participant and his or her Business Leader and Executive Sponsor. A study trip to Southeast Asia was added to the program, to complement the time spent in Boston and Silicon Valley, and a module at INSEAD was added in 1999. Thus, although geographic coverage was extended, considerable effort was expended to make it a more cost-effective program. Cost per participant dropped from $100,000 to about $50,000 when the program was brought in-house.

Internal management of the CAP by SNI proved short-lived. In October 1998, SNI was fully integrated into the parent company, Siemens AG, and ceased to exist. Siemens had become exasperated with the perceived underperformance of its computer subsidiary and absorbed all of its activities. With this transition, the culture change program came to an end, as did Gerhard Schulmeyer's champion's role. It was decided, however, to continue the CAP under the auspices of the newly formed division—Information and Communication (I&C)—at Siemens while retaining the same internal program team. A strong content program was delivered in 1999, with significant individual benefits resulting. Unfortunately, the raison d'être of inculcating the whole corporation with culture change had been lost because most senior managers at Siemens showed little interest in learning from either the project results or the enhanced skills of participants. Interestingly, one or two business units did continue to encourage the CAs to act as change catalysts, with positive results in terms of both behavior and performance. The program was run again in 2000, when mid-level managers rather than high-potential participants were chosen. By this time, the focus had changed to become more of a leadership excellence program. Because of these shifts in the environmental and political situation, the official CAP was terminated at the end of 2000.

Questions

1. Critique the change process initiated and executed by Gerhard Schulmeyer. What do you see as the strengths and weaknesses of his efforts?

2. Assume that the head of the Information and Communication division at Siemens contacts you after receiving a variety of emails and voice mails supporting and questioning the CAP program. A request is made for you to conduct an evaluation of the CAP program. Based on the above information, design and justify an evaluation process, including the contracting terms or "essential wants" that you think are critical in carrying out the assessment, the interview and/or survey questions you would ask, and the sampling design you would use.

Source: *Adapted and excerpted with permission from Philip Dover, "Change Agents at Work: Lessons from Siemens Nixdorf," Journal of Change Management, (2003) vol. 3, no. 3, 243–57. http://www.tandf.co.uk/journals/titles/14697017.asp.*

Initiating Change in the Manufacturing and Distribution Division of PolyProd

Information management has become a critical competency in modern high-technology firms. These companies simply cannot afford to waste time reinventing or re-justifying existing methodologies, and costly errors—even injuries—can result from not having and following appropriate operating procedures. Yet, the burgeoning quantity of data, information, and knowledge that must be retrieved and used has begun to tax some companies' abilities to keep up. In addition, many of the people within these organizations are not trained properly or willing to deal with formal information systems.

You are Roberta Jackson, a concerned, experienced first-level project manager working at the headquarters site of the manufacturing and distribution division (M&DDiv) of PolyProd, a corporation that develops, markets, and manufactures a variety of high technology products for industry and home use. You are convinced, based on your experience and some informal information that you have collected, that failing to improve the current information management practices will cost PolyProd millions of dollars in direct expenses and could contribute to long-term market share declines in PolyProd products. As a result, you believe that it is necessary to change M&DDiv's documentation processes and procedures. These processes govern the creation and use of the specifications and formal procedures required by the manufacturing organization.

You anticipate that the undertaking will involve change and project management techniques traditional in large engineering firms, and that it should proceed along well-trodden paths: you will plan the project, "sell" it to management and obtain the authority to begin, and then allocate resources and monitor progress until you can declare victory. The following sections describe the M&DDiv's organization, the documentation system, and other factors contributing to the current situation.

THE M&DDIV ORGANIZATION AND CULTURE

M&DDiv manufactures and distributes a small but lucrative subset of PolyProd's products and has five locations around the world. The headquarters organization is located in the United States. It centrally manages the other four sites in Canada, Asia, Africa, and Europe, but also allows them a lot of autonomy in decision-making. Each location houses both manufacturing and distribution processes.

The variety and complexity of M&DDiv's products have increased markedly, as have the speed, intricacy, and expense of the unique high-volume automated manufacturing processes that produce the products. As a result, M&DDiv has been growing rapidly during its entire 11-year history, experiencing exponential increases in locations, sales, capital equipment, product lines, and personnel. Support systems, such as the information and knowledge management system, have struggled to keep up with the growth. Moreover, the required hiring of many inexperienced or temporary personnel has stretched the ability of M&DDiv to maintain the culture of PolyProd. These trends are expected to continue unabated for the foreseeable future.

The company's business strategy charters the headquarters site with designing products and their manufacturing methodologies, and then with transferring the maturing manufacturing processes offshore to take advantage of the lower tax rates and cheaper labor at the four production locations. The key success factors for the headquarters site are rapid design innovation and time-to-volume-manufacturability. The priorities of the production sites are shippable-product volume, quality, and cost-effectiveness.

Over the last several years, the friction developing between headquarters and the other locations has been increasing. The sites are generally dissatisfied with what they regard as a patronizing and demanding attitude, and resent policies and assignments unilaterally sent out by headquarters. Headquarters, in turn, resents the fierce and sometimes unnecessary individualism of the other locations. Throughout M&DDiv, there is a subtle but strong resistance to large-scale or externally initiated change. This is especially true when the change involves converging all sites to a single process or technology. Much of this is due to the pressures of maintaining high production levels; unproven change is simply too risky. Historically, any attempt to institute a change by dictate has been doomed to failure. For example, announced changes typically take three to five years to institutionalize, and even after that time, there is considerable residual resistance or malicious compliance. It is not uncommon for otherwise successful projects to wither and die due to lack of implementation support.

Headquarters has its own internal issues. First, it has a long-standing tradition of conservatism and hardened reluctance to change. Second, it is still reeling from the rapid growth that has transformed it from a small, independent factory into the hub of a global business. Finally, it is suffering from a discontinuity in its own cultural history: Rapid hiring and promotion, insufficient mentoring, heavy outsourcing and downsizing of certain competencies, and extensive use of a temporary workforce in non-engineering areas has put extreme pressures on the once homogenous and intensely loyal culture.

In a static and stable environment, the relationship between headquarters and the other locations might be considered an acceptable cost of doing business. In M&DDiv, however, the stakes are far too high to allow it to continue. The anticipated continued growth will magnify all problems exponentially, and the seriousness of the problems could very well inhibit or halt that growth. Because M&DDiv's revenue represents a significant portion of PolyProd's bottom line, much of PolyProd's total growth is contingent on M&DDiv's continued expansion. If M&DDiv falters, PolyProd could well follow.

THE DOCUMENTATION PROBLEM

In PolyProd, quality is everything. The company simply cannot allow bad products to reach the customer, but neither can it afford to scrap good products that may have failed too-stringent tests. The precision high-volume manufacturing processes used by all M&DDiv sites utilize rigorous quality control procedures to ensure the highest yield of good products and the lowest scrap. This is achieved by statistical analyses of interim results and by standardizing tasks and tooling as much as possible. This, in turn, hinges on a huge quantity of documentation, including material and process specifications, operating instructions, maintenance information, replication data (bills of materials, assembly and checkout instructions, etc.), and the like. In summary, good products require either good documentation or expensive workarounds and corrections.

- *The documentation system.* The documentation "system" consists of a number of components: an electronic "vault" where a variety of documents are kept, the computer systems and networks that allow access to the vault, the documents (electronic files) themselves, the protocols for routing and approving revisions, and perhaps most critical and most dangerous, all of the people who interact with these components. To be effective, a documentation system has to be carefully developed, actively maintained, and closely protected from inappropriate alteration. Since products and their production equipment migrate between sites, the documentation must also be portable and useable without extensive revision.

When a new product design is initiated, a suite of drawings and other specifications is created immediately and remains with the project for its whole life. The design engineer's early sketches and notes are entered into an electronic "vault" where they are protected against loss and inadvertent change. As experiments are done and prototypes are created, test results and design refinements are added to the vault. As the design moves into the pre-manufacturing stage, parts lists, materials specifications, assembly instructions, test procedures, and quality criteria are added to the file. When the automated equipment to produce the product in volume is designed, its information joins the product's information in the vault.

The vault provides functions other than safekeeping. Accessed through workstations throughout the site, the vault allows engineers to "sign out" documents for revision, printing, or on-line viewing. Every time a change is made, the vault's software tracks the differences between the old and new versions, records who made the changes, and routes the revised documentation by e-mail through an approval team. Once approved, the revised document replaces the original version, which is then automatically archived to provide an audit trail. Throughout its life, a document may be entirely electronic and viewed only on-line, printed and bound, printed when needed and then discarded, or some combination of these media.

Virtually every department in the factory uses these documents. R&D designs the product, manufacturing engineering uses the product specifications to design production equipment, materials engineering uses the same specifications to select the plastics and metals used to make the product, materials procurement uses the materials engineering documents to order the supplies for the production line, capital purchasing uses the manufacturing engineering documents to get contracts for the production lines, technical writing groups use all of these documents to create user manuals and other printed materials to ship with the final product, and traffic combs through the data to estimate the number and types of shipping containers and vehicles that will be needed. When the product is actually manufactured, the production departments continuously refer to the documentation for instructions on how to operate, test, and repair their equipment; how to order and load raw materials into the machinery; how to test the products; and how to judge the product's quality.

When headquarters prepares to send a product and its production equipment to one of the other locations, the documentation is supposed to be sent first. The documentation is used at the new location to train employees, to guide the preparation of the new facility, and to ensure that all of the supply chain components are in place to provide raw materials and outbound shipping. Much of the documentation is translated into the local language for use by semi-skilled production workers once the production line is running at the new location.

Every department at every location is both a consumer and a producer of documentation, and all are completely interdependent. A single error in a specification can cascade into a multimillion dollar disaster in the form of incorrect raw materials, a product that passes tests but doesn't work for the customer, a production line that won't fit inside the factory building, or a huge fine from US Customs for mistakenly exporting restricted technology.

- *The current situation*. Various departments within M&DDiv have invested heavily in the human resources, tools, and time needed to create and maintain the documentation process. Despite this investment, M&DDiv's documentation is still regarded as unsatisfactory by the majority of employees and management. For example, there is widespread dissatisfaction with the documentation system in the design departments at headquarters. Because of past bad experiences with outdated or incorrect documentation, users distrust all documentation's accuracy, and find the vault hard to access. The quality department is distressed by the delays in the correction and update cycle. Technical writers are unhappy with the general usability of the required word processors, graphics programs, and the vault; they also feel artistically constrained when asked to use standard templates or designs for their documents. They get little cooperation from the subject matter experts and reviewers they rely on for information, and feel that creating a finished document can take four to five times as much time and effort as it should take.

  The headquarters document control supervisors and technical-writing supervisors also are frustrated. Their personal workloads have ballooned to unmanageable levels as they added staff to keep up with the increasing documentation requirements of M&DDiv's growing number of products. At the same time, they are permitted to hire only temporary resources; qualified candidates became increasingly hard to find, and they take everything they have learned away with them when their finite-length contracts end.

  The production sites share all these concerns and have unique issues of their own. They are frustrated by their inability to get correct and complete documentation when a manufacturing process transfers from headquarters, even though the documentation is supposed to arrive long before the manufacturing process. They often must convert unusual file formats or struggle to rewrite United States-idiomatic information to meet the needs of their local users. They also often feel that they need to invent their own document designs because global designs are still pending or are too specific to another location's needs.

CONTRIBUTING FACTORS

As your early interest in overcoming these problems increased, you conducted an informal analysis based on interviews and observations at all five locations. You have concluded that there are a number of interrelated causes producing M&DDiv's documentation problems.

The primary issue is the lack of an overriding vision or strategy to guide the creation of a full and robust documentation system. To be fair, several years ago, M&DDiv's senior management chartered a documentation quality effort. However, this was only partially implemented, and the project lost momentum after some early successes. This sent a signal—to both the headquarters site and the production locations—that documentation was not really so important after all, much to the relief of those who considered documentation-related tasks a distraction from their "real work." As the rigor of document-creation and -maintenance rules began to wane, the quality of the documents and the processes they supported began to deteriorate again. This continuing gradual slide at each of the locations is exacerbated by the lack of coordination between them. Decisions are made independently, based on local or perceived larger-scope needs, or occasionally on policies that were developed during the short-lived documentation-quality project. Few people consider a time horizon farther out than one year, and even fewer look forward with a global perspective.

There are severe integration problems between the different locations. The production entities are concerned with document control and simplicity. Headquarters has difficulty in simply collecting the information in the first place, and with keeping it up-to-date and complete as the subject matter rapidly evolves during the design and tuning phases. Headquarters often uses the documentation as repositories of historical or justification information; this serves only to confuse and annoy the production sites, which require only the minimum information necessary to manufacture products.

There also are internal integration problems within each individual location. Responsibility for different aspects of the documentation falls within several organizations: creation and storage technology in one, the formal processes for acquisition and control in another, best practice consulting in a third, and technical writers scattered throughout several other departments with their "customers" (e.g., some writers sit within R&D, some work with manufacturing engineering, and still others are in the quality department). There are no rewards for communicating or collaborating, and the groups frequently develop similar or conflicting solutions to what turn out to be common problems.

Day-to-day operation is also less than optimal. The majority of involved personnel have little or no training or experience in the field of documentation. This has led to quality problems, arbitrary decision-making, inappropriate prioritizing of tasks and objectives, and several "blind alley" projects (i.e., projects that start successfully but then run into insurmountable barriers and are abandoned). Many writers and document controllers are former production line operators who show little interest or aptitude during times of high need. Few of the external temporary personnel have formal technical writing experience; most are recently graduated English majors or journalists. The technical writing supervisors all moved laterally from production, and received no special training or mentoring; this results in inefficiency and quality problems within their departments.

Generally, each of the problems and frustrations outlined above is restricted to the immediately affected departments. The various symptoms are highly distributed, are frequently noticeable only at the lowest levels of the organization, and are often concealed beneath their effects. For example, raw material rejection in the receiving department might increase without anyone questioning whether the inspection checklist itself was incorrect, or growing headcount in the support department might not be linked with a particular manufacturing location's use of an obsolete adjustment procedure. These problems would usually be examined by the immediate department supervisor without regard to a larger context, and would seldom be escalated to a point of visibility to upper management or someone with a less parochial viewpoint.

Until you began talking with people at all sites, most people were aware only of their own difficulties with the documentation, and were surprised by your interest. You found that the overall sense of "shared pain" in the organization was very low, and that upper management was completely unaware of the magnitude, frequency, and very real cost of the issues.

Aside from a few informal networks and councils, there are no worldwide activities working to resolve these problems from a system perspective. Most of the separate organizations do recognize the local aspects of the problems, and some have projects in place to improve their own processes in isolation. However, there is no movement toward a larger-scale solution.

It is clear that M&DDiv is in a state of uneasy stasis and that external stimulus—you—will be needed to begin a resolution.

YOUR PLAN TO INITIATE CHANGE

You have decided to conduct an informal discussion with Stewart Jones, the M&DDiv executive you deem to be the most likely potential sponsor for the project, to get a preliminary opinion on whether your project would be worth proposing formally. You have planned your approach carefully.

Because of the engineering-intense environment in M&DDiv, you know that you must follow a defined, rational project management methodology—overt "touchy-feely" techniques would be rejected out of hand. However, you also understand that changing the documentation process will be equal parts cultural change and process improvement.

You also understand the dynamics of M&DDiv management: They seem powerless to force change upon the different geographical locations, and they also are unable and unwilling to spend much time attempting to reach a consensus on the need for standardizing anything. "Going to the top" won't help. Because you are dealing with many branches of a very large organization you must face a "Catch-22" situation: when you appeal up the organization chart to a level that has the power to command all relevant organizations, that individual is so removed from the problem that he or she is unwilling to consider it unless it has huge demonstrable impact.

Questions

1. What is your assessment of your (Roberta's) efforts to date?

2. How will you convince Stewart Jones to allow you to proceed with the project? What arguments might you use?

3. Describe how you will develop a change process and the critical issues you will face in managing the change.

Source: ©2000 by Clarity and Brian B. Egan.

PART
3

Human Process Interventions

Chapter 12   Individual, Interpersonal, and Group
                     Process Approaches

Chapter 13   Organization Process Approaches

Selected Cases   The Metric Division Case
                     Gulf States Metals, Inc

12

Individual, Interpersonal, and Group Process Approaches

This chapter discusses change programs relating to individuals, interpersonal relations, and group dynamics. These interventions are among the earliest ones devised in OD and the most popular. They represent attempts to improve individual performance as well as people's working relationships with one another. The interventions are aimed at helping individuals develop skills, and members of groups assess their interactions and devise more effective ways of working. These change programs represent a basic skill requirement for an OD practitioner.

Individual approaches, including coaching and training, focus on the skills, knowledge, and capabilities of an organization member. Coaching attempts to improve an individual's ability to set and meet goals, improve interpersonal relations, handle conflict, or address leadership style. Training and development, a large field in its own right, is an educational intervention that attempts to transfer knowledge and skill to many individuals at once. Both coaching and training are important elements of most leadership development programs.

Interpersonal and group process approaches, including process consultation, third-party interventions, and team building, are among the most enduring OD interventions. Process consultation helps group members understand, diagnose, and improve their behaviors. Through process consultation, the group should become better able to use its own resources to identify and solve interpersonal problems that often block the solving of work-related problems. Third-party interventions focus directly on dysfunctional interpersonal conflict. This approach is used only in special circumstances and only when both parties are willing to engage in the process of direct confrontation. Team building is aimed both at helping a team perform its tasks better and at satisfying individual needs. Through team-building activities, group goals and norms become clearer. In addition, team members become better able to confront difficulties and problems and to understand the roles of individuals within the team. Among the specialized team-building approaches presented are interventions with ongoing teams and temporary teams such as project teams and task forces.

COACHING

Coaching involves working with organizational members, typically managers and executives, on a regular basis to help them clarify their goals, deal with potential stumbling blocks, and improve their performance. This intervention is highly personal and generally involves a one-on-one relationship between the OD practitioner and the client. Coaching helps managers gain perspective on their dilemmas and transfer their learning into organizational results; it increases their leadership skill and effectiveness.[1]

Coaching is itself a skill that any OD practitioner or manager can develop.[2] It involves using guided inquiry, active listening, reframing, and other techniques to help individuals see new or different possibilities[3] and to direct their efforts toward what matters most to them. When done well, coaching improves personal productivity and builds capacity in individuals to lead more effectively. Unfortunately, despite growing professionalism in the coaching field, the process can be technique driven, especially when formulas, tools, and advice are substituted for good judgment, facilitation, and compassion.

Coaching can be seen as a specialized form of OD, one that is focused on using the principles of applied behavioral science to increase the capacity and effectiveness of individuals as opposed to groups or organizations. It is one of the fastest-growing areas of OD practice. The International Coach Federation (http://www.coachfederation.org), founded in 1995, grew to over 5,500 members in 2002, doubling in size between 2000 and 2002. CoachVille (http://www.coachville.com), the largest professional network and trainer of coaches worldwide has over 30,000 members. These two bodies are actively creating coaching certification programs and standards to professionalize the field.

What Are the Goals?

Coaching typically addresses one or more of the following goals: assisting an executive to more effectively execute some transition, such as a merger integration or downsizing; addressing a performance problem; or developing new behavioral skills as part of a leadership development program. In any case, coaching is often confused with therapy.[4] Most coaching approaches acknowledge that coaching is not therapy. While both coaching and therapy focus on personal development, coaching assumes that the client is healthy rather than suffering from some pathology. Coaching is also primarily future and action oriented rather than focused on the past, as are many therapeutic models. Coaching involves helping clients understand how their behaviors are contributing to the current situation. Such understanding is often difficult to achieve and often deeply personal. Therefore, the limits of a coach's skills and abilities must be acknowledged. Many coaching failures have been attributed to working too far from the practical application of behavioral principles, or too close to the boundaries of therapy, and to the failure of the coach to understand the difference.

Application Stages

The coaching process closely follows the process of planned change outlined in Chapter 2, including entry and contracting, assessment, debriefing (feedback), action planning, intervention, and assessment.[5]

1. **Establish the principles of the relationship.** The initial phases of a coaching intervention involve establishing the goals of the engagement; the parameters of the relationship, such as schedules, resources, and compensation; and ethical considerations.

2. **Conduct an assessment.** This process can be personal or systemic. In a personal assessment, the client is guided through an assessment framework.[6] It can involve a set of interview questions that elicit development opportunities or a more formal personal-style instrument, such as the Myers–Briggs Type Indicator, the FIRO-B, or DISC profile. Other instruments, including the Hogan's battery of tests, the Minnesota Multiphasic Personality Inventory (MMPI), or the "Big 5" instrument, can also be used, but they require extensive training and certification. OD practitioners should carefully consider the ethics of using different instruments and their qualifications for administering and interpreting the results. In a systemic assessment, the client's team, peers, and relevant others are engaged in the process. The most common form of systemic assessment involves a 360-degree feedback process.

3. **Debrief the results.** The coach and client review the assessment data and agree on a diagnosis. The principles of data feedback outlined in Chapter 8

apply here. The purpose of the feedback session is to get the client to move to action. In light of the assessment data, intervention goals can be further refined and revised if necessary.

4. **Develop an action plan.** The specific activities the client and coach will engage in are specified. These can include new actions that will lead to goal achievement, learning opportunities that build knowledge and skill, or projects to demonstrate competence. Developing an action plan can be the most difficult part of the process because the client must own the results of the assessment and begin to see new possibilities for action. The action plan should also include methods and milestones to monitor progress and to evaluate the effectiveness of the coaching process.

5. **Implement the action plan.** In addition to the elements of the action plan listed above, much of the coaching process involves one-on-one meetings between the coach and client. In these sessions, the coach supports and encourages the client to act on her/his intentions. A considerable amount of skill is required to confront, challenge, and facilitate learning.

6. **Assess the results.** At appropriate intervals, the results of the client's actions are reviewed and evaluated. Based on this information, the goals or action plans can be revised, or the process can be terminated.

The Results of Coaching

Although coaching has been practiced for many years, few studies have assessed its effectiveness. Most of the evidence is anecdotal and case based. Benefits cited are diverse and depend on the nature of the client's objectives. Two studies of coaching effectiveness are suggestive of the intervention's results. One found that coaching improved personal productivity, quality, working relationships, and job satisfaction. The return was estimated to be 5.7 times the initial investment.[7] The other study noted improvements in productivity and employee satisfaction, and identified specific financial benefits. The estimated return on investment was 529%, although the method for calculating this figure was not explained. Clearly, more rigorous studies are necessary to judge the effectiveness of coaching interventions.[8]

TRAINING AND DEVELOPMENT

Training and development interventions are among the oldest strategies for organizational change.[9] They provide new or existing organization members with the skills and knowledge they need to perform work. The focus of training interventions has broadened from classroom methods aimed at hourly workers to varied methods, including simulations, action learning, computer-based or on-line training, and case studies, intended for all levels and types of organization members.

Training and development is a large practice area with growing importance in organizations. The American Society of Training and Development (ASTD) (http://www.astd.org), the largest professional organization, has over 70,000 members worldwide. According to its most recent state of the industry report, U.S. companies spent about $54.2 billion on training in 2002[10], an increase from almost $50 billion that was spent in 2000.[11] Training and development represents an important organization investment accounting for about 2% of a company's payroll.[12] A recent survey by the Center for Creative Leadership and *Chief Executive* magazine reported that about 79% of the 756 executives who responded saw leadership development as either "the most" important or "one of the top five" factors in achieving competitive advantage.[13] This section describes the purpose and goals of training and development interventions, the application steps and conditions for transfer, and the research support for this intervention.

What Are the Goals?

The term *training* is typically used when the goal is development of the workforce, while the terms *management development* or *leadership development* are normally applied when the goal is development of the organization's management and executive talent. There is a wide range of training and development interventions, and not all involve OD. For training to be considered an OD intervention, it must focus on changing the skills and knowledge of a group of organization members to improve their effectiveness or to build the capabilities of an organization system.[14] For example, a new employee training program that provides information about the organization's health care benefits would not qualify as an OD intervention.

Application Stages

Training and development interventions generally follow a process of needs assessment, setting instructional objectives and design, delivery, and evaluation.[15]

1. **Perform a needs assessment.** Similar to the diagnostic process in the general model of planned change, a needs assessment determines what training, if any, is necessary. It involves gathering data on the organization, the work, and the individual.[16] The *organization assessment* focuses on the systems that may affect the ability to transfer training back to the organization. For transfer to occur, participants must be provided with the opportunity and appropriate conditions to apply their new skills, knowledge, and abilities to the work situation. The organization assessment determines whether the necessary support exists in the organization to make training and development worthwhile. For example, if managers are generally unwilling to send their supervisors to learn how to administer a new performance management system, then the organization assessment would suggest addressing management's readiness for change before implementing the training. The *work assessment* involves understanding the tasks, activities, and decisions that participants should perform better after training. In the case of technical training, such as completing an assembly task, working on a computer program, or fulfilling a customer request, there exists a large body of tools, techniques, and processes for performing this analysis.[17] For managerial and leadership development efforts, this step is much more difficult because there is little agreement on what skills, knowledge, and abilities constitute "management." The final element, *individual assessment,* aims to understand the existing level of skills, knowledge, and abilities of the individuals who are eligible to participate in the training.

2. **Develop the objectives and design of the training.** This step first establishes outcome objectives for the training and development intervention. These objectives should describe the quality and quantity of performance a participant should be able to demonstrate to be considered competent. An appropriate objective for a customer-service training program might be "to be able to successfully handle 95% of all customer requests." For a leadership development program, an appropriate objective might be "to produce an acceptable strategic plan for the participant's department" or "to increase participants' commitment to the strategic direction of the corporation."

   The design of the training involves making choices from among a wide variety of techniques, including on-the-job training, audiovisual methods, computer-based or Internet-based approaches, or more traditional methods, such as classroom lectures, simulations, case studies, or experiential exercises. A recent study suggests that although instructor-led methods still dominate, the use of technology in various training and development interventions is increasing.[18]

3. **Deliver the training.** This stage implements the training and development. Participants are invited or apply to attend the training, complete the activities included in its design, and return to their normal work routines.

4. **Evaluate the training.** This final step assesses the training to determine whether it met its objectives. The four criteria most commonly used to evaluate training effectiveness are reaction, learning, behavior, and results.[19] *Reaction* is the most commonly used evaluation criterion and refers simply to the participants' initial judgment about the training's usefulness. It is often assessed via questionnaires completed immediately following the training activity. The *learning* criterion refers to whether or not participants acquired the knowledge that should have been transferred during the training; it stops short of assessing performance or behavior on the job. This can be assessed via interview or questionnaire. The *behavior* criterion assesses whether new skills and abilities gained in the training are actually applied to job activities. These data can be collected through observation or through interviews with the participant's manager. The final criterion, *results,* determines whether or not the training can be credited with improvements in the participant's or the system's effectiveness.

Application 12.1 describes a management development program at Microsoft Corporation. The company was interested in building the strategic competence of its middle managers and making the organization more capable.

The Results of Training

Despite the prevalence of training and development interventions in the workplace, most of the evaluation research consists of only reactions, the weakest measure of effectiveness.[20] Reaction data tend to correlate only weakly with other measures of training effectiveness.[21] Several more rigorous assessments, however, provide evidence about training effects. For example, a training program at Cyprus Sierrita Corporation yielded an annualized savings of $1.9 million after accounting for the cost of training, including the opportunity costs of employees' attendance, trainer costs, equipment idle time, and overtime premiums.[22] A broader study of 40 companies from multiple industries indicated that companies with higher average training expenditures per employee also had higher profits per employee.[23] There are few published studies on the effectiveness of leadership development programs, and their increased use warrants further research.

PROCESS CONSULTATION

Process consultation (PC) is a general framework for carrying out helping relationships.[24] Schein defines process consultation as "the creation of a relationship that permits the client to perceive, understand, and act on the process events that occur in [his or her] internal and external environment in order to improve the situation as defined by the client."[25] The process consultant does not offer expert help in the form of solutions to problems, as in the doctor–patient model. Rather, the process consultant works to help managers, employees, and groups assess and improve *human processes,* such as communication, interpersonal relations, decision making, and task performance. Schein argues that effective consultants and managers should be good helpers, aiding others in getting things done and in achieving the goals they have set.[26] Thus, PC is as much a philosophy as a set of techniques aimed at performing this helping relationship. The philosophy ensures that those who are receiving the help own their problems, gain the skills and expertise to diagnose them, and solve them themselves. PC is an approach to helping people and groups help themselves.

LEADING YOUR BUSINESS AT MICROSOFT CORPORATION

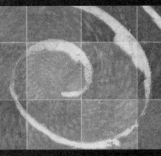

Microsoft is the largest software development organization and one of the most successful businesses in the world. In its relatively short history, growth has characterized almost every aspect of the company. Growth fueled not only Microsoft's reputation and no small number of millionaires, but it also demanded that the Microsoft organization mature. As technologies, products, markets, and revenues grew, so did the opportunities for professional advancement. Software development engineers that wanted to guide, shape, and manage the organization's growth found plenty of chances to become managers, directors, and vice presidents.

After years of double-digit growth, senior management at Microsoft worried that promotion of the young and brilliant technologists it had recruited was occurring too fast. While they understood technology, they were ill prepared to manage strategy, structure, people, and change. Interviews with successful and unsuccessful Microsoft managers about the competencies necessary to lead a business confirmed these suspicions. CEO Steve Ballmer believed that the speed of change in the software industry demanded leadership from the middle of the organization where people were closest to the technology and customers. He commissioned Microsoft's Management Development Group (MDG) to create a series of workshops aimed at developing the future leaders of the organization. Three courses were envisioned for the series, including one focused on strategic thinking and strategic change.

The MDG group contacted an OD practitioner with a background in educational interventions, strategy, and large-scale systems change. Together with internal OD practitioners and other members of the MDG organization, the OD practitioner interviewed additional managers, discussed program philosophy and company culture, shared strategy and strategic change concepts, and proposed a variety of methods to transfer the topics of strategic leadership to the participants.

After several weeks of discussions, a 2-day workshop design began to emerge. It consisted of a variety of learning technologies and was based on a principle and philosophy of self-managed learning. That is, the OD practitioner and the MDG consultants assumed that the participants, already having achieved a middle-management position, would possess a broad range of experiences and knowledge. The purpose of the workshop would be to marry that experience with the concepts from strategy and change. A number of delivery methods, including lectures, videos, experienctial exercises, and case studies, were used to expose the participants to certain topics, such as goals and goal setting, distinctive competencies, environmental scanning, strategy, and strategy implementation. At the beginning of the workshop, the participants would be allowed to form "peer consulting teams" and, following an input module, the teams would work individually and then in groups to apply the concepts to their own business. In this way, the participants actually left the workshop with a roughed-out strategic plan.

The design was "beta tested" with a group of about 20 middle managers and their comments, reactions, and suggestions were used to make adjustments in different parts of the workshop design. For example, the peer consulting groups turned out to be a very powerful idea and all of the groups wanted more time at the beginning of the workshop to explain their business so that the other members of the group had a good understanding of the competitive issues. After the beta workshop, the program was marketed to all middle managers at the Redmond, Washington, headquarters. Eventually, middle managers in Asia, Canada, and Europe were included. Over 2 years, about 500 of Microsoft's most important future leaders went through the workshop.

Ten days after the workshop, an evaluation was emailed to all participants for the reactions and feedback. This provided an ongoing database to ensure that the program continued to meet the needs of the middle managers. In addition, a qualitative study of the workshop's impact was conducted about a year into the program. A variety of information about how participants had used the workshop was gathered. Most participants rated the course highly, found the materials relevant and useful, had applied many of the frameworks and models in their day-to-day work, and appreciated the opportunity to stop and think about their business. The most highly rated feature of the class was the peer-to-peer learning and the business view the participants gained, there were few examples of direct impact on the organization. However, Only a few cases of dramatic success were found, including a substantial increase in strategic focus, clarity, and profitability within one of the Microsoft Office groups; a merger between two groups that was conceived during the workshop and then executed successfully after the program; and the launching of a new strategy within groups of the MSN and Xbox organizations. In each of these cases, the managers reported taking the ideas and plans worked out in the workshop and involving their direct reports in additional discussions. These additional inputs along with the original plans became the basis for implementing changes.

As a philosophy of helping in relationships, Schein proposes 10 principles to guide the process consultant's actions.[27]

- **Always try to be helpful.** Process consultants must be mindful of their intentions, and each interaction must be oriented toward being helpful.

- **Always stay in touch with the current reality.** Each interaction should produce diagnostic information about the current situation. It includes data about the client's opinions, beliefs, and emotions; the system's current functioning; and the practitioner's reactions, thoughts, and feelings.

- **Access your ignorance.** An important source of information about current reality is the practitioner's understanding of what is known, what is assumed, and what is not known. Process consultants must use themselves as instruments of change.

- **Everything you do is an intervention.** Any interaction in a consultative relationship generates information as well as consequences. Simply conducting preliminary interviews with group members, for example, can raise members' awareness of a situation and help them see it in a new light.

- **The client owns the problem and the solution.** This is a key principle in all OD practice. Practitioners help clients solve their own problems and learn to manage future change.

- **Go with the flow.** When process consultants access their own ignorance, they often realize that there is much about the client system and its culture that they do not know. Thus, practitioners must work to understand the client's motivations and perceptions.

- **Timing is crucial.** Observations, comments, questions, and other interventions intended to be helpful may work in some circumstances and fail in others. Process consultants must be vigilant to occasions when the client is open (or not open) to suggestions.

- **Be constructively opportunistic with confrontive interventions.** Although process consultants must be willing to go with the flow, they also must be willing to take appropriate risks. From time to time and in their best judgment, practitioners must learn to take advantage of "teachable moments." A well-crafted process observation or piece of feedback can provide a group or individual with great insight into their behavior.

- **Everything is information; errors will always occur and are the prime source for learning.** Process consultants never can know fully the client's reality and invariably will make mistakes. The consequences of these mistakes, the unexpected and surprising reactions, are important data that must be used in the ongoing development of the relationship.

- **When in doubt, share the problem.** The default intervention in a helping relationship is to model openness by sharing the dilemma of what to do next.

Group Process

Process consultation deals primarily with the interpersonal and group processes that describe how organization members interact with each other. Such social processes directly and indirectly affect how work is accomplished. When group process promotes effective interactions, groups are likely to perform tasks successfully.[28] Group process includes:

- **Communications.** One of the process consultant's areas of interest is the nature and style of communication, or the process of transmitting and receiving thoughts, facts, and feelings. Communication can be overt—who talks to whom, about what, for how long, and how often. It can include body language, including facial expressions, fidgeting, posture, and hand gestures.[29] Communication can also be covert, as when a manager says, "I'm not embarrassed" as his or her face turns scarlet. Covert communication is "hidden" and the process consultant often seeks to find the best way to make the message more explicit.

- **The functional roles of group members.** The process consultant must be keenly aware of the different roles individual members take on in a group. Both upon entering and while remaining in a group, individuals must address and understand their self-identity, influence, and power that will satisfy personal needs while working to accomplish group goals. In addition, group members must take on roles that enhance: (a) task-related activities, such as giving and seeking information and elaborating, coordinating, and evaluating activities; and (b) group-maintenance actions, directed toward holding the group together as a cohesive team, including encouraging, harmonizing, compromising, setting standards, and observing. Most ineffective groups perform little group maintenance, and this is a primary reason for bringing in a process consultant.

- **Group problem solving and decision making.** To be effective, a group must be able to identify problems, examine alternatives, and make decisions. For example, one way of making decisions is to ignore a suggestion, as when one person makes a suggestion and someone else offers another before the first has been discussed. A second method is to give decision-making power to the person in authority. Sometimes decisions are made by minority rule, the leader arriving at a decision and turning for agreement to several people who will comply. Frequently, silence is regarded as consent. Decisions can also be made by majority rule, consensus, or unanimous consent. The process consultant can help the group understand how it makes decisions and the consequences of each decision process, as well as help diagnose which type of decision process may be the most effective in a given situation. Decision by unanimous consent or consensus, for example, may be ideal in some circumstances but too time-consuming or costly in other situations.

- **Group norms.** Especially if a group of people works together over a period of time, it develops group norms or standards of behavior about what is good or bad, allowed or forbidden, right or wrong. The process consultant can be very helpful in assisting the group to understand and articulate its own norms and to determine whether those norms are helpful or dysfunctional. By understanding its norms and recognizing which ones are helpful, the group can grow and deal realistically with its environment, make optimum use of its own resources, and learn from its own experiences.[30]

- **The use of leadership and authority.** A process consultant needs to understand processes of leadership and how different leadership styles can help or hinder a group's functioning. In addition, the consultant can help the leader adjust his or her style to fit the situation.

Basic Process Interventions

For each of the interpersonal and group processes described above, a variety of interventions may be used. In broad terms, these are aimed at making individuals and groups more effective.[31]

Individual Interventions

These interventions are designed primarily to help people be more effective in their communication with others. For example, the process consultant can provide feedback to one or more individuals about their overt behaviors during meetings. At the covert or hidden level of communication, feedback can be more personal and is aimed at increasing the individual's awareness of how their behavior affects others. A useful model for this process has been developed by Luft in what is called the *Johari Window.*[32] Figure 12.1, a diagram of the Johari Window, shows that some personal issues are perceived by both the individual and others. This is the "open" window. In the "hidden" window, people are aware of their behavior, motives, and issues, but they conceal them from others. People with certain feelings about themselves or others in the work group may not share with others unless they feel safe and protected; by not revealing reactions they feel might be hurtful or impolite, they lessen the degree of communication.

The "blind" window comprises personal issues that are unknown to the individual but that are communicated clearly to others. For example, one manager who made frequent business trips invariably told his staff to function as a team and to make decisions in his absence. The staff, however, consistently refused to do this because it was clear to them, and to the process consultant, that the manager was really saying, "Go ahead as a team and make decisions in my absence, but be absolutely certain they are the exact decisions I would make if I were here." Only after the manager participated in several meetings in which he received feedback was he able to understand that he was sending a double message. Thereafter, he tried both to accept decisions made by others and to use management by objectives with his staff and with individual managers. Finally, the "unknown" window represents those personal aspects that are unknown to either the individual or others. Because such areas are outside the realm of the process consultant and the group, focus is typically on the other three cells.

Individual interventions encourage people to be more open with others and to disclose their views, opinions, concerns, and emotions, thus reducing the size of the

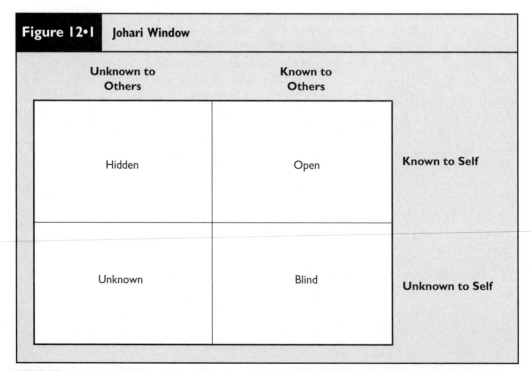

Figure 12•1   Johari Window

	Unknown to Others	Known to Others	
Known to Self	Hidden	Open	
Unknown to Self	Unknown	Blind	

SOURCE: Adapted by permission of the publisher from J. Luft, "The Johari Window," *Human Relations Training News* 5 (1961): 6–7.

hidden window. Further, the consultant can help individuals give feedback to others, thus reducing the size of the blind window. Reducing the size of these two windows helps improve the communication process by enlarging the open window, the "self" that is open to both the individual and others.

Before process consultants give individual feedback, they first must observe relevant events, ask questions to understand the issues fully, and make certain that the feedback is given to the client in a usable manner.[33] The following are guidelines[34] for effective feedback:

- The giver and receiver must have consensus on the receiver's goals.
- The giver should emphasize description and appreciation.
- The giver should be concrete and specific.
- Both giver and receiver must have constructive motives.
- The giver should not withhold negative feedback if it is relevant.
- The giver should own his or her observations, feelings, and judgments.
- Feedback should be timed to when the giver and receiver are ready.

Group Interventions

These interventions are aimed at the process, content, or structure of the group. *Process interventions* sensitize the group to its own internal processes and generate interest in analyzing them. Interventions include comments, questions, or observations about relationships between and among group members; problem solving and decision making; and the identity and purpose of the group. For example, process consultants can help by suggesting that some part of each meeting be reserved for examining how these decisions are made and periodically assessing the feelings of the group's members. As Schein points out, however, the basic purpose of the process consultant is not to take on the role of expert but to help the group share in its own diagnosis and do a better job in learning to diagnose its own processes: "It is important that the process consultant encourage the group not only to allocate time for diagnosis but to take the lead itself in trying to articulate and understand its own processes."[35]

Content interventions help the group determine what it works on. They include comments, questions, or observations about group membership; agenda setting, review, and testing procedures; interpersonal issues; and conceptual inputs on task-related topics.

Finally, *structural interventions* help the group examine the stable and recurring methods it uses to accomplish tasks and deal with external issues. They include comments, questions, or observations about inputs, resources, and customers; methods for determining goals, developing strategies, accomplishing work, assigning responsibility, monitoring progress, and addressing problems; and relationships to authority, formal rules, and levels of intimacy.

Application 12.2 presents an example of process consultation with the top-management team of a manufacturing firm.[36]

Results of Process Consultation

Although process consultation is an important part of organization development and has been widely practiced over the past 40 years, only a modest amount of research addresses its effect on improving the ability of groups to accomplish work. The few studies that have been conducted have produced little hard evidence of effectiveness. Research findings on process consultation are unclear, especially when the findings relate to task performance.

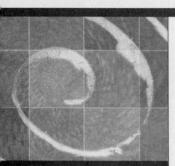

PROCESS CONSULTATION AT ACTION COMPANY

This application, a story often told by Ed Schein and documented in several of his books about process consultation and culture, involves the senior management team of an organization that he worked with over several years. It illustrates well several of the principles of process consultation, such as accessing your ignorance, always trying to be helpful, and understanding that errors are the prime source of learning.

The Action Company was a large and innovative high-technology organization. One salient feature of their executive committee meetings was long and loud discussions. Members interrupted each other constantly, often got into shouting matches, drifted off the subject, and moved from one agenda point to another without any clear sense of what had been decided. Based on his beliefs about the nature of effective groups and his experiences with group dynamics training, the process consultant made several initial interventions as an "expert" consultant. For example, whenever he saw an opportunity, he would ask the group to consider the consequences of interrupting each other repeatedly. This had the effect of communicating his belief that their process was "bad" and interfered with the group's task and effectiveness. He pointed out how important ideas were being lost and potentially important ideas were not getting a full discussion. The group invariably responded with agreement and a resolution to do better, but within 10 minutes were back to the same pattern.

As the process consultant reflected on these early interventions, he noticed that he was imposing on the group his own beliefs about what an ideal team should look like and how it should behave. This group, on the other hand, was clearly on a different path. Over time, he discovered that this group had a different set of shared assumptions that were driving their behaviors. In short, the group was trying to arrive at the "truth." Their assumption was that truth was revealed in ideas and actions that could withstand argument and debate. If an idea could survive intense scrutiny, it must be true and was worth pursuing.

Once he understood this basic premise, the process consultant asked himself what he could do that would be more helpful to the group. His answer was to work within the group's assumptions that were driving their behavior rather than imposing his beliefs on them. He had to learn that the primary task of the group, as they saw it, was to develop ideas that were so sound they could afford to bet the company on them. Generating ideas and evaluating them were therefore the two most crucial functions that they worked on in meetings.

Two kinds of interventions grew out of this insight. First, he noticed that ideas were in fact being lost because so much information was being processed so rapidly. Partly for his own sake and partly because he thought it might help, he went to the flipchart and wrote down the main ideas as they came out.

These ideas, incomplete or undeveloped because the presenter had been interrupted, led to the second kind of intervention. Instead of punishing the group for its "bad" behavior, as he had done in the early stages of the consultation, he looked for opportunities to turn the conversation back over to the person with the idea. For example, he would say, "John, you were trying to make a point. Did we get all of that?" This created the opportunity to get the idea out without drawing unnecessary attention to the reason why it had not gotten out in the first place. The combination of these two kinds of interventions focused the group on the ideas that were not on the flipchart and helped them navigate through their complex agenda. Ideas that were about to be lost were written down, resurrected, and given a fair chance.

The lesson was clear. Until the process consultant understood what the group really was trying to do, he could not focus on the right processes and he did not know how to intervene helpfully. He had to sense what the primary task was and where the group was getting stuck (incomplete idea formulation and too-quick evaluation) before he could determine what kind of intervention would be "facilitative."

A number of difficulties arise in trying to measure performance improvements as a result of process consultation. One problem is that most process consultation is conducted with groups performing mental tasks (for example, decision making); the outcomes of such tasks are difficult to evaluate. A second difficulty with measuring PC's effects occurs because in many cases process consultation is combined with other interventions in an ongoing OD program. Isolating the impact of process consultation from other interventions is difficult.

Kaplan's review of process consultation studies underscored the problems of measuring performance effects.[37] It examined published studies in three categories: (1) reports in which process intervention is the causal variable but performance is measured inadequately or not at all, (2) reports in which performance is measured but process consultation is not isolated as the independent variable (the case in many instances), and (3) research in which process consultation is isolated as the causal variable and performance is adequately measured. The review suggests that process consultation has positive effects on participants, according to self-reports of greater personal involvement, higher mutual influence, group effectiveness, and similar variables. However, very little, if any, research clearly demonstrates that objective task effectiveness was increased. In most cases, either the field studies did not directly measure performance or the effect of process intervention was confounded with other variables.

A third problem with assessing the performance effects of process consultation is that much of the relevant research has used people's perceptions rather than hard performance measures as the index of success.[38] Although much of this research shows positive results, these findings should be interpreted carefully until further research is done using more concrete measures of performance.

THIRD-PARTY INTERVENTIONS

Third-party interventions focus on conflicts arising between two or more people within the same organization. Conflict is inherent in groups and organizations and can arise from a variety of sources, including differences in personality, task orientation, goal interdependence, and perceptions among group members, as well as competition for scarce resources. To emphasize that conflict is neither good nor bad per se is important. Conflict can enhance motivation and innovation and lead to greater understanding of ideas and views. On the other hand, it can prevent people from working together constructively, destroying necessary task interactions among group members. Consequently, third-party interventions are used primarily in situations in which conflict significantly disrupts necessary task interactions and work relationships among members.

Third-party interventions vary considerably depending on the kind of issues underlying the conflict. Conflict can arise over substantive issues, such as work methods, pay rates, and conditions of employment, or it can emerge from interpersonal issues, such as personalities and misperceptions. When applied to substantive issues, conflict resolution interventions often involve resolving labor–management disputes through arbitration and mediation. The methods used in such substantive interventions require considerable training and expertise in law and labor relations and generally are not considered part of OD practice. For example, when union and management representatives cannot resolve a joint problem, they can call upon the Federal Mediation and Conciliation Service to help them resolve the conflict. In addition, "alternative dispute resolution" (ADR) practices increasingly are offered in lieu of more expensive and time-consuming court trials.[39] Conflicts also may arise at the boundaries of the organization, such as between suppliers and the company, between a company and a public-policy agency, or between multiple organizations or groups.[40]

When conflict involves interpersonal issues, however, OD has developed approaches that help control and resolve it. These third-party interventions help the parties interact with each other directly, facilitating their diagnosis of the conflict and its resolution. The ability to facilitate conflict resolution is a basic skill in OD and applies to all of the process interventions discussed in this chapter. Consultants, for example, frequently coach clients through a conflict or help organization members resolve interpersonal conflicts that invariably arise during process consultation and team building.

Third-party interventions cannot resolve all interpersonal conflicts in organizations, nor should they. Many times, interpersonal conflicts are not severe or disruptive enough to warrant attention. At other times, they simply may burn themselves out. Evidence also suggests that other methods may be more appropriate under certain conditions. For example, managers tend to control the process and outcomes of conflict resolution actively when they are under heavy time pressures, when the disputants are not expected to work together in the future, and when the resolution of the dispute has a broad impact on the organization.[41] Under those conditions, the third party may resolve the conflict unilaterally with little input from the conflicting parties.

An Episodic Model of Conflict

Interpersonal conflict often occurs in iterative, cyclical stages known as "episodes." An episodic model is shown in Figure 12.2. At times, issues underlying a conflict are latent and do not present any manifest problems for the parties. Then something triggers the conflict and brings it into the open. For example, a violent disagreement or frank confrontation can unleash conflictual behavior. Because of the negative consequences of that behavior, the unresolved disagreement usually becomes latent again. And again, something triggers the conflict, making it overt, and so the cycle continues with the next conflict episode.

Conflict has both costs and benefits to the antagonists and to those in contact with them. Unresolved conflict can proliferate and expand. An interpersonal conflict may be concealed under a cause or issue that serves to make the conflict appear more legitimate. Frequently, the overt conflict is only a symptom of a deeper problem.

The episodic model identifies four strategies for conflict resolution. The first three attempt to control the conflict, and only the last approach tries to change the basic issues underlying it.[42] The first strategy is to prevent the ignition of conflict by arriving at a clear understanding of the triggering factors and thereafter avoiding or blunting them when the symptoms occur. For example, if conflict between the research and production managers is always triggered by new-product introductions, then senior executives can warn them that conflict will not be tolerated during the introduction of the latest new product. However, this approach may not always be functional and may merely drive the conflict underground until it explodes. As a control strategy, however, this method may help to achieve a temporary cooling-off period.

The second control strategy is to set limits on the form of the conflict. Conflict can be constrained by informal gatherings before a formal meeting or by exploration of

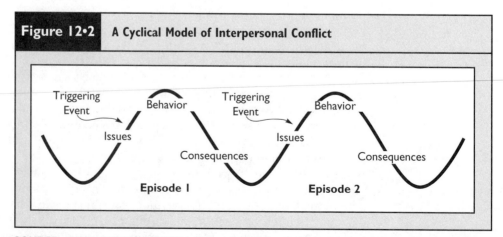

Figure 12•2   A Cyclical Model of Interpersonal Conflict

SOURCE: MANAGING CONFLICT 2/E by Walton, © 1987. Reprinted by permission of Pearson Education, Inc., Upper Saddle River, NJ.

other options. It also can be limited by setting rules and procedures specifying the conditions under which the parties can interact. For example, a rule can be instituted that union officials can attempt to resolve grievances with management only at weekly grievance meetings.

The third control strategy is to help the parties cope differently with the consequences of the conflict. The third-party consultant may work with the people involved to devise coping techniques, such as reducing their dependence on the relationship, ventilating their feelings to friends, and developing additional sources of emotional support. These methods can reduce the costs of the conflict without resolving the underlying issues.

The fourth method is an attempt to eliminate or to resolve the basic issues causing the conflict. As Walton points out, "There is little to be said about this objective because it is the most obvious and straightforward, although it is often the most difficult to achieve."[43]

Facilitating the Conflict Resolution Process

Walton has identified a number of factors and tactical choices that can facilitate the use of the episodic model in resolving the underlying causes of conflict.[44] The following ingredients can help third-party consultants achieve productive dialogue between the disputants so that they examine their differences and change their perceptions and behaviors: mutual motivation to resolve the conflict; equality of power between the parties; coordinated attempts to confront the conflict; relevant phasing of the stages of identifying differences and of searching for integrative solutions; open and clear forms of communication; and productive levels of tension and stress.

Among the tactical choices identified by Walton are those having to do with diagnosis, the context of the third-party intervention, and the role of the consultant. One of the tactics in third-party intervention is the gathering of data, usually through preliminary interviewing. Group-process observations can also be used. Data gathering provides some understanding of the nature and the type of conflict, the personality and conflict styles of the individuals involved, the issues and attendant pressures, and the participants' readiness to work together to resolve the conflict.

The context in which the intervention occurs is also important. Consideration of the neutrality of the meeting area, the formality of the setting, the appropriateness of the time for the meeting (that is, a meeting should not be started until a time has been agreed on to conclude or adjourn), and the careful selection of those who should attend the meeting are all elements of this context.

In addition, the third-party consultant must decide on an appropriate role to assume in resolving conflict. The specific tactic chosen will depend on the diagnosis of the situation. For example, facilitating dialogue of interpersonal issues might include initiating the agenda for the meeting, acting as a referee during the meeting, reflecting and restating the issues and the differing perceptions of the individuals involved, giving feedback and receiving comments on the feedback, helping the individuals diagnose the issues in the conflict, providing suggestions or recommendations, and helping the parties do a better job of diagnosing the underlying problem.

Third-party consultants must develop considerable skill at diagnosis, intervention, and follow-up, and be highly sensitive to their own feelings and to those of others. They must recognize that some tension and conflict are inevitable and that although there can be an optimum amount and degree of conflict, too much conflict can be dysfunctional for both the people involved and the larger organization. The third-party consultant must be sensitive to the situation and able to use a number of different intervention strategies and tactics when intervention appears to be useful. Finally, he or she must have professional expertise in third-party intervention and must be seen by the parties as neutral or unbiased regarding the issues and outcomes of the conflict resolution.

Application 12.3 describes an attempt to address conflict in an information technology unit.[45] How does this description fit with the process described above? What would you have done differently?

TEAM BUILDING

Team building refers to a broad range of planned activities that help groups improve the way they accomplish tasks and help members enhance their interpersonal and problem-solving skills. Organizations comprise many different types of groups including permanent work groups, temporary project teams, and virtual teams. Team building is an effective approach to improving teamwork and task accomplishment in such environments. It can help problem-solving groups make maximum use of members' resources and contributions. It can help members develop a high level of motivation to implement group decisions. Team building also can help groups overcome specific problems, such as apathy and general lack of member interest; loss of productivity; increasing complaints within the group; confusion about assignments; low participation in meetings; lack of innovation and initiation; increasing complaints from those outside the group about the quality, timeliness, and effectiveness of services and products; and hostility or conflicts among members.

It is equally important that team building can facilitate other OD interventions, such as employee involvement, work design, restructuring, and strategic change. Those change programs typically are designed by management teams and implemented through various committees and work groups. Team building can help the groups design high-quality change programs and ensure that the programs are accepted and implemented by organization members. Indeed, most technostructural, human resources management, and strategic interventions depend on some form of team building for effective implementation.

The importance of team building is well established, and its high use is expected to continue in the coming years. Management teams are encountering issues of greater complexity and uncertainty, especially in such fast-growing industries as software and hardware development, entertainment, and health and financial services. Team building can provide the kind of teamwork and problem-solving skills needed to tackle such issues. When the team represents the senior management of an organization, team building can be an important part of establishing a coherent corporate strategy, and can promote the kind of close cooperation needed to implement complex strategies and new forms of governance.[46] As manufacturing and service technologies continue to develop—for example, just-in-time inventory systems, lean manufacturing, robotics, and service quality concepts—there is increasing pressure on organizations to implement team-based work designs. Team building can assist in the development of group goals and norms that support high productivity and quality of work life. The globalization of work and organizations implies that people from different cultures and geographic locations will increasingly interact over complex management and operational tasks using a variety of information and communication technologies. Team-building activities for these "virtual" teams has increased substantially over the past several years.[47] It can help virtual teams to examine cross-cultural issues and their impact on decision making and problem solving, facilitate communication processes where tone and body language clues are absent, and build trust. Finally, mergers and acquisitions, restructurings, and strategic alliances continue to proliferate. The success of these endeavors depends partly on getting members from different organizations to work together effectively. Team building can facilitate the formation of a unified team with common goals and procedures.

In the OD literature, team building is not clearly differentiated from process consultation. This confusion exists because most team building includes process consultation—helping the group diagnose and understand its own internal processes.

CONFLICT MANAGEMENT AT BALT HEALTHCARE CORPORATION

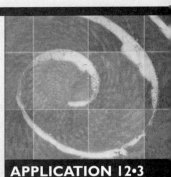

APPLICATION 12·3

Pete Brooks and Dan Gantman were managers in an IT department that was part of the information services group at Balt Healthcare Corporation, a large organization that provided health care products to a global market. Brooks was the general manager of the IT department and had been working in the unit for most of his 16 years with Balt. The IT department had global responsibility for developing and maintaining the organization's intranets, Web sites, and internal networks. Brooks ran his department with a traditional and formal management style where communication traveled vertically through the hierarchy.

Gantman recently had been assigned to Brooks's department to operate a small experimental group charged with developing E-commerce solutions for the organization and the industry. This was state-of-the-art development work with enormous future implications for the organization as it explored the possibility of sales, business-to-business, and other supply-chain opportunities on the Internet. Gantman, in contrast to Brooks, had a management style that stressed the value of open communication channels to promote teamwork and collaboration.

The biggest challenge in Gantman's work was managing the transition from design into production. Senior management at Balt believed that by assigning Gantman's team to Brooks's organization, the resources required to manage this transition would be more readily available to Gantman's group. In fact, it was generally agreed that Brooks's strengths complemented Gantman's weaknesses. Whereas Gantman was a better designer, Brooks had operational expertise that would help in bringing Gantman's ideas on-line.

Unfortunately, the trouble started almost as soon as the assignment was announced. Although in front of their bosses Brooks had agreed to work with Gantman to make the project a success, his support was lukewarm at best. Gantman and Brooks had a history of conflict in the organization. Neither one respected the other's style, and prior conflicts had been swept under the carpet, creating a considerable amount of pent-up animosity. Operationally, when Gantman's group needed resources to bring an idea on-line, Brooks announced that all of his people were busy and that he couldn't assign anyone to help. Similarly, anytime Gantman needed access to a piece of hardware within the IT unit, Brooks made it complicated to get that access. Gantman became increasingly frustrated by Brooks's lack of cooperation and he was quite open about his feelings of being sabotaged. His complaints reached the highest levels of management as well as other members of the information services staff.

After several frustrating attempts to speak with Brooks about the situation, Gantman consulted Marilyn Young, the vice president for information services. Young, like others in the organization, was aware of the conflict. She requested assistance from the human resources manager and an organization development specialist. The OD specialist met with Brooks and Gantman separately to understand the history of the conflict and each individual's contribution to it. Although different styles were partly to blame, the differences in the two work processes were also contributing to the problem. Brooks's organization was primarily routine development and maintenance tasks that allowed for considerable preplanning and scheduling of resources. Gantman's project, however, was highly creative and unpredictable. There was little opportunity to give Brooks advance notice regarding the experimental team's needs for equipment and other resources.

The OD specialist recommended several strategies to Young, including a direct confrontation, the purchase of additional hardware and software, and mandating the antagonists' cooperation. Young responded that there was no available budget for purchasing new equipment and admitted that she did not have any confidence in her ability to facilitate the needed communication and leadership for her staff. She asked the OD specialist to facilitate a more direct process. Agreements were made in writing about how the process would work, including Young meeting with Gantman and Brooks to discuss the problem between them and how it was affecting the organization. But Young did not follow through on the agreement. She never met with Brooks and Gantman at the same time and, as a result, the messages she sent to each were inconsistent. In fact, during their separate conversations, it appeared that Young began supporting Brooks and criticizing Gantman. Gantman began to withdraw, productivity in both groups suffered, and he became more hostile, stubborn, and bitter.

In the end, Gantman felt sabotaged not only by Brooks but by Young as well. He took a leave of absence based on Young's advice. His project was left without a leader and he ended up leaving the organization. Brooks stayed on, but staff at all levels of the organization were upset that his behavior had not been questioned. Similarly, the organization lost a lot of respect for Young's ability to address conflict. Losses in productivity and morale among staff in many areas in the organization resulted from the conflict between two employees.

However, process consultation is a more general approach to helping relationships than is team building. Team building focuses explicitly on helping groups perform tasks and solve problems more effectively. Process consultation, on the other hand, is concerned with establishing effective helping relationships in organizations. It is seen as key to effective management and consultation and can be applied to any helping relationship, from subordinate development to interpersonal relationships to group development. Thus, team building consists of process consultation plus other, more task-oriented interventions.

Team building is applicable in a large number of situations, from starting a new team, to resolving conflicts among members, to revitalizing a complacent team. Dyer has developed a checklist for identifying whether a team-building program is needed and whether the organization is ready to start such a program (Table 12.1).[48] If the problem is a structural or technical one, an intergroup issue, an administrative mistake, or a conflict between only two people, team building would not be an appropriate change strategy.

Team-Building Activities

A team is a group of interdependent people who share a common purpose, have common work methods, and hold each other accountable.[49] The nature of that interdependence varies, creating the following types of teams: groups reporting to the same supervisor, manager, or executive; groups involving people with common organizational goals; temporary groups formed to do a specific, one-time task; groups consisting of people whose work roles are interdependent; and groups whose members have no formal links in the organization but whose collective purpose is to achieve tasks they cannot accomplish alone. Another important variable in teams is location. When team members are in close proximity, a traditional team exists; when members are geographically dispersed and their interaction is mediated by information technology, a virtual team exists.

Several factors can affect the outcomes of any specific team-building activity: the length of time allocated to the activity, the team's willingness to look at its processes, the length of time the team has been working together, and the team's permanence. Consequently, the results of team-building activities can range from comparatively modest changes in the team's operating mechanisms (for example, meeting more frequently or gathering agenda items from more sources) to much deeper changes (for example, modifying team members' behavior patterns or the nature and style of the group's management, or developing greater openness and trust).

As shown in Table 12.2 (on page 235), team-building activities can be classified according to their level and orientation. Team-building activities can focus on the following levels: (1) one or more individuals; (2) the group's operation and behavior; or (3) the group's relationship with the rest of the organization. They also can be classified according to whether their orientation is (1) diagnostic or (2) development. A particular team-building activity can overlap these categories, and, on occasion, a change in one area will have negative results in other areas. For example, a very cohesive team may increase its isolation from other groups, leading to intergroup conflict or other dysfunctional results, which in turn can have a negative impact on the total organization unless the team develops sufficient diagnostic skills to recognize and deal with such problems.

Activities Relevant to One or More Individuals

People come into groups and organizations with varying needs for achievement, inclusion, influence, and belonging. These needs can be supported and nurtured by the team's structure and process or they can be discouraged. Diagnostic interviews and survey instruments can help members to better understand their motivations,

Table 12•1	Team-Building Checklist

I. Problem identification: To what extent is there evidence of the following problems in your work unit?

	LOW EVIDENCE		SOME EVIDENCE		HIGH EVIDENCE
1. Loss of production or work-unit output	1	2	3	4	5
2. Grievances or complaints within the work unit	1	2	3	4	5
3. Conflicts or hostility between unit members	1	2	3	4	5
4. Confusion about assignments or unclear relationships between people	1	2	3	4	5
5. Lack of clear goals or low commitment to goals	1	2	3	4	5
6. Apathy or general lack of interest or involvement of unit members	1	2	3	4	5
7. Lack of innovation, risk taking, imagination, or taking initiative	1	2	3	4	5
8. Ineffective staff meetings	1	2	3	4	5
9. Problems in working with the boss	1	2	3	4	5
10. Poor communications: people afraid to speak up, not listening to each other, or not talking together	1	2	3	4	5
11. Lack of trust between boss and members or between members	1	2	3	4	5
12. Decisions are made that people do not understand or agree with	1	2	3	4	5
13. Good work is not recognized or rewarded	1	2	3	4	5
14. Lack of encouragement for working together in a better team effort	1	2	3	4	5

Scoring: Add the scores for the 14 items. If your score is between 14 and 28, there is little evidence your unit needs team building. If your score is between 29 and 42, there is some evidence but no immediate pressure, unless two or three items are very high. If your score is between 43 and 56, you should think seriously about planning the team-building program. If your score is over 56, team building should be top priority for your work unit.

II. Are you (or your manager) prepared to start a team-building program? Consider the following statements. To what extent do they apply to you or your department?

	LOW		MEDIUM		HIGH
1. You are comfortable in sharing organizational leadership and decision making with subordinates and prefer to work in a participative atmosphere.	1	2	3	4	5
2. You see a high degree of interdependence as necessary among functions and workers in order to achieve your goals.	1	2	3	4	5
3. The external environment is highly variable or changing rapidly, and you need the best thinking of all your staff to plan for these conditions.	1	2	3	4	5
4. You feel you need the input of your staff to plan major changes or develop new operating policies and procedures.	1	2	3	4	5
5. You feel that broad consultation among your people as a group in goals, decisions, and problems is necessary on a continuing basis.	1	2	3	4	5

Continued on page 234

Table 12•1	Team-Building Checklist, *(continued)*					
		LOW		**MEDIUM**		**HIGH**
6.	Members of your management team are (or can become) compatible with each other and are able to create a collaborative rather than a competitive environment.	1	2	3	4	5
7.	Members of your team are located close enough to meet together as needed.	1	2	3	4	5
8.	You feel you need to rely on the ability and willingness of subordinates to resolve critical operating problems directly and in the best interest of the company or organization.	1	2	3	4	5
9.	Formal communication channels are not sufficient for the timely exchange of essential information, views, and decisions among your team members.	1	2	3	4	5
10.	Organization adaptation requires the use of such devices as project management, task forces, or ad hoc problem-solving groups to augment conventional organization structure.	1	2	3	4	5
11.	You feel it is important to bring out and deal with critical, albeit sensitive, issues that exist in your team.	1	2	3	4	5
12.	You are prepared to look at your own role and performance with your team.	1	2	3	4	5
13.	You feel there are operating or interpersonal problems that have remained unsolved too long and need the input from all group members.	1	2	3	4	5
14.	You need an opportunity to meet with your people to set goals and develop commitment to these goals.	1	2	3	4	5

Scoring: If your total score is between 50 and 70, you probably are ready to go ahead with the team-building program. If your score is between 35 and 49, you probably should talk the situation over with your team and others to see what would need to be done to get ready for team building. If your score is between 14 and 34, you probably are not prepared to start team building.

SOURCE: W. G. Dyer, *Team Building: Issues and Alternatives*, pages 42–46. Copyright © 1987. Reprinted by permission of the Estate of W. G. Dyer.

style, or emotions in the group context. It results in one or more of the members gaining a better understanding of the way inclusion, emotions, control, and power affect problem solving and other group processes, and provide choices about their degree of involvement and commitment. Such activities provide information so that people have a clearer sense of how their needs and wants can or will be supported.

Developmental activities that address one or more members of the group include coaching, 360-degree feedback, and assistance with conflict. These interventions attempt to alter the group's ongoing processes by focusing on the behaviors and attitudes of individual members. For example, one team's typical decision-making process included the leader having several agenda items for discussion. Each of the items, however, had a predetermined set of actions that she wanted the group to take. Most members were frustrated by their inability to influence the conclusions. The team-building process consisted of coaching the team leader and group members about ways to change this process. The leader received feedback about specific

Table 12·2	A Classification of Team-building Activity	
	Orientation of Activity	
LEVEL OF ACTIVITY	**DIAGNOSTIC**	**DEVELOPMENT**
One or more individuals	Instruments, interviews, and feedback to understand style and motivations of group members	Coaching 360-degree feedback Third-party interventions
Group operations and behavior	Surveys, interviews, and team meetings to understand the group's processes and procedures	Role clarification Mission and goal development Decision-making processes Normative change
Relationships with the organization	Surveys and interviews to understand how the group relates to its organization context	Strategic planning Stakeholder analysis

examples of her not-so-subtle manipulation to arrive at preconceived decisions and how group members felt about it. At the next meeting, the leader acknowledged the feedback and indicated her willingness to be challenged about such preconceived decisions. Team members expressed their increased willingness to engage in problem-solving discussions, their trust in the leader, and their ability to make the challenge without fear of reprisal.

Activities Oriented to the Group's Operation and Behavior

The most common focus of team-building activities is behavior related to task performance and group process. In an effective team, task behavior and group process must be integrated with each other as well as with the needs and wants of the people making up the group. Diagnostic activities involve gathering data through the use of questionnaires or, more commonly, through interviews. The nature of the data gathered will vary depending on the purpose of the team-building program, the consultant's knowledge about the organization and its culture, and the people involved. The consultant already may have obtained a great deal of data by sitting in as a process observer at staff and other meetings. The data gathered also will depend on what other OD efforts have taken place in the organization. By whatever method obtained, however, the data usually include information on leadership styles and behavior; goals, objectives, and decision-making processes; organizational culture, communication patterns, and interpersonal relationships and processes; barriers to effective group functioning; and task and related technical problems. Diagnostic activities often establish a framework within which further work can be done.

Developmental activities aim to improve the group's process and functioning. French and Bell have defined team development as "an inward look by the team at its own performance, behavior, and culture for the purposes of dropping out dysfunctional behaviors and strengthening functional ones."[50]A variety of team development activities and exercises have been described by different authors.[51] They include role clarification, improving goal clarity and member commitment, modifying the decision-making or problem-solving process, changing norms, increasing risk taking and trust, and improving communication.

Application 12.4 presents an example of a team-building meeting involving a top-management team.

APPLICATION 12•4

BUILDING THE EXECUTIVE TEAM AT CAESARS TAHOE

Caesars Tahoe is a casino, hotel, and entertainment complex on the south shore of Lake Tahoe, Nevada. As part of the Caesars World chain, including Caesars Palace in Las Vegas, Caesars in Atlantic City, and the riverboat Caesars Indiana, Caesars Tahoe enjoys a reputation as a "high-end" experience. Its history is laced with stories of celebrities, athletes, and some of the wealthiest people in the world winning and losing millions of dollars gambling in its casinos. Originally established as an alternative to the Las Vegas desert, Caesars Tahoe is the third-largest facility in town in terms of casino floor space and number of rooms, but it has the largest showroom for headline talent, the highest gambling limits, and the highest proportion of table games such as craps, blackjack, and roulette.

In 1995, the Caesars World organization was purchased by the ITT conglomerate, was spun off into the Starwood Resorts organization when ITT reorganized in 1997, and then was sold to Park Place Entertainment when Starwood decided to focus on nongaming properties. As of late 1999, the Caesars World corporate office was waiting for the transaction with Park Place to be closed formally.

The executive team at Caesars Tahoe consisted of an executive vice president and general manager (GM) for the property and seven direct reports. The marketing function was divided into three segments, each headed by a vice president. Far East marketing was responsible for recruiting "million-dollar players" from the South Pacific region; national marketing was responsible for working with other Caesars properties to ensure that "high rollers" from the United States were well attended to; and casino marketing handled the more traditional promotion activities of advertising, special-events coordination, entertainment bookings, and convention marketing. The hotel vice president was responsible for the front desk, housekeeping, maintenance, food and beverage service, and so on. The casino operations vice president managed all gambling operations. In addition, there was a vice president for human resources and a chief financial officer. The vice presidents for casino marketing and casino operations had been with the property for 10 and 20 years, respectively. No other member of the team had been with the property more than 2 years. In fact, the current GM was the 13th in 20 years.

The GM contacted an external OD consultant to help the executive team improve teamwork and clarify the core values of the organization. General changes in the gaming industry, higher than normal turnover levels in the hotel and

casino, concerns over whether the Caesars "brand" had suffered in all the corporate portfolio adjustments, and conflicts among his senior managers prompted his call. His own vision for the property included growing the property, reestablishing the Caesars brand, and investing in human resources. Interviews with the members of executive committee confirmed his initial descriptions about the team and the organization's situation.

In consultation with the GM, the corporate OD consultant, and the human resources vice president, an agenda was developed that addressed the goals and vision for the property, team processes and roles, and action plans for the future. A 2-day off-site meeting was arranged at a local resort.

The workshop kicked off on the evening before the meeting with a welcome and overview of the agenda by the GM and a stakeholder mapping exercise that clarified the current mission of the property. Team members were excused for the evening with the thoughts of the exercise fresh in their minds. On the morning of the first day, executive-committee members were encouraged to share their expectations for the meeting and to develop specific norms that would guide their behaviors during the 2-day meeting. This process was aided by an exercise in which the group members shared their experiences about the best team they had ever worked on and in that way identified characteristics of effective teams. The norms and characteristics were placed on flipcharts and hung on the wall of the meeting room. All members agreed to behave according to the norms and to assess periodically how well the norms were being followed. The consultant agreed to provide feedback on norm compliance during the session.

The group then participated in a problem-solving exercise that prompted members to collaborate on a task. The task generated important data about the group's functioning. Those observations were discussed, as were insights about the team gleaned from the results of an interpersonal style instrument completed by members prior to the meeting. The nature of the conflicts among members also was discussed. From this new basis of group understanding, the executive committee began to discuss their hopes and visions for the property. The first day ended with several unfinished lists of value statements, core purposes, and thoughts about the strategies and markets served by the organization. An evaluation of the day asked for an overall rating and comments about what the group should stop, start, and continue to do.

The next day began by feeding back the data from the evaluation, which suggested that most people were satisfied with the accomplishments of the first day but that important issues still needed to be addressed. Although the agenda called for a flow similar to that of the day before, moving back and forth between teamwork-related activities and discussions about the property's future, the consultant wrote several important topics on a flipchart and asked the group to identify the most important agenda items. Quickly they decided that they wanted to finish the core-values work and then discuss their core purpose.

The consultant facilitated the conversation that was now clearly under the control of the group members. Within a couple of hours, the group had produced a list of core values, developed a process for involving the rest of the organization in creating a final list of values, and crafted a core purpose that described the essence of the organization. Based on this work, the group moved to some initial discussions about its vision for the future. In addition, the group generated a list of key action items necessary to realize that vision. This was especially tricky given the uncertain demands of the new owner, but the group decided that it was important to have a clear strategy for themselves so that any demands from the new parent could be evaluated. Members also reasoned that the parent might ask them what they thought was possible and they wanted to be ready.

The meeting ended with the completion of a responsibility chart to clarify task completion expectations and accountabilities among the team members. A final evaluation of the meeting included process observations by the team members about how they had worked together and statements about their satisfaction with the results of the meeting. They all agreed that they had made important decisions and were leaving with substantial results.

Activities Affecting the Group's Relationship with the Rest of the Organization

As a team gains a better understanding of itself and becomes better able to diagnose and solve its own problems, it focuses on its role within the organization. A group's relationship to the larger organizational context is an important aspect of group effectiveness.[52] Diagnostic activities focus on understanding the group's organizational role, how its goals support the larger organization, or how the group interacts with other groups.

Developmental activities involve actions that improve or modify the group's contribution to the organization, how it acquires resources, or alters its outputs in terms of cost, quality, and quantity. Sometimes, the team may recognize a need for more collaboration with other parts of the organization and may try to establish a project team that crosses the boundaries of existing teams.

As the team becomes more cohesive, it usually exerts a stronger influence on other groups within the organization. This can lead to intergroup conflict. Because that is one area in which team building can have negative effects, the process consultant must help the group understand its role within the larger organization, develop its own diagnostic skills, and examine alternative action plans so that intergroup tensions and conflicts do not expand.

The Manager's Role in Team Building

Ultimately, the manager is responsible for team functioning, although this responsibility obviously must be shared by the group itself. Therefore, it is management's task to develop a work group that can regularly analyze and diagnose its own effectiveness and work process. With the team's involvement, the manager must diagnose the group's effectiveness and take appropriate actions if it shows signs of operating difficulty or stress.

Many managers, however, have not been trained to perform the data gathering, diagnosis, planning, and action necessary to maintain and improve their teams continually. Thus, the issue of who should lead a team-building session is a function of managerial capability. The initial use of an OD consultant usually is advisable if a manager is aware of problems, feels that he or she may be part of the problem, and believes that some positive action is needed to improve the operation of the team, but is not sure how to go about it. Dyer has provided a checklist for assessing the need for a consultant (Table 12.3). Some of the questions ask the manager to examine problems and establish the degree to which he or she feels comfortable in trying out new and different things, the degree of knowledge about team building, whether the boss might be a major source of difficulty, and the openness of group members.

Basically, the role of the OD consultant is to work closely with the manager (and members of the team) to a point at which the manager is capable of engaging in team development activities as a regular and ongoing part of overall managerial responsibilities. Assuming that the manager wants and needs a consultant, the two should work together in developing the initial program, keeping in mind that (1) the manager ultimately is responsible for all team-building activities, even though the consultant's resources are available; and (2) the goal of the consultant's presence is to help the manager learn to continue team development processes with minimum consultant help or without the ongoing help of the consultant.

Thus, in the first stages, the consultant might be much more active in data gathering, diagnosis, and action planning, particularly if a 1- to 3-day off-site workshop is considered. In later stages, the consultant takes a much less active role, with the manager becoming more active and serving as both manager and team developer.

The Results of Team Building

The research on team building's effectiveness has produced inconsistent results. Some studies have reported positive results across a range of variables including

Table 12•3	Assessing the Need for a Consultant

SHOULD YOU USE AN OUTSIDE CONSULTANT TO HELP IN TEAM BUILDING? (Circle the appropriate response.)

1. Does the manager feel comfortable in trying out something new and different with the staff?	Yes	No	?
2. Is the staff used to spending time in an outside location working on issues of concern to the work unit?	Yes	No	?
3. Will group members speak up and give honest data?	Yes	No	?
4. Does your group generally work together without a lot of conflict or apathy?	Yes	No	?
5. Are you reasonably sure that the boss is not a major source of difficulty?	Yes	No	?
6. Is there a high commitment by the boss and unit members to achieving more effective team functioning?	Yes	No	?
7. Is the personal style of the boss and his or her management philosophy consistent with a team approach?	Yes	No	?
8. Do you feel you know enough about team building to begin a program without help?	Yes	No	?
9. Would your staff feel confident enough to begin a team-building progam without outside help?	Yes	No	?

Scoring: If you have circled 6 or more "yes" responses, you probably do not need an outside consultant. If you have circled 4 or more "no" responses, you probably do need a consultant. If you have a mixture of "yes," "no," and ? responses, invite a consultant to talk over the situation and make a joint decision.

SOURCE: W. G. Dyer, *Team Building: Issues and Alternatives,* pages 42–46. Copyright © 1987. Reprinted by permission of the Estate of W. G. Dyer.

feelings, attitudes, and measures of performance.[53] For example, one review showed that team building improves process measures, such as employee openness and decision making, about 45% of the time and improves outcome measures, such as productivity and costs, about 53% of the time.[54] Another review revealed that team building positively affects hard measures of productivity, employee withdrawal, and costs about 50% of the time.[55]

Other studies have shown less positive outcomes.[56] In general, the research supports a pattern of positive changes in attitudes or satisfaction.[57] However, less powerful research designs and short time frames prohibit drawing strong conclusions linking performance improvements to team development efforts.[58] For example, one review of 30 studies found that only 10 tried to measure changes in performance. Although these changes were generally positive, the studies' research designs were relatively weak, reducing confidence in the findings.[59] Moreover, team building rarely occurs in isolation. Usually it is carried out in conjunction with other interventions leading to or resulting from team building itself. For this reason it is difficult to separate the effects of team building from those of the other interventions.[60]

Buller and Bell have attempted to differentiate the effects of team building from the effects of other interventions that occur along with team building.[61] Specifically, they tried to separate the effects of team building from the effects of goal setting, an intervention aimed at setting realistic performance goals and developing action plans for achieving them. In a rigorous field experiment, Buller and Bell examined the differential effects of team building and goal setting on productivity measures of underground miners. The results showed that team building affects the quality of performance and goal setting affects the quantity of performance. This differential impact was explained in terms of the nature of the mining task. The task of improving the quality of performance was more complex, unstructured, and interdependent than was the task of achieving quantity. This suggests that team building can improve group performance, particularly on tasks that are complex, unstructured, and interdependent. That the advantages of combining both interventions were inconclusively identified in the Buller and Bell study suggests the need for additional studies of the differential impact of team building and other interventions such as goal setting.

Finally, Boss has presented evidence to support the effectiveness of personal management interviews (PMIs) in sustaining the long-term effects of off-site team building.[62] A PMI is a follow-up intervention that arrests the potential fade-out effects of off-site team building.[63] A team leader negotiates roles with each member and then holds regular meetings with each team member to resolve problems and increase personal accountability. He compared the long-term effects of team building in 10 teams that had engaged in off-site team building, and a control group with no intervention. The data showed that all teams having off-site team building improved their effectiveness as measured soon after the intervention. However, only those teams subsequently engaged in PMIs were able to maintain those effectiveness levels; the other teams showed a substantial regression of effects over time. The data further showed that PMIs can help to maintain the level of group effectiveness over a 3-year period.

■ SUMMARY

In this chapter, we presented human process interventions aimed at individuals, interpersonal relations, and group dynamics. Among the earliest interventions in OD, these change programs help people gain individual skills and knowledge, interpersonal competence, work through interpersonal conflicts, and develop effective groups. Coaching and training and development interventions are aimed mainly at individuals. They seek to improve personal competence and are important aspects of leadership development programs.

Process consultation is used not only as a way of helping groups become effective but also as a means whereby groups learn to diagnose and solve their own problems and continue to develop their competence and maturity. Important areas of activity include communications, roles of group members, difficulties with problem-solving and decision-making norms, and leadership and authority. The basic difference between process consultation and third-party intervention is that the latter focuses on interpersonal dysfunctions in social relationships between two or more individuals within the same organization and is targeted toward resolving direct conflict between those individuals.

Team building is directed toward improving group effectiveness and the ways in which members of teams work together. Teams may be permanent or temporary or traditional or virtual, but their members have either common organizational aims or work activities. The general process of team building, like process consultation, tries to equip a team to handle its own ongoing problem solving.

■ NOTES

1. M. O'Neill, *Executive Coaching with Backbone and Heart: A Systems Approach to Engaging Leaders with Their Challenges* (San Francisco: Jossey-Bass, 2000); T. Crane, *The Heart of Coaching* (San Diego: FTA Press, 2001); M. Goldsmith, L. Lyons, A. Freas, and R. Witherspoon (eds.), *Coaching for Leadership: How the World's Greatest Coaches Help Leaders Learn* (San Francisco: Jossey-Bass, 2000); C. Fitzgerald and J. Berger (eds.), *Executive Coaching: Practices and Perspectives* (Palo Alto, Calif.: Davies-Black Publisher, 2002).

2. R. Heckler, *The Anatomy of Change: A Way to Move Through Life's Transition* (Berkeley, Calif.: North Atlantic Books, 1993); L. Whitworth, H. House, P. Sandahl, and H. Kimsey-House, *Co-active Coaching: New Skills for Coaching People Toward Success in Work and Life* (Palo Alto, Calif.: Davies-Black Publishing, 1998).

3. R. Hargrove, *Masterful Coaching: Extraordinary Results by Impacting People and the Way They Think and Work Together* (San Diego: Pfeiffer and Co., 1995).

4. International Coaching Federation Web site (http://www.coachfederation.org) "Coaching Core Competencies," accessed on February 5, 2002.

5. Ibid.

6. J. Flaherty, *Coaching: Evoking Excellence in Others* (Burlington, Mass.: Butterworth-Heinemann, 1998).

7. L. Miller, "Coaching Pays Off," *HRMagazine* (March 2001): 16.

8. M. Anderson, "Executive Briefing: Case Study on the Return on Investment of Executive Coaching" (2001), http://www.metrixglobal.net accessed on February 5, 2003.

9. R. Chin and K. Benne, "General Strategies for Effecting Changes in Human Systems," in *The Planning of Change,* 3d ed., eds. W. Bennis, K. Benne, and R. Chin (New York: Holt, Rinehart and Winston, 1976).

10. T. Galvin, "2002 Industry Report," *Training* 39 (2002): 24–52.

11. R. Fulmer and M. Goldsmith, *The Leadership Investment: How the World's Best Organizations Gain Strategic Advantage Through Leadership Development.* (New York: AMACOM, 2000).

12. C. Thompson, E. Koon, W. Woodwell, and J. Beauvais, "Training for the Next Economy: An ASTD State of the Industry Report on Trends in Employer-provided Training in the U.S.," American Society of Training and Development, 2002.

13. What CEOs Think: A Leadership Survey from CCL and Chief Executive Magazine (October 2002). *CCL'S E-Newsletter.* Retrieved August 7, 2003 from http://www.Ccl.Org/Connected/Enews/Articles/1002chiefexecmag.htm

14. C. Worley and A. Feyerherm, "Reflections on the Future of OD," *Journal of Applied Behavioral Science* 39 (2003): 97–115.

15. I. Goldstein, "Training in Work Organizations," in *Handbook of Industrial and Organizational Psychology,* ed. M. Dunnette (Chicago: Rand McNally, 1976), 507–619; G. Dessler, *Essentials of Human Resource Management* (Upper Saddle River, N.J.: Prentice Hall, 1999); C. Greer, *Strategic Human Resource Management* (Upper Saddle River, N.J.: Prentice Hall, 2001).

16. Goldstein, "Training in Work Organizations."

17. Ibid.

18. M. Van Buren and W. Erskine, "State of the Industry: ASTD's Annual Review of Trends in Employer-Provided

Training in the United States," http://www.astd.org/virtual_community/research/pdf/2002_sir_executive_summary.pdf.

19. D. Kirkpatrick, "Techniques for Evaluating Training Programs," *Journal of the American Society of Training Directors* 13 (1959): 21–26.

20. L. Ralphs and E. Stephan, "HRD in the Fortune 500," *Training and Development Journal* 40 (1986): 69–76.

21. A. Alliger and E. Janak, "Kirkpatrick's Levels of Training Criteria: Thirty Years Later," *Personnel Psychology* 42 (1989): 331–41.

22. C. Jones, "Financial Benefits of Training at Cyprus Sierrita," *Mining Engineering* 50 (1998): 20–43.

23. L. Bassi and D. McMurrer, "Training Investments Can Mean Financial Performance," *Training and Development* 52 (1998): 40–42.

24. E. Schein, *Process Consultation Volume II: Lessons for Managers and Consultants* (Reading, Mass.: Addison-Wesley, 1987).

25. E. Schein, *Process Consultation Revisited* (Reading, Mass.: Addison-Wesley, 1998), 20.

26. Schein, *Process Consultation Volume II*, 5–17.

27. Schein, *Process Consultation Revisited*.

28. M. Marks, J. Mathieu, and S. Zaccaro, "A Temporally Based Framework and Taxonomy of Team Processes," *Academy of Management Review* 26 (2001): 356–78.

29. J. Fast, *Body Language* (Philadelphia: Lippincott, M. Evans, 1970).

30. N. Clapp, "Work Group Norms: Leverage for Organizational Change, Theory and Application" (undated working paper, Block Petrella Weisbord, Plainfield, N.J); R. Allen and S. Pilnick, "Confronting the Shadow Organization: How to Detect and Defeat Negative Norms," *Organizational Dynamics* (Spring 1973): 3–18.

31. Schein, *Process Consultation Revisited*, 147.

32. J. Luft, "The Johari Window," *Human Relations Training News* 5 (1961): 6–7.

33. C. Seashore, E. Seashore, and G. Weinberg, *What Did You Say?: The Art of Giving and Receiving Feedback* (Columbia, Md.: Bingham House Books, 2001).

34. J. Gibb, "Defensive Communication," *Journal of Communication* 11 (1961): 141–48; Schein, *Process Consultation Revisited*; Seashore, Seashore, and Weinberg, *What Did You Say?*

35. E. Schein, *Process Consultation: Its Role in Organization Development* (Reading, Mass.: Addison-Wesley, 1969), 44.

36. Schein, *Process Consultation Revisited*, 167–68; E. Schein, *Organization Culture and Leadership*, 2d ed. (San Francisco: Jossey-Bass, 1992).

37. R. Kaplan, "The Conspicuous Absence of Evidence That Process Consultation Enhances Task Performance," *Journal of Applied Behavioral Science* 15 (1979): 346–60.

38. G. Lippitt, *Organizational Renewal* (New York: Appleton-Century-Crofts, 1969); C. Argyris, *Organization and Innovation* (Homewood, Ill.: Richard D. Irwin, 1965).

39. People interested in finding assistance might want to contact The Society of Professionals in Dispute Resolution (SPIDR) at http://www.acrnet.org.

40. D. Kolb and associates, *When Talk Works: Profiles of Mediators* (San Francisco: Jossey-Bass, 1994); R. Saner and L. Yiu, "External Stakeholder Impacts on Third-Party Interventions in Resolving Malignant Conflicts: The Case of a Failed Third-Party Intervention in Cyprus," *International Negotiation* 6 (2001): 387–416.

41. R. Lewicki and B. Sheppard, "Choosing How to Intervene: Factors Affecting the Use of Process and Outcome Control in Third-Party Dispute Resolution," *Journal of Occupational Behavior* 6 (January 1985): 49–64; H. Prein, "Strategies for Third-Party Intervention," *Human Relations* 40 (1987): 699–720; P. Nugent, "Managing Conflict: Third-Party Interventions for Managers," *Academy of Management Executive* 16 (2002):139–54.

42. R. Walton, *Managing Conflict: Interpersonal Dialogue and Third-Party Roles*, 2d ed. (Reading, Mass.: Addison-Wesley, 1987); Nugent, "Managing Conflict."

43. Walton, *Managing Conflict*, 81–82.

44. Ibid., 83–110.

45. This application was developed by Christine Mattos. Her contribution is gratefully acknowledged.

46. T. Patten, *Organizational Development Through Team Building* (New York: John Wiley & Sons, 1981), 2; D. Stepchuck, "Strategies for Improving the Effectiveness of Geographically Distributed Work Teams" (unpublished master's thesis, Pepperdine University, 1994).

47. C. Gibson and S. Cohen (Eds.), *Virtual Teams That Work: Creating Conditions for Virtual Team Effectiveness* (San Francisco: Jossey-Bass, 2003).

48. W. Dyer, *Team Building: Issues and Alternatives*, 2d ed. (Reading, Mass.: Addison-Wesley, 1987).

49. J. Katzenbach and D. Smith, *The Wisdom of Teams* (Boston: Harvard Business School Press, 1993).

50. French and Bell, *Organization Development*, 115.

51. Dyer, *Team Building*; Clapp, "Work Group Norms"; Katzenbach and Smith, *Wisdom of Teams*; C. Torres, D.

Fairbanks, and R. Roe, eds., *Teambuilding: The ASTD Trainer's Sourcebook* (New York: McGraw-Hill, 1996); L. Offermann and R. Spiros, "The Science and Practice of Team Development: Improving the Link," *Academy of Management Journal* 44 (2001): 376–93.

52. D. Ancona and D. Caldwell, "Bridging the Boundary: External Activity and Performance in Organizational Teams," *Administrative Science Quarterly* 37 (1992): 634–65; S. Cohen, "Designing Effective Self-Managing Work Teams" (paper presented at the Theory Symposium on Self-Managed Work Teams, Denton, Tex., June 4–5, 1993).

53. G. Bushe and G. Coetzer, "Appreciative Inquiry as a Team-Development Intervention: A Controlled Experiment," *Journal of Applied Behavioral Science* 31 (1995): 13–30; P. Walsh, C. Garbs, M. Goodwin, and E. Wolff, "An Impact Evaluation of a VA Geriatric Team Development Program," *Gerontology & Geriatrics Education*, 15(1995): 19–35.

54. J. Porras and P. O. Berg, "The Impact of Organization Development," *Academy of Management Review* 3 (April 1978): 249–66.

55. J. Nicholas, "The Comparative Impact of Organization Development Interventions on Hard Criteria Measures," *Academy of Management Review* 7 (October 1982): 531–42.

56. D. Eden, "Team Development: A True Field Experiment at Three Levels of Rigor," *Journal of Applied Psychology* 70 (1985): 94–100.

57. G. Neuman, J. Edwards, and N. Raju, "Organizational Development Interventions: A Meta-Analysis of Their Effects on Satisfaction and Other Attitudes," *Personnel Psychology* 42 (1989): 461–89; R. Woodman and S. Wayne, "An Investigation of Positive-Finding Bias in Evaluation of Organization Development Interventions," *Academy of Management Journal* 28 (December 1985): 889–913.

58. de Meuse and Liebowitz, 1981; R. Woodman and J. Sherwood, "The Role of Team Development in Organizational Effectiveness: A Critical Review," *Psychological Bulletin* 88 (July-Nov. 1980).

59. Woodman and Sherwood, "Role of Team Development."

60. Woodman and Sherwood, "Role of Team Development"; R. Guzzo and M. Dickson, "Teams in Organizations: Recent Research on Performance and Effectiveness," in *Annual Review of Psychology*, vol. 47, J. Spence, J. Darley, and J. Foss, eds., (Palo Alto, Calif.: Annual Reviews, 1996): 307–38; Wellins, Byham, and Wilson, 1991.

61. R. Buller and C. Bell, Jr., "Effects of Team Building and Goal Setting: A Field Experiment," *Academy of Management Journal* 29 (1986): 305–28.

62. R. W. Boss, "Team Building and the Problem of Regression: The Personal Management Interview as an Intervention," *Journal of Applied Behavioral Science* 19 (1983): 67–83.

63. Ibid.

Organization Process Approaches

13

In Chapter 12, we presented interventions aimed at improving individual, interpersonal, and group processes. This chapter describes systemwide process interventions—change programs directed at improving such processes as organizational problem solving, leadership, visioning, and task accomplishment between groups—for a major subsystem or for an entire organization.

The first type of intervention, the organization confrontation meeting, is among the earliest organizationwide process approaches. It helps mobilize the problem-solving resources of a major subsystem or whole organization by encouraging members to identify and confront pressing issues.

The second organization process approach is called intergroup relations. It consists of two interventions: the intergroup conflict resolution meeting and microcosm groups. Both interventions are aimed at diagnosing and addressing important organization-level processes, such as conflict, the coordination of organizational units, and diversity. The intergroup conflict intervention is specifically oriented toward conflict processes, whereas the microcosm group is a more generic systemwide change strategy.

The third and final systemwide process approach, the large-group intervention, has received considerable attention recently and is one of the fastest-growing areas in OD. Large-group interventions get a "whole system into the room"[1] and create processes that allow a variety of stakeholders to interact simultaneously. A large-group intervention can be used to clarify important organizational values, develop new ways of looking at problems, articulate a new vision for the organization, solve cross-functional problems, restructure operations, or devise an organizational strategy. It is a powerful tool for addressing organizational problems and opportunities and for accelerating the pace of organizational change.

ORGANIZATION CONFRONTATION MEETING

The *confrontation meeting* is an intervention designed to mobilize the resources of the entire organization to identify problems, set priorities and action targets, and begin working on identified problems. Originally developed by Beckhard,[2] the intervention can be used at any time but is particularly useful when the organization is in stress and when there is a gap between the top and the rest of the organization (such as when a new top manager joins the organization). General Electric's "Work-Out" program is an example of how the confrontation meeting has been adapted to fit today's organizations.[3] Although the original model involved only managerial and professional people, it has since been used successfully with technicians, clerical personnel, and assembly workers.

Application Stages

The organization confrontation meeting typically involves the following steps:

1. A group meeting of all those involved is scheduled and held in an appropriate place. Usually the task is to identify problems about the work environment and the effectiveness of the organization.

2. Groups are appointed representing all departments of the organization. Thus, each group might have one or more members from sales, purchasing, finance, operations, and quality assurance. For obvious reasons, a subordinate should not be in the same group as his or her boss, and top management should form its own group. Group size can vary from 5 to 15 members, depending on such factors as the size of the organization and available meeting places.

3. The point is stressed that the groups are to be open and honest and to work hard at identifying problems they see in the organization. No one will be criticized for bringing up problems and, in fact, the groups will be judged on their ability to do so.

4. The groups are given an hour or two to identify organization problems. Generally, an OD practitioner goes from group to group, encouraging openness and assisting the groups with their tasks.

5. The groups then reconvene in a central meeting place. Each group reports the problems it has identified and sometimes offers solutions. Because each group hears the reports of all the others, a maximum amount of information is shared.

6. Either then or later, the master list of problems is broken down into categories. This can be done by the participants, by the person leading the session, or by the manager and his or her staff. This process eliminates duplication and overlap and allows the problems to be separated according to functional or other appropriate areas.

7. Following problem categorization, participants are divided into problem-solving groups whose composition may, and usually does, differ from that of the original problem-identification groups. For example, all operations problems may be handled by people in that subunit. Or task forces representing appropriate cross sections of the organization may be formed.

8. Each group ranks the problems, develops a tactical action plan, and determines an appropriate timetable for completing this phase of the process.

9. Each group then periodically reports its list of priorities and tactical plans of action to management or to the larger group.

10. Schedules for periodic (frequently monthly) follow-up meetings are established. At these sessions, the team leaders report either to top management, to the other team leaders, or to the group as a whole regarding their team's progress and plans for future action. The formal establishment of such follow-up meetings ensures both continuing action and the modification of priorities and timetables as needed.

Application 13.1 presents the Work-Out process at General Electric Medical Systems business. It shows how the basic framework of a confrontation meeting can be adapted to address organizational problems such as productivity and employee involvement.[4]

Results of Confrontation Meetings

Because organization confrontation meetings often are combined with other approaches, such as survey feedback, determining specific results is difficult. In many cases, the results appear dramatic in mobilizing the total resources of the organization

A WORK-OUT MEETING AT GENERAL ELECTRIC MEDICAL SYSTEMS BUSINESS

APPLICATION 13•1

As part of the large-scale change effort, former CEO Jack Welch and several managers at General Electric devised a method for involving many organization members in the change process. Work-Out is a process for gathering the relevant people to discuss important issues and develop a clear action plan. The program has four goals: to use employees' knowledge and energy to improve work, to eliminate unnecessary work, to build trust through a process that allows and encourages employees to speak out without being fearful, and to engage in the construction of an organization that is ready to deal with the future.

At GE Medical Systems (GEMS), internal consultants conducted extensive interviews with managers throughout the organization. The interviews revealed considerable dissatisfaction with existing systems, including performance management (too many measurement processes, not enough focus on customers, unfair reward systems, and unrealistic goals), career development, and organizational climate. Managers were quoted as saying:

I'm frustrated. I simply can't do the quality of work that I want to do and know how to do. I feel my hands are tied. I have no time. I need help on how to delegate and operate in this new culture.

The goal of downsizing and delayering is correct. The execution stinks. The concept is to drop a lot of "less important" work. This just didn't happen. We still have to know all the details, still have to follow all the old policies and systems.

In addition to the interviews, Jack Welch spent some time at GEMS headquarters listening and trying to understand the issues facing the organization.

Based on the information compiled, about 50 GEMS employees and managers gathered for a 5-day Work-Out session. The participants included the group executive who oversaw the GEMS business, his staff, employee relations managers, and informal leaders from the key functional areas who were thought to be risk takers and who would challenge the status quo. Most of the work during the week was spent unraveling, evaluating, and reconsidering the structures and processes that governed work at GEMS. Teams of managers and employees addressed business problems. Functional groups developed visions of where their operations were headed. An important part of the teams' work was to engage in "bureaucracy busting" by identifying CRAP (Critical Review APpraisals) in the organization. Groups were asked to list needless approvals, policies, meetings, and reports that stifled productivity. In an effort to increase the intensity of the work and to encourage free thinking, senior managers were not a part of these discussions.

At the end of the week, the senior management team listened to the concerns, proposals, and action plans from the different teams. During the presentations, senior GEMS managers worked hard to understand the issues, communicate with the organization members, and build trust by sharing information, constraints, and opportunities. Most of the proposals focused on ways to reorganize work and improve returns to the organization. According to traditional Work-Out methods, managers must make instant, on-the-spot decisions about each idea in front of the whole group. The three decision choices are (1) approval; (2) rejection with clear reasons; and (3) need more data, with a decision to be made within a month.

The 5-day GEMS session ended with individuals and functional teams signing close to a hundred written contracts to implement the new processes and procedures or drop unnecessary work. The contracts were between people, between functional groups, and between levels of management. Other organizational contracts affected all GEMS members. One important outcome of the Work-Out effort at GEMS was a decision to involve suppliers in its internal email network. Through that interaction, GEMS and a key supplier eventually agreed to build new-product prototypes together, and their joint efforts have led to further identification of ways to reduce costs, improve design quality, or decrease cycle times.

Work-Out at GE has been very successful but hard to measure in dollar terms. Since 1988, hundreds of Work-Outs have been held, and the concept has continued to evolve into best-practice investigations, process mapping, and change-acceleration programs. The Work-Out process, however, clearly is based on the confrontation meeting model, where a large group of people gathers to identify issues and plan actions to address problems.

for problem identification and solution. Beckhard cites a number of specific examples in such different organizations as a food products manufacturer, a military products manufacturer, and a hotel.[5] Positive results also were found in a confrontation meeting with 40 professionals in a research and development firm.[6]

The organization confrontation meeting is a classic approach for mobilizing organizational problem solving, especially in times of low performance. Although the results of its use appear impressive, little systematic study of this intervention has been done. There is a clear need for evaluative research.

INTERGROUP RELATIONS INTERVENTIONS

The ability to diagnose and understand intergroup relations is important for OD practitioners because (1) groups often must work with and through other groups to accomplish their goals; (2) groups within the organization often create problems and place demands on each other; and (3) the quality of the relationships between groups can affect the degree of organizational effectiveness. Two OD interventions—microcosm groups and intergroup conflict resolution—are described here. A microcosm group uses members from several groups to help solve organizationwide problems. Intergroup issues are explored in this context, and then solutions are implemented in the larger organization. Intergroup conflict resolution helps two groups work out dysfunctional relationships. Together, these approaches help improve intergroup processes and lead to organizational effectiveness.

Microcosm Groups

A microcosm group consists of a small number of individuals who reflect the issue being addressed.[7] For example, a microcosm group composed of members representing a spectrum of ethnic backgrounds, cultures, and races can be created to address diversity issues in the organization. This group, assisted by OD practitioners, can create programs and processes targeted at specific issues. In addition to addressing diversity problems, microcosm groups have been used to carry out organization diagnoses, solve communications problems, integrate two cultures, smooth the transition to a new structure, and address dysfunctional political processes.

Microcosm groups work through "parallel processes," which are the unconscious changes that take place in individuals when two or more groups interact.[8] After groups interact, members often find that their characteristic patterns of roles and interactions change to reflect the roles and dynamics of the group with whom they were relating. Put simply, groups seem to "infect" and become "infected" by the other groups. The following example given by Alderfer[9] helps to clarify how parallel processes work:

> An organizational diagnosis team had assigned its members to each of five departments in a small manufacturing company. Members of the team had interviewed each department head and several department members, and had observed department meetings. The team was preparing to observe their first meeting of department heads and were trying to anticipate the group's behavior. At first they seemed to have no "rational" basis for predicting the top group's behavior because they "had no data" from direct observation. They decided to role-play the group meeting they had never seen. Diagnostic team members behaved as they thought the department heads would, and the result was uncanny. Team members found that they easily became engaged with one another in the simulated department-head meeting; emotional involvement occurred quickly for all participants. When the team actually was able to observe a department-head meeting, they were amazed at how closely the simulated meeting had approximated the actual session.

Thus, if a small and representative group can intimately understand and solve a complex organizational problem for themselves, they are in a good position to recommend action to address the problem in the larger system.

Application Stages

The process of using a microcosm group to address organizationwide issues involves the following five steps:

1. **Identify an issue.** This step involves finding a systemwide problem to be addressed. This may result from an organizational diagnosis or may be an idea generated by an organization member or task force. For example, one microcosm group charged with improving organizational communications was started by a division manager. He was concerned that the information provided by those reporting directly to him differed from the data he received from informal conversations with people throughout the division.

2. **Convene the group.** Once an issue is identified, the microcosm group can be formed. The most important convening principle is that group membership needs to reflect the appropriate mix of stakeholders related to the issue. If the issue is organizational communication, then the group should contain people from all hierarchical levels and functions, including staff groups and unions, if applicable. If the issue is integrating two corporate cultures following a merger, the microcosm group should contain people from both organizations who understand their respective cultures. Following the initial setup, the group itself becomes responsible for determining its membership. It will decide whether to add new members and how to fill vacant positions.

    Convening the group also draws attention to the issue and gives the group status. Members need to be perceived as credible representatives of the problem. This will increase the likelihood that organization members will listen to and follow the suggestions they make.

3. **Provide group training.** Once the microcosm group is established, training is provided in group problem solving and decision making. Team-building interventions also may be appropriate. Group training focuses on establishing a group mission or charter, working relationships among members, group decision-making norms, and definitions of the problem to be addressed.

    From a group-process perspective, OD practitioners may need to observe and comment on how the group develops. Because the group is a microcosm of the organization, it will tend, through its behavior and attitudes, to reflect the problem in the larger organization. For example, if the group is addressing communication problems in the organization, it is likely to have its own difficulties with communication. Recognizing within the group the problem or issue it was formed to address is the first step toward solving the problem in the larger system.

4. **Address the issue.** This step involves solving the problem and implementing solutions. OD practitioners may help the group diagnose, design, implement, and evaluate changes. A key issue is gaining commitment in the wider organization to implementing the group's solutions. Several factors can facilitate such ownership. First, a communication plan should link group activities to the organization. This may include publishing minutes from team meetings; inviting organization members, such as middle managers, union representatives, or hourly workers, into the meetings; and making presentations to different organizational groups. Second, group members need to be visible and accessible to management and labor. This can ensure that the appropriate support and resources are developed for the recommendations. Third, problem-solving processes should include an appropriate level of participation by organization members. Different data collection methods can be used to gain member input and to produce ownership of the problem and solutions.

5. **Dissolve the group.** The microcosm group can be disbanded following successful implementation of changes. This typically involves writing a final report or holding a final meeting.

Results of Microcosm Groups

The microcosm group intervention derives from an intergroup relations theory developed by Alderfer, who has applied it to communications and race-relations problems. A microcosm group that addressed communications issues improved the way meetings were conducted; developed a job posting, career development, and promotion program; and conducted new-employee orientations.[10] In addition, the group assisted in the development, administration, and feedback of an organization-wide employee opinion survey. Alderfer also reported 7 years of longitudinal data on a race-relations advisory group in a large organization.[11] Over time, white members showed significant improvements in their race-relations perceptions; African Americans consistently perceived more evidence of racism in the organization; and attendance at the meetings varied both over time and by race. In addition to the intragroup data, the case documented several changes in the organization, including the development of a race-relations competency document, the implementation of a race-relations workshop, and the creation of an upward-mobility policy.

A dearth of research exists on microcosm groups, partly because it is difficult to measure parallel processes and associate them with measures of organizational processes. More research on this intervention is needed.

Resolving Intergroup Conflict

The intergroup conflict intervention is designed specifically to help two groups or departments within an organization resolve dysfunctional conflicts. Intergroup conflict is neither good nor bad in itself, and in some cases, conflict among departments is necessary and productive for organizations.[12] This applies where there is little interdependence among departments and conflict or competition among them can spur higher levels of productivity. For example, organizations structured around different product lines might want to promote competition among the product groups. This might increase each group's productivity and add to the overall effectiveness of the firm.

In other organizations, especially those with very interdependent departments, conflict may become dysfunctional.[13] Two or more groups may grow polarized, and their continued conflict may result in the development of defensiveness and negative stereotypes of the other group. Polarization can be revealed in such statements as: "Any solution they come up with is wrong," "We find that nobody in that group will cooperate with us," or "What do you expect of those idiots?" Particularly when intergroup communication is necessary, the amount and quality of communication usually drops off. Groups begin seeing the others as "the enemy" rather than in positive or even neutral terms. As the amount of communication decreases, the amount of mutual problem solving falls off as well. The tendency increases for one group to sabotage the efforts of the other group, either consciously or unconsciously.

Application Stages

A basic strategy for improving interdepartmental or intergroup relationships is to change the perceptions (perhaps, more accurately, misperceptions) that the two groups have of each other. One formal approach for accomplishing this, originally described by Blake and his associates, consists of a 10-step procedure.[14]

1. A consultant external to the two groups obtains their agreement to work directly on improving intergroup relationships. (The use of an outside consul-

tant is highly recommended because without the moderating influence of such a neutral third party, it is almost impossible for the two groups to interact without becoming deadlocked and polarized in defensive positions.)

2. A time is set for the two groups to meet—preferably away from their normal work situations.

3. The consultant, together with the managers of the two groups, describes the purpose and objectives of the meeting: to develop better mutual relationships, explore the perceptions the groups have of each other, and formulate plans for improving the relationship. The two groups are presented the following or similar questions: "What qualities or attributes best describe our group?" "What qualities or attributes best describe the other group?" and "How do we think the other group will describe us?" Then, the two groups are encouraged to establish norms of openness for feedback and discussion.

4. The two groups are assigned to separate rooms and asked to write their answers to the three questions. Usually, an outside consultant works with each group to help the members become more open and to encourage them to develop lists that accurately reflect their perceptions, both of their own image and of the other group.

5. After completing their lists, the two groups reconvene. A representative from each group presents the written statements. Only the two representatives are allowed to speak. The primary objective at this stage is to make certain that the images, perceptions, and attitudes are presented as accurately as possible and to avoid the arguments that might arise if the two groups openly confronted each other. Questions, however, are allowed to ensure that both groups clearly understand the written lists. Justifications, accusations, or other statements are not permitted.

6. When it is clear that the two groups thoroughly understand the content of the lists, they separate again. By this point, a great number of misperceptions and discrepancies have been brought to light.

7. The task of the two groups (almost always with a consultant as a process observer) is to analyze and review the reasons for the discrepancies. The emphasis is on solving the problems and reducing the misperceptions. The actual or implicit question is not whether the perception of the other group is right or wrong but rather "How did these perceptions occur? What actions on the part of our group may have contributed to this set of perceptions?"

8. When the two groups have worked through the discrepancies, as well as the areas of common agreement, they meet to share both the identified discrepancies and their problem-solving approaches to those discrepancies. Because the primary focus is on the behavior underlying the perceptions, free, open discussion is encouraged between the two groups, and their joint aim is to develop an overall list of remaining and possible sources of friction and isolation.

9. The two groups are asked to develop specific plans of action for solving specific problems and for improving their relationships.

10. When the two groups have gone as far as possible in formulating action plans, at least one follow-up meeting is scheduled so that the groups can report on actions that have been implemented, identify any further problems that have emerged, and, where necessary, formulate additional action plans.

In addition to this formal approach to improving interdepartmental or intergroup relationships there are a number of more informal procedures. Beckhard asks each of the two groups to develop a list of what irritates or exasperates them about the other group and to predict what they think the other group will say about them.[15] A more simplified approach, although perhaps not as effective, is to bring the two groups together, dispense with the written lists developed in isolation, and discuss only common problems and irritations. Finally, based on their experience at TRW Systems, Fordyce and Weil developed a modified approach whereby each group builds three lists—one containing "positive feedback" items (those things the group values and likes about the other group), a "bug" list (those things the group dislikes about the other group), and an "empathy" list (predictions about what the other group's list contains).[16] When the groups come together, they build a master list of major concerns and unresolved problems, which are assigned priorities and developed into an agenda. When they have completed the task, the subgroups report the results of their discussions to the total group, which then develops a series of action steps for improving the relations between the groups and commits itself to following through. For each action step, specific responsibilities are assigned, and an overall schedule is developed for prompt completion of the action steps.

Different approaches to resolving intergroup conflict form a continuum from behavioral solutions to attitudinal change solutions.[17] Behavioral methods are oriented to keeping the relevant parties physically separate and specifying the limited conditions under which interaction will occur. Little attempt is made to understand or change how members of each group see the other. Conversely, attitudinal methods, such as exchanging group members or requiring intense interaction with important rewards or opportunities clearly tied to coordination, are directed at changing how each group perceives the other. Here, it is assumed that perceptual distortions and stereotyping underlie the conflict and need to be changed to resolve it.

Most of the OD solutions to intergroup conflict reviewed in this section favor attitudinal change strategies. However, such interventions typically require considerably more skill and time than do the behavioral solutions. Changing attitudes is difficult in conflict situations, especially if the attitudes are deep-seated and form an integral part of people's personalities. Attitudinal change interventions should be reserved for those situations in which behavioral solutions might not work.

Behavioral interventions seem most applicable in situations in which task interdependence between the conflicting groups is relatively low and predictable. For example, the task interaction between the production and maintenance departments might be limited to scheduled periodic maintenance on machines. Here, higher management can physically separate the departments and specify the limited conditions under which they should interact. Where the shared task requires only limited interaction, that interaction can be programmed and standardized.

Attitudinal change interventions seem necessary when task interdependence between the conflicting groups is high and unpredictable, such as might be found between the research and production departments during a new-product introduction. Here, the two departments need to work together closely, often at unpredictable times and with novel, complex issues. When conflicts arise because of misperceptions, they must be worked through in terms of people's perceptions and attitudes. The shared task does not permit physical separation or limited, specific interaction. It is in these highly interdependent and unpredictable task situations that the conflict resolution interventions discussed in this section are most appropriate.

Application 13.2 presents an example of intergroup conflict resolved by an attitudinal change intervention.[18] The method reflects a variation on the traditional process described above and also places the intervention in a planned change context.

IMPROVING INTERGROUP RELATIONSHIPS IN JOHNSON & JOHNSON'S DRUG EVALUATION DEPARTMENT

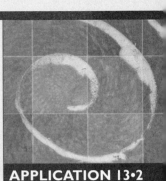

Johnson & Johnson (J&J) is one of the world's largest manu-facturers of health care products. The fundamental objective of the company is to provide scientifically sound, high-quality products and services to help heal the sick, cure disease, and improve the quality of life. In mid-2000, J&J made a strategic decision to merge two research and development organiza-tions in the Pharmaceuticals Group. Departments in the Robert Wood Johnson Pharmaceutical Research Institute, headquartered in New Jersey, and the Janssen Research Foundation, headquartered in Belgium, were integrated to create a leading-edge global function called the Drug Evalua-tion (DE) organization. DE's purpose is to rapidly generate data that allows J&J to make the best investment decisions about the drug portfolio. In the overall R&D process, the group is the bridge between discovery of new compounds and full development of a new drug. As a group, they are re-sponsible for investigating all compounds that may be poten-tial new products and making data-driven decisions in collaboration with the discovery and full development groups. The highest quality and highest potential discovery compounds are quickly and efficiently moved through pre-clinical development and into initial human trials. DE employ-ees experience a genuine and unique opportunity to shape the R&D pipeline in J&J and ultimately influence patient well-being. It is an exciting and challenging place to be.

Most of the first half of 2001 was spent in merger and in-tegration activity with the groups, while moving compounds through the pipeline. The DE management team has overall responsibility for the organization and consists of the global head of DE and seven direct reports representing chemical pharmaceuticals, clinical drug evaluation, clinical operations, and portfolio planning and resource management (PPRM), among others.

One of the groups, the PPRM group, was a new function created to improve the efficiency of DE processes. They al-lowed the DE management team to accurately track com-pounds as they moved through the process and provided information in a consistent manner across the organization. The group consisted of project champions, portfolio plan-ners, resource managers, and support staff. Project champi-ons were the core of the PPRM group. When a compound is accepted into DE, the project champion leads a project team consisting of representatives from the different functions. This team is responsible for planning and executing the DE plan for their compound. The project champion works closely with all of the functions to ensure the compound progresses on schedule through the different stages of the process and ultimately on the handoff to full development.

The Clinical Drug Evalua-tion group was responsible for developing clinical plans that would take the new drug com-pound into human trials. The group consisted primarily of clinical scientists, MDs who were responsible for focusing on the key questions to be identified to achieve DE deliverables. Clinical scientists were also responsible for communicating these questions and the results from the clinical aspects of the project to the rest of the project team. The quality of the data depends on asking the right questions, so this role is critical to delivering busi-ness benefits of the compound.

In the fall of 2001, the DE management team expressed concern that there were many issues surfacing about the na-ture of the work, roles and responsibilities, and the general cohesion within DE. This was particularly true with the clini-cal scientists and the project champions. They worried that a conflict between the schedule-oriented project champions and the quality-oriented clinical specialists was hurting de-partment morale. The DE management team asked an OD practitioner to help with understanding and addressing these issues. As part of the process, the practitioner conducted di-agnostic interviews with various members of the PPRM and Clinical Drug Evaluation groups. She found that opinions var-ied widely as to the nature of the problem and its character-istics. For example, some people did not perceive a problem, others believed it had nothing to do with the interaction of the project champions and the clinical scientists, and others believed it was a lack of clear roles and responsibilities. Overall, seven different themes emerged from the data, al-though no single issue dominated. Faced with this lack of agreement on the issue and its causes, the practitioner, in collaboration with the different groups, proposed a 3-day off-site meeting to work through the data and concerns.

The meeting was held in January 2002 in Villars, Switzer-land (selected for its neutrality), and consisted of exercises to improve communications and an intergroup conflict meet-ing process. Members of the PPRM and Clinical Drug Evalua-tion groups were asked to address the following questions:

- What do we want from you?
- What don't we want from you?
- What do we offer/give you?
- What we don't offer/give you?

Each group was asked to discuss and come to consensus about their perceptions of the other group. Reflecting the diagnostic data, there was a lively discussion within each group as perceptions were shared, discussed, and resolved.

When each group presented their results, typical responses included: We want your expertise; we want everyone to be a part of the team; we want input, support and agreement, adequate time, and frequent interaction. The groups did not want surprise decisions, delayed or filtered information, and responsibility for another's job. These themes were consistent across both groups.

The practitioner then opened the floor for a large group discussion of the presentations. Although a variety of issues were discussed and clarified, the groups noticed that they were in 90% agreement. The key issue that needed to be resolved was the decision-making process. The practitioner then facilitated a discussion of how the two groups should make decisions and they agreed on a method to do so.

As a result of the meeting, the two groups reported improved relations and increased trust because of an increased understanding of each other's perspectives. They developed positive, cooperative attitudes toward the other group, understood how different cultural backgrounds and working styles were contributing to the strained decision-making process, and were able to reach agreement on a variety of important roles and responsibilities. In addition, a few weeks after the meeting, the participants said they realized the importance of setting the time aside to work through the issues. They gained an appreciation for a need to have consistency in methods and tools for the teams. The DE management team was pleased with the results.

Results of Intergroup Conflict Interventions

A number of studies have been done on the effects of intergroup conflict resolution. Positive results have been reported by Blake,[19] Bennis,[20] Golembiewski and Blumberg,[21] French and Bell,[22] Huse and Beer,[23] and Huse[24] in a variety of settings, including union–management relations, an Indian tribal council, government organ-izations, and for-profit firms. The results include attitudinal changes such as improved perceptions, increased trust, and less stereotyping in addition to improved operational results. For example, Huse found that bringing representatives of different groups together to work on common work-related problems had a marked effect, not only on relationships among a number of different manufacturing groups but also on the quality of the product, which increased 62%.[25]

The technology for improving intergroup relations is promising. A greater distinction between attitudinal and behavioral changes needs to be made in planning effective intergroup interventions. A greater variety of interventions that addresses the practical difficulties of bringing two groups together also is necessary. Finally, more knowledge is needed about how culture affects intergroup conflict and how interventions need to be adjusted in cross-cultural situations.[26] Growing knowledge and theory suggest that conflict can be either functional or dysfunctional, depending on the circumstances. Further research is needed to identify when conflict should be intensified and when it should be reduced.

LARGE-GROUP INTERVENTIONS

The third systemwide process intervention is called large-group intervention. Such change programs have been referred to variously as "search conferences," "open-space meetings," "open-systems planning," "world cafés," and "future searches."[27] They focus on issues that affect the whole organization or large segments of it, such as developing new products or services, responding to environmental change, or introducing new technology. The defining feature of large-group intervention is the bringing together of large numbers of organization members and other stakeholders, often more than a hundred, for a 2- to 4-day meeting or conference. Here, conference attendees work together to identify and resolve organizationwide problems, to design new approaches to structuring and managing the firm, or to propose future directions for the organization. Large-group interventions are among the fastest-growing OD applications.

Large-group interventions can vary on several dimensions, including purpose, size, length, structure, and number. The purpose of these change methods can range from solving particular organizational problems to envisioning future strategic directions. Large-group interventions have been run with groups of less than 50 to more than 2,000 participants and have lasted between 1 and 5 days. Some large-group processes are relatively planned and structured; others are more informal.[28] Some interventions involve a single large-group meeting; others include a succession of meetings to accomplish systemwide change in a short period of time.[29]

Despite these differences, most large-group interventions have similar conceptual foundations and methods. These interventions have evolved over the past 30 years and represent a combination of open-systems applications and "futuring" and "visioning" exercises. Open-systems approaches direct attention to how organizations interact with and are shaped by their environments. They suggest that an organization's current state is the result of the intentional and unintentional interaction among many groups and individuals both inside and outside the organization. Changing the organization's vision, structure, strategy, or work therefore requires the deliberate, face-to-face coordination of these groups. Four key assumptions[30] underlie this approach.

1. **Organization members' perceptions play a major role in environmental relations.** They determine which parts of the environment are attended to or ignored as well as what value is placed on those parts. Such perceptions provide the basis for planning and implementing specific actions in relation to the environment.

2. **Organization members must share a common view of the environment to permit coordinated action toward it.** Without a shared view of the environment, conflicts can arise about what parts of the environment are important and about what value should be placed on different parts. Such perceptual disagreements make planning and implementing a coherent strategy difficult.[31]

3. **Organization members' perceptions must accurately reflect the condition of the environment if organizational responses are to be effective.** Members can misinterpret environmental information, ignore important forces, or attend to negligible events. Such misperceptions can render organizational responses to the environment inappropriate or ineffective. For example, managers at Coca-Cola misperceived the market for soft drinks and introduced New Coke. Sales failed to meet expectations, and New Coke had to be withdrawn from the market.

4. **Organizations cannot only adapt to their environment; they must create it proactively.** Organizations often are discussed in terms of their dependency on environments and on how they should adapt to environmental forces. But it also is possible for organizations to plan proactively for a desired environment and then take action against the existing environment to move it in the desired direction. For example, when Alcoa first started to manufacture aluminum building materials, there was little demand for them. Rather than wait to see whether the market developed, Alcoa entered the construction business and pioneered the use of aluminum building materials.

Futuring and visioning exercises help guide members in creating "images of potential" toward which the organization can grow and develop.[32] Focusing on the organization's potential rather than its problems is aligned with the positive models of planned change described in Chapter 2. It can increase members' energy for change and build a broad consensus toward a new future.

Application Stages

Conducting a large-group intervention generally involves preparing for the meeting, conducting it, and following up on outcomes. These activities are described below.

Preparing for the Large-Group Meeting

A design team comprising OD practitioners and several organization members is formed to organize the event. The team generally addresses three key ingredients for successful large-group meetings: a compelling meeting theme, appropriate participants, and relevant tasks to address the theme.

1. **Compelling meeting theme.** Large-group interventions require a compelling reason or focal point for change. Although "people problems" can be an important focus, more powerful reasons for large-group efforts include managing impending mergers or reorganizations, responding to environmental threats and opportunities, or proposing radical organizational changes.[33] Whatever the focal point for change, senior leaders need to make clear to others the purpose of the large-group meeting. Ambiguity about the reason for the intervention can dissipate participants' energy and commitment to change. For example, a large-group meeting that successfully envisioned a hospital's future organization design was viewed as a failure by a few key managers who thought that the purpose was to cut costs from the hospital's budget. Their subsequent lack of support stalled the change effort.

2. **Appropriate participants.** A fundamental goal of large-group interventions is to "get the whole system in the room." This involves inviting as many people as possible who have a stake in the conference theme and who are energized and committed to conceiving and initiating change. Senior managers, suppliers, union leaders, internal and external customers, trade group representatives, government and regulatory officials, and organization members from a variety of jobs, genders, races, and ages are potential participants.

3. **Relevant tasks to address the conference theme.** As described below, these tasks typically are assigned to several subgroups responsible for examining the theme and drawing conclusions for action. Generally, participants rely on their own experience and expertise to address systemwide issues, rather than drawing on resources from outside of the large-group meeting. This ensures that the meeting can be completed within the allotted time and that members can participate fully as important sources of information.

Conducting the Meeting

The flow of events in a large-group meeting can vary greatly, depending on its purpose and the framework adopted. Most large-group processes, however, fit within two primary frameworks: open-systems methods and open-space methods.

Open-Systems Methods. A variety of large-group approaches, such as search conferences, open-systems planning, and real-time strategic change, have their basis in open-systems methods. These approaches help organizations assess their environments systematically and develop strategic responses to them. They help organization members develop a strategic mission for relating to the environment and influencing it in favorable directions. Open-systems methods begin with a diagnosis of the existing environment and how the organization relates to it. They proceed to develop possible future environments and action plans to bring them about.[34] These steps are described below.

1. **Map the current environment surrounding the organization.** In this step, the different domains or parts of the environment are identified and prioritized. This involves listing all external groups directly interacting with the organization, such as customers, suppliers, or government agencies, and ranking them in importance. Participants then are asked to describe each domain's expectations for the organization's behavior.

2. **Assess the organization's responses to environmental expectations.** This step asks participants to describe how the organization currently addresses the environmental expectations identified in step 1.

3. **Identify the core mission of the organization.** This step helps to identify the underlying purpose or core mission of the organization, as derived from how it responds to external demands. Attention is directed at discovering the mission as it is revealed in the organization's behavior, not as it is pronounced in the organization's official statement of purpose. This is accomplished by examining the organization and environment transactions identified in steps 1 and 2 and then assessing the values that seem to underlie those interactions. These values provide clues about the actual identity or mission of the organization.

4. **Create a realistic future scenario of environmental expectations and organization responses.** This step asks members to project the organization and its environment into the near future, assuming no real changes in the organization. It asks participants to address the question, "What will happen if the organization continues to operate as it does at present?" Participant responses are combined to develop a likely organization future under the assumption of no change.

5. **Create an ideal future scenario of environmental expectations and organization responses.** Members are asked to create alternative, desirable futures. This involves going back over steps 1, 2, and 3 and asking what members ideally would like to see happen in the near future in both the environment and the organization. People are encouraged to fantasize about desired futures without worrying about possible constraints.

6. **Compare the present with the ideal future and prepare an action plan for reducing the discrepancy.** This last step identifies specific actions that will move both the environment and the organization toward the desired future. Planning for appropriate interventions typically occurs in three timeframes: tomorrow, 6 months from now, and 2 years from now. Participants also decide on a follow-up schedule for sharing the flow of actions and updating the planning process.

There are a number of variations on this basic model, each of which follows a similar pattern of creating common ground, discussing the issues, and devising an agenda for change. For example, search conferences begin with an exercise called "appreciating the past," which asks participants to examine the significant events, milestones, and highlights of the organization's previous 30 years (or less, in the case of newer organizations).[35] It demonstrates that participants share a common history, although they may come from different organizations, departments, age groups, or hierarchical levels.

Once common ground is established, members can discuss the systemwide issue or theme. To promote widespread participation, members typically organize into subgroups of 8 to 10 people representing as many stakeholder viewpoints as possible. The subgroups may address a general question (for example, "What are the opportunities for new business in our global market?") or focus on a specific issue (for example, "How can we improve quality and cut costs on a particular product line?"). Subgroup members brainstorm answers to these questions, record them on flipchart paper, and share them with the larger group. The whole group compares responses from the subgroups and identifies common themes. Other methods, such as presentations to the large group, small-group meetings on particular aspects of the conference theme, or spontaneous meetings of interest to the participants, are used to discuss the conference theme and distribute information to members.

The final task of large-group meetings based on open-systems methods is creating an agenda for change. Participants are asked to reflect on what they have learned at the meeting and to suggest changes for themselves, their department, and the whole organization. Members from the same department often are grouped together to discuss their proposals and decide on action plans, timetables, and accountabilities. Action items for the total organization are referred to a steering committee that addresses organizationwide policy issues and action plans. At the conclusion of the large-group meeting, the departmental subgroups and the steering committee report their conclusions to all participants and seek initial commitment to change.

Application 13.3 describes a large-group intervention to address the complex issue of how to manage forests in North America.[36] The Seventh American Forest Congress followed an open-systems model to design and implement its large-group meeting.

Open-Space Methods. The second approach to large-group interventions is distinguished by its lack of formal structure. Open-space methods temporarily restructure or "self-organize" participants around interests and topics associated with the conference theme. They generally follow these steps:[37]

1. **Set the conditions for self-organizing.** In the first step, the OD practitioner or manager responsible for the large-group intervention sets the stage by announcing the theme of the session and the norms that will govern it. In addition, participants are informed that the meeting will consist of small-group discussions convened by the participants and addressing any topic they believe critical to the theme of the conference. Two sets of norms govern how open-space methods are applied, and although the norms may sound ambiguous, they are critical to establishing the conditions for a successful meeting.

   The first set of norms concerns the "Law of Two Feet." It encourages people to take responsibility for their own behavior—to go to meetings and discussions where they are learning, contributing, or in some way remaining interested. Moving from group to group is legitimized by the roles of "butterflies" and "bumblebees." Butterflies attract others into spontaneous conversations and, in fact, may never attend a formal meeting. Bumblebees go from group to group and sprinkle knowledge, information, or new ideas into different meetings.

   The second set of norms is labeled the "Four Principles." The first principle is "whoever comes is the right people." It is intended to free people to begin conversations with anyone at any time. It also signals that the quality of a conversation is what's most important, not who's involved. The second principle, "Whatever happens is the only thing that could have," infuses the group with responsibility, encourages participants to be flexible, and prepares them to be surprised. "Whenever it starts is the right time" is the third principle and is aimed at encouraging creativity and following the natural energy in the group. The final principle, "When it is over, it is over," allows people to move on and not feel like they have to meet for a certain time period or satisfy someone else's requirements.

THE SEVENTH AMERICAN FOREST CONGRESS

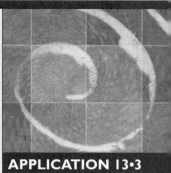

APPLICATION 13•3

The use and management of America's forests traditionally have been governed by regular Forest Congresses that were convened by a friendly but somewhat exclusive group of landowners, government agencies, timber companies, and recreational users. Legislation and government regulation followed from the advice of the congresses. The congresses of 1882 and 1905 established, respectively, the National Forest System and the U.S. Forest Service. A third congress, in 1946, considered reforestation issues after significant stands of timber were used for the war effort. The Fourth, Fifth, and Sixth Congresses met at intervals of about a decade (1953, 1963, and 1975), mostly to refine the multiple-use policy that governed forest use. Changes in the timber industry and government policy, increasing product demand, a confusing maze of court rulings, and the proliferation of groups with an interest in forest policy polarized a once-workable system for mediating differences. As a result, no congress was called in the 1980s, and not until 1994 were steps made to find a new way to bring stakeholders together to hammer out the increasingly problematic issues of forest use.

In 1994, a small group of diverse stakeholders met to commit together to a new path. That group's recommendation was to move away from the failed approaches of the past that stressed listening to or pleading with experts seated together on a stage and left groups talking past one another. The complex issues, elusive answers, and sharpening conflict demanded a wholly different paradigm. The steering group's executive committee, what became known as the Seventh American Forest Congress's board of directors, devised a core vision that called for high participation of very diverse groups talking with each other in a process that encouraged brand-new forms of much more open communication and ways of working together. The board also acknowledged that deeply rooted problems required a process rather than a solution and a new means for empowering the system of conflicting interests to resolve its own problems.

Out of this initial effort came detailed plans that would make the Seventh American Forest Congress in February 1996 a midpoint in a broad process of large-scale change among forestry's diverse interests. From July 1995 until late January 1996, about 90 local meetings were arranged to feed the eventual work of the congress. Roundtable sessions were organized in local areas to collect opinions and mirrored the expected mix of demographics, professions, and interests. Fifty-one of these roundtable sessions were conducted with the assistance of experienced facilitators, and each lasted at least a day. Thirty-nine collaborative meetings were con-

ducted by individual interested parties (for example, professional groups, timber producers, and communities). Both types of pre-congress groups were required to develop common ground (not necessarily consensus) in three areas: a new vision for forest use, principles for achieving that vision, and essential next steps for moving toward the vision. The results of these local sessions provided the working raw materials for the large, diverse, and inclusive Seventh Congress.

From the outset, organizers stressed just how different the Seventh Congress would be. The program brochure promised that "this will not be like any convention you have attended previously." It was to be clearly purposeful and would use the latest methods in large-group facilitation: "Together, you will agree on a shared vision for the future of America's forests, a set of guiding principles, and the next steps necessary to realize the vision based on principles. This will be accomplished through interaction sessions using state-of-the-art methods in large-group facilitation." Rather than throttle voices, the congress specifically embraced and celebrated the diversity of interests around forest-use policy. It was to be a citizen's congress with no delegates, no invitations, and no maximum level of attendance. Anyone who wished to attend the congress could register. Of course, congress organizers had prepared to conduct a large-scale interactive process event. A design team selected by the board of directors attended six 2-day sessions to put together a process and assemble the logistics for carrying out the congress.

The 1,500 participants were placed at tables of no more than 10 people each. Table members were selected to maximize the diversity of interests represented at the congress. The design team created a "script" that would lead table members through a process of refining a vision for America's forests and the principles for the use and care of those forests. Members then would consider the next steps to be taken by the system of interests to achieve the common vision both at the national level and in local environments. The congress would finish by obtaining the individual commitments of every participant to put congress outcomes into practice. The keys to success included the creation of effective teams out of highly diverse table members; the use of processes that explicitly took into account the explosive potential for conflict and hence kept interest focused on talking with tablemates and not talking at the congress as a whole;

and finally congress leaders' and facilitators' taking no substantive stance on the issues but letting the congress find and empower itself through the process.

In the first day's activities, the process and goals were outlined, table teams were built, members worked toward refining a common vision, and table members participated in different "concurrent dialogue sessions" that brought back emerging views and principles to their tables. The real key to the first session was the building of the table teams. Ten diverse people with passionately held points of view were put together and given tasks that forced them to seek and cultivate common bonds. Before moving on to working with more substantive issues, table members shared information about themselves and established commitments to each other that would carry their work through the congress. In the first round of activity, each table had a trained facilitator. After the first round, tablemates chose facilitators and recorders from their own ranks. Once table members established commitments to each other, they began the process of creating a common database for the congress. The first task was to brainstorm the items that made each member feel good and not so good about what is happening to America's forests. From the very start, table members had to deal face-to-face with the hottest issues of the congress.

With dissatisfaction out in the open and systematically identified, table members turned their attention to developing the vision. Vision elements were taken from the prior work of the roundtables and collaborative meetings. Every table was asked to react to each of those elements. Each member could express her or his reaction by giving the statement a green light for solid agreement, a yellow light indicating less than full support but willingness to go along, or a red light for complete disagreement. Table members were asked to tally their responses to more than a dozen of these vision statement elements and to focus their discussion on finding common ground.

In the afternoon of the first day, table members could choose to attend breakout groups called concurrent dialogue sessions. The topics of those sessions had been predefined based on inputs from the roundtables. Table teams sent members to the sessions to bring back ideas and points of view emerging elsewhere. In each dialogue session a trained facilitator helped the group broaden various perspectives on forest issues. At the end of the day, team members reported the results of the dialogue sessions to their tables.

The second day's work began with a second round of concurrent dialogue sessions and feedback about the results of the first day's activities, especially congresswide tallies of vision statements and views about what was and was not

working in America's forests. With this context established, table members refined the principles by which the common vision could be achieved. Table members attended concurrent dialogue sessions on particular principles, much like the sessions of the previous day. The purpose of these sessions was to revise the principles and supporting statements and to generate principles that were missing after the roundtable process. The work of the dialogue sessions was reported to the whole congress on the following day.

In the last phases of the congress, participants began to feel empowered by the process. Instead of holding to a rigid schedule, the design team restructured the last day-and-a-half of the congress based on real-time feedback from the participants. Congress members worked first at their tables to develop advice to the board of directors for steps to be taken at the national level. Afterward, the now highly practiced participants decided to go to their "back-home" teams—formed by zip-code membership—to work out ways to translate the vision and principles into realities at the local level, the resources needed to do so, and the kinds of processes needed to link the work of the congress to the local areas. In addition, the early commitment to the process even thwarted an attempt to organize a walkout: Two of the more vocal members, advocating personal agendas, failed to divide and disrupt the congress. Another indicator of the acceptance of the process was that literally thousands of actions were developed to support the principles.

Early reactions to the vision elements resulted in a large percentage of "red" or complete-disagreement votes. But the final tally of the congress recorded that of the 13 considered pieces to the vision statement, more than a third of them received green lights from more than 80% of the participants. For example, 90% of the participants agreed that in the future the forests would be held in a variety of public, private, tribal, land-grant, and trust ownerships by owners whose rights, objectives, and expectations would be respected and who would understand and accept their responsibilities as stewards. Key statements of principle also received strong support. Back-home steps included reconvening local meetings within 60 days to review the results of the congress and to share the process of how those results were obtained. Advice to the congress board of directors reflected a deep interest in the new process that had been used. In fact, most of the comments dealt not with the contentious substantive issues, but with how to make the process run even more smoothly in the future. This, of course, was a key lesson: Members were taking back process, not the better-honed conflict that had characterized traditional methods of dealing with forest policy.

2. **Create the agenda.** The second step in open-space interventions is to develop a road map for the remainder of the conference. This is accomplished by asking participants to describe a topic related to the conference theme that they have passion for and interest in discussing. This topic is written on a large piece of paper, announced to the group, and then posted on the community bulletin board where meeting topics and locations are displayed.[38] The person announcing the topic agrees to convene the meeting at the posted time and place. This process continues until everyone who wants to define a topic has been given the chance to speak. The final activity in this step asks participants to sign up for as many of the sessions as they have interest in. The open-space meeting begins with the first scheduled sessions.

3. **Coordinate activity through information.** During an open-space session, there are two ways to coordinate activities. First, each morning and evening a community meeting is held to announce new topics that have emerged for which meeting dates and times have been assigned, or to share observations and learnings. Second, as the different meetings occur, the conveners produce 1-page summaries of what happened, who attended, what subjects were discussed, and what recommendations or actions were proposed. Typically, this is done on computer in a room dedicated for this purpose. These summaries are posted near the community bulletin board in an area often labeled "newsroom." Participants are encouraged to visit the newsroom and become familiar with what other groups have been discussing. The summaries also can be printed and copied for conference participants.

Application 13.4 provides a more detailed description of how an open-space meeting is conducted.[39] The consultant organization believed the open-space design allowed them to discuss a variety of issues in a flexible format and gave them the opportunity to network with colleagues in ways that a normal annual meeting would not have supported.

Following up on Meeting Outcomes

Follow-up efforts are vital to implementing the action plans from large-scale interventions. These efforts involve communicating the results of the meeting to the rest of the organization, gaining wider commitment to the changes, and structuring the change process. In those cases where all the members of the organization were involved in the large-group meeting, implementation can proceed immediately according to the timetable included in the action plans.

Results of Large-Group Interventions

In the past decade, the number of case studies describing the methods and results of large-group interventions has increased dramatically. Such interventions have been conducted widely, at Hewlett-Packard, AT&T, AMI Presbyterian St. Luke's Hospital, Boeing, Kodak, Microsoft, and Rockport, among other companies; around a variety of themes or issues, including natural resources conservation, community development, and strategic change; and in a variety of countries, including Pakistan, Australia, England, Mexico, and India.[40] Despite the proliferation of practice, however, little systematic research has been done on the interventions' effects. Because these change efforts often set the stage for subsequent OD interventions, it is difficult to isolate their specific results from those of the other changes. Anecdotal evidence from practitioners suggests the following benefits from large-group interventions: increased energy toward organizational change, improved feelings of community, ability to see "outside the box," increased speed of change, and improved relationships with stakeholders.[41] Clearly, systematic research is needed on this important systemwide process intervention.

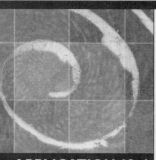

OPEN-SPACE MEETING AT A CONSULTING FIRM

A worldwide consulting organization used an open-space design to address the future of the organization as part of its annual meeting. The meeting began with a day of traditional reports on past performance, market trends, and awards for outstanding consultants. The next morning, the 320 principals assembled in the conference center ballroom.

Day One

When people walked into the room, 320 chairs were arranged in three concentric circles. Many paused at the door as they arrived, looked around with raised eyebrows, and tried to decide where to sit. The open-space event was opened by the general manager, who spoke about the organization's future and how it might be positioned for success. During his talk, he made several comments about how unusual it was for the organization to try this kind of meeting.

He then introduced a consultant who described what they would be doing and how they would do it. He told them that they would create their own agenda and run their own meetings for the next 2 days around issues that they really cared about. He described the importance of a few simple principles and laws (the Law of Two Feet and the Four Principles). Side murmurs and appreciative laughter were heard as he spoke.

The consultant then invited participants to think about issues related to the future of the organization about which they were passionate and willing to initiate a conversation. Participants were asked to come to the center of the circle, write their issue on a piece of paper and sign it, and announce their topic and their name to the group. Then they were instructed to go to the wall labeled "Community Bulletin Board," select a time and location for their meeting from the available openings, and hang their topic on the wall in that space. The community bulletin board had been arranged so that each meeting would last about an hour at a particular meeting place in the conference center. Eight time slots and 15 meeting spaces were available in the 2 days after the first morning, creating 120 meeting spaces.

There was a long pause, but after some time, someone rose, picked up a piece of paper, and began to write on it. Others followed and soon a dozen people were writing and announcing their topic and their name. When the initial flow waned, people who had been hesitating were urged to take the plunge and a number did. In about 15 minutes, more than 50 topics were announced and posted. After being given a final opportunity to propose a topic, the participants were asked to go to the community bulletin board and sign their names to any and all topics that they wanted to attend. People sat around and chatted until there was space at the wall and then went over to sign their names. In another 15 minutes most of the topics had some names on them; a number were of high interest and attracted many signatures.

Once a person declared a topic and picked a time and place, his or her responsibility was to show up and convene the meeting. After the meeting was over, this person was to type up a summary of who was there and what happened on one of the 15 computers arranged around the other walls of the ballroom. Following this initial set of instructions and agenda-setting activities, the participants were dismissed to start their meetings. The consultant was available to help with any problems, but the program was simple and self-instructing.

Some groups were clearly led by the convener; others had free-flow give-and-take. One group of six or seven took to working out a complex technical problem. Another group of 20 debated the necessity for certain corporate policies and appropriate actions to take. A third group was inventing new processes for integrating and educating midcareer hires. The groups were relatively stable, with people occasionally joining or leaving. One group that didn't have time to decide on the action steps it wanted after a lively discussion noted that a similar topic was being discussed on the next day and agreed to show up in that time space. Other small groups of people, in central gathering places, were meeting and working intently, apparently on business issues. The annual meeting convened attendees from many countries, and this was the one time during the year when they were all together. The open-space design provided a lot of agenda flexibility and time and space for easy networking.

During the afternoon, reports were filed, printed, and posted on a wall near the ballroom entrance. As people discovered them, the readers began to collect and converse. The page-length reports were numbered in order of their printing and posting, so that on subsequent visits to this "newsroom," it was easy to remember what had been read. The "Evening News," or final session of the first day, held in the ballroom at 5:45 p.m., was brief. A few announcements were made, along with a reminder about the next day's "Morning News" session. No activities were planned for the evening, and people went off to do whatever they wished.

Day Two

The second day began as the first had ended, in the large circles in the ballroom. The consultant asked if people wished to raise any new topics. After a long pause, one man came out to write on the newsprint. Several people followed him and another 8 to 10 topics were posted. The consultant then explained that a book summarizing all the discussions would be published and in their hands the next morning. The only requirement was that meeting conveners had to submit their summary reports before 6:30 that evening.

The second day was similar to the first, but with a more relaxed flow. Groups were meeting all over the place and this way of working was becoming familiar. People regularly checked in at the wall to see where they wanted to go or to read the long list of reports. At the Evening News, some announcements were made and the consultant explained that the next day would be spent prioritizing the 67 issues that had been reported out. At 6:30 p.m., when the computers shut down, 102 pages were printed with a table of contents, a 1-page description of the event that produced the book, and a simple ballot for voting on the top 10 priorities. This went off to the copy center, where it was reproduced and bound with a cover page overnight.

Day Three

The next morning, the 320 attendees assembled to start the day's schedule. First, they picked up a copy of the book of reports, read and selected their 10 most important issues, and then keyed in their votes on the computers. Second, after a short break, they returned to the ballroom to hear the results. The overall frequency distribution was displayed for the group. The titles of the 15 top priorities were written on flipcharts and posted around the ballroom and adjoining anteroom space. People were given an opportunity to visit any or all of the stations and record two types of information on them: (1) any other related issues and (2) action steps that they wanted to see occur. The person who convened each of the top-priority sessions was asked to record the comments of those who came by. The final event of this open-space assembly was a commentary by the firm's manager about each issue, what had been written about it, and how the action items would be carried out.

■ SUMMARY

This chapter described three types of systemwide process interventions: confrontation meetings, intergroup interventions, and large-group interventions. The organization confrontation meeting is a way of mobilizing resources for organizational problem solving and seems especially relevant for organizations undergoing stress. The intergroup relations approaches are designed to help solve a variety of organizational problems. Microcosm groups can be formed to address particular issues and use parallel processes to diffuse group solutions to the organization. The intergroup conflict resolution approach involves a method for mitigating dysfunctional conflicts between groups or departments. Conflict can be dysfunctional in situations in which groups must work together. It may, however, promote organizational effectiveness when departments are relatively independent of each other. Large-group interventions are designed to focus the energy and attention of a "whole system" around organizational processes such as a vision, strategy, or culture. It is best used when the organization is about to begin a large-scale change effort or is facing a new situation. These three process interventions represent important, time-honored, and successful methods of introducing change in organizations.

■ NOTES

1. M. Weisbord, *Productive Workplaces* (San Francisco: Jossey-Bass, 1987).

2. R. Beckhard, "The Confrontation Meeting," *Harvard Business Review* 4 (1967): 149–55.

3. B. B. Bunker and B. Alban, *Large Group Interventions* (San Francisco: Jossey-Bass, 1997); N. Tichy and S. Sherman, *Control Your Destiny or Someone Else Will* (New York: HarperCollins, 1993).

4. This application was adapted from material in Bunker and Alban, *Large Group Interventions,* and in Tichy and Sherman, *Control Your Destiny.*

5. R. Beckhard, *Organization Development: Strategies and Models* (Reading, Mass.: Addison-Wesley, 1969).

6. W. Bennis, *Organization Development: Its Nature, Origins, and Prospects* (Reading, Mass.: Addison-Wesley, 1969), 7.

7. C. Alderfer, "An Intergroup Perspective on Group Dynamics," in *Handbook of Organizational Behavior*, ed. J. Lorsch (Englewood Cliffs, N.J.: Prentice Hall, 1987), 190–222; C. Alderfer, "Improving Organizational Communication Through Long-Term Intergroup Intervention," *Journal of Applied Behavioral Science* 13 (1977): 193–210; C. Alderfer, R. Tucker, C. Alderfer, and L. Tucker, "The Race Relations Advisory Group: An Intergroup Intervention," in *Organizational Change and Development*, vol. 2, eds. W. Pasmore and R. Woodman (Greenwich, Conn.: JAI Press, 1988), 269–321.

8. Alderfer, "Intergroup Perspective."

9. Ibid., p. 210.

10. Alderfer, "Improving Organizational Communication."

11. Alderfer et al., "Race Relations Advisory Group."

12. K. Jehn, "A Multimethod Examination of the Benefits and Detriments of Intragroup Conflict," *Administrative Science Quarterly* 40 (1995): 256–83.

13. D. Tjosvold, "Cooperation Theory and Organizations," *Human Relations* 37 (1984): 743–67.

14. R. Blake, H. Shepard, and J. Mouton, *Managing Intergroup Conflict in Industry* (Houston, Tex.: Gulf, 1954).

15. Beckhard, *Organization Development.*

16. J. Fordyce and R. Weil, *Managing WITH People* (Reading, Mass.: Addison-Wesley, 1971).

17. E. Neilson, "Understanding and Managing Intergroup Conflict," in *Organizational Behavior and Administration*, eds. P. Lawrence, L. Barnes, and J. Lorsch (Homewood, Ill.: Richard D. Irwin, 1976), 291–305.

18. This application was written and submitted by Marianne Tracy, who served as the OD practitioner in this case.

19. Blake, Shepard, and Mouton, *Managing Intergroup Conflict.*

20. Bennis, *Organization Development.*

21. R. Golembiewski and A. Blumberg, "Confrontation as a Training Design in Complex Organizations: Attitudinal Changes in a Diversified Population of Managers," *Journal of Applied Behavioral Science* 3 (1967): 525–47.

22. W. French and C. Bell, *Organization Development: Behavioral Science Interventions for Organization Improvement* (Englewood Cliffs, N.J.: Prentice Hall, 1978).

23. E. Huse and M. Beer, "Eclectic Approach to Organizational Development," *Harvard Business Review* 49 (1971): 103–13.

24. E. Huse, "The Behavioral Scientist in the Shop," *Personnel* 44 (May-June 1965): 8–16.

25. Ibid.

26. A. Hubbard, "Cultural and Status Differences in Intergroup Conflict Resolution: A Longitudinal Study of a Middle East Dialogue Group in the United States," *Human Relations* 52 (1999): 303–23.

27. Weisbord, *Productive Workplaces;* M. Weisbord, *Discovering Common Ground* (San Francisco: Berrett-Koehler, 1993); Bunker and Alban, *Large Group Interventions;* H. Owen, *Open Space Technology: A User's Guide* (Potomac, Md.: Abbott, 1992); J. Brown, D. Isaacs, and the World Café Pioneers, "The World Café: Living Knowledge Through Conversations That Matter," in *The Systems Thinker* (Cambridge, Mass.: Pegasus Communications, June/July 2001) (http://www.theworldcafe.com/resources.html#articles).

28. Owen, *Open Space Technology.*

29. D. Axelrod, "Getting Everyone Involved," *Journal of Applied Behavioral Science* 28 (1992): 499–509.

30. T. Cummings and S. Srivastva, *Management of Work: A Socio-Technical Systems Approach* (San Diego: University Associates, 1977), 112–16.

31. L. Bourgeois, "Strategic Goals, Perceived Uncertainty, and Economic Performance in Volatile Environments," *Academy of Management Journal* 28 (1985): 548–73; C. West Jr. and C. Schwenk, "Top Management Team Strategic Consensus, Demographic Homogeneity, and Firm Performance: A Report of Resounding Nonfindings," *Academy of Management Journal* 17 (1996): 571–76.

32. F. Emery and E. Trist, *Towards a Social Ecology* (New York: Plenum Publishing, 1973); R. Beckhard and R. Harris, *Organizational Transitions: Managing Complex Change*, 2d ed. (Reading, Mass.: Addison-Wesley, 1987); R. Lippitt, "Future Before You Plan," in *The NTL Manager's Handbook* (Arlington, Va.: NTL Institute, 1983), 38–41.

33. Weisbord, *Productive Workplaces.*

34. C. Krone, "Open Systems Redesign," in *Theory and Method in Organization Development: An Evolutionary Process*, ed. J. Adams (Arlington, Va.: NTL Institute for Applied Behavioral Science, 1974), 364–91; G. Jayaram, "Open Systems Planning," in *The Planning of Change*, 3d ed., eds. W. Bennis, K. Benne, R. Chin, and K. Corey (New York: Holt, Rinehart and Winston, 1976), 275–83; R. Beckhard and R. Harris, *Organizational Transitions: Managing Complex Change*, 2d ed. (Reading, Mass.: Addison-Wesley, 1987); Cummings and Srivastva, *Management of Work.*

35. Weisbord, *Productive Workplaces.*

36. This application was submitted by Roland Sullivan, designer and co-lead facilitator of the Seventh American Forest Congress.

37. Bunker and Alban, *Large Group Interventions;* Owen, *Open Space Technology.*

38. Owen, *Open Space Technology.*

39. Adapted from an example provided in Bunker and Alban, *Large Group Interventions.*

40. Weisbord, *Common Ground;* Owen, *Open Space Technology;* M. Manning and J. DelaCerda, "Building Organizational Change in an Emerging Economy: Whole Systems Change Using Large Group Interventions in Mexico," in *Research in Organization Change and Development,* W. Pasmore and R. Woodman (Oxford: JAI Press, 2003), 51–98.

41. R. Purser, S. Cabana, M. Emery, and F. Emery, "Search Conferencing: Accelerating Large-Scale Strategic Planning," in *Fast Cycle Organization Development,* ed. M. Anderson (Cincinnati, Ohio: South-Western College Publishing, 2000); D. Coghlan, "The Process of Change through Interlevel Dynamics in a Large-Group Intervention for a Religious Organization," *Journal of Applied Behavioral Science* 34 (1998): 105–20.

The Metric Division Case

You are a member of the corporate OD staff of a large conglomerate of companies manufacturing household hardware goods. As is typical of your work, you have been asked to make a presentation to a management team in one of the companies concerning the different kinds of management development programs and activities that the corporation offers. The contact in this case comes from the personnel manager of the Metric Division. This division has recently been reorganized so that it is now totally responsible for an entire product line. The top-management staff has been in place for 5 months, and the division president is interested in the available options for management development of his subordinates. Joan, the personnel manager, has also shared with you her perception that Joe, the division head, wants to get off to a good start in the new structure and is looking for "perks" for his people: programs they can attend to increase their knowledge, skills, and so on.

At a staff meeting of Metric Division management, you presented the various kinds of training programs, consultation services, and so on that your corporate group offers. The presentation covered individual skill-oriented programs as well as on-site action-research or OD interventions, including team development. During a brief discussion of the kinds of things that enhance team effectiveness, the national sales manager, Don, commented that some of the ideas you were covering might be helpful to the staff. You discussed the need to do some diagnosis before launching into a developmental program. Don further stated that he thought it would be very helpful to have someone interview all the members of the staff to determine what could be done to help them work together more effectively. A more general discussion ensued; everyone, including Joe, agreed verbally to have you conduct a diagnosis to help them decide whether some special developmental effort was warranted.

You proceeded to interview each member of the staff for about one to one and a half hours each over the next 10 days. Your contract around the interviews included:

1. *Anonymity:* They should use names only if it was all right for others to see that name in some paraphrase of their comments.

2. *Feedback:* You would provide a summary of the interview data for the team to look at together in order to decide collectively whether there was sufficient need to spend time on particular issues to improve their functioning.

3. *Action planning:* The staff has agreed to one 3-hour session to look at your feedback summary and to decide whether or not to go ahead with any developmental efforts.

It is now 3 days before the scheduled feedback meeting. The following information is the summary of the interviews with each staff member, including Joe.

SUMMARY OF VERBATIM RESPONSES TO QUESTIONS

What does this staff do well as a team?

Not a team yet but does have common thread of loyalty to Joe—doesn't function as a team on group decisions, however. We don't listen, though we talk a hell of a lot and say little. In crisis we band together. One-on-ones don't contribute to team concept.

Share information well. Have mutual and high regard for one another.

Not too much as a team yet—mainly a source of information from each other. Effective in information sharing.

Cope fairly well with business situations, such as profit position—good willingness to recognize others' problems.

Bring keen interest and desire to do well, but not that many things done well as a team. There's a question of functional as opposed to division responsibility.

What does this staff not do well as a team?

Nothing really as a team—"Don't really know what we do well."

Identify and solve or decide on issues of divisional nature (things like examining ourselves as a division—how we operate, how we function as management group within a division). Not agreed as a staff that we should even do that.

Might be unreal, but I don't feel the staff does very well at solving problems. We don't address issues, clarify data, or go for resolution very well. All problems are treated alike, and we need ground rules for the kinds of problems to be solved by the group at the right time and by the right people. We're less effective as a team than we are in pairs or in one-to-one situations.

Where we have tried to problem-solve, I think we've been less effective than we could have been—not too much practice at it.

Deal in abstract matters—tendency not to resolve such issues but rather to let them disappear. We're a business-oriented group that deals best with dollars and things.

We don't question one another—don't feel we're open to looking at each other's worlds—don't have overriding sense of owning division-wide problems—still some functionalism present. Look to Joe for decisions.

As a team, we haven't come to grips with anything of great relevance to the business decision-making process—probably have avoided it.

Haven't learned to resolve issues quickly and provide input to areas outside our area.

We don't routinely as a group discuss division problems, only in a crisis when we're trying to put out a fire. Do a lot of one-on-one in staff meeting, especially sales and marketing, while rest of us sit there not knowing what's going on or how to contribute. Subjects get so specific you're out in center field. We don't discuss business needs like development—we as staff don't know what's going on in any depth.

We debate and discuss a subject forever—for example, name tags discussion. Joe lets discussion ramble. Someone ought to be process observer and pull us up short if wasting time.

How effective do you feel staff meetings are?

Semieffective—information mode—do well. However, when a specific problem arises, we don't do as well. Don't attack a problem in an orderly way. We would like a more systematic approach. Must utilize staff time more effectively.

Don't feel everyone's on board. Issues of new versus old still present and get in the way. We are more just a group of functional heads around the table. Staff meeting not effective at all. Question about how to conduct a staff meeting—never complete an agenda. What should these meetings be—information sharing, decision making, or what? What does Joe really want?

Meetings seem to be a waste of time in terms of moving the business ahead, but helpful as a learning device. There's not a lot of building, and we talk to Joe, rather than each other. Heavy loading of marketing people probably skews perspective of staff. Must decide on how we want to use the staff. Are we really going to be a problem-solving group, or just an information-sharing team? We should agree to define our role if we are serious about it.

Not very effective if you expect problem solving or decision making, but effective as information sharing—depends on question of role. I'd like it to be a problem-solving group for division—size might make it difficult.

Compared with my previous experiences, I think they're more effective; however, we seem unable to generate agenda items and deal with them.

Staff meetings are pretty ineffective. No one questions why we're there.

Relatively ineffective. Misapplication of time for majority of people there. We wait for our issue to come up. We should deal with issues that transcend total division—convene relevant staff on business issues.

We confirm previously made decisions and disguise this as decision making.

We don't discriminate between major and minor issues; we handle them the same way—from a million-dollar problem to name tags for a sales meeting.

Staff expertise could be productive if applied to bigger, longer-range problems instead of this being done by individuals.

Staff meetings ramble. Joe likes everyone to have an opportunity to talk. I like meetings crisp and to the point; we are better organized with agendas and minutes and follow-up. Size of staff affects this also—in long run we should reduce size.

How effective do you feel the organization structure of the division is in facilitating getting the work done?

Has some problems—the untraditional marketing organization gives me some concerns. I don't see any real negatives though.

Very effective. We've gotten along very well as a division in an operating business fashion. Feel more strongly about our unit as opposed to former structure.

My only other comment would be about the number of marketing people on the staff, which may risk tilting the direction toward marketing too much.

Reasonably effective.

I'm pleased with it. We do fundamental things well, but administratively we're not that effective (except controller's function).

Not bad. Some communication problem between operations and marketing. Size of staff might make forming a team more difficult.

We're set up the way we should be, but having nine people report to Joe may preclude us from dealing with things as a staff. We might have to trim the number to operate truly as a staff team.

We should improve interaction of staff—not confine to staff meetings—and improve productive exchange between members.

We should (1) identify people relevant to decision; (2) clearly identify others as resource; (3) get primary options out quickly; (4) avoid continual competitiveness and dwelling on minor aspects, such as name tags.

If I had responsibility for all aspects of business and could get all people working together as a team, I'd do even a better job.

We should be organized to maximize development, and I don't think we are. Development is not fully coordinated but is going on in several separate areas.

In the long run, the division should be organized around our businesses. Our division should be organized so that a person responsible for a given product line should have all aspects: research, operations, marketing, and so forth.

With three marketing jobs, I have concern we have too many people on staff—eleven people cut air time for each. I have to deal with three guys instead of one to get job done, which takes time.

Present structure requires several people in each function to zero in on work direction, and this is time consuming.

What are the goals or priorities of this staff, and how do you feel about them?

None that explicit. Implicit goals to learn how to function under this kind of structure. What is our role? We could use explicit goals and priorities.

What goals? We still don't have the clear-cut goals I'd like to see.

We have some clear-cut goals and priorities as a division, and each function is contributing separately. Staff should help achieve them in a synergistic fashion.

We don't have goals as a group, but individually we probably do. One commonly shared goal might be to move staff meetings along more expeditiously.

No specific set of goals for staff aside from business objectives.

Not come to grips yet—no list, but a goal could be the establishment of process (climate) and relationship that would lead to accomplishment of our business objectives.

Absence of goals and priorities linked to plan and to how we solve issues. As raw materials costs rise, goals should be defined. Everybody keeps asking what the goals and objectives are. They want the boss to restate them: (1) to achieve the profit objectives—most important; (2) make products x and y successful new businesses; (3) increase the profitability of business; (4) weave us into an effective operating division.

Goals have not been communicated to staff accurately and emphatically enough. We develop strategies for top management, but we don't discuss them. They are developed between marketing and Joe. We don't develop them jointly and therefore have to run to find out what they are.

We don't talk in staff about priorities—we decide in our own minds. Joe never says exactly what we are going to do. Joe should go off and lay out plan and come back and we will critique; instead, it's taken for granted. Joe's a great guy, however; don't get me wrong.

Goals and priorities not fully coordinated—for example, where we stand on the new generation of products. Is anyone working on them, and if not, shouldn't we be?

What helps you get your job done?

The learning part of my job has clearly been helped by the staff, and exposure to individuals has helped me to work more effectively with them.

They're still bringing me on board. Very helpful efforts to bring me up to date. Willingness to help has been gratifying.

Fair exchange of information among ourselves, facilitated by personal respect. Posting from staff is important—extent to which they get involved in my work is important.

Timely provision of information in an easily disgested form capable of being passed on—"completed staff work"—we're getting better, but I'm still rewriting a lot. Lack of organizational status; for example, when marketing doesn't dominate the business to an unhealthy degree.

When staff involves and uses me as a resource and they do it early enough.

Complete confidence of boss, accessibility of other levels within organization and other functions (point of relevant information), plus effective support of other functions. Resource application from other functional heads is very important, and that deployment is critical.

Staff's commitment to giving me resources to do my job. They have restraints.

Pete, Dick—less exchange or help from them. They are too into their own bag. We could counsel each other better, but we don't.

If division does well and I don't, I suffer. If division does not do well and I do, I suffer.

Support of staff to make new products division successful is very helpful.

Joe is a leader and very supportive, is trusting and stays cool in face of problems. Without that kind of boss my job would be twice as difficult.

Helps—knowing what total decision is and knowing Joe's on board so I can go ahead with money, time, and so on, knowing I have authority once decision is made.

Joe's saying that you have authority and responsibilities—he does not nitpick things. He leaves you on your own to run your job.

Question is how to make my organization to fit into overall operation of division.

What gets in the way of getting your job done?

Not having it clear in our minds what our individual roles and responsibilities are—"Where should we be getting into the act?"

One-to-one decisions as opposed to those that have impacts on other areas—time restraints, schedules, time demands. Inability to sit down and make decisions together quickly.

Tendency of senior marketing personnel to delegate market research could create problems for me. Question of trust and respect of market research professionalism raises a concern.

Not enough interaction between functions; for example, development guys across units don't interchange their knowledge and take advantage of individual capabilities.

Not getting into a situation until it's cast in concrete—it becomes more difficult to be of constructive help then.

What would you like your boss to do more or less of?

Continue leaning on me for input—more leadership in staff meetings and more decisiveness when there are disagreements among us. Less detail orientation on some items, as it could be a waste of his time.

Be more available to each of the functions. Work at continuing interface relationships. Fewer one-on-one decisions where decision makes impact on my area.

Get himself away from details of day-to-day business. Ask more often, "What do you need or want from me?" Keep himself oriented to how business is operating and just trust staff more for their functional expertise. He gets problems transferred to him.

Apply decisive leadership abilities more—he's hedging to be nice right now. More appreciation/involvement in developing aspects of business and in long-term issues transcending all groups. Less orientation to brand detail.

Boss—as a resource; give more of his time. Less of sending signals to rest of organization (my area of organization) without touching base with me first, for example, discussing with agency what he feels is working with our advertising program. Express where he thinks business is capable of going—his assessment. What he thinks we can and should be doing.

Joe must recognize that president's job is different; principal function is to mold different functions together toward common objective. Need to find his philosophy and express to group what the role of president is.

Could reach out more to staff to do and define his job. Perhaps staff should tell him how we see his role.

What would you like your peers to do more or less of?

I wish the staff as a totality would become less sensitive to people running across functional lines to get information from individuals directly involved. We're too compartmentalized.

Would like group to be more sensitive to the sales organization situation and help us to become more effective as a line function. In other words, use us more. I would hope individuals would resolve possible disagreements before meetings to avoid taking up others' time.

Make me more aware of their planning needs earlier. Be less independent of each other.

Set climate in their organization that would allow all expertise regardless of level to surface. Give their people more lead time.

Help discipline staff to allocate appropriate amount of time to big versus little issues.

Give me more time to discuss my business with them.

Like more opportunity to participate in their business and broader aspects of business; for example, I'd like to feel people are tapping me for my expertise in technical research and development.

Express goals and strategies for business and functional areas more. Not in detail, but overview.

More working as team and less perpetuating one-on-one interaction, especially when subject cuts across many functions.

Which, if any, of your relationships with members of this staff do you feel could be improved? How would you start to do this?

Relations with production could be worked on. Communications between functions at plant levels could be improved. Division professional services, too—have started discussions on this with Don. We're defining the problem now.

We've done some fence mending with Harold and are off to a good start with technical research, financial, and sales. Have innate rivalries with new-products development group, and Pete and I would have to work on and set the right climate. Could be sharing of ideas and data that we are both developing.

Harold and I have good workaday relationship. George and I still sorting out our different styles—I'm too loose and we're in process of bending. Don's fine, still fending his way—Dick and I have good relationship, he keeps me aware and involved but doesn't always respond to things I'd like to see done; he must keep me aware of things I need to know—Pete and I still working on relationships, I think he believes I intrude into nuts and bolts too much. Ray believes I don't spend enough time with him and his function. Fred and I have clear understanding. I have little contact with Kurt and would like more participation and counseling in staff meetings. Pleased with relationship with Joan—would like a stronger functional voice at times.

Relationship between Dick and me one of standard politeness; don't get along, contribute little to each other.

My best relationship is with Fred.

I could improve my relationship with George. I have to get his confidence that I'm not managing the numbers to make them look better than they are.

Harold and I have a good relationship. He makes it clear that I should handle relationships with his subs through him. We could keep each other posted more.

Dick—slightly strained relationship. We are hesitant to give each other advice. I get the feeling of a competitive relationship.

Joan and I are fine, and George and Don also.

Initially, there was an old-guard and new-guard feeling with Dick and Sid, who have been with the company for years—I believe that's going away.

Dick is obviously smart and ambitious; he's willing to speak long and articulately on any and all subjects. I feel he overwhelms organization and shuts off many because it turns into a philosophical discussion between Joe and Dick. Pete is not about to let Dick be crown prince and throws in his points also; this cuts off air time for others. They love to debate. Don also takes his share of air time.

Pete's feeling of competition and of being alone in getting new product off the ground getting in way.

Sid undecided about whether or not he is coming back and so on is getting in way. Dick has fine connections and pushes through decisions. Sid always plays it cagy.

Questions

1. What are the major issues you think the team is facing?

2. What would you do next with the data? Who would see them? In what form?

3. Assuming the team agreed, what course of action would you recommend after the feedback meeting?

Source: *Reprinted by permission of the publisher from M. Plovnick, R. Fry, and W. Burke,* Organization Development: Exercises, Cases, and Readings *(Boston: Little, Brown, 1982), 109–17. This case is an adoption of a teaching case developed by James Shonk, President, J. H. Shonk & Associates, Ridgefield, Conn.*

Gulf States Metals, Inc.

CURRENT SITUATION

Gulf States Metals, Inc. (GSM) is a large nickel refining plant located in the southeastern United States. In addition to nickel, it also produces copper, cobalt, and ammonia sulfate. GSM was created 10 years ago by the parent company, International Metals, Inc. (IMI) to take advantage of a strong market for nickel. IMI purchased an existing plant and GSM spent 2 years refurbishing the equipment before the plant was opened. GSM has been in operation now for 8 years.

IMI expected GSM to lose money the first 2 years of operation. After that, it was expected to be highly profitable. In fact, GSM has not yet shown a profit, losing $1 million last year. The poor financial performance has been blamed on a variety of factors, including decreased demand for nickel and copper, the condition of the equipment, and labor problems. IMI did not anticipate the dramatic change in demand for GSM's products. The substitution of less expensive materials for nickel and copper has significantly affected the market price of these products. In addition, GSM is in the ninth year of a 20-year raw materials contract that had been negotiated for terms they thought were very favorable. With the current price for nickel and copper, the cost of raw material makes it very difficult to show a profit. Reducing operating expenses appears to be the only hope for profitability.

Two years ago, GSM had a union walkout that lasted 9 months. The walkout almost closed the plant permanently. GSM ran the plant with nonunion staff and cross-overs. Since that time, antimanagement feelings of nonunion employees have been even stronger. The strike was precipitated by a "get tough" policy initiated 4 years ago. At that time, the current GSM general manager was hired as plant manager. Several other new managers were also hired. Three years ago, IMI hired a New York consulting firm to restructure GSM. The result was a 30% reduction in work force.

ORGANIZATION STRUCTURE

The senior executive of GSM is the General Manager who reports to a Group Vice President at the corporate level. The Plant Manager reports directly to the General Manager and is the second in command at the plant. Reporting to the Plant Manager is the Director of Operations, Director of Engineering, and the Director of Administration.

Reporting to the Director of Operations is the Production Manager. Under the Production Manager are the area production supervisor and shift supervisors. There are area production supervisors over material (mat) handling, copper extraction, cobalt extraction, ammonia sulphate extraction, and nickel extraction. The shift supervisors oversee the overall production operation on the swing, graveyard, and weekend shifts.

The Director of Engineering is responsible for equipment and facilities maintenance, quality control, plant engineering, process control, and the parts and equipment warehouse. Reporting to the Director of Engineering is the Maintenance Manager, Process Control Manager, Industrial Engineer, and the Plant Engineer. Under the Maintenance Manager are area maintenance supervisors, shift maintenance supervisors, and the warehouse supervisor. The area and shift supervisors are assigned in a similar fashion to the production supervisors. The Process Control Manager is responsible for chemical process control and product quality control. The chemical status of the "slur" (see the description of the production process below) determines product quality and the flow of the slur through the system. The Plant Engineer is responsible for plant utilities and for facility construction and maintenance, but not equipment maintenance. The Industrial Engineer conducts research in areas such as productivity and safety.

The Director of Administration is responsible for accounting, data processing, industrial relations, safety, purchasing, and shipping and receiving. Reporting to him are the accounting manager and the industrial relations manager. The data processing supervisor, purchasing supervisor, and shipping and receiving supervisor report to the accounting manager. The safety supervisor and an industrial relations supervisor report to the industrial relations manager. The Director of Administration has been with GSM for 9 years. He was responsible for setting up the plant administrative function prior to the opening of the plant.

PRODUCTION PROCESS

The refining of nickel is a continuous flow process. The raw material (mat) is first crushed and then put into a solution referred to as "slur." The slur then is pumped through a series of extraction stations with each of the products sequentially removed from the slur. Stoppage of the flow of the slur, even for a short time, causes the equipment to become clogged. Because of this, the plant is operated 24 hours a day, 7 days a week. Equipment maintenance is performed without stopping the refining process.

The process is monitored through the readings of gauges located throughout the production system and through the analysis of samples testing in the quality control lab. The Process Control Department is responsible for making adjustments in the process to ensure quality and flow.

PLANT ENVIRONMENT

The physical environment of the plant can best be described as "rough." Buildings and equipment are old and corroded. The atmosphere smells of chemicals. Leaky valves and pipes spray chemicals and vapors into the air. Chemicals drip from overhead pipes. The operations area is covered by a roof but is an outdoor environment. Operators work in the cold in the winter and in the heat in the summer. The paint and the chrome on the cars in the parking lot show the effect of the air quality around the plant. Hard hats and safety goggles are required. Most people wear the hard hat, but few wear goggles.

The operators are "rough necks." They work hard and drink hard. Their language is filled with profanities. Their attitudes toward women, minorities, management, "Yankees," and "people with fancy theories instead of common sense" are easily observed.

AN OPPORTUNITY FOR OD

IMI has given GSM 2 years to show a profit. Six months ago, the plant manager was promoted to general manager. IMI is looking to him to turn the plant around.

The human resource (HR) manager at IMI has contacted you about the possibility of an OD project at GSM to reduce operating cost in a way that will ensure long-term operating effectiveness. Your meeting with the corporate HR manager yields the following additional information.

The corporate office believes that the current problem at GSM is a result of poor management by the former general manager. It has been made very clear to the new GM that his job and the future of the plant depend upon his ability to turn the plant around. Although they have set 2 years as the timetable for the turnaround, the GM does not have any guarantee about how long he will be retained. IMI expects immediate results from him.

The corporate HR manager has talked with the GM about the possibility of an OD project at GSM. The GM appears to be interested and wants to meet with some consultants to see what they have to offer. No one at GSM has ever been involved in anything resembling OD. In fact, no one at GSM has ever had any training in management. Everything they've learned about management has been learned on the job.

DIAGNOSTIC ACTIVITIES AND INFORMATION

Following an introductory meeting with the corporate HR manager and GSM's general manager, you contract to perform an initial diagnosis, to meet with the key managers at GSM to familiarize yourself with the organization, and to get a feel for the potential for an OD effort at GSM. A series of confidential individual interviews and a plant tour produce the following diagnostic information.

Interviews with Top Plant Managers

The general manager, plant manager, and director of operations are carbon copies of each other. Each of them was promoted to their current position at the same time about 6 months ago. Each is highly autocratic. They tend to look for technical solutions to problems and expect their managers to be tough on people to get the job done. Not surprisingly, they see the plant's problems in identical terms. Interviews with these three individuals produced the following perceptions of the situation:

1. A major reason for the lack of profitability is that the cost of mat is too high in relation to the market price of nickel.

2. Middle managers and supervisors are incapable or unwilling to "get tough" with their people to "make this work."

3. The plant could run effectively and efficiently if people would do their job.

4. Supervisors cannot be trusted to make decisions. When they are left on their own, the place falls apart.

5. The equipment is a problem, but not an insurmountable problem. Replacement of equipment is not an option right now, so we have to make do with what we have to do the job.

6. The director of engineering needs to be replaced. Technically, he is outstanding, but he is much too soft on his people. He is the major reason that the maintenance staff is not responsive to the needs of the production management.

The Director of Engineering has been with the organization since the beginning and was responsible for the original plant refurbishment. He thinks the major problem is the management style of the GM, Director of Operations, and the Production Manager. He reported that the production supervisors are totally intimidated by their managers and are oriented to protecting themselves rather than focused on correcting production problems. In addition, he believes there is plenty of technical expertise within GSM that could be used to solve the production problems, but it is not being utilized. And finally, production needs to understand that the equipment will not hold up to the demands being placed on it. Production needs to be willing to slow down the production process on a scheduled basis so that preventive maintenance can be performed.

The Industrial Relations Manager has been with the plant for 8 years. He has very good relations with the union representatives and feels that he has a good knowledge of what was going on in the plant. He feels that the plant could be much more productive and efficient by giving the supervisors authority and responsibility commensurate with their positions, improving the working relationships between production and maintenance, and allowing maintenance to perform scheduled preventive maintenance to reduce unscheduled work stoppages caused by equipment breakdowns. He is particularly concerned that management is ignoring the resources they have in the production supervisors.

Your impressions from the interviews with other top managers include the following. The Production Manager has attitudes and beliefs very similar to the top three executives. He too has been in his job for only 6 months. The Director of Administration feels that the three primary problems are the cost of the mat, costly dumb mistakes in the plant, and poor maintenance which results in frequent equipment failure. He appears to have a rather laissez-faire management style. The Maintenance Manager, promoted 2 years ago, is a hard-nosed, tough-minded manager who feels that the primary problem in the plant is the breakdown of production equipment caused by the unwillingness of operations to allow adequate maintenance of equipment.

Interviews with Middle Managers and Supervisors

As part of the diagnosis, you also interviewed several production managers and supervisors, as well as several maintenance managers and supervisors. The production people reported the following:

1. "We really aren't managers. We are never allowed to make decisions or change anything. If we change something and it goes wrong, we really are in trouble, so we don't correct problems if it means going against an order. We see a problem coming, but we don't dare do anything about it. Even if we bring the potential problem to the attention of management, we probably will be criticized. All decisions are made at the top."

2. "We think we could help a lot. We are all well trained and experienced. We are never given an opportunity to contribute."

3. "We don't want to see the plant close. We don't think it has to. We think it can be salvaged. If management will give us a chance, we will pull it through."

4. "We never know what is going on around here. Management never tells us anything. We usually find out about things from our direct reports, or from other departments."

5. "The director of operations, the production manager, and even the GM and plant manager give direct orders to our people and don't even bother to tell us about it. If they are in the work area and see something they don't like, they just start ordering people around. If we aren't in the area, we don't find out about it until our people tell us."

6. "Maintenance is really a mess. They don't know what they are doing. They want to shut down the flow to pull preventative

maintenance. We can't do that and meet our production goals. When something breaks, you can never find them. When they finally show up, they don't have the right part or the right tool."

Interviews with the maintenance manager and supervisors revealed the following:

1. "Production is screwed up. They think they can run the equipment forever without pulling maintenance on it. If they would shut down for scheduled maintenance, they wouldn't have so many unscheduled shutdowns."

2. "When something breaks down, production expects miracles from us. We're not magicians. We don't know what tools or parts we're going to need until we get the equipment apart."

3. "Management ought to let the production supervisors do their jobs. We'd be a lot better off if they did."

4. "I wouldn't trust management any further than I could throw an elephant. All you have to do to get fired is question one of their orders."

5. "We can save this place if management will let us."

6. "This equipment is so old. It'll never last another 2 years. We can't keep up with the breakdowns."

7. "The production operators are so angry at management that they sabotage the equipment or don't report problems until they cause a shutdown."

8. "The production supervisors are closer to the operators than they are to their bosses."

Questions

1. How would you summarize the diagnostic information? What are, from your perspective, the key drivers of the issues at GSM?

2. What are the potential OD interventions that could be used here? What intervention makes the most sense to you and why?

3. Provide an outline of your preferred intervention.

Source: Adapted with permission from Walter L. Ross.

PART 4

Technostructural Interventions

Chapter 14   Restructuring Organizations

Chapter 15   Employee Involvement

Chapter 16   Work Design

Selected Cases   Sullivan Hospital System
City of Carlsbad (A)

14 Restructuring Organizations

In this chapter, we begin to examine technostructural interventions—change programs focusing on the technology and structure of organizations. Increasing global competition and rapid technological and environmental changes are forcing organizations to restructure themselves from rigid bureaucracies to leaner, more flexible designs. These new forms of organizing are highly adaptive, innovative, and cost efficient. They often result in fewer managers and employees and in streamlined work flows that break down functional barriers.

Interventions aimed at structural design include moving from more traditional ways of dividing the organization's overall work, such as functional, divisional, and matrix structures, to more integrative and flexible forms, such as process and network structures. Diagnostic guidelines help determine which structure is appropriate for particular organizational environments, technologies, and conditions.

Downsizing seeks to reduce costs and bureaucracy by decreasing the size of the organization. This reduction in personnel can be accomplished through layoffs, organization redesign, and outsourcing, which involves moving functions that are not part of the organization's core competence to outside contractors. Successful downsizing is closely aligned with the organization's strategy.

Reengineering radically redesigns the organization's core work processes to give tighter linkage and coordination among the different tasks. This work-flow integration results in faster, more responsive task performance. Reengineering often is accomplished with new information technology that permits employees to control and coordinate work processes more effectively.

STRUCTURAL DESIGN

Organization structure describes how the overall work of the organization is divided into subunits and how these subunits are coordinated for task completion. Based on a contingency perspective shown in Figure 14.1, organization structures should be designed to fit with at least five factors: the environment, organization size, technology, organization strategy, and worldwide operations. Organization effectiveness depends on the extent to which its structures are responsive to these contingencies.[1]

Organizations traditionally have structured themselves into one of three forms: functional departments that are task specialized; self-contained divisional units that are oriented to specific products, customers, or regions; or matrix structures that combine both functional specialization and self-containment. Faced with accelerating changes in competitive environments and technologies, however, organizations increasingly have redesigned their structures into more integrative and flexible forms. These more recent innovations include process structures that design subunits around the organization's core work processes, and network-based structures that link the organization to other, interdependent organizations. The advantages, disadvantages, and contingencies of the different structures are described below.

The Functional Structure

Perhaps the most widely used organizational structure in the world today is the basic *functional structure*, depicted in Figure 14.2. The organization usually is divided into functional units, such as marketing, operations, research and development, human resources, and finance. This structure is based on early management theories

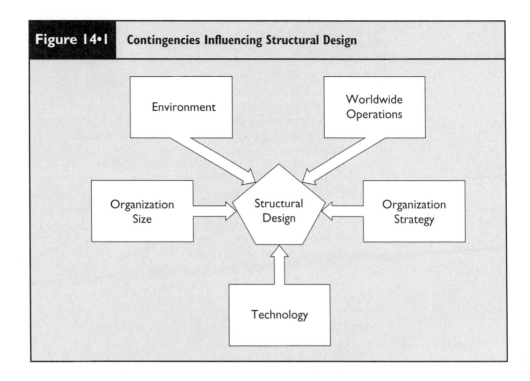

Figure 14•1   Contingencies Influencing Structural Design

regarding specialization, line and staff relations, span of control, authority, and responsibility.[2] The major functional units are staffed by specialists from such disciplines as engineering and accounting. It is considered easier to manage specialists if they are grouped together under the same head and if the head of the department has training and experience in that particular discipline.

Table 14.1 lists the advantages and disadvantages of functional structures. On the positive side, functional structures promote specialization of skills and resources by grouping people who perform similar work and face similar problems. This grouping facilitates communication within departments and allows specialists to share their expertise. It also enhances career development within the specialty, whether it be accounting, finance, engineering, or sales. The functional structure reduces duplication of services because it makes the best use of people and resources.

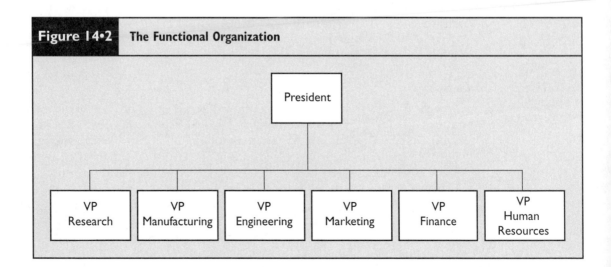

Figure 14•2   The Functional Organization

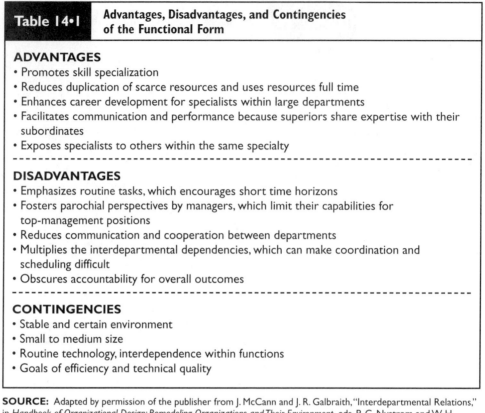

Table 14•1	Advantages, Disadvantages, and Contingencies of the Functional Form

ADVANTAGES
- Promotes skill specialization
- Reduces duplication of scarce resources and uses resources full time
- Enhances career development for specialists within large departments
- Facilitates communication and performance because superiors share expertise with their subordinates
- Exposes specialists to others within the same specialty

DISADVANTAGES
- Emphasizes routine tasks, which encourages short time horizons
- Fosters parochial perspectives by managers, which limit their capabilities for top-management positions
- Reduces communication and cooperation between departments
- Multiplies the interdepartmental dependencies, which can make coordination and scheduling difficult
- Obscures accountability for overall outcomes

CONTINGENCIES
- Stable and certain environment
- Small to medium size
- Routine technology, interdependence within functions
- Goals of efficiency and technical quality

SOURCE: Adapted by permission of the publisher from J. McCann and J. R. Galbraith, "Interdepartmental Relations," in *Handbook of Organizational Design: Remodeling Organizations and Their Environment,* eds. P. C. Nystrom and W. H. Starbuck, vol. 2 (New York: Oxford University Press, 1981), p. 61.

On the negative side, functional structures tend to promote routine tasks with a limited orientation. Department members focus on their own tasks, rather than on the organization's total task. This can lead to conflict across functional departments when each group tries to maximize its own performance without considering the performances of other units. Coordination and scheduling among departments can be difficult when each emphasizes its own perspective. As shown in Table 14.1, the functional structure tends to work best in small- to medium-size firms in environments that are relatively stable and certain. These organizations typically have a small number of products or services, and coordination across specialized units is relatively easy. This structure also is best suited to routine technologies in which there is interdependence within functions, and to organizational goals emphasizing efficiency and technical quality.

The Divisional Structure

The *divisional structure* represents a fundamentally different way of organizing. Also known as a product or self-contained-unit structure, it was developed at about the same time by General Motors, Sears, Standard Oil of New Jersey (now ExxonMobil), and DuPont.[3] It groups organizational activities on the basis of products, services, customers, or geography. All or most of the resources and functions necessary to accomplish a specific objective are set up as a division headed by a product or division manager. For example, General Electric has plants that specialize in making jet engines and others that produce household appliances. Each plant manager reports to a particular division or product vice president, rather than to a manufacturing vice president. In effect, a large organization may set up smaller (sometimes temporary) special-purpose organizations, each geared to a specific product, service,

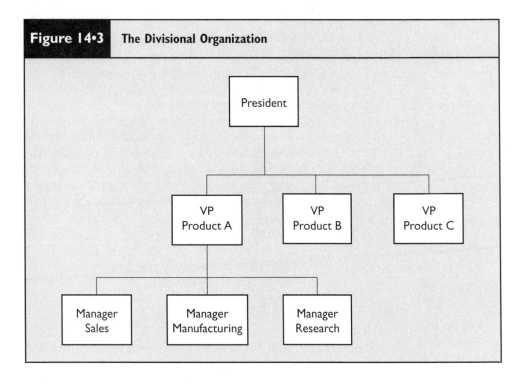

Figure 14•3   The Divisional Organization

customer, or region. A typical division structure is shown in Figure 14.3. It is interesting to note that the formal structure within a self-contained unit often is functional in nature.

Table 14.2 lists the advantages and disadvantages of divisional structures. These organizations recognize key interdependencies and coordinate resources toward an

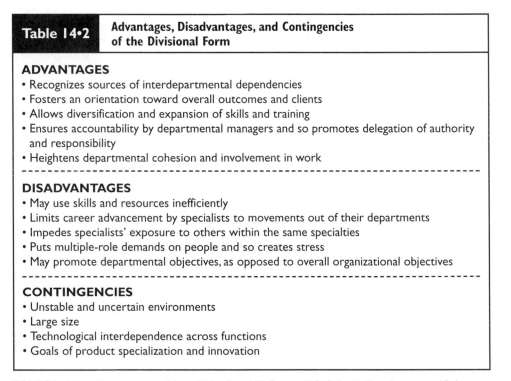

Table 14•2   Advantages, Disadvantages, and Contingencies of the Divisional Form

ADVANTAGES
- Recognizes sources of interdepartmental dependencies
- Fosters an orientation toward overall outcomes and clients
- Allows diversification and expansion of skills and training
- Ensures accountability by departmental managers and so promotes delegation of authority and responsibility
- Heightens departmental cohesion and involvement in work

DISADVANTAGES
- May use skills and resources inefficiently
- Limits career advancement by specialists to movements out of their departments
- Impedes specialists' exposure to others within the same specialties
- Puts multiple-role demands on people and so creates stress
- May promote departmental objectives, as opposed to overall organizational objectives

CONTINGENCIES
- Unstable and uncertain environments
- Large size
- Technological interdependence across functions
- Goals of product specialization and innovation

SOURCE: Adapted by permission of the publisher from J. McCann and J. R. Galbraith, "Interdepartmental Relations," in *Handbook of Organizational Design: Remodeling Organizations and Their Environment,* eds. P. C. Nystrom and W. H. Starbuck, vol. 2 (New York: Oxford University Press, 1981), p. 61.

overall outcome. This strong outcome orientation ensures departmental accountability and promotes cohesion among those contributing to the product. These structures provide employees with opportunities for learning new skills and expanding knowledge because workers can move more easily among the different specialties contributing to the product. As a result, divisional structures are well suited for developing general managers.

Divisional structures do have certain problems. They may not have enough specialized work to use people's skills and abilities fully. Specialists may feel isolated from their professional colleagues and may fail to advance in their career specialty. The structures may promote allegiance to department rather than organization objectives. They also place multiple demands on people, thereby creating stress.

The divisional structure works best in conditions almost the opposite of those favoring a functional organization, as shown in Table 14.2. The organization needs to be relatively large to support the duplication of resources assigned to the units. Because each unit is designed to fit a particular niche, the structure adapts well to uncertain conditions. Divisional units also help to coordinate technical interdependencies falling across functions and are suited to goals promoting product or service specialization and innovation.

The Matrix Structure

Some OD practitioners have focused on maximizing the strengths and minimizing the weaknesses of both the functional and the divisional structures, and this effort has resulted in the *matrix structure*.[4] It superimposes a lateral structure that focuses on product or project coordination on a vertical functional structure, as shown in Figure 14.4. Matrix organizational designs originally evolved in the aerospace industry where changing customer demands and technological conditions caused managers to focus on lateral relationships between functions to develop a flexible and adaptable system of resources and procedures, and to achieve a series of project objectives. Matrix structures now are used widely in manufacturing, service, nonprofit, governmental, and professional organizations.[5]

Every matrix organization contains three unique and critical roles: the top manager, who heads and balances the dual chains of command; the matrix bosses (functional, product, or area), who share subordinates; and the "two-boss" managers, who report to two different matrix leaders. Each of these roles has its own unique requirements. For example, functional matrix leaders are expected to maximize their respective technical expertise within constraints posed by market realities. Two-boss managers, however, must accomplish work within the demands of supervisors who want to achieve technical sophistication on the one hand, and to meet customer expectations on the other. Thus, a matrix organization has more than its matrix structure. It also must be reinforced by matrix processes, such as performance management systems that get input from both functional and project bosses, by matrix leadership behavior that operates comfortably with lateral decision making, and by a matrix culture that fosters open conflict management and a balance of power.[6]

Matrix organizations, like all organization structures, have both advantages and disadvantages, as shown in Table 14.3. On the positive side, this structure allows multiple orientations. Specialized, functional knowledge can be applied to all projects. New products or projects can be implemented quickly by using people flexibly and by moving between product and functional orientations as circumstances demand. Matrix structures can maintain consistency among departments and projects by requiring communication among managers. For many people, matrix structures are motivating and exciting.

On the negative side, these organizations can be difficult to manage. To implement and maintain them requires heavy managerial costs and support. When peo-

Figure 14•4   The Matrix Organization

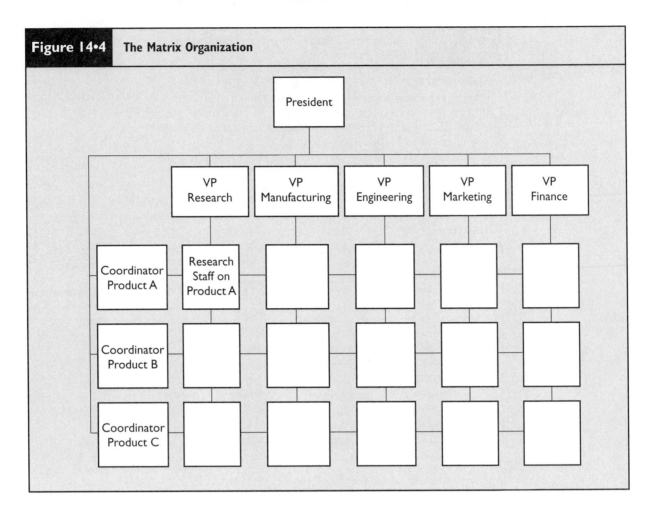

ple are assigned to more than one department, there may be role ambiguity and conflict, and overall performance may be sacrificed if there are power conflicts between functional departments and project structures. To make matrix structures work, organization members need interpersonal and conflict management skills. People can get confused about how the matrix works, and that can lead to chaos and inefficiencies.

As shown in Table 14.3, matrix structures are appropriate under three important conditions.[7] First, there must be real outside pressures for a dual focus. For example, a matrix structure works well when there are many customers with unique demands on the one hand and strong requirements for technical sophistication on the other. The OD practitioner must work with the client system to determine whether there is real pressure for a dual focus. Managers often agree, without carefully testing the assumption, that both are important. Second, a matrix organization is appropriate when the organization must process a large amount of information. Circumstances requiring such capacity are few and include the following: when external environmental demands change unpredictably; when the organization produces a broad range of products or services, or offers those outputs to a large number of different markets; when the relevant technologies evolve quickly; and when there is reciprocal interdependence among the tasks in the organization's technical core. In each case, there is considerable complexity in decision making and pressure on communication and coordination systems. Third, and finally, there must be pressures for shared resources. When customer demands vary greatly and

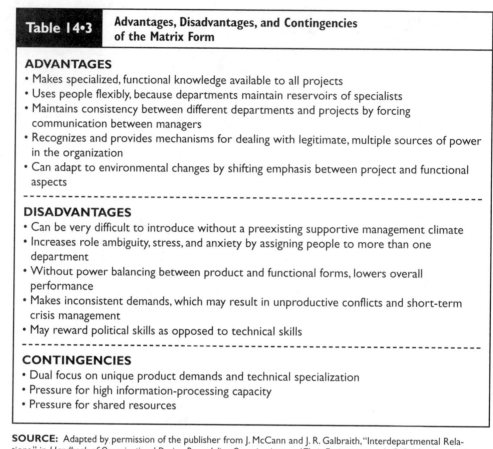

Table 14•3	Advantages, Disadvantages, and Contingencies of the Matrix Form

ADVANTAGES
- Makes specialized, functional knowledge available to all projects
- Uses people flexibly, because departments maintain reservoirs of specialists
- Maintains consistency between different departments and projects by forcing communication between managers
- Recognizes and provides mechanisms for dealing with legitimate, multiple sources of power in the organization
- Can adapt to environmental changes by shifting emphasis between project and functional aspects

DISADVANTAGES
- Can be very difficult to introduce without a preexisting supportive management climate
- Increases role ambiguity, stress, and anxiety by assigning people to more than one department
- Without power balancing between product and functional forms, lowers overall performance
- Makes inconsistent demands, which may result in unproductive conflicts and short-term crisis management
- May reward political skills as opposed to technical skills

CONTINGENCIES
- Dual focus on unique product demands and technical specialization
- Pressure for high information-processing capacity
- Pressure for shared resources

SOURCE: Adapted by permission of the publisher from J. McCann and J. R. Galbraith, "Interdepartmental Relations," in *Handbook of Organizational Design: Remodeling Organizations and Their Environment,* eds. P. C. Nystrom and W. H. Starbuck, vol. 2 (New York: Oxford University Press, 1981), p. 61.

technological requirements are strict, valuable human and physical resources are likely to be scarce. The matrix works well under those conditions because it facilitates the sharing of scarce resources. If any one of the foregoing conditions is not met, a matrix organization is likely to fail.

The Process Structure

A radically new logic for structuring organizations is to form multidisciplinary teams around core processes, such as product development, order fulfillment, sales generation, and customer support.[8] As shown in Figure 14.5, *process-based structures* emphasize lateral rather than vertical relationships.[9] All functions necessary to produce a product or service are placed in a common unit usually managed by a role labeled a "process owner." There are few hierarchical levels, and the senior executive team is relatively small, typically consisting of the chair, the chief operating officer, and the heads of a few key support services such as strategic planning, human resources, and finance.

Process structures eliminate many of the hierarchical and departmental boundaries that can impede task coordination and slow decision making and task performance. They reduce the enormous costs of managing across departments and up and down the hierarchy. Process-based structures enable organizations to focus most of their resources on serving customers, both inside and outside the firm.

The use of process-based structures is growing rapidly in a variety of manufacturing and service companies. Typically referred to as "horizontal," "boundaryless,"

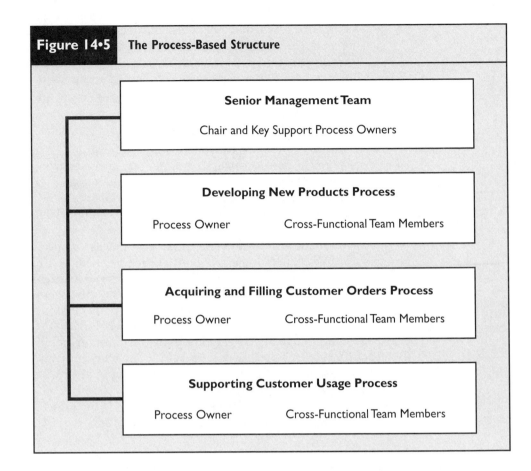

Figure 14•5   The Process-Based Structure

> **Senior Management Team**
>
> Chair and Key Support Process Owners

> **Developing New Products Process**
>
> Process Owner   Cross-Functional Team Members

> **Acquiring and Filling Customer Orders Process**
>
> Process Owner   Cross-Functional Team Members

> **Supporting Customer Usage Process**
>
> Process Owner   Cross-Functional Team Members

or "team-based" organizations, they are used to enhance customer service at such firms as American Express Financial Advisors, American Healthways, Johnson & Johnson, BP/Amoco, 3M, Xerox, General Electric Capital Services, and the National & Provincial Building Society in the United Kingdom. Although there is no one right way to design process-based structures, the following features characterize this new form of organizing:[10]

- **Processes drive structure.** Process-based structures are organized around the three to five key processes that define the work of the organization. Rather than products or functions, processes define the structure and are governed by a "process owner." Each process has clear performance goals that drive task execution.

- **Work adds value.** To increase efficiency, process-based structures simplify and enrich work processes. Work is simplified by eliminating nonessential tasks and reducing layers of management, and it is enriched by combining tasks so that teams perform whole processes.

- **Teams are fundamental.** Teams are the key organizing feature in a process-based structure. They manage everything from task execution to strategic planning, are typically self-managing, and are responsible for goal achievement.

- **Customers define performance.** The primary goal of any team in a process-based structure is customer satisfaction. Defining customer expectations and designing team functions to meet those expectations command much of the team's attention. The organization must value this orientation as the primary path to financial performance.

- **Teams are rewarded for performance.** Appraisal systems focus on measuring team performance against customer satisfaction and other goals, and then provide real recognition for achievement. Team-based rewards are given as much, if not more, weight than is individual recognition.

- **Teams are tightly linked to suppliers and customers.** Through designated members, teams have timely and direct relationships with vendors and customers to understand and respond to emerging concerns.

- **Team members are well informed and trained.** Successful implementation of a process-based structure requires team members who can work with a broad range of information, including customer and market data, financial information, and personnel and policy matters. Team members also need problem-solving and decision-making skills and abilities to address and implement solutions.

Table 14.4 lists the advantages and disadvantages of process-based structures. The most frequently mentioned advantage is intense focus on meeting customer needs, which can result in dramatic improvements in speed, efficiency, and customer satisfaction. Process-based structures remove layers of management, and consequently information flows more quickly and accurately throughout the organization. Because process teams comprise different functional specialties, boundaries between departments are removed, thus affording organization members a broad view of the work flow and a clear line of sight between team performance and organization effectiveness. Process-based structures also are more flexible and adaptable to change than are traditional structures.

A major disadvantage of process structures is the difficulty of changing to this new organizational form. These structures typically require radical shifts in mind-

Table 14•4	Advantages, Disadvantages, and Contingencies of the Process-Based Form

ADVANTAGES
- Focuses resources on customer satisfaction
- Improves speed and efficiency, often dramatically
- Adapts to environmental change rapidly
- Reduces boundaries between departments
- Increases ability to see total work flow
- Enhances employee involvement
- Lowers costs because of less overhead structure

DISADVANTAGES
- Can threaten middle managers and staff specialists
- Requires changes in command-and-control mindsets
- Duplicates scarce resources
- Requires new skills and knowledge to manage lateral relationships and teams
- May take longer to make decisions in teams
- Can be ineffective if wrong processes are identified

CONTINGENCIES
- Uncertain and changing environments
- Moderate to large size
- Nonroutine and highly interdependent technologies
- Customer-oriented goals

sets, skills, and managerial roles—changes that involve considerable time and resources and can be resisted by functional managers and staff specialists. Moreover, process-based structures may result in expensive duplication of scarce resources and, if teams are not skilled adequately, in slower decision making as they struggle to define and reach consensus. Finally, implementing process-based structures relies on properly identifying key processes needed to satisfy customer needs. If critical processes are misidentified or ignored altogether, performance and customer satisfaction are likely to suffer.

Table 14.4 shows that process structures are particularly appropriate for highly uncertain environments where customer demands and market conditions are changing rapidly. They enable organizations to manage nonroutine technologies and coordinate work flows that are highly interdependent. Process-based structures generally appear in medium- to large-size organizations having several products or projects. They focus heavily on customer-oriented goals and are found in both domestic and global organizations.

Application 14.1 describes the process-based structure proposed as part of the structural change process at American Healthways.[11]

The Network Structure

A *network structure* manages the diverse, complex, and dynamic relationships among multiple organizations or units, each specializing in a particular business function or task.[12] Organizations that utilize network structures include shamrock organizations and virtual, modular, or cellular corporations.[13] Less formally, they have been described as "pizza" structures, spiderwebs, starbursts, and cluster organizations. Some of this confusion over the definition of a network was clarified by a typology describing four basic types of networks.[14]

- An *internal market network* exists when a single organization establishes each subunit as an independent profit center that is allowed to buy and sell services and resources from each other as well as from the external market. Asea Brown Boveri's (ABB) 50 worldwide businesses consist of 1,200 companies organized into 4,500 profit centers that conduct business with each other.

- A *vertical market network* is composed of multiple organizations linked to a focal organization that coordinates the movement of resources from raw materials to end consumer. Nike, for example, has its shoes manufactured in different plants around the world and then organizes their distribution through retail outlets.

- An *intermarket network* represents alliances among a variety of organizations in different markets and is exemplified by the Japanese *keiretsu*, the Korean *chaebol*, and the Mexican *grupos*.

- An *opportunity network* is the most advanced form of network structure. It is a temporary constellation of organizations brought together to pursue a single purpose. Once accomplished, the network disbands. Li and Fung is a Hong Kong–based trading company that pulls together a variety of specialist supplier organizations to design and manufacture a wide range of private-label clothing.

These types of networks can be distinguished from one another in terms of whether they are single or multiple organizations, single or multiple industry, and stable or temporary.[15] For example, an internal market network is a stable, single-organization, single-industry structure; an opportunity network is a temporary, multiple-organization structure that can span several different industries.

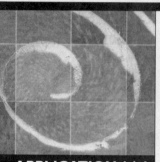

AMERICAN HEALTHWAYS' PROCESS STRUCTURE

As part of American Healthways' (http://www.americanhealthways.com) structural change effort, the initial organization design and development task force (the ODD group) recommended a process-based organization structure to the senior leadership group. The organization was described in terms of five core processes: understand the market and plan the business, acquire and retain customers, build value solutions, deliver solutions and add value, and manage the business (Figure 14.7).

- The *understand-the-market process* was responsible for scanning AMHC's external environment for business opportunities, trends, regulatory changes, and competitive intelligence. The process was also responsible for generating new product ideas, based on their environmental scanning activities, and for developing and driving the strategic planning process of the organization.

- Based on the outputs of the understand-the-market process, the *build-value-solutions process* was responsible for translating business or product opportunities into reproducible products. This organization was responsible for more fully developing the business case initially identified by the understand-the-market process, developing performance metrics, product development and testing, and the development of marketing materials.

- The *acquire-and-retain-customers process* involved the sales and marketing organization. It was responsible for finalizing marketing materials, identifying new customers, selling and signing contracts, developing relationships with key stakeholders, implementing marketing plans, and responding to requests for proposals.

- The *deliver-solutions-and-add-value process* was responsible for delivering on contractual commitments, account management and upselling, maintaining product integrity, and building delivery capacity.

- In the *manage-the-business process,* the small corporate headquarters staff was responsible for human resources, financial governance, information technology standards, medical leadership, and corporate image and branding. It was to act as a shared services organization supporting the value-adding process organizations.

Each process was to be staffed with an appropriate mix of functional experts. That is, the operational basis of the new organization was a cross-functional team that could represent the different perspectives at each stage of the business. For example, the acquire-and-retain-customers process included not only sales and marketing expertise, but functional expertise in account management, information technology, finance, medical and clinical specialties, and product development. In recommending that a core process be staffed with the appropriate mix of functional expertise, the task force was also suggesting that the structure within a core process be team based. That is, the acquire-and-retain-customers process could flexibly organize cross-functional teams to address a specific customer's requirements and then recombine resources to pursue a different customer.

In addition, appropriate metrics for monitoring the effectiveness of each process as well as the relationships between any two processes in the organization were specified. In terms of effectiveness metrics, the key outcome for all processes was customer satisfaction. That is, the acquire-customer process was judged primarily on the extent to which it produced customers and contracts that the deliver-solutions group believed could be managed. In terms of relationships, any new business opportunities identified by the understand-the-market process required certain approvals by senior management before being handed off to the build-value-solutions process. This "go-no go" decision assured that the organization had sufficient investment resources to fund new business or product development and that good opportunities, not just a lot of opportunities, were being forwarded to the build-value-solutions process.

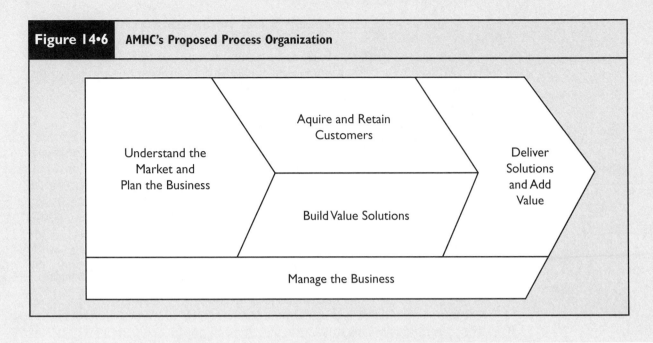

Figure 14•6   AMHC's Proposed Process Organization

Understand the Market and Plan the Business

Aquire and Retain Customers

Build Value Solutions

Deliver Solutions and Add Value

Manage the Business

As shown in Figure 14.7, the network structure redraws organizational boundaries and links separate business units to facilitate task interaction. The essence of networks is the relationships among organizations that perform different aspects of work. In this way, organizations do the things that they do well; for example, manufacturing expertise is applied to production, and logistical expertise is applied to distribution. Network organizations use strategic alliances, joint ventures, research and development consortia, licensing agreements, and wholly owned subsidiaries to design, manufacture, and market advanced products, enter new international

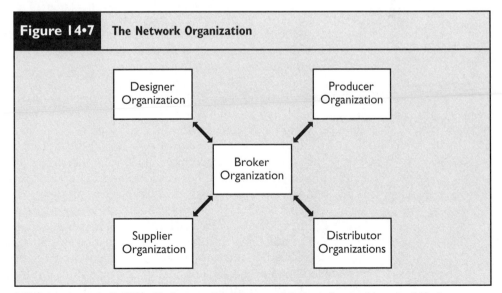

Figure 14•7   The Network Organization

Designer Organization

Producer Organization

Broker Organization

Supplier Organization

Distributor Organizations

markets, and develop new technologies. Companies such as Apple Computer, Benetton, Sun Microsystems, Liz Claiborne, MCI, and Merck have implemented fairly sophisticated vertical market and intermarket network structures. Opportunity networks also are commonplace in the construction, fashion, and entertainment industries, as well as in the public sector.[16]

Network structures typically have the following characteristics:

- **Vertical disaggregation.** This refers to the breaking up of the organization's business functions, such as production, marketing, and distribution, into separate organizations performing specialized work. In the film industry, for example, separate organizations providing transportation, cinematography, special effects, set design, music, actors, and catering all work together under a broker organization, the studio. The particular organizations making up the opportunity network represent an important factor in determining its success.[17] More recently, disintermediation, or the replacement of whole steps in the value chain by information technology—specifically the Internet—has fueled the development and numbers of network structures.

- **Brokers.** Networks often are managed by broker organizations or "process orchestrators" that locate and assemble member organizations. The broker may play a central role and subcontract for needed products or services, or it may specialize in linking equal partners into a network. In the construction industry, the general contractor typically assembles and manages drywall, mechanical, electrical, plumbing, and other specialties to erect a building.

- **Coordinating mechanisms.** Network organizations generally are not controlled by hierarchical arrangements or plans. Rather, coordination of the work in a network falls into three categories: informal relationships, contracts, and market mechanisms. First, coordination patterns can depend heavily on interpersonal relationships among individuals who have a well-developed partnership. Conflicts are resolved through reciprocity; network members recognize that each likely will have to compromise at some point. Trust is built and nurtured over time by these reciprocal arrangements. Second, coordination can be achieved through formal contracts, such as ownership control, licensing arrangements, or purchase agreements. Finally, market mechanisms, such as spot payments, performance accountability, technology standards, and information systems, ensure that all parties are aware of each other's activities and can communicate with each other.

Network structures have a number of advantages and disadvantages, as shown in Table 14.5.[18] They are highly flexible and adaptable to changing conditions. The ability to form partnerships with different organizations permits the creation of a "best-of-the-best" company to exploit opportunities, often global in nature. They enable each member to exploit its distinctive competence. They can accumulate and apply sufficient resources and expertise to large, complex tasks that single organizations cannot perform. Perhaps most important, network organizations can have synergistic effects whereby members build on each other's strengths and competencies, creating a whole that exceeds the sum of its parts.

The major problems with network organizations are in managing such complex structures. Galbraith and Kazanjian describe network structures as matrix organizations extending beyond the boundaries of single firms but lacking the ability to appeal to a higher authority to resolve conflicts.[19] Thus, matrix skills of managing lateral relations across organizational boundaries are critical to administering network structures. Most organizations, because they are managed hierarchically, can be expected to have difficulties managing lateral relations. Other disadvantages of

Table 14•5	Advantages, Disadvantages, and Contingencies of the Network-Based Form

ADVANTAGES
- Enables highly flexible and adaptive response to dynamic environments
- Creates a "best-of-the-best" organization to focus resources on customer and market needs
- Enables each organization to leverage a distinctive competency
- Permits rapid global expansion
- Can produce synergistic results

DISADVANTAGES
- Managing lateral relations across autonomous organizations is difficult
- Motivating members to relinquish autonomy to join the network is troublesome
- Sustaining membership and benefits can be problematic
- May give partners access to proprietary knowledge/technology

CONTINGENCIES
- Highly complex and uncertain environments
- Organizations of all sizes
- Goals of organizational specialization and innovation
- Highly uncertain technologies
- Worldwide operations

network organizations include the difficulties of motivating organizations to join such structures and of sustaining commitment over time. Potential members may not want to give up their autonomy to link with other organizations and, once linked, they may have problems sustaining the benefits of joining together. This is especially true if the network consists of organizations that are not the "best of breed." Finally, joining a network may expose the organization's proprietary knowledge and skills to others.

As shown in Table 14.5, network organizations are best suited to highly complex and uncertain environments where multiple competencies and flexible responses are needed. They seem to apply to organizations of all sizes, and they deal with complex tasks or problems involving high interdependencies across organizations. Network structures fit with goals that emphasize organization specialization and innovation. They also fit well in organizations with worldwide operations.

Application 14.2 describes how Amazon.com's network structure was configured to align with its strategy and how relationships are managed.[20]

DOWNSIZING

Downsizing refers to interventions aimed at reducing the size of the organization.[21] This typically is accomplished by decreasing the number of employees through lay-offs, attrition, redeployment, or early retirement or by reducing the number of organizational units or managerial levels through divestiture, outsourcing, reorganization, or delayering. In practice, downsizing generally involves layoffs where a certain number or class of organization members is no longer employed by the organization. Although traditionally associated with lower-level workers, downsizing increasingly has claimed the jobs of staff specialists, middle managers, and senior executives.

An important consequence of downsizing has been the rise of the contingent workforce. In companies like Cisco or Motorola, less expensive temporary or permanent part-time workers often are hired by the same organizations that just laid

AMAZON.COM'S NETWORK STRUCTURE

Amazon.com (http://www.amazon.com) was launched in mid-1995 as the "Earth's Biggest Bookstore." It offered more than 1 million titles to on-line buyers, more than three times the number offered at traditional bookstores. Since then, it has evolved into a powerful network structure involving both other Internet retailers as well as more traditional retailers, including other bookstores. At the center of it all is Amazon's massive Web site, Amazon.com. By pairing Amazon's state-of-the-art technology, built-in traffic, and industry-leading fulfillment and customer service processes with its partners' products and their own strengths, a complex network of organizations is working together to make everyone more successful.

The company went public in the first quarter of 1997 riding the dot.com wave, and revenues have grown from $147.8 million in 1997 to over $3.93 billion in fiscal year 2002. Sales increased 26% over fiscal year 2001. Despite this impressive sales growth, there was increasing pressure to deliver profits, which occurred for the first time in fiscal year 2002. From at least one point of view, the development of Amazon's network structure is an important reason.

From the beginning, Amazon has operated as a virtual organization and leveraged the network structure. For example, it developed and operated its Amazon.com Web site to draw in customers and learn about creating an effective on-line customer experience. But the company owned little or no inventory, warehouses, distribution centers, or customer service operations. Early on, order fulfillment was left to Ingram Book Distributors, one of the largest book wholesalers, who also contracted out delivery to third-party vendors, such as UPS.

In June of 1998, Amazon began selling CDs, and added DVDs and videos in November 1998. It added electronic products, toys, software, and video games in 1999, and tools, health and beauty products, kitchen products, and photo services in 2000. It has also expanded internationally, opening up the United Kingdom and German markets in 1999 and Japan and France in 2000. Amazon's first West Coast distribution center was built in 1996 and an East Coast distribution center was added in 1997. In 1999, in anticipation of the Christmas rush, Amazon built five warehouse and distribution facilities and several customer service centers to improve its order fulfillment capabilities.

Amazon's initial forays into a broader network began in 1999 but were compartmentalized on the Web site. Non-Amazon products, such as used books or individuals auctioning off different products, were not allowed to infiltrate Amazon's millions of book, CD, and DVD pages. Third-party products were put under "tabs" that roughly described the kind of commerce to be conducted, such as the "auction" tab or the "zShops" tab that contained a variety of vendor products. Thus, traditional Amazon products were separated from products offered by others. Continued profit pressure, however, forced the organization to look at relationships differently.

Jeff Bezos, company founder and CEO, stated:

> We realized that what was most important to the marketplace sellers was demand—access to prospective buyers. So, the idea of the "single store" was to give them a level of access equal to our own—listing their goods right alongside ours.

As a result, a Web page describing Amazon's product—say a DVD with the product's image and other information—was altered to contain product offerings and descriptions from other vendors, such as used DVDs, DVD players from Circuit City, and used soundtrack CDs from another partner.

With the "single store" strategy, Amazon.com transformed itself from an Internet retailer to a platform for commerce. Small businesses and individuals, which used to be in the Auctions or zShops section, were given the opportunity to place their products on Amazon's most visited sites. In exchange for this visibility, Amazon developed a contract that included a fee schedule and described the responsibilities and activities that each organization would perform.

Larger organizations had more options, including the Merchants@amazon.com arrangement, the merchants.com program, the syndicated stores program, as well as more traditional marketing relationships. The Merchants@amazon.com arrangement gave partner organizations, such as Office Depot, Circuit City, Borders Books, and Toys "R" Us, access to Amazon's customer base and Web site while retaining ownership of the inventory and the ability to set prices. Amazon got a service fee and commission on sales. For example, Amazon created a 3-year partnership with Circuit City that allowed Amazon to generate revenue on people who performed product research on-line and then made purchases at the store. Amazon began by selling a limited assortment of Circuit City products for in-store pickup, and then expanded its selection of Circuit City products in 2002, including products that duplicated Amazon's product mix.

The Toys "R" Us relationship is an excellent example of how networks operate to the advantage of both companies. Traditional retailers often get 60% of their annual sales in the final 2 months of the year; in Toys "R" Us's case, it was more like 75%. In 1999, the Toys "R" Us Christmas season nearly ruined the company. As with many retailers, Toys "R" Us hoped to take advantage of the Internet shopping trend and opened toysrus.com. But their inability to fill customer orders produced such a large volume of customer complaints that the company was fined by the Federal Trade Commission for violating mail and telephone order rules. By partnering with Amazon, there was no need for Toys "R" Us to invest in an infrastructure that was going to be used only for 8 weeks.

The Toys "R" Us case is a 10-year agreement where Amazon houses toy inventory, ships toys to customers, processes payments, and performs post-sale customer service. Toys "R" Us retains responsibility for buying and pricing products. This relationship was based on an understanding of the strengths of Amazon and Toys "R" Us. Bezos noted that:

> There are things we'll never be able to do that partners can do effortlessly. Likewise, we bring certain skills and a customer base to the table that would be very difficult for partners to acquire. The toys category is a good example.

Amazon was building key capabilities in personalizing the customer experience, making it possible to suggest additional purchases based on information provided by the buyer and previous purchases. For example Amazon's "customer filtering" software tracks a consumer's purchases and finds other consumers in the database who have made similar purchases. It then recommends additional products assuming that the on-line customer has similar tastes. Other technologies that Amazon can bring include payment systems and Web customer assistance technologies.

On the other hand, Toys "R" Us is an incredibly large buyer, and the Internet sales unit enjoys the same purchasing power

as its parent. As Christmas approaches and particular toys or categories of toys attract attention, the larger buyers are more likely to get the last-minute shipments that come in from overseas manufacturers. The partnership works well for both.

In the merchants.com program, Amazon operated third-party Web sites on behalf of the merchant. For example, Amazon offered its know-how to operate Target's Web site (http://www.target.com), took inventory into its distribution centers, and completed most fulfillment functions. In exchange, Target paid Amazon a fixed fee and commissions on sales. The syndicated store option was similar to the Merchants.com program in that Amazon operated the Web site. The difference was that Amazon offered a completely outsourced solution, taking responsibility for Web site development, buying, stocking, pricing, shipping, and servicing the customer.

Finally, Amazon also engaged in more traditional marketing arrangements where the Amazon.com Web site served as a marketing vehicle for other companies. From the Amazon Web site, users were transferred over to the vendor's Web site and Amazon received a fee based on the number of customers exposed to the vendor's marketing message or on the number of customers referred. Amazon made its first set of partnerships with Drugstore.com, Living.com, and Wine.com among others. As Amazon affiliates, they paid Amazon placement and referral fees for advertising on the Amazon Web site. This was called the Amazon Commerce Network.

By excelling at particular aspects of retailing in the Internet environment, Amazon has been able to leverage those competencies into a powerful network of alliances and partnerships. The network structure is one important reason Amazon is one of the few Internet startups to actually post a profit.

off thousands of employees. A study by the American Management Association found that nearly a third of the 720 firms in the sample had rehired recently terminated employees as independent contractors or consultants because the downsizings had not been matched by an appropriate reduction in or redesign of the workload.[22] Overall cost reduction was achieved by replacing expensive permanent workers with a contingent workforce.

Over the past decade, most major U.S. corporations and government agencies have engaged in downsizing activities. For example, a recent study by Mercer Consulting found that 71% of their respondents had a reduction in force since January 2001 and another study of more than 3,500 companies found that 59% had fired at least 5% of their workers at least once between 1980 and 1994, and one-third of those companies downsized more than 15% of their workforce at least once.[23] In addition, more than 138,000 people were laid off in February 2003, and more than 132,000 layoffs were announced in January 2003.[24]

Other organizations have downsized through redeploying workers from one function or job to another. For example, AT&T, IBM, Boeing, Sears, and Xerox cut nearly a quarter-million jobs in 1993 and hired more than 63,000 in 1996.[25] Similarly, in 1996 IBM laid off more than 69,000 people but increased its workforce by 16,000 that same year as its demand was shifting from hardware to software and services.[26]

Downsizing is generally a response to at least four major conditions. First, it is associated increasingly with mergers and acquisitions. One in nine job cuts during 1998 were the result of the integration of two organizations.[27] Second, it can result from organization decline caused by loss of revenues and market share and by technological and industrial change. As a result of fuel oil prices, terrorism, and other changes, the airline industry has reduced its workforce by more than 10% between early 2002 and early 2003.[28] Third, downsizing can occur when organizations implement one of the new organizational structures described above. For example, creation of network-based structures often involves outsourcing work that is not essential to the organization's core competence. Fourth, downsizing can result from beliefs and social pressures that smaller is better.[29] In the United States, there is strong conviction that organizations should be leaner and more flexible. Hamel and Prahalad warned, however, that organizations must be careful that downsizing is not a symptom of "corporate anorexia."[30] Organizations may downsize for their own sake and not think about future growth. They may lose key employees who are necessary for future success, cutting into the organization's core competencies and leaving a legacy of mistrust among members. In such situations, it is questionable whether downsizing is developmental as defined in OD.

Application Stages

Successful downsizing interventions tend to proceed by the following steps:[31]

1. *Clarify the Organization's Strategy.* As a first step, organization leaders specify corporate and business strategy and communicate clearly how downsizing relates to it. They seek to inform members that downsizing is not a goal in itself, but a restructuring process for achieving strategic objectives. Leaders need to provide visible and consistent support throughout the process. They can provide opportunities for members to voice their concerns, ask questions, and obtain counseling if necessary.

2. *Assess Downsizing Options and Make Relevant Choices.* Once the strategy is clear, the full range of downsizing options can be identified and assessed. Table 14.6 describes three primary downsizing methods: workforce reduction, organization redesign, and systemic change. A specific downsizing strategy may use elements of all three approaches. Workforce reduction is aimed at reducing the number of employees, usually in a relatively short timeframe. It can include attrition, retirement incentives, outplacement services, and layoffs. Organization redesign attempts to restructure the firm to prepare it for the next stage of growth. This is a medium-term approach that can be accomplished by merging organizational units, eliminating management layers, and redesigning tasks. Systemic change is a longer-term option aimed at changing the culture and strategic orientation of the organization. It can involve interventions that alter the responsibilities and work behaviors of everyone in the organization and that promote continual improvement as a way of life in the firm.

    Case, a manufacturer of heavy construction equipment, used a variety of methods to downsize, including eliminating money-losing product lines; narrowing the breadth of remaining product lines; bringing customers to the company headquarters to get their opinions of new product design (which surprisingly resulted in maintaining, rather than changing, certain preferred features, thus holding down redesign costs); shifting production to outside vendors; restructuring debt; and spinning off most of its 250 stores. Eventually,

Table 14•6	Three Downsizing Tactics	
DOWNSIZING TACTIC	**CHARACTERISTICS**	**EXAMPLES**
Workforce reduction	Aimed at headcount reduction Short-term implementation Fosters a transition	Attrition Transfer and outplacement Retirement incentives Buyout packages Layoffs
Organization redesign	Aimed at organization change Moderate-term implementation Fosters transition and, potentially, transformation	Eliminate functions Merge units Eliminate layers Eliminate products Redesign tasks
Systemic redesign	Aimed at culture change Long-term implementation Fosters transformation	Change responsibility Involve all constituents Foster continuous improvement and innovation Simplification Downsizing: a way of life

SOURCE: K. Cameron, S. Freeman, and A. Mishra, "Best Practices in White-Collar Downsizing: Managing Contradictions," *Academy of Management Executive* 5 (1991), 62.

these changes led to closing five plants and to payroll reductions of almost 35%.[32] The number of jobs lost would have been much greater, however, if Case had not implemented a variety of downsizing methods.

Unfortunately, organizations often choose obvious solutions for downsizing, such as layoffs, because they can be implemented quickly. This action produces a climate of fear and defensiveness as members focus on identifying who will be separated from the organization. Examining a broad range of options and considering the entire organization rather than only certain areas can help allay fears that favoritism and politics are the bases for downsizing decisions. Moreover, participation of organization members in such decisions can have positive benefits. It can create a sense of urgency for identifying and implementing options to downsizing other than layoffs. Participation can provide members with a clearer understanding of how downsizing will proceed and can increase the likelihood that whatever choices are made are perceived as reasonable and fair.

3. *Implement the Changes.* This stage involves implementing methods for reducing the size of the organization. Several practices characterize successful implementation. First, downsizing is best controlled from the top down. Many difficult decisions are required, and a broad perspective helps to overcome people's natural instincts to protect their enterprise or function. Second, identify and target specific areas of inefficiency and high cost. The morale of the organization can be hurt if areas commonly known to be redundant are left untouched. Third, link specific actions to the organization's strategy. Organization members need to be reminded consistently that restructuring activities are part of a plan to improve the organization's performance. Finally, communicate frequently using a variety of media. This keeps people informed, lowers their anxiety over the process, and makes it easier for them to focus on their work.

4. ***Address the Needs of Survivors and Those Who Leave.*** Most downsizing eventually involves reduction in the size of the workforce, and it is important to support not only employees who remain with the organization but also those who leave. When layoffs occur, employees are generally asked to take on additional responsibilities and to learn new jobs, often with little or no increase in compensation. This added workload can be stressful, and when combined with anxiety over past layoffs and possible future ones, it can lead to what researchers have labeled the "survivor syndrome."[33] This syndrome involves a narrow set of self-absorbed and risk-averse behaviors that can threaten the organization's survival. Rather than working to ensure the organization's success, survivors often are preoccupied with whether additional layoffs will occur, with guilt over receiving pay and benefits while co-workers are struggling with termination, and with the uncertainty of career advancement.

   Organizations can address these survivor concerns with communication processes that increase the amount and frequency of information provided. Communication should shift from explanations about who left or why to clarification of where the company is going, including its visions, strategies, and goals. The linkage between employees' performance and strategic success is emphasized so that remaining members feel they are valued. Organizations also can support survivors through training and development activities that prepare them for the new work they are being asked to perform. Senior management can promote greater involvement in decision making, thus reinforcing the message that people are important to the future success and growth of the organization.

   Given the negative consequences typically associated with job loss, organizations have developed an array of methods to help employees who have been laid off. These include outplacement counseling, personal and family counseling, severance packages, office support for job searches, relocation services, and job retraining. Each service is intended to assist employees in their transition to another work situation.

5. ***Follow Through with Growth Plans.*** This final stage of downsizing involves implementing an organization renewal and growth process. Failure to move quickly to implement growth plans is a key determinate of ineffective downsizing.[34] For example, a study of 1,020 human resource directors reported that only 44% of the companies that had downsized in the previous 5 years shared details of their growth plans with employees; only 34% told employees how they would fit into the company's new strategy.[35] Organizations must ensure that employees understand the renewal strategy and their new roles in it. Employees need credible expectations that, although the organization has been through a tough period, their renewed efforts can move it forward.

   Application 14.3 describes the process of a strategically focused downsizing effort at Delta Air Lines.[36] It demonstrates how, even in crisis, an organization can view the downsizing process strategically and align its restructuring with human resource and other competitive advantages in mind.

Results of Downsizing

The empirical research on downsizing is mostly negative. A review conducted by the National Research Council concluded, "From the research produced thus far, downsizing as a strategy for improvement has proven to be, by and large, a failure."[37] A number of studies have documented the negative productivity and employee consequences. One survey of 1,005 companies that used downsizing to reduce costs reported that fewer than half of the firms actually met cost targets. Moreover, only 22% of the companies achieved expected productivity gains, and consequently about 80% of the firms needed to rehire some of the same people that

STRATEGIC DOWNSIZING PROCESS AT DELTA AIR LINES

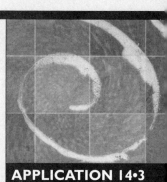

APPLICATION 14•3

Delta Air Lines (http://www.delta.com) is the third largest U.S. airline and is favorably viewed by industry analysts for its conservative financial practices and largely union-free workforce. Not having union organizations between Delta management and employee work groups provides more direct and efficient interaction that translates into greater productivity, improved communication and employee participation, and greater organizational agility. For example, Delta is able to more quickly shift marginally performing markets to its lower-cost affiliates because they do not have to engage in lengthy contract negotiations with multiple unions. In fact outside of the Pilots and Dispatchers, all employee groups including flight attendants, mechanics, airport workers, and reservation agents are non-union. Similarly, Delta is able to test new practices, products, and services more efficiently than airlines where these are impeded by work rules and union negotiations. This competitive advantage has a positive impact on Delta's revenues and operating costs and is a strategic capability of the airline. Although this advantage is somewhat offset by low-cost competitors' lower wage structures, such as Southwest or Jet Blue, workforce flexibility continues to be viewed by industry analysts as a competitive advantage for Delta, especially when compared to the other major airlines.

Already suffering from bad industry fundamentals, such as excess capacity, cost increases in excess of revenue growth, and the inability to accurately anticipate and manage the volatility of fuel prices, the attacks of September 11, 2001, pushed the airline industry over the edge. For at least 3 days, the airspace over the United States was quiet; no civilian or commercial aircraft were allowed in the air. Faced with the same environmental jolt, all airlines were forced to reduce capacity, service, and staffing. In the months that followed, the major U.S. carriers cut costs by $14 billion. Over 70,000 people or 16% of the workforce were laid off and 267 aircraft or 15% of the industry's capacity were grounded. Carriers with collective bargaining agreements in place were able to manage staff reductions according to their contracts, in most cases furloughing staff, starting with the most junior and continuing up through seniority lists until the staff reduction targets were achieved. But not all airlines approached the task the same way, providing important insights into the relationships among strategies, priorities, and management styles.

Delta Air Line's downsizing efforts were different from the others and reflected their deep commitment to people and their strategic advantage. Delta has been known for decades for a quote of founder C. E. Woolman, "All airlines are alike, it's people that make Delta different." Although Delta had the ability to mimic carriers with mostly organized labor, they chose to utilize this crisis as an opportunity to de-velop policies, processes, and tools consistent with their strategy of maintaining workforce flexibility and remaining union-free. To maintain employee belief that dealing directly with management was better than indirectly through a labor union, Delta would have to manage the downsizing process differently from airlines with organized labor.

The evaluation and management of Delta's downsizing actions fell primarily on its human resources department. Delta was able to leverage its recent investment in upgrading its HR organization from the outside (including companies like GE, Pepsi, and Coke) and called them into action. A "core team" was quickly created for this purpose. It was led by the chief learning officer and included other HR disciplines: organization development, recruitment and staffing, global rewards and recognition, learning services, and client-based HR leaders from each operating area. A "war room" was created as the headquarters for this core team and meetings were held at the beginning and end of each day to communicate progress and coordinate next steps. The core team members routinely worked 12- to 15-hour days with few days off in the 6 weeks following September 11th. The work of the core team was to collect and analyze company, industry, and market information, obtain employee and management input, develop procedures, and manage reductions in a fair and balanced manner. This effort included a change plan to effectively communicate and implement the changes with key stakeholders and employee groups, and measure results to ensure organization objectives were achieved.

Under the overall leadership of Bob Colman, Executive Vice President of Human Resources, the core team quickly evaluated how to balance the short-term need to reduce operating expenses, the desire to give employees choices, and the long-term opportunities. Like its competitors, Delta believed that the market would recover in 12 to 18 months. However, Delta wanted to look beyond the short-term tactical responses of simple cost cutting. Carriers that could most quickly add capacity as demand returned had an opportunity to gain market share. As a result, Delta's strategy was to build a workforce reduction program with flexibility to effectively manage the crisis while ensuring ability to seize anticipated opportunities.

The core team developed three programs, under the umbrella called Delta Workforce Programs (DWP), which gave employees the choice of an enhanced early retirement, leave of absence, or severance. Variations of these programs were created providing employees with six voluntary programs to consider. These programs included 1-, 2-, 3-, and 5-year leave programs where employees would be given flight privileges, pension credit time for the leave period upon their return, and ability to bid for jobs while on leave. The intent was to keep connectivity of employees to Delta and the communities it served. At the time, these voluntary options were expected to garner half of the staffing reductions needed. Furlough and involuntary severance programs were also developed and would be used to achieve the remaining staff reductions, if required. In the end, over 98% of employee reductions were met through voluntary leave programs, and anyone affected by an involuntary separation was eligible to apply for open positions elsewhere in the company.

While the core team focused on creating programs and processes that would meet staff reduction targets while not jeopardizing Delta's employee-related advantages, the Change Management group, under the leadership of Chief Learning Officer, Bill Kline, addressed sustainability. It developed tools to assist managers in evaluating their processes, job designs, and organization structures and to identify and implement changes in alignment with reduced staffing levels. The Change Management staff then provided the Human Resources generalist staff with training to prepare them to subsequently train the managers in their client groups on using the tools, including a knowledge capture process. The generalists then supported their client managers through the change process.

Finally, collaboration between the core team and corporate communications produced a new "leader-led" communication strategy. The human resources group trained company managers on the new programs and procedures and then supported them as they communicated these to their direct reports. Previous employee surveys indicated that organization members wanted their immediate manager to be the primary source of communication, and the communication strategy supported this preference.

This approach produced a new partnership between members of the HR team and the managers they supported. Managers were seen by their employees as the individuals they could rely on to inform them about the business, as those with general knowledge of all areas that impacted them. Human Resources became viewed as a support area, rather than control area, a place where managers and employees could go to get detailed information. Communication programs were put in place to facilitate the leader-led communications and included frequent field visits and interaction by executives, open-forum call-ins with department and division executives, and frequent meetings with frontline managers. Additional communication choices for employees included ability to replay executive messages and call-ins, as well as ability to access company communications via telephone, Internet, email, and newsletters. At the same time two groups, the Airport Customer Service workers and Flight Attendants, developed Web sites to connect to employees who took leave programs or might have been furloughed. Again, multiple channels of access and choices were provided to employees so that they could select a method that matched their needs and preferences.

Delta leadership made a commitment to create the DWP programs and policies before implementing workforce reductions in balancing the need to maintain workforce flexibility and meet short-term economic requirements. The intensity of the 4-week period before implementing reductions can not be described other than to say it represented a significant investment of resources at a time when all other major airlines were making layoffs happen immediately, without employee engagement. The decision to provide employee choices via innovative leave programs was branded as "The Delta Difference," and positioned Delta as the industry leader in strategically managing staff reductions that would be followed in the next downsizing of the airline industry during late 2002 and early 2003.

they had previously terminated. Fewer than 33% of the companies surveyed reported that profits increased as much as expected, and only 21% achieved satisfactory improvements in shareholder return on investment.[38] Another survey of 1,142 downsized firms found that only about a third achieved productivity goals.[39] In addition, the research points to a number of problems at the individual level, including increased stress and illness, loss of self-esteem, reduced trust and loyalty, and marriage and family disruptions.[40]

Research on the effects of downsizing on financial performance also shows negative results. One study examined an array of financial performance measures, such as return on sales, assets, and equity, in 210 companies that announced layoffs.[41] It found that increases in financial performance in the first year following the layoff announcements were not followed by performance improvements in the next year.

In no case did a firm's financial performance after a layoff announcement match its maximum levels of performance in the year before the announcement. These results suggest that layoffs may result in initial improvements in financial performance, but such gains are temporary and not sustained at even pre-layoff levels. In a similar study of 16 firms that wrote off more than 10% of their net worth in a 5-year period, stock prices, which averaged 16% below the market average before the layoff announcements, increased on the day that the restructuring was announced but then began a steady decline. Two years after the layoff announcements, 10 of the 16 stocks were trading below the market by 17% to 48%, and 12 of the 16 were below comparable firms in their industries by 5 to 45%.[42]

These research findings paint a rather bleak picture of the success of downsizing. The results must be interpreted cautiously, however, for three reasons. First, many of the survey-oriented studies received responses from human resources specialists who might have been naturally inclined to view downsizing in a negative light. Second, the studies of financial performance may have included a biased sample of firms. If the companies selected for analysis had been poorly managed, then downsizing alone would have been unlikely to improve financial performance. There is some empirical support for this view because low-performing firms are more likely to engage in downsizing than are high-performing firms.[43]

Third, disappointing results may be a function of the way downsizing was implemented. A number of organizations, such as Florida Power and Light, General Electric, Motorola, Texas Instruments, Boeing, DaimlerChrysler, and Hewlett-Packard, have posted solid financial returns following downsizing.[44] A study of 30 downsized firms in the automobile industry showed that those companies that implemented effectively the process described above scored significantly higher on several performance measures than did firms that had no downsizing strategy or that implemented the steps poorly.[45] Several studies have suggested that where downsizing programs adopt appropriate OD interventions or apply strategies similar to the process outlined above, they generate more positive individual and organizational results.[46] Thus, the success of downsizing efforts may depend as much on how effectively the intervention is applied as on the size of the layoffs or the amount of delayering.

REENGINEERING

The final restructuring intervention is *reengineering*—the fundamental rethinking and radical redesign of business processes to achieve dramatic improvements in performance.[47] Reengineering transforms how organizations traditionally produce and deliver goods and services. Beginning with the Industrial Revolution, organizations have increasingly fragmented work into specialized units, each focusing on a limited part of the overall production process. Although this division of labor has enabled organizations to mass-produce standardized products and services efficiently, it can be overly complicated, difficult to manage, and slow to respond to the rapid and unpredictable changes experienced by many organizations today. Reengineering addresses these problems by breaking down specialized work units into more integrated, cross-functional work processes. This streamlines work processes and makes them faster and more flexible; consequently, they are more responsive to changes in competitive conditions, customer demands, product life cycles, and technologies.[48]

As might be expected, reengineering requires an almost revolutionary change in how organizations design their structures and their work. It addresses fundamental issues about why organizations do what they do, and why do they do it in a particular way. Reengineering identifies and questions the often unexamined assumptions underlying how organizations perform work. This effort typically results in radical changes in thinking and work methods—a shift from specialized jobs, tasks, and structures to integrated processes that deliver value to customers. Such revolutionary change differs considerably from incremental approaches to performance improvement, such as continuous improvement and total quality management (Chapter 15), which emphasize incremental changes in existing work processes. Because reengineering radically alters the status quo, it seeks to produce dramatic increases in organization performance.

In radically changing business processes, reengineering frequently takes advantage of new information technology. Modern information technologies, such as teleconferencing, expert systems, shared databases, and wireless communication, can enable organizations to reengineer. They can help organizations to break out of traditional ways of thinking about work and embrace entirely new ways of producing and delivering products. At IBM Credit, for example, an integrated information system with expert systems technology enables one employee to handle all stages of the credit-delivery process. This eliminates the handoffs, delays, and errors that derived from the traditional work design, in which different employees performed sequential tasks.

Whereas new information technology can enable organizations to reengineer themselves, existing technology can thwart such efforts.[49] Many reengineering projects fail because existing information systems do not provide the data needed to operate integrated business processes. The systems do not allow interdependent departments to interface with each other; they often require new information to be entered by hand into separate computer systems before people in different work areas can access it. Given the inherent difficulty in trying to support process-based work with specialized information systems, organizations have sought to develop information technologies that are more suited to reengineered work. The most popular software system, SAP, was developed by a German company of the same name. With SAP, firms can standardize their information systems because the software processes data on a range of tasks and links it all together, thus integrating the information flow among different parts of the business. Because they believe that SAP may be the missing technological link to reengineering, many of the largest consulting firms that provide reengineering services, such as Deloitte Touche and Accenture, have developed their own SAP consultants.

Reengineering also is associated with interventions having to do with downsizing, the shift from functional to process-based structures, and work design (Chapter 16). Although these interventions have different conceptual and applied backgrounds, they overlap considerably in practice. Reengineering can result in production and delivery processes that require fewer people and fewer layers of management. Conversely, downsizing may require subsequent reengineering interventions. When downsizing occurs without fundamental changes in how work is performed, the same tasks simply are being performed with a smaller number of people. Thus, expected cost savings may not be realized because lower salaries and fewer benefits are offset by lower productivity.

Reengineering also can be linked to transformation of organization structures and work design. Its focus on work processes helps to break down the vertical orientation of functional and divisional organizations. The endeavor identifies and assesses core business processes and redesigns work to account for key task interdependencies running through them. That typically results in new jobs or teams that emphasize multifunctional tasks, results-oriented feedback, and employee empowerment—characteristics associated with motivational and sociotechnical approaches to work design. Regrettably, reengineering initially failed to apply these approaches' attention to individual differences in people's reactions to work to its own work-design prescriptions. It advocated enriched work and teams, without consideration for the wealth of research that shows that not all people are motivated to perform such work.[50]

Application Stages

Early reengineering efforts emphasized identifying which business processes to reengineer and technically assessing the work flow. More recent efforts have extended reengineering practice to address issues of managing change, such as how to deal with resistance to change and how to manage the transition to new work processes.[51] The following application steps are included in most reengineering efforts, although the order may change slightly from one situation to another:[52]

1. *Prepare the Organization.* Reengineering begins with clarification and assessment of the organization's context, including its competitive environment, strategy, and objectives. This effort establishes the need for reengineering and the strategic direction that the process should follow. Changes in an organization's competitive environment can signal a need for radical change in how it does business. As preparation for reengineering at GTE Telephone Operations, for example, executives determined that although deregulation had begun with coin-operated telephones and long-distance service, it soon would spread to the local network. They concluded that this would present an enormous competitive challenge and that the old way of doing business, reinforced by years of regulatory protection, would seriously saddle the organization with high costs.[53]

2. *Specify Organization Strategy and Objectives.* The business strategy determines the focus of reengineering and guides decisions about the business processes that are essential for strategic success. In the absence of such information, the organization may reengineer extraneous processes or ones that could be outsourced. GTE executives recognized that the keys to the firm's success in a more competitive environment were low costs and customer satisfaction. Consequently, they set dramatic goals of doubling revenues while halving costs and reducing product development time by 75%. Defining these objectives gave the reengineering effort a clear focus.

   A final task in this preparation step is to communicate clearly throughout the organization why reengineering is necessary and the direction it will take. GTE's communications program lasted a year and a half, and helped ensure that members understood the reasons underlying the program and the magnitude of the changes to be made. Senior executives were careful to communicate, both verbally and behaviorally, that they were fully committed to the change effort. Demonstration of such unwavering support seems necessary if organization members are to challenge their traditional thinking about how business should be conducted.

3. *Fundamentally Rethink the Way Work Gets Done.* This step lies at the heart of reengineering and involves these activities: identifying and analyzing core business processes, defining their key performance objectives, and designing new processes. These tasks are the real work of reengineering and typically are performed by a cross-functional team who is given considerable time and resources to accomplish them.[54]

   a. **Identify and analyze core business processes.** Core processes are considered essential for strategic success. They include activities that transform inputs into valued outputs. Core processes typically are assessed through development of a process map that lists the different activities required to deliver an organization's products or services. GTE determined that its core processes could be characterized as "choose, use, and pay." Customers first choose a telephone carrier, use its services, and then pay for them. GTE developed a process map for these core processes that included the work flow for getting customers to choose, use, and pay for the firm's service.

Analysis of core business processes can include assigning costs to each of the major phases of the work flow to help identify costs that may be hidden in the activities of the production process. Traditional cost-accounting systems do not store data in process terms; they identify costs according to categories of expense, such as salaries, fixed costs, and supplies.[55] This method of cost accounting can be misleading and can result in erroneous conclusions about how best to reduce costs. For example, the material control department at a Dana Corporation plant in Plymouth, Minnesota, changed from a traditional to a process-based accounting system.[56] The traditional accounting system showed that salaries and fringe benefits accounted for 82% of total costs—an assessment that suggested workforce downsizing was the most effective way to lower costs. The process-based accounting system revealed a different picture, however: it showed that 44% of the department's costs involved expediting, resolving, and reissuing orders from suppliers and customers. In other words, almost half of their costs were associated with reworking deficient orders.

Business processes also can be assessed in terms of value-added activities—the amount of value contributed to a product or service by a particular step in the process. For example, as part of its invoice collection process, Corky's Pest Control, a small service business dependent on a steady stream of cash payments, provides its customers with a self-addressed, stamped envelope. Although this adds an additional cost to each account, it more than pays for itself in customer loyalty and retention, and reduced accounts receivables and late-payments handling. Conversely, organizations often engage in process activities that have little or no added value. For instance, in a Denver hospital an employee on each workshift checked a pump that circulated oxygen. Eight years earlier, the pump had failed and caused a death. Since that time, a new pump had been installed with fault-protection equipment and control sensors that no longer required the physical inspection. Yet because of habit, the checking process remained in place and drained resources that could be used more productively in other areas.

b. **Define performance objectives.** Challenging performance goals are set in this step. The highest possible level of performance for any particular process is identified, and dramatic goals are set for speed, quality, cost, or other measures of performance. These standards can derive from customer requirements or from benchmarks of the best practices of industry leaders. For example, at Andersen Windows, the demand for unique window shapes pushed the number of different products from 28,000 to more than 86,000 in 1991.[57] The pressure on the shop floor for a "batch of one" resulted in 20% of all shipments containing at least one order discrepancy. As part of its reengineering effort, Andersen set targets for ease of ordering, manufacturing, and delivery. Each retailer and distributor was sold an interactive, computerized version of its catalogue that allowed customers to design their own windows. The resulting design is then given a unique "license plate number" and the specifications are sent directly to the factory. By 1995, new sales had tripled at some retail locations, the number of products had increased to 188,000, and fewer than 1 in 200 shipments had a discrepancy.

c. **Design new processes.** The last task in this third step of reengineering is to redesign current business processes to achieve breakthrough goals. It often starts with a clean sheet of paper and addresses the question "If we were starting this company today, what processes would we need to create a sustainable competitive advantage?" These essential processes are then designed according to the following guidelines:[58]

- Begin and end the process with the needs and wants of the customer.
- Simplify the current process by combining and eliminating steps.
- Use the "best of what is" in the current process.
- Attend to both technical and social aspects of the process.
- Do not be constrained by past practice.
- Identify the critical information required at each step in the process.
- Perform activities in their most natural order.
- Assume the work gets done right the first time.
- Listen to people who do the work.

An important activity that appears in many successful reengineering efforts is implementing "early wins" or "quick hits." Analysis of existing processes often reveals obvious redundancies and inefficiencies for which appropriate changes may be authorized immediately. These early successes can help generate and sustain momentum in the reengineering effort.

4. *Restructure the Organization Around the New Business Processes.* This last step in reengineering involves changing the organization's structure to support the new business processes. This endeavor typically results in the kinds of process-based structures that were described earlier in this chapter. An important element of this restructuring is implementing new information and measurement systems that reinforce a shift from measuring behaviors, such as absenteeism and grievances, to assessing outcomes, such as productivity, customer satisfaction, and cost savings. Moreover, information technology is one of the key drivers of reengineering because it can drastically reduce the cost and time associated with integrating and coordinating business processes.

Reengineered organizations typically have the following characteristics:[59]

- **Work units change from functional departments to process teams.** The Principal Financial Group's Individual Insurance Department was structured according to product lines, such as life, health, and auto insurance.[60] Following reengineering, the department organized around cross-functional presale teams aimed at developing and building customer relationships and postsale teams that maintained them.

- **Jobs change from simple tasks to multidimensional work.** The postsale team was responsible for a field-support process called licensing and contracting. Under the old structure, this was a 16-step effort that involved nine people in different departments and on different floors in Principal's home office. Following reengineering, the process consists of only six steps and involves only three people who are cross-trained to perform the various tasks.

- **People's roles change from controlled to empowered.** At Hallmark Circuits, the reengineering effort resulted not only in changed jobs and processes, but in increased employee involvement as well. Production teams meet twice daily to discuss problems; hiring decisions are made by a four-person team of employees; major equipment purchases are jointly de-termined by management and employees; and the manufacturing group plays a big role in deciding whether to bid on or take new jobs.[61]

- **The focus of performance measures and compensation shifts from activities to results.** Reengineered organizations routinely collect and re-port measures of customer satisfaction, operating costs, and productivity to all teams and then tie these measures to pay. In this way, teams and their members are rewarded for working smarter, not harder.

- **Organization structures change from hierarchical to flat.** As de-scribed earlier, the favored structure of the reengineered organization is process based. Rather than having layers of management, the organization has empowered, cross-functional, and well-educated process teams that collect information, make decisions about task execution, and monitor their performance.

- **Managers change from supervisors to coaches; executives change from scorekeepers to leaders.** In process-based structures, the role of management and leadership changes drastically. A new set of skills is re-quired, including facilitation, resource acquisition, information sharing, sup-porting, and problem solving.

Application 14.4 describes the reengineering efforts at Honeywell's Industrial Au-tomation and Control business. It highlights the importance of mapping current processes, aligning the rest of the organization to support the change, especially in-formation technology.[62]

Results from Reengineering

The results from reengineering vary widely. Industry journals and the business press regularly contain accounts of dramatic business outcomes attributable to reengi-neering. On the other hand, the best-selling book on reengineering reported that as many as 70% of the efforts failed to meet their cost, cycle time, or productivity ob-jectives.[63] One study polled 497 companies in the United States and 1,245 compa-nies in Europe, and found that 60% of U.S. firms and 75% of European firms had engaged in at least one reengineering project. Eighty-five percent of the firms re-ported little or no gain from the efforts.[64] Despite its popularity, reengineering is only beginning to be evaluated systematically, and there is little research to help un-ravel the disparate results.[65]

One evaluation of business process reengineering examined more than one hundred companies' efforts.[66] In-depth analyses of 20 reengineering projects found that 11 cases had total business unit cost reductions of less than 5%, whereas 6 cases had total cost reductions averaging 18%. The primary difference was the scope of the business process selected. Reengineering key value-added processes significantly affected total business unit costs; reengineering narrow business processes did not.

Similarly, performance improvements in particular processes were associated strongly with changes in six key levers of behavior, including structure, skills, infor-mation systems, roles, incentives, and shared values. Efforts that addressed all six levers produced average cost reductions in specific processes by 35%; efforts that af-fected only one or two change levers reduced costs by 19%. Finally, the percentage reduction in total unit costs was associated with committed leadership. Similarly, a survey of 23 "successful" reengineering cases found that they were characterized by a clear vision of the future, specific goals for change, use of information technology, top management's involvement and commitment, clear milestones and measure-ments, and the training of participants in process analysis and teamwork.[67]

HONEYWELL IAC'S TOTALPLANT™ REENGINEERING PROCESS

Honeywell (http://www.honeywell.com) is a diversified technology and manufacuring organization that serves customers worldwide with aerospace products and services; control technologies for buildings, homes, and industry; automotive products; and specialty materials. Its industrial automation and control (IAC) business unit in Phoenix, Arizona, is responsibile for the design, manufacture, and configuration of world-class process control equipment marketed as the TDC 3000X family of systems. Their customer base includes refineries, chemical plants, and paper mills around the world.

In response to declining performance results, IAC management set out to implement an ISO 9000 certified quality program named TotalPlant™ as part of an effort to optimize global customer satisfaction. The objectives of this initiative were reducing defects, minimizing production cycles, and optimizing resource management. The TotalPlant™ initiative was a business process reengineering intervention based upon four principles: process mapping, fail-safing, teamwork, and communication. Cross-functional multiskilled teams were created and given responsibility for an entire module or product line. Each team member was then educated in each of the principles and empowered to enact them to create improvements within their work groups.

Process mapping is a methodology that converts any business activity into a graphical form. It creates a common visual language that can be used to enhance an employee's ability to see beyond the boundaries of their work process. It is also the basis of radical change in business processes. As part of the TotalPlant™ initiative, process mapping consisted of eight major stages.

- The first three stages were to select the process to be reviewed, identify all customers, and set the boundaries of the process. Through consensus decision making, these simple steps kept the participants focused on the process being mapped. In addition, the team reviewed its composition to ensure that all appropriate functions were represented.

- Fourth, the team developed an "as is" map. This required them to outline and document the existing process. By creating a visual map the team was able to identify the flow of both the product and the information related to the process. Cross-functional decision points and dependencies became visually apparent through the process. Fifth, the "as is" map was used by the team to calculate cycle times, the elapsed times between the start of a process and the conclusion of a process, as well as the distance the product travels during that cycle. Both the mean and the range were calculated for each process cycle time.

- Sixth, the team identified areas of improvement that did not require additional costs or resources. Non-value-added steps, extended approval processes, and processes with highly variant cycle times were analyzed and either streamlined or completely eliminated. Following this step, the seventh stage was to develop a "should be" map that described the improved process.

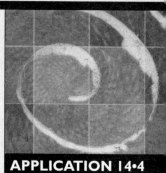

APPLICATION 14•4

- Finally, the eighth step directed the team to develop a process implementation plan, establish confirmation from a steering committee, and then implement it. New goals were established and results tracked for each of the process steps.

The second major component of the TotalPlant™ process was the *fail-safing process*. Fail-safing was a five-step process intended to create a product that is defect free by identifying and analyzing defects, and understanding their root causes. A root cause has three characteristics: (1) it is defined as being the cause of the defect; (2) it is possible to change the cause; and (3) if eliminated, the defect will be eliminated or at least significantly reduced. Once the root cause is identified, a set of alternative solutions is developed to eliminate the defect in future product. Each alternative is evaluated for ease of implementation, cost, and time to implement.

Once a solution is agreed upon, the team implements the PDCA (Plan, Do, Check, Act) process to move the solution forward. Planning includes developing a full implementation plan, which include areas impacted, timing, resource requirements, and costs. This becomes a living document outlining the action items needed to implement the change. "Doing" consists of executing against the implementation plan. Once the new process has been implemented, the results are "checked" to ensure that they are in line with the desired results. Finally, the team must "act" to determine the next steps for continuous improvement.

Teamwork was the critical third piece of the TotalPlant™ process. Honeywell realized that the transition to a team environment needed to happen gradually. Through the process mapping and fail-safing process, they gave people real problems to solve and systematic tools with which to solve them. With the addition of education and training around teams, these "hard-skill" activities became the fertile soil for team development. As team members were asked to own the whole process, an environment that fosters teamwork was created. Creativity, innovation, and risk taking were rewarded and the values of the organization moved to trust, respect, and empowerment. Managers were educated to support the teams not run them in order to further enrich the team environment.

The final and foundational element of the TotalPlant™ process was *communication*. Top management's successful communication of the TotalPlant™ paradigm shift was pivotal to the initiative's success. Through their everyday actions, top management lived the values of open communication throughout the organization. In addition, teams were given training in conflict resolution, problem solving, and listening skills to enhance the overall effectiveness of communication within the teams. The creation of a positive, open environment became critical to the success of the change initiative being undertaken. Top management understood that the environment needed to shift to consistently support teamwork, creativity, and "new thinking." The major challenges within the process took the form of middle-management resistance. The new team concepts took managers who had been functional or process experts and moved them outside their comfort zone by requiring them to look at processes across functions and broaden their view of success. Top management was required to move from command and control to a more facilitative and empowering approach to support this type of behavior change.

In addition to the four major components of the TotalPlant™ process, Honeywell made significant changes in the technology strategy to support the business strategy. The information systems group was converted into an information technology shop where all technology was developed in direct support of the plant and its operations. All systems were fully integrated to optimize the timeliness and accuracy of information.

After 3 years, performance results indicated a reduction in defects of 70%, customer rejects declined by 57%, and there was a 46% reduction in inventory investments. Honeywell's execution against their vision is what set this business process reengineering apart from others. Top management did not just speak the vision, they lived and supported it through active participation in the entire change process. Another critical component was that the organizational structure was redesigned to align with the new processes and strategies. Top management at Honeywell understood that change of this magnitude takes time and therefore were able to set the organization's expectations accordingly. Additionally, they committed appropriate levels of training and financial resources to make the initiative a success.

The Honeywell case provides some excellent learnings for making a reengineering initiative successful. First, people are the key enablers of change. They must be trained, developed, and rewarded to support the change process. Second, people must be able to question all of their assumptions. Nothing can be sacred as each process is deconstructed and then rebuilt. Third, process mapping provides people with a systematic process for analyzing and improving existing systems and processes. Next, management must be able to create dissatisfaction with the existing process and allow the teams to own the solution. An environment conducive to change must be created and supported by management's attitudes and behaviors. This includes active participation at all stages of the process.

However, while support and participation from the top is important, implementation should take place by empowering decision makers at the level where the work is being done. Honeywell also demonstrated that reengineering must be a business-driven and continuous process. Initiatives like failsafing demonstrated the need to continuously challenge the status quo. Stretch goals must be set throughout the process to keep employees motivated. Finally, the most critical component of a successful reengineering initiative is the ability to actively implement and execute against the plan. By keeping their eye on the end goal, Honeywell was able to successfully optimize their customer satisfaction through this process.

■ SUMMARY

This chapter presented interventions aimed at restructuring organizations. Several basic structures, such as the functional structure, the divisional structure, and the matrix configuration, dominate most organizations. Two newer forms, process-based and network-based structures, were also described. Each of these structures has corresponding strengths and weaknesses, and supportive conditions must be assessed when determining which structure is an appropriate fit with the organization's environment.

Two restructuring interventions were described: downsizing and reengineering. Downsizing decreases the size of the organization through workforce reduction or organizational redesign. It generally is associated with layoffs where a certain number or class of organization members are no longer employed by the organization. Downsizing can contribute to organization development by focusing on the organization's strategy, using a variety of downsizing tactics, addressing the needs of all organization members, and following through with growth plans. Reengineering is the fundamental rethinking and radical redesign of business processes to achieve dramatic improvements in performance. It seeks to transform how organizations traditionally produce and deliver goods and services. A typical reengineering project prepares the organization, rethinks the way work gets done, and restructures the organization around the newly designed core processes.

■ NOTES

1. P. Lawrence and J. Lorsch, *Organization and Environment: Managing Differentiation and Integration* (Cambridge: Harvard Graduate School of Business, Administration Division of Research, 1967); J. R. Galbraith, *Designing Organizations* (San Francisco: Jossey-Bass, 2002).

2. L. Gulick and L. Urwick, eds., *Papers on the Science of Administration* (New York: Institute of Public Administration, Columbia University, 1937); M. Weber, *The Theory of Social and Economic Organization*, eds. A. Henderson and T. Parsons (Glencoe, Ill.: Free Press, 1947).

3. A. Chandler, *Strategy and Structure: Chapters in the History of the Industrial Enterprise* (Cambridge: MIT Press, 1962).

4. S. Davis and P. Lawrence, *Matrix* (Reading, Mass.: Addison-Wesley, 1977); H. Kolodny, "Managing in a Matrix," *Business Horizons* 24 (March-April 1981): 17–35.

5. Davis and Lawrence, *Matrix.*

6. W. Joyce, "Matrix Organization: A Social Experiment," *Academy of Management Journal* 29 (1986): 536–61; C. Worley and C. Teplitz, "The Use of 'Expert Power' as an Emerging Influence Style within Successful U.S. Matrix Organizations," *Project Management Journal* (1993): 31–36.

7. Davis and Lawrence, *Matrix.*

8. J. Byrne, "The Horizontal Corporation," *Business Week* (20 December 1993): 76–81; S. Mohrman, S. Cohen, and A. Mohrman, *Designing Team-Based Organizations* (San Francisco: Jossey-Bass, 1995); R. Ashkenas, D. Ulrich, T. Jick, and S. Kerr, *The Boundaryless Organization* (San Francisco: Jossey-Bass, 1995).

9. J. Galbraith, E. Lawler, and associates, *Organizing for the Future: The New Logic for Managing Complex Organizations* (San Francisco: Jossey-Bass, 1993).

10. Byrne, "Horizontal Corporation"; Mohrman, Cohen, and Mohrman, *Designing Team-based Organization.*

11. This application is part of the series of snapshots into the change process at American Healthways Corporation.

12. J. Brown, S. Durchslag, and J. Hagel, "Loosening Up: How Process Networks Unlock the Power of Specializa-

tion," *McKinsey Quarterly* (6 August 2002) (downloaded from Dow Jones Interactive); W. Halal, "From Hierarchy to Enterprise: Internal Markets Are the New Foundation of Management," *Academy of Management Executive* 8, 4 (1994): 69–83; C. Snow, R. Miles, and H. Coleman Jr., "Managing 21st Century Network Organizations," *Organizational Dynamics* 20 (1992): 5–19; S. Tully, "The Modular Corporation," *Fortune* (8 February 1993): 106–14; R. Rycroft, "Managing Complex Networks: Key to 21st Century Innovation Success," *Research-Technology Management* (May-June 1999): 13–18.

13. W. Davidow and M. Malone, *The Virtual Corporation: Structuring and Revitalizing the Corporation of the 21st Century* (New York: Harper Business, 1992); J. Bryne, R. Brandt, and O. Port, "The Virtual Corporation," *Business Week* (8 February 1993): 98–102; Tully, "The Modular Corporation"; R. Keidel, "Rethinking Organizational Design," *Academy of Management Executive* 8 (1994): 12–30; C. Handy, *The Age of Unreason* (Cambridge: Harvard Business School Press, 1989); R. Miles, C. Snow, J. Mathews, G. Miles, and H. Coleman, "Organizing in the Knowledge Age: Anticipating the Cellular Form," *Academy of Management Executive* 11 (1997): 7–20.

14. R. Chisolm, *Developing Network Organizations: Learning from Theory and Practice* (Reading, Mass.: Addison-Wesley, 1998); R. Achrol, "Changes in the Theory of Interorganizational Relations in Marketing: Toward a Network Paradigm," *Journal of the Academy of Marketing Science* 25 (1997): 56–71.

15. C. Snow, "Twenty-First Century Organizations: Implications for a New Marketing Paradigm," *Journal of the Academy of Marketing Science* 25 (1997): 72–74.

16. W. Powell, "Neither Market Nor Hierarchy: Network Forms of Organization," in *Research in Organizational Behavior*, vol. 12, eds. B. Staw and L. Cummings (Greenwich, Conn.: JAI Press, 1990), 295–336; M. Lawless and R. Moore, "Interorganizational Systems in Public Service Delivery: A New Application of the Dynamic Network Framework," *Human Relations* 42 (1989): 1167–84; M. Gerstein, "From Machine Bureaucracies to Networked

Organizations: An Architectural Journey," in *Organizational Architecture*, eds. D. Nadler, M. Gerstein, R. Shaw, and associates (San Francisco: Jossey-Bass, 1992), 11–38.

17. D. Tapscott, *The Digital Economy* (New York: McGraw-Hill, 1996); Bryne, Brandt, and Port, "Virtual Corporation."

18. Bryne, Brandt, and Port, "Virtual Corporation"; G. Dess, A. Rasheed, K. McLaughlin, and R. Priem, "The New Corporate Architecture," *Academy of Management Executive* 9 (1995): 7–20.

19. J. Galbraith and R. Kazanjian, *Strategy Implementation: Structure, Systems and Process,* 2d ed. (St. Paul: West, 1986), 159–60.

20. Anonymous, "Amazon Alliances Create Next-gen E-tail Model," *DSN Retailing Today* 41 (2002): 47; T. Kemp, "Partnerships R Us—Toysrus.com Is Building a Sustainable E-retail Business by Drawing on the Strengths of Its Two Giant Business Partners," *InternetWeek* 882 (15 October 2001): 14, 15+; S. Leschly, M. Roberts, and W. Sahlman, "Amazon.com—2002," *Harvard Business School Case 9-803-098,* 2003; S. Kotha, "Amazon.com: Expanding Beyond Books," University of Washington Business School, 1998, downloaded at http://us.badm. washington.edu/kotha/cases.htm on May 9, 2003.

21. W. Cascio, "Downsizing: What Do We Know? What Have We Learned?" *Academy of Management Executive* 7 (1993): 95–104.

22. J. Laabs, "Has Downsizing Missed Its Mark?" *Workforce* (April 1999): 30–37.

23. A summary of the Mercer Study can be found at http://www.mercerhr.com. J. Morris, W. Cascio, and C. Young, "Downsizing after All These Years: Questions and Answers about Who Did It, How Many Did It, and Who Benefited from It," *Organizational Dynamics* (Winter 1999): 78–87.

24. "Unemployment at 5.8% for February, Planned Layoffs Rise Slightly," *HR Focus* (April 2003): 8.

25. Laabs, "Has Downsizing Missed Its Mark?"

26. Ibid.

27. Ibid.

28. A. Pasztor, "Airline Layoffs Raise Concerns about Safety," *Wall Street Journal* (8 April 2003): D1.

29. W. McKinley, C. Sanchez, and A. Schick, "Organizational Downsizing: Constraining, Cloning, Learning," *Academy of Management Executive* 9 (1995): 32–44.

30. G. Hamel and C. Prahalad, *Competing for the Future* (Cambridge: Harvard Business School Press, 1994).

31. K. Cameron, S. Freeman, and A. Mishra, "Best Practices in White-Collar Downsizing: Managing Contradictions," *Academy of Management Executive* 5 (1991): 57–73;

K. Cameron, "Strategies for Successful Organizational Downsizing," *Human Resource Management* 33 (1994): 189–212; R. Marshall and L. Lyles, "Planning for a Restructured, Revitalized Organization," *Sloan Management Review* 35 (1994): 81–91; N. Polend, "Downsizing and Organization Development: An Opportunity Missed, but Not Lost" (unpublished senior project, The Union Institute, 1999).

32. K. Kelly, "Case Digs Out from Way Under," *Business Week* (14 August 1995).

33. J. Brockner, "The Effects of Work Layoffs on Survivors: Research, Theory and Practice," in *Research in Organizational Behavior,* vol. 10, eds. B. M. Staw and L. L. Cummings (Greenwich, Conn.: JAI Press, 1989), 213–55; J. Byrne, "The Pain of Downsizing," *Business Week* (9 May 1994).

34. Marshall and Lyles, "Planning for a Restructured, Revitalized Organization."

35. J. E. Rogdon, "Lack of Communication Burdens Restructurings," *Wall Street Journal* (2 November 1992): B1.

36. This application was contributed by Jay Greaves.

37. D. Druckman, J. Singer, and H. Van Cott, eds., *Enhancing Organizational Performance* (Washington, D.C.: National Academy Press, 1997).

38. A. Bennett, "Downsizing Doesn't Necessarily Bring an Upswing in Corporate Profitability," *Wall Street Journal* (6 June 1991): B1; Cascio, "Downsizing."

39. R. Henkoff, "Getting beyond Downsizing," *Fortune* (1 October 1994): 58.

40. A. Roan, G. Lafferty, and R. Loudoun, "Survivors and Victims: A Case Study of Organisational Restructuring in the Public Health Sector," *New Zealand Journal of Industrial Relations* (June 2002): 151; R. Cole, "Learning from Learning Theory: Implications for Quality Improvements of Turnover, Use of Contingent Workers, and Job Rotation Policies," *Quality Management Journal* 1 (1993): 1–25; K. Kozlowski, G. Chao, E. Smith, and J. Hedlund, "Organizational Downsizing: Strategies, Interventions, and Research Implications," in *International Review of Industrial and Organizational Psychology* (New York: John Wiley & Sons, 1993); Druckman, Singer, and Van Cott, eds., *Enhancing Organizational Performance;* B. Luthans and S. Sommer, "The Impact of Downsizing on Workplace Attitudes," *Group and Organization Management* (March 1999): 46–55.

41. W. McKinley, A. G. Schick, J. L. Sun, and A. P. Tang, "The Financial Environment of Layoffs: An Exploratory Study" (working paper, Southern Illinois University at Carbondale, 1994).

42. Cascio, "Downsizing."

43. Morris, Cascio, and Young, "Downsizing."

44. J. Byrne, "There Is an Upside to Downsizing," *Business Week* (9 May 1994).

45. Cameron, Freeman, and Mishra, "Best Practices."

46. Cameron, Freeman, and Mishra, "Best Practices"; Kozlowski et al., "Organizational Downsizing"; J. Davy, A. Kinicki, and C. Schreck, "Developing and Testing a Model of Survivor Responses to Layoffs," *Journal of Vocational Behavior* 38 (1991): 302–17; K. Labich, "How to Fire People and Still Sleep at Night," *Fortune* (10 June 1996): 65–72; D. Feldman and C. Leana, "Better Practices in Managing Layoffs," *Human Resource Management Journal* 33 (1995): 239–60; J. Byrne, "Why Downsizing Looks Different These Days," *Business Week* (10 October 1994).

47. M. Hammer and J. Champy, *Reengineering the Corporation* (New York: HarperCollins, 1993); T. Stewart, "Reengineering: The Hot New Managing Tool," *Fortune* (23 August 1993): 41–48; J. Champy, *Reengineering Management* (New York: HarperCollins, 1994).

48. R. Kaplan and L. Murdock, "Core Process Redesign," *McKinsey Quarterly* 2 (1991): 27–43.

49. Tapscott, *Digital Economy.*

50. J. Moosbruker and R. Loftin, "Business Process Redesign and Organizational Development: Enhancing Success by Removing the Barriers," *Journal of Applied Behavioral Science* (September 1998): 286–97; T. Davenport, L. Prusak, and J. Wilson, "Reengineering Revisited," *Computerworld* 37 (2003): 48–49.

51. M. Miller, "Customer Service Drives Reengineering Effort," *Personnel Journal* 73 (1994): 87–93.

52. Kaplan and Murdock, "Core Process Redesign"; R. Manganelli and M. Klein, *The Reengineering Handbook* (New York: AMACOM, 1994).

53. D. P. Allen and R. Nafius, "Dreaming and Doing: Reengineering GTE Telephone Operations," *Planning Review* (June-July 1993): 28–31.

54. J. Katzenbach and D. Smith, "The Rules for Managing Cross-Functional Reengineering Teams," *Planning Review* (March-April 1993): 12–13; A. Nahavandi and E. Aranda, "Restructuring Teams for the Re-Engineered Organization," *Academy of Management Executive* 8 (1994): 58–68.

55. M. O'Guin, *The Complete Guide to Activity Based Costing* (Englewood Cliffs, N.J.: Prentice Hall, 1991); H. Johnson and R. Kaplan, *Relevance Lost: The Rise and Fall of Management Accounting* (Cambridge: Harvard Business School Press, 1987).

56. T. P. Pare, "A New Tool for Managing Costs," *Fortune* (14 June 1993): 124–29.

57. J. Martin, "Are You as Good as You Think You Are?" *Fortune* (30 September 1996): 142–52.

58. Hammer and Champy, *Reengineering the Corporation.*

59. Ibid.

60. C. Rohm, "The Principal Insures a Better Future by Reengineering Its Individual Insurance Department," *National Productivity Review* 12 (1992): 55–65.

61. R. Riggs, "Employees Re-Engineer Firm," *San Diego Union Tribune* (23 October 1993): C1–C2.

62. This application was written and submitted by Ann McCloskey based on information adapted from D. Paper, J. Rodger, and P. Pendharker, "A BPR Case Study at Honeywell," *Business Process Management Journal* 7 (2001): 85–99.

63. Hammer and Champy, *Reengineering the Corporation.*

64. CSC Index, "State of Reengineering Report, 1994," *Economist* (2 July 1994): 6.

65. Champy, *Reengineering Management;* K. Jensen, "The Effects of Reengineering on Injury Frequency" (unpublished master's thesis, Pepperdine University, 1993); Druckman, Singer, and Van Cott, eds., *Enhancing Organizational Performance;* D. Rigby, "Management Tools and Techniques: A Survey," *California Management Review* 34 (2001): 139–160.

66. G. Hall, J. Rosenthal, and J. Wade, "How to Make Reengineering Really Work," *Harvard Business Review* (November-December 1993): 119–31.

67. J. Dixon, "Business Process Reengineering: Improving in New Strategic Directions," *California Management Review* 36 (1994): 93–108.

15

Employee Involvement

Faced with competitive demands for lower costs, higher performance, and greater flexibility, organizations are increasingly turning to employee involvement (EI) to enhance the participation, commitment, and productivity of their members. This chapter presents OD interventions aimed at moving decision making downward in the organization, closer to where the actual work takes place. This increased employee involvement can lead to quicker, more responsive decisions, continuous performance improvements, and greater employee flexibility, commitment, and satisfaction.

Employee involvement is a broad term that has been variously referred to as "empowerment," "participative management," "work design," "industrial democracy," and "quality of work life." It covers diverse approaches to gaining greater participation in relevant workplace decisions. Organizations such as General Mills, AT&T, and Intel have enhanced worker involvement through enriched forms of work; others, such as Verizon and Ford, have increased participation by forming employee involvement teams that develop suggestions for improving productivity and quality; Southwest Airlines, Shell Oil, and Nucor Steel have sought greater participation through union–management cooperation on performance and quality-of-work-life issues; and still others, such as Texas Instruments, Solar Turbines, 3M, the IRS, and Motorola, have improved employee involvement by emphasizing participation in quality improvement approaches.

As described in Chapter 1, current EI approaches evolved from earlier quality-of-work-life efforts in Europe, Scandinavia, and the United States. The terms *employee involvement* and *empowerment* gradually have replaced the designation *quality of work life,* particularly in the United States. A current definition of EI includes four elements that can promote meaningful involvement in workplace decisions: power, information, knowledge and skills, and rewards. These components of EI combine to exert powerful effects on productivity and employee well-being.

Major EI applications discussed in this chapter are parallel structures, including cooperative union–management projects and quality circles; high-involvement organizations; and total quality management. Two additional EI approaches, work design and reward system interventions, are discussed in Chapters 16 and 17, respectively.

EMPLOYEE INVOLVEMENT: WHAT IS IT?

Employee involvement is the current label used to describe a set of practices and philosophies that started with the quality-of-work-life movement in the late 1950s. The phrase *quality of work life* was used to stress the prevailing poor quality of life at the workplace.[1] As described in Chapter 1, both the term *QWL* and the meaning attributed to it have undergone considerable change and development. In this section, we provide a working definition of EI, document the growth of EI practices in the United States and abroad, and clarify the important and often misunderstood relationship between EI and productivity.

A Working Definition of Employee Involvement

Employee involvement seeks to increase members' input into decisions that affect organization performance and employee well-being.[2] It can be described in terms of four key elements that promote worker involvement:[3]

1. **Power.** This element of EI includes providing people with enough authority to make work-related decisions covering various issues such as work methods, task assignments, performance outcomes, customer service, and employee selection. The amount of power afforded employees can vary enormously, from simply asking them for input into decisions that managers subsequently make, to managers and workers jointly making decisions, to employees making decisions themselves.

2. **Information.** Timely access to relevant information is vital to making effective decisions. Organizations can promote EI by ensuring that the necessary information flows freely to those with decision authority. This can include data about operating results, business plans, competitive conditions, new technologies and work methods, and ideas for organizational improvement.

3. **Knowledge and skills.** Employee involvement contributes to organizational effectiveness only to the extent that employees have the requisite skills and knowledge to make good decisions. Organizations can facilitate EI by providing training and development programs for improving members' knowledge and skills. Such learning can cover an array of expertise having to do with performing tasks, making decisions, solving problems, and understanding how the business operates.

4. **Rewards.** Because people generally do those things for which they are recognized, rewards can have a powerful effect on getting people involved in the organization. Meaningful opportunities for involvement can provide employees with internal rewards, such as feelings of self-worth and accomplishment. External rewards, such as pay and promotions, can reinforce EI when they are linked directly to performance outcomes that result from participation in decision making. (Reward systems are discussed more fully in Chapter 17.)

Those four elements—power, information, knowledge and skills, and rewards—contribute to EI success by determining how much employee participation in decision making is possible in organizations. The further that all four elements are moved downward throughout the organization, the greater the employee involvement. Furthermore, because the four elements of EI are interdependent, they must be changed together to obtain positive results. For example, if organization members are given more power and authority to make decisions but do not have the information or knowledge and skill to make good decisions, then the value of involvement is likely to be negligible. Similarly, increasing employees' power, information, and knowledge and skills but not linking rewards to the performance consequences of changes gives members little incentive to improve organizational performance. The EI methods that will be described in this chapter vary in how much involvement is afforded employees. Parallel structures, such as union–management cooperative efforts and quality circles, are limited in the degree that the four elements of EI are moved downward in the organization; high-involvement organizations and total quality management provide far greater opportunities for involvement.

The Diffusion of Employee Involvement Practices

The number of organizations using employee involvement practices is growing in both the United States and Europe. In the most comprehensive, long-term study of EI applications, Lawler and his colleagues at the Center for Effective Organizations at the University of Southern California have surveyed the *Fortune* 1000 every 3 years between 1987 and 2003.[4] Their data show positive trends in EI use among these firms over that time period, including both a growing number of firms applying EI and a greater percentage of the workforce included in such programs. Despite these positive trends, however, their research reveals that the scope and depth of EI interventions are relatively modest. Across a range of EI applications, from employee suggestion systems to self-managed work teams, the 2003 data suggested about half of the companies involved fewer than 20% of employees in these applications. Thus, although many large organizations are using EI practices, there is considerable room for their diffusion across organizations and throughout the workforce.

Similarly, EI has prospered outside of the United States. Countries using EI in western Europe include France, Germany, Denmark, Ireland, Sweden, Norway, Holland, Italy, and Great Britain.[5] Although the tremendous changes currently taking place in countries such as Russia, Bulgaria, the Philippines, and the People's Republic of China may have dampened EI efforts, several programs are actively under way.[6] Canada, Mexico, India, Australia, New Zealand, Hong Kong, and Japan also are using EI. Internationally, EI may be considered a set of processes directed at changing the structure of the work situation within a particular cultural environment and under the influence of particular values and philosophies. As a result, in some instances EI has been promoted by unions; in others, by management. In some cases, it has been part of a pragmatic approach to increasing productivity; in other cases, it has been driven by socialist values.[7]

How Employee Involvement Affects Productivity

An assumption underlying much of the EI literature is that such interventions will lead to higher productivity. Although this premise has been based mainly on anecdotal evidence and a good deal of speculation, there is now a growing body of research findings to support that linkage.[8] Studies have found a consistent relationship between EI practices and such measures as productivity, financial performance, customer satisfaction, labor hours, and waste rates.

Attempts to explain this positive linkage traditionally have followed the idea that giving people more involvement in work decisions raises their job satisfaction and, in turn, their productivity. There is growing evidence that this satisfaction-causes-productivity premise is too simplistic and sometimes wrong.

A more realistic explanation for how EI interventions can affect productivity is shown in Figure 15.1. EI practices, such as participation in workplace decisions, can improve productivity in at least three ways.[9] First, such interventions can improve communication and coordination among employees and organizational departments, and help integrate the different jobs or departments that contribute to an overall task.

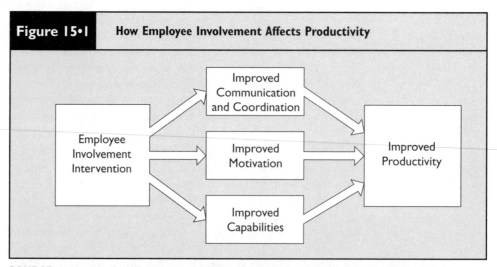

Figure 15•1   How Employee Involvement Affects Productivity

SOURCE: Lawler & Ledford, "Productivity and QWL," *National Productivity Review* 1, 1 (Winter 1981–82). Copyright 1982 by Executive Enterprises, Inc., Reprinted by permission of John Wiley & Sons, Inc.

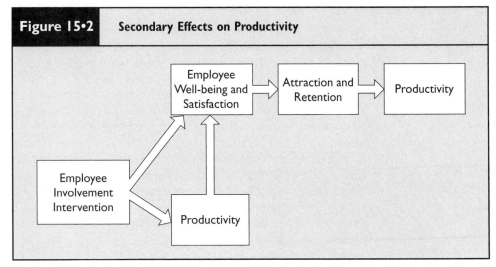

Figure 15•2   **Secondary Effects on Productivity**

SOURCE: Lawler & Ledford, "Productivity and QWL," *National Productivity Review* 1, 1 (Winter 1981–82). Copyright 1982 by Executive Enterprises, Inc., Reprinted by permission of John Wiley & Sons, Inc.

Second, EI interventions can improve employee motivation, particularly when they satisfy important individual needs. Motivation is translated into improved performance when people have the necessary skills and knowledge to perform well and when the technology and work situation allow people to affect productivity. For example, some jobs are so rigidly controlled and specified that individual motivation can have little impact on productivity.

Third, EI practices can improve the capabilities of employees, thus enabling them to perform better. For example, attempts to increase employee participation in decision making generally include skill training in group problem solving and communication.

Figure 15.2 shows the secondary effects of EI. These practices increase employee well-being and satisfaction by providing a better work environment and a more fulfilling job. Improved productivity also can increase satisfaction, particularly when it leads to greater rewards. Increased employee satisfaction, deriving from EI interventions and increased productivity, ultimately can have a still greater impact on productivity by attracting good employees to join and remain with the organization.

In sum, EI interventions are expected to increase productivity by improving communication and coordination, employee motivation, and individual capabilities. They also can influence productivity by means of the secondary effects of increased employee well-being and satisfaction. Although a growing body of research supports these relationships,[10] there is considerable debate over the strength of the association between EI and productivity.[11] Recent data support the conclusion that relatively modest levels of EI produce moderate improvements in performance and satisfaction and that higher levels of EI produce correspondingly higher levels of performance.[12]

EMPLOYEE INVOLVEMENT APPLICATIONS

This section describes three major EI applications that vary in the amount of power, information, knowledge and skills, and rewards that are moved downward through the organization (from least to most involvement): parallel structures, including cooperative union–management projects and quality circles; high-involvement organizations; and total quality management.

Parallel Structures

Parallel structures involve members in resolving ill-defined, complex problems and build adaptability into bureaucratic organizations.[13] Also known as "collateral structures," "dualistic structures," or "shadow structures,"[14] parallel structures operate in conjunction with the formal organization. They provide members with an alternative setting in which to address problems and to propose innovative solutions free from the existing, formal organization structure and culture. For example, members may attend periodic off-site meetings to explore ways to improve quality in their work area or they may be temporarily assigned to a special project or facility to devise new products or solutions to organizational problems. Parallel structures facilitate problem solving and change by providing time and resources for members to think, talk, and act in completely new ways. Consequently, norms and procedures for working in parallel structures are entirely different from those of the formal organization. This section describes the application steps associated with the two most common parallel structures, cooperative union–management projects and quality circles, and reviews the research on their effectiveness.

Application Stages

Cooperative union–management projects and quality circle interventions fall at the lower end of the EI scale. Member participation and influence typically are restricted to making proposals and to offering suggestions for change because subsequent decisions about implementing the proposals are reserved for management. Membership in parallel structures also tends to be limited, primarily to volunteers and to numbers of employees for which there are adequate resources. Management heavily influences the conditions under which parallel structures operate. It controls the amount of authority that members have in making recommendations, the amount of information that is shared with them, the amount of training they receive to increase their knowledge and skills, and the amount of monetary rewards for participation. Because parallel structures offer limited amounts of EI, they are most appropriate for organizations with little or no history of employee participation, top-down management styles, and bureaucratic cultures.

Cooperative union–management and quality circle programs typically are implemented in the following steps:[15]

1. ***Define the Purpose and Scope.*** This first step involves defining the purpose for the parallel structure and initial expectations about how it will function. Organizational diagnosis can help clarify which specific problems and issues to address, such as productivity, absenteeism, or service quality. In addition, management training in the use of parallel structures can include discussions about the commitment and resources necessary to implement them; the openness needed to examine organizational practices, operations, and policies; and the willingness to experiment and learn.

2. ***Form a Steering Committee.*** Parallel structures typically use a steering committee composed of acknowledged leaders of the various functions and constituencies within the formal organization. For example, in cooperative union–management projects, the steering committee would include key representatives from management, such as a president or chief operating officer, and each of the unions and employee groups involved in the project, such as local union presidents. This committee performs the following tasks:

   • Refining the scope and purpose of the parallel structure

   • Developing a vision for the effort

- Guiding the creation and implementation of the structure
- Establishing the linkage mechanisms between the parallel structure and the formal organization
- Creating problem-solving groups and activities
- Ensuring the support of senior management

OD practitioners can play an important role in forming the steering committee. First, they can help to establish the team and select appropriate members. Second, they can assist in developing and maintaining group norms of learning and innovation. These norms set the tone for problem solving throughout the parallel structure. Third, they can help the committee create a vision statement that refines the structure's purpose and promotes ownership of it. Fourth, they can help committee members develop and specify objectives and strategies, organizational expectations and required resources, and potential rewards for participation in the parallel structure.

3. ***Communicate with Organization Members.*** The effectiveness of a parallel structure depends on a high level of involvement from organization members. Communicating the purpose, procedures, and rewards of participation can promote that involvement. Moreover, employee participation in developing a structure's vision and purpose can increase ownership and visibly demonstrate the "new way" of working. Continued communication concerning parallel structure activities can ensure member awareness.

4. ***Form Employee Problem-solving Groups.*** These groups are the primary means of accomplishing the purpose of the parallel learning structure. Their formation involves selecting and training group members, identifying problems for the groups to work on, and providing appropriate facilitation. Selecting group members is important because success often is a function of group membership.[16] Members need to represent the appropriate hierarchical levels, expertise, functions, and constituencies that are relevant to the problems at hand. This allows the parallel structure to identify and communicate with the formal structure. It also provides the necessary resources to solve the problems. Ad hoc committees may also be formed as when workers and managers initiate action to address an issue of interest to the parallel organization. Ad hoc teams are typically charged with a particular task and have a limited lifetime.

   Once formed, the groups need appropriate training. This may include discussions about the vision of the parallel structure, the specific problems to be addressed, and the way those problems will be solved. As in the steering committee, group norms promoting openness, creativity, and integration need to be established.

   Another key resource for parallel structures is facilitation for the problem-solving groups. Although this can be expensive, it can yield important benefits in problem-solving efficiency and quality. Group members are being asked to solve problems by cutting through traditional hierarchical and functional boundaries. Facilitators can pay special attention to processes that require disparate groups to cooperate. They can help members identify and resolve problem-solving issues within and between groups.

5. ***Address the Problems and Issues.*** Generally, groups in parallel structures solve problems by using an action research process. They diagnose specific problems, plan appropriate solutions, and implement and evaluate them. Problem solving can be facilitated when the groups and the steering committee relate effectively to each other. This permits the steering committee to direct problem-solving efforts in an appropriate manner, to acquire the necessary resources and support,

and to approve action plans. It also helps ensure that the groups' solutions are linked appropriately to the formal organization. In this manner, early attempts at change will have a better chance of succeeding.

6. ***Implement and Evaluate the Changes.*** This step involves implementing appropriate organizational changes and assessing the results. Change proposals need the support of the steering committee and the formal authority structure. As changes are implemented, the organization needs information about their effects. This lets members know how successful the changes have been and if they need to be modified. In addition, feedback on changes helps the organization learn to adapt and innovate.

Application 15.1 presents a classic example of a cooperative union–management program at GTE of California.[17]

Results of Parallel Structure Approaches

A large body of literature exists on the implementation and impact of parallel structure approaches to EI. The business and popular press are full of glowing reports about the benefit of union–management cooperative projects, quality circles, and other parallel structure interventions. For many people, especially lower-level employees, this opportunity to influence the formal organization leads to increased work satisfaction and task effectiveness.[18] Among the reported results are reductions in costs, improvements in the quality and quantity of production, and increased member skill development, motivation, organizational commitment, and satisfaction.[19] There are also many classic case studies of parallel structures, including General Motors' central foundry division; the Harman plant in Bolivar and the Rockwell International plant in Battle Creek, Michigan (a joint UAW–GM effort); the Rushton Mines in Pennsylvania; and more recently, the Magma Copper Company (now BHP Copper) in Arizona. These types of studies, however, often raise more questions than they answer about the ability of EI interventions to affect organizational outcomes, and they often challenge the validity of the reported successes.[20]

Early large-sample evaluations of parallel structures typically reported mixed results.[21] For example, the most extensive assessment of union–management cooperative projects was conducted by researchers from the University of Michigan's Institute for Social Research (ISR).[22] Over a period of at least 3 years, the ISR studied eight major projects implemented during the 1970s. Although the projects showed some improvements in employee attitudes, only two projects showed improvements in productivity. The ISR researchers explained the meager productivity results in terms of the projects' mistakes. All of the projects were pioneering efforts and hardly could be expected to avoid mistakes during implementation. Similarly, in a review of more than a hundred citations, Ledford, Lawler, and Mohrman concluded that the existing research showed no clear positive or negative trend in the productivity effects of quality circles.[23] Although the evidence of attitudinal effects was more extensive than that of productivity effects, the studies reviewed still showed mixed results for attitudinal changes. For example, in one study using a rigorous research design, participation in a quality circle was positively related to measures of personal competence and interpersonal trust but was not related to an increased sense of participation.[24]

More recent union–management cooperative projects seem to be doing better: "The newer projects tend to be much better linked to the management and union hierarchies, receive better assistance from a widening circle of experienced consultants, have more realistic goals, and use more sharply focused organizational change strategies."[25] Similarly, more recent data suggest stronger relationships between employee participation and direct performance outcomes, such as productivity,

UNION–MANAGEMENT COOPERATION AT GTE OF CALIFORNIA

GTE of California (GTEC) and the Communications Workers of America embarked on a cooperative union–management project in response to deregulation of the telecommunications industry. Over time, the deregulation of the industry would remove the protective shield of guaranteed returns on investment, monopoly territories, and "cradle-to-grave" employment that had characterized operations.

Under the new conditions, GTEC management and union leadership believed strongly that the company's usual way of operating in the regulatory environment would need to change. The traditional approach to managing the business was characterized by centralized decision making and work planning, lackadaisical service orientation, and little cross-functional teamwork. The advent of deregulation was coupled with tremendous technological changes in information processing and service delivery and a broadening of the belief that workers should have more say in decisions that affect them. The old way of managing produced low morale and mediocre service in this changing environment. Consequently, management and union officials felt the need for improved adaptability and productivity and a more customer-oriented workforce.

For some time, union leadership had been researching worker participation and union–management cooperation at its national office in Washington, D.C. This research was limited, however, because no one had implemented such interventions during a period of rapid deregulation. At the same time, GTEC senior management had been meeting with other telephone companies to discuss how to meet the challenges posed by deregulation, technological change, and increased worker sophistication. These discussions consistently pointed out that effective organizations in deregulated environments were more decentralized in their decision making. But, given decades of regulatory tradition, the means to accomplish such an organizational change were not clear.

Working with OD consultants from the University of Southern California's Center for Effective Organizations, senior managers and union leaders began discussing how to increase worker participation and decentralize decision making without treading on traditional collective bargaining issues. These discussions resulted in a cooperative union–management partnership called Employee Involvement. The purpose of the EI process was to improve employees' quality of working life and productivity. The group of senior managers and union officials became the steering committee for the project and developed a vision of the EI process and its objectives.

The steering committee established a parallel structure to guide implementation of the EI process with the 26,000 employees at GTEC. It comprised three area coordinating committees responsible for implementing the EI process in their respective geographic regions. Each coordinating committee created support committees for the functional areas in its region. The support committees, in turn, established

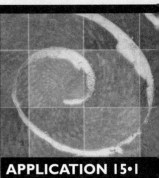

APPLICATION 15•1

EI teams that would identify and solve work-related problems in the different units of the company. Each committee and team was staffed with both union and management personnel as appropriate.

As part of the early implementation activities, all organization members attended a 2-hour orientation meeting that described the goals, structure, and implementation of the EI process. This orientation was conducted by both GTEC management and local union presidents. In addition, a 3-day union–management training program was conducted for all supervisors and union officials (local presidents and stewards). During the first 2 days of training, union leaders and GTEC managers were trained separately in their respective roles and responsibilities in the EI process. On the third day, the managers and union officials were brought together to discuss how the implementation of EI would proceed in their particular departments. Members of the support committees and employee involvement teams attended a 5-day training program focusing on meeting-management skills, problem-solving techniques, and group dynamics. They were also provided with internal facilitators if needed.

Over the next several months, the EI teams focused on quality-of-work-life issues, such as the provision of bottled drinking water, rather than on productivity-related changes. Responsible committees were concerned about this limited focus and modified the process to align it more closely with EI's productivity objectives. For example, the problem-solving training was changed to emphasize performance issues. In addition, the composition and responsibilities of the different committees were revised to increase senior management and union leadership involvement and accountability. At the organizational level, a new incentive compensation system was initiated. This system rewarded cross-functional teamwork and generated many ideas for employee involvement. Finally, facilitators were assigned permanently to functional areas to focus on operating problems.

The EI process produced many successes. One team worked for more than 2 years to simplify the way field employees reported their time at work. These efforts produced savings of more than $3 million by increasing the amount of productive time that employees spent in the field and by consolidating several offices that had been used to collect, collate, and report work-time information. Over a 2-year period, an evaluation of the EI process concluded that the program had produced a net savings (after the costs of training and dedicated personnel) of more than $1 million. In addition, 5 years after the implementation of the EI effort, GTEC surpassed its competition in measures of customer satisfaction for large- and medium-size businesses to become the benchmark for others, and several cost measures also decreased significantly. The EI program survived through two union contract negotiations and massive corporate changes that reduced the size of the workforce by consolidating work functions and business units and standardizing systems and equipment.

customer satisfaction, quality, and speed; profitability; and employee satisfaction[26] and a 1994 study by the Commission on the Future of Worker–Management Relations supported that conclusion. It found that systematically implemented programs often improve productivity and almost always increase investment in employee skills and knowledge.[27]

Several studies have attempted to discover which parallel structure intervention features contribute most to program success. The findings support several conclusions.[28] First, members should have access to the necessary skills and knowledge to address problems systematically; formalized meetings and record keeping; and separate communication channels. Second, the parallel organization must eventually integrate both horizontally and vertically with the rest of the company and become a regular part of the formal organization, rather than a special or extraparallel set of activities. Third, parallel structures are highly dependent on group members having sufficient group process, problem-solving, and presentation skills and adequate task-relevant information. Fourth, lower-level managers need to support the program and have participatory leadership styles if workers are to gain the necessary freedom to engage in problem solving. Fifth, top-management support is necessary both to start the program and to implement many of the subsequent solutions. Unless management is willing to authorize necessary resources to make suggested improvements, circle members are likely to become disenchanted, seeing the program more as window dressing than as meaningful participation.

Finally, court rulings in the early 1990s challenged the legality of some EI approaches under provisions of the National Labor Relations Act (NLRA). This law, passed by Congress in 1935, gives employees the right to form labor unions and decrees that employers must bargain in good faith with representatives of those organizations. In protecting employees' rights to collective bargaining, the NLRA precludes certain employer unfair labor practices, one of which is aimed at employer domination of a labor organization. Under the law, a committee or team of workers that meets to address issues related to wages, hours, or conditions of work can be considered a "labor organization." If management creates the team, provides it with resources, or influences it in any way, then management may be found to dominate this so-called labor organization. In two legal cases involving Electromation, Inc., and DuPont, the court ruled that, in setting up employee teams or committees to address such issues as communication, cost cutting, and safety, the companies had created labor organizations and had dominated them unfairly. Although the NLRA does not outlaw EI teams per se, such interventions may be legally questionable in situations where teams address issues traditionally reserved for bargaining and where management influences or controls the teams. In response to these rulings, Congress passed legislation in 1996 to amend the National Labor Relations Act. The Teamwork for Employees and Management Act of 1995 preserves legitimate employee involvement programs without infringing on the rights of employees to bargain collectively.

High-Involvement Organizations

Over the past several years, an increasing number of employee involvement projects have been aimed at creating high-involvement organizations (HIOs). These interventions create organizational conditions that support high levels of employee participation. What makes HIOs unique is the comprehensive nature of their design process. Unlike parallel structures that do not alter the formal organization, in HIOs almost all organization features are designed jointly by management and workers to promote high levels of involvement and performance, including structure, work design, information and control systems, physical layout, personnel policies, and reward systems.

Features of High-Involvement Organizations

High-involvement organizations are designed with features congruent with one another. For example, in HIOs employees have considerable influence over decisions. To support such a decentralized philosophy, members receive extensive training in problem-solving techniques, plant operation, and organizational policies. In addition, both operational and issue-oriented information is shared widely and is obtained easily by employees. Finally, rewards are tied closely to unit performance, as well as to knowledge and skill levels. These disparate aspects of the organization are mutually reinforcing and form a coherent pattern that contributes to employee involvement. Table 15.1 (on page 316) presents a list of compatible design elements characterizing HIOs,[29] and most such organizations include several if not all of the following features:

- **Flat, lean organization structures** contribute to involvement by pushing the scheduling, planning, and controlling functions typically performed by management and staff groups toward the shop floor. Similarly, minienterprise, team-based structures that are oriented to a common purpose or outcome help focus employee participation on a shared objective. Participative structures, such as work councils and union–management committees, create conditions in which workers can influence the direction and policies of the organization.

- **Job designs** that provide employees with high levels of discretion, task variety, and meaningful feedback can enhance involvement. They enable workers to influence day-to-day workplace decisions and to receive intrinsic satisfaction by performing work under enriched conditions. Self-managed teams encourage employee responsibility by providing cross-training and job rotation, which give people a chance to learn about the different functions contributing to organizational performance.

- **Open information systems** that are tied to jobs or work teams provide the necessary information for employees to participate meaningfully in decision making. Goals and standards of performance that are set participatively can provide employees with a sense of commitment and motivation for achieving those objectives.

- **Career systems** that provide different tracks for advancement and counseling to help people choose appropriate paths can help employees plan and prepare for long-term development in the organization. Open job posting, for example, makes employees aware of jobs that can further their development.

- **Selection** of employees for high-involvement organizations can be improved through a realistic job preview providing information about what it will be like to work in such situations. Team member involvement in a selection process

Table 15•1	Design Features for a Participative System

☐ ORGANIZATIONAL STRUCTURE

1. Flat
2. Lean
3. Minienterprise oriented
4. Team based
5. Participative council or structure

☐ JOB DESIGN

1. Individually enriched
2. Self-managing teams

☐ INFORMATION SYSTEM

1. Open
2. Inclusive
3. Tied to jobs
4. Decentralized; team-based
5. Participatively set goals and standards

☐ CAREER SYSTEM

1. Tracks and counseling available
2. Open job posting

☐ SELECTION

1. Realistic job preview
2. Team based
3. Potential and process-skill oriented

☐ TRAINING

1. Heavy commitment
2. Peer training
3. Economic education
4. Interpersonal skills

☐ REWARD SYSTEM

1. Open
2. Skill based
3. Gain sharing or ownership
4. Flexible benefits
5. All salaried workforce
6. Egalitarian perquisites

☐ PERSONNEL POLICIES

1. Stability of employment
2. Participatively established through representative group

☐ PHYSICAL LAYOUT

1. Around organizational structure
2. Egalitarian
3. Safe and pleasant

SOURCE: Reproduced by permission of the publisher from Edward E. Lawler III, "Increasing Worker Involvement to Enhance Organizational Effectiveness: Design Features for a Participation System" in *Change in Organizations*, eds. P. S. Goodman and associates (San Francisco: Jossey-Bass, 1982), p. 298–99.

oriented to potential and process skills of recruits can facilitate a participative climate.

- **Training** employees for the necessary knowledge and skills to participate effectively in decision making is a heavy commitment in HIOs. This effort includes education on the economic side of the enterprise, as well as interpersonal skill development. Peer training is emphasized as a valuable adjunct to formal, expert training.

- **Reward systems** can contribute to employee involvement when information about them is open and the rewards are based on acquiring new skills, as well as sharing gains from improved performance. Similarly, participation is enhanced when people can choose among different fringe benefits and when reward distinctions among people from different hierarchical levels are minimized.

- **Personnel policies** that are participatively set and encourage stability of employment provide employees with a strong sense of commitment to the organization. People feel that the policies are reasonable and that the firm is committed to their long-term development.

- **Physical layouts** of organizations also can enhance employee involvement. Physical designs that support team structures and reduce status differences among employees can reinforce the egalitarian climate needed for employee participation. Safe and pleasant working conditions provide a physical environment conducive to participation.

These HIO design features are mutually reinforcing. "They all send a message to people in the organization that says they are important, respected, valued, capable of growing, and trusted and that their understanding of and involvement in the total organization is desirable and expected."[30] Moreover, these design components tend to motivate and focus organizational behavior in a strategic direction, and thus can lead to superior effectiveness and competitive advantage, particularly in contrast to more traditionally designed organizations.[31]

Application Factors

At present, there is no universally accepted approach to implementing the high-involvement features described here. The actual implementation process often is specific to the situation, and little systematic research has been devoted to understanding the change process itself.[32] Nevertheless, at least two distinct factors seem to characterize how HIOs are implemented. First, implementation generally is guided by an explicit statement of values that members want the new organization to support. Typically, such values as teamwork, equity, quality, and empowerment guide the choice of specific design features. Values that are strongly held and widely shared by organization members can provide the energy, commitment, and direction needed to create high-involvement organizations. A second feature of the implementation process is its participative nature. Managers and employees take active roles in choosing and implementing the design features. They may be helped by OD practitioners, but the locus of control for the change process resides clearly within the organization. This participative change process is congruent with the high-involvement design being created. In essence, high-involvement design processes promote high-involvement organizations.

Results of High-Involvement Organizations

A number of studies provide support for the high-involvement model. For example, a survey of 98 HIOs showed that about 75% of them perceived their performance relative to competitors as better than average on quality of work life, customer service, productivity, quality, and grievance rates.[33] Voluntary turnover was 2%, substantially below the national average of 13.2%; return on investment was almost four times greater than industry averages; and return on sales was more than five times greater. Another study of the financial performance of U.S. companies from 1972 to 1992 revealed that the five top-performing firms—Plenum Publishing, Circuit City, Tyson Foods, Wal-Mart, and Southwest Airlines—all relied heavily on EI practices for competitive advantage rather than on those factors typically associated with financial success, such as market leadership, profitable industries, unique technology, and strong barriers to entry.[34] More recently, a study of more than 160 firms in New Zealand supported a positive relationships between high-involvement practices and productivity measured in terms of sales per employee.[35]

Such results cannot be expected in all situations.[36] The following situational contingencies seem to favor high-involvement organizations: interdependent technologies, small organization size, new plant start-ups, and conditions under which quality is an important determinant of operating effectiveness.

Application 15.2 presents an example of how DaimlerChrysler applied high-involvement principles to its Neon automobile.[37] The Neon drew critical acclaim for its short design time and was introduced in Japan to compete with Toyota's and Honda's popular subcompacts.

Total Quality Management[38]

Total quality management (TQM) is the most recent and, along with high-involvement organizations, the most comprehensive approach to employee involvement. Also known as "continuous process improvement," "continuous quality," and "six-sigma," TQM grew out of a manufacturing emphasis on quality control and represents a long-term effort to orient all of an organization's activities around the concept of quality. Quality is achieved when organizational processes reliably produce products and services that meet or exceed customer expectations. Although it is possible to implement TQM without employee involvement, member participation in the change process increases the likelihood that it will become part of the organization's culture. Quality improvement processes were popular in the 1990s, and many organizations, including Morton Salt, Weyerhaeuser, Xerox, Boeing's Airlift and Tanker Programs, Motorola, and Analog Devices, incorporated TQM interventions. Today, a continuous quality improvement capability is essential for global competitiveness.

Like high-involvement designs, TQM increases workers' knowledge and skills through extensive training, provides relevant information to employees, pushes decision-making power downward in the organization, and ties rewards to performance. When implemented successfully, TQM also is aligned closely with a firm's overall business strategy and attempts to change the entire organization toward continuous quality improvement.[39]

The principles underlying TQM can be understood by examining the careers of W. Edwards Deming and Joseph M. Juran, the fathers of the modern quality movement. They initially introduced TQM to U.S. companies during World War II, but in an odd twist of fate following the war, they found their ideas taking hold more in Japan than in the United States.[40] Based on the pioneering work of Walter A. Shewhart of Bell Laboratories, Deming applied statistical techniques to improve product quality at defense plants. When the war ended, U.S. businesses turned to mass-production techniques and emphasized quantity over quality to satisfy postwar demand. Deming was known for his statistical and sampling expertise, and General Douglas MacArthur asked him to conduct a census of the Japanese population. During his work in Japan, Deming began discussions with Japanese managers about rebuilding their manufacturing base. He advocated a disciplined approach of "plan–do–check–adjust" to identify and improve manufacturing processes that affected product quality. For example, he suggested that ensuring the quality of inputs was a better way of minimizing deviations in an operating process than inspecting finished goods. With such an approach, the Japanese could produce world-class-quality products and restore their country economically. Deming's ideas eventually were codified into the "Fourteen Points" and the "Seven Deadly Sins" of quality summarized in Table 15.2 (on page 320). In honor of the ideas that helped rejuvenate the Japanese economy, the Union of Japanese Scientists and Engineers (JUSE) created the Deming Award to distinguish annually the best in quality manufacturing.

At about the same time, Juran's publication of the *Quality Control Handbook* in 1951 identified two sources of quality problems: avoidable and unavoidable costs. Avoidable costs included hours spent reworking defective products, processing complaints, and scrapping otherwise useful material. Unavoidable costs included work associated with inspection and other preventive measures. He suggested that when organizations focused on unavoidable costs to maintain quality, an important

CHRYSLER CORPORATION MOVES TOWARD HIGH INVOLVEMENT

In 1989, Chrysler Corporation decided to build the new Neon subcompact at its Belvidere, Illinois, plant and discontinue the Horizon Omni and Sundance Shadow. Although important differences exist, Neon was to be to Chrysler what the Saturn was to General Motors, a totally new American car with the quality and price that would rival similar Japanese models. It also represented Chrysler's first strong implementation of high-involvement principles; the cornerstone concept to the design, engineering, and production of the Neon was worker participation. The major impetus behind the project was top management's belief that high-involvement concepts would provide the kind of well-trained, flexible workforce needed to produce high-quality cars efficiently at low cost. In addition, Chrysler's 1.35-defects-per-car quality rating was well above industry leader Toyota, which reported only .74 defects per car. The high-involvement transformation was expected to make significant improvements in Chrysler quality.

By 1992, seven permanent "process teams," each with approximately 35 hourly workers and managers, were established from the Belvidere plant. The teams went to Chrysler's Technology Center in Auburn Hills, Michigan, to assist in the design of the car, its parts, the production process, and the production tools. This involved working with design and process engineers on prototypes, engines, and assembly. Almost half of the plant's workers went to the Technology Center during the design phase.

This design process was a significant deviation from the traditional method. Under the old way, engineering design was completely separated from manufacturing and production. Each new car was elegantly conceived and then handed over to manufacturing to produce. More often than not, the design was not producible. If manufacturing had a problem, the engineering group might consider alterations in the design if there was sufficient time before production was scheduled. Otherwise, it was manufacturing's problem.

But under Chrysler's "platform" approach, designers, assembly line workers, fabricators, suppliers, and managers all came together in the same room. Not surprisingly, there was a considerable amount of resistance. The engineers' status was threatened by hourly workers telling a professional what couldn't be done. Similarly, the hourly worker felt uncomfortable because the engineers rarely listened to, let alone implemented, any suggestions from the plant. Several meetings were required to build the trust necessary for complete collaboration.

As a result of the early cooperation between production and engineering, the production ramp-up process went more smoothly. In one case, workers showed the engineers how a particular part could not be attached because the bumper assembly blocked the air gun; the engineers redesigned the bumper. Together, the engineers and the assembly workers designed the Neon in just 31 months, 5 months ahead of schedule and tying Honda for the fastest vehicle development time.

The design and development process was supported by a high-involvement communications and suggestion program, more egalitarian structures and processes, and extensive training for the Belvidere workers. For example, worker suggestions pass through an Individual Quality Participation process. Under a prior, neglected system, suggestions struggled through a slow and bureaucratic structure, and employees rarely were given credit when their ideas were implemented. Under the new system, each suggestion goes to a manager who has 1 day to get it to someone who can act on it. The second person has 2 days to respond. By day 4, the worker who made the suggestion is given feedback on the status of the idea. Millions of dollars have been saved by these suggested changes that ranged from small process improvements, like how to reduce the number of times a worker needs to replenish the bolts from inventory, to larger ones, like changing from cardboard shipping containers to reusable plastic ones.

Egalitarian structure and process changes were evident as well, although they were not radical departures from the old governance principles. Within Chrysler, the Neon organization followed a traditional, but considerably flatter, functional structure. Belvidere's organization structure was relatively flat, with only three levels separating the plant manager from the workers. Supervisors coordinated interactions with other workers and across different shifts. They treated workers more as colleagues than as subordinates; they involved them in decision making and helped them develop appropriate skills. Workers were empowered and customer focused, and they used principles of total quality management. Under the United Auto Workers' contract, the Belvidere plant workers kept their narrowly defined jobs, although production workers in the stamping plant had only one classification and performed 15 different jobs. However, in the rest of the plant, workers were given much more ability to rotate to different positions, and there was a strong attempt to fit the employee to the work that best suited his or her talents and personality.

Other processes also supported worker involvement in ongoing plant operations. For example, everyone at the Belvidere plant punches a time clock—even the plant manager—and all of Neon's 3,200 workers share in the company's profits. In an important symbolic change, the plant manager spends a large amount of time on the factory floor interacting with workers. Under the old plant regime, workers were told what to do and to keep their mouths shut. Now, says one 28-year veteran, there's a "little bit of listen. I ain't saying it's 100% yet. I'd be lying if I said it was. But it's a lot better than it used to be." What makes the symbolism work is a direct and open climate. People talk openly to the plant manager and to each other about the current defects that have been found. More important, the conversation often centers on how the customer will never see the defect because it was found and fixed, and how processes were implemented to ensure that it will not occur again.

One of the biggest enablers of worker involvement in the design and production effort was worker education. Every worker, hourly and salaried, attended a variety of training sessions. Early orientation sessions, for example, featured descriptions of the new car and introduced the new emphasis on quality. Videos of the plant manager and local union president talking about the Neon project were followed by presentations on quality and exercises to practice with the new tools. More specialized training was also offered. Eight coordinators from the plant worked with the production personnel and engineers to design and deliver the focused training modules. All in all, more than 948,000 labor-hours of training were designed and delivered by factory workers.

The results from the new design and production process were impressive. Annual grievances declined from about 3,000 before worker involvement to just 51 in 1993. The car was a critical success before it was commercially available; it was named 1994 Car of the Year by *Automobile* magazine. The first Neon rolled off the assembly line on November 10, 1993, but it was known as the 1995 Neon because it met 1995 federal safety and emission standards. Finally, consultants and industry analysts familiar with the Belvidere plant were impressed by the differences in employee attitudes and the participative climate.

opportunity was being missed, and he advocated that an organization focus on avoidable costs that could be found in any process or activity, not just in manufacturing.

The popularity of TQM in the United States can be traced to a 1980 NBC television documentary titled, "If Japan Can . . . Why Can't We?" The documentary

Table 15·2	Deming's Quality Guidelines

THE FOURTEEN POINTS	THE SEVEN DEADLY SINS
1. Create a constancy of purpose	1. Lack of constancy of purpose
2. Adopt a new philosophy	2. Emphasizing short-term profits and immediate dividends
3. End the practice of purchasing at lowest prices	3. Evaluation of performance, merit rating, or annual review
4. Institute leadership	4. Mobility of top management
5. Eliminate empty slogans	5. Running a company only on visible figures
6. Eliminate numerical quotas	6. Excessive medical costs
7. Institute on-the-job training	7. Excessive costs of warranty
8. Drive out fear	
9. Break down barriers between departments	
10. Take action to accomplish the transformation	
11. Improve constantly and forever the process of production and service	
12. Cease dependence on mass inspection	
13. Remove barriers to pride in workmanship	
14. Retrain vigorously	

chronicled Deming's work with the Japanese and his concern that U.S. companies would not listen to him after the war. The documentary had a powerful impact on firms facing severe competition, particularly from the Japanese, and many companies, including Ford Motor Company, General Motors, Dow Chemical, and Hughes Aircraft, quickly sought Deming's advice. Another important influence on the TQM movement in the United States was Philip Crosby's book *Quality Is Free*.[41] He showed that improved quality can lower overall costs, dispelling the popular belief that high quality means higher total costs for the organization. With fewer parts reworked, less material wasted, and less time spent inspecting finished goods, the organization's total costs actually can decline. Deming also believed that if the principles of quality were put in place, reduced costs would be a natural by-product of increased quality.

In 1987, Congress established the Malcolm Baldrige National Quality Award. It recognizes large and small organizations in business, education, and health care for quality achievement along seven dimensions: leadership; strategic planning; customer and market focus; measurement, analysis, and knowledge management; human resources focus; process management; and business results. Competition for the award has grown enormously. Some large organizations have spent large sums to prepare for the contest; others have applied just to receive the extensive feedback from the board of examiners on how to improve quality; and still others feel compelled to apply because customers insist that they show progress in process improvement.

In 1992, the Rochester Institute of Technology and *USA Today* started the annual Quality Cup to honor quality improvement teams of 5 to 20 people.[42] Providian Financial was the 2001 award winner in the service category. The winning team made over 200 changes in telemarketing sales techniques and direct mail in a redesigned customer satisfaction program. According to their results, the total number of accounts serviced increased 60% while customer complaints dropped 40%. Unfortunately, the RIT/*USA Today* Quality Cup competition was discontinued in 2001. Another quality award is the Shingo Prize (http://www.shingoprize.org/) for companies that achieve highly efficient production methods. The 2003 award winners included plants from Mexico and the United States representing the Delphi Corporation, Texas Instruments, Medtronics, and Lockheed Martin. For example, Delphi Corporation's Delnosa 1-4 plant in Reynosa, Mexico, was able to increase its productivity by 34%, decrease customer defects by 35%, and achieve 25 million man-hours without a lost workday.[43] Numerous states have initiated their own quality awards. At the national level, the Carey Award is given to federal agencies and the Hammer Awards are given as part of the National Performance Review for innovation and quality improvement in the federal government.

TQM is a growing industry itself, with consulting firms, university courses, training programs, and professional associations related to quality improvement diffusing rapidly across industrial nations. The quality approach is supported by at least four major associations: the American Society for Quality (ASQ: *http://www.asq.org*), the Association for Quality and Participation (AQP: *http://www.aqp.org*) (formerly the International Quality Circle Association), the American Productivity and Quality Center (APQC: *http://www.apqc.org*), and the International Society of Six-sigma Professionals (ISSSP: *http://www.isssp.org*). The ASQ has more than 100,000 members, and the AQP has more than 1,800 members. These associations actively support TQM by sponsoring quality training workshops and conferences and serving as clearinghouses for important information on TQM programs. The APQC, for example, has assembled a database of best-practices information so that organizations can compare their processes against the best in the world. AQP is an excellent source of information and training in employee involvement, union partnerships, and quality tools. ASQ has gained prominence as the administrator of the Malcolm Baldrige Award and is known for its course offerings in TQM. The International Organization for Standardization (ISO) also supports TQM. Its ISO 9000 standard applies to quality systems, and certification requires firms to document key goals and processes, to demonstrate compliance, and to create processes for improvement.

Application Stages

TQM typically is implemented in five major steps. With the exception of gaining senior management commitment, most of the steps can occur somewhat concomitantly.

1. *Gain Long-term Senior Management Commitment.* This stage involves helping senior executives understand the importance of long-term commitment to TQM. Without a solid understanding of TQM and the key success factors for implementation, managers often believe that workers are solely responsible for quality. Yet only senior executives have the authority and larger perspective to address the organization-wide, cross-functional issues that hold the greatest promise for TQM's success.

   Senior managers' role in TQM implementation includes giving direction and support throughout the change process. For example, establishing organization-wide TQM generally takes 3 or more years, although technical improvements to the workflow can be as quick as 6 to 8 months. The longer-term and more difficult parts of implementation, however, involve changes in the organization's support systems, such as customer service, finance, sales, and human resources. Often these systems are frozen in place by old policies and norms that can interfere with the new approach. Senior managers have to confront those practices and create new ones that support TQM and the organization's strategic orientation.

   Top executives also must be willing to allocate significant resources to TQM implementation, particularly to make large investments in training. For example, as part of its Baldrige Award preparation, Motorola developed Motorola University, a training organization that teaches in 27 languages. Departments at Motorola allocate at least 1.5% of their budgets to education, and every employee must take a minimum of 40 hours of training a year. This effort supports Motorola's goal of "six-sigma" quality (a statistical measure of product quality that implies 99.9997% perfection) and of having a workforce that is able to read, write, solve problems, and do math at the seventh-grade level or above. When several business units within Motorola achieved the six-sigma target, the company demonstrated its commitment to continuously improving quality with a new target of tenfold improvement in key goals.

   Finally, senior managers need to clarify and communicate throughout the organization a totally new orientation to producing and delivering products and services. At Volvo, for example, CEO Leif Johansson affirms the company's three core values—quality, environmental concern and, especially, safety. The organization challenges its managers to create a climate "where people can use their analytical skills and their creativity to continuously improve the organization's overall effectiveness and efficiency."

2. *Train Members in Quality Methods.* TQM implementation requires extensive training in the principles and tools of quality improvement. Depending on the organization's size and complexity, such training can be conducted in a few weeks to more than 2 years. Members typically learn problem-solving skills and simple statistical process control (SPC) techniques, usually referred to as the seven tools of quality. At Cedar-Sinai Hospital in Los Angeles, all employees take

a 3-day course on the applicability of brainstorming, histograms, flowcharts, scatter diagrams, Pareto charts, cause-and-effect diagrams, control charts, and other problem-solving procedures. This training is the beginning of a long-term process in continuous improvement. The knowledge gained is used to understand variations in organizational processes, to identify sources of avoidable costs, to select and prioritize quality improvement projects, and to monitor the effects of changes on product and service quality. By learning to analyze the sources of variation systematically, members can improve the reliability of product manufacturing or service delivery. For example, HCA's West Paces Ferry Hospital used TQM methods to reduce direct costs attributable to antibiotic waste.[44] It used flowcharts, fishbone diagrams, and Pareto charts to determine the major causes of unused intravenous preparations. Changes in the antibiotic delivery process resulted in reduced costs of antibiotics to the hospital of 44.5% and to patients of 45%.

3. ***Start Quality Improvement Projects.*** In this phase of TQM implementation, individuals and work groups apply the quality methods to identify the few projects that hold promise for the largest improvements in organizational processes. They identify output variations, intervene to minimize deviations from quality standards, monitor improvements, and repeat this quality improvement cycle indefinitely. Identifying output variations is a key aspect of TQM. Such deviations from quality standards typically are measured by the percentage of defective products or, in the case of customer satisfaction, by on-time delivery percentages or customer survey ratings. For example, VF Corporation, a leading retail apparel firm, found that retailers were out of stock on 30% of their items 100% of the time. In response, VF revamped its systems to fill orders within 24 hours 95% of the time.

    TQM is concerned not only with variations in the quality of finished products and services but also with variations in the steps of a process that produce a product or service and the levels of internal customer satisfaction. For example, Eastman Chemical Company established a patent process improvement team to enhance the relationship between scientists and lawyers in applying for patent approvals. The team, made up of inventors, lab managers, and attorneys, doubled the number of patent attorneys and relocated their offices near the labs. Attorneys now meet with scientists during the experimental phase of research to discuss ways to increase the chances of yielding a patentable product or process. Patent submissions have increased by 60%, and the number of patents issued to the company has doubled.[45]

    Based on the measurement of output variations, each individual or work group systematically analyzes the cause of variations using SPC techniques. For example, product yields in a semiconductor manufacturing plant can go down for many reasons, including a high concentration of dust particles, small vibrations in the equipment, poor machine adjustments, and human error. Quality improvement projects often must determine which of the possible causes is most responsible, and, using that information, run experiments and pilot programs to determine which adjustments will cause output variations to drop and quality to improve. Those adjustments that do reduce variations are implemented across the board. Members continue to monitor the quality process to verify improvement and then begin the problem-solving process again for continuous improvement.

4. ***Measure Progress.*** This stage of TQM implementation involves measuring organizational processes against quality standards. Knowing and analyzing the competition's performance are essential for any TQM effort because it sets minimum standards of quality, cost, and service and ensures the organization's

position in the industry over the short run. For the longer term, such analytical efforts concentrate on identifying world-class performance, regardless of industry, and creating stretch targets, also known as *benchmarks*. Benchmarks represent the best in organizational achievements and practices for different processes and generally are accepted as "world class." For example, Alaska Airlines is considered the benchmark of customer service in the airline industry, while Disney's customer-service orientation is considered a world-class benchmark.

The implied goal in most TQM efforts is to meet or exceed a competitor's benchmark. Alcoa's former chairman, Paul H. O'Neill, charged all of the company's business units with closing the gap between Alcoa and its competitor's benchmarks by 80% within 2 years.[46] In aluminum sheet for beverage cans, for example, Japan's Kobe Steel, Ltd. was the benchmark, and Wall Street estimated that achieving O'Neill's goal would increase Alcoa's earnings by one dollar per share. The greatest leverage for change often is found in companies from unrelated industries, however. For example, Alcoa might look to Alaska Airlines or Disney to get innovative ideas about customer service. Understanding benchmarks from other industries challenges an organization's thinking about what is possible and promotes what is referred to as "out-of-the-box thinking."

5. ***Rewarding Accomplishment.*** In this final stage of TQM implementation, the organization links rewards to improvements in quality. TQM does not monitor and reward outcomes that are normally tracked by traditional reward systems, such as the number of units produced. Such measures do not necessarily reflect product quality and can be difficult to replace because they are ingrained in the organization's traditional way of doing business. Rather, TQM rewards members for "process-oriented" improvements, such as increased on-time delivery, gains in customers' perceived satisfaction with product performance, and reductions in cycle time—the time it takes a product or service to be conceived, developed, produced, and sold. Rewards usually are designed initially to promote finding solutions to the organization's key problems. The linkage between rewards and process-oriented improvements reinforces the belief that continuous improvements, even small ones, are an important part of the new organizational culture associated with TQM. According to a survey of 500 firms in four countries, conducted by Ernst and Young and the American Quality Foundation, more than half of the U.S. companies studied linked executive pay to improving quality and achieving benchmarks.[47]

TQM has continued to evolve in most industrialized countries. Early adopters of this intervention focused on trying to identify and solve the key problems facing the organization to improve performance and customer satisfaction. Organizations with mature TQM programs have shifted their attention from retrospective problem solving to proactive problem anticipation and prevention. For example, one of the Conference Board's longest-running quality councils held a 2-day workshop using TQM principles to forecast the needs of human resources management. The council, which is made up of organizations with mature TQM systems, examined how human resources planning could integrate career planning, training, and management succession. It also discussed how the human resources function could evolve to a more strategic role in organization change. This shift from reaction to anticipation seems to be a hallmark of mature, successful TQM programs.

Another important evolution has been the recent emergence of six-sigma programs. Based on the principles of TQM, large organizations, such as GE, Motorola, May Co., and Sun Microsystems, are attempting to drive out important sources of variation and achieving near perfection in the execution of critical processes. Application 15.3 describes one such six-sigma effort at GE Financial Services.[48]

SIX-SIGMA SUCCESS STORY AT GE FINANCIAL

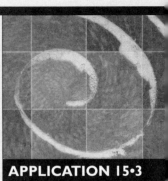

APPLICATION 15•3

GE Financial, the consumer insurance and investment arm of the General Electric Company, helps individuals create and preserve wealth, protect assets, and enhance their lifestyles through products like insurance, annuities, mutual funds, and other personal-finance methods. Today's competitive environment requires that companies delight their customers and relentlessly look for new ways to exceed expectations. How does GE do this? Through six sigma. It is not a secret society, a slogan, or a cliché. Six sigma refers to a highly disciplined methodology that helps GE businesses focus on developing and delivering ever-improving products and services. Why "six sigma"? This methodology borrows the term "sigma" from statistics. In six sigma, the term describes the capability of a process to meet the key customer's requirements. The higher the sigma, the better the process. When a process fails to meet the customer's requirement, it is counted as a defect. The central idea behind six sigma is that if you can measure how many "defects" you have in a process, you can systematically figure out how to eliminate them. To illustrate how GE Financial uses six sigma, we begin with a short description of the background of GE Financial, and a description of how six sigma was applied to a typical project called "Optimization."

GE Financial is a business that grew quickly by acquiring two to three different companies annually between 1996 and 2001. Managing this growth required an enormous amount of consolidation and integration of people, technologies, and processes. Six sigma helped drive both speed and success in these areas. Recently, GE Financial recognized an opportunity to improve a critical process called *optimization*. Optimization refers to the process that routinely occurs as an insurance company manages its investments. When a customer purchases an insurance policy, their premiums are invested by the insurance company in instruments, such as bonds, of varying yields and maturities. The insurance company's goals are to pick the best combination of investments that will ensure that the premium will grow sufficiently to repay a customer's future claim and to provide a profit to the insurer. To ensure the ability to meet the investment goals, the investment managers fine-tune the portfolio. The goal of this fine-tuning, or optimization, is to maximize desirable characteristics, such as yield, while minimizing undesirable characteristics, such as credit default and interest rate risk. The project at GE Financial was focused on improving the process of how optimization of the investment portfolio occurred.

A key internal customer on the GE Financial team knew that that the current optimization process could be more ef-

fective if it reflected the most current market conditions. The team measured how long it took to complete a typical cycle of optimization. The cycle time of the process, a measure of the time from the start of a process until the output was delivered to the internal customer, took, on average, 84 working days. The team realized that to meet the customer's requirement for an optimization that reflects current market condition meant they needed to reduce the cycle time from 84 days to, at most, 5 days. To drive the cycle down to an acceptable level, a six-sigma quality "Black Belt" (a GE Financial associate with a high level of expertise) was assigned. The Black Belt's role is similar to that of a consultant, facilitating the team through changes and providing expertise in six-sigma methodology. A brief description of the steps involved in driving the process improvement follows.

In the first phase, the Black Belt and process improvement team gathered information to understand the current process and the requirements of key stakeholders and customers. Interviews with the Chief Investment Officer and investment analysts resulted in greater understanding of the requirements for a successful project. These requirements included the previously mentioned reduction in cycle time from 84 days to 5 days; improving scalability by creating the ability to optimize multiple portfolios; and lastly, improving functionality by adding the ability to analyze several different types of risk.

As part of first phase, the team also determined the project boundaries and how to allocate proper resources for an on-time project completion. Together, the customers and the improvement team reached a consensus on how to proceed. The portfolio optimization project team divided the project into three generations of related projects. For example, the first-generation project would focus on reducing cycle time by 30% for the optimization of the investment portfolio. The latter-generation projects would then focus on improving scalability and capability, and they would require long-term technological investments in research and development. By developing a consensus definition of expectations for the project, the team defined a long-term course for improvement, based on the customer's requirements. The project team set off and determined how best to precisely measure the existing process and collect data.

Once measures were collected, the Black Belt helped the team analyze the data to identify the possible causes behind the existing cycle time for the process. While many causes were investigated, the ones that were determined to be statistically significant and had the greatest impact on cycle time were further analyzed. The in-depth analysis of the process highlighted a number of areas, including inefficient hand-offs, time lags, and repetitive steps. Through discussions with the process experts, the team identified potential root causes impacting cycle time and ultimately narrowed down to a "vital few" drivers of variation in the cycle time for the portfolio optimization.

Upon understanding the drivers of the existing cycle time, the improvement team, the stakeholders, and the process owners discussed potential improvement opportunities. Ultimately, the team devised specific improvements for each key driver. Some simply required a change in process and procedure, while others required moderate changes to systems and structures. For example, during the analysis, the team determined that different data formats drove cycle-time variation. A dollar amount may have been quoted as: $100,000,000 or 100000000 or $100,000,000.00, depending on the source. This inconsistency forced the receiver to rework the formatting of multitudes of data prior to inputting the data into the optimization tool. This formatting inconsistency caused significant time delays and introduced a possibility for error. The solution was to clearly specify and communicate to data suppliers both the particular data requirement and the format for the data as well. To facilitate the appropriate formatting, data templates were created and distributed to the data suppliers. This was a relatively simple solution, but nonetheless it translated to significant impact on the cycle time for the process. For those changes that required a process and procedure change, the adjustments were documented and communicated. The changes to systems and structures required that well-defined project plans be submitted to a team from the Information Technology organization for programming actual changes to the systems. Throughout this project phase, the improvement team kept the stakeholders and process owners aware of the improvement plans, timelines, and any issues that prevented goal achievement.

When various improvements were being designed and eventually completed, the team communicated the changes in process, procedure, and technology to the associates involved in this optimization process. A small-scale pilot program was developed to take associates through the new process ensuring clear understanding of the new process and methods. The close relationship and constant communication between the team and those who worked the process was a key to the success of the project.

At the conclusion of the first project, the goal was not only achieved, but also exceeded. The 30% cycle-time reduction goal, from 84 days to 59 days, was actually reduced to 42 days. This result equated to a 50% reduction in cycle time. Besides that improvement, the project team had a better sense of the process and their customer's requirements. This clarity will lead to a speedier implementation of the next generations of project where the team will seek to achieve the overall goal of a 95% reduction equating to the 5-day cycle-time goal.

This case serves to illustrate three key concepts in the six-sigma problem-solving methodology. First, consistent interaction between the project team and the stakeholders and process owners allowed for realistic project expectations and set the stage for project success. Second, having appropriate project scoping and project phasing allowed for the setting of realistic goals and timelines. And third, the robust use of qualitative and quantitative data to properly identify root causes will ensure that the "right" solutions are undertaken.

Results of Total Quality Management

TQM's emergence in the United States and the variation in how it is applied across organizations have made rigorous evaluation of results difficult. Much of the evidence is anecdotal. For example, the 2002 Malcolm Baldrige award winners, Motorola Commerical's Government and Industrial Solutions Sector in the business category, Branch-Smith Printing Division in the small-business category, and SSM Health Care in the health care category, can each point to significant accomplishments. Branch Smith Printing experienced a 72% growth in sales and an 83% increase in customer accounts over a 4-year period.[49] Similarly, as part of Motorola's 1988 award, its manufacturing organization reduced the number of parts in its cellular phones by 70% and cut the time required to build a cellular phone from 40 hours to 4; it reduced defects by 80% and saved $962 million in inspection and reworking costs; it set a goal of tenfold improvement in quality within 5 years and exceeded that goal within 3 years.[50] The U.S. Commerce Department's National Institute of Standards and Technology routinely tracks the stock performance of Baldrige Award winners compared to a Standard & Poor's 500 index fund. On the one hand, the Baldrige winners outperformed the index fund by a ratio of 2.6 to 1 and outperformed the S&P 500 significantly between 1994 and 1999.[51] More recently, however, the award recipients between 1992 and 2001 underperformed the S&P 500 by a ratio of 1 to 1.9. Finally, a study of hospitals provided empirical support for the Baldrige framework.[52] Significant relationships were identified between hospitals' adherence to the Baldrige Criteria and their performance in the areas of patient and customer satisfaction, staff and work systems, and organization-specific results. However, the relationships between hospital quality systems and financial/market performance or health care outcomes was not significant. The authors recommend more longitudinal research because of the likely time lags between implementation and manifestation of financial or health-related outcomes.

A 1999 survey of the *Fortune* 1000 companies showed that about 75% have implemented some form of TQM.[53] Furthermore, 87% of the companies rated their TQM experience as either positive or very positive, up from 76% in 1993. The research also found that TQM is often associated with the implementation of other EI interventions. As organizations enact process improvements, they may need to make supporting changes in reward systems and work design.[54] Finally, the study revealed that TQM was positively associated with performance outcomes, such as productivity, customer service, product/service quality, and profitability, as well as with human outcomes, such as employee satisfaction and quality of work life.

Other studies also suggest positive TQM results. In a Conference Board study of 149 large organizations, more than 30% reported improved financial performance. Another study of the 20 highest-point-scorers in the Baldrige competition reported improved employee relations, product quality, and customer satisfaction and lowered costs compared with other Baldrige applicants.[55] These results should be interpreted cautiously, however, because most of the studies lack sufficient scientific rigor.

A more balanced picture of TQM effects is provided by a study of 54 firms of different sizes, both adopters and nonadopters of TQM. It found that TQM firms significantly outperformed non-TQM firms. The source of the performance advantage was not the tools and techniques of TQM, however, but the culture, empowerment, and commitment that came from successful implementation. The study concluded that "these tacit resources, and not TQM tools and techniques, drive TQM success," and that "organizations that acquire them can outperform competitors with or without the accompanying TQM ideology."[56] Similarly, a study of Swedish quality award winners was compared with their primary competitors. The award winners consistently outperformed their competitors on measures of sales and profitability.[57]

Although reports of TQM success are plentiful in the popular literature, there are also reports of problems.[58] At Florida Power and Light, executives were divided over whether TQM actually had helped the organization, and a new CEO's interviews with employees found widespread resentment toward the process. There appears to be good and improving evidence of TQM's impact on organization effectiveness, but it is clear that the relationship between these variables is complex. For example, Boeing's experience with TQM has suggested that the biggest organizational gains have come through the integration of TQM concepts with other business and strategic initiatives. TQM has helped Boeing be a better all-around company. More systematic research is needed to assess when and why positive outcomes are valid and how TQM affects the entire organization.

SUMMARY

This chapter described employee involvement interventions. These technostructural change programs are aimed at moving organization decision making downward to improve responsiveness and performance and to increase member flexibility, commitment, and satisfaction. Different approaches to EI can be described by the extent to which power, information, knowledge and skills, and rewards are shared with employees.

The relationship between EI and productivity can be oversimplified. Productivity can be increased through improved employee communication, motivation, and skills and abilities. It also can be affected through increased worker satisfaction, which in turn results in productive employees joining and remaining with the organization.

Major EI interventions are parallel structures, including cooperative union–management projects and quality circles; high-involvement designs; and TQM. The results of these approaches tend to be positive, and the quality of research supporting these interventions is increasing.

NOTES

1. L. Davis, "Enhancing the Quality of Work Life: Developments in the United States," *International Labour Review* 116 (July-August 1977): 53–65.

2. D. Glew, A. O'Leary-Kelly, R. Griffin, and D. Van Fleet, "Participation in Organizations: A Preview of the Issues and Proposed Framework for Future Analysis," *Journal of Management* 21, 3 (1995): 395–421.

3. E. Lawler III, *High-Involvement Management* (San Francisco: Jossey-Bass, 1986).

4. E. Lawler, *Organizing for High Performance: Employee Involvement, TQM, Re-engineering, and Knowledge Management in the Fortune 1000* (San Francisco: Jossey-Bass, 2001); E. Lawler III, S. Mohrman, and G. Ledford, *Strategies for High-Performance Organizations* (San Francisco: Jossey-Bass, 1998).

5. M. Marchington, A. Wilkinson, and P. Ackers, "Understanding the Meaning of Participation: Views from the Workplace," *Human Relations* 47, 8 (1994): 867–94; C. Goulden, "Supervisory Management and Quality Circle Performance: An Empirical Study," *Journal of Management Development* 14, 7 (1995): 15–27.

6. D. Welsh, F. Luthans, and S. Sommer, "Managing Russian Factory Workers: The Impact of U.S.-Based Behavioral and Participative Techniques," *Academy of Management Journal* 36, 1 (1993): 58–79; D. Jones, "Employee Participation During the Early Stages of Transition: Evidence from Bulgaria," *Economic and Industrial Democracy* 16, 1 (1995): 111–35.

7. E. Poutsma, J. Hendrickx, and F. Huijgen, "Employee Participation in Europe: In Search of the Participative Workplace," *Economic and Industrial Democracy* 24 (2003): 45–77; J. Wimalasiri and A. Kouzmin, "A Comparative Study of Employee Involvement Initiatives in Hong Kong and the USA," *International Journal of Manpower* 21 (2000): 614–32; C. Cooper and E. Mumford, *The Quality of Working Life in Western and Eastern Europe* (Westport, Conn.: Greenwood Press, 1979); P. Sorenson, T. Head, T. Yaeger, and D. Cooperrider, *Global and Internation Organization Development,* 3d ed. (Champaign, Ill.: Stipes, 2001).

8. M. Kizilos, "The Relationship Between Employee Involvement and Organization Performance" (unpublished Ph.D. diss., University of Southern California, 1995); M. Huselid, "The Impact of Human Resource Management Practices on Turnover, Productivity, and Corporate Financial Performance," *Academy of Management Journal* 38 (1995): 635–72; M. Kizilos, T. Cummings, and A. Strickstein, "Achieving Superior Customer Service Through Employee Involvement," *Academy of Management Best Paper Proceedings* (1994): 197–201; J. Arthur, "Effects of Human Resources Systems on Manufacturing Performance and Turnover," *Academy of Management Journal* 37 (1994): 670–87; A. Kalleberg and J. Moody, "Human Resource Management and Organizational Performance," *American Behavioral Scientist* 37 (1994): 948–62; D. Denison, *Corporate Culture and Organizational Effectiveness* (New York: John Wiley & Sons, 1990); G. Hansen and B. Wernerfelt, "Determinates of Firm Performance: The Relative Importance of Economic and Organizational Factors," *Strategic Management Journal* 10 (1989): 399–411.

9. E. Lawler III and G. Ledford, "Productivity and the Quality of Work Life," *National Productivity Review* 2 (Winter 1981–82): 23–36.

10. Glew et al., "Participation in Organizations"; J. Wagner, "Participation's Effects on Performance and Satisfaction: A Reconsideration of Research Evidence," *Academy of Management Review* 19 (1994): 312–30.

11. G. Ledford and E. Lawler, "Research on Employee Participation: Beating a Dead Horse?" *Academy of Management Review* 19 (1994): 633–36.

12. Lawler, Mohrman, and Ledford, *Strategies,* p. 150.

13. G. Bushe and A. Shani, "Parallel Learning Structure Interventions in Bureaucratic Organizations," in *Research in Organizational Change and Development,* vol. 4, eds. W. Pasmore and R. Woodman (Greenwich, Conn.: JAI Press, 1990), 167–94.

14. D. Zand, "Collateral Organization: A New Change Strategy," *Journal of Applied Behavioral Science* 10 (1974): 63–89; S. Goldstein, "Organizational Dualism and Quality Circles," *Academy of Management Review* 10 (1985): 504–17; V. Schein and L. Greiner, "Can Organization Development Be Fine Tuned to Bureaucracies?" *Organizational Dynamics* (Winter 1977): 48–61.

15. D. Zand, *Information, Organization, and Power: Effective Management in the Knowledge Society* (New York: McGraw-Hill, 1981), 57–88; G. Bushe and A. Shani, *Parallel Learning Structures: Increasing Innovation in Bureaucracies* (Reading, Mass.: Addison-Wesley, 1991).

16. C. Worley and G. Ledford, "The Relative Impact of Group Process and Group Structure on Group Effectiveness" (paper presented at the Western Academy of Management, Spokane, Wash., April 1992).

17. C. Worley, "Implementing Strategic Change at GTE of California" (working paper, Pepperdine University, 1993).

18. Zand, *Collateral Organization.*

19. A. Honeycutt, "The Key to Effective Quality Circles," *Training and Development Journal* 43 (May 1989): 81–84; E. Yager, "The Quality Circle Explosion," *Training and Development Journal* 35 (April 1981): 93–105; "A Quality Circle Nets a Nice Round Figure," *Supervisory Management* 40 (1995): 7.

20. E. Miller, "The Parallel Organization Structure at General Motors—An Interview with Howard C. Carlson," *Personnel* (September-October 1978): 64–69; M. Barrick and R. Alexander, "A Review of Quality Circle Efficacy and the Existence of Positive-Findings Bias," *Personnel Psychology* 40 (1987): 579–92; J. Vogt and B. Hunt, "What Really Goes Wrong with Participative Groups," *Training and Development Journal* 42 (May 1988): 96–100; R. Steel and G. Shane, "Evaluation Research on Quality Circles: Technical and Analytical Implications," *Human Relations* 39 (1986): 449–68; M. Duckles, R. Duckles, and M. Maccoby, "The Process of Change at Bolivar," *Journal of Applied Behavioral Science* 13 (1977): 387–499.

21. Bushe, "Developing Cooperative Labor–Management Relations in Unionized Factories: A Multiple Case Study of Quality Circles and Parallel Organizations Within Joint Quality of Work Life Projects," *Journal of Applied Behavioral Science* 24 (1988): 129–50; H. Katz, T. Kochan, and M. Weber, "Assessing the Effects of Industrial Relations Systems and Efforts to Improve the Quality of Working Life on Organizational Effectiveness," *Academy of Management Journal* 28 (1985): 509–26.

22. Lawler and Ledford, "Productivity."

23. G. Ledford Jr., E. Lawler III, and S. Mohrman, "The Quality Circle and Its Variations," in *Enhancing Productivity: New Perspectives from Industrial and Organizational Psychology,* eds. J. P. Campbell and J. R. Campbell (San Francisco: Jossey-Bass, 1988), 225–94.

24. R. Steel and R. Lloyd, "Cognitive, Affective, and Behavioral Outcomes of Participation in Quality Circles: Conceptual and Empirical Findings," *Journal of Applied Behavioral Science* 24 (1988): 1–17.

25. Lawler and Ledford, "Productivity," 35.

26. Lawler, Mohrman, and Ledford, *Strategies,* 112–13; D. Tjosvold, "Making Employee Involvement Work: Cooperative Goals and Controversy to Reduce Costs," *Human Relations* 51 (1998): 210–14.

27. "Employee Participation and Labor–Management Cooperation in American Workplaces," *Challenge* 38 (1995): 38–46.

28. S. Mohrman and G. Ledford Jr., "The Design and Use of Effective Employee Participation Groups," *Human Resource Management* 24 (1985): 413–28; E. Lawler III and S. Mohrman, "Quality Circles after the Fad," *Harvard Business Review* 85 (1985): 64–71; Mohrman and Ledford Jr., "Design and Use"; D. Collins, "Self-Interests and Group Interests in Employee Involvement Programs: A Case Study," *Journal of Labor Research* 16 (1995): 57–79; R. Callahan, "Quality Circles: A Program for Productivity Improvement Through Human Resource Development" (unpublished paper, Albers School of Business, Seattle University, 1982); C. Worley, "Implementing Participation Strategies in Hospitals: Correlates of Effective Problem-Solving Teams," *Public Administration and Management: An Interactive Journal* 5 (2000): 1–27 (http://www.pamij.com).

29. Lawler, *High-Involvement Management.*

30. E. Lawler III, "Increasing Worker Involvement to Enhance Organizational Effectiveness," in *Change in Organizations,* ed. P. Goodman (San Francisco: Jossey-Bass, 1982), 299; R. Walton, "From Control to Commitment in the Workplace," *Harvard Business Review* 63 (1985): 76–84.

31. Lawler, *High-Involvement Management;* E. Lawler, *The Ultimate Advantage* (San Francisco: Jossey-Bass, 1992).

32. Glew et al., "Participation in Organizations."

33. G. Ledford, "High-Involvement Organizations" (working paper, Center for Effective Organizations, University of Southern California, 1992).

34. J. Pfeffer, "Producing Sustainable Competitive Advantage Through the Effective Management of People," *Academy of Management Executive* 9, 1 (1995): 55–69.

35. J. Guthrie, "High-Involvement Work Practices, Turnover, and Productivity: Evidence from New Zealand," *Academy of Management Journal* 44 (2001): 180–91.

36. R. Forrester, "Empowerment: Rejuvenating a Potent Idea," *Academy of Management Executive* 14 (2000): 67–81.

37. This application was adapted from information provided in M. Hequet, "Worker Involvement Lights up Neon," *Training* 31 (1994): 23–29.

38. The authors wish to thank Miriam Y. Lacey, associate professor of Applied Behavioral Science, Pepperdine University, and Debbie Collard, director, Continuous Quality Improvement, Airlift and Tanker Programs, Boeing, for their helpful comments on this section.

39. Y. Shetty, "Product Quality and Competitive Strategy," *Business Horizons* (May-June 1987): 46–52; D. Garvin, "Competing on the Eight Dimensions of Quality," *Harvard Business Review* (November-December 1987): 101–09; D. Garvin, *Managing Quality: The Strategic and Competitive Edge* (New York: Free Press, 1988); "The Quality Imperative," *Business Week,* Special Issue (25 October 1991): 34.

40. W. Deming, *Quality, Productivity, and Competitive Advantage* (Cambridge: MIT Center for Advanced Engineering Study, 1982); W. Deming, *Out of the Crisis* (Cambridge: MIT Press, 1986); J. Juran, *Quality Control Handbook,* 3d ed. (New York: McGraw-Hill, 1974); J. Juran, *Juran on the Leadership for Quality: An Executive Handbook* (New York: Free Press, 1989).

41. P. Crosby, *Quality Is Free* (New York: McGraw-Hill, 1979); P. Crosby, *Quality Without Tears* (New York: McGraw-Hill, 1984).

42. J. Hillkirk, "New Award Cites Teams with Dreams," *USA Today* (10 April 1992): 1, 4, 5b; http://www.qualitycup.org.

43. Information on the Shingo Prize and the recipients can be found at http://www.shingoprize.com.

44. C. Caldwell, J. Mceachern, and V. Davis, "Measurement Tools Eliminate Guesswork," *Healthcare Forum Journal* (July-August 1990): 23–27.

45. "Quality Imperative," *Business Week,* p. 152.

46. Ibid., 14.

47. Ibid., 14.

48. This application was written and submitted by Maureen Donahue and F. Antonio Munoz, both of GE's Asset Management organization. Their efforts are greatly appreciated.

49. Data was gathered from the Malcolm Baldrige Web site: http://www.nist.gov/public affairs/releases/mbnqa052103.htm. It was accessed on 3 June 2003.

50. R. Shaffer, "Why Motorola Is Expensive—And Still a Bargain," *Forbes* 146 (1990): 102; E. Segalla, "All for Quality, and Quality for All," *Training and Development Journal* 43 (1989): 36–45; B. Avishai and W. Taylor, "Customers Drive a Technology-Driven Company: An Interview with George Fisher," *Harvard Business Review* 67 (1989): 106–14; K. Bhote, "Motorola's Long March to the Malcolm Baldrige National Quality Award," *National Productivity Review* 8 (1989): 365–75; "Quality at Motorola," various internal company documents from January 1988 to June 1990.

51. "Betting to Win on the Baldie Winners," *Business Week* (18 October 1993): 8; additional information about this study can be found at http://www.nist.gov/public affairs/stockstudy.htm.

52. S. Goldstein and S. Schweikhart, "Empirical Support for the Baldrige Award Framework in U.S. Hospitals," *Health Care Management Review* 27(2002): 62–75.

53. Lawler, *Organizing for High Performance.*

54. T. Douglas and W. Judge Jr., "Total Quality Management Implementation and Competitive Advantage: The Role of Structural Control and Exploration," *Academy of Management Journal* 44 (2001): 158–70; R. Allen and R. Kilmann, "The Role of the Reward System for a Total Quality Management Based Strategy," *Journal of Organizational Change Management,* 14 (2001): 110–32.

55. U.S. General Accounting Office, *Management Practices: U.S. Companies Improve Performance Through Quality Efforts* (Gaithersburg, Md.: Author, 1991).

56. T. Powell, "Total Quality Management as a Competitive Advantage: A Review and Empirical Study," *Strategic Management Journal* 16 (1995): 15–37.

57. J. Hansson and H. Eriksson, "The Impact of TQM on Financial Performance," *Measuring Business Excellence* 6(2002): 44–54.

58. "Is the Baldrige Overblown?" *Fortune* (1 July 1991): 62–65.

Work Design

This chapter is concerned with work design—creating jobs and work groups that generate high levels of employee fulfillment and productivity. This technostructural intervention can be part of a larger employee involvement application, or it can be an independent change program. Work design has been researched and applied extensively in organizations. Recently, organizations have tended to combine work design with formal structure and supporting changes in goal setting, reward systems, work environment, and other performance management practices. These organizational factors can help structure and reinforce the kinds of work behaviors associated with specific work designs. (How performance management interventions can support work design is discussed in Chapter 17.)

This chapter examines three approaches to work design. The *engineering approach* focuses on efficiency and simplification, and results in traditional job and work group designs. Traditional jobs involve relatively routine and repetitive forms of work, where little interaction among people is needed to produce a service or product. Call center operators, data-entry positions, and product support representatives are examples of this job design. Traditional work groups are composed of members performing routine yet interrelated tasks. Member interactions are typically controlled by rigid work flows, supervisors, and schedules, such as might be found on assembly lines.

A second approach to work design rests on *motivational theories* and attempts to enrich the work experience. Job enrichment involves designing jobs with high levels of meaning, discretion, and knowledge of results. A well-researched model focusing on job attributes has helped clear up methodological problems with this important intervention.

The third and most recent approach to work design derives from *sociotechnical systems methods,* and seeks to optimize both the social and the technical aspects of work systems. This method has led to a popular form of work design called "self-managed teams," which are composed of multiskilled members performing interrelated tasks. Members are given the knowledge, information, and power necessary to control their own task behaviors with relatively little external control. New support systems and supervisory styles are needed to manage them.

The chapter describes each of these perspectives on work design, and then presents a contingency framework for integrating the approaches based on personal and technical factors in the workplace. When work is designed to fit these factors, it is both satisfying and productive.

THE ENGINEERING APPROACH

The oldest and most prevalent approach to designing work is based on engineering concepts and methods. It proposes that the most efficient work designs can be determined by clearly specifying the tasks to be performed, the work methods to be used, and the work flow among individuals. The engineering approach is based on the pioneering work of Frederick Taylor, the father of scientific management. He developed methods for analyzing and designing work and laid the foundation for the professional field of industrial engineering.[1]

The engineering approach scientifically analyzes workers' tasks to discover those procedures that produce the maximum output with the minimum input of energies and resources.[2] This generally results in work designs with high levels of specialization and specification. Such designs have several benefits: They allow workers to learn tasks rapidly; they permit short work cycles so performance can take place with little or no mental effort; and they reduce costs because lower-skilled people can be hired and trained easily and paid relatively low wages.

The engineering approach produces two kinds of work design: traditional jobs and traditional work groups. When the work can be completed by one person, such as with bank tellers and telephone operators, traditional jobs are created. These jobs tend to be simplified, with routine and repetitive tasks having clear specifications concerning time and motion. When the work requires coordination among people, such as on automobile assembly lines, traditional work groups are developed. They are composed of members performing relatively routine yet related tasks. The overall group task is typically broken into simpler, discrete parts (often called jobs). The tasks and work methods are specified for each part, and the parts are assigned to group members. Each member performs a routine and repetitive part of the group task. Members' separate task contributions are coordinated for overall task achievement through such external controls as schedules, rigid work flows, and supervisors.[3] In the 1950s and 1960s, this method of work design was popularized by the assembly lines of American automobile manufacturers and was an important reason for the growth of American industry following World War II.

The engineering approach to job design is less an OD intervention than a benchmark in history. Critics of the approach argue that the method ignores workers' social and psychological needs. They suggest that the rising educational level of the workforce and the substitution of automation for menial labor point to the need for more enriched forms of work in which people have greater discretion and are more challenged. Moreover, the current competitive climate requires a more committed and involved workforce able to make on-line decisions and to develop performance innovations. Work designed with the employee in mind is more humanly fulfilling and productive than that designed in traditional ways. However, it is important to recognize the strengths of the engineering approach. It remains an important work design intervention because its immediate cost savings and efficiency can be measured readily, and because it is well understood and easily implemented and managed.

THE MOTIVATIONAL APPROACH

The motivational approach to work design views the effectiveness of organizational activities primarily as a function of member needs and satisfaction, and seeks to improve employee performance and satisfaction by enriching jobs. The motivational method provides people with opportunities for autonomy, responsibility, closure (that is, doing a complete job), and performance feedback. Enriched jobs are popular in the United States at such companies as AT&T Universal Card, TRW, Dayton Hudson, and GTE.

The motivational approach usually is associated with the research of Herzberg and of Hackman and Oldham. Herzberg's two-factor theory of motivation proposed that certain attributes of work, such as opportunities for advancement and recognition, which he called *motivators*, help increase job satisfaction.[4] Other attributes, which Herzberg called *hygiene factors*, such as company policies, working conditions, pay, and supervision, do not produce satisfaction but rather prevent dissatisfaction—

important contributors because only satisfied workers are motivated to produce. Successful job enrichment experiments at AT&T, Texas Instruments, and Imperial Chemical Industries helped to popularize job enrichment in the 1960s.[5]

Although Herzberg's motivational factors sound appealing, increasing doubt has been cast on the underlying theory. Motivation and hygiene factors are difficult to put into operation and measure, and that makes implementation and evaluation of the theory difficult. Furthermore, important worker characteristics that can affect whether people will respond favorably to job enrichment were not included in his theory. Finally, Herzberg's failure to involve employees in the job enrichment process itself does not suit most OD practitioners today. Consequently, a second, well-researched approach to job enrichment has been favored. It focuses on the attributes of the work itself and has resulted in a more scientifically acceptable theory of job enrichment than Herzberg's model. The research of Hackman and Oldham represents this more recent trend in job enrichment.[6]

The Core Dimensions of Jobs

Considerable research has been devoted to defining and understanding core job dimensions.[7] Figure 16.1 summarizes the Hackman and Oldham model of job design. Five core dimensions of work affect three critical psychological states, which in turn produce personal and job outcomes. These outcomes include high internal work

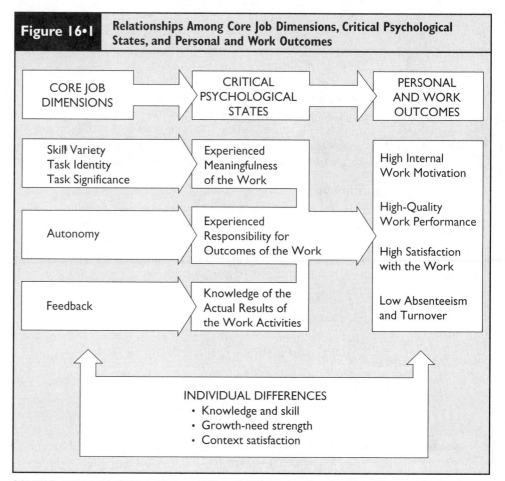

Figure 16•1   Relationships Among Core Job Dimensions, Critical Psychological States, and Personal and Work Outcomes

CORE JOB DIMENSIONS → CRITICAL PSYCHOLOGICAL STATES → PERSONAL AND WORK OUTCOMES

Skill Variety
Task Identity
Task Significance → Experienced Meaningfulness of the Work

Autonomy → Experienced Responsibility for Outcomes of the Work

Feedback → Knowledge of the Actual Results of the Work Activities

High Internal Work Motivation

High-Quality Work Performance

High Satisfaction with the Work

Low Absenteeism and Turnover

INDIVIDUAL DIFFERENCES
• Knowledge and skill
• Growth-need strength
• Context satisfaction

SOURCE: WORK REDESIGN by Hackman/Oldham, © 1980. Reprinted by permission of Pearson Education, Inc., Upper Saddle River, NJ.

motivation, high-quality work performance, satisfaction with the work, and low absenteeism and turnover. The five core job dimensions—skill variety, task identity, task significance, autonomy, and feedback from the work itself—are described below and associated with the critical psychological states that they create.

Skill Variety, Task Identity, and Task Significance

These three core job characteristics influence the extent to which work is perceived as meaningful. *Skill variety* refers to the number and types of skills used to perform a particular task. Employees at Lechmere's, a retail chain in Florida, can work as warehouse stock clerks, cashiers, or salespeople. The more tasks an individual performs, the more meaningful the job becomes. When skill variety is increased by moving a person from one job to another, a form of job enrichment called *job rotation* is accomplished. However, simply rotating a person from one boring job to another is not likely to produce the outcomes associated with a fully enriched job.

Task identity describes the extent to which an individual performs a whole piece of work. For example, an employee who completes an entire wheel assembly for an airplane, including the tire, chassis, brakes, and electrical and hydraulic systems, has more task identity and will perceive the work as more meaningful than someone who only assembles the braking subsystem. *Job enlargement,* another form of job enrichment that combines increases in skill variety with task identity, blends several narrow jobs into one larger, expanded job. For example, separate machine setup, machining, and inspection jobs might be combined into one. This method can increase meaningfulness, job satisfaction, and motivation when employees comprehend and like the greater task complexity.

Task significance represents the impact that the work has on others. In jobs with high task significance, such as nursing, consulting, or manufacturing something like sensitive parts for the space shuttle, the importance of successful task completion creates meaningfulness for the worker.

Experienced meaningfulness is expressed as an average of these three dimensions. Thus, although it is advantageous to have high amounts of skill variety, task identity, and task significance, a strong emphasis on any one of the three dimensions can, at least partially, make up for deficiencies in the other two.

Autonomy

This refers to the amount of independence, freedom, and discretion that the employee has to schedule and perform tasks. Salespeople, for example, often have considerable autonomy in how they contact, develop, and close new accounts, whereas assembly line workers often have to adhere to work specifications clearly detailed in a policy-and-procedure manual. Employees are more likely to experience responsibility for their work outcomes when high amounts of autonomy exist.

Feedback from the Work Itself

This core dimension represents the information that workers receive about the effectiveness of their work. It can derive from the work itself, as when determining whether an assembled part functions properly, or it can come from such external sources as reports on defects, budget variances, customer satisfaction, and the like. Because feedback from the work itself is direct and generates intrinsic satisfaction, it is considered preferable to feedback from external sources.

Individual Differences

Not all people react in similar ways to job enrichment interventions. Individual differences—among them, a worker's knowledge and skill levels, growth-need strength, and satisfaction with contextual factors—moderate the relationships among core dimensions, psychological states, and outcomes. "Worker knowledge and skill" refers to the education and experience levels characterizing the workforce. If employees lack the appropriate skills, for example, increasing skill variety may not improve a job's meaningfulness. Similarly, if workers lack the intrinsic motivation to grow and develop personally, attempts to provide them with increased autonomy may be resisted. (We will discuss growth needs more fully in the last section of this chapter.) Finally, contextual factors include reward systems, supervisory style, and co-worker satisfaction. When the employee is unhappy with the work context, attempts to enrich the work itself may be unsuccessful.

Application Stages

The basic steps for job enrichment as described by Hackman and Oldham include making a thorough diagnosis of the situation, forming natural work units, combining tasks, establishing client relationships, vertical loading, and opening feedback channels.[8]

Making a Thorough Diagnosis

The most popular method of diagnosing a job is through the use of the Job Diagnostic Survey (JDS) or one of its variations.[9] An important output of the JDS is the motivating potential score, which is a function of the three psychological states—experienced meaningfulness, autonomy, and feedback. The survey can be used to profile one or more jobs, to determine whether motivation and satisfaction are really problems or whether the job is low in motivating potential, and to isolate specific job aspects that are causing difficulties. Figure 16.2 shows two jobs. Job A in

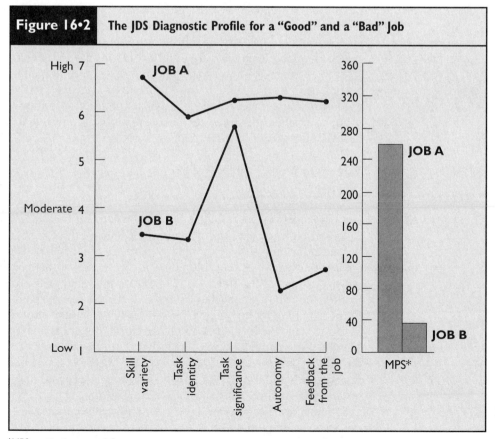

Figure 16•2   The JDS Diagnostic Profile for a "Good" and a "Bad" Job

*MPS, motivating potential score.

engineering maintenance is high on all of the core dimensions. Its motivating potential score is 260 (motivating potential scores average about 125). Job B, the routine and repetitive task of processing checks in a bank, has a motivating potential score of 30. The score is well below average and would be even lower except for the job's relatively high task significance. This job could be redesigned and improved.

The JDS also indicates how ready employees are to accept change. Employees who have high growth needs will respond more readily to job enrichment than will those with low or weak growth needs. A thorough diagnosis of the existing work system should be completed before implementing actual changes. The JDS measures satisfaction with pay, co-workers, and supervision. If there is high dissatisfaction with one or more of these areas, other interventions might be more helpful prior to work redesign.

Forming Natural Work Units

As much as possible, natural work units should be formed. Although there may be a number of technological constraints, interrelated task activities should be grouped together. The basic question in forming natural work units is "How can one increase 'ownership' of the task?" Forming such natural units increases two of the core dimensions—task identity and task significance—that contribute to the meaningfulness of work.

Combining Tasks

Frequently, divided jobs can be put back together to form a new and larger one. In the Medfield, Massachusetts, plant of Corning Glass Works, the task of assembling laboratory hotplates was redesigned by combining a number of previously separate tasks. After the change, each hotplate was completely assembled, inspected, and shipped by one operator, resulting in increased productivity of 84%. Controllable rejects dropped from 23% to less than 1%, and absenteeism dropped from 8% to less than 1%.[10] A later analysis indicated that the change in productivity was the result of the intervention.[11] Combining tasks increases task identity and allows a worker to use a greater variety of skills. The hotplate assembler can identify with a product finished for shipment, and self-inspection of his or her work adds greater task significance, autonomy, and feedback from the job itself.

Establishing Client Relationships

When jobs are split up, the typical worker has little or no contact with, or knowledge of, the ultimate user of the product or service. Improvements often can be realized simultaneously on three of the core dimensions by encouraging and helping workers to establish direct relationships with the clients of their work. For example, when an individual from a support pool is assigned to a particular department, feedback increases because of the additional opportunities for praise or criticism of his or her work. Because of the need to develop interpersonal skills in maintaining the client relationship, skill variety may increase. If the worker is given personal responsibility for deciding how to manage relationships with clients, autonomy is increased.

Three steps are needed to create client relationships: (1) The client must be identified; (2) the contact between the client and the worker needs to be established as directly as possible; and (3) criteria and procedures are needed by which the client can judge the quality of the product or service received and relay those judgments back to the worker. For example, even customer-service representatives and data-entry operations can be set up so that people serve particular clients. In the hotplate department, personal nametags can be attached to each instrument. The Indiana Bell Telephone Company found substantial improvements in satisfaction and performance when telephone directory compilers were given accountability for a specific geographic area.[12]

Vertical Loading

The intent of vertical loading is to decrease the gap between *doing* the job and *controlling* the job. A vertically loaded job has responsibilities and controls that formerly were reserved for management. Vertical loading may well be the most crucial of the job-design principles. Autonomy is invariably increased. This approach should lead to greater feelings of personal accountability and responsibility for the work outcomes. For example, at an IBM plant that manufactures circuit boards for personal computers, assembly workers were trained to measure the accuracy and speed of production processes and to test the quality of finished products. Their work is more "whole," they are more autonomous, and the engineers who used to measure and test are free to design better products and more efficient ways to manufacture them.[13]

Loss of vertical loading usually occurs when someone has made a mistake. Once a supervisor steps in, the responsibility may be removed indefinitely. For example, many skilled machinists have to complete forms to have maintenance people work on a machine. The supervisor automatically signs the slip rather than allowing the machinist either to repair the machine or ask directly for maintenance support.

Opening Feedback Channels

In almost all jobs, approaches exist to open feedback channels and help people learn whether their performance is remaining at a constant level, improving, or deteriorating. The most advantageous and least threatening feedback occurs when a worker learns about performance as the job is performed. In the hotplate department at Corning Glass Works, assembling the entire instrument and inspecting it dramatically increased the quantity and quality of performance information available to the operators. Data given to a manager or supervisor often can be given directly to the employee. Computers and other automated operations can be used to provide people with data not currently accessible to them. Many organizations simply have not realized the motivating impact of direct, immediate feedback.

Application 16.1 presents an example of job enrichment in a large data-entry operation where workers were not directly involved in the redesign process and where supervisors developed and implemented the changes.[14] Although the results were extremely positive, research suggests that employee participation in the change program might have produced even more beneficial outcomes.[15]

Barriers to Job Enrichment

As the application of job enrichment has spread, a number of obstacles to significant job restructuring have been identified. Most of these barriers exist in the organizational context within which the job design is executed. Other organizational systems and practices, whether technical, managerial, or personnel, can affect both the implementation of job enrichment and the lifespan of whatever changes are made.

At least four organizational systems can constrain the implementation of job enrichment:[16]

1. **The technical system.** The technology of an organization can limit job enrichment by constraining the number of ways jobs can be changed. For example, long-linked technology like that found on an assembly line can be highly programmed and standardized, thus limiting the amount of employee discretion that is possible. Technology also may set an "enrichment ceiling." Some types of work, such as continuous-process production systems, may be naturally enriched so there is little more that can be gained from a job enrichment intervention.

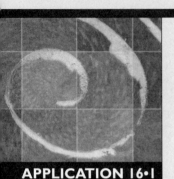

JOB ENRICHMENT AT THE TRAVELERS INSURANCE COMPANIES

APPLICATION 16•1

A job enrichment program took place in a data-entry operation of the Travelers Insurance Companies. Before the intervention, the department was ineffective: Due dates and schedules frequently were missed, and absenteeism was higher than average. The department consisted of 98 data-entry clerks and verifiers, plus 7 assignment clerks and a supervisor. The jobs were split up and highly standardized, providing workers with little opportunity for discretion, skill variety, and feedback. Typically, assignment clerks received jobs from user departments, reviewed the work for obvious errors, and put acceptable work into batches that could be completed in about an hour. If the clerks found errors, they gave the work to the supervisor, who usually handled the problem by dealing with the user department. The data-entry clerks who were given the batches were told to enter only what they saw and not to correct any errors, no matter how obvious. All data entry was 100% verified, a separate task that resembled the original data-entry task and took almost as long. Errors detected in verification were given randomly to data-entry operators to be corrected.

Management and consultants felt that the problems experienced by the data-entry department were motivational. The supervisor spent most of his time responding to crises. He dealt almost daily with employee complaints, especially their apathy or outright hostility toward their jobs. Further diagnosis using the JDS showed that the data-entry and verifying jobs had extremely low motivating potential. Skill variety was low because operators used only a single skill—the ability to input or verify the data adequately. Task identity and task significance were not apparent. People did not perform a whole identifiable job, nor did they have any knowledge about the job's meaning to the user department or the ultimate customer. Autonomy was nonexistent because workers had no freedom to schedule work, to resolve problems, or even to correct obvious errors. Feedback about results was low because an operator who finished a batch of work rarely saw evidence of its quality.

Realizing the low motivating potential of the jobs, management decided to undertake a job enrichment program. First, the consultants conducted an educational session with the supervisor, who was introduced to Hackman and Oldham's approach to job enrichment. Relevant job changes were designed using the following five implementation concepts:

1. **Natural work units.** Each operator was assigned continuing responsibility for certain accounts, rather than receiving batches at random.
2. **Task combination.** Some planning and controlling functions were combined with the task of data entry or verifying.
3. **Client relationships.** Each operator was given several channels of direct contact with clients. The operators inspected their incoming documents for correctness; when mistakes were found, they resolved them directly with the user departments.
4. **Feedback.** Operators received direct feedback about their work from clients and the computer department, including a weekly record of productivity and errors.
5. **Vertical loading.** Operators were permitted to correct obvious data errors and set their own schedules as long as they met department schedules. Some competent operators were given the option of not verifying their work and of making certain program changes.

The results of the job enrichment program were outstanding. The number of operators declined from 98 to 60, primarily through attrition, transfers to other departments, and promotions to higher-paying jobs. The quantity of work increased 39.6%, while the percentage of operators performing poorly declined from 11.1% to 5.5%. Absenteeism declined 24.1%, and employee satisfaction increased significantly. Because of these improvements, management permitted operators to work with fewer external controls. Perhaps more important, the supervisor no longer had to spend his time supervising behavior and dealing with crises, but could devote time to developing feedback systems, setting up work modules, and leading the job enrichment effort.

2. **The personnel system.** Personnel systems can constrain job enrichment by creating formalized job descriptions that are rigidly defined and limit flexibility in changing people's job duties. For example, many union agreements include such narrowly defined job descriptions that major renegotiation between management and the union must occur before jobs can be significantly enriched.

3. **The control system.** Control systems, such as budgets, production reports, and accounting practices, can limit the complexity and challenge of jobs within the system. For example, a company working on a government contract may have such strict quality control procedures that employee discretion is effectively curtailed.

4. **The supervisory system.** Supervisors determine to a large extent the amount of autonomy and feedback that subordinates can experience. To the extent that supervisors use autocratic methods and control work-related feedback, jobs will be difficult, if not impossible, to enrich.

Once these implementation constraints have been overcome, other factors determine whether the effects of job enrichment are strong and lasting.[17] Consistent with the contingency approach to OD, the staying power of job enrichment depends largely on how well it fits and is supported by other organizational practices, such as those associated with training, compensation, and supervision. These practices need to be congruent with and to reinforce jobs having high amounts of discretion, skill variety, and meaningful feedback.

Results of Job Enrichment

Hackman and Oldham reported data from the JDS on more than a thousand people in about a hundred different jobs in more than a dozen organizations.[18] In general, they found that employees whose jobs were high on the core dimensions were more satisfied and motivated than were those whose jobs were low on the dimensions. The core dimensions also were related to such behaviors as absenteeism and performance, although the relationship was not strong for performance. In addition, they found that responses were more positive for people with high growth needs than for those with weaker ones. Similarly, recent research has shown that enriched jobs are strongly correlated with mental ability.[19] Enriching the jobs of workers with low growth needs or with low knowledge and skills is more likely to produce frustration than satisfaction.

An impressive amount of research has been done on Hackman and Oldham's approach to job enrichment. In addition, a number of studies have extended and refined their approach, including a modification of the original JDS instrument to produce more reliable data[20] and the incorporation of such other moderators as the need for achievement and job longevity.[21] In general, research has supported the proposed relationships between job characteristics and outcomes, including the moderating effects of growth needs, knowledge and skills, and context satisfaction.[22] In regard to context satisfaction, for example, research indicates that employee turnover, dissatisfaction, and withdrawal are associated with dark offices, a lack of privacy, and high worker densities.[23]

Reviews of the job enrichment research also report positive effects. An analysis of 28 studies concluded that the job characteristics are positively related to job satisfaction, particularly for people with high growth needs.[24] Another review concluded that job enrichment is effective at reducing employee turnover.[25] A different examination of 28 job enrichment studies reported overwhelmingly positive results.[26] Improvements in quality and cost measures were reported slightly more frequently than improvements in employee attitudes and quantity of production. However, the studies suffered from methodological weaknesses that suggest that the positive findings should be viewed with some caution. Another review of 16 job enrichment studies showed mixed results.[27] Thirteen of the programs were developed and implemented solely by management. These studies showed significant reduction in absenteeism, turnover, and grievances, and improvements in production quality in only about half of the cases where these variables were measured. The three studies with high levels of employee participation in the change program showed improvements in these variables in all cases where they were measured. Although it is difficult to generalize from such a small number of studies, employee participation in the job enrichment program appears to enhance the success of such interventions.

Finally, a comprehensive meta-analysis of more than 75 empirical studies of the Hackman and Oldham model found modest support for the overall model.[28] Although some modifications to the model appear warranted, the studies suggested that many of the more substantive criticisms were unfounded. For example, research supported the conclusion that the relationships between core job characteristics and psychological outcomes were stronger and more consistent than the relationships between core job dimensions and work performance, although these latter relationships did exist and were meaningful. The researchers also found support for the proposed linkages among core job dimensions, critical psychological states, and psychological outcomes. It is interesting that the job feedback dimension emerged as the strongest and most consistent predictor of both psychological and behavioral work outcomes. The researchers suggested that of all job characteristics, increasing feedback had the most potential for improving work productivity and satisfaction. The role of growth-need strength as a moderator was also supported, especially between core dimensions and work performance. Clearly, research supporting the job enrichment model is plentiful. Although the evidence suggests that the model is not perfect, it does appear to be a reasonable guide to improving the motivational outcomes of work.

THE SOCIOTECHNICAL SYSTEMS APPROACH

The *sociotechnical systems (STS) approach* currently is the most extensive body of scientific and applied work underlying employee involvement and innovative work designs. Its techniques and design principles derive from extensive action research in both public and private organizations across diverse national cultures. This section reviews the conceptual foundations of the STS approach and then describes its most popular application: self-managed work teams.

Conceptual Background

Sociotechnical systems theory was developed originally at the Tavistock Institute of Human Relations in London and has spread to most industrialized nations in a little more than 50 years. In Europe and particularly Scandinavia, STS interventions are almost synonymous with work design and employee involvement. In Canada and the United States, STS concepts and methods underlie many of the innovative work designs and team-based structures that are so prevalent in contemporary organizations. Intel Corporation, United Technologies, General Mills, and Procter & Gamble are among the many organizations applying the STS approach to transforming how work is designed and performed.

STS theory is based on two fundamental premises: that an organization or work unit is a combined, social-plus-technical system (sociotechnical), and that this system is open in relation to its environment.[29]

Sociotechnical System

The first assumption suggests that whenever human beings are organized to perform tasks, a joint system is operating—a sociotechnical system. This system consists of two independent but related parts: a social part including the people performing the tasks and the relationships among them, and a technical part—the tools, techniques, and methods for task performance. These two parts are independent of each other because each follows a different set of behavioral laws. The social part operates according to biological and psychosocial laws, whereas the technical part functions according to mechanical and physical laws. Nevertheless, the two parts are related because they must act together to accomplish tasks. Hence, the term *sociotechnical* signifies the joint relationship that must occur between the social and technical parts, and the word *system* communicates that this connection results in a unified whole.

Because a sociotechnical system is composed of social and technical parts, it follows that it will produce two kinds of outcomes: products, such as goods and services; and social and psychological consequences, such as job satisfaction and commitment. The key issue is how to design the relationship between the two parts so that both outcomes are positive (referred to as *joint optimization*). Sociotechnical practitioners design work and organizations so that the social and technical parts work well together, producing high levels of product and human satisfaction. This effort contrasts with the engineering approach to designing work, which focuses on the technical component, worries about fitting people in later, and often leads to mediocre performance at high social costs. The STS approach also contrasts with the motivational approach, which views work design in terms of human fulfillment and that can lead to satisfied employees but inefficient work processes.

Environmental Relationship

The second major premise underlying STS theory is that such systems are open to their environments. As discussed in Chapter 5, open systems must interact with their environments to survive and develop. The environment provides the STS with necessary inputs of energy, raw materials, and information, and the STS provides the environment with products and services. The key issue here is how to design the interface between the STS and its environment so that the system has sufficient freedom to function while exchanging effectively with the environment. In what is typically called *boundary management*, STS practitioners structure environmental relationships both to protect the system from external disruptions and to facilitate the exchange of necessary resources and information. This enables the STS to adapt to changing conditions and to influence the environment in favorable directions.

In summary, STS theory suggests that effective work systems jointly optimize the relationship between their social and technical parts. Moreover, such systems effectively manage the boundary separating and relating them to the environment. This allows them to exchange with the environment while protecting themselves from external disruptions.

Self-Managed Work Teams

The most prevalent application of the STS approach is self-managed work teams.[30] Alternatively referred to as self-directed, self-regulating, or high-performance work teams, these work designs consist of members performing interrelated tasks.[31] Self-managed teams typically are responsible for a complete product or service, or a major part of a larger production process. They control members' task behaviors and make decisions about task assignments and work methods. In many cases, the team sets its own production goals within broader organizational limits and may be responsible for support services, such as maintenance, purchasing, and quality control. Team members generally are expected to learn many if not all of the jobs within the team's control and frequently are paid on the basis of knowledge and skills rather than seniority. When pay is based on performance, team rather than individual performance is the standard.

Self-managed work teams are being implemented at a rapid rate across a range of industries and organizations, such as Intel, Sherwin-Williams, General Mills, Quantum, General Electric, and Motorola. A 2001 survey of *Fortune* 1000 companies found that 70% of these firms were using self-managed work teams, a nearly 50% increase from 1987.[32] Although this work design typically does not cover a majority of the workforce, this represents an impressive increase in the use of self-managed teams.

Figure 16.3 is a model explaining how self-managed work teams perform. It summarizes current STS research and shows how teams can be designed for high performance. Although the model is based mainly on experience with teams that perform the daily work of the organization (work teams), it also has relevance to other team designs, such as problem-solving teams, management teams, cross-functional integrating teams, and employee involvement teams.[33] The model shows that team performance and member satisfaction follow directly from how well the team functions: how well members communicate and coordinate with each other, resolve conflicts and problems, and make and implement task-relevant decisions. Team functioning, in turn, is influenced by three major inputs: team task design, team process interventions, and organization support systems. Because these inputs affect how well teams function and subsequently perform, they are key intervention targets for designing and implementing self-managed work teams.

Team Task Design

Self-managed work teams are responsible for performing particular tasks; consequently, how the team is designed for task performance can have a powerful influence on how well it functions. Task design generally follows from the team's mission and goals that define the major purpose of the team and provide direction for task achievement. When a team's mission and goals are closely aligned with corporate strategy and business objectives, members can see how team performance contributes to organization success. This can increase member commitment to team goals.

Team task design links members' behaviors to task requirements and to each other. It structures member interactions and performances. Three task design elements are necessary for creating self-managed work teams: task differentiation, boundary control, and task control.[34] *Task differentiation* involves the extent to which the team's task is autonomous and forms a relatively self-completing whole. High levels of task differentiation provide an identifiable team boundary and a

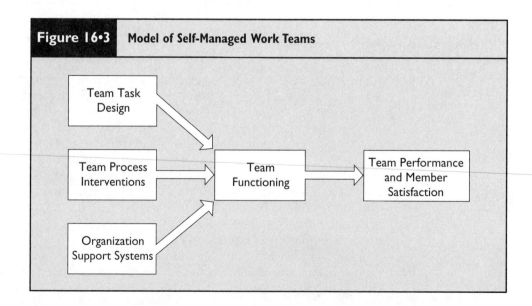

| Figure 16•3 | Model of Self-Managed Work Teams |

clearly defined area of team responsibility. At Johnsonville Sausage, for example, self-managed teams comprise 7 to 14 members each. Each team is large enough to accomplish a set of interrelated tasks but small enough to allow face-to-face meetings for coordination and decision making. In many hospitals, self-managed nursing teams are formed around interrelated tasks that together produce a relatively whole piece of work. Thus, nursing teams may be responsible for particular groups of patients, such as those in intensive care or undergoing cancer treatments, or they may be accountable for specific work processes, such as those in the laboratory, pharmacy, or admissions office.

Boundary control involves the extent to which team members can influence transactions with their task environment—the types and rates of inputs and outputs. Adequate boundary control includes a well-defined work area; group responsibility for boundary-control decisions, such as quality assurance (which reduces dependence on external boundary regulators, such as inspectors); and members sufficiently trained to perform tasks without relying heavily on external resources. Boundary control often requires deliberate cross-training of team members to take on a variety of tasks. This makes members highly flexible and adaptable to changing conditions. It also reduces the need for costly overhead because members can perform many of the tasks typically assigned to staff experts, such as those in quality control, planning, and maintenance.

Task control involves the degree to which team members can regulate their own behavior to provide services or to produce finished products. It includes the freedom to choose work methods, to schedule activities, and to influence production goals to match both environmental and task demands. Task control relies heavily on team members having the power and authority to manage equipment, materials, and other resources needed for task performance. This "work authority" is essential if members are to take responsibility for getting the work accomplished. Task control also requires that team members have accurate and timely information about team performance to allow them to detect performance problems and make necessary adjustments.

Task control enables self-managed work teams to observe and control technical variances as quickly and as close to their source as possible. Technical variances arise from the production process and represent significant deviations from specific goals or standards. In manufacturing, for example, abnormalities in raw material, machine operation, and work flow are sources of variance that can adversely affect the quality and quantity of the finished product. In service work, out-of-the-ordinary requests, special favors or treatment, or unique demands create variances that can place stress on the process. Technical variances traditionally are controlled by support staff and managers, but this can take time and add greatly to costs. Self-managed work teams, on the other hand, have the freedom, skills, and information needed to control technical variances on-line when they occur. This affords timely responses to production problems and reduces the amount of staff overhead needed.

Team Process Interventions

A second key input to team functioning involves team process interventions. As described in Chapter 12, teams may develop ineffective social processes that impede functioning and performance, such as poor communication among members, dysfunctional roles and norms, and faulty problem solving and decision making. Team process interventions, such as process consultation and team building, can resolve such problems by helping members address process problems and moving the team to a more mature stage of development. Because self-managed work teams need to be self-reliant, members generally acquire their own team process skills. They may attend appropriate training programs and workshops or they may learn on the job by working with OD practitioners to conduct process interventions on their own teams. Although members' process skills generally are sufficient to resolve most of the team's process problems, OD experts occasionally may need to supplement the team's skills and help members address problems that they are unable to resolve.

Organization Support Systems

The final input to team functioning is the extent to which the larger organization is designed to support self-managed work teams. The success of such teams clearly depends on support systems that are quite different from traditional methods of managing.[35] For example, a bureaucratic, mechanistic organization is not highly conducive to self-managed teams. An organic structure, with flexibility among units, relatively few formal rules and procedures, and decentralized authority, is much more likely to support and enhance the development of self-managed work teams. This explains why such teams are so prevalent in high-involvement organizations (described in Chapter 15). Their different features, such as flat, lean structures, open information systems, and team-based selection and reward practices, all reinforce teamwork and responsible self-management.

A particularly important support system for self-managed work teams is the external leadership. Self-managed teams exist along a spectrum from having only mild influence over their work to near-autonomy. In many circumstances, such teams take on a variety of functions traditionally handled by management. These can include assigning members to individual tasks, determining the methods of work, scheduling, setting production goals, and selecting and rewarding members. These activities do not make external supervision obsolete, however. That leadership role usually is changed to two major functions: working with and developing team members, and assisting the team in managing its boundaries.[36]

Working with and developing team members is a difficult process and requires a different style of managing than do traditional systems. The team leader (often called a team facilitator) helps team members organize themselves in a way that allows them to become more independent and responsible. He or she must be familiar with team-building approaches and must assist members in learning the skills to perform their jobs. Recent research suggests that the leader needs to provide expertise in self-management.[37] This may include encouraging team members to be self-reinforcing about high performance, to be self-critical of low performance, to set explicit performance goals, to evaluate goal achievement, and to rehearse different performance strategies before trying them.

If team members are to maintain sufficient autonomy to control variance from goal attainment, the leader may need to help them manage team boundaries. Where teams have limited control over their task environment, the leader may act as a buffer to reduce environmental uncertainty. This can include mediating and negotiating with other organizational units, such as higher management, staff experts, and related work teams. Research suggests that better managers spend more time in lateral interfaces.[38]

These new leadership roles require new and different skills, including knowledge of sociotechnical principles and group dynamics, understanding of both the task environment and the team's technology, and ability to intervene in the team to help members increase their knowledge and skills. Leaders of self-managed teams also should have the ability to counsel members and to facilitate communication among them.

Many managers have experienced problems trying to fulfill the complex demands of leading self-managed work teams. The most typical complaints mention ambiguity about responsibilities and authority, lack of personal and technical skills and organizational support, insufficient attention from higher management, and feelings of frustration in the supervisory job.[39] Attempts to overcome these problems have been made in the following areas:[40]

1. **Recruitment and selection.** Recruitment has been directed at selecting team leaders with a balanced mixture of technical and social skills. Those with extensive technical experience have been paired with more socially adept leaders so that both can share skills and support each other.

2. **Training.** Extensive formal and on-the-job training in human relations, group dynamics, and leadership styles have been instituted for leaders of self-managed work teams. Such training is aimed at giving leaders concepts sfor understanding their roles, as well as hands-on experience in team building, process consultation, and third-party intervention (see Chapter 12).

3. **Evaluation and reward systems.** Attempts have been made to tie team leader rewards to achievements in team development. Leaders prepare developmental plans for individual workers and the team as a whole, and set measurable benchmarks for progress. Performance appraisals of leaders are conducted within a group format, with feedback supplied by team members, peers, and higher-level management.

4. **Leadership support systems.** Leaders of self-managed work teams have been encouraged to develop peer support groups. Team leaders can meet off-site to share experiences and to address issues of personal and general concern.

5. **Use of freed-up time.** Team leaders have been provided with a mixture of strategies to apply their talents beyond the immediate work team. A team leader has more time when the team has matured and taken on many managerial functions. In those cases, team leaders have been encouraged to become involved in such areas as higher-level planning and budgeting, companywide training and development, and individual career development.

Application Stages

STS work designs have been implemented in a variety of settings, including manufacturing firms, hospitals, schools, and government agencies. Although the specific implementation strategy is tailored to the situation, a common method of change underlies many of these applications. It generally involves high worker participation in work design and implementation. Such participative work design allows employees to translate their special knowledge of the work situation into relevant designs, and employees with ownership over the design process are likely to be highly committed to implementing the outcomes.[41]

STS applications generally proceed in six steps:[42]

1. *Sanctioning the Design Effort.* At this step, workers receive the necessary protection and support to diagnose their work system and to create an appropriate work design. In many unionized situations, top management and union officials jointly agree to suspend temporarily the existing work rules and job classifications so that employees have the freedom to explore new ways of working. Management also may provide workers with sufficient time and external help to diagnose their work system and devise alternative work structures. In cases of redesigning existing work systems, normal production demands may be reduced during the redesign process. Also, workers may be given some job and wage security so that they feel free to try new designs without fear of losing their jobs or money.

2. *Diagnosing the Work System.* This step includes analyzing the work system to discover how it is operating. Knowledge of existing operations (or of intended

operations, in the case of a new work system) is the basis for creating an appropriate work design. STS practitioners have devised diagnostic models applicable to work systems that make products or deliver services. The models analyze a system's technical and social parts and assess how well the two fit each other. The task environment facing the system also is analyzed to see how well it is meeting external demands, such as customer quality requirements.

3. ***Generating Appropriate Designs.*** Based on the diagnosis, the work system is redesigned to fit the situation. Although this typically results in self-managed work teams, it is important to emphasize that the diagnosis may reveal that tasks are not very interdependent and that an individual-job work design, such as an enriched job, might be more appropriate. Two important STS principles guide the design process.

   The first principle, *compatibility,* suggests that the process of designing work should fit the values and objectives underlying the approach. For example, the major goals of STS design are joint optimization and boundary management. A work-design process compatible with those objectives would be highly participative, involving those having a stake in the work design, such as employees, managers, engineers, and staff experts. They would jointly decide how to create the social and technical components of work, as well as the environmental exchanges. This participative process increases the likelihood that design choices will be based simultaneously on technical, social, and environmental criteria. How well the compatibility guideline is adhered to can determine how well the work design subsequently is implemented.[43]

   The second design principle is called *minimal critical specification*. It suggests that STS designers should specify only those critical features needed to implement the work design. All other features of the design should be left free to vary with the circumstances. In most cases, minimal critical specification identifies what is to be done, not how it will be accomplished. This allows employees considerable freedom to choose work methods, task allocations, and job assignments to match changing conditions.

   The output of this design step specifies the new work design. In the case of self-managed teams, this includes the team's mission and goals, an ideal work flow, the skills and knowledge required of team members, a plan for training members to meet those requirements, and a list of the decisions the team will make now as well as the ones it should make over time as members develop greater skills and knowledge.

4. ***Specifying Support Systems.*** As suggested above, organizational support systems may have to be changed to support new work designs. When self-managed teams are designed, for example, the basis for pay and measurement systems may need to change from individual to team performance to facilitate necessary task interaction among workers.

5. ***Implementing and Evaluating the Work Designs.*** This stage involves making necessary changes to implement the work design and evaluating the results. For self-managing teams, implementation generally requires a great amount of training so that workers gain the necessary technical and social skills to perform multiple tasks and to control task behaviors. It also may entail developing the team through various team-building and process-consultation activities. OD consultants often help team members carry out these tasks with a major emphasis on helping them gain competence in this area. Evaluation of the work design is necessary both to guide the implementation process and to assess the overall effectiveness of the design. In some cases, the evaluation information suggests the need for further diagnosis and redesign efforts.

6. ***Continual Change and Improvement.*** This last step points out that STS design-ing never is complete but rather continues as new things are learned and new conditions are encountered. Thus, the ability to design and redesign work con-tinually needs to be built into existing work designs. Members must have the skills and knowledge to assess their work unit continually and to make neces-sary changes and improvements. From this view, STS designing rarely results in a stable work design but instead provides a process for modifying work contin-ually to fit changing conditions and to make performance improvements.

Application 16.2 describes how one of ASEA Brown Boveri's plants implemented self-managed teams.[44] It clearly demonstrates the importance of aligning the sys-tems to support self-management as well as the process of gradually increasing the team's autonomy and responsibility.

Results of Self-Managed Teams

Research on STS design efforts is extensive. For example, a 1994 bibliography by re-searchers at Eindhoven University of Technology in The Netherlands found 3,082 English-language studies.[45] As with reports on job enrichment, most of the pub-lished reports on self-managed teams show favorable results.[46]

A series of famous case studies at General Foods' Gaines Pet Food/Topeka plant, the Saab-Scania engine assembly plant, and Volvo's Kalmar and Uddevalla plants provide one set of positive findings. The Gaines Pet Food plant operated at an over-head rate that was 33% below that of traditional plants.[47] It reported annual vari-able cost savings of $600,000, one of the best safety records in the company, turnover rates far below average, and high levels of job satisfaction. A long-term, external evaluation of the groups at the Gaines plant attributed savings related to work innovation at about $1 million a year, and despite a variety of problems, pro-ductivity increased in every year but one over a decade of operation.[48] The plant has maintained one of the highest product quality ratings at General Foods since its opening.

Extensive research on self-managing groups has been done by Saab-Scania.[49] The first group was established in 1969, and 4 years later there were 130 produc-tion groups. These groups have generally shown improvements in production and employee attitudes and decreases in unplanned work stoppages and turnover rates. It is interesting that workers from the United States who have visited Saab's engine assembly plant reported that work was too fast and that lunch breaks were too short.[50] A Saab executive commented that the visitors had not stayed long enough to understand the design fully, causing their complaint that the pace was too fast.

The widely publicized use of self-managing groups at Volvo's automotive plant in Kalmar, Sweden, also has shown positive results.[51] The Kalmar factory opened in July 1974 and by the following year it was operating at 100% efficiency. As a refer-ence point, highly productive automobile plants normally operate at about 80% of engineering standards. Interviews with workers and union officials indicated that the quality of work life was considerably better than in assembly jobs that they had held in the past. Volvo's Uddevalla plant also reported significant quality improve-ments and higher productivity than comparable plants.[52]

A second set of studies supporting the positive impact of sociotechnical design teams comes from research comparing self-managed teams with other interventions. For example, probably one of the most thorough assessments of self-managing groups is a longitudinal study conducted in a midwestern U.S. food-processing plant.[53] Self-managed groups were created as part of an overall revamping of a

MOVING TO SELF-MANAGED TEAMS AT ABB

The ASEA Brown Boveri (ABB) Industrial Systems plant in Columbus, Ohio, was part of ABB's Industrial and Building Systems division. It produced low-volume, made-to-order industrial process and quality control systems. A single system included mechanical and hydraulic machinery, high-speed computer processors, and high-speed/high-accuracy measurement sensors that incorporated infrared, microwave, and other optical technologies packaged for severe environments. Customers for these control systems included the pulp and paper, chemical, petrochemical, pharmaceutical, metals, textiles, and food industries.

Overall demand for industrial control systems expanded steadily during the 1980s. But in 1990, demand dropped sharply and competition from international manufacturers increased. Ken Morris became vice president of manufacturing at the Columbus plant in 1991. Unfortunately, Morris arrived at a time when the manufacturing performance at the Columbus plant had not kept pace with the global market. Overhead costs above industry averages and low quality of suppliers' products combined to produce a net loss for 4 straight years. Morris recognized another sign of trouble when he repeatedly observed employees from different departments meeting separately with the same customers and not communicating with the other departments about the discussions they had with their mutual customers. "We had a silo-based organization. No one knew what the other was doing," Morris explained.

Based on this and other information, Morris's original idea was to create more flexibility for employees to work with customers and suppliers. "I had done a lot of reading about teams," he said, "and I knew that a lot of folks in the industry were talking about moving to total quality management or teams over the next few years. But I wasn't interested in teaming for teaming's sake. Whatever we did had to keep us alive, and I didn't have years to do it. I had to do something now." Morris laid out a change plan that would radically reshape the structure and systems that governed the Columbus plant. At the center of the reorganization was the concept of the high-performance work system. Eventually, 19 teams—12 production process teams and 7 continuous improvement teams—would be the fundamental work units of the 186-employee plant.

ABB's move to a high-performance, team-based work system proceeded in a stepwise fashion, each step building on the previous one. Morris began the effort by preparing both his leadership team and the plant's employees for the coming changes. An off-site meeting was used to educate members of his leadership staff on the basics of team-based organizations and to gain their ownership in the plant's new direction. One output of the retreat was the formation of a "high-performance work system" design team that worked for 6 months to create a change plan. Another important output was the new mission for the ABB Columbus plant: "To become recognized as the best time-based competitor in the world" by developing a customer-focused environment with a passion for process management and waste reduction, and a desire to unleash the power of people. Morris also began to hold quarterly meetings with all plant employees and to share information with them about competitors, the industry, planning, and financial conditions. For most employees, the inaugural quarterly meeting was the first time they had heard that the plant was operating at a loss.

Implementing the high-performance work system at ABB Columbus was formally initiated by adopting a set of industry benchmarks for products and processes in 1991. These quality measurements became the first goals for the plant's production system. In this way, Morris and his team hoped to get the manufacturing and supply processes under control. Implementation continued with technical changes in the work flow, including adoption of a just-in-time production process and installation of a new, fully integrated management information system. These changes dramatically increased the interdependency between steps in the work flow. The organization structure was changed from functional silos to a process-based structure in November 1993.

As the structure evolved, ABB emphasized training as a key to its success. "Education and training shifted us to the paradigm we wanted. Without that investment, we would have only seen incremental improvements," said Morris. "The quantum improvements we achieved were possible because we created a new vision of what was possible and then taught ourselves how to achieve it." Every ABB employee participated in a rigorous program of high-performance work systems, just-in-time manufacturing systems, conflict resolution, and ISO 9000 standards and processes. As noted by human resources internal consultant Mari Jo Cary, "The high-performance work system created a business environment to produce a quality product and on-time delivery at the right price for our customers." Plant employees continued to spend 4.5% of their time on training and education. These preparatory changes allowed for establishing the first process teams and process improvement teams following the restructuring.

The movement toward a team-based organization was slow and frustrating. The changes came at a time of falling production that increased unit costs and of rising turnover at all levels of the organization. Furthermore, negative attitudes toward teams surfaced in the 1992 employee survey. Employee complaints continued to rise about the frequency of meetings, team goals that seemed unreachable, and the time it took to operate as a team.

The 12 process teams were formed around three key product lines and five support processes, such as supply management, engineering, metal fabrication, traffic management, and financial and human resources support. Each team consisted of 6 to 15 members who, in addition to their manufacturing responsibilities, could serve as a coordinator for one of the seven team functions: time management, quality, safety, just-in-time processes, supply management, communications, and continuous improvement. Each team was chartered by its process owner—a senior-level manager for that product line who was responsible for two or three teams. Each charter described the team's purpose and vision, the roles and responsibilities of team members, processes for selection and dismissal, and norms of team member behavior.

While the production and support process teams were charged with meeting the benchmark standards for cycle time, quality, and cost, the seven process improvement teams worked to enhance efficiency and effectiveness within and across the production process teams. For example, a supply management process improvement team initiated a supplier excellence certification process. Each supplier was rated on a "report card." Those who didn't rate well were eliminated from the list of eligible suppliers; those who rated well received contracts. Eventually, continuous improvement in the supply management process led to elimination of all inspections of incoming material, the direct delivery of supplies to the point of use rather than into inventory, the elimination of a 115,000-square-foot storage facility, and the creation of a planner/supply management expert role for each production process team.

A key feature of ABB's transition to a fully self-managed team environment was the teams' gradual adoption of more and more responsibility and decision-making authority. ABB developed 24 "points of implementation," outlining responsibilities common to all teams. These 24 key team functions ranged from simple tasks (for example, housekeeping, equipment maintenance, and control of scrap material), to more difficult functions (for example, vacation scheduling, control of materials and inventory, and job design), to advanced team functions (for example, conflict resolution, selection of new members, and, ultimately, compensation decisions). Initially, all teams were assigned a low level of accountability and empowerment

(level 1) for each of the 24 points. At that stage, the team had little ownership for the function. Although the process owner worked with the team, accountability for team behaviors rested with that owner. Higher levels of empowerment increased the amounts of responsibility, authority, and accountability over key functions. At level 4, the team developed and implemented plans without review, and team accountability rested with team members. Boundary management and compensation decisions were shared with the process owner.

To reach the highest level of autonomy and accountability (level 4), a team first had to be introduced to the meaning and concept of the particular function. The team's next step was to take the function and create a plan to implement and perform ongoing management of that function. The third step was to demonstrate that it had the ability to implement the plan and manage the function without assistance. As the final step in becoming accountable for a function, the process owner signified that the team was fully empowered for future actions within this function. These points of implementation laid out a clear road map for each team and provided it with clear boundaries regarding its level of autonomy, responsibility, and accountability.

By 1995, each team was completely self-managed. All functions traditionally conducted by a manager or team leader were handled by the team. Teams answered directly to their process owner and customers, and in 1996 began conducting their own performance evaluations using a 360-degree process. When the teams required knowledge or skills outside of their existing capabilities, they called upon subject-matter experts within the plant who provided support in such areas as order management, price/cost quoting, material sourcing and control, production, inventory control, product quality, packing, and invoicing.

The results of ABB's effort were impressive. By 1994, the Columbus plant had achieved the following performance improvements:

- Warranty costs had been reduced by 74%.
- Revenue generated per person was up 212%.
- Work-in-progress turnover was up 222%.
- Total cycle time had been reduced from 16.2 weeks to 4.3 weeks, a 73% reduction.
- Seven managers and 25 supervisors had been replaced with five process owners.

By 1995, the Columbus plant had posted a profit for the first time since 1990, and all key financial and performance objectives were met or exceeded. In addition, its 95.3% on-time-to-customer rating was recognized as a best-in-class benchmark, and the plant was named among Industry Week's top 10 plants.

major part of the plant's production facilities. The effects of the intervention were extremely positive. One year after start-up, production was 133% higher than originally planned, while start-up costs were 7.7% lower than expected. Fewer workers were needed to operate the plant than engineers had projected, with an annual savings in fixed-labor expense of $264,000. Employee attitudes were extremely positive toward the group design. These positive effects did not result solely from the self-managing design, however. The intervention also included survey feedback for diagnostic purposes and changes in technology, the physical work setting, and management. These kinds of changes, common in self-managing group projects, facilitate the development of self-managed teams.

This study also permitted a comparison of self-managing groups with job enrichment, which occurred in another department of the company. Both interventions included survey feedback. The self-managing project involved technological changes, whereas the job enrichment program did not. The results showed that the interventions had similar positive effects in terms of employee attitudes, but only the self-managing project had significant improvements in productivity and costs. Again, the productivity improvements cannot be attributed solely to the self-managed teams but also were the result of the technological changes.

More recently, a rigorous field experiment in a telecommunications company compared self-managed teams with traditionally designed work groups performing the same types of tasks. The study found significant differences between the two groups in job satisfaction, growth-needs satisfaction, social-needs satisfaction, and group satisfaction. Self-managing group members and higher-level managers perceived group performance as superior to traditionally managed groups. In contrast to these overall findings, however, objective measures of service quality and customer satisfaction did not differ between the two types of groups.[54]

A third set of positive results comes from reviews, or meta-analyses, of other studies. One review examined 16 studies and showed that when productivity, costs, and quality were measured, improvements occurred in more than 85% of the cases.[55] Significant reductions in employee turnover and absenteeism rates and improvements in employee attitudes were reported in about 70% of the cases where these variables were measured. Certain methodological weaknesses in the studies suggest, however, that the positive results should be viewed carefully. Another review of 12 studies of self-managed groups showed improvements in hard performance measures in about 67% of the cases where such measures were taken.[56] Both of these reviews also included job enrichment studies, as reported earlier in this chapter. The relative impact of self-managing groups seems about equal to that of job enrichment, especially when the latter includes worker participation in the design process.

Three more recent meta-analyses also provide general support for self-managed teams. In a review of all STS work design studies conducted in the 1970s, researchers found a strong positive relationship between the installation of self-managed teams and attitudinal and economic gains.[57] These designs were found to increase employee satisfaction; to reduce production costs through group member innovations; and to decrease absenteeism, turnover, and accident rates. The researchers reported little evidence for claims of increased productivity primarily because of the lack of sufficient reported data. In a technical and comprehensive meta-analysis, researchers concluded that self-managed teams do produce increases in productivity and reductions in escape behavior, such as absenteeism, but that these effects varied widely. Higher results were associated with high levels of work-group autonomy, supporting changes in the reward system, interventions that did not include technological changes, and applications outside of the United States.[58]

Finally, a detailed and comprehensive meta-analysis of 131 North American field experiments reported that work innovations, such as autonomous and semiautonomous work groups, were more likely to have a positive impact on financial-performance measures, including costs, productivity, and quality, than were behavioral or attitudinal variables.[59] Considerable variation in the size of the positive effect, however, led the researchers to suggest that organization change was risky. Only when other organizational features such as reward systems, information systems, and performance appraisal systems changed simultaneously was the probability of positive results increased.

Although the majority of studies report positive effects of self-managing groups, some research suggests a more mixed assessment. A field experiment studying the long-term effects of self-managed groups showed improvements in job satisfaction but no effects on job motivation, work performance, organizational commitment, mental health, or voluntary turnover.[60] The company did lower indirect overhead costs, however, by reducing the number of supervisors. This study, which received an award from the Academy of Management for quality research, concluded that the major benefits of self-managed teams are economic, deriving from the need for less supervision. Another study found that the introduction of self-managed teams into an independent insurance agency threatened the personal control and autonomy of individual employees.[61] The groups that were implemented without employee participation exerted strong pressures to follow rigid procedures. Group leaders focused on the concerns of younger, inexperienced employees and ignored older workers' requests for less red tape and more freedom. The older employees felt that the groups undermined their individual discretion, autonomy, and initiative. The study concluded that unless self-managed teams are implemented and managed properly, individual members' autonomy and motivation can be constrained inadvertently.

DESIGNING WORK FOR TECHNICAL AND PERSONAL NEEDS

This chapter has described three approaches to work design: engineering, motivational, and sociotechnical. Trade-offs and conflicts among the approaches must be recognized. The engineering approach produces traditional jobs and work groups and focuses on efficient performance. It downplays employee needs and emphasizes economic outcomes. The motivational approach designs jobs that are stimulating and demanding and highlights the importance of employee need satisfaction. Research suggests, however, that increased satisfaction may not generate improvements in productivity. Finally, the sociotechnical systems approach integrates social and technical aspects, but it has not produced consistent research results on its success. In this final section, we attempt to integrate the three perspectives by providing a contingency framework that suggests that any of the three approaches can be effective when applied in the appropriate circumstances. Work design involves creating jobs and work groups for high levels of employee satisfaction and productivity. A large body of research shows that achieving such results depends on designing work to match specific factors operating in the work setting, factors that involve the technology for producing goods and services and the personal needs of employees. When work is designed to fit or match these factors, it is most likely to be both productive and humanly satisfying.

The technical and personal factors affecting work design success provide a contingency framework for choosing among the four different kinds of work designs discussed in the chapter: traditional jobs, traditional work groups, enriched jobs, and self-managed teams.

Technical Factors

Two key dimensions can affect change on the shop floor: technical interdependence, or the extent to which cooperation among workers is required to produce a product or service; and technical uncertainty, or the amount of information processing and decision making employees must do to complete a task.[62] In general, the *degree of technical interdependence* determines whether work should be designed for individual jobs or for work groups. When interdependence is low and there is little need for worker cooperation—as, for example, in field sales and data entry—work can be designed for individual jobs. Conversely, when interdependence is high and employees must cooperate—as in production processes like coal mining, assembly lines, and writing software—work should be designed for groups composed of people performing interacting tasks.

The second dimension, *technical uncertainty,* determines whether work should be designed for external forms of control, such as supervision, scheduling, or standardization, or for worker self-control. When technical uncertainty is low and little information has to be processed by employees, work can be designed for external control, such as might be found on assembly lines and in other forms of repetitive work. On the other hand, when technical uncertainty is high and people must process information and make decisions, work should be designed for high levels of employee self-control, such as might be found in professional work and troubleshooting tasks.

Figure 16.4 shows the different types of work designs that are most effective, from a purely technical perspective, for different combinations of interdependence and uncertainty. In quadrant 1, where technical interdependence and uncertainty are both low, such as might be found in data entry, jobs should be designed traditionally with limited amounts of employee interaction and self-control. When task interdependence is high but uncertainty is low (quadrant 2), such as work occurring on assembly lines, work should be designed for traditional work groups in which employee interaction is scheduled and self-control is limited. In quadrant 3, where technical interdependence is low but uncertainty is high, such as in field

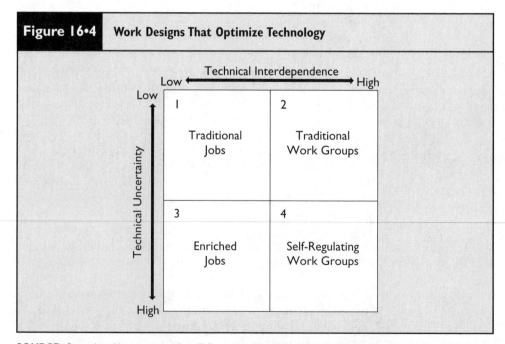

Figure 16•4   **Work Designs That Optimize Technology**

Technical Interdependence

Low ← → High

Technical Uncertainty — Low / High

1	2
Traditional Jobs	Traditional Work Groups
3	4
Enriched Jobs	Self-Regulating Work Groups

SOURCE: Reproduced by permission from T. Cummings, "Designing Work for Productivity and Quality of Work Life," *Outlook* 6 (1982): 39.

sales, work should be structured for individual jobs with internal forms of control, such as in enriched jobs. Finally, when both technical interdependence and uncertainty are high (quadrant 4), such as might be found in a continuous-process chemical plant, work should be designed for self-managed teams in which members have the multiple skills, discretion, and information necessary to control their interactions around the shared tasks.

Personal-Need Factors

Most of the research identifying individual differences in work design has focused on selected personal traits. Two types of personal needs can influence the kinds of work designs that are most effective: social needs, or the desire for significant social relationships; and growth needs, or the desire for personal accomplishment, learning, and development.[63] In general, the degree of *social needs* determines whether work should be designed for individual jobs or work groups. People with low needs for social relationships are more likely to be satisfied working on individualized jobs than in interacting groups. Conversely, people with high social needs are more likely to be attracted to group forms of work than to individualized forms.

The second individual difference, *growth needs*, determines whether work designs should be routine and repetitive or complex and challenging. People with low growth needs generally are not attracted to jobs offering complexity and challenge (that is, enriched jobs) but are more satisfied performing routine forms of work that do not require high levels of decision making. On the other hand, people with high growth needs are satisfied with work offering high levels of discretion, skill variety, and meaningful feedback. Performing enriched jobs allows them to experience personal accomplishment and development.

It is often difficult for OD practitioners to accept that some people have low social and growth needs, particularly in light of the social and growth values underlying much OD practice. It is important to recognize, however, that individual differences do exist. Assuming that all people have high growth needs or want high levels of social interaction can lead to inappropriate work designs. For example, a new manager of a clerical support unit was astonished to find six members using typewriters, even though a significant portion of the work consisted of retyping memos and reports that were produced frequently but changed very little from month to month. In addition, the unit had a terrible record of quality and on-time production. The manager quickly ordered new word processors and redesigned the work flow to increase interaction among members. Worker satisfaction declined, interpersonal conflicts increased, and work quality and on-time performance remained poor. An assessment of the effort revealed that all six of the staff members had low growth needs and low needs for inclusion in group efforts. In the words of one worker, "All I want is to come into work, do my job, and get my paycheck."

It is important to emphasize that people who have low growth or social needs are not inferior to those placing a higher value on those factors; they simply are different. It is necessary also to recognize that people can change their needs through personal growth and experience. OD practitioners must be sensitive to individual differences in work design and careful not to force their own values on others. Many consultants, eager to be seen on the cutting edge of practice, recommend self-managed teams in all situations, without careful attention to technological and personal considerations.

Figure 16.5 (on page 354) shows the different types of work designs that are most effective for the various combinations of social and growth needs. When employees have relatively low social and growth needs (quadrant 1), traditional jobs are most effective. In quadrant 2, where employees have high social needs but low growth needs, traditional work groups, such as might be found on an assembly line,

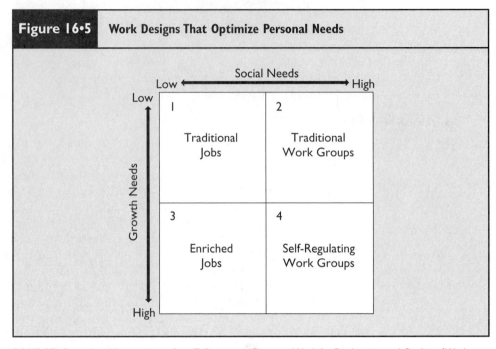

Figure 16•5   Work Designs That Optimize Personal Needs

SOURCE: Reproduced by permission from T. Cummings, "Designing Work for Productivity and Quality of Work Life," *Outlook* 6 (1982): 40.

are most appropriate. These allow for some social interaction but limited amounts of challenge and discretion. When employees have low social needs but high growth needs (quadrant 3), enriched jobs are most satisfying. Here, work is designed for individual jobs that have high levels of task variety, discretion, and feedback about results. A research scientist's job is likely to be enriched, as is that of a skilled craftsperson. Finally, in quadrant 4, where employees have high social and growth needs, work should be designed for self-managed teams that offer significant social interaction around complex and challenging tasks. A team of astronauts in a space shuttle resembles a self-managed work group, as does a group managing the control room of an oil refinery or a group of nurses in a hospital unit.

Meeting Both Technical and Personal Needs

Jointly satisfying technical and human needs to achieve work-design success is likely to occur only in limited circumstances. When the technical conditions of a company's production processes (as shown in Figure 16.4) are compatible with the personal needs of its employees (as shown in Figure 16.5), the respective work designs combine readily and can satisfy both. On General Motors' assembly lines, for example, the technology is highly interdependent but low in uncertainty (quadrant 2 in Figure 16.4). Much of the production is designed around traditional work groups in which task behaviors are standardized and interactions among workers are scheduled. Such work is likely to be productive and fulfilling to the extent that General Motors' production workers have high social needs and low growth needs (quadrant 2 in Figure 16.5).

When technology and people are incompatible—for example, when an organization has quadrant 1 technology and quadrant 4 worker needs—at least two kinds of changes can be made to design work that satisfies both requirements.[64] One strategy is to change technology or people to bring them more into line with each other. This is a key point underlying sociotechnical systems approaches. For example, technical interdependence can be reduced by breaking long assembly lines into more discrete groups. In Sweden, Volvo redesigned the physical layout and technology for assembling automobiles and trucks to promote self-managed teams. Modifying people's needs is more complex and begins by matching new or existing workers to available work designs. For example, companies can assess workers' needs through standardized paper-and-pencil tests and use the information gleaned from them to counsel employees and help them locate jobs compatible with their needs. Similarly, employees can be allowed to volunteer for specific work designs—a common practice in STS projects. This matching process is likely to require high levels of trust and cooperation between management and workers, as well as a shared commitment to designing work for high performance and employee satisfaction.

A second strategy for accommodating both technical and human requirements is to leave the two components unchanged and create compromise work designs that only partially fulfill the demands of either component. The key issue is to decide to what extent one contingency will be satisfied at the expense of the other. For example, when capital costs are high relative to labor costs, such as in highly automated plants, work design is likely to favor the technology. Conversely, in many service jobs where labor is expensive relative to capital, organizations may design work for employee motivation and satisfaction at the risk of shortchanging their technology. These examples suggest a range of possible compromises based on different weightings of technical and human demands. Careful assessment of both types of contingencies and of the cost–benefit trade-offs is necessary to design an appropriate compromise work design.

Clearly, the strategy of designing work to bring technology and people more into line with each other is preferable to the compromise work design strategy. Although the latter approach seems necessary when there are heavy constraints on changing the contingencies, in many cases those constraints are more imagined than real. The important thing is to understand the technical and personal factors existing in a particular situation and to design work accordingly. Traditional jobs and traditional work groups will be successful in certain situations (as shown in Figures 16.4 and 16.5); in other settings, enriched jobs and self-managed teams will be more effective.

◼ SUMMARY

In this chapter, we discussed three different approaches to work design and described a contingency framework to determine the approach most likely to result in high productivity and worker satisfaction. The contingency framework reconciles the strengths and weaknesses of each approach. The engineering approach produces traditional jobs and traditional work groups. Traditional jobs are highly simplified and involve routine and repetitive forms of work, rather than coordination among people to produce a product or service. Traditional jobs achieve high productivity and worker satisfaction in situations characterized by low technical uncertainty and interdependence and low growth and social needs.

Traditional work groups are composed of members who perform routine yet interrelated tasks. Member interactions are controlled externally, usually by rigid work flows, schedules, and supervisors. Traditional work groups are best suited to conditions of low technical uncertainty but high technical interdependence. They fit people with low growth needs but high social needs.

The motivational approach produces enriched jobs involving high levels of skill variety, task identity, task significance, autonomy, and feedback from the work itself. Enriched jobs achieve good results when the technology is uncertain but does not require high levels of coordination and when employees have high growth needs and low social needs.

Finally, the sociotechnical systems approach is associated with self-managed teams. These groups are composed of members performing interrelated tasks. Members are given the multiple skills, autonomy, and information necessary to control their own task behaviors with relatively little external control. Many OD practitioners argue that self-managed teams represent the work design of the 2000s because high levels of technical uncertainty and interdependence are prevalent in today's workplaces and because today's workers often have high growth and social needs.

■ NOTES

1. F. Taylor, *The Principles of Scientific Management* (New York: Harper & Row, 1911).

2. Ibid.

3. T. Cummings, "Self-Regulating Work Groups: A Socio-Technical Synthesis," *Academy of Management Review* 3 (1978): 625–34; G. Susman, *Autonomy at Work* (New York: Praeger, 1976); J. Slocum and H. Sims, "A Typology of Technology and Job Redesign," *Human Relations* 33 (1983): 193–212.

4. F. Herzberg, B. Mausner, and B. Snyderman, *The Motivation to Work* (New York: John Wiley & Sons, 1959); F. Herzberg, "The Wise Old Turk," *Harvard Business Review* 52 (September-October 1974): 70–80; F. Herzberg and Z. Zautra, "Orthodox Job Enrichment: Measuring True Quality in Job Satisfaction," *Personnel* 53 (September-October 1976): 54–68.

5. M. Myers, *Every Employee a Manager* (New York: McGraw-Hill, 1970); R. Ford, *Motivation Through the Work Itself* (New York: American Management Association, 1969); W. Paul, K. Robertson, and F. Herzberg, "Job Enrichment Pays Off," *Harvard Business Review* 45 (March-April 1969): 61–78.

6. J. Hackman and G. Oldham, *Work Redesign* (Reading, Mass.: Addison-Wesley, 1980).

7. A. Turner and P. Lawrence, *Industrial Jobs and the Worker* (Cambridge: Harvard Graduate School of Business Administration, Division of Research, 1965); J. Hackman and G. Oldham, "Development of the Job Diagnostic Survey," *Journal of Applied Psychology* 60 (April 1975): 159–70; H. Sims, A. Szilagyi, and R. Keller, "The Measurement of Job Characteristics," *Academy of Management Journal* 19 (1976): 195–212.

8. Hackman and Oldham, *Work Redesign*; J. Hackman, G. Oldham, R. Janson, and K. Purdy, "A New Strategy for Job Enrichment," *California Management Review* 17 (Summer 1975): 57–71; R. Walters, *Job Enrichment for Results: Strategies for Successful Implementation* (Reading, Mass.: Addison-Wesley, 1975); J. Hackman, "Work Design," in *Improving Life at Work: Behavioral Science Approaches to Organizational Change*, eds. J. Hackman and L. L. Suttle (Santa Monica, Calif.: Goodyear, 1977), 96–163.

9. J. Hackman and G. Oldham, *The Diagnostic Survey: An Instrument for the Diagnosis of Jobs and the Evaluation of Job Redesign Projects*, Technical Report No. 4 (New Haven, Conn.: Yale University, Department of Administrative Sciences, 1974); Sims, Szilagyi, and Keller, "Measurement"; M. Campion, "The Multimethod Job Design Questionnaire," *Psychological Documents* 15 (1985): 1; J. Idaszak and F. Drasgow, "A Revision of the Job Diagnostic Survey: Elimination of a Measurement Artifact," *Journal of Applied Psychology* 72 (1987): 69–74.

10. E. Huse and M. Beer, "Eclectic Approach to Organizational Development," *Harvard Business Review* 49 (September-October 1971): 103–12.

11. A. Armenakis and H. Field, "Evaluation of Organizational Change Using Nonindependent Criterion Measures," *Personnel Psychology* 28 (Spring 1975): 39–44.

12. R. Ford, "Job Enrichment Lessons from AT&T," *Harvard Business Review* 51 (January-February 1973): 96–106.

13. R. Henkoff, "Make Your Office More Productive," *Fortune* (25 February 1991): 84.

14. Hackman et al., "New Strategy."

15. I. Seeborg, "The Influence of Employee Participation in Job Redesign," *Journal of Applied Behavioral Science* 14 (1978): 87–98.

16. G. Oldham and J. Hackman, "Work Design in the Organizational Context," in *Research in Organizational Behavior*, vol. 2, eds. B. Staw and L. Cummings (Greenwich, Conn.: JAI Press, 1980), 247–78; J. Cordery and T. Wall, "Work Design and Supervisory Practice: A Model," *Human Relations* 38 (1985): 425–41.

17. Hackman and Oldham, *Work Redesign*.

18. Ibid.

19. M. Campion, "Interdisciplinary Approaches to Job Design: A Constructive Replication with Extensions," *Journal of Applied Psychology* 73 (1988): 467–81.

20. C. Kulik, G. Oldham, and P. Langner, "Measurement of Job Characteristics: Comparison of the Original and the Revised Job Diagnostic Survey," *Journal of Applied Psychology* 73 (1988): 426–66; Idaszak and Drasgow, "Revision of the Job Diagnostic Survey."

21. R. Steers and D. Spencer, "The Role of Achievement Motivation in Job Design," *Journal of Applied Psychology* 62 (1977): 472–79; J. Champoux, "A Three-Sample Test of Some Extensions to the Job Characteristics Model," *Academy of Management Journal* 23 (1980): 466–78; R. Katz, "The Influence of Job Longevity on Employee Reactions to Task Characteristics," *Human Relations* 31 (1978): 703–25.

22. R. Zeffane, "Correlates of Job Satisfaction and Their Implications for Work Redesign," *Public Personnel Management* 23 (1994): 61–76.

23. G. Oldham and Y. Fried, "Employee Reactions to Workspace Characteristics," *Journal of Applied Psychology* 72 (1987): 75–80.

24. B. Loher, R. Noe, N. Moeller, and M. Fitzgerald, "A Meta-Analysis of the Relation of Job Characteristics to Job Satisfaction," *Journal of Applied Psychology* 70 (1985): 280–89.

25. B. McEvoy and W. Cascio, "Strategies for Reducing Employee Turnover: A Meta-Analysis," *Journal of Applied Psychology* 70 (1985): 342–53.

26. T. Cummings and E. Molloy, *Improving Productivity and the Quality of Work Life* (New York: Praeger, 1977).

27. J. Nicholas, "The Comparative Impact of Organization Development Interventions on Hard Criteria Measures," *Academy of Management Review* 7 (1982): 531–42.

28. Y. Fried and G. Ferris, "The Validity of the Job Characteristics Model: A Review and Meta-Analysis," *Personnel Psychology* 40 (1987): 287–322.

29. E. Trist, B. Higgin, H. Murray, and A. Pollock, *Organizational Choice* (London: Tavistock, 1963); T. Cummings and S. Srivastva, *Management of Work: A Socio-Technical Systems Approach* (San Diego: University Associates, 1977); A. Cherns, "Principles of Sociotechnical Design Revisited," *Human Relations* 40 (1987): 153–62.

30. Cummings, "Self-Regulating Work Groups"; J. Hackman, *The Design of Self-Managing Work Groups*, Technical Report No. 11 (New Haven, Conn.: Yale University, School of Organization and Management, 1976); Cummings and Srivastva, *Management of Work*; Susman, *Autonomy at Work*; H. Sims and C. Manz, "Conversations within Self-Managed Work Groups," *National Productivity Review* 1 (Summer 1982): 261–69; T. Cummings, "Designing Effective Work Groups," in *Handbook of Organizational Design: Remodeling Organizations and Their Environments*, vol. 2, eds. P. C. Nystrom and W. H. Starbuck (New York: Oxford University Press, 1981), 250–71.

31. C. Manz, "Beyond Self-Managing Teams: Toward Self-Leading Teams in the Workplace," in *Research in Organizational Change and Development*, vol. 4, eds. W. Pasmore and R. Woodman (Greenwich, Conn.: JAI Press, 1990), 273–99; C. Manz and H. Sims Jr., "Leading Workers to Lead Themselves: The External Leadership of Self-Managed Work Teams," *Administrative Science Quarterly* 32 (1987): 106–28.

32. E. Lawler, *Organizing for High Performance: Employee Involvement, TQM, Re-engineering, and Knowledge Management in the Fortune 1000* (San Francisco: Jossey-Bass, 2001); E. Lawler, S. Mohrman, and G. Ledford, *Strategies for High-Performance Organizations* (San Francisco: Jossey-Bass, 1998).

33. B. Dumaine, "The Trouble with Teams," *Fortune* (5 September 1994): 86–92.

34. Cummings, "Self-Regulating Work Groups."

35. Cummings, "Self-Regulating Work Groups"; J. Pearce II and E. Ravlin, "The Design and Activation of Self-Regulating Work Groups," *Human Relations* 40 (1987): 751–82; J. R. Hackman, "The Design of Work Teams," in *Handbook of Organizational Behavior*, ed. J. Lorsch (Englewood Cliffs, N.J.: Prentice Hall, 1987), 315–42.

36. Ibid.

37. C. Manz and H. Sims, "The Leadership of Self-Managed Work Groups: A Social Learning Theory Perspective" (paper delivered at meeting of National Academy of Management, New York, August 1982); C. Manz and H. Sims Jr., "Searching for the 'Unleader': Organizational Member Views on Leading Self-Managed Groups," *Human Relations* 37 (1984): 409–24.

38. H. Mintzberg, *The Nature of Managerial Work* (New York: Harper & Row, 1973); L. Sayles, *Managerial Behavior: Administration in Complex Organizations* (New York: McGraw-Hill, 1964).

39. R. Walton and L. Schlesinger, "Do Supervisors Thrive in Participative Work Systems?" *Organizational Dynamics* 8 (Winter 1979): 25–38.

40. Ibid.

41. M. Weisbord, "Participative Work Design: A Personal Odyssey," *Organizational Dynamics* (1984): 5–20.

42. T. Cummings, "Socio-Technical Systems: An Intervention Strategy," in *New Techniques in Organization Development*, ed. W. Burke (New York: Basic Books, 1975), 228–49; Cummings and Srivastva, *Management of Work*; Cummings and Molloy, *Improving Productivity*.

43. Cherns, "Sociotechnical Design Revisited."

44. This application was submitted by Joseph Whittinghill of Rayner and Associates, Freeland, Washington.

45. F. van Eijnatten, S. Eggermont, G. de Goffau, and I. Mankoe, *The Socio-Technical Systems Design Paradigm*

(Eindhoven, The Netherlands: Eindhoven University of Technology, 1994).

46. P. Goodman, R. Devadas, and T. Hughson, "Groups and Productivity: Analyzing the Effectiveness of Self-Managing Teams," in *Productivity in Organizations*, eds. J. Campbell, R. Campbell, and associates (San Francisco: Jossey-Bass, 1988), 295–325.

47. R. Walton, "How to Counter Alienation in the Plant," *Harvard Business Review* 12 (November-December 1972): 70–81.

48. R. Schrank, "On Ending Worker Alienation: The Gaines Pet Food Plant," in *Humanizing the Workplace*, ed. R. Fairfield (Buffalo, N.Y.: Prometheus Books, 1974), 119–20, 126; R. Walton, "Teaching an Old Dog Food New Tricks," *Wharton Magazine* 4 (Winter 1978): 42; L. Ketchum, "Innovating Plant Managers Are Talking About. . ." (presentation at the International Conference on the Quality of Working Life, Toronto, August 30–September 3, 1981): 2–3; H. Simon et al., "General Foods Topeka: Ten Years Young" (presentation at the International Conference on the Quality of Working Life, Toronto, August 30–September 3, 1981): 5–7.

49. J. Norsted and S. Aguren, *The Saab-Scania Report* (Stockholm: Swedish Employer's Confederation, 1975).

50. "Doubting Sweden's Way," *Time* (10 March 1975): 40.

51. P. Gyllenhammèr, *People at Work* (Reading, Mass.: Addison-Wesley, 1977), 15–17, 43, 52–53; B. Jünsson, "Corporate Strategy for People at Work—The Volvo Experience" (presentation at the International Conference on the Quality of Working Life, Toronto, August 30–September 3, 1981); N. Tichy and J. Nisberg, "When Does Work Restructuring Work? Organizational Innovations at Volvo and GM," *Organizational Dynamics* 5 (Summer 1976): 73.

52. J. Kapstein and J. Hoerr, "Volvo's Radical New Plant: The Death of the Assembly Line?" *Business Week* (28 August 1989): 92–93.

53. W. Pasmore, "The Comparative Impacts of Sociotechnical System, Job-Redesign, and Survey-Feedback Interventions," in *Sociotechnical Systems: A Source Book*, eds. W. Pasmore and J. Sherwood (San Diego: University Associates, 1978), 291–300.

54. S. Cohen and G. Ledford Jr., "The Effectiveness of Self-Managing Teams: A Quasi-Experiment," *Human Relations* 47 (1994): 13–43.

55. Cummings and Molloy, *Improving Productivity*.

56. Nicholas, "Comparative Impact."

57. Pearce and Ravlin, "Design and Activation."

58. R. Beekun, "Assessing the Effectiveness of Sociotechnical Interventions: Antidote or Fad?" *Human Relations* 42 (1989): 877–97.

59. B. Macy, P. Bliese, and J. Norton, "Organizational Change and Work Innovation: A Meta-Analysis of 131 North American Field Experiments—1961–1990," in *Research in Organizational Change and Development*, vol. 7, eds. R. Woodman and W. Pasmore (Greenwich, Conn.: JAI Press, 1994).

60. T. Wall, N. Kemp, P. Jackson, and C. Clegg, "Outcomes of Autonomous Workgroups: A Long-Term Field Experiment," *Academy of Management Journal* 29 (June 1986): 280–304.

61. C. Manz and H. Angle, "Can Group Self-Management Mean a Loss of Personal Control: Triangulating a Paradox," *Group and Organization Studies* 11 (December 1986): 309–34.

62. T. Cummings, "Self-Regulating Work Groups"; Susman, *Autonomy at Work*; Slocum and Sims, "Typology of Technology"; M. Kiggundu, "Task Interdependence and Job Design: Test of a Theory," *Organizational Behavior and Human Performance* 31 (1983): 145–72.

63. Hackman and Oldham, *Work Redesign*; K. Brousseau, "Toward a Dynamic Model of Job–Person Relationships: Findings, Research Questions, and Implications for Work System Design," *Academy of Management Review* 8 (1983): 33–45; G. Graen, T. Scandura, and M. Graen, "A Field Experimental Test of the Moderating Effects of Growth Needs Strength on Productivity," *Journal of Applied Psychology* 71 (1986): 484–91.

64. T. Cummings, "Designing Work for Productivity and Quality of Work Life," *Outlook* 6 (1982): 35–39.

The Sullivan Hospital System

PART I

At the Sullivan Hospital System (SHS), CEO Donald Fulton expressed concern over market share losses to other local hospitals over the past 6 to 9 months and declines in patient satisfaction measures. To him and his senior administrators, the need to revise the SHS organization was clear. It was also clear that such a change would require the enthusiastic participation of all organizational members, including nurses, physicians, and managers.

At SHS, the senior team consisted of the top administrative teams from the two hospitals in the system. Fulton, CEO of the system and President of the larger of the two hospitals, was joined by Mary Fenton, President of the smaller hospital. Their two styles were considerably different. Whereas Fulton was calm, confident, and mild-mannered, Fenton was assertive, enthusiastic, and energetic. Despite these differences in style, both administrators demonstrated a willingness to lead the change effort. In addition, each of the direct reports was enthusiastic about initiating a change process and was clearly taking whatever initiative Fulton and Fenton would allow or empower them to do.

You were contacted by Donald Fulton to conduct a 3-day retreat with the combined management teams and kick off the change process. Based on conversations with administrators from other hospitals and industry conferences, the team believed that Total Quality Management (TQM) would be an appropriate intervention for two primary reasons. First, they believed that improving patient care would give physicians a good reason to use the hospital thus improving market share. Second, the primary regulatory body, the Joint Commission on Accreditation of Healthcare Organizations (JCAHO) had enacted policies some time ago encouraging hospitals to adopt continuous improvement principles. The team readily agreed that they lacked the adequate skills and knowledge associated with implementing a TQM process. This first meeting was to gather together to hear about the history of TQM and the issues that would need to be addressed if TQM were to be implemented. In addition, you guided them through several exercises get the team to examine methods of decision making, how teams solved problems using TQM processes, and to explore their understanding of the hospital's current mission, goals, and strategies.

Although you were concerned about starting the process with a workshop that explored a solution rather than understanding the problem, you remembered Roger Harrison's consulting rule, "Start where your client is at," and agreed to conduct the workshop. You were assured by Fulton that the hospital system was committed to making substantive changes and that this was only the first step. In addition, and in support of this commitment, Fulton tells you that he has already agreed in principle to begin a work redesign process in a few of the nursing units at each hospital and has begun to finalize a contract with a large consulting firm to do the work. The workshop was highly praised and you convinced the team to hold off long enough to conduct a diagnosis of the system.

Following the retreat, your diagnosis of the SHS organization employed a variety of data collection activities including interviews with senior managers from both hospitals as well as a sampling of middle managers and staff (for example, nurses, ancillary professionals, and environmental services providers). Questions about the hospital's mission garnered the most consensus and passion. There was almost unanimous commitment to the breadth of services provided and the values that played a prominent role in the delivery of those services by a Catholic-sponsored health care organization such as SHS. A mission and values statement was clearly posted throughout the hospital and many of the items in that statement were repeated almost verbatim in the interviews.

From there, however, answers about the organization's purpose and objectives became more diverse. With respect to goals and objectives, different stakeholder groups saw them differently. Senior administrators were fairly clear about the goals listed in the strategic plan. These goals included increasing measurements of patient satisfaction, decreasing the amount of overtime, and increasing market share. However, among middle managers and supervisors, there was little awareness of hospital goals or how people influenced their accomplishment. A question about the hospital's overall direction or how the goals were being achieved yielded a clear split in people's perceptions. Some believed the hospital achieved its objectives through its designation as the area's primary trauma center. They noted that if someone's life were in danger, the best chance of survival was to go to SHS. The problem, respondents joked, was that "after we save their life, we tend to forget about them." Many, however, held beliefs that could be labeled "low cost." That is, objectives were achieved by squeezing out every penny of cost no matter how that impacted patient care.

Opinions about the policies governing the hospital's operation supported a general belief that the organization was too centralized. People felt little empowerment to make decisions. There also were a number of financial policies that were seen as dictated from the corporate office, where "shared services" existed, including finance, marketing, information systems, and purchasing. Further, several policies limited a manager's ability to spend money, especially if it wasn't allocated in budgets.

In addition to the managerial sample, a variety of individual contributors and supervisors were interviewed either individually or in small groups to determine the status and characteristics of different organization design factors. The organization's policy and procedure manuals, annual reports, organization charts, and other archival information were also reviewed. This data collection effort revealed the following organization design features:

- *The hospitals' structures were more bureaucratic than organic.* Each hospital had a functional structure with a chief executive officer and from two to five direct reports. Both hospitals had directors of nursing services and professional services. The larger hospital had additional directors in special projects, pastoral care, and other staff functions that worked with both hospitals. Traditional staff functions, such as finance, procurement, human resources, and information services, were centralized at the corporate office. There were a number of formal policies regarding spending, patient care, and so on.

- *The basic work design of the hospitals could be characterized as traditional.* Tasks were narrowly defined (janitor, CCU nurse, admissions clerk, and so on). Further, despite the high levels of required interdependency and complexity involved in patient care, most jobs were individually based. That is, job descriptions detailed the skills, knowledge, and activities required of a particular position. Whenever any two departments needed to coordinate their activities, the work was controlled by standard operating procedures, formal paperwork, and tradition.

- *Information and control systems were old and inflexible.* From the staff's perspective, and to some extent even middle management's, little, if any, operational information (that is, about costs, productivity, or levels of patient satisfaction) was shared. Cost information in terms of budgeted versus actual spending was available to middle managers and their annual performance reviews were keyed to meeting budgeted targets. Unfortunately, managers knew the information in the system was grossly inaccurate. They felt helpless in affecting change, since the system was centralized in the corporate office. As a result, they devised elaborate methods for getting the "right" numbers from the system or duplicated the system by keeping their own records.

- *Human resource systems, also centralized in the corporate office, were relatively generic.* Internal job postings were updated weekly (there was a shortage of nurses at the time). There was little in the way of formal training opportunities beyond the required, technical educational requirements to maintain currency and certification. Reward systems consisted mainly of a merit-based pay system that awarded raises according to annual performance appraisal results. Raises over the previous few years, however, had not kept pace with inflation. There also were various informal recognition systems administered by individual managers.

Questions

1. Assemble the diagnostic data into a framework and prepare feedback to the senior administrators of the hospitals. What's your sense of the organization's current structure and employee involvement issues?

2. What changes would you recommend? Is a total quality management intervention appropriate here? What alternatives would you propose?

3. Design an implementation plan for your preferred intervention.

PART II

This diagnostic data was discussed and debated among the senior team. A steering committee composed of physicians, managers, nurses, and other leaders from both hospitals was convened and creating a vision for the system and the change effort became one of their first tasks.

The steering committee spent hours poring over vision statements from other organizations, discussing words and phrases that described what they thought would be an exciting outcome from interacting with the hospital, and trying to satisfy their own needs for something unique and creative. When the first draft of a statement emerged, they spent several months sharing and discussing it with a variety of stakeholders. To their dismay, the initial version was roundly rejected by almost everyone as boring, unimaginative, or unreal. The group discussed the input gathered during these discussions and set about the task of revising the vision. After several additional iterations and a lot of wordsmithing, a new and more powerful vision statement began to emerge. The centerpiece of the vision was the belief that the organization should work in such a way that the patient felt like they were the "center of attention." Such an orientation to the vision became a powerful rallying point since many of the hospitals' management teams readily understood that there was an existing perception of poor service that needed to be turned around.

The 3 months spent working and adapting the vision statement was well worth it. As it was presented to people in small meetings and workshops, each word and phrase took on special meaning to organizational members and generated commitment to change.

Questions

1. Critique SHS's visioning process.

2. What implications does the visioning process have for the intervention you want to implement? How can you take advantage of the process in your action plan?

City of Carlsbad, California
Restructuring the Public Works Department (A)

OVERVIEW

In 1995, the City of Carlsbad, California, an oceanfront community of about 75,000 people, was emerging from the worst recession in its history. In response to a call from the City Council and nationwide efforts to operate governments in a more businesslike manner, the City Manager led the organization through a comprehensive strategic planning process. Through highly participative methods, including focus groups and a large-group community visioning process, a new city mission and vision (Exhibit 1) and a set of values to guide decision making (Exhibit 2) were developed. In addition, several important strategic initiatives, including a new information system and a revised performance appraisal and incentive compensation process were started.

These strategic initiatives and the City Manager's assessment of the organization's design pointed to misalignments in the city's structure. He convened a small representative task force of managers to design a new structure. The result was a reorganization of the city into five major service areas (MSAs), such as community development, safety services (e.g., fire, police), and public works.

An evaluation of the entire strategic change effort suggested that a large majority of the internal

Exhibit 1	City of Carlsbad Mission and Vision Statement

Our mission is to provide top-quality services to our citizens and customers in a manner that enhances the quality of life for all who live, work, and play in Carlsbad.

and external stakeholders viewed the changes positively and believed that they had improved customer focus and employee commitment. The results also promised to reduce operating costs and to create an organization that could absorb the expected growth in demand for new and better services.

THE PUBLIC WORKS DEPARTMENT

The largest of the new MSAs, Public Works, consisted of six previously independent departments responsible for engineering services; parks, streets, facilities, and fleet maintenance; and a legally separate water district owned by the city (Exhibit 3). The new organization was expected to design, construct, and maintain the infrastructure for the growing city. The new Public Works Director was excited about the prospect of designing his new MSA according to the vi-

Exhibit 2	City of Carlsbad Values

We believe these values are important to achieve our desired future as employees for the City of Carlsbad. They are chosen freely, prized publicly, and acted upon again and again.

Integrity—An organization and workforce distinguished by sound moral and ethical character

Trust—A workplace characterized by widespread belief in the integrity, reliability, and ability of employees

Competence—A workplace characterized by employees who have the skills and training to do their jobs

Accountability—An environment characterized by employees who are willing to be responsible

Teamwork—A workplace that encourages the use of teams to accomplish organizational goals and objectives

Quality—An environment characterized by employees with passion for excellence

Empowerment—Employees who have the authority, responsibility and accountability to decide and act

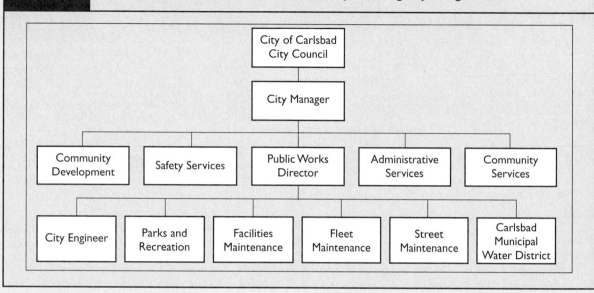

sion and values created by the city during its strategic change efforts. In line with those values, he saw the opportunity to implement the new design in participative and empowering ways, and he wanted to take advantage of the city's general plan that called for new buildings to house the engineering staff and the public works yard.

In consultation with an OD consultant, diagnostic interviews and focus groups with a variety of employees and other stakeholders were commissioned. The data can be summarized as follows:

- *Each of the previously independent departments had their own way of doing things.* They were suspicious of the reasons for the structural change. The water district employees were particularly cohesive.

- *Many of the work processes in each department were similar.* For example, the buildings, parks, and street departments each had equipment and work assignments involving the maintenance of restrooms, painting, landscaping, and light construction. The engineering department for the water district was largely redundant with the engineering department in the City, and the both the City and the water district owned several pieces of large and expensive equipment.

- *Each department had members with both long and short tenures.*

- *Most of the departments lacked formal goals and planning processes.*

- *The current Public Works Director was also acting as the City Engineer.*

- *The engineering department was anticipating an increased workload over the next 10 years as the City continued growing.* Conversely, workloads in the maintenance groups were expected to grow over time but lag the growth rates in engineering.

- *Almost all of the employees enjoyed working for the City of Carlsbad and intended to stay.*

Based on these data, the Public Works Director and the OD consultants worked together to understand the implications of the data and to design an action plan to describe and refine the new structure.

Questions:

1. What is your diagnosis of the situation in the Public Works Department?

2. How would you proceed from this point?

3. What interventions would you recommend and why?

4. For your preferred intervention, develop an action plan for implementation.

PART 5

Human Resources Management Interventions

Chapter 17   Performance Management

Chapter 18   Developing and Assisting Members

Selected Cases   Employee Benefits at
                           HealthCo
                        Sharpe BMW

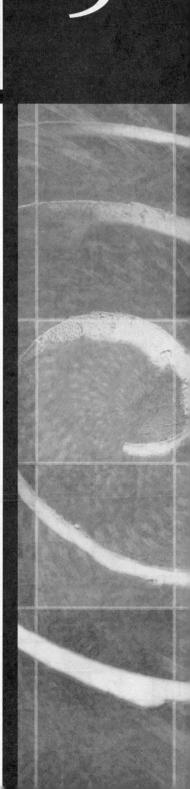

17

Performance Management

In this chapter, we discuss human resources management interventions concerned with managing individual and group performance. Performance management involves goal setting, performance appraisal, and reward systems that align member work behavior with business strategy, employee involvement, and workplace technology. Goal setting describes the interaction between managers and employees in jointly defining member work behaviors and outcomes. Orienting employees to the appropriate kinds of work outcomes can reinforce the work designs described in Chapter 16 and support the organization's strategic objectives. Goal setting can clarify the duties and responsibilities associated with a particular job or work group. When applied to jobs, goal setting can focus on individual goals and can reinforce individual contributions and work outcomes. When applied to work groups, it can be directed at group objectives and can reinforce members' joint actions and overall group outcomes. One popular and classic approach to goal setting is called management by objectives.

Performance appraisal involves collecting and disseminating performance data to improve work outcomes. It is the primary human resources management intervention for providing performance feedback to individuals and work groups. Performance appraisal is a systematic process of jointly assessing work-related achievements, strengths, and weaknesses. It also can facilitate career counseling, provide information about the strength and diversity of human resources in the company, and link employee performance with rewards.

Reward systems are concerned with eliciting and reinforcing desired behaviors and work outcomes. They can support goal setting and feedback systems by rewarding the kinds of behaviors required to implement a particular work design or support a business strategy. Like goal setting, rewards systems can be oriented to individual jobs and goals or to group functions and objectives. Moreover, they can be geared to traditional work designs that require external forms of control or to enriched, self-regulating designs that require employee self-control. Several innovative and effective reward systems are used in organizations today.

Performance management interventions traditionally are implemented by the human resources department within organizations, whose managers have special training in these areas. Because of the breadth and depth of knowledge required to carry out these kinds of change programs successfully, practitioners tend to specialize in one part of the human resources function, such as performance appraisal or compensation.

The interest in integrating human resources management with organization development continues unabated. In many companies, such as AG Communication Systems, BP, Microsoft, Intel, Colgate-Palmolive, and Johnson & Johnson, organization development is a separate function of the human resources department. As OD practitioners increasingly have become involved in organization design and employee involvement, they have realized the need to bring human resources practices more in line with the new designs and processes. Consequently, personnel specialists now frequently help initiate OD projects. For example, a large electronics firm expanded the role of compensation specialists to include initiation of work design projects. The compensation people at this firm, who traditionally were consulted by OD practitioners *after* the work design had taken place, were dissatisfied with this secondary role and wanted to be more proactive. In most cases, personnel practitioners continue to specialize in their respective areas, but they become more sensitive to and competent in organization development. Similarly, OD practitioners continue to focus on planned change while becoming more knowledgeable about human resources management.

We begin by describing a performance management model. It shows how goal setting, performance appraisal, and rewards are closely linked and difficult to separate in practice, but how each element is distinct and has its own dynamics. Following the model, each aspect of performance management is discussed and its impact on performance evaluated.

A MODEL OF PERFORMANCE MANAGEMENT

Performance management is an integrated process of defining, assessing, and reinforcing employee work behaviors and outcomes.[1] Organizations with a well-developed performance management process often outperform those without this element of organization design.[2] As shown in Figure 17.1, performance management includes practices and methods for goal setting, performance appraisal, and reward systems. These practices jointly influence the performance of individuals

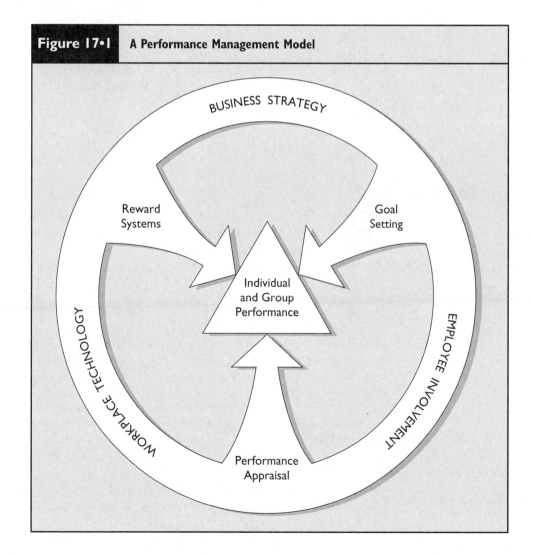

Figure 17•1   A Performance Management Model

and work groups. Goal setting specifies the kinds of performances that are desired; performance appraisal assesses those outcomes; reward systems provide the reinforcers to ensure that desired outcomes are repeated. Because performance management occurs in a larger organizational context, at least three contextual factors determine how these practices affect work performance: business strategy, workplace technology, and employee involvement.[3] High levels of work performance tend to occur when goal setting, performance appraisal, and reward systems are aligned jointly with these contextual factors.

Business strategy defines the goals and objectives, policies, and intended relationships between the organization and its environment to compete successfully, and performance management focuses, assesses, and reinforces member work behaviors toward those objectives and intentions. This ensures that work behaviors are strategically driven.

Workplace technology affects whether performance management practices should be based on the individual or the group. When technology is low in interdependence and work is designed for individual jobs, goal setting, performance appraisal, and reward systems should be aimed at individual work behaviors. Conversely, when technology is highly interdependent and work is designed for groups, performance management should be aimed at group behaviors.[4]

Finally, the level of employee involvement in an organization should determine the nature of performance management practices. When organizations are highly bureaucratic, with low levels of participation, then goal setting, performance appraisal, and reward systems should be formalized and administered by management and staff personnel. In high-involvement situations, on the other hand, performance management should be heavily participative, with both management and employees setting goals and appraising and rewarding performance. In high-involvement organizations, for example, employees participate in all stages of performance management, and are heavily involved in both designing and administering its practices.

GOAL SETTING

Goal setting involves managers and subordinates in jointly establishing and clarifying employee goals. In some cases, such as management by objectives, it also can facilitate employee counseling and support. In other cases, such as the *balanced scorecard*, it generates goals in several defined categories, at different organizational levels, to establish clear linkages with business strategy.[5] The process of establishing challenging goals involves managing the level of participation and goal difficulty. Once goals have been established, the way they are measured is an important determinant of member performance.[6]

Goal setting can affect performance in several ways. It influences what people think and do by focusing their behavior in the direction of the goals, rather than elsewhere. Goals energize behavior, motivating people to put forth the effort to reach difficult goals that are accepted, and when goals are difficult but achievable, goal setting prompts persistence over time. Goal-setting interventions have been implemented in such organizations as GE, 3M, AT&T Universal Card, and Occidental Petroleum's subsidiary Oxy-USA.

Characteristics of Goal Setting

An impressive amount of research underlies goal-setting interventions and practices;[7] it has revealed that goal setting works equally well in both individual and group settings.[8] This research has identified two major processes that affect positive outcomes: establishment of challenging goals and clarification of goal measurement.

Establishing Challenging Goals

The first element of goal setting concerns establishing goals that are perceived as challenging but realistic and to which there is a high level of commitment. This can be accomplished by varying the goal difficulty and the level of employee participation in the goal-setting process. Increasing the difficulty of employee goals, also known as *"stretch goals,"* can increase their perceived challenge and enhance the amount of effort expended to achieve them.[9] Thus, more difficult goals tend to lead to increased effort and performance, as long as they are seen as feasible. If goals are set too high, however, they may lose their motivating potential and employees will give up when they fail to achieve them. An important method for increasing the acceptance of a challenging goal is to collect benchmarks or best-practice referents. When employees see that other people, groups, or organizations have achieved a specified level of performance, they are more motivated to achieve that level themselves.

Another aspect of establishing challenging goals is to vary the amount of participation in the goal-setting process. Having employees participate can increase motivation and performance, but only to the extent that members set higher goals than those typically assigned to them. Participation also can convince employees that the goals are achievable and can increase their commitment to achieving them.

All three contextual factors play an important role in establishing challenging goals. First, there must be a clear "line of sight" between the business strategy goals and the goals established for individuals or groups. This is a key strength of the balanced scorecard approach to goal setting. When the group is trying to achieve goals that are not aligned with the business strategy, performance can suffer and organization members can become frustrated. Second, employee participation in goal setting is more likely to be effective if employee involvement policies in the organization support it. Under such conditions, participation in goal setting is likely to be seen as legitimate, resulting in the desired commitment to challenging goals. Third, when tasks are highly interdependent and work is designed for groups, group-oriented participative goal setting tends to increase commitment.[10]

Clarifying Goal Measurement

The second element in the goal-setting process involves specifying and clarifying the goals. When given specific goals, workers perform higher than when they are simply told to "do their best" or when they receive no guidance at all. Specific goals reduce ambiguity about expectations and focus the search for appropriate behaviors.

To clarify goal measurement, objectives should be operationally defined. For example, a group of employees may agree to increase productivity by 5%—a challenging and specific goal. But there are a variety of ways to measure productivity, and it is important to define the goal operationally to be sure that the measure can be influenced by employee or group behaviors. For example, a productivity goal defined by sales per employee may be inappropriate for a manufacturing group.

Clarifying goal measurement also requires that employees and supervisors negotiate the resources necessary to achieve the goals—for example, time, equipment, raw materials, and access to information. If employees cannot have appropriate resources, the targeted goal may have to be revised.

Contextual factors also play an important role in the clarifying process. Goal specification and clarity can be difficult in high-technology settings where the work often is uncertain and highly interdependent. Increasing employee participation in clarifying goal measurement can give employees ownership of a nonspecific but challenging goal. Employee involvement policies also can impact the way goals are clarified. The entire goal-setting process can be managed by employees and work teams when employee involvement policies and work designs favor it. Finally, the process of specifying and clarifying goals is extremely difficult if the business strategy is unclear. Under such conditions, attempting to gain consensus on the measurement and importance of goals can lead to frustration and resistance to change.

Application Stages

Based on these features of the goal-setting process, OD practitioners have developed specific approaches to goal setting. The following steps characterize those applications:

1. ***Diagnosis.*** The first step is a thorough diagnosis of the job or work group, of employee needs, and of the three context factors, business strategy, workplace technology, and level of employee involvement. This provides information about the nature and difficulty of specific goals, the appropriate types and levels, of participation, and the necessary support systems.

2. ***Preparation for Goal Setting.*** This step prepares managers and employees to engage in goal setting, typically by increasing interaction and communication between managers and employees, and offering formal training in goal-setting methods. Specific action plans for implementing the program also are made at this time.

3. ***Setting of Goals.*** In this step challenging goals are established and methods for goal measurement are clarified. Employees participate in the process to the extent that contextual factors support such involvement and to the extent that they are likely to set higher goals than those assigned by management.

4. ***Review.*** At this final step the goal-setting process is assessed so that modifications can be made, if necessary. The goal attributes are evaluated to see whether the goals are energizing and challenging and whether they support the business strategy and can be influenced by the employees.

Management by Objectives

A common form of goal setting used in organizations is *management by objectives* (MBO). This method is chiefly an attempt to align personal goals with business strategy by increasing communications and shared perceptions between the manager and subordinates, either individually or as a group, and by reconciling conflict where it exists.

All organizations have goals and objectives; all managers have goals and objectives. In many instances, however, those goals are not stated clearly, and managers and subordinates have misunderstandings about what those objectives are. MBO is an approach to resolving these differences in perceptions and goals. MBO is characterized by systematic and periodic manager–subordinate meetings designed to accomplish organizational goals by joint planning of the work, periodic reviewing of accomplishments, and mutual solving of problems that arise in the course of getting the job done.

MBO has its origin in two different backgrounds: organizational and developmental. The organizational root of MBO was developed by Drucker, who emphasized that organizations need to establish objectives in eight key areas: "market standing; innovation; productivity; physical and financial resources; profitability; manager performance and development; worker performance and attitude; and public responsibility."[11] Drucker's work was expanded by Odiorne, whose first book on MBO stressed the need for quantitative measurement.[12]

According to Levinson,[13] MBO's second root is found in the work of McGregor, who stressed the qualitative nature of MBO and its use for development and growth on the job.[14] McGregor attempted to shift emphasis from identifying weaknesses to analyzing performance in order to define strengths and potentials. He believed that this shift could be accomplished by having subordinates reach agreement with their bosses on major job responsibilities; then, individuals could develop short-term performance goals and action plans for achieving those goals, thus allowing them to appraise their own performance. Subordinates then would discuss the results of this self-appraisal with their supervisors and develop a new set of performance goals and plans. This emphasis on mutual understanding and performance rather than personality would shift the supervisor's role from judge to helper, thereby reducing both role conflict and ambiguity. The second root of MBO reduces role ambiguity by making goal setting more participative and transactional, by increasing communication between role incumbents, and by ensuring that both individual and organizational goals are identified and achieved.

An MBO program often goes beyond the one-on-one, manager–subordinate relationship to focus on problem-solving discussions involving work teams as well. Setting goals and reviewing individual performance are considered within the larger context of the job. In addition to organizational goals, the MBO process gives attention to individuals' personal and career goals and tries to make those and the organizational goals more complementary. The target-setting procedure allows real (rather than simulated) subordinate participation in goal setting, with open, problem-centered discussions among team members, supervisors, and subordinates.

There are six basic steps in implementing an MBO process.[15]

1. **Work group involvement.** In the first step of MBO, the members of the primary work group define overall group and individual goals and establish action plans for achieving them. If this step is omitted or if organizational goals and strategies are unclear, the effectiveness of an MBO approach may be greatly reduced over time.

2. **Joint manager–subordinate goal setting.** Once the work group's overall goals and responsibilities have been determined, attention is given to the job duties and responsibilities of the individual role incumbents. Roles are carefully examined in light of their interdependence with the roles of others outside the work group.

3. **Establishment of action plans for goals.** The subordinate develops action plans for goal accomplishment, either in a group meeting or in a meeting with the immediate manager. The action plans reflect the individual style of the subordinate, not that of the supervisor.

4. **Establishment of criteria, or yardsticks, of success.** At this point, the manager and subordinate agree on the success criteria for the goals that have been established—criteria that are not limited to easily measurable or quantifiable data. A more important reason for jointly developing the success criteria is to ensure that the manager and subordinate have a common understanding of the task and what is expected of the subordinate. Frequently, the parties involved discover that they have not reached a mutual understanding. The subordinate and the manager may have agreed on a certain task, but in discussing how to measure its success, they find that they have not been communicating clearly. Arriving at joint understanding and agreement on success criteria is the most important step in the entire MBO process.

5. **Review and recycle.** Periodically, the manager reviews work progress, either in the larger group or with the subordinate. There are three stages in this review process. First, the subordinate takes the lead, reviewing progress and discussing achievements and the obstacles faced. Next, the manager discusses work plans and objectives for the future. Last, after the action plans have been made, a more general discussion covers the subordinate's future ambitions and other factors of concern. In this final phase, a great deal of coaching and counseling usually takes place.

6. **Maintenance of records.** In many MBO programs, the working documents of the goals, criteria, yardsticks, priorities, and due dates are forwarded to a third party. Although the evidence is indirect, it is likely that the MBO program, as an OD effort, suffers when the working papers are reviewed regularly by a third party, such as higher management or the personnel department. Experience shows that when the working papers routinely are passed on, they are less likely to reflect open, honest communication within the supervisor–subordinate pair or the work group. Often they represent instead an effort to impress the third party or to comply with institutionalized rules and procedures.

Application 17.1 describes how a performance management process was designed at Monsanto Company. It shows how goal-setting processes can be linked with business strategies and performance appraisal processes.[16]

Effects of Goal Setting and MBO

The impact of goal setting has been researched extensively and shown to be a particularly effective OD intervention. The research results on MBO generally are positive but less consistent than are the findings on goal setting.

Goal setting appears to produce positive results over a wide range of jobs and organizations. It has been tested on data-entry operators, logging crews, clerical workers, engineers, and truck drivers, and it has produced performance improvements of between 11% and 27%.[17] Moreover, four meta-analyses of the extensive empirical evidence supporting goal setting concluded that the proposed effects of goal difficulty, goal specificity, and participation in goal setting generally are substantiated across studies and with both groups and individuals.[18] Longitudinal analyses support the conclusion that the gains in performance are not short-lived.[19] A field study of the goal-setting process, however, failed to replicate the typical positive linear relationship between goal difficulty and performance, raising some concern about the generalizability of the method from the laboratory to practice.[20] Additional research has attempted to identify potential factors moderating the results of goal setting, including task uncertainty, amount and quality of planning, personal need for achievement, education, past goal successes, and supervisory style.[21] Some support for the moderators has been found. For example, when the technical context is uncertain, goals tend to be less specific and people need to engage in more search behavior to establish meaningful goals.

The existing research on MBO effectiveness is large but mixed.[22] However, it suggests that a properly designed MBO program can have positive organizational results. Carroll and Tosi conducted a long-term study of an MBO program at Black & Decker,[23] first evaluating the program and then using those data to help the company revise and improve it. This resulted in greater use of and satisfaction with the program. The researchers concluded that top-management support of MBO is the most important factor in implementing such programs. Many programs are short-lived, however, and wither on the vine because they have been installed without adequate diagnosis of the context factors. In particular, MBO can focus too much on *vertical alignment* of individual and organizational goals and not enough on the *horizontal issues* that exist when tasks or groups are interdependent.

PERFORMANCE APPRAISAL

Performance appraisal is a feedback system that involves the direct evaluation of individual or work group performance by a supervisor, manager, or peers. Most organizations have some kind of evaluation system that is used for performance feedback, pay administration, and, in some cases, counseling and developing employees.[24]

THE PERFORMANCE ENHANCEMENT PROCESS AT MONSANTO

The Chemical Group of the Monsanto Company is a global provider of chemicals, plastics, and fibers. Previously the centerpiece in Monsanto's corporate strategy, the Chemical Group's role was changing as Monsanto restructured its business from commodity and specialty chemicals to biotechnology-based products and health care. As part of that role change, the business was asked to become a cash generator with a workforce that had been through divestitures, downsizings, and other dramatic changes.

In 1991, the human resources department was reorganized into a development group and an administration group. The development group's first assignment was to redesign the performance management system in light of the Chemical Group's new role and the existing workforce. A task force was formed to design a long-range human resources strategy where the new performance management system would be the key implementation vehicle.

Interviews with more than 1,500 organization members, a literature review on performance management, and a review of best practices at other firms resulted in several key conclusions. First, human resources management practices can have a major impact on organization performance. Second, performance management systems typically constrain rather than promote employee contributions to performance. Third, traditional MBO processes were ineffective, contrary to empowerment values, and focused more on past accomplishments than on future development. Based on this diagnosis, the task force recommended adopting a *Performance Enhancement Process* (PEP) based on the following design principles:

- Focus on development rather than judgment.
- Focus employee effort on continuous improvement of work processes.
- Simplify goal setting.
- Shift the focus from individuals to teams, from supervisory judgment to supervisory coaching.
- Clarify roles and increase the amount of feedback.

The designed PEP process included direction setting and performance planning, individual development, and continual coaching. Direction setting and performance planning initiate the PEP process and occur at the beginning of a yearly performance management cycle. The supervisor and employee meet to establish job accountabilities and goals, and they agree on a competency profile that the employee is expected to demonstrate in his or her current job. Job accountabilities are the actual behaviors that directly contribute to achieving the organization's objectives. They define the reason why the job exists. Work goals are the specific accomplishments to be achieved during the year. The PEP process suggests that there should be no more than five goals and that one of them should be related to the development of the employee.

APPLICATION 17•1

Direction setting and performance planning ensure that employees have a clear line of sight between their work and the achievement of the organization's objectives. In addition, this part of the PEP process is designed to be developmental and future oriented. It tries to avoid the negative dynamics of setting low goals that are not challenging, using fuzzy language that allows differing interpretations of accomplishments, or specifying a long list of assumptions about what might go wrong that would prevent a fair appraisal. Rather, through discussion, the employee and supervisor understand and agree on the direction the employee's work should take.

Finally, a competency expectation profile is developed. The task force defined competency as a combination of knowledge, skills, and behaviors that drive performance, and identified 12 core competencies that all employees should develop, such as commitment to task, appreciating differences, and customer focus. Each competency was defined differently depending on a particular stage in a person's career. Together, the supervisor and employee decide on the competencies the employee needs to demonstrate during the performance appraisal cycle.

Individual development and continual coaching are the next components of the PEP process. The key to the success of these components is the transformed role of the supervisor from judge to coach. First, the employee evaluates his or her performance according to the stated accountabilities, goals, and competencies. The supervisor cannot edit this form, the employee is asked to sign the self-assessment, and it becomes a part of the employee's permanent record. The supervisor's input to the self-assessment is a "coaching dialogue" that occurs over time and clarifies the supervisor's view of the employee's performance. Second, the supervisor and employee agree on a list of peers, colleagues, internal customers, and others, who provide feedback from multiple viewpoints to the employee on the demonstration of his or her competencies. The feedback is summarized and given to the employee, who compares the feedback with the self-assessment and the competency profile developed at the beginning of the cycle. The employee notes discrepancies and uses them in developing the next competency profile.

The supervisor facilitates the feedback process. He or she helps identify raters, collects the data, and is available to the employee for help in interpretation. The data do not go into the employee's permanent file. The supervisor is removed from being the omniscient observer, and a more structured and developmental approach to feedback is achieved.

Thus, performance appraisal represents an important link between goal-setting processes and reward systems. One recent survey of over 300 North American companies, for example, found that 65% reported a link between performance ratings and rewards, 46% used the system equally for performance development and decision making, and 53% of the organizations believed the system was aligned with organizational values and priorities.[25]

Abundant evidence, however, indicates that organizations do a poor job appraising employees.[26] As one study put it, "The appraisal of performance appraisals is not good. . . . In fact, our review indicates that, regardless of a program's stated purpose, few studies show positive effects."[27] Another study found that only 55% believed the appraisal process adequately distinguished between poor, average, and good performers.[28] Consequently, a growing number of firms have sought ways to improve performance appraisal. Some innovations have been made in enhancing employee involvement, balancing organizational and employee needs, and increasing the number of raters.[29] These newer forms of appraisal are being used in such organizations as AT&T, Raychem, Levi Strauss, Intel, and Monsanto.

The Performance Appraisal Process

Table 17.1 summarizes several common elements of performance appraisal systems.[30] For each element, two contrasting features are presented, representing traditional bureaucratic approaches and newer, high-involvement approaches. Performance appraisals are conducted for a variety of purposes, including affirmative action, pay and promotion decisions, and human resources planning and development. Because each purpose defines what performances are relevant and how they should be measured, separate appraisal systems are often used. For example, appraisal methods for pay purposes are often different from systems that assess employee development or promotability. Employees also have a variety of reasons for wanting appraisal, such as receiving feedback for career decisions, getting a raise, and being promoted. Rather than trying to meet these multiple purposes with a few standard appraisal systems, the new appraisal approaches are more tailored to balance the multiple organizational and employee needs. This is accomplished by actively involving the appraisee, co-workers, and managers in assessing the purposes

Table 17·1	Performance Appraisal Elements	
ELEMENTS	**TRADITIONAL APPROACHES**	**HIGH-INVOLVEMENT APPROACHES**
Purpose	Organizational, legal Fragmented	Developmental Integrative
Appraiser	Supervisor, managers	Appraisee, co-workers, and others
Role of appraisee	Passive recipient	Active participant
Measurement	Subjective Concerned with validity	Objective and subjective
Timing	Periodic, fixed, administratively driven	Dynamic, timely, employee- or work-driven

of the appraisal at the time it takes place and adjusting the process to fit that purpose. Thus, at one time the appraisal process might focus on pay decisions, another time on employee development, and still another time on employee promotability. Actively involving all relevant participants can increase the chances that the purpose of the appraisal will be correctly identified and understood and that the appropriate appraisal methods will be applied.

The new methods tend to expand the appraiser role beyond managers to include multiple raters, such as the appraisee, peers or co-workers, and direct reports and others having direct exposure to the manager's or employee's performance. Also known as *360-degree feedback*, this broader approach is used more for member development than for compensation purposes.[31] This wider involvement provides a number of different views of the appraisee's performance. It can lead to a more comprehensive assessment of the employee's performance and can increase the likelihood that both organizational and personal needs will be taken into account. The key task is to form an overarching view of the employee's performance that incorporates all of the different appraisals. Thus, the process of working out differences and arriving at an overall assessment is an important aspect of the appraisal process. This improves the appraisal's acceptance, the accuracy of the information, and its focus on activities that are critical to the business strategy.

The newer methods also expand the role of the appraisee. Traditionally, the employee is simply a receiver of feedback. The supervisor unilaterally completes a form concerning performance on predetermined dimensions, usually personality traits, such as initiative or concern for quality, and presents its contents to the appraisee. The newer approaches actively involve appraisees in all phases of the appraisal process. The appraisee joins with superiors and staff personnel in gathering data on performance and identifying training needs. This active involvement increases the likelihood that the content of the performance appraisal will include the employee's views, needs, and criteria, along with those of the organization. This newer role for employees increases their acceptance and understanding of the feedback process.

Performance measurement is typically the source of many problems in appraisal because it is seen as subjective. Traditionally, performance evaluation focused on the consistent use of prespecified traits or behaviors. To improve consistency and validity of measurement, considerable training is used to help raters (supervisors) make valid assessments. This concern for validity stems largely from legal tests of performance appraisal systems and leads organizations to develop measurement approaches, such as the *behaviorally anchored rating scale* (BARS) and its variants. In newer approaches, validity is not only a legal or methodological issue but a social issue as well; all appropriate participants are involved in negotiating acceptable ways of measuring and assessing performance. Increased participation in goal setting is a part of this new approach. All participants are trained in methods of measuring and assessing performance. Because it focuses on both objective and subjective measures of performance, the appraisal process is more understood, accepted, and accurate.

The timing of performance appraisals traditionally is fixed by managers or staff personnel and is based on administrative criteria, such as yearly pay decisions. Newer approaches increase the frequency of feedback. In 1997, 78% of appraisals were performed annually; in 2003, over 40% of companies surveyed conducted appraisals two times per year.[32] Although it may not be practical to increase the number of formal appraisals, the frequency of informal feedback can increase, especially when strategic objectives change or when the technology is highly uncertain. In those situations, frequent performance feedback is necessary for appropriate adaptations in work behavior. The newer approaches to appraisal increase the timeliness of feedback and give employees more control over their work.

Application Stages

The process of designing and implementing a performance appraisal system has received increasing attention. OD practitioners have recommended the following six steps:[33]

1. *Select the Right People.* For political and legal reasons, the design process needs to include human resources staff, legal representatives, senior management, and system users. Failure to recognize performance appraisal as part of a complex performance management system is the single most important reason for design problems. Members representing a variety of functions need to be involved in the design process so that the essential strategic and organizational issues are addressed.

2. *Diagnose the Current Situation.* A clear picture of the current appraisal process is essential to designing a new one. Diagnosis involves assessing the contextual factors (business strategy, workplace technology, and employee involvement), current appraisal practices and satisfaction with them, work design, and the current goal-setting and reward system practices. This information is used to define the current system's strengths and weaknesses.

3. *Establish the System's Purposes and Objectives.* The ultimate purpose of an appraisal system is to help the organization achieve better performance. Managers, staff, and employees can have more specific views about how the appraisal process can be used. Potential purposes can include serving as a basis for rewards, career planning, human resources planning, and performance improvement or simply giving performance feedback.

4. *Design the Performance Appraisal System.* Given the agreed-upon purposes of the system and the contextual factors, the appropriate elements of an appraisal system can be established. These should include choices about who performs the appraisal, who is involved in determining performance, how performance is measured, and how often feedback is given. Criteria for designing an effective performance appraisal system include timeliness, accuracy, acceptance, understanding, focus on critical control points, and economic feasibility.

    First, the timeliness criterion recognizes the time value of information. Individuals and work groups need to get performance information before evaluation or review. When the information precedes performance evaluation, it can be used to engage in problem-solving behavior that improves performance and satisfaction. Second, the information contained in performance feedback needs to be accurate. Inaccurate data prevent employees from determining whether their performance is above or below the goal targets and discourage problem-solving behavior. Third, the performance feedback must be accepted and owned by the people who use it. Participation in the goal-setting process can help to ensure this commitment to the performance appraisal system. Fourth, information contained in the appraisal system needs to be understood if it is to have problem-solving value. Many organizations use training to help employees understand the operating, financial, and human resources data that will be fed back to them. Fifth, appraisal information should focus on critical control points. The information received by employees must be aligned with important elements of the business strategy, employee performance, and reward system. For example, if the business strategy requires cost reduction but workers are measured and rewarded on the basis of quality, the performance management system may produce the wrong kinds of behavior. Finally, the economic feasibility criterion suggests that an appraisal system should meet a simple cost–benefit test. If the costs associated with collecting and feeding back performance information exceed the benefits derived from using the information, then a simpler system should be installed.

5. ***Experiment with Implementation.*** The complexity and potential problems associated with performance appraisal processes strongly suggest using a pilot test of the new process to spot, gauge, and correct any flaws in the design before it is implemented systemwide.

6. ***Evaluate and Monitor the System.*** Although the experimentation step may have uncovered many initial design flaws, ongoing evaluation of the system once it is implemented is important. User satisfaction from human resources staff, manager, and employee viewpoints is an essential input. In addition, the legal defensibility of the system should be tracked by noting the distribution of appraisal scores against age, sex, and ethnic categories.

Application 17.2 describes the redesign of a performance appraisal process for the Washington State Patrol agency. It demonstrates the importance of a pilot test and integrating the appraisal process with context factors and other organizational initiatives.[34]

Effects of Performance Appraisal

Despite the poor track record organizations have in implementing appraisal processes well, the research supports the linkage between feedback and performance.[35] Early studies concluded that objective feedback as a means for improving individual and group performance has been "impressively effective"[36] and has been supported by a large number of literature reviews over the years.[37] Another researcher concluded that "objective feedback does not usually work, it virtually always works."[38] In field studies where performance feedback contained behavior-specific information, median performance improvements were over 47%; when the feedback concerned less-specific information, median performance improvements were over 33%. In a meta-analysis of performance appraisal interventions, feedback was found to have a consistently positive effect across studies.[39] In addition, although most appraisal research has focused on the relationship between performance and individuals, several studies have demonstrated a positive relationship between group performance and feedback.[40]

REWARD SYSTEMS

Organizational rewards are powerful incentives for improving employee and work group performance. As pointed out in Chapter 16, rewards also can produce high levels of employee satisfaction. OD traditionally has relied on intrinsic rewards, such as enriched jobs and opportunities for decision making, to motivate employee performance. Early quality-of-work-life interventions were based mainly on the intrinsic satisfaction derived from performing challenging, meaningful types of work. More recently, OD practitioners have expanded their focus to include extrinsic rewards: pay; various incentives, such as stock options, bonuses, and gain sharing; promotions; and benefits. They have discovered that both intrinsic and extrinsic rewards can enhance performance and satisfaction.[41]

OD practitioners increasingly are attending to the design and implementation of reward systems. This recent attention to rewards has derived partly from research in organization design and employee involvement. These perspectives treat rewards as an integral part of an organization.[42] They hold that rewards should be congruent with other organizational systems and practices, such as the organization's structure, top management's human relations philosophy, and work designs. Many reward system features contribute to both employee fulfillment and organizational

CHANGING THE APPRAISAL PROCESS IN THE WASHINGTON STATE PATROL

The Washington State Patrol (WSP) is a law enforcement agency of over 2,200 people. Its officers' long tradition of courtesy and professionalism has won the agency a consistent set of high marks in citizen surveys. Also by tradition, the WSP bureaucracy functioned according to an "expert, autonomous" model rather than a more current "community policing" model. It lacked strong incentive to change. The organization's performance appraisal process was also conventional and limited. It included an annual appraisal form and interview for troopers and sergeants, but no formal appraisal for lieutenants or captains. The appraisal meeting focused on individual past performance, with little consideration of work unit context or tie to any direction of the agency; appraisals were often viewed as having little meaning or consequence.

By 1997 the pressures for change had increased. Internal discontent about the agency's lack of direction, an executive staff interested in agency improvement, a governor encouraging agencies to implement *total quality management* (TQM) practices, and a nationwide shift toward community policing provided the impetus to develop an agency strategic plan. It included objectives, action plans, and accountabilities; a community policing program called Problem Oriented Public Safety (POPS); and the infrastructure to implement TQM.

To ensure alignment with these strategic initiatives, a committee was formed in 1998 to develop a new appraisal form and process. The design process was highly collaborative and included input and participation from 13 officers, ranging from trooper through captain. Eight of the 13 officers were field officers, and several represented the Troopers and Sergeants Association. As the committee completed its diagnosis, it struggled to ensure the clarity of the appraisal process's purpose, to develop good performance measures, and to differentiate between effort and outcomes. With regard to the system's purpose, the old appraisal process was independent of the promotions process. Eligibility and readiness were traditionally assessed through exams and assessment center results. Some argued that the agency should be able to "leverage" the appraisal data as another input to promotion decisions. After many hours of discussion, the decision was made not to keep the appraisal process separate from promotion decisions. With regard to measuring performance, WSP administrators argued for a testing and coaching approach while others were concerned with the legal complications of documenting test results on key skills and thought such a system would detract from the appraisal's pri-

mary developmental and compensation purposes. Ultimately, a modified testing protocol was adopted that allowed managers to note improvements in skills and knowledge rather than deficiencies.

The third issue the committee struggled with was outcome vs. effort measurement. For example, the new appraisal form sought feedback data in three sections. Section 1 combined core value dimensions, such as courtesy and integrity, with TQM and POPS-oriented dimensions, such as continuous improvement skills and interest/knowledge of citizen groups. These dimensions intended to apply to all levels of officers. Section 2 reported on the officer's contributions to the achievement of local field objectives and linked to the agency's strategic plans. Section 3 documented tested knowledge of important job practices.

In developing the new form, the committee realized the agency culture had emphasized a fairly outcome- or activity-oriented standard. Performance in terms of contacts made or citations written was more impressive than effective improvement efforts, such as helping to relieve traffic congestion. The strategic initiatives wanting to encourage officers to solicit citizen input and to identify and deal effectively with local problems conflicted with the existing agency culture. As a result, the committee believed that many officers would be confused by the new system. Most importantly, the committee worried that the state legislature and other stakeholders, used to hearing about performance in outcome terms, would be supportive of this new approach. In fact, the switch to POPS-oriented activities might actually result in short-term increases in accidents and other items traditionally reported. The committee discussed these concerns with the agency's executives and was advised to proceed in the direction in which it was headed. In the meantime, this new direction would be discussed with legislators and other stakeholders.

When the committee was ready for implementation, it requested the participation of two districts to introduce and pilot-test the new appraisal process. Based on preparation discussions, a training module was developed by officers in one of the test districts. It included a pre-appraisal work group meeting where employees discussed and agreed on complementary roles and expectations and applied these toward common objectives. This training focused as much on the agency's new developments as on the new appraisals and showed how they fit together. The presenters encouraged operational questions about shifting to the new approach. In effect, these training sessions served to resolve operational issues regarding the new approach, as well as train officers on the new appraisals.

At about the same time as the pilot training and process testing, the appraisal committee and other groups working on the different initiatives realized that an additional intervention was necessary to address the cultural conflict and really make the new approaches happen. The committee found and adapted a practice used by the New York Police Department that involved presenting operational improvement activities and outcomes to peers and higher-level managers. The approach asked district/division managers to give presentations every 6 months on issues and efforts to implement TQM and POPS, and on quality efforts toward objectives more than toward outcomes. The range of issues to be addressed was to be sent out well in advance of the presentation date. The presentations would be structured and visible and were expected to generate discussion and debates about the key issues facing the organization. The agency named the presentation event the Strategic Advancement Forum (SAF). The first SAF presentations were held in early 2000, several months after managers received SAF orientation and a list of issues to be addressed in their presentations. Each district/division manager gave a 30- to 40-minute presentation, followed by 20–30 minutes of questions/discussion with peers and executives. A follow-up survey of presenters indicated they felt the SAF format was useful for reporting efforts and improving communication with executives and peers. In effect, SAF became an important adjunct to the appraisal process by motivating and guiding performance efforts of mid-managers and employees toward desired agency ends. SAF's more public format, including peers and executive managers, may be more interesting than the traditional performance appraisal format but the one-on-one sessions are more appropriate for discussing and coaching individual areas needing attention.

The pilot appraisal process was conducted in early 2000, after which it was fine-tuned. The new process was reviewed and accepted by the Troopers and Sergeants Association. Designated individuals in the other six districts then received "train the trainer" instruction and subsequently trained officers in their respective districts. Following this, the new appraisal process was implemented agency-wide in July 2000. Troopers and sergeants were evaluated with the new appraisals for the first time in 2001.

effectiveness. In this section, we describe the structural features of a reward system and how rewards affect individual and group performance; discuss four specific rewards, including skill-based pay, performance-based pay, gain sharing, and promotions; and the process issues involved in establishing and administrating reward systems.

Structural and Motivational Features of Reward Systems

A reward system is an important part of an organization's design and must be aligned with the strategy, structure, employee involvement, and work. The design features of a reward system are summarized in Table 17.2 (on page 380).[43]

- **Person/job Based vs. Performance Based.** One of the first and most important design choices is the focus or basis of the reward system. The most prevalent system is the job-based system. Here, job descriptions are created for each position in the organization and a value is attached to the work performed. Pay is based on that valuation process. More recently, reward systems have been crafted around the person in the job and the value brought by their skills and knowledge. Skill-based pay and knowledge-based pay are important examples of this system. The other major alternative is to base rewards on the performance achieved by a job or person. In this system, pay is contingent on the outcomes produced.

- **Internal and External Equity.** Member satisfaction and motivation can be influenced by design features that ensure that the organization's pay policies are equitable or fair. Internal equity concerns comparison of individual rewards to those holding similar jobs or performing similarly in the organization. Internal inequities typically occur when employees are paid a similar salary or hourly wage regardless of their position or level of performance. Many organizations

Table 17.2	Reward System Design Features

DESIGN FEATURE	DEFINITION
Person/Job Based vs. Performance Based	The extent to which rewards and incentives are based on the person in a job, the job itself, or the outcomes of the work
Market Position (External Equity)	The relationship between what an organization pays and what other organizations pay
Internal Equity	The extent to which people doing similar work in an organization are rewarded the same
Hierarchy	The extent to which people in higher positions get more and varied types of rewards than people lower in the organization
Centralization	The extent to which reward system design features, decisions, and administration are standardized across an organization
Rewards Mix	The extent to which different types of rewards are available and offered to people
Security	The extent to which work is guaranteed
Seniority	The extent to which rewards are based on length of service

work hard to establish practices to ensure that people who are doing similar kinds of activities have similar levels of compensation. External equity involves comparing the organization's rewards with those of other organizations in the same labor market. Most human resources policies commit to a rewards and compensation system relative to the market. Organizations can decide to pay below, at, or above market rates. In their quest for attracting and retaining scarce human resource talent, many organizations have had to commit to above-market pay schemes. When an organization's reward level does not compare favorably with the level of other organizations, employees are likely to feel inequitably rewarded and may leave.

- **Hierarchy.** Although not often a formal policy, many organizations offer different types of rewards based on a position's level in the organization structure. The recent concerns over CEO pay reflect the increasing prevalence of hierarchical reward systems.[44] In hierarchical systems, senior managers have access to a variety of perquisites, such as reserved parking, corporate transportation, financial aid, or health benefits that others do not.

- **Centralization.** Organizations can choose to design and administer reward systems through a centralized or decentralized process. When a reward system is centralized, there is a strong preference for standardized job descriptions, performance appraisal processes, promotion protocols, and pay practices.

- **Rewards Mix.** This design feature involves specifying the extent to which different types of rewards are included in the overall reward strategy. These rewards can include pay in various forms, including base salary, bonuses, commissions, and stock; benefits, such as health care, insurance, child care, leaves, and education; and perquisites, including preferred office space, cell phones, cars, or health club memberships. Although pay receives most of the attention in reward systems, the contribution of other rewards, such as benefit programs and status incentives, should not be underestimated. For example, rising health care costs and increasing interest in retaining important skills and competencies have resulted in a variety of benefit innovations to increase the value of this reward.[45]

- **Security.** Organizations, such as IBM and AT&T, once offered organization members lifetime employment as a formal policy. Today, the rapid expansion and contraction of markets and the realities of downsizing have dramatically altered the psychological employment contract. Instead of job security, a more instrumental relationship has emerged. However, organizations can and do make commitments to people and job security and this remains an important feature of reward systems.

- **Seniority.** Many reward systems include an implicit or explicit policy concerning the value of longevity. Organizations, especially unionized companies covered by a collective bargaining agreement, often have built-in rewards for increasing lengths of service.

The structural features of a reward system represent important design choices available to human resources and other senior managers. These features interact with work design and employee involvement practices to produce goal-directed behavior and task performance. Considerable research has been done on how different rewards and reward system features affect individual and group performance. The most popular model describing this relationship is value expectancy theory. In addition to explaining how performance and rewards are related, it suggests requirements for designing and evaluating reward systems.

The *value expectancy model*[46] posits that employees will expend effort to achieve performance goals that they believe will lead to outcomes that they value. This effort will result in the desired performance goals if the goals are realistic, if employees fully understand what is expected of them, and if they have the necessary skills and resources. Ongoing motivation depends on the extent to which attaining the desired performance goals actually results in valued outcomes. Consequently, key objectives of reward systems interventions are to identify the intrinsic and extrinsic outcomes (rewards) that are highly valued and to link them to the achievement of desired performance goals.

Based on value expectancy theory, the ability of rewards to motivate desired behavior depends on these five factors:[47]

1. **Availability.** For rewards to reinforce desired performance, they must be not only desired but also available. Too little of a desired reward is no reward at all. For example, pay increases are often highly desired but unavailable. Moreover, pay increases that are below minimally accepted standards may actually produce negative consequences.[48]

2. **Timeliness.** Like effective performance feedback, rewards should be given in a timely manner. A reward's motivating potential is reduced to the extent that it is separated in time from the performance it is intended to reinforce.

3. **Performance contingency.** Rewards should be closely linked with particular performances. If the goal is met, the reward is given; if the target is missed, the reward is reduced or not given. The clearer the linkage between performance and rewards, the better able rewards are to motivate desired behavior. Unfortu-

nately, this criterion often is neglected in practice. About 40% of employees nationwide believe that there is no linkage between pay and performance.[49] If salary increases are concentrated at certain levels, almost everyone, regardless of performance level, is getting about the same raise.

4. **Durability.** Some rewards last longer than others. Intrinsic rewards, such as increased autonomy and pride in workmanship, tend to last longer than extrinsic rewards. Most people who have received a salary increase realize that it gets spent rather quickly.

5. **Visibility.** To leverage a reward system, it must be visible. Organization members must be able to see who is getting the rewards. Visible rewards, such as placement on a high-status project, promotion to a new job, and increased authority, send signals to employees that rewards are available, timely, and performance contingent.

Reward systems interventions are used to elicit and maintain desired levels of performance. To the extent that rewards are available, durable, timely, visible, and performance contingent, they can support and reinforce organizational goals, work designs, and employee involvement. The next sections describe four types of rewards. Skill-based pay, pay for performance, gain sharing, and promotions can be used to reward individual, team, or organization performance. Each system represents a flexible intervention that is effective in improving employee performance and satisfaction.

Skill-Based Pay Systems

The most traditional reward system is job based. The characteristics of a particular job are determined, and pay is made comparable to what other organizations pay for jobs with similar characteristics. Pay increases are primarily a function of cost-of-living adjustments (COLA) or small merit pools that are awarded with little relationship to performance. This job evaluation and reward method tends to result in pay systems with high external and internal equity. However, it fails to reward employees for all of the skills that they have, discourages people from learning new skills, and results in a view of pay as an entitlement.[50]

Some organizations, such as General Mills, Northern Telecom, United Technologies, and General Foods, have worked to resolve these problems by designing pay systems according to people's skills and abilities. A recent survey found that almost 25% of the Fortune 1000 use skill-based pay to at least some extent.[51] By focusing on the individual, rather than the job, skill-based pay systems reward learning and growth.

Skill-based pay systems must first establish the skills needed for effective operations, identify the optimal skill profile and number of employees needed with each skill, price each skill and skill set, develop rules to sequence and acquire skills, and develop methods to measure member skill acquisition.[52] Typically, employees are paid according to the number of different jobs that they can perform. For example, in General Mill's Squeeze-It plant, new employees are paid a starting wage at the low end of the skilled worker wage rate for premium employers in the community. They are then assigned to any one of four skill blocks corresponding to a particular set of activities in the production process. For each skill block there are three levels of skill. Pay is based on the level of skill in each of the skill blocks; the more proficient the skill in each block and the more blocks one is proficient at, the higher the pay. After all skill blocks are learned at the highest level, the top rate is given.[53] This progression in skills typically takes 2 years to complete, and employees are given support and training to learn the new jobs.

Skill-based pay systems have a number of benefits. They contribute to organizational effectiveness by providing a more flexible workforce and by giving employees a broad perspective on how the entire plant operates. This flexibility can result in leaner staffing and fewer problems with absenteeism, turnover, and work disruptions. Skill-based pay can lead to durable employee satisfaction by reinforcing individual development and by producing an equitable wage rate.[54]

The two major drawbacks of skill-based pay schemes are the tendency to "top out," the expense, and the lack of performance contingency. Top-out occurs when employees learn all the skills there are to learn and then run up against the top end of the pay scale, with no higher levels to attain. Some organizations have resolved this topping-out effect by installing a gain-sharing plan after most employees have learned all relevant jobs. *Gain sharing,* discussed later in this section, ties pay to organizational effectiveness, allowing employees to push beyond previous pay ceilings. Other organizations have resolved this effect by making base skills obsolete and adding new ones, thus raising the standards of employee competence. Skill-based pay systems also require a heavy investment in training, as well as a measurement system capable of telling when employees have learned the new jobs. They typically increase direct labor costs, as employees are paid highly for learning multiple tasks. In addition, because pay is based on skill and not performance, the workforce could be highly paid and flexible but not productive.

Like most new personnel practices, limited evaluative research exists on the effectiveness of these interventions. Long-term assessment of the Gaines Pet Food plant revealed that the skill-based pay plan contributed to both organizational effectiveness and employee satisfaction. Several years after the plant opened, workers' attitudes toward pay were significantly more positive than those of people working in other similar plants that did not have skill-based pay. Gaines workers reported much higher levels of pay satisfaction, as well as feelings that their pay system was fairly administered.[55]

A national survey of skill-based pay plans sponsored by the U.S. Department of Labor concluded that such systems increase workforce flexibility, employee growth and development, and product quality and quantity while reducing staffing needs, absenteeism, and turnover.[56] These results appear contingent on management commitment to the plan and having the right kind of people, particularly those with interpersonal skills, motivation, and a desire for growth and development. This study also showed that skill-based pay is applicable across a variety of situations, including both manufacturing and service industries, production and staff employees, new and old sites, and unionized and nonunionized settings. Finally, in a 1996 survey of 212 Fortune 1000 companies, 42% indicated that skill-based pay systems were successful or very successful, down from 52% in 1993.[57]

Performance-Based Pay Systems

In addition to person- or job-based reward systems, organizations have devised many ways of linking pay to performance,[58] making it the fastest-growing and most popular segment of pay-based reward systems. One study estimated that almost two-thirds of businesses have some form of performance-based or variable pay system.[59] They are used in such organizations as American Express, Herman Miller, and Corning. Pay-for-performance plans tend to vary along three dimensions: (1) the organizational unit by which performance is measured for reward purposes—an individual, group, or organization basis; (2) the way performance is measured—the subjective measures used in supervisors' ratings or objective measures of productivity, costs, or profits; and (3) what rewards are given for good performance—salary increases, stock, or cash bonuses. Table 17.3 (on page 384) lists different types of performance-based pay systems varying along these dimensions and rates them in terms of other relevant criteria.

Table 17•3	Ratings of Various Pay-for-Performance Plans*				

		TIE PAY TO PERFORMANCE	PRODUCE NEGATIVE SIDE EFFECTS	ENCOURAGE COOPERATION	EMPLOYEE ACCEPTANCE
SALARY REWARD					
Individual plan	Productivity	4	1	1	4
	Cost-effectiveness	3	1	1	4
	Superiors' rating	3	1	1	3
Group	Productivity	3	1	2	4
	Cost-effectiveness	3	1	2	4
	Superiors' rating	2	1	2	3
Organization-wide	Productivity	2	1	3	4
	Cost-effectiveness	2	1	2	4
STOCK/BONUS REWARD					
Individual plan	Productivity	5	3	1	2
	Cost-effectiveness	4	2	1	2
	Superiors' rating	4	2	1	2
Group	Productivity	4	1	3	3
	Cost-effectiveness	3	1	3	3
	Superiors' rating	3	1	3	3
Organization-wide	Productivity	3	1	3	4
	Cost-effectiveness	3	1	3	4
	Profit	2	1	3	3

*Ratings: 1 = lowest rating, 5 = highest rating.

SOURCE: Reproduced by permission of the publisher from E. Lawler III, "Reward Systems," in *Improving Life at Work*, eds. J. Hackman and J. Suttle (Santa Monica, Calif.: Goodyear, 1977), p. 195.

In terms of linking pay to performance, individual pay plans are rated highest, followed by group plans and then organization plans. The last two plans score lower on this factor because pay is not a direct function of individual behavior. At the group and organization levels, an individual's pay is influenced by the behavior of others and by external market conditions. Generally, stock and bonus plans tie pay to performance better than do salary plans. The amount of awarded stock may vary sharply from year to year, whereas salary increases tend to be more stable because organizations seldom cut employees' salaries. Finally, objective measures of performance score higher than subjective measures. Objective measures, such as profit or costs, are more credible, and people are more likely to see the link between pay and objective measures.

Most of the pay plans in Table 17.3 do not produce negative side effects, such as workers falsifying data and restricting performance. The major exceptions are individual bonus plans. These plans, such as piece-rate systems, tend to result in negative effects, particularly when trust in the plan is low. For example, if people feel that piece-rate quotas are unfair, they may hide work improvements for fear that quotas may be adjusted higher.

As might be expected, group- and organization-based pay plans encourage cooperation among workers more than do individual plans. Under the former, it is generally to everyone's advantage to work well together because all share in the financial rewards of higher performance. The organization plans also tend to promote cooperation among functional departments. Because members from different departments feel that they can benefit from each others' performance, they encourage and help each other make positive contributions.

From an employee's perspective, Table 17.3 suggests that the least acceptable pay plans are individual bonus programs. Employees tend to dislike such plans because they encourage competition among individuals and because they are difficult to administer fairly. Such plans may be inappropriate in some technical contexts. For example, technical innovations typically lead engineers to adjust piece-rate quotas upward because employees should be able to produce more with the same effort. Workers, on the other hand, often feel that the performance worth of such innovations does not equal the incremental change in quotas, thus resulting in feelings of pay inequity. Table 17.3 suggests that employees tend to favor salary increases to bonuses. This follows from the simple fact that a salary increase becomes a permanent part of a person's pay, but a bonus does not.

The overall ratings in Table 17.3 suggest that no one pay-for-performance plan scores highest on all criteria. Rather, each plan has certain strengths and weaknesses that depend on a variety of contingencies. As business strategies, organization performance, and other contingencies change, the pay-for-performance system also must change. At Lincoln Electric, a longtime proponent and model for incentive pay, growth into international markets, poor managerial decisions, and other factors have put pressure on the bonus plan. In one instance, a poor acquisition decision hurt earnings and left the organization short of cash for the bonus payout. The organization borrowed money rather than risk losing employees' trust. Financially weakened by the acquisition, and in combination with the other changes, Lincoln Electric has initiated a planned change effort to examine its pay-for-performance process and recommend a new approach.[60]

When all criteria are taken into account, however, the best performance-based pay systems seem to be group and organization bonus plans that are based on objective measures of performance and individual salary-increase plans. These plans are relatively good at linking pay to performance. They have few negative side effects and at least modest employee acceptance. The group and organization plans promote cooperation and should be used where there is high task interdependence among workers, such as might be found on assembly lines. The individual plan promotes competition and should be used where there is little required cooperation among employees, such as in field sales jobs.

Gain-Sharing Systems

As the name implies, *gain sharing* involves paying employees a bonus based on improvements in the operating results of an organization. Although not traditionally associated with employee involvement, gain sharing increasingly has been included in comprehensive employee involvement projects. Many organizations, such as Dana, Eaton, Weyerhaeuser, and 3M, are discovering that when designed correctly, gain-sharing plans can contribute to employee motivation, involvement, and performance.

Developing a gain-sharing plan requires making choices about the following design elements:[61]

- **Process of design.** The success of a gain-sharing system depends on employee acceptance and cooperation. Recommended is a participative approach that involves a cross section of employees to design the plan and be trained in gain-sharing concepts and practice. The task force should include people who are credible and represent both management and nonmanagement interests.

- **Organizational unit covered.** The size of the unit included in the plan can vary widely, from departments or plants with less than 50 employees to companies with several thousand people. A plan covering the entire plant would be ideal in situations where there is a freestanding plant with good performance measures and an employee size of less than 500. When the number of employees exceeds 500, multiple plans may be installed, each covering a relatively discrete part of the company.

- **Bonus formula.** Gain-sharing plans are based on a formula that generates a bonus pool, which is divided among those covered by the plan. Although most plans are custom-designed, there are two general considerations about the nature of the bonus formula. First, a standard of performance must be developed that can be used as a baseline for calculating improvements or losses. Some plans use past performance to form a historical standard, whereas others use engineered or estimated standards. When available, historical data provide a relatively fair standard of performance; engineer-determined data can work, however, if there is a high level of trust in the standard and how it is set. Second, the costs included in arriving at the bonus must be chosen. The key is to focus on those costs that are most controllable by employees. Some plans use labor costs as a proportion of total sales; others include a wider range of controllable costs, such as those for materials and utilities.

- **Sharing process.** Once the bonus formula is determined, it is necessary to decide how to share gains when they are obtained. This decision includes choices about what percentage of the bonus pool should go to the company and what percentage to employees. In general, the company should take a percentage low enough to ensure that the plan generates a realistic bonus for employees. Other decisions about dividing the bonus pool include who will share in the bonus and how the money will be divided among employees. Typically, all employees included in the organizational unit covered by the plan share in the bonus. Most plans divide the money on the basis of a straight percentage of total salary payments.

- **Frequency of bonus.** Most plans calculate a bonus monthly. This typically fits with organizational recording needs and is frequent enough to spur employee motivation. Longer payout periods generally are used in seasonal businesses or where there is a long production or billing cycle for a product or service.

- **Change management.** Organizational changes, such as new technology and product mixes, can disrupt the bonus formula. Many plans include a steering committee to review the plan and to make necessary adjustments, especially in light of significant organizational changes.

- **The participative system.** Many gain-sharing plans include a participative system that helps to gather, assess, and implement employee suggestions and improvements. These systems generally include a procedure for formalizing suggestions and different levels of committees for assessing and implementing them.

Although gain-sharing plans are tailored to each situation, three major plans are used most often: the Scanlon plan, the Rucker plan, and Improshare. The most popular program is the Scanlon plan, used in such firms as Donnelly Corporation, De Soto, Midland-Ross, and Dana Corporation. The incentive part of the Scanlon plan generally includes a bonus formula based on a ratio measure comparing total sales volume to total payroll expenses. This measure of labor cost efficiency is relatively responsive to employee behaviors and is used to construct a historical base rate at the beginning of the plan. Savings resulting from improvements over this base make up the bonus pool. The bonus is often split equally between the company and employees, with all members of the organization receiving bonuses of a percentage of their salaries. The Rucker plan and Improshare use different bonus formulas and place less emphasis on worker participation than does the Scanlon plan.[62]

More recently, *goal-sharing* plans have also emerged. Like gain sharing, goal-sharing plans pay bonuses when performance exceeds a standard, but differ in that goal-sharing plans are not based on historical and well-understood performance measures. Rather, goal-sharing plans use changing strategic objectives as the primary standard of performance. Thus, goal sharing is a more flexible reward system than gain sharing.

Gain-sharing plans tie the goals of workers to the organization's goals. It is to the financial advantage of employees to work harder, to cooperate with each other, to make suggestions, and to implement improvements. Reviews of the empirical literature and individual studies suggest that when such plans are implemented properly, organizations can expect specific improvements.[63] A study sponsored by the General Accounting Office found that plans in place more than 5 years averaged annual savings of 29% in labor costs;[64] there also is evidence to suggest that they work in 50% to 80% of the reported cases.[65] A report on four case studies in manufacturing and service settings noted significant increases in productivity (32% in manufacturing and 11% in services), as well as in several other measures.[66] A longitudinal field study employing experimental and control groups supports gain sharing's positive effect over time and even after the group's bonus was discontinued.[67] Other reported results include enhanced coordination and teamwork; cost savings; acceptance of technical, market, and methods changes; demands for better planning and more efficient management; new ideas as well as effort; reductions in overtime; more flexible union–management relations; and greater employee satisfaction.[68]

Gain-sharing plans are better suited to certain situations than to others, and Table 17.4 (on page 389) lists conditions favoring such plans. In general, gain sharing seems suited to small organizations with a good market, simple measures of historical performance, and production costs controllable by employees. Product and market demand should be relatively stable, and employee–management relations should be open and based on trust. Top management should support the plan, and support services should be willing and able to respond to increased demands. The workforce should be interested in and knowledgeable about gain sharing and should be technically proficient in its tasks.

Application 17.3 describes the reward system at Lands' End Direct Merchants.[69] It describes a variety of reward system design features as well as how a number of different types of rewards can be mixed together to produce an overall reward system.

Promotion Systems

Like decisions about pay increases, many decisions about promotions and job movements in organizations are made in a top-down, closed manner: Higher-level managers decide whether lower-level employees will be promoted. This process can be secretive, with people often not knowing that a position is open, that they are being considered for promotion, or the reasons why some people are promoted but others are not. Without such information, capable people who might be interested in a new job may be overlooked. Furthermore, because employees may fail to see the connection between good performance and promotions, the motivational potential of promotions is reduced.

Fortunately, this is changing. Most organizations today have tried to reduce the secrecy surrounding promotions and job changes by openly posting the availability of new jobs and inviting people to nominate themselves.[70] Although open job posting entails extra administrative costs, it can lead to better promotion decisions.

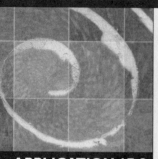

REVISING THE REWARD SYSTEM AT LANDS' END

Lands' End Direct Merchants is an international catalogue retailer employing a seasonal workforce that varies between 5,500 and 8,500 full- and part-time staff. It is widely recognized as one of the best companies to work for as a result of its participative culture, employment practices, and rewards. The company operates through a simple belief in employees "doing the right thing." This philosophy has helped to make the company an employer of choice.

The organization has been proactively rethinking and implementing specific aspects of its reward system over a 4-year period to help Lands' End stay ahead of other companies. The reward system is composed of a mix of competitive pay, innovative benefits, work-life initiatives, and a variety of internal opportunities that encourage organization members to progress.

The firm's reward strategy is guided by principles such as maintaining direct and clear communication channels regarding any aspect of employment practice; encouraging the free exchange of information, ideas, and suggestions; and where possible, eliminating any causes and conditions that lead to inequities, complaints, or employee dissatisfaction. For example, an employee job-evaluation committee annually reviews and analyzes pay rates in different organizations and industries. This task force, composed of a variety of employees, then assigns specific wage levels to work positions. As a result, rates are perceived as fair by individuals while Lands' End itself learns more about how to value jobs and work based on predefined factors such as knowledge, skills, environment, and responsibility.

In the area of pay, one of the key changes has been a shift from rewarding a job population to rewarding the person. For example, under the old reward system, all salaried people used to receive a cash bonus based on sales volume and profits for the entire company. Now, each job is assigned an annual-incentive-plan target expressed as a percentage of base salary. Payouts on the plan are dependent on actual pretax profit performance for the whole company and the business-units-against-performance goals established each year by the board. Individual bonuses are based 50% on business-unit performance and 50% by corporate performance, thus linking individual effort to both local and organizational results.

In addition to the above changes in the pay system, the organization is piloting a gain-sharing-style bonus plan designed by a departmental task force for a small 20-person unit. It is being progressively deployed across the operations organization. Five operations departments have so far designed plans to link people's effort and knowledge to business-unit results—in both cost and quality terms. Each operations department has its own performance measures. For example, employees in the order-filling department are measured on a cost-per-piece and quality basis. These changes are being made to introduce group- or departmental-level performance rewards in addition to individual pay and annual-incentive-plan bonuses.

An individual reward system for the large hourly workforce supplements the bonus system. The inputs to the system are the employee job-evaluation committee's assignment of wage grades to jobs. Each grade has a minimum and maximum hourly rate, with six steps in between. Full- and part-time employees can progress through these six steps and increase their pay by completing a required number of hours in the job and satisfactorily meeting four generic performance standards that are specifically interpreted for each job and function. The four performance standards are:

- **Service:** helpfulness and support for customers and colleagues
- **Quality:** how well the job is done
- **Quantity:** a measure of individual productivity
- **Reliability:** a measure of dependability

These four performance standards are reviewed during performance reviews with immediate supervisors throughout the year. An individual's ratings are based on achieving jointly set personal goals that are tied to:

- The four performance standards
- Job responsibilities and competencies
- Personal aspirations
- Business-unit objectives
- The spirit of Lands' End principles of doing business

Pay increases within a grade are given automatically until the maximum within grade rate is achieved. Then annual company increases only are received until the employee enters a new grade. The system is based on giving credit for hours worked in each grade, although individuals can be promoted to a higher grade and begin the process again. Hourly employees can also receive an annual performance bonus based on annual-incentive-plan computations that is typically between 2% and 4% of earnings.

Lands' End is also attempting to repackage work-life benefits to suit individual preferences, and so get greater value from its significant investments in this area. The main elements of the work-life benefits are:

- Plans for health care and additional retirement health care

- Child-care leave, summer camps, and provision of an on-site day-care center
- Health promotion and sports facilities
- A range of time-off-with-pay schemes, for matters ranging from family member illness to child adoption
- Employee-assistance programs to support life changes or crises
- Flexible working hours
- Education opportunities with financial support
- Job share and a six-week "try a job" work-experience scheme
- An emergency fund to help employees who suffer loss because of fire, tornado, or flood

Lands' End also offers between $35 and $1,000 to employees who recommend people who subsequently come to work for the company. More than half of job applicants from outside the company are usually referrals.

The guiding principle in Lands' End's thinking to pay the person rather than a given job population, repackage incentives and not reinvent them, and manage individuals rather than the compensation plan or system itself for best results has been simplicity. Through the reward system revision process, the organization has learned the importance of (1) involving and educating leaders and top managers to gain the confidence of business partners; (2) clearly stating the business case; (3) listening to others and inviting feedback on the basis of engagement and respect; (4) continually challenging yourself to stay abreast of new developments or options that are emerging in the areas of compensation and benefits; and (5) achieving a level of change with which people feel comfortable to encourage participation in ongoing dialogue.

Table 17•4	Conditions Favoring Gain-Sharing Plans
ORGANIZATIONAL CHARACTERISTIC	**FAVORABLE CONDITION**
Size	Small unit, usually less than 500 employees
Age	Old enough that the learning curve has flattened and standards can be set based on performance history
Financial measures	Simple, with a good history
Market for output	Good, can absorb additional production
Product costs	Controllable by employees
Organizational climate	Open, high level of trust
Style of management	Participative
Union status	No union, or one that is favorable to a cooperative effort
Overtime history	Limited to no use of overtime in past
Seasonal nature of business	Relatively stable across time
Work floor interdependence	High to moderate interdependence
Capital investment plans	Little investment planned
Product stability	Few design changes
Comptroller/chief financial officer	Trusted, able to explain financial measures
Communication policy	Open, willing to share financial results
Plant manager	Trusted, committed to plan, able to articulate goals and ideals of plan
Management	Technically competent, supportive of participative management style, good communication skills, able to deal with suggestions and new ideas
Corporate position (if part of larger organization)	Favorable to plan
Workforce	Technically knowledgeable, interested in participation and higher pay, financially knowledgeable and interested
Plant support services	Maintenance and engineering groups competent, willing, and able to respond to increased demands

SOURCE: PAY AND ORGANIZATION DEVELOPMENT by Lawler, © 1981. Reprinted by permission of Pearson Education, Inc., Upper Saddle River, NJ.

Open posting increases the pool of available personnel by ensuring that interested people will be considered for new jobs and that capable people will be identified. Open posting also can increase employee motivation by showing that a valued reward is available and contingent on performance.

Some organizations have increased the accuracy and equity of job-change decisions by including peers and subordinates in the decision-making process. Peer and subordinate judgments about a person's performance and promotability help bring all relevant data to bear on promotion decisions. Such participation can increase the accuracy of these decisions and can make people feel that the basis for promotions is equitable. In many self-regulating work teams, for example, the group interviews and helps select new members and supervisors. This helps ensure that new people will fit in and that the group is committed to making that happen. Evidence from high-involvement plants suggests that participation in selecting new members can lead to greater group cohesiveness and task effectiveness.[71]

Reward-System Process Issues

Thus far, we have discussed different reward systems and assessed their strengths and weaknesses. Considerable research has been conducted on the process aspect of reward systems. Process refers to how pay and other rewards typically are administered in the organization. At least two process issues affect employees' perceptions of the reward system: who should be involved in designing and administering the reward system, and what kind of communication should exist with respect to rewards.[72]

Traditionally, reward systems are designed by top managers and compensation specialists and are simply imposed on employees. Although this top-down process may result in a good system, it cannot ensure that employees will understand and trust it. In the absence of trust, workers are likely to have negative perceptions of the reward system. There is growing evidence that employee participation in the design and administration of a reward system can increase employee understanding and can contribute to feelings of control over and commitment to the plan.

Lawler and Jenkins described a small manufacturing plant where a committee of workers and managers designed a pay system, after studying alternative plans and collecting salary survey data.[73] This resulted in a plan that gave control over salaries to members of work groups. Team members behaved responsibly in setting wage rates. They gave themselves 8% raises, which fell at the 50th percentile in the local labor market. Moreover, the results of a survey administered 6 months after the start of the new pay plan showed significant improvements in turnover, job satisfaction, and satisfaction with pay and its administration. Lawler attributed these improvements to employees having greater information about the pay system. Participation led to employee ownership of the plan and feelings that it was fair and trustworthy.

Communication about reward systems also can have a powerful impact on employee perceptions of pay equity and on motivation. Most organizations maintain secrecy about pay rates, especially in the managerial ranks. Managers typically argue that secrecy is preferred by employees. It also gives managers freedom in administering pay because they do not have to defend their judgments. There is evidence to suggest, however, that pay secrecy can lead to dissatisfaction with pay and to reduced motivation. Dissatisfaction derives mainly from people's misperceptions about their pay relative to the pay of others. Research shows that managers tend to overestimate the pay of peers and of people below them in the organization and that they tend to underestimate the pay of superiors. These misperceptions contribute to dissatisfaction with pay because regardless of a manager's pay level, it will seem small in comparison to the perceived pay level of subordinates and peers. Perhaps worse, potential promotions will appear less valuable than they actually are.

Secrecy can reduce motivation by obscuring the relationship between pay and performance. For organizations having a performance-based pay plan, secrecy prevents employees from testing whether the organization is actually paying for performance; employees come to mistrust the pay system, fearing that the company has something to hide. Secrecy can also reduce the beneficial impact of accurate performance feedback. Pay provides people with feedback about how they are performing in relation to some standard. Because managers overestimate the pay of peers and subordinates, they will consider their own pay low and thus perceive performance feedback more negatively than it really is. Such misperceptions about performance discourage those managers who are actually performing effectively.

For organizations having a history of secrecy, initial steps toward an open reward system should be modest. For example, an organization could release information on pay ranges and median salaries for different jobs. Organizations with unions generally publish such data for lower-level jobs, and extending that information to all jobs would not be difficult. Once organizations have established higher levels of trust about pay, they might publicize information about the size of raises and who receives them. Finally, as organizations become more democratic, with high levels of trust among managers and workers, they can push toward complete openness about all forms of rewards.

It is important to emphasize that both the amount of participation in designing reward systems and the amount of frankness in communicating about rewards should fit the rest of the organization design and managerial philosophy. Clearly, high levels of participation and openness are congruent with democratic organizations. It is questionable whether authoritarian organizations would tolerate either one.

■ SUMMARY

This chapter presented three types of human resources management interventions: goal setting, performance appraisal, and rewards systems. Although all three change programs are relatively new to organization development, they offer powerful methods for managing employee and work group performance. They also help enhance worker satisfaction and support work design, business strategy, and employee involvement practices.

Principles contributing to the success of goal setting include establishing challenging goals and clarifying measurement. These are accomplished by setting difficult but feasible goals, managing participation in the goal-setting process, and being sure that the goals can be measured and influenced by the employee or work group. The most common form of goal setting—management by objectives—depends on top-management support and participative planning to be effective.

Performance appraisals represent an important link between goal setting and reward systems. As part of an organization's feedback and control system, they provide employees and work groups with information they can use to improve work outcomes. Appraisals are becoming more participative and developmental. An increasing number of people are involved in collecting performance data, evaluating an employee's performance, and determining how the appraisee can improve.

Reward systems interventions elicit, reinforce, and maintain desired performance. They can be oriented to individual jobs, work groups, or organizations and affect both performance and employee well-being. In addition to traditional job-based compensation systems, the major reward systems interventions in use today are skill-based pay, pay for performance, gain sharing, and promotions. Each of the plans has strengths and weaknesses when measured against criteria of performance contingency, equity, availability, timeliness, durability, and visibility. The critical process of implementing a reward system involves decisions about who should be involved in designing and administering it and how much information about pay should be communicated.

■ NOTES

1. A. Mohrman, S. Mohrman, and C. Worley, "High-Technology Performance Management," in *Managing Complexity in High-Technology Organizations,* eds. M. Von Glinow and S. Mohrman (New York: Oxford University Press, 1990), 216–36.

2. D. McDonald and A. Smith, "A Proven Connection: Performance Management and Business Results," *Compensation and Benefits Review* 27 (1995): 59–64; F. Luthans and A. Stajkovic, "Reinforce for Performance: The Need to Go Beyond Pay and Even Rewards," *Academy of Management Executive* 13 (1999): 49–58; P. Bernthal, R. Sumlin, P. Davis, and R. Rogers, *Performance Management Practices Survey Report,* New York: Development Dimensions International, 1997; Hewitt Associates, *The Impact of Performance Management on Organizational Success,* New York: Hewitt Associates LLC, 1994.

3. J. Riedel, D. Nebeker, and B. Cooper, "The Influence of Monetary Incentives on Goal Choice, Goal Commitment, and Task Performance," *Organizational Behavior and Human Decision Processes* 42 (1988): 155–80; P. Earley, T. Connolly, and G. Ekegren, "Goals, Strategy Development, and Task Performance: Some Limits on the Efficacy of Goal Setting," *Journal of Applied Psychology* 74 (1989): 24–33; N. Perry, "Here Come Richer, Riskier Pay Plans," *Fortune* (19 December 1988): 50–58; E. Lawler III, *High-Involvement Management* (San Francisco: Jossey-Bass, 1986); A. Mohrman, S. Resnick-West, and E. Lawler III, *Designing Performance Appraisal Systems* (San Francisco: Jossey-Bass, 1990).

4. Mohrman, Mohrman, and Worley, "High-Technology Performance Management."

5. R. Kaplan and D. Norton, "Transforming the Balanced Scorecard from Performance Measurement to Strategic Management—Part II," *Accounting Horizons* 15 (2001): 147–61.

6. E. Locke and G. Latham, *A Theory of Goal Setting and Task Performance* (Englewood Cliffs, N.J.: Prentice Hall, 1990).

7. Locke and Latham, *Theory of Goal Setting;* E. Locke, R. Shaw, L. Saari, and G. Latham, "Goal Setting and Task Performance: 1969–1980," *Psychological Bulletin* 97 (1981): 125–52; M. Tubbs, "Goal Setting: A Meta-Analytic Examination of the Empirical Evidence," *Journal of Applied Psychology* 71 (1986): 474–83.

8. A. O'Leary-Kelly, J. Martocchio, and D. Frink, "A Review of the Influence of Group Goals on Group Per-

formance," *Academy of Management Journal* 37 (1994): 1285–1301.

9. S. Sherman, "Stretch Goals: The Dark Side of Asking for Miracles," *Fortune* (13 November 1995): 231–32; S. Tully, "Why to Go for Stretch Targets," *Fortune* (14 November 1994): 145–58.

10. D. Crown and J. Rosse, "Yours, Mine, and Ours: Facilitating Group Productivity Through the Integration of Individual and Group Goals," *Organizational Behavior and Human Decision Processes* 64, 2 (1995): 138–50.

11. P. Drucker, *The Practice of Management* (New York: Harper & Row, 1954), 63.

12. G. Odiorne, *Management by Objectives* (New York: Pittman, 1965).

13. H. Levinson, "Management by Objectives: A Critique," *Training and Development Journal* 26 (1972): 410–25.

14. D. McGregor, "An Uneasy Look at Performance Appraisal," *Harvard Business Review* 35 (May-June 1957): 89–94.

15. E. Huse and E. Kay, "Improving Employee Productivity Through Work Planning," in *The Personnel Job in a Changing World,* ed. J. Blood (New York: American Management Association, 1964), 301–15; R. Byrd and J. Cowan, "MBO: A Behavioral Science Approach," *Personnel* 51 (March-April 1974): 42–50.

16. This application was adapted from T. Jones, "Performance Management in a Changing Context: Monsanto Pioneers a Competency-Based, Developmental Approach," *Human Resource Management* 34 (1995): 425–42.

17. Locke and Latham, *Theory of Goal Setting.*

18. Tubbs, "Goal Setting"; R. Guzzo, R. Jette, and R. Katzell, "The Effects of Psychologically Based Intervention Programs on Worker Productivity: A Meta-Analysis," *Personnel Psychology* 38 (1985): 275–91; A. Mento, R. Steel, and R. Karren, "A Meta-Analytic Study of the Effects of Goal Setting on Task Performance: 1966–1984," *Organizational Behavior and Human Decision Processes* 39 (1987): 52–83; O'Leary-Kelly, Martocchio, and Frink, "Influence of Group Goals."

19. C. Pearson, "Participative Goal Setting as a Strategy for Improving Performance and Job Satisfaction: A Longitudinal Evaluation with Railway Track Maintenance Gangs," *Human Relations* 40 (1987): 473–88; R. Pritchard,

S. Jones, P. Roth, K. Stuebing, and S. Ekeberg, "Effects of Group Feedback, Goal Setting, and Incentives on Organizational Productivity," *Journal of Applied Psychology* 73 (1988): 337–58.

20. S. Yearta, S. Maitlis, and R. Briner, "An Exploratory Study of Goal Setting in Theory and Practice: A Motivational Technique That Works?" *Journal of Occupational and Organizational Psychology* 68 (1995): 237–52.

21. R. Steers, "Task-Goal Attributes: Achievement and Supervisory Performance," *Organizational Behavior and Human Performance* 13 (1975): 392–403; G. Latham and G. Yukl, "A Review of Research on the Application of Goal Setting in Organizations," *Academy of Management Journal* 18 (1975): 824–45; R. Steers and L. Porter, "The Role of Task-Goal Attributes in Employee Performance," *Psychological Bulletin* 81 (1974): 434–51; Earley, Connolly, and Ekegren, "Goals"; J. Hollenbeck and A. Brief, "The Effects of Individual Differences and Goal Origin on Goal Setting and Performance," *Organizational Behavior and Human Decision Processes* 40 (1987): 392–414.

22. Huse and Kay, "Improving Employee Productivity," 301–15; A. Raia, "Goal Setting and Self-Control: An Empirical Study," *Journal of Management Studies* 2 (1965): 34–53; A. Raia, "A Second Look at Management Goals and Controls," *California Management Review* 8 (1965): 49–58; D. Terpstra, P. Olson, and B. Lockeman, "The Effects of MBO on Levels of Performance and Satisfaction Among University Faculty," *Group and Organization Studies* 7 (1982): 353–66.

23. S. Carroll and W. Tosi Jr., *Management by Objectives* (New York: Macmillan, 1973), 23.

24. G. Latham and R. Wexley, *Increasing Productivity Through Performance Appraisal* (Reading, Mass.: Addison-Wesley, 1981).

25. L. Holsinger, "Effective Performance Management Practices," Mercer Human Resource Consulting, New York, October, 2002.

26. Mohrman, Resnick-West, and Lawler, *Designing Performance Appraisal Systems*; Anonymous, "Employees Say Companies Must Improve Performance Management," *HR Focus* 80 (2003): 9; J. Smither (ed.). *Performance Appraisal* (San Francisco: Jossey-Bass, 1998).

27. H. Bernardin, C. Hagan, J. Kane, and P. Villanova, "Effective Performance Management," in *Performance Appraisal*, ed. J. Smither (San Francisco: Jossey-Bass, 1998), 348–64.

28. Anonymous, "Companies Must Improve."

29. G. Yukl and R. Lepsinger, "How to Get the Most Out of 360-Degree Feedback," *Training* 32, 21 (1995): 45–50; G. Roberts, "Employee Performance Appraisal System Participation: A Technique that Works," *Public Personnel Management* 32 (2003): 89–97.

30. Mohrman et al., "Quality of Work Life"; S. Scott and W. Einstein, "Strategic Performance Appraisal in Team-Based Organizations: One Size Does Not Fit All," *Academy of Management Executive* 15 (2001): 107–17.

31. W. Tornow and M. London, *Maximizing the Value of 360-Degree Feedback: A Process for Successful Individual and Organizational Development* (San Francisco: Jossey-Bass, 1998); B. O'Reilly, "360 Feedback Can Change Your Life," *Fortune* (17 October 1994): 93–100.

32. Anonymous, "Performance Management Systems Are Quickly Becoming Popular," *HR Focus* 80 (2003): 8–10.

33. Mohrman, Resnick-West, and Lawler, *Designing Performance Appraisal Systems*; E. Lawler, "Performance Management: The Next Generation," *Compensation and Benefits Review* 26, 3 (1994): 16–19.

34. This case was adapted from D. Cederblom and D. Pemerl, "From Performance Appraisal to Performance Management: One Agency's Experience," *Public Personnel Management* 21 (2002): 131–41.

35. L. Pettijohn, R. Parker, C. Pettijohn, and J. Kent, "Performance Appraisals: Usage, Criteria, and Observations," *The Journal of Management Development* 20 (2001): 754–72.

36. J. Fairbank and D. Prue, "Developing Performance Feedback Systems," in *Handbook of Organizational Behavior Management*, ed. L. Frederiksen (New York: John Wiley & Sons, 1982).

37. R. Ammons, *Knowledge of Performance: Survey of Literature, Some Possible Applications and Suggested Experimentation*, USAF WADC Technical Report 5414 (Wright-Patterson Air Force Base, Ohio: Wright Air Development Center, Aero Medical Laboratory, 1954); J. Adams, "Response Feedback and Learning," *Psychology Bulletin* 70 (1968): 486–504; J. Annett, *Feedback and Human Behavior* (Baltimore: Penguin, 1969); J. Sassenrath, "Theory and Results on Feedback and Retention," *Journal of Educational Psychology* 67 (1975): 894–99; F. Luthans and T. Davis, "Behavioral Management in Service Organizations," in *Service Management Effectiveness*, eds. D. Bowen, R. Chase, and T. Cummings (San Francisco: Jossey-Bass, 1989): 177–210.

38. R. Kopelman, *Managing Productivity in Organizations* (New York: McGraw-Hill, 1986).

39. Guzzo, Jette, and Katzell, "Psychologically Based Intervention Programs."

40. D. Nadler, "The Effects of Feedback on Task Group Behavior: A Review of the Experimental Research,"

Organizational Behavior and Human Performance 23 (1979): 309–38; D. Nadler, C. Cammann, and P. Mirvis, "Developing a Feedback System for Work Units: A Field Experiment in Structural Change," *Journal of Applied Behavioral Science* 16 (1980): 41–62; J. Chobbar and J. Wallin, "A Field Study on the Effect of Feedback Frequency on Performance," *Journal of Applied Psychology* 69 (1984): 524–30.

41. W. Scott, J. Farh, and P. Podsakoff, "The Effects of 'Intrinsic' and 'Extrinsic' Reinforcement Contingencies on Task Behavior," *Organizational Behavior and Human Decision Processes* 41 (1988): 405–25; E. Lawler III, *Strategic Pay* (San Francisco: Jossey-Bass, 1990); A. Stajkovic and F. Luthans, "Differential Effects of Incentive Motivators on Work Performance," *Academy of Management Journal* 44 (2001): 580–90.

42. E. Lawler, *Rewarding Excellence: Pay Strategies for the New Economy* (San Francisco: Jossey-Bass, 2000).

43. Ibid.

44. J. Useem, "Have They No Shame," *Fortune* (14 April 2003): 57–63.

45. J. Bruner, "The Next Big Thing in Health Benefits: Consumer Choice," *Benefits Quarterly* 18 (2002): 49–53.

46. J. Campbell, M. Dunnette, E. Lawler III, and K. Weick, *Managerial Behavior, Performance, and Effectiveness* (New York: McGraw-Hill, 1970).

47. S. Kerr, "Risky Business: The New Pay Game," *Fortune* (22 July 1996): 94–96.

48. C. Worley, D. Bowen, and E. Lawler III, "On the Relationship Between Objective Increases in Pay and Employees' Subjective Reactions," *Journal of Organization Behavior* 13 (1992): 559–71.

49. Anonymous, "Performance Management Systems Are Quickly Becoming Popular."

50. V. Gibson, "The New Employee Reward System," *Management Review* (February 1995): 13–18.

51. E. Lawler, *Organizing for High Performance: Employee Involvement, TQM, Re-engineering, and Knowledge Management in the Fortune 1000* (San Francisco: Jossey-Bass, 2001).

52. Lawler, *Rewarding Excellence.*

53. G. Ledford and G. Bergel, "Skill-Based Pay Case Number 1: General Mills," (Skill-based pay seminar materials, American Compensation Association, Scottsdale, Ariz., 1990).

54. E. Lawler, *Pay and Organization Development* (Reading, Mass.: Addison-Wesley, 1981): 66; E. Lawler and G. Ledford Jr., "Skill-Based Pay," *Personnel* 62 (1985): 30–37; Lawler, *From the Ground Up.*

55. Lawler, *Pay and Organization Development*, 66.

56. N. Gupta, G. D. Jenkins Jr., and W. Curington, "Paying for Knowledge: Myths and Realities," *National Productivity Review* (Spring 1986): 107–23.

57. E. Lawler III, S. Mohrman, and G. Ledford, *Strategies for High-Performance Organizations* (San Francisco: Jossey-Bass, 1998).

58. Lawler, *Rewarding Excellence.*

59. F. Lyons and D. Ben-Ora, "Total Rewards Strategy: The Best Foundation of Pay for Performance," *Compensation and Benefits Review* (March/April, 2002): 34–40.

60. Z. Schiller, "A Model Incentive Plan Gets Caught in a Vise," *Business Week* (22 January 1996): 89–90.

61. Lawler, *Pay and Organization Development*, 134–43; M. Schuster, J. Schuster, and M. Montague, "Excellence in Gainsharing: From the Start to Renewal," *Journal for Quality and Participation* 17, 3 (1994): 18–25; D. Band, G. Scanlon, and C. Tustin, "Beyond the Bottom Line: Gainsharing and Organization Development," *Personnel Review* 23, 8 (1994): 17–32; J. Belcher, "Gainsharing and Variable Pay: The State of the Art," *Compensation and Benefits Review* 26, 3 (1994): 50–60.

62. Lawler, *Pay and Organization Development*, 146–54.

63. J. Ramquist, "Labor–Management Cooperation: The Scanlon Plan at Work," *Sloan Management Review* (Spring 1982): 49–55; T. Cummings and E. Molloy, *Improving Productivity and the Quality of Work Life* (New York: Praeger, 1977), 249–60; R. J. Bullock and E. Lawler III, "Gainsharing: A Few Questions, and Fewer Answers," *Human Resource Management* 23 (1984): 23–40; C. Miller and M. Schuster, "A Decade's Experience with the Scanlon Plan: A Case Study," *Journal of Occupational Behavior* 8 (April 1987): 167–74; T. Welbourne and L. Gomez-Meija, "Gainsharing: A Critical Review and a Future Research Agenda," *Journal of Management* 21, 3 (1995): 559–609; W. Imberman, "Is Gainsharing the Wave of the Future," *Management Accounting* 77 (1977): 35–40; D. Collins, *Gainsharing and Power: Lessons from Six Scanlon Plans* (Ithaca, N.Y.: ILR Press of Cornell University Press, 1998).

64. General Accounting Office, *Productivity Sharing Programs: Can They Contribute to Productivity Improvement?* (Washington, D.C.: Author, 1981).

65. Bullock and Lawler, "Gainsharing"; C. O'Dell, *People, Performance, and Pay* (Houston, Tex.: American Productivity Center, 1987).

66. E. Doherty, W. Nord, and J. McAdams, "Gainsharing and Organization Development: A Productive Synergy," *Journal of Applied Behavioral Science* 25 (1989): 209–29.

67. S. Hanlon, D. Meyer, and R. Taylor, "Consequences of Gainsharing: A Field Experiment Revisited," *Group and Organization Management* 19, 1 (1994): 87–111.

68. E. Lawler III, "Gainsharing Theory and Research: Findings and Future Directions," in *Organizational Change and Development*, vol. 2, eds. W. Pasmore and R. Woodman (Greenwich, Conn.: JAI Press, 1988), 323–44.

69. This application was adapted from C. Ashton, "Lands' End Rethinks Pay for Performance," *Human Resource Management International Digest* 8 (2000): 18–21.

70. E. Lawler III, "Reward Systems," in *Improving Life at Work*, eds. J. Hackman and J. Suttle (Santa Monica, Calif.: Goodyear, 1977), 176.

71. R. Walton, "How to Counter Alienation in the Plant," *Harvard Business Review* 50 (November-December 1972): 70–81.

72. Lawler, *Rewarding Excellence*, 57–59.

73. E. Lawler III and G. Jenkins, *Employee Participation in Pay Plan Development* (unpublished technical report to U.S. Department of Labor, Ann Arbor; Institute for Social Research, University of Michigan, 1976).

18 Developing and Assisting Members*

This chapter presents three human resources management interventions concerned with developing and assisting the well-being of organization members. First, organizations have had to adapt their career planning and development processes to a variety of trends. For example, people have different professional needs and concerns as they progress through their career and life stages; people want to have a healthy work–life balance between professional and personal (home, family, and community) responsibilities; technological changes have altered organizational structures and systems dramatically; and global competition has forced organizations to redefine how work gets done. These processes and concerns have forced individuals and organizations to redefine the social contract that binds them together. Career planning and development interventions can help deal effectively with the issues affecting the social contracts binding employees and organizations. Second, increasing workforce diversity provides an especially challenging environment for human resources management. The mix of age, gender, race, sexual orientation, disabilities, and culture and value orientations in the modern workforce is increasingly varied. Management's perspectives, strategic responses, and implementation approaches can help address pressures posed by this diversity. Finally, wellness interventions, such as work–life balance programs and stress management programs, including employee assistance programs (EAPs), are addressing several important social trends, such as the relationship and interaction between professional and personal roles and lives, fitness and health consciousness, and drug and alcohol abuse.

CAREER PLANNING AND DEVELOPMENT INTERVENTIONS

Career planning and development have been receiving increased attention in organizations. Growing numbers of managers and professional staff are seeking more control over their work lives. Organization members are not willing to have their careers "just happen" and are taking an active role in planning and managing them. This is particularly true for women, midcareer employees, and college recruits, who are increasingly asking for career planning assistance.[1] For example, a study by the Hay Group found that technology professionals were willing to leave their jobs for better career development opportunities.[2] On the other hand, organizations are becoming more and more reliant on their "intellectual capital." Providing career planning and development opportunities for organization members helps to recruit and retain skilled and knowledgeable workers. Many talented job candidates, especially minorities and women, are showing a preference for employers who offer career advancement opportunities.

Many organizations—General Electric, Xerox, Intel, Ciba-Geigy, Cisco Systems, Quaker Oats, and Novotel UK, among others—have adopted career planning and development programs. These programs have attempted to improve the quality of work life for managers and professionals, enhance their performance, increase employee retention, and respond to equal employment and affirmative action legisla-

*The authors would like to gratefully acknowledge the contribution of Karen Whelan-Berry, Utah Valley State College, for her revision of this chapter.

tion. Companies have discovered that organizational growth and effectiveness require career development programs to ensure that needed talent will be available. Competent managers are often the scarcest resource. Many companies also have experienced the high costs of turnover among recent college graduates, including MBAs; the turnover can reach 50% after 5 years. Career planning and development help attract and hold such highly talented people and can increase the chances that their skills and knowledge will be used.

Recent legislation and court actions have motivated many firms to set up career planning and development programs for minority and female employees, who are in short supply at the middle- and upper-management levels. Organizations are discovering that the career development needs of women and minorities often require special programs and the use of nontraditional methods, such as integrated systems for recruitment, placement, and development. Similarly, age-discrimination laws have led many organizations to set up career programs aimed at older managers and professionals. Thus, career planning and development are increasingly being applied to people at different ages and stages of development—from new recruits to those nearing retirement age.

Career planning is concerned with individuals choosing occupations, organizations, and positions at each stage of their careers. *Career development* involves helping employees attain career objectives.[3] Although both of these interventions generally are aimed at managerial and professional employees, a growing number of programs are including lower-level employees, particularly those in white-collar jobs.

Career Stages

A career consists of a sequence of work-related positions occupied by a person during the course of a lifetime.[4] Early research on careers has been devoted to understanding how aging and experience affect people's careers. This research built on the extensive work done on adult growth and development[5] and adapted that developmental perspective to work experience.[6] Results suggest that employees progress through at least four distinct career stages as they mature and gain experience. Each stage has unique concerns, needs, and challenges. While initially linked with life stages, which are discussed below, career stages may repeat and or be compressed if an individual changes careers at midlife.

1. **The establishment stage (ages 21–26).** This phase is the outset of a career when people are generally uncertain about their competence and potential. They are dependent on others, especially bosses and more experienced employees, for guidance, support, and feedback. At this stage, people are making initial choices about committing themselves to a specific career, organization, and job. They are exploring possibilities while learning about their own capabilities.

2. **The advancement stage (ages 26–40).** During this phase, employees become independent contributors who are concerned with achieving and advancing in their chosen careers. They have typically learned to perform autonomously and need less guidance from bosses and closer ties with colleagues. This settling-down period also is characterized by attempts to clarify the range of long-term career options.

3. **The maintenance stage (ages 40–60).** This phase involves leveling off and holding on to career successes. Many people at this stage have achieved their greatest advancements and are now concerned with helping less-experienced subordinates. For those who are dissatisfied with their career progress, this period can be conflictual and depressing, as characterized by the term "midlife crisis." People often reappraise their circumstances, search for alternatives, and redirect their career efforts. Success in these endeavors can lead to continuing growth, whereas failure can lead to early decline.

4. **The withdrawal stage (age 60 and above)**. This final stage is concerned with leaving a career. It involves letting go of organizational attachments and getting ready for greater leisure time and retirement. The employee's major contributions are imparting knowledge and experience to others. For those people who are generally satisfied with their careers, this period can result in feelings of fulfillment and a willingness to leave the career behind.

The different career stages represent a broad developmental perspective on people's jobs. They provide insight about the personal and career issues that people are likely to face at different career phases. These issues can be potential sources of stress. Employees are likely to go through the phases at different rates, and to experience personal and career issues differently at each stage. For example, one person may experience the maintenance stage as a positive opportunity to develop less-experienced employees; another person may experience the maintenance stage as a stressful leveling off of career success.

Life stage, which has traditionally been defined by age, also can impact the experience of the various career stages. Adult life stages include early life (ending sometime between 35 and 45), midlife (ending somewhere between 50 and 55), and finally, late life. Each stage is bridged by a transition phase. However, chronological age may no longer be the best indicator of life stage or a transition point. In the past, life and career stages tended to follow a parallel progression, especially for men. That is, the early life stage coincided with establishment and advancement, midlife with maintenance, and late life with withdrawal. This was not as true for women who entered the workforce after bearing and raising children.[7] Today, life and career stage may not be parallel at all. This can occur for both men and women through significant early career success, as happened with the "dot-com" boom period, through major career changes after early life, or through leaving organizational for self-employment. Life stage and career stage can impact the interventions described in this chapter.

More recent work on careers suggests that careers will be more "protean." That is, careers will be driven by the individual and involve greater personal and less organizational responsibility for their progress. This emphasizes that life age or stage will matter less than career age and the ability to perform.[8] Such a view of careers provides another lens through which to view an individual's overall and career development. For purposes of discussing career planning and development, we use the career stage model.

Career Planning

Career planning involves setting individual career objectives. It is highly personalized and generally includes assessing one's interests, capabilities, values, and goals; examining alternative careers; making decisions that may affect the current job; and planning how to progress in the desired direction. This process results in people choosing occupations, organizations, and jobs. It determines, for example, whether individuals will accept or decline promotions and transfers and whether they will stay or leave the company for another job or for retirement.

Individual responsibility for careers and career planning has increased significantly, and recent estimates project that an individual career beginning now will involve an average of eight major job and/or organization changes. One survey indicates organizations are experiencing average annual turnover of 15%.[9] Further, as organizations downsize and restructure, there is less trust in the organization to provide job security. In the past, when employees more frequently spent their entire career in one organization, careers were judged in terms of advancement and promotion upward in the organizational hierarchy. Today, they are defined in more holistic ways to include a person's attitudes, experiences, and ability to perform. For example, individuals may make numerous job changes to acquire additional responsibilities, skills, and knowledge within or across organizations, or they can remain in the same job, acquiring and developing new skills, and have a successful career. Similarly, people may move horizontally through a series of jobs in different functional areas of the firm. Although they may not be promoted upward in the hierarchy, their broadened job experiences constitute a successful career.

The four career stages can be used to make career planning more effective. Table 18.1 shows the different career stages and the career planning issues relevant at each phase. (As noted earlier, career and life stage might not be parallel.) Applying the table to a particular employee involves first diagnosing the person's existing career stage—establishment, advancement, maintenance, or withdrawal. Next, available career planning resources are used to help the employee address pertinent issues.[10] Career planning programs include some or all of the following resources:

- Communication about career opportunities and resources available to employees within the organization
- Workshops to encourage employees to assess their interests, abilities, and job situations and to formulate career development plans
- Career counseling by managers or human resources personnel
- Self-development materials, such as books, videotapes, and other media, directed toward identifying life and career issues
- Assessment programs that provide various tests of vocational interests, aptitudes, and abilities relevant to setting career goals

Table 18•1	Career Stages and Career Planning Issues
CAREER STAGE	**CAREER PLANNING ISSUES**
Establishment	What are alternative occupations, organizations, and jobs? What are my interests and capabilities? How do I get the work accomplished? Am I performing as expected? Am I developing the necessary skills for advancement?
Advancement	Am I advancing as expected? How can I advance more effectively? What long-term options are available? How do I get more exposure and visibility? How do I develop more effective peer relationships? How do I better integrate career choices with my personal life?
Maintenance	How do I help others become established and advance? Should I reassess myself and my career? Should I redirect my actions?
Withdrawal	What are my interests outside of work? What post-retirement work options are available to me? How can I be financially secure? How can I continue to help others?

According to Table 18.1, employees who are just becoming established in careers can be stressed by concerns for identifying alternatives, assessing their interests and capabilities, learning how to perform effectively, and finding out how they are doing. In terms of life stage, employees are most commonly transitioning to early adulthood, especially new college graduates. Men and women may make decisions about when to have children, although this a more complex decision for women. Establishing a home and family, separate from parents' home, is a key task.

At this stage, the company should provide considerable communication and counseling about available career paths and the skills and abilities needed to progress in them. Workshops, self-development materials, and assessment techniques should be aimed at helping employees assess their interests, aptitudes, and capabilities and at linking that information to possible careers and jobs. Considerable attention should be directed to giving employees continual feedback about job performance and to counseling them about how to improve it. The supervisor–subordinate relationship is especially important for these feedback and development activities.

People at the advancement stage are mainly concerned with getting ahead, discovering long-term career options, and integrating career choices, such as transfers or promotions, with their personal lives. In terms of life stage, individuals may be dealing with children ranging from toddlers to adolescents, and aging parents may interfere with the ability to balance self, family, and work. It is at this stage that individuals may begin to or fully experience the midlife transition. This transition can be quite different for men and women. Early research indicated that the midlife could be a time of crisis as individuals faced mortality, reconciled dreams with actual achievement, and revised life goals. More recent research does not support the consistency of this crisis for men, and women experience more of a transition involving a recalibration of life's guiding values or principles. Organizationally, members should be provided with communication and counseling about challenging assignments and possibilities for more exposure and demonstration of skills. This communication and counseling should help clarify the range of possible long-term career options and provide members with some idea about where they stand in achieving them. Workshops, developmental materials, and assessment methods should be aimed at helping employees develop wider collegial relationships, join with effective mentors and sponsors, and develop more creativity and innovation. These activities also should help people assess both career and personal life spheres and integrate them more successfully.

At the maintenance stage, individuals may be concerned with helping newer employees become established and grow in their careers. This phase also may involve a reassessment of self and career and a possible redirection to something more rewarding. In terms of life stage, individuals progress through the midlife transition to midlife itself, and may begin the late life transition. This involves children leaving home, the ongoing care of parents, or grieving their death. Research shows that employees at the maintenance career stage who have been high achievers in earlier career stages seek ongoing opportunities for high achievement during maintenance and even during withdrawal.[11] The firm should provide individuals with communications about the broader organization and how their desires and roles might fit into it. Workshops, developmental materials, counseling, and assessment techniques should be aimed at helping employees to assess and develop skills to train and coach others.

Employees who are at the withdrawal stage can experience stress about disengaging from work and establishing a secure leisure life. Individuals have typically moved through the late life transition to late life and begin focusing on personal interests and enjoying life. Here, the company should provide communications and counseling about options for post-retirement work and financial security, and it should convey the message that the employee's experience in the organization is

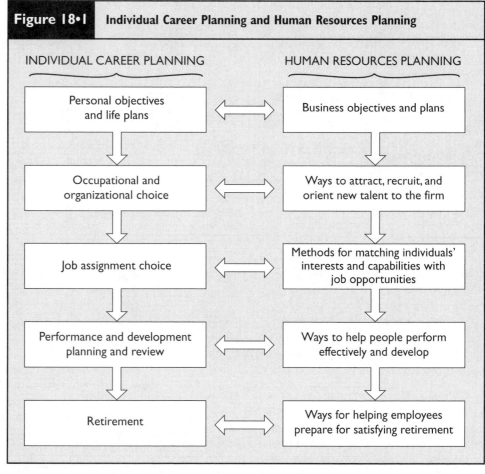

Figure 18•1   Individual Career Planning and Human Resources Planning

INDIVIDUAL CAREER PLANNING

HUMAN RESOURCES PLANNING

Personal objectives and life plans	⟺	Business objectives and plans
Occupational and organizational choice	⟺	Ways to attract, recruit, and orient new talent to the firm
Job assignment choice	⟺	Methods for matching individuals' interests and capabilities with job opportunities
Performance and development planning and review	⟺	Ways to help people perform effectively and develop
Retirement	⟺	Ways for helping employees prepare for satisfying retirement

SOURCE: Reprinted with permission from BUSINESS HORIZONS, 16(1). Copyright © 1973 by The Trustees at Indiana University, Kelley School of Business.

still valued. Retirement planning workshops and materials can help employees gain the skills and information necessary to make a successful transition from work to nonwork life. They can prepare people to shift their attention away from the organization to other interests and activities.[12]

Effective career planning and development requires a comprehensive program integrating both corporate business objectives and employee career needs. As shown in Figure 18.1, this is accomplished through human resources planning aimed at developing and maintaining a workforce to meet business objectives. It includes recruiting new talent, matching people to jobs, helping them develop careers and perform effectively, and preparing them for satisfactory retirement. Career planning activities feed into and support career development and human resources planning activities.

Application 18.1 describes how Colgate-Palmolive, an international consumer-products company, revised career planning to integrate better with business strategy and human resources planning.[13]

Career Development

Career development interventions help individuals achieve their career objectives. Career development follows closely from career planning and includes organizational practices that help employees implement those plans. Career development

LINKING CAREER PLANNING, HUMAN RESOURCES PLANNING, AND STRATEGY AT COLGATE-PALMOLIVE

Colgate-Palmolive Co. is a global manufacturer and marketer of consumer products, with about 70% of its annual $9 billion in sales of personal and house-hold-care products deriving from international markets. To support its global business strategy, the company organized into five worldwide business units in 1989: oral care, personal care, hard-surface care, fabric care, and pet nutrition. However, it soon discovered a significant gap between its business strategy and the human resources necessary to implement it. Consequently, a Global Human Resources Strategy (GHRS) team was formed to devise ways to integrate business strategy with human resources planning and career planning.

The GHRS team's first task was to articulate a human resources vision based on three key values needed to compete globally: care, teamwork, and continuous improvement. This effort resulted in the following vision statement:

We care about people. Colgate people, consumers, shareholders, and our business partners. We are committed to act with compassion, integrity, and honesty in all situations, to listen with respect to others and to value cultural differences. We are also committed to protect our global environment and enhance the local communities where we work.

We are all part of a global team, committed to working together across functions, across countries, and throughout the world. Only by sharing ideas, technologies, and talents can we sustain profitable growth.

We are committed to getting better every day in all we do, as individuals and as teams. By better understanding consumers' and customers' expectations, and by continuously working to innovate and improve our products, services, and processes, we will "become the best."

The GHRS team circulated the vision statement among the firm's senior executives. After extensive discussion, they revised and approved it. Based on principles espoused in the vision, the team then worked on crafting a human resources strategy that would align with business objectives. First, they interviewed managers from Colgate businesses around the world. "The line managers provided invaluable perspective and insight as to the needs of the organization and the role of HR in achieving business goals," said Brian Smith, director of global human resource strategy.

The interviews revealed the need for human resources support in several areas, including career planning, educa-tion and training, and strategy implementation. Colgate needed a comprehensive career planning system so that sufficient numbers of managers with the right skills would be available to fill forecasted job openings. Employees, on the other hand, needed a meaningful career planning system to help them determine what experiences and skills they would need to achieve their own career objectives. Colgate also needed education and training programs that could be applied across business units around the world to reduce the waste and redundancy of the current approach to train-ing where each business unit developed unique programs. Finally, to implement product strategies, the business units needed certain reservoirs of talent, skills, and knowledge. This would require career planning and development on a global scale.

Based on the interview data, the GHRS team coordinated the design of human resources practices for each of the major business functions in the firm. To that end the team created functional design teams, each chaired by the senior manager of the respective business function and including line managers from the business functions as well as appropriate human resources specialists. The design teams first identified global competencies needed to perform the different business functions at Colgate and then designed appropriate career paths and training programs that would allow employees to acquire those competencies.

The manufacturing design team, for example, headed by the manufacturing vice president, identified three sets of global manufacturing competencies: functional/technical, managerial, and leadership. The functional/technical cluster comprised skills and knowledge associated with financial analysis, safety, and production management. The managerial competencies included expertise in negotiation, relationship build-ing, and innovation. The leadership skills involved mobilizing and inspiring people toward a common vision and strategy. To gain the job experiences necessary to learn these competencies, the manufacturing team identified three career paths: functional/technical competencies could be learned in entry-level positions; managerial competencies could be acquired through job rotation, promotion, and special job assignments both domestically and globally; leadership competencies could be gained with experience in higher-level director and vice president positions. To support these career paths, the manufacturing team designed appropriate training programs as well as performance management processes to monitor and reward learning and performance for each level in the career tracks.

At the conclusion of the functional design teams' efforts, the GHRS team sponsored a Global Human Resources Conference to launch implementation of the human resources strategy and practices throughout Colgate. More than 200 human resources leaders from business units around the world attended the weeklong conference. Also present were Colgate's chairman, president, chief operating officer, division presidents, and global business leaders. The conference described the new human resources strategy and practices and linked them directly to business strategy and objectives. It reaffirmed senior management's commitment to the human resources vision, and resulted in specific plans to implement the functional career paths, training programs, and performance management systems across business units worldwide. Colgate's human resources leaders left the conference with renewed energy for the human resources strategy and with clear directions for implementing it across the global businesses.

can be integrated with people's career needs by linking it to different career stages. As described earlier, employees progress through distinct career stages, each with unique issues relevant to career planning: establishment, advancement, maintenance, and withdrawal. Career development interventions help members implement these plans. Table 18.2 identifies career development interventions, lists the career stages to which they are most relevant, and defines their key purposes and intended outcomes. It shows that career development practices may apply to one or more career stages. Performance feedback and coaching, for example, is relevant to all stages, but especially in establishment and advancement stages. Career development interventions also can serve a variety of purposes, such as helping members identify a career path or providing feedback on career progress and work effectiveness. They can contribute to different organizational outcomes such as lowering turnover and costs and enhancing member satisfaction.

Career development interventions traditionally have been applied to younger employees who have a longer time period to contribute to the firm than do older members. Managers often stereotype older employees as being less creative, alert, and productive than younger workers and consequently provide them with less career development support. However, the aging of the workforce has focused new attention on older workers, including a focus on the pace and organization of work, physical and psychological factors, and ergonomic factors.[14] Table 18.2 (on page 404) suggests that the OD field has been relatively lax in developing methods for helping older members cope with the withdrawal stage because only 2 of the 11 interventions presented there apply to the withdrawal stage: consultative roles and phased retirement. This relative neglect can be expected to change in the near future, however, as the U.S. workforce continues to gray. To sustain a highly committed and motivated workforce, organizations increasingly will have to address the career needs of older employees. They will have to recognize and reward the contributions that older workers make to the company. Workforce diversity interventions, discussed later in this chapter, are a positive step in that direction.

Role and Structure Interventions

Role and structure interventions involve programs and processes that focus on the design, the structure and scheduling of work, and the sequencing of assignments to build employee knowledge and leadership potential.

Realistic Job Preview. This intervention provides applicants with credible expectations about the job during the recruitment process. It provides recruits with information about whether the job is likely to be consistent with their needs and career plans. From an organizational perspective, realistic job previews can affect job acceptance in both positive and negative ways; recent research indicates that realistic job previews decrease job acceptance if the applicant has previous exposure to the job, and increase job acceptance if the applicant does not have previous exposure.[15]

Table 18•2	Career Development Interventions

INTERVENTION	CAREER STAGE	PURPOSE	INTENDED OUTCOMES
ROLE & STRUCTURE INTRVENTIONS			
Realistic job preview	Establishment Maintenance Advancement	To provide members with an accurate expectation of work requirements	Reduce turnover Reduce training costs Increase commitment
Job rotation and challenging assignments	Establishment Advancement Maintenance	To provide members with interesting work assignments leading to career objective	Reduce turnover Build organizational knowledge Increase job satisfaction Maintain member motivation
Consultative roles	Maintenance Withdrawal	To help members fill productive roles later in their careers	Increase problem-solving capacity Increase job satisfaction
Phased retirement	Withdrawal	To assist members in moving into retirement	Increase job satisfaction Lower stress during transition
INDIVIDUAL EMPLOYEE DEVELOPMENT			
Assessment centers	Establishment Advancement Maintenance Withdrawal	To select and develop members for managerial and technical jobs	Increase person–job fit Identify high-potential candidates
Mentoring	Establishment Advancement Maintenance	To link a less-experienced member with a more-experienced member for member development	Increase job satisfaction Increase member motivation Increase diversity in upper management & leadership
Developmental training	Establishment Advancement Maintenance Withdrawal	To provide education and training opportunities that help members achieve career goals	Increase organizational capacity
PERFORMANCE FEEDBACK & COACHING			
	Establishment Advancement Maintenance Withdrawal	To provide members with knowledge about their career progress and work effectiveness	Increase productivity Increase job satisfaction Monitor human resources development
WORK LIFE BALANCE			
	Establishment Advancement Maintenance	To help members balance work and personal goals	Improve quality of life Increase productivity & morale Increase organizational commitment Decrease absenteeism
	Withdrawal		Decrease turnover

Knowledge resulting from realistic job previews can be especially useful during the establishment stage, when people are most in need of full and balanced information about organizations and jobs. It also can help employees during the advancement stage, when job changes are likely to occur because of promotion. Research suggests that people may develop unrealistic expectations about the organization and job.[16] They can suffer from "reality shock" when those expectations are not fulfilled and may leave the organization or stay and become disgruntled and unmotivated. To overcome these problems, organizations such as Texas Instruments, Prudential Insurance, and Johnson & Johnson provide new recruits with information about both the positive and negative aspects of the company and the job. They furnish recruits with booklets, talks, and site visits showing what organizational life is really like. Such information reduces the chances that employees will develop unrealistic job expectations, become disgruntled, and leave the company, especially when their tenure is viewed over the long term.[17] This can lead to reduced turnover and training costs, and increased organizational commitment and job satisfaction.[18]

Job Rotation and Challenging Assignments. The purpose of these interventions is to provide employees with the experience and visibility needed for career advancement or with the challenge needed to revitalize a stagnant career at the maintenance stage. A more formalized approach to job rotation is called *job pathing,* which specifies a sequence of jobs to reach a career objective, although the notion of a job path in the new economy is being challenged.[19] Job rotation and challenging assignments are less planned and may not be as oriented to promotion opportunities.

Job rotation helps members in the establishment and advancement stages of their careers by helping them develop new skills, knowledge, and competencies in new jobs. Organization members in the advancement stage may be moved into new job areas after they have demonstrated competence in a particular work specialty. Research suggests that employees who receive challenging job assignments early in their careers do better in later jobs.[20] Companies such as Corning Glass Works, Hewlett-Packard, American Crystal Sugar Company, and Fidelity Investments identify "comers" (managers under 40 years old with potential for assuming top management positions) and "hipos" (high-potential candidates) and provide them with cross-divisional job experiences during the advancement stage. These job transfers provide managers with a broader range of skills and knowledge as well as opportunities to display their managerial talent to a wider audience of corporate executives. Such exposure helps the organization identify members who are capable of handling senior executive responsibilities; it helps the members decide whether to seek promotion to higher positions or to particular departments. Retaining "hipos" is seen as critical to success in today's highly competitive labor market.[21] To reduce the risk of transferring employees across divisions or functions, some firms, such as Procter & Gamble, Heublein, and Continental Can, have created "fallback positions." These jobs are identified before the transfer, and employees are guaranteed that they can return to them without negative consequences if the transfers or promotions do not work out. Fallback positions reduce the risk that employees in the advancement stage will become trapped in a new job assignment that is neither challenging nor highly visible in the company.

In the maintenance stage, challenging assignments or job pathing can help revitalize veteran employees by providing them with new challenges and opportunities for learning and contribution. Research on enriched jobs suggests that people are most responsive to them during the first 1 to 3 years on a job, when enriched jobs are likely to be seen as challenging and motivating.[22] People who have leveled off and remain on enriched jobs for 3 years or more tend to become unresponsive to them, and may no longer be motivated and satisfied by enriched jobs. One way to prevent this loss of job motivation—especially among midcareer employees who are likely to remain on jobs for longer periods of time than are people in the establishment and advancement phases—is to rotate workers to new, more challenging jobs at about 3-year intervals, or to redesign their jobs at those times. Such job changes would keep employees responsive to challenging jobs and sustain motivation and satisfaction during the maintenance phase.[23]

A growing body of research suggests that "plateaued employees" (those with little chance of further advancement) can still have satisfying and productive careers if they accept their new role in the company and are given challenging assignments with high performance standards.[24] Planned rotation to jobs requiring new skills can provide that challenge. However, a firm's business strategy and human resources philosophy must reinforce lateral (as opposed to strictly vertical) job changes if plateaued employees are to adapt effectively to their new jobs.[25] Firms with business strategies emphasizing stability and efficiency of operations, such as the U.S. Post Office and McDonald's, are likely to have more plateaued employees at the maintenance stage than are companies with strategies promoting development and growth, such as Microsoft and Intel.

Consultative Roles. This role involves opportunities to apply wisdom and knowledge to helping others develop in their careers and solve organizational problems, and is most frequently offered to late-career employees. Such roles, which can be structured around specific projects or problems, involve offering advice and expertise to those responsible for resolving the issues, thus increasing the organization's problem-solving abilities. For example, a large aluminum-forging manufacturer was having problems developing accurate estimates of the cost of producing new products. The sales and estimating departments lacked the production experience to make accurate bids for potential new business, thus either losing customers or losing money on products. The company temporarily assigned an old-line production manager who was nearing retirement to consult with the salespeople and estimators about bidding on new business. The consultant applied his years of forging experience to help the sales and estimating people make more accurate estimates. In about a year, the sales staff and estimators gained the skills and invaluable knowledge necessary to make more accurate bids. Perhaps equally important, the preretirement production manager felt that he had made a significant contribution to the company—something he had not experienced for years.

In contrast to mentoring roles (discussed below), consultative roles are not focused directly on guiding or sponsoring younger employees' careers. They are directed at helping others deal with complex problems or projects. Similarly, in contrast to managerial positions, consultative roles do not include the performance evaluation and control inherent in being a manager. They are based more on wisdom and experience than on authority. Consequently, consultative roles provide an effective transition for moving preretirement managers into more support-staff positions. They free up managerial positions for younger employees while allowing older managers to apply their experience and skills in a more supportive and less threatening way than might be possible from a strictly managerial role.

Phased Retirement. This provides older employees with an effective way of withdrawing from the organization and establishing a productive leisure life, by gradually reducing work hours and moving to full retirement.[26] A recent study of women over 35 indicates a strong interest for phased retirement plans, which may put new demands on related human resource management programs.[27] Employees gradually devote less of their time to the organization and more time to leisure pursuits (which to some might include developing a new career). For example, people may use the extra time off work to take courses, to gain new skills and knowledge, and to create opportunities for productive leisure. IBM, for example, once offered tuition rebates for courses on any topic taken within 3 years of retirement.[28] Many IBM preretirees used this program to prepare for second careers.

Equally important, phased retirement lessens the reality shock often experienced by those who retire all at once. It helps employees grow accustomed to leisure life and withdraw emotionally from the organization. A growing number of companies have some form of phased retirement. Pepperdine University and the University of Southern California, for example, implemented a phased retirement program for professors, which allows them some choice about part-time employment starting at age 55. The program is intended to provide more promotional positions for younger academics and to give older professors greater opportunities to establish a leisure life and still enjoy many benefits of the university.

Individual Employee Development Interventions

Three other interventions focus on career development by developing the organization member directly: assessment centers, mentoring, and training.

Assessment Centers. This intervention was traditionally designed to help organizations select and develop employees with high potential for managerial jobs. More recently, assessment centers have been extended to career development and to selection of people to fit new work designs, such as self-managing teams.[29] Assessment centers are popular in both Europe and the United States; more than 70% of large organizations in the United Kingdom and more than 2,000 U.S. companies have some form of assessment center.[30] When used to evaluate managerial capability, assessment centers typically process 12 to 15 people at a time and require them to spend 2 to 3 days on site. Participants are given a comprehensive interview, take several tests of mental ability and knowledge, and participate in individual and group exercises intended to simulate managerial work. An assessment team consisting of experienced managers and human resources specialists observes the behaviors and performance of each candidate. This team arrives at an overall assessment of each participant's managerial potential, including a rating on several items believed to be relevant to managerial success in the organization, and pass the results to management for use in making promotion decisions.

Assessment centers have been applied to career development as well, where the emphasis is on feedback of results to participants. Trained staff help participants hear and understand feedback about their strong and weak points. They help participants become clearer about career advancement and identify training experiences and job assignments to promote that progress. When used for developmental purposes, assessment centers can provide employees with the support and direction needed for career development. They can demonstrate that the company is a partner rather than an adversary in that process. Although assessment centers can help people's careers at all stages of development, they seem particularly useful at the advancement stage, when employees need to assess their talents and capabilities in light of long-term career commitments. Research suggests that assessment centers can promote career advancement to the extent that participants are willing to work on the center's recommendations for development.[31] When participants develop themselves in such areas as clarity about career motivation and ability to work with others, their probability of promotion increases.

Mentoring. One of the most useful ways to help employees advance in their careers is sponsorship.[32] This involves establishing a close link between a manager or someone more experienced and another organization member who is less experienced. Mentoring is a powerful intervention that assists members in the establishment, advancement, and maintenance stages of their careers. For those in the establishment stage, a sponsor or mentor takes a personal interest in the employee's career and guides and sponsors it. This ensures that a person's hard work and skill translate into actual opportunities for promotion and advancement.[33] For older employees in the maintenance stage, mentoring provides opportunities to share knowledge and experience with others who are less experienced. Older managers may mentor younger employees who are in the establishment and advancement career stages. Mentors do not have to be the direct supervisors of the younger employees but can be hierarchically or functionally distant from them. Other mentoring opportunities include temporarily assigning veteran managers to newer managers to help them gain managerial skills and knowledge.

Several of Boeing's divisions have well-developed mentoring processes. High-potential members are identified and paired with a corporate manager who volunteers to be a mentor. The mentor helps the employee gain the skills, experience, and visibility necessary for advancement in the company. Senior executives strongly support the mentoring program and believe that "mentoring improves the pool of talent for management and technical jobs and helps to shape future leaders. It is also an effective vehicle for moving knowledge through the organization from the people who have the most experience."[34]

Research suggests that mentoring is relatively prevalent in organizations. About two-thirds of top executives report having a mentor or sponsor during their early career stages, when learning, growth, and advancement were most prominent. Effective mentors were willing to share knowledge and experience, were knowledgeable about the company and the use of power, and were good counselors. Mentored executives, in contrast to executives who did not have mentors, received slightly more compensation, had more advanced college degrees, had engaged in career planning prior to mentoring, and were more satisfied with their careers and their work.[35]

Research also shows that mentoring is critical for minority and female employees. One recent study of mentoring minorities stresses that a strong network of mentors is critical to advancement, and that the mentor of minorities must understand the challenges that race presents to career development and advancement.[36] Similarly, women face unique challenges, and must address some of the same issues. While more women than men tend to seek mentors, a female mentor is not always available due to the limited numbers of women in executive positions, a phenomenon that is also true for minorities. Cross-gender mentoring relationships can involve a number of potential issues, including sexual harassment and misperceptions of the relationships.[37] Some organizations have used mentoring teams, although individual mentoring is considered more effective.[38]

Although research shows that mentoring can have positive outcomes, artificially creating such relationships when they do not occur naturally is difficult.[39] Some organizations have developed workshops in which managers are trained to become effective mentors. Others, such as IBM and AT&T, include mentoring as a key criterion for paying and promoting managers.

Developmental Training. This intervention helps employees gain the skills and knowledge for training and coaching others. It may include workshops and training materials oriented to human relations, communications, active listening, and mentoring. It can also involve substantial investments in education, such as tuition reimbursement programs that assist members in achieving advanced degrees. As described in Chapter 12, developmental training interventions generally are aimed at increasing the organization's reservoir of skills and knowledge, and can be related to increased retention and performance.[40] This enhances its capability to implement personal and organizational strategies.

A large number of organizations offer developmental training programs, including Procter & Gamble, Cisco Systems, IBM, Microsoft, and Hewlett-Packard. Many of these efforts are directed at midcareer managers who generally have good technical skills but only rudimentary experience in coaching others. Classroom learning is often rotated with on-the-job experiences, and there is considerable follow-up and recycling of learning. Numerous consulting firms also offer workshops and structured learning materials on developmental training, and an extensive practical literature exists in this area.[41]

Performance Feedback and Coaching Interventions

One of the most effective interventions during the establishment and advancement phases includes feedback about job performance and coaching to improve performance. As suggested in the discussions of goal setting and performance appraisal interventions (Chapter 17), employees need continual feedback about goal achievement as well as necessary support and coaching to improve their performances. Feedback and coaching are particularly relevant when employees are establishing careers. They have concerns about how to perform the work, whether they are performing up to expectations, and whether they are gaining the necessary skills for advancement. A manager can facilitate career establishment by providing feedback on performance, coaching, and on-the-job training. These activities can help employees get the job done while meeting their career development needs. Companies such as Intel and Monsanto, for example, use performance feedback and coaching for employee career development. They separate the career development aspect of performance appraisal from the salary review component, thus ensuring that employees' career needs receive as much attention as salary issues. Feedback and coaching interventions can increase employee performance, satisfaction, and morale, and provide a systematic way to monitor the development of human resources in the firm, at little or no cost.[42]

Work–Life Balance Interventions

This relatively new OD intervention helps employees better integrate and balance work and home life. Restructuring, downsizing, and increased global competition have contributed to longer work hours and more stress. Baby-boomers approaching 50 years of age and others are rethinking their priorities and seeking to restore some balance in a work-dominated life. Organizations from a variety of industries, such as Edward Jones in financial services, The Container Store in retailing, and the law firm of Alston & Bird topped *Fortune*'s 2003 "100 Best Companies to Work For," and they are responding to these concerns so they can attract, retain, and motivate the best workforce.[43] In addition, many cities, such as Boston, San Francisco, Denver, and Birmingham, are identifying and publishing a "Best Companies" list.[44] More balanced work and family lives can benefit both employees and the company through increased creativity, morale, and effectiveness, and reduced absenteeism and turnover.[45] Early work–life balance programs started with a focus on women with young children in the workforce, but now these programs serve men and women, all ages, and all family and life situations. Work life programs continue to focus on dependent care of both children and elders, but they also focus on job scheduling and flexibility, paid and unpaid leaves, employee wellness, concierge services, and others. Work–life balance planning helps members better manage the interface between work or paid employment and all the work and responsibilities associated with a person's life.

A related issue in the worklife arena involves dual-career accommodation practices in situations where both the employee and their spouse or significant other pursue full-time careers. The U.S. Department of Labor reports that more than 80% of all marriages involve dual careers,[46] and dual-career households are more likely to give each individual's career equal weighting in decisions than to give one career precedence over the other.[47]

Because partners' careers can affect the recruitment and advancement of employees, organizations are devising policies to accommodate dual-career employees. A survey of companies reported offering recognition of problems in dual careers, help with relocation, flexible working hours, counseling for dual-career employees, family day-care centers, improved career planning, and policies making it easier for two members of the same family to work in the same organization or department.[48] Some companies have also established cooperative arrangements with other firms to provide sources of employment for the other partner.[49] General Electric, for example, has created a network with other firms to share information about job opportunities for dual-career couples. (Chapter 19 describes interventions aimed at interorganizational networking.)

Although these interventions can apply to all career stages, they are especially relevant during advancement. One of the biggest problems created by dual careers is job transfers, which are likely to occur during the advancement stage. Transfer to another location usually means that the working partner must also relocate. In many cases, the company employing the partner must either lose the employee or arrange a transfer to the same location. Dual careers also impact expatriate assignments, and being able to facilitate or accommodate a spouse or partner's wish to work may make the difference in terms of an employee accepting such an assignment. Similar problems can occur in recruiting employees. A recruit may not join an organization if its location does not provide career opportunities for the partner.

WORKFORCE DIVERSITY INTERVENTIONS

Several profound trends are shaping the labor markets of modern organizations. Researchers suggest that contemporary workforce characteristics are radically different from what they were just 20 years ago. Employees represent every ethnic background and color; range from highly educated to illiterate; vary in age from 18 to 80; may appear perfectly healthy or may have a terminal illness; may be single parents or part of dual-income, divorced, same-sex, or traditional families; and may be physically or mentally challenged.

Workforce diversity is more than a euphemism for cultural or racial differences. Such a definition is too narrow and focuses attention away from the broad range of issues that a diverse workforce poses. Diversity results from people who bring different resources and perspectives to the workplace and who have distinctive needs, preferences, expectations, and lifestyles.[50] Organizations must design human resources systems that account for these differences if they are to attract and retain a productive workforce and if they want to turn diversity into a competitive advantage.[51]

Figure 18.2 presents a general framework for managing diversity in organizations.[52] First, the model suggests that an organization's diversity approach is a func-

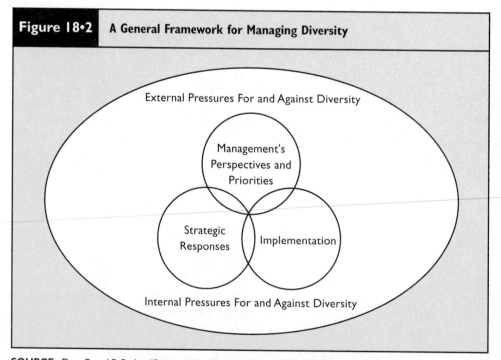

| **Figure 18•2** | **A General Framework for Managing Diversity** |

External Pressures For and Against Diversity

Management's Perspectives and Priorities

Strategic Responses

Implementation

Internal Pressures For and Against Diversity

SOURCE: Dass, P., and B. Parker, "Strategies for Managing Human Resource Diversity: From Resistance to Learning," *Academy of Management Executive*, 13 (1999), p. 69. Permission conveyed via Copyright Clearance Center.

tion of *internal and external pressures* for and against diversity. Pro-diversity forces argue that organization performance is enhanced when the workforce's diversity is embraced as an opportunity. But diversity is often discouraged by those who fear that too many perspectives, beliefs, values, and attitudes dilute concerted action. Second, management's *perspective and priorities* with respect to diversity can range from resistance to active learning and from marginal to strategic. For example, organizations can resist diversity by implementing only legally mandated policies such as affirmative action, equal employment opportunity, or Americans with Disabilities Act requirements. On the other hand, a learning and strategic perspective can lead management to view diversity as a source of competitive advantage. For example, a health care organization with a diverse customer base can improve perceptions of service quality with physician diversity. Third, within management's priorities, the organization's *strategic responses* can range from reactive to proactive. Diversity efforts at Texaco and Denny's had little momentum until a series of embarrassing race-based events forced a response. Fourth, the organization's *implementation style* can range from episodic to systemic. A diversity approach will be most effective when the strategic responses and implementation style fit with management's intent and internal and external pressures.

Unfortunately, organizations have tended to address workforce diversity pressures in a piecemeal fashion; only 5% of more than 1,400 companies surveyed thought they were doing a "very good job" of managing diversity.[53] As each trend makes itself felt, the organization influences appropriate practices and activities. For example, as the percentage of women in the workforce increased, many organizations simply added maternity leaves to their benefits packages; as the number of physically challenged workers increased and when Congress passed the Americans with Disabilities Act in 1990, organizations changed their physical settings to accommodate wheelchairs. Demographers warn, however, that these trends are not only powerful by themselves but will likely interact with each other to force organizational change. Thus, a growing number of organizations, such as SBC Communications, McDonald's, PepsiCo, Procter & Gamble, and Southern California Edison, are taking bolder steps. They are not only adopting learning perspectives with respect to diversity, but systemically weaving diversity-friendly values and practices into the cultural fabric of the organization.

Many of the OD interventions described in this book can be applied to the strategic responses and implementation of workforce diversity, as shown in Table 18.3 (on page 412). It summarizes several of the internal and external pressures facing organizations, including age, gender, race, disability, culture and values, and sexual orientation.[54] The table also reports the major trends characterizing those dimensions, organizational implications and workforce needs, and specific OD interventions that can address those implications.

Age

The average age of the U.S. workforce is rising and changing the distribution of age groups. Between 1998 and 2008, the category of workers aged 25 to 54 will grow 5.5%, and the 55-and-over age category is expected to increase almost 48%. This skewed distribution is mostly the result of the baby boom between 1946 and 1964. As a result, organizations will face a predominantly middle-aged and older workforce. Even now, many organizations are reporting that the average age of their workforce is over 40. Such a distribution will place special demands on the organization.

For example, the personal needs and work motivation of the different cohorts will require differentiated human resources practices. Older workers place heavy demands on health care services, are less mobile, and will have fewer career advancement opportunities. This situation will require specialized work designs that account for physical capabilities of older workers, career development activities that

Table 18•3	Work Diversity Dimensions and Interventions		
WORKFORCE DIFFERENCES	**TRENDS**	**IMPLICATIONS AND NEEDS**	**INTERVENTIONS**
Age	Median age up Distribution of ages changing	Health care Mobility Security	Wellness program Job design Career planning and development Reward systems
Gender	Percentage of women increasing Dual-income families	Child care Maternity/paternity leave Single parents	Job design Fringe benefit rewards
Disability	The number of people with disabilities entering the workforce is increasing	Job challenge Job skills Physical space Respect and dignity	Performance management Job design Career planning and development
Culture and values	Rising proportion of immigrant and minority-group workers Shift in rewards	Flexible organizational policies Autonomy Affirmation Respect	Career planning and development Employee involvement Reward systems
Sexual orientation	Number of single-sex households up More liberal attitudes toward sexual orientation	Discrimination	Equal employment opportunities Fringe benefits Education and training

address and use their experience, and benefit plans that accommodate their medical and psychological needs. Demand for younger workers, on the other hand, will be intense. To attract and retain this more mobile group, jobs will have to be more challenging, advancement opportunities more prevalent, and an enriched quality of work life more common.

Organization development interventions, such as work design, wellness programs (discussed below), career planning and development, and reward systems must be adapted to these different age groups.[55] For the older employee, work designs can reduce the physical components or increase the knowledge and experience components of a job. At Builder's Emporium, a chain of home improvement centers, the store clerk job was redesigned to eliminate heavy lifting by assigning night crews to replenish shelves and emphasizing sales ability instead of strength. Younger workers will likely require more challenge and autonomy. Wellness programs can be used to address the physical and mental health of both generations. Career-planning and development programs will have to recognize the different career stages of each cohort and offer resources tailored to that stage. Finally, reward system interventions may offer increased health benefits, time off, and other perks for the older worker while using promotion, ownership, and pay to attract and motivate the scarcer, younger workforce.

Gender

Another important trend is the increasing percentage of female workers in the labor force. By the year 2008, almost 48% of the U.S. workforce will be women, and they will represent more than half of the new entrants between 1998 and 2008. However, women represented only 10% of senior managers in the *Fortune* 500, and less than 3% of top corporate earners in 2000.[56] Three-quarters of all working women are in their childbearing years, and more than half of all mothers work. The organizational implications of these trends are sobering. Demands for child care, maternity and paternity leaves, and flexible working arrangements will place pressure on work systems to maintain productivity and teamwork. From a management perspective, there will be more men and women working together as peers, more women entering the executive ranks, greater diversity of management styles, and changing definitions of managerial success.

Work design, reward systems, and career development are among the more important interventions for addressing issues arising out of the gender trend. For example, jobs can be modified to accommodate the special demands of working mothers. A number of organizations, such as Digital Equipment, Steelcase, and Hewlett-Packard, have instituted job sharing, by which two people perform the tasks associated with one job. The firms have done this to allow their female employees to pursue both family and work careers. Reward system interventions, especially fringe benefits, can be tailored to offer special leaves to mothers and fathers, child-care options, flexible working hours, and health and wellness benefits. Career development interventions help maintain, develop, and retain a competent and diverse workforce. Organizations such as Hoechst Celanese and Ameritech have instituted challenging assignments and mentoring programs to retain key female members. Recent research on career development programs suggests that organizations consider the assumptions embedded in their career development programs to ensure programs are not biased toward masculine experiences and worldviews, especially those related to careers.[57]

Unfortunately, many programs over the last several years have tended to focus more on the symptoms, as opposed to sources of gender inequity.[58] Recent research suggests that once an organization recognizes the problem, diagnosis through interviews with employees is critical to addressing the sources of gender inequity. The research further suggests that using a strategy of small interventions, "small wins," or small initiatives that combine behavior and understanding and that target the organization's specific issues are more effective. For example, one European retail company discovered upon interviewing its employees that a key issue in turnover among female employees was the company's lack of discipline regarding time. Last-minute scheduling, meeting overruns, and tardiness wreaked havoc for female employees trying to manage work and home responsibilities. Company leadership began a more disciplined approach to time, resulting in greater efficiency and effectiveness. Resolving such issues requires careful and organization-specific diagnosis and intervention.

Race/Ethnicity

Race continues to be a critical area in diversity management programs. While minorities represent large segments of the workforce, they represent only a fraction of top management and senior executives. For example, African Americans make up approximately 12% of the American population, but comprise, respectively, only 5% and less than 1% of management and senior executive ranks.[59] Minority populations in the United States continue to grow, especially the Hispanic population.

Several trends are impacting race as an aspect of diversity management. While many companies and their leaders demonstrate excellent intentions, several recent legal rulings indicate potential issues. For example, although Texaco recently agreed to pay $140 million in settlement of a racial-discrimination lawsuit,[60] one study showed that newly hired black clerical employees in a large commercial bank were four times more likely than were white clerical employees to be assigned to a black supervisor after 5 months on the job.[61] Research has also noted that often qualifications and experience of minority employees are overlooked, with leaders and fellow employees focusing instead on "skin color" and seeing minorities as representing their race and/or ethnicity.[62]

Such trends suggest that diversity interventions must continue to address race as a key aspect of diversity management, especially as organizations work to increase diversity among top leadership and board members. Sensitivity training can increase the likelihood that effective diversity management programs rely on data (not impressions or perceptions) and are responsive, move beyond eliminating obvious racism to eradicating more subtle forms as well, eliminate vague selection and promotion criteria which can let discrimination persist, link diversity management to individual performance appraisals, and develop and enforce appropriate rules.[63] For example, 46% of new hires for SBC (Southwestern Bell Corp.) were minorities, along with 48% of participants in their leadership development program; Wyndham Hotels established a diversity officer position that reports to the CEO, and J.P. Morgan annually reviews their "Diversity Scorecards."[64] Mentoring programs can ensure that minorities in the advancement stage get the appropriate coaching and that successful minority managers and executives get the chance to share their wisdom and experience with others.

Sexual Orientation

Diversity in sexual and affectional orientation, including gay, lesbian, and bisexual individuals and couples, increasingly is affecting the way that organizations think about human resources. Accurate data on the number of gays and lesbians in the workforce are difficult to obtain because laws and social norms do not support self-disclosure of a person's sexual orientation. However, related data suggest that this dimension of workforce diversity is gaining in significance. A 1998 U.S. Census report showed the number of same-sex-partner households as 1.67 million, and a number of studies have estimated the number of gays and lesbians at between 6% and 10% of the population.

The primary organizational implication of sexual orientation diversity is discrimination. Gay men and lesbians often are reticent to discuss how organizational policies can be less discriminatory because they fear their openness will lead to unfair treatment. People can have strong emotional reactions to sexual orientation. When these feelings interact with the gender, culture, and values trends described in this section, the likelihood of both overt and unconscious discrimination is high. An important aspect to this discrimination is the misperceived relationship between sexual orientation and AIDS/HIV. Overall, although 47,000 new cases of HIV and AIDS were reported in the 12 months ending July 1999, the data suggest that the growth of AIDS/HIV is lowest within the gay and lesbian community and highest among drug users and teenagers. The common perception, however, does not fit the facts. In addition, from an intervention perspective, it is important to note that AIDS/HIV is protected under the Americans with Disabilities Act (ADA) discussed later in this chapter.

Interventions aimed at this dimension of workforce diversity are relatively new in OD and are being developed as organizations encounter sexual orientation issues in the workplace. The most frequent response is education and training. This intervention increases members' awareness of the facts and decreases the likelihood of overt discrimination. While sexual orientation is not protected under federal equal employment opportunity (EEO) laws, some cities and states have passed legislation protecting sexual orientation. Human resources practices having to do with equal employment opportunity (EEO) and fringe benefits also can help to address sexual orientation parity issues. Some organizations have modified their EEO statements to address sexual orientation, including 61% of *Fortune* 500 companies.[65] Firms such as Advanced Micro Devices, Fujitsu, Ben & Jerry's, and Dow Chemical have communicated strongly to members and outsiders that decisions with respect to hiring, promotion, transfer, and so on cannot (and will not) be made with respect to a person's sexual orientation. Similarly, organizations are increasingly offering domestic-partner benefit plans, and now over 5,000 employers offer domestic partner benefits.[66] Companies such as Wal-Mart, Microsoft, and Apple as well as governments and universities have extended health care and other benefits to the same-sex partners of their members.

Disability

A fifth trend is the increasing number of men and women with disabilities entering the workforce. The workforce of the 21st century will comprise people with a variety of physical and mental disabilities. For example, the high school dropout rate remained above 4% throughout the 1990s, and approximately 21% of the population over age 16 had only rudimentary reading and writing skills. In a world of knowledge work, the lack of education or an inability to learn is a profoundly debilitating condition. More and more organizations will employ physically handicapped people, especially as the number of younger workers declines, creating a great demand for labor. In 1990, the federal Americans with Disabilities Act banned all forms of discrimination on the basis of physical or mental disability in the hiring and promotion process. It also required many organizations to modify physical plants and office buildings to accommodate people with disabilities.

The organizational implications of the disability trend represent both opportunity and adjustment. The productivity of physically and mentally disabled workers often surprises managers. Training is required to increase managers' awareness of this opportunity and to create a climate where accommodation requests can be made without fear.[67] Employing disabled workers, however, also means a need for more comprehensive health care, new physical workplace layouts, new attitudes toward working with the disabled, and challenging jobs that use a variety of skills.

OD interventions, including work design, career planning and development, and performance management, can be used to integrate the disabled into the workforce. For example, traditional approaches to job design can simplify work to permit physically handicapped workers to complete an assembly task. Career planning and development programs need to focus on making disabled workers aware of career opportunities. Too often these employees do not know that advancement is possible, and they are left feeling frustrated. Career tracks need to be developed for these workers.

Performance management interventions, including goal setting, monitoring, and coaching performance, aligned with the workforce's characteristics are important. At Blue Cross and Blue Shield of Florida, for example, a supervisor learned sign language to communicate with a deaf employee whose productivity was low but whose quality of work was high. Two other deaf employees were transferred to that supervisor's department, and over a 2-year period, the performance of the deaf workers improved 1,000% with no loss in quality.

Culture and Values

Immigration into the United States from the Pacific Rim, South America, Europe, the Middle East, and the former Soviet states will drastically alter the cultural diversity of the workplace. Between 1998 and 2008, the U.S. civilian labor force will increase by 12%, while the Asian and Hispanic population in the United States will increase by 40% and 37%, respectively. Approximately 600,000 people will immigrate (legally and illegally) into the United States, mostly from Latin America and Asia, and about two-thirds of those immigrants will enter the workforce. In

California, 50% of the population will be people of color by the year 2005, and they will speak more than 80 languages.

Cultural diversity has broad organizational implications. Different cultures represent a variety of values, work ethics, and norms of correct behavior. Not all cultures want the same things from work, and simple, piecemeal changes in specific organizational practices will be inadequate if the workforce is culturally diverse. Management practices will have to be aligned with cultural values and support both career and family orientations. English is a second language for many people, and jobs of all types (processing, customer contact, production, and so on) will have to be adjusted accordingly. Finally, the organization will be expected to satisfy both extrinsic and monetary needs, as well as intrinsic and personal growth needs.

Several planned change interventions, including employee involvement, reward systems, and career planning and development, can be used to adapt to cultural diversity. Employee involvement practices can be adapted to the needs for participation in decision making. People from certain cultures, such as Scandinavia, are more likely to expect and respond to high-involvement policies; other cultures, such as Latin America, view participation with reservation. (See the discussion of cultural values in Chapter 21.) Participation in an organization can take many forms, from suggestion systems and attitude surveys to high-involvement work designs and performance management systems. Organizations can maximize worker productivity by basing the amount of power and information workers have on cultural and value orientations.

Reward systems can focus on increasing flexibility. For example, flexible working hours enable employees to meet personal obligations without sacrificing organizational objectives. Many organizations have implemented this innovation, and most report that the positive benefits outweigh the costs. Work locations also can be varied. Many organizations, including McKesson, Texas Instruments, Hewlett-Packard, and BP, allow workers to spend part of their time telecommuting from home. Other flexible benefits, such as floating holidays, allow people from different cultures to match important religious and family occasions with work schedules.

Child-care and dependent-care assistance also support different lifestyles. For example, at Stride Rite Corporation, the Stride Rite Intergenerational Day Care Center houses 55 children between the ages of 15 months and 6 years as well as 24 elders over 60 years old. The center was established after an organizational survey determined that 25% of employees provided some sort of elder care and that an additional 13% anticipated doing so within 5 years.

Finally, career planning and development programs can help workers identify advancement opportunities that are in line with their cultural values. Some cultures value technical skills over hierarchical advancement; others see promotion as a prime indicator of self-worth and accomplishment. By matching programs with people, job satisfaction, productivity, and employee retention can be improved.

Workforce diversity interventions are growing rapidly in OD. A national survey revealed that 75% of firms either have, or plan to begin, diversity efforts.[68] Research suggests that diversity interventions are especially prevalent in large organizations with diversity-friendly senior management and human resources policies.[69] Although existing evidence shows that diversity interventions are growing in popularity, there is still ambiguity about the depth of organizational commitment to such practices and the contingencies that moderate the relationship between commitment and performance.[70] A great deal more research is needed to understand these newer interventions and their outcomes.

Application 18.2 describes a workforce diversity intervention at Baxter Exports, showing how diversity can exist in many areas and how organizations can employ a range of interventions to make the workplace more flexible.[71]

EMBRACING EMPLOYEE DIVERSITY AT BAXTER EXPORT

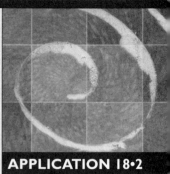

APPLICATION 18•2

Baxter Export Corporation is an 85-person unit responsible for international logistics at Baxter Healthcare, a $5.4 billion maker of health care products. Their diversity practices are the first steps in response to an 18-month study by Baxter International. A survey of 1,000 employees found that among salaried employees, most work–life tensions were driven by the need for greater balance and the desire for flexibility.

Work–life tensions are prevalent at Baxter Export. The pressures of a globally competitive business require analysts, who make around $40,000 annually, to manage the flow of catheters, dialysis solutions, intravenous tubes, and other products to subsidiaries and customers around the world. As a result, many two-income families have been forced into intensive arrangements.

One analyst's day ends with emails and voicemails from Saudi Arabia, Oman, and Panama; a conference call that runs over the allotted time; and the anxiety from expectations that dinner should be ready by 5:30. An on-time dinner is important because her husband, who has picked up their 3-year-old from day care and their 7-year-old from grade school, has to leave for one of his two night jobs. The week will also include a Cub Scout meeting, grocery shopping, other kids' activities, and errands. "We're kind of used to it . . . it's our life," the analyst says.

Another employee's day begins at 6:30 a.m. because it's easier to communicate with customers in South Africa and New Zealand, and she can pick up her daughter from day care by 4 p.m. Getting home sooner is also important because of the full-time care required by her mother-in-law, who recently was diagnosed with cancer. "I was working overtime, often until 7 p.m.," she explains. "I'd get home in time to give my daughter her bottle, then put her to sleep. I said: 'this is ridiculous.'" The flexible work hours and at least one day a week spent telecommuting ease the burden.

At Baxter Export, 30% of its employees use telecommuting, job-sharing, or working part-time to build flexibility into their schedules. John Linder, the manager who oversees the analysts, is convinced that acknowledging and easing tensions in the workplace is good business. Although he doesn't work at home himself, he believes that his people are 10% more productive on the days they telecommute. Baxter's willingness to accommodate problems, he adds, also pays off in higher commitment. Still, telecommuters are held to rules that limit disruption. They can't work more than 2 days a week out of the office. Any more than that and it begins to affect the cohe-

siveness of the group. In addition, everyone has to be in on Wednesdays for meetings, and they must pay for call-waiting on their home phones (Latin American customers, especially, don't like voicemail).

With all their flexibility, however, Baxter Export employees still struggle to find balance. Most spend 45 to 50 hours a week on the job. There is a solution, but it is no easy fix: The division is entering a thorough restructuring that is altering not just its own jobs and processes but also those throughout the corporation.

Griff Lewis, the executive vice president who oversees Baxter Export, notes that the unit's volume is growing at 12% to 15% per year, and he does not have the budget to add corresponding staff. Just to keep people's hours reasonable, never mind reducing them, he has to find ways to lift productivity—rethinking processes, redesigning jobs, and eliminating unnecessary tasks.

Over the next 5 years, therefore, Baxter will have to move to an automated allocation system that requires overseas customers, rather than Baxter Export analysts, to prepare demand forecasts and enter orders. That system would route orders directly to U.S. warehouses and, as a result, decrease each analyst's workload by 3 days per month within 2 years. Also, Lewis expects to standardize processes across the 120 countries his department services, eliminating extraneous tasks and allowing employees to address mostly exceptional orders and higher-level issues.

Already, such schemes have relieved the 60-hour weeks that were commonplace a few years ago. Lewis's restructuring is complicated by his division's web of relationships with the many units of its global parent. Baxter's U.S. manufacturing division, for instance, maintains as little inventory as possible. When demand overseas exceeds expectations, Lewis's analysts cannot always find product easily. If managers in Brazil cram in last-minute orders to meet quarterly quotas, someone at Baxter Exports has to work late to meet requirements on time.

The attempts to build flexibility into the work schedules and think systemically about reducing the hours worked at Baxter Export is one of the reasons Baxter Healthcare ranked nineteenth on *Business Week*'s 1997 annual survey of work and family strategies in corporate America.

EMPLOYEE STRESS AND WELLNESS INTERVENTIONS

In the past decade, organizations have become increasingly aware of the relationship between employee wellness and productivity.[72] The estimated cost to industry from stress-related ailments is more than $200 billion per year[73] and is an increasingly global phenomenon. In the United Kingdom, stress and stress-related illness cost industry and taxpayers £12 *billion* each year.[74] Stress management and wellness interventions, including employee assistance programs (EAPs), have grown because organizations are interested in retaining a skilled workforce and concerned for the welfare of their employees. Companies such as Johnson & Johnson, Weyerhaeuser, Federal Express, Quaker Oats, and Abbott Laboratories are sponsoring a wide range of fitness, wellness, and stress management programs.

Individual well-being or wellness comprises "the various life/non-work satisfactions enjoyed by individuals, work/job-related satisfactions, and general health."[75] Health is a subcomponent of well-being and includes both mental/psychological and physical/physiological factors. In addition, a person's work setting, personality traits, and stress coping skills affect overall well-being. In turn, well-being impacts personal and organizational outcomes, including absenteeism, productivity, and health insurance costs.[76]

Two major types of wellness interventions—work leaves, including vacation, sabbaticals, and paid and unpaid leaves, and stress management, including employee assistance programs (EAPs)—are presented. Work leaves focus on paid and unpaid time the employee has to maintain employee wellness and to have a break from job, career, and/or organizational responsibilities. Stress management, both proactive and reactive, is concerned with helping employees alleviate or cope with the negative consequences of stress at work.

Work Leaves

In the United States, employees work more hours and take less time off than in most other developed countries. For example, Americans worked an average of 1,878 hours per year while workers in the United Kingdom averaged 1,711, France averaged 1,532, and German workers averaged 1,467. Korean employees worked more than Americans, and Japanese workers averaged about the same number of hours. Similarly, other countries offer longer and more flexible work leave arrangements, with vacation minimums often subject to government mandate. The United States and Japan average 10 days annual vacation, and the U.K., France, and Germany average 22, 25, and 24 days, respectively.[77] While some differences can be explained by cultural values or government policies, the potential to affect wellness through work leaves should not be ignored.

As organizations struggle to minimize the effects of work stress, paid and unpaid work leaves are receiving increasing attention. Paid leaves include vacation, holidays, personal days, as well as maternity and paternity leaves. The comparative statistics suggest that globalization may create increasing pressure on vacation allowances. As with vacation time, the United States lags behind other countries in regards to maternity and paternity leave. Although the Family Medical Leave Act (FMLA) guarantees parents 12 weeks unpaid leave, and more people are taking advantage of FMLA unpaid leave, many employees cannot afford to take it, and firms at the top of *Fortune*'s "Best Companies to Work For" list have responded with paid maternity and paternity leave.[78] Another key work leave intervention is paid sabbaticals, typically received after a specified tenure of service. For example, Perkins Coie, a Seattle law firm with approximately 1,400 employees, offers 8-week paid sabbaticals. In one recent survey, 19% of companies, including Microsoft and Intel, offered sabbaticals, but only 5% with pay.[79] Sabbaticals are a way of avoiding burnout and renewing employee creativity and commitment.

Unpaid leaves, or leaves of absence, also offer employees a chance to renew and to bring new experiences to the organization, while guaranteeing a job for them upon their return. For example, personal growth leaves or social service leaves may allow an employee to explore an individual interest or cause. Such a leave is an exchange, offering the employee a chance for time off, renewal, and pursuit of a given interest, while retaining a valued employee for the organization.

Stress Management Programs

Concern has been growing in organizations about managing the dysfunction caused by stress. Stress has been linked to hypertension, heart attacks, diabetes, asthma, chronic pain, allergies, headache, backache, various skin disorders, cancer, immune system weakness, and decreases in the number of white blood cells and changes in their function. It can also lead to alcoholism and drug abuse, two problems that are reaching epidemic proportions in organizations and society. For organizations, these personal effects can result in costly health benefits, absenteeism, turnover, and low performance. One study reported that one in three workers said they have thought about quitting because of stress; one in two workers said job stress reduced their productivity; and one in five workers said they took sick leave in the month preceding the survey because of stress.[80] Another study estimates that each employee who suffers from a stress-related illness loses an average of 16 days of work per year.[81] Finally, the Research Triangle Institute estimated the annual cost to the U.S. economy from stress-related disorders at $187 billion. Other estimates are more conservative, but they invariably run into the billions of dollars.[82]

Like other human resources management interventions, stress management is often facilitated by practitioners with special skills and knowledge—typically psychologists, physicians, and other health professionals specializing in work stress. Recently, some OD practitioners have gained competence in this area, and there has been a growing tendency to include stress management as part of larger OD efforts. The concept of stress is best understood in terms of a model that describes the organizational and personal conditions contributing to the dysfunctional consequences of stress. Two key types of stress management interventions may be used: those aimed at the diagnosis or awareness of stress and its causes, and those directed at changing the causes and helping people cope with stress.

Definition and Model

Stress refers to the reaction of people to their environments. It involves both physiological and psychological responses to environmental conditions, causing people to change or adjust their behaviors. Stress is generally viewed in terms of the fit of people's needs, abilities, and expectations with environmental demands, changes, and opportunities.[83] A good person–environment fit results in positive reactions to stress; a poor fit leads to the negative consequences already described. Stress is generally positive when it occurs at moderate levels and contributes to effective motivation, innovation, and learning. For example, a promotion is a stressful event that is experienced positively by most employees. On the other hand, stress can be dysfunctional when it is excessively high (or low) or persists over a long period of time. It can overpower a person's coping abilities and cause physical and emotional exhaustion. For example, a boss who is excessively demanding and unsupportive can cause subordinates undue tension, anxiety, and dissatisfaction. Those factors, in turn, can lead to withdrawal behaviors, such as absenteeism and turnover; to ailments, such as headaches and high blood pressure; and to lowered performance. Situations in which there is a poor fit between employees and the organization produce negative stress consequences.

A tremendous amount of research has been conducted on the causes and consequences of work stress. Figure 18.3 identifies specific occupational stressors, potential dysfunctional consequences, and interventions to address stress. People's individual differences determine the extent to which the stressors are perceived negatively. For example, people with strong social support experience the stressors as less stressful than those who do not have such support. This greater perceived stress can lead to such negative consequences as anxiety, poor decision making, increased blood pressure, and low productivity.

The stress model shows that almost any dimension of the organization, including the physical environment, structure, roles, or relationships, can cause negative stress. This suggests that much of the material covered so far in this book provides knowledge about work-related stressors, and implies that virtually all of the OD interventions included in the book can play a role in stress management. Team building, employee involvement, reward systems, and career planning and devel-

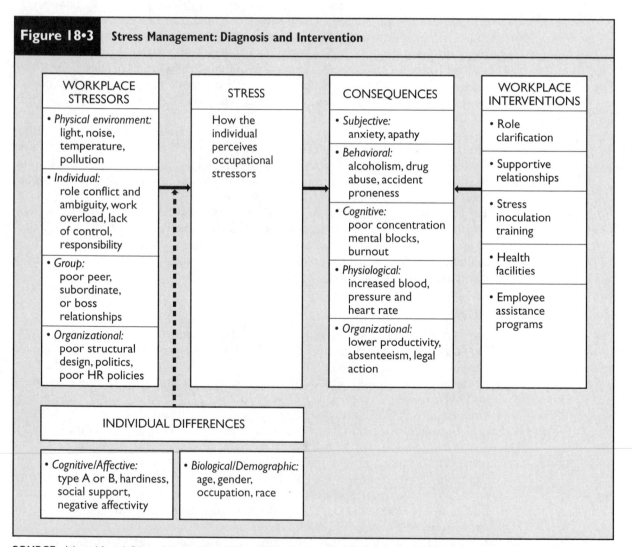

Figure 18•3   Stress Management: Diagnosis and Intervention

WORKPLACE STRESSORS	STRESS	CONSEQUENCES	WORKPLACE INTERVENTIONS
• *Physical environment:* light, noise, temperature, pollution • *Individual:* role conflict and ambiguity, work overload, lack of control, responsibility • *Group:* poor peer, subordinate, or boss relationships • *Organizational:* poor structural design, politics, poor HR policies	How the individual perceives occupational stressors	• *Subjective:* anxiety, apathy • *Behavioral:* alcoholism, drug abuse, accident proneness • *Cognitive:* poor concentration mental blocks, burnout • *Physiological:* increased blood, pressure and heart rate • *Organizational:* lower productivity, absenteeism, legal action	• Role clarification • Supportive relationships • Stress inoculation training • Health facilities • Employee assistance programs

INDIVIDUAL DIFFERENCES

• *Cognitive/Affective:* type A or B, hardiness, social support, negative affectivity	• *Biological/Demographic:* age, gender, occupation, race

SOURCE: Adapted from J. Gibson, J. Ivancevich, and J. Donnelly Jr., *Organizations: Behaviors, Structure, Processes,* 8th ed. (Plano, Texas: Business Publications, 1994), p. 266. Reproduced with permission of The McGraw-Hill Companies.

opment all can help alleviate stressful working conditions. Thus, to some degree stress management has been under discussion throughout this book. Here, the focus is on those occupational stressors and stress management techniques that are unique to the stress field and that have received the most systematic attention from stress researchers.

Occupational Stressors. Figure 18.3 identifies several organizational sources of stress, including the physical environment, individual situations, group pressures, and organizational conditions. Extensive research has been done on three key individual sources of stress: the individual items related to work overload, role conflict, and role ambiguity.

Work overload can be a persistent source of stress, especially among managers and white-collar employees having to process complex information and make difficult decisions. Quantitative overload consists of having too much to do in a given time period. Qualitative overload refers to having work that is too difficult for one's abilities and knowledge. A review of the research suggests that work overload is highly related to managers' needs for achievement and so it may be partly self-inflicted.[84] Research relating workload to stress outcomes reveals that both too much or too little work can have negative consequences. Apparently, when the amount of work is in balance with people's abilities and knowledge, stress has a positive impact on performance and satisfaction, but when workload either exceeds employees' abilities (overload) or fails to challenge them (underload), people experience stress negatively. This negative experience can lead to lowered self-esteem and job dissatisfaction, nervous symptoms, increased absenteeism, and reduced participation in organizational activities.[85]

People's roles at work also can be a source of stress. A role can be defined as the sum total of expectations that the individual and significant others have about how the person should perform a specific job. The employee's relationships with peers, supervisors, vendors, customers, and others can result in diverse expectations about how a particular role should be performed. The employee must be able to integrate these expectations into a meaningful whole to perform the role effectively. Problems arise when there is role ambiguity and the person does not clearly understand what others expect of him or her, or when there is role conflict and the employee receives contradictory expectations that cannot be satisfied at the same time.[86]

Extensive studies of role ambiguity and conflict suggest that both conditions are prevalent in organizations, especially among managerial jobs where clarity often is lacking and job demands often are contradictory.[87] For example, managerial job descriptions typically are so general that it is difficult to know precisely what is expected on the job. Similarly, managers spend most of their time interacting with people from other departments, and opportunities for conflicting demands abound in these lateral relationships. Role ambiguity and conflict can cause severe stress, resulting in increased tension, dissatisfaction, and withdrawal, and reduced commitment and trust in others. Some evidence suggests that role ambiguity has a more negative impact on managers than does role conflict. In terms of individual differences, people with a low tolerance for ambiguity respond more negatively to role ambiguity than others do; introverts and people who are more flexible react more negatively to role conflict than others do.[88]

Individual Differences. Figure 18.3 identifies several individual differences affecting how people respond to occupational stressors: hardiness, social support, age, education, occupation, race, negative affectivity, and Type A behavior patterns. Much research has been devoted to the Type A behavior pattern, which is characterized by impatience, competitiveness, and hostility. Type A personalities (in contrast to Type B's) invest long hours working under tight deadlines. They put themselves under extreme time pressure by trying to do more and more work in less and less time. Type B personalities, on the other hand, are less hurried, aggressive, and hostile than Type A's. Extensive research shows that Type A people are especially prone to stress. For example, a longitudinal study of 3,500 men found that Type A's had twice as much heart disease, five times as many second heart attacks, and twice as many fatal heart attacks as did Type B's.[89] Researchers explain Type A susceptibility to stress in terms of an inability to deal with uncertainty, such as might occur with qualitative overload and role ambiguity. To work rapidly and meet pressing deadlines, Type A's need to be in control of the situation. They do not allocate enough time for unforeseen disturbances and consequently experience extreme tension and anxiety when faced with unexpected events.[90]

Unfortunately, the proportion of Type A managers in organizations may be quite large. One study showed that 60% of the managers were clearly Type A and only 12% were distinctly Type B.[91] In addition, a short questionnaire measuring Type A behaviors and given to members of several MBA classes and executive programs has found that Type A's outnumber Type B's by about five to one. These results are not totally surprising because many organizations (and business schools) reward aggressive, competitive, workaholic behaviors. Indeed, Type A behaviors can help managers achieve rapid promotion in many companies. Ironically, however, those same behaviors may be detrimental to effective performance at top organizational levels where tasks and decision making require the kind of patience, tolerance for ambiguity, and attention to broad issues often neglected by Type A's.

Diagnosis and Awareness of Stress and Its Causes

Stress management is directed at preventing negative stress outcomes either by changing the organizational conditions causing the stress or by enhancing employees' abilities to cope with them. This preventive approach starts from a diagnosis of the current situation, including employees' self-awareness of their own stress and its sources. This diagnosis provides the information needed to develop an appropriate stress management program.[92] There are two methods for diagnosing stress.

Charting Stressors. Such charting involves identifying organizational and personal stressors operating in a particular situation. It is guided by a conceptual model like that shown in Figure 18.3, and it measures potential stressors affecting employees negatively. Data can be collected through questionnaires and interviews about environmental and personal stressors. Researchers at the University of Michigan's Institute for Social Research have developed standardized instruments for measuring most of the stressors shown in Figure 18.3. It is important to obtain perceptual measures because people's cognitive appraisal of the situation makes a stressor stressful. Most organizational surveys measure dimensions potentially stressful to employees, such as work overload, role conflict and ambiguity, promotional issues, opportunities for participation, managerial support, and communication. Similarly, there are specific instruments for measuring the individual differences, such as hardiness, social support, and Type A or B behavior pattern. In addition to perceptions of stressors, it is necessary to measure stress consequences, such as subjective moods, performance, job satisfaction, absenteeism, blood pressure, and cholesterol level. Various instruments and checklists have been developed for obtaining people's perceptions of negative consequences, and these can be supplemented with hard measures taken from company records, medical reports, and physical examinations.

Once measures of the stressors and consequences are obtained, the two sets of data must be related to reveal which stressors contribute most to negative stress in the situation under study. For example, a relational analysis might show that qualitative overload and role ambiguity are highly related to employee fatigue, absenteeism, and poor performance, especially for Type A employees. This kind of information points to specific organizational conditions that must be improved to reduce stress. Moreover, it identifies the kinds of employees who may need special counseling and training in stress management. Organizations such as AT&T, the U.S. Department of Defense, and the Los Angeles Police Department periodically chart stressors to assess the health of their employees and to make necessary improvements.

Health Profiling. This method is aimed at identifying stress symptoms so that corrective action can be taken. It starts with a questionnaire asking people for their medical history; personal habits; current health; and vital signs, such as blood pressure, cholesterol level, and triglyceride levels. It also may include a physical examination if some of the information is not readily available. Information from the questionnaire and physical examination is then analyzed, usually by a computer that calculates the individual's health profile. This profile compares the individual's characteristics with those of an average person of the same gender, age, and race. The profile identifies the person's future health prospect, typically by placing him or her in a health-risk category with a known probability of fatal disease, such as cardiovascular risk. The health profile also indicates how the health risks can be reduced by making personal and environmental changes such as dieting, exercising, or traveling.

Many firms cannot afford to do their own health profiling and contract with health firms to do it on a fee basis per employee. Other firms have extensive in-house health and stress management programs. At one program, health profiling was an initial diagnostic step. Each participant first went through a rigorous physical and medical history examination to determine personal health risks and to establish a basis for prescribing an individualized health program. Company officials reported that the program had positive results: "It has generated good public interest, helped recruiting efforts, and provided better all-around fitness for participants in the program. Individual health screening has uncovered six cases of early-stage cancer and a number of cases of high blood pressure and heart disease."[93]

Alleviating Stressors and Coping with Stress

After diagnosing the presence and causes of stress, the next step in stress management is to do something about it. OD interventions for reducing negative stress tend to fall into two groups: those aimed at changing the organizational conditions causing stress and those directed at helping people to cope better with stress. Because stress results from the interaction between people and the environment, both strategies are needed for effective stress management.

Two methods for alleviating stressful organizational conditions include role clarification and supportive relationships. These efforts are aimed at decreasing role ambiguity and conflict and improving poor relationships, key sources of managerial stress. Two interventions aimed at helping people to cope more positively with stress are stress inoculation training and health and fitness facilities. These can help employees alleviate stress symptoms and prepare themselves for handling stressful situations. Finally, an employee assistance program addresses both organizational conditions and the individual.

Role Clarification. This involves helping employees better understand the demands of their work roles. A manager's role is embedded in a network of relationships with other managers, each of whom has specific expectations about how the manager should perform the role. Role clarification is a systematic process for revealing others' expectations and arriving at a consensus about the activities constituting a particular role. There are several role clarification methods, among them job expectation technique (JET) and role analysis technique (RAT)[94] and they follow a similar strategy. First, the people relevant to defining a particular role are identified (e.g., members of a managerial team, a boss and subordinate, and members of other departments relating to the role holder) and brought together at a meeting, usually in a location away from the organization.

Second, the role holder discusses his or her perceived job duties and responsibilities and the other participants are encouraged to comment on and to agree or disagree with the role holder's perceptions. An OD practitioner may act as a process consultant to facilitate interaction and reduce defensiveness. Third, when everyone has reached consensus on defining the role, the role holder is responsible for writing a description of the activities that are seen now as constituting the role. A copy of the role description is distributed to all participants to ensure that they fully understand and agree with the role definition. Fourth, the participants periodically check to see whether the role is being performed as intended and make modifications if necessary.

Role clarification can be used to define a single role or the roles of members of a group. It has been used in such companies as Alcoa, Sherwin-Williams, Johnson & Johnson, and Honeywell to help management teams arrive at agreed-upon roles for members. The process is generally included as part of initial team-building meetings for new management teams starting high-involvement plants. Managers share perceptions and negotiate about one another's roles as a means of determining areas of discretion and responsibility. Role clarity is particularly important in new plant situations where managers are trying to implement participative methods. The ambiguity of such settings can be extremely stressful, and role clarification can reduce stress by helping managers translate such ambiguous concepts as "involvement" and "participation" into concrete role behaviors.

Research on role clarification supports these benefits. One study found that it reduced stress and role ambiguity and increased job satisfaction.[95] Another study reported that it improved interpersonal relationships among group members and contributed to improved production and quality.[96] These findings should be interpreted carefully, however, because both studies had weak research designs and used only perceptual measures.

Supportive Relationships. This involves establishing trusting and genuinely positive relationships among employees, including bosses, subordinates, and peers. Supportive relations have been a hallmark of organization development and are a major part of such interventions as team building, intergroup relations, employee involvement, work design, goal setting, and career planning and development. Considerable research shows that supportive relationships can buffer people from stress.[97] When people feel that relevant others really care about what happens to them and are willing to help, they can cope with stressful conditions. The pioneering coal mining studies which gave rise to sociotechnical systems theory found that miners needed the support from a cohesive work group to deal effectively with the stresses of underground mining.

Research on the boss–subordinate relationship suggests that a supportive boss can provide subordinates with a crucial defense against stress. A study of managers at an AT&T subsidiary undergoing turmoil because of the company's corporate breakup showed that employees who were under considerable stress but felt that their boss was supportive suffered half as much illness, depression, impaired sexual performance, and obesity as employees reporting to an unsupportive boss. A study of U.S. Defense Department employees at air force bases in the Midwest showed that the single organizational dimension accounting for higher levels of cholesterol was having a boss who was too bossy.[98]

This research suggests that organizations must become more aware of the positive value of supportive relationships in helping employees cope with stress. They may need to build supportive, cohesive work groups in situations that are particularly stressful, such as introducing new products, solving emergency problems, and handling customer complaints. For example, firms such as Procter & Gamble and BP have recognized that internal OD consultation can be extremely stressful, and so they have encouraged internal OD practitioners to form support teams to help each other cope with the demands of the role. Equally important, organizations need to direct more attention to ensuring that managers provide the support and encouragement necessary to help subordinates cope with stress. For example, the University of Southern California's executive programs often include a module on helping subordinates cope with stress, and firms are training managers to be more sensitive to stress and more supportive and helpful to subordinates.

Stress Inoculation Training. Companies have developed programs to help employees acquire the skills and knowledge to cope more positively with stressors. Participants are first taught to understand stress warning signals, such as difficulty in making decisions, disruption in sleeping and eating habits, and greater frequencies of headaches and backaches. Then they are encouraged to admit that they are overstressed (or understressed) and to develop a concrete plan for coping with the situation. One strategy is to develop and use a coping self-statement procedure. Participants verbalize a series of questions or statements each time they experience negative stress. The following sample questions or statements[99] are addressed to the four stages of the stress-coping cycle:

- Preparation (What am I going to do about these stressors?)
- Confrontation (I must relax and stay in control.)
- Coping (I must focus on the present set of stressors.)
- Self-reinforcement (I handled it well.)

Stress inoculation training is aimed at helping employees cope with stress rather than at changing the stressors themselves. Its major value is sensitizing people to the presence of stress and preparing them to take personal action. Self-appraisal and self-regulation of stress can free people from total reliance on others for stress management. Given the multitude of organizational conditions that can cause stress, such self-control is a valuable adjunct to interventions aimed at changing the conditions themselves.

Health Facilities. A growing number of organizations are providing facilities for helping employees cope with stress. Elaborate exercise facilities are maintained by such firms as Xerox, Weyerhaeuser, and PepsiCo. Similarly, more than 500 companies operate corporate cardiovascular fitness programs. Before starting such programs, employees must take an exercise tolerance test and have the approval of either a private or a company doctor. Each participant is then assigned a safe level of heart response to the various parts of the fitness program. Preliminary evidence suggests that fitness programs can reduce absenteeism and coronary risk factors, such as high blood pressure, body weight, percentage of body fat, and triglyceride levels.[100] A review of the research, however, suggests that fitness programs primarily result in better mental health and resistance to stress and that such organizational improvements as reduced absenteeism and turnover and improved performance are more uncertain.[101]

In addition to exercise facilities, some companies, such as McDonald's and Equitable Life Assurance Society, provide biofeedback facilities in which managers take relaxation breaks using biofeedback devices to monitor respiration and heart rate.

Feedback of such data helps managers lower their respiration and heart rates. Some companies provide time for employees to meditate, and other firms have stay-well programs that encourage healthy diets and lifestyles.

Employee Assistance Programs. This final stress and wellness intervention is an organizational intervention and a method for helping individuals directly. EAPs help identify, refer, and treat workers whose personal problems affect their performance.[102] While some large companies still provide an in-house EAP, most outsource their EAP programs. Initially started in the 1940s to combat alcoholism, these programs have expanded to deal with emotional, family, marital, and financial problems, and, more recently, drug abuse. For example, the 2002 National Survey on Drug Use and Health suggested that 71% of current illicit drug users 18 years or older were working full- or part-time. Another study of workplace-related drug testing showed a decline in workplace drug use from 1998 to 1999, but a slight increase from 1999 to 2000.[103] Alcohol and drug use costs U.S. business an estimated $102 billion per year in lost productivity, accidents, and turnover.[104] Britain's Royal College of Psychiatrists suggested that up to 30% of employees in British companies would experience mental health problems and that 115 million workdays were lost each year as a result of depression.[105] Other factors, too, have contributed to increased problems: altered family structures, the growth of single-parent households, the increase in divorce, greater mobility, and changing modes of child rearing are all fairly recent phenomena that have added to the stress experienced by employees. These trends indicate that an increasing number of employees need assistance with personal problems, and the research suggests that EAP use increases during downsizing and restructuring.[106]

When other stress management interventions are not effective or when employees have particular types of wellness and or health issues, employee assistance programs provide a means of responding to employee wellness problems including extreme or chronic stress, drug and alcohol abuse, problems with child and or elder care, grief, and financial problems.[107] Central to the philosophy underlying EAPs is the belief that although the organization has no right to interfere in the private lives of its employees, it does have a right to impose certain standards of work performance and to establish sanctions when these are not met. Anyone whose work performance is impaired because of a personal problem is eligible for admission into an EAP program. Successful EAPs have been implemented at General Motors, Johnson & Johnson, Motorola, Burlington Northern Railroad, and Dominion Foundries and Steel Company. Although limited, some research has demonstrated that EAPs can positively affect absenteeism, turnover, and job performance.[108] At AT&T, for example, 59 employees who were close to losing their jobs were enrolled in an EAP and successfully returned to work. Hiring and training replacements would have been much more costly than the expense of the EAP.[109]

Numerous Web sites, including the Employee Assistance Professionals Association, share or provide at minimal cost detailed guidelines on establishing an EAP. These steps include developing an appropriate EAP policy, deciding to insource or outsource the program, communicating the program to organization members, and providing training on EAP use. Recent changes in health care privacy as a result of the Health Insurance Portability and Privacy Act (HIPAA) impact EAPs, related health insurance benefits, data requirements, and how such data and information can be used and shared.[110]

Application 18.3 describes the evolution of an EAP and wellness program at Johnson & Johnson and demonstrates how such programs can be implemented in large, decentralized organizations.[111]

JOHNSON & JOHNSON'S HEALTH AND WELLNESS PROGRAM

Johnson & Johnson (J&J) is the most diversified health care corporation in the world. It grosses more than $36 billion a year and employs approximately 101,800 people at 190 companies in 51 countries. The J&J companies are decentralized and directly responsible for their own operations. Corporate management is committed to this structure because of the many proven advantages to the businesses and people involved, such as the development of general managers, faster product development, and a closer connection with the customer. Its philosophy is embodied in a document called "Our Credo," a section of which makes a commitment to the welfare of its employees.

J&J has a long history of commitment to health, wellness, and stress management programs. For example, based on a successful pilot project in its Ethicon division during the 1970s, J&J top management decided to implement EAPs throughout the rest of the company. The J&J EAPs were in-house treatment programs that offered employees and family members confidential, professional assistance for problems related to alcohol and drug abuse, as well as marital, family, emotional, and mental health difficulties. The major goal was to help clients assume responsibility for their own behavior and, if it was destructive to themselves or others, to modify it. Employees could enter an EAP by self-referral or by counseling from their supervisor. The program emphasized the necessity of maintaining complete confidentiality when counseling the employee or family member to protect both the client's dignity and job.

The EAPs were implemented between 1980 and 1985 in three phases. The first phase consisted of contacting the managers and directors of personnel for each of the decentralized divisions and assessing their divisions' EAP needs. An educational process was initiated to inform managers and directors about the employee assistance program. This EAP training then was conducted in each of the personnel departments of the divisions. The second phase included a formal presentation to the management board of each division. It included information about the EAP and about an alcohol and drug component for executives. In the third phase, cost estimates were developed for EAP use and for employment of an EAP administrator to implement the program in each division. In addition, the corporate director of assistance programs established a quality assurance program to review all EAP activities biennially.

Eventually, more than 90% of all domestic employees had direct access to an EAP, and the remaining employees had telephone access. There were employee assistance programs at all major J&J locations throughout the United States, Puerto Rico, and Canada. Programs also operated in Brazil

and England. A study of J&J's EAP in the New Jersey area showed that clients with drug abuse, emotional, or mental health problems who availed themselves of EAP services were treated at substantial savings to the company.

APPLICATION 18•3

The EAPs were ultimately integrated with J&J's original wellness program known as Live for Life. This program was initiated by the chairman of the board in 1979, when he committed to provide all employees and their families with the opportunity to become the healthiest employees of any corporation in the world. The program brought together experts in health care education, behavior change, and disease management to create a program to improve the health and productivity of workers. The Live for Life program offered classes in nutrition, weight reduction, and smoking cessation. In addition, small gymnasiums with workout equipment, aerobics rooms, and swimming pools were made available. In the late 1980s and 1990s the combined programs became known as Live for Life Assistance programs. Health, safety, benefits, wellness, and employee assistance programs worked together to promote employee well-being in the workplace.

The current Johnson & Johnson Health and Wellness Program is an outgrowth of those early programs. It has undergone several transformations in the past two decades to respond to shifting business requirements and changing employee health needs. The Johnson & Johnson Health and Wellness Program includes disability management, occupational health, employee assistance, work–life programs, and wellness and fitness programs. The program is often studied by other corporations because of its integrated service deliveries.

In 1995, Johnson & Johnson's health and fitness group took a simple step that catapulted participation in the company's wellness program from 26% to 90%. Patricia Flynn, vice president of Johnson & Johnson's health care system, described how J&J offered every employee a $500 health-benefits credit in exchange for completing an annual health-risk assessment before enrolling in the plan. Although the company had offered the assessment optionally for years as part of its wellness program, it was not until the incentive was attached that employees flocked to it. "People think they are fit and might not want to bother with an assessment," Flynn says. "This incentive got them to do it."

In the past, organization members were given incentives for participating in various wellness programs, but the company's focus has shifted all of its incentive dollars toward risk assessment. "We are confident that once employees know what their risks are, then we can make a positive impact on their health," says Jennifer Bruno, director of business planning. Early studies conducted at the company showed that even those employees who took the assessment but had no follow-up support through wellness programs showed improvements in their health.

But for Johnson & Johnson, the assessment is just the beginning. The aggregate data helps the health care group choose the right wellness programs for the exact needs of the population, Bruno says. The program developers aren't guessing at employees' health interests or expecting them to know what programs they will benefit from, she says. They use the hard data to guide their wellness program choices. "We are making better use of our health care dollars, thanks to the assessment information."

For example, the initial assessment showed that the employees had three areas of risk: high cholesterol, high blood pressure, and inactivity. The company now regularly offers exercise and counseling programs to help employees reduce cholesterol and blood pressure and manage weight. Bruno says there are also subtle additions to the workplace environment that contribute to a healthy culture, such as nutritious choices in the cafeteria, scales in all of the bathrooms, and a nonsmoking environment.

Since the assessment and resulting wellness programs were implemented, costs have decreased significantly at Johnson & Johnson. Between 1995 and 1999, medical care costs decreased by $225 per person due to lower administrative and medical utilization, an annual total savings of $8.5 million. Participating employees had significantly lower medical expenses and improved health-risk factors in categories such as high cholesterol, high blood pressure, and smoking. Importantly, the savings grew over time, with most of the savings attained in the third or fourth year after the program's inception. For those employees who were discovered to be at high risk for a disease and then reduced their risk, the savings was $390 per year.

Johnson & Johnson's Health and Wellness program demonstrates a long-term commitment to its strategy, its industry, and its people. The execution and coordination of the different wellness components has paid off handsomely for many stakeholders.

SUMMARY

This chapter presented three major human resources interventions: career planning and development, workforce diversity interventions, and employee stress and wellness interventions. Although these kinds of change programs generally are carried out by human resources specialists, a growing number of OD practitioners are gaining competence in these areas and the interventions are increasingly being included in OD programs.

Career planning involves helping people choose occupations, organizations, and jobs at different stages of their careers. Employees typically pass through four different career stages—establishment, advancement, maintenance, and withdrawal—with different career planning issues relevant to each stage. Major career planning practices include communication, counseling, workshops, self-development materials, and assessment programs. Career planning is a highly personalized process that includes assessing one's interests, values, and capabilities; examining alternative careers; and making relevant decisions.

Career development helps employees achieve career objectives. Effective efforts in that direction include linking corporate business objectives, human resources needs, and the personal needs of employees. Different career development needs and practices exist and are relevant to each of the four stages of people's careers.

Workforce diversity interventions are designed to adapt human resources practices to an increasingly diverse workforce. Age, gender, race, sexual orientation, disability, and culture and values trends point to a more complex set of human resources demands. Within such a context, OD interventions (e.g., job design, performance management, and employee involvement practices) have to be adapted to a diverse set of personal preferences, needs, and lifestyles.

Employee stress and wellness interventions, such as work leaves and stress management, recognize the important link between worker health and organizational productivity. Work leaves offer opportunities for organization members to rejuvenate over extended periods of time before returning to work. Stress management is concerned with helping employees to cope with the negative consequences of stress at work. The concept of stress involves the fit of people's needs, abilities, and expectations with environmental demands, changes, and opportunities. A good person–environment fit results in positive reactions to stress, such as motivation and innovation, and a poor fit results in negative effects, such as headaches, backaches, and cardiovascular disease. A model for understanding work-related stress includes occupational stressors; individual differences, which affect how people respond to the stressors; stress outcomes; and interventions to increase wellness or decrease stress. The two main steps in stress management are diagnosing stress and its causes, and alleviating stressors and helping people to cope with stress. Two methods for diagnosing stress are charting stressors and health profiling. Techniques for alleviating stressful conditions include role clarification and supportive relationships. Means for helping workers cope with stress are stress inoculation training and participation in activities at health and fitness facilities. Finally, EAPs identify, refer, and treat employees and their families for such problems as marital difficulties, drug and alcohol abuse, emotional disturbances, and financial crises. EAPs preserve the dignity of the individual but also recognize the organization's right to expect certain work behaviors.

■ NOTES

1. J. Fierman, "Beating the Midlife Career Crisis," *Fortune* (6 September 1993): 52–62; L. Richman, "How to Get Ahead in America," *Fortune* (16 May 1994): 46–54; D. Hall, "Protean Careers of the 21st Century," *Academy of Management Journal* 10 (1996): 8–16.

2. "IT Workers Expect Career Development and Job Satisfaction," *HR Focus* (1 August 1999): 4.

3. G. Bohlander and S. Snell, *Managing Human Resources* (Cincinnati, Ohio: South-Western College Publishing, 2004).

4. D. Feldman, *Managing Careers in Organizations* (Glenview, Ill.: Scott, Foresman, 1988).

5. E. Erikson, *Childhood and Society* (New York: W.W. Norton and Co., 1963); G. Sheehy, *Passages: Predictable Crises of Adult Life* (New York: E. P. Dutton, 1974); D. Levinson, *Seasons of a Man's Life* (New York: Alfred A. Knopf, 1978); R. Gould, *Transformations: Growth and Change in Adult Life* (New York: Simon & Schuster, 1978); D. Levinson, *Seasons of a Woman's Life* (New York: Alfred A. Knopf, 1996).

6. D. Super, *The Psychology of Careers* (New York: Harper & Row, 1957); D. T. Hall, *Careers in Organizations* (Santa Monica, Calif.: Goodyear, 1976); E. Schein, *Career Dynamics: Matching Individual and Organizational Needs* (Reading, Mass.: Addison-Wesley, 1978); L. Baird and K. Kram, "Career Dynamics: The Superior/Subordinate Relationship," *Organizational Dynamics* 11 (Spring 1983): 46–64; J. Slocum and W. Cron, "Job Attitudes and Performance During Three Career Stages" (working paper, Edwin L. Cox School of Business, Southern Methodist University, Dallas, Tex., 1984).

7. Sheehy, *Passages;* Levinson, *Seasons of a Man's Life;* Gould, *Transformations;* Levinson, *Seasons of a Woman's Life;* M. Lachman and J. James, *Multiple Paths of Midlife Development* (Chicago: University of Chicago Press, 1997); J. Gordon, J. Beatty, and K. Whelan-Berry, "The Midlife Transition of Professional Women with Children," *Women in Management Review* 77 (2002): 328–41.

8. Hall, "Protean Careers."

9. D. Stafford, "Enticing Workers to Stay is Harder Than It Used to Be," *Kansas City Star* (15 June 1998): B-6; Hall, "Protean Careers."

10. J. Clausen, *The Life Course: A Sociological Perspective.* (Englewood Cliffs, N.J.: Prentice-Hall, 1986); Sheehy, *Passages;* Levinson, *Seasons of a Man's Life;* Gould, *Transformations;* Levinson, *Seasons of a Woman's Life;* Lachman and James, *Multiple Paths of Midlife Development;* J. R. Gordon and K. S. Whelan-Berry, "Women at Midlife: Changes, Challenges, and Contributions," in *Supporting Women's Career Advancement*, eds. R. Burke and M. Mattis (in press).

11. J. Gordon and K. Whelan-Berry, "Successful Professional Women at Midlife: How Organizations Can More Effectively Understand and Respond to the Challenges," *Academy of Management Executive* 12 (1998): 8–24.

12. Clausen, *The Life Course;* Sheehy, *Passages;* Levinson, *Seasons of a Man's Life;* Gould, *Transformations;* Levinson, *Seasons of a Woman's Life;* Lachman and James, *Multiple Paths of Midlife Development;* Gordon and Whelan-Berry, "Women at Midlife."

13. D. Anfuso, "Colgate's Global HR Unites Under One Strategy," *Personnel Journal* 74, 10 (1995): 44–48; D. McNamara, "Developing Global Human Resource Competencies" (presentation to the Conference Board Quality Council II, Chicago, April 11, 1996).

14. B. Rosen and T. Jerdee, "Too Old or Not Too Old," *Harvard Business Review* 55 (November-December 1977): 97–106; N. Munk, "Finished at Forty," *Fortune* (1 February 1999): 50–66; Anonymous, "How to Prepare for the Coming Older Workforce," IOMA's Safety Director's Report, 1, April 2001.

15. B. Meglino, "A Meta-Analytic Examination of Realistic Job Preview Effectiveness: A Test of Three Counterintuitive Propositions," *Human Resource Management* 10 (2000): 407–34.

16. J. Wanous, "Realistic Job Previews for Organizational Recruitment," *Personnel* 52 (1975): 58–68.

17. J. Wanous, "Effects of a Realistic Job Preview on Job Acceptance, Job Attitudes, and Job Survival," *Journal of Applied Psychology* 58 (1973): 327–32; J. Wanous, "Realistic Job Previews: Can a Procedure to Reduce Turnover Also Influence the Relationship Between Abilities and Performance?" *Personnel Psychology* 31 (Summer 1978): 249–58; S. Premack and J. Wanous, "A Meta-Analysis of Realistic Job Preview Experiments," *Journal of Applied Psychology* 70 (1985): 706–19.

18. B. Meglino, A. DeNisi, S. Youngblood, and K. Williams, "Effects of Realistic Job Previews: A Comparison Using an Enhancement and a Reduction Preview," *Journal of Applied Psychology* 73 (1988): 259–66; J. Vandenberg and V. Scarpello, "The Matching Method: An Examination of the Processes Underlying Realistic Job Previews," *Journal of Applied Psychology* 75 (1990): 60–67.

19. L. Thurow, "Building Wealth," *Atlantic Monthly* (June 1999): 57–69.

20. D. Bray, R. J. Campbell, and D. Grant, *Formative Years in Business: A Long Term AT&T Study of Managerial Lives* (New York: John Wiley & Sons, 1974).

21. B. Kaye and S. Jordan-Evans, "From Assets to Investors," *Training & Development* 57 (2003): 40–46.

22. R. Katz, "Time and Work: Towards an Integrative Perspective," in *Research in Organizational Behavior*, vol. 2, eds. B. Staw and L. Cummings (New York: JAI Press, 1979), 81–127.

23. K. Brousseau, "Toward a Dynamic Model of Job-Person Relationships: Findings, Research Questions, and Implications for Work System Design," *Academy of Management Review* 8 (January 1983): 33–45.

24. J. Carnazza, A. Korman, T. Ference, and J. Stoner, "Plateaued and Non-Plateaued Managers: Factors in Job Performance," *Journal of Management* 7 (1981): 7–27.

25. J. Slocum, W. Cron, R. Hansen, and S. Rawlings, "Business Strategy and the Management of the Plateaued Performer," *Academy of Management Journal* 28 (1985): 133–54.

26. Allerton, "Trend Watch," *Training & Development* 54, 1 (January 2000): 11.

27. J. Gordon, L. Litchfield, and K. Whelan-Berry, *Women at Midlife and Beyond: A Glimpse into the Future* (Chestnut Hill, Mass.: Boston College Center for Work & Family, 2003).

28. J. Ivancevich and W. Glueck, *Foundations of Personnel/Human Resource Management*, 3d ed. (Plano, Tex.: Business Publications, 1986), 541.

29. G. Thornton, *Assessment Centers* (Reading, Mass.: Addison-Wesley, 1992); A. Engelbrecht and H. Fischer, "The Managerial Performance Implications of a Developmental Assessment Center Process," *Human Relations* 48 (1995): 387–404.

30. Thornton, *Assessment Centers;* P. Griffiths and P. Goodge, "Development Centres: The Third Generation," *Personnel Management* 26, 6 (1994): 40–43; P. Geradus, W. Jansen, and F. DeJongh, *Assessment Centres: A Practical Handbook* (New York: John Wiley & Sons, 1998).

31. R. Jones and M. Whitmore, "Evaluating Developmental Assessment Centers as Interventions," *Personnel Psychology* 48 (1995): 377–88.

32. J. Clawson, "Mentoring in Managerial Careers," in *Family and Career,* ed. C. B. Derr (New York: Praeger, 1980); K. Kram, *Mentoring at Work* (Glenview, Ill.: Scott, Foresman, 1984); A. Geiger-DuMond and S. Boyle, "Mentoring: A Practitioner's Guide," *Training and Development* (March 1995): 51–54; G. Shea, *Mentoring: How to Develop Successful Mentor Behaviors* (Menlo Park, Calif. Crisp Publications, 1998).

33. E. Collins and P. Scott, "Everyone Who Makes It Has a Mentor," *Harvard Business Review* 56 (July-August 1978): 100; M. Murray, *Beyond the Myths and Magic of Mentoring* (San Francisco: Jossey-Bass, 1991).

34. Geiger-DuMond and Boyle, "Mentoring," 51.

35. G. Roche, "Much Ado About Mentors," *Harvard Business Review* 57 (January-February 1979): 14–28.

36. D. Thomas, "The Truth About Mentoring Minorities: Race Matters," *Harvard Business Review* 79 (April 2001): 98–107.

37. E. Fagensen and G. Baugh, "Career Paths, Networking, and Mentoring," in *Women at Work*, ed. D. Smith (Saddle River, N.J.: Prentice-Hall, 2000).

38. Ibid.

39. Bohlander and Snell, *Managing Human Resources.*

40. S. Wager, "Retention Update," *Training & Development,* 55 (2001): 63–66.

41. See, for example, D. Kolb, D. Rubin, and J. McIntyre, *Organizational Psychology: Readings on Human Behavior in Organizations,* 4th ed. (New York: Prentice-Hall, 1984).

42. F. Balcazar, B. Hopkins, and Y. Suarez, "A Critical Objective Review of Performance Feedback," *Journal of Organizational Behavior Management* 7 (1986): 65–89; J. Chobbar and J. Wallin, "A Field Study on the Effect of Feedback Frequency on Performance," *Journal of Applied Psychology* 69 (1984): 524–30; R. Waldersee and F. Luthans, "A Theoretically Based Contingency Model of Feedback: Implications for Managing Service Employees," *Journal of Organizational Change Management* 3 (1990): 46–56; P. Swinburne, "How to Use Feedback to Improve Performance," *People Management* 7 (2001): 11.

43. R. Levering and M. Moskowitz, "100 Best Companies to Work For," *Fortune* (20 January 2003): 127–52.

44. For an example, see S. Merkner, ed., *Birmingham's Best Companies for Working Families 2000 Annual Report,* (Birmingham: Child Times, Inc., 2003).

45. Anonymous, "Absence Makes the Business Run Slower," *Journal of Business Strategy* 22 (2001): 3

46. R. Karanbayya and A. Reilly, "Dual Earner Couples: Attitudes and Actions in Restructuring Work for Family," *Journal of Organizational Behavior* 13 (1992): 585–603; J. Schneer and F. Reitman, "Effects of Alternate Family Structures on Managerial Careers," *Academy of Management Journal* 36 (1993): 830–43.

47. P. Kruger, "The Good News About Working Couples," *Parenting,* 12 (1998a): 69; P. Kruger, "The Job-Home Juggle & Dads," *Parenting,* 12 (1998b): 68–71; Gordon and Whelan-Berry, "Women at Midlife."

48. D. T. Hall and M. Morgan, "Career Development and Planning," in *Contemporary Problems in Personnel,* 3d ed., eds. K. Pearlman, F. Schmidt, and W. C. Hamnek (New York: John Wiley & Sons, 1983), 232–33.

49. M. Bekas, "Dual-Career Couples—A Corporate Challenge," *Personnel Administrator* (April 1984): 37–44.

50. D. Jamieson and J. O'Mara, *Managing Workforce 2000* (San Francisco: Jossey-Bass, 1991).

51. F. Rice, "How to Make Diversity Pay," *Fortune* (8 August 1994): 78–86; R. Thomas Jr., "From Affirmative Action to Affirming Diversity," *Harvard Business Review* (March-April 1990): 107–17; K. Labich, "Making Diversity Pay," *Fortune* (9 September 1996): 177–80.

52. P. Dass and B. Parker, "Strategies for Managing Human Resource Diversity: From Resistance to Learning," *Academy of Management Executive* 13 (1999): 68–80.

53. Rice, "How to Make Diversity Pay," 79.

54. This section benefited greatly from the advice and assistance of Pat Pope, president of Pope and Associates, Cincinnati, Ohio. Much of the data and many examples cited in support of each trend can be found in the following references and Web sites: Munk, "Finished at Forty"; M. Galen, "Equal Opportunity Diversity: Beyond the Numbers Game," *Business Week* (14 August 1995): 60–61; K. Hammon and A. Palmer, "The Daddy Trap," *Business Week* (21 September 1998): 56–64; H. Kahan and D. Mulryan, "Out of the Closet," *American Demographics* (May 1995): 40–47; http://stats.bls.gov; http://nces.ed.gov;http://census.gov; http://cdc.gov.

55. Anonymous, "How to Prepare for the Coming Older Workforce," *IOMA's Safety Director's Report,* 1(03), April 2001. See also World Health Organization information on aging of the workforce.

56. D. Meyerson and J. Fletcher, "A Modest Manifesto for Breaking the Glass Ceiling," *Harvard Business Review* (January-February 2000): 127–135.

57. E. Cook, M. Heppner, and K. O'Brien, "Career Development of Women of Color and White Women: Assumptions, Conceptualizations, and Interventions from an Ecological Perspective," *Career Development Quarterly* 50 (2002): 291–305.

58. Meyerson and Fletcher, "A Modest Manifesto."

59. A. Brief, R. Buttram, R. Reizenstein, D. Pugh, J. Callahan, R. McCline, and J. Vaslow, "Beyond Good Intentions: The Next Steps Toward Racial Equality in the American Workplace," *Academy of Management Executive* 11(1997): 59–72; K. Caver and A. Livers, "Dear White Boss," *Harvard Business Review* 80 (November 2002): 76–81.

60. Brief, et al., "Beyond Good Intentions".

61. Ibid.

62. Caver and Livers, "Dear White Boss."

63. Brief et al., "Beyond Good Intentions."

64. J. Hickman, C. Tkaczyk, E. Florian, J. Stemple, and D. Vazquez, "50 Best Companies for Minorities," *Fortune* (7 July 2003): 103–9.

65. Anonymous, "More Employers Cover Domestic Partners," *Employee Benefit News* 17, 8 (June 15, 2003): 30.

66. Ibid.

67. D. Baldrige and J. Veiga, "Toward a Greater Understanding of the Willingness to Request an Accommodation: Can Requesters' Beliefs Disable the Americans with Disabilities Act?" *Academy of Management Review* 26 (2001): 85–99.

68. Towers Perrin, *Workforce 2000 Today: A Bottom-Line Concern—Revisiting Corporate Views on Workforce Change* (New York: Author, 1992).

69. S. Rynes and B. Rosen, "A Field Survey of Factors Affecting the Adoption and Perceived Success of Diversity Training," *Personnel Psychology* 48 (1995): 247–70; K. Labich, "Making Diversity Pay."

70. M. Kwak, The Paradox of Effects of Diversity," *Sloan Management Review* 44 (Spring 2003): 7–8

71. This application was adopted from material in K. Hammonds, "Case Study: One Company's Delicate Balancing Act," *Business Week* (15 September 1997): 102–4.

72. J. Blair and M. Fotter, *Challenges in Health Care Management* (San Francisco: Jossey-Bass, 1990).

73. K. Warner, T. Wickizer, R. Wolfe, J. Schildroth, and M. Samuelson, "Economic Implications of the Workplace Health Promotion Programs: Review of the Literature," *Journal of Occupational Medicine* 30 (1988): 106–12; G. Pfeiffer, WorkCare Group, information found at http://www.jps.net/dkgamow/clarsrch.htm, accessed on January 15, 2000; additional data can be found at the National Institute of Drug Abuse, http://www.nida.hih.gov/.

74. These data were found at http://www.successunlimited.co.uk/costs.htm, accessed January 14, 2000. The results have since been moved to http://www.bullyonline.org/workbully/costs.htm, accessed on October 1, 2003.

75. K. Danna and R. Griffin, "Health and Well-Being in the Workplace: A Review and Synthesis of the Literature," *Journal of Management* 25(1999): 357–84.

76. Ibid.

77. M. Peak, "I Think I'll Go to Work in France," *Management Review* 84 (1995): 7; U.S. Department of Labor, (http://www.dol.gov/ilab), Chart 19, "Annual Hours Worked per Employed Person 1990 and 2001."

78. Levering and Moskowitz,"100 Best Companies to Work For."

79. T. Gunter, "The Pause That Refreshes," *Business Week* (19 November 2001): 138.

80. T. O'Boyle, "Fear and Stress in the Office Take Toll," *Wall Street Journal* (6 November 1990): B1, B3; A. Riecher, "Job Stress: What It Can Do to You," *Bryan-College Station Eagle* (15 August 1993): D1.

81. D. Allen, "Less Stress, Less Litigation," *Personnel* (January 1990): 32–35; D. Hollis and J. Goodson, "Stress: The Legal and Organizational Implications," *Employee Responsibilities and Rights Journal* 2 (1989): 255–62.

82. D. Ganster and J. Schaubroeck, "Work Stress and Employee Health," *Journal of Management* 17 (1991): 235–71; T. Stewart, "Do You Push Your Employees Too Hard?" *Fortune* (22 October 1990): 121–28.

83. T. Cummings and C. Cooper, "A Cybernetic Framework for Studying Occupational Stress," *Human Relations* 32 (1979): 395–418.

84. J. French and R. Caplan, "Organization Stress and Individual Strain," in *The Failure of Success*, ed. A. Morrow (New York: AMACOM, 1972).

85. Ibid.

86. R. Kahn, D. Wolfe, R. Quinn, J. Snoek, and R. Rosenthal, *Organizational Stress* (New York: John Wiley & Sons, 1964).

87. C. Cooper and J. Marshall, "Occupational Sources of Stress: A Review of the Literature Relating to Coronary Heart Disease and Mental Ill Health," *Journal of Occupational Psychology* 49 (1976): 11–28; C. Cooper and R. Payne, *Stress at Work* (New York: John Wiley & Sons, 1978).

88. Cooper and Marshall, "Occupational Sources."

89. R. Rosenman and M. Friedman, "The Central Nervous System and Coronary Heart Disease," *Hospital Practice* 6 (1971): 87–97.

90. D. Glass, *Behavior Patterns, Stress and Coronary Disease* (Hillsdale, N.J.: Lawrence Erlbaum, 1977); V. Price, *Type A Behavior Pattern* (New York: Academic Press, 1982).

91. J. Howard, D. Cunningham, and P. Rechnitzer, "Health Patterns Associated with Type A Behavior: A Managerial Population,"*Journal of Human Stress* 2 (1976): 24–31.

92. See, for example, the Addison-Wesley series on occupational stress: L. Warshaw, *Managing Stress* (Reading, Mass.: Addison-Wesley, 1982); A. McClean, *Work Stress* (Reading, Mass.: Addison-Wesley, 1982); A. Shostak, *Blue-Collar Stress* (Reading, Mass.: Addison-Wesley, 1982); L. Moss, *Management Stress* (Reading, Mass.: Addison-Wesley, 1982); L. Levi, *Preventing Work Stress* (Reading, Mass.: Addison-Wesley, 1982); J. House, *Work Stress and Social Support* (Reading, Mass.: Addison-Wesley, 1982).

93. J. Ivancevich and M. Matteson, "Optimizing Human Resources: A Case for Preventive Health and Stress Management," *Organizational Dynamics* 9 (Autumn 1980): 7–21.

94. E. Huse and C. Barebo, "Beyond the T-Group: Increasing Organizational Effectiveness," *California Management Review* 23 (1980): 104–17; I. Dayal and J. Thomas, "Operation KPE: Developing a New Organization," *Journal of Applied Behavioral Science* 4 (1968): 473–506.

95. Huse and Barebo, "Beyond the T-Group."

96. Dayal and Thomas, "Operation KPE."

97. House, *Work Stress and Social Support.*

98. D. Goleman, "Stress: It Depends on the Boss," *International Herald Tribune* 10 (February 1984).

99. Ivancevich and Matteson, "Optimizing Human Resources," 19.

100. Zuckerman, "Keeping Managers in Good Health," *International Management* 34 (January 1979): 40.

101. L. Falkenberg, "Employee Fitness Programs: Their Impact on the Employee and the Organization," *Academy of Management Review* 12 (1987): 511–22.

102. Bohlander and S. Snell, *Managing Human Resources.*

103. Anonymous, "What Does the Renewed Rise in Employee Drug Use Mean to HR?," *HR Focus,* 79, 2 (February 2002): 7–8.

104. S. Savitz, "Mental Health Plans Help Employees, Reduce Costs," *Best's Review* 96, 3 (1995): 60–62.

105. C. Hodges, "Growing Problem of Stress at Work Alarms Business," *People Management* 1 (1995): 14–15.

106. W. Lissy and M. Morgenstern, "Employees Turn to EAPs During Downsizing," *Compensation and Benefits Review* 27, 3 (1995): 16.

107. K. Blassingame, "Providers Offer Bereaved Employees Counseling Options," *BenefitNews.com* (1 September 2003): 51.

108. M. Shain and J. Groenveld, *Employee Assistance Programs: Philosophy, Theory, and Practice* (Lexington, Mass.: D. C. Heath, 1980).

109. Ivancevich and Glueck, *Foundations of Personnel,* 706.

110. K. Bakich and K. Pestaina, "HIPAA Mean Changes for Human Resources," *Employee Relations Law Journal* 28 (2002): 29–54; K. Bakich and K. Pestaina, "HIPAA Mean Changes for Human Resources—Part II: Addressing the Most Challenging HR Issues," *Employee Relations Law Journal* 28 (2003): 47–64.

111. Adapted from T. Desmond, "An Internal Broadbrush Program: J & J's Live for Life Assistance Program," in *The EAP Solution,* ed. J. Spicer (Center City, Minn.: Hazelden, 1987), 148–56; L. Paetsch, "Wellness Program Saves Johnson and Johnson $8.5 Million in Health Care Costs," *Employee Benefit Plan Review* 56 (2002): 31–32; S. Gale, "Selling Health to High-Risk Workers," *Workforce* 81 (2002): 74–76; and the company's Web site http://www.jnj.com

Employee Benefits at HealthCo

Scenario #1

"Pat, I just can't do it. I know you want me to go to New York tonight, but I can't make a trip like this at the last minute."

"Chris, you are the best attorney we have for these negotiations—we need you."

"I appreciate the compliment, but I can't arrange the care for my mother and my daughter on four hours notice. I told you during my performance appraisal about the demands I am under—in terms of carrying my own workload and part of Sidney's [a co-worker] during this parental leave time. In addition, like I said, I have two elderly parents, one needing daily care, my toddler daughter, and I am moving next week. I know you want me to progress and I appreciate it, but you know I work hard—I work overtime every week—but I can't do what you want this time. I'm sorry. I'll talk to you later."

Pat hangs up the phone and thinks, "Okay, I know I am asking a lot, but how do I resolve these issues? It's frustrating that Sidney is out on twelve weeks leave—geez!!!—and it's only going to get worse. Chris is my best person . . . why isn't Chris more committed? And doesn't Sidney know that twelve weeks off creates hardships for everyone else? How can I get them to do more?"

Chris walks to the parking lot thinking, "Boy, I thought I made a good move in coming here. But Pat is worse than the partners I used to work for. What am I going to do? Oh well, at least the job market for attorneys is good."

Scenario #2

"Francis, I appreciate your help these last few weeks. I never could have exceeded all my goals or facilitated my team exceeding its goal if you hadn't connected me with Kyle's Elder Care Referral Service. I feel like I would have had to take at least five to seven days off to gather the same information that Kyle had immediately available. And then I would have spent another week or two—not two days—getting my dad settled. I don't know why he decided to retire to Ireland, but he is delighted with the arrangements, and is doing well."

"That's okay, Blair, I'm happy to help. Thank you for the excellent job you've been doing. I really appreciate it. Let's talk about next month's key goals."

Blair had been the project lead during the implementation of a new quality process in the laboratory, and despite an above-average workload the last month, had successfully met the project's objectives. Francis thought, "It was touch and go when Blair's dad suddenly wanted to retire to Ireland, and wanted to move immediately. Thank heaven I remembered reading about Kyle and the Elder Care Referral Service."

Blair left Francis' office with a smile, thinking, "Francis is great to work for . . . I can't even consider any of the calls I'm getting from other hospitals or headhunters. It's just great to work for someone who understands that work is just one part of life."

Scenario #3

Robin, department head for pediatrics at HealthCo's second largest hospital, had asked to meet with Mercer, the director of pediatrics for HealthCo.

"Mercer, thanks for your time. As you know I'm fifty-six this year, and I want to talk to you about my retirement. I have many interests beyond my medical practice, and also want more time with my family and community. What I would like to do is begin working part-time after this first year. What I'm thinking is that I would work thirty hours a week for two years, still holding clinic hours two days week. Then the next three to five years I would like to transition to full-time retirement. What I would like is to work twenty or so hours per week for those years, working with medical school students and on research projects."

"Well, Robin, as you know, we don't have any formal retirement policy except to fully retire. I'm going to have to talk to HR about this. You have extensive experience and expertise, and I don't want to lose that. I'm just not sure what HR or the Physicians' Council will say."

"I understand. My first choice is to remain with HealthCo, but I know there are organizations that would be interested in my working part-time. When can you get back to me?"

"Give me a couple of weeks, Robin."

"Okay."

Mercer began to think about Robin's request, already hearing HR raise issues like benefits, ongoing participation in retirement funding, and precedents being set. But Mercer didn't want to lose Robin's expertise. And Robin's idea of working with the medical students might let HealthCo create a unique internship and residency experience, which would let HealthCo attract the top students.

BACKGROUND

The people in these three scenarios work for HealthCo, a fully integrated, nonprofit health care organization with nine major medical centers and thirty-six affiliated clinics, rehabilitation units, therapy facilities, hospice and geriatric units, and other highly specialized centers. Located in the eastern United States, HealthCo has about 6,700 employees. Like other health care companies, it employs a disproportionate number of women, especially in nursing and patient care, allied health services, and support staff. The backgrounds of Pat, Francis, and Mercer, all managers at HealthCo, are provided below.

Pat is the chief counsel of HealthCo's internal legal department. Pat has worked for HealthCo for five years, after fifteen years in a major law firm in Washington, D.C. It has been a difficult transition from the "do-anything, 24/7" pace of the firm to the "slower, less professional" pace of HealthCo. Pat is married and has three kids. Pat's spouse is also an attorney. Pat's staff is primarily full-time and works "nine to five." The department is very busy, often with a workload that significantly exceeds the day-to-day capacity of the staff.

Francis serves as the director of laboratory services for the largest hospital. The laboratory is staffed around the clock and can be called on to perform routine and emergency procedures at any time. The new quality process that Blair helped to implement was critical to the lab supporting the hospital's status as the primary emergency and critical-care facility in the region. Francis, who had started in a research lab prior to joining HealthCo, felt the pressure of staffing a 24/7 lab. Having never married, Francis could not imagine juggling marriage and children in addition to the demands of having two parents

and five siblings and their families living nearby. Francis tried to help the lab's employees with family or life demands, but did so on a personal basis, and not because the hospital had many such benefits available.

Mercer is a nationally known pediatrician with fifteen years experience, and was recently hired to head HealthCo's pediatrics organization. Mercer's expertise and management capabilities were stretched in a positive way by the demands of such a large and comprehensive pediatric practice. Thriving on that challenge, Mercer had been very successful since taking over the organization. Marrying after medical school to another physician, Mercer felt grateful for being able to work the hours required to fully learn and understand this new position. Mercer knew a number of people on the pediatric staff, including a number of the pediatricians. Many of them felt Mercer worked way too much, and moreover, worried Mercer expected the same of them. Mercer knew that younger physicians weren't as keen on the 24/7 doctor lifestyle that Mercer's father had lived.

RECENT EVENTS

A couple of weeks after Pat's conversation with Chris, Francis' with Blair, and Mercer's with Robin, a senior staff meeting was called to discuss current issues and the coming year's strategic initiatives. The CEO, Dr. Palmer, recently had became focused on employee retention, after Human Resources reported that HealthCo's turnover was 1.5 times the industry average. While HealthCo was competitive about salary, benefits seemed to be an area needing improvement. Further, the recent issue of *Fortune*, which identified the "Best Companies to Work For," raised Dr. Palmer's awareness of the growing importance of work–life programs and policies.

Dr. Palmer realized that HealthCo did not provide many of the benefits offered by these "best companies." In fact, very few health care companies made the list. Palmer conceded that the twenty-four hours a day, seven days a week nature of health care organizations probably complicated the provision of work–life benefits. However, Palmer also saw a potential competitive advantage in being a leader in providing such benefits, especially when combined with the competitive salary and merit structure HealthCo offered. Dr. Palmer remembered that a survey had been done of HealthCo female employees by an outside research team, and that one area of the survey was work–life issues. A review of the data revealed a number of benefits seen as important to the female employees of HealthCo (see Table 1). The research also had suggested that the immediate supervisor played a vital role in the employee's ability to successfully balance work and life, and the employee's satisfaction with her work–life balance. An immediate supervisor's direct support of work–life balance was significantly linked to other important outcomes, such as job satisfaction, organizational commitment, and intent to leave the organization.

Dr. Palmer raised the question of offering work–life benefits at the senior staff meeting. Dr. Palmer noted that while funding was not unlimited, of course, HealthCo's recent financial performance would permit budget allocations to such benefits, and might also be offset by reduced turnover costs or improved productivity.

Pat immediately stated, "I can barely get my staff together now with all the work we have

Table I	Rank-Order Importance of Work–Life Benefits for Female Employees at HealthCo	
BENEFIT	**RANK**	**CURRENTLY OFFERED BY HEALTHCO**
Maternity/Paternity and Family Leave Includes paid maternity and paternity leave, extended paid leave for family issues, and unpaid leave for family issues with the ability to return to work.	I	HealthCo pays six weeks maternity and paternity leave, after the employees has been with the company for one year. Employees can take another six weeks unpaid. No extended leave.
Sabbatical/Extended Leave Paid extended leave after working for a specified time with the company.	2	Not offered by HealthCo.
Fitness Includes on-site fitness facilities, and/or paid health club memberships.	3	Not offered by HealthCo.
Flextime Includes part-time work schedules, flextime, and telecommuting.	4	Flextime, with two-hour flex offered in some departments.
Work–Life Task Force Employee committee that oversees work–life issues.	5	Currently overseen by HR.
Concierge Services Includes services such as on-site takeout, dry cleaning, auto service, and other similar services.	6	Not offered except at corporate headquarters.
Child Care Includes on-site child care, vacation programs, and before and after school care.	7	Sick-child care offered at some of the medical centers.
Referral Services Includes child care, elder care, and other referral services.	8	Not offered by HealthCo.
Paid Health Insurance Premiums	*	HealthCo pays the employee's premium.

* Payment of health insurance premium not rank-ordered, but included in survey information.

going on. And, I certainly can't hold their hands. They would never be coddled this way in a law firm. People work the hours needed, no questions asked." Francis said, "I can see the difference such benefits would make, but how do I make this work in a 24/7 department? While Legal might see it as difficult, I see it as impossible, especially any movement away from traditional shifts." A nursing director commented thoughtfully, "Some hospitals are considering shorter, split shifts, and longer shifts to create flexibility—there might be something to that." A number of departments immediately argued such scheduling was a leader's nightmare, and that the company's existing two hours of flextime in a number of departments created serious issues. The V.P. of finance for the hospital spoke up, "I don't see why people with children should be treated differently—it's their choice to have children. I have a life, too, and you don't see me asking for special arrangements. I have employees asking me to work from home—how do I appraise their performance if they primarily work at home?" Mercer thought about Robin's request, wondering if other baby-boomer employees would soon be making similar requests.

Dr. Palmer listened to what was quickly becoming a heated discussion, noting the varied and complicated reactions of the different directors, vice presidents, and other top leaders of the organization. Dr. Palmer commented, "We say in our recruiting materials that our employees *are* HealthCo, that it is individual care in all areas of the company—from nursing to accounting—that makes us different. How can we expect our employees to give individual care if we, as an organization, don't care about them and their lives?

"I'd like a team of four to six volunteers to put together a plan for becoming a top company in terms of work–life benefits. Please identify the key issues in serving all employees with such a set of benefits, and any related issues."

Questions

1. How would you conduct a diagnosis of the situation at HealthCo?

2. Based on the information provided in the scenarios and the case, what is your own diagnosis of the situation?

3. What do you see as the key issues in HealthCo becoming a top company in terms of work–life benefits?

Source: This case was prepared by Professor Karen Whelan-Berry of Utah Valley State College for classroom discussion. It is published with permission of the author.

Sharpe BMW

Tom Dunn was the newly appointed service manager for Sharpe BMW, a Grand Rapids, Michigan, BMW dealership. After the previous service manager left, the service department's revenues and the dealership's customer satisfaction index (CSI) ratings fell. In an effort to correct these problems, Bob Deshane, the service director of the dealership, submitted a new plan to owner George Sharpe. The plan called for a change in the way service technicians were compensated. Upon approval by the owner, Deshane handed the plan to Dunn and asked him to implement it.

As Dunn looked at the new plan, he realized that in implementing the plan he was going to initiate a major change in the service department. He wondered what specific steps he could take to ensure that the new plan achieved the results that he and his organization were hoping for.

THE AUTOMOTIVE DEALERSHIP INDUSTRY

According to the National Automobile Dealers Association (NADA), profits from the sale of new vehicles accounted for 29 percent of total dealership profits in 1998. Typically, new vehicle sales were a break-even proposition for dealerships. However, in 1998, due to strong new unit sales, good expense control, and increased productivity, profitability reached its highest level in ten years. Used vehicle sales contributed 24 percent of overall profits in 1998. This was a slight improvement since the more than 40 percent plunge in profits in 1995 and the subsequent slow recovery. NADA attributed the improved used vehicle sales profitability to the increased willingness of financial institutions to lend money at attractive rates for purchase of used vehicles. Total service and parts profits rose 5 percent in 1998, reaching a record high. Service and parts department profits accounted for 47 percent of overall dealer profits. NADA forecasted a growth in service and parts revenue even as dealers continued to compete with an increased number of independent service outlets and quick-lube centers. To maintain customer satisfaction, franchised dealers invested heavily

Exhibit I	Dealerships' Service Sales (in billions of dollars)		
	1997	1998	% Change
Service labor sales			
Customer mechanical	$10.54	$11.14	5.7%
Customer body	3.77	3.68	−2.3
Warranty	5.13	5.27	2.6
Sublet	2.73	2.73	0.0
Internal	3.41	3.5	2.6
Other	1.72	1.8	4.7
Total service labor	$27.31	$28.13	3.0%

SOURCE: National Automobile Dealers Association

in the parts and service operations, primarily by adding service bays and carrying a larger inventory of parts. NADA estimated that in 1998, 60 percent of dealership service departments offered evening and/or weekend hours and were, on an average, open for business 53 hours a week. Exhibit 1 breaks down the components of dealerships' service revenue, and Exhibit 2 provides a financial profile of the dealership's service and parts operation.

SHARPE BMW

Sharpe BMW was part of the Serra Automotive Group, which was a family of nineteen automobile dealerships in the states of Michigan, Ohio, Georgia, Tennessee, Colorado, and California. Sharpe BMW was the only BMW dealership in the group, with the other dealerships selling a wide range of automobiles manufactured primarily by General Motors and Ford.

Sharpe BMW was the only Grand Rapids BMW dealer (Exhibit 3 contains the dealership's organization chart). The two closest BMW dealers were in Kalamazoo (located fifty miles southwest of Grand Rapids) and Lansing (about seventy miles east of Grand Rapids). According to Dunn, neither of the two was as big as Sharpe BMW. He

Exhibit 2	Profile of the Dealership's Service and Parts Operation	
		Average dealership
Total service and parts sales		$2,845,520
Total gross profit as percentage of service and parts sales		44.0 percent
Total net profit as percentage of service and parts sales		5.7 percent
Total number of repair orders written		9,847
Total service and parts sales per customer repair order		$174
Total service and parts sales per warranty repair order		$203
Number of technicians (including body shop)		11.4
Number of service bays (excluding body shop)		16.3
Total parts inventory		$221,300
Average customer mechanical labor rate		$55

SOURCE: National Automobile Dealers Association

Exhibit 3	Sharpe BMW Organization Chart

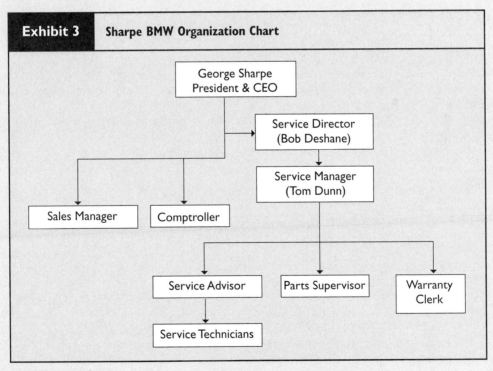

SOURCE: Sharpe BMW

had this to say about competing for service jobs in the market area:

> We offer pick-up and drop-off service to those customers who live far away. The service is also extended to whoever purchases a vehicle from us. To some customers, we have a "virtual" service department. They never see the inside of the service department—their cars are always picked up and brought back to them. This feature is used as a heavy sales tool to lure business from the Kalamazoo and Lansing dealers.

Service departments are an integral part of the revenue stream for auto dealerships. Deshane put the importance of service departments in the proper perspective:

> The average auto dealership service department maintains about an 82 percent absorption rate. This means that the profit from the service department pays 82 percent of all of the dealership's overhead. Good service departments are closer to 100 percent, leaving all dollars from car sales as pure profit. We currently fall between the average and 100 percent.

SERVICE DEPARTMENT REPAIRS

Sharpe BMW's service department had grown sizably in the last three years, primarily by increasing sales of vehicles to local customers and by aggressively seeking business from the Kalamazoo and Lansing areas. When the BMW dealership was first opened, its service department shared facilities with a Buick dealership that was also part of the Serra group. As BMW service revenues grew, a separate and dedicated service facility was built.

In Sharpe BMW's service department, two types of jobs were performed. The first type, "customer pay," occurred when the customer paid for the repair, after the warranty period expired on the car. For customer pay jobs, the customer was charged BMW's hourly labor rate of $69 times the number of hours specified by the *Mitchell Guide to Car Repairs*—a standard guide used by most major car dealerships. The *Guide* listed average time per repair for most types of automotive repair work. For example, the repair time to replace a water pump on a 1993 BMW 740I, according to the *Guide*, was 3.5 hours. The customer, thus, was charged $69 times 3.5 hours, or $241.50. This was the charge to the customer regardless of the actual time to do the repair. At Sharpe BMW, the techni-

cian who performed the repair job was paid his hourly wage rate times the *Guide*'s time for the job. For example, a technician making $13 an hour would make 13 times 3.5 hours, or $47.25, for that job.

When the vehicle was still covered by warranty, BMW paid the dealership for the repair work, known as "warranty pay." BMW had its own flat-rate book in which average hours for a specific job were often much lower than that listed in the *Mitchell Guide*. For example, the water pump repair was a 2.1-hour job for BMW. Repairing a water pump while the car was covered by warranty generated revenues of $69 times 2.1 hours, or $144.90, for the dealership, and $13 times 2.1 hours, or $27.30, for the technician. Service technicians' compensation, thus, depended upon whether they were working on a customer pay or a warranty pay job. Exhibit 4 provides an illustration of a service technician's pay for the two types of jobs.

CUSTOMER SATISFACTION INDEX

BMW surveyed all its customers, both when they bought cars and when they went to the dealership for warranty repairs. Only scores from customers who went to a dealer for warranty repairs, however, formed the CSI score for the dealership. A total of eight questions on the CSI survey were for service jobs (see Exhibit 5), of which one ("Satisfaction with work performed") related to the technician performing the repair. The others related to the function of the service manager and other dealer personnel who interacted with the customer.

Dunn had this to say about CSI:

> CSI is extremely important to dealers. It governs their flexibility with the manufacturer and is compared regionally and nationally with other dealers. BMW rewards the dealer financially the higher its CSI score is. It can also affect delivery of cars. For example, BMW is to introduce a new sports activity vehicle (SAV). If the dealer's overall CSI (a weighted score with 40 percent weight for sales CSI and 60 percent for service CSI) is below the standard, they will not receive any SAVs for the first year of production. In most cases, if your CSI is okay, as a manager you can do no wrong. Revenues are important, but I would rather be called into a meeting where revenues were low than one in which CSI was low. Ninety-one percent is

Exhibit 4	Example of Calculation of Average Weekly Pay for Service Technician

In both examples, it is assumed that the only service job performed by the technician is replacement of a water pump on a 1993 BMW 740I, and that it takes the technician two actual hours to finish the job. In a forty-hour week, the service technician performs twenty such jobs.

Example 1: Customer pay/warranty split: 12/8 jobs

Repair time per the *Mitchell Guide* is 3.5 hours
Repair time per BMW is 2.1 hours

Technician's compensation for 12 customer pay jobs	$12 \times 3.5 = 42$ hours
Technician's compensation for 8 warranty jobs	$8 \times 2.1 = 16.8$ hours
Total compensation	58.8 hours $\times$ \$13 per hour = \$764.40

Example 2: Customer pay/warranty split: 8/12 jobs

Technician's compensation for 8 customer pay jobs	$8 \times 3.5 = 28$ hours
Technician's compensation for 12 warranty jobs	$12 \times 2.1 = 25.2$ hours
Total compensation	53.2 hours $\times$ \$13 per hour = \$691.60

SOURCE: Sharpe BMW and case writer's estimates

the industry average CSI score (while our peer group of ten Midwest BMW dealerships had a 92.1 average last year) and about the minimum allowable score that Sharpe will tolerate. Our dealership's score in the last year was below the peer-group and the national average.

Exhibit 5	Customer Satisfaction Index Questions: Warranty Repair Orders

1. Ease of obtaining a service appointment.
2. Greeted promptly when vehicle dropped off.
3. Respectful and courteous treatment.
4. Vehicle ready at time promised.
5. Waited on promptly at vehicle pick up.
6. Paperwork completed/accurate at pick up.
7. Explanation of service work performed.
8. Satisfaction with work performed.

The questions are rated on the following scale:

Excellent	100 points
Good	80 points
Fair	60 points
Poor	0 points

SOURCE: Sharpe BMW

Since the previous service manager left, both service department revenues and CSI ratings declined. The average CSI score for the previous year (before Dunn's appointment) was 88 and the scores for the three most recent months were 90.4, 86, and 88. Deshane, the service director, identified the problem in the service department to be the differential rate of compensation paid to technicians for the two types of jobs. While customer pay repair work paid the technician more, the dealership's CSI score depended on the quality of the warranty work.

Dunn summed up his feelings about the CSI:

The dealership can't change the questions on the CSI, nor ask BMW to consider certain questions only for bonus purposes. In short, we have very little control over the index. I don't like some questions, but what I really don't like about the CSI is that if a customer responds "good" to any question, we get a score of only 80, which would really hurt us. To maintain our ratings, the customer has to rank us "excellent" (worth 100 points) on the majority of questions. BMW contracts with an independent agency, Sky Allend, to administer the survey over the telephone. All automobile manufacturers have CSI ratings, but we really can't compare them even within the Serra Group because the questions are very different for each manufacturer. We can only compare our performance with other BMW dealers.

SERVICE TECHNICIANS' LABOR MARKET

Good technicians were difficult to recruit and retain. According to Dunn:

Experience and certification determine the qualifications of service technicians. The state of Michigan requires that a technician be state-certified in the area in which he or she does repair work on a vehicle. For example, a technician would need to be state-certified in HVAC to do air-conditioning work or have a certification in brake repair to do brake work. Certification is received via passing written tests administered by the Secretary of State. Some technicians receive additional certification through ASE [Automotive Service Excellence]. These certifications are much more difficult to achieve and carry weight when negotiating hourly wage. Repair shops boast often that ASE-certified technicians perform repairs.

After talking about auto service technicians in general, Dunn spoke about technicians employed by BMW dealers:

To work at a dealership such as BMW, a technician would go regularly to school for training. Usually one to two times a year, the technician would go, at the dealer's expense, to Chicago for training that would range from two to five days at a time. The complexity of repairs and the specific tools and computer equipment that are needed to repair BMWs highlight the need for proper schooling. The manufacturer requires that dealer technicians attend a certain amount of schooling each year. The cost of educating technicians is expensive for the dealer. Yes, for BMW it would require a lot of training and time until a new hire could perform to the level of the person being replaced. The technician also knows this. Good technicians can quit one job and get another at least equally as good the same day. Unfortunately, this makes discipline and loyalty a problem.

At Sharpe BMW, a service technician's typical weekly workload was 60:40 in favor of customer pay jobs. The dealership paid higher wages than those in aftermarket repair outlets such as Sears and Montgomery Ward's. In addition, Sharpe BMW tried to decrease technician turnover by emphasizing factory training, as well as access to BMW's repair hotline, the latest equipment, and ongoing training. According to Dunn, all automobile dealerships faced the problem of disparity between customer pay and warranty pay wages for technicians, and to date, neither individual dealerships nor the NADA had attempted a systematic response to this problem. Aftermarket repair shops that were not associated with a manufacturer had an advantage over dealerships because they did not have the disparity problem between customer pay and warranty pay jobs, and paid their technicians a single standard hourly wage rate.

THE NEW PLAN

Deshane's plan called for a monthly bonus to be paid to a service technician if the technician's individual CSI rating were above 91 percent. Since each technician's repairs were linked to a CSI report, an individual technician's repair effectiveness could be easily determined. The bonuses ranged from 2 to 3 percent of the hourly pay. Four technicians were employed by the dealership. Two were senior and had obtained ASE certification in a number of areas, one was ASE-certified in a small number of areas, and the fourth, the least experienced technician, had no ASE certification. Deshane summed up his proposed bonus plan in the following words:

Though this does not seem to be a significant amount of bonus money paid, it is a radical change for Sharpe BMW and one that is not very common in the industry. The bonus plan shows dealer commitment to CSI results.

DUNN'S CHALLENGE

Dunn had worked his entire career in the auto service industry. After college, he worked as a manager of a tire store, after which he managed a small automotive repair shop. He then joined the Serra Group, where he worked as a service manager at the group's other dealerships before his present position. While at Serra, Dunn completed his MBA at a nearby regional university. At Sharpe BMW, Dunn's pay was tied to the CSI ratings. His bonus was based on the dealership achieving the national average score of 91 and increased till the score hit 93, when it reached its maximum level of 20 percent of basic pay.

Dunn had worked for Deshane earlier, who had handpicked him for the current job because of his favorable impression of him. Dunn maintained that he had an excellent working relationship with both Sharpe and Deshane. In addition, he felt that the entire service department worked as a team and that he shared a positive rapport with the service technicians.

As Dunn read the details of the new plan, he realized that the plan neatly dovetailed with the charge that management had given him when he was hired: to improve the dealership's CSI rating and increase the service department's revenues. Given his charge and the possibility that the new plan (even though it had a marginal economic benefit to the technicians) would help him achieve it, he wanted to make sure that the new plan was implemented effectively. He realized that the new plan involved bringing a change in the service department and that organizational change situations had to be handled carefully. He had informally talked about the bonus plan to two of his service technicians.

Peter Jackson* was a level-one technician—the highest level a technician could achieve in the automotive service industry. He had worked five years with Sharpe and over twenty years in the industry. Jackson felt that the bonus was in the right direction, in that it did show that management was more understanding of how hard technicians worked. He told Dunn that the amount of the bonus was not enough, however, and that he could make more money by working fast on warranty work.

Jack Sycamore* was a level-two technician with three years of tenure at Sharpe and twenty years overall in the industry. He was more optimistic about the bonus plan. He felt that though the CSI score depended on too many things beyond his control, it did show that man-

agement was doing something beyond a pat-on-the-back or a thank-you. It did make him more satisfied to know that money was attached.

Dunn realized that his job was made more difficult by the fact that the bonus money that technicians would get from the plan was meager. There was no guarantee that the plan would be successful upon implementation and that everyone would be happy. Dunn knew that both Sharpe and Deshane would measure the success of the plan by the improvement in the dealership's overall CSI scores.

Tom Dunn knew that the new bonus plan was important to his career. The automotive dealership industry had wrestled with the differential-pay problem without finding a solution to it. This might be his chance to have an impact, both in the dealership as well as in his industry, by providing a solution to this recurring problem. But to achieve that, Dunn realized that he had to carefully implement the bonus plan.

He had given this issue a great deal of thought. What if the plan does not result in improved CSI scores? Will the fault be ascribed to the plan or, as seemed more likely, to its implementation?

Questions

1. What do you see as the pros and cons of the proposed bonus plan?

2. Based on the information in the case, prepare an implementation plan for Dunne to follow.

Source: This case was prepared by Professor Ram Subramanian from Grand Valley State University for classroom discussion. It is not intended to illustrate either effective or ineffective handling of a managerial situation. Reprinted by permission from the Case Research Journal. Copyright 2002 by Ram Subramanian and the North American Case Research Association. All rights are reserved.

---

*disguised name

PART

6

Strategic Change Interventions

Chapter 19   Competitive and Collaborative
                    Strategies

Chapter 20   Organization Transformation

Selected Cases Rondell Data Corporation
                    Fourwinds Marina

19

Competitive and Collaborative Strategies

This chapter describes interventions that help organizations implement strategies for both competing and collaborating with other organizations. These change programs are relatively recent additions to the OD field. They focus on helping organizations position themselves strategically in their social and economic environments and achieve a better fit with the external forces affecting goal achievement and performance. Practitioners are discovering that additional knowledge and skills in such areas as marketing, finance, economics, political science, and complexity theory are necessary to implement these strategic interventions.

Organizations are open systems and must relate to their environments. They must acquire the resources and information needed to function, and they must deliver products or services that customers value. An organization's strategy—how it acquires resources and delivers outputs—is shaped by particular aspects and features of the environment. For example, cigarette manufacturers faced with increasing regulation and declining demand in the United States increased distribution to other countries and diversified into other industries, such as foods, beverages, and consumer products. Thus, organizations can devise a number of competitive and collaborative responses for managing environmental interfaces. Competitive responses, such as creating or clarifying mission statements and goals, developing new strategies, or creating special units to respond to the environment, help the organization to outperform rivals. Collaborative responses, such as forming strategic alliances with other organizations and developing networks, seek to improve performance by joining with others.

The interventions described in this chapter help organizations gain a comprehensive understanding of their environments and devise appropriate responses to external demands. The chapter begins with an elaboration of the organizational environments discussion started in Chapter 5. Then, two categories of interventions are described: competitive strategies and collaborative strategies.

Competitive strategies include integrated strategic change, mergers, and acquisitions. Integrated strategic change is a comprehensive OD intervention aimed at a single organization or business unit. It suggests that business strategy and organization design must be aligned and changed together to respond to external and internal disruptions. A strategic change plan helps members manage the transition between the current strategic orientation and the desired future strategic orientation. Mergers and acquisitions represent a second strategy of competition. These interventions seek to leverage the strengths (or shore up the weaknesses) of one organization by combining with another organization. This complex strategic change involves integrating many of the interventions previously discussed in this text, including human process, technostructural, and human resources management interventions. Research and practice in mergers and acquisitions strongly suggest that OD practices can contribute to implementation success.

Collaborative strategies include alliances and networks. Alliance interventions, including joint ventures, franchising, and long-term contracts, help to develop the relationship between two organizations that believe the benefits of cooperation outweigh the costs of lowered autonomy and control. These increasingly common arrangements require each organization to understand its goals and strategy in the relationship, build and leverage trust, and ensure that it is receiving the expected benefits. Finally—and building on the knowledge of alliances—network development interventions are concerned with helping sets of three or more organizations engage in relationships to perform tasks or to solve problems that are too complex and multifaceted for a single organization to resolve. These multiorganization systems abound in today's environment and include research and development consortia, public–private partnerships, and constellations of profit-seeking organizations. They tend to be loosely coupled and nonhierarchical, and consequently they require methods different from most traditional OD interventions that are geared to single organizations. These methods involve helping organizations recognize the need for partnerships and developing coordinating structures for carrying out multiorganization activities.

ENVIRONMENTAL FRAMEWORK

This section provides a framework for understanding how environments affect organizations. The framework is based on the concept, described in Chapter 5, that organizations and their subunits are *open systems* existing in environmental contexts. Environments can be described in two ways. First, there are different types of environments consisting of specific components or forces. To survive and grow, organizations must understand these different environments, select appropriate parts to respond to, and develop effective relationships with them. A manufacturing firm, for example, must understand raw materials markets, labor markets, customer segments, and production technology alternatives. It then must select from a range of raw material suppliers, applicants for employment, customer demographics, and production technologies to achieve desired outcomes effectively. Organizations are thus dependent on their environments. They need to manage external constraints and contingencies and take advantage of external opportunities. They also need to influence the environment in favorable directions through such methods as political lobbying, advertising, and public relations.

Second, several useful dimensions capture the nature of organizational environments. Some environments are rapidly changing and complex, and so require organizational responses different from those in environments that are stable and simple. For example, chewing gum manufacturers face a stable market and use well-understood production technologies. Their strategy and organization design issues are radically different from those of software developers, which face product life cycles measured in months instead of years, where labor skills are rare and hard to find, and where demand can change drastically overnight.

In this section, we first describe different types of environments that can affect organizations. Then we identify environmental dimensions that influence organizational responses to external forces. This material provides an introductory context for describing two kinds of interventions, competitive strategies and collaborative strategies, that represent different ways organizations can respond to their environments.

Environmental Types

Organizational environments are everything beyond the boundaries of organizations that can indirectly or directly affect performance and outcomes. There are two classes of environments, the general environment and the task environment.[1] We will also describe the enacted environment, which reflects members' perceptions of the general and task environments.

As described in Chapter 5, the *general environment* consists of all external forces that can influence an organization. It can be categorized into technological, legal and regulatory, political, economic, social, and ecological components. Each of these forces can affect the organization in both direct and indirect ways. For example, the outbreak of SARS (severe acute respiratory syndrome) directly affected the demand for tourism, airline, and other industries in Singapore, Hong Kong, Beijing, and Toronto. Cathay Pacific and Singapore Airlines had to ground much of their fleet as demand plummeted. The general environment also can affect organizations indirectly by virtue of the linkages between external agents. Any business that was dependent on tourism or travel was also affected by the SARS outbreak. Similarly, an organization may have trouble obtaining raw materials from a supplier because the supplier is embroiled in a labor dispute with a national union, a lawsuit with a government regulator, or a boycott by a consumer group. Thus, components of the general environment can affect the organization without having any direct connection to it.

The *task environment* consists of the specific individuals and organizations that interact directly with the organization and can affect goal achievement: customers, suppliers, competitors, producers of substitute products or services, labor unions, financial institutions, and so on. These direct relationships are the medium through which organizations and environments mutually influence one another. Customers, for example, can demand changes in the organization's products, and the organization can try to influence customers' tastes and desires through advertising.[2]

The *enacted environment* consists of the organization members' perception and representation of its general and task environments. Weick suggested that environments must be perceived before they can influence decisions about how to respond to them.[3] Organization members must actively observe, register, and make sense of the environment before it can affect their decisions about what actions to take. Thus, only the enacted environment can affect which organizational responses are chosen. The general and task environments, however, can influence whether those responses are successful or ineffective. For example, members may perceive customers as relatively satisfied with their products and may decide to make only token efforts at developing new products. If those perceptions are wrong and customers are dissatisfied with the products, the meager product development efforts can have disastrous organizational consequences. As a result, an organization's enacted environment should accurately reflect its general and task environments if members' decisions and actions are to be effective.

Environmental Dimensions

Environments also can be characterized along dimensions that describe the organization's context and influence its responses. One perspective views environments as information flows and suggests that organizations need to process information to discover how to relate to their environments.[4] The key dimension of the environment affecting information processing is *information uncertainty*, or the degree to which environmental information is ambiguous. Organizations seek to remove uncertainty from the environment so that they know best how to transact with it. For example, organizations may try to discern customer needs through focus groups and surveys and attempt to understand competitor strategies through press releases, sales force behaviors, and knowledge of key personnel. The greater the uncertainty, the more information processing is required to learn about the environment. This is particularly evident when environments are complex and rapidly changing. These kinds of environments pose difficult information processing problems for organizations. For example, global competition, technological change, and financial markets have created highly uncertain and complex environments for many multinational firms and have severely strained their information processing capacity.

Another perspective views environments as consisting of resources for which organizations compete.[5] The key environmental dimension is *resource dependence*, or the degree to which an organization relies on other organizations for resources. Organizations seek to manage critical sources of resource dependence while remaining as autonomous as possible. For example, firms may contract with several suppliers of the same raw material so that they are not overly dependent on one vendor. Resource dependence is extremely high for an organization when other organizations control critical resources that cannot be obtained easily elsewhere. Resource criticality and availability determine the extent to which an organization is dependent on the environment and must respond to its demands. An example is the tight labor market for information systems experts experienced by many firms in the late 1990s.

These two environmental dimensions—information uncertainty and resource dependence—can be combined to show the degree to which organizations are constrained by their environments and consequently must be responsive to their demands.[6] As shown in Figure 19.1, organizations have the most freedom from external forces when information uncertainty and resource dependence are both low. In such situations, organizations do not need to respond to their environments and can behave relatively independently of them. U.S. automotive manufacturers faced these conditions in the 1950s and operated with relatively little external constraint or threat. Organizations are more constrained and must be more responsive to external demands as information uncertainty and resource dependence increase. They must perceive the environment accurately and respond to it appropriately. As described in Chapter 1, organizations such as financial institutions, high-technology firms, and health care facilities are facing unprecedented amounts of environmental uncertainty and resource dependence. Their existence depends on recognizing external challenges and responding quickly and appropriately to them.

Organizations must have the capacity to monitor and make sense of their environments if they are to respond appropriately. They must identify and attend to those environmental factors and features that are highly related to goal achievement

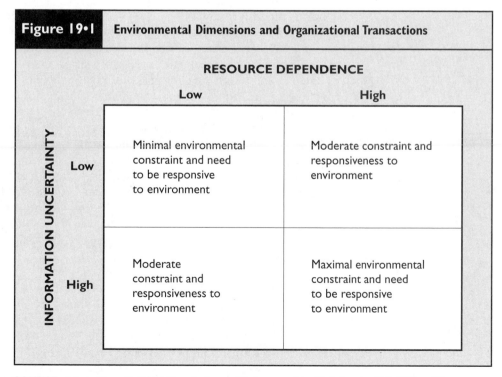

Figure 19•1	**Environmental Dimensions and Organizational Transactions**

RESOURCE DEPENDENCE

	Low	**High**
INFORMATION UNCERTAINTY — **Low**	Minimal environmental constraint and need to be responsive to environment	Moderate constraint and responsiveness to environment
High	Moderate constraint and responsiveness to environment	Maximal environmental constraint and need to be responsive to environment

SOURCE: Adapted from H. Aldrich, *Organizations and Environments* (New York: Prentice-Hall, 1979), p. 133.

and performance. Moreover, they must have the internal capacity to develop effective responses. Organizations employ a number of methods to influence and respond to their environments, to buffer their technology from external disruptions, and to link themselves to sources of information and resources. These responses are generally designed by senior executives responsible for setting corporate strategy and managing external relationships. To respond to environmental pressures and opportunities, OD practitioners can help organizations implement competitive and collaborative responses.

The two types of interventions discussed in this chapter derive from this environmental framework. Competitive interventions, such as integrated strategic change and mergers and acquisitions, focus on sets of administrative and competitive responses to help an individual organization improve its performance. Collaborative interventions, such as alliances and networks, utilize a variety of collective responses to coordinate the actions of multiple organizations.

COMPETITIVE STRATEGIES

These interventions are concerned with choices organizations can make to improve their competitive performance. They include integrated strategic change and mergers and acquisitions. Competitive strategies use a variety of responses to better align the organization with pressing environmental demands. To establish a competitive advantage, organizations must achieve a favored position vis-à-vis their competitors or perform internally in ways that are unique, valuable, and difficult to imitate.[7] Although typically associated with for-profit firms, these competitive criteria can also apply to nonprofit and governmental organizations. Activities that are unique, valuable, and difficult to imitate enhance the organization's performance by establishing a competitive advantage over its rivals.

Uniqueness. A fundamental assumption in competitive strategies is that all organizations possess a unique bundle of resources and processes. Individually or in combination, they represent the source of competitive advantage. An important task in any competitive strategy is to understand these unique organizational features. For example, resources can be financial, such as access to low-cost capital; reputational, such as brand image or a history of product quality; technological, such as patents, know-how, or a strong research and development department; and human, such as excellent labor–management relationships or scarce and valuable skill sets. Bill Gates's knowledge of IBM's need for an operating system on the one hand and the availability of the disk operating system (DOS) on the other hand represent a powerful case for how resources alone can represent a unique advantage.

An organization's processes—regular patterns of organizational activity involving a sequence of tasks performed by individuals[8]—use resources to produce goods and services. For example, a software development process combines computer resources, programming languages, typing skills, knowledge of computer languages, and customer requirements to produce a new software application. Other organizational processes include new product development, strategic planning, appraising member performance, making sales calls, fulfilling customer orders, and the like. When resources and processes are formed into capabilities that allow the organization to perform complex activities better than others, a distinctive competence or "hedgehog concept" is identified.[9] Collins found that a key determinant in an organization's transition from "good to great" was a clear understanding and commitment to the one thing an organization does better than anyone else.

Value. Organizations achieve competitive advantage when their unique resources and processes are arranged in such a way that products or services either warrant a higher-than-average price or are exceptionally low in cost. Both advantages are valuable according to a performance/price criterion. Products and services with highly desirable features or capabilities, although expensive, are valuable because of their ability to satisfy customer demands for high quality or some other performance dimension. BMW automobiles are valuable because the perceived benefits of superior handling exceed the price paid. On the other hand, outputs that cost little to produce are valuable because of their ability to satisfy customer demands at a low price. Hyundai automobiles are valuable because they provide basic transportation at a low price. BMW and Hyundai are both profitable, but they achieve that outcome through different value propositions.

Difficult to Imitate. Finally, competitive advantage is sustainable when unique and valuable resources and processes are difficult to mimic or duplicate by other organizations.[10] Organizations have devised a number of methods for making imitation difficult. For example, they can protect their competitive advantage by making it difficult for other firms to identify their distinctive competence. Disclosing unimportant information at trade shows or forgoing superior profits can make it difficult for competitors to identify an organization's strengths. Organizations also can aggressively pursue a range of opportunities, thus raising the cost for competitors who try to replicate their success. Finally, organizations can seek to retain key human resources through attractive compensation and reward practices like those described in Chapter 17, thereby making it more difficult and costly for competitors to attract such talent.

The success of a competitive strategy depends on organization responses that result in unique, valuable, and difficult-to-imitate advantages. This section describes two OD interventions that can assist individual organizations in developing these advantages and managing strategic change.

Integrated Strategic Change

Integrated strategic change (ISC) is a recent intervention that extends traditional OD processes into the content-oriented discipline of strategic management. It is a deliberate, coordinated process that leads gradually or radically to systemic realignments between the environment and a firm's strategic orientation, and that results in improvement in performance and effectiveness.[11]

The ISC process was developed in response to managers' complaints that good business strategies often are not implemented. Research suggests that too little attention is given to the change process and human resources issues necessary to execute strategy.[12] The predominant paradigm in strategic management—formulation and implementation—artificially separates strategic thinking from operational and tactical actions; it ignores the contributions that planned change processes can make to implementation.[13] In the traditional process, senior managers and strategic planning staff prepare economic forecasts, competitor analyses, and market studies. They discuss these studies and rationally align the firm's strengths and weaknesses with environmental opportunities and threats to form the organization's strategy.[14] Implementation occurs as middle managers, supervisors, and employees hear about the new strategy through memos, restructuring announcements, changes in job responsibilities, or new departmental objectives. Consequently, because participation has been limited to top management, there is little understanding of the need for change and little ownership of the new behaviors, initiatives, and tactics required to achieve the announced objectives.

Key Features

ISC, in contrast, was designed to be a highly participative process. It has three key features:[15]

1. The relevant unit of analysis is the organization's *strategic orientation* comprising its strategy and organization design. Strategy and the design that supports it must be considered as an integrated whole.

2. Creating the strategic plan, gaining commitment and support for it, planning its implementation, and executing it are treated as one integrated process. The ability to repeat such a process quickly and effectively when conditions warrant is valuable, rare, and difficult to imitate. Thus, a strategic change capability represents a sustainable competitive advantage.[16]

3. Individuals and groups throughout the organization are integrated into the analysis, planning, and implementation process to create a more achievable plan, to maintain the firm's strategic focus, to direct attention and resources on the organization's key competencies, to improve coordination and integration within the organization, and to create higher levels of shared ownership and commitment.

Application Stages

The ISC process is applied in four phases: performing a strategic analysis, exercising strategic choice, designing a strategic change plan, and implementing the plan. The four steps are discussed sequentially here but actually unfold in overlapping and integrated ways. Figure 19.2 displays the steps in the ISC process and its change components. An organization's existing strategic orientation, identified as its current strategy (S_1) and organization design (O_1), are linked to its future strategic orientation (S_2/O_2) by the strategic change plan.

1. ***Performing the Strategic Analysis.*** The ISC process begins with a diagnosis of the organization's readiness for change and its current strategy and organization (S_1/O_1). The most important indicator of readiness is senior management's willingness and ability to carry out strategic change. Greiner and Schein suggest that the two key dimensions in this analysis are the leader's willingness and commitment to change and the senior team's willingness and ability to follow the leader's initiative.[17] Organizations whose leaders are not willing to lead and whose senior managers are not willing and able to support the new strategic direction when necessary should consider team-building processes to ensure their commitment.

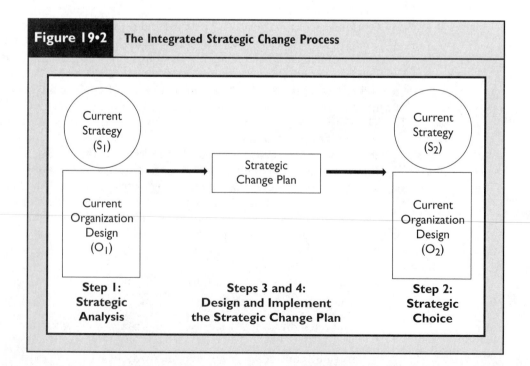

| **Figure 19•2** | **The Integrated Strategic Change Process** |

Current
Strategy
(S_1)

Current
Organization
Design
(O_1)

Step 1:
Strategic
Analysis

Strategic
Change Plan

Steps 3 and 4:
Design and Implement
the Strategic Change Plan

Current
Strategy
(S_2)

Current
Organization
Design
(O_2)

Step 2:
Strategic
Choice

The second stage in strategic analysis is understanding the current strategy and organization design. The process begins with an examination of the organization's industry as well as its current financial performance and effectiveness. This information provides the necessary context to assess the current strategic orientation's viability. Porter's model of industry attractiveness[18] as well as the environmental framework introduced at the beginning of this chapter are the two most relevant models for analyzing the environment.

Next, the current strategic orientation is described to explain current levels of performance and human outcomes. Several models for guiding this diagnosis exist.[19] For example, the organization's current strategy, structure, and processes can be assessed according to the model and methods introduced in Chapter 5. A metaphor or other label that describes how the organization's mission, goals and objectives, intent, and business policies lead to improved performance best represents strategy. 3M's traditional strategy of "differentiation" aptly summarizes its mission to solve unsolved problems innovatively, its goal of having a large percentage of current revenues come from products developed in the last 5 years, and policies that support innovation, such as encouraging engineers to spend up to 15% of their time on new projects. An organization's objectives, policies, and budgets signal which parts of the environment are important, and allocate and direct resources to particular environmental relationships.[20] Intel's new-product development objectives and allocation of more than 20% of revenues to research and development signal the importance of its linkage to the technological environment.

The organization's design is described by the structure, work design, information system, and human resource system. Other models for understanding the organization's strategic orientation include the competitive positioning model[21] and other typologies.[22] These frameworks assist in assessing customer satisfaction; product and service offerings; financial health; technological capabilities; and organizational culture, structure, and systems.

The strategic analysis process actively involves organization members. Large group conferences; employee focus groups; interviews with salespeople, customers, and purchasing agents; and other methods allow a variety of employees and managers to participate in the diagnosis and increase the amount and relevance of the data collected. This builds commitment to and ownership of the analysis; should a strategic change effort result, members are more likely to understand why and be supportive of it.

2. ***Exercising Strategic Choice.*** Once the existing strategic orientation is understood, a new one must be designed. For example, the strategic analysis might reveal misfits among the organization's environment, strategic orientation, and performance. These misfits can be used as inputs to workshops where the future strategy and organization design are crafted. Based on this analysis, senior management formulates visions for the future and broadly defines two or three alternative sets of strategies and objectives for achieving those visions. Market forecasts, employees' readiness and willingness to change, competitor analyses, and other projections can be used to develop the alternative future scenarios.[23] The different sets of strategies and objectives also include projections about the organization design changes that will be necessary to support each alternative. Although participation from other organizational stakeholders is important in the alternative generation phase, choosing the appropriate strategic orientation ultimately rests with top management and cannot easily be delegated. Senior executives are in the unique position of viewing strategy from a general-management position. When major strategic decisions are given to lower-level managers, the risk of focusing too narrowly on a product, market, or technology increases.

This step determines the content or "what" of strategic change. The desired strategy (S_2) defines the products or services to offer, the markets to be served, and the way these outputs will be produced and positioned. The desired organization design (O_2) specifies the organization structures and processes necessary to support the new strategy. Aligning an organization's design with a particular strategy can be a major source of superior performance and competitive advantage.[24]

3. ***Designing the Strategic Change Plan.*** The strategic change plan is a comprehensive agenda for moving the organization from its current strategy and organization design to the desired future strategic orientation. It represents the process or "how" of strategic change. The change plan describes the types, magnitude, and schedule of change activities, as well as the costs associated with them. It also specifies how the changes will be implemented, given power and political issues, the nature of the organizational culture, and the current ability of the organization to implement change.[25]

4. ***Implementing the Strategic Change Plan.*** The final step in the ISC process is the actual implementation of the strategic change plan. This draws heavily on knowledge of motivation, group dynamics, and change processes. It deals continuously with such issues as alignment, adaptability, teamwork, and organizational and personal learning. Implementation requires senior managers to champion the different elements of the change plan. They can, for example, initiate action and allocate resources to particular activities, set high but achievable goals, and provide feedback on accomplishments. In addition, leaders must hold people accountable to the change objectives, institutionalize the changes that occur, and be prepared to solve problems as they arise. This final point recognizes that no strategic change plan can account for all of the contingencies that emerge. There must be a willingness to adjust the plan as implementation unfolds to address unforseen and unpredictable events and to take advantage of new opportunities.

Application 19.1 describes an integrated strategic change process at Microsoft Canada and demonstrates how the process was refined over time as the organization builds capability in strategic management.

Mergers and Acquisitions

Mergers and acquisitions (M&As) involve the combination of two organizations. The term *merger* refers to the integration of two previously independent organizations into a completely new organization; *acquisition* involves the purchase of one organization by another for integration into the acquiring organization. M&As are distinct from the strategies of collaboration described later in this chapter because at least one of the organizations ceases to exist. The stressful dynamics associated with M&As led one researcher to call them the "ultimate change management challenge."[26]

M&A Rationale

Organizations have a number of reasons for wanting to acquire or merge with other firms, including diversification or vertical integration; gaining access to global markets, technology, or other resources; and achieving operational efficiencies, improved innovation, or resource sharing.[27] As a result, M&As have become a preferred method for rapid growth and strategic change. In 2002, for example, over 6,900 M&A deals worth $458.7 billion were conducted in the United States; globally, over 23,500 deals worth $1.4 trillion were registered according to the Dealogic market research firm.[28] Recent large transactions include Oracle and Peoplesoft, HP and Compaq, AOL and Time/Warner, Chrysler and Daimler-Benz, Ford and Volvo, and Boeing and McDonnell Douglas. Despite M&A popularity, they have a questionable

MANAGING STRATEGIC CHANGE AT MICROSOFT CANADA

Microsoft Canada is a subsidiary of the Microsoft Corporation responsible for the marketing, sales, and service of the full range of software products, including the Window's operating systems, the Office productivity suite, a variety of .Net products, and the Xbox game console. The organization marketed to a variety of segments, such as software application developers, small and medium business, and large enterprises, through a broad range of partners that worked directly with the client organizations to install and optimize the software's use. A small service organization provided consulting support to clients with the partner.

Prior to 2001, Microsoft Canada had been part of the North American subsidiary. Under this structure, the large U.S. market was clearly the focus of attention for Microsoft's server, desktop, and other software products. However, Frank Clegg, President of Microsoft Canada, argued that the Canadian market was different and underdeveloped. It had a different mix of customers than did the United States, different competitors, and different growth opportunities. Moreover, software sales and personal computer shipments as a percentage of the market's size and growth were below worldwide averages. These differences, Clegg argued, warranted a specialized strategy.

As the fiscal year ended, Clegg and his newly appointed Director of Strategic Planning, Sandra Palmero, wanted to seize the opportunity to define a uniquely Canadian strategy. Prior to becoming Director of Strategic Planning, Palmero had been Director of Marketing and Corporate Communications in Microsoft Canada. There, with Richard Reynolds, her senior marketing manager, they had crafted and implemented a participative process of strategic planning. Palmero contacted the OD practitioner who had worked with them and contracted to design and implement a strategic planning process for the Canadian organization. Over a 2-month period Palmero conceived of a series of workshops involving the Canadian Leadership Team (CLT). This team represented a broad cross section of the organization including representatives from the legal staff, human resources, Microsoft's consulting and service business, marketing managers, customer support, and managers responsible for different segments of Microsoft's business, including enterprise customers, small and medium business, Xbox, and the Microsoft Network (MSN).

The strategic analysis phase consisted of preliminary work by several members of the CLT as well as initial exercises during the first workshop. Members of the CLT each prepared an analysis of their respective area of responsibility. For example, the enterprise sales manager provided historical growth rates in revenues, developed forecasts for market growth and Microsoft's share, described current levels of cus-

tomer satisfaction, and a technology road map of products being developed by the Redmond headquarters organization. In addition to these specific analyses, Palmero contracted with a market research

APPLICATION 19•1

firm to provide overall descriptions of the Canadian information technology market. Finally, a competitor analysis was performed to develop an understanding of likely strategies, goals, and initiatives from key competitors such as IBM, Oracle, and Sun Microsystems as well as the competitive threat posed by the Linux operating system software.

During the first workshop, the CLT used the prework data to perform an environmental scan. They discussed, debated, and ultimately came to some agreements about the trends affecting the organization. Based on that scan, the group engaged in a vision and value formulation exercise and set out an initial list of short- and long-term goals. These activities led to several important decisions for the new marketing organization. For example, the vision and values exercise produced important insights about what the Canadian organization stood for, its uniqueness compared to other marketing subsidiaries within the Microsoft organization, and its strengths in competing as a Canadian organization. The values also informed discussions about future goals and the strategy for achieving them. Importantly, the Canadian leadership realized that customer loyalty would and should become a driving force for the organization. This realization led to passionate discussions about the relative emphasis in the organization on revenues versus customer satisfaction and loyalty. It also led to the development of a Big Hairy Audacious Goal (BHAG) that the members of the CLT believed would be challenging but achievable.

The first workshop ended with a number of assignments, unresolved issues, and excitement about the future. In between the first and second workshops, members of the CLT worked with their own organizations. Issues, decisions, and questions that were addressed within the CLT were discussed throughout the organization. The most important discussion concerned the BHAG and the relative emphasis of revenues and customer loyalty over the short and the long term. A consensus began to emerge that the right and proper strategy for Microsoft Canada was to argue for a slower growth rate in revenues in the short term, invest in customer satisfaction and loyalty, and then leverage that loyalty for a more secure stream of revenues in the future.

Frank Clegg took this idea to the executives in Redmond and discussed the implications of this strategy, including revenue projections, budget implications, the risks involved, and how the strategy aligned with corporate and other marketing organizations' initiatives. The results of these conversations became the subject of opening discussions at the second workshop.

The cautious but positive support from the corporate organization allowed the CLT to move forward on its strategic intent. In the second workshop, the organization's mission and values were finalized, year-by-year revenue goals were agreed upon to achieve the BHAG, and these goals were broken down and assigned to specific groups and managers. Finally, key customer and partner loyalty programs were established and outlined. Ownership for the different initiatives was assigned and a strategic change plan emerged. Clegg pressed the group on its decision to emphasize customer loyalty and challenged the group with several scenarios that tempted them to trade off satisfaction for revenue. These scenarios helped cement the CLT's commitment to their strategy.

An important part of the strategic change plan that emerged was a discussion and decision to tie the individual performance appraisals of CLT members to the achievement of both revenue and customer satisfaction goals. The CLT as a whole also staked their end-of-fiscal-year bonuses to the achievement of customer satisfaction, rather than revenue goals.

The strategic change efforts at Microsoft Canada are important for several reasons. First, the Canadian organization's realization of the importance of customer satisfaction and loyalty was influential in moving the larger Microsoft Corporation to examine its values in this area. *Business Week* reported on the changes Steve Ballmer was making in the organization; they reflected the increased importance of customer loyalty in Microsoft's strategy and structure changes. Second, the organization learned how to organize a strategic planning effort. In the 2 years since this effort began, Sandra Palmero has built a stronger strategic planning organization and taken more and more responsibility for driving the strategic planning process. Even as the corporate Microsoft organization was making important changes in its reporting structure, financial systems, and business processes, the Canadian organization was able to adapt using its own resources and knowledge. Finally, the BHAG has become an institutionalized part of the organization that drives thinking and decision making in the organization.

record of success.[29] Among the reasons commonly cited for merger failure are inadequate due diligence processes, lack of a compelling strategic rationale, unrealistic expectations of synergy, paying too much for the transaction, conflicting corporate cultures, and failure to move quickly.[30]

M&A interventions typically are preceded by an examination of corporate and business strategy. *Corporate strategy* describes the range of businesses within which the firm will participate, and *business strategy* specifies how the organization will compete in any particular business. Organizations must decide whether their corporate and strategic goals should be achieved through strategic change, such as ISC, a merger or acquisition, or a collaborative response, such as alliances or networks. Mergers and acquisitions are preferred when internal development is considered too slow, or when alliances or networks do not offer sufficient control over key resources to meet the firm's objectives.

In addition to the OD issues described here, M&As are complex strategic changes that involve legal and financial knowledge beyond the scope of this text. OD practitioners are encouraged to seek out and work with specialists in these other relevant disciplines. The focus here is on how OD can contribute to M&A success.

Application Stages

Mergers and acquisitions involve three major phases as shown in Table 19.1: precombination, legal combination, and operational combination.[31] OD practitioners can make substantive contributions to the precombination and operational combination phases as described below.

Precombination Phase

This first phase consists of planning activities designed to ensure the success of the combined organization. The organization that initiates the strategic change must

Table 19•1	Major Phases and Activities in Merger and Acquisitions	
MAJOR M&A PHASES	**KEY STEPS**	**OD AND CHANGE MANAGEMENT ISSUES**
Precombination	• Search for and select candidate • Create M&A team • Establish business case • Perform due diligence assessment • Develop merger integration plans	• Ensure that candidates are screened for cultural as well as financial, technical, and physical asset criteria • Define a clear leadership structure • Establish a clear strategic vision, competitive strategy, and systems integration potential • Specify the desirable organization design features • Specify an integration action plan
Legal combination	• Complete financial negotiations • Close the deal • Announce the combination	
Operational combination	• Day 1 activities • Organizational and technical integration activities • Cultural integration activities	• Implement changes quickly • Communicate • Solve problems together and focus on the customer • Conduct an evaluation to learn and identify further areas of integration planning

identify a candidate organization, work with it to gather information about each other, and plan the implementation and integration activities. The evidence is growing that precombination activities are critical to M&A success.[32]

1. ***Search For and Select Candidate.*** This involves developing screening criteria to assess and narrow the field of candidate organizations, agreeing on a first-choice candidate, assessing regulatory compliance, establishing initial contacts, and formulating a letter of intent. Criteria for choosing an M&A partner can include leadership and management characteristics, market access resources, technical or financial capabilities, physical facilities, and so on. OD practitioners can add value at this stage of the process by encouraging screening criteria that include managerial, organizational, and cultural components as well as technical and financial aspects. In practice, financial issues tend to receive greater attention at this stage, with the goal of maximizing shareholder value. Failure to attend to cultural and organizational issues, however, can result in diminished shareholder value during the operational combination phase.[33]

   Identifying potential candidates, narrowing the field, agreeing on a first choice, and checking regulatory compliance are relatively straightforward activities. They generally involve investment brokers and other outside parties who have access to databases of organizational, financial, and technical information. The final two activities, making initial contacts and creating a letter of intent, are aimed at determining the candidate's interest in the proposed merger or acquisition.

2. ***Create an M&A Team.*** Once there is initial agreement between the two organizations to pursue a merger or acquisition, senior leaders from the respective organizations appoint an M&A team to establish the business case, to oversee the due diligence process, and to develop a merger integration plan.[34] This team typically comprises senior executives and experts in such areas as business valuation, technology, organization, and marketing. OD practitioners can facilitate formation of this team through human process interventions, such as team building and process consultation, and help the team establish clear goals and action strategies. They also can help members define a leadership structure, apply relevant skills and knowledge, and ensure that both organizations are represented appropriately. The group's leadership structure, or who will be accountable for the team's accomplishments, is especially critical. In an acquisition, an executive from the acquiring firm is typically the team's leader. In a merger of equals, the choice of a single individual to lead the team is more difficult, but essential. The outcome of this decision and the process used to make it form the first outward symbol of how this strategic change will be conducted.

3. ***Establish the Business Case.*** The purpose of this activity is to develop a prima facie case that combining the two organizations will result in a competitive advantage that exceeds their separate advantages.[35] It includes specifying the strategic vision, competitive strategy, and systems integration potential for the M&A. OD practitioners can facilitate this discussion to ensure that each issue is fully explored. If the business case cannot be justified on strategic, financial, or operational grounds, the M&A should be revisited, terminated, or another candidate should be sought.

   Strategic vision represents the organizations' combined capabilities. It synthesizes the strengths of the two organizations into a viable new organization. For example, AT&T had a clear picture of its intentions in acquiring NCR: to "link people, organizations, and their information in a seamless global computer network."

   Competitive strategy describes the business model for how the combined organization will add value in a particular product market or segment of the value chain, how that value proposition is best performed by the combined organization (compared with competitors), and how it will be difficult to imitate. The purpose of this activity is to force the two organizations to go beyond the rhetoric of "these two organizations should merge because it's a good fit." The AT&T and NCR acquisition struggled, in part, because NCR management was told simply to "look for synergies."[36]

   Systems integration specifies how the two organizations will be combined. It addresses how and if they can work together. It includes such key questions as: Will one firm be acquired and operated as a wholly owned subsidiary? Does the transaction imply a merger of equals? Are layoffs implied, and if so, where? On what basis can promised synergies or cost savings be achieved?

4. ***Perform a Due Diligence Assessment.*** This involves evaluating whether the two organizations actually have the managerial, technical, and financial resources that each assumes the other possesses. It includes a comprehensive review of each organization's articles of incorporation, stock option plans, organization charts, and so on. Financial, human resources, operational, technical, and logistical inventories are evaluated along with other legally binding issues. The discovery of previously unknown or unfavorable information can halt the M&A process.

   Although due diligence assessment traditionally emphasizes the financial aspects of M&As, this focus is increasingly being challenged by evidence that culture clashes between two organizations can ruin expected financial gains.[37]

Thus, attention to the cultural features of M&As is becoming more prevalent in due diligence assessment. For example, Abitibi-Price applied a cultural screen as part of its due diligence activities along with financial and operational criteria. The process sought to identify the fit between Abitibi's values and those of possible merger candidates. Stone Consolidated emerged as both a good strategic and cultural fit with Abitibi. This cultural assessment contributed heavily to the success of the subsequent merger.

The scope and detail of due diligence assessment depend on knowledge of the candidate's business, the complexity of its industry, the relative size and risk of the transaction, and the available resources. Due diligence activities must reflect symbolically the vision and values of the combined organizations. An overly zealous assessment, for example, can contradict promises of openness and trust made earlier in the transaction. Missteps at this stage can lower or destroy opportunities for synergy, cost savings, and improved shareholder value.[38]

5. ***Develop Merger Integration Plans.*** This stage specifies how the two organizations will be combined.[39] It defines integration objectives; the scope and timing of integration activities; organization design criteria; Day 1 requirements; and who does what, where, and when. The scope of these plans depends on how integrated the organizations will be. If the candidate organization will operate as an independent subsidiary with an "arm's-length" relationship to the parent, merger integration planning need only specify those systems that will be common to both organizations. A full integration of the two organizations requires a more extensive plan.

   Merger integration planning starts with the business case conducted earlier and involves more detailed analyses of the strategic vision, competitive strategy, and systems integration for the M&A. For example, assessment of the organizations' markets and suppliers can reveal opportunities to serve customers better and to capture purchasing economies of scale. Examination of business processes can identify best operating practices; which physical facilities should be combined, left alone, or shut down; and which systems and procedures are redundant. Capital budget analysis can show which investments should be continued or dropped. Typically, the M&A team appoints subgroups composed of members from both organizations to perform these analyses. OD practitioners can conduct team-building and process-consultation interventions to improve how those groups function.

   Next, plans for designing the combined organization are developed. They include the organization's structure, reporting relationships, human resources policies, information and control systems, operating logistics, work designs, and customer-focused activities.

   The final task of integration planning involves developing an action plan for implementing the M&A. This specifies tasks to be performed, decision-making authority and responsibility, and timelines for achievement. It also includes a process for addressing conflicts and problems that will invariably arise during the implementation process.

Legal Combination Phase

This phase of the M&A process involves the legal and financial aspects of the transaction. The two organizations settle on the terms of the deal, register the transaction with and gain approval from appropriate regulatory agencies, communicate with and gain approval from shareholders, and file appropriate legal documents. In some cases, an OD practitioner can provide advice on negotiating a fair agreement, but this phase generally requires knowledge and expertise beyond that typically found in OD practice.

Operational Combination Phase

This final phase involves implementing the merger integration plan. In practice, it begins during due diligence assessment and may continue for months or years following the legal combination phase.[40] M&A implementation includes the three kinds of activities described below.

1. ***Day 1 Activities.*** These include communications and actions that officially start the implementation process. For example, announcements may be made about key executives of the combined organization, the location of corporate headquarters, the structure of tasks, and areas and functions where layoffs will occur. M&A practitioners pay special attention to sending important symbolic messages to organization members, investors, and regulators about the soundness of the merger plans and those changes that are critical to accomplishing strategic and operational objectives.[41]

2. ***Operational and Technical Integration Activities.*** These involve the physical moves, structural changes, work designs, and procedures that will be implemented to accomplish the strategic objectives and expected cost savings of the M&A. The merger integration plan lists these activities, which can be large in number and range in scope from seemingly trivial to quite critical. For example, American Airlines's acquisition of Reno Air involved changing Reno's employee uniforms, the signage at all airports, marketing and public relations campaigns, repainting airplanes, and integrating the route structures, among others. When these integration activities are not executed properly, the M&A process can be set back. American's poor job of clarifying the wage and benefit programs caused an unauthorized pilot "sickout" that cancelled many flights and left thousands of travelers stranded. Integrating the reservation, scheduling, and pricing systems was also a critical activity. Failure to execute this task quickly could have caused American tremendous logistical problems, increased safety risks, and further alienated customers.

3. ***Cultural Integration Activities.*** These tasks are aimed at building new values and norms in the combined organization. Successful implementation melds both the technical and cultural aspects of the combined organization. For example, members from both organizations can be encouraged to solve business problems together, thus addressing operational and cultural integration issues simultaneously.[42]

    The M&A literature contains several practical suggestions for managing the operational combination phase. First, the merger integration plan should be implemented sooner rather than later, and quickly rather than slowly. Integration of two organizations generally involves aggressive financial targets, short timelines, and intense public scrutiny.[43] Moreover, the change process is often plagued by culture clashes and political fighting. Consequently, organizations need to make as many changes as possible in the first hundred days following the legal combination phase.[44] Quick movement in key areas has several advantages: It preempts unanticipated organization changes that might thwart momentum in the desired direction; it reduces organization members' uncertainty about when things will happen; and it reduces members' anxiety about the M&A's impact on their personal situation. All three of these conditions can prevent desired collaboration and other benefits from occurring.

    Second, integration activities must be communicated clearly and in a timely fashion to a variety of stakeholders, including shareholders, regulators, customers, and organization members. M&As can increase uncertainty and anxiety about the future, especially for members of the involved organizations who often inquire: Will I have a job? Will my job change? Will I have a new boss? These kinds of questions can dominate conversations, reduce productive work, and spoil opportunities for collaboration. To reduce ambiguity, organizations can provide concrete answers through a variety of channels including company newsletters, email and intranet postings, press releases, video and in-person presentations, one-on-one interaction with managers, and so on.

Third, members from both organizations need to work together to solve implementation problems and to address customer needs. Such coordinated tasks can clarify work roles and relationships; they can contribute to member commitment and motivation. Moreover, when coordinated activity is directed at customer service, it can assure customers that their interests will be considered and satisfied during the merger.

Fourth, organizations need to assess the implementation process continually to identify integration problems and needs. The following questions can guide the assessment process:[45]

- Have savings estimated during precombination planning been confirmed or exceeded?
- Has the new entity identified and implemented shared strategies or opportunities?
- Has the new organization been implemented without loss of key personnel?
- Was the merger and integration process seen as fair and objective?
- Is the combined company operating efficiently?
- Have major problems with stakeholders been avoided?
- Did the process proceed according to schedule?
- Were substantive integration issues resolved?
- Are people highly motivated (more so than before)?

Mergers and acquisitions are among the most complex and challenging interventions facing organizations and OD practitioners. Application 19.2 describes several of the key issues in the M&A process at Dow Chemical and Union Carbide. It clearly demonstrates the importance of cultural issues in mergers and the role that OD can play in the process.[46]

COLLABORATIVE STRATEGIES

In the prior section, we explored strategies of competition, OD interventions that helped individual organizations cope with environmental dependence and uncertainty by managing their internal resources to achieve competitive advantage and improve performance. Organizations also can cope with environmental pressures by collaborating with other organizations. This section discusses collaborative strategies where two or more organizations agree to work together to achieve their objectives. This represents a fundamental shift in strategic orientation because the strategies, goals, structures, and processes of two or more organizations become interdependent and must be coordinated and aligned.

The rationale for collaboration is discussed first. Then we describe the process of forming and developing alliances and networks. *Alliance interventions* focus on the relationship between two organizations, while *network interventions* involve three or more organizations. As the number of organizations increases, the scope and complexity of the problems and issues that need to be addressed increase. Alliances can be building blocks for networks, however, and the lessons learned there can be applied to the development of network arrangements.

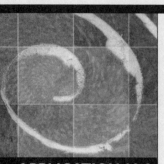

LESSONS LEARNED FROM THE DOW CHEMICAL COMPANY AND UNION CARBIDE MERGER

APPLICATION 19·2

The Dow Chemical Company (http://www.dow.com) announced on February 5, 2001, that it had received clearance from the U.S. Federal Trade Commission for its merger with Union Carbide. On a combined basis, the Dow and Union Carbide organization had revenues of $28.4 billion, earnings before interest and taxes of $3.1 billion, and assets valued at over $36 billion. Union Carbide had 11,569 employees in 40 countries and Dow had 39,200 employees in 32 countries worldwide. As a result of the merger, Dow became the world's leading supplier of chemicals, plastics, and agricultural products.

In the 1990s, Dow set out to establish itself as a premier, sustainable growth company. A globalized economy, demanding customers, and aggressive competitors led Dow to focus its strategy on four elements, including (1) improved productivity; (2) a restructured business portfolio in favor of higher growth, less cyclical performance businesses; (3) an owner-investor culture and mindset, and (4) increased revenues through new products, new markets, and acquisitions. The announcement of the proposed merger with Union Carbide in 1998 marked a milestone. Union Carbide had spent the years following the 1984 Bhopal disaster fighting off a hostile takeover by GAF and was looking for an acceptable buyer and a marriage that "fit." Dow President and CEO Mike Parker told employees, "We are committed to becoming a better and bigger company. The completion of our merger with Union Carbide accelerates our growth strategy, which is underpinned by our financial objective of growing earnings per share by 10% per year across the cycle. This merger increases Dow's scale, breadth, and depth, all of which will allow us to continue to create more value for our shareholders."

In addition to clearance from the U.S. Federal Trade Commission, Dow also had to receive necessary regulatory clearance for the merger from the European Union, the Canadian Competition Bureau, and other jurisdictions around the world. Global competitors pushed hard to block or modify the deal. The antitrust review and regulatory approval process required Dow to make certain actions or "remedies" to avoid monopolistic or anticompetitive situations. For example, Dow had to divest certain plants and businesses that might have given it too prominent a position and to license certain intellectual property to other companies. Dow managers had to ensure that these divestitures and licenses would not prevent the organization from leveraging its corporate strategy. This phase, prior to sealing the deal, was called the planning or "Transaction Phase."

The transaction phase was expected to produce the following deliverables:

1. Agreement that the merger met the underlying corporate strategy for value creation
2. Development and delivery of high level, multiphased integration plans by business, function, and region
3. Performance of a cultural due diligence process that ensured that this integration issue was understood and addressed
4. Assurance that the two great chemical companies would stay focused on environmental, health, and safety performance throughout the change and beyond
5. Programs to give Union Carbide and Dow customers top priority and no reasonable cause to go elsewhere
6. Identification and plans to capture (a) synergies in cost reduction, (b) operational and work process integration, and (c) opportunities to position the company for accelerated revenue growth.

Planning for the merger of two world-scale companies such as Dow and Union Carbide was a Herculean task in terms of resources, employee populations, and level of complexity. Temporary teams of top executives, Mergers and Acquisitions (M&A) staff from the Program Management Office (PMO), the Organization Effectiveness wing of human resources, business unit managers, and legal staff were formed to plan the integration of product portfolios, people systems, R&D projects, technology, hard assets and facilities, territories, markets, and regions. Organization development professionals assisted in the creation of the plans and interventions at a high level (e.g., communications, change readiness surveys, focus groups, project plans) and the facilitation of planning and integration teams at the local implementation level in geographies, businesses, functions, and sites.

Synergies, for example, were the near-term and long-term drivers of the merger. Cost savings were achieved by reducing redundancy in support structures, leveraging the most appropriate systems, and standardizing on best practices. These structures, systems, and practices included human resources, information technology, research and development, purchasing, legal, finance, and manufacturing. Additional cost savings and growth opportunities came from bargaining power over raw materials prices, backward and forward integration opportunities, new technology applications, and new market growth opportunities. Prior to closing the deal in the Transaction Phase, a clear picture of and agreements in principle on structures, systems, and identity were reached.

The output of the teams in the Transaction Phase became input into the second phase, called "Integration." This phase was led by five Integration Leadership Teams (ILTs) formed with members from both companies. The ILTs were tasked with developing and producing integration project plans that reconciled limited resources, integration initiatives, and short- and long-term business initiatives. Plans were put in place to achieve the objectives according to a timeline with a set of milestones called a "state-of-being" document. Course corrections were enabled by regular performance and progress reviews. ILT activities began at "Boot Camp" at Dow's corporate headquarters where the master integration plan and functional integration plans were first communicated. "Boot Camp" resumed at a Dow location in Eastern Europe. Here the integration teams, facilitated by OD experts called "change leaders," put together detailed project plans for training, communication, redesign, and combining all functional plans into a single plan. Boot Camp was a phase in which both companies built a common foundation; aligned with a common purpose and set of plans; and built teamwork and cultural understanding just prior to actual implementation.

The speed and amount of change that was to impact employees when the integration project plans were launched, in addition to the stress of working with a different corporate culture, was tremendous. As a result, a set of "enabling" processes and systems were created to support the ILTs. Change readiness surveys, continuous communications, leaders who modeled Dow Core Values in their behavior, and change leaders trained and experienced in change management methodologies all enabled the project plans to be achieved. By tailoring leadership style to integration processes and interventions based on high levels of employee participation, employee "buy-in" and the probability for successful outcomes were enhanced. The integration leadership

and change leaders charged managers at all levels of the organization with rising to the occasion by providing the tools, training, and processes to quickly put practices in place and assist employees through transitions.

The Dow Chemical Company and Union Carbide merger was economically driven. In the short run, both companies gained tremendous opportunities from combining their businesses, technology, and markets. The success of the merger was measured in numbers. Initially those measurements were called "synergies" that reduced costs by reducing redundancies and created new growth opportunities by combining complementary assets. For example, Dow announced estimated merger synergies of $500 million on August 4, 1999, and then on February 7, 2001, Dow CEO Mike Parker announced to Wall Street that "Achieving these synergies will be critical to ensure that this merger creates value for our shareholders. Savings will begin immediately and will be fully realized in two years." By February of 2003 synergies of over $1.5 billion were achieved. In the long run, valuations of the merger will be measured in economic profit, shareholder value, stock price, price–earnings ratios, net worth, and value-based market share.

As a result of the merger process, members of the new organization learned a set of valuable lessons. They included: (1) mergers ultimately must meet strategic and financial criteria; (2) not underestimating the complexity of the legal approval process, the response of competitors to a proposed merger, or the negative impact on employees, customers, and communities; (3) creation of detailed but flexible plans before the merger is finalized using the best data available; (4) engagement of OD practitioners in planning and integrating phases to ensure alignment with corporate plans, high levels of employee participation, and transition assistance; and (5) the importance of moving quickly once plans are in place.

Collaboration Rationale

More and more, organizations are collaborating with other organizations to achieve their objectives. These collaborative strategies can provide additional resources for large-scale research and development; spread the risks of innovation; apply diverse expertise to complex problems and tasks; make information or technology available to learn and develop new capabilities; position the organization to achieve economies of scale or scope; or gain access to new, especially international, marketplaces.[47] For example, pharmaceutical firms form strategic alliances to distribute noncompeting medications and avoid the high costs of establishing sales organizations; firms from different countries form joint ventures to overcome restrictive trade barriers; and high-technology firms form research consortia to undertake significant and costly research and development for their industries.

More generally, however, collaborative strategies allow organizations to perform tasks that are too costly and complicated for single organizations to perform.[48] These tasks include the full range of organizational activities, including purchasing raw materials, hiring and compensating organization members, manufacturing and service delivery, obtaining investment capital, marketing and distribution, or strategic planning. The key to understanding collaborative strategies is recognizing that these individual tasks must be coordinated with each other. Whenever a good or service from one of these tasks is exchanged between two units (individuals, departments, or organizations), a *transaction* occurs. Transactions can be designed and managed internally within the organization's structure, or externally between organizations. For example, organizations can acquire a raw materials provider and operate these tasks as part of internal operations or they can collaborate with a raw material supplier through long-term contracts in an alliance.

Economists and organization theorists have spent considerable effort investigating when collaborative strategies are preferred over competitive strategies. They have developed frameworks, primarily transaction cost theory and agency theory, that are useful for understanding the interventions described in this chapter.[49] As a rule, collaborative strategies work well when transactions occur frequently and are well understood. Many organizations, for example, outsource their payroll tasks because the inputs, such as hours worked, pay rates, and employment status; the throughputs, such as tax rates and withholdings; and the outputs occur regularly and are governed by well-known laws and regulations. Moreover, if transactions involve people, equipment, or other assets that are unique to the task, then collaboration is preferred over competition. For example, Microsoft works with a variety of value-added resellers, independent software vendors, and small and large consulting businesses to bring their products to customers ranging in size from individual consumers to the largest business enterprises in the world. An internal sales and service department to handle the unique demands of each customer segment would be much more expensive to implement and would not deliver the same level of quality as the partner organizations. In general, relationships between and among organizations become more formalized as the frequency of interaction increases, the type of information and other resources that are exchanged become more proprietary, and the number of different types of exchanges increases.[50]

Cummings has referred to groups of organizations that have joined together for a common purpose, including alliances and networks, as *transorganizational systems* (TSs).[51] TSs are functional social systems existing intermediately between single organizations on the one hand and societal systems on the other. These multiorganization systems can make decisions and perform tasks on behalf of their member organizations, although members maintain their separate organizational identities and goals. This separation distinguishes TSs from mergers and acquisitions.

In contrast to most organizational systems, TSs tend to be underorganized: Relationships among member organizations are loosely coupled; leadership and power are dispersed among autonomous organizations, rather than hierarchically centralized; and commitment and membership are tenuous as member organizations act to maintain their autonomy while jointly performing. These characteristics make creating and managing TSs difficult.[52] Potential member organizations may not perceive the need to join with other organizations. They may be concerned with maintaining their autonomy or have trouble identifying potential partners. U.S. firms, for example, are traditionally "rugged individualists" preferring to work alone rather than to join with other organizations. Even if organizations decide to join together, they may have problems managing their relationships and controlling joint performances. Because members typically are accustomed to hierarchical forms of control, they may have difficulty managing lateral relations among independent organizations. They also may have difficulty managing different levels of commitment and motivation among members and sustaining membership over time.

Alliance Interventions

An alliance is formal agreement between two organizations to pursue a set of private and common goals through the sharing of resources, including intellectual property, people, capital, technology, capabilities, or physical assets.[53] They are an important strategy for such organizations as British Petroleum, Eli Lilly, Corning Glass, Federal Express, IBM, Starbucks, Cisco Systems, Millennium Pharmaceuticals, and Siebel Systems. The term *alliance* generally refers to any collaborative effort between two organizations, including licensing agreements, franchises, long-term contracts, and joint ventures. Franchising is a common collaborative strategy. Companies such as McDonald's, Kinko's, or Holiday Inn license their name and know-how to independent organizations that deliver the service and leverage the brand name for marketing. A *joint venture* is a special type of alliance where a third organization, jointly owned and operated by two (or more) organizations, is created. Joint ventures between domestic and foreign firms, such as Fuji-Xerox, can help overcome trade barriers and facilitate technology transfer across nations. The New United Motor Manufacturing, Inc., in Fremont, California, for example, is a joint venture between General Motors and Toyota to produce automobiles using Japanese teamwork methods.

Application Stages

The development of effective alliances generally follows a process of strategy formulation, partner selection, alliance structuring and start-up, and alliance operation and adjustment.

1. ***Alliance Strategy Formulation.*** The first step in developing alliances is to clarify the business strategy and understand why an alliance is an appropriate method to implement it. About one-half to two-thirds of alliances fail to meet their financial objectives, and the number one reason for that failure is the lack of a clear strategy.[54] For example, Collins found that alliance success was heavily influenced by the alignment of the partner to the company's "hedgehog concept."[55] If the organization understood its passion, distinctive capabilities, and economic drivers, it was more likely to develop alliances that supported its strategy. Thus, it is important to pursue alliances according to a "collaboration logic."[56] The alliance must be seen as a more effective way of organizing and operating than developing new capabilities to perform the work in-house; acquiring or merging with another organization; or buying the capabilities from another organization in a transactional relationship.

2. ***Partner Selection.*** Once the reasons for an alliance are clear, the search for an appropriate partner begins. Alliances always involve a cost/benefit trade-off; while the organization typically gains access to new markets or new capabilities, it does so at the cost of yielding some autonomy and control over its activities.

   Similar to identifying merger and acquisition candidates discussed previously, this step involves developing screening criteria, agreeing on candidates, establishing initial contacts, and formulating a letter of intent. A good alliance partnership will leverage both similarities and differences to create competitive advantage. Compatible management styles or cultures, goals, information technologies, or operations are important similarities that can smooth alliance formation and implementation. However, different perspectives, technologies, capabilities, and other resources can complement existing ones and be good sources of learning and value in the partnership. These differences can also be a source of frustration for the alliance. OD practitioners can add value at this stage of the process by ensuring that the similarities and differences among potential alliance partners are explored and understood. In addition, the way the alliance begins and proceeds is an important ingredient in building trust, a characteristic of successful alliances explored more fully in the next step.

3. ***Alliance Structuring and Start-up.*** Following agreement to enter into an alliance, the focus shifts to how to structure the partnership and build and leverage trust in the relationship. First, an appropriate governance structure must be chosen and can include medium-to-long-term contracts, minority equity investments, equal equity partnerships, or majority equity investments. As the proportion of equity investment increases, the costs, risk, and amount of required management attention also increase.[57] In general, partners need to know how expenses, profits, risk, and knowledge will be shared.

   Second, research increasingly points to "relational quality" as a key success factor of long-term alliances.[58] Alliances shift the nature of the relationship from the simple exchange of goods, services, or resources with no necessary expectation of a future relationship to one where there is a clear expectation of future exchange. The parties in the relationship must act in good faith to ensure the future. This requires trust, "a psychological state comprising the intention to accept vulnerability based upon positive expectations of the intentions or behavior" of another firm or individual representing the organization. It implies an expectation that the organization will subordinate its self-interest to the "joint interest" of the alliance under most conditions.[59]

   Trust can increase or decrease over the life of the alliance. Early in the alliance formation process, it can serve as an initial reservoir of comfort and confidence based on perceptions of the organization's reputation, prior success, and other sources. These same factors can also contribute to a lack of initial trust. Trust can be increased or decreased by new assessments of the other's capabilities, competence, and ethical behavior. OD practitioners can assist in this initial start-up phase by making implicit perceptions of trust explicit and getting both parties to set appropriate expectations.[60] During the structuring and start-up phase, trust can increase through direct activities as a function of the number, frequency, and importance of interactions; differences between expectations and reality; the nature of mistakes and how they are resolved; and attributions made about partners' behavior.

4. ***Alliance Operation and Adjustment.*** Once the alliance is functioning, the full range of OD interventions described in this text can be applied. Team building, conflict resolution, large-group interventions, work design, employee involvement, strategic planning, and culture change efforts have all been reported in alliance work.[61] OD practitioners should pay particular attention to helping each partner in the alliance clarify the capabilities contributed, the lessons learned, and the benefits received.

   Diagnosing the state of the alliance and making the appropriate adjustments is a function of understanding whether the environment has changed in ways that make collaboration unnecessary, whether partner goals and capabilities have changed the nature of the relationship and interdependence, and whether the alliance is successfully generating outcomes. The long-term success of the Fuji-Xerox joint venture, for example, has been due to the willingness and ability of the two organizations to adjust the relationship in terms of ownership, profit sharing, new product development responsibilities, and market access.[62]

Network Interventions

Networks involve three or more organizations that have joined together for a common purpose; their use is increasing rapidly in today's highly competitive, global environment. In the private sector, research and development consortia, for example, allow companies to share resources and risks associated with large-scale research efforts. Networks among airlines with regional specializations can combine to provide worldwide coverage; Japanese *keiretsu*, Korean *chaeobols*, or Mexican *grupos* can enable different organizations to take advantage of complementary capabilities among them. In the public sector, partnerships between government and business provide the resources and initiative to undertake complex urban renewal projects, such as Baltimore's Inner Harbor Project and Pittsburgh's Neighborhood Housing Services. Networks of business, labor, government, education, finance, community organizations, and economic development agencies, such as the New Baldwin Corridor Coalition, can help coordinate services, promote economies, and avoid costly overlap and redundancy.[63]

Managing the development of multiorganization networks involves two types of change: (a) creating the initial network and (b) managing change within an established network. Both change processes are complex and not well understood. First, the initial creation of networks recognizes their underorganized nature. Forming them into a more coherent, operating whole involves understanding the relationships among the participating organizations and their roles in the system, as well as the implications and consequences of organizations leaving the network, changing roles, or increasing their influence. Second, change within existing networks must account for the relationships among member organizations as a whole system.[64] The multiple and complex relationships involved in networks produce emergent phenomena that cannot be fully explained by simply knowing the parts. Each organization in the network has goals that are partly related to the good of the network and partly focused on self-interest. How the network reacts over time is even more difficult to capture and is part of the emerging science of complexity.[65]

Creating the Network

OD practitioners have evolved a unique form of planned change aimed at creating networks and improving their effectiveness. In laying out the conceptual boundaries of network development, also known as *transorganization development,* Cummings described the practice as following the phases of planned change appropriate for underorganized systems (see Chapter 2).[66] The four stages are shown in Figure 19.3 (on page 468), along with key issues that need to be addressed at each stage. The stages and issues are described below.

1. ***Identification Stage.*** This initial stage of network development involves identifying existing and potential member organizations best suited to achieving their collective objectives. Identifying potential members can be difficult because organizations may not perceive the need to join together or may not know enough about each other to make membership choices. These problems are typical when trying to create a new network. Relationships among potential members may be loosely coupled or nonexistent; thus, even if organizations see the need to form a network, they may be unsure about who should be included.

   The identification stage is generally carried out by one or a few organizations interested in exploring the possibility of creating a network. OD practitioners work with these initiating organizations to clarify their own goals, such as product or technology exchange, learning, or market access, and to understand the trade-off between the loss of autonomy and the value of collaboration. Change agents also help specify criteria for network membership and identify organizations meeting those standards. Because networks are intended to perform specific tasks, a practical criterion for membership is how much organizations can contribute to task performance. Potential members can be identified and judged in terms of the skills, knowledge, and resources that they bring to bear on the

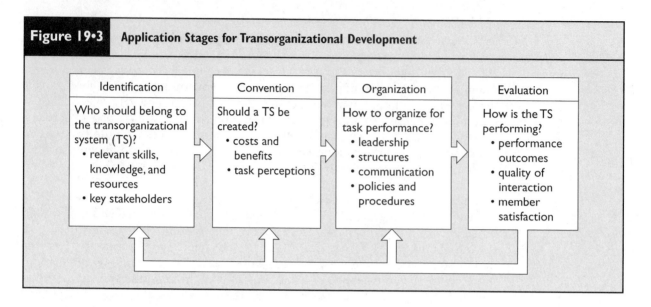

Figure 19•3 | **Application Stages for Transorganizational Development**

Identification	Convention	Organization	Evaluation
Who should belong to the transorganizational system (TS)? • relevant skills, knowledge, and resources • key stakeholders	Should a TS be created? • costs and benefits • task perceptions	How to organize for task performance? • leadership • structures • communication • policies and procedures	How is the TS performing? • performance outcomes • quality of interaction • member satisfaction

network task. Practitioners warn, however, that identifying potential members also should take into account the political realities of the situation.[67] Consequently, key stakeholders who can affect the creation and subsequent performance of the network are identified as possible members.

An important difficulty at this stage can be insufficient leadership and cohesion among participants to choose potential members. In these situations, OD practitioners may need to adapt a more activist role in creating the network.[68] They may need to bring structure to a group of autonomous organizations that do not see the need to join together or may not know how to form relationships. In several cases of network development, change agents helped members create a special leadership group that could make decisions on behalf of the participants.[69] This leadership group comprised a small cadre of committed members and was able to develop enough cohesion among members to carry out the identification stage. The activist role requires a good deal of leadership and direction. For example, change agents may need to educate potential network members about the benefits of joining together. They may need to structure face-to-face encounters aimed at sharing information and exploring interaction possibilities.

2. *Convention Stage.* Once potential network members are identified, the convention stage is concerned with bringing them together to assess whether formalizing the network is desirable and feasible. This face-to-face meeting enables potential members to explore mutually their motivations for joining and their perceptions of the joint task. They work to establish sufficient levels of motivation and task consensus to form the network.

Like the identification stage, this phase of network creation generally requires considerable direction and facilitation by OD practitioners. Existing stakeholders may not have the legitimacy or skills to perform the convening function, and practitioners can serve as conveners if they are perceived as legitimate and credible by the attending organizations. However, change agents need to maintain a neutral role, treating all members alike.[70] They need to be seen by members as working on behalf of the total system, rather than as being aligned with particular members or views. When practitioners are perceived as neutral, network members are more likely to share information with them and to listen to their inputs. Such neutrality can enhance change agents' ability to mediate conflicts among members. It can help them uncover diverse views and interests and forge agreements among stakeholders. OD practitioners, for example, can act as mediators, ensuring that members' views receive a fair hearing and that disputes are equitably resolved. They can help to bridge the different views and interests and achieve integrative solutions. In many cases, practitioners came from research centers or universities with reputations for neutrality and expertise in networks.[71] Because participating organizations tend to have diverse motives and views and limited means for resolving differences, change agents may need to structure and manage interactions to facilitate airing of differences and arriving at consensus about forming the network. They may need to help organizations work through differences and reconcile self-interests with those of the larger network.

3. *Organization Stage.* When the convention stage results in a decision to create a network, members then begin to organize themselves for task performance. This involves developing the structures and mechanisms that promote communication and interaction among members and that direct joint efforts to the task at hand.[72] It includes the organizations to be involved in the network and the roles each will play; the communication and relationships among them; and the control system that will guide decision making and provide a mechanism for monitoring performance. For example, members may create a coordinating council to manage the network and a powerful leader to head it. They might choose to formalize exchanges among members by developing rules, policies, and formal operating procedures. When members are required to invest large amounts of resources in the network, such as might occur in an industry-based research consortium, the organizing stage typically includes voluminous contracting and negotiating about members' contributions and returns. Here, corporate lawyers and financial analysts play key roles in specifying the network structure. They determine how costs and benefits will be allocated among member organizations as well as the legal obligations, decision-making responsibilities, and contractual rights of members. OD practitioners can help members define competitive advantage for the network as well as the structural requirements necessary to support achievement of its goals.

4. *Evaluation Stage.* This final stage of creating a network involves assessing how the network is performing. Members need feedback so that they can identify problems and begin to resolve them. Feedback data generally include performance outcomes and member satisfactions, as well as indicators of how well members are interacting jointly. Change agents can periodically interview or survey member organizations about various outcomes and features of the network and feed that data back to network leaders. Such information will enable leaders to make necessary operational modifications and adjustments. It may signal the need to return to previous stages in the process to make necessary corrections, as shown by the feedback arrows in Figure 19.3.

Managing Network Change

In addition to developing new networks, OD practitioners may need to facilitate change within established networks. Planned change in existing networks derives from an understanding of the "new sciences," including complexity, nonlinear systems, catastrophe, and chaos theories. From these perspectives, organization networks are viewed as complex systems displaying the following properties:[73]

1. The behavior of a network is sensitive to small differences in its initial conditions. How the network was established and formed—the depth and nature of

trust among the partners, who was selected (and not selected) to be in the network, and how the network was organized—play a key role in its willingness and ability to change.

2. Networks display "emergent" properties or characteristics that cannot be explained through an analysis of the parts: "Given the properties of the parts and the laws of their interaction, it is not a trivial matter to infer the properties of the whole."[74] The tools of systems thinking and the understanding of emergence in complex systems is still being developed and applied.[75]

3. A variety of network behaviors and patterns, both expected and unexpected, can emerge from members performing tasks and making decisions according to simple rules to which everyone agreed. This is amply demonstrated in Senge's "beer game" simulation where a retailer, a wholesaler, and a brewery each acts according to the simple rule of maximizing its own profit. Participants in the simulation routinely end up with enormous inventories of poor-selling beer, delayed deliveries, excess capacity, and other problems. Without an understanding of the "whole" system, the nature of interdependencies within the system, and timely and complete information, each part, acting in its own self-interest, destroys itself.[76] Apparently random changes in networks may simply be chaotic patterns that are not understood. These patterns cannot be known in advance but represent potential paths of change that are the result of the complex interactions among members in the network.

The process of change in complex systems such as networks involves creating instability, managing the tipping point, and relying on self-organization. These phases roughly follow Lewin's model of planned change described in Chapter 2. Change in a network requires an unfreezing process where the system becomes unstable. Movement in the system is described by the metaphor of a "tipping point" where changes occur rapidly as a result of information processing. Finally, refreezing involves self-organization. The descriptions below represent rudimentary applications of these concepts to networks; our understanding of them is still in a formative stage.

1. *Create Instability in the Network.* Before change in a network can occur, relationships among member organizations must become unstable. A network's susceptibility to instability is a function of members' motivations for structure versus agency.[77] *Structure* refers to the organization's expected role in the network and represents a source of stability. All things being equal, network members tend to behave and perform according to their agreed-upon roles. For example, most routine communications among the network members are geared toward increasing stability and working together. A manufacturing plant in Nike's network is expected to produce a certain number of shoes at a certain cost with certain features. Nike headquarters in Beaverton, Oregon, plans on the plant behaving this way. On the other hand, *agency* involves self-interest which can create instability in the network. Each member of the network is trying to maximize its own performance in the context of the network. Changes in member goals and strategies, the ratio of costs and benefits in network membership, and so on, can affect the willingness and ability of members to contribute to network performance. When a plant in Nike's network grows to a sufficient size, it may decide to alter its role in the network. As the ratio of agency to structure increases, the instability of the network rises, thus enabling change to occur.

   OD practitioners can facilitate instability in a network by changing the pattern of communication among members. They can, for example, encourage organizations to share information. Technology breakthroughs, new product introductions, changes in network membership, or changes in the strategy of a network member all represent fluctuations that can increase the susceptibility of the network to change. Another important aspect of changing the pattern of information is to ask who should get the information. Understanding and creating instability is difficult because the nature of members' connectedness also influences the system's susceptibility. Some organizations are more connected than others; most organizations are closely connected to several others, but relatively unconnected to many. This makes creating a sense of urgency for change difficult. Diagnosis of the relationships among member organizations can provide important information about organizations that are central to network communications.[78]

2. *Manage the Tipping Point.* Although instability provides the impetus and opportunity for change, the direction, type, and process of change are yet to be determined. An unstable network can move to a new state of organization and performance or it can return to its old condition. At this point, network members, individually and collectively, make choices about what to do. OD practitioners can help them through this change period. Recent studies suggest the following guides for facilitating network change:[79]

    a. *The Law of the Few.* A new idea, practice, or other change spreads because of a relatively few but important roles in the network. Connectors, mavens, and salespeople help an innovation achieve sufficient awareness and credibility throughout the network to be considered viable. *Connectors* are individuals who occupy central positions in the network and are able to tap into many different network audiences. They have "Rolodex" power; they are quickly able to alert and connect with a wide variety of people in many organizations. *Mavens* are "information sinks." They passionately pursue knowledge about a particular subject and are altruistically willing to tell anyone who is interested everything they know about it. The key to the maven's role is trust. People who speak to mavens know that they are getting unbiased information, that there is no "hidden agenda," just good data. Finally, *salespeople* are the champions of change and are able to influence others to try new ideas, do new things, or consider new options. Thus, the first key factor in changing a network is the presence of communication channels occupied by connectors, mavens, and salespeople.

    OD practitioners can fill any of these roles. They can, if appropriate, be mavens on a particular subject and act as a source of unbiased information about a new network practice, aspects of interpersonal relationships that network members agree is slowing network response, or ideas about information systems that can speed communication. Less frequently, OD practitioners can be connectors, ensuring that any given message is seeded throughout the network. This is especially true if the change agent was part of the network's formation. In this case, the practitioner might have the relationships with organizations in the network. Thus, networking skills, such as the ability to manage lateral relations among autonomous organizations in the relative absence of hierarchical control, are indispensable to practitioners of network change. Change agents must be able to span the boundaries of diverse organizations, link them together, and facilitate exchanges among them.[80] The OD practitioner can also play the role of salesperson. Although it is in line with the "activist" role described earlier in the practice of network creation, it is not a traditional aspect of OD practice. The wisdom of having a change agent as the champion of an idea rather than a key player in the organization network is debatable. The change agent and network members must understand the trade-offs in sacrificing the OD practitioner's neutrality for influence. If that trade-off is made, the change agent will need the political competence to understand and resolve the conflicts of interest and value dilemmas inherent in systems made up of multiple organizations, each seeking to maintain autonomy while jointly interacting. Political savvy can help change agents manage their own roles and values in respect to those power dynamics.

b. *Stickiness.* The second ingredient in network change is stickiness. For a new idea or practice to take hold, the message communicated by the connectors, mavens, and salespeople must be memorable. A memorable or sticky message is not a function of typical communication variables, such as frequency of the message, loudness, or saliency. Stickiness is often a function of small and seemingly insignificant characteristics of the message, such as its structure, format, and syntax, as well as its emotional content, practicality, or sequencing with other messages. OD practitioners can also help network members develop sticky messages. Brainstorming alternative phrases, using metaphors to symbolize meaning, or enlisting the help of marketing and communications specialists can increase the chance of developing a sticky message. Since the ingredients of stickiness are often not obvious, several iterations of a message's structure with focus groups or different audiences may be necessary to understand what gets people's attention.

c. *The Power of Context.* Finally, a message must be meaningful. This is different from stickiness and refers to the change's relevance to network members. The source of meaning is in the context of the network. When network members are feeling pressure to innovate or move quickly in response to a customer request, for example, messages about new cost-cutting initiatives or new and exciting information systems that will allow everyone to see key financial data are uninteresting and can get lost. On the other hand, a message about how a new information system will speed up customer communication is more likely to be seen as relevant. When OD practitioners understand the network's current climate or "conversation," they can help members determine the appropriate timing and relevance of any proposed communication.[81]

When the right people communicate a change, present and package it appropriately, and distribute it in a timely fashion, the network can adopt a new idea or practice quickly. In the absence of these ingredients, there is not enough information, interest, or relevance and the change stalls.

3. **Rely on Self-Organization.** Networks tend to exhibit "self-organizing" behavior. Network members seek to reduce uncertainty in their environment, while the network as a whole drives to establish more order in how it functions. OD practitioners can rely on this self-organizing feature to refreeze change. Once change has occurred in the network, a variety of controls can be leveraged to institutionalize it. For example, communication systems can spread stories about how the change is affecting different members, diffusing throughout the network, or contributing to network effectiveness. This increases the forces for stability in the network. Individual organizations can communicate their commitment to the change in an effort to lower agency forces that can contribute to instability. Each of these messages signifies constraint and shows that the different parts of the network are not independent of each other.

Application 19.3 describes the behaviors of organizations within the Toyota network in response to a crisis. The application demonstrates the fragility of collaborative networks, their robust and responsive capabilities, and the importance of the law of the few, stickiness, and context.[82]

FRAGILE AND ROBUST—NETWORK CHANGE IN TOYOTA MOTOR CORPORATION

The Toyota Motor Corporation is one of the best car companies in the world. It is efficient, flexible, and routinely produces many of the world's best-engineered cars with the lowest costs in the industry. However, Toyota is not one company but a Japanese *keiretsu*, a group of about 200 companies united in supplying Toyota with everything from dashboards to headlights. The network is integrated by the Toyota Production System (TPS), a collection of total quality management, just-in-time inventory systems, and concurrent engineering processes that have been adopted by most Japanese and American firms. But Toyota's system is different because of the close-knit family culture that supports TPS and explains why costs are kept so low to insure global competitiveness. Members of the *keiretsu* routinely exchange personnel, share intellectual property, and assist each other at the cost of their own time and resources, all without the requirement of formal contracts or detailed record keeping.

One of the *keiretsu* members, Aisin Seiki, produces P-valves, a part that helps to prevent skidding by controlling pressure on the rear brakes. The fist-size P-valves are not complicated, but require precision manufacturing in specialized facilities using custom-designed drills and gauges because their role is so critical to safety. By 1997, Aisin was producing all but 1% of the P-valves for Toyota's 20 plants because of its efficiency, costs, and quality. Aisin's only P-valve manufacturing factory, the Kariya plant, produced 32,500 valves a day, and because of the success of their just-in-time system, Toyota held between 4 hours' and 2 days' worth of P-values in stock. Production at the Kariya plant was, therefore, a critical element of Toyota's supply chain. As Duncan Watts succinctly stated, "No factory, no P-valves. No P-valves, no brakes. No brakes, no cars." Toyota's general manager of production control conceded that depending on a single source and holding essentially no inventory was a calculated risk, but it also kept Toyota's production lean.

Network Fragility

On Saturday, February 1, 1997, the Kariya plant burned down. By 9:00 a.m., the fire had destroyed most of the factory's 506 highly specialized machines and all the production lines for P-valves. Toyota estimated that more than 2 weeks would be needed just to restore a few milling machines to partial production, and 6 months to order new machines.

At the time, Toyota's auto plants were operating at full capacity to meet strong domestic demand and serve the U.S. market. About 30 production lines were producing more than 15,000 cars a day. By Wednesday, February 5, all production had ceased. Across the entire Kobe industrial zone, Toyota's

own plants, and the facilities and workers supplying them, were closed. Economists estimated that Toyota's shutdown would damage Japan's annual industrial output by 0.1 percentage point each day. The brittleness of the

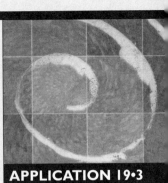

APPLICATION 19•3

system to such a relatively small failure points to the fragility of networks and networked organizations.

But the rapidity with which the system responded and recovered also points to the robustness and adaptability of networks. Although many experts thought Toyota couldn't recover for weeks or months, its car factories started up again within 5 days after the fire, and by the following Thursday, 36 different suppliers, aided by more than 150 other subcontractors, had nearly 50 separate lines producing small batches of P-valves. As soon as Thursday, February 6, two of Toyota's plants had reopened, and by the following Monday, little more than a week after the crisis had begun, production of almost 14,000 cars a day had been restored. A week after that, the daily volume was right back at its pre-disaster level.

The speed of the recovery is especially amazing given that none of individual firms in the Toyota group that helped Aisin had had the capability to do so. Very few firms that became emergency producers of P-valves, or the firms involved indirectly as suppliers, had any prior experience making the valves, nor did they have access to the kind of specialized tools that had been destroyed in the fire. The interesting question, therefore, is not why did they stage so dramatic a recovery, but how?

Network Robustness

Aisin and Toyota managers realized immediately that the recovery task was beyond their capabilities as an individual firm and beyond the capabilities of their immediate suppliers. A much broader effort would be required, and one over which they would have little direct control. Before the fire was out, Aisin officials organized a committee to assess the damage, notify customers and labor unions and, following Japanese custom, visit neighbors to apologize. Over 300 cellular phones, 230 extra phone lines, and several dozen sleeping bags were ordered.

At 8:00 a.m., Aisin asked Toyota to help. Kosuke Ikebuchi, a Toyota senior managing director, set up a "war room" at Toyota headquarters to direct the damage-control operation. Toyota also sent more than 400 engineers to Aisin. Later that morning, having set up an emergency response headquarters, Aisin sent out a distress call to other *keiretsu* members, defining the problem broadly and asking for help. Within hours, they had begun making blueprints for the valve, improvising tooling systems, and setting up makeshift production lines.

On Saturday afternoon, Toyota and Aisin invited some of their major parts suppliers to a second war room, at Aisin headquarters. It quickly became a hectic scene, with officials shouting out for copies of the blueprints of different P-valves while Toyota executives divvied up valve-making assignments. Despite the face-to-face meeting of several companies, being helpful wasn't easy. The firms involved in the recovery effort lacked the tools and expertise specific to P-valve production. As a result, they were forced to invent novel manufacturing procedures in real time, and to solve both design and production problems simultaneously. To make matters worse, Aisin's expertise rested largely with its own processes; it was often of little help in overcoming technical obstacles. And finally, Aisin became extremely difficult to contact. Even after installing hundreds of additional phone lines, so much information was flowing in and out in the form of queries, suggestions, solutions, and new problems, that the company was often unreachable, leaving the makeshift supply chain largely on its own.

Unfortunately, the capacity of this initial group of suppliers was insufficient. So Toyota purchasing officials called more parts makers to a Sunday afternoon meeting. These officials, like those who had met on Saturday, were also part of the Toyota family. "It was crucial because we knew each other, we knew the face of the people," Mr. Ikebuchi says. For example, Masakazu Ishikawa, a former Toyota manager whose division had designed Toyota P-valves, was now Executive Vice President of Somic Ishikawa Inc., a supplier of brake parts and suspension ball joints. Mr. Ishikawa called Somic's top production engineers and asked them to meet at the office at 8:00 p.m. Sunday. They stayed there until after midnight plotting to hire out some of their current factory work to free up machines to make the Toyota parts.

At 6:00 a.m. Monday, Somic's four designers began an eight-stage design process. Staying up 40 hours, the engineers designed jigs, and then they called in some favors from Somic's chain of suppliers. For example, Somic got a machine-tool maker, Meiko Machinery Co., to turn down other orders and put 30 workers on round-the-clock shifts to make the jigs it needed. Somic drafted technical and administrative staffers to help man the machines. On February 6, right on schedule, it delivered its first P-valves to Toyota.

The above example provides an important glimpse into the many different problem-solving and network-related activities that were taking place. Other examples included the Taiho Kogyo Co., a bearing maker that searched nationwide for special machine tools and still delivered 500 P-valves on Thursday, and Brother, a sewing and fax machine maker that had never made car parts, which spent about 500 man-hours refitting a milling machine to make just 40 valves a day.

Early in the week after the fire, even Toyota's Mr. Ikebuchi had doubts about the goal of resuming production in all plants by Friday. But the supplier group came through. Trucks bearing the first 1,000 usable P-valves rolled in late Wednesday. On Thursday, 3,000 more arrived, and on Friday, 5,000. Slowly, Toyota's assembly lines started up again.

The recovery story demonstrates how all the years of experience with the TPS paid off. All the companies involved possessed a common understanding of how problems should be approached and solved. To them, simultaneous design and engineering was an everyday activity, and because Aisin knew this, they were able to specify their requirements to a minimum level of detail, allowing potential suppliers the greatest possible latitude in deciding how to proceed. Even more important, while the particular situation was unfamiliar, the idea of cooperating was not. Because many of the firms involved in the recovery effort had previously exchanged personnel and technical information with Aisin, and also with each other, they could make use of lines of communication, information resources, and social ties that were already established. They understood and trusted each other, an arrangement that facilitated not only the rapid dissemination of information (including seven descriptions of their mistakes) but also the mobilization and commitment of resources.

In effect then, the companies of the Toyota group managed to pull off two recovery efforts simultaneously. First, they redistributed the stress of a major failure from one firm to hundreds of firms, thus minimizing the damage to any one member of the group. And second, they recombined the resources of those same firms in multiple distinct and original configurations to produce an equivalent output of P-valves. They did all this without generating any additional breakdowns, with very little central direction, and almost completely in the absence of formal contracts. And they did it in just 3 days.

SUMMARY

In this chapter, we presented interventions aimed at implementing competitive and collaborative strategies. Organizations are open systems that exist in environmental contexts and they must establish and maintain effective linkages with the environment to survive and prosper. Three types of environments affect organizational functioning: the general environment, the task environment, and the enacted environment. Only the last environment can affect organizational choices about behavior, but the first two impact the consequences of those actions. Two environmental dimensions, information uncertainty and resource dependence, affect the degree to which organizations are constrained by their environments and the need to be responsive to them. For example, when information uncertainty and resource dependence are high, organizations are maximally constrained and need to be responsive to their environments.

Integrated strategic change is a comprehensive intervention for responding to complex and uncertain environmental pressures. It gives equal weight to the strategic and organizational factors affecting organization performance and effectiveness. In addition, these factors are highly integrated during the process of assessing the current strategy and organization design, selecting the desired strategic orientation, developing a strategic change plan, and implementing it.

Mergers and acquisitions involve combining two or more organizations to achieve strategic and financial objectives. The process generally involves three phases: precombination, legal combination, and operational combination. The M&A process has been dominated by financial and technical concerns, but experience and research strongly support the contribution that OD practitioners can make to M&A success.

Collaborative strategies are a form of planned change aimed at helping organizations create partnerships with other organizations to perform tasks or to solve problems that are too complex and multifaceted for single organizations to carry out. Alliance interventions describe the technical and organizational issues involved when two organizations choose to work together to achieve common goals.

Network development interventions must address two types of change. First, because multiorganization systems tend to be underorganized, the initial development of the network follows the stages of planned change relevant to underorganized systems: identification, convention, organization, and evaluation. Second, the management of change within a network also must acknowledge the distributed nature of influence and adopt methods of change that rely on the law of the few, the power of context, and the stickiness factor.

NOTES

1. R. Miles, *Macro Organization Behavior* (Santa Monica, Calif.: Goodyear, 1980); R. Daft, *Organization Theory and Design*, 8th ed. (Cincinnati, Ohio: South-Western College Publishing, 2004).

2. J. Cummings and J. Doh, "Identifying Who Matters: Mapping Key Players in Multiple Environments," *California Management Review* (2000): 83–104.

3. K. Weick, *The Social Psychology of Organizing*, 2d ed. (Reading, Mass.: Addison-Wesley, 1979).

4. J. Galbraith, *Competing with Flexible Lateral Organizations*, 2d ed. (Reading, Mass.: Addison-Wesley, 1994); P. Evans and T. Wurster, "Strategy and the New Economics of Information," *Harvard Business Review* 75 (1997): 70–83.

5. J. Pfeffer and G. Salancik, *The External Control of Organizations: A Resource Dependence Perspective* (New York: Harper & Row, 1978).

6. H. Aldrich, *Organizations and Environments* (New York: Prentice-Hall, 1979); L. Hrebiniak and W. Joyce, "Organizational Adaptation: Strategic Choice and Environmental Determinism," *Administrative Science Quarterly* 30 (1985): 336–49.

7. J. Barney, *Gaining and Sustaining Competitive Advantage* (Reading, Mass.: Addison-Wesley, 1996).

8. R. Nelson and S. Winter, *An Evolutionary Theory of Economic Change* (Cambridge, Mass.: Belknap Press, 1982).

9. P. Selznick, *Leadership in Administration* (New York: Harper & Row, 1957); M. Peteraf, "The Cornerstones of Competitive Advantage: A Resource-Based View," *Strategic Management Journal* 14 (1993): 179–92; J. Collins, *Good to Great* (New York: HarperCollins, 2001).

10. R. Grant, *Contemporary Strategy Analysis*, 4th ed. (Malden, Mass.: Blackwell, 2001); Barney, *Competitive Advantage*.

11. L. Greiner and A. Bhambri, "New CEO Intervention and the Dynamics of Strategic Change," *Strategic Management Journal* 10 (1989): 67–87.

12. M. Jelinek and J. Litterer, "Why OD Must Become Strategic," *Organizational Change and Development*, vol. 2, eds. W. Pasmore and R. Woodman (Greenwich, Conn.: JAI Press, 1988), 135–62; A. Bhambri and L. Pate, "Introduction—The Strategic Change Agenda: Stimuli, Processes, and Outcomes," *Journal of Organization Change Management* 4 (1991): 4–6; D. Nadler, M. Gerstein, R. Shaw, and associates, eds., *Organizational Architecture* (San Francisco: Jossey-Bass, 1992); C. Worley, D. Hitchin, and W. Ross, *Integrated Strategic Change: How Organization Development Builds Competitive Advantage* (Reading, Mass.: Addison-Wesley, 1996).

13. C. Worley, D. Hitchin, R. Patchett, R. Barnett, and J. Moss, "Unburn the Bridge, Get to Bedrock, and Put Legs on the Dream: Looking at Strategy Implementation with Fresh Eyes" (paper presented to the Western Academy of Management, Redondo Beach, Calif., March 1999).

14. H. Mintzberg, *The Rise and Fall of Strategic Planning* (New York: Free Press, 1994).

15. Worley, Hitchin, and Ross, *Integrated Strategic Change*.

16. P. Senge, *The Fifth Discipline* (New York: Doubleday, 1990); E. Lawler, *The Ultimate Advantage* (San Francisco: Jossey-Bass, 1992); Worley, Hitchin, and Ross, *Integrated Strategic Change*.

17. L. Greiner and V. Schein, *Power and Organization Development* (Reading, Mass.: Addison-Wesley, 1988).

18. M. Porter, *Competitive Strategy* (New York: Free Press, 1980).

19. Grant, *Contemporary Strategy Analysis*.

20. C. Hofer and D. Schendel, *Strategy Formulation: Analytic Concepts* (St. Paul, Minn.: West Publishing, 1978).

21. M. Porter, *Competitive Advantage* (New York: Free Press, 1985).

22. R. Miles and C. Snow, *Organization Strategy, Structure, and Process* (New York: McGraw-Hill, 1978); M. Tushman and E. Romanelli, "Organizational Evolution: A Metamorphosis Model of Convergence and Reorientation," in *Research in Organizational Behavior*, vol. 7, eds. L. Cummings and B. Staw (Greenwich, Conn.: JAI Press, 1985).

23. J. Naisbitt and P. Aburdene, *Reinventing the Corporation* (New York: Warner Books, 1985); A. Toffler, *The Third Wave* (New York: McGraw-Hill, 1980); A. Toffler, *The Adaptive Corporation* (New York: McGraw-Hill, 1984); M. Weisbord, *Productive Workplaces* (San Francisco: Jossey-Bass, 1987).

24. E. Lawler, *The Ultimate Advantage* (San Francisco: Jossey-Bass, 1992); M. Tushman, W. Newman, and E. Romanelli, "Convergence and Upheaval: Managing the Unsteady Pace of Organizational Evolution," *California Management Review* 29 (1987): 1–16; Nadler et al., *Organizational Architecture*; R. Buzzell and B. Gale, *The PIMS Principles* (New York: Free Press, 1987).

25. L. Hrebiniak and W. Joyce, *Implementing Strategy* (New York: Macmillan, 1984); J. Galbraith and R. Kazanjian, *Strategy Implementation: Structure, Systems, and Process*, 2d ed. (St. Paul, Minn.: West Publishing, 1986).

26. T. Galpin and D. Robinson, "Merger Integration: The Ultimate Change Management Challenge," *Mergers and Acquisitions* 31(1997): 24–29.

27. M. Marks and P. Mirvis, *Joining Forces: Making One Plus One Equal Three in Mergers, Acquisitions, and Alliances* (San Francisco: Jossey-Bass, 1998).

28. G. Dixon, "Merger and Acquisition Activity in Canada, World Continues to Decline in 2002," *The Canadian Press* (6 January 2003), accessed at http://www.factiva.com on 12 June 2003.

29. A variety of studies have questioned whether merger and acquisition activity actually generates benefits to the organization or its shareholders, including M. Porter, "From Competitive Advantage to Corporate Strategy," *Harvard Business Review* (May-June 1978): 43–59; "Merger Integration Problems," *Leadership and Organization Development Journal* 19 (1998): 59–60; "Why Good Deals Miss the Bull's-Eye: Slow Integration, Poor Communication Torpedo Prospects for Creating Value," *Mergers and Acquisitions* 33 (1999): 5; T. Brush, "Predicted Change in Operational Synergy and Post-Acquisition Performance of Acquired Businesses," *Strategic Management Journal* 17 (1996): 1–24; and P. Zweig with J. Perlman, S. Anderson, and K. Gudridge, "The Case Against Mergers," *Business Week* (30 October 1995): 122–30. The research includes an A. T. Kearney study of 115 multibillion-dollar, global mergers between 1993 and 1996 where 58% failed to create "substantial returns for shareholders," measured by tangible returns in the form of dividends and stock price appreciation; a Mercer Management Consulting study of all mergers from 1990 to 1996 where nearly half "destroyed" shareholder value; a PriceWaterhouseCoopers study of 97 acquirers that com-

pleted deals worth $500 million or more from 1994 to 1997 and where two-thirds of the buyer's stocks dropped on announcement of the transaction and "a year later" a third of the losers still were lagging the levels of peer-company shares or the stock market in general; and a European study of 300 companies that found that planning for restructuring was poorly thought out and underfunded. Similarly, despite the large amount of writing on the subject, a large proportion of firms involved in mergers have not gotten the message that postmerger integration is the key to success. For example, in the A. T. Kearny study, only 39% of the cases had set up a management team in the first hundred days and only 28% had a clear vision of corporate goals when the acquisition began.

30. Zweig et al., "Case Against Mergers."

31. Marks and Mirvis, *Joining Forces;* R. Ashkenas, L. De-Monaco, and S. Francis, "Making the Deal Real: How GE Capital Integrates Acquisitions," *Harvard Business Review* (January-February 1998); B. Brunsman, S. Sanderson, and M. Van de Voorde, "How to Achieve Value Behind the Deal During Merger Integration," *Oil and Gas Journal* 96 (1998): 21–30; A. Fisher, "How to Make a Merger Work," *Fortune* (24 January 1994): 66–70; K. Kostuch, R. Malchione, and I. Marten, "Post-Merger Integration: Creating or Destroying Value?" *Corporate Board* 19 (1998): 7–11; A. Kruse, "Merging Cultures: How OD Adds Value in Mergers and Acquisitions" (presentation to the ODNetwork meeting, San Diego, Calif., October 1999); M. Sirower, "Constructing a Synergistic Base for Premier Deals," *Mergers and Acquisitions* 32 (1998): 42–50; D. Jemison and S. Sitkin, "Corporate Acquisitions: A Process Perspective," *Academy of Management Review* 11 (1986): 145–63.

32. Ashkenas, DeMonaco, and Francis, "Making the Deal Real"; G. Ledford, C. Siehl, M. McGrath, and J. Miller, "Managing Mergers and Acquisitions" (working paper, Center for Effective Organizations, University of Southern California, Los Angeles, 1985).

33. Ledford et al., "Managing Mergers and Acquisitions"; B. Blumenthal, "The Right Talent Mix to Make Mergers Work," *Mergers and Acquisitions* (September-October 1995): 26–31; A. Buono, J. Bowditch, and J. Lewis, "When Cultures Collide: The Anatomy of a Merger," *Human Relations* 38 (1985): 477–500; D. Tipton, "Understanding Employee Views Regarding Impending Mergers to Minimize Integration Turmoil" (unpublished master's thesis, Pepperdine University, 1998).

34. Marks and Mirvis, *Joining Forces*; Ashkenas, DeMonaco, and Francis, "Making the Deal Real."

35. Sirower, "Constructing a Synergistic Base"; Brunsman, Sanderson, and Van de Voorde, "How to Achieve Value."

36. Sirower, "Constructing a Synergistic Base."

37. Ledford et al., "Managing Mergers and Acquisitions."

38. S. Elias, "Due Diligence," http://www.eliasondeals. com/duedilig.html, 1998.

39. Brunsman, Sanderson, and Van de Voorde, "How to Achieve Value."

40. Ashkenas, DeMonaco, and Francis, "Making the Deal Real."

41. Ashkenas, DeMonaco, and Francis, "Making the Deal Real"; Brunsman, Sanderson, and Van de Voorde, "How to Achieve Value."

42. Galpin and Robinson, "Merger Integration."

43. Ibid.

44. Ashkenas, DeMonaco, and Francis, "Making the Deal Real."

45. Kostuch, Malchione, and Marten, "Post-Merger Integration."

46. This application was developed by Michael Krup. His contribution is gratefully acknowledged.

47. A. Tsai, "A Note on Strategic Alliances," 9-298-047 (Boston: Harvard Business School, 1997); B. Gomes-Casseres, "Managing International Alliances: Conceptual Framework," 9-793-133 (Boston: Harvard Business School, 1993); J. Bamford, B. Gomes-Casseres, and M. Robinson, *Mastering Alliance Strategy* (New York: John Wiley and Sons, 2002).

48. Aldrich, *Organizations and Environments.*

49. O. Williamson, *Markets and Hierarchies* (New York: Free Press, 1975); O. Williamson, *The Economic Institutions of Capitalism* (New York: Free Press, 1985); J. Barney and W. Ouchi, *Organizational Economics* (San Francisco: Jossey-Bass, 1986); K. Eisenhardt, "Agency Theory: An Assessment and Review," *Academy of Management Review* 14 (1989): 57–74.

50. P. Kenis and D. Knoke, "How Organizational Field Networks Shape Interorganizational Tie-Formation Rates," *Academy of Management Review* 27 (2002): 275–93.

51. T. Cummings, "Transorganizational Development," in *Research in Organizational Behavior,* vol. 6, eds. B. Staw and L. Cummings(Greenwich, Conn.: JAI Press, 1984), 367–422.

52. B. Gray, "Conditions Facilitating Interorganizational Collaboration," *Human Relations* 38 (1985): 911–36; K. Harrigan and W. Newman, "Bases of Interorganization Co-Operation: Propensity, Power, Persistence," *Journal of Management Studies* 27 (1990): 417–34; Cummings, "Transorganizational Development."

53. A. Arino, J. de la Torre, and P. Ring, "Relational Quality: Managing Trust in Corporate Alliances," *California*

Management Review 44 (2001): 109–31; M. Hitt, R. Ireland, and R. Hoskisson, *Strategic Management* (Cincinnati, Ohio: South-Western College Publishing, 1999).

54. Bamford, Gomes-Casseres, and Robinson, *Mastering Alliance Strategy.*

55. Collins, *Good to Great.*

56. Gomes-Casseres, "Managing International Alliances"; J. Child and D. Faulkner, *Strategies of Co-operation: Managing Alliances, Networks, and Joint Ventures* (New York: Oxford University Press, 1998).

57. Bamford, Gomes-Casseres, and Robinson, *Mastering Alliance Strategy.*

58. A. Arino, J. de la Torre, and P. Ring, "Relational Quality."

59. C. Rousseau, S. Sitkin, R. Burt, and C. Camerer, "Not So Different After All: A Cross-discipline View of Trust," *Academy of Management Review* 23 (1998): 395.

60. M. Hutt, E. Stafford, B. Walker, and P. Reingen, "Case Study Defining the Social Network of a Strategic Alliance," *Sloan Management Review,* Winter (2000): 51–62.

61. Marks and Mirvis, *Joining Forces;* Child and Faulkner, *Strategies of Cooperation.*

62. K. McQuade and B. Gomes-Casseres, "Xerox and Fuji-Xerox" 9-391-156 (Boston: Harvard Business School, 1991).

63. R. Chisholm, *Developing Network Organizations* (Reading, Mass.: Addison-Wesley, 1998).

64. D. Watts, *Six Degrees* (New York: W.W. Norton and Co., 2003).

65. S. Strogatz, "Exploring Complex Networks," *Nature* 410 (March 2001): 268–76.

66. Cummings, "Transorganizational Development"; C. Raben, "Building Strategic Partnerships: Creating and Managing Effective Joint Ventures," in *Organizational Architecture,* eds. Nadler et al., (San Francisco: Jossey-Bass, 1992), 81–109; B. Gray, *Collaborating: Finding Common Ground for Multiparty Problems* (San Francisco: Jossey-Bass, 1989); Harrigan and Newman, "Bases of Interorganization Co-operation"; P. Lorange and J. Roos, "Analytical Steps in the Formation of Strategic Alliances," *Journal of Organizational Change Management* 4 (1991): 60–72; B. Gomes-Casseres, "Managing International Alliances."

67. D. Boje, "Towards a Theory and Praxis of Transorganizational Development: Stakeholder Networks and Their Habitats" (working paper no. 79-6, Behavioral and Organizational Science Study Center, Graduate School of

Management, University of California, Los Angeles, February 1982); B. Gricar, "The Legitimacy of Consultants and Stakeholders in Interorganizational Problems" (paper presented at annual meeting of the Academy of Management, San Diego, Calif., August 1981); T. Williams, "The Search Conference in Active Adaptive Planning," *Journal of Applied Behavioral Science* 16 (1980): 470–83; B. Gray and T. Hay, "Political Limits to Interorganizational Consensus and Change," *Journal of Applied Behavioral Science* 22 (1986): 95–112.

68. Cummings, "Transorganizational Development."

69. E. Trist, "Referent Organizations and the Development of Interorganizational Domains" (paper presented at annual meeting of the Academy of Management, Atlanta, August 1979).

70. Cummings, "Transorganizational Development."

71. Ibid.

72. Raben, "Building Strategic Partnerships"; C. Baldwin and K. Clark, "Managing in an Age of Modularity," in *Managing in the Modular Age,* eds. R. Garud, A. Kumaraswamy, and R. Langlois (Malden, Mass.: Blackwell Publishing Ltd., 2003), 149–60.

73. P. Anderson, "Complexity Theory and Organization Science," *Organization Science* 10 (1999): 216–32.

74. H. Simon, "The Architecture of Complexity," in *Managing in the Modular Age,* eds. R. Garud, A. Kumaraswamy, and R. Langlois (Malden, Mass.: Blackwell Publishing Ltd., 2003), 15–37.

75. P. Senge, *The Fifth Discipline* (New York: Doubleday, 1990); B. Lichtenstein, "Emergence as a Process of Self-Organizing: New Assumptions and Insights from the Study of Non-Linear Dynamic Systems," *Journal of Organizational Change Management* 13 (2000): 526–46.

76. Senge, *The Fifth Discipline.*

77. Watts, *Six Degrees.*

78. P. Monge and N. Contractor, *Theories of Communication Networks* (New York: Oxford University Press, 2003).

79. This section relies on information in M. Gladwell, *The Tipping Point* (Boston: Little, Brown, 2000).

80. B. Gricar and D. Brown, "Conflict, Power, and Organization in a Changing Community," *Human Relations* 34 (1981): 877–93.

81. P. Shaw, *Changing Conversations in Organizations: A Complexity Approach to Change* (London: Routledge, 2002).

82. Adapted from material presented in D. Watts, *Six Degrees;* V. Reitman, "Toyota Motor Shows Its Mettle After Fire Destroys Parts Plant," *Wall Street Journal* (8 May 1997): A-1.

Organization Transformation

This chapter presents interventions aimed at transforming organizations. It describes activities directed at changing the basic character or culture of the organization. These interventions bring about important alignments among the organization's strategies, design elements, and culture, and between the organization and its competitive environment.[1] They are directed mostly at the culture or dominant paradigm within the organization. These frame-breaking and sometimes revolutionary interventions typically go beyond improving the organization incrementally, focusing instead on changing the way it views itself and its environment.

Organization transformations can occur in response to or in anticipation of major changes in the organization's environment or technology. In addition, these changes often are associated with significant alterations in the firm's business strategy, which, in turn, may require modifying corporate culture as well as internal structures and processes to support the new direction. Such fundamental change entails a new paradigm for organizing and managing organizations. It involves qualitatively different ways of perceiving, thinking, and behaving in organizations. Movement toward this new way of operating requires top managers to take an active leadership role. The change process is characterized by considerable innovation and learning and continues almost indefinitely as organization members discover new ways of improving the organization and adapting it to changing conditions.

Organization transformation is a recent advance in organization development, and there is some confusion about its meaning and definition. This chapter starts with a description of several major features of transformational change. Against this background, three kinds of interventions are discussed: culture change, self-design, and organization learning and knowledge management.

An organization's culture is the pattern of assumptions, values, and norms that are more or less shared by organization members. A growing body of research has shown that culture can affect strategy formulation and implementation as well as the firm's ability to achieve high levels of performance. Culture change involves helping senior executives and administrators diagnose existing culture and make necessary alterations in the basic assumptions and values underlying organizational behaviors.

Self-designing organizations are those that have gained the capacity to alter themselves fundamentally. Creating them is a highly participative process in which multiple stakeholders set strategic directions, design appropriate structures and processes, and implement them. This intervention includes considerable innovation and learning as organizations design and implement significant changes.

Organization learning and knowledge management refer to the capacity of an organization to change and improve.[2] Distinct from individual learning, this intervention helps the organization move beyond solving existing problems and gain the capability to improve continuously. It results in the development of a learning organization where empowered members take responsibility for strategic direction.

CHARACTERISTICS OF TRANSFORMATIONAL CHANGE

In the past decade, a large number of organizations radically altered how they operate and relate to their environments. Increased foreign or global competition forced many industries to downsize or consolidate and become leaner, more efficient, and flexible. Deregulation pushed organizations in the financial services, telecommunications, and airline industries to rethink business strategies and reshape how they operate. Public demand for less government and lowered deficits forced public sector agencies to streamline operations and to deliver more for less. Rapid changes in technologies rendered many organizational practices obsolete, pushing firms to be continually innovative and nimble.

Organization transformation implies radical changes in how members perceive, think, and behave at work. These changes go far beyond making the existing organization better or fine-tuning the status quo. They are concerned with fundamentally altering the organizational assumptions about its functioning and how it relates to the environment. Changing these assumptions entails significant shifts in corporate philosophy and values and in the numerous structures and organizational arrangements that shape members' behaviors. Not only is the magnitude of change greater, but the change fundamentally alters the qualitative nature of the organization.

Organization transformation interventions are recent additions to OD and still are in a formative stage of development. For example, organization learning was originally discussed in the late 1950s but did not reach prominence until the early 1990s. Examination of the rapidly growing literature on the topic suggests, however, the following distinguishing features of these revolutionary change efforts.

Change Is Triggered by Environmental and Internal Disruptions

Organizations are unlikely to undertake transformational change unless significant reasons to do so emerge. Power, sentience, and expertise are vested in the existing organizational arrangements, and when faced with problems, members are more likely to fine-tune those structures than to alter them drastically. Thus, in most cases, organizations must experience or anticipate a severe threat to survival before they will be motivated to undertake transformational change.[3] Such threats arise when environmental and internal changes render existing organizational strategies and designs obsolete. The changes threaten the very existence of the organization as it presently is constituted.

In studying a large number of organization transformations, Tushman, Newman, and Romanelli showed that transformational change occurs in response to at least three kinds of disruption:[4]

1. **Industry discontinuities**—sharp changes in legal, political, economic, and technological conditions that shift the basis for competition within an industry
2. **Product life cycle shifts**—changes in product life cycle that require different business strategies
3. **Internal company dynamics**—changes in size, corporate portfolio strategy, or executive turnover

These disruptions severely jolt organizations and push them to question business strategy and, in turn, their mission, values, structure, systems, and procedures.

Change Is Systemic and Revolutionary

Transformational change involves reshaping the organization's culture and design elements. These changes can be characterized as systemic and revolutionary because the entire nature of the organization is altered fundamentally. Typically driven by senior executives, change may occur rapidly so that it does not get mired in politics, individual resistance, and other forms of organizational inertia.[5] This is particularly pertinent to changing the different features of the organization, such as structure, information systems, human resources practices, and work design. These features tend to reinforce one another, thus making it difficult to change them in a piecemeal manner.[6] They need to be changed together and in a coordinated fashion so that they can mutually support each other and the new cultural values and assumptions.[7] Transformational change, however, is distinguished from other types of strategic change by its attention to the people side of the organization. For a change to be labeled transformational, a majority of individuals in an organization must change their behavior.[8]

Long-term studies of organizational evolution underscore the revolutionary nature of transformational change.[9] They suggest that organizations typically move through relatively long periods of smooth growth and operation. These periods of convergence or evolution are characterized by incremental changes. At times, however, most organizations experience severe external or internal disruptions that render existing organizational arrangements ineffective. Successful firms respond to these threats to survival by transforming themselves to fit the new conditions. These periods of total system and quantum changes represent abrupt shifts in the organization's structure, culture, and processes. If successful, the shifts enable the organization to experience another long period of smooth functioning until the next disruption signals the need for drastic change.[10]

These studies of organization evolution and revolution point to the benefits of implementing transformational change as rapidly as possible. The faster the organization can respond to disruptions, the quicker it can attain the benefits of operating in a new way. Rapid change enables the organization to reach a period of smooth growth and functioning sooner, thus providing it with a competitive advantage over those firms that change more slowly.

Change Demands a New Organizing Paradigm

Organizations undertaking transformational change are, by definition, involved in second-order or gamma types of change.[11] *Gamma change* involves discontinuous shifts in mental or organizational frameworks.[12] Creative metaphors, such as "organization learning" or "continuous improvement," often are used to help members visualize the new paradigm.[13] During the 1980s, increases in technological change, concern for quality, and worker participation led to at least one shift in organizing paradigm. Characterized as the transition from a "control-based" to a "commitment-based" organization, the features of the new paradigm included leaner, more flexible structures; information and decision making pushed down to the lowest levels; decentralized teams and business units accountable for specific products, services, or customers; and participative management and teamwork. This new organizing paradigm is well suited to changing conditions.

Change Is Driven by Senior Executives and Line Management

A key feature of organization transformation is the active role of senior executives and line managers in all phases of the change process.[14] They are responsible for the strategic direction and operation of the organization and actively lead the transformation. They decide when to initiate transformational change, what the change should be, how it should be implemented, and who should be responsible for directing it. Because existing executives may lack the talent, energy, and commitment to undertake these tasks, they may be replaced by outsiders who are recruited to lead the change. Research on transformational change suggests that externally recruited executives are three times more likely to initiate such change than are existing executive teams.[15]

The critical role of executive leadership in transformational change is clearly emerging. Lucid accounts of transformational leaders describe how executives, such as Jack Welch at General Electric, Max DuPree at Herman Miller, and Sir Colin Marshall at British Airways, actively manage both the organizational and personal dynamics of transformational change.[16] The work of Nadler, Tushman, and others points to three key roles for executive leadership of such change:[17]

1. **Envisioning.** Executives must articulate a clear and credible vision of the new strategic orientation. They also must set new and difficult standards for performance, and generate pride in past accomplishments and enthusiasm for the new strategy.

2. **Energizing.** Executives must demonstrate personal excitement for the changes and model the behaviors that are expected of others. Behavioral integrity, credibility, and "walking the talk" are important ingredients.[18] They must communicate examples of early success to mobilize energy for change.

3. **Enabling.** Executives must provide the resources necessary for undertaking significant change and use rewards to reinforce new behaviors. Leaders also must build an effective top-management team to manage the new organization and develop management practices to support the change process.

Continuous Learning and Change

Transformational change requires considerable innovation and learning.[19] Organizational members must learn how to enact the new behaviors required to implement new strategic directions. This typically is a continuous learning process of trying new behaviors, assessing their consequences, and modifying them if necessary. Because members usually must learn qualitatively different ways of perceiving, thinking, and behaving, the learning process is likely to be substantial and to involve much unlearning. It is directed by a vision of the future organization and by the values and norms needed to support it. Learning occurs at all levels of the organization, from senior executives to lower-level employees.

Because the environment itself is likely to be changing during the change process, transformational change rarely has a delimited time frame but is likely to persist as long as the firm needs to adapt to change. Learning how to manage change in a continuous manner can help the organization keep pace with a dynamic environment. It can provide the built-in capacity to fit the organization continually to its environment.

CULTURE CHANGE

The topic of organization culture has become extremely important to American companies in the past 10 years, and culture change is the most common form of organization transformation. The number of culture change interventions has grown accordingly. Organization culture is also the focus of growing research and OD application and has spawned a number of bestselling management books starting with *Theory Z, The Art of Japanese Management,* and *In Search of Excellence* and, more recently, *Built to Last* and *Corporate Culture and Performance.*[20] Organization culture is seen as a major strength of such companies as Herman Miller, Intel, PepsiCo, Motorola, Hewlett-Packard, Southwest Airlines, and Levi Strauss. A growing number of managers appreciate the power of corporate culture in shaping employee beliefs and actions. A well-conceived and well-managed organization culture, closely linked to an effective business strategy, can mean the difference between success and failure in today's demanding environments.

Concept of Organization Culture

Despite the increased attention and research devoted to corporate culture, there is still some confusion about what the term *culture* really means when applied to organizations.[21] Martin argues that culture can be viewed from an integrated, a differentiated, or a fragmented perspective. The integrated view focuses on culture as an organizationally shared phenomenon; it represents a stable and coherent set of beliefs about the organization and its environment. In contrast to the integrated perspective, the differentiated view argues that culture is not monolithic but that it is best seen in terms of subcultures that exist throughout the organization. While each subculture is locally stable and shared, there is much that is different across the subcultures. Finally, the fragmented view holds that culture is always changing and is dominated by ambiguity and paradox. Summarizing an organization's culture from a fragmented viewpoint is somewhat meaningless.

Despite these different cultural views, there is some agreement about the elements or features of culture that are typically measured. They include the artifacts, norms, values, and basic assumptions that are more or less shared by organization members. The meanings attached to these elements help members make sense out of everyday life in the organization. The meanings signal how work is to be done and evaluated, and how employees are to relate to each other and to significant others, such as customers, suppliers, and government agencies.

As shown in Figure 20.1, organization culture includes four major elements existing at different levels of awareness:[22]

1. **Artifacts.** Artifacts are the highest level of cultural manifestation. These are the visible symbols of the deeper levels of culture, such as norms, values, and basic assumptions. They include observable behaviors of members, such as clothing

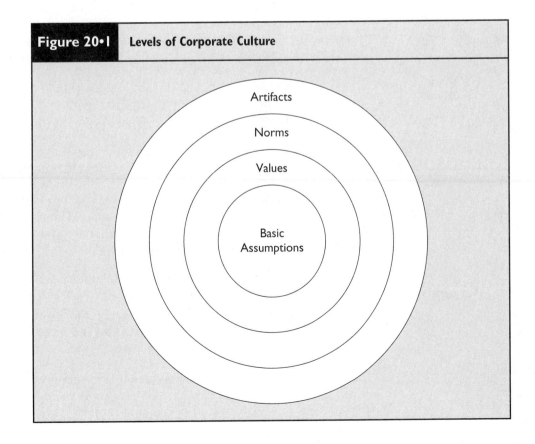

Figure 20•1   Levels of Corporate Culture

Artifacts

Norms

Values

Basic Assumptions

and language; the structures, systems, procedures, and rules; and physical aspects of the organization, such as décor, space arrangements, and noise levels. At Nordstrom, a high-end retail department store, the policy and procedure manual is rumored to be one sentence, "Do whatever you think is right." In addition, stores promote from within; pay commissions on sales to link effort and compensation; provide stationery for salespeople to write personal notes to customers; and expect buyers to work as salespeople to better understand the customer's expectations. By themselves, artifacts can provide a great deal of information about the real culture of the organization because they often represent the deeper assumptions. The difficulty in their use during cultural analysis is interpretation; an outsider (and even some insiders) has no way of knowing what the artifacts represent, if anything.

2. **Norms.** Just below the surface of cultural awareness are norms guiding how members should behave in particular situations. These represent unwritten rules of behavior. At Nordstrom, norms dictate that it's okay for members to go the extra mile to satisfy customer requests, and it's not okay for salespeople to process customers who were working with another salesperson.

3. **Values.** The next-deeper level of awareness includes values about what ought to be in organizations. Values tell members what is important in the organization and what deserves their attention. Because Nordstrom values customer service, the sales representatives pay strong attention to how well the customer is treated. Obviously, this value is supported by the norms and artifacts.

4. **Basic assumptions.** At the deepest level of cultural awareness are the taken-for-granted assumptions about how organizational problems should be solved. These basic assumptions tell members how to perceive, think, and feel about things. They are nonconfrontable and nondebatable assumptions about relating to the environment and about human nature, human activity, and human relationships. For example, a basic assumption at Nordstrom is the belief in the fundamental dignity of people; it is morally right to treat customers with extraordinary service so that they will become loyal and frequent shoppers.

In summary, culture is defined as the pattern of artifacts, norms, values, and basic assumptions about how to solve problems that works well enough to be taught to others.[23] Culture is a process of social learning; it is the outcome of prior choices about and experiences with strategy and organization design. It is also a foundation for change that can either facilitate or hinder organization transformation. For example, the cultures of many companies (e.g., IBM, JCPenney, Sony, Disney, Microsoft, and Hewlett-Packard) are deeply rooted in the firm's history. They were laid down by strong founders and have been reinforced by top executives and corporate success into customary ways of perceiving and acting. These customs provide organization members with clear and often widely shared answers to such practical issues as "what really matters around here," "how do we do things around here," and "what we do when a problem arises."

Organization Culture and Organization Effectiveness

The interest in organization culture derives largely from its presumed impact on organization effectiveness. Considerable speculation and increasing research support suggest that organization culture has both direct and indirect relationships with effectiveness.

Indirectly, culture affects performance through its influence on the organization's ability to implement change. A particular pattern of values and assumptions that once was a source of strength for a company can become a major liability in successfully implementing a new strategy.[24] The case evidence of organizational transformations is full of accounts where the change failed because the culture didn't support the new strategy, including AT&T's failed integration of NCR, Daimler-Benz's troubles with Chrysler, and Prudential Insurance's difficulties in diversifying into other financial services.

The growing appreciation that culture can play a significant role in implementing new strategy has fueled interest in the topic, especially in those firms needing to adapt to turbulent environments. A number of practitioners and academics have focused on helping firms implement new strategies by bringing culture more in line with the new direction.[25] Indeed, much of the emphasis in the 1970s on formulating business strategy shifted to organization culture in the 1980s as firms discovered cultural roadblocks to implementing a strategy. Along with this emerging focus on organization culture, however, came the sobering reality that cultural change is an extremely difficult and long-term process. Some experts doubt whether large firms actually can bring about fundamental changes in their cultures; those who have accomplished such feats estimate that the process takes from 6 to 15 years.[26] For example, Alberto-Culver's performance in its core business was suffering, and senior management, with the help of an employee opinion survey, realized that the culture was not aligned with the changing business needs. Beginning with the commitment of influential top managers, a management restructuring, explicit values, and new roles and practices, Alberto-Culver began a culture change effort that took over 7 years. Its efforts have been rewarded with increased sales and pretax profit growth.[27]

Directly, evidence suggests that, in addition to affecting the implementation of business strategy, corporate culture can affect organization performance. Comparative studies of Japanese and American management methods suggest that the relative success of Japanese companies in the 1980s could be partly explained by their strong corporate cultures emphasizing employee participation, open communication, security, and equality.[28] One study of American firms showed a similar pattern of results.[29] Using survey measures of culture and Standard & Poor's financial ratios as indicators of organizational effectiveness, the results showed that firms whose cultures support employee participation in decision making, adaptable work methods, sensible work designs, and reasonable and clear goals perform significantly higher (financial ratios about twice as high) than do companies scoring low on those factors. Moreover, the employee participation element of corporate culture only showed differences in effectiveness among the firms after 3 years; the other measures of culture showed differences in all 5 years. This suggests that changing some parts of corporate culture, such as participation, should be considered as a long-term investment.

Another study of 207 firms in 22 different industries examined relationships between financial performance and the strength of a culture, the strategic appropriateness of a culture, and the adaptiveness of a culture.[30] First, there were no significant performance differences between organizations with widely shared values and those with little agreement around cultural assumptions. Second, there was a significant relationship between culture and performance when the organization emphasized the "right" values—values that were critical to success in a particular industry. Finally, performance results over time supported cultures that emphasized anticipating and adapting to environmental change.

These findings suggest that the strength of an organization's culture can be both an advantage and a disadvantage. Under stable conditions, widely shared and strategically appropriate values can contribute significantly to organization performance. However, if the environment is changing, strong cultures can be a liability. Unless they also emphasize adaptiveness, the organization may experience wide swings in performance during transformational change. This line of thought was recently given empirical support.[31] In a study of over 150 large, publicly traded companies from 19 industries, organizations with strong cultures had more reliable performance outcomes—that is, the strength of the culture was related to the predictability of performance. However, when the environment was more uncertain and dynamic, this reliability faded. In stable environments, strong cultures provide efficiency in decision making and operations. In volatile environments, the strength of the culture becomes a weakness because it stunts creativity. Organizations with strong cultures are less able to exploit new environmental opportunities.

Diagnosing Organization Culture

Culture change interventions generally start by diagnosing the organization's existing culture to assess its fit with current or proposed business strategies. This requires uncovering and understanding the shared assumptions, values, norms, and artifacts that characterize an organization's culture. OD practitioners have developed a number of useful approaches for diagnosing organization culture. These fall into three different yet complementary perspectives: the behavioral approach, the competing values approach, and the deep assumption approach. Each diagnostic perspective focuses on particular aspects of organization culture, and together the approaches can provide a comprehensive assessment of these complex phenomena.

The Behavioral Approach

This method of diagnosis emphasizes the surface level of organization culture—the pattern of behaviors that produce business results.[32] It is among the more practical approaches to culture diagnosis because it assesses key work behaviors that can be observed.[33] The behavioral approach provides specific descriptions about how tasks are performed and how relationships are managed in an organization. For example, Table 20.1 summarizes the organization culture of an international banking division as perceived by its managers. In this classic case, the data were obtained from a series of individual and group interviews asking managers to describe "the way the game is played," as if they were coaching a new organization member. Managers were asked to give their impressions in regard to four key relationships—company-wide, boss–subordinate, peer, and interdepartment—and in terms of six managerial tasks—innovating, decision making, communicating, organizing, monitoring, and appraising/rewarding. These perceptions revealed a number of implicit norms for how tasks are performed and relationships managed at the division.

Cultural diagnosis derived from a behavioral approach can also be used to assess the cultural risk of trying to implement organizational changes needed to support a new strategy. Significant cultural risks result when changes that are highly important to implementing a new strategy are incompatible with the existing patterns of behavior. Knowledge of such risks can help managers determine whether implementation plans should be changed to manage around the existing culture, whether the culture should be changed, or whether the strategy itself should be modified or abandoned.

The Competing Values Approach

This perspective assesses an organization's culture in terms of how it resolves a set of value dilemmas.[34] The approach suggests that an organization's culture can be understood in terms of two important "value pairs"; each pair consists of contradictory values placed at opposite ends of a continuum, as shown in Figure 20.2. The two value pairs are (1) internal focus and integration versus external focus and differentiation and (2) flexibility and discretion versus stability and control. Organizations continually struggle to satisfy the conflicting demands placed on

Table 20•1	Summary of Corporate Culture at an International Banking Division

RELATIONSHIPS	CULTURE SUMMARY
Companywide	Preserve your autonomy. Allow area managers to run the business as long as they keep the profit budget.
Boss–subordinate	Avoid confrontations. Smooth over disagreements. Support the boss.
Peer	Guard information; it is power. Be a gentleman or lady.
Interdepartment	Protect your department's bottom line. Form alliances around specific issues. Guard your turf.

TASKS	CULTURE SUMMARY
Innovating	Consider it risky. Be a quick second.
Decision making	Handle each deal on its own merits. Gain consensus. Require many sign-offs. Involve the right people. Seize the opportunity.
Communicating	Withhold information to control adversaries. Avoid confrontation. Be a gentleman or lady.
Organizing	Centralize power. Be autocratic.
Monitoring	Meet short-term profit goals.
Appraising and rewarding	Reward the faithful. Choose the best bankers as managers. Seek safe jobs.

SOURCE: Reprinted from *Organizational Dynamics*, Summer/1981. © 1981 American Management Association International with permission from Elsevier.

them by these competing values. For example, when faced with the competing values of internal versus external focus, organizations must choose between attending to the integration problems of internal operations or the competitive issues in the external environment. Too much emphasis on the environment can result in neglect of internal efficiencies. Conversely, too much attention to the internal aspects of organizations can result in missing important changes in the competitive environment.

The competing values approach commonly collects diagnostic data about the competing values with a survey designed specifically for that purpose.[35] It provides measures of where an organization's existing values fall along each of the dimensions. When taken together, these data identify an organization's culture as falling into one of the four quadrants shown in Figure 20.2 (on page 488): clan culture, adhocracy culture, hierarchical culture, and market culture. For example, if an organization's

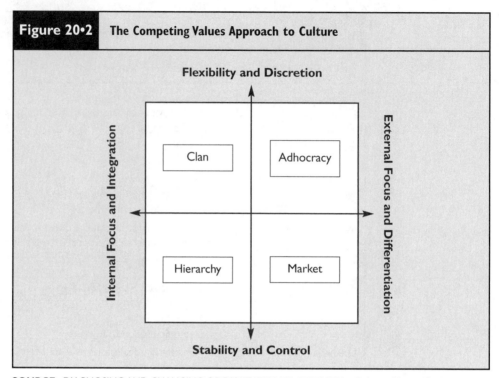

| **Figure 20·2** | **The Competing Values Approach to Culture** |

SOURCE: DIAGNOSING AND CHANGING ORGANIZATIONAL CULTURE by Cameron/Quinn, © 1999. Adapted by permission of Pearson Education, Inc., Upper Saddle River, NJ.

values are focused on internal integration issues and emphasize innovation and flexibility, it manifests a clan culture. On the other hand, a market culture characterizes values that are externally focused and emphasize stability and control.

The Deep Assumptions Approach

This final diagnostic approach emphasizes the deepest levels of organization culture—the generally unexamined, but tacit and shared assumptions that guide member behavior and that often have a powerful impact on organization effectiveness. Diagnosing culture from this perspective typically begins with the most tangible level of awareness and then works down to the deep assumptions.

Diagnosing organization culture at the deep assumptions level poses at least three difficult problems for collecting pertinent information.[36] First, culture reflects the more or less shared assumptions about what is important, how things are done, and how people should behave in organizations. People generally take cultural assumptions for granted and rarely speak of them directly. Rather, the company's culture is implied in concrete behavioral examples, such as daily routines, stories, rituals, and language. This means that considerable time and effort must be spent observing, sifting through, and asking people about these cultural outcroppings to understand their deeper significance for organization members. Second, some values and beliefs that people espouse have little to do with the ones they really hold and follow. People are reluctant to admit this discrepancy, yet somehow the real assumptions underlying idealized portrayals of culture must be discovered. Third, large, diverse organizations are likely to have several subcultures, including countercultures going against the grain of the wider organization culture. Assumptions may not be shared widely and may differ across groups in the organization. This means that focusing on limited parts of the organization or on a few select individuals may provide a distorted view of the organization's culture and subcultures. All relevant groups in the organization must be discovered and their cultural assumptions sampled. Only then can practitioners judge the extent to which assumptions are shared widely.

OD practitioners emphasizing the deep assumptions approach have developed a number of useful techniques for assessing organization culture.[37] One method involves an iterative interviewing process involving both outsiders and insiders.[38] Outsiders help members uncover cultural elements through joint exploration. The outsider enters the organization and experiences surprises and puzzles that are different from what was expected. The outsider shares these observations with insiders, and the two parties jointly explore their meaning. This process involves several iterations of experiencing surprises, checking for meaning, and formulating hypotheses about the culture. It results in a formal written description of the assumptions underlying an organizational culture.

A second method for identifying the organization's basic assumptions brings together a group of people for a culture workshop—for example, a senior management team or a cross section of managers, old and new members, labor leaders, and staff.[39] The group first brainstorms a large number of artifacts, such as behaviors, symbols, language, and physical space arrangements. From this list, the values and norms that would produce such artifacts are deduced. In addition, the values espoused in formal planning documents are listed. Finally, the group attempts to identify the assumptions that would explain the constellation of values, norms, and artifacts. Because they generally are taken for granted, they are difficult to articulate. A great deal of process consultation skill is required to help organization members see the underlying assumptions.

Application Stages

There is considerable debate over whether changing something as deep-seated as organization culture is possible.[40] Those advocating culture change generally focus on the more superficial elements of culture, such as norms and artifacts. These elements are more changeable than the deeper elements of values and basic assumptions. They offer OD practitioners a more manageable set of action levers for changing organizational behaviors. Some would argue, however, that unless the deeper values and assumptions are changed, organizations have not really changed the culture.

Those arguing that implementing culture change is extremely difficult, if not impossible, typically focus on the deeper elements of culture (values and basic assumptions). Because these deeper elements represent assumptions about organizational life, members do not question them and have a difficult time envisioning anything else. Moreover, members may not want to change their cultural assumptions. The culture provides a strong defense against external uncertainties and threats.[41] It represents past solutions to difficult problems. Members also may have vested interests in maintaining the culture. They may have developed personal stakes, pride, and power in the culture and may strongly resist attempts to change it. Finally, cultures that provide firms with a competitive advantage may be difficult to imitate, thus making it hard for less successful firms to change their cultures to approximate the more successful ones.[42]

Given the problems with cultural change, most practitioners in this area suggest that changes in corporate culture should be considered only after other, less difficult and less costly solutions have been applied or ruled out.[43] Attempts to overcome cultural risks when strategic changes are incompatible with culture might include ways to manage around the existing culture. Consider, for example, a single-product organization with a functional focus and a history of centralized control that is considering an ambitious product-diversification strategy. The firm might manage around its existing culture by using business teams to coordinate functional specialists around each new product. Another alternative to changing culture is to modify strategy to bring it more in line with culture. The single-product organization just mentioned might decide to undertake a less ambitious strategy of product diversification.

Despite problems in changing corporate culture, large-scale cultural change may be necessary in certain situations: if the firm's culture does not fit a changing environment; if the industry is extremely competitive and changes rapidly; if the company is mediocre or worse; if the firm is about to become a very large company; or if the company is smaller and growing rapidly.[44] Organizations facing these conditions need to change their cultures to adapt to the situation or to operate at higher levels of effectiveness. They may have to supplement attempts at cultural change with other approaches, such as managing around the existing culture and modifying strategy.

Although knowledge about changing corporate culture is in a formative stage, the following practical advice can serve as guidelines for cultural change:[45]

1. ***Formulate a Clear Strategic Vision.*** Effective cultural change should start from a clear vision of the firm's new strategy and of the shared values and behaviors needed to make it work.[46] This vision provides the purpose and direction for cultural change. It serves as a yardstick for defining the firm's existing culture and for deciding whether proposed changes are consistent with core values of the organization. A useful approach to providing clear strategic vision is development of a statement of corporate purpose, listing in straightforward terms the firm's core values. For example, Johnson & Johnson calls its guiding principles "Our Credo." It describes several basic values that guide the firm, including "We believe our first responsibility is to the doctors, nurses and patients, to mothers and all others who use our products and services"; "Our suppliers and distributors must have an opportunity to make a fair profit"; "We must respect [employees'] dignity and recognize their merit"; and "We must maintain in good order the property we are privileged to use, protecting the environment and natural resources."[47]

2. ***Display Top-management Commitment.*** Cultural change must be managed from the top of the organization. Senior managers and administrators have to be strongly committed to the new values and need to create constant pressures for change. They must have the staying power to see the changes through.[48] For example, when Jack Welch was CEO at General Electric, he enthusiastically pushed a policy of cost cutting, improved productivity, customer focus, and bureaucracy busting for more than 10 years to every plant, division, group, and sector in his organization. His efforts were rewarded with a *Fortune* cover story lauding his organization for creating more than $52 billion in shareholder value during his tenure.[49]

3. ***Model Culture Change at the Highest Levels.*** Senior executives must communicate the new culture through their own actions. Their behaviors need to symbolize the kinds of values and behaviors being sought. In the few publicized cases of successful culture change, corporate leaders have shown an almost missionary zeal for the new values; their actions have symbolized the values forcefully.[50] For example, when the Four Seasons hotel chain agreed to operate the George V hotel in Paris, it not only remodeled the hotel; it had to implement a culture consistent with its corporate brand and strategy, which were both "North American" in nature. Didier Le Calvez, General Manager of the Four Seasons George V, made a number of controversial decisions, including agreeing to the 35-hour work week, hiring an executive chef, and implementing a performance appraisal process. The nature of these decisions symbolized his understanding of French culture on the one hand and the importance of the Four

Seasons's standards on the other. In addition, Le Calvez was very visible on the property, meeting the French union officials for lunch, finding constructive ways to correct behavior in line with the Four Seasons's service expectations, and participating in the interview and selection of all employees.[51]

4. ***Modify the Organization to Support Organizational Change.*** Cultural change generally requires supporting modifications in organizational structure, human resources systems, information and control systems, and management styles. These organizational features can help to orient people's behaviors to the new culture.[52] They can make people aware of the behaviors required to get things done in the new culture and can encourage performance of those behaviors. For example, Carol Lavin Bernick, President of Alberto-Culver North American, created the "growth development leader" or GDLs to support the cultural imperatives of honesty, ownership, trust, commitment, and teamwork. Each of the 70 GDLs mentors about a dozen key people in the organization to ensure they create and follow through on their "individual economic value-add" (IEV) statements. In turn, Ms. Bernick meets with the GDLs every 6 weeks to symbolize the importance of their work.[53]

5. ***Select and Socialize Newcomers and Terminate Deviants.*** One of the most effective methods for changing corporate culture is to change organizational membership. People can be selected and terminated in terms of their fit with the new culture. This is especially important in key leadership positions, where people's actions can significantly promote or hinder new values and behaviors. For example, Gould, in trying to change from an auto parts and battery company to a leader in electronics, replaced about two-thirds of its senior executives with people more in tune with the new strategy and culture. Jan Carlzon of Scandinavian Airlines (SAS) replaced 13 out of 15 top executives in his turnaround of the airline. Another approach is to socialize newly hired people into the new culture. People are most open to organizational influences during the entry stage, when they can be effectively indoctrinated into the culture. For example, companies with strong cultures like Samsung, Procter & Gamble, and 3M attach great importance to socializing new members into the company's values.

6. ***Develop Ethical and Legal Sensitivity.*** Cultural change can raise significant tensions between organization and individual interests, resulting in ethical and legal problems for practitioners. This is particularly pertinent when organizations are trying to implement cultural values promoting employee integrity, control, equitable treatment, and job security—values often included in cultural change efforts. Statements about such values provide employees with certain expectations about their rights and about how they will be treated in the organization. The organization needs to follow through with behaviors and procedures supporting and protecting these implied rights, or risk violating ethical principles and, in some cases, legal employment contracts. Recommendations for reducing the chances of such ethical and legal problems include setting realistic values for culture change and not promising what the organization cannot deliver; encouraging input from throughout the organization in setting cultural values; providing mechanisms for member dissent and diversity, such as internal review procedures; and educating managers about the legal and ethical pitfalls inherent in cultural change and helping them develop guidelines for resolving such issues.

Application 20.1 presents an example of culture change at Washington Mutual. The example illustrates how important cultural principles are used to shape behavior during a period of organizational growth and how culture can be used to facilitate merger and acquisition integration processes.[54]

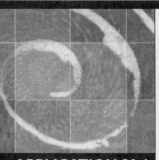

WASHINGTON MUTUAL: LEVERAGING CULTURE AS COMPETITIVE ADVANTAGE

APPLICATION 20•1

Washington Mutual, Inc. (http://www.wamu.com) is one of the nation's leading and fastest growing financial services companies. In 2003, it was rated by *Fortune* as one of the top 20 companies for minorities, by *Business Week* as the thirteenth best-performing company, and by *Fast Company* as one of the 25 most innovative companies in the world. Washington Mutual (WaMu) serves the broad middle market, including consumers and small- to midsize businesses. Its business strategy is to provide a higher level of personalized customer service than its competitors. WaMu's CEO, Kerry Killinger, summarized their business philosophy as follows:

> Washington Mutual has learned what other masters of the middle market have: Delivering what customers value, becoming an efficient provider and shooting for the sort of friendly service that builds long-lasting relationships and leads to satisfied customers—service high on courtesy, helpfulness, and efficiency—are what the middle market wants. And the broad middle market is where the greatest long-term profit potential lies.

One of the important ingredients in WaMu's success has been the way it has driven its cultural values and brand promise throughout the organization. When asked by columnist Lou Dobbs about how to institutionalize a set of values in an organization of over 50,000 employees, Killinger remarked:

> First, you need very clear statements about what the corporate values are. It's important to have those down. The top one is always integrity. Then we have respect for people, the individual. Next is encouraging teamwork. We also place value on innovation and excellence, where we have very high performance standards.

As a result, two guideposts drive the strategy and organization design at WaMu:

1. The brand promise of great value with friendly service for everyone and the associated brand attributes of fair, caring, human, dynamic, and driven.
2. The corporate values that guide decision making at all levels are:
   - Ethics—All actions are guided by absolute honesty, integrity, and fairness.
   - Respect—People are valued and appreciated for their contribution.
   - Teamwork—Cooperation, trust, and shared objectives are vital to success.
   - Innovation—New ideas are encouraged, and sound strategies implemented with enthusiasm.
   - Excellence—High standards for service and performance are expected and rewarded.

Strategically, the values and brand promise infuse its external relations and acquisitions process. For example, the organization's products and advertising are innovative, capture WaMu's personality, and focus on the customer. Similarly, a partnership with Magic Johnson's development company helps WaMu deliver its "Power of Yes" home loan brand to underserved communities. Moreover, employees are encouraged to volunteer and can use up to 4 paid hours per month to give back to the community.

In addition, the values and brand promise underpin the way WaMu conducts its acquisition process. Even though acquisitions have a poor track record in general, WaMu has successfully completed 32 acquisitions since 1983, and 5 since 2001. Seven principles guide the acquisition process: (1) Pick targets that will make you a market leader; (2) Work with sellers whose values match yours; (3) Make blunt decisions about who will run the show; (4) Get everyone involved in fitting all of the pieces together; (5) Close your deals quickly; (6) Go all out to win your new employees' trust; and (7) Don't ever stop growing internally. Five of the seven principles are clearly linked to WaMu's values. For example, WaMu seeks organizations that share its values; and blunt decision making and winning employee trust are supported by ethics/integrity, respect, and excellence.

The brand promise and cultural values also support the organization's structure, performance management systems, communications, and training and development practices. Structurally, the organization supports the values and brand promise with 75 "brand ambassadors" named by the executive committee for their knowledge and embodiment of the company's message, and with branches designed more like retail department stores than conservative banking establishments. For example, a branch office puts tellers in front of the customer rather than behind a glass wall or counter; concierge "greeters" dressed in khaki pants and bright golf shirts meet customers; and a children's play area is provided. The performance management system sets and reinforces high performance standards during appraisals, rewards eligible employees with stock options that are expensed, and hands out promotions based on performance.

Corporate and internal communications are also aligned with the promise and the values. For example, to reinforce the company's brand promise of caring and fair, and to support the values of ethics, respect, and innovation, the company revamped the way it communicates with delinquent loan customers. Under the old practice, letters sent out following a missed payment included cold language that threatened negative actions if payment was not received. The letter was revised to include a message acknowledging that difficulties can happen and that if the customer will call, WaMu will do everything it can to help out. Internally, Killinger underscores and reinforces the values in all of the company communications. He believes they anchor the organization's past and provide a compass to the future, and he stresses how they translate into value for the customer. In response to a recent enterprisewide employee survey, Killinger sent a message letting everyone know what had been improved and what still needs improving. And he has followed up those messages with monthly reminders about the importance of performance and the resources the organization is putting behind improvement.

Finally, training and leadership development programs are also designed to explicitly reinforce the company values. For example, companywide competencies were released in 2003 for the professional members of the organization, and, as part of the validation process, the proposed competencies were tested against the brand promise and values. The competencies are being used to design a leadership development program, and the board of directors is following up on its progress as part of an initiative to bring more rigor into the talent management process.

More recently, Killinger has continued to reinforce the brand promise and values with the launch of his "one vision, one company" message. Historically, the organization has had difficulty integrating the silos and subcultures in different parts of the organization. For example, the loan division and the consumer banking division operate with different time orientations, technologies, and even customers. In line with the one vision, one company message, product strategies, policies, and management practices are beginning to shift. If the brand promise and values are to result in higher performance, cross-selling customers from one product to another is crucial, and the one vision, one company message is intended to improve integration.

SELF-DESIGNING ORGANIZATIONS

A growing number of researchers and practitioners have called for self-designing organizations that have the built-in capacity to transform themselves to achieve high performance in today's competitive and changing environment.[55] Mohrman and Cummings have developed a self-design change strategy that involves an ongoing series of designing and implementing activities carried out by managers and employees at all levels of the firm.[56] The approach helps members translate corporate values and general prescriptions for change into specific structures, processes, and behaviors suited to their situations. It enables them to tailor changes to fit the organization and helps them continually to adjust the organization to changing conditions.

The Demands of Transformational Change

Mohrman and Cummings developed the self-design strategy in response to a number of demands facing organizations engaged in transformational change. These demands strongly suggest the need for self-design, in contrast to more traditional approaches to organization change that emphasize ready-made programs and quick fixes. Although organizations prefer the control and certainty inherent in programmed change, the five requirements for organizational transformation reviewed below argue against this strategy:

1. Transformational change generally involves altering most features of the organization and achieving a fit among them and with the firm's strategy. This suggests the need for a systemic change process that accounts for these multiple features and relationships.

2. Transformational change generally occurs in situations experiencing heavy change and uncertainty. This means that changing is never totally finished, as new structures and processes will continually have to be modified to fit

changing conditions. Thus, the change process needs to be dynamic and iterative, with organizations continually changing themselves.[57]

3. Current knowledge about transforming organizations provides only general
    prescriptions for change. Organizations need to learn how to translate that in-
    formation into specific structures, processes, and behaviors appropriate to their
    situations. This generally requires considerable on-site innovation and learning
    as members learn by doing—trying out new structures and behaviors, assessing
    their effectiveness, and modifying them if necessary. Transformational change
    needs to facilitate this organizational learning.[58]

4. Transformational change invariably affects many organization stakeholders, in-
    cluding owners, managers, employees, and customers. These different stake-
    holders are likely to have different goals and interests related to the change
    process. Unless the differences are revealed and reconciled, enthusiastic support
    for change may be difficult to achieve. Consequently, the change process must
    attend to the interests of multiple stakeholders.[59]

5. Transformational change needs to occur at multiple levels of the organization if
    new strategies are to result in changed behaviors throughout the firm. Top ex-
    ecutives must formulate a corporate strategy and clarify a vision of what the or-
    ganization needs to look like to support it. Middle and lower levels of the
    organization need to put those broad parameters into operation by creating
    structures, procedures, and behaviors to implement the strategy.[60]

Application Stages

The self-design strategy accounts for these demands of organization transformation. It
focuses on all features of the organization (for example, structure, human resources
practices, and technology) and designs them to support the business strategy mutually. It is a dynamic and an iterative process aimed at providing organizations with the
built-in capacity to change and redesign themselves continually as the circumstances
demand. The approach promotes organizational learning among multiple stakeholders at all levels of the firm, providing them with the knowledge and skills needed to
transform the organization and continually improve it.

Figure 20.3 outlines the self-design approach. Although the process is described
in three stages, in practice the stages merge and interact iteratively over time. Each
stage is described below:

1. *Laying the Foundation.* This initial stage provides organization members with
    the basic knowledge and information needed to get started with organization

Figure 20•3   The Self-Design Strategy

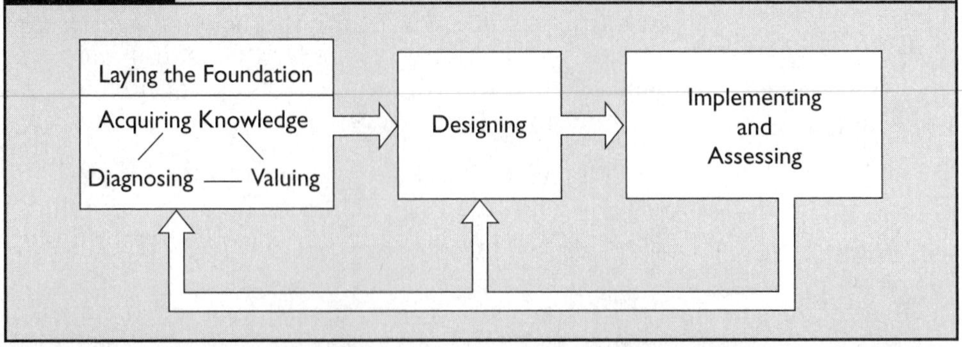

SOURCE: SELF-DESIGNING ORGANIZATIONS by Mohrman/Cummings, © 1989. Adapted by permission of
Pearson Education, Inc., Upper Saddle River, NJ.

transformation. It involves three kinds of activities. The first is acquiring knowledge about how organizations function, about organizing principles for achieving high performance, and about the self-design process. This information is generally gained through reading relevant material, attending in-house workshops, and visiting other organizations that successfully have transformed themselves. This learning typically starts with senior executives or with those managing the transformation process and cascades to lower organizational levels if a decision is made to proceed with self-design. The second activity in laying the foundation involves valuing—determining the corporate values that will guide the transformation process. These values represent those performance outcomes and organizational conditions that will be needed to implement the corporate strategy. They are typically written in a values statement that is discussed and negotiated among multiple stakeholders at all levels of the organization. The third activity is diagnosing the current organization to determine what needs to be changed to enact the corporate strategy and values. Organization members generally assess the different features of the organization, including its performance. They look for incongruities between its functioning and its valued performances and conditions. In the case of an entirely new organization, members diagnose constraints and contingencies in the situation that need to be taken into account in designing the organization.

2. *Designing.* In this second stage of self-design, organization designs and innovations are generated to support corporate strategy and values. Only the broad parameters of a new organization are specified; the details are left to be tailored to the levels and groupings within the organization. Referred to as minimum specification design, this process recognizes that designs need to be refined and modified as they are implemented throughout the firm.

3. *Implementing and Assessing.* This last stage involves implementing the designed organization changes. It includes an ongoing cycle of action research: changing structures and behaviors, assessing progress, and making necessary modifications. Information about how well implementation is progressing and how well the new organizational design is working is collected and used to clarify design and implementation issues and to make necessary adjustments. This learning process continues not only during implementation but indefinitely as members periodically assess and improve the design and alter it to fit changing conditions. The feedback loops shown in Figure 20.3 suggest that the implementing and assessing activities may lead back to affect subsequent designing, diagnosing, valuing, and acquiring knowledge activities. This iterative sequence of activities provides organizations with the capacity to transform and improve themselves continually.

The self-design strategy is applicable to existing organizations needing to transform themselves, as well as to new organizations. It is also applicable to changing the total organization or subunits. The way self-design is managed and unfolds can also differ. In some cases, it follows the existing organization structure, starting with the senior executive team and cascading downward across organizational levels. In other cases, the process is managed by special design teams that are sanctioned to set broad parameters for valuing and designing for the rest of the organization. The outputs of these teams then are implemented across departments and work units, with considerable local refinement and modification. Application 20.2 continues our description of the change process at American Healthways. The application describes how the structural change effort used the self-design approach on an overall basis as well as the basis for each of the task forces.

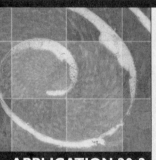

SELF-DESIGN AT AMERICAN HEALTHWAYS CORPORATION

APPLICATION 20•2

Prior applications of the American Healthways (AMHC) change process have described the entry and contracting process (Application 4.1 and 4.2), the gathering of diagnostic data (Application 7.1), and a description of the process-based structure they adopted (Application 14.1). In this application, we step back and take a broader look at the overall self-design change strategy employed by the organization.

As described in Application 4.1, the senior leaders at AMHC clearly sensed a need to look at the organization's design in the context of the expected rapid growth of the health plan business. AMHC had identified an important and growing niche (proactive disease management) in the growing health care industry. They had crafted an impressive strategy but recognized that the current structure was insufficient to the task.

The university-based OD practitioner initially recommended a task force and a series of workshops to choose an appropriate organization design for the company. The task force and workshop idea was guided by a self-design philosophy. As described in the entry and contracting process, the organization knew its structure was inadequate and that it needed a new way of operating, but it did not have a broad range of skills or experience in operating a large organization. This led the OD practitioner to believe that the self-design model would be the best approach. As the organization considered what structure to implement, it also needed to learn and build the capacity to change itself.

To date, there have been three organization design and development (ODD) task forces, and each one has been guided by the self-design strategy. The first ODD task force was dedicated to laying the foundation; their output was the recommendation to pursue a process-based structure. The second ODD task force was responsible for designing; they were charged with putting "meat on the bones" of the approved structure. The third ODD task force began implementing the new design as well as developing more sophisticated long-term implementation templates.

The first ODD task force's activities were dominated by laying the foundation activities. Members of the task force, representing most of the organization's key functional areas, read extensively on organization design, interviewed other organizations who had adopted different structures, and studied alternative change processes. As a result of the knowledge acquired through this process, the task force became aware that the organization lacked a clear vision and

"big hairy audacious goal" (BHAG) that most change management frameworks listed as a key success factor. This insight led the task force to instigate a vision and strategy effort to clarify the organization's purpose, to forecast revenues, and to understand the organization's strategic intent. Within the context of a clearer strategy, the task force was able to examine the pros and cons of alternative structures and to ground their recommendation in business terms. The first ODD task force also engaged in diagnostic activities as outlined in Application 7.1. This process allowed the group to better understand the current organization's strengths and weaknesses, to test the initial draft of the BHAG, to alert the organization to the task force's activities, and to ensure that the new organization aligned with the organization's culture. Finally, the task force spent a considerable amount of time discussing and debating the values that would guide the new organization. A culture initiative was proceeding concomitantly with the ODD task force and the outputs of their work were an important input to these discussions.

The first ODD task force used the knowledge and information generated in the laying-the-foundation phase to design three alternative structures that they believed would meet the needs of the future organization. Each of the alternative structures was formalized with high-level charts, pros and cons, and a business case rationale. The group discussed the structures and debated their relative strengths and weaknesses in the context of the diagnostic information, values, and strategy of the organization. The design phase concluded with a recommendation to senior management to adopt the process-based structure. The recommendation of the first ODD task force was debated and approved by members of AMHC's senior management team, several of whom had been on the task force. The senior team recommended that another task force be created to expand on the recommended structure.

The second ODD task force's activities were predominantly focused on the design phase of the self-design strategy. In addition to a few original task force members, the second task force consisted of organization members representing a broader range of functions and levels in the organization. This ensured that knowledge and understanding of the process-based structure generated in the first task force would be passed along to a larger set of managers in the organization. More importantly, the second task force was expected to model the type of cross-functional team that would be the centerpiece of the new structure. As a result, the laying-the-foundation phase of the second task force included acquiring knowledge about cross-functional and self-managed teams and continuous improvement processes. The rationale for the process-based structure was reviewed and the values guiding the structural choice were discussed by the team. However, the primary work of the second ODD task force was to add detail to each of the core processes, conceptualize and define the corporate office organization, create design principles to aid managers in understanding why functions and processes were assigned in certain ways, create financial statements reflecting expected operating expenses in the new design, and create additional timelines and implementation templates to guide execution of the new structure. The second task force ended with a presentation of roles, reporting relationships, metrics, and control and reward mechanisms to the senior management team.

As the organization debated how to implement the structure, learnings from the first two task forces were applied. That is, both groups had developed important insights about the operation of a process-based organization and recommended that the next group to manage the change process had to be the senior management team itself. As a result, the COO appointed the senior management team to be the third ODD task force. The primary focus of this group would be implementation, the third phase of the self-design strategy. Despite several senior managers' participation on the first two task forces, the entire senior management team was not intimately familiar with the logic and operation of the process-based organization, nor had this group operated as a cross-functional team. By having the COO's direct reports operate as a cross-functional team, ownership for the new structure would be placed squarely on the shoulders of those who would guide its implementation and an important symbol of the new organization structure would be established. Early in the life of the third task force, and based on its recommendation, the COO and CEO renamed and replaced the old senior management team with the executive leadership group structure that would be responsible for operating the new organization. In addition, several key process owners were named to begin the implementation. The third ODD task force also developed more detailed implementation guidelines, including a variety of measures to monitor the success of the structure's implementation and methods to keep the organization's focus on meeting customer needs during the transition.

The design and implementation of the process-based structure at AMHC has been driven by the philosophy and logic of the self-design strategy. It has produced important insights and changes in the way managers at the organization viewed its strategy, culture, and operations. Most importantly, the process itself has built capacity and knowledge into the system. A variety of managers in different functions and levels of the organization have a deeper understanding of the structure's rationale and important experiences working on cross-functional teams. This knowledge and experience will serve the organization well as it implements the process-based structure.

ORGANIZATION LEARNING AND KNOWLEDGE MANAGEMENT

The third organizational transformation intervention is aimed at helping organizations develop and use knowledge to change and improve themselves continually. It includes two interrelated change processes: organization learning (OL), which enhances an organization's capability to acquire and develop new knowledge, and knowledge management (KM), which focuses on how that knowledge can be organized and used to improve performance. Both OL and KM are crucial in today's complex, rapidly changing environments. They can be a source of strategic renewal, and they can enable organizations to acquire and apply knowledge more quickly and effectively than competitors, thus establishing a sustained competitive advantage.[61] Moreover, when knowledge is translated into new products and services, it can become a key source of wealth creation for organizations.[62] OL and KM are among the most widespread and fastest-growing interventions in OD. They are the focus of an expanding body of research and practice, and have been applied in such diverse firms as McKinsey, L.L. Bean, the Canadian Broadcasting Corporation, Allegheny-Ludlum Steel, Boeing, Microsoft, and the U.S. Army.

Conceptual Framework

Like many new interventions in OD, there is some ambiguity about the concepts underlying OL and KM. Sometimes the terms "organization learning" and "knowledge management" are used interchangeably to apply to the broad set of activities through which organizations learn and organize knowledge; other times, they are used separately to emphasize different aspects of learning and managing knowledge. This confusion derives in part from the different disciplines and applications traditionally associated with OL and KM.

OL interventions emphasize the organizational structures and social processes that enable employees and teams to learn and to share knowledge. They draw heavily on the social sciences for conceptual grounding and on OD interventions, such as team building, structural design, and employee involvement, for practical guidance. In organizations, OL change processes typically are associated with the human resources function and may be assigned to a special leadership role, such as chief learning officer.

KM interventions, on the other hand, focus on the tools and techniques that enable organizations to collect, organize, and translate information into useful knowledge. They are rooted conceptually in the information and computer sciences and, in practice, emphasize electronic forms of knowledge storage and transmission such as intranets, data warehousing, and knowledge repositories. Organizationally, KM applications often are located in the information systems function and may be under the direction of a chief technology officer.

There is also confusion about the concept of organization learning itself, about whether it is an individual- or organization-level process. Some researchers and practitioners describe OL as individual learning that occurs within an organization context; thus, it is the aggregate of individual learning processes occurring within an organization.[63] Others characterize it in terms of organization processes and structures; they emphasize how learning is embedded in routines, policies, and organization cultures.[64] Snyder has proposed an integration of the two perspectives that treats organization learning as a relative concept.[65] Individuals do learn in organizations but that learning may or may not contribute to organization learning. Learning is organizational to the extent that

- It is done to achieve organization purposes.
- It is shared or distributed among members of the organization.
- Learning outcomes are embedded in the organization's systems, structures, and culture.

To the extent that these criteria are met, organization learning is distinct from individual learning. Thus, it is possible for individual members to learn while the organization does not. For example, a member may learn to serve the customer better without ever sharing such learning with other members. Conversely, it is possible for the organization to learn without individual members learning. Improvements in equipment design or work procedures, for example, reflect OL, even if these changes are not understood by individual members. Moreover, because organization learning serves the organization's purposes and is embedded in its structures, it stays with the organization, even if members change.

A key premise underlying much of the literature on OL and KM is that such interventions will lead to higher organization performance. Although their positive linkage to performance is assumed, the mechanisms through which OL and KM translate into performance improvements are rarely identified or explained. Understanding those mechanisms, however, is essential for applying these change processes in organizations.

Based on existing research and practice, Figure 20.4 provides an integrative framework for understanding OL and KM interventions,[66] summarizing the elements of these change processes and showing how they combine to affect organization performance. This framework suggests that specific characteristics, such as structure and hu-

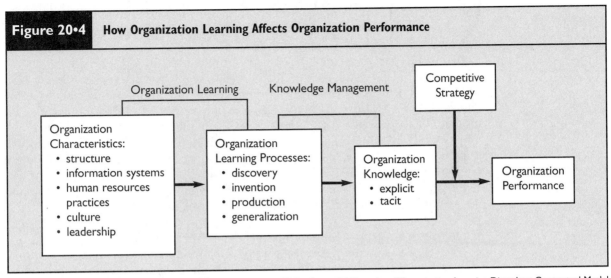

Figure 20•4   How Organization Learning Affects Organization Performance

SOURCE: Reprinted by permission of Sage Publications Ltd. from W. Snyder and T. Cummings, "Organization Learning Disorders: Conceptual Model and Intervention Hypotheses," *Human Relations* 51 (1998): 873–95. © The Tavistock Institute, 1998.

man resources systems, influence how well organization learning processes are carried out. These learning processes affect the amount and kind of knowledge that an organization possesses; that knowledge, in turn, directly influences performance outcomes, such as product quality and customer service. As depicted in Figure 20.4, the linkage between organization knowledge and performance depends on the organization's competitive strategy. Organization knowledge will lead to high performance to the extent that it is both relevant and applied effectively to the strategy. For example, customer-driven organizations require timely and relevant information about customer needs. Their success relies heavily on members having that knowledge and applying it effectively in their work with customers.

Figure 20.4 also shows how OL and KM are interrelated. OL interventions address how organizations can be designed to promote effective learning processes, and how those learning processes themselves can be improved. KM interventions focus on the outcomes of learning processes, on how strategically relevant knowledge can be effectively organized and used throughout the organization. Each of the key elements of OL and KM—organization characteristics, organization learning processes, and organization knowledge—are described below along with the interventions typically associated with them.

Characteristics of a Learning Organization

As shown in Figure 20.4, there are several organization features that can promote effective learning processes including structure, information systems, human resources practices, culture, and leadership. Consequently, many of the interventions described in this book can help organizations develop more effective learning capabilities. Human resources management interventions—performance appraisal, reward systems, and career planning and development—can reinforce members' motivation to gain new skills and knowledge. Technostructural interventions, such as process-based and network structures, self-managing work teams, and reengineering, can provide the kinds of lateral linkages and teamwork needed to process, develop, and share diverse information and knowledge. Human process changes, including team building, search conferences, and intergroup relations interventions, can help members develop the kinds of healthy interpersonal relationships that underlie effective OL. Strategic interventions, such as integrated strategic change and alliances, can help organizations gain knowledge about their environments and develop values and norms that promote OL.

OL practitioners have combined many of these interventions into the design and implementation of what is commonly referred to as the learning organization. It is an organization "skilled at creating, acquiring, interpreting, transferring, and retaining knowledge, and at purposefully modifying its behavior to reflect new knowledge and insights."[67] Much of the literature on the learning organization is prescriptive and proposes how organizations should be designed and managed to promote effective learning. Although there is relatively little systematic research to support these premises, there is growing consensus among researchers and practitioners about specific organizational features that characterize the learning organization.[68] These qualities are mutually reinforcing and fall into five interrelated categories:

- **Structure**—Organization structures emphasize teamwork, few layers, strong lateral relations, and networking across organizational boundaries both internal and external to the firm. These features promote the information sharing, involvement in decision making, systems thinking, and empowerment.

- **Information systems**—Organization learning involves gathering and processing information, and consequently, the information systems of learning organizations provide an infrastructure for OL. These systems facilitate rapid acquisition, processing, and sharing of rich, complex information and enable people to manage knowledge for competitive advantage.

- **Human resources practices**—Human resources, including appraisal, rewards, and training, are designed to account for long-term performance and knowledge development; they reinforce the acquisition and sharing of new skills and knowledge.

- **Organization culture**—Learning organizations have strong cultures that promote openness, creativity, and experimentation among members. These values and norms provide the underlying social support needed for successful learning. They encourage members to acquire, process, and share information; they nurture innovation and provide the freedom to try new things, to risk failure, and to learn from mistakes.

- **Leadership**—Like most interventions aimed at organization transformation, OL and KM depend heavily on effective leadership throughout the organization. The leaders of learning organizations actively model the openness, risk taking, and reflection necessary for learning. They also communicate a compelling vision of the learning organization and provide the empathy, support, and personal advocacy needed to lead others in that direction.

Organization Learning Processes

The organization characteristics described above affect how well members carry out organization learning processes. As shown in Figure 20.4, these processes consist of four interrelated activities: discovery, invention, production, and generalization.[69] Learning starts with discovery when errors or gaps between desired and actual conditions are detected. For example, sales managers may discover that sales are falling below projected levels and set out to solve the problem. Invention is aimed at devising solutions to close the gap between desired and current conditions; it includes diagnosing the causes of the gap and creating appropriate solutions to reduce it. The sales managers may learn that poor advertising is contributing to the sales problem and may devise a new sales campaign to improve sales. Production processes involve implementing solutions, and generalization includes drawing conclusions about the effects of the solutions and extending that knowledge to other relevant situations. For instance, the new advertising program would be implemented, and if successful, the managers might use variations of it with other product lines. Thus, these four learning processes enable members to generate the knowledge necessary to change and improve the organization.

Organizations can apply the learning processes described above to three types of learning.[70] First, *single-loop learning* or *adaptive learning* is focused on improving the status quo. This is the most prevalent form of learning in organizations and enables members to reduce errors or gaps between desired and existing conditions. It can produce incremental change in how organizations function. The sales managers described above engaged in single-loop learning when they looked for ways to reduce the difference between current and desired levels of sales.

Second, *double-loop learning* or *generative learning* is aimed at changing the status quo. It operates at a more abstract level than does single-loop learning because members learn how to change the existing assumptions and conditions within which single-loop learning operates. This level of learning can lead to transformational change, where the status quo itself is radically altered. For example, the sales managers may learn that sales projections are based on faulty assumptions and models about future market conditions. This knowledge may result in an entirely new conception of future markets with corresponding changes in sales projections and product development plans. It may lead the managers to drop some products that had previously appeared promising, develop new ones that were not considered before, and alter advertising and promotional campaigns to fit the new conditions.

The third type of learning is called *deuterolearning*, which involves learning how to learn. Here learning is directed at the learning process itself and seeks to improve how organizations perform single- and double-loop learning. For example, the sales managers might periodically examine how well they perform the processes of discovery, invention, production, and generalization. This could lead to improvements and efficiencies in how learning is conducted throughout the organization.

Practitioners have developed change strategies designed specifically for organization learning processes. Although these interventions are relatively new in OD and do not follow a common change process, they tend to focus on cognitive aspects of learning and how members can become more effective learners. In describing these change strategies, we draw heavily on the work of Argyris and Schon and of Senge and his colleagues because it is the most developed and articulated work in OL practice.[71]

From this perspective, organization learning is not concerned with the organization as a static entity but as an active process of sense making and organizing. Based in the interpretive model of change (Chapter 2), members socially construct the organization as they continually act and interact with each other and learn from those actions how to organize themselves for productive achievement. This active learning process enables members to develop, test, and modify mental models or maps of organizational reality. Called *theories in use*, these cognitive maps inform member behavior and organizing.[72] They guide how members make decisions, perform work, and organize themselves. Unfortunately, members' theories in use can be faulty, resulting in ineffective behaviors and organizing efforts. They can be too narrow and fail to account for important aspects of the environment; they can include erroneous assumptions that lead to unexpected negative consequences. Effective OL can resolve these problems by enabling members to learn from their actions how to detect and correct errors in their mental maps, and thus it can promote more effective organizing efforts.

The predominant mode of learning in most organizations is ineffective, however, and may even intensify errors. Referred to as *Model I learning*, it includes values and norms that emphasize unilateral control of environments and tasks, and protection of oneself and others from information that may be hurtful.[73] These norms result in a variety of defensive routines that inhibit learning, such as withholding information and feelings, competition and rivalry, and little public testing of theories in use and the assumptions underlying them. Model I is limited to single-loop learning, where existing theories in use are reinforced.

A more effective approach to learning, called *Model II,* is based on values promoting valid information, free and informed choice, internal commitment to the choice, and continuous assessment of its implementation.[74] This results in minimal defensiveness with greater openness to information and feedback, personal mastery and collaboration with others, and public testing of theories in use. Model II applies to double-loop learning, where theories in use are changed, and to deuterolearning, where the learning process itself is examined and improved.

OL interventions are aimed at helping organization members learn how to change from Model I to Model II learning. Like all learning, this change strategy includes the learning processes of discovery, invention, production, and generalization. Although the phases are described linearly below, in practice they form a recurrent cycle of overlapping learning activities.

1. ***Discover Theories in Use and Their Consequences.*** This first step involves uncovering members' mental models or theories in use and the consequences that follow from behaving and organizing according to them. Depending on the size of the client system, this may directly involve all members, such as a senior executive team, or it may include representatives of the system, such as a cross section of members from different levels and areas.

   OL practitioners have developed a variety of techniques to help members identify their theories in use. Because these theories generally are taken for granted and rarely examined, members need to generate and analyze data to infer the theories' underlying assumptions. One approach is called *dialogue,* a variant of the human process interventions described in Chapter 12.[75] It involves members in genuine exchange about how they currently address problems, make decisions, and interact with each other and relevant others, such as suppliers, customers, and competitors. Participants are encouraged to be open and frank with each other, to behave as colleagues, and to suspend individual assumptions as much as possible. OL practitioners facilitate dialogue sessions using many of the human process tools described in Chapter 12, such as process consultation and third-party intervention. As a result, group members are encouraged to inquire into their own and others' ways of thinking, to advocate for certain beliefs, and to reflect on the assumptions that lead to those beliefs. Dialogue can result in clearer understanding of existing theories in use and their behavioral consequences and enable members to uncover faulty assumptions that lead to ineffective behaviors and organizing efforts.

   A second method of identifying theories in use involves constructing an *action map* of members' theories and their behavioral consequences.[76] OL practitioners typically interview members about recurrent problems in the organization, explanations of why they are occurring, actions that are taken to resolve them, and outcomes of those behaviors. Based on this information, an action map is constructed showing interrelationships among the values underlying theories in use, the action strategies that follow from them, and the results of those actions. Such information is fed back to members so that they can test the validity of the map, assess the effectiveness of their theories in use, and identify factors that contribute to functional and dysfunctional learning in the organization.

A third technique for identifying theories in use and revealing assumptions is called the *left-hand, right-hand column*.[77] It starts with each member selecting a specific example of a situation where he or she was interacting with others in a way that produced ineffective results. The example is described in the form of a script and is written on the right side of a page. For instance, it might include statements such as, "I told Larry that I thought his idea was good." "Joyce said to me that she did not want to take the assignment because her workload was too heavy." On the left-hand side of the page, the member writes what he or she was thinking but not saying at each phase of the exchange. For example, "When I told Larry that I thought his idea was good, what I was really thinking is that I have serious reservations about the idea, but Larry has a fragile ego and would be hurt by negative feedback." "Joyce said she didn't want to take the assignment because her workload is too heavy, but I know it's because she doesn't want to work with Larry." This simple yet powerful exercise reveals hidden assumptions that guide behavior and can make members aware of how erroneous or untested assumptions can undermine work relationships.

A fourth method that helps members identify how mental models are created and perpetuated is called the *ladder of inference*, as shown in Figure 20.5.[78] It demonstrates how far removed from concrete experience and selected data are the assumptions and beliefs that guide our behavior. The ladder shows vividly how members' theories in use can be faulty and lead to ineffective

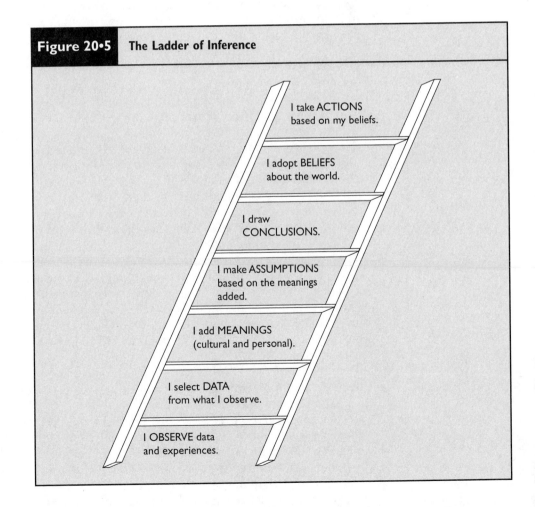

Figure 20•5   The Ladder of Inference

I take ACTIONS based on my beliefs.

I adopt BELIEFS about the world.

I draw CONCLUSIONS.

I make ASSUMPTIONS based on the meanings added.

I add MEANINGS (cultural and personal).

I select DATA from what I observe.

I OBSERVE data and experiences.

actions. People may draw invalid conclusions from limited experience; their cultural and personal biases may distort meaning attributed to selected data. The ladder of inference can help members understand why their theories in use may be invalid and why their behaviors and organizing efforts are ineffective. Members can start with descriptions of actions that are not producing intended results and then back down the ladder to discover the reasons underlying those ineffective behaviors. For example, a service technician might withhold from management valuable yet negative customer feedback about product quality, resulting in eventual loss of business. Backing down the ladder, the technician could discover an untested belief that upper management does not react favorably to negative information and may even "shoot the messenger." This belief may have resulted from assumptions and conclusions that the technician drew from observing periodic layoffs and from hearing widespread rumors that the company is out to get troublemakers and people who speak up too much. The ladder of inference can help members understand the underlying reasons for their behaviors and help them confront the possibility that erroneous assumptions are contributing to ineffective actions.

2. *Invent and Produce More Effective Theories in Use.* Based on what is discovered in the first phase of this change process, members invent and produce theories in use that lead to more effective actions and that are more closely aligned with Model II learning. This involves double-loop learning as members try to create and enact new theories. In essence, members learn by doing; they learn from their invention and production actions how to invent and produce more effective theories in use. As might be expected, learning how to change theories in use can be extremely difficult. There is a strong tendency for members to revert to habitual behaviors and modes of learning. They may have trouble breaking out of existing mindsets and seeing new realities and possibilities. OL practitioners have developed both behavioral and conceptual interventions to help members overcome these problems.

   Behaviorally, practitioners help members apply the values underlying Model II learning—valid information, free choice, and internal commitment—to question their experience of trying to behave more consistently with Model II.[79] They encourage members to confront and talk openly about how habitual actions and learning methods prevent them from creating and enacting more effective theories. Once these barriers to change are discussed openly, members typically discover that they are changeable. This shared insight often leads to the invention of more effective theories for behaving, organizing, and learning. Subsequent experimentation with trying to enact those theories in the workplace is likely to produce more effective change because the errors that invariably occur when trying new things now can be discussed and hence corrected.

   Conceptually, OL practitioners teach members *systems thinking* to help them invent more effective theories in use.[80] It provides concepts and tools for detecting subtle but powerful structures that underlie complex situations. Learning to see such structures can help members understand previously unknown forces operating in the organization. This information is essential for developing effective theories for organizing, particularly in today's complex, changing world.

   Systems thinking generally requires a radical shift in how members view the world: from seeing parts to seeing wholes; from seeing linear cause–effect chains to seeing interrelationships; from seeing static entities to seeing processes of change. Practitioners have developed a variety of exercises and tools to help members make this conceptual shift. These include systems diagrams for displaying circles of influence among system elements; system archetypes describing recurrent structures that affect organizations; computerized microworlds where new strategies can be tried out under conditions that permit experimentation and learning; and games and experiential exercises demonstrating systems principles.[81]

3. ***Continuously Monitor and Improve the Learning Process.*** This final stage involves deuterolearning—learning how to learn. As described earlier, learning is directed at the learning process itself and at how well Model II learning characteristics are reflected in it. This includes assessing OL strategies and the organizational structures and processes that contribute to them. Members assess periodically how well these elements facilitate single- and double-loop learning. They generalize positive findings to new or changing situations and make appropriate modifications to improve OL. Because these activities reflect the highest and most difficult level of OL, they depend heavily on members' capability to do Model II learning. Members must be willing to question openly their theories in use about OL; they must be willing to test publicly the effectiveness both of their learning strategies and of the wider organization.

Organization Knowledge

The key outcome of organization learning processes is organization knowledge. It includes what members know about organizational processes, products, customers, and competitive environments. Such knowledge may be explicit and exist in codified forms such as documents, manuals, and databases; or it may be tacit and reside mainly in members' skills, memories, and intuitions.[82] Fueled by innovations in information technology, KM interventions have focused heavily on codifying organization knowledge so it can be readily accessed and applied to organizational tasks. Because tacit knowledge is difficult if not impossible to codify, attention also has been directed at how such knowledge can be shared informally across members and organizational units.

Organization knowledge contributes to organization performance to the extent that it is relevant and applied effectively to the organization's competitive strategy, as shown in Figure 20.4. Moreover, organization knowledge is particularly valuable when it is unique and cannot easily be obtained by competitors.[83] Thus, organizations seek to develop or acquire knowledge that distinctly adds value for customers and that can be leveraged across products, functions, business units, or geographical regions. For example, Wal-Mart excels at managing its unique distribution system across a wide variety of regional stores. Honda is particularly successful at leveraging its competence in producing motors across a number of product lines, including automobiles, motorcycles, generators, outboard motors, and lawn mowers.[84]

Because organization knowledge plays a crucial role in linking organization learning processes to organization performance, increasing attention is being directed at how firms can acquire and use it effectively. Studies have demonstrated how many Japanese companies and such American firms as Hewlett-Packard and Motorola achieve competitive advantage through building and managing knowledge effectively.[85] These knowledge capabilities have been described as "core competencies,"[86] "invisible assets,"[87] and "intellectual capital,"[88] thus suggesting their contribution to organization performance.

There is growing emphasis both in the accounting profession and in many industries on developing measures that capture knowledge capital.[89] For many organizations, the value of intellectual assets far exceeds the value of physical and financial assets; intellectual assets are usually worth three to four times tangible book value.[90] Moreover, the key components of cost in many of today's organizations are research and development, intellectual assets, and services rather than materials and labor, which are the focus of traditional cost accounting. Dow Chemical, for example, has developed a process for measuring and managing intellectual capital.[91] The method first defines the role of knowledge in the firm's business strategy, then assesses current knowledge assets and deficiencies, and finally assembles a knowledge portfolio. This process enables Dow to manage knowledge almost as rigorously as it manages its tangible assets.

KM interventions are growing rapidly in OD and include a range of change strategies and methods. Although there is no universal approach to KM, these change processes address the essential steps for generating, organizing, and distributing knowledge within organizations:

1. *Generating Knowledge.* This stage involves identifying the kinds of knowledge that will create the most value for the organization and then creating mechanisms for increasing that stock of knowledge. It starts with examination of the organization's competitive strategy—how it seeks to create customer value to achieve profitable results. Strategy provides the focus for KM; it identifies those areas where knowledge is likely to have the biggest payoff. For example, competitive strategies that emphasize customer service, such as those found at McKinsey and Nordstrom, place a premium on knowledge about customer needs, preferences, and behavior. Strategies favoring product development, like those at Microsoft and Hoffman-LaRoche, benefit from knowledge about technology, research, and development. Strategies focusing on operational excellence, such as those at Motorola and Chevron, value knowledge about manufacturing and quality improvement processes.

   Once the knowledge required for competitive strategy is identified, organizations need to devise mechanisms for acquiring or creating that knowledge. Externally, organizations can acquire other companies that possess the needed knowledge, or they can rent it from knowledge sources such as consultants and university researchers.[92] Internally, organizations can facilitate communities of practice—informal networks among employees performing similar work who share expertise and solve problems together.[93] They can also create more formal groups for knowledge generation, such as R&D departments, corporate universities, and centers of excellence. Organizations can bring together people with different skills, ideas, and values to generate new products or services. Called creative abrasion, this process breaks traditional frames of thinking by having diverse perspectives rub creatively against each other to develop innovative solutions.[94]

2. *Organizing Knowledge.* This phase includes putting valued knowledge into a form that organizational members can use readily. It also may involve refining knowledge to increase its value to users. KM practitioners have developed tools and methods for organizing knowledge that form two broad strategies: codification and personalization.[95]

   Codification approaches rely heavily on information technology. They categorize and store knowledge in databases where it can be accessed and used by appropriate members. This strategy works best for explicit forms of knowledge that can be extracted from people, reports, and other data sources, and then organized into meaningful categories called "knowledge objects" that can be reused for various purposes. The economic rationale underlying this strategy is to invest once in a knowledge asset and then to reuse it many times. Management consulting firms such as McKinsey and Bain extract key knowledge objects from consulting reports, benchmark data, and market segmentation analyses, and then place them in an electronic repository for people to use. This enables them to apply knowledge assets across various projects and clients, thus achieving scale in knowledge reuse to grow their business.

Personalization strategies for organizing knowledge focus on the people who develop knowledge and on how they can share it person-to-person. This approach emphasizes tacit knowledge, which cannot be codified and stored effectively in computerized information systems. Such knowledge is typically accessed through personal conversations, direct contact, and ongoing dialogue with the people who possess it. Thus, KM practitioners have developed a variety of methods for facilitating personal exchanges between those with tacit knowledge and those seeking it. For example, Bain and Company fosters networking among its employees through transferring people across offices, encouraging the prompt return of phone calls from colleagues, brainstorming sessions, and cross-functional project teams. Hughes, Microsoft, and Time-Life have created "knowledge maps" that identify valued competencies, skills, and knowledge and show people where to go and whom to contact to access them.[96]

3. **Distributing Knowledge.** This final stage of KM creates mechanisms for members to gain access to needed knowledge. It overlaps with the previous phase of KM and involves making knowledge easy for people to find and encouraging its use and reuse. KM practitioners have developed a variety of methods for distributing knowledge, generally grouped as three approaches: self-directed distribution, knowledge services and networks, and facilitated transfer.[97]

Self-directed methods rely heavily on member control and initiative for knowledge distribution. They typically include databases for storing knowledge and locator systems for helping members find what they want. Databases can include diverse information such as articles, analytical reports, customer data, and best practices. Locator systems can range from simple phone directories to elaborate search engines. Self-directed knowledge transfer can involve either "pull" or "push" systems.[98] The former lets members pull down information they need, when they need it; the latter makes knowledge available to members by sending it out to them. Fluor Corporation, for example, placed job requirements and career ladder information on its intranet and let employees access the information on an "as needed" basis.

Knowledge services and networks promote knowledge transfer by providing specific assistance and organized channels for leveraging knowledge throughout the organization. KM services include a variety of support for knowledge distribution, such as help desks, information systems, and knowledge packages. They also may involve special units and roles that scan the flow of knowledge and organize it into more useful forms, such as "knowledge departments," "knowledge managers," or "knowledge integrators."[99] Knowledge networks create linkages among organizational members for sharing knowledge and learning from one another. These connections can be electronic, such as those occurring in chat rooms, intranets, and discussion databases, or they may be personal like those taking place in talk rooms, knowledge fairs, and communities of practice.

Facilitated transfer of organization knowledge involves specific people who assist and encourage knowledge distribution. These people are trained to help members find and transmit knowledge as well as gain access to databases and other knowledge services. They also may act as change agents helping members implement knowledge to improve organization processes and structures. For example, BP's "Shared Learning Program" includes dedicated practitioners, called "quality/progress professionals," who coach employees in best practices and how to use them.[100]

Application 20.3 describes how KM interventions helped BP revitalize itself. It shows how KM can facilitate organization transformation and contribute to performance improvements.[101]

KNOWLEDGE MANAGEMENT AT BP

APPLICATION 20•3

BP is one of the most profitable oil companies in the world today. In the past decade, it has changed from a large, stodgy bureaucracy with mediocre performance and enormous debt to a much smaller, flexible organization with drastically reduced costs and debt and surging oil reserves, production output, and profits. To accomplish this radical transformation, BP downsized and restructured itself into a learning organization where people, teams, and informal networks generate and share knowledge to add value to what they do.

BP's change process began in 1992 under CEO David Simon and was subsequently led by John Browne, who became CEO in 1995. Browne was a strong advocate of OL and KM and sought ways to foster their application throughout the firm. To spearhead this effort, Browne asked Kent Greenes to head a team charged with improving performance by sharing best practices, reusing knowledge, and accelerating learning. The team first assembled a portfolio of 15 projects where KM was likely to have the greatest payoffs. These included helping BP enter the Japanese retail market, reducing downtime at a polyethylene plant, and cutting the costs of a refinery turnaround—a scheduled shutdown and refurbishment— in Holland. To ensure success, projects were sponsored by specific business units that agreed to pay for them. Moreover, project outcomes were tied to the business units' "performance contracts" for financial, environmental, and other results. In BP's culture, these agreements are considered unbreakable, and executives will do almost anything to fulfill them.

Greenes's team used a number of KM tools to facilitate the projects. The Dutch refinery, for example, received a "peer assist" from other refineries having experience in turnarounds. This consisted of a 2-day meeting where people with refinery turnaround experience shared their knowledge with the Dutch employees before the project began. It resulted in a $9 million savings. Another technique was adapted from the U.S. Army. Called "after-action reviews," it consists of answering the following questions after taking action: What was supposed to happen? What actually happened? Why is there a difference? What can we learn and do from this? A more elaborate version of this process, "the retrospect," was also applied at BP. The outcomes of these learning tools were used to develop a Web-based folder of information and knowledge including email hyperlinks to people with expertise to share.

Greenes's team also used information technology to enable employees to connect, communicate, and share knowledge. One method, called "connect," is a voluntary intranet directory listing people's expertise; about 12,000 BP employees initially put themselves into this database. Another tool, "virtual team network," enables people from BP's different geographic locations to work together. It includes desktop videoconferencing, multimedia email, and a real-time shared whiteboard.

In 1999, 2 years after the start of BP's KM projects, documented savings were $260 million with another $400 million anticipated. Perhaps more important, about one-third of the firm's 90 business units had applied KM tools and ideas, and more were becoming involved rapidly. More than 300 employees had become part-time knowledge managers, expanding greatly the work of Greenes's team.

Outcomes of OL and KM

Given the current popularity of OL and KM interventions, research about their effects in organizations is growing. The Society for Organizational Learning (SoL: http://www.solonline.org) at MIT is engaged in a variety of research efforts that focus on capacity building, dialogue, and other aspects of OL processes. For example, Volvo and IKEA applied learning processes in their implementation of environmentally sustainable organization designs. Other organizations claim considerable success with the ladder of inference, the left-hand/right-hand column tool, and systems thinking. The Canadian Broadcasting Corporation, for example, used the left-hand/right-hand column to increase collaboration between the English and French Radio and TV organizations and to create a new vocabulary for sharing resources. Despite these success stories, there appears to be considerable room for improving OL interventions. A longitudinal analysis of Royal Dutch Shell described its rise and fall as a "premier learning organization" and questioned whether such a strategy could be institutionalized.[102] Argyris and Schon state that they are unaware of any organization that has fully implemented a double-loop learning (Model II) system.[103]

A recent study of KM in 431 U.S. and European firms also suggests that organizations may have more problems implementing KM practices than is commonly reported in the popular media.[104] Only 46% of the companies reported above-average performance in "generating new knowledge." Ratings were even lower for "embedding knowledge in processes, products, and/or services" (29%) and "transferring existing knowledge into other parts of the organization" (13%). Another study of 31 KM projects across 20 organizations revealed that KM contributed to the fundamental transformation of only 3 of the firms studied.[105] Many of the companies, however, reported operational improvements in product development, customer support, software development, patent management, and education and training. Studies of transfer of best practices and KM by the American Productivity & Quality Center reveal a number of performance improvements in such companies as Buckman Laboratories, Texas Instruments, CIGNA Property & Casualty, and Chevron.[106] Among the reported outcomes were increases in new product sales, manufacturing capacity, and corporate profits, as well as reductions in costs, service delivery time, and start-up time for new ventures. Because most of the existing reports of OL and KM outcomes are case studies or anecdotal reports, more systematic research is need to assess the effects of these popular interventions.

◼ SUMMARY

In this chapter, we presented interventions for helping organizations transform themselves. These changes can occur at any level in the organization, but their ultimate intent is to change the total system. They typically happen in response to or in anticipation of significant environmental, technological, or internal changes. These changes may require alterations in the firm's strategy, as described in Chapter 19, but are mostly aimed at altering corporate culture, vision, and mental models within the organization.

Organization culture includes the pattern of basic assumptions, values, norms, and artifacts shared by organization members. It influences how members perceive, think, and behave at work. Culture affects whether firms can implement new strategies and whether they can operate at high levels of excellence. Culture change interventions start with diagnosing the organization's existing culture. This can include assessing the cultural risks of making organizational changes needed to implement strategy. Changing corporate culture can be extremely difficult and requires clear strategic vision, top-management commitment, symbolic leadership, supporting organizational changes, selection and socialization of newcomers and termination of deviants, and sensitivity to legal and ethical issues.

A self-design change strategy helps a firm gain the built-in capacity to design and implement its own organizational transformation. Self-design involves multiple levels of the firm and multiple stakeholders and includes an iterative series of activities: acquiring knowledge, valuing, diagnosing, designing, implementing, and assessing.

Organization learning and knowledge management interventions help organizations develop and use knowledge to change and improve themselves continually. Organization learning interventions address how organizations can be designed to promote effective learning processes and how those learning processes themselves can be improved. An organization designed to promote learning over a sustained period of time is called a learning organization. Knowledge management focuses on how that knowledge can be organized and used to improve organization performance.

NOTES

1. C. Lundberg, "On Organizational Learning: Implications and Opportunities for Expanding Organizational Development," in *Research in Organizational Change and Development*, vol. 3, eds. W. Pasmore and R. Woodman (Greenwich, Conn.: JAI Press, 1989), 61–82.

2. M. Fiol and M. Lyles, "Organizational Learning," *Academy of Management Review* 10 (1985): 803–13; J. March and H. Simon, *Organizations* (New York: John Wiley & Sons, 1958).

3. A. Grove, "Churning Things Up," *Fortune* (11 August 2003): 115–18; J. Sorensen, "The Strength of Corporate Culture and the Reliability of Firm Performance," *Administrative Science Quarterly* 47 (2002): 70–91; G. Young, "Managing Organizational Transformations: Lessons from the Veterans Health Administration," *California Management Review* 43 (2000): 66–82.

4. M. Tushman, W. Newman, and E. Romanelli, "Managing the Unsteady Pace of Organizational Evolution," *California Management Review* (Fall 1986): 29–44.

5. Ibid.

6. A. Meyer, A. Tsui, and C. Hinings, "Guest Co-Editors Introduction: Configurational Approaches to Organizational Analysis," *Academy of Management Journal* 36 (1993): 1175–95.

7. D. Miller and P. Friesen, *Organizations: A Quantum View* (Englewood Cliffs, N.J.: Prentice-Hall, 1984).

8. B. Blumenthal and P. Haspeslagh, "Toward a Definition of Corporate Transformation," *Sloan Management Review* 35 (1994): 101–07.

9. Tushman, Newman, and Romanelli, "Managing the Unsteady Pace"; L. Greiner, "Evolution and Revolution as Organizations Grow," *Harvard Business Review* (July-August 1972): 37–46.

10. M. Tushman and E. Romanelli, "Organizational Evolution: A Metamorphosis Model of Convergence and Reorientation," in *Research in Organizational Behavior*, vol. 7, eds. L. Cummings and B. Staw (Greenwich, Conn.: JAI Press, 1985), 171–222.

11. J. Bartunek and M. Louis, "Organization Development and Organizational Transformation," in *Research in Organizational Change and Development*, vol. 2, eds. W. Pasmore and R. Woodman (Greenwich, Conn.: JAI Press, 1988), 97–134.

12. R. Golembiewski, K. Billingsley, and S. Yeager, "Measuring Change and Persistence in Human Affairs: Types of Changes Generated by OD Designs," *Journal of Applied Behavioral Science* 12 (1975): 133–57.

13. J. Sackmann, "The Role of Metaphors in Organization Transformation," *Human Relations* 42 (1989): 463–85.

14. R. Eisenbach, K. Watson, and R. Pillai, "Transformational Leadership in the Context of Organization Change," *Journal of Organizational Change Management* 12 (1999): 80–89; R. Waldersee, "Becoming a Learning Organization: The Transformation of the Workplace," *Journal of Management Development* 16 (1997): 262–74; A. Pettigrew, "Context and Action in the Transformation of the Firm," *Journal of Management Studies* 24 (1987): 649–70; Tushman and Romanelli, "Organizational Evolution."

15. M. Tushman and B. Virany, "Changing Characteristics of Executive Teams in an Emerging Industry," *Journal of Business Venturing* (1986): 37–49; L. Greiner and A. Bhambri, "New CEO Intervention and Dynamics of Deliberate Strategic Change," *Strategic Management Journal* 10 (Summer 1989): 67–86.

16. N. Tichy and M. Devanna, *The Transformational Leader* (New York: John Wiley & Sons, 1986); M. DuPree, *Leadership Jazz* (New York: Doubleday, 1992); Blumenthal and Haspeslagh, "Corporate Transformation"; N. Tichy and S. Sherman, *Control Your Destiny or Someone Else Will* (New York: Doubleday, 1993).

17. P. Nutt and R. Backoff, "Facilitating Transformational Change," *Journal of Applied Behavioral Science* 33 (1997): 490–508; M. Tushman, W. Newman, and D. Nadler, "Executive Leadership and Organizational Evolution: Managing Incremental and Discontinuous Change," in *Corporate Transformation: Revitalizing Organizations for a Competitive World*, eds. R. Kilmann and T. Covin (San Francisco: Jossey-Bass, 1988): 102–30; W. Bennis and B. Nanus, *Leaders: The Strategies for Taking Charge* (New York: Harper & Row, 1985); Pettigrew, "Context and Action."

18. J. Kouzes and B. Posner, *The Leadership Challenge*, 3d ed. (San Francisco: Jossey-Bass, 2002); T. Simons, "Behavioral Integrity as a Critical Ingredient for Transformational Leadership," *Journal of Organizational Change Management* 12 (1999): 89–105.

19. T. Cummings and S. Mohrman, "Self-Designing Organizations: Towards Implementing Quality-of-Work-Life Innovations," in *Research in Organizational Change and Development*, vol. 1, eds. R. Woodman and W. Pasmore (Greenwich, Conn.: JAI Press, 1987), 275–310.

20. W. Ouchi, *Theory Z: How American Business Can Meet the Japanese Challenge* (Reading, Mass.: Addison-Wesley, 1979); R. Pascale and A. Athos, *The Art of Japanese Management* (New York: Simon & Schuster, 1981); T. Deal and A. Kennedy, *Corporate Cultures* (Reading, Mass.: Addison-Wesley, 1982); T. Peters and R. Waterman, *In Search of Excellence* (New York: Harper & Row, 1982); T. Peters and

N. Austin, *A Passion for Excellence* (New York: Random House, 1985); J. Pfeffer, *Competitive Advantage Through People* (Cambridge, Mass.: Harvard Business School, 1994); J. Collins and J. Porras, *Built to Last* (New York: Harper Business, 1994); J. Kotter and J. Heskett, *Corporate Culture and Performance* (New York: Free Press, 1992).

21. J. Martin, *Organization Culture* (Newbury Park, Calif.: Sage Publications, 2002); D. Meyerson and J. Martin, "Cultural Change: An Integration of Three Different Views," *Journal of Management Studies* 24 (1987): 623–47; D. Denison and G. Spreitzer, "Organizational Culture and Organizational Development: A Competing Values Approach," in *Research in Organizational Change and Development*, vol. 5, eds. R. Woodman and W. Pasmore (Greenwich, Conn.: JAI Press, 1991), 1–22; E. Schein, *Organizational Culture and Leadership*, 2d ed. (San Francisco: Jossey-Bass, 1992).

22. Schein, *Organizational Culture*; R. Kilmann, M. Saxton, and R. Serpa, eds., *Gaining Control of the Corporate Culture* (San Francisco: Jossey-Bass, 1985).

23. Schein, *Organizational Culture*.

24. E. Abrahamson, and C. J. Fombrun, "Macrocultures: Determinants and Consequences," *Academy of Management Journal* 19 (1994): 728–55; B. Dumaine, "Creating a New Company Culture," *Fortune* (15 January 1990): 127–31.

25. B. Uttal, "The Corporate Culture Vultures," *Fortune* (17 October 1983): 66–72; C-M Lau, L. Kilbourne, and R. Woodman, "A Shared Schema Approach to Understanding Organizational Culture Change," in *Research on Organizational Change and Development*, vol. 14, eds. W. Pasmore and R. Woodman (Greenwich, Conn.: JAI Press, 2003), 225–56.

26. Ibid., 70.

27. C. Bernick, "When Your Culture Needs a Makeover," *Harvard Business Review* (June 2001): 5–11.

28. Ouchi, Theory Z; Pascale and Athos, *Japanese Management*.

29. D. Denison, "The Climate, Culture, and Effectiveness of Work Organizations: A Study of Organizational Behavior and Financial Performance" (Ph.D. diss., University of Michigan, 1982.

30. Kotter and Heskett, *Corporate Culture*.

31. J. Sorensen, "The Strength of Corporate Culture and the Reliability of Firm Performance," *Administrative Science Quarterly* 47 (2002): 70–91.

32. D. Hanna, *Designing Organizations for High Performance* (Reading, Mass.: Addison-Wesley, 1988).

33. H. Schwartz and S. Davis, "Matching Corporate Culture and Business Strategy," *Organizational Dynamics* (Summer 1981): 30–48; S. Davis, *Managing Corporate Culture* (Cambridge, Mass.: Ballinger, 1984).

34. K. Cameron and R. Quinn, *Diagnosing and Changing Organizational Culture* (Reading, Mass.: Addison-Wesley, 1999); Denison and Spreitzer, "Organizational Culture"; R. E. Quinn, *Beyond Rational Management: Mastering the Paradoxes and Competing Demands of High Performance* (San Francisco: Jossey-Bass, 1988).

35. R. Quinn and G. Spreitzer, "The Psychometrics of the Competing Values Culture Instrument and an Analysis of the Impact of Organizational Culture on Quality of Life," in *Research in Organizational Change and Development*, vol. 5, eds. R. Woodman and W. Pasmore (Greenwich, Conn.: JAI Press, 1991), 115–42.

36. Schein, *Organizational Culture*.

37. R. Zammuto and J. Krakower, "Quantitative and Qualitative Studies of Organizational Culture," in *Research in Organizational Change and Development*, vol. 5, eds. R. Woodman and W. Pasmore (Greenwich, Conn.: JAI Press, 1991), 83–114; Quinn and Spreitzer, "Psychometrics."

38. Schein, *Organizational Culture*.

39. E. Schein, *The Corporate Culture Survival Guide* (San Francisco: Jossey-Bass, 1999).

40. P. Frost, L. Moore, M. Louis, C. Lundberg, and J. Martin, eds., *Organizational Culture* (Beverly Hills, Calif.: Sage, 1985), 95–196; Martin, *Organizational Culture*.

41. Meyerson and Martin, "Cultural Change."

42. J. Barney, "Organizational Culture: Can It Be a Source of Sustained Competitive Advantage?" *Academy of Management Review* 11 (1986): 656–65.

43. Uttal, "Corporate Culture Vultures."

44. Ibid., 70.

45. Schein, *Corporate Culture Survival Guide*; Schwartz and Davis, "Matching Corporate Culture"; Uttal, "Corporate Culture Vultures"; Davis, *Managing Corporate Culture*; Kilmann, Saxton, and Serpa, *Gaining Control*; Frost et al., *Organizational Culture*; V. Sathe, "Implications of Corporate Culture: A Manager's Guide to Action," *Organizational Dynamics* (Autumn 1983): 5–23; B. Drake and E. Drake, "Ethical and Legal Aspects of Managing Corporate Cultures," *California Management Review* (Winter 1988): 107–23.

46. C. Worley, D. Hitchin, and W. Ross, *Integrated Strategic Change* (Reading, Mass.: Addison-Wesley, 1996); R. Beckhard and W. Pritchard, *Changing the Essence* (San Francisco: Jossey-Bass, 1992).

47. F. Aguilar and A. Bhambri, *Johnson and Johnson* (A) (Boston: HBS Case Services, 1983).

48. Dumaine, "Creating a New Company Culture"; C. O'Reilly, "Corporations, Culture, and Commitment:

Motivation and Social Control in Organizations," *California Management Review* 31 (Summer 1989): 9–25; Pettigrew, "Context and Action."

49. Tichy and Sherman, *Control Your Destiny*; B. Morris, "The Wealth Builders," *Fortune* (11 December 1995): 80–96.

50. Dumaine, "Creating a New Company Culture."

51. R. Hallowell, D. Bowen, and C. Knoop, "Four Seasons Goes to Paris," *Academy of Management Executive* 16 (2002): 7–24.

52. Tichy and Sherman, *Control Your Destiny*.

53. C. Bernick, "When Your Culture Needs a Makeover."

54. The support of Julie Rubenstein in writing this application is gratefully acknowledged. In addition, the following references were consulted: K. Allers, "A New Banking Model: Washington Mutual is Using a Creative Retail Approach to Turn the Banking World Upside Down," *Fortune* (31 March 2003): 102; L. Mandaro, "Wamu Rallies the Troops, Literally," *American Banker* (11 November 2002): no page numbers; G. Anders, "7 Lessons from WaMu's Playbook," *Fast Company* 54 (January 2002): 102; L. Dobbs, "The Lou Dobbs Money Letter," *Premier Issue* (May 2003): 1–5; K. Killinger, "Middle-Market Mortgages . . . Then More," in *Investing Under Fire: Winning Strategies from the Masters for Bulls, Bears, and the Bewildered*, ed. A. Ackerman (New York: Bloomberg Press, 2003).

55. B. Hedberg, P. Nystrom, and W. Starbuck, "Camping on Seesaws: Prescriptions for a Self-Designing Organization," *Administrative Science Quarterly* 21 (1976): 41–65; K. Weick, "Organization Design: Organizations as Self-Designing Systems," *Organizational Dynamics* 6 (1977): 30–46.

56. S. Mohrman and T. Cummings, *Self-Designing Organizations: Learning How to Create High Performance* (Reading, Mass.: Addison-Wesley, 1989); Cummings and Mohrman, "Self-Designing Organizations."

57. P. Lawrence and D. Dyer, *Renewing American Industry* (New York: Free Press, 1983).

58. C. Argyris, R. Putnam, and D. Smith, *Action Science* (San Francisco: Jossey-Bass, 1985); C. Lundberg, "On Organizational Learning: Implications and Opportunities for Expanding Organizational Development," in *Research on Organizational Change and Development*, vol. 3, eds. R. Woodman and W. Pasmore (Greenwich, Conn.: JAI Press, 1989), 61–82; P. Senge, *The Fifth Discipline* (New York: Doubleday, 1990).

59. M. Weisbord, *Productive Workplaces* (San Francisco: Jossey-Bass, 1987); R. Freeman, *Strategic Management* (Boston: Ballinger, 1984).

60. Miller and Friesen, *Organizations*.

61. T. Lant, "Organization Learning: Creating, Retaining, and Transferring Knowledge," *Administrative Science Quarterly* (Winter, 2000): 622–43; M. Crossan, H. Lane, and R. White, "An Organizational Learning Framework: From Intuition to Institution," *Academy of Management Review* 24 (1999): 522–37; S. Prokesch, "Unleashing the Power of Learning: An Interview with British Petroleum's John Browne," *Harvard Business Review* (September-October 1997): 147–68; J.-C. Spender, "Making Knowledge the Basis of a Dynamic Theory of the Firm," *Strategic Management Journal* 17 (1996): 45–62; R. Strata, "Organizational Learning: The Key to Management Innovation," *Sloan Management Review* 30 (1989): 63–74.

62. D. Teece, "Capturing Value from Knowledge Assets: The New Economy, Market for Know-How, and Intangible Assets," *California Management Review* 40 (Spring 1998): 55–79.

63. C. Argyris and D. Schon, *Organizational Learning: A Theory of Action Perspective* (Reading, Mass.: Addison-Wesley, 1978); C. Argyris and D. Schon, *Organizational Learning II: Theory, Method, and Practice* (Reading, Mass.: Addison-Wesley, 1996); Senge, *Fifth Discipline*.

64. P. Adler and R. Cole, "Designed for Learning: A Tale of Two Auto Plants," *Sloan Management Review* 34 (1993): 85–94; S. Cook and D. Yanow, "Culture and Organizational Learning," *Journal of Management Inquiry* 2 (1993): 373–90; G. Huber, "The Nontraditional Quality of Organizational Learning," *Organization Science* 2 (1991): 88–115.

65. W. Snyder, "Organization Learning and Performance: An Exploration of the Linkages Between Organizational Learning, Knowledge, and Performance" (unpublished Ph.D. diss., University of Southern California, Los Angeles, 1996).

66. This framework draws heavily on the work of W. Snyder and T. Cummings, "Organization Learning Disorders: Conceptual Model and Intervention Hypotheses," *Human Relations* 51 (1998): 873–95.

67. D. Garvin, *Learning in Action* (Cambridge: Harvard Business School Press, 2000).

68. M. McGill, J. Slocum, and D. Lei, "Management Practices in Learning Organizations," *Organizational Dynamics* (Autumn 1993): 5–17; E. Nevis, A. DiBella, and J. Gould, "Understanding Organizations as Learning Systems," *Sloan Management Review* (Winter 1995): 73–85.

69. J. Dewey, *How We Think* (Boston: D.C. Heath, 1933).

70. Argyris and Schon, *Organizational Learning*; Argyris and Schon, *Organizational Learning II*; Senge, *Fifth Discipline*.

71. Argyris and Schon, *Organizational Learning II*; Senge, *Fifth Discipline*; P. Senge, C. Roberts, R. Ross, B. Smith, and A. Kleiner, *The Fifth Discipline Fieldbook: Strategies for Building a Learning Organization* (New York: Doubleday, 1995).

72. Argyris and Schon, *Organizational Learning II*.

73. Ibid.

74. Argyris and Schon, *Organizational Learning II*; C. Argyris, *Intervention Theory and Method* (Reading, Mass.: Addison-Wesley, 1970).

75. Senge, *Fifth Discipline*.

76. Argyris and Schon, *Organizational Learning II*.

77. Argyris and Schon, *Organizational Learning II*; Senge et al., *Fifth Discipline Fieldbook*; B. Dumaine, "Mr. Learning Organization," *Fortune* (17 October 1994): 147–57.

78. Senge et al., *Fifth Discipline Fieldbook*.

79. Argyris and Schon, *Organizational Learning II*; Argyris, *Intervention Theory and Method*.

80. Senge, *Fifth Discipline*.

81. Ibid.

82. M. Polanyi, *The Tacit Dimension* (New York: Doubleday, 1966); I. Nonaka and H. Takeuchi, *The Knowledge-Creating Company: How Japanese Companies Foster Creativity and Innovation for Competitive Advantage* (New York: Oxford University Press, 1995).

83. M. Sarvary, "Knowledge Management and Competition in the Consulting Industry" *California Management Review* 41 (1999): 95–107; J. Barney, "Looking Inside for Competitive Advantage," *Academy of Management Executive* 9 (4, 1995): 49–61; M. Peteraf, "The Cornerstones of Competitive Advantage," *Strategic Management Journal* 14, 3 (1993): 179–92; Worley, Hitchin, and Ross, *Integrated Strategic Change*.

84. Snyder, "Organization Learning."

85. D. Leonard-Barton, *Wellsprings of Knowledge: Building and Sustaining the Sources of Innovation* (Boston: Harvard Business School Press, 1995); Nonaka and Takeuchi, *Knowledge Creating*.

86. C. Prahalad and G. Hamel, "The Core Competencies of the Corporation," *Harvard Business Review* 68 (1990): 79–91.

87. H. Itami, *Mobilizing for Invisible Assets* (Cambridge, Mass.: Harvard University Press, 1987).

88. L. Edvinsson and M. Malone, *Intellectual Capital: Realizing Your Company's True Value by Finding Its Hidden Brainpower* (New York: Harper Business, 1997); T. Stewart, *Intellectual Capital: The New Wealth of Organizations* (New York: Doubleday, 1997); J. Nahapiet and S. Ghoshal, "Social Capital, Intellectual Capital, and the Organizational Advantage," *Academy of Management Review* 23 (1998): 242–66.

89. Edvinsson and Malone, *Intellectual Capital*; Stewart, *Intellectual Capital*; R. Kaplan and D. Norton, *The Balanced Scorecard* (Boston: Harvard Business School Press, 1996); K. Svieby, *The New Organizational Wealth: Managing and Measuring Knowledge-Based Assets* (San Francisco: Berrett-Koehler, 1977).

90. Edvinsson and Malone, *Intellectual Capital*; C. Handy, *The Age of Unreason* (Boston: Harvard Business School Press, 1991).

91. T. Stewart, "Intellectual Capital," *Fortune* (3 October 1994): 68–74.

92. V. Anand, C. Manz, and W. Glick, "An Organizational Memory Approach to Information Management," *Academy of Management Review* 23 (1998): 796–809.

93. E. Wenger, *Communities of Practice: Learning, Meaning, and Identity* (Cambridge, Eng.: Cambridge University Press, 1999); J. Brown and P. Duguid, "Organizational Learning and Communities of Practice: Towards a Unified View of Working, Learning, and Innovation," *Organization Science* 2 (1991): 40–57.

94. Leonard-Barton, *Wellsprings of Knowledge*; D. Leonard-Barton and S. Sensiper, "The Role of Tacit Knowledge in Group Innovation," *California Management Review* 40 (Spring 1998): 112–32.

95. M. Hansen, N. Nohria, and T. Tierney, "What's Your Strategy for Managing Knowledge?" *Harvard Business Review* (March–April 1999): 106–16.

96. T. Davenport and L. Prusak, *Working Knowledge: How Organizations Manage What They Know* (Boston: Harvard Business School Press, 1998).

97. C. O'Dell and C. Grayson, *If Only We Knew What We Know* (New York: Free Press, 1998).

98. D. Garvin and A. March, *A Note on Knowledge Management* (Boston: Harvard Business School Publishing, 1997).

99. O'Dell and Grayson, *If Only We Knew*.

100. Ibid.

101. Prokesch, "Unleashing the Power"; T. Stewart, "Telling Tales at BP Amoco," *Fortune* (7 June 1999): 220–24.

102. E. Boyle, "A Critical Appraisal of the Performance of Royal Dutch Shell as a Learning Organization in the 1990's," *The Learning Organization* 9 (2002): 6–18.

103. Argyris and Schon, *Organizational Learning II*, 112.

104. R. Ruggles, "The State of the Notion: Knowledge Management in Practice," *California Management Review* 40 (Spring 1998): 80–89.

105. Davenport and Prusak, *Working Knowledge*.

106. O'Dell and Grayson, *If Only We Knew*.

Rondell Data Corporation

"Goddamn it, he's done it again!" Frank Forbus threw the stack of prints and specifications on his desk in disgust. The Model 802 wide-band modulator, released for production the previous Thursday, had just come back to Frank's engineering services department with a caustic note that began, "This one can't be produced, either. . . . " It was the fourth time production had returned the design.

Forbus, director of engineering for the Rondell Data Corporation, was normally a quiet person. But the Model 802 was stretching his patience; it was beginning to appear like other new products that had hit delays and problems in the transition from design to production during the eight months Frank had worked for Rondell. These problems were nothing new at the sprawling, old Rondell factory. Frank's predecessor in the engineering job had run afoul of them, too, and had finally been fired for protesting too vehemently about the other departments. But the Model 802 should have been different. Frank had met two months earlier (on July 3, 1988) with the firm's president, Bill Hunt, and with the factory superintendent, Dave Schwab, to smooth the way for the new modulator design. He thought back to the meeting . . .

"Now, we all know there's a tight deadline on the 802," Bill Hunt said, "and Frank's done well to ask us to talk about its introduction. I'm counting on both of you to find any snags in the system, and to work together to get that first production run out by October 2. Can you do it?"

"We can do it in production if we get a clean design two weeks from now, as scheduled," answered Dave Schwab, the grizzled factory superintendent. "Frank and I have already talked about that, of course. I'm setting aside time in the card room and the machine shop, and we'll be ready. If the design goes over schedule, though, I'll have to fill in with other runs, and it will cost us a bundle to break in for the 802. How does it look in engineering, Frank?"

"I've just reviewed the design for the second time," Frank replied. "If Ron Porter can keep the salespeople out of our hair, and avoid any more last-minute changes, we've got a shot. I've pulled the draftspersons off of three other overdue jobs to get this one out. But, Dave, that means we can't spring engineers loose to confer with your production people on manufacturing problems."

"Well Frank, most of those problems are caused by the engineers, and we need them to resolve the difficulties. We've all agreed that production bugs come from both of us bowing to sales pressure, and putting equipment into production before the designs are really ready. That's just what we're trying to avoid on the 802. But I can't have five hundred people sitting on their hands waiting for an answer from your people. We'll have to have *some* engineering support."

Bill Hunt broke in, "So long as you two can talk calmly about the problem I'm confident you can resolve it. What a relief it is, Frank, to hear the way you're approaching this. With Kilmann [the previous director of engineering], this conversation would have been a shouting match. Right, Dave?" Dave nodded and smiled.

"Now there's one other thing you should both be aware of," Hunt continued. "Doc Reeves and I talked last night about a new filtering technique, one that might improve the signal-to-noise ratio of the 802 by a factor of two. There's a chance Doc can come up with it before the 802 reaches production, and if it's possible, I'd like to use the new filters. That would give us a real jump on the competition."

Four days after that meeting, Frank found that two of his key people on the 802 design had been called to production for an emergency consultation about a problem in final assembly: Two halves of a new data transmission interface wouldn't fit together, because recent changes in the front end required a different chassis design for the rear end.

One week later, Doc Reeves proudly walked into Frank's office with the new filter design. "This won't affect the other modules of the 802 much," Doc had said. "Look, it takes three new cards, a few connectors, some changes in the wiring harness, and some new shielding, and that's all."

Frank had tried to resist the last-minute design changes, but Bill Hunt had stood firm. With considerable overtime by the engineers and draftspersons, engineering services should still be able to finish the prints in time.

Two engineers and three draftspersons went onto twelve-hour days to get the 802 ready, but the prints were still five days late reaching Dave Schwab. Two days later, the prints came back to Frank, heavily annotated in red. Schwab had worked all day Saturday to review the job and had found more than a dozen discrepancies in the prints—most of them caused by the new filter design and insufficient checking time before release. Correction of these design faults gave rise to a new generation of discrepancies; Schwab's cover note on the second return of the prints indicated that he had had to release the machine capacity reserved for the 802. On the third iteration, Schwab committed his photo and plating capacity to another rush job. The 802 would be at least one month late getting into production. Ron Porter, the vice president for sales, was furious. His customer needed one hundred units *now*. Rondell was the customer's only late supplier.

"Here we go again," thought Forbus.

COMPANY HISTORY

Rondell Data Corporation traced its lineage through several generations of electronics technology. Its founder, Bob Rondell, launched the firm in 1930 as Rondell Equipment Company to manufacture several electrical testing devices he had invented as an engineering faculty member at a large university. The firm entered radio broadcasting equipment in 1957 and data transmission equipment in the early 1960s. A well-established corps of direct sales representatives, mostly engineers, called on industrial, scientific, and government accounts but concentrated heavily on original equipment manufacturers. In this market, Rondell had a long-standing reputation as a source of high-quality, innovative designs. The firm's salespeople fed a continual stream of challenging problems into the engineering department, where the creative genius of Doc Reeves and several dozen other engineers "converted problems to solutions" (as the sales brochure bragged). Product design formed the spearhead of Rondell's growth.

By 1988, Rondell offered a wide range of products in its two major lines. Broadcast equipment sales had benefited from the growth of UHF television and FM radio; it now accounted for 35 percent of company sales. Data transmission had blossomed and, in its field, an increasing number of orders called for unique specifications, ranging from specialized display panels to entirely untried designs.

The company had grown from one hundred employees in 1957 to more than eight hundred in 1988. (Exhibits 1 and 2 show the current organization chart and the backgrounds of key employees.) Bill Hunt, who had been a student of the company's founder, had presided over most of that growth and took great pride in preserving the family spirit of the old organization. Informal relationships between Rondell's veteran employees formed the backbone of the firm's day-to-day operations. All managers relied on personal contact, and Hunt often insisted that the absence of bureaucratic red tape was a key factor in recruiting outstanding engineering talent. The personal management approach extended throughout the factory. All exempt employees were paid a straight salary and a share of the profits. Rondell boasted an extremely loyal group of senior employees, and very low turnover in nearly all areas of the company.

The highest-turnover job in the firm was director of engineering services. Forbus had joined Rondell in January 1988, replacing Jim Kilmann, who had lasted only ten months. Kilmann, in turn, had replaced Tom MacLeod, a talented engineer who had made a promising start but had taken to drinking after a year in the job. MacLeod's predecessor had been a genial old timer, who retired at seventy, after thirty years in charge of engineering. (Doc Reeves had refused the directorship in each of the recent changes, saying, "Hell, that's no promotion for a bench man like me. I'm no administrator.")

For several years, the firm had experienced a steadily increasing number of disputes between research, engineering, sales, and production people. Disputes generally centered on the problem of new-product introduction. Quarrels between departments became more numerous under MacLeod, Kilmann, and Forbus. Some managers associated these disputes with the company's recent decline in profitability—a decline that, despite higher sales and gross revenues, was beginning to bother people in 1987. Hunt commented:

> Better cooperation, I'm sure, could increase our output by 5 to 10 percent. I'd hoped Kilmann could solve the problems, but pretty obviously he was too young—too arrogant.

Exhibit I   Rondell Data Corporation—Organizational Chart, 1978

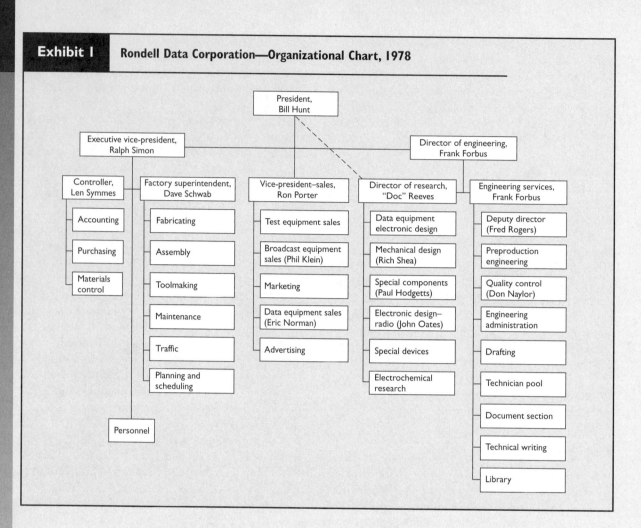

People like him—that conflict type of personality—bother me. I don't like strife, and with him it seemed I spent all my time smoothing out arguments. Kilmann tried to tell everyone else how to run their departments, without having his own house in order. That approach just wouldn't work here at Rondell. Frank Forbus, now, seems much more in tune with our style of organization. I'm really hopeful now.

Still, we have just as many problems now as we did last year. Maybe even more. I hope Frank can get a handle on engineering services soon.

ENGINEERING DEPARTMENT: RESEARCH

According to the organization chart, Forbus was in charge of both research (the product development function) and engineering services (engineering support). To Forbus, however, the relationship with research was not so clear-cut:

Doc Reeves is one of the world's unique people, and none of us would have it any other way. He's a creative genius. Sure, the chart says he works for me, but we all know Doc does his own thing. He's not the least bit interested in management routines, and I can't count on him to take any responsibility in scheduling projects, or checking budgets, or what-have-you. But as long as Doc is director of research, you can bet this company will keep on leading the field. He has more ideas per hour than most people have per year, and he keeps the whole engineering staff fired up. Everybody loves Doc—and you can count me in on that, too. In a way, he works for me, sure. But that's not what's important.

Doc Reeves—unhurried, contemplative, casual, and candid—tipped his stool back against the wall of his research cubicle and talked about what *was* important:

Exhibit 2   **Background of Selected Executives**

EXECUTIVE	POSITION	AGE	BACKGROUND
Bill Hunt	President	63	Engineering graduate of an Ivy League college. Joined the company in 1946 as an engineer. Worked exclusively on development for over a year and then split his time between development and field sales work until he became assistant to the president in 1956. Became president in 1960. Together, Hunt and Simon hold enough stock to command effective control of the company.
Ralph Simon	Executive vice president	65	Joined company in 1945 as a traveling representative. In 1947 became Rondell's leading salesperson for broadcast equipment. In 1954 was made treasurer but continued to spend time selling. In 1960 was appointed executive vice president with direct responsibility for financial matters and production.
Ron Porter	Vice president of sales	50	BS in engineering. Joined the company in 1957 as a salesperson. Was influential in establishing the data transmission product line and did early selling himself. In 1967 was made sales manager. Extensive contacts in trade associations and industrial shows. Appointed vice president of sales in 1974.
Dave Schwab	Production manager	62	Trade school graduate; veteran of both World War II and Korean War. Joined Rondell in 1955. Promoted to production manager seven months later after exposure of widespread irregularities in production and control deparatments. Reorganized production department and brought a new group of production specialists to the company.
Frank Forbus	Director of engineering	40	Master's degree in engineering. Previously division director of engineering in large industrial firm. Joined the company in 1977 as director of engineering, replacing an employee who had been dismissed because of an inability to work with sales and production personnel. As director of engineering, had administrative responsibility for research personnel and complete responsibility for engineering services.
Ed Reeves	Director of research	47	Joined Rondell in 1960. Worked directly with Hunt to develop major innovations in data transmission equipment. Appointed director of research in 1967.
Les Symmes	Controller	43	Joined company in 1955 while attending business college. Held several jobs, including production scheduling, accounting and cost control. Named controller in 1972.

Development engineering. That's where the company's future rests. Either we have it there, or we don't have it.

There's no kidding ourselves that we're anything but a bunch of Rube Goldbergs here. But that's where the biggest kicks come from—from solving development problems and dreaming up new ways of doing things. That's why I so look forward to the special contracts we get involved in. We accept them not for the revenue they represent but be-cause they subsidize the basic development work that goes into all our basic products.

This is a fantastic place to work. I have a great crew and they can really deliver when the chips are down. Why, Bill Hunt and I [he gestured toward the neighboring cubicle, where the president's name hung over the door] are likely to find as many people here at work at 10 P.M. as at 3 P.M. The important thing here is the relationships between people; they're based on mutual respect, not on policies and procedures. Administrative red tape is a pain. It takes away from development time.

Problems? Sure, there are problems now and then. There are power interests in production, where they sometimes resist change. But I'm not a fighting man, you know. I suppose if I were, I might go in there and push my weight around a little. But I'm an engineer, and can do more for Rondell sitting right here, or working with my own people. That's what brings results.

Other members of the research department echoed these views and added additional sources of satisfaction from their work. They were proud of the personal contacts built with customers' technical staffs—contacts that increasingly involved travel to the customers' factories to serve as expert advisors in preparation of overall system design specifications. The engineers were also delighted with the department's encouragement of their personal development, continuing education, and independence on the job.

But there were problems, too. Rich Shea, of the mechanical design section, noted:

In the old days I really enjoyed the work— and the people I worked with. But now there's a lot of irritation. I don't like someone breathing down my neck. You can be hurried into jeopardizing the design.

John Oates, head of the radio electronic design section, was another designer with definite views:

Production engineering is almost nonexistent in this company. Very little is done by the preproduction section in engineering services. Frank Forbus has been trying to get preproduction into the picture, but he won't succeed because you can't start from such an ambiguous position. There have been three directors of engineering in three years. Frank can't hold his own against the others in the company. Kilmann was too aggressive. Perhaps no amount of tact would have succeeded.

Paul Hodgetts was head of special components of the R&D department. Like the rest of the department, he valued bench work. But he complained of engineering services:

The services don't do things we want them to do. Instead, they tell *us* what they're going to do. I should probably go to Frank, but I don't get any decisions there. I know I should

go through Frank, but this holds things up, so I often go direct.

ENGINEERING SERVICES DEPARTMENT

The engineering services department (ESD) provided ancillary services to R&D and served as liaison between engineering and the other Rondell departments. Among its main functions were drafting, management of the central technicians' pool, scheduling and expediting engineering products, documentation and publication of parts lists and engineering orders, preproduction engineering (consisting of the final integration of individual design components into mechanically compatible packages), and quality control (including inspection of incoming parts and materials, and final inspection of subassemblies and finished equipment). Top management's description of the department included the line, "ESD is responsible for maintaining cooperation with other departments, providing services to the development engineers, and freeing more valuable people in R&D from essential activities that are diversions from and beneath their main competence."

Many of the seventy-five ESD employees were located in other departments. Quality control people were scattered through the manufacturing and receiving areas, and technicians worked primarily in the research area or the prototype fabrication room. The remaining ESD personnel were assigned to leftover nooks and crannies near production or engineering sections. Forbus described his position:

My biggest problem is getting acceptance from the people I work with. I've moved slowly rather than risk antagonism. I saw what happened to Kilmann, and I want to avoid that. But although his precipitate action had won over a few of the younger R&D people, he certainly didn't have the department's backing. Of course, it was the resentment of other departments that eventually caused his discharge. People have been slow accepting me here. There's nothing really overt, but I get a negative reaction to my ideas.

My role in the company has never been well-defined, really. It's complicated by Doc's unique position, of course, and also by the fact that ESD sort of grew by itself over the years, as the design engineers concentrated more and more on the creative parts of product development. I wish I could be more involved in the technical side. That's been my training, and it's a lot of fun. But in our setup, the technical side is the least necessary for me to be involved in.

Schwab is hard to get along with. Before I came and after Kilmann left, there were six months when no one was really doing any scheduling. No workloads were figured, and unrealistic promises were made about releases. This puts us in an awkward position. We've been scheduling way beyond our capacity to manufacture or engineer.

Certain people within R&D, for instance John Oates, understand scheduling well and meet project deadlines, but this is not generally true of the rest of the R&D department, especially the mechanical engineers, who won't commit themselves. Most of the complaints come from sales and production department heads because items, such as the 802, are going to production before they are fully developed, under pressure from sales to get out the unit, and this snags the whole process. Somehow, engineering services should be able to intervene and resolve these complaints, but I haven't made much headway so far.

I should be able to go to Hunt for help, but he's too busy most of the time, and his major interest is the design side of engineering, where he got his own start. Sometimes he talks as though he's the engineering director as well as president. I have to put my foot down; there are problems here that the front office just doesn't understand.

Salespeople were often observed taking their problems directly to designers, while production frequently threw designs back at R&D, claiming they could not be produced and demanding the prompt attention of particular design engineers. The latter were frequently observed in conference with production supervisors on the assembly floor. Frank continued:

The designers seem to feel they're losing something when one of us tries to help. They feel it's a reflection on them to have someone take over what they've been doing. They seem to want to carry a project right through to the final stages, particularly the mechanical people. Consequently, engineering services people are used below their capacity to contribute, and our department is denied functions it should be performing. There's not as much use made of engineering services as there should be.

An ESD technician supervisor added his comments:

Production picks out the engineer who'll be the "bum of the month." They pick on every little detail instead of using their heads and making the minor changes that have to be made. The people with fifteen to twenty years of experience shouldn't have to prove their ability anymore, but they spend four hours defending themselves and four hours getting the job done. I have no one to go to when I need help. Frank Forbus is afraid. I'm trying to help him but he can't help me at this time. I'm responsible for fifty people and I've got to support them.

Fred Rodgers, whom Forbus had brought with him to the company as an assistant, gave another view of the situation:

I try to get our people in preproduction to take responsibility but they're not used to it, and people in other departments don't usually see them as best qualified to solve the problem. There's a real barrier for a newcomer here. Gaining people's confidence is hard. More and more, I'm wondering whether there really is a job for me here. [Rodgers left Rondell a month later.]

Another subordinate of Forbus gave his view:

If Doc gets a new product idea, you can't argue. But he's too optimistic. He judges that others can do what he does—but there's only one Doc Reeves. We've had nine hundred production change orders this year—they changed two thousand five hundred drawings. If I were in Frank's shoes, I'd put my foot down on all this new development. I'd look at the reworking we're doing and get production set up the way I wanted it. Kilmann was fired when he was doing a good job. He was getting some system in the company's operations. Of course, it hurt some people. There is no denying that Doc is the most important person in the company. What gets overlooked is that Hunt is a close second, not just politically but in terms of what he contributes technically and in customer relations.

This subordinate explained that he sometimes went out into the production department but that Schwab, the production head, resented this. Production personnel said that Kilmann had failed to show respect for oldtimers and was always meddling in other departments' business. This was the reason for his being fired, they contended. Don Taylor, in charge of quality control, commented:

> I am now much more concerned with administration and less with work. It is one of the evils you get into. There is tremendous detail in this job. I listen to everyone's opinion. Everybody is important. There shouldn't be distinctions—distinctions between people. I'm not sure whether Frank has to be a fireball like Kilmann. I think the real question is whether Frank is getting the job done. I know my job is essential—I want to supply service to the more talented people and give them information so they can do their jobs better.

SALES DEPARTMENT

Ron Porter was angry. His job was supposed to be selling, but instead it had turned into settling disputes inside the plant and making excuses to waiting customers. He jabbed a finger toward his desk:

> You see that telephone? I'm actually afraid nowadays to hear it ring. Three times out of five, it will be a customer who's hurting because we've failed to deliver on schedule. The other two calls will be from production or ESD, telling me some schedule has slipped again.
>
> The Model 802 is typical. Absolutely typical. We padded the delivery date by six weeks to allow for contingencies. Within two months, the slack had evaporated. Now it looks like we'll be lucky to ship it before Christmas. [It was now November 28.] We're *ruining* our reputation in the market. Why, just last week one of our best customers—people we've worked with for fifteen years—tried to hang a penalty clause on their latest order.
>
> We shouldn't have to be after the engineers all the time. They should be able to see what problems they create without our telling them.

Phil Klein, head of broadcast sales under Porter, noted that many sales decisions were made by top management. He thought that sales was understaffed and had never really been able to get on top of the job:

> We have grown further and further away from engineering. The director of engineering does not pass on the information that we give him. We need better relationships there. It is very difficult for us to talk to customers about

development problems without technical help. We need each other. The whole of engineering is now too isolated from the outside world. The morale of ESD is very low. They're in a bad spot—they're not well-organized.

> People don't take much to outsiders here. Much of this is because the expectation is built by top management that jobs will be filled from the bottom. So it's really tough when an outsider like Frank comes in.

Eric Norman, order and pricing coordinator for data equipment, talked about his relationships with the production department:

> Actually, I get along with them fairly well. Oh, things could be better, of course, if they were more cooperative generally. They always seem to say, "It's my bat and my ball, and we're playing by my rules." People are afraid to make production mad; there's a lot of power in there.
>
> But you've got to understand that production has its own set of problems. And nobody in Rondell is working any harder than Dave Schwab to try to straighten things out.

PRODUCTION DEPARTMENT

Schwab had joined Rondell just after the Korean War, in which he had seen combat duty at the Yalu River and intelligence duty at Pyong Yang. Both experiences had been useful in his first year of civilian employment at Rondell. The wartime factory superintendent and several middle managers had apparently been engaging in highly questionable side deals with Rondell's suppliers. Schwab gathered the evidence, revealed the situation to Hunt, and had stood by the president in the ensuing unsavory situation. Seven months after joining the company, Schwab was named factory superintendent.

Schwab's first move had been to replace the fallen managers with a new team from outside the corporation. This group did not share the traditional Rondell emphasis on informality and friendly personal relationships and had worked long and hard to install systematic manufacturing methods and procedures. Before the reorganization, production had controlled purchasing, stock control, and final quality control (where final assembly of products in cabinets was accomplished). Because of the wartime events, management decided on a checks-and-balance system of organization and removed these three departments from production jurisdiction. The new production managers felt they had been unjustly penalized by this reorganization, particularly since they had uncovered the behavior that was detrimental to the company in the first place.

By 1988, the production department had grown to five hundred employees, of whom 60 percent worked in the assembly area—an unusually pleasant environment that had been commended by *Factory* magazine for its colorful decoration, cleanliness, and low noise level. Another 30 percent of the workforce, mostly skilled machinists, staffed the finishing and fabrication department. The remaining employees performed scheduling, supervisory, and maintenance duties. Production workers were not union members, were paid by the hour, and participated in both the liberal profit-sharing program and the stock purchase plan. Morale in production was traditionally high, and turnover was extremely low.

Schwab commented:

To be efficient, production has to be a self-contained department. We have to control what comes into the department and what goes out. That's why purchasing, inventory control, and quality ought to run out of this office. We'd eliminate a lot of problems with better control there. Why, even Don Naylor of QC, would rather work for me than for ESD; he's said so himself. We understand his problems better.

The other departments should be self-contained, too. That's why I always avoid the underlings, and go straight to the department heads with any questions. I always go down the line.

I have to protect my people from outside disturbances. Look what would happen if I let unfinished, half-baked designs in here—there'd be chaos. The bugs have to be found before the drawings go into the shop, and it seems I'm the one who has to find them. Look at the 802, for example. [Dave had spent most of Thanksgiving Day (it was now November 28) red-pencilling the latest set of prints.] ESD should have found every one of those discrepancies. They just don't check drawings properly. They change most of the things I flag, but then they fail to trace through the impact of those changes on the rest of the design. I shouldn't have to do that.

And those engineers are tolerance crazy. They want everything to a millionth of an inch. I'm the only one in the company who's had any experience with actually machining

things to a millionth of an inch. We make sure that the things that engineers say on their drawings actually have to be that way and whether they're obtainable from the kind of raw material we buy.

That shouldn't be production's responsibility, but I have to do it. Accepting bad prints wouldn't let us ship the order any quicker. We'd only make a lot of junk that had to be reworked. And that would take even longer.

This way, I get to be known as the bad guy, but I guess that's just part of the job. [Schwab paused and smiled wryly.] Of course, what really gets them is that I don't even have a degree.

Schwab had fewer bones to pick with the sales department, because he said that they trusted him:

When *we* give Ron Porter a shipping date, he knows the equipment will be shipped *then*.

You've got to recognize, though, that all of our new-product problems stem from sales making absurd commitments on equipment that hasn't been fully developed. That *always* means trouble. Unfortunately, Hunt always backs sales up, even when they're wrong. He always favors them over us.

Ralph Simon, executive vice president of the company, had direct responsibility for Rondell's production department. He said:

There shouldn't really be a dividing of departments among top management in the company. The president should be czar over all. The production people ask me to do something for them, and I really can't do it. It creates bad feelings between engineering and production, this special attention that they [R&D] get from Bill. But then Hunt likes to dabble in design. Schwab feels that production is treated like a poor relation.

EXECUTIVE COMMITTEE

At the executive committee meeting of December 6, it was duly recorded that Schwab had accepted the prints and specifications for the Model 802 modulator and had set December 29 as the shipping date for the first ten pieces. Hunt, as chairperson, shook his head and changed the subject quickly when Forbus tried to initiate discussion of interdepartmental coordination.

The executive committee itself was a brainchild of Rondell's controller, Len Symmes, who was well aware of the disputes that plagued the company. Symmes had convinced Hunt and Simon to meet every two weeks with their department heads; the meetings were formalized with Hunt, Simon, Porter, Schwab, Forbus, Reeves, Symmes, and the personnel director attending. Symmes explained his intent and the results:

> Doing things collectively and informally just doesn't work as well as it used to. Things have been gradually getting worse for at least two years now. We had to start thinking in terms of formal organization relationships. I did the first organization chart, and the executive committee was my idea, too—but neither idea is contributing much help, I'm afraid. It takes top management to make an organization click. The rest of us can't act much differently until the top people see the need for us to change.

> I had hoped the committee especially would help get the department managers into a constructive planning process. It hasn't worked out that way, because Mr. Hunt really doesn't see the need for it. He uses the meetings as a place to pass on routine information.

MERRY CHRISTMAS

"Frank, I didn't know whether to tell you now, or after the holiday." It was December 22, and Forbus was standing awkwardly in front of Hunt's desk.

"But I figured you'd work right through Christmas Day if we didn't have this talk, and that just wouldn't have been fair to you. I can't understand why we have such poor luck in the engineering director's job lately. And I don't think it's entirely your fault. But . . ."

Frank heard only half of Hunt's words, and said nothing in response. He'd be paid through February 28. . . . He should use the time for searching. . . . Hunt would help all he could. . . . Jim Kilmann was supposed to be doing well at his own new job, and might need more help.

Frank cleaned out his desk and numbly started home. The electronic carillon near his house was playing a Christmas carol. Frank thought again of Hunt's rationale: conflict still plagued Rondell— and Frank had not made it go away. Maybe somebody else could do it.

"And what did Santa Claus bring you, Frankie?" he asked himself. "The sack. Only the empty sack."

Questions

1. What is your diagnosis of the strategy and organization design at Rondell? How well does Rondell's strategic orientation fit with its external environment?

2. How would you work with Bill Hunt and the executive committee to bring about strategic change at Rondell?

Source: Reprinted with permission. Copyright © 1981 by John A. Seeger, Professor of Management at Bentley College, Waltham, Mass.

Fourwinds Marina

Jack Keltner had just completed his first day as general manager of the Fourwinds Marina. It was mid-August and though the marina slip rentals ran until October 30, business always took a dramatic downturn after Labor Day. It would be unwise to change any of the current operations in the next three weeks, but he would have to move swiftly to implement some of the changes he had been considering, and at the same time would have the better part of a year to develop and implement some short-range and long-range plans that were sorely needed if the marina was to survive.

The day before, Jack had been called in by Sandy Taggart, president of the Taggart Corporation, owners of the Fourwinds Marina and the Inn of the Fourwinds. Leon McLaughlin had just submitted his resignation as general manager of the marina. McLaughlin and Taggart had disagreed on some compensation McLaughlin felt was due him. Part of the disagreement concerned McLaughlin's wife, who had been hired to work in the parts department but had spent little time there due to an illness.

McLaughlin had been the fifth manager in as many years that the marina had been in operation. He had fifteen years of marine experience before being hired to manage the marina. His experience, however, consisted of selling and servicing boats and motors in Evansville, Indiana, not in marina management. He took pride in running a "tight ship" and felt that the marina had an excellent chance to turn around after some hard times. It was fairly easy to keep the marina staffed because the resort atmosphere was so attractive, and his goal was to have the majority of the staff on a full-time basis year-round. Even though the marina is closed from November until April there is a considerable amount of repair work on boats needed during those months. McLaughlin was told when hired that he had a blank check to get the marina shaped up. This open policy, however, was later rescinded. He and his wife have a mobile home near the marina, but maintain a permanent residence in Evansville. For the most part he put in six full days a week, but had an aversion to working on Sunday. McLaughlin was an effective organizer, but weak in the area of employee and customer relations.

Keltner had no experience in marina management, but was considered a hard worker willing to take on tremendous challenges. He had joined the Taggart Corporation after four years as a CPA for Ernst and Ernst, an accounting firm. Functioning as controller of the corporation, he found that there was a tremendous volume of work demanded, necessitating late hours at the office and a briefcase full of work to take home with him most evenings. At this point, Keltner lived in a small community near the marina, but still had to commute frequently to the home office of the Taggart Corporation in Indianapolis, an hour and a half drive from Lake Monroe. He had indicated that he hoped to move the offices to Lake Monroe, site of the marina and inn, as soon as possible. Handling the accounting for the marina, the inn, and the other Taggart Corporation interests could be done effectively at the marina. The inn and the marina comprise 90 percent of the corporation.

Much of the explanation for the heavy workload lay in the fact that there had been virtually no accounting system when he first joined Taggart. He had, however, set up six profit centers for the marina and generated monthly accounting reports.

The other principal investors involved in the Taggart Corporation besides Sandy (A. L. Taggart III) were William Brennan, president of one of the state's largest commercial and industrial real estate firms, and Richard DeMars, president of Guepel-DeMars, Inc., the firm that designed both the marina and the inn.

Sandy Taggart is a well-known Indianapolis businessman who is Chairman of the Board of Colonial Baking Company. This organization is one of the larger bakeries serving the Indianapolis metropolitan area and surrounding counties. He did his undergraduate work at Princeton and completed Harvard's A.M.P. program in 1967. He is an easygoing man and appears not to let problems upset him easily. He maintains his office at the Taggart Corporation in Indianapolis, but tries to get to the marina at least once every week. He kept in daily contact with Leon McLaughlin, and continues to do the same with Keltner. He enjoys being a part of the daily decision making and problem solving that goes on at the marina and feels that he needs to be aware of all decisions due to their weak financial position. Taggart feels current problems stem from a lack of knowledge of the marina business and lack of experienced general managers when they began operation some six years ago. He also admits that their lack of expertise in maintaining accurate cost data and controlling their costs hurt them, but feels Keltner has already gone a long way in correcting this problem.

Keltner has been intimately involved in the operation and feels that at a minimum the following changes should be made over the next twelve-month period.

1. Add eighty slips on E, F, and G docks and put in underwater supports on these docks to deter breakage from storms. Cost $250–300,000. Annual profits if all slips are rented: $75,000+.

2. Add a second employee to assist the present secretary-receptionist bookkeeper. This will actually be a savings if the Indianapolis office is closed. Savings: $300+/month.

3. Reorganize the parts department and put in a new inventory system. Cost: $3,000. Savings: $2,500–3,000/year.

4. Keep the boat and motor inventory low. Boat inventory as of mid-August is approximately $125,000. It has been over $300,000.

5. Reduce the workforce through attrition if a vacated job can be assumed by someone remaining on the staff.

6. Use E, F, and G for winter storage with the improved and more extensive bubbling system. Profits to be generated are difficult to estimate.

7. Light and heat the storage building so repair work can be done at night and in the winter. Cost will be $12,000, which he estimates probably would be paid for from the profits in two winters.

Each of these changes would add to the effectiveness and profitability of the marina operation, and that was his prime concern. The operation of the inn was under the control of another general manager, and functioned as a separate corporate entity. Keltner was responsible only for the accounting procedures of the inn.

As he reviewed the structure, background, and development of the inn and the marina, he realized the problems that faced him in his new role of general manager—and at the same time controller of Taggart Corporation. Managing the marina was a full-time, seven-day-a-week job, particularly during the season. The questions uppermost in his mind were 1) what would be the full plan he would present to Taggart for the effective, efficient, and profitable operation of the marina, and 2) how would it be funded? The financial statements presented a fairly glum picture, but he had the available backup data to analyze for income per square foot on most of the operations, payroll data, etc., as well as the knowledge he had gleaned working with the past general managers and observing the operation of the marina. (See Exhibits 3, 4, and 5 for the organizational structure and financial statements of the marina.)

BACKGROUND DATA ON FOURWINDS MARINA

The Setting

The Fourwinds Marina and the Inn of the Fourwinds are located on Lake Monroe, a manmade reservoir over ten thousand acres in size nestled in the hills of southern Indiana. Both facilities are owned and operated by the Taggart Corporation, but are operated as totally distinct and separate facilities. They cooperate in promoting business for each other.

The inn occupies some 71,000 square feet on 30 acres of land. It is designed to blend into the beautifully wooded landscape and is constructed of rustic and natural building materials. It is designed to appeal to a broad segment of the population with rooms priced from $21 to $33 for a double room. The inn is comprised of 150 sleeping rooms, singles, doubles, and suites, and has meeting rooms to appeal to the convention and sales meetings clientele. The largest meeting room will seat 300 for dining and 350 for conferences. Recreation facilities include an indoor-outdoor swimming pool, tennis courts, sauna, whirlpool bath, a recreation room with pool tables, and other games. Additional facilities include two dining rooms and a cocktail lounge. The inn is open year-round with heavy seasonal business in the summer months.

It is the first lodge of its nature built on state property by private funds. By virtue of the size of its food service facilities (in excess of $100,000 per annum) it qualifies under Indiana State Law for a license to serve alcoholic beverages on Sunday.

A brief description of the Pointe is also in order as its development promises a substantial boost to the marina's business. The Pointe, located three miles from the marina, consists of 384 acres on the lake. It is a luxury condominium development designed to meet the housing needs of primary and secondary home buyers. Currently seventy units are under construction. Twenty of these have been sold and the down-payment has been received on eighty more. These condominiums range from $25,000 to $90,000, with an average price of $60,000. Approval has been secured for the construction of 1,900 living units over a seven-year period. The development has a completed eighteen-hole golf course. Swimming pools and tennis courts are now under construction. The Pointe is a multimillion-dollar development by Indun Realty, Inc., Lake Monroe Corporation, and Reywood, Inc. Indun Realty is a wholly owned subsidiary of Indiana National Corp., parent firm of Indiana National Bank, the state's largest fiduciary institution.

The Fourwinds Marina occupies four acres of land and is one of the most extensive and complete marinas of its type in the United States. It is comprised of the boat docks, a sales room for boats and marine equipment, an indoor boat storage facility, and marine repair shop (see Exhibit 1).

There are seven docks projecting out from a main connecting dock that runs parallel to the shore line. The seven parallel docks extend out from 330 to 600 feet into the lake at a right angle to the connecting dock. The center dock houses a large building containing a grocery store, snack bar, and restrooms and a section of docks used as mooring for rental boats.

At the end of the dock is an office for boat rental, five gasoline pumps, and pumping facilities for removing waste from the houseboats and larger cruisers.

The three docks to the right of the center dock (facing toward the lake) are docks A, B, and C and are designed for mooring smaller boats—runabouts, fishing boats, etc. A bait shop is on A dock. A, B, and C slips are not always fully rented. The three docks to the left are the prime slips (E, F, G) and are designed for berthing houseboats, large cruisers, etc.[1] There are a total of 460 rentable slips priced from $205 to $775 for uncovered slips and $295 to $1,125 for covered slips per season (April 1–October 30). Seventy-five percent of all the slips are under roof and are in the more desirable location, hence they are rented first. Electric service is provided to all slips, and the slips on E and F docks have water and trash removal provided at no extra cost. To the left of the prime slips are 162 buoys, renting for $150 per season. This rental includes shuttle boat service to and from the moored craft. Buoys are not considered to be a very profitable segment. The buoys shift and break loose occasionally, requiring constant attention. Time is required to retrieve boats that break loose at night or during storms.

Lake Monroe, the largest lake in Indiana, is a 10,700-acre reservoir developed by the U.S. Army Corps of Engineers in conjunction with and under the jurisdiction of the Indiana Department of Natural Resources. With the surrounding public lands (accounting for some 80 percent of the 150-mile shore line) the total acreage is 26,000. It is a multipurpose project designed to provide flood control, recreation, water supply, and flow augmentation benefits to the people of Indiana.

The Reservoir is located in the southwestern quadrant of the state, about nine miles or a fifteen-minute drive southwest of Bloomington, Indiana, home of Indiana University, and a ninety-minute drive from Indianapolis. The Indianapolis metropolitan area has a population of over one million with some $3.5 billion dollars to spend annually. It is considered a desirable site for future expansion by many of the nation's top industrial leaders, as reported in a recent *Fortune* magazine survey. The city is the crossroads of the national interstate highway system, with more interstate highways converging here than in any other section of the United States. Its recently enlarged airport can accommodate any of the jet aircraft currently in operation, and is served by most of the major airlines. The per capita effective buying income is $4,264 as contrasted with $3,779 for the United States as a whole, with almost half of the households falling in the annual income bracket of

---

(1) E, F, and G are the most profitable slips and are fully rented. There is a waiting list to get into these slips.

Exhibit 1 **General Layout of the Marina**

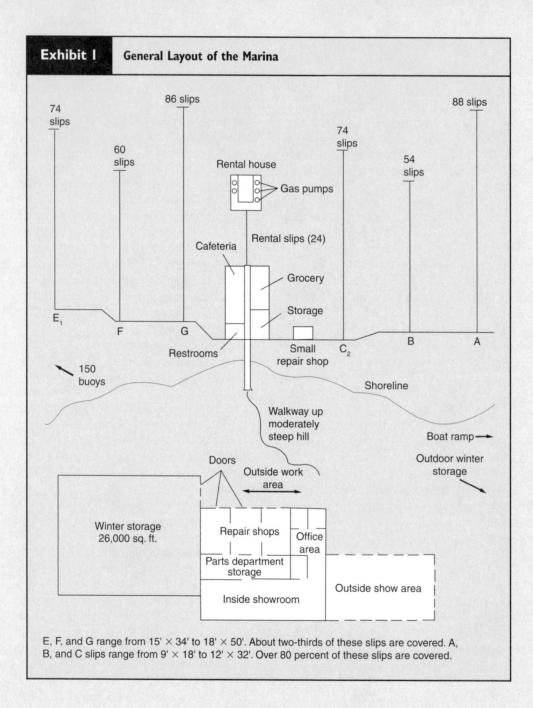

74 slips

86 slips

88 slips

60 slips

74 slips

54 slips

Rental house

Gas pumps

Rental slips (24)

Cafeteria

Grocery

Storage

E₁

F

G

Restrooms

Small repair shop

C₂

B

A

150 buoys

Shoreline

Walkway up moderately steep hill

Boat ramp →

Outdoor winter storage

Doors

Outside work area

Winter storage 26,000 sq. ft.

Repair shops

Office area

Parts department storage

Inside showroom

Outside show area

E, F, and G range from 15' × 34' to 18' × 50'. About two-thirds of these slips are covered. A, B, and C slips range from 9' × 18' to 12' × 32'. Over 80 percent of these slips are covered.

$10,000 and above. While approximately 75 percent of the customers of the marina for boat dockage, etc., come from the Indianapolis area, it is estimated that there is a total potential audience of some 2.9 million inhabitants within a 100-mile radius of Bloomington (see Exhibit 2).

The thirty-four acres of land on which the Fourwinds complex is located are leased to the corporation by the state of Indiana. In 1968 a prospectus was distributed by the Indiana Department of Natural Resources asking for bids on a motel and marina on the selected site. Of the eight to ten bids submitted, only one other bidder qualified. The proposal submitted by the Taggart Corporation was accepted primarily based on the economic strength of the individuals who composed the group, as well as the actual content of the bid.

The prospectus specified a minimum rental for the land of $10,000. Taggart Corporation offered

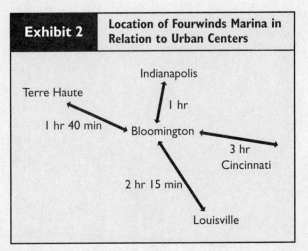

Exhibit 2 | **Location of Fourwinds Marina in Relation to Urban Centers**

in their bid a guarantee of $2,000 against the first $100,000 in marina sales and income and 4 percent of all income over that amount. For the inn, they guaranteed $8,000 against the first $400,000 of income plus 4 percent of all room sales and 2 percent of all food and beverage sales over that amount.

An initial lease of thirty-seven years was granted to Taggart with two options of thirty years each. At the termination of the contract, all physical property reverts to the state of Indiana and personal property to Taggart. The entire dock structure is floating and is considered under the personal property category.

Prior to tendering a bid, the corporation visited similar facilities at Lake of the Ozarks, Lake Hamilton in Hot Springs, and the Kentucky Lakes operations. They received a considerable amount of information from the Kentucky Lakes management.

Construction of the initial phase of the marina began in May 1969 and the first one hundred slips were opened in August under a speeded-up construction schedule. The inn had its formal opening in November of 1972.

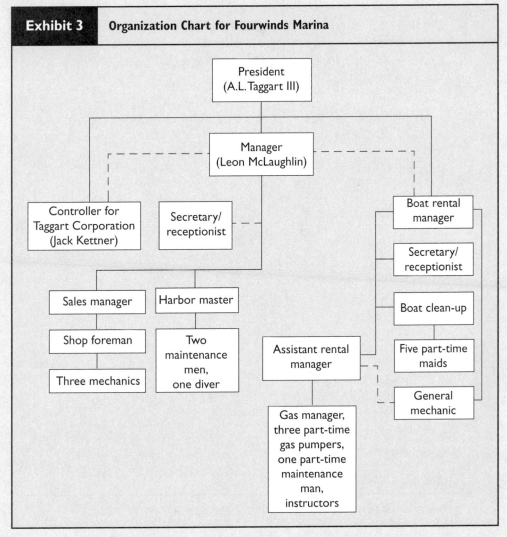

Exhibit 3 | **Organization Chart for Fourwinds Marina**

Exhibit 4 Profit and Loss Statement (Fiscal Year Ending March 31, 1974)

REVENUE

Sale of new boats	$774,352	
Sale of used boats	179,645	
Sale of rental boats	17,051	
Total Sales		$971,048

Other Income

Service and repair	$128,687	
Gasoline and oil	81,329	
Ship store	91,214	
Slip rental	174,808	
Winter storage	32,177	
Boat rental	99,895	
Other income		608,110
Total Income		$1,579,158

EXPENSES

Fixed Costs

Cost of boats	$798,123	
Cost of repair equipment	56,698	
Ship store costs	64,405	
Cost of gasoline	51,882	
Boat rental costs	8,951	
Total Fixed Costs		$980,059

Operating Expenses

Wages and salaries	$228,154	
Taxes	23,725	
Building rent	58,116	
Equipment rent	8,975	
Utilities	18,716	
Insurance	25,000	
Interest on loans	209,310	
Advertising	30,105	
Legal expenses	19,450	
Bad debt expenses	8,731	
Miscellaneous	39,994	
Total Operating Expenses		670,321
Total Costs		$1,650,380
Operating Loss		**$71,222**
Depreciation		**122,340**
TOTAL LOSS[1]		**$193,562**

(1) This represents the total operating loss of the Fourwinds Marina in the fiscal year ending March 31, 1974. Fourwinds sold a subsidiary in 1973 (boat sales firm in Indianapolis), on which they wrote off a loss of $275,580.

Exhibit 5	Balance Sheet (March 31, 1974)

ASSETS

Current Assets

Cash	$31,858
Accounts receivable	70,632
New boats	199,029
Used boats	60,747
Parts	53,295
Ship store	2,471
Gas/oil	2,626
Total Current Assets	$420,928

Fixed Assets

		Less depr.
Buoys and docks	$984,265	$315,459
Permanent bldgs.	201,975	17,882
Office furniture	3,260	704
Houseboats	139,135	15,631
Work boats	40,805	7,987
Equipment	72,420	38,742
	$1,441,860	$396,396
Net Fixed Assets	$1,045,464	

Other Assets

Prepaid expense	$2,940
Deferred interest exp.	25,231
	$28,261
Total Assets	**$1,494,653**

LIABILITIES

Current Liabilities

Accounts payable	$89,433
Intercompany payables	467,091
Accrued salary expense	8,905
Accrued interest expense	20,383
Accrued tax expense	43,719
Accrued lease expense	36,190
Prepaid dock rental	178,466
Boat deposits	4,288
Current bank notes	177,600
Mortgage (current)	982,900
Note payable to floor plan	225,550
Note on rental houseboats	71,625
Notes to stockholders	515,150
Dealer reserve liability	13,925
Total Current Liabilities	$2,835,225
Long-term note on houseboats	117,675
Common stock—1,000 shares at par value $1/share	1,000
Retained earnings deficit	−990,105
Loss during year ending March 31, 1974[1]	−469,142
Total Liabilities	**$1,494,653**

(1) Loss during year ended March 31, 1974, is composed of an operating loss of $71,222 plus depreciation of $122,340, and a write-off loss of a sold subsidiary of $275,580.

SOURCES OF INCOME

Note: The Indiana Department of Natural Resources exercises total control over the rates that can be charged on slip rental as well as room rates at the inn.

Slip Rental

Reservations for slips must be made by November 15 of each year or the slip is subject to sale on a first-come basis. Ordinarily all slips are rented for the year. The rental period runs from April 1 to October 30, and rental amounts vary from $205 to $1,125, depending on the size of slip and whether or not it is covered.

Buoy Rental

One hundred and sixty-two buoys are rented for the same April 1 to October 30 season at a rate of

$150. Shuttle boat service for transporting boat owners to and from their craft moored at the buoy area is operative twenty-four hours a day. It is not a scheduled service, but operates as the demand occurs. This requires the primary use of a runabout and driver. The charge for the service is included in the buoy rental fee for the season. As long as the buoy field is in existence, the shuttle service must operate on a twenty-four-hour basis in season.

Boat Storage—Winter

It is more expensive to remove a boat from the water than to allow it to remain moored at the dock all winter. The prime rate for storage is based on the charge for storage in the covered area of the main inside storage building. This area is not heated or lighted so repair work cannot be done in this building. An investment of about $12,000 would afford lighting and spot heating to overcome this drawback. When boats are stored, they are not queued according to those needing repair and those not needing service. As a result, time is lost in rearranging boats to get to those on which work must be performed. The storage facility is not utilized in the summer months. The addition of lights in the facility would allow display of used boats for sale, which are currently stored out of doors. Rates for storage charges are:

100 percent base rate—inside storage

70 percent of base rate—bubbled area of docks covered

60 percent of base rate—bubbled area of docks open

50 percent of base rate—open storage areas out of water

Storage rate is computed by the size of the boat. A six-foot-wide boat has a rate of $7. This is multiplied by the boat length to determine the total rate. So a twenty-foot-long boat seven feet wide would cost $140. Last winter the storage facility was filled. One hundred boats were stored, with the average size somewhat larger than the seven by twenty example given above. This rate does not include charges (approximately $75) for removing the boat from the water and moving it to either inside or outside storage areas. In the past there has been vandalism on the boats stored in the more remote areas of the uncovered, out-of-water storage. The marina claims no responsibility for loss, theft, or damage.

Boat and Motor Rental

Available equipment is up-to-date and well maintained. It consists of:

15 houseboats—rental Monday to Friday $300; Friday to Monday $300

10 pontoon boats—hourly rental $20 for 3 hours; $35 for 6 hours

6 runabouts for skiing—$15–$20 per hour

12 fishing boats—$12 for 6 hours; $18 for 12 hours

Maximum hourly rental is thirteen hours per day during the week and fifteen hours per day on Saturday and Sunday (the rental rate does not include gasoline).

It is not uncommon to have all fifteen houseboats out all week long during the height of the season. (Season height is from Memorial Day weekend to Labor Day weekend.) Pontoons are about 50 percent rented during the week. Utilization of runabouts is 50 percent, while fishing boats is approximately 40 percent. The man who operates the boat and motor rental for the marina has a one-third interest in all of the boat rental equipment. The marina holds the balance. Funds for the purchase of the equipment were contributed on the same one-third to two-thirds ratio. Net profits after payment of expenses, maintenance, depreciation, etc., are split between the two owners according to the same ratio. The area utilized by the rental area could be converted to slips in the $500 range as a possible alternate use for the dock space. Rental income after expenses, but before interest and depreciation, was slightly less than $20,000 last season.

Small-Boat Repair Shop

A small-boat repair shop is located between C and D docks. It is well equipped with mechanical equipment and a small hoist for removing small boats from the water for repair at the docks. This facility is currently standing idle. One qualified mechanic could operate it.

Grocery Store

The grocery store is subleased and is effectively operated. Prices are those expected at a small grocery catering to a predominantly tourist clientele. Income on the leased operation is approximately $500 month.

Snack Bar

The snack bar is operated by the Inn of the Fourwinds and returns a 5 percent commission to the marina on food sales. Currently it is felt that the manager of the snack bar is not doing a reliable job in operating the unit. The snack bar is sometimes closed for no apparent reason. Food offered for sale includes hot sandwiches, pizza, snack food, soft drinks, milk, and coffee. Prices are high and general quality is rated as good.

Gasoline Sales

Five pumps are located around the perimeter of the end of the center dock. They are manned thirteen hours per day, from seven A.M. to eight P.M., seven days a week. The pumps for the removal of waste from the houseboats and other large craft are located in this area. It takes an average of five minutes to pump out the waste and there is no charge. These gasoline pumps are the only ones available on the lake, permitting access from the water to the pump.

Boat and Boat Accessory Sales Room

A glass-enclosed showroom occupying approximately 1,500 square feet of floor space is located at the main entrance to the marina property. Major boat lines Trojan Yacht, Kingscraft, Burnscraft, Harris Flote Boat, and Signa, as well as Evinrude motors, are offered for sale. In addition, quality lines of marine accessories are available. The sales room building also houses the executive offices of the marina and the repair and maintenance shops. Attached to the building is the indoor storage area for winter housing of a limited number of boats. Last year total boat sales were $971,048. The boat inventory has been reduced from last year's $300,000, removing some lines while concentrating on others that offered higher profit on sales.

Fourwinds Marina is the only operation in the state that stocks the very large boats. It is also the only facility in Indiana with large slips to accommodate these boats. With E, F, and G slips filled and a waiting list to get in, selling the larger, more profitable boats has become nearly impossible.

MARINA DOCKING AREA FACTS

Dock Construction

The entire section is of modular floating construction. Built-in smaller sections that can be bolted together, the construction is of steel frameworks with poured concrete surfaces for walking upon and plastic foam panels in the side for buoyancy. In the event of damage to a section, a side can be replaced easily, eliminating repair of the entire segment of dock. Electrical conduits and water pipes are inside the actual dock units. The major damage to the plastic foam dock segments comes from ducks chewing out pieces of the foam to make nests, and from gasoline spillage that literally "eats" the plastic foam. An antigas coating is available. Damage from boats to the dock is minimal. The docks require constant attention. A maze of cables underneath the sections must be kept at the proper tension or the dock will buckle and break up. Three people are involved in dock maintenance. If properly maintained, the docks will have twenty to thirty more years of use. Original cost of the entire dock and buoy system was $984,265.

Winter Storage

Winter storage can be a problem at a marina located in an area where a freeze-over of the water occurs. It is better for the boat if it can remain in the water. Water affords better and more even support to the hull. By leaving the craft in the water, possible damage from hoists used to lift boats and move them to dry storage is avoided. These factors, however, are not common knowledge to the boat owner and require an educational program.

A rule of the marina prohibits any employee from driving any of the customers' boats. Maintaining a duplicate set of keys for each boat and the cost of the insurance to cover the employee are the prime reasons for this ruling. This means, however, that all boats must be towed, with possibility of damage to the boats during towing.

Bubbling Process

To protect boats left in the water during the winter season, Fourwinds Marina has installed a bubbling system. The system, simple in concept, consists of hoses that are weighted and dropped to the bottom of the lake around the individual docks and along a perimeter line surrounding the entire dock area. Fractional horsepower motors operate compressors that pump air into the submerged hose. The air escaping through tiny holes in the hose forces warmer water at the bottom of the lake up to the top, preventing freezing of the surface (or melting ice that might have frozen before the compressors were started). The lines inside the dock areas protect the boats from being damaged by ice formations, while the perimeter line prevents major damage to the entire dock area from a pressure ridge that might build up and be jammed against the dock and boats in high wind.

Source: This is a classic case in the strategic management literature. Copyright 1974 by W. Harvey Hegarty, Indiana University, and Harry Kelsy, Jr., California State College. Reprinted with permission.

Questions

1. What are the marina's strengths, weaknesses, opportunities, and threats?

2. How would you describe the marina's strategy and organization, and what do you think of Keltner's list of actions?

3. Assume Keltner asked you for some help in thinking through the changes. Where would you start, whom would you involve, and what might you propose?

Special Applications of Organization Development

Chapter 21   Organization Development in
                  Global Settings

Chapter 22   Organization Development in
                  Nonindustrial Settings: Health Care,
                  Family Businesses, School Systems and
                  the Public Sector

Chapter 23   Future Directions in Organization
                  Development

Integrative Cases   B.R. Richardson Timber Products
                      Corporation
                  Managing Strategy at Caesars Tahoe
                  Black & Decker International:
                      Globalization of the Architectural
                      Hardware Line

21

Organization Development in Global Settings

This chapter describes the practice of organization development in international settings. It presents the contingencies and practice issues associated with OD in organizations outside the United States, in worldwide organizations, and in global social change organizations. The applicability and effectiveness of OD in countries and cultures outside of the United States is the subject of intense debate, however. Because OD was developed predominantly by American and Western European practitioners, its practices and methods are heavily influenced by the values and assumptions of industrialized cultures. Thus, the traditional approaches to planned change may promote management practices that conflict with the values and assumptions of other societies. Will Chinese cultural values, for example, be preserved or defended as an increasing number of European and American organizations establish operations in that country? On the other hand, some practitioners believe that OD can result in organizational improvements in any culture.[1] Despite different points of view on this topic, the practice of OD in international settings can be expected to expand dramatically. The rapid development of foreign economies and firms, along with the evolution of the global marketplace, is creating organizational needs and opportunities for change.

In designing and implementing planned change for organizations operating outside the United States, OD practice must account for two important contingencies: alignment between the cultural values of the host country and traditional OD values, and the host country's level of economic development. Preliminary research suggests that failure to adapt OD interventions to these cultural and economic contingencies can produce disastrous results.[2] For example, several OD concepts, including dialogue, truthfulness, and performance management, do not always work in all countries.[3] Dialogue assumes that "all differences can be bridged if you get people together in the right context." However, mediation, arbitration, or traditional negotiation are more acceptable in some cultures. Similarly, truthfulness, a very North American notion, is culturally relativistic and as a value depends on whether you are American, Asian, Middle Eastern, or from some other culture. Finally, the process and content of performance evaluation can also depend on culture.[4]

In worldwide organizations, OD is used to help firms operate in multiple countries. Referred to as international, global, multinational, or transnational corporations, these firms must fit their organizational strategies, structures, and processes to different cultures. OD can help members gain the organizational skills and knowledge needed to operate across cultural boundaries, enhancing organizational effectiveness through better alignment of people and systems with international strategy.

Finally, OD is playing an increasingly important role in global social change. Practitioners using highly participative approaches are influencing the development of evolving countries, providing a voice to underrepresented social classes, and bridging the gap between cultures facing similar social issues. The application of planned change processes in these settings represents one of the newest and most exciting areas of OD.

ORGANIZATION DEVELOPMENT OUTSIDE THE UNITED STATES

Organization development is being practiced increasingly in organizations outside of the United States.[5] Survey feedback interventions have been used at Air New Zealand and at the Air Emirates (United Arab Republic); work design interventions have been implemented in Gamesa (Mexico); structural interventions have been completed at Neusoft Corporation (China); and merger and acquisition integration interventions have been used in Korea, The Netherlands, and Europe.[6] This international diffusion of OD derives from three important trends: the rapid development of foreign economies, the increasing worldwide availability of technical and financial resources, and the emergence of a global economy.[7]

The dramatic restructuring of socialist economies and the rapid economic growth of developing countries are numbing in scope and impact. Initial World Bank estimates of world gross domestic product growth averaging about 3.5% between 1996 and 2005 have been scaled back to average increases of 2.8% between 2001 and 2004 because of the global economic slowdown. However, projected growth rates in East Asia and Pacific and South Asia remain strong. The European Union continues its push for integration through fiscal policies, the admission of new countries, and the rationalizing of economic standards. Political transformations in the Middle East, China, Russia, and South Africa will produce both uncertainty and new growth-oriented economies.

Organizations operating in these rejuvenated or newly emerging economies are increasingly turning to OD practices to embrace opportunities and improve effectiveness. In China, for example, economic reforms are breaking up the "work units"—operational business units organized with housing, health care, education, food service, and other infrastructure organizations—that used to dominate the Chinese economy. As these work units are disbanded so that the operational unit can address "market facing" issues, the social fabric of China is severely shocked. A variety of nongovernmental organizations have formed to help China develop a "civil society." Many of these organizations, such as Global Village of Beijing, Friends of the Earth, and the Green Earth Volunteers, are using appreciative inquiry interventions to identify best practices and what gives life to their work. Ways of working together are being developed and networks of these nongovernmental organizations are coming together to provide assistance to the homeless, build environmental awareness, and deliver child care. Other interventions, including work design, survey feedback, and leadership development, represent efforts to increase ownership, commitment, and productivity in Chinese organizations.

The second trend contributing to OD applications in global settings is the unprecedented availability of technological and financial resources on a worldwide scale. The development of the Internet, the World Wide Web, and E-commerce has increased foreign governments' and organizations' access to enormous information resources and fueled growth and development. The increased availability of capital and technology, for example, was cited as a primary reason for the rise of Chilean firms in the 1980s.[8] Information technology, in particular, is making the world "smaller" and more interdependent. As organizations outside the United States adopt new technology, the opportunity increases to apply techniques that facilitate planned change. OD interventions can smooth the transition to a new reporting structure, clarify roles and relationships, and reduce the uncertainty associated with implementing new techniques and practices.

The final trend fueling international OD applications is the emergence of a global economy. The continued difficulties of Japan's economy, the advent of terrorism on a worldwide basis, and the spread of the SARS virus aptly demonstrate how interdependent the world's markets have become. Many foreign organizations are maturing and growing by entering the global business community. This international expansion is aided by lowered trade barriers, deregulation, and privatization. The established relationships and local knowledge that once favored only a small number of worldwide organizations no longer are barriers to entry into many countries.[9] As organizations expand globally, they are faced with adapting structures, information systems, coordinating processes, and human resources practices to worldwide operations in a variety of countries. This has led to OD interventions geared to planned change across different cultures and economies.

The success of OD in settings outside the United States depends on two key contingencies: cultural context and economic development. First, OD interventions need to be responsive to the cultural values and organizational customs of the host country if the changes are to produce the kinds of positive results shown in the United States.[10] For example, team-building interventions in Latin American countries can fail if there is too much emphasis on personal disclosure and interpersonal relationships. Latin Americans typically value masculinity and a devotion to family, avoid conflict, and are status conscious. They may be suspicious of human process interventions that seek to establish trust, openness, and equality, and consequently they may resist them actively. The more a country's cultural values match the traditional values of OD, the less likely it is that an intervention will have to be modified. Second, a country's economic development can affect the success of OD interventions.[11] For example, organizations operating in countries with moderate levels of economic development may need business-oriented interventions more than OD kinds of changes. Indeed, little may be gained from addressing interpersonal conflict in a top-management team if the organization has difficulty getting products shipped or delivering service.

Cultural Context

Researchers have proposed that applying OD in different countries requires a "context-based" approach to planned change.[12] This involves fitting the change process to the organization's cultural context, including the values held by members in the particular country or region. These beliefs inform people about behaviors that are important and acceptable in their culture. Cultural values play a major role in shaping the customs and practices that occur within organizations as well, influencing how members react to phenomena having to do with power, conflict, ambiguity, time, and change.

There is a growing body of knowledge about cultural diversity and its effect on organizational and management practices.[13] Researchers have identified five key values that describe national cultures and influence organizational customs: context orientation, power distance, uncertainty avoidannce, achievement orientation, and individualism (Table 21.1).[14]

Context Orientation

This value describes how information is conveyed and time is valued in a culture. In low-context cultures, such as Scandinavia and the United States, information is communicated in words and phrases. By using more specific words, more meaning is expressed. In addition, time is viewed as discrete and linear—as something that can be spent, used, saved, or wasted. In high-context cultures, on the other hand, the communication medium reflects the message more than the words, and time is a fluid and flexible concept. For example, social cues in Japan and Venezuela provide as much, if not more, information about a particular situation than do words alone. Organizations in high-context cultures emphasize ceremony and ritual. How one behaves is an important signal of support and compliance with the way things are done. Structures are less formal in high-context cultures; there are few written

		ORGANIZATION CUSTOMS WHEN THE VALUE IS AT	
VALUE	**DEFINITION**	**ONE EXTREME**	**REPRESENTATIVE COUNTRIES**
Context	The extent to which words carry the meaning of a message; how time is viewed	Ceremony and routines are common. Structure is less formal; fewer written policies exist. People are often late for appointments.	*High:* Asian and Latin American countries *Low:* Scandinavian countries, United States
Power distance	The extent to which members of a society accept that power is distributed unequally in an organization	Decision making is autocratic. Superiors consider subordinates as part of a different class. Subordinates are closely supervised. Employees are not likely to disagree. Powerful people are entitled to privileges.	*High:* Latin American and Eastern European countries *Low:* Scandinavian countries
Uncertainty avoidance	The extent to which members of an organization tolerate the unfamiliar and unpredictable	Experts have status/authority. Clear roles are preferred. Conflict is undesirable. Change is resisted. Conservative practices are preferred.	*High:* Asian countries *Low:* European countries
Achievement orientation	The extent to which organization members value assertiveness and the acquisition of material goods	Achievement is reflected in wealth and recognition. Decisiveness is valued. Larger and faster are better. Gender roles are clearly differentiated.	*High:* Asian and Latin American countries, South Africa *Low:* Scandinavian countries
Individualism	The extent to which people believe they should be responsible for themselves and their immediate families	Personal initiative is encouraged. Time is valuable to individuals. Competitiveness is accepted. Autonomy is highly valued.	*High:* United States *Low:* Latin American and Eastern European countries

Table 21•1   Cultural Values and Organization Customs

policies and procedures to guide behavior. Because high-context cultures view time as fluid, punctuality for appointments is less a priority than is maintaining relationships.

Power Distance

This value concerns the way people view authority, status differences, and influence patterns. People in high power-distance regions, such as Latin America and Eastern Europe, tend to favor unequal distributions of power and influence, and consequently autocratic and paternalistic decision-making practices are accepted. Organizations in high power-distance cultures tend to be highly centralized with several hierarchical levels and a large proportion of supervisory personnel. Subordinates in these organizations represent a lower social class. They expect to be supervised closely and believe that power holders are entitled to special privileges. Such practices would be inappropriate in low power-distance regions, such as Scandinavia, where participative decision making and egalitarian methods prevail.

Uncertainty Avoidance

This value reflects a preference for conservative practices and familiar and predictable situations. People in high uncertainty-avoidance regions, such as Asia, prefer stable routines, resist change, and act to maintain the status quo. They do not like conflict and believe that company rules should not be broken. In regions where uncertainty avoidance is low, such as in many European countries, ambiguity is less threatening. Organizations in these cultures tend to favor fewer rules, higher levels of participation in decision making, more organic structures, and more risk taking.

Achievement Orientation

This value concerns the extent to which the culture favors the acquisition of power and resources. Employees from achievement-oriented cultures, such as Asia and Latin America, place a high value on career advancement, freedom, and salary growth. Organizations in these cultures pursue aggressive goals and have high levels of stress and conflict. Organizational success is measured in terms of size, growth, and speed. On the other hand, workers in cultures where achievement is less of a driving value, such as those in Scandinavia, prize the social aspects of work including working conditions and supervision, and typically favor opportunities to learn and grow at work.

Individualism

This value is concerned with looking out for oneself as opposed to one's group or organization. In high-individualism cultures, such as the United States and Canada, personal initiative and competitiveness are valued strongly. Organizations in individualistic cultures often have high turnover rates and individual rather than group decision-making processes. Employee empowerment is supported when members believe that it improves the probability of personal gain. These cultures encourage personal initiative, competitiveness, and individual autonomy. Conversely, in low individualism countries, such as China, Japan, and Mexico, allegiance to one's group is paramount. Organizations operating in these cultures tend to favor cooperation among employees and loyalty to the company.

Economic Development

In addition to cultural context, an important contingency affecting OD success internationally is a country's level of industrial and economic development. For example, although long considered an industrial economy, Russia's political and economic transformation, and the concomitant increases in uncertainties over infrastructure, corruption, cash flow, and exchange rates, has radically altered assumptions underlying business practices. Thus, economic development can be judged from social, economic, and political perspectives.[15] For example, it can be reflected in a country's management capability as measured by information systems and skills; decision-making and action-taking capabilities; project planning and organizing abilities; evaluation and control technologies; leadership, motivational, and reward systems; and human selection, placement, and development levels. The United Nations' Human Development Programme has created a Human Development Index that assesses a country's economic development in terms of life expectancy, educational attainment, and adjusted real income.

Subsistence Economies

Countries such as Pakistan, Nepal, Nigeria, Uganda, and Rwanda have relatively low degrees of development and their economies are primarily agriculturally based. Their populations consume most of what they produce, and any surplus is used to barter for other needed goods and services. A large proportion of the population is unfamiliar with the concept of "employment." Working for someone else in exchange for wages is not common or understood, and consequently few large organizations exist outside of the government. In subsistence economies, OD interventions emphasize global social change and focus on creating conditions for sustainable social and economic progress. These change methods are described in the last section of this chapter.

Industrializing Economies

Malaysia, Venezuela, India, Turkey, the Philippines, Iran, and the People's Republic of China are moderately developed and tend to be rich in natural resources. An expanding manufacturing base that accounts for increasing amounts of the country's gross domestic product fuels economic growth. The rise of manufacturing also contributes to the formation of a class system including upper-, middle-, and low-income groups. Organizations operating in these nations generally focus on efficiency of operations and revenue growth. Consequently, OD interventions address strategic, structural, and work design issues.[16] They help organizations identify domestic and international markets, develop clear and appropriate goals, and structure themselves to achieve efficient performance and market growth.

Industrial Economies

Highly developed countries, such as Sweden, Japan, France, and the United States, emphasize nonagricultural industry. In these economies, manufactured goods are exported and traded with other industrialized countries; investment funds are available both internally and externally; the workforce is educated and skilled; and technology often is substituted for labor. Because the OD interventions described in this book were developed primarily in industrial economies, they can be expected to have their strongest effects in those contexts. Their continued success cannot be ensured, however, because these countries are advancing rapidly to postindustrial conditions. Here, OD interventions will need to fit into economies driven by information and knowledge, where service outpaces manufacturing, and where national and organizational boundaries are more open and flexible.

How Cultural Context and Economic Development Affect OD Practice

The contingencies of cultural context and economic development can have powerful effects on the way OD is carried out in various countries.[17] They can determine whether change proceeds slowly or quickly; involves few or many members; is directed by hierarchical authority or by consensus; and focuses on business, organizational, or human process issues. For example, planned change processes in Russia require more clarity in roles, the development of common understandings, changes in how an organization's vision is communicated, and the insightful use of symbols and signals.[18] When the two contingencies are considered together, they reveal four different international settings for OD practice, as shown in Figure 21.1 (on page 540). These different situations reflect the extent to which a country's culture fits with traditional OD values of direct and honest communication, sharing power, and improving their effectiveness and the degree to which the country is economically developed.[19] In Figure 21.1, the degree of economic development is restricted to industrializing and highly industrialized regions. Subsistence economies are not included because they afford little opportunity to practice traditional OD; in those contexts, a more appropriate strategy is global social change, discussed later in this chapter. In general, however, the more developed the economy, the more OD is applied to the organizational and human process issues described in this book. In less developed situations, OD focuses on business issues, such as procuring raw materials, producing efficiently, and marketing successfully.[20] On the other hand, when

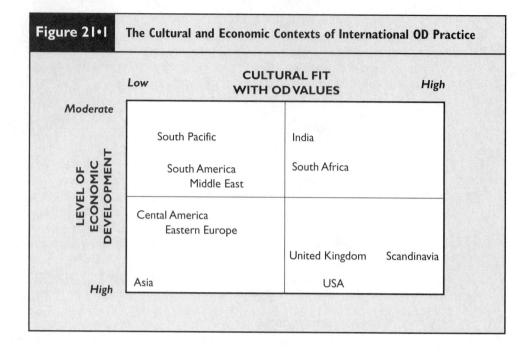

Figure 21•1 The Cultural and Economic Contexts of International OD Practice

the country's culture supports traditional OD values, the planned change process can be applied with only small adjustments.[21] The more the cultural context differs from OD's traditional values profile, the more the planned change process will need to be modified to fit the situation.

Low Cultural Fit, Moderate Industrialization

This context is least suited to traditional OD practice. It includes industrializing economies with cultural values that align poorly with OD values, including many Middle East nations, such as Iraq, Iran, and the United Arab Republic; the South Pacific region, including Malaysia and the Philippines; and certain South American countries, such as Brazil, Ecuador, Guatemala, and Nicaragua. These regions are highly dependent on their natural resources and have a relatively small manufacturing base. They tend to be high-context cultures with values of high power distance and achievement orientation and of moderate uncertainty avoidance. They are not a bad fit with OD values because these cultures tend toward moderate or high levels of collectivism, especially in relation to family.

These settings require change processes that fit local customs and that address business issues. As might be expected, little is written on applying OD in these countries, and there are even fewer reports of OD practice. Cultural values of high power distance and achievement are inconsistent with traditional OD activities emphasizing openness, collaboration, and empowerment. Moreover, executives in industrializing economies frequently equate OD with human process interventions, such as team building, training, and conflict management. They perceive OD as too soft to meet their business needs. For example, Egyptian and Filipino managers tend to be autocratic, engage in protracted decision making, and focus on economic and business problems. Consequently, organizational change is slow paced, centrally controlled, and aimed at achieving technical rationality and efficiency.[22]

Not all organizations are influenced similarly by these contextual forces. A recent study of 20 large-group interventions in Mexico suggests that culture may not be as constraining as has been hypothesized.[23] Similarly, in an apparent exception to the rule, the president of Semco S/A (Brazil), Ricardo Semler, designed a highly participative organization.[24] Most Semco employees set their own working hours and approved hires and promotions. Information flowed downward through a relatively flat hierarchy, and strategic decisions were made participatively by companywide vote. Brazil's cultural values are not as strong on power distance and masculinity as in other Latin American countries, and that may explain the apparent success of this high-involvement organization. It suggests that OD interventions can be implemented within this cultural context when strongly supported by senior management.

High Cultural Fit, Moderate Industrialization

This international context includes industrializing economies with cultures that align with traditional OD values. Such settings support the kinds of OD processes described in this book, especially technostructural and strategic interventions that focus on business development. According to data on economic development and cultural values, relatively few countries fit this context. India's industrial base is growing rapidly and may fit this contingency. Similarly, South Africa's recent political and cultural changes make it one of the most interesting settings in which to practice OD.[25]

South Africa is an industrializing economy. Its major cities are the manufacturing hubs of the economy, although agriculture and mining still dominate in rural areas. The country's values are in transition and may become more consistent with OD values. South Africans customarily have favored a low-context orientation; relatively high levels of power distance; and moderate levels of individualism, uncertainty avoidance, and achievement orientation. Organizations typically have been bureaucratic with authoritarian management, established career paths, and job security primarily for Caucasian employees. These values and organizational conditions are changing, however, as the nation's political and governance structures are transformed. Formerly, apartheid policies reduced uncertainty and defined power differences among citizens. Today, free elections and the abolishment of apartheid have increased uncertainty drastically and established legal equality among the races. These changes are likely to move South Africa's values closer to those underlying OD.[26] If so, OD interventions should become increasingly relevant to that nation's organizations.

A study of large South African corporations suggests the directions that OD is likely to take in that setting.[27] The study interviewed internal OD practitioners about key organizational responses to the political changes in the country, such as the free election of Nelson Mandela, abolishment of apartheid, and the Reconstruction and Development Program. Change initiatives at Spoornet, Eskom, and Telkom, for example, centered around two strategic and organizational issues. First, the political changes opened up new international markets, provided access to new technologies, and exposed these organizations to global competition. Consequently, these firms initiated planned change efforts to create corporate visions and identify strategies for entering new markets and acquiring new technologies. Second, the political changes forced corporations to modify specific human resources and organizational practices. The most compelling change was mandated affirmative action quotas. At Spoornet, Eskom, and Telkom, apartheid was thoroughly embedded in the organizations' structures, policies, and physical arrangements. Thus, planned change focused on revising human resources policies and practices. Similarly, organizational structures that had fit well within the stable environment of apartheid were outmoded and too rigid to meet the competitive challenges of international markets. Planned changes for restructuring these firms were implemented as part of longer-term strategies to change corporate culture toward more egalitarian and market-driven values.

Low Cultural Fit, High Industrialization

This international setting includes industrialized countries with cultures that fit poorly with traditional OD values. Many countries in Central America, Eastern Asia, and Eastern Europe fit this description. Reviews of OD practice in those regions suggest that planned change includes all four types of interventions described in this book, although the change process itself is adapted to local conditions.[28] For example, Mexico, Venezuela, China, Japan, and Korea are high-context cultures where knowledge of local mannerisms, customs, and rituals is required to understand the meaning of communicated information.[29] To function in such settings, OD practitioners not only must know the language but the social customs as well. Similarly, cultural values emphasizing high levels of power distance, uncertainty avoidance, and achievement orientation foster organizations where roles, status differences, and working conditions are clear; where autocratic and paternalistic decisions are expected; and where the acquisition of wealth and influence by the powerful is accepted. OD interventions that focus on social processes and employee empowerment are not favored naturally in this cultural context and consequently need to be modified to fit the situations.

Asian organizations, such as Matsushita, Nissan, Toyota, Fujitsu, NEC, and Hyundai, provide good examples of how OD interventions can be tailored to this global setting. These firms are famous for continuous improvement and TQM practices; they adapt these interventions to fit the Asian culture. Roles and behaviors required to apply TQM are highly specified, thereby holding uncertainty to a relatively low level. Teamwork and consensus decision-making practices associated with quality improvement projects also help to manage uncertainty. When large numbers of employees are involved, information is spread quickly and members are kept informed about the changes taking place. Management controls the change process by regulating the implementation of suggestions made by the problem-solving groups. Because these interventions focus on work processes, teamwork and employee involvement do not threaten the power structure. Moreover, TQM and continuous improvement do not alter the organization radically but produce small, incremental changes that can add up to impressive gains in long-term productivity and cost reduction.

In these cultures, OD practitioners also tailor the change process itself to fit local conditions. Mexican companies, for example, expect OD practitioners to act as experts and to offer concrete advice on how to improve the organization. To be successful, OD practitioners need sufficient status and legitimacy to work with senior management and to act in expert roles.[30] Status typically is associated with academic credentials, senior management experience, high-level titles, or recommendations by highly placed executives and administrators. As might be expected, the change process in Latin America is autocratic and driven downward from the top of the organization. Subordinates or lower-status people generally are not included in diagnostic or implementation activities because inclusion might equalize power differences and threaten the status quo. Moreover, cultural norms discourage employees from speaking out or openly criticizing management. There is relatively little resistance to change because employees readily accept changes dictated by management.

In Asia, OD is an orderly process, driven by consensus and challenging performance goals. Organizational changes are implemented slowly and methodically, so trust builds and change-related uncertainty is reduced. Changing too quickly is seen as arrogant, divisive, and threatening. At the China Association for the International Exchange of Personnel, the move from a government bureau to a "market-facing" organization has been gradual but consistent. Managers have been encouraged to contact more and more foreign organizations, to develop relationships and contracts, and to learn marketing and organization development skills. Because Asian values promote a cautious culture that prizes consensus, dignity, and respect, OD tends to be impersonal and to focus mainly on work-flow improvements. Human process issues are rarely addressed because people are expected to act in ways that do not cause others to "lose face" or to bring shame to the group.

Application 21.1 describes an action research project in China designed to increase the capacity of human resource and training departments. The OD practitioners, who were from Switzerland, and the participants report on the learnings they had as a result of the program. As you look at the design and implementation of the program, what do you see as the pros and cons of their work?[31]

High Cultural Fit, High Industrialization

This last setting includes industrialized countries with cultural contexts that fit well with traditional OD values. Much of the OD practice described in this book was developed in these situations, particularly in the United States.[32] To extend our learning, we will focus on how OD is practiced in other nations in this global setting, including the Scandinavian countries—Sweden, Norway, Finland, and Denmark—and countries with a strong British heritage, such as Great Britain, Northern Ireland, Australia, and New Zealand.

Scandinavians enjoy a high standard of living and strong economic development.[33] Because their cultural values most closely match those traditionally espoused in OD, organizational practices are highly participative and egalitarian. OD practice tends to mirror these values. Multiple stakeholders, such as managers, unionists, and staff personnel, actively are involved in all stages of the change process, from entry and diagnosis to intervention and evaluation. This level of involvement is much higher than that typically occurring in the United States. It results in a change process that is heavily oriented to the needs of shop-floor participants. Norwegian labor laws, for example, give unionists the right to participate in technological innovations that can affect their work lives. Such laws also mandate that all employees in the country have the right to enriched forms of work.

Given this cultural context, Scandinavian companies pioneered sociotechnical interventions to improve productivity and quality of work life.[34] Sweden's Saab and Volvo restructured automobile manufacturing around self-managed work groups. Denmark's Patent Office and Norway's Shell Oil demonstrated how union–management cooperative projects can enhance employee involvement throughout the organization. In many cases, national governments were involved heavily in these change projects by sponsoring industrywide improvement efforts. The Norwegian government, for example, was instrumental in introducing industrial democracy to that nation's companies. It helped union and management in selected industries implement pilot projects to enhance productivity and quality of work life. The results of these sociotechnical experiments were then diffused throughout the Norwegian economy. In many ways, the Scandinavian countries have gone further than other global regions in linking OD to national values and policies.

Countries associated with the United Kingdom tend to have values consistent with a low-context orientation, moderate to high individualism and achievement orientation, and moderate to low power distance and uncertainty avoidance. This cultural pattern results in personal relationships that often seem indirect to Americans. For example, a British subordinate who is told to think about a proposal is really being told that the suggestion has been rejected. These values also promote organizational policies that are steeped in formality, tradition, and politics. The United Kingdom's long history tends to reinforce the status quo, and consequently resistance to change is high.

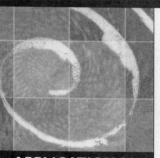

MODERNIZING CHINA'S HUMAN RESOURCE DEVELOPMENT AND TRAINING FUNCTIONS

APPLICATION 21•1

The economic, political, and cultural changes sweeping through the People's Republic of China (PRC) are complex in both scope and breadth. China has evolved from an isolated and underdeveloped country to an economic growth engine. Since 1979, China's GDP has more than quadrupled as a result of its transition to a "market-facing" economy. Despite clear intentions to conduct the transition in ways that honor, support, and reinforce the Chinese culture, balancing these changes has not been easy. For example, the 70,000 state-owned enterprises have been forced to reinvent themselves through financial restructuring, massive downsizings, and upgrading the competencies of their employees. In the mid-1990s, the capability to manage the human resource consequences of breaking up the old work units, downsizing various parts of the organization, and developing managers just didn't exist inside the country. China's training and human resource development departments were ill prepared to respond to these demands. As a context for OD, China represents a set of cultural values that are very different from Europe and North America.

In an effort to assist in the development of China's human resource development capacity, OD practitioners from the Center for Socio-Eco-Nomic Development (CSEND) in Switzerland were called in to act as technical advisors to a unit of the Chinese Communist Party's (CCP) Organization Department. A separate training institute called the China Training Centre for Senior Personnel Management Officials (CTCSPMO) was established and initial institution building efforts were financed by the United Nations Development Program (UNDP).

One output of the CTCSPMO was the Sino-Swiss bilateral project (SSBP), a program designed to increase the institutional capacity of Chinese public administrators to manage change. The strategy was to work with a small group of experienced training managers and trainers to apply the concepts and techniques of modern management training and organization development. The Chinese participants were to form the vanguard of a new generation of Chinese public management trainers and HRD managers and to act as a catalyst in bringing about the institutional development of their respective organizations.

In designing the program, the Chinese and Swiss partners had to ensure that the skills and knowledge of human resource and organization development would be transferred not only to the participants but to the administrative systems and training institutions involved in the program. Based on observations and interviews with Chinese government officials, communist party members, faculty members at different Chinese educational institutions, and training and human resource managers in Chinese organizations, the OD practitioners recommended a combination of *action learning* (AL) and *action research* (AR) methods. AR and AL were seen as appropriate techniques because they had not been tried before in China, offered viable tools for developing internal capacity for continuous improvement and for systemwide multilevel intervention, and were centrally concerned with transferring capacity to the client system. These action-based approaches constituted a pioneering attempt of international know-how transfer.

During the initial preparatory phase between September 1993 and March 1994, the 60 selected participants were given intensive English-language courses. Then, beginning in March 1994, the program began with a series of "programmed learning" workshops followed by a "workplace application" experience. The cycle of programmed learning and workplace application was then repeated. Following each workplace application period, a conference was organized to review the project work and its findings, to exchange experiences, and to reflect on the learnings generated. The two cycles were completed in December 1996.

The programmed learning workshops covered 10 different topic areas, such as comparative public administration, human resource management, organizational theory and development, adult learning theories and methods, and training management. These topics were taught in the classrooms by foreign experts in Beijing. The workplace application projects involved creating groups of participants from similar provincial areas or functional responsibilities to address actual human resource, training and development, or organizational change issues. The project organization consulted with the Chinese partner organization, CTCSPMO, to approve a variety of learning projects, including the redesign of a management development program for senior party officials in Beijing, developing a training program for managers guiding large infrastructure projects, and research on human resources and motivation practices in state-owned enterprises.

In addition to the project work, the workplace application groups were instructed to meet every 2 weeks either face-to-face or by phone. Practically, most of the meetings were by phone due to physical distance. The purpose of these meetings was to reflect on the project's progress, review how topics from the learning workshop were being applied, and to capture personal learnings. The participants were also asked to keep a journal and the group was assigned a facilitator to work with them.

In reviewing the first two rounds of learning and action, several observations were made. First, the Chinese participants learned:

- to participate actively in the learning process and take responsibility for the relevance of their learning;
- to redefine the role of a "good" trainer/teacher;
- to question each other and the trainer/teacher's statements as "facts," "opinion," or "truth";
- to challenge the widely held belief that "the bird who raise its head will be shot first"; and
- to perceive the social process and group dynamics of learning as beneficial, not chaotic or lacking discipline.

In addition, the OD practitioners learned:

- to question and to reflect on their own assumptions concerning Chinese culture, organizations, human relations, and management theories;
- to confront their own cultural biases in a foreign environment that had its own logic in getting things done;
- to find ways to work as a team with the Chinese facilitators, who had different ways of relating;
- to refrain from assuming responsibility for the Chinese partners;

- to facilitate rather than dominate; and
- to sustain the interest and commitment of the CTC-SPMO and facilitators to the action research and action learning approach.

Reactions from different stakeholders, including the Deputy Directors of the provincial organization department of the CCP, the Deputy Commissioner of the State Commission of the Nationalities, the Academic Dean of the Central Party School, and the Directors of Training of the Ministry of Personnel and the State Economic and Trade Commission, were in general positive. They found the results of the action research informative and the recommended solutions helpful. A reportedly high rate of project recommendation implementation was later verified by a team of international independent reviewers, and a final project evaluation conducted in October 1997 confirmed the initial positive assessment.

The SSBP program allowed the Chinese government and the CCP to acquire cutting edge know-how in management development and training. At the same time, they were able to review the various training programs being provided for senior government officials, enterprise executives, and party officials in China. Based on the findings from action learning projects, the training department of the CCP revised their training requirements, adjusted their training approach, and added more skill-based topics to the curriculum.

OD practice in the United Kingdom parallels the cultural pattern described above. In Great Britain, for example, sociotechnical systems theory was developed by practitioners at the Tavistock Institute of Human Relations.[35] Applications, such as self-managed work groups, however, have not readily diffused within British organizations. The individualistic values and inherently political nature of this culture tend to conflict with interventions emphasizing employee empowerment and teamwork. In contrast, the Scandinavian cultures are far more supportive of sociotechnical practice and have been instrumental in diffusing it worldwide.

The emergence of the European Union has served as a catalyst for change in many organizations. Companies such as Akzo Nobel, Airbus, BMW, and Credit Lyonnais are actively engaged in strategic change interventions. At L'Oreal, CEO Lindsay Owen-Jones is implementing an aggressive strategy of acquiring and integrating cosmetic firms, driving the international business, and building its brand.[36] More limited interventions, such as team building, conflict resolution, and work redesign, are being carried out in such organizations as Unilever and Smithkline Beecham.

WORLDWIDE ORGANIZATION DEVELOPMENT

An important trend facing many business firms is the emergence of a global marketplace. Driven by competitive pressures, lowered trade barriers, and advances in information technologies, the number of companies offering products and services in multiple countries is increasing rapidly. The organizational growth and complexity associated with managing worldwide operations is challenging. Executives must choose appropriate strategic orientations for operating across cultures and geographical locations, and under diverse governmental and environmental requirements. They must be able to adapt corporate policies and procedures to a range of local conditions. Moreover, the tasks of controlling and coordinating operations in different nations place heavy demands on information and control systems and on managerial skills and knowledge.

Worldwide organization development applies to organizations that are operating across multiple geographic and cultural boundaries. This contrasts with OD in organizations that operate outside the United States but within a single cultural and economic context. This section describes the emerging practice of OD in worldwide organizations, a relatively new but important area of planned change.

Worldwide Strategic Orientations

Worldwide organizations can be defined in terms of three key facets.[37] First, they offer products or services in more than one country and actively manage substantial direct investments in those countries. Consequently, they must relate to a variety of demands, such as unique product requirements, tariffs, value-added taxes, governmental regulations, transportation laws, and trade agreements. Second, worldwide firms must balance product and functional concerns with geographic issues of distance, time, and culture. American tobacco companies, for example, face technological, moral, and organizational issues in determining whether to market cigarettes in less-developed countries, and if they do, they must decide how to integrate manufacturing and distribution operations on a global scale. Third, worldwide companies must carry out coordinated activities across cultural boundaries using a wide variety of personnel, including expatriates, short-term and extended business travelers, and local employees. Workers with different cultural backgrounds must be managed in ways that support the overall goals and image of the organization.[38] The company must therefore adapt its human resources policies and procedures to fit the culture and accomplish operational objectives. From a managerial perspective, selecting executives to head foreign operations is an important decision in worldwide organizations.

How these three facets of products/services, organization, and personnel are arranged enable firms to compete in the global marketplace.[39] Worldwide organizations can offer certain products or services in some countries and not in others; they can centralize or decentralize operations; and they can determine how to work with people from different cultures. Despite the many possible combinations of characteristics, researchers have found that two dimensions are useful in guiding decisions about choices of strategic orientation. As shown in Figure 21.2, managers need to assess two key success factors: the degrees to which there is a need for global integration or for local responsiveness. *Global integration* refers to whether or not business success requires tight coordination of people, plants, equipment, products, or service delivery on a worldwide basis. For example, semiconductor makers often design chips in one or more countries, manufacture the chips in a variety of locations, assemble and test the finished products in different countries, and then ship the chips to customers. All of this activity must be coordinated carefully. *Local responsiveness*, on the other hand, is the extent to which business success is dependent on customizing products, services, support, packaging, and other aspects of operations to local conditions. Based on that information, worldwide organizations generally implement one of four types of strategic orientations: international, global, multinational, or transnational. Table 21.2 presents these orientations in terms of the diagnostic framework described in Chapter 5. Each strategic orientation is geared to specific market, technological, and organizational requirements. OD interventions that support each orientation also are included in Table 21.2.

| Figure 21•2 | The Integration-Responsiveness Framework |

Need for Global Integration

High
- Global Orientation
- Transnational Orientation

Low
- International Orientation
- Multinational Orientation

Need for Local Responsiveness — Low ... High

| Table 21•2 | Characteristics and Interventions for Worldwide Strategic Orientations |

WORLDWIDE STRATEGIC ORIENTATION	STRATEGY	STRUCTURE	INFORMATION SYSTEM	HUMAN RESOURCES	OD INTERVENTIONS
International	Existing Products Goals of increased foreign revenues	Centralized international division	Loose	Volunteer	Cross-cultural training Strategic planning
Global	Standardized products Goals of efficiency through volume	Centralized, balanced, and coordinated activities Global product division	Formal	Ethnocentric selection	Career planning Role clarification Employee involvement Senior management team building Conflict management
Multinational	Tailored products Goals of local responsiveness through specialization	Decentralized operations; centralized planning Global geographic divisions	Profit centers	Regiocentric or polycentric selection	Intergroup relations Local management team building Management development Reward systems Strategic alliances
Transnational	Tailored products Goals of learning and responsiveness through integration	Decentralized, worldwide coordination Global matrix or network	Subtle, clan-oriented controls	Geocentric selection	Extensive selection and rotation Cultural development Intergroup relations Building corporate vision

The International Strategic Orientation

The international orientation exists when the key success factors of global integration and local responsiveness are low. This is the most common label given to organizations making their first attempts at operating in non-host-country markets. The primary required coordination is between the parent company and the small number of foreign sales and marketing offices in chosen countries. Similarly, local responsiveness is low because the organization exports the same products and services offered domestically. When an organization has decided to expand internationally, it has most often determined that:

- other country-markets appear to offer specific advantages large enough to exceed the tangible and intangible costs of implementing a new strategy,
- the organization's products, services, and value propositions are sufficiently powerful to counteract the initial disadvantages of operating in a foreign location, and
- the organizational capabilities exist to extract value from the foreign operations in excess of simpler contracting or licensing of the organization's technology, products, or services in the foreign location.[40]

Characteristics of the International Design

The goal of the international orientation is to increase total sales by adding revenues from nondomestic markets. By using existing products/services, domestic operating capacity is extended and leveraged. As a result, most domestic companies will enter international markets by extending their product lines first into nearby countries and then expanding to more remote areas. For example, most U.S.-based companies first offer their products in Canada or Mexico. After a certain period of time, they begin to set up operations in other countries.

To support this goal and operations strategy, an "international division" is given responsibility for marketing, sales, and distribution, although it may be able to set up joint ventures, licensing agreements, distribution territories/franchises, and in some cases, manufacturing plants. The organization basically retains its original structure and operating practices. The information system governing the division is typically looser, however. While expecting returns on its investment, the organization recognizes the newness of the venture and gives the international division some "free rein" to establish an international presence.

Finally, roles in the new international organization are staffed with volunteers from the parent company, often with someone who has appropriate foreign language training, experience living overseas, or eagerness for an international assignment. Little training or orientation for the position is offered as the organization is generally unaware of the requirements for being successful in international business.

Implementing the International Orientation

Changing from a domestic to an international organization represents an incremental shift in scope for most firms, and is typically handled as a simple extension of the existing strategy into new markets. Despite the logic of such thinking, the shift is neither incremental nor simple and OD can play an important role in making the transition smoother and more productive.

Strategic planning, technostructural, and human resource interventions can help to implement an international orientation. Managers can use integrated strategic change to design and manage the transition from the old strategic orientation to the new one. Environmental scans, competitor analyses, and market studies can be done to calibrate expectations about revenue goals and determine the levels of investment necessary to support the division. Team building and large-group interventions, such as search conferences, can aid the process through which senior executives gather appropriate information about international markets, distinctive competencies, and culture, and then choose a strategic orientation. Similarly, managers can apply technostructural interventions to design an appropriate organization structure, to define new tasks and work roles, and to clarify reporting relationships between corporate headquarters and foreign-based units. Based on these decisions, OD interventions can help the organization to implement the change.

Managers and staff also can apply human resources management interventions to train and prepare managers and their families for international assignments and to develop selection methods and reward systems relevant to operating internationally.[41] Since these are the organization's first experiences with international business, OD practitioners can alert key managers and potential candidates for the international assignments to the need for cultural training. Candidates can be directed to outsourced offerings on cross-cultural skills, local country customs, and legal/regulatory conditions. OD practitioners also can assist the human resource organization to design or modify existing compensation and benefits packages, or set up policies around housing, schooling, and other expenses associated with the relocation.

This initial movement into the international arena enables domestic organizations to learn about the demands of the global marketplace, thus providing important knowledge and experience with the requirements for success in more sophisticated strategies.

The Global Strategic Orientation

This orientation exists when the need for global integration is high but the need for local responsiveness is low. The global orientation is characterized by a strategy of marketing standardized products in different countries. It is an appropriate orientation when there is little economic reason to offer products or services with special features or locally available options. Manufacturers of office equipment, consumer goods, computers and semiconductors, tires, and containers, for example, can offer the same basic product in almost any country.

Characteristics of the Global Design

The goal of efficiency dominates this orientation. Production efficiency is gained through volume sales and a small number of large manufacturing plants, and managerial efficiency is achieved by centralizing product design, manufacturing, distribution, and marketing decisions. Global integration is supported by the close physical proximity of major functional groups and formal control systems that balance inputs, production, and distribution with worldwide demand. Many Japanese firms, such as Honda, Sony, NEC, and Matsushita, used this strategy in the 1970s and early 1980s to grow in the international economy. In Europe, Nestlé exploits economies of scale in marketing by advertising well-known brand names around the world. The increased number of microwaves and two-income families, for example, allowed Nestlé to push its Nescafé coffee and Lean Cuisine low-calorie frozen dinners to dominant market-share positions in Europe, North America, Latin America, and Asia. Similarly, a Korean noodle maker, Nong Shim Company, avoided the 1999 financial crisis by staying focused on efficiency. Yoo Jong Suk, Nong Shim's head of strategy, went against recommendations to diversify and stated, "All we want is to be globally recognized as a ramyon maker."[42]

In the global orientation, the organization tends to be centralized with a global product structure. Presidents of each major product group report to the CEO and form the line organization. Each of these product groups is responsible for worldwide operations. Information systems in global orientations tend to be quite formal with local units reporting sales, costs, and other data directly to the product president. The predominant human resources policy integrates people into the organization through ethnocentric selection and staffing practices. These methods seek to fill key foreign positions with personnel from the home country where the corporation headquarters is located.[43] Key managerial jobs at Volvo, Siemens, Nissan, and Michelin, for example, are often occupied by Swedish, German, Japanese, and French citizens, respectively.[44] Ethnocentric policies support the global orientation because expatriate managers are more likely than host-country nationals to recognize and comply with the need to centralize decision making and to standardize processes, decisions, and relationships with the parent company. Although many Japanese automobile manufacturers have decentralized production, Nissan's global strategy has been to retain tight, centralized control of design and manufacturing, ensure that almost all of its senior foreign managers are Japanese, and have even low-level decisions emerge from face-to-face meetings in Tokyo.[45]

Implementing the Global Orientation

OD interventions can be used to refine and support the global strategic orientation as well as assist in the transition from an international orientation.

1. *Planned Change in the Global Orientation.* Several OD interventions support the implementation of this orientation. Career planning, role clarification, employee involvement, conflict management, and senior management team building help the organization achieve improved operational efficiency. For example, role clarification interventions, such as job enrichment or goal setting, and conflict management can formalize and standardize organizational activities. This ensures that each individual knows specific details about how, when, and why a job needs to be done. As a result, necessary activities are described and efficient transactions and relationships are created. Similarly, Intel has used training interventions to ensure consistent implementation of a variety of company-standard business practices, such as meeting protocols, performance management processes, and reporting accountability.

   Senior management team building can improve the quality of strategic decisions. Centralized policies make the organization highly dependent on this group and can exaggerate decision-making errors. In addition, interpersonal conflict can increase the cost of coordination or cause significant coordination mistakes. Process interventions at this level can help improve the speed and quality of decision making and improve interpersonal relationships.

   Career planning can help home-country personnel develop a path to senior management by including foreign subsidiary experiences and cross-functional assignments as necessary qualifications for advancement. At the country level, career planning can emphasize that advancement beyond regional operations is limited for host-country nationals. OD can help here by developing appropriate career paths within the local organization or in technical, nonmanagerial areas. Finally, employee empowerment can support efficiency goals by involving members in efforts at cost reduction, work standardization, and minimization of coordination costs.

2. *The Transition to a Global Orientation.* In addition to fine tuning this strategic orientation, OD can help the organization transition from an international to a global strategic orientation. The organization's experience with the international strategic orientation has helped to build basic knowledge and skills in international business. The successful transition to a global strategy assumes that managers believe global integration is more important than local responsiveness

and that the organization has strong centralized operating capabilities. If either the assessment of key success factors or the organization's competencies are inaccurate, implementation will be more difficult and performance will suffer.

The decision to favor global integration over local responsiveness must be rooted in a strong belief that the worldwide market is relatively homogenous in character. That is, that products and services, support, distribution, or marketing activities can be standardized without negatively affecting sales or customer loyalty. This decision should not be made lightly, and OD practitioners can help to structure rigorous debate and analysis of this key success factor.

In addition to information about the market, organizations must take into account their distinctive competencies when choosing a global strategy. The key organizational and operational competence necessary for success in a global strategy is the ability to coordinate a complex, worldwide organization. The global strategy is facilitated when culture and core competencies are more suited for centralized decision making, when the organization has experience with supply-chain management, and when it is comfortable with enterprise resource and material resource planning processes. Centralization favors a global orientation because the orientation favors tight, global coordination.

Once companies develop a strategic orientation for competing internationally, they create an organization design to support it. Information like that found in Table 21.2 is useful for designing structures, information systems, and personnel practices for specific strategic orientations. OD practitioners can help to design change management programs to implement these features.

The Multinational Strategic Orientation

This strategic orientation exists when the need for global integration is low, but the need for local responsiveness is high. It represents a strategy that is conceptually quite different from the global strategic orientation.

Characteristics of the Multinational Design

A multinational strategy is characterized by a product line that is tailored to local conditions and is best suited to markets that vary significantly from region to region or country to country. At American Express, for example, charge card marketing is fitted to local values and tastes. The "Don't leave home without it" and "Membership has its privileges" themes seen in the United States were translated to "Peace of mind only for members" in Japan.[46]

The multinational orientation emphasizes a decentralized, global division structure. Each region or country is served by a divisional organization that operates autonomously and reports to headquarters. This results in a highly differentiated and loosely coordinated corporate structure. Operational decisions, such as product design, manufacturing, and distribution, are decentralized and tightly integrated at the local level. For example, laundry soap manufacturers offer product formulas, packaging, and marketing strategies that conform to the different environmental regulations, types of washing machines, water hardness, and distribution channels in each country. On the other hand, planning activities often are centralized at corporate headquarters to achieve important efficiencies necessary for worldwide coordination of emerging technologies and of resource allocation. A profit-center control system allows local autonomy as long as profitability is maintained. Examples of multinational corporations include Hoechst and BASF of Germany, IBM and Merck of the United States, and Honda of Japan. Each of these organizations encourages local subsidiaries to maximize effectiveness within their geographic region.

People are integrated into multinational firms through polycentric or regiocentric personnel policies because these firms believe that host-country nationals can understand native cultures most clearly.[47] By filling positions with local citizens who appoint and develop their own staffs, the organization aligns the needs of the market with the ability of its subsidiaries to produce customized products and services. The distinction between a polycentric and a regiocentric selection process is one of focus. In a polycentric selection policy, a subsidiary represents only one country; in the regiocentric selection policy, a slightly broader perspective is taken and key positions are filled by regional citizens (that is, people who might be called Europeans, as opposed to Belgians or Italians).

Implementing the Multinational Orientation

The decentralized and locally coordinated multinational orientation suggests the need for a complex set of OD interventions. When applied to a subsidiary operating in a particular country or region, the OD processes described earlier in the chapter for organizations outside the United States are relevant. The key is to tailor OD to fit the specific cultural and economic context where the subsidiary is located.

1. *Planned Change in the Multinational Orientation.* When OD is applied across different regions and countries, interventions must account for differences in cultural and economic conditions that can affect its success. Appropriate interventions for multinational corporations include intergroup relations, local management team building, sophisticated management selection and development practices, and changes to reward systems. Team building remains an important intervention. Unlike team building for senior management in global orientations, the local management team requires attention in multinational firms. This presents a challenge for OD practitioners because polycentric selection policies can produce management teams with different cultures at each subsidiary. Thus, a program developed for one subsidiary may not work with a different team at another subsidiary, given the different cultures that might be represented.

   Intergroup interventions to improve relations between local subsidiaries and the parent company are also important for multinational companies. Decentralized decision making and regiocentric selection can strain corporate–subsidiary relations. Local management teams, operating in ways appropriate to their cultural context, may not be understood by corporate managers from another culture. OD practitioners can help both groups understand these differences by offering training in cultural diversity and appreciation. They also can smooth parent–subsidiary relationships by focusing on the profit-center control system or other criteria as the means for monitoring and measuring subsidiary effectiveness.

   Management selection, development, and reward systems also require special attention in multinational firms. Managerial selection for local or regional subsidiaries requires finding technically and managerially competent people who also possess the interpersonal competence needed to interface with corporate headquarters. Because these people may be difficult to find, management development programs can teach these cross-cultural skills and abilities. Such programs typically involve language, cultural awareness, and technical training; they also can include managers and staff from subsidiary and corporate offices to improve communications between the two areas. Finally, reward systems need to be aligned with the decentralized structure. Significant proportions of managers' total compensation could be tied to local profit performance, thereby aligning reward and control systems.

2. *The Transition to Multinational.* Organization development activities can also help to facilitate the transition from an international to a multinational orienta-

tion. Much of the recommended activity in transitioning to a global orientation applies here as well except that it must be customized to the issues facing a multinational strategy. For example, the successful transition to a multinational strategy assumes that managers believe local responsiveness is more important than global integration and that the organization is comfortable with the ambiguity of managing decentralized operations.

The decision to favor local responsiveness over global integration must be made with the same analytic rigor described earlier. In this case, the analysis must support the belief that the worldwide market is relatively heterogeneous in character. That is, that products and services, support, distribution, or marketing activities must be customized and localized to drive overall sales. Similarly, the organization must have the managerial, technical, and organizational competence to achieve profit margins from businesses operating around the globe. The multinational strategy is facilitated when culture and core competencies are more suited for decentralized decision making, and when the organization can manage high amounts of ambiguity and complexity.

Once companies develop a strategic orientation for competing internationally, they create an organization design to support it. Information like that found in Table 21.2 is useful for designing structures, information systems, and personnel practices for specific strategic orientations. OD practitioners can help to design change management programs to implement these features.

Application 21.2 describes the challenges Campbell Soup Company faced in moving to a worldwide strategy.[48] The story provides an opportunity to apply your knowledge of worldwide OD. What is their current strategic orientation? What strategic orientation do you think Campbell should pursue? What OD interventions can help the firm compete in new markets?

The Transnational Strategic Orientation

This orientation exists when the need for global integration and local responsiveness are both high. It represents the most complex and ambitious worldwide strategic orientation and reflects the belief that any product or service can be made anywhere and sold everywhere.[49]

Characteristics of the Transnational Design

The transnational strategy combines customized products with both efficient and responsive operations; the key goal is learning. This is the most complex worldwide strategic orientation because transnationals can manufacture products, conduct research, raise capital, buy supplies, and perform many other functions wherever in the world the job can be done optimally. They can move skills, resources, and knowledge to regions where they are needed.

The transnational orientation combines the best of global and multinational orientations and adds a third attribute—the ability to transfer resources both within the firm and across national and cultural boundaries. Otis Elevator, a division of United Technologies, developed a new programmable elevator using six research centers in five countries: a U.S. group handled the systems integration; Japan designed the special motor drives that make the elevators ride smoothly; France perfected the door systems; Germany created the electronics; and Spain produced the small-geared components.[50] Other examples of transnational firms include General Electric, Asea Brown Boveri, Motorola, Electrolux, and HP.

Transnational firms organize themselves into global matrix and network structures especially suited for moving information and resources to their best use. In the matrix structure, local divisions similar to the multinational structure are crossed

CAMPBELL SOUP COMPANY MOVES TO A WORLDWIDE STRATEGIC ORIENTATION

Campbell's soup is an American tradition. Its red-and-white label represents one of the strongest brands in the United States, although Campbell markets many other consumer products, such as V-8 juice, Pepperidge Farm baked goods, and Swanson's frozen foods. The company was started in 1869 by Joseph Campbell and Abram Anderson, but its initial growth was spurred by John Dorrance's technological innovation of canning condensed soup. The Dorrance family still owns more than 50% of the company.

Many of Campbell's products have enjoyed a dominant market share and solid financial performance over time. That performance has been supported by a divisional structure focused on each basic product line, plus an international division whose sales accounted for 18% to 20% of total revenues in the mid-1980s and less than 25% in 1993. Marketing and new product development have always been strengths of the Campbell organization. For example, between 1984 and 1986 the company introduced more than 290 new products, and it led the domestic prepared foods industry in establishing regionalized marketing in the late 1980s. Finally, under the Dorrance family, the company always has possessed a strong, conservative, and almost secretive culture.

Like many domestic industries, however, Campbell's main markets have both matured and experienced increased competition. Campbell's sales have flattened in the United States, increasing only about 3% per year between 1990 and 1993. Canned soup, the company's mainstay, has lost ground to fresh and frozen foods, which are more in tune with today's health-conscious marketplace, forcing Campbell to introduce new products in this category. At the same time, Campbell's other products face tough competition. H.J. Heinz and General Foods, for example, have imitated Campbell's regionalized marketing strategy and caused Campbell to undertake large increases in advertising and marketing expenses.

In response to these issues, Campbell began a strategic change effort to implement a worldwide strategy. CEO David Johnson began devising the foreign strategy almost as soon as he took over the top job at Campbell in 1990. Johnson is well qualified to lead the change; he has plenty of overseas experience to help him. His career has included assignments as a marketing executive in South Africa for Colgate-Palmolive Co., and he ran WarnerLambert Co.'s Parke-Davis Group in Hong Kong. His initial actions at Campbell focused on earnings problems by cutting operating costs and closing or

selling 20 plants. But he clearly believed that global growth was Campbell's ticket out of stagnation and announced that international sales should supply more than half of Campbell's revenues by the year 2000.

However, prepared foods are difficult to market globally. First, prepared foods are not as universal or as easily marketed as soap, cigarettes, or soda, which have allowed such domestic players as Procter & Gamble, Philip Morris, and Coca-Cola to expand abroad. Prepared foods may be the toughest products to sell overseas because of the broad range of items, and many of Campbell's products have difficulty in foreign markets. Italians, not surprisingly, look down on canned pasta, so Franco-American SpaghettiOs cannot be offered there. Similarly, the average Pole consumes five bowls of soup a week—three times the American average—but 98% of Polish soups are homemade, and "Mom is one tough competitor." Second, Campbell faces several large competitors that have been active in the global market for years. For example, CPC International Inc. and H.J. Heinz Co. already have built healthy market shares abroad. CPC has established brands, such as Knorr powdered soups, in most of the foreign markets that Campbell would like to enter, and it owns 80% of the market in Argentina. Last year, 60% of CPC's $6.6 billion in sales originated outside North America. Similarly, Heinz is the dominant canned-soup maker in Britain.

Still, with the flat sales in the United States, Johnson has had little choice but to make the change, which includes acquisitions, new product development, and marketing. Despite its domestic strength in marketing and new product development, the organization faces uphill struggles. Its acquisition history has been spotty. One of the company's biggest overseas ventures, the $400 million acquisition of Britain's Freshbake Foods Group PLC in 1988, was disappointing. Freshbake products lacked brand appeal and did not excite British consumers. More recently, Johnson tried to acquire Australia's Arnotts Ltd. As he saw it, the two companies were a natural fit. The $485-million-a-year cookie maker was a household name throughout Australia; Johnson was born in Australia; Arnotts was run by a Campbell's veteran; and Johnson believed that the cookie maker could benefit from Campbell's marketing competencies. In addition, Campbell already owned one-third of Arnotts' stock—a purchase dating back to 1985. Unfortunately for Campbell, what followed was a painful, costly, 4-month struggle. Along the way, the local press painted Johnson and the company as Ugly Americans. When Campbell finally was allowed to increase its holdings to 58% in February 1993, it was at a cost of more than $200 million.

Johnson indicated that Campbell may increase its pace of acquisitions to fill in its emerging global network. He also suggested that he would be willing to borrow funds to make the acquisitions happen. Increasing debt would be quite a break from Campbell's past conservative, debt-averse culture.

Marketing and product development initiatives, however, have gone better. In Western Europe, the company's Pepperidge Farm cookies, renamed Biscuits Maison to appeal to continental palates, are fast gaining a following. In addition, Campbell's soup is being shipped to Asia, and a Hong Kong taste kitchen and research and development operation is testing new recipes for that market. In some markets, Campbell's intent is to create new products that appeal to distinctly regional tastes. Early results include a fiery cream of chile poblano soup for Mexico and a watercress and duck gizzard soup for Hong Kong.

Campbell also has managed to overcome competitive and cultural obstacles in some countries. It has attacked Knorr's powdered soups in Argentina with advertisements that tout its Sopa de Campbell as "the Real Soup" and stress its list of fresh ingredients. Less than a year after introducing nine varieties of red-and-white-labeled soup in Buenos Aires, the company now claims 10% of the country's $50 million soup market. In Poland, Campbell advertises to working Polish mothers looking for convenience. But it acknowledges that learning what works best will take time. In many regions, consumers know nothing about Campbell or its products—a legacy of the company's insular history.

Johnson's biggest problem, however, is Campbell's culture. Conservative and paternalistic, the organization had a long-standing policy during the 1970s that no new product could be introduced unless it could show a profit within a year. Under the previous CEO, Gordon McGovern, some of the more stifling artifacts of the culture were changed. He permitted members to eat and drink coffee at their desks; he began wandering through the hallways without his suit coat on; he appointed the first two women vice presidents; and he changed several of the benefits, including the establishment of a daycare center and the creation of an allowance for employees who adopted children. Still, the organization's culture remained stodgy.

One of the most important problems Johnson faces is that, because of acquisition and operating problems in the past, managers in the organization have avoided taking assignments in foreign countries, and few Campbell executives now have any substantive overseas experience.

with product groups at the headquarters office. The network structure treats each local office, including headquarters, product groups, and production facilities, as self-sufficient nodes that coordinate with each other to move knowledge and resources to their most valued place. Because of the heavy communication and logistic demands needed to operate these structures, transnationals have sophisticated information systems. State-of-the-art information technology is used to move strategic and operational information throughout the system rapidly and efficiently. Organizational learning and knowledge management practices (Chapter 20) gather, organize, and disseminate the knowledge and skills of members who are located around the world.

People are integrated into transnational firms through a geocentric selection policy that staffs key positions with the best people, regardless of nationality.[51] This staffing practice recognizes that the distinctive competence of a transnational firm is its capacity to optimize resource allocation on a worldwide basis. Unlike global and multinational firms, which spend more time training and developing managers to fit the strategy, the transnational firm attempts to hire the right person from the beginning. Recruits at any of HP's foreign locations, for example, are screened not only for technical qualifications but for personality traits that match the company's cultural values.[52]

Implementing the Transnational Orientation

1. *Planned Change in the Transnational Orientation.* Transnational companies require OD interventions that can improve their ability to achieve efficient global integration under highly decentralized decision-making conditions. These interventions include extensive management selection and development

practices in support of the geocentric policies described above, intergroup relations, and development and communication of a strong corporate vision and culture. Knowledge management interventions help develop a worldwide repository of information that enables members' learning.

Effective transnational firms have well-developed vision and mission statements that communicate the values and beliefs underlying the firm's culture and guide its operational decisions. ABB's mission statement, for example, went through a multicultural rewriting when the company recognized that talking about profit was an uncomfortable activity in some cultures.[53] OD processes that increase member participation in the construction or modification of these statements can help members gain ownership of them. Research into the development of corporate credos at the British computer manufacturer ICL, SAS, and Apple Computer showed that success was more a function of the heavy involvement of many managers than the quality of the statements themselves.[54]

Once vision and mission statements are crafted, management training can focus on clarifying their meaning, the values they express, and the behaviors required to support those values. This process of gaining shared meaning and developing a strong culture provides a basis for social control. Because transnationals need flexibility and coordination, they cannot rely solely on formal reports of sales, costs, or demand to guide behavior. This information often takes too much time to compile and distribute. Rather, the corporate vision and culture provide transnational managers with the reasoning and guidelines for why and how they should make decisions.

This form of social control supports OD efforts to improve management selection and development, intergroup relationships, and strategic change. The geocentric selection process can be supplemented by a personnel policy that rotates managers through different geographical regions and functional areas to blend people, perspectives, and practices. At such organizations as GE, ABB, Coca-Cola, and Colgate, a cadre of managers with extensive foreign experience is being developed. Rotation throughout the organization also improves the chances that when two organizational units must cooperate, key personnel will know each other and make coordination more likely. The corporate vision and culture can also become important tools in building cross-functional or interdepartmental processes for transferring knowledge, resources, or products. Moreover, they can provide guidelines for formulating and implementing strategic change, and serve as a social context for designing appropriate structures and systems at local subsidiaries.

2. *The Transition to the Transnational Orientation.* In addition to implementing planned changes that support the development of the transnational orientation, OD can help firms make the complex transition to a transnational strategy. Although many firms take on the international orientation, a much smaller number of firms are large enough to become global or multinational. The requirements for successfully operating a transnational orientation—global integration and local responsiveness—are sufficiently restrictive and demanding that only a small fraction of organizations should pursue this strategy. As a result, knowledge about the transition to transnational is still being developed.

    Global and multinational organizations tend to evolve into a transnational orientation because of changes in the organization's environment, markets, or technologies.[55] In the global orientation, for example, environmental changes can reduce the need for centralized and efficient operations. The success of Japanese automobile manufacturers employing a global strategy caused employment declines in the U.S. auto industry and overall trade imbalances. Consumer and government reactions forced Japanese firms to become more responsive to local conditions. Conversely, consumer preference changes can reduce the needs for tailored products and locally responsive management that are characteristic of the multinational strategy. The typical response is to centralize many decisions and activities.

Thus, the evolution to a transnational orientation is a complex strategic change effort requiring the acquisition of two additional capabilities. First, global organizations need to learn to trust distant operations, and multinational organizations need to become better at coordination. Second, both types of organizations need to acquire the ability to transfer resources efficiently around the world. Much of the difficulty in evolving to a transnational strategy lies in developing these additional capabilities.

In the transition from a global to a transnational orientation, the firm must acquire the know-how to operate a decentralized organization and learn to transfer knowledge, skills, and resources among disparate organizational units operating in different countries. In this situation, the administrative challenge is to encourage creative over centralized thinking and to let each functional area operate in a way that best suits its context. For example, if international markets require increasingly specialized products, then manufacturing needs to operate local plants and flexible delivery systems that can move raw materials to where they are needed, when they are needed. OD interventions that can help this transition include training efforts that increase the tolerance for differences in management practices, control systems, performance appraisals, and policies and procedures; reward systems that encourage entrepreneurship and performance at each foreign subsidiary; and efficient organization designs at the local level.

The global orientation strives to achieve efficiency through centralization and standardization of products and practices. In the case of organizational systems, this works against the establishment of highly specialized and flexible policies and resists the movement of knowledge, skills, and resources. Training interventions that help managers develop an appreciation for the different ways that effectiveness can be achieved will aid the global organization's move toward transnationalism.

Changes in reward systems also can help the global firm evolve. By changing from a highly quantitative, centralized, pay-for-performance system characteristic of a global orientation, the organization can reward people who champion new ideas and provide incentives for decentralized business units. This more flexible reward system promotes coordination among subsidiaries, product lines, and staff groups. In addition, the transition to a transnational orientation can be aided by OD practitioners working with individual business units, rather than with senior management at headquarters. Working with each subsidiary on issues relating to its own structure and function sends an important message about the importance of decentralized operations.

Finally, changing the staffing policy is another important signal to organization members that a transition is occurring. Under the global orientation, an ethnocentric policy supported standardized activities. By staffing key positions with the best people, rather than limiting the choice to just parent-country individuals, the symbols of change are clear and the rewards for supporting the new orientation are visible.

In moving from a multinational to a transnational orientation, products, technologies, and regulatory constraints can become more homogeneous and require more efficient operations. The competencies required to compete on a transnational basis, however, may be located in many different geographic areas.

The need to balance local responsiveness against the need for coordination among organizational units is new to multinational firms. They must create interdependencies among organizational units through the flow of parts, components, and finished goods; the flow of funds, skills, and other scarce resources; or the flow of intelligence, ideas, and knowledge. For example, as part of Ford's transition to a transnational company, the redesign of the Tempo automobile was given to one person, David Price, an Englishman. He coordinated all features of the new car for both sides of the Atlantic and used the same platform, engines, and other parts. Ford used teleconferencing and computer links, as well as extensive air travel, to manage the complex task of meshing car companies on two continents.[56]

In such situations, OD is an important activity because complex interdependencies require sophisticated and nontraditional coordinating mechanisms.[57] OD interventions, such as intergroup team-building or cultural awareness and interpersonal skills training, can help develop the communication linkages necessary for successful coordination. In addition, the inherently "matrixed" structures of worldwide firms and the cross-cultural context of doing business in different countries tend to create conflict. OD interventions, such as role clarification, third-party consultation, and mediation techniques, can help to solve such problems.

The transition to a transnational firm is difficult and threatens the status quo. Under the multinational orientation, each subsidiary is encouraged and rewarded for its creativity and independence. Transnational firms, however, are effective when physically or geographically distinct organizational units coordinate their activities. The transition from independent to interdependent business units can produce conflict as the coordination requirements are worked through. OD practitioners can help mitigate the uncertainty associated with the change by modifying reward systems to encourage cooperation and spelling out clearly the behaviors required for success.

GLOBAL SOCIAL CHANGE

The newest and perhaps most exciting applications of organization development in international settings are occurring in global social change organizations (GSCOs).[58] These organizations generally are not for profit and nongovernmental. They typically are created at the grassroots level to help communities and societies address such important problems as unemployment, race relations, sustainable development, homelessness, hunger, disease, and political instability. In international settings, GSCOs are heavily involved in the developing nations. Examples include the World Conservation Union, the Hunger Project, the Nature Conservancy, the Mountain Forum, International Physicians for the Prevention of Nuclear War, International Union for the Conservation of Nature and Natural Resources, and the Asian Coalition for Agrarian Reform and Rural Development. Many practitioners who help create and develop these GSCOs come from an OD background and have adapted their expertise to fit highly complex, global situations. This section describes global social change organizations and how OD is practiced in them.

Global Social Change Organizations

Global social change organizations are part of a social innovation movement to foster the emergence of a global civilization.[59] They exist under a variety of names, including development organizations (DOs), international nongovernmental organizations (INGOs), social movement organizations (SMOs), international private voluntary organizations, and bridging organizations.[60] They exist to address complex social problems, including overpopulation, ecological degradation, the increasing concentration of wealth and power, the lack of management infrastructures to facilitate growth, and the lack of fundamental human rights. The efforts of many GSCOs to raise awareness and mobilize resources toward solving these problems culminated in the United Nations' Conference on Environment and Development in Rio de Janeiro in June 1992, where leaders from both industrialized and less-developed countries met to discuss sustainable development.[61] More recently, the Kyoto Protocol has focused attention on global warming and how countries and organizations can cooperate to address climatic concerns.

GSCOs have the following characteristics:[62]

- They assert, as their primary task, a commitment to serve as an agent of change in creating environmentally and socially sustainable world futures; their transformational missions are articulated around the real needs of people and the earth.

- They have discovered and mobilized innovative social-organizational architectures that make possible human cooperation across previously polarizing or arbitrarily constraining boundaries.

- They hold values of empowerment, or people-centered forms of action, in the accomplishment of their global change mission, emphasizing the central role of people as both means and ends in any development process.

- They are globally and locally linked in structure, membership, or partnership and thereby exist, at least in identity and practice (maybe not yet legally), as entities beyond the nation-state.

- They are multiorganizational and often cross-sectoral. They can be business, governmental, or not for profit. Indeed, many of the most significant global change organizing innovations involve multiorganization partnerships bridging sectoral boundaries in new hybrid forms of business, intergovernmental, and private voluntary sectors.

GSCOs therefore differ from traditional for-profit firms on several dimensions.[63] First, they typically advocate a mission of social change—the formation and development of better societies and communities. "Better" typically means more just (Amnesty International, Hunger Project), peaceful (International Physicians for the Prevention of Nuclear War), or ecologically conscious (Nature Conservancy, the Global Village of Beijing, the Mountain Forum, International Union for the Conservation of Nature and Natural Resources, World Wildlife Fund). Second, the mission is supported by a network structure. Most GSCO activity occurs at the boundary or periphery between two or more organizations.[64] Unlike most industrial firms that focus on internal effectiveness, GSCOs are directed at changing their environmental context. For example, World Vision coordinated the efforts of more than a hundred organizations to address the human consequences of Ceausescu's Romanian government.[65] Third, GSCOs generally have strong values and ideologies that justify and motivate organization behavior. These "causes" provide intrinsic rewards to GSCO members and a blueprint for action.[66] The ideological position that basic human rights include shelter has directed Habitat for Humanity to erect low-cost homes in Tijuana, Mexico, and other underdeveloped communities. Fourth, GSCOs interact with a broad range of external and often conflicting constituencies. To help the poor, GSCOs often must work with the rich; to save the ecology, they must work with developers; to empower the masses, they must work with the powerful few. This places a great deal of pressure on GSCOs to reconcile pursuit of a noble cause with the political reality of power and wealth. Fifth, managing these diverse external constituencies often creates significant organizational conflict. On the one hand, GSCOs need to create specific departments to serve and represent particular stakeholders. On the other hand, they are strongly averse to bureaucracy and desire collegial and consensus-seeking cultures. The conflicting perspectives of the stakeholders, the differentiated departments, and the ideological basis of the organization's mission can produce a contentious internal environment. For example, the International Relief and Development Agency was created to promote self-help projects in Third World countries using resources donated from First World countries. As the agency grew, departments were created to represent different stakeholders: a fund-raising group handled donors, a projects department worked in the Third World, a public relations department directed media exposure, and a policy information department lobbied the government. Each department adapted to fit its role. Fund-raisers and lobbyists dressed more formally, took more moderate political positions, and managed less participatively than did the projects departments. These differences were often interpreted in political and ideological terms, creating considerable internal conflict.[67] Sixth, GSCO membership often is transitory. Many people are volunteers, and the extent and depth of their involvement varies over time and by issue. Turnover is quite high.

Application Stages

Global social change organizations are concerned with creating sustainable change in communities and societies. This requires a form of planned change in which the practitioner is heavily involved, many stakeholders are encouraged and expected to participate, and "technologies of empowerment" are used.[68] Often referred to as "participatory action research,"[69] planned change in GSCOs typically involves three types of activities: building local organization effectiveness, creating bridges and linkages with other relevant organizations, and developing vertical linkages with policymakers.

Building the Local Organization

Although GSCOs are concerned primarily with changing their environments, a critical issue in development projects is recognizing the potential problems inherent in the GSCO itself. Because the focus of change is their environment, members of GSCOs are often oblivious to the need for internal development. Moreover, the complex organizational arrangements of a network make planned change in GSCOs particularly challenging.

OD practitioners focus on three activities in helping GSCOs build themselves into viable organizations: using values to create the vision, recognizing that internal conflict is often a function of external conditions, and understanding the problems of success. For leadership to function effectively, the broad purposes of the GSCO must be clear and closely aligned with the ideologies of its members. Singleness of purpose can be gained from tapping into the compelling aspects of the values and principles that the GSCO represents. For example, the Latin American Division of the Nature Conservancy held annual 2-day retreats. Each participant prepared a white paper concerning his or her area of responsibility: the issues, challenges, major dilemmas or problems, and ideas for directions the division could take. Over the course of the retreat, participants actively discussed each paper. They had broad freedom to challenge the status quo and to question previous decisions. By the end of the retreat, discussions produced a clear statement about the course that the division would take for the following year. People left with increased clarity about and commitment to the purpose and vision of the division.[70]

Developing a shared vision results in the alignment of individual and organizational values. Because most activities occur at the boundary of the organization, members often are spread out geographically and are not in communication with each other. A clearly crafted vision allows people in disparate regions and positions to coordinate their activities. At the Hunger Project, for example, OD practitioners asked organization members, "What is your job or task in this organization?" The GSCO president responded, "That is simple. My work is to make the end of hunger an idea whose time has come." A receptionist answered, "My task in this organization is to end hunger. I don't just answer phones or set up meetings. In everything I do, I am working to end hunger."[71] Because of the diverse perspectives of the different stakeholders, GSCOs often face multiple conflicts. In working through them, the organizational vision can be used as an important rallying point for discovering how each person's role contributes to the GSCO's purpose. The affective component of the vision is what allows GSCO members to give purpose to their lives and work.[72]

Another way to manage conflict is to prevent its occurrence. At the Hunger Project, the "committed listener" and "breakthrough" processes give GSCO members an opportunity to seek help before conflict becomes dysfunctional. Every member of the organization has a designated person who acts as a committed listener. When things are not going well, or someone is feeling frustrated in his or her ability to accomplish a goal, he or she can talk it out with this colleague. The role of the committed listener is to listen intently, to help the individual understand the issues, and to think about framing or approaching the problem in new ways. This new perspective is called a "breakthrough"—a creative solution to a potentially conflictual situation.

Finally, a GSCO's success can create a number of problems. The very accomplishment of its mission can take away its reason for existence, thus causing an identity crisis. For example, a GSCO that succeeds in creating jobs for underprivileged youth can be dissolved because its funding is redirected toward organizations that have not yet met their goals, because its goals change, or simply because it has accomplished its purpose. During these times, the vital social role that these organizations play needs to be emphasized. GSCOs often represent bridges between the powerful and powerless, between the rich and poor, and between the elite and oppressed, and as such may need to be maintained as legitimate parts of the community.

Another problem can occur when GSCO success produces additional demands for greater formalization. New people must be hired and acculturated; greater control over income and expenditures has to be developed; new skills and behaviors have to be learned. The need for more formal systems often runs counter to ideological principles of autonomy and freedom and can produce a profound resistance to change. Employees' participation during diagnosis and implementation can help them commit to the new systems. In addition, new employment opportunities, increased job responsibilities, and improved capabilities to carry out the GSCO's mission can be used to encourage commitment and reduce resistance to the changes.

Alternatively, the organization can maintain its autonomy through structural arrangements. The Savings Development Movement (SDM) of Zimbabwe was a grassroots effort to organize savings clubs, the proceeds of which helped farmers buy seed in volume. Its success in creating clubs and helping farmers lower their costs caused the organization to grow very rapidly. Leaders chose to expand SDM not by adding staff but by working with the Ministry of Agriculture to provide technical support to the clubs and with the Ministry of Community Development and Women's Affairs to provide training. The savings clubs remained autonomous and locally managed. This reduced the need for formal systems to coordinate the clubs with government agencies. The SDM office staff did not grow, but the organization remained a catalyst, committed to expanding participation rather than providing direct services.[73]

Creating Horizontal Linkages

Successful social change projects often require a network of local organizations with similar views and objectives. Such projects as creating a civil society in China, turning responsibility for maintenance and control over small irrigation systems to local water users in Indonesia, or teaching leadership skills in South Africa require that multiple organizations interact.[74] Consequently, an important planned change activity in GSCOs is creating strong horizontal linkages to organizations in the community or society where the development project is taking place. The China Brief (http://www.chinadevelopmentbrief.com), for example, publishes a newsletter describing the activities of different NGOs focused on environmental, child welfare, and other issues. Like-minded NGOs can then contact each other and support common interests. Similarly, GSCOs aimed at job development not only must recruit, train, and market potential job applicants but also must develop relationships with local job providers and government authorities. The GSCO must help these organizations commit to the GSCO's vision, mobilize resources, and create policies to support development efforts.

The ability of GSCOs to sustain themselves depends on establishing linkages with other organizations whose cooperation is essential to preserving and expanding their efforts. Unfortunately, members of GSCOs often view local government officials, community leaders, or for-profit organizations as part of the problem. Rather than interacting with these stakeholders, GSCOs often "protect" themselves and their ideologies from contamination by these outsiders. Planned change efforts to overcome this myopia are similar to the transorganizational development interventions discussed in Chapter 19. GSCO members are helped to identify, convene, and organize these key external organizations. For example, following the earthquakes in Mexico City in 1985, the Committee of Earthquake Victims was established to prevent the government and landlords from evicting low-income tenants from their destroyed housing. The committee formed relationships with other GSCOs concerned with organizing the poor or with responding to the disaster. The committee also linked up with local churches, universities, charitable organizations, and poor urban neighborhood organizations. It bargained with the government and appealed to the media to scuttle attempts at widespread eviction proceedings. This pressure culminated in agreement around a set of principles for reconstruction in Mexico City.[75]

Developing Vertical Linkages

GSCOs also must create channels of communication and influence upward to governmental and policy-level decision-making processes. These higher-level decisions often affect the creation and eventual success of GSCO activities. For example, the Global Village of Beijing (GVB) is a nongovernmental organization that raises the environmental consciousness of people in China. GVB leveraged its relationships with journalists and the government to produce a weekly television series on government channels to discuss and promote environmentally friendly practices, such as recycling, and to expose the Chinese people to environmental projects in different countries. When the Chinese government proposed new environmental regulations and policies as part of the World Trade Organization admission process, GVB helped assess the proposals.[76] More recently, GVB's founder, Liao Xiaoyi, sat on Beijing's successful 2008 summer Olympics Committee and drafted a "green Olympics movement" proposal that addressed concerns about Beijing's pollution.[77]

Vertical linkages also can be developed by building on a strong record of success. The Institute of Cultural Affairs (ICA) is concerned with the "application of methods of human development to communities and organizations all around the world." With more than 100 offices in 39 nations, ICA trains and consults with small groups, communities, organizations, and voluntary associations, in addition to providing leadership training for village leaders, conducting community education programs, and running ecological preservation projects. Its reputation has led to recognition and credibility: It was given consultative status by the United Nations in 1985, and it has category II status with the Food and Agriculture Organization, working relation status with the World Health Organization, and consultative status with UNICEF.[78]

Application 21.3 describes the work of Floresta and gives a brief account of how the organization operates, including the process of change and development.[79] The opening of Floresta's Mexico program provides important clues about the development of vertical and horizontal linkages and how GSCOs work within a clear vision.

Change Agent Roles and Skills

Planned change in global social change organizations is a relatively new application of organization development in international settings. The number of practitioners is small but growing, and the skills and knowledge necessary to carry out OD in these situations are being developed. The grassroots, political, and ideological natures of many international GSCOs require change agent roles and skills that are quite different from those in more formal, domestic settings.[80] GSCO change agents typically occupy stewardship and bridging roles. The *steward* role derives from the ideological and grassroots activities associated with GSCOs. It asks the change agent to be a co-learner or co-participant in achieving global social change. This type of change is "sustainable," or ecologically, politically, culturally, and economically balanced. Change agents must therefore work from an explicit value base that is aligned with GSCO activities. For example, change agents are not usually asked, "What are your credentials to carry out this project?" Instead, practitioners are asked, "Do you share our values?" or "What do you think of the plight of the people we are serving?" Stewardship implies an orientation toward the development of sustainable solutions to local and global problems.

The second role, bridging, derives from the grassroots and political activities of many GSCOs. *Bridging* is an appropriate title for this role because it metaphorically reflects the core activities of GSCOs and the change agents who work with them. Both mainly are concerned with connecting and integrating diverse elements of societies and communities toward sustainable change, and with transferring ideas among individuals, groups, organizations, and societies.

Carrying out the steward and bridging roles requires communication, negotiation, and networking skills. Communication and negotiation skills are essential for GSCO change agents because of the asymmetrical power bases extant in grassroots development efforts. GSCOs are relatively powerless compared with governments, wealthy upper classes, and formal organizations. Given the diverse social systems involved, there often is no consensus about a GSCO's objectives. Moreover, different constituencies may have different interests, and there may be histories of antagonism among groups that make promulgation of the development project difficult. The steward and bridging roles require persuasive articulation of the GSCO's ideology and purpose at all times, under many conditions, and to everyone involved.

The change agent also must be adept at political compromise and negotiation.[81] Asymmetrical power contexts represent strong challenges for stewardship and bridging. To accomplish sustainable change, important trade-offs often are necessary. The effective change agent needs to understand the elements of the ideology that can and cannot be sacrificed and when to fight or walk away from a situation.

Networking skills represent a significant part of the action research process as applied in GSCO settings. Networking takes place at two levels. First, in the steward role, practitioners bring to the GSCO specific knowledge of problem solving,

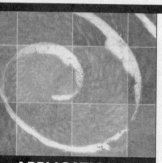

SOCIAL AND ENVIRONMENTAL CHANGE AT FLORESTA

Floresta is a nongovernmental organization founded on the premise that many environmental and social problems can be addressed effectively by harnessing basic economic forces. Its mission is to attack the economic problems in developing countries that cause and are caused by deforestation. Deforestation can be stemmed if it is economically advantageous for people to change their practices and take care of their environment. Similarly, poverty can be addressed optimally by providing long-term opportunities for people to change their own situations.

Floresta brings hope and long-term opportunity to the people affected by these problems through technically appropriate, business-based programs that lead to self-sufficiency. This fundamental vision has remained unchanged for 17 years.

Originally developed to meet the environmental, economic, and spiritual needs of the rural people of the Dominican Republic, Floresta provides local farmers with a loan of several thousand dollars each over a 7-year period through the Agroforestry Revolving Loan Fund. These loans are used to establish agroforests consisting of fast-growing trees that are harvested for wood products, as well as fruit trees and more traditional short-term crops. The loans are not a handout. The farmers begin to pay back their loans with their first tree harvest. That money is used to enter more farmers in the program. This process offers significant economic gains to the farmers (often up to a 500% or 600% increase in income) while healing environmental scars.

Although the loan fund is the heart of Floresta's program, farmers also receive technical training and marketing assistance. For example, agroforestry is different from traditional farming, and involves much more than simply planting trees. Each farmer must learn to plant, care for, and eventually harvest his or her trees in a sustainable manner. In addition, farmers receive training in soil care, harvesting, and marketing as well as financial planning assistance for the first surplus money they earn. Finally, a common problem faced by subsistence farmers is market access. The individual beneficiary must have not only a market for his or her products but also an economical way to get those products to that market. Floresta provides services in both of those areas.

More than 300 families have benefited or are benefiting from Floresta's program in the Dominican Republic. Of these, 20 have completed repayment of their loans and now have self-sufficient, 6-acre agroforestry farms that are producing at several times the rate of their former subsistence farms. They no longer have any obligation to Floresta, and the money that was loaned to them is now available to other needy farmers. The farmers, however, frequently are eager to continue their relationship with Floresta because of Floresta's marketing services and the community spirit that Floresta engenders. The farmers' achievements validate the Floresta model, supporting it with real-life success.

Scott Sabin, executive director of Floresta, described his approach to social and environmental change as he brought the program into Mexico:

I first met the people in the Mixtec village of El Oro in 1996, and for the past year our team had been working closely with them to diagnose some of the economic and environmental problems of the region, and to begin to develop solutions. We have become quite comfortable with many of the local people and several of them typically accompany us as we visit some of the other villages in the municipality of Santo Domingo Nuxaa. The makeup of the team varies, but usually consists of representatives from AMEXTRA, government forestry offices, local municipalities, and several other consultants. I represent Floresta. Over the past 2 years and many visits, we had built up quite a feeling of camaraderie.

Floresta partnered with the Mexican agency, AMEXTRA, to bring this team together and to ensure that Floresta's agroforestry program in Oaxaca would be well thought out and appropriate. Floresta has considerable experience in the Dominican Republic, but the mountains of Mexico are completely different ecologically, economically, and culturally. It is a big mistake to assume that the identical solution can work everywhere.

Working with the people of El Oro, we studied the local problems from both the community and technical perspectives. We worked to incorporate the community itself into the data collection and the investigation. For example, the Mixtec people tend to be cautious around outsiders. They also tend to be very communal, and every step along the way they voted as to whether or not they wished to continue working with us. So far we have passed all the votes unanimously, but stories of other development workers who had not been so fortunate always made me uneasy. Now we are working on implementing solutions and with promoters from El Oro, sharing these ideas with other communities.

Firewood and charcoal are the biggest sources of income for most of the villages. For example, I once observed and interviewed five family members, ranging in age from the mid-60s to 6, making charcoal. It was the primary source of income for the family. They had crops, too, but in years when there was drought, they were forced to rely more on charcoal. They were able to sell 25-kilogram bags of charcoal for 14 pesos a bag, or less than 2 dollars each. They made 30 bags of charcoal at a time and they did it about three times a year. Roughly calculated, this family of five subsisted on about 160 dollars per year.

The problem faced by the family is one of poverty, and tragically, the solution that they have chosen, the only solution they can choose, is leading toward their own ultimate demise and the destruction of the mountains around them. That is, an important cause of deforestation in the tropics is the subsistence farmer who must continually move to find fertile soil and who sells wood for fuel. Deforestation is a product of desperation and hunger, rather than of greed. Farmers are faced daily with the need to cut trees for their immediate survival. It quickly becomes a vicious cycle, as the treeless hillsides erode at an alarming rate and the topsoil pollutes rivers and streams. Without vegetation, the hills no longer hold water and quickly become unproductive. Rural families are often left with no alternative but migration to overcrowded cities. Any solution to deforestation must address their needs first.

In the Mixteca, Floresta has helped the community of El Oro to establish nine agroforestry demonstration farms, a community tree nursery, and an Agroforestry Development Committee. It also is establishing connections between the local church and churches in the United States. A sawmill and community-based reforestation and forest management plan is being implemented. This will replace the concessions that currently are being sold to large logging companies. Together with the Mixtec people, who already realize the precarious nature of the situation, Floresta is helping to diversify and improve the rural economy.

technologies of empowerment using processes that socially construct and make sense of the surrounding conditions, and organization design.[82] The participants bring local knowledge of political players, history, culture, and ecology. A "cogenerative dialogue" or "collective reflection" process emerges when these two frames of reference interact to produce new ideas, possibilities, and insights.[83] When both the practitioner and the participants contribute to sustainable solutions, the stewardship role is satisfied.

Second, in the bridging role, networking skills create conditions that enable diverse stakeholders to interact and solve common problems or address common issues. Change agents must be able to find common ground so that different constituencies can work together. Networking requires the capability to tap multiple sources of information and perspective, often located in very different constituencies. Action becomes possible through these networks.

But bridging also implies making linkages among individual, group, GSCO, and social levels of thought. Ideas are powerful fuel in international grassroots development projects. Breakthrough thinking by individuals to see things in new ways can provide the impetus for change at the group, GSCO, social, and global levels. This was demonstrated by U2's Bono and U.S. Treasury secretary Paul O'Neill during their 2002 visit to understand and develop solutions to poverty in Africa. The change agent in international GSCO settings must play a variety of roles and use many skills. Clearly, stewardship and bridging roles are important in facilitating GSCO accomplishment. Other roles and skills will likely emerge over time. Change agents, for example, are finding it increasingly important to develop "imaginal literacy" skills—the ability to see the possibilities, rather than the constraints, and the ability to develop sustainable solutions by going outside the boxes to create new ideas.[84]

SUMMARY

This chapter has examined the practice of international organization development in three areas. In organizations outside the United States, traditional approaches to OD need to be adapted to fit the cultural and economic development context in which they are applied. This adaptation approach recognizes that OD practices may be culture-bound: What works in one culture may be inappropriate in another. The cultural contexts of different geographical regions were examined in terms of five values: context orientation, power distance, uncertainty avoidance, achievement orientation, and individualism. This approach also recognizes that not all OD interventions may be appropriate. The prevailing economic situation may strongly favor business-oriented over process-oriented interventions. The process of OD under different cultural and economic conditions was also described, although the descriptions are tentative. As OD matures, its methods will become more differentiated and adaptable.

OD activities to improve international, global, multinational, and transnational strategic orientations increasingly are in demand. Each of these strategies responds to specific environmental, technological, and economic conditions. Interventions in worldwide organizations require a strategic and organizational perspective on change to align people, structures, and systems.

Finally, the OD process in global social change organizations was discussed. This relatively new application of OD promotes the establishment of a global civilization. Strong ideological positions regarding the fair and just distribution of wealth, resources, and power fuel this movement. By strengthening local organizations, building horizontal linkages with other like-minded GSCOs, and developing vertical linkages with policy-making organizations, a change agent can help the GSCO become more effective and alter its external context. To support roles of stewardship and bridging, change agents need communication, negotiation, and networking skills.

NOTES

1. S. Camden-Anders, and T. Knott, "Contrasts in Culture: Practicing OD Globally," in *Global and International Organization Development,* eds. P. Sorensen, T. Head, T. Yaeger, and D. Cooperrider (Chicago: Stipes Publishing, 2001).

2. L. Bourgeois and M. Boltvinik, "OD in Cross-Cultural Settings: Latin America," *California Management Review* 23 (Spring 1981): 75–81; L. Brown, "Is Organization Development Culture Bound?" *Academy Of Management Newsletter* (Winter 1982); P. Evans, "Organization Development in the Transnational Enterprise," in *Research in Organizational Change and Development,* vol. 3, eds. R. Woodman and W. Pasmore (Greenwich, Conn.: JAI Press, 1989): 1–38; R. Marshak, "Lewin Meets Confucius: A Re-View of the OD Model of Change," *Journal of Applied Behavioral Science* 29 (1997): 400–402; A. Chin and C. Chin, *Internationalizing OD: Cross-Cultural Experiences Of NTL Members* (Alexandria, Va.: NTL Institute, 1997); A. Shevat, "Practicing OD with a Technology-driven Global Company," *OD Practitioner* 33, 1 (2001): 28–35.

3. Shevat, "Practicing OD."

4. J. Schmuckler, "Cross-cultural Performance Feedback," *OD Practitioner* 33(2001): 15–20.

5. P. Sorensen Jr., T. Head, T. Yaeger, and D. Cooperrider, eds., *Global and International Organization Development* (Champaign, Ill.: Stipes Publishing, 2001); D. Berlew and W. LeClere, "Social Intervention in Curaçao: A Case Study," *Journal of Applied Behavioral Science* 10 (1974): 29–52; B. Myers and J. Quill, "The Art of O.D. in Asia: Never Take Yes for an Answer," *Proceedings of the O.D. Network Conference, Seattle* (Fall 1981): 52–58; R. Boss and M. Mariono, "Organization Development in Italy," *Group and Organization Studies* 12 (1987): 245–56.

6. B. Moore, "The Service Profit Chain—A Tale of Two Airlines" (unpublished master's thesis, Pepperdine University, 1999); the other examples come from fieldwork projects in Pepperdine University's Master of Science in Organization Development program.

7. T. Peters, "Prometheus Barely Unbound," *Academy of Management Executive* 4 (1990): 70–84; Evans, "Organization Development," 3–23; L. Thurow, *The Future of Capitalism* (New York: Morrow, 1996).

8. C. Fuchs, "Organizational Development Under Political, Economic, and Natural Crisis," in *Global and International Organization Development*, Sorensen et al., 248–58.

9. "A Survey of Multinationals: Big Is Back," *Economist* 24 (June 1995).

10. Evans, "Organization Development," 8–11; Brown, "Is Organization Development Culture Bound?"; Bourgeois and Boltvinik, "OD in Cross-Cultural Settings"; W. Ouchi, *Theory Z* (Reading, Mass.: Addison-Wesley, 1981).

11. T. Head and J. Cicarelli, "The Role of a Country's Economic Development in Organization Development Implementation," in *Global and International Organization Development*, 3d ed., eds. Sorensen et al., 25–34; W. Woodworth, "Privatization in Belarussia: Organizational Change in the Former USSR," *Organization Development Journal* 3 (1993): 53–59.

12. E. Schein, *Organization Culture and Leadership*, 2d ed. (San Francisco: Jossey-Bass, 1992); Evans, "Organization Development," 11.

13. G. Hofstede, *Culture's Consequences* (Beverly Hills, Calif.: Sage Publications, 1980); A. Jaeger, "Organization Development and National Culture: Where's the Fit?" *Academy of Management Journal* 11 (1986): 178–90; N. Margulies and A. Raia, "The Significance of Core Values on the Theory and Practice of Organizational Development," *Journal of Organizational Change and Management* 1 (1988): 6–17; A. Francesco and B. Gold, *International Organizational Behavior* (Upper Saddle River, N.J.: Prentice-Hall, 1998); R. Hodgetts and F. Luthans, *International Management: Culture, Strategy, and Behavior* (Boston: Irwin McGraw-Hill, 2000).

14. Hofstede, *Culture's Consequences*; E. Hall and M. Hall, "Key Concepts: Understanding Structures of Culture" in *International Management Behavior*, 3d ed., eds. H. Lane, J. DiStefano, and M. Maznevski, 4th ed. (Cambridge: Blackwell, 2000); F. Kluckhohn and F. Strodtbeck, *Variations in Value Orientations* (Evanston, Ill.: Peterson, 1961); F. Trompenaars, *Riding the Waves of Culture* (London: Economist Press, 1993).

15. K. Murrell, "Management Infrastructure in the Third World," in *Global Business Management in the 1990s*, ed. R. Moran (New York: Beacham, 1990); S. Fukuda-Parr, N. Woods, and N. Birdsall, *Human Development Report 2002* (New York: United Nations Development Program, 2002) (http://www.undp.org); P. Kotler, *Marketing Management*, 9th ed. (Englewood Cliffs, N.J.: Prentice-Hall, 1997).

16. B. Webster, "Organization Development: An International Perspective" (unpublished master's thesis, Pepperdine University, 1995).

17. Jaeger, "Organization Development and National Culture."

18. S. Michailova, "Contrasts in Culture: Russian and Western Perspectives in Organization Change," *Academy of Management Executive* 14 (2000): 99–112.

19. The dearth of published empirical descriptions of OD in particular countries and organizations necessitates a regional focus. The risk is that these descriptions may generalize too much. Practitioners should take great care in applying these observations to specific situations.

20. Woodworth, "Privatization in Belarussia."

21. K. Johnson, "Estimating National Culture and O. D. Values," in *Global and International Organization Development*, 3d ed., eds. Sorensen et al., 329–44; Jaeger, "Organization Development and National Culture."

22. A. Shevat, "The Practice of Organizational Development in Israel," in *Global and International Organization Development*, 3d ed., eds. Sorensen et al., 237–41; W. Fisher, "Organization Development in Egypt," in *Global and International Organization Development*, 3d ed., eds. Sorensen et al., 241–49.

23. M. Manning and J. Delacerda, "Building Organization Change in an Emerging Economy: Whole Systems Change Using Large Group Methods in Mexico," in *Research in Organization Change and Development*, vol. 14, eds. W. Pasmore and R. Woodman (Oxford, England: JAI Press, 2003), 51–97.

24. R. Semler, "All for One, One for All," *Harvard Business Review* (September-October 1989): 76–84.

25. J. Preston, L. DuToit, and I. Barber, "A Potential Model of Transformational Change Applied to South Africa," in *Research in Organizational Change and Development*, vol. 9, eds. R. Woodman and W. Pasmore (Greenwich, Conn.: JAI Press, 1998); G. Sigmund, "Current Issues in South African Corporations: An Internal OD Perspective" (unpublished master's thesis, Pepperdine University, 1996).

26. Johnson, "Estimating National Culture."

27. Sigmund, "Current Issues."

28. Webster, "Organization Development"; I. Perlaki, "Organization Development in Eastern Europe," *Journal of Applied Behavioral Science* 30 (1994): 297–312; J. Putti, "Organization Development Scene in Asia: The Case of Singapore," in *Global and International Organization Development*, 3d ed., eds. Sorensen et al., 275–84; J. Reeder, "When West Meets East: Cultural Aspects of Doing Business in Asia," *Business Horizons* (January-February 1987): 69–74; Myers and Quill, "Art of O.D."; I. Nonaka, "Creating Organizational Order Out of Chaos: Self-Renewal in Japanese Firms," *California Management Review* (Spring 1988): 57–73; S. Redding, "Results-Orientation and the Orient: Individualism as a Cultural Determinant of Western Managerial Techniques," *International HRD Annual*,

vol. 1 (Alexandria, Va.: American Society for Training & Development, 1985); K. Johnson, "Organizational Development in Venezuela," in *Global and International Organization Development*, 3d ed., eds. Sorensen et al., 305–10; Fuchs, "Organizational Development"; R. Babcock and T. Head, "Organization Development in the Republic of China (Taiwan)," in *Global and International Organization Development*, 3d ed., eds. Sorensen et al., 285–92; R. Marshak, "Training and Consulting in Korea," *OD Practitioner* 25 (Summer 1993): 16–21.

29. Babcock and Head, "Organization Development"; Johnson, "Organizational Development."

30. Johnson, "Organizational Development"; A. Mueller, "Successful and Unsuccessful OD Interventions in a Venezuelan Banking Organization: The Role of Culture" (unpublished master's thesis, Pepperdine University, 1995).

31. This application was based on material in R. Saner and L. Yiu, "Building Internal Capacities for Change in China," in *Action Learning Worldwide: Experiences of Leadership and Organizational Development*, ed. J. Boshyk (New York: Plagrave Macmillan, 2002), 293–310; and L. Yiu, and R. Saner, "Use of Action Learning as a Vehicle for Capacity Building in China," *Performance Improvement Quarterly* 11, 1 (1998): 129–48.

32. Webster, "Organization Development"; B. Gustavsen, "The LOM Program: A Network-based Strategy for Organization Development in Sweden," in *Research in Organizational Change and Development*, vol. 5, eds. R. Woodman and W. Pasmore (Greenwich, Conn.: JAI Press, 1991): 285–316; P. Sorensen Jr., H. Larsen, T. Head, and H. Scoggins, "Organization Development in Denmark," in *Global and International Organization Development*, 3d ed., eds. Sorensen et al., 95–112; A. Derefeldt, "Organization Development in Sweden," in *Global and International Organization Development*, 3d ed., eds. Sorensen et al., 113–22; J. Norsted and S. Aguren, *The Saab-Scania Report* (Stockholm: Swedish Employer's Confederation, 1975); B. Jonsson, "Corporate Strategy for People at Work—The Volvo Experience" (paper presented at the International Conference on the Quality of Working Life, Toronto, Canada, August 30–September 3, 1981).

33. Johnson, "Estimating National Culture."

34. Norsted and Aguren, *Saab-Scania Report*; Jonsson, "Corporate Strategy."

35. E. Trist, "On Socio-Technical Systems," in *The Planning of Change*, 2d ed., eds. W. Bennis, K. Benne, and R. Chin (New York: Holt, Rinehart & Winston, 1969), 269–72; A. Cherns, "The Principles of Sociotechnical Design," *Human Relations* 19 (1976): 783–92; E. Jacques, *The Changing Culture of a Factory* (New York: Dryden, 1952).

36. R. Tomlinson, "L'Oreal's Global Makeover," *Fortune* (15 August 2002): http://www.fortune.com/fortune/ceo/articles/0,15114,372136,00.html accessed on 18 November 2003.

37. C. Bartlett and S. Ghoshal, *Transnational Management*, 3d ed. (Boston: Irwin McGraw-Hill, 2000).

38. H. Lancaster, "Global Managers Need Boundless Sensitivity, Rugged Constitutions," *Wall Street Journal* (13 October 1998): B1.

39. Bartlett and Ghoshal, *Transnational Management*; D. Heenan and H. Perlmutter, *Multinational Organization Development* (Reading, Mass.: Addison-Wesley, 1979); Evans, "Organization Development," 15–16; Y. Doz, *Strategic Management in Multinational Companies* (Oxford, England: Pergamon Press, 1986); C. Bartlett, Y. Doz, and G. Hedlund, *Managing the Global Firm* (London: Routledge, 1990).

40. Bartlett and Ghoshal, *Transnational Management*.

41. R. Tung, "Expatriate Assignments: Enhancing Success and Minimizing Failure," *Academy of Management Executive* (Summer 1987): 117–26; J. Roure, J. Alvarez, C. Garcia-Pont, and J. Nueno, "Managing Internationally: The International Dimensions of the Managerial Task," *European Management Journal* 11 (1993): 485–92; A. Mamman, "Expatriate Adjustment: Dealing with Hosts' Attitudes in a Foreign Assignment," *Journal of Transitional Management Development* 1 (1995).

42. M. Ihlwan, "Doing a Bang-up Business," *Business Week* (18 May 1999): 50.

43. Heenan and Perlmutter, *Multinational Organization Development*, 13.

44. A. Borrus, "The Stateless Corporation," *Business Week* (14 May 1990): 103.

45. Ibid., 105.

46. J. Main, "How to Go Global—And Why," *Fortune* (28 August 1989): 76.

47. Heenan and Perlmutter, *Multinational Organization Development*, 20.

48. This application was derived from J. Weber, "Campbell: Now It's M-M-Global," *Business Week* (15 March 1993): 52–54; C. Dugas, "Marketing's New Look," *Business Week* (26 June 1987): 64–69; J. Weber, "M'm M'm Bad: Trouble at Campbell Soup," *Business Week* (September 1989): 68–70.

49. Thurow, *The Future of Capitalism*.

50. Borrus, "Stateless Corporation," 101.

51. Heenan and Perlmutter, *Multinational Organization Development*, 20.

52. Evans, "Organization Development."

53. T. Stewart, "A Way to Measure Worldwide Success," *Fortune* (15 March 1999): 196–98.

54. Evans, "Organization Development."

55. C. Bartlett and S. Ghoshal, "Organizing for Worldwide Effectiveness: The Transnational Solution," *California Management Review* (Fall 1988): 54–74.

56. Main, "How to Go Global," 73.

57. Evans, "Organization Development in the Transnational Enterprise."

58. L. Brown and J. Covey, "Development Organizations and Organization Development: Toward an Expanded Paradigm for Organization Development," in *Research in Organizational Change and Development,* vol. 1, eds. R. Woodman and W. Pasmore (Greenwich, Conn.: JAI Press, 1987), 59–88; P. Tuecke, "Rural International Development," in *Discovering Common Ground,* ed. M. Weisbord (San Francisco: Berrett-Koehler, 1993).

59. P. Freire, *Pedagogy of the Oppressed* (Harmondsworth, England: Penguin, 1972); H. Perlmutter and E. Trist, "Paradigms for Societal Transition," *Human Relations* 39 (1986): 1–27; F. Westley, "Bob Geldof and Live Aid: The Affective Side of Global Social Innovation," *Human Relations* 44 (1991): 1011–36; D. Cooperrider and W. Pasmore, "Global Social Change: A New Agenda for Social Science," *Human Relations* 44 (1991): 1037–55; H. Perlmutter, "On the Rocky Road to the First Global Civilization," *Human Relations* 44 (1991): 897–920; E. Boulding, "The Old and New Transnationalism: An Evolutionary Perspective," *Human Relations* 44 (1991): 789–805; P. Johnson and D. Cooperrider, "Finding a Path with a Heart: Global Social Change Organizations and Their Challenge for the Field of Organizational Development," in *Research in Organizational Change and Development,* vol. 5, eds. R. Woodman and W. Pasmore (Greenwich, Conn.: JAI Press, 1991), 223–84.

60. D. Cooperrider and T. Thachankary, "Building the Global Civic Culture: Making Our Lives Count," in *Global and International Organization Development,* eds. Sorensen et al., 282–306; Brown and Covey, "Development Organizations."

61. E. Smith, "Growth vs. Environment," *Business Week* (11 May 1992): 66–75.

62. D. Cooperrider and J. Dutton, *Organizational Dimensions of Global Change* (Newbury Park, Calif.: Sage Publications, 1999), 12.

63. L. Brown, "Bridging Organizations and Sustainable Development," *Human Relations* 44 (1991): 807–31; Johnson and Cooperrider, "Finding a Path"; Cooperrider and Thachankary, "Building the Global Civil Culture."

64. L. D. Brown and D. Ashman, "Social Capital, Mutual Influence, and Social Learning in Intersectoral Problem Solving in Africa and Asia," in *Organizational Dimensions of Global Change,* eds. Cooperrider and Dutton (Newbury Park, Calif.: Sage Publications, 1999), 139–167.

65. W. Pasmore, "OD and the Management of Global Social Change: Implications and Opportunities," *ODC Newsletter* (Winter 1994): 8–11.

66. F. Westley, "Not on Our Watch," in *Organizational Dimensions of Global Change,* eds. Cooperrider and Dutton, 88–113.

67. Brown and Covey, "Development Organizations."

68. Johnson and Cooperrider, "Finding a Path"; Cooperrider and Thachankary, "Building the Global Civic Culture."

69. P. Reason and H. Bradbury (eds.), *Handbook of Action Research* (Newbury Park, CA: Sage Publications, 2001).

70. Johnson and Cooperrider, "Finding a Path," 240–41.

71. Ibid., 237.

72. P. Vaill, "The Purposing of High Performing Organizations," *Organization Dynamics* 11 (Autumn 1982): 23–39; J. Collins and J. Porras, *Built to Last* (New York: HarperCollins, 1994).

73. M. Bratton, "Non-Governmental Organizations in Africa: Can They Influence Public Policy?" *Development and Change* 21 (1989): 81–118.

74. Brown and Ashman, "Social Capital"; L. DuToit, "Leadership for the Future: A Large Systems OD Intervention in South Africa," in *Global and International Organization Development,* eds. Sorensen et al. (Champaign, Ill.: Stipes Publishing, 1995), 203–14; L. DuToit, "Large Systems Change: Corporate Reaction to Transnational Demands in South Africa" (presentation to the 1995 OD Network, Seattle, Wash., 1995).

75. S. Annis, "What Is Not the Same about the Urban Poor: The Case of Mexico City," in *Strengthening the Poor: What Have We Learned?* ed. J. Lewis (Washington, D.C.: Overseas Development Council, 1988), 138–43.

76. Personal communication with members of the Global Village of Beijing, March 28, 2000.

77. Article posted in the China Brief Web site, http://www.chinadevelopmentbrief.com/brief.asp?art=112, and accessed on June 5, 2003.

78. Johnson and Cooperrider, "Finding a Path."

79. Information for this application was drawn from personal experience with the organization, their Web site, http://www.floresta.org, and links to various articles.

80. L. Brown and J. Covey, "Action Research for Grassroots Development: Collective Reflection and Development NGOS in Asia" (presentation at the Academy of Management, Miami, 1990).

81. R. Saner and L.Yiu, "Porous Boundary and Power Politics: Contextual Constraints of Organization Development Change Projects in the United Nations Organizations," *Gestalt Review* 6 (2002): 84–94.

82. D. Cooperrider and S. Srivastva, "Appreciative Inquiry in Organizational Life," in *Research in Organizational Change and Development*, vol. 1, eds. R. Woodman and W. Pasmore (Greenwich, Conn.: JAI Press, 1987), 129–69; Cooperrider and Dutton, *Organizational Dimensions of Global Change*.

83. Brown and Covey, "Action Research"; M. Elden and M. Levin, "Cogenerative Learning: Bringing Participation into Action Research," in *Participatory Action Research*, ed. W. Whyte (Newbury Park, Calif.: Sage Publications, 1991), 127–42.

84. E. Boulding, *Building a Global Civic Culture: Education for an Interdependent World* (Syracuse, N.Y.: Syracuse University Press, 1988).

Organization Development in Nonindustrial Settings: Health Care, Family Businesses, School Systems, and the Public Sector

22

Organization development is practiced in various types of organizations in both the private and public sectors. In recent years we also have seen growing applications of OD in service industries. Traditionally, however, the published material on OD has focused on applications in industrial and manufacturing organizations. This raises an issue of how relevant much of that knowledge is to other kinds of organizations, such as hospitals, family businesses, schools, and government agencies. There is considerable speculation and some evidence that traditional applications of OD may need to be modified if they are to extend beyond the narrow industrial model.

This chapter presents broad applications of OD in nonindustrial settings. In previous editions of this book, a person with knowledge and experience in OD in a particular kind of organization was asked to contribute a section for this chapter. For this edition, we asked Carol Gausz-Mandelberg of Blue Heron Associates and Foster Mobley of Organization Technologies to examine OD in health care; Rachel Mickelson of DHV Family Business Advisors to report on OD in family businesses; Paul Spittler, a former high school teacher, to describe how OD is applied in school systems; and Ray Patchett, city manager for the City of Carlsbad, California, to discuss OD applications in the public sector. Each author stresses the similarities and differences between OD as it is traditionally practiced in industrial organizations and how it applies in these nonindustrial settings. Their conclusions suggest the need for a greater diversity of diagnostic methods, interventions, and values when using OD in nonindustrial environments.

ORGANIZATION DEVELOPMENT IN HEALTH CARE*

Health care is a dynamic and complex industry facing significant growth and change. By 2011, health care expenditures are expected to account for 17% of GDP. The debates affecting the eventual definition of care, care delivery, financing, and access to care are being held in the halls of Congress, the boardrooms of large and small employers, and intensively in the countless daily interactions between care providers and those they serve. The health care industry represents a challenging context within which to practice OD. For example, compared to other industries, such as software development, manufacturing, or retail, health care differs along several dimensions:

- Consumers are often insulated from the economic consequences of their major health care decisions, including which hospital to go to and where to get outpatient

---

* Written by Carol Gausz-Mandelberg (Blue Heron Associates) and Foster W. Mobley (Organizational Technologies).

services. Access to the health care system and the cost of care is mostly determined by insurance provided through Medicare (a federally funded program for the elderly and disabled), Medicaid (a combined federal/state–funded program for the poor), or private insurance, the majority of which is provided through employers.

- The key providers of care are not all connected through an employment agreement. While there is a formal process to apply for "privileges" to work at a hospital or other care setting, physicians are not typically *employed* by them and often do not exclusively work at one hospital or outpatient facility.

- Hospitals, a key component of the health care system, are primarily not for profit and are faced with several challenges related to their ability to create sustainable revenue to support operations. They are heavily regulated by government and dependent on them for their revenue base. For example, Medicare accounts for an average of 38% of hospital revenues, while Medicaid accounts for 13%. In addition, hospitals are required to care for all patients regardless of the patient's ability to pay, prompting the need to grow revenue in other areas. In those areas, however, they are often in competition with physicians and entrepreneurs.

During the 1990s, mergers and alliances among different health care providers were common. Payers (insurance companies) exerted extraordinary pressure on providers (physicians and hospitals) to cut costs. This was due to pressure payers received from employers to contain the cost of insurance and to pressure from the payers' stockholders to increase profits. As a result, large "full service" organizations serving a broad geographic region were favored. Providers also responded with re-engineering efforts and delayed facility and equipment investments. It was a time of redefinition and shifting control. Now, however, for a number of different reasons, health care organizations are returning to their more traditional roles—providers caring for people in hospitals and outpatient facilities and insurance companies paying the bills.

Environmental Trends in Health Care

Health care practitioners and leaders acknowledge several important trends. They include imbalanced supply and demand, severe workforce shortages and the need for increased diversity, growing attention to patient safety and accountability, continued investment in technology and applications, persistent financial pressures and concerns, and eroding trust in, and among, health care providers and payers.

Imbalanced Supply and Demand. There is a renewed increase in the demand for health care brought on by an aging population, immigration, technology, and medicines that prolong life. For example, the baby-boomer bulge is rapidly reaching the age where their demands on inpatient and outpatient services will be greatest, and every state experienced population growth from 1990 to 2000 as did 80% of all U.S. counties.[1]

On the other hand, hospitals concerned with excess capacity in the 1990s, due to years of declining utilization rates, are now faced with meeting growing demand in outdated and undersized facilities. Providers must also work with limited capital for the facility and technology expansion needed to serve the increased demand. Similarly, there are projections of severe shortages in several critical medical specialties because of malpractice concerns, regulation, and quality-of-work-life issues. As a result, some providers can focus only on those programs and services of highest priority to their population, eliminating those of secondary importance. This could result in focused downsizing and the need for retraining or redeployment. Moreover, although certain outpatient services could provide revenue-generating opportunities for hospitals, physicians, and entrepreneurs, it increases stress on the hospital–physician relationship by placing them in competition.

Severe Workforce Shortages and Little Diversity. Health care is facing a widespread and long-term workforce shortage, especially in nursing but also in areas such as pharmacy, radiology, and medical records coding. Over 88% of CEOs[2] and more than 84% of Chief Nursing Officers[3] report a significant number of unfilled positions. The sheer numbers of patients, an aging workforce, opportunities in other settings and industries, and little interest in stressful, low-paying jobs have fueled the shortage. For example, nurses average 46 years of age and many cut back their time or retire after age 50. Nurses often have other demands on their time such as aging parents and/or young children, and there is little economic incentive to remain at the bedside rather than move into management. Moreover, women choosing health care careers now enter medicine more frequently than nursing.[4]

The health care workforce lacks diversity. While there is a rapidly growing racial and ethnic minority population, minorities are underrepresented in health care. For example, racial and ethnic minorities currently comprise more than one-fourth of the U.S. population and are expected to comprise nearly 40% by the year 2020. Yet, more than 90% of the RNs in the U.S. are white females.[5] A culturally diverse nursing workforce is more likely to meet the health care needs of a diverse nation's population. Minority populations have higher rates of certain diseases, lower rates of successful treatment, and in some cases, shorter life expectancies than do majority populations. They are also more likely to reside in areas with chronic shortages of health care providers.[6] Increasing the diversity of the nursing workforce will more accurately reflect the needs of patients.

Increasing Calls for Patient Safety and Accountability. Medical errors are a leading cause of death in America. There are more deaths in hospitals each year from preventable medical mistakes than there are from vehicle accidents, breast cancer, or AIDS.[7] This number does not include the mistakes made in outpatient health care settings. In 1999 a comprehensive report by the Institute of Medicine (IOM)[8] called attention to the significant problems of patient safety in the U.S health system and increased calls for accountability. In response to the problems, the Leapfrog Group was formed by a national association of Fortune 500 CEOs. It includes more than 140 public and private organizations that provide health care benefits and is dedicated ". . . to help save lives and reduce preventable medical mistakes by mobilizing employer purchasing power to initiate breakthrough improvements in the safety of health care and by giving consumers information to make more informed hospital choices."[9] The Leapfrog Group is backing the IOM's most recent recommendation of a billion-dollar investment in safety technology.[10]

The Joint Commission on Accreditation of Health Care Organizations has linked workforce shortages to medical errors.[11] A study by the American Nursing Association (ANA) found that 75% of RNs feel that the quality of care at their facilities has declined over the past 2 years, and 40% of ANA members would not feel comfortable having a family member or someone close to them be cared for in their facility.[12] This comes at the time of a national malpractice crisis in which the doubling of insurance premiums is prompting some physicians to leave their specialties and others to launch work stoppages. The crisis is decreasing patient access to emergency care, as physicians increasingly refuse to accept back-up call for emergency patients; straining the relationship between physicians, hospital leadership, and boards; and could result in a shortage of physicians in high-risk specialties such as OB, neurosurgery, and anesthesiology.

The impact of increasing accountability through government regulation is exacerbating the workforce challenges. The American Hospital Association (AHA) suggested that hospitals were in a "straitjacket." Regulations force them to direct more and more time and effort to paperwork than to direct patient care. The AHA notes that hospitals and other health care providers must comply with more than 132,000 pages of requirements governing Medicare and Medicaid programs, over three times the size of the IRS Code and its federal tax regulations.[13]

Increasing Technology Acquisition and Application. Health care providers and payers are increasingly adopting technology for clinical, administrative, and financial needs. The recent implementation of regulations related to the Health Insurance Portability and Accountability Act of 1996 increased the demand and attention on information technology and the processes surrounding it to assure confidentiality of patient information. Wireless, point of care, voice recognition, and handheld technologies hold promise for more virtual team collaboration, personal and organizational knowledge management, and streamlined record keeping enabling staff more time for interaction with the patient and their coworkers. But these new technologies also pose challenges of affordability, process change, and information security.

Continuing Financial Challenges. During the 1990s, a period of robust economic growth, hospitals, physicians, and other providers faced significant cost-cutting pressure and decreasing payments from all types of payers. Private payers, for example, faced criticism from consumers regarding decreased access to providers. At the same time, they faced pressure from employers, who fund most health insurance policies, regarding the need to decrease costs. With the return of the federal deficit, new efforts to decrease payment to health care providers, similar to the Balanced Budget Act of 1997, could result in deficits, restructurings, and provider exits from the industry. Similarly, state financial challenges—45 states reported budget deficits in 2002[14]—could prompt decreased Medicaid payments to providers. Physicians unwilling to serve Medicare and Medicaid patients could increase stress on emergency rooms as the last source of care for some patients.

The cost of providing care continues to increase, and for many providers it outpaces the revenue gain from volume increases. Major sources of expense growth include: pharmaceuticals, labor, technology, and legislative/regulatory requirements. Cost containment will be increasingly difficult, as many hospitals have already gone through numerous re-engineering cycles.[15] Private payers already pay a larger proportion of the pharmaceutical costs than the consumer, and these expenses are growing three times as fast as overall expense growth.

Finally, the economic downturn in 2001–2003 has contributed to an increase in the number of uninsured. Two million people lost employer sponsored coverage in 2001 and another 1.5 to 2 million are expected to lose it or decide they can no longer afford the increasing premiums or co-pay. Data from the U.S. census shows that nearly two-thirds of the 40 million uninsured had household incomes of $25,000 or more.[16]

Eroding Trust in the Health Care System. The public's trust in the health care system is eroding. Medical errors, reports of Medicare fraud, unethical health care industry executives and board members, and health care workers who make decisions for financial gain over quality care contribute to the mistrust. In addition, trust among the various parties involved (e.g., physicians, Boards, administrators, nurses, payers, etc.) is strained by the changing competitive and financial dynamics. Boards are increasing their scrutiny of financial records and practices. Hospitals and physicians compete for the outpatient care market. The lack of respect nurses receive from physicians contributes significantly to dissatisfaction in their work environment[17] and the restructuring of the 1990s eroded health care employees' trust in and respect for leadership.

Opportunities for Organization Development Practice

Despite the mostly negative and difficult trends facing the industry, organization development practitioners can positively influence the process and outcomes of change in the health care environment. The opportunities include creating effective cultures; creating systems and services that cost effectively differentiate and meet needs; job and process redesign to maximize effective use of expertise; and restoring trust in and among stakeholders.

Creating Effective Cultures. The past decade's focus on mergers and alliances may still require some cultural integration, human systems development, and work process improvement. However, the focus now needs to shift to creating effective cultures that attract and retain key stakeholders and promote patient safety. The workforce shortage and need to restore trust prompt the need for attention to cultures that welcome, support, and engage commitment from all stakeholders. Health systems that enable consumers, physicians, and employees to feel a sense of belonging and trust will achieve a sustainable competitive advantage. Alignment of recruitment, orientation, performance management, and other systems with the culture will be critical to success.

Recent articles about the workforce challenges cite the importance of attention to culture. An American Hospital Association commission studying the workforce issue suggested that culture changes and fostering meaningful work are as important as compensation for the long term.[18] Ideas for making the best of scarce resources include creation of mid-level professionals and increasing teamwork designs. Recommendations from the landmark "Magnet Hospital" study of the 1980s by the American Academy of Nursing, which outlined approaches that successful hospitals were using to serve as a "magnet" in attracting and retaining qualified nurses, are being cited as relevant and needed today. All but two relate to opportunities for OD, including:

- A philosophy of caring from top management that pervades the patient care environment
- Leaders that are visible and accessible
- Participatory management with practicing nurses engaged in decision making at the unit, departmental, and hospital levels
- Directors that interact frequently with nursing staff one-on-one
- Quality assurance programs that identify and resolve problem situations
- Nursing administration that recognizes the autonomy of the professional nurse
- Leadership that encourages the nurses in their continuing self-development[19]

Cultivating a culture of openness and learning, as opposed to blame, is important for addressing the increased focus on patient safety and accountability. Employees and physicians need to feel encouraged to raise safety problems, to find appropriate solutions to preserve patient safety, and to restore public trust in health systems.

High Quality, Cost Effective Human Resource Systems. OD practitioners can contribute to the creation of systems and services that strengthen the health care employers' ability to attract and retain qualified workers. This could include strong and unique training and development programs, career tracks that provide training and work opportunities enabling increased responsibility, mentoring programs to support new employees, work/family programs, diversity-friendly policies, and flexible scheduling and/or work assignment options. Efforts and programs devoted to new employees are especially important in retention.

Serving the increasing patient demand amidst human, facility, and financial capacity constraints results in significant, negative costs to the people involved. Although stress, burnout, and voluntary termination are frequent topics in industry journals today, the human and social issues of morale, job satisfaction, commitment, quality of work life, and worker productivity and performance are equally important.[20] For example, one study found that 68% of health care executives see burnout as a serious problem, 64% are physically exhausted by the end of the day, and 58% say emotional exhaustion is common.[21] The work environment for the practice of nursing has long been cited as one of the most demanding across all types of work settings and it is increasingly described as highly stressful and professionally unfulfilling.[22] The quality of work life for people in health care is under intense attack, and work performance may be a casualty of industry change. OD interventions that increase employee involvement and assist members in coping with stress clearly will be needed.

Effective Job and Work Designs. According to a national survey, the number one concern of nurses is their increased daily workload.[23] Another survey on worker retention showed that the primary reason people leave is the inability to use their skills and abilities.[24] Job redesign may be needed to tailor jobs for an aging workforce and one with multiple work/family demands; to address the increasingly challenging workload; and to enable most effective use of expertise. Job design and process design will also be important to address changes that may occur with the adoption of new clinical or information technology. Simply automating existing approaches to work will not achieve the optimal benefits from the capital and human cost of technology acquisition. OD practitioners can make a significant contribution in assuring that work streamlining in one area (e.g., pharmacy) does not increase workload in another (e.g., nursing). Team development will also be increasingly important to address the high patient demand and the issues around patient safety.

Application 22.1 describes a longitudinal effort at work redesign in an intensive care unit of a medical center. The application demonstrates the importance of involving people in decisions that affect them, basing interventions in data, and responding to strategic issues.[25]

Restoring Trust in and among Stakeholders. Trust has a significant impact on workplace relationships and performance. Healthy relationships need trust, and the stronger the level of trust, the stronger the relationship.[26] Trust is needed for constructive relationships among stakeholders (e.g., physicians, nurses, Board, leadership, payers, etc.) and to restore public confidence in health care organizations. It is crucial for opening dialogue and conflict on the ideas needed to address patient safety issues and strategic decisions. Individuals who trust each other are more inclined to speak openly about difficult issues. Open dialogue facilitates commitment, accountability, and ultimately greater performance results. Trust is also important to tap the knowledge and contribution of all workers, especially amidst workforce shortages. Research demonstrates that organizations with a high level of trust have four times the level of employee commitment and significantly more favorable financial results than their competitors.[27]

OD practitioners can contribute in assessment of the current state of relationships and assist in surfacing and resolving differences. Skills in conflict resolution and restoration of trust will be critical to address challenges from past interactions; to maximize effective use of limited talent; and to address societal issues of mistrust in public institutions.

Success Principles for OD in Health Care

A set of principles and beliefs that describe effective OD interventions and OD practitioners in health care are posed as future challenges to the practice and practitioner of OD in health care.

WORK REDESIGN AT HAMOT MEDICAL CENTER

APPLICATION 22•1

In the mid-1990s, the 467-bed Hamot Medical Center in Erie, Pennsylvania, believed that changing reimbursement regulations and decreasing utilization of the hospital required a $30 million expenses reduction. Among the different departments in a hospital, the critical care units are among the most expensive to operate because of the specialized materials, equipment, and labor. In fact, labor costs are often over 94% of total expenses. Two of the critical care units at Hamot Medical Center, the 15-bed medical intensive care unit (MICU) and the 16-bed surgical intensive care unit (SICU), were charged with producing more than $300,000 in savings. After discussions among a variety of stakeholders, a work redesign initiative was chosen as the best way to approach the problem.

As part of the diagnostic efforts, nursing managers and medical center executives adopted a two-part philosophy. First, the process should be data driven. Toward that end, the nurse managers created data collection sheets for the units' employees, including the nurse manager, registered nurses (RNs), patient care assistants (PCAs), unit secretaries, and housekeepers. During a 1-week period, ICU employees recorded and summarized their activity in 5-minute blocks of time. Those activities that did not occur in the patient care areas, such as accounting, marketing, and medical credentialing, were not included on the form. Staff summarized their activities at the end of each day and again at the end of the week. The unit managers closely audited each staff member's sheet to ensure that each tool was properly completed.

Second, the change process should be evaluated, designed, and implemented by those closest to the work. After analyzing each unit's data, nursing managers for each unit assembled their own work redesign team. The teams scrutinized the data and developed their own strategies for improving quality, while decreasing costs.

The data analysis and feedback took a variety of forms. For example, the top 10 activities for both the RNs and PCAs were placed on a grid and provided a quick visual assessment of role overlap and time spent in key activities. The RN data were further analyzed by career ladder levels. A significant amount of time also was spent identifying the percentage of RN time in RN-focused or mandated activities, as well as the percentage of RN time in activities that did not have to be done by an RN. The time spent performing components of the nursing process, case management, patient education, and professional education activities was placed in the RN-focus category. Documenting patient care, administering medications, making rounds with physicians, discharge planning, and participating in patient-family conferences were identified as valued and/or legally mandated RN activities. The 21 activities placed in this category were valued components of the RN role.

All of the RN time in each unit (by career ladder level and the unit's global average) was further sorted into one of two categories: RN time and non-RN time. Defining non-RN activity generated some debate and was somewhat unit-specific. Consensus was quickly achieved: Toileting, bathing, and changing linens were generally non-RN activities—specifically, those activities that could be performed by someone other than an RN at a potentially reduced cost. More than 40 activities were identified and placed in the non-RN category.

Other activities proved more difficult to categorize, such as taking vital signs on patients coming out of surgery or unstable patients that clearly required an RN's expertise. As a compromise, half of the RN's time spent gathering vital signs, intake and output, and responding to patient requests was placed in both categories. A number of activities did not belong in either category, including attending meetings, paid breaks, and analyzing staffing and committee work. RN time spent in management and education activities was analyzed but was a minor focus of data analysis.

The MICU's results are summarized here. During the first data collection period, the MICU staff had just hired a new nurse manager, and the unit was facing a number of challenges, including a high number of RN vacancies that were difficult to fill, high RN turnover rates, and job dissatisfaction. The new nurse manager gathered a team that reflected all levels of the career ladder and began to change the unit's culture and climate, improve patient care, and save money.

The MICU was historically staffed with 100% RNs. Occasionally, a student nurse acted as a floating PCA. Accordingly, the first data collection effort reflected a 100% RN skills mix. On the whole, the RNs were spending 33% of their time in non-RN activity, with the new graduate nurses spending 42% of their time in those activities. Furthermore, the RNs were using only 41% of their time in valued activities, e.g., assessing the patient.

This first team drafted 12 proposals to improve care and the quality of work life in the unit. In response to the unit's high percentage of non-RN time, PCAs were introduced and the unit's skill mix ratio was designed to meet a 75% RN target. Initially, four PCAs were hired and RN positions were slowly lost through attrition. Other initiatives included a case management pilot, a shared governance model, integration of the ICU nurses into the hospital's home health program, and charting-by-exception.

After a year of implementation, the diagnostic process was repeated. Members of the MICU organization, during a 1-week period, collected data on the activities of the different job classifications. The results suggested that the percentage of RNs in the unit had decreased to 84%. The four PCAs had been utilized in a care partner approach with nurses that increased task identity and reduced the amount of time RNs spent on non-RN activities to 24%. RN-focused time increased to 47%. A new team was assembled to evaluate the skills mix and activities percentages. The design changes were labeled a success. The team reset the RN skills mix percentage to 80% and determined that the unit would not drop below this figure to maintain quality patient care. In addition, they fine-tuned efficiencies found in charting, reporting, and the care partner relationship.

In the third year, the evaluation process was again repeated, and the RN percentage remained approximately the same (83%), but the percentage of non-RN time in non-RN activities had dropped to a unit average of 15%. The new graduate nurses continued to perform these activities (22%)

as the data reflected good differentiation of activity and focus along the career ladder. The unit's nurses were now spending 59% of their time in RN-valued activities. The care partner approach was working well and it was now difficult to see further opportunities for great changes. Only three work re-design strategies were submitted and reflected the earlier focus on refining the shared governance model, case management, and integration of the ICU nurses into a congestive heart failure home health program.

In the fourth year, the evaluation results showed some slippage in efficiencies that disappointed MICU members. The unit's percentage of non-RN time rose from 15% to 18%, while the RN focus dropped from 59% to 54%. Role overlap between RNs and PCAs was reemerging, and teamwork was again an issue. A large, highly committed group closely analyzed the data and developed strategies to put the unit back on course. A half-day retreat allowed the entire staff to work on teamwork and the care partner relationship. A goal for the next evaluation snapshot was to clearly link patient satisfaction and patient outcomes with RN percentages and care delivery systems. Meanwhile, changes in professional mix and care delivery continue as managers and staff closely watch the quality of care delivered.

Demonstrate the Relevance of the Subject to Strategic Performance. A central debate in OD is whether it should be focused only on quality-of-work-life issues or if performance and systems improvement issues should be of equal importance. The challenge of keeping up with demand while addressing workforce shortages and tenuous financial conditions strongly suggests that any organizational intervention that is not linked to strategic performance risks being labeled irrelevant. In the health care industry, OD interventions must be linked clearly to issues of the organization's strategic performance—those things that help the organization achieve and sustain competitive advantage, such as cost position, clinical excellence, and market share. OD interventions must not be seen as irrelevant or inconsequential to the life-and-death matters in operating a health care organization.

Linking OD efforts to issues of strategic importance will require two things: the practitioner's ability to understand the business of health care and how OD skills and knowledge can impact organizational performance, and the careful identification of the issues selected for action. The increasingly connected relationships among external strategy, structural integration, and human systems enhancement will have to be the expanded domain of the OD practitioner in health care.

Demonstrate the Importance of Depth for Sustainability. Health care's life-and-death focus, coupled with the crisis of insufficient capacity (i.e., human, facility, and financial) to care for the increased patient demand could prompt interest in quick fixes, or reactions rather than solutions to more systemic problems. OD practitioners must be able to make a compelling case for attention on deeper systemic issues for sustainable change such as cultures built on trust and learning, rather than shorter term "feel good" training and development.

Demonstrate Competence. The changes taking place within health care will require constant reevaluation and redefinition of competences in a particular field or discipline. This will be as true for medical professionals and health care managers as for OD practitioners. That may include enhanced knowledge and skill for leaders in intervention technologies, exposure to important trends and regulatory issues, and practice in the principles of large-scale change. Leading health systems and hospitals already are providing skills and awareness training to managers in areas of leadership, strategy, restructuring clinical care, human resources issues, and change management.[28]

Facilitate Integration among and between the Diverse Parts of the System. A universal theme of the practice of OD in health care today is integration among traditional and nontraditional stakeholder groups. For example, medical staffs, physician offices, community agencies, and insurance companies typically are untouched by OD processes. Now, in addition to new opportunities for improving the health and performance within each of those groups, significant efforts are necessary to facilitate their integration to improve health care delivery and effectively deploy limited resources. A good example is in the practice of community building currently under way among stakeholder groups such as medical practices, citizens, employers, and hospitals. The purpose of this intervention is to craft a common vision for what constitutes health for the entire community, across all health care providers. OD practitioners are uniquely qualified to assist in developing such a vision. Many have the skills and knowledge to work in network settings and possess the technologies of large-group intervention to create such a process.

Conclusions

The health care industry offers unprecedented challenges and opportunities. OD practitioners can influence positive growth and development by linking their efforts to the strategies of the organization, demonstrating competence and integrity, and being able to facilitate integration of people and processes across traditional departmental and organizational boundaries.

This opportunity comes with a challenge. At a time when each dollar and every resource in health care is being closely scrutinized, the inherent value of the OD approach is being tested for validity. Clients, under increasing pressure to demonstrate the added value of key activities, will, in turn, subject OD practitioners and their change interventions to the same testing. The practitioner must seek a balance between responsiveness and relevance while maintaining a commitment to the core values that have defined OD—namely the equal importance of human needs and the creation of a work environment that allows growth, fulfillment, and performance.[29]

ORGANIZATION DEVELOPMENT IN FAMILY-OWNED BUSINESSES*

Family businesses, such as Levi Strauss, Cargill, and Kikkoman (founded in 1630), are among the most diverse and least understood types of organizations. They are often thought of as "mom and pop" operations, yet 40% of the *Fortune* 500, including Wal-Mart and McGraw-Hill, are owned or controlled by family members. Moreover, family businesses comprise the single largest demographic segment—between 65% and 80% of all worldwide businesses—and they generate half of the U.S. domestic product and employ 50% of the workforce.[30]

Professional advisors, such as accountants, lawyers, and financial planners, have been serving this market for years. However, organization development practition-

---

*Written by Rachel Mickelson.

ers have only recently recognized this opportunity. This section explores the definition and model of the family business system, outlines critical issues facing family firms, and describes a typical planned change process.

The Family Business System

The most common definition of a family business is an organization where ownership and/or management control rests with a family (or families).[31] Accordingly, family firms have several potential competitive advantages that other organizations do not. These include higher employee loyalty (family and nonfamily), the ability to quickly move in and out of market niches due to their flexible form of organization, their long-term (vs. short-term) orientation that is often termed "patient capital," a higher attention to quality due to the family's reputation and their strong interest in their communities, and, finally, the benefits of being privately owned, as other firms find it difficult to determine a family firm's distinctive capabilities.

A family business system model is shown in Figure 22.1. It helps to understand the differences between family firms and more traditional businesses, and how OD practice must be modified. The family business system is composed of three different subsystems: the business, the shareholder, and the family. For each subsystem, there is an implicit or explicit plan that determines how the objectives will be achieved and a governance structure that represents the people in that system. In the case of a small family business, there can be complete overlap in the membership of the family council, the shareholder forum, and the board of directors.

Business, Shareholder, and Family Systems

The *business system* consists of family and nonfamily organization members, the strategic business plan, and a governance structure represented by a board of advisors or directors. The strategic plan outlines the business goals, objectives, strategies, and organization design. The board of advisors or directors counsels the business's leader(s) on strategy implementation, organization form, and other key business policy decisions.

The *shareholder system* consists of the business's owners, the shareholder plan, and a governance structure represented by the shareholder forum. The shareholder plan outlines the owners' business goals and objectives including risk tolerance, return on investment, and liquidity. The shareholder forum consists of owners who meet to develop and oversee the shareholder plan. Shareholder assumptions, including the buy-sell agreement, ownership succession, dividend policies, and investment options for business proceeds are relevant topics for this forum. Shareholders are responsible for reviewing the family plan (discussed below) and determining the relevant goals and policies to represent at the board of advisors/directors.

Finally, the *family system* consists of all family members, including those who have married into the family, their plan, and their governance structure, the family council. The family plan outlines the family's philosophy, goals and objectives for the business as well as other family activities, such as community service, family gatherings, and philanthropy. The Family Council represents the relevant group of family members and plans for discussions on such topics as educating family members on responsible ownership, developing policies on family membership in the business, communications and conflict resolution, and education about family business financials.

Values

At the center of the family business system model is a set of core values. They represent a key integration point for aligning the three subsystems listed above. How-

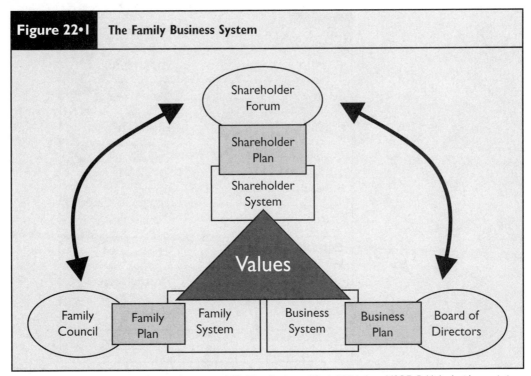

Figure 22•1 **The Family Business System**

SOURCE: The Healthy Family Business System model by Tom Starko and Rachel Mickelson, MSOD. Published with permission by DHV Family Business Advisors, http://www.dhvadvisors.com, 2000.

ever, values also best illustrate the differences between family and nonfamily firms. The complexity of the family business is a function of not only the interplay among the family, business, and shareholder systems, but the different (and often opposing) values that lie at the core of each system. For example, family and business system values are shown in Table 22.1.

The family system is dominated by values of security and equality. There is a strong inward focus on the family's dynamics, strong goals of keeping the system in equilibrium (even if it's an unhealthy equilibrium), and strong interest in maintaining unity and support. The family's continuity, even if the business does not prosper, produces a preference for stability and risk aversion. Relationships are most important, there is a great deal of emotion built into decisions, and one can only be born into (or married into) this system. Businesses hire the person that best fits the organization's needs based on knowledge, skills, and abilities; however, there's no job description to be a good family member. The family system places high import on family and business privacy. Families tend to covet financial, family dynamics, and business information; often they do not want business information shared even *within* the family.

On the other hand, the business system is interested in risk and equitability in the organization. Change, competition, results, transparency, and an outward orientation characterize business system values. Ideally, decisions are made rationally and objectively, and the system is composed of an often-changing mix of people who are hired into (or severed from) the organization. While 85% of those family firms who have identified a successor say they want it to be a family member,[32] how many of those family leaders would *objectively* fit the profile of the kind of leader the company needs based on its goals and strategy?

Thus, value dilemmas lie at the heart of how family businesses work. A family involved in a business can pursue its own objectives even when these are at odds

Table 22•1	Family vs. Business System Values
FAMILY	**BUSINESS**
Security	Risk
Equality	Equitability
Inward orientation	Outward orientation
Status quo/equilibrium	Change
Unity & Support	Competitive
Relationship based	Results based
Emotion based	Rationally based
Born into	Hired into
Secrecy	Transparency

with generally accepted business practices. Compensation, dividends, treatment of family and business expenses, performance evaluation and promotion, and the budget process are practices that can be influenced by family factors. Similarly, tensions in the business can be the result of the emotional relations in the family. Family relations are personal, often complex, and the result of a lifetime of positive and negative experiences. These relations influence business decisions overtly and covertly, as every family member is, in part, defined by their relationship to the business. Moreover, families often structure their business relationships in ways that fill a void in their family relationship outside of the business.[33] OD practitioners often have to consider such issues as:

- Should the chronic underperforming son or daughter be kept on in their business role and for how long?
- How much conflict should the family (and nonfamily) business members have to endure between two siblings in rivalry?
- When the business is suffering, will the family member's significantly higher compensation be addressed?

In sum, the family business system model provides an effective diagnostic tool and helps to explain some of the reasons why OD in family firms can be difficult.

Critical Issues in Family Business

The interaction of the family, shareholder, and business systems is more easily managed when they stay separate, as in nonfamily firms. However, when the systems overlap as family members come together in business, there are potential interface issues, potential problems, and dilemmas. Critical issues in family businesses are discussed next.

Entering or Leaving the Business as a Family Member. Family members often report choosing the family business as a place to work with comments like "It just happened" or "I fell into it." Family members are a convenient workforce, but businesses that successfully integrate family members do not base selection practices only on genetics. Policies on entering the family business, options for career paths, and multiple points of exposure to the family firm are a few of the critical practices.[34] There must be clear roles, recruiting processes, training and development, and a continued awareness of the family–business balance. Moreover, the business strategy and organization structure should influence selection, although only 37% of family firms report having a written strategic plan.[35] Most importantly, every family member should feel they have the opportunity to "opt out" of the family business, without the risk of losing the unconditional love of the family. To that point, many founders find it impossible to leave; close to 88% of family business respondents said that the family will continue to control the firm in 5 years.[36] Too often a family member's identity is largely derived from the family business they began, and many strive to keep the status quo at all costs instead of welcoming change, another values dilemma.

Conflicts and Rivalry in the Business. Conflicts and rivalries are common in family firms and are often the result of values dilemmas.[37] If a family is relationship based and a business is results based, how is the family member to be evaluated? If equality is valued in the family system, how do you choose a business successor? Family member compensation, roles and responsibilities, authority, and opportunity are some of the critical issues that ignite conflict between family members. The family system is an emotional one, and when placed together in a business setting, family members often revert back to the family roles they played growing up. Another source of conflict lies in the secret nature of families. Substance abuse problems, for example, are much more likely to be kept quiet in the family business[38] and only 62% of significant shareholders report knowing the senior generation's share transfer intentions.[39] The complexity of the family business system requires additional structures, practices, and processes to ensure open communications, conflict resolution, and business performance.

Ownership Transfer and Estate Planning. In addition to distinguishing between family and business roles, members of the family system may have a third role to play, that of "owner" or "shareholder." Owners' rights and responsibilities are different from family and business ones. Ownership rights typically include electing directors, creating bylaws, voting on specified major business decisions, and realizing a fair return on investment. Typical responsibilities include making informed decisions, creating and keeping agreements, respecting limits of authority, and developing business competencies to adequately fulfill their role as a shareholder.[40]

One value dilemma evidenced in the owner arena has to do with "equal vs. equitable." When ownership transfer issues arise, members of the shareholder group often struggle between transferring family business stock to members of the entire family vs. only those family members who are active in the business. The former option creates challenges between active vs. inactive owners, as active owners have growth goals, whereas inactive owners have value goals. Often, this dilemma is resolved by "equalizing" the total estate. For example, a family with two active and two inactive business members of the next generation all receive an equal share of the total estate, yet the two active members receive 100% of the business assets and the estate is "equalized" by transferring more of the nonbusiness assets to the inactive siblings.

Selecting a New Leader. The vast majority of family firms, 85% according to one survey, choose successors that are family members.[41] In addition, 39% of family firms will change leadership within the next 5 years and of those, 42% have not chosen a successor. Many families avoid the topic altogether due to its emotional intensity.[42] Some of the key reasons include a founder/owner who won't "let go" of the business, the lack of competency in the next generation, rivalry among siblings for key leadership positions, succession timing, incongruent business visions of the current and successor generation, and pressures from various family branches. Forward-thinking family business leaders spend the time to identify the optimum type of leader needed to take the business into the future. This can only happen after creating a shared business vision and strategy and then identifying the best leadership candidates. Once the current leaders have accepted the need for change, decisions can to be made as to where the potential candidates will come from. Will the next leader be a family or nonfamily member? If the choice is the former (and it typically is), what mentoring and development will ensure the family candidate is successful? Business is about risk and change, yet family is about stability and status quo, which explains part of the reason why choosing a new leader creates difficulties. Succession is marked by a shift of power and influence, followed by a period of shared power[43] and for many leaders, the proposed transition is met with great resistance.

Business Growth and Family Wealth.   Most family businesses struggle to transition the generations. Fewer than 30% of first generation family businesses survive to the second generation and only 12% survive to the third generation.[44] No successors, family assets too concentrated in the business, family conflict, passive vs. active owners, empire building, lack of professional management, or the absence of a shared vision and sustainable business model can all contribute to a family business's demise. When the business fails, there is little chance for the family's wealth to grow.

To grow the business and the family's wealth requires careful thought and strategic planning.[45] The company must move from an entrepreneurial business to a professionally managed firm, develop governance structures, formalize systems and processes, and recruit talent (from inside and outside of the family). Owners must continually develop assets independent of the business. As the business grows, so do liquidity options such as venture capital, debt or equity financing, internal stock sale, sale of the company, or employee stock ownership plans (ESOPs).[46]

OD Interventions in Family Business System

For a consultant working with family businesses, complexity is the norm, a result of the interconnectedness of the family, business, and shareholder systems. Necessarily addressing the entire family business system is a key difference from the work of a nonfamily business practitioner. The skill set required for a family business advisor is comprehensive and includes OD competencies (e.g., behavioral sciences, systems thinking, strategy, and organization design), family systems knowledge (e.g., life cycle development, birth order issues, and family dynamics), conflict resolution skills, and family meeting facilitation. In addition, the family business consultant should acquire working knowledge in the areas of estate and financial planning, legal forms of organization, exit strategies, family philanthropy, family offices, financial analysis, and multidisciplinary (professional) teaming.

Perhaps the key to the success of a family business consultant is the ability to establish a trusting, caring relationship with the client system, to accurately surface the issues and dynamics at the heart of the family business dilemmas, and to effect positive, sustainable change. Consultants must know their own values, ethics, goals, and personal development areas, including their beliefs about families and families in business and insight into their own family system issues and dynamics. Such awareness increases the family business consultant's ability to handle issues that arise in a family firm engagement.

In addition, given the many demands and diversity of the family business system, it can be beneficial to use a team consulting approach in certain cases. For example, a 60-year-old founder may relate best to a senior advisor perceived as an "equal," while younger next-generation leaders may connect better with someone closer to their age who has worked with other clients with similar experiences. If significant conflicts exist in the family, including an advisor with expertise and qualifications in individual and family therapy may be a valuable asset to the team.

Entering and Contracting. The special entry and contracting issues involved in family businesses include the need to quickly create a safe emotional environment, asking sensitive questions related to the family systems early in the engagement, getting permission to recontract as issues emerge, getting permission to work with other family members, and being clear about the requirements of collaboration. Unlike nonfamily firms, the "client" in a family business is the entire family business system. The mission of an OD practitioner dictates a systems approach, so any relationships begun in this phase must integrate family issues around the business issues. The contract will typically be with the major shareholders of the family firm; threfore additional efforts are required up front to ensure buy-in and collaboration in the process. Trust must be established early on for the rest of the process to have a chance of moving successfully.

Diagnosing the Organization. Diagnosing the family-run organization requires the particular tasks and skills necessary to understand the family system in addition to the business system. "Presenting" issues and problems that appear to be business related often require careful probing and unbundling to get an accurate picture of "what is." Trust building, begun in the entry phase, continues in the diagnosis stage by bringing the family together for an orientation meeting. This meeting, often the first time the family has congregated around business issues, helps them to understand they are not alone in the dilemmas they face, affords time for establishing trust within the family and between family members and the OD practitioner, and builds communications skills. Tools to help gather data include confidential interviews of a range of stakeholders, individual and business profiles, and a *genogram*, which is a visual representation of the family history, similar to an organization chart.[47] The genogram enables the practitioner to understand the intergenerational dynamics and to analyze how the family came to be who they are by identifying the patterns and issues have been passed down. The individual, confidential interview is perhaps the most powerful tool for gathering data and intervening in the system. It is critical to assess not only the pressing business issues, but those that are in the family system and the shareholder arena, as well as determining what boundaries exist between the subsystems, including how communications flow.

Key questions for understanding the family business system include:

1. Describe what long-term "personal success" means to you and your own personal vision of the future.

2. What is most important to your family?

3. Tell me about the best time that you've had with the family. Looking at the entire experience, recall a time when you felt most alive, most involved, most excited. What made it a great experience? Describe the event in detail.

4. Describe what "business success" for your company means to you. For example, what would your company look like if it was operating at its very best? What is getting in the way of that success? What is your role?

5. As a shareholder in this business, what do you want most from your investment?

6. How much agreement (alignment) exists between the family, the business leaders, and the shareholders about the vision, values, policies, goals, and strategy for the family business?

Feedback and Planning. Providing feedback to family business members often includes a 1- to 2-day off-site session to review a "discussion guide" (as opposed to a completed document) that summarizes key issues, priorities, and recommendations.

This session should be the *second* time the group has come together and can be viewed as an opportunity to facilitate the practices of good communications, group decision making, and conflict resolution. The more the practitioner can help those in the system build competency in these areas, the stronger and more sustainable the family business system will be. Among the typical issues found in diagnostic results and the discussion guides are lack of role clarity; lack of shared vision for the family, the shareholders, and the business; a dearth of communications; conflict between family members; and systems, processes, and structure deficiencies. The goal for the meeting is for the family to identify and agree on key issues, priorities, and next steps. Building good communication practices (e.g., regular family meetings) and resolving conflict are two common starting points for work with family firms. These interventions are good places to begin to "name" the particular value dilemmas inherent in the particular system.

Table 22.2 identifies the most common interventions in family business systems today.

Table 22•2	Typical Family Business Intervention Areas		
TYPE OF INTERVENTION	**BUSINESS**	**FAMILY**	**SHAREHOLDER**

Strategy	• Vision, mission, values
	• Goals and strategic initiatives
	• Organization capabilities
		• Mission, values, goals
		• Policies
		• Activities
			• Values, goals
			• Policies regarding
			  Risk tolerance
			  Dividends
			  Exit strategies
			  Investment and ROI
			  Liquidity

System	• Human resource • Technical • Information/ management • Culture	• Communications • Education • Social • Succession • Compensation • Philanthropy	• Shareholder agreement • Estate plan • Ownership succession • Communications
Structure	• Management team • Board of advisors or directors	• Family council	• Shareholder forum
Process	• Coaching founder/ current leader • Coaching next generation leaders/ leadership teams • Management team building • Conflict resolution • Role clarity • Board development • Board policies	• Conflict resolution • Communication planning • Family business education • Family/business roles, responsibilities, and boundaries • Meeting management • Family charter • Family policies	• Forum development • Forum policies • Communication planning • Shareholders' roles, responsibilities, and boundaries • Conflict resolution

1. **Strategic.** Strategic interventions, including mission and vision development, capability identification, and goal setting, are an appropriate place to begin work with a family business system as many family business issues stem from a lack of alignment around shared vision and values. Members of each subsystem—the business, family, and shareholders—need to dialogue and create a shared view of the future and an appropriate set of goals. In reality, there is a good amount of overlap between members of each subsystem so the family business OD practitioner must continually clarify roles, responsibilities, and boundaries. Strategic business planning is appropriate only after the family and shareholder subsystems have aligned on a set of values, goals, and shared vision for the family business. In addition, the process should be an iterative one with open communications between the appropriate family and shareholder governance structures.

2. **Systems.** System interventions include traditional OD approaches in the business, such as human resource policies and procedures, technical operations, information/ management systems, and organization culture. Many family firms can benefit from formalizing their business systems, including performance management, succession planning, leadership development, rewards, core process improvement, information technology implementation, and recruiting. Family and shareholder systems tend to be less formal. Interventions in the family subsystem can focus on communications, education, family succession, compensation, and philanthropy while shareholder agreements, estate planning, ownership succession, and communications are appropriate in the shareholder subsystem.

3. **Structure.** Governance structures are necessary for all three subsystems so that effective communications and coordination can occur among these complex systems. The business system benefits from a professional management team, led by a qualified CEO who reports to a board of advisors or board of directors. Outside board members should be roughly balanced with inside board members; the former should be skilled at earning the trust of the family and working with members of the both the senior and junior generation.[48] The shareholders' subsystem requires its own governance structure—a shareholders' forum. Here, active and inactive shareholders can meet to develop their goals, review the performance of their investment and make important decisions about family ownership. Finally, the governance structure for the family—the family council—is a place for the family to plan for their future, to nurture and develop its members, and to continually determine to what extent the business will be able to fulfill their needs.

4. **Process.** Process interventions can be very effective with family firms. This is especially true if the source or resolution of the client's problem is unknown and the nature of the problem is such that the client would benefit from involvement in its diagnosis.[49] Process interventions in the business system include coaching both the founder/current leader and the next generation leader, team-building, conflict resolution, and board development. Typical family process interventions include conflict resolution, communications and family meeting facilitation, and family charter development. The shareholder subsystem requires process interventions in the areas of forum development, communications/boundary management, and conflict resolution.

Application 22.2 describes a typical OD engagement with a family firm. Note how the three systems are entwined and in particular, how the family's issues override many of the business demands.

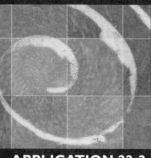

OD IN THE ROSS FAMILY BUSINESS

Don had founded a food manufacturing and distribution business in 1970 that amply provided for his family over the years and grew to annual revenues of $25 million by 2001. The company has steady growth and above-average profitability. Don's wife Jean was involved in the business on a part-time basis since its inception, and their two sons, David and Jeff, had occupied management roles for the last 10 years. Their daughter, Emily, managed the family's real estate investments. Despite all the good news, Jean and Don were distraught and ready to sell the business because of their sons' intense competition in the business and general resentment for each other. Not having any confidence in the management model for the next generation, Don and Jean feared that they might not be able to retire the following year, as planned. While they had gifted some nonvoting stock to their sons over the years, Jean and Don remained the majority shareholders and would not make any plans for further ownership transfer until this issue was resolved. Jean contacted Ed, an OD practitioner who also had a degree in family therapy, and asked if he could help. Ed and his partner Shelly initially met with the founder and his wife. Following that meeting, Ed and Shelly held confidential interviews with all siblings, the firm's CPA and lawyer, nonfamily managers, and a couple of members from their advisory board. In addition, they administered a set of assessment instruments that described the management style and decision-making preferences of key members of the management team.

The diagnostic efforts yielded the following information for the shareholder, business, and family subsystems. Within the shareholder subsystem, Don and Jean wanted to retire in 2003 but they expected to receive a continuing income from the business operations. They decided that transferring ownership and voting control of the business to the sons would be conditional (and were currently on hold) upon management's effectiveness and performance going forward. The sons believed they were entitled to their parent's shares sooner than later and wanted a guarantee. Finally, Emily was angry with her brothers for treating her parents with disrespect and wanted nothing to do with the business.

Within the business subsystem, the organization had grown to a level such that human and organizational constraints were preventing growth. There were strong indications that until the organizational structure and management models were changed, the organization would probably flounder. Importantly, there was no vision, mission, or strategic plan for the business, and one customer accounted for a large portion of the firm's revenues. Organizationally, the flow of communications among executives was inadequate and was not just limited to the relationship between David and Jeff; few people understood how decisions were made and the roles family and nonfamily members played. Finally, it was not clear that Don, David, and Jeff had the appropriate skills, interests, and abilities to lead the organization nor was there any plan for the development of these leadership and management skills.

Within the family subsystem, Ed and Shelly noted that family communications were infrequent, surface, and strained; issues that could be discussed openly were instead discussed between smaller groups. Family members rarely expressed appreciation and support of each other and the boundaries between the family and the business were blurred. The business strain between the brothers has affected their wives' and families' relations, and family gatherings have decreased as a result. Finally, records indicated that family members were being compensated at a rate two-and-a-half times similar positions in other companies.

The family was brought together to discuss the challenges family businesses face in general, and their family business system strengths and challenges, in particular. Spouses of the brothers and Emily and her husband attended the meeting. Although tensions were high, most members at the meeting appreciated the opportunity to discuss some important issues. The agenda included discussions of the diagnostic data, exercises to address communication within the family, and opportunities to discuss next steps. When disagreements and emotions became strong, Ed and Shelly intervened at teachable moments to model and explain communication and conflict resolution practices. The consultants made sure that no family member was left out of the process and worked to build trust with each person in the room.

As a result of the meeting, the following action plan was developed collaboratively with the family:

1. Establish family business meetings with Don, Jean, David, and Jeff (in pairs and together) to:
   a. Discuss and resolve outstanding interpersonal issues/conflicts
   b. Share their vision for their personal future
   c. Agree, as shareholders, on ownership succession
   d. Agree, as managers, on the current management model (roles, responsibilities, accountabilities, authorities)

2. Concurrent with the first action item, begin leadership coaching and communication skills development

   a. 1:1 leadership coaching with David and with Jeff

   b. Build management communications by holding and running effective management meetings. An outside facilitator would be used until family members gained sufficient skill to run the meeting themselves.

3. Schedule regular family meetings

4. Begin a strategic planning process, once the first two action items were well underway

With the above plan and family member cooperation, Ed and Shelly were able to help stabilize the family business system.

Communications improved, and better role definition resulted in fewer conflicts and better business performance. After leadership assessment and coaching, it became clear that Jeff was a better candidate to lead the company. David carved out a management niche for himself in the sales and marketing area, which better fit his personality and talents, while Don and Jean began easing away from the business and preparing for retirement. With a strategic plan in place they were better positioned to take the business into the future. Jeff and David eventually received the majority of the shares in the company and agreed on their goals for the future, which included strong business growth.

Implementing and Evaluating Change. There are various levels of consultant involvement in implementation. It is important to understand where involvement will support intervention success, where organization members can be "coached," and where members can take primary responsibility for implementation. High involvement is almost always needed in the first stages of implementation, where activities typically include establishing goals and milestones, creating a shared vision, establishing boundaries for family and business roles, and facilitating productive communications. Also in the early stages, the OD practitioner can communicate the importance of establishing and keeping to an implementation timetable and meeting regularly to resolve the many family business–interface issues that arise. Once the implementation phase is well underway, a 6-month or annual retreat can help to assess change process and effectiveness, reconnect with the family, and create plans around new family, business and/or ownership transitions. The continual transitions that occur in a family business provide a unique opportunity for an OD practitioner to become a long-term, trusted advisor.

ORGANIZATION DEVELOPMENT IN SCHOOL SYSTEMS*

Mark Twain once said, "In the first place God made idiots. This was for practice. Then He made school boards." Fortunately, modern critics of public schools are kinder in their analysis. Driven by greater social complexity and increasingly competitive demands of a global economy, societal pressure to improve educational effectiveness has increased during the past 20 years. Shifting demographics, for example, have produced a culturally diverse and multilingual student population. Other societal trends, such as increased rates of divorce and dual-career families, manifest themselves in children who arrive at school poorly prepared and lacking the supportive and active involvement of their parents. Schools are being asked to do more under more difficult circumstances.

In response to the challenges facing public education today, reformers advocate changes in all aspects of the bureaucratic network that constitutes and

---

* Written by Paul Spittler.

surrounds public education. Educational reform focuses on the individual school site as well as on the complex policy-making machinery that directs and simultaneously constrains schools. Reformers seek higher standards for all children, more demanding curricular content and instructional methodology, smaller class sizes, authentic measurement systems and greater accountability, comprehensive special education plans, and more effective school organizations. In short, it asks school personnel to attain higher standards, carry out their tasks differently, and organize differently to do so.[50]

As organizations, schools are regarded by educators as completely unique, distinct from other organizational types. However, practitioners of organizational change view schools as typical bureaucratic systems, not unlike other kinds of organizations. Comparative studies indicate that there is some validity in both these views. Schools share certain characteristics with all open systems and can be diagnosed and changed along variables common to all organizations. At the same time, schools differ from other organizations with respect to such things as the tasks they perform and the technologies they use to accomplish those tasks. Considering both the similarities and differences between schools and business organizations, OD programs designed for business and industry are neither entirely suited to nor entirely inappropriate for educational systems. OD techniques developed for other organizations can be used constructively in schools but only if they are refocused and modified to be responsive to the special needs of these systems.[51]

After exploring the characteristics of school systems and the implications for planned change processes, several high-involvement interventions that are currently being implemented in school are described.

Some Unique Characteristics of Schools

Schools differ from private-sector firms in their tasks and technologies, environments, members, and structures. The primary task carried out by schools is the transformation of young people through learning. This task differs from that of most business organizations in that it focuses on people, rather than on nonliving systems. Educating children is a complex and uncertain task. There is, for example, considerable ambiguity and disagreement concerning educational content of the required curriculum and little public consensus as to valid measures authenticating mastery of that curriculum.[52] Further, the technologies or methods used to carry out this task are ambiguous, particularly in their effectiveness. The impact of a particular teaching strategy may be difficult to discern, and its applicability may vary for students with different characteristics. These uncertainties create problems for the individual teacher as well as for the school as a whole.[53]

Not unlike business organizations, public schools are highly dependent on and vulnerable to their environments. Their enrollments rise and fall with birth and immigration rates, and their funding base erodes as citizens demand lower taxes. In addition, their customers are characterized by different and often mutually exclusive sets of interests. They are subject to close public scrutiny and to occasional "crises" that may arise within their communities.[54] Unfortunately, school administrators react to these forces by retrenching and defending, and their schools evolve into reactive, rather than proactive, organizations.[55]

However, public schools enjoy near-monopoly status and generally lack an environmental force for change matching that of competitive pressure. Although private schools have increased in number, their total share of the market is slight, accessible only to a relatively small percentage of the population.

Schools also are somewhat unique with respect to the qualifications and characteristics of their members. Teachers generally are better educated than are the people dealing with clients or working on the line in business or industrial organizations.[56]

Teachers probably take a greater interest in their jobs than do people in many other organizations and derive more satisfaction from the intrinsic rewards of their work.[57] Teachers believe that it is their responsibility to solve many task-related problems—in some cases, autonomously in their own classrooms and, in other cases, cooperatively in communities and faculty senates.[58]

Although some structural differences exist between schools and other organizations, these differences are not always very great.[59] The administrative structures of schools originally were modeled after those of business organizations,[60] and schools have been characterized by their centrality of decision making and their standardization of activities.[61] However, schools also have been called "loosely structured"[62] and "loosely coupled"[63] organizations. Those labels have been applied partly because teachers carry out their work in self-contained classrooms; are highly autonomous; and are weakly interconnected in influence, interpersonal support, and the flow of information. Thus, the administrative (or vertical) structures of schools are well developed, but collegial (or horizontal) structures tend to be weak. Although these structural characteristics are similar to those of many business organizations, they are not entirely appropriate for schools, given the uncertainties of their tasks and technologies. Better-developed collegial structures would be particularly useful in schools for solving the problems experienced by those directly responsible for carrying out the primary tasks of the organization.[64]

Implications for OD in Schools

The organizational characteristics of schools have important implications for the design of OD programs. First, schools traditionally have highly developed administrative structures that enable them to interact with their environments, although not necessarily in a proactive manner. For example, all schools are subject to public oversight concerning the academic achievement of their students. As a result, these sophisticated structures are quite good at collecting and reporting on the students' academic progress. Yet, despite the repetitive nature of annual standardized testing, few states have sought to achieve public consensus regarding the test instrument in advance of public criticism.

Second, the tasks performed by schools are somewhat uncertain. This uncertainty can create difficulties in task performance and can complicate other problems, including those of coordinating activities and allocating resources, that routinely must be solved by all organizations. In states with high levels of immigration, for example, the number of non-English-speaking students may change dramatically from one year to the next. Although teachers and other members of the school community may be able to solve some of these problems by relying on traditional authority structures, other problems may be resolved only through the use of collaborative decision-making structures which often do not exist.

Third, teachers committed to their work are likely to receive greater intrinsic rewards if task-related issues are resolved properly. However, teachers typically do not have access to structures for collaborative problem solving or do not possess the skills needed to use such structures effectively should they exist.[65]

Finally, despite their obvious bureaucratic characteristics, schools paradoxically may be regarded as underorganized systems (see Chapter 2). Communication among teachers is typically fragmented, curricular responsibilities between and within grade levels are frequently unclear, and the output requirements of the system are somewhat ambiguous. Correspondingly, many school districts exhibit characteristics of transorganizational systems (see Chapter 19). Schools within a given district can be said to be loosely coupled because leadership and power are typically dispersed among principals at largely autonomous school sites.

Those four points explain why many OD programs for schools focus heavily on creating collaborative decision-making structures that include teachers and parents and on helping participants develop the skills necessary to use such structures. These interventions can provide the school community with a base for identifying and solving problems that involve task and technological issues and that require the collective expertise of the entire school staff as well as the active support and involvement of parents.[66] Furthermore, they can provide a base for change initiation within schools[67] and can make them more proactive vis-à-vis their environments. And although the appropriateness of collaborative structures depends on the precise nature of the organization's environment and tasks,[68] substantial evidence suggests that collaborative decision-making structures are needed in most schools.[69]

High-Involvement Management in Schools

School reform stressing greater collaboration in decision making as a means of improving organizational performance is based on the principles of high-involvement management—a systemic change model that creates an environment where employees are motivated and empowered to become active in improving organizational performance.[70] The basic goal of high-involvement management applied to schools is to create an alternative to the traditional control-oriented hierarchy in which school district superintendents and school principals at the top are responsible for strategy, direction, and organizational performance and in which teachers feel victimized and constrained by a bureaucracy they cannot influence.[71] High-involvement management diffuses control throughout the organization such that all organizational stakeholders—including parents—can influence decisions, contribute to strategy and direction, and participate in improving organizational performance.

The high-involvement framework entails increasing the presence of four key organizational resources at the technical core of the organization: power, information, knowledge and skills, and rewards. These resources are believed to be closely linked to employees' capability and motivation to contribute to enhanced organizational performance.[72] Ideally, a high-involvement approach in schools would enable parents and teachers to influence the content of the curriculum, the delivery of that content, and the evaluation of student performance; it would allow them to participate in the creation of school district strategy and mission and specific educational goals; it would enable them to develop the skills necessary to use cooperative decision-making structures and to collect and assess performance data; it would provide them with ongoing task feedback; and it would reward teachers based on the improved academic performance of their students as well as on the development of their individual capabilities.

High-involvement principles have been found to be particularly appropriate in settings where the work is nonroutine, where organizational inputs are of a wide variety, and where the results of the task technologies are uncertain. Educational organizations fit these characteristics: Work cannot be entirely preprogrammed, and teachers are called on to employ their judgment to tailor approaches to individual students.[73] High involvement is also appropriate where interdependence among various task contributors is high and where their activities must be coordinated in a manner that cannot be fully anticipated.[74] For example, the work of one high school teacher has a reciprocal impact on the work of another and vice versa.

Most important for educators, the effectiveness of high-involvement management has already been demonstrated. In private-sector service and manufacturing organizations, implementing high-involvement practices has had a positive influence on many organizational conditions, including levels of work quality, innovation, introduction of new technology, customer satisfaction, and quality of decision making; employee outcomes such as quality of work life and satisfaction; and financial outcomes such as efficiency and competitiveness.[75]

Two broad-based trends in educational management incorporate the principles of high-involvement management: total quality management (TQM) and school-based management (SBM). Successful examples of both frameworks focus not only on the creation of collaborative decision-making structures, which include teachers and parents in addition to administrators, but also on the development of the requisite skills necessary to use such structures.

Total Quality Management

This intervention is the most recent and perhaps the most comprehensive approach to employee involvement (see Chapter 15). It is a long-term effort that orients all of an organization's activities around the concept of quality. TQM pushes decision-making power downward in the organization, provides relevant information to all employees, increases workers' knowledge and skills through extensive training, and ties rewards to organizational performance.

For Deming, a central figure in TQM, the key problem in American education is the absence of quality—meeting and exceeding the customer's needs and expectations and then continuing to improve. For him, the responsibility for quality lies with school administration, not with the student. Through evaluation systems that off-load the responsibility for quality onto the student, administrators abdicate their primary role of defining quality and improving work processes, and instead induce conflict, reduce cooperation, destroy intrinsic motivation, and cause morale and quality to suffer.[76]

Total quality initiatives have been ongoing in a variety of educational settings for nearly a decade. Deming's own *Out of the Crisis*[77] specifically identified public education as a service provider for which his "14 Points" would be appropriate. That same year, California's Sacramento County Office of Education began the first K–12 public education, organizationwide application of quality concepts in the United States, based on Deming's approach. Simultaneously, education literature began to appear that noted the parallels between independent research on improving school effectiveness and the Deming approach.[78] Further, beginning about 1989, Deming commenced annual seminars aimed especially at teachers. In 1990 Myron Tribus reported on the applications of Deming's principles in a Native American "alternative" school in Sitka, Alaska, and the American Association of School Administrators began its official study of the applicability of TQM to schools.[79] By 1994 more than 135 school districts were engaged in formal TQM programs nationally.[80]

In practice, successful TQM programs tend to be leader initiated, long term, and iterative in nature. Implementation of TQM typically is dependent on a number of team-based structures that operate parallel to traditional administrative authority. The teams arrive at decisions through group consensus, ground recommendations for action on valid data, determine valid criteria and strategies for measuring progress, and enjoy some degree of co-governance or collaborative decision making with the formal administrative leadership. In addition, extensive training is provided in a variety of areas to match the needs of the implementation process. In the early phases of implementation, training focuses on building an awareness of the quality philosophy. Then, as the organization moves forward, participants receive group process training and team-building assistance. Later, training in specific statistical tools is introduced in preparation for ongoing data gathering and analysis.[81]

TQM calls for total transformation rather than incremental movement in the pursuit of its objectives.[82] Its assumptions regarding human nature and behavior fit naturally with the assumptions of many educators.[83] In addition, the changes envisioned by the principles of TQM align closely with counterpart proposals in educational research for increasing educational effectiveness.[84] But, despite its popularity and track record of success in industrial, service, and governmental settings, little compelling evidence exists linking TQM with increased student achievement.[85]

School-based Management

This intervention, also known as *site-based management*, involves the formal alteration of school governance structures. It is a form of decentralization that identifies the individual school as the primary unit of improvement and relies on the redistribution of decision-making authority to achieve and sustain educational improvements. Some formal authority to make decisions regarding budget, personnel, and educational programs is commonly distributed among site-level participants so that they can become directly involved in schoolwide decision making.[86]

Site-based management has almost as many variations as locations claiming to be site based, and they differ along every important dimension—who initiates it, who is involved, what they control, and whether they are accountable to an outside authority. Site-based management may be instituted by state law or administrative action, by a district, or by a school. It may or may not be linked to an accountability system with consequences tied to student performance. But, in all its iterations, school-based management is an attempt to transform schools into individual communities in which appropriate people participate constructively in major decisions that affect them.[87]

Most variants of SBM involve some sort of representative decision-making body that shares authority with the principal or acts in an advisory capacity. The composition of these councils, committees, or boards may vary tremendously and can include principals, teachers, and parents, as well as students, community residents, and business representatives. States or districts may specify the constituencies that must be represented on the councils or simply leave it to individual schools. The state of Kentucky and the city of Chicago, for example, require virtually every school to have a school-based council, specify their makeup, and endow councils with extensive fiscal and policy authority. Maryland and Texas require schools to have school-based decision-making teams but, in contrast, do not specify their composition or legally transfer authority from the district to the school. These are only a few examples. According to one study, one-third of all school districts had some version of SBM between 1986 and 1990, and since 1990 at least five additional states have required it in some form.[88] During that same period, more than 20 states have passed legislation to permit the creation of "charter" schools, individual schools that are de facto school-based although they carry another title.[89]

Power and its delegation are central to SBM. In typically centralized school districts, many administrative decisions are made at the central office.[90] By contrast, school-based programs delegate decision-making authority to the school level, namely to principals, teachers, and parents, under the assumption that school-level actors are better positioned than district or state officials to make decisions for their organizations.[91]

Despite the current popularity of SBM, however, evidence of its impact on student performance is not compelling. A comprehensive literature review[92] concludes that there is little evidence that SBM has significantly enhanced conditions in schools and districts or improved students' academic performance, and a more recent Rand Corporation study reached the same conclusion.[93]

Classroom Interventions

Although not OD interventions per se, two instructional trends—integrated curriculum and cooperative learning—incorporate many of the principles of high-involvement management, altering the nature of power, information, knowledge and skills, and rewards within the classroom. Typically a team-based approach, integrated curriculum breaks down the traditional barriers among academic departments. Rather than viewing mathematics, science, language arts, fine arts, and social sciences as isolated subjects, integrated curriculum produces lessons that cut horizontally across departments, reintegrating and enriching student work. Similarly, cooperative learning specifically adopts a team-based approach to classroom work design and student learning.[94] Students work in cooperative learning teams and, to varying degrees, are evaluated based on the team's performance. Both of these instructional trends are project oriented, and students produce whole, identifiable pieces of work. Ideally, both approaches redefine the roles of teacher and student. Rather than delivering educational content to passive observers, the teacher becomes a facilitator for student-designed projects, and students take a more responsible role in the design of their own learning.

Conclusions

Reformers have called for large-scale change in educational systems that may require schools to become high-involvement organizations, capable of tapping the vast underutilized potential of teachers, parents, and the community to find better ways to educate children. Principals, teachers, and parents are not being asked simply to do their jobs better; they are being asked to do different jobs.

Principals are being asked to lead organizational transformation at a time when the task of educating children is more difficult than ever. Teachers are being asked to participate in improving the quality and performance of the school; to collectively solve problems and generate new and more effective approaches to teaching and learning; and to demonstrate new ways of relating to each other, to students, and to the community. Parents are being asked to participate more fully in the decisions affecting the direction, content, and delivery of their children's education.

This transformation process requires establishing new and effective structures and processes to promote broader participation in school governance, organizational improvement, and enhanced delivery of service; creating systems to measure results and share information; developing broader and deeper skills and knowledge through extensive training; and establishing appropriate systems to reward improvement.

A number of factors in schools make change of this magnitude especially difficult and present special challenges. The loose coupling of various aspects of schools and the isolated functioning of teachers conspire against a systemic approach to change. Schools do not have a tradition of strategy formulation and goal setting, nor are accountability and performance management systems well developed or accepted there. School participants will have to get used to examining results, talking about goals and how to achieve them, watching trends collectively, solving problems, and being held accountable.

There is a pressing need for additional experimentation and evaluation of new forms of school organization. In response, a number of demonstration schools have exhibited high-involvement characteristics,[95] including the School Development Program schools,[96] Accelerated Schools,[97] Essential Schools,[98] and the Pinellas County Schools.[99] SBM schools having success in reforming their approaches to teaching and learning are characterized by decentralized influence in decision making, broad information sharing, and high levels of knowledge and skills development.[100]

Much more research is required to test fully the efficacy of high-involvement approaches to school reform, and much of this will have to be action research. In particular, future researchers must consider how specific programs incorporate each of the four elements of high-involvement management. Most important, the connection between high involvement and enhanced student performance must be established convincingly.

ORGANIZATION DEVELOPMENT IN THE PUBLIC SECTOR*

Public-sector organizations, such as federal, state, and local governments, operate in an environment of competing political, social, and economic forces. Calls for the government to become more citizen focused and to operate in a more businesslike manner are common. Legislation and programs aimed at improving government accountability, quality, and effectiveness are being introduced and adopted at all levels of government.[101] For example, the 1993 National Performance Review (NPR) initiative created by former President Bill Clinton and run by former Vice President Al Gore called for national agencies to transform themselves into high-quality, low-cost service providers[102] and outlined 384 recommendations for improvement. At the state level, initiatives to curb government revenues or taxing authority, such as California's Proposition 13 (adopted by voters in 1978), continue to be introduced.

In addition, public-sector organizations face increasingly complex and significant challenges in responding to citizens, crafting public policy, and providing public services. Their record of success has been spotty at best, with trust in government falling dramatically. In 1964, 75% of Americans said that they trusted the federal government to do the right thing "just about always" or "most of the time." By 1999, that percentage had dropped to 29%.[103] In the face of economic recession, terrorism, and war these numbers are unlikely to improve. Similarly, public participation, once the hallmark of the American democratic process, is suffering. Voter turnout in presidential elections has dropped from more than 62% in 1964 to 51% in 2000.[104] As a result, public-sector organizations are engaging in a variety of efforts focused on increasing citizen participation and involvement in hopes of developing greater public trust and confidence in government as they move further into the twenty-first century.

For example, many governments are supporting community building and neighborhood involvement initiatives that engage citizens. At the same time, they are attempting to be more productive, efficient, and effective by downsizing and privatizing public services and introducing technology to increase effectiveness and productivity.[105] The International City/County Management Association and the Innovation Group have introduced nationwide performance measurement initiatives aimed at improving public-sector effectiveness. City governments, such as Phoenix, Arizona, and San Diego, California, are competing with the private sector through managed competition programs. Other cities, such as Carlsbad and Irvine, California, are implementing performance management compensation systems that reward employees based on competencies and the achievement of goals. All are being introduced to translate legislative mandates into measurable results and outcomes, such as citizen satisfaction and service quality.

These types of changes suggest a vital and important OD role in the public sector. Planned organization change efforts in the public sector can be as successful as those in private organizations,[106] and OD interventions are becoming more common and accepted in government. For example, community-visioning processes are being conducted to connect government with its citizens; technology is being introduced to help governments operate electronically and be more effective; team building is being conducted for elected officials and staff at all levels of the organization; and performance management and compensation programs are being implemented. These OD interventions, and others included in this book, are helping public-sector organizations respond to the citizenry and trans-

---

*Written by Raymond R. Patchett, City Manager, City of Carlsbad, California.

form themselves into citizen-focused, customer-driven, results-oriented public-sector organizations.

Although public-sector OD applications are becoming more common, they face a unique set of circumstances, including a complex political and administrative environment. Interventions often are conducted in the public arena among a number of stakeholders, each of whom has legitimate standing in the policymaking process—and often in the decision-making process. The climate and support for OD is complicated further by the structure of public-sector organizations. Although the legislative and political arena is interdependent with the administrative and staff domain, it is highly unlikely that both will be involved in the same OD intervention. If they are, each domain has a different role and operates based on different and sometimes competing values. To conduct planned change initiatives effectively, OD practitioners must recognize and appreciate these differences. This section highlights some key differences between the public and private sectors and discusses some of the implications for applying OD in public-sector organizations.

Comparing Public- and Private-Sector Organizations

Public sector OD initiatives need to recognize the political nature of government and be aware of the differences between public- and private-sector organizations. This discussion draws on the writing and research of Bob Golembiewski, John Bryson, H. George Frederickson, and John Nalbandian. Public- and private-sector organizations differ along four key dimensions: values and structure, the multiplicity of decision makers, stakeholder diversity and access, and the extent of intergovernmental relationships. Each of these differences is discussed along with its implications for OD practice.

Values and Structure

Public- and private-sector organizations differ in important ways with respect to their values and structures. In private-sector companies, the key values are profitability and the creation of competitive advantage. The board of directors, who represent the shareholders, and the management team, who are tasked with implementing a strategy, share these values. Although public-sector organizations share a similar structural arrangement of representation and implementation, there are crucial differences in purpose and role that hold important implications for OD practice.

In contrast to the private sector, the overarching purpose of public-sector organizations is to govern toward greater public good and demonstrate responsiveness to public wants and needs. The public good is addressed through the adoption of laws and policies and the establishment of public services and programs that support a broad array of citizen needs that must, by law, be discussed and adopted in an open public meeting. Responsiveness is reflected in demands for representation, efficiency, individual rights, and social equity.[107] In service of these values and purposes, public sector organizations also adopt a representation–implementation structural form. The representative function is known as the political or legislative domain, and the implementation function is known as the administrative domain.

The political–administrative structure reflects the values and roles inherent in government organizations. In the classic theory of public administration, the political domain is led by elected representatives who pass legislation and enabling statutes in service of the public good. In turn, they delegate implementation of programs and statutes to administrative agencies.[108] The political domain includes both elected and politically appointed officials, and the administrative group includes the merit-based civil service and certain executives, such as city managers, who are appointed on the basis of professional rather than political criteria.[109] This structure mirrors the private sector's distinction between a board of directors and management.

Unlike private-sector organizations, however, the purposes and values within public-sector organizations are not shared necessarily by the political and administrative functions. For example, politicians serve at the pleasure of the public. Although private-sector board members are elected representatives of the shareholders, their elections are not as open and public as are those of political office-holders. Politicians must compete to get elected and continue to posture and compete to get reelected. As a result, political values of responsiveness, representation, social equity, and efficiency, and the ever present political survival value are reflected in an open and public process where the particular interests and values of a diverse set of constituencies are brought together to produce a common view of the public good. Clearly, politics is the art and science of government.[110]

Moreover, the political function is responsible for the establishment and oversight of an organization that is designed to implement the outcomes of the legislative process. Generally, the mission of the administrative function is implementation and enforcement of the laws and delivery of public services or goods. The legislative mandates, rules, and procedures established to address public wants and needs make public-sector organizations less flexible than most private-sector organizations and constrain their ability to act outside of their legislative framework. Thus, the administrative function values partisan neutrality; selection and promotion on the basis of merit, specialization, and expertise; the use of information for analyzing public policy issues; recordkeeping for purposes of continuity; application of the work ethic; and the justification of decisions based on efficiency (achieving the most productivity for the money available) or economy (achieving a given level of productivity for as little money as possible) or both.[111] When elected officials are responding to the citizenry or setting policy, the political domain's values of responsiveness and representation may override the administrative values of functional expertise and economy. When such value conflicts occur, administrators are often caught in the tension between politics and their mandate to run an efficient organization.

These value differences, along with government's regulatory and taxation role, have contributed to the perception of government as a bureaucracy, which simply refers to the administration of a government through bureaus staffed with non-elected officials. Perceptions of bureaucracy are often negative, however, and include indifferent people exercising power through strict adherence to inflexible policies, rules, and procedures. Although public- and private-sector organizations can take on the characteristics of a bureaucracy, such as departmentalization, vertical decision-making processes, and many formal rules and procedures, the characteristics are more pronounced in government organizations. A critical reason for this phenomenon is that government organizations are legislated into existence, giving the organization or agency life until it is legislated out of existence. As a result, the organization receives funding that sustains its existence regardless of performance. Although budgets at all levels of government are reviewed and adopted annually, the complete elimination of a public-sector agency or organization is rare. The effect is that public-sector organizations, despite their purpose, can be much less responsive to citizens and customers than private-sector organizations because they aren't directly reliant on the customer for funding to sustain their existence.

The political nature of the legislative and representation process and the functional expert and efficiency orientation of the administrative process produce important tensions in a public-sector organization. OD practitioners must be aware of these tensions and of the implications they have for OD practice. First, OD practitioners must understand that a public-sector organization's primary mission, unlike private-sector organizations, is set by law, and major changes can only occur through additional legislative action. Even so, appointed officials and staff have much flexibility and discretion on how to implement government services and programs. The implication for OD is that many of the interventions used to help private sector organizations, such as strategic goal setting, business process re-engineering, total quality management, large-group interventions, and team-building, can be used successfully in the public sector.

Second, public-sector interventions often require approval and funding from an elected board. This increases the probability that the design, especially one for citizen and neighborhood-focused initiatives, will be scrutinized and challenged to ensure its efficacy. OD practitioners need to be ready to provide evidence of success for particular interventions in public-sector organizations.

Third, OD processes that support elected officials in citizen-focused initiatives or in enacting policy must consider the public environment in which they are being conducted. Public-sector organizations are subject to greater direct public access, media coverage, and a much broader array of responsibilities and more distributed power than are most private sector organizations. As a result, most policy-level OD and citizen-focused applications will be conducted in public. OD practitioners must select processes that create a constructive environment on the one hand and allow for public participation and review on the other. In addition, OD interventions must account for the vulnerability that elected officials, and sometimes public administrators, experience. For example, the results of a community-visioning process may serve as the political platform for candidates seeking the same public office that the incumbents leading the visioning process currently hold. OD practitioners need to be aware of this possibility as interventions are designed and implemented.

Fourth, the values of the political domain may differ from traditional OD values. The win–lose dynamics associated with passing legislation, mediating competing interests and political trade-offs, and balancing scarce resources can conflict with OD values of collaboration, teamwork, and efficiency. Improving organization effectiveness is an OD value often at odds with the political process. Last, administrative values and OD values are more likely to be aligned. As such, the OD practitioner may find more affinity for the administrative domain than for the political domain. To be effective, an OD practitioner must appreciate the tensions found in these differences.

Multiplicity of Decision Makers

The public sector operates in an environment of largely unlimited access to multiple authoritative decision makers, a phenomenon designed to ensure that "public business gets looked at from a variety of perspectives."[112] The public expectation of government is full and legitimate access to all decision makers at every level. As a result, access to the decision-making process is broader and accountability is more dispersed than in private-sector organizations, where such access is uncommon and responsibility is more clear-cut.[113] Further complicating the public-sector decision-making process is that different organizations are responsible for different steps in the governmental process, often making it confusing and difficult for citizens, clients, customers, and even public officials and staff to understand who is responsible for what decision and accountable for what product.

In addition, Golembiewski noted that decision making by public officials, "tends to favor patterns of delegation that maximize their sources of information and minimize the control exercised by subordinates."[114] Specifically, the goal was to have all decisions brought to their level for action and review. While this may have been the case in the past, most public-sector organizations today are just as embroiled as the private sector in the task of evolving from a command-and-control decision-making structure to one of empowered workers. Within the constraints of the legal mandates and regulations governing the organization, public officials can delegate decision-making responsibility and accountability to the public worker closest to the citizen and customer if they want to and if it is in alignment with their leadership philosophy. The implication is that OD values that seek to expand worker self-control and move decision making closest to the point of service are consistent with many government transformation efforts currently underway.

This multiplicity of decision makers results in additional implications for OD interventions. First, multiple decision makers make it difficult to determine the identity of the client and the expected results. For example, a legislative body may adopt a policy, such as pay-for-performance, and direct staff to design and implement the program. In this example, both the legislative body and the staff are accountable and responsible for different parts of the intervention. Because of the interdependence of the policy and administrative decision-making process, the OD practitioner may be unable to gain the same level of clarity about who is the client, their authority, and an understanding of their responsibilities that is possible in the private sector.

Second, approval, support, and funding for OD interventions may be more difficult to obtain. Operating at multiple levels of the same organization or with multiple agencies, adds a degree of difficulty relative to approval and support for OD interventions that is greater than private-sector organizations. The implication for OD practitioners is most direct when entering and contracting. The project may require staff support for the intervention and legislative approval and funding for the project. As a result of the public approval process, OD practitioners must be able to explain the process and outcomes that will result and must expect that the public or politicians resisting the project may challenge the efficacy of the intervention(s).

Stakeholder Access

As described earlier, a stakeholder is any group or individual who is affected by or who can affect the policies and operations of the public-sector organization—citizens, customers, political parties, corporations, employees, other governments, interest groups, critics, and so forth.[115] In contrast to private industry, the public sector conducts business in open public meetings and involves a "greater variety of individuals and groups with different and often mutually exclusive sets of interests, reward structures, and values."[116] In addition, citizens and interest groups have full access to public reports, documents, plans, and other background information via public records, public notices, and the Internet. OD practitioners must recognize that all stakeholders have legitimate entry into the public policy and administrative processes and bring different values, goals, or proposed solutions to public issues. For example, stakeholders supporting the goals inherent in the Americans with Disabilities Act must compete for funding with stakeholders supporting the objectives inherent in the Endangered Species Act and its programs. Such diversity of interests and access creates a broad array of challenges for OD. Foremost among the challenges is helping diverse groups of people with different and competing interests to collaborate with each other in developing a common goal that may represent an unpopular compromise to any individual group.

All citizens have access to and may influence the policymaking process. Such broad access may exist in the private sector with respect to certain types of information, but is much more restricted with respect to influence over decisions and activities. Such access and responsibility complicate the roles of politicians and administrators and politicize their position. Thus, the role demands of an elected official are much broader than the role demands of a private-sector board member. In addition, public-sector administrators, who are responsible for implementing public policy, have a duty to respond to the citizens, elected officials, and the staff that work for them. The implications of this web of roles and responsibilities for OD practitioners is that anybody can make a demand to be involved in the process at virtually any level of a public organization and the likelihood is that the individual or group will have legitimate standing to do so.

In addition, public-sector employees are stakeholders as a result of their legal right to form unions to represent them on matters concerning wages, hours, and working conditions. Because collective bargaining laws are structured for managing disagreement, a challenge for OD practitioners, if involved, is to help facilitate the process in a way where all parties perceive their interests have been considered and they feel heard. A poor labor relations environment and poor employee morale will make it difficult, if not impossible, to implement OD interventions successfully. Importantly, OD practitioners must understand that, in contrast to the private sector, it is difficult to arrange stakeholder interests and expectations behind a common goal. Even so, practitioners must appreciate that "attention to stakeholder concerns is crucial because the key to success in public and nonprofit organizations is the satisfaction of key stakeholders."[117]

Intergovernmental Relations

Government comprises a latticework of interrelated government agencies and organizations providing different public services to the same citizens and customers. The result is an intergovernmental relations environment where federal, state, and local government share power, responsibility and, in some cases, resources.[118] These intergovernmental relationships raise several considerations for public-sector OD applications.

First, issues of coordination and power may emerge out of the sharing of responsibility across public-sector organizations in the provision of public services. Although the services may appear to be provided by "the government," the reality is that a number of public organizations often are responsible for different aspects of the same public service. For example, providing an integrated transportation system requires federal, state, special district, private developer, and local government participation. The federal government and special districts work together to provide train and bus service. The state works with federal and local governments to provide interstate and state highways. Local governments provide the local road system with financial assistance from development, federal, and state agencies. OD practitioners working on intergovernmental relations projects must utilize a network perspective that makes explicit these differences with the intention of reaching agreement about overarching outcomes, responsibility, and shared resources.

Second, governments often work together on intergovernmental projects involving two or more public-sector organizations. In such cases, it is common to find that a federal policy, such as the Clean Water Act or the Endangered Species Act, sets the goals and objectives for state and local government organizations working together to implement the law. The resulting questions about what agency is responsible for what services or programs and what level of government pays for those services or programs have important OD implications. For example, a network development intervention would recognize the existing transorganizational system and help all agencies, each with a different degree of power, achieve reasonable agreement in addressing legislative goals and implementation issues. As with the private sector, however, reaching agreement often involves differing positions and conflict. Since different levels of government have different degrees of power, the OD practitioner could facilitate a positive result to the process by getting early agreement between the organizations on how decision making and conflict will be managed. Such an intervention is complex, however, because of the tendency of governmental agencies to participate while limiting their financial and resource responsibility. Appreciation for the mission and power relationships among agencies is critical in designing effective network development interventions.

Clearly, there are important differences between public and private organizations, and in many instances, the public-sector organization is more complex. In addition, one must appreciate the distinctions between the political domain and the administrative domain to consult or work in public organizations. With this understanding and an appreciation of the political arena in which public organizations operate, application of OD programs and techniques can be successful.

Recent Research and Innovations in Public Sector Organizational Development

The comparisons between the public and private sectors described above suggest that OD has a role in government and not-for-profit organizations. OD practitioners need to appreciate the inherent differences and understand that OD applications in the public sector are conducted in a complex political and organizational environment. Moreover, the unique features of public organizations—the values and structures, the multiplicity of decision makers, stakeholder diversity, and the intergovernmental relations environment—make OD applications challenging but not impossible.

Despite these challenges to OD practice in the public sector, there is growing evidence that OD interventions in government are successful, even when compared with change efforts in private industry. One review of 574 OD applications across the two sectors showed a similar pattern of predominantly positive results in both government and private industry.[119] Another study of 154 quality circle interventions in public and private organizations concluded that, although the highest levels of success occurred in private firms, overall success rates were substantial in both sectors.[120] A recent and particularly rigorous review of 52 OD interventions in government and industry confirmed these conclusions. The findings suggested that OD interventions were similarly successful in the two sectors, and led the researchers to conclude that the results "serve to contradict the common notion that planned change is likely to be less successful in the public sector."[121]

In addition to these promising findings, recent innovations in government point to the continued growth and success of OD in the public sector. At the federal level, for example, both Congress and the Clinton administration enacted legislation and reforms to create a twenty-first-century government designed to "get results Americans care about" with the overarching goal to "restore trust in America's government." In 1993, former President Bill Clinton created the National Performance Review, which was later renamed as the National Partnership for Reinventing Government. This program was discontinued in early 2001, but produced impressive results, including the creation of more than 4,000 customer service standards, the introduction of the Hammer Award for federal employees who reinvented their part of the government, and the passage of 34 laws enacting recommendations needing legislation. In addition, there have been over $136 billion in cost savings, more than

16,000 pages of reduced regulation, a reduction of 351,000 positions, and 83,000 laws enacting NPR recommendations.[122] These results have been achieved through interventions aimed at creating learning organizations (Chapter 20) and high-involvement organizations (Chapter 15), reengineering projects aimed at streamlining work flows and response times (Chapter 14), and, perhaps most difficult of all, efforts to change the civil service system so that the federal workforce is more flexible, development oriented, and performance driven.

These national reforms have their complement in state and local governments. Faced with similar pressures to reform, become more focused on citizens and customers, and operate in a more businesslike manner, state and local governments are introducing initiatives to become more productive and efficient while providing top-quality services. For example, a national survey of 987 state agencies found that 60% of them were using some type of strategic planning.[123] Another national survey found that all but three states have performance-based budgeting requirements,[124] and almost every state has enacted quality awards based on the Hammer Award and Malcolm Baldrige National Quality Award criteria.[125] In addition, local governments have conducted a variety of OD activities, such as team-building, leadership development, large-group interventions, and total quality management programs, to become more effective.[126]

Application 22.3 describes an OD effort in the City of Carlsbad to redefine and implement an orientation program for new employees. The involvement of a number of different constituencies aptly demonstrates several of the differences in public-sector OD.

Finally, nongovernmental organizations are working to help improve government. The National Innovations in American Government Awards, cosponsored by the Ford Foundation, the John F. Kennedy School of Government at Harvard University, and the Council for Excellence in Government, recognize examples of creative problem solving in the public sector. The National Civic League's All-America City Award recognizes exemplary community problem solving and is given to communities that cooperatively tackle challenges and achieve results. The Alliance for Redesigning Government of the National Academy of Public Administration is a national network for all levels of government that advocate performance-based, results-driven governance. The Innovation Groups is a national network and clearinghouse of local government organizations with the mission of innovation in the provision of public services, sustaining meaningful connections, and renewing passion for public service.

Conclusions

OD applications have proven to be effective in public-sector organizations. Faced with many of the same pressures as private industry and some that are unique to government, public organizations will continue to use OD applications and interventions to transform themselves into citizen- and customer-driven, high-performance, results-oriented organizations. But to be effective, practitioners helping government must appreciate the differences incumbent in public-sector values and organization structure; the differences in public and private organizations; and the mindsets of elected officials and government workers. OD practitioners need to understand public-sector organizations and tailor interventions to fit highly diverse, politicized situations where elected officials and bureaucrats struggle with moving toward a new emphasis on continuous improvement, teamwork, customer focus, employee development, and learning. Although public-sector OD is difficult and challenging, the successes cited in this chapter illustrate that OD is an invaluable tool in helping public-sector organizations provide top-quality services.

APPROACHING EMPLOYEE ORIENTATION AS A CULTURAL EXPERIENCE

APPLICATION 22·3

Like many organizations, the City of Carlsbad, California, had offered new employees a minimal orientation to the organization at the start of their employment. The focus of the orientation was primarily on explaining compensation and benefit plans.

In the spring of 1998, propelled by the City Manager's urging and the high degree of employee interest manifest at the city's large-scale organizational Futuring Conference 2 years prior, the manager and his leadership team began a series of discussions focusing on how orientation could be "something more." Over the course of several months the team members had a series of discussions, facilitated by an internal OD consultant, exploring both their preconceived notions of employee orientation processes and the outcomes they hoped to achieve as a result of doing "something more."

Two conclusions emerged from those discussions. First, the group developed a much more expansive view of the objectives, structure, and content of "employee orientation." Second, they decided to use a "diagonal slice" of employees from all branches and all levels in a strategic initiative team (SIT) to design a new process. The SIT symbolized that responsibility for employee orientation would not belong to one department (i.e., Human Resources) or one group (i.e., management); that it was to be shared by all members of the workforce.

The leadership team engaged the SIT in developing a statement of outcomes from what was referred to as "orientation-Plus." It included the city's vision is shared by people at all levels; employees regard public service as a noble and important purpose; and policies, practices, and people all send the same message (about the organization's commitment to service). The outcome statements served as the heart of the design team's charter and its frame of reference throughout the design development process.

In addition, the SIT and the leadership team co-created both task and process goals, again expressed as outcomes, for the development effort. The task goals were to develop (1) a process to orient, integrate, invest and *re-invest* all employees in the city's public service mission, and (2) plans for implementation, continuing improvement, and ongoing development of that process. Three process goals were defined, including (1) the orientation-Plus process is owned by the organization, (2) the city's capabilities and knowledge are extended, and (3) cross-functional teamwork is reinforced. The

same internal consultant who had worked with the leadership team helped craft a design and development process for the SIT and facilitated its work throughout.

The design and development plan included a learning phase with two elements. The first was an internally focused appreciative inquiry through which team members and other volunteer inquirers gained insights into the positive core of the city organization—that which energizes those who work within it. The second element, termed "Global Learning," included research on the orientation practices of organizations—public and private—recognized for excellence in their fields. The objective of this research was not to discover practices that Carlsbad could copy as much as it was to inspire the team to think more creatively about approaches they might recommend.

The end result of the team's effort, initiated in February 2000, was an employee *engagement* process called *Experience*Carlsbad. The process is an interrelated series of activities, events, and procedures designed to give participants an *experience* of the city imbued with the values, mission, and vision articulated by employees in the 1996 Futuring Conference. For new employees, the *Experience* begins before they are even hired through a new emphasis on the city's mission, vision, and values in the recruitment process. It continues after hiring with welcoming letters from the City Manager and the senior executives responsible for the employees' work units. Both letters focus explicitly on the same mission-oriented themes while tacitly underscoring the importance of the individual as an organization value.

The next step in the *Experience* is a human resources compensation and benefits review with a twist: The review characterizes compensation and benefits as direct manifestations of the city's mission, values, and vision. In addition, a new employee meets with a "PAL"—a city designated Peer-Advisor-Liaison. The PAL's job is to orient newcomers to the city's many facilities and locations and to begin the process of introducing them to coworkers, particularly those who are outside their immediate work unit but with whom they will have significant interactions. The PAL's role as a networking facilitator and general source of support extends for weeks or longer.

Within the first few months of their employment, new staff members join their longer-term counterparts as participants in a half-day *Leadership Conversation*. In this session the City Manager, City Attorney, and the executives heading the city's operating divisions meet and talk with employees. They trace the origins of the mission, vision, and values; share a "big picture" perspective on the city's organization and functions;

and emphasize their commitments to sustain and enhance top quality services. Informal, roundtable "break-out" sessions, in which leaders participate, foster conversation and help draw together those involved. The sessions purposefully blend people, old and new, from all parts and levels of the organization. Employee feedback, systematically gathered after each session, consistently and enthusiastically applauds the powerful, positive message delivered by senior managers' active participation.

Following their conversation with city leaders, employees attend two citizen, and customer, service, focused workshops. Significantly, both workshops are presented, not by professional trainers, but by teams of employee volunteers coached for the role and supported by a consultant. Having the city's service message come from peers, fellow line employees—including two uniformed police officers and a firefighter—is part of what makes *Experience*Carlsbad so unique.

Instead of being a static program, *Experience*Carlsbad continues to develop as the culture of the organization changes.

A recent addition to *Experience*Carlsbad is a workshop on "Creating a Respectful Workplace," focusing on increasing the workforce's consciousness of diversity and gender issues. Participants in the *Experience*Carlsbad program have also suggested the addition of a third customer service workshop. Ideas for improvement are solicited as a regular part of each session.

*Experience*Carlsbad is regarded internally as an investment in high-performance culture. It accelerates employees' assimilation into the workplace and facilitates their ability to operate across departmental lines when necessary to meet customer needs. The *Experience* introduces them firsthand to the community they serve and to the places and people that comprise the organization. It provides an overview of the how the city works so that they can help both themselves and their customers. It delivers and repeatedly reinforces the mission-centered message of commitment to citizens and customers and supports the message with service skill-building opportunities.

◼ SUMMARY

Traditionally, the published material in organization development has focused on applications in industrial organizations. This chapter presented broad applications of OD in nonindustrial organizations, such as hospitals, family businesses, schools, and government agencies. The results of these change programs to date suggest that OD is being applied but also needs a greater range of customized diagnostic methods and interventions, and it must be clear about the values in use when it is applied to nonindustrial settings.

Carol Gausz-Mandelberg and Foster Mobley pointed out how dramatic changes in the health care industry are affecting the practice of OD in that setting. They noted how changes in the nature of the health care product, the way it is delivered, and how it is paid for are altering fundamentally the industry's structure and making it more difficult to identify the target of change. To be effective under these new conditions, OD practitioners will be under considerable pressure to demonstrate their competence in areas, such as culture, alliances and networks, and organization design. Change projects likely will be focused on integrating a diverse set of previously uncoordinated stakeholders. They will be more reactive than proactive; more solution oriented than people oriented.

Rachel Mickelson presented a family business system model to underscore the important differences between traditional organizations and family businesses. The family, business, and shareholder subsystems hold distinct and often conflicting values that make diagnosis and intervention in family businesses complex. The model also served as a diagnostic framework to guide inquiry into a family business. Effective OD interventions must account for these three subsystems, the relationships among them, and be sensitive to the family interpersonal dynamics that are likely to pervade the entire effort.

Paul Spittler pointed out that school systems are different from industrial firms because they are not subject to the same types of competitive pressures, are subject to close public scrutiny from multiple stakeholders, and are loosely structured at the horizontal level. Their vertical structures, however, are sophisticated and bureaucratic. As a result, recent interventions are aimed at developing structures to support better collegial problem solving. Programs such as high-involvement management and total quality management are producing important improvements in the quality of both educational outcomes and teachers' quality of work life.

Ray Patchett's section suggested that the public-sector is more bureaucratic and adheres more strongly to bureaucratic norms than does the private sector. Thus, differences between the two sectors stem largely from differences in underlying value structures that encourage people to behave in different ways. He indicated that many of the differences between the public and private sectors may be a matter of degree, rather than kind. Further, the public-sector has multiple access by multiple decision makers, which can make it difficult to know who is really at the top of the organization. Thus, OD interventions in the public-sector focus more on technostructural interventions, such as work flow design and structure, than on process-oriented interventions, such as team-building. Despite these differences, OD interventions in the public-sector have an admirable track record of success, nearly equal to the success rate in industrial settings.

◼ NOTES

1. R. Coile, "Futurescan 2003: A Forecast of Healthcare Trends 2003–2007." Presented by the Society for Healthcare Strategy and Market Development of the American Hospital Association, the American College of Healthcare Executives, and Superior Consulting Company, Inc., p. 4.

2. American Hospital Association Commission on Workforce for Hospitals and Health Systems, *In Our Hands, How Hospital Leaders Can Build a Thriving Workforce* (Chicago: American Hospital Association, April 2002).

3. B. Kimball and E. O'Neill, *Health Care's Human Crisis: The American Nursing Shortage* (Princeton, N.J.: The Robert Wood Johnson Foundation, April 2002.)

4. R. Coile, "Magnet Hospitals Use Culture, Not Wages, to Solve Nursing Shortage," *Journal of Healthcare Management* (July/August 2001): 224–27.

5. National Advisory Council on Nurse Education and Practice, *Report to the Secretary of Health and Human Services and Congress, A National Agenda for Nursing Workforce Racial/Ethnic Diversity* (Rockville, Md.: U.S. Department of Health and Human Services, Health Resources and Services Administration, 2000), 18.

6. Ibid, vii.

7. This information can be found at http://www.leapfroggroup.org, and was accessed on 2 September 2003.

8. Institute of Medicine, *To Err is Human: Building a Safer Health System* (Washington, D.C.: National Academy Press, 1999).

9. This information can be found at http://www.leapfroggroup.org, and was accessed on 2 September 2003.

10. R. Coile, "Futurescan 2003," 25.

11. Joint Commission on Healthcare Organizations, *Healthcare at the Crossroads: Strategies for Addressing the Evolving Nursing Crisis* (Oakbrook Terrace, Ill: JCAHO, 2002).

12. R. Coile, "Magnet Hospitals Use Culture," 224.

13. American Hospital Association, *Strengthening the Workforce: Easing Regularly Burdens* (http://www.aha.org), p. 1.

14. R. Coile, "Futurescan 2003," p. 20.

15. M. Arrick, S. Rodgers, S. Gigante, L. Sweeney, and S. Hill, "Special Report: Health Care at a Crossroads." Reprinted from *Ratings Direct, Standard & Poor's Corporate Ratings*, October 19, 2000. http://www.standardandpoors.com, p. 4.

16. U.S. Census Bureau, *Health Insurance Coverage: 2002* (Washington, D.C.: U.S. Government Printing Office, 2002).

17. B. Kimball and E. O'Neill, *Health Care's Human Crisis: The American Nursing Shortage*.

18. AHA Commission on Workforce for Hospitals and Health Systems.

19. R. Coile, "Magnet Hospitals Use Culture," 226.

20. M. Sashkin and W. Warner Burke, "Organization Development in the 1980's," in *Advances in Organization Development*, vol. 1, ed. F. Massarik (Norwood, N.J.: Abelex, 1992).

21. A. Nordhaus-Bike, "The Battle Against Burnout," *Hospitals and Health Networks* (20 May 1995): 36–40.

22. American Association of Colleges of Nursing, *AACN White Paper: Hallmarks of the Professional Nursing Practice Environment* (Washington, D.C.: American Association of Colleges of Nursing, January 2002).

23. B. Kimball and E. O'Neill, *Health Care's Human Crisis: The American Nursing Shortage*.

24. Hay Group, Inc., *The Retention Dilemma, Why Productive Workers Leave—Seven Suggestions for Keeping Them* (Philadelphia: Hay Group, 2001).

25. This application was adapted from A. Pedersen and M. Antoon, "A 4-year History of Work Redesign in Two ICU's," *Nursing Management* 28 (1997): 32–36.

26. D. S. Reina and M.L. Reina, *Trust and Betrayal in the Workplace: Building Effective Relationships in Your Organization* (San Francisco: Berrett-Koehler, 1999).

27. Watson Wyatt Worldwide, *Human Capital Index 2000* (Washington, D.C., 2000).

28. F. Cerne, "Learning to Survive," *Hospitals and Health Networks* 5 (September 1995): 47–50.

29. N. Margulies and A. Raia, "The Significance of Core Values," in *Advances in Organization Development*, vol. 1, ed. F. Massarik (Norwood, N.J.: Ablex, 1992).

30. K. Gersick, J. Davis, M. Hampton, and I. Lansberg, *Generation to Generation* (Boston: Harvard Business School Press, 1997).

31. J. Ward and C. Aronoff, "Just What Is a Family Business?" in *Family Business Sourcebook II*, eds. C. E. Aronoff, J. H. Astrachan, & J. L. Ward (Atlanta: Business Owners Resources, 1996), 2–3.

32. Raymond Institute, "American Family Business Survey" (Alfred, N.Y.: Raymond Institute/Mass Mutual Financial, 2003). The report can be downloaded at http://www.raymondinstitute.org.

33. I. Lansberg, *Succeeding Generations: Realizing the Dream of Families in Business* (Boston: Harvard Business School Press, 1999).

34. Ibid.

35. Raymond Institute, "American Family Business Survey."

36. Ibid.

37. J. Ward, *Keeping the Family Business Healthy: How to Plan for Continuing Growth, Profitability, and Family Leadership* (San Francisco: Jossey-Bass, 1987).

38. D. Bork, D. Jaffe, S. Lane, L. Dashew, and Q. Heisler, *Working with Family Businesses* (San Francisco: Jossey-Bass 1996).

39. Raymond Report, "American Family Business Survey."

40. E. Doud, Jr. and L. Hausner, *Hats Off to You: Balancing Roles and Creating Success in Family Business* (Los Angeles: DHV Family Business Advisors, 2000).

41. Raymond Report, "American Family Business Survey."

42. Ward, *Keeping the Family Business Healthy*.

43. Bork, Jaffe, Lane, Dashew, and Heisler, *Working with Family Businesses*.

44. J. Hilburt-Davis and W. G. Dyer, Jr. *Consulting to Family Business: A Practical Guide to Contracting, Assessment, and Implementation* (San Francisco: Jossey-Bass/Pfeiffer, 2003).

45. R. Mickelson and C. Worley, "M & As: A Strategic Choice for Family-Owned Firms," *Family Business Journal* (in press).

46. E. Doud, Jr., *Evolution of Family Business and Wealth* (Los Angeles: DHV Family Business Advisors, 2003).

47. Bork, Jaffe, Lane, Dashew, and Heisler, *Working with Family Businesses*.

48. I. Lansberg, *Succeeding Generations*.

49. E. Schein, *Process Consultation Revisited* (Reading, Mass.: Addison-Wesley, 1999); T. Cummings and C. Worley, *Organization Development and Change*, 7th ed. (Cincinnati, Ohio: South-Western College Publishing, 2001).

50. National Commission on Excellence in Education, *A Nation at Risk: The Imperative for Educational Reform* (Washington, D.C.: U.S. Government Printing Office, 1983); S. Mohrman and E. Lawler, "Motivation for School Reform" (working paper, Center for Effective Organizations, University of Southern California, Los Angeles, 1995).

51. R. Cooke, "Organization Development in Schools," in *Organization Development and Change*, 5th ed., eds. T. Cummings and C. Worley (St. Paul, Minn.: West, 1993).

52. L. Lezotte, (personal interview, Poway, Calif., April 1995); P. Spittler, "Total Quality Management: Applications in Public Education" (unpublished master's thesis, Pepperdine University, 1995).

53. Cooke, "Organization Development in Schools."

54. Ibid.

55. C. Derr, "OD Won't Work in Schools," *Education and Urban Society* 8 (1976): 227–41.

56. Cooke, "Organization Development in Schools."

57. D. Lortie, *Schoolteacher: A Sociological Study* (Chicago: University of Chicago Press, 1975).

58. J. Savedoff, "The Distribution of Influence and Its Relationship to Relevance, Expertise and Interdependence in Educational Organizations" (Ph.D. diss., University of Michigan, 1978).

59. Cooke, "Organization Development in Schools."

60. C. Flynn, "Collaborative Decision Making in a Secondary School: An Experiment," *Education and Urban Society* 8 (1976): 172–92.

61. W. Hawley, "Dealing with Organizational Rudity in Public Schools" (undated manuscript, Yale University).

62. C. Bidwell, "The School as a Formal Organization," in *Handbook of Organizations,* ed. J. March (Chicago: Rand McNally, 1965).

63. K. Weick, "Educational Organizations as Loosely Coupled Systems," *Administrative Science Quarterly* 21 (1976): 1–79.

64. Cooke, "Organization Development in Schools."

65. Ibid.

66. Ibid.

67. Spittler, "Total Quality Management"; J. Kingsley, "Cause for Hope: A Strategic Change Case Study of Bowling Green Elementary School" (unpublished master's thesis, Pepperdine University, 1994).

68. T. Cummings, "Designing Work for Productivity and Quality of Work Life," *Outlook* 6 (1982): 35–39; J. Gabarro, "Diagnosing Organization–Environment Fit: Implications for Organization Development," *Education and Urban Society* 3 (1974): 18–29.

69. Cooke, "Organization Development in Schools."

70. E. Lawler, *High-Involvement Management* (San Francisco: Jossey-Bass, 1986).

71. Mohrman and Lawler, "Motivation for School Reform."

72. Ibid.

73. B. Rowan, "Commitment and Control: Alternative Strategies for the Organizational Design of Schools," in *Review of Research in Education,* ed. E. Cazden (Washington D.C.: American Educational Research Association, 1990); B. Rowan, S. Rauderbush, and Y. Cheong, "Teaching as a Non-Routine Task: Implications for Management of Schools," *Education Administration Quarterly* 29 (1993): 479–500.

74. S. Mohrman, E. Lawler, and A. Mohrman, "Applying Employee Involvement in Schools," *Educational Policy Analysis* 14 (1992): 31–57.

75. E. Lawler, S. Mohrman, and G. Ledford, *Creating High-Performance Organizations: Practices and Results of Employee Involvement and Total Quality Management in Fortune 1000 Companies* (San Francisco: Jossey-Bass, 1995).

76. W. Glasser, *Control Theory in the Classroom* (New York: Perennial Library, 1986); A. Kohl, *No Contest—The Case Against Competition* (Boston: Houghton-Mifflin, 1986); W. Deming, "Foundation for Management of Quality in the Western World" (paper delivered at a meeting of the Institute of Management Sciences, Osaka, Japan, 1990).

77. W. Deming, *Out of the Crisis* (Cambridge: Massachusetts Institute of Technology, 1986).

78. J. Stampen, "Improving the Quality of Education: W. Edwards Deming and Effective Schools," *Contemporary Education Review* 3 (1987): 423–33.

79. M. Tribus, "The Application of Quality Management Principles in Education at Mt. Edgecumbe High School, Sitka, Alaska," in *An Introduction to Total Quality for Schools,* ed. American Association of School Administrators (Arlington, Va.: American Association of School Administrators, 1991), 30.

80. American Society for Quality Control, "Fourth Annual Quality in Education Listing," *Quality Progress* 27, 9 (1994): 27.

81. Spittler, "Total Quality Management."

82. Deming, "Foundation for Management."

83. American Association of School Administrators, ed., *An Introduction to Total Quality for Schools* (Arlington, Va.: American Association of School Administrators, 1991); Stampen, "Improving the Quality of Education."

84. Stampen, "Improving the Quality of Education."

85. Spittler, "Total Quality Management."

86. B. Malen, R. Ogawa, and J. Kranz, "What Do We Know about School-Based Management? A Case Study of the Literature—A Call for Research," in *Choice and Control in Education,* eds. W. Clune and J. Witte (Philadelphia: Falmer Press, 1990), 289–342.

87. J. David, "The Who, What, and Why of Site-Based Management," *Educational Leadership* 53 (1995): 4–9.

88. R. Ogawa and P. White, "School-Based Management: An Overview," in *School-Based Management—Organizing for High Performance,* eds. A. Mohrman and P. Wohlstetter (San Francisco: Jossey-Bass, 1994).

89. David, "Who, What, and Why."

90. R. Campbell, L. Cumnningham, R. Nystrand, and D. Usdan, *The Organization and Control of American Schools,* 5th ed. (Columbus, Ohio: Charles E. Merrill, 1985).

91. P. Hill and J. Bonan, *Decentralization and Accountability in Public Education* (Santa Monica, Calif.: Rand Corporation, 1991).

92. Malen, Ogawa, and Kranz, "What Do We Know?"

93. B. Bimber, *Decentralization Mirage: Comparing Decision Making Arrangements in Four High Schools* (Santa Monica, Calif.: Institute on Education and Training, Rand Corporation, 1994).

94. S. Sharan, ed., *Cooperative Learning Theory and Research* (New York: Praeger, 1990).

95. P. Wohlstetter and R. Smyer, "Models of High-Performance Schools," in *School-Based Management—Organizing for High Performance,* eds. A. Mohrman and P. Wohlstetter (San Francisco: Jossey-Bass, 1994).

96. J. Comer, *School Power* (New York: Free Press, 1980).

97. H. Levin, "Accelerated Schools for Disadvantaged Students," *Educational Leadership* 44, 6 (1987): 19–29.

98. T. Sizer, *Horace's School: Redesigning the American High School* (Boston: Houghton-Mifflin, 1984).

99. Spittler, "Total Quality Management."

100. P. Robertson, P. Wohlstetter, and S. Mohrman, "Generating Curriculum and Instructional Innovations Through School-Based Management," *Educational Administration Quarterly* 31 (1995): 257–76.

101. M. G. Popovich, *Creating High-Performance Government Organizations* (San Francisco: Jossey-Bass, 1998).

102. *From Red Tape to Results: Creating a Government That Works Better and Costs Less* (Washington D.C.: U.S. Government Printing Office, September 1993); *Common Sense Government Works Better and Costs Less* (Washington, D.C.: U.S. Government Printing Office, September 1995); *Reinvention's Next Steps: Governing in a Balanced Budget World* (Washington, D.C.: U.S. Government Printing Office, March, 1996).

103. KPMG LLP, *Transforming State and Local Government: The Critical Role of Public Management* (Montvale, N.J.: 1999); P. Hart and R. Teeter, "America Unplugged: Citizens and Their Government." (Washington, D.C.: The Council for Excellence in Government, 1999): http://www.excelgov.org/displayContent.asp?Keyword= ppp070199, accessed on August 31, 2003.

104. This information was found at http:www.hmco. com/college/polisci/psn/index.html, and was accessed in December 1999; additional information was found at http://www.fairvote.org/turnout/preturn.htm and accessed on September 1, 2003.

105. R. Dilger, R. Moffett, and L. Struyk, "Privatization of Municipal Services in America's Largest Cities," *Public Administration Review* 57 (1997): 21–26.

106. P. Robertson and S. Seneviratne, "Outcomes of Planned Organizational Change in the Public Sector: A Meta-Analytic Comparison to the Private Sector," *Public Administration Review* 55 (1995): 547–58.

107. J. Nalbandian, "City Council–City Manager Partnerships" (presentation to the California City Managers Conference, 1998).

108. H. G. Frederickson, *The Spirit of Public Administration* (San Francisco: Jossey-Bass, 1997).

109. Ibid., 164.

110. Frederickson, *Spirit of Public Administration;* W. Morris, *The American Heritage Dictionary of the English Language* (Boston: Houghton-Mifflin, 1981); P. Appleby, "Government Is Different," in *Classics of Public Administration*, eds. J. Shafritz and A. Hyde (Oak Park, Ill., Moore, 1978): 101–07.

111. Frederickson, *Spirit of Public Administration.*

112. R. Golembiewski, "Organization Development in Public Agencies: Perspectives on Theory and Practice," *Public Administration Review* 29 (July-August 1969): 370.

113. Popovich, *Creating High-Performance Government Organizations*, p. 29; Golembiewski, "Organization Development in Public Agencies."

114. Golembiewski, "Organization Development."

115. Bryson, *Strategic Planning;* T. Cummings and C. Worley, *Organization Development and Change*, 6th ed. (Cincinnati, Ohio: South-Western College Publishing, 1997), 163; Golembiewski, "Organization Development," 370.

116. Golembiewski, "Organization Development," 370.

117. Bryson, *Strategic Planning.*

118. Ibid., 246.

119. R. Golembiewski, C. Proehl, and D. Sink, "Success of OD Applications in the Public Sector: Toting up the Score for a Decade, More or Less," *Public Administration Review* 41 (1981): 679–82; R. Golembiewski, C. Proehl, and D. Sink, "Estimating the Success of OD Applications," *Training and Development Journal* 72 (April 1982): 86–95.

120. S. Park, "Estimating Success Rates of Quality Circle Programs: Public and Private Experiences," *Public Administration Quarterly* 15 (1991): 133–46.

121. Robertson and Seneviratne, "Outcomes."

122. Information on the National Partnership for Reinventing Government (formerly the National Performance Review) can be found on the Web site, http://www.fedgate.org/fg_npr.htm.

123. F. Berry and B. Wechsler, "State Agencies' Experience with Strategic Planning: Findings from a National Survey," *Public Administration Review* 55 (1995): 159–68.

124. J. Melkers and K. Willoughby, "The State of the States: Performance-Based Budgeting Requirements in 47 out of 50," *Public Administration Review* 58 (1998): 66–73.

125. H. Hill and K. Shook, "Virginia's Results Manager," *New Public Innovator* (1998): 30–33.

126. Robertson and Seneviratne, "Outcomes"; E. M. Berman and J. P. West, "Municipal Commitment to Total Quality Management: A Survey of Recent Progress," Public Administration Review 55 (1995): 57–66; K. Parry, "Enhancing Adaptability: Leadership Strategies to Accommodate Change in Local Government Settings," *Journal of Organizational Change Management,* 12 (1999): 134–148; L. White, "Changing the 'Whole System' in the Public Sector," *Journal of Organizational Change Management,* 13 (2000): 162–178.

Future Directions in Organization Development

The field of organization development continues to grow. New theories and concepts are being developed, more complex and rigorous research is being conducted, new methods and interventions are being applied, and organizations from more diverse countries and cultures are becoming involved. Because so much change has occurred in a relatively brief period, predicting the future of OD is risky if not foolhardy. On the other hand, the field is also maturing and it is useful to look at the forces influencing how OD is likely to evolve. This knowledge can enable OD practitioners, managers, and researchers to more readily affect a relevant OD future. The chapter first identifies three trends within the OD field that are pushing it toward different futures. The implications of these trends are discussed. The chapter then describes trends in the larger context within which OD operates including economic, workforce, technology, and organization trends. It concludes with a discussion of how these trends are likely to influence future OD practice.

TRENDS WITHIN ORGANIZATION DEVELOPMENT

In updating an OD bibliography (http://www.cba.bgsu.edu/mod/html/od_bibliography.html), Varney noted that recent writings in OD focused more on the status of the field than evaluations of practice or research on the processes of change.[1] Reviews of the literature, conversations within Internet listservs, and the diversity in OD education and training opportunities suggest three trends occurring within OD—characterized as traditional, pragmatic, and scholarly.[2] Each trend has a different vision of what OD can and should be, and although they are presented separately, they are not mutually exclusive or independent. On the contrary, the future of OD will no doubt emerge from their integration. Figure 23.1 (on page 612) summarizes the trends and their likely implications for OD's future.

Traditional

The first trend has to do with increasing calls for a return to OD's traditional values and practices. Championed by the National Training Laboratories (NTL) and others, traditionalists argue that OD should be driven by long-established values of human potential, equality, trust, and collaboration. The major objective of OD should be to promulgate these root values through interventions that humanize work and organizations, help employees balance work and family life, promote diversity and spirituality at the workplace, and champion the self actualization of organization members.[3] Thus, traditionalists propose that OD should do what is "right" by assuring that organizations promote positive social change and corporate citizenship.

The traditional trend is also characterized by an increased focus on process interventions. OD's key purpose, according to this view, is to ensure that organizational processes are transparent, possess integrity, treat people with dignity, and serve diverse stakeholders. Thus, OD's primary goal is to help organizations create such

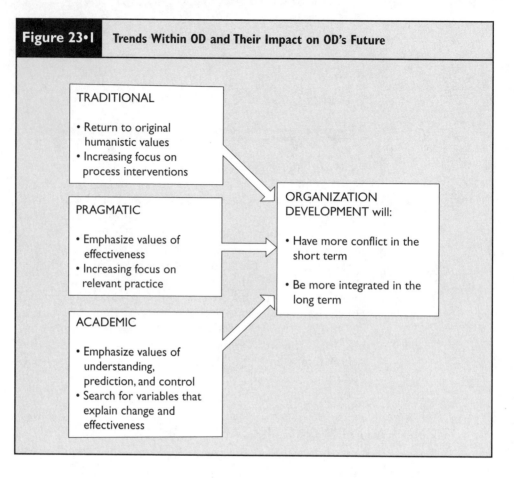

Figure 23·1   Trends Within OD and Their Impact on OD's Future

processes; whether they subsequently lead to performance outcomes is of secondary importance.

Pragmatic

The second trend within OD is related to increasing demands for professionalization of the field and an emphasis on relevance. Championed by the change management practices at large consulting firms and some OD professional associations, pragmatists argue that OD practitioners should be certified like most other professionals.[4] This drive to professionalize OD is in response to a growing number of people marketing themselves as OD practitioners without any formal training or education in the field, as well as a lack of consistency in applying OD's core theories, skills, and interventions. As a result, distinguishing between qualified and unqualified OD practitioners can be a difficult challenge for organizations, and professionalization of the field can help to remedy that problem.[5]

To become a profession, according to pragmatists, OD should require certification of members, create a common body of knowledge, define minimum levels of competencies, and institute other regulatory infrastructure. Certification would create boundaries between who is (and is not) an OD professional, and what is (and is not) OD practice.

The pragmatic trend is also distinguished by an emphasis on change technologies, typically under the banner of "change management." In contrast to OD's "soft" reputation, change management is viewed as a highly relevant and applied practice, much like medicine, engineering, or accounting.[6] It focuses on helping organizations implement change and adapt to turbulent environments. Relevance, a minor chord among traditionalists, is a major theme among pragmatists, who value the performance outcomes of OD work. Thus, process interventions are not seen as ends in themselves but as means for implementing change and achieving those results.

Scholarly

The third trend within OD has to do with the increasing number of people making research contributions to our understanding of change. Championed by universities and applied research centers, such as USC's Center for Effective Organizations and MIT's Society of Organization Learning, scholars propose a "research agenda" for OD that includes: (1) how multiple contexts and levels of analysis affect organizational change; (2) the inclusion of time, history, process, and action in theories of change; (3) the link between change processes and organization performance; (4) the comparative analysis of international and cross-cultural OD interventions; (5) the study of receptivity, customization, sequencing, pace, and episodic versus continuous change processes; and (6) the partnership between scholars and practitioners in studying organizational change.[7]

The scholarly perspective focuses on understanding, predicting, and controlling change. It is far less concerned about how OD is defined, what its values are, how it is practiced, or whether an OD practitioner was involved except as potential explanations for change success. OD is just one of several ways organizations can be changed. Unlike traditionalists and pragmatists, scholars are concerned with creating valid knowledge, and with generalizing conclusions about how change occurs, how it is triggered, under what conditions it works well, and so on. Similar to the traditional and pragmatic trends, however, the scholarly trend is connected to the actors involved in change; its favored methodology is action research but from a more distant and detached perspective than the other two trends.

Implications for OD's Future

The three trends are likely to have important consequences for OD's future. In the short term, they will likely continue on their separate paths with periodic and perhaps intense conflicts among them. In the longer term, however, there should be increasing attempts at reconciling these differences and generating a more integrative view of OD.

OD Will Have More Conflicts in the Short Term

Current views and debates about OD values and professionalization are likely to continue at least in the near term. The traditional and pragmatic trends hold different and often conflicting views of how the field should evolve. Traditionalists fear that OD is becoming too corporate and may unwittingly collude with powerful stakeholders to promote goals that are inconsistent with OD's social responsibility and humanistic values. For example, corporate strategies can concentrate wealth and ignore cultural diversity. Technology can isolate people and alienate them. The traditionalists therefore advocate for a stronger focus on the central values of the field. Pragmatists, on the other hand, worry that relying too heavily on traditional values will reinforce OD's "touchy-feely" orientation. They argue that focusing on human potential exclusively will doom OD to irrelevance in today's highly competitive organizations. Thus, in the short term, the battle over values within the field is likely to continue. Symbolic of the struggle, no fewer than three formal projects are under way to clarify OD's values. Each effort is championed by a different institutional sponsor, relies on a different set of OD practitioners, and argues that their results will clarify this important issue for the field. The ongoing conflict in the field is therefore likely to continue and may become even more intense as additional values, such as ecological sustainability and economic equality, enter the OD field.

OD is also likely to face more disagreement over professionalization. The debate over values discussed above demonstrates how difficult it will be to gain agreement about standards, competencies, enforcement mechanisms, and oversight. Unless a groundswell of support for a common set of OD values emerges, judgments about qualifications will likely become caught up in conflicts between the traditional and pragmatic perspectives. Several prior attempts to professionalize the field or to accredit practitioners have had limited success, and provide ample evidence of the difficulty of resolving such differences.

OD Will Become More Integrated in the Long Term

Despite the conflicts likely to continue in the short run, there is considerable common ground among the diverse trends within OD, and the emergence of a more integrated view of the field seems likely in the long term. For example, both the traditional and pragmatic trends agree that applying behavioral science to organization can improve effectiveness and increase member satisfaction. Both trends believe that knowledge and skill should be transferred to a client system, and all three trends believe that a body of theory and practice underlie the process of change in organizations. Given OD's history, its long-term future is likely to be some blend of practitioner values-in-use (traditional trend), professional change practice (pragmatic trend), and change theory (scholarly trend). The field is not likely to be completely pragmatic; there is little likelihood that it will return to its purely traditional roots; and the subject of change is too important and personal to be left to research alone. A more limited integration is also problematic. A pragmatic and research-driven OD would be cold and impersonal; a traditional and research-driven field would be naïve and irrelevant to economic realities; and a traditional and pragmatic-driven OD would be intuitive and noncumulative. An integration of the three trends, on the other hand, will assure that OD has moral purpose, drives sustainable bottom lines, and represents a healthy balance of art and science.

A set of integrated values, including participation and effectiveness but recognizing the tension between them, will drive the traditional and pragmatic trends to exploit the common ground in theory and practice. For example, the theories of change underlying traditional action research; positive scholarship and practice; contemporary approaches to change, such as network models, complexity and chaos theories; and the evolution of underorganized systems can be integrated. The practical benefits of traditional objective approaches and the traditional values reflected in a social constructionist view hold promise for a new view of OD. This integrated view will challenge the field to redefine existing views of work, competition, culture, and organizations; to see them not only as objects with inertia, structure, resistance, and permanence, but as social processes produced, maintained, and changed through conversations that are flexible, aspirational, and changeable.[8] A positive view of organizations and their members' potential aligns well with the traditional trend; it supports values of basic human rights, social responsibility, democracy, and ecological sustainability. This view of organizations also supports the pragmatic trend; it recognizes the importance of economic viability, the time value of activity, and the opportunities that growth conveys. If carefully applied, an integrated objective and socially constructed perspective can be an influential voice in OD's future.

TRENDS IN THE CONTEXT OF ORGANIZATION DEVELOPMENT

As summarized in Figure 23.2, several interrelated trends are affecting the context within which OD will be applied in the near future. They concern various aspects of the economy, the workforce, technology, and organizations. In some cases, the

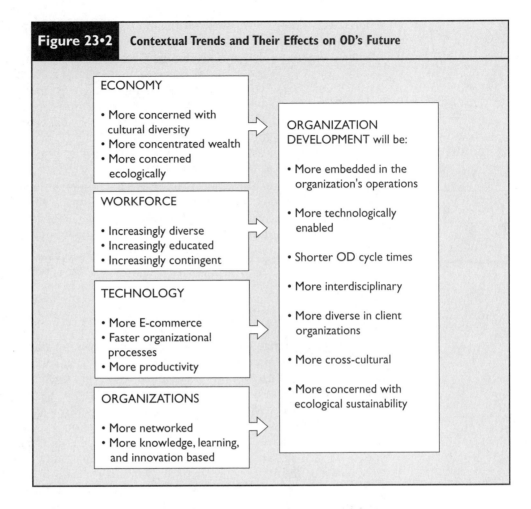

Figure 23•2   Contextual Trends and Their Effects on OD's Future

ECONOMY

- More concerned with cultural diversity
- More concentrated wealth
- More concerned ecologically

WORKFORCE

- Increasingly diverse
- Increasingly educated
- Increasingly contingent

TECHNOLOGY

- More E-commerce
- Faster organizational processes
- More productivity

ORGANIZATIONS

- More networked
- More knowledge, learning, and innovation based

ORGANIZATION DEVELOPMENT will be:

- More embedded in the organization's operations

- More technologically enabled

- Shorter OD cycle times

- More interdisciplinary

- More diverse in client organizations

- More cross-cultural

- More concerned with ecological sustainability

trends will directly affect OD practice. Technology trends, such as Internet portals, telephone over the Internet, and wireless networks, will no doubt influence how OD practitioners communicate with organization members, facilitate teams, and manage change. Other trends, such as the increasing concentration of wealth, represent important contextual forces that will indirectly affect OD through their interaction with other trends.[9]

The Economy

Researchers and futurists have described a variety of economic scenarios, and there is substantial agreement that the world's economy is undergoing an important transition from the industrial age that characterized much of the twentieth century.[10] Although these scenarios differ in their particulars, they all fit under the rubric of *globalization,* and many of the same trends are identified as drivers—including technology, workforce, and organization, which will be discussed separately.

The fall of the Berlin Wall, the end of Apartheid, the breakup of the former Soviet Union, the creation of the European Union, and the opening of China are key events in the transition to a global economy. Organizations from around the world are increasingly able to shift their manufacturing from high- to low-labor-cost countries, execute international mergers and acquisitions, and build worldwide service businesses. Today, almost any product or service can be made, transported, and bought anywhere in the world. Globalization can help companies reduce costs, gain resources, expand markets, and develop new products and practices more quickly.

The emergence of a global economy is well under way, but the promise and rationalization of that process is far from complete. The initial steps toward a globalization have fueled real price decreases in many consumer products, provided employment for people in lower developed nations, and driven revenue growth in a variety of industries. However, the transition to a global economy is for the most part unmanaged, and there is increasing concern over its social and ecological consequences.[11] This raises troublesome questions about three key issues: *cultural diversity*, *income distribution*, and *ecological sustainability*.

First, transitioning to a global economy is a complex and daunting process that involves organizations, technology, people, and countries. The role and function of national governments and the importance of cultural diversity in the process is not well understood and there are few generally accepted guidelines.[12] Governments must face the difficult choice of preserving their culture at the risk of being left out of the global economy or sacrificing their culture to participate in greater wealth. For example, the Chinese government is trying diligently to preserve its cultural and political underpinnings while facing a rapid influx of capitalist goods and services,[13] and many other developing nations face pressures to move to a Western capitalism model despite questions about whether it is appropriate for their cultures.[14] Organizations implementing global strategies (Chapter 21) prefer standardized approaches; they often see little practical incentive to account for cultural or governmental differences. Pursing both cultural preservation and economic participation is possible, but it is a complex task; the short-term financial benefits often appear much larger than the long-term social consequences; and the required leadership and management capabilities are not widely available. The decisions governments make to resolve this dilemma will dramatically shape the character of the global economy.

Second, globalization of the economy is closely related to an increasing concentration of wealth in relatively few individuals, corporations, and nations. Over the past two decades, for example, the ratio of CEO compensation to that of the average employee grew from 35:1 to 150:1 in large U.S. firms,[15] and the median compensation for CEOs rose 14% to $13.2 million in 2002, even as the total return for the S&P 500 declined 22.1%.[16] Between 1979 and 1999, the number of billionaires in the world increased over 14-fold,[17] although there was a decline in 2001 and 2002 due to the economic recession.[18] In 2003, the world's largest multinational corporations accounted for 80% of the world's industrial output, and the 500 largest corporations accounted for 90% of the world's foreign direct investment.[19] Similarly, the largest 500 transnational corporations employ 0.05 of 1% of the world's population;[20] and of the largest 100 economies in the world, 49 are corporations.[21] At the same time, 5.2 billion of the world's 6.2 billion people live in low and moderate income countries, and these same people exist on about $3 a day.[22] The CIA's report, *Global Trends, 2015*, concluded that globalization will create "an even wider gap between regional winners and losers than exists today. [Its] evolution will be rocky, marked by chronic volatility and a widening economic divide . . . deepening economic stagnation, political instability, and cultural alienation. [It] will foster political, ethnic, ideological, and religious extremism, along with the violence that often accompanies it."[23]

The concentration of wealth may be a natural outcome of capitalism facing imperfectly competitive markets, but it can also contribute to misallocation of resources, environmental degradation, and short-term thinking.[24] For example, Wall Street's current focus on quarterly earnings can skew decision-making criteria to delay preventive maintenance or safety initiatives, to postpone implementation of necessary environmental-protection equipment, or to forego important long-term capital investments. The concentration of wealth can also contribute to social conflict driven by fears that the wealthy will act in their own self-interest at the expense of those who are financially less fortunate. The bloody demonstrations that occurred at the December 1999 meeting of the World Trade Organization in Seattle derived in part from such fear and people's willingness to act on it. And more recently, the 2003 WTO meetings in Cancun, Mexico, were cancelled because developing nations banded together against developed countries who were accused of not listening to requests for modifications in trade agreements.

Third, there are increasingly clear warnings that the ecosystem no longer can be treated as a factor of production, and that success cannot be defined as the accumulation of wealth and material goods at the expense of the environment. There are strong pressures to fuel economic growth, for example, by exploring and developing oil fields in sensitive and protected areas such as the Arctic National Wildlife Refuge. Yet, sport-utility vehicle (SUV) demand remains strong despite concerns over safety and low gas mileage. If SUVs complied with the same fuel-economy standards as ordinary cars, the United States would save 1 million barrels of oil a day, more than the Arctic National Wildlife Refuge could produce at peak volumes.[25] These concerns arise in part from the proliferation of capitalism, but also from the growing realization that free and open markets can have negative unintended consequences for the global ecosystem. Studies suggest that industrialization is a controversial but probable cause of global warming,[26] and several traditional organizations, such as BP and Royal Dutch/Shell, are reversing long-held opinions about their contribution to environmental decay by setting aggressive goals to reduce greenhouse gases.[27] Unfortunately, many developing economies, including China, the Philippines, and Mexico, continue to operate with loose environmental controls. As a result, there are more calls for change in the values underlying capitalism—from consumption to investment,[28] from open to mindful markets,[29] and from wealth accumulation as an end in itself to an examination of the return on living capital.[30] Some observers note that such value shifts are already under way in many nations and organizations. For example, traditional business models that assume labor scarcity and natural resource abundance are being tempered by models that emphasize the abundance of knowledge and the scarcity of natural resources. IKEA, the Swedish household furnishings retailer/manufacturer, has altered its environmental policies and practices radically to reduce emissions, waste, and environmental degradation and increase sustainability, profits, and customer satisfaction.[31]

The Workforce

The workforce is becoming more diverse, educated, and contingent. Chapter 18 documented the diversity trend and suggested that organizations, whether they operate primarily in their home country or abroad, will need to develop policies and operating styles that embrace the changing cultural, ethnic, gender, and age diversity of the workforce.

The workforce is also becoming more educated. The 2002 U.S. Census data, for example, report that 84.1% of adults over 25 years of age have completed high school and that 28.5% have a bachelor's or higher degree. Both of those numbers represent significant increases over 1997 and 2000 data. A more educated workforce is likely to demand higher wages, more involvement in decision making, and continued investment in knowledge and skills. For example, the current half-life of information systems personnel is about 2 years and requires continual updating of their knowledge and skills to remain competent in these jobs. In response, organizations are increasing their training and management development budgets significantly.[32] They are investing far more in corporate universities and corporate–university partnerships, and many organizations, such as Motorola, 3M, and Xerox, have policies outlining the minimum hours of technical and managerial training that each employee will receive yearly.

Finally, the continued high rate of downsizings, re-engineering efforts, and mergers and acquisitions described in Chapters 14 and 19 is forcing the workforce to become more contingent and less loyal. The number of "free-agent" workers, including temporary and contract employees, freelancers, independent professionals, and consultants made up 22% of the workforce in 1998 and increased to 28%, or 30 million workers, in 2002.[33] The implicit psychological contract that governs relationships between employers and employees is being rewritten with new assumptions about long-term employment and rewards in exchange for commitment and loyalty. For example, a study by the National Association of Temporary and Staffing Services found that 90% of companies use temporary help.[34] Other studies have suggested that the personnel supply services industry, about 90% of which is involved with providing contingent employees, will be among the top five fastest growing. One study predicted 53% growth between 1996 and 2006, while another study predicated an average annual growth rate of 4.1% through 2010.[35]

Technology

By almost any measure, information technology is a significant and increasingly common fact of life. For example, an estimated 150.9 million worldwide Internet users in 1998 grew to 605.6 million in 2002, and will surely exceed the initial predictions of more than 717 million by 2005.[36] The Internet is the backbone of a global economy, and although the technology sector suffered recent financial setbacks, few people doubt its future importance.

At the core of information technology is E-commerce, an economy that knows no boundaries.[37] E-commerce involves buying and selling products and services over the Internet, and ranges from withdrawing cash from an automatic teller machine to more complex transactions such as purchasing products and services from a Web site. Worldwide E-commerce sales in the second quarter of 2003 were $858.8 billion, a 4.9% increase over the same period in 2002. According to the most recent data available, the value of E-commerce transactions in the United States increased 700% between 1996 and 2001, and is expected to grow from $100 billion in 1999 to between $2 and $3 trillion by 2005.[38]

Two types of E-commerce seem particularly relevant to OD's future: business-to-consumer and business-to-business. The business-to-consumer market garners much attention and awareness because it is how the public participates in E-commerce. This market, which includes E-tailers such as Amazon.com and Fandango.com, is expected to grow to over $184 billion in revenues by 2004. The business creations and transformations fueled by information technology are likely to be a big part of OD in the future. Dell Computer, for instance, sells custom-made computers to consumers and businesses, but it started out as a mail-order company advertising in the back of magazines. Today, more than 25% of its computer sales come through the Internet. The shift in organization structures, labor skill sets, work designs, and work processes in the transformation from a mail-order business to an E-commerce leader represents the kind of change that many organizations will face and the challenges OD practitioners must meet.

The organizational issues in the business-to-business market are even more complex. Estimates suggest that this form of E-commerce will grow to over $2.7 trillion by 2004. A good example of the implications and potential of this market is the online store being created by the global automobile industry. Covisint was formed by DaimlerChrysler, Ford, General Motors and Renault-Nissan in 2000, and since its inception, PSA Peugeot Citroen has also joined the initiative. It represents the first major migration of an entire industry's supply chain onto the Internet, and will re-engineer radically the way businesses interact with each other. This virtual marketplace will handle $250 billion in parts and supplies purchased from 60,000 suppliers each year, automate routine transactions, and streamline the bidding process for everything from car windows to paper clips. Web-based transactions will replace the inefficient phone, mail, and face-to-face sales call processes that dominated this industry for decades. Such business-to-business marketplaces are expected to be adopted by other automakers as well as other industries, such as aerospace, construction, and office supplies.[39]

In addition to providing the infrastructure for E-commerce, technology is also changing and enabling a variety of organizational processes. New technologies such as SAP or PeopleSoft drive changes in how information and work processes are coordinated and managed; they also require modification in the way productivity is measured. For example, the implementation of enterprise resource systems and supply-chain management programs must integrate with existing work processes and the competencies of organization members. This requires adjustments in the entire sociotechnical system and how it interfaces with customers, suppliers, regulators, and other stakeholders.

Finally, we are gaining a clearer picture of the way technology affects productivity. For example, for years, economists were puzzled by a "productivity paradox." Despite a 30-year, $2 trillion investment in computers and technology, productivity rose very slowly during the 1980s and early 1990s. But in 1999, productivity rose 2.9% in the United States (and 5% in the last 6 months of 1999), nearly twice the 1.5% average annual gains seen since the early 1970s. The biggest gains were in manufacturing, but service businesses such as transportation, trade, and finance also started to see a payoff from new technology investments. This productivity lag apparently resulted from the relatively long time it took for organizations to adopt the new technology and to learn how to apply it.[40] For example, Countrywide Home Loans, one of the largest mortgage lenders in the United States, has been experimenting with technology solutions since the late 1980s. But only recently have the benefits of technology paid off. The 1997 implementation of an automated information system in its customer service center has helped reduce the average cost per call from $4 to less than $0.60 on more than 20,000 calls per day. The increased productivity has not cost jobs; Countrywide nearly doubled its workforce between 1996 and 1999.

Organizations

The final trend likely to shape OD's future involves the increasingly networked and knowledge-based nature of organizations. The interventions described in this book help organizations become more streamlined and flexible, more capable of improving themselves continuously in response to economic and other trends, and more effective. A large proportion of organizations are not aware of these practices, however, and still others resist applying them.[41] Despite the attention to them in the business press, only a small percentage of organizations use self-managed work teams, are organized into networks, successfully manage strategic alliances, or have organization learning programs. But these organizations are harbingers of the future, and they will invent entirely new, entrepreneurial structures capable of exploiting new ideas and technologies quickly.

Clearly, organizations are becoming more networked. As explained in Chapters 14 and 19, network structures rely on collaborative strategies and allow single organizations to partner with other organizations to develop, manufacture, and distribute goods and services.[42] More than any other organization form, networks hold the promise of realizing the economic opportunities presented by globalization without the negative social consequences of large multinational corporations.[43] Large organizations that gain economies of scale in manufacturing, distribution, and marketing can also become rigid and slow, and indifferent to unintended social and ecological consequences. These latter outcomes can be disastrous in today's rapidly changing environments and cannot easily be remedied in the future. Networks, on the other hand, enable small organizations to access the advantages of scale and scope traditionally reserved for large firms. Small, focused firms that perform particular tasks with excellence can align with organizations that have complementary resources and expertise. These networks are highly adaptable and can disband and reform along different task or market lines as the circumstances demand. To succeed, organizations are learning how to assess quickly whether they are compatible with network partners and whether the joint product/service is successful. They are gaining competence to form and end networks swiftly, thus enabling them to exploit product/market opportunities rapidly and to "fail quickly" when the network is unproductive.[44] Because each network node (organization) is small and local, resident cultures and ecosystems are more likely to be preserved.

Finally, in an organizational world that is technically enabled, fast-paced, and networked, there will be a premium placed on learning and knowledge management. This increasingly important source of organizational capability and competitive advantage will require unprecedented amounts of innovation and coordination. Multiple stakeholders representing a diversity of interests will come together to envision a shared future and to learn how to enact it. Because this process typically leads into uncharted waters, both organizational members and OD practitioners will be joint learners, exploring new territory together. Moreover, implementing new organizational innovations will require significant amounts of experimentation as members try out new ways of operating, assess progress, and make necessary adjustments. In essence, they will learn from their actions how to create a new strategy, organization, or product/service. Such collaborative learning is capable of implementing radically new possibilities and ways of functioning that could not be envisioned beforehand. It is a process of *innovation*, not of detection and correction of errors. In turn, the new structures and systems will increase feedback and information flow to the organization, thereby improving its capacity to learn and adapt to a rapidly changing environment. They will transcend both internal and external organizational boundaries, remove barriers to learning, and facilitate how employees acquire, organize, and disseminate knowledge assets.

Implications for OD's Future

The economic, workforce, technology, and organization trends outlined above have significant implications for how OD will be conceived and practiced. Figure 23.2 summarizes them. A global economy populated with flexible, networked organizations and driven by information technology and a diverse workforce will require OD to be more embedded in the organization's operations, more technologically enabled, shorter in cycle time, more interdisciplinary, applied to more diverse clients, more cross-cultural, and more focused on sustainability.

OD Will Be More Embedded in the Organization's Operations

As the global economy and information technology enable and push for faster, more flexible organizations, the ability to manage change continuously will become a key source of competitive advantage. This suggests that OD practices will become more embedded in the organization's normal operating routines. OD skills, knowledge, and competencies can and should become part of the daily work of managers and employees.[45] This will diffuse change capabilities throughout the organization rather than limit them to a special function or role. It will permit faster and more flexible reactions to challenges faced by the organization. In addition to embedding OD skills into managerial roles, OD interventions themselves will be integrated into core business processes, such as product development, strategic planning, and order fulfillment. This should provide a closer linkage between OD and business results.

This does not mean that the role of the professional OD practitioner will go away. Professionals will be needed to help organization members gain change management competencies. Small, entrepreneurial firms will need specialized assistance in bringing on new members rapidly and organizing their efforts. Organizations involved in strategic alliances, mergers, and acquisitions will need professional help managing interorganizational interfaces and integrating diverse corporate cultures and business practices. OD professionals also will be needed to assist in the implementation of new technologies, particularly knowledge management practices. As supported by the contingent workforce trends, the demand for skilled OD practitioners is likely to increase rather than decrease. For example, there is some anecdotal evidence to suggest that as line and senior managers learn more about the knowledge and skills associated with OD practice, their requests for assistance in formulating change processes increase. Managers will look more frequently for a partner and coach to help them lead and facilitate organization change.

OD Processes Will Be More Technologically Enabled

Information technology is pervasive and will have a significant affect on OD practice. First, it will enable OD processes to be both synchronous and asynchronous (anytime, anywhere) as well as more virtual and less face-to-face. In global organizations, members can work in a variety of locations, cultures, and time zones. OD interventions, such as team-building, employee involvement, and strategic change, will have to be planned and implemented in ways that encourage contributions from a variety of stakeholders at times that are convenient or at times when creative ideas emerge. Information technology, such as email and listservs, enable organization members to make these contributions at any time they are ready. In addition, groupware technologies allow members to discuss issues in chat rooms and portals, in Web and video conferences, and on the more traditional telephone conference.

As a result, the process of OD is likely to change. For example, using these technologies to exchange ideas, discuss policies, or decide on change processes will produce different types of group dynamics from those found in face-to-face meetings. OD practitioners will need to be comfortable with this technology and to develop virtual facilitation skills that recognize these dynamics. In many cases, a more structured and assertive approach will be necessary to ensure that all members have an opportunity to share their ideas. The effect of these technically mediated exchanges on work satisfaction, productivity, and quality is not yet known. In addition, processes of visioning, diagnosis, data feedback, and action planning will have to be reengineered to leverage new information technologies.

Second, information technology will provide much more data about the organization to a greater number of participants in a shorter period of time. OD processes will be adapted to recognize that members have more information at their fingertips. For example, organization intranets provide members with an information channel that is richer, more efficient, more interactive, and more dynamic than such traditional channels as newsletters and memos. Thus, intranets can provide a timely method for collecting data on emerging issues, to provide performance feedback on key operational measures, and to involve members in key decisions.

OD Cycle Times Will Be Shorter

Trends in the economy and technology are shortening product, organization, and industry life cycles. Pressures to reduce the cycle time of OD activities are also likely to increase. To be seen as relevant, OD practitioners must be mindful of opportunities to quicken the pace of key change processes, and simultaneously to remain aware of the practices and processes that cannot be hurried.

New information technologies will expedite certain steps in the change process. For example, a large-scale organization diagnosis involving member interviews and surveys used to take as long as 6 months. By the time the data were ready, many of the pressing issues had faded because of new developments in the marketplace, turnover in personnel, or proactive management. Today, with electronic surveys and large-group designs, organization diagnosis can be completed in as little as a few hours. In coming years, new technologies, such as groupware and video conferencing, will increasingly be used to bring more people together faster than ever before. In short, there is real potential to reduce dramatically the time required to perform many OD practices.

There are physical and psychological limits to reductions in the OD change cycle, however, and it is not realistic to expect change to be instantaneous.[46] For example, managers are often disturbed by estimates that major structural or cultural changes take 2 to 5 years. A new organization chart or a new vision and values statement hung on members' office walls often gives the illusion that change has occurred, but the working relationships, process improvements, and other aspects of fully implementing these large-scale changes often take longer than expected. Similarly, most organization members are not capable of dropping a well-known and understood set of behaviors one day and picking up a new set of behaviors the next with the same level of efficiency. Members can face a steep learning curve when they are asked to change their routines, and thus there are likely minimums with respect to the speed of change in individual behavior.

OD Will Be More Interdisciplinary

OD will continue to become more interdisciplinary and rely on different perspectives and approaches to develop and change organizations. Historically, the focus of OD expanded from small groups and social process to organization structures and work design, and more recently, to strategic and global social change.[47] Along the way, different disciplines were applied to OD practice, including organization theory, industrial engineering, labor relations, comparative management, and corporate strategy. Technology, workforce diversity, and other trends are broadening the focus of OD further and making other social sciences more relevant to planned change. This enlarged sphere of practice will require new approaches to planned change informed by such fields as information systems, international relations, social ecology, and the "new sciences," including complexity, chaos, and network theories. Fortunately, many of these disciplines are expanding their boundaries as well and becoming more aware of the contributions that OD can make to them.

Recent developments in complexity science and chaos theory, for example, provide fascinating new frameworks and metaphors for OD practice and theory.[48] Concepts such as *emergence, instability, phase transitions, bifurcation, self-organization*, and *strange attractors* can be used to describe systems change and may yield new insights into the change process. The application of these concepts in physical systems is well underway and their use as a metaphor for organization change is gaining ground. Their development into practical interventions is still in its infancy, however. Similarly, the popularity of describing network structures in the business press overestimates our understanding of network dynamics. Research and practice into organizational networks is only just beginning, and concepts such as *small-worlds, connectedness, synchrony, cascades*, and *interaction rules*[49] have yet to be translated into frameworks that are useful for OD practitioners and their clients.

Despite our lack of knowledge about networks and complexity—or maybe because of it—these subjects hold promise for entirely new kinds of OD interventions.

As described in Chapter 19, our ability to create and change networks is a skill that will be in increasing demand. Technological infrastructures and network organizations are making different parts of the world more interdependent. As the members of a network increase their interdependency, the network becomes more, not less, fragile. In 2003 alone, electrical blackouts in the northeastern United States and Canada, the diffusion of worm viruses through the Internet, and the waves of financial and social consequences resulting from the SARS epidemic provided ample evidence that understanding networks will increase our ability to manage complex change in the future.

As OD becomes more interdisciplinary, the prospects for integration described earlier seem even more promising. Ideally, an integrated and interdisciplinary OD perspective will balance human fulfillment and economic performance, provide a fuller recognition of the systemic and dynamic nature of organizations, and develop improved techniques for managing large-scale, transformational change within and across national cultures. For OD practice, the benefit will be organizations where all members think strategically, and are guided jointly by self-interest, organizational efficiency, and ecological welfare.

OD Will Be Applied to More Diverse Organizations

The changes occurring in OD's context suggest that in the future, planned change will be applied to a more diverse client base. Traditionally, OD focused on large business organizations, but three other types of organizations increasingly will become targets of planned change: *small entrepreneurial start-ups, government organizations,* and *global social change organizations*. Small, entrepreneurial start-ups are an important and underserved market for OD. Many of these organizations are at the forefront of the technology trends cited earlier. Because they are operating on scarce and finite venture capital, time is their most valuable asset and the one most critical to their success. As a result, entrepreneurial firms generally have a clear action orientation, little perceived need to reflect and learn, and few structures and systems to guide behaviors and decisions.[50] This is a context that can be well served by fast, flexible change processes orienting new people quickly to the business strategy, integrating them rapidly into new work roles, increasing the efficiency of work processes, and helping founders and key managers think about how the market, competitors, and technology are changing. Entrepreneurs are not inclined to think about nor are they trained to examine these issues. OD can help them gain needed competence to address such matters.

Chapter 22 described the differences between public- and private-sector organizations and the implications of those differences for the practice of OD. The economic, workforce, technology, and organization trends also are pushing government organizations to become more efficient, flexible, and networked. Consequently, government is increasingly applying OD interventions such as strategic planning, employee involvement, and performance management, and we expect that the demand for change management expertise in the public sector will grow. Moreover, governments will become more proactive in managing the effects of global economic development. Public–private partnerships, a form of collaborative strategy, are also likely to flourish. They will require the assistance of OD practitioners who are sensitive to the differences between these two types of organizations and to the demands the partnerships will be under, such as environmental protection, corporate citizenship, and taxation.

Similarly, Chapter 21 described the application of OD in global social change organizations. The increasing concentration of wealth and globalization of the economy will create a plethora of opportunities for OD to assist developing countries, disadvantaged citizens, and the ecology. In China, for example, as the government breaks up the old "work unit" structure and creates market-facing enterprises, the need for nongovernment organizations to take over delivery of social services is likely to increase. For example, the Global Village of Beijing has begun campaigns to involve the Chinese people in pro-environment practices and to develop leaders for other nongovernment organizations; the China Brief has cataloged NGOs and provided a forum for their communication; and the World Wildlife Fund (WWF) is partnering with corporations to initiate environmentally friendly policies. OD can help these organizations achieve their objectives, manage their resources, and improve their functioning through such interventions as team-building, strategic planning, and alliance building.

OD Will Become More Cross-Cultural

As organizations and the economy become more global, the recent growth of OD practice in international and cross-cultural situations will continue. However, we know relatively little about planned change processes in cross-cultural settings. Traditionally, OD has been practiced in organizations within specific cultures: British-trained OD practitioners helped British organizations in Great Britain; Mexican OD practitioners helped Latin American organizations; and so on. But the current trends clearly point to the need for OD applications that work across cultures. Team-building interventions need to be modified to help a team composed of Americans, Indians, Chinese, Koreans, and French Canadians who have never met face-to-face but are charged with developing a new product in a short period of time. The merger-and-acquisition process needs to be adapted to help a Japanese and a U.S. firm implement a new organization structure that honors both cultures. Because the number of organizations operating in multiple countries is growing rapidly, opportunities for OD in these situations seem endless: interorganizational and network relationships between subsidiaries, operating units, and headquarters organizations; team building across cultural boundaries; working out global logistic and supply-chain processes; implementing diversity-centric values in ethnocentric cultures; designing strategic planning exercises at multiple levels. Moreover, OD is likely to find increased opportunities in GSCO organizations that are often part of an international network. Alliance development processes and network structure interventions adapted for cross-cultural contexts have yet to be developed and will have important applications in the future.

OD Will Focus More on Ecological Sustainability

OD will become increasingly concerned with ecological sustainability. Limits to the world's ecosystem, including its capacity to absorb population growth, function with a depleted ozone layer, and operate with polluted waters, provide serious challenges to the traditional business model. New concepts, frameworks, and philosophies, including the Coalition for Environmentally Responsible Economics (CERES) principles, ISO 14000, The Natural Step, and natural capitalism, represent opportunities to make ecological sustainability a more deliberate and intentional value of organizational growth. The natural capitalism model, for example, suggests that business strategies built around the productive use of natural resources can solve environmental problems at a profit.[51] Most sustainability models go beyond ecological concerns to promote a multidimensional view called the *triple bottom line*. It proposes that organization change and globalization should be guided by the economic, social, and ecological value that is added or destroyed. These three values provide a framework for measuring and reporting corporate performance. They can also guide how organizations go about minimizing harm or maximizing benefits through their decisions and actions. This involves being clear about the company's purpose and taking into consideration the needs of all stakeholders—shareholders, customers, employees, business partners, governments, the ecology, local communities, and the public.

OD interventions to promote ecological sustainability are just being developed. The Natural Step, for example, proposes a set of guidelines for development and a process of change that aligns with an OD perspective.[52] It begins with a simple premise: Current economic models based on growth cannot reconcile the increasing demand for and decreasing supply of finite and fundamental natural resources. The sooner this incompatibility is recognized and addressed, the larger the number of available and socially acceptable solutions. The Natural Step utilizes four "system conditions" to guide an organization's strategic decisions: (1) Substances from within the earth must not systematically increase in the ecosphere, (2) substances produced by society must not systematically increase in the ecosphere, (3) the physical ability of nature to renew itself must not be diminished, and (4) the basic human needs of all people need to be met with fairness and efficiency. Implementing these guidelines starts with building organizational awareness and knowledge of sustainability concepts and conducting a baseline assessment. Then a vision and strategic plan are created and necessary changes are supported one step at a time.

Ecological sustainability interventions represent important and growing influences on global organizations. More and more organizations on the path to globalizing their business or rationalizing their existing worldwide strategy are including sustainability as one of their values. IKEA, Interface, and Motorola among others, provide positive examples of alternative business models in practice. For example, Interface, a manufacturer of carpet products, has pioneered the idea of "leasing" its carpets. Under its "Evergreen Lease," they accept responsibility for keeping the carpet clean and fresh in exchange for a monthly fee. By installing carpet tiles instead of large rolls, and because only a small fraction of carpeting actually gets used, they can replace the tiles and save approximately 80% of the cost of carpeting materials. The model adds service revenues to the core business model and increases margins to its product line while radically reducing the organization's ecological footprint.

SUMMARY

In this concluding chapter, we described three trends within OD and four trends driving change in OD's context. OD's future is likely to be the result of the interactions among the traditional, pragmatic, and academic trends as well as how the global economy evolves, technology develops, workforces are engaged, and organizations structure themselves. To be relevant, OD practitioners and the field as a whole must act together to influence the future they prefer or adjust to the future that is coming. Moving OD toward rigor and relevance requires more than simple extensions of existing theory and practice. OD's ability to contribute to an organization's success, to shape globalization, or unite the trends within OD will depend on its ability to generate new and more powerful interventions that draw on new models and integrated values. Our hope is that this text was able to inform and equip the reader with the skills, knowledge, and value awareness necessary to shape the future.

NOTES

1. G. Varney, personal conversation, Academy of Management Conference, Seattle, Wash., August 1, 2003.

2. C. Worley, "Defining OD," *ODC Newsletter* (Summer 2003), http://www.aom.pace.edu/odc/newsletters/SUM03.htm#def.

3. J. Milliman, J. Ferguson, D. Trickett, and B. Condemi, "Spirit and Community at Southwest Airlines: An Investigation of a Spiritual Values-Based Model," *Journal of Organizational Change Management* 12 (1999): 221–33; W. Gellerman, M. Frankel and R. Ladenson, *Values and Ethics*

in Human Systems Development (San Francisco: Jossey-Bass, 1990); D. Maier, B. Levan, and D. Orr-Alfeo, "A Values Statement on OD: An Interview with Practitioner-Scholar Dr. Allan Church," *Organization Development Journal* 19 (Fall, 2001): 69–75.

4. C. Weidner and O. Kulick, "The Professionalization of Organization Development: A Status Report and Look to the Future," in *Organizational Change and Development*, vol. 12, eds. W. Pasmore and R. Woodman (Oxford, England: JAI Press, 1999); A. Church, "The Professionalization of Organization Development: The Next Step in an Evolving Field," in *Organizational Change and Development*, vol. 13, eds. R. Woodman and W. Pasmore (Oxford, England: JAI Press, 2001), 1–42.

5. L. Forcella, "Marketing Competency and Consulting Competency for External OD Practitioners," (unpublished master's thesis, Pepperdine University, 2003).

6. N. Worren, K. Ruddle, and K. Moore, "From Organizational Development to Change Management: The Emergence of a New Profession," *Journal of Applied Behavioral Science* 35(1999): 273–86; H. Hornstein, "Organizational Development and Change Management: Don't Throw the Baby Out with the Bath Water," *Journal of Applied Behavioral Science*, 37(2001): 223–26; M. Davis, "OD and Change Management Consultants: An Empirical Examination and Comparison of their Values and Interventions" (working paper, Harry F. Byrd, Jr. School of Business, Shenandoah University, 2002).

7. A. Pettigrew, R. Woodman, and K. Cameron, "Studying Organizational Change and Development: Challenges for Future Research," *Academy of Management Journal* 44 (2001): 697–714.

8. P. Berger and T. Luckman, *The Social Construction of Reality* (New York: Anchor Books, 1967); K. Gergen, "The Social Constructionist Movement in Modern Psychology," *American Psychologist* 40 (1985): 266–75; D. Cooperrider, "Positive Image, Positive Action: The Affirmative Basis for Organizing," in *Appreciative Management and Leadership*, eds. S. Srivastva, D. Cooperrider, and Associates (San Francisco: Jossey-Bass, 1990); D. Maines, "Charting Futures of Sociology: Culture and Meaning: The Social Construction of Meaning," *Contemporary Sociology* 29 (2000): 577–84.

9. B. Nixon, "The Big Issues—The Challenge for OD Practitioners," *OD Practitioner* 34 (2002): 16–19; K. Eisenhardt, K. Eisenhardt, "Has Strategy Changed?", *Sloan Management Review* 43 (2002): 88–91.

10. D. Bell, *The Coming of Post-Industrial Society: A Venture in Social Forecasting* (New York: Basic Books, 1973); A. Toffler, *The Third Wave* (New York: William Morrow, 1980); D. Korten, *When Corporations Rule the World* (West Hartford, Conn.: Kumarian Press; San Francisco: Berrett-Koehler, 1995); L. Thurow, *The Future of Capitalism* (New York: William Morrow, 1996); The International Forum on Globalization, *Alternatives to Economic Globalization* (San Francisco: Berrett-Koehler, 2002).

11. Eisenhardt, "Has Strategy Changed?"; The International Forum on Globalization, *Alternatives to Economic Globalization*.

12. R. Wright, "The New Mantra of Globalization: Inclusion Conference," *Los Angeles Times*, 8 February 2000, A-10; Thurow, *Future of Capitalism*.

13. T. Carrel, "Beijing: New Face for the Ancient Capital," *National Geographic* 197 (2000): 116–37.

14. International Forum on Globalization, *Alternatives to Economic Globalization*.

15. L. Thurow, "Building Wealth," *Atlantic Monthly* (June 1999): 57–69; R. Senser, "Loaded at the Top: The Growing Inequalities in Wealth and Income in the United States," http://www.senser.com/loaded.htm, accessed on December 11, 1999. The article, in a slightly different form, first appeared in *Commonweal* (1 December 1995).

16. J. Useem, "Have They No Shame?" *Fortune* (14 April 2003): 57–63.

17. Thurow, "Building Wealth."

18. CBSNews.com, "Bad Year for Billionaires," (1 March 2002): http://www.cbsnews.com/stories/2002/03/01/national/main502573.shtml accessed on September 26, 2003.

19. A. Jarblad, "The Global Political Economy of Transnational Corporations," Department of Business Administration and Social Science, Lulea University of Technology, Lulea, Sweden, 2003, http://ebubl.luth.se/1402-1773/2003/047/LTU-CUPP-03047-SE.pdf.

20. Korten, *When Corporations Rule*.

21. Data are from the "Mapping the Global Corporations Project" and can be found at http://www.bigpicture-smallworld.com/Global%20Inc%202/pgs/i ntro.html accessed on November 11, 2003.

22. The data here was collected from the World Bank Web site: http://www.worldbank.org/data, accessed on October 20, 2003.

23. Central Intelligence Agency, *Global Trends, 2015*. (Langley, Va.: Central Intelligence Agency, 2000) as cited in The International Forum on Globalization, *Alternatives to Economic Globalization* (San Francisco: Berrett-Koehler, 2002).

24. Thurow, *Future of Capitalism*; Korten, *When Corporations Rule*; N. Mankiw, *Principles of Economics* (Fort Worth, Tex.: Dryden Press, 1997).

25. C. Murphy, "The Next Big Thing," *FSB* (June, 2003): 64–70.

26. U. McFarling, "Climate Is Warming at Steep Rate Study Says," *Los Angeles Times*, 23 February 2000, A1.

27. J. Guyon, "A Big Oil Man Gets Religion," *Fortune* (6 March 2000): F87–F89.

29. Thurow, *Future of Capitalism*.

30. Korten, *When Corporations Rule*.

31. Information on IKEA's transformation can be found at http://www.naturalstep.org/event/cases.

32. C. Thompson, E. Koon, W. Woodwell, and J. Beauvais, "Training for the Next Economy: An Astd State of the Industry Report on Trends in Employer-Provided Training in the U.S.," American Society of Training and Development, 2002.

33. S. Berchem, "ASA's Annual Economic Analysis of the Staffing Industry," http://www.staffingtoday.net/staffstats/annualanalysis03.htm accessed on 15 November 2003.

34. R. Melchionno, "The Changing Temporary Work Force," *Occupational Outlook Quarterly* (Spring 1999), http://www.bls.gov/opub/ooq/1999/Spring/art03.pdf accessed on 13 November 2003.

35. Melchionno, "The Changing Temporary Work Force"; Berchem, "ASA's Annual Economic Analysis."

36. Information gathered at http://cyberatlas.internet.com/ accessed on 4 October 2003.

37. P. Drucker, "Beyond the Information Revolution," *Atlantic Monthly* (October 1999). 47–57.

38. D. Marshall and R. Morales, "FTAA-Joint Government-Private Sector Committee of Experts on Electronic Commerce," http://www.ecommerce.gov/PressRelease/ecom-01.htm, accessed 16 December 1999.

39. A. Dunn and J. O'Dell, "Auto Makers Plan Behemoth E-Business," *Los Angeles Times*, 26 February 2000, A-1.

40. E. Sanders, "Tech-Driven Efficiency Spurs Economic Boom," *Los Angeles Times*, 22 February 2000, A-1.

41. G. Colvin, "Managing in the Info Era," *Fortune* (6 March 2000): F6–F9.

42. Institute for the Future, "21st Century Organizations: Reconciling Control and Empowerment," http://www.iftf.org, accessed 4 December 1999; J. Child and D. Faulkner, *Strategies of Co-operation: Managing Alliances, Networks, and Joint Ventures* (New York: Oxford University Press, 1998); J. Bamford, B. Gomes-Casseres, and M. Robinson, *Mastering Alliance Strategy* (New York: John Wiley and Sons, 2002).

43. M. Piore and C. Sabel, *The Second Industrial Divide* (New York: Basic Books, 1984); D. Watts, *Six Degrees* (New York: W.W. Norton and Co., 2003).

44. From remarks of Kirby Dyess, vice president for business development, Intel, in a speech at Pepperdine University's MSOD alumni conference, Watsonville, Calif., July 1999.

45. N. Tichy, "The Death and Rebirth of Organizational Development," in *Organization 21C*, ed. S. Chowdhury (Upper Saddle River, N.J.: Financial Times Prentice Hall, 2002), 155–74.

46. C. Worley and R. Patchett, "Myth and Hope Meet Reality: The Fallacy of and Opportunities for Reducing Cycle Time in Strategic Change," in M. Anderson, *Fast-Cycle Organization Development* (Cincinnati, Ohio: South-Western College Publishing, 2000); C. Worley, T. Cummings, and P. Monge, "A Critique, Test, and Refinement of the Punctuated Equilibrium Model of Strategic Change" (working paper, Pepperdine University, 1999).

47. R. Jacobs, *Real Time Strategic Change* (San Francisco: Berrett-Koehler, 1994): C. Worley, D. Hitchin, and W. Ross, *Integrated Strategic Change* (Reading, Mass.: Addison-Wesley, 1996); J. Preston, L. DuToit, and I. Barber, "A Potential Model of Transformational Change Applied to South Africa" in *Research in Organizational Change and Development*, vol. 9, eds. R.Woodman and W. Pasmore (Greenwich, Conn.: JAI Press, 1998).

48. M. Wheatley, *Leadership and the New Science: Learning about Organization from an Orderly Universe* (San Francisco: Berrett-Koehler, 1992).

49. Watts, *Six Degrees*; A. Barabasi, *Linked* (Cambridge, Mass.: Perseus, 2002).

50. K. Chee, "Strategic and Organization Development Challenges Faced by High-Technology Startup Chief Executive Officers" (unpublished master's thesis, Pepperdine University, 1999).

51. A. Lovins, L. Lovins, P. Hawken, "A Road Map for Natural Capitalism," *Harvard Business Review* (May-June, 1999): 145–58; information on the Natural Step can be found at http://www.naturalstep.org.

52. H. Bradbury and J. Clair, "Promoting Sustainable Organization's with Sweden's Natural Step," *Academy of Management Executive* 13 (1999): 63–74.

B. R. Richardson Timber Products Corporation

Jack Lawler returned to his desk with a fresh cup of coffee. In front of him was a file of his notes from his two visits to the B. R. Richardson Timber Products Corporation. As Lawler took a sip of coffee and opened the file, he was acutely aware that he had two tasks. In a week, he was to meet with the company president, B. R. Richardson, and the industrial relations officer, Richard Bowman, to make a presentation on his findings with regard to the lamination plant and his recommendations for what might be done. Lawler knew he had a lot of preparation to do, starting with a diagnosis of the situation. It wouldn't be easy. Taking another sip from his mug, he leaned back in his chair and recalled how this project had begun.

MAKING A PROPOSAL

It was about 2:30 P.M. when the office intercom buzzed. Lawler's secretary said there was a Richard Bowman calling from Papoose, Oregon. Lawler knew that Papoose was a small community about a hundred and fifty miles south, a town with three or four lumber mills lying in the mountain range of western Oregon. When Lawler picked up his telephone, Bowman introduced himself as being in charge of industrial relations for the B. R. Richardson Timber Products Corporation. He was calling because a friend of his in a regional association for training and development persons had recommended Lawler, and Bowman had heard of Lawler's management training and consulting reputation. Bowman said he was searching for someone to conduct a "motivation course" for the blue-collar employees of the lamination plant. Morale in the plant was very low, there had been a fatality in the plant a few months before, and the plant manager was "a bit authoritative." Given the gravity of the plant situation, Bowman wanted to conduct the course within the next few months.

Lawler asked if the plant manager was supportive of the course idea. Bowman replied that he hadn't asked him but had gotten approval from B. R. Richardson, the founder and president of the firm. Lawler then stated that he really didn't have enough information on which to design such a course nor enough information to determine whether such a course was appropriate.

He suggested a meeting with Bowman and Richardson the next week; he would be able to stop by Papoose in the late afternoon on his way home from another engagement. Bowman immediately accepted his proposal and gave Lawler directions.

Taking another sip of coffee, Jack Lawler continued to reminisce, visualizing the road winding past two very large lumber and plywood plants and over a small hill, and recalling his first sight of the B. R. Richardson Timber Products Corporation. It was much smaller than its neighbors, consisting of a one-story office building, a medium-size lumber mill, open storage yards, an oblong, hangarlike structure, dirt connecting roads, lumber and log piles seemingly scattered around, and cars and pickup trucks parked at random. The office building entryway was paneled with photographs showing the company buildings as they had changed over many years.

Bowman greeted Lawler, led him to a carpeted and paneled conference room, and introduced him to Ben Richardson. "BR" was a man in his late fifties, dressed in western apparel. The subsequent conversation was one in which the company as a whole was outlined and information was presented about the plant workers. Lawler described his preferred ways of working (essentially, diagnosis before training or other action). BR and Bowman shared their concerns that the plant manager, Joe Bamford, was getting out the work but wasn't sensitive to the workers. Bowman then took Lawler on a tour of the lamination plant. The meeting ended cordially, with Lawler promising to write a letter in a few days in which he would outline his thoughts on going forward.

Jack Lawler opened the file in front of him on his desk and smiled as he found the copy of the letter he had sent:

Mr. Richard Bowman
B. R. Richardson Timber Corporation
P.O. Box 66
Papoose, Oregon

Dear Mr. Bowman:

When I departed from your office about a week ago, I promised a letter outlining my thoughts on some next steps regarding the laminating plant.

Let me sketch some alternatives:

1. One is for me to put you in touch with someone in your immediate region who could design and/or present the "motivation" course for the laminating workers that you originally had in mind.

2. Second is for me to be engaged as a consultant. Recall the experience I described with the plywood plant in northern California in which I facilitated an approach called "action research." You'll remember that it basically involved a process wherein the concerned parties were helped to identify noncontrolled problems and plan to overcome them. This would begin with a diagnosis conducted by myself.

3. Third, you'll also recall that I teach part-time at State University. This relationship leads to two ways graduate students might become involved:

   I believe I could get a colleague in personnel management training to create a student team to design and conduct the motivation course.

   I can have a student team in my change seminar do a diagnosis of the laminating plant and provide you with their analyses and recommendations.

I believe I was clear during my visit that I think a diagnosis is needed first, regardless of next steps. When you and Mr. Richardson have thought about these alternatives, give me a call. I'll be prepared to outline what I see as the costs of alternatives 2 and 3.

Thanks for the opportunity to visit. I enjoyed meeting you and beginning to learn about your company.

Sincerely,

Jack Lawler
Partner
Oregon Consulting Associates

VISITING THE PLANT

Lawler remembered that six weeks went by before Bowman called. He had shown Lawler's letter to B. R. Richardson, and they agreed that a more adequate diagnosis was probably a useful first step. Bowman was quite clear that Richardson did not want to invest much money but also wanted Lawler's expertise. In the ensuing conversation, Bowman and Lawler worked out an initial plan in which he would utilize several of his graduate students in a one-day visit to the company to gather information. Lawler would then analyze it and make a presentation to BR and Bowman. The use of the graduate students would substantially reduce his time as well as provide the students with some useful experience. They agreed that he would bill for three days of his time plus the expenses incurred when he and the students visited.

The next week when Lawler went to campus to teach his evening seminar called "The Management of Change" at the Graduate School of Business, he shared with the class the opportunity for some relevant fieldwork experience. He and four students could do the observing and interviewing in one day by leaving very early in the morning to drive to Papoose and arriving home by midevening. The information gained would be the focus of a subsequent class in which all seminar participants performed the diagnosis. When he asked his seminar who was interested in the information-gathering day, six students volunteered. When particular dates for the trip to Papoose were discussed, however, most of the six had conflicting schedules. Only Mitch and Mike, two second-year MBA students, were available on one of the days that Lawler's schedule permitted.

Having constituted the field team, Lawler suggested that the seminar invest some time that evening in two ways. He wanted to share with the class some information he had gained on his first visit to B. R. Richardson Timber and suggested that the class could help prepare Mitch and Mike for the experience in the field. He then drew an organization chart on the blackboard that showed the various segments of the corporation and the lamination business, including the personnel and main work groups. He further drew a layout of the laminating plant on the board. Exhibits 1 and 2 show these sketches. While doing this, Lawler spoke of his understanding of the technology,

Exhibit 1   **Organizational Chart**

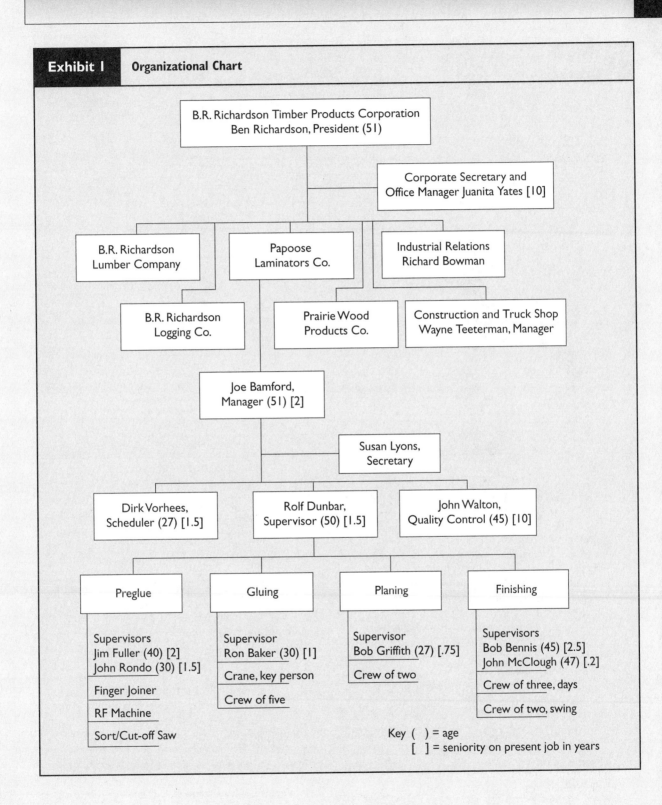

B.R. Richardson Timber Products Corporation
Ben Richardson, President (51)

Corporate Secretary and
Office Manager Juanita Yates [10]

B.R. Richardson
Lumber Company

Papoose
Laminators Co.

Industrial Relations
Richard Bowman

B.R. Richardson
Logging Co.

Prairie Wood
Products Co.

Construction and Truck Shop
Wayne Teeterman, Manager

Joe Bamford,
Manager (51) [2]

Susan Lyons,
Secretary

Dirk Vorhees,
Scheduler (27) [1.5]

Rolf Dunbar,
Supervisor (50) [1.5]

John Walton,
Quality Control (45) [10]

Preglue

Gluing

Planing

Finishing

Supervisors
Jim Fuller (40) [2]
John Rondo (30) [1.5]

Finger Joiner

RF Machine

Sort/Cut-off Saw

Supervisor
Ron Baker (30) [1]

Crane, key person

Crew of five

Supervisor
Bob Griffith (27) [.75]

Crew of two

Supervisors
Bob Bennis (45) [2.5]
John McClough (47) [.2]

Crew of three, days

Crew of two, swing

Key ( ) = age
     [ ] = seniority on present job in years

Exhibit 2   **Laminating Plant**

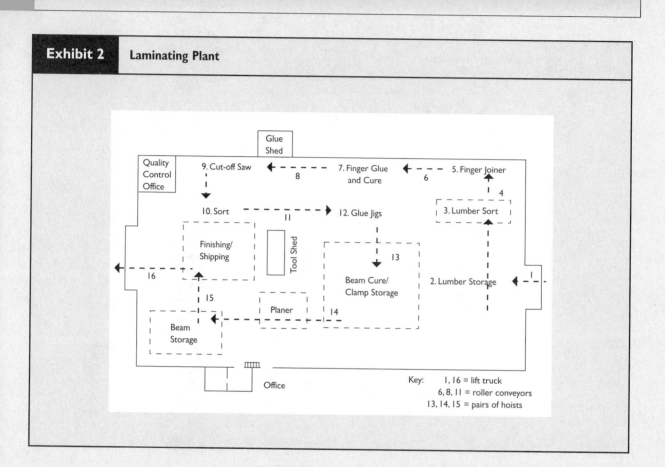

work flow, and product of the laminating plant as follows:

It's a family-held corporation. It's composed of four small companies, divisions really, three in Papoose—a logging operation, a lumber mill, and the laminating plant—and a mill over in eastern Oregon. The head office, the mill, and the lam plant are on the edge of Papoose, which is a very small logging town about six or seven miles from the interstate highway. The lam plant looks like a long airplane hangar, the type with a curved roof. Rich Bowman took me on a tour, safety helmet on, and explained the activities as we went along.

Now, the end products are long, laminated wood roof trusses or beams like you sometimes see in supermarkets and arenas. These are built up out of many layers of two-by-fours, two-by-sixes, and two-by-eights glued together end to end and then side to side. So in one end of the plant come lift trucks of lumber, which is stacked up to a height of twelve to fifteen feet. According to orders—and all beams are made to customer

order—the lumber is sorted and then hand-placed on a machine that cuts deep notches in the ends of the lumber. These go along one wall of the plant where the notched ends, called fingers, are glued together to make really long pieces.

These then go on along the roller conveyor, to the other end of the plant almost, where they are cut to the correct length, and sets of these long pieces are grouped together—the right number of the right length to make up a beam. This set then goes to a work station where there is a metal jig. The pieces are put in the jig one at a time, the glue is applied, and they are tapped down by hand. When the beam is fully assembled, clamps are put on every little way. This rough, clamped beam, running anywhere from twenty to, say, seventy-eight feet in length and from one to three-plus feet high, obviously very, very heavy, is marked, then picked out of the jig by two small hoists and stacked up to cure (dry). The curing piles have cross sticks and must be fifteen to eighteen feet high in some places.

These beams cure and eventually are picked out of the stack with the hoists and maneuvered so that they are fed into the planer, which is set to plane the rough beam to exact thickness dimensions. After planing, the beam is stored until the finishing crew gets to it. This crew cuts the beam to length, patches minor surface blemishes, and wraps plastic around it for shipping. These beams then sometimes go directly onto a truck for shipment or into the yard until a load is ready.

The plant is noisy from saws, conveyors and hoists, and especially the planer. There are glue drippings, sawdust, and ends everywhere. The aisles tend to disappear in tools and piles. Above the plant offices of the manager, supervisor, and secretary is a lunchroom and another office for the scheduler. The company's head office is about fifty yards away in one direction and the mill about the same distance in another. The yard is graveled, with lumber of all kinds piled up and cars parked around the edges.

The class was encouraged to visualize the laminating plant and its working conditions. Lawler then divided the class into two groups around Mike and Mitch for the task of preparing for their visit to B. R. Richardson Timber. It was important to clarify what information might be usefully sought and how informal interviewing on the work floor might be accomplished.

On the next Wednesday, the trio drove to Papoose, stopping for breakfast along the way. When they arrived at the Richardson head office, they were met by Richard Bowman. Lawler initially interviewed Juanita Yates while Bowman took Mike and Mitch to the lamination plant and introduced them to Joe Bamford, the manager. At lunch time, Lawler and his students drove into Papoose and ate at a cafe. They summarized what they had learned in the morning. Each of them had been jotting some notes, and Lawler encouraged even more. He reminded Mike and Mitch that they would dictate their information during the drive home but that notes were needed as cues. At 4:30 P.M., the three met at Bowman's office, turned in their safety helmets, thanked him, and left. The first hour of the drive was filled with the sharing of anecdotes from each other's day. After a dinner stop, they took turns in the back seat dictating their notes.

REVIEWING THE NOTES

Jack Lawler's reverie was broken by the office intercom. His secretary announced a long-distance telephone call from a potential client. After the call, Jack turned his attention to the Richardson file. He realized that his forthcoming meeting with Ben Richardson and Richard Bowman would take place before his graduate seminar met to diagnose the laminating plant situation, and so he had best get to work himself. He decided to review the notes he and his students had created.

Jack's Notes

Current Lam schedule: Breakout crew 2:00 A.M. to 12:00 noon. Finish end 3:30 A.M. on. Joe typically works 7:00 A.M. to 6:00 P.M.

Ben Richardson (Juanita): "In the beginning he was very authoritarian, still is somewhat. Seen as a perfectionist." "Not quite a workaholic." "Has been, for several years, politically active—that is to say, locally." "When there is a cause, he throws his energies and resources behind it." Example, workers' compensation is currently a thorn in his side, and he has encouraged Rich to fight. "In the last few years, Ben has listened a little more and seems slightly more open." The last couple of years has had consultant Chuck Byron from Eugene, who has pushed the idea of a management team. Rich is the first real outsider hired as a professional. Ben has a "conservative philosophy." Will not have safety meetings on company time. Appreciates and rewards loyalty and dedication. Example, December 1978 Christmas party—a couple of twenty-year men were given $1,000 checks and plane tickets to Hawaii for themselves and families—it surprised everybody.

Who's influential (Rich): Juanita Yates, office manager and secretary, has been with Ben ten years. When Ben is away, he calls her once or twice a day. Second-most influential is Wayne Teeterman, also ten years with Richardson. Heads construction and truck shop. Formerly ran the sawmill. Ben's ear to the mill. Rich is a distant third in influence. Mostly via Nita. "Ben sees Joe, manager of lam plant, as an enigma—almost canned him a couple of times." However, Joe is seen as dedicated, mostly because of the long hours put in.

Overall business pretty good (Rich): "Ben keeps thinking the other shoe will drop one of these days." "Ben used to be able to predict the lumber market. This is getting more difficult." Right now the economy is stable enough regarding lumber and lumber products. Richardson mill sales of clear-cut high grade are pretty much cutting to order. Laminating plant growing ever since it was started. It's very profitable, busy, and active—probably has the largest margin of all Richardson companies.

Laminating plant (Rich): Laminating plant has six- to seven-week delivery dates now.

Timber purchases (Rich): Timber purchases from Forest Service and BLM. One to two year's cutting is now available. Last year needed to cut only half of year's sales because of fortunate other purchases. Last year, half of timber requirements were from private ground. "Costs of cutting, however, go up, and it makes Ben nervous."

Laminating plant lumber (Rich): "Approximately 70 percent of laminating plant lumber purchased outside—30 percent from Richardson mill." This material is in the middle of the quality range. Outside purchases are primarily from Oregon companies—Weyerhaeuser, Bohemia, Georgia-Pacific, and smaller ones. Joe does the purchasing for lam plant. "He likes to do this."

Recent changes (Juanita): "Turnover has consistently been high and continues. For the company as a whole it is around 72 to 76 percent. In the lam plant there was 100 percent turnover last year" (among operators). "Right now this year it is down 50 percent."

Rolf (Juanita): Rolf was formerly industrial relations manager. A year ago April, he was appointed supervisor in the lam plant. Rolf's predecessor in lam plant ineffectual; gone from company. Rolf did not do a good job with personnel. Fatality in lam plant happened two months before Rolf went down there. It was in the breakdown area—several people quit at that time. There has been a constant concern for the height of stacking in the lam plant. "Joe has had a positive impact on morale—started a softball team in a community league."

Reward system (Juanita): "Nine paid holidays, hourly wage, liberal vacation plan, life insurance,

no pension, no bonus except for those people who report directly to Ben (Nita, Wayne, Joe, and Rich). Joe has not had a bonus yet."

Incentives for safety: Joe and Rolf have introduced incentives for safety. Competition for groups about lost time. Joe gave a fishing outfit last month for the first time that a safety target was met.

Hiring (Rich): Hiring was traditionally done by division managers. At present, Rich has taken over that. He now goes into background more deeply.

Interaction with middle management (Rich): Normally when Ben is in Papoose, he and Joe interact a couple times a week, which is about the same as Ben interacts with other division or company managers.

Ben's style (Juanita): "He focuses on a problem. He will write a list and go over it with the manager item by item. Pretty much forcing his way. Later, he will pull out that list to check up with." He often wants Rich to play intermediary between top management and the lam plant. Rich tries to resist.

Rolf (Rich): "Fairly introverted, basically a nice guy. He finds it hard to be tough. Doesn't think he could do Joe's job." His folks were missionaries.

Dirk (Rich): "His goal is to get into sales. Ben has given okay, and he is supposed to look into local sales. Joe has agreed but has not given Dirk time to do any of this. Dirk probably has no long-run commitment to the company." He has a degree in forestry.

John Walton (Juanita): In charge of quality control. "Very loyal to the company. Very dedicated to quality. Member of national organization. Never gets very distressed. Seems well liked by crews. Not afraid to pitch in when they are a man short or behind."

Jim Fuller (Rich): "Ben doesn't like him." Had EMT training recently sponsored by the companies. Ben questions Jim's commitment. Jim gets into lots of community activities, has been a disc jockey on Sunday mornings, and is very active in community organizations with youth. "Not perceived as a real strong leadership type, but knowledgeable and pretty well liked in the lam plant."

John Rondo (Rich): "Dedicated, works hard. Pushes the men, too. Ben sees him as having future management promise." From an old logging family in the area. "Much more leadership oriented."

Ron Baker (Rich): Gluing supervisor. "Businesslike, could be sour. Likes to impress others."

John McClough (Rich): "Failing as a finishing supervisor. Originally from California. Worked in Roseburg area as carpenter; does excellent work by himself. He is a flop and probably won't last much longer."

Bob Bennis (Rich): Finishing supervisor. "Not really a pusher." "Time has made him knowledgeable about the work." "Willing to be directed." He has had a number of family conflicts and has been in financial trouble. "Overall, a nice guy."

Bob Griffith (Rich): Planer. Came to Richardson out of the service. Started in gluing, then in breakdown, then gluing. Finally, planer's job opened up, and he took it. "Still learning the job. Generally a good worker; some question about his leadership."

Supervisors summary (Rich): "In general, the supervisors all kind of plod along."

Jim Fuller (Juanita): Is lam plant safety committee representative.

General reputation in community (Rich): "Not good from employees' point of view. Matter of turnover, accidents, and the fatality. Seems to be turning around somewhat over the last year. The company, as a whole economically, has a successful image. It's made money, survived downturns, and so forth."

Summer: During summer, fill-ins are hired for vacationers—sometimes college or high school students. The supervisor spots are filled in by key men on the crew.

Communication: Bulletin board outside of lam office has safety information, vacation schedule, and production information. Blackboard in lunchroom has jokes, congratulations, etc.

Reports: Daily production is scheduled by Dirk. Daily report from lam plant to office is compared against that. Production and lam's information reported daily. Joe keeps records on productivity by lam plant area. This duplicates Susan's records. Quality control turns in three sheets a day: on finger-joint testing, glue spread and temperature, and finished-product tests. Also Walton keeps cumulative information on block shear (where a core is drilled and stressed) and delamination tests made (where product is soaked and then stressed).

Records: A few years ago, 18,000 board feet was the high for preglue. May 9, daily was 16,406 board feet. Swing shift is consistently higher than the day shift preglue. Gluing, Ben expects 30,000 feet. On May 9, it was 27,815 feet.

Overtime (Juanita): "Is approximately 6 percent over the year. Right now lam plant is higher than that."

April (Juanita): Bids for the month were $8,166,000. Orders received for the month were $648,600. Shipped in April: $324,400. When $400,000 is shipped, that is an excellent month, according to Nita. Joe does all the bidding. Sue actually may do the calls, however. "The margin is significantly higher than the sawmill or planing mill."

History of lam plant (Juanita): "In 1968 Wayne Lauder started it. He had lots of prior experience." "The property that Richardson stands on had just been purchased. Wayne came to Joe with a proposition. Ended up with Wayne having stock in the Papoose Laminators Company." Original crew was eight to ten men. "In fact Wayne taught Ben all Ben knows about the laminating plant." "Got into lamination business at a very good time." "In the early days, there were no accidents and no turnover." "Wayne had hired old friends, largely married family types." "Walton is the only one left from those days." In the spring of 1973, Wayne went to South Africa on a missionary call. Between then and Joe, there have been four managers and four or five supervisors. Ben has an image of Wayne that successive managers cannot live up to. Joe, in Ben's eyes, has done better than anyone since Wayne. The supervisor's job was started under Wayne; since then it is not clear what they do. At one time, there was an experiment to move the lam office up to the main office so that the supervisor was forced to see the manager up there. This did not work. With Joe, the office moved back to the plant.

Sue (Juanita): Secretary in lam plant. Now handextending the data. Could use a computer. It is programmed; she has computer skills. "Computer never used for lam bidding since Sue came two years ago." Phone coverage is awkward. To get copies of things means Sue has to come to the office.

Market conditions: Market conditions have been good since Joe became manager.

Joe's ability (Juanita): Highly questioned around planning. Example: "Sue away; he knew it beforehand; it was a day he wanted to be away. This left the head office trying to get someone to cover for the phone." "Clearly sales is Joe's strong area. Get excellent reports back from customers. But Joe doesn't follow up, so payables are very weak. We still haven't got a ninety-day payment and are likely to ship the next load to the customer anyway."

Lack of communication (Juanita): "Lack of communication with us about cash flow is another weak spot of Joe's. Lack of supervision over key people like Sue and Rolf. Seems to just let them go. Certainly doesn't supervise them. Sue gets to set her own hours." Example offered by Nita of misbidding because Sue didn't get the bid back to the customer. "Joe just wasn't aware of the timing—hadn't planned for it." Another example: "Sue runs out of invoice paper, which means we have to scurry around."

Sue's wages (Juanita): "At one time, Sue was all riled up about wages and upset the secretaries in the main office. She got no pay increase last year. Ben upset. Joe went to bat for her. Joe almost put his job on the line for her."

Sue's performance (Juanita): "Sue does sloppy work. Not very efficient. Poor letters; late; missing deadlines. Joe allows or accepts, or perhaps doesn't know." Nita is supposed to be responsible for Sue on quality matters. In general, to make sure that her backup is there. "Sue now works ten to fifteen hours a week overtime." Nita cannot see the reason for this.

Rolf's attitude (Rich/Juanita): Rolf's attitude changing. Seems more cooperative to both Rich and Nita. Nita thinks Rolf is a very intelligent man. Neither are clear exactly on what Rolf does. Company policy is to send out invoices each workday and that invoices should be sent

and dated on the day shipped. Sue doesn't send them.

After Wayne, a lot of lam workers were hippies, had long hair, etc. Part of that is the reason why Rich now hires. Why is Ben down on Jim Fuller? Nita says because of time lost with accidents. "Ben knows his family and all about the radio station. Doesn't think he is committed to the lumber company. There have been financial problems, too. There were garnishments in the past. He's quit or been laid off, or was fired about three years ago. Some things stick in Ben's throat. Now Jim is out of debt; they sold the home and moved; his wife works; they do an awful lot of volunteer work at the school. Ben sees this and wonders why he can't give that energy to the company."

John Rondo (Juanita): From a local logging family. He is a nephew of Butch (someone from a logging company). "Notorious redneck." Once called Ben from a bar when he was drunk and swore to Ben about his paycheck. "Ben doesn't forget those things."

Sue hired by Joe: Does all the paperwork in the lam plant. Doesn't really have to interact with any of the men except Joe. Takes care of the purchase orders, invoices, and daily records.

Glue used in lam plant: Twenty-two thousand pounds at 60 cents per pound; that's nearly $10,000 a month.

Maintenance man: Leon replacing rails and turning chair at preglue. "Had help until noon. Don't know where they took off to." It's really a two-person job. Also said that they're probably six to eight months overdue with this job.

Hoists: Planer and helper talking at break that it is awkward and sometimes have to wait either on the finish end or breakdown side of planing because of competition for hoists. Believe the roof could hold more hoists. Can't understand why Ben won't spring for a couple of more hoists on each side. In the lunchroom, the planer was coaching a breakdown/finish helper on how to undo clamps efficiently. Says that the "whole operation has to be speeded up." 1:05 P.M.—lunchroom. The planer approaches Joe: "Can we get off a little early? We've been working lots of ten-hour days." Joe responds, "If you get that 57 job done, maybe we'll see." As Joe turns to leave, the other finish man, who helps the planer, says, "Hey, Joe, I want to talk to you later." Joe says, "Okay." The man turns to me and says, "He thinks we should be working harder. I want to tell him what's what."

Rolf put in lam plant by Ben: Probably consulted with Joe, but still he did it.

Goals for lam plant (Rich): Joe and Ben both have some goals in their heads, of course, and talk on occasion. "Probably not very systematically written down."

Jim Fuller, preglue supervisor: Swing shift now. Three men work directly under him. First work position is a lumber grading cut-off saw. A nine-teen- to twenty-year-old tends to work here. "You need a big reach." Then there is a cut-off saw that feeds a finger-joiner cut. Then the ends are glued. "Young men tend to be in this position, too. Need to have a lot of manual dexterity and a sense of rhythm." Then there is the radio frequency curing machine. It gives an eight- to ten-second jolt at 109; then the hardest job comes along. The lumber is stopped, set to length, and cut three inches longer than order and then put in stacks on rollers. "You need to visually check ahead, grade lumber, and everything else." This position has to be communicated back up to preglue line for amount.

Production scheduling (Rich/Jim): "Rolf is so-called production supervisor. However, if Joe has his druthers, he'd do that, too." Supposed to have orders from Joe to Dirk to Jim. Needs to be scheduling. This mostly happens, but sometimes he gets a message from Joe himself. Actually Jim says, "Both Rolf and Joe more or less equally give me orders." Jim confirms that the majority of materials come from external sources and suppliers. He thinks Joe is a "sharp bargainer." "If he can save $100 per thousand on eight- or ten-footers, he may buy them. Of course, this means they have to do a lot more cutting and gluing." Somehow it's known that thirty thousand feet a day per shift is what the lam plant is to produce. It takes two preglue shifts to get that. A few years ago, Jim reports, a production quota for the plant

was eighteen to twenty thousand feet per day. "Joe is really production-minded, a real pusher."

Asking about problems (Jim): He quickly responds with "confusion" and elaborates that it has to do with scheduling. "Sometimes Dirk has to work on the line and get inaccurate figures, or we don't get them in time." Nonetheless, he thinks Dirk is a good man and tries hard. Another problem has to do with stacking. There is not enough room to handle items where beams are curing, particularly in the finishing area. He makes a big point about the difference between architectural and other grades. There are 15 percent of the former in general, but it takes more layout space in the finish end to handle it.

The most inexperienced crew, in Jim's opinion, is in the breakdown area (unclamping beams for planing). There seems to be a bottleneck around the planer. "The crew tries hard but is somewhat inexperienced. His helpers couldn't care a damn." Planing is to a tolerance of plus or minus 1/16-inch. He gives an example of large beams for Los Angeles that were overplaned, and those beams now sit in the yard until they can be worked into some later order for someone.

Another problem, according to Fuller, has to do with Paul, an electrician who works under Wayne. Has strong sawmill preference. Can never find him. For example, the RF machine is only half rebuilt. "People who do this work for Wayne will probably never get it done."

Age of workers (Jim): Mostly young—"means that they don't really care about working, aren't very responsible. They take off when they feel like it; hence, there is a lot of personnel being shuffled around. Both Walton and Dirk, and even Joe, pitch in sometimes, not that this makes it really more efficient." "Personnel is shuffled too much." Fuller gives an example. He was hit by a beam and was off for seven weeks. Jay replaced him. There was stacking in the breakdown area on the main two. Jay tried to move a ceiling air hose; it came back; two top beams fell and "snuffed him out just like that." Maintenance men have to fill in on lines, too. This cuts into maintenance being done on time. The whole program is behind. It's sort of down to what Fuller calls "band-aid work." Also, major replacements are done poorly.

Example: glue area where pipes come right down in the middle of the preglue line when they should have been run down the wall. Bruce did this.

Ben's approach (Jim): "Ben used to visit the laminating plant twice a week a few years ago. I haven't seen Ben through here for more than a month now. Ben likes to use a big-stick approach." He gives example of Ben looking at maintenance work in gluing shop and insisting that the millwright come in on Saturday to get it done, "or else."

Those who report to Ben: Rich, industrial relations; Wayne, construction; Juanita, who is secretary and office manager; and managers of three companies. Richardson Lumber, which has 110 employees, was founded in 1951. Papoose Laminators started in 1968, and Prairie Wood Products started in about 1976, with forty-five employees. There is a logging company, too, which is for buying.

Mitch's Notes

Jack, Mike, and I arrive at B. R. Richardson. We enter through the main building into the office and are seated in a conference room located at the back of the main office, which is located up on a hill overlooking the rest of the plant.

Rich enters; after formal introductions, proceeds to talk about Joe, or I should say, describes Joe.

Describes Joe in the following way. Says that Joe is aware the training program was a possibility. Stated that Joe had had military experience, that he (Joe) believes he knows about management, that there are some possible resentful feelings toward our intrusion upon the plant, that he is aware of us and the fact that we are from State University.

Rich, Mike, and I leave the main office and go down to the plant to be introduced to Joe.

Rich introduces us to Joe by saying that we are with Jack and that we are down looking around at the plant, etc.—seemed awkward. Communication not straightforward. Not a lot of eye-to-eye contact. Rich is leaning up against the wall; he looks uncomfortable and leaves rather abruptly.

Joe immediately questions us as to what we are doing, why we are here, and what we are

looking for. My perception is that he is resentful. In talking to Joe, I perceive that he felt the workers were good, that with the proper knowledge of the task they could lead themselves. He also stated they were "multicapacity"—that "they had many functions which they performed," and that it wasn't that specialized down on the floor. He mentioned that his functions were bidding, managing, and engineering. He made a comment toward work team functions ("work team crap"), and then he corrected himself. He also remarked that "theories come and theories go."

At one point, Joe stressed the use of communication as a tool in management. He showed Mike and me a little exercise and seemed to be impressed with it.

In looking on the walls of his office, he had approximately five awards or merits for leadership or worker participation.

His assistant Rolf had a desk right next to his, which was in an office off the side of the secretarial room serving as the entrance to his building.

Joe's background included working in many plants, primarily in forestry—that is my understanding. He said he preferred working at B. R. Richardson's mainly because it was a "small and nonpolitical plant." He likes leadership, and he enjoys working there. He stated, as we were walking through the plant, that he felt a high degree of frustration about the plant because the size was too small at times and the seasonal rush (which is beginning right now as of May) for summer building puts a crunch on things. He stated that production is up 10 percent from last year; that there have been scheduling problems—they received some wood in February, and it wasn't until May that they could use it and laminate it and get it out the other side, so it's been stacked taking up space. He stated that if they fall behind, they have no chance to catch up and that they are working at full capacity right now.

Later on that afternoon, I went back and talked to Joe. I asked him what his specific duties were. He replied in the following way: His duties were to take orders, to plan the shipping, to make bids on orders, and to manage the plant. His typical day was to arrive about 7:00 to 7:15 A.M., to look over the plant, to look at the new orders of the day, and to take care of any emergencies. Lately, he stated that he was making engineering drawings. When asked if this was common, he said it usually was done by the customers, but he felt it was a service he could render them. He stated, "It's foolishness because it takes too much time." However, he continued to work on that project. He stated that he liked the work, that he didn't mind long hours. When asked about the scheduling, he said that after he makes a bid and fills the order, it goes to Dirk, who schedules the work to be done, which goes to Ron, who is either in preglue or the gluing operation. I'm not sure, but I felt he was talking about the gluing operation. And he stated that Ron's job was very specific, that he had to coordinate the people to get the wood clamped up, to get the glue on, and to get it organized in a rather specified manner. (I think it is interesting to check Ron's description that I include later on.)

My personal comment on Joe is that he seemed very friendly with the workers, that it was a buddy-buddy relationship. At one time, we were in the lunchroom with Joe, and he was talking openly about the problems of the shop; it was kind of like "we all suffer through this too, don't we?" He seemed to enjoy his work, he likes to work hard, he was proud of the fact that production was up, he was supportive of the men down there, and he was also apprehensive of Mike's and my presence. I think it is interesting to note the roles that Mike and I took. Mike took the role of a person interested in design, more or less, and I took the role, as I stated to Joe, that I was interested in seeing what it was like to be a manager in this situation and to learn any knowledge he might have to offer. Many times during our encounter, he asked me what my background was and also about what I wanted to do when I got through school. He seemed very interested in my studies and my goals.

Joe's secretary, while I did not talk to her, seemed to play an important role in the organization. At one point, I was talking to Joe when the secretary answered the phone and interrupted our conversation to tell Joe about a possible bid. Joe then made the bid based on the board footage, and the secretary questioned him on this

bid, at which point Joe thought a minute and said, "Yeah, I want to keep the bid the way it is." The secretary then asked him, "Are you sure?" and Joe said, "Yes," at which point the secretary completed the preliminary parts of the bid over the phone.

At one point when we were walking through the plant with Joe, I made mental notes on safety aspects of the plant—this was something in question. Some of the things I noted are as follows.

There seemed to be many metal spacers or clamps by the glue section. This section wasn't in use, so I don't know if this was normal or not. It was very crowded and difficult to walk around. As we walked through the plant, I saw at least two different types of band saws with no guarding whatsoever—a very dangerous situation in my opinion. There were no safety signs around the plant—at least not outside the lunchroom. One worker did not have a safety helmet on. I also noticed that the safety helmets that they gave us were of very low quality. I base this on past experience in wearing them; they were the cheapest I have seen. I did see a safety insignia on one gentleman's lunch box. (I wonder how they meet OSHA standards.) Also because of the crowdedness of the facility, it was very difficult to move around, and with things going on, I could see how it would be difficult not to get hurt. The workers at one point asked Joe about another worker (I think his name was Bob). It seems that Bob was going down the highway and was reaching for a speaker wire and hit the center rail on Highway I-5 and totaled his truck. He seemed to be okay with a mild concussion. The workers were very concerned. A group of about three of them asked Joe how Bob was doing.

I had a chance to talk to Ron, the team leader in gluing. His comment about his job was that there were long hours, that these were typically ten or more per day, and that he received overtime for the long hours provided that in total they were over forty hours per week. Each hour over the forty minimum would be paid at 1.5 times the normal rate. For Ron, the normal rate was about $8 an hour, $12 an hour overtime. His comments about his job and his attitude toward the plant were "sweatshop," "Richardson won't spend money," and "everyone's worked at BR's at one time or another before." "They have plans for expansion of the plant, but they don't want to spend the money on it." At one point, he said he didn't really know what he was doing in terms of how to be a supervisor, how to be a leader. When I questioned him some more, he really didn't know what the supervisor did, in this case Rolf. He had just finished his first year, as far as experience on the job.

Ron had a major complaint about his job in that the glue person also had to prepare the glue and was responsible for getting all the boards and clamps in the right direction. He seemed to think maybe an extra glue prepare person would help. It seems to be a major job for him. There seemed to be quite a bit of dissatisfaction about Rolf in his mind. He stated that when overtime or a certain amount of board footage was needed to meet a quota, this created work unrest, which led to accidents. He said that Rolf was always the one who initiated or told the workers that they had to work overtime. When asked about the death that had occurred, he stated that everybody was pretty upset about it, that it was bound to happen. I asked him what happened that day. He said that a guy got hurt, and yet management still wanted them to work even after the guy died. This seemed to upset Ron.

Ron mentioned that they (the workers) had a softball team; that he felt frustrated about it because he couldn't always play because the games were at six or seven o'clock and many times they were working until late in the evening trying to make a quota. He also stated that accidents were very high around here, that it was not uncommon to get a finger smashed or something, and that management didn't seem to care too much. He stated that he liked Joe, the manager, that he was okay but that he was maybe more production-oriented than necessary. He stated that the work is very hard and the need for better methods is evident. He stated that most men had bad backs, hernias, and broken fingers or toes, and he seemed to be kind of embarrassed. He did state that they had medical insurance.

Ron stated that one of the biggest causes of unrest, he felt, was due to overtime, and his own personal frustration was that in a year he had obtained probably the highest vertical level on the management structure, that of supervisor. He stated that the next job would probably be to take Joe's job. He said that wouldn't happen, so there seems to be a lack of job mobility in his eyes. He stated that workers do almost anything, any task at any time; that what needs to be done, needs to be done, and they do it. He also stated that in the summertime, when it is warmer, the metal building that they work in gets really hot, and it's not uncommon for men to lose five or more pounds in one shift, which would be in an eight-hour period. When asked if it was possible to ventilate the building a little bit more, he said it would be hard, that even if they could, management wouldn't spend the money to do it.

Ron said he didn't have enough time for his home life. He also stated that Rolf and Joe, who were the supervisor and manager, would come out and help when they had the time. He said they would actually end up losing a half-hour of production time that way and would be better off if they would just stay in their offices. Ron seemed to express a great amount of displeasure with Rolf, and he said most of the workers agreed that Rolf was a "thorn." When Rolf would give orders, men would get upset and throw things around, and this would cause accidents. When asked about new members, he said they don't last more than a couple of days, and very rarely do they last over a year. Ron stated that one of the jobs they gave new workers was to bang beams in the gluing job with a weight that was on a pole that is picked up and bounced up and down off the wood. It weighed anywhere from forty-five to one hundred pounds; very grueling work. He laughed a little bit and said that they usually hurt their back the first day, and it takes them a couple of weeks to learn how to do it, to learn the right technique, but he said "there is no other way to learn the job, other than just jumping up there and doing it."

My own personal opinion of Ron was that while somewhat upset at the conditions down there, he was dedicated, he did enjoy his role as a leader, and he was looked up to by the fellow workers. He mentioned at one time that the record of total board footage was broken by his crew, and he seemed very proud of that fact. He did not seem to think that any of our suggestions would make any waves around there, that "I would not be listened to." He was enjoyable to talk to, and he was more than willing to help me obtain the information I needed.

Marty, who like Ron has been there for over a year, was "key person" of the glue team. However, Ron acted as the leader. They seemed to be good friends and went home together that afternoon. Marty had been there the longest. He had stated that the work is hard, that there are long hours, and that he had been right next to the man who was killed. He stated that he was no more than three to six feet from his friend (I guess he was his friend) when it happened. He was the one to fill out the accident report for the police and insurance people. He stated that they wanted to stop work and that the plant, and he didn't say specifically who, didn't want to shut down but wanted to complete the work that was started. It seemed that most of the workers there did not want to work that day. That was the extent of my talking to Marty.

When the workers were leaving, it seems they had set up a bet for a keg of beer if the planer Griffith could plane all the beams that were set out in front of him, which from the comments of the men, was quite a chore. But Griffith seemed pretty confident that he could get the work out. He did say that he was looking to go to pharmacy school as soon as he got his hernia fixed, and when asked about the hernia, he said he got it some time ago. He said he got it working while picking up some stuff in the plant. Again, this seemed to be common.

I had a chance to talk to a couple of the preglue persons; there is a total of three. I believe Jack had talked to the leader, and I talked to the two workers. They pretty much agreed that a union would be nice; however, BR, the owner, would not allow one to come in. He said, "Work long hours, or you get fired." There seemed to be a lot of stress as far as meeting their quota, and they could not go home until they met the quota

for the day. They stated that the job was okay, but that they didn't have much time for their families. One said, "I go home, I sleep, I get up, I go to work, and I go back home and go to sleep again." When asked about their salary, he stated that they're paying, in his opinion, 60 cents per hour lower than the unions around here, and he said further, "The unions will get a 65-cent-per-hour raise, and we'll get a 45-cent-per-hour raise."

I also had a chance to talk to some of the guys in the finish area. This seemed to be a typical eight-hour shift that consisted primarily of watching the beams run through the planer. They go back and clean it up so that it can be packaged and shipped out. One man's biggest complaint was that he was upset about the lunch-break change, which he stated was initiated by Rolf. It consisted of taking their one-hour lunch break and cutting it down to a half-hour. He stated that Rolf felt production would be increased by cutting down the lunch break. He seemed upset about this. I don't know his name. He lived five blocks away from the plant and didn't have time to go home to eat and then come back (on a half-hour break). He seemed to have a high degree of resentment toward Rolf, and he had no knowledge of what Rolf does.

I had an opportunity to meet with John, the quality-control man. He seemed like a very nice man. No real quotes. He was just there for a few minutes. He had had an eye operated on: I guess a new lens was put in. He seemed to talk with Joe very well. When I asked Joe about John, Joe stated John was officially to report to him; however, John reported to Rich, and that worked out for the best because quality control should really be removed from production somewhat. Joe seemed to see no conflict in that.

Mike's Notes

Mitch and I had a morning interview with Joe. Some of the quotes on management style were: "I don't know about this work team crap, oops, stuff," "Theories come and theories go," "I believe in giving my workers explicit instructions; perceptions differ, and you have to be sure they understand," and "I didn't like the politics of larger plants I've worked in." Also, Joe mentioned frustration over the lack of plant space. To a worker he mentioned, "You are frustrated, aren't you, Bill?"

During our tour, Joe set a brisk pace. He seemed to have quite a competent manner.

When Rich approached Joe about taking Mitch and me under his wing for a tour, I think Rich was intimidated by Joe. Rich had his back against the wall sideways to Joe, and he shifted his eyes from Joe to Mitch and me during the conversation.

Joe was more than a bit curious in regard to our plant visit objective. I said it was for a class project. Joe replied, "Oh, then it's theory." I explained we covered all the theories equally. Another quote from Joe: "A day's production lost is a day lost," delivered with a hint of frustration and impatience.

Joe's office contained numerous good-worker awards. One prominent sign contained a message roughly to the effect that "I am right in the end." My impression of the plant—there were no safety glasses on the workers. One worker had no helmet; there were no band-saw safety devices. Seemed pretty lackadaisical. During our initial interview with Joe, Darrell, a truck driver, was in the office. He talked good-naturedly with Joe, and he seemed to like Joe in general. Later on in the day I had an interview alone with Dirk. Dirk is the scheduler. Dirk has a master's in forestry from the University of Washington. Dirk mentioned that he spends half his time filling in various positions. He says one of the major problems is the transition between shifts. This is in regard to mistakes. One of Dirk's quotes: "There is no communication between shifts. Mainly people don't want to take the blame for mistakes." During the course of the interview, Dirk's manner was fidgety; he moved around a bit, but he seemed fairly open. A quote from Dirk: "The men change jobs so much that it is hard to train them. Everyone has to know what is needed in beams." This implies that workers weren't really trained well enough to know what was needed in beams. "Production people go home after the quota." That was his perception of the amount of overtime worked. "Repairs after gluing are costly and difficult. Double checking is needed before they

are glued together. Average beam is six thousand board feet, or approximately $840. I currently have seventy-five bastard beams I have to find a home for." Then Dirk went on to an example of mistakes made. A tapecloth shrunk two inches. They used this tape for quite some time before they finally found the mistake. He also mentioned there were frequent mixups between the $1\frac{3}{16}$-inch and $1\frac{1}{4}$-inch strips for laminated beams. Dirk's quote on the workers: "A few are incompetent; they just get soft warnings. Management should be harder on them."

Item on bidding or posting for jobs: seniority or ability (whoever they think will do best) decides who gets the job. On the workers: Morale is low. Safety and overtime are the main causes. On Rich, industrial relations: "The only contact I've had with him is when he came down and asked about people." I asked, "Who, what people?" and Dirk said, "I'd rather not say." On safety, he mentioned there are no physicals required. Later on in the interview, I asked why he didn't try to change things, seeing as he has a master's and seems to have his head together. Dirk mentioned, "Go up the line. Joe would listen." I said, "Listen?" and Dirk said, "Yeah, Joe would listen." At this point, Bruce, a bubbling and brassy guy who is a millwright in charge of special-projects maintenance, came in. The interview with Dirk was about thirty minutes under way; the next twenty minutes I spent with Dirk, he mentioned Ben Richardson, the president. I asked, "Do men like to see BR?" Dirk responded, "No, BR is bad news in the laminating plant." He also mentioned that in the year he has been there, BR had been down to the laminating plant only five times.

Item from Bruce: "I've had thirty projects in the year I've been here; I only finished one. Joe keeps jerking me around. As I get something operating but not all the kinks out, I'm on to something else." Bruce also mentioned that he is on emergency call every other week. He splits it with the other maintenance person.

The beam stacks before and after planing were mentioned as being in terrible disarray. Bruce mentioned that the Roseburg plants had a computer and a big yard with designated areas to organize their stacks. He said that this company should take a bulldozer and knock out the field to expand the outside stack area.

Item from Bruce: "Antiquated machinery. Maintenance is costly and time-consuming." Bruce commented on BR: "Joe thinks labor is cheap; we don't have that many benefits. An example of BR's attitude: one of his right-hand men got in a flap over the 3:30 A.M. shift parking down here instead of in the muddy, rutted parking lot an eighth of a mile up the road. Christ, they had a caterpillar running up there, and they didn't even smooth it out. Anyway, this guy tells Rolf, the super, if these guys are too lazy to walk down from the workers' parking lot, they can go work somewhere else." This was mentioned right in front of some of the men. Bruce went on to say, "It really makes us feel wanted." I then asked who was this guy, BR's right-hand man, and Bruce said, "I don't want to say. . . . What the hell, I'm quitting this heap in a while anyway. It was Wayne Teeterman, BR's special-projects director." During most of Bruce's spiel, Dirk appeared to be quite happy with what Bruce was saying; I'm sure he was glad he didn't have to say it himself.

It was mentioned that the sawmill didn't have a lunchroom, so the laminated plant felt favored. Also, Rolf mentioned that the bathroom was one of the best in BR's operations.

Bruce on Rolf: "He, Rolf, is a nice guy. Nobody respects him, though."

Dirk and Bruce mentioned that there are only six or seven men who have made it ten years in all of BR's five companies.

Dirk on Joe: "Joe does too much. He keeps it all in his head. He is efficient. It would take two people to replace him. He's overworked, he doesn't like the hours, and he's just trying to keep his job." Bruce concurred on the above points.

Bruce: "Stacks of beams are too high. Two of them fell last week. Damned near got me and another guy." I noted that the accidental death last year and its details were repeated to me three times during the day.

Bruce mentioned that he recently organized a softball team. "The first thing this plant has ever had. It's hard practicing and playing games with all the overtime. We went to BR to ask him for $700 to start it up. He gave us $250. There's fourteen teams in our league, and the minimum anyone else has gotten is $700."

Dirk mentioned that the workers peak out at $8 an hour after one year. He seemed to think that money was a big motivating factor.

In response to my query why there was no union, Bruce and Dirk mentioned that hearsay has it that when union representatives came, BR said, "Fine, if you want a union, I'll just close the place down."

Dirk: "Communication is the main problem. Joe schedules some changes, and I never hear about them."

Bruce, on the foremen meetings with BR: "Hell, the foremen will have their say, and in the end BR will stand up and say, 'This is the way it's going to be because I pay the checks.' "

About five minutes before the session ended, Joe came in and with a friendly greeting said, "There you are," to Bruce and indirectly to Dirk. Dirk got up as if getting ready to go back to work. Bruce stalled. Bruce then said that he didn't know how BR made any money on the operation. Dirk giggled lightly and nodded his head.

In the afternoon, I spent an hour and a half to two hours with Rolf, the superintendent. About an hour of this talking was Rolf trying to prove his competence by divulging intricate, technical, and totally useless details of the plant. I got some tasty stuff anyway, and here it is:

Me: "What does Joe do?"

Rolf: "So doggone many things, I don't know." Then he went on to mention he is a general manager in charge of scheduling and raw materials procurement and to rattle off two or three more. I said, "What's your working relationship with Joe?" Rolf said, "I implement his schedules. Dirk, the head of the finishing and planing department, and I get Joe's schedules. Joe will skip me whenever he wants to make changes—goes right to planing and finishing. Then I have to go see what's going on." I asked him if he thought it would be more efficient if Joe went through him. Rolf said, "No, we get along well. Joe saves time by going directly to the workers. We spend a lot of time after the shift going over and discussing what happened and planning for the next day and weeks ahead."

Rolf mentioned that there are often schedule changes when customers' trucks pick up their orders. I wondered if maybe they could get tougher with the customers, and Rolf said, "No, we'd lose them."

Rolf mentioned that the company deals with brokers, not contractors. He said that customers sometimes cancel their orders.

On Bruce's idea of bulldozing a pasture to expand finish-beam storage, Rolf said that in the winter it was tough enough to keep the field clear with the current area.

Rolf on equipment: "BR gives us the junkiest stuff to work with." He went on to mention one particular piece of machinery that has four wheels and five feet of clearance (I don't know what it is called): "It has no brakes and no shut-off; you have to idle it to kill it."

On Joe: "Joe's good; he and I go to bat for the guys."

Me: "You must have a pretty little bat; I hear BR is a tough guy to get through to."

Rolf: "Yeah, he picks his battles."

On Dirk: "Effective, will improve with time; he doesn't always see the opportunities for utilizing stock beams. He has his master's degree in glue technology."

On John: "Quality control marginal." That's all he said.

On Nita, BR's secretary: "She doesn't always use her power right."

On Sue, Joe's secretary: "She does the work of two people. Has lots of customer respect; they often comment on her."

On Joe: "He's too intelligent for the job. I don't know why he does not get something better. I guess he likes to work."

On Rich: "Rich does his job well."

On the workforce: "There are three types of guys. One is eight to five and a paycheck—never volunteers or does anything extra—50 percent of the workforce. Second are the ones who use workers' compensation to get time off all the time; this is 20 percent. Workers' compensation is the biggest deterrent to an effective workforce,"

he went on to comment. "And third, the ones who try, 30 percent."

Rolf mentioned that 15 to 20 percent of the work hours were spent trying to unsort the beam piles, pre- and postplaner.

Rolf mentioned that architectural beams, 7 to 12 percent of the output, took three times as long to process as the plain beams.

On Joe again: "Joe does a good job of scheduling and customer relations."

On BR: "BR is secretive; he should keep the guys informed."

Rolf often has to juggle men around on their tasks and catches a lot of flack for this. I asked his criteria for deciding which men would go on which jobs. They were (1) how well the man will do the job and (2) how easy it is to replace him at his original task.

Rolf said overtime is a big problem. It's necessary to go through the jobs in order. Men never know how long they'll have to work. Lock-ups have to be finished. He mentioned that a good lock-up will take an hour, a bad one, one and a half to two hours. (A lock-up is essentially gluing and clamping the beam into a form.)

Rolf said he used to spend three hours a day on the glue crew. He doesn't do this anymore; he has a good crew. Eighty percent of the glue crew are good workers, in Rolf's opinion. He mentioned that two of the bad ones quit because they didn't want overtime. Also, Rolf noted that it was possible to avoid overtime by scheduling good or easy lock-ups. This was done when the glue crew had been putting in too much overtime.

Rolf stated that the overall problem with the operation was that everyone knows that "BR doesn't give a shit about them." I asked him if there was anything he liked about working for the company, and he said, "I like working for Joe." We ended the interview with Rolf saying, "Overall, it's not a bad place to work; the checks don't bounce."

PREPARING THE DIAGNOSIS

Jack Lawler leaned back in his chair and stretched. It had all come back. Now he needed a plan for working. It seemed that the first step was to determine what ideas, models, or theories would be useful in ordering and understanding the information he had. Then he would have to do a diagnosis and, finally, think about what to say to Ben Richardson and Richard Bowman. After buzzing his secretary to say that he didn't want to be interrupted, Lawler rolled up his sleeves and began to work.

Questions

1. How would you assess Jack Lawler's entry and contracting process at B. R. Richardson? Would you have done anything differently?

2. What theories or models would you use to make sense out of the diagnostic data? How would you organize the information for feedback to Ben Richardson and Richard Bowman? How would you carry out the feedback process?

3. What additional information would you have liked Jack Lawler and his team to collect? Discuss.

Source: Printed by permission of Craig C. Lundberg, Cornell University. Events described are not intended to illustrate either effective or ineffective managerial behavior.

Managing Strategy at Caesars Tahoe

Caesars Tahoe General Manager David Attaway prepared to face his executive committee. While the sun was shining on the perfect Lake Tahoe morning, the information he was about to present was anything but a fair-weather forecast. He had just received the property's 1997 financial goal from the parent company, Caesars World, and he knew it would be a tough goal to meet given the challenges that 1996 had presented. Caesars World consisted of four properties, including Caesars Palace in Las Vegas, Caesars in Atlantic City, another property in Canada, and Caesars Tahoe. Additionally, the parent of Caesars World, ITT Corporation, was placing increasing emphasis on cash flow and sustained earnings improvement. Attaway knew that some carefully formulated strategic plans were needed for Caesars Tahoe to meet its aggressive financial goal for 1997. Moreover, sustaining earnings improvement in subsequent years would continue to be a challenge at Caesars Tahoe.

For the past eight years, the Lake Tahoe tourism market had been flat, with no change in sight. Increased competition from Las Vegas and nearby Reno only added to the ongoing challenge. The situation would be an easier one to remedy if the tough regulatory environment would allow the company to expand its facilities. How easy it would be if Tahoe were like Las Vegas, where hotel room additions could be had for the capital expense and could potentially add ten-fold to revenues. But Tahoe was not Las Vegas, so there would be no new hotel rooms at Caesars Tahoe to help meet the financial goals.

Since entering the gaming industry, Attaway had watched it grow from a business with a colorful history of underworld involvement, owned primarily by private concerns and centered in Las Vegas, to a widely-respected and accepted industry, operated by public corporations in twenty-five states, and with annual gross revenues of $39.4 billion. Indeed, with the acquisition by ITT Corporation, Caesars World had a parent among the blue-chip corporations in the United States.

With the industry's rapid expansion, customers had many choices. The various gaming venues, particularly in Las Vegas, offered an "experience" to the increasingly sophisticated customer. Erupting volcanoes, giant pyramids, live street shows, and other "WOW" attractions drew visitors from around the world. Additionally, hotel expansions provided opportunities for great room and package values.

Among the new entrants in the market each year were major hotel companies, riverboat operations, cruise ships, and Native American reservations. In addition, the traditional sources of revenue were shifting. Slot machine revenue was increasing at a stronger pace than table games, such as blackjack and craps, proving that customer mix and preference had shifted. In addition, at some of the new Las Vegas properties, gaming was no longer the major revenue source. As much as 60 percent of revenues were coming from retail operations, food, beverage, and hotel room sales. This represented a major shift in thinking and operating.

Attaway decided that the first issues the executive committee would need to tackle were the strategic challenges, including an understanding of the market drivers and the specific elements facing Caesars Tahoe.

CAESARS TAHOE—A HISTORIC PERSPECTIVE

Caesars Tahoe has been in business for seventeen years. The property was built in 1978 and leased by Caesars World from the property owner in 1979. It was the last of the four major Lake Tahoe properties to be built. Different from most lease situations, Caesars World was responsible for financing the completion of construction on the building. The lease is for a period of twenty-five years, expiring in 2004, with two twenty-five-year renewal options.

Since opening, there have been ten chief operating officers and numerous changes in strategic focus. To illustrate, the first five years of operation were marked by major financial losses, and the property's business focus was exclusively on the volatile high-end customer. Any long-term focus was sacrificed for short-term gains. Local business was not cultivated and, as a result, the property had to work hard at generating local clientele.

What resulted was a general lack of direction and confusion among the staff.

LAKE TAHOE—A NATIONAL TREASURE

Lake Tahoe lies between two cities: Reno, with an area population of 250,000, is ninety minutes away by car; and Sacramento, with a population of 1.7 million, is a two-hour drive to the west. The lake is twenty-two miles long and twelve miles wide. The surface of the lake is 6,229 feet above sea level. Surrounding mountains form what is considered the Lake Tahoe basin, with the highest peak at about eleven thousand feet. Temperatures range from a low of 16° F in the winter to a high of about 80° in the summer.

Caesars Tahoe's location on the south shore of Lake Tahoe is at once an asset and a liability. As a popular tourist area, with a year-round population of thirty-five thousand and annual visitors numbering over 2 million, the natural beauty of the area is the major attraction. But that same scenic beauty is also highly regulated by environmental restrictions that had virtually stopped growth at the lake. Attractions could not be built due to these restrictions, leaving the lake's natural attraction the most significant source of tourism.

Summer and winter are the lake's biggest seasons in terms of visitor volumes, with summer busier on a week-to-week basis. However, the period from June through September typically accounts for 40 percent of the annual gaming revenue. During both seasons, weekends and holidays attract the lion's share of visitors to the area. In the "shoulder" months—those falling between the summer and winter seasons—visitor counts decrease significantly. These months continue to be a time of great challenge for local business.

THE COMPETITIVE ENVIRONMENT

Overview

Caesars Tahoe's competition on the south shore is, for the most part, limited to the three other major casino properties: Harrah's, Harvey's, and the Horizon. These properties, along with Cae-

sars, are located within a several-block area of one another, an area commonly referred to as the "casino core." There is also a stand-alone Harrah's satellite casino called Bill's located between Harrah's and Caesars, as well as a small hotel/casino, the Lakeside Inn, located just outside the casino core. The total rooms available within the casino core is 2,350.

The Embassy Suites, along with several other midsize properties, are the only other notable hotel properties on the south shore, and there are few national motel chains. Most of the motels are small, individually owned operations. Rooms available on the California side total seven thousand, many of which are old and in disrepair.

The competition outside the basin is fierce. With more rooms than customers and hotel occupancy rates declining, Reno attracts business with value packages and low room rates. On average, Reno room rates are in the $50 to $60 range, less than half of Caesars Tahoe's average room rate.

Las Vegas, just an hour by air from Reno, San Francisco, and Los Angeles, offers value and an "experience." Unsurpassed growth and the ability to offer thrills and attractions have made Las Vegas one of the top travel destinations in the United States. Las Vegas rooms number approximately one hundred thousand with ten thousand more rooms planned in the next several years. In 1995, 30 million people visited Las Vegas. While questions have arisen about the sustainability of such incredible growth, visitors keep coming and the city keeps booming.

In California, gaming concerns are represented by Native Americans, most notably Cache Creek, just outside of Sacramento. There are also plans for a casino outside of Placerville, which is located approximately ninety miles from Lake Tahoe.

The Competitors

Harrah's Tahoe is Caesars Tahoe's toughest competitor. Harrah's has been in business on the south shore for forty years. Its location as the most accessible casino property for California visitors has only added to its sustained success, and walk-in business comprises a large portion of its clientele. Reported operating income for 1995 was $37.5 million on revenues of $160 million (compared with an operating income of $11.4 million on $107.2 million in revenue for Caesars). Its continued growth in a flat market appears to be supported by an aggressive approach to controlling expenses.

The company is known for its consistency and is often considered "the McDonald's" of the industry. Harrah's customers have come to expect reasonably priced products and services in a clean and friendly environment. With multiple properties throughout the United States, Harrah's vast marketing network allows it to service the mid-market customer extremely well. Customers are loyal, and Harrah's markets its properties in a way that encourages repeat visits.

In Lake Tahoe, Harrah's has the only buffet with a view of the lake. There are 535 guest rooms and approximately ninety thousand square feet of casino space. For the past decade, the Harrah's Tahoe target market has been the dollar-plus slot player. Their ratio of table-game revenues to slot revenues is 0.6:1, compared to 1.4:1 for Caesars. While Harrah's Tahoe is no longer an official five-star property according to the Mobile travel guide, the customer perception of five-star still endures.

Harvey's, located directly across the street from Harrah's, is the largest of the casino core properties, with 744 guest rooms and 100,000 feet of casino space. Their ratio of table-game revenues to slot revenues is 0.4:1. It is connected via underground tunnel to Harrah's. Family-owned for fifty years, Harvey's went public in 1994, and had 1995 operating income of $22.6 million on revenues of $130.6 million. They have several other properties outside of Lake Tahoe, most notably a joint venture with the Hard Rock Cafe in Las Vegas.

Despite Harvey's mass-marketing approach, the company is not considered a strong marketer and is associated with a lack of identity. Recently, several members of top management at Harrah's moved over to Harvey's, which may strengthen its position in the future. To date, the company appears to have failed to take advantage of its size relative to its position in the market.

The *Horizon*, located across the street from Caesars Tahoe, is owned and operated by a hotel holding company and is associated with no other identifiable casino company. The property, which has 537 rooms and a forty-thousand-square-foot casino, is barely surviving financially. There was an operating loss of $2.5 million in 1995 on revenues of $36.5 million. The Horizon competes through somewhat desperate measures, such as unusual betting options and low price, and the company depends heavily on the walk-in business such options generate. At one time or another, all three major properties—Harrah's, Harvey's, and Caesars—have considered purchasing the Horizon, both individually and as a group. That remains a viable option but no one has moved forward to date because of perceived cost and the current lease agreement with the same property owner that leases Caesars Tahoe.

Political and Regulatory Environment

The south shore of Lake Tahoe is located in both Nevada and California, and presents a unique governmental structure, unlike any other in the nation. One city and two county governments oversee the area, governed by the Tahoe Regional Planning Agency (TRPA), a bi-state agency created by the U.S. Congress. The TRPA oversees all building, signage, land usage, transportation, and general development issues to ensure that environmental standards are maintained.

Casinos in the region may do nothing that expands current cubic volume, and noncasino hotel growth must be mitigated by the retirement of 1.3 existing rooms for every new room constructed. The focus of the TRPA does appear to be changing. The addition of Steve Wynn, chairman of the Mirage and part-time Lake Tahoe resident, to the TRPA board may be the beginning of an agency more focused on environmental priorities as opposed to micromanaging local business growth. But until the law that governs the TRPA changes, the high level of regulation will continue to prevail.

Two chambers of commerce support the south shore: the Tahoe-Douglas Chamber and the South Lake Tahoe Chamber. Few of the small businesses associated with the chambers have the dollars available for additional marketing. Local business is also supported by the Lake Tahoe Visitors Authority, a community marketing organization, and the South Tahoe Gaming Alliance

(STGA), a committee comprised of all the local gaming concerns. The STGA's function is to consolidate all gaming issues and maintain a unified front with various agencies.

The Infrastructure

Transportation to and from the Tahoe basin is extremely difficult. For example, the most common route into the south shore from northern California, U.S. Highway 50, is often reduced to a two-lane highway in the winter. During major snowstorms, which are not unusual, the road is closed completely. Highway 50 continues north toward Reno and is the main route for visitors from the Reno area. In the early 1980s, three-quarters of a million passengers passed through the South Lake Tahoe Airport annually. Today, that number is virtually zero because the airport no longer serves commercial carriers, due to legal battles over environmental restrictions, inability to compete on a low-cost basis, and general uncertainty in the market. The Reno Tahoe International Airport, located in Reno, is a ninety-minute drive.

The budget squeeze that has hit many local governments has affected Lake Tahoe as well. The poor condition of sidewalks, roads, and other city and county areas is testimony to the lack of funds available. There is a redevelopment plan in place for rejuvenating selected areas of the city. Financed primarily through private funding, the plan has three phases, two of which—the Ski Run and Park Avenue projects—are TRPA-approved. None of the three projects provide for additional hotel rooms. Significant upscaling of existing rooms, however, will be allowed.

- The Ski Run project, located approximately one and a half miles from Caesars and about a quarter-mile from the base of Heavenly Valley Ski Resort, is under way and scheduled for completion in 1997. It includes construction of a new hotel and general rejuvenation of the intersection.

- The Park Avenue project, scheduled to begin in 1997 and to be completed in 1999, covers a fourteen-acre area just three blocks from Caesars Tahoe. It includes a central transportation area, with a gondola to and from Heavenly Valley, an ice rink, a multiplex movie theater, shops, and seven hundred upscale hotel rooms. For the purposes of the Ski Run and Park Avenue projects, the TRPA has allowed for one-to-one room replacement instead of the current 1.3 rooms retired for every new room constructed. As yet, funding has not been secured for this project.

- A third project is still pending approval. It is to be located directly across the street from the Park Avenue project. The proposal for Project Three includes a convention center, additional retail space, an information building, a park with a "miniature" Lake Tahoe, and replacement of existing rooms with upscale rooms. There are mixed opinions on the probable success of Project Three. To date, no approvals have been awarded.

THE CAESARS TAHOE CUSTOMER

For the past decade, an increasing trend away from visits driven solely by gaming activities has developed. As gaming proliferates across the country, visitors to northern Nevada seek a more diversified experience. Much like guests aboard cruise ships, more and more visitors approach gaming as another amenity, along with food, entertainment, and retail opportunities. The Caesars Tahoe experience appears to be similar, with customer revenues generated by food and beverage, hotel, and entertainment sales, as well as the casino.

Customers at Caesars Tahoe, as in most casino operations, are ranked by earning potential, or EP, the mathematical probability expressed as the amount of money the casino will win based on the type of game, length of time, and amount of average bet played by a particular individual. For example, if John Doe plays blackjack and bets an average of $100 for one hour, the calculation of his EP would be as follows:

- $100 × 90 bets (the average number of blackjack hands per hour) = $9,000

- $9,000 × 1.5 percent (the theoretical win percentage ascribed to blackjack) = $135 per hour played

This means that the amount the casino should theoretically win (EP) per hour from John Doe would be $135. Each customer's EP is calculated based on his or her individual play and is an estimate derived from observed behavior. In most cases, the estimated total time played—in John Doe's case, total hours of play at all games—is used to determine trip earning potential.

The calculation of EP is important because it serves as a guideline for determining what level of free services or "complimentaries" a customer receives from the property. Complimentaries or "comps" are used as a marketing tool to support a guest's visit with free hotel rooms, food, beverage, transportation to and from the property, and, in some cases, discounts on losses. The complimentary amount provided is determined as a percentage of the customer's EP. As a general rule, comps represent 30 to 40 percent of earning potential at Caesars Tahoe.

While the margins on the high-roller business can be great, comps still represent a significant portion of the expense associated with obtaining and maintaining business from a particular customer. Because of the significant opportunities to realize a greater margin on certain customers, there is tremendous pressure within the industry to attract qualified players. The trends are toward continually raising the bar with extra benefits to the customer in an attempt to attract him or her to the property. Without the volumes to support the escalating expense, Caesars Tahoe will have a more difficult time competing in the high-roller marketplace in the future.

While the "comped" customer is a significant revenue source for Caesars Tahoe, the importance of walk-in business cannot be overlooked. Each year, over a million people walk through the doors of Caesars Tahoe. The trends show that they are younger, looking for entertainment, and tend to spend less time on gaming. When they are involved in gaming, they tend to prefer slot machines to table games. They are more price and value conscious, loyal only to the extent that a good deal is available.

Unlike Las Vegas, where visitors come from many diverse markets, visitors from northern California represent 68 percent of the south shore's total numbers. Additionally, convention and wholesale business continues to provide revenue opportunities. Convention business, like the rest of the Tahoe market, has been flat for years. Convention room nights in 1995 totaled 15,000, and wholesale room nights numbered 17,649. Caesars Tahoe just completed a $500,000 renovation on the convention area, including audiovisual and decorative upgrades. The largest convention business segment comes from the West Coast, followed by the East Coast and Midwest respectively. The sales staff is looking forward to developing a strong relationship with ITT Sheraton for the opportunities it may provide for Caesars Tahoe to tap into its national market resources.

Hotel business has been flat to declining overall, with total room nights in the hotel off by 7,000 between 1995 and 1996 year to date. Regular cash sale room nights totaled 61,397 in 1995, with comp sales at 37,354 room nights. The average day room rate (ADR) for Caesars Tahoe in 1995 was $113.08, compared to $104.07 for the south shore. There has been an effort to increase the ADR at Caesars Tahoe.

THE RESOURCE BASE

The Physical Plant

Caesars Tahoe has 440 rooms, forty thousand square feet of casino space, a fifteen-thousand-square-foot convention center, three gourmet restaurants, a twenty-four-hour coffee shop and room service, a health spa/pool area, and a shopping galleria with approximately ten leased retail outlets. In addition, there is a wedding chapel located on property operated by a leasee. Planet Hollywood, the popular restaurant chain, opened at Caesars Tahoe in 1994, turning a previously under-performing area (a cabaret bar) into a performing asset. Nero's 2000, Caesars Tahoe's own nightclub, provided additional operating income of $1 million in 1995. Plans for 1996 include the renovation of the twenty-four-hour coffee shop into a 250-seat buffet.

Caesars Tahoe itself operates the building as a leasee to the property owner. There is a fixed payment of approximately $4 million per year plus 20 percent of any pretax net profit (earnings before interest and taxes). The lease is up for renewal in the year 2004.

Human Resources

There are approximately eighteen hundred employees who work full-time for Caesars Tahoe. Turnover is high—around 60 percent annually—and is consistent with the other Lake Tahoe resort properties. High turnover is partly the result of seasonality and partly due to resort living, which couples low-wage, entry-level positions with a relatively high cost of living. The average starting wage at Caesars Tahoe is about $6.00 per hour. While turnover is high, there is still a core group of long-term employees. Close to 50 percent of the Caesars Tahoe employee base has been with the company for more than five years. While this stable employee base is beneficial in some ways, it tends to create pockets of low morale and motivation. In some departments, there is little management depth. Lake Tahoe, like many resort areas, has an extremely limited labor pool. The majority of Caesars employees live in California. The average residency is three years. Much of the hiring for the summer months is accomplished through college student recruiting outside of Lake Tahoe. Attracting and retaining good employees has always been and continues to be a challenge for all of the Lake Tahoe casino properties.

Reputation

Caesars Tahoe's brand image—the Roman theme—is both an asset and a liability. The Caesars brand is recognized worldwide. Although mostly associated with Caesars Palace in Las Vegas, the reputation of high-rollers, sports figures, and entertainers extends to all of its properties. The theme and reputation allow the company to differentiate itself in the Tahoe marketplace because no other area casino has the same distinctive brand image. The theme's image of grandeur, luxury, and wealth, however, has also proven intimidating for guests. For this reason, Caesars Tahoe has been inconsistent in its use of the brand during its seventeen years in Lake Tahoe.

THE CAESARS TAHOE EXECUTIVE COMMITTEE CHALLENGE

Refocusing his executive team on the key strategic issues was Attaway's foremost objective. Many questions needed answers. What services should Caesars Tahoe offer? Should the company change its scope and customer focus? Which market segments were working well and which still needed targeting: high-rollers or customers with smaller gaming budgets, or both? What about the company's current basis for competing? How should Caesars Tahoe differentiate itself, both locally and within other markets such as Reno and Las Vegas? What are additional revenue sources? How can the company gain from its relationship with its parent, Caesars World? With ITT Sheraton and ITT Corporation? How best to deliver the earnings goals to the parents? And, perhaps most troubling to Attaway, what were the strategic issues that he and his team had failed to identify? With information and questions in hand, Attaway prepared to face his executive committee.

Questions

1. Perform a strategic analysis of the Caesars Tahoe organization. What are the key issues (opportunities and constraints) facing this property?

2. Design a strategic change process that you would propose to Attaway.

Source: "The Executive Committee Challenge," by Barbara Falvey and David Attaway, 1997. The case was adapted and reproduced with permission of Barbara Falvey.

Black & Decker International: Globalization of the Architectural Hardware Line

If you don't know where you're going, any road will take you there. . . .

—Theodore Levitt

In March 1990, Fred Grunewald was reviewing the presentation he had prepared for top management of the Black & Decker Company. Mr. Grunewald was vice president of product and market development for the international group (Power Tools & Home Improvement Group); his job was to act as the catalyst for developing the company's businesses from local or regional entities into global players. A perfect opportunity for dramatic changes and profit growth was presented by Black & Decker's recent acquisition of the Emhart Corporation, which brought with it an architectural hardware (locks and locksets) business. Mr. Grunewald believed that capitalizing on the opportunity would require both restructuring the way the acquired companies went to market, as well as rethinking how the various parts of the businesses could be integrated on a global scale.

The bottom line of his opening transparency read, "We intend to create a global Black & Decker lock business." Substantial work lay ahead, however, to make this intention a reality—not only in coordinating the management of the acquired entities (with the risk of alienating and losing some key managers) but also in finishing marketing research, simplifying production design and engineering, rationalizing distribution channels, and overcoming regional differences. On top of these tasks, his proposal, which called for the addition of new personnel, would inevitably add to overhead costs at a time when the company's earnings were being squeezed by the costs of financing the Emhart acquisition.

This job would be one of the more challenging jobs Mr. Grunewald had faced in his 18 months with the company, but he had developed considerable global knowledge as he had worked with the operating divisions to build strategic plans and to set development priorities. He believed he would also be helped by the globalization momentum that had won the company much favorable publicity in recent times. Because the presentation of his recommendations was scheduled for next week, he set about thinking through the logic and implications of his report one more time.

BLACK & DECKER[1]

Four years ago, Black & Decker was a struggling industrial also-ran that was in serious trouble. We made a commitment to turn the company around, and we have met that commitment. Today, Black & Decker has been transformed into a global marketing power that has rewritten nearly every performance record in its history. . . . The company's resurgence has been driven by a four-part strategy that concentrated all of our resources and energies on a set of clear objectives: build core profitability; strengthen management; improve return on equity; and broaden the earnings base.

—1989 *Annual Report*

Founded in 1917, Black & Decker manufactured and sold a wide line of electric and battery-powered power tools (and accessories), household products, outdoor products, locks and hardware, plumbing products, and mechanical fastening systems. Net sales for fiscal year (FY) 1989 were $3.2 billion, up from $2.3 billion in FY 1988; net earnings were $30 million, down from $97 million. Part of the sales increase and earnings decrease were attributable to the acquisition of Emhart Corporation in 1989.

This case was made possible through the cooperation of the Black & Decker Company. Some of the data are disguised and should thus not be used for research purposes. Case material is intended as a basis for class discussion rather than to illustrate either effective or ineffective handling of an administrative situation. Copyright © 1990 by the Darden Graduate Business School Foundation, Charlottesville, VA.

---

[1]Material for this section comes from "The New Power in Black & Decker," *Fortune,* January 2, 1989, pp. 89–92, and from the company's 1989 *Annual Report.*

In 1985, Nolan Archibald became chief executive officer of a Black & Decker company that had disjointed international product lines and policies, dissatisfied customers, and a tarnished reputation. While the Black & Decker name still had a loyal following [in England, a do-it-yourself (DIY) hobbiest would be "Black & Deckering"; a French person who was socially "plugged in" would be "*très Black & Decker*"], the main product lines were losing to Asian global competition (especially Japan's Makita) and to strong local competitors in all parts of the world.

Two of Mr. Archibald's key actions had been to develop a worldwide view toward the markets for the company's products and to reduce drastically the number of models needed to fill those global markets. As part of this, the company reverse-engineered its competition's products and established just-in-time, continuous-flow production processes. Mr. Archibald hired new top managers, who began an active program of new-product development (sixty new or redesigned power tools; 40 percent of household products less than three years old).

As of early 1990, the organization was still in a period of fluid change, an outcome of the shift to looking at global rather than local manufacturing and design opportunities. The organization was a mixture of three forms—functional units, product categories (or strategic business units), and geographical units. Three main divisions, each under a group president, were Power Tools & Home Improvement, Household Products, and Commercial & Industrial Products (see Exhibit 1 for a partial organization chart). Within the Power Tools & Home Improvement Group was a mix of product and geographical divisions; the U.S. Power Tools, Europe, International, Hardware & Home Improvement, and Power Tool Accessories divisions each had a president.

Within the Power Tools Group, the Europe Division, in addition to having full marketing and manufacturing facilities for power tools, was also responsible for sales of the Households Products and for the products of the Hardware and Home Improvement Division and the Power Tool Accessories Division. Moreover, the International Division had responsibility for two plants manufacturing household products in Brazil and Mexico, along with sales responsibilities for all

company products in the world outside of Europe and the United States. Mr. Grunewald, under the president of International, had product- and market-development responsibility for all but the North American and European businesses. The Power Tool Accessories Division sold its products in the United States but also had responsibility for plants and engineering design centers in Europe. Finally, the full-functioned Household Products Group had the responsibility for U.S. sales of its own products, for a housewares plant in Singapore, and for sales of all Black & Decker products in Canada.

A new position of president under the Hardware and Home Improvement Division had just been established and filled from outside the company. This new president of the Hardware and Security Products Section, a full-functioned marketing/production/finance operation, would be charged with rationalizing the acquired lock companies into one integrated business.

FRED GRUNEWALD

Mr. Grunewald had been recruited to Black & Decker in late 1988 to the staff position of vice president, product and market development, as a key resource in the globalization initiative at Black & Decker. Along with ten years experience at General Electric in sales, product management, marketing, and strategic planning, Mr. Grunewald commented on his credentials:

> It seems as if I have the background for international marketing: I was born of German parents, raised in Latin America, nearly completed a Ph.D. in Chinese studies, and got my MBA at Michigan! It helps that my office is located in the same building as those of the group and divisional presidents. That fact, my knowledge about what's going on in the rest of the world (being on the road 25 percent of the year and constantly asking for information from the field), and an intellectual instinct to view things from a central perspective helps to build a knowledge base and perspective that helps my credibility with the operating managers.

Examples of his job included developing strategic plans, working with field managers to develop market research, and functioning as a critical resource in top-management meetings to set strategic product priorities. As he viewed

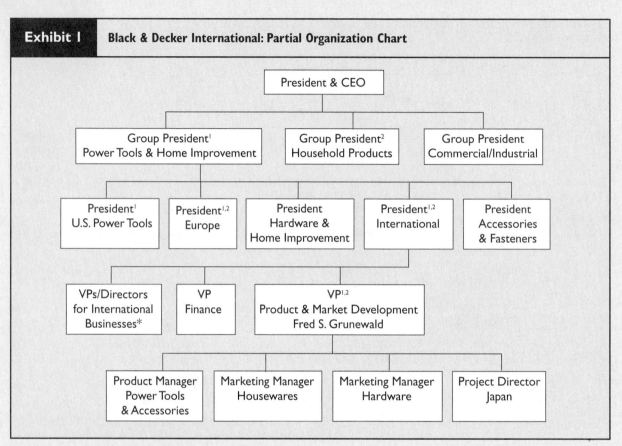

*"International" included Mexico, Latin America, the Middle East, Africa, and Australasia.
[1]Included in the quarterly strategic reviews for the power tools businesses.
[2]Included in the quarterly strategic reviews for the housewares businesses.
SOURCE: Company documents

Black & Decker's "strategy for the '90s," he believed that it was important to leverage the company's solid international base in power tools into housewares and other Black & Decker products that were not as well known. He believed building a global base for housewares—basically, a "metal-bending and plastics moldings business"—was especially important to move the company out of the "no-win" box of the middle market in which the low-cost operators won on cost and the high-end niche players won on gross margin. An interesting question to resolve at the international level, he thought, was how well the brand name might transfer from "basement [power tools] to kitchen [housewares]" in non-U.S. cultures. He believed that his part of the world, especially the Pacific rim, was crucial for Black & Decker's future growth: it currently comprised

the smallest share of the company's sales (16 percent), yet was growing the fastest (21 percent in 1989) with much larger potential for the future.

He had concluded that the company's businesses would continue to become more diversified—and the complexities increase—as the company pursued its global imperative. Japan remained a particularly elusive market, and one that exemplified the different demands that different cultures placed on quality and attention to detail, requiring one to adjust to a myriad of local regulations and customs. He illustrated this as follows:

> These two faxes I got from the Far East, just yesterday, are a timely example of what I mean. I had just received this two-page fax from [X country] complaining about the five things that went wrong with a recent product launch. When this message cleared, I got another from our agent in

Japan, who had counted our shipment of 3,098 items to find that we had sent only 3,096, and gave us a *credit* of ¥60 [30¢]—the fax cost more than that! You can see the need to be flexible from culture to culture and yet stay above the minutiae of local situations that can threaten to drown you.

Despite such differences, however, the company had succeeded in drastically paring the number of different product designs. For example, in the case of power tools, the number of motor designs was reduced from over one hundred in 1985 to a planned five in 1989; the change was implemented by creating four key design centers for all power tools (DIY tools in the U.K., woodworking tools in West Germany, and similar specialties in Italy and in the United States).

GLOBAL PRODUCT PLANNING AND REVIEW

Black & Decker operationalized its global approach to the identification and development of world products through a process of *strategic, managerial,* and *operational* activities. This approach had developed over the past few years as a way to set priorities for new-product projects and to review their status on a regular basis. In the past, managers tended to look at product-line planning—its depth and breadth—on a purely country-by-country basis, but now a given product line—dubbed by company managers "the product road"—was under a regular cycle of research, evaluation, goal setting, and review.

For the Power Tools and the Household Products groups, *strategic* product-road reviews were held quarterly, attended by key management and engineering/manufacturing personnel (see Exhibit 1). These day-long meetings were held at company headquarters in the United States. Based on extensive research of the market, competitors, etc., these meetings would set the capital-budgeting priorities for new product types, approve major new-product programs, and review and adjust the progress of previously approved programs. The data for these meetings were developed by product managers in the U.S. and Europe with input from the international group. Depending on how fast a market seemed to be evolving, a product (e.g., a commercial power drill, a cordless screwdriver) would be reviewed on a twelve-month, eighteen-month, or twenty-four-month cycle.

Similar quarterly *managerial* meetings were held at the four design centers in which key engineering and marketing personnel tracked the progress of major product programs. Invaluable by-products of these meetings were exchanges of information and ideas on emerging market trends and on problem solving ("If we could use the three-meter European cord standard in all markets, look what we would save . . .").

An additional *operational* activity, which Mr. Grunewald called "product-road bashing," took place continually among product managers at the same levels in the organization but in different groups in different parts of the world. Under constant encouragement from top management, the product manager for, say, angle-grinders in the Power Tools Division and his/her counterpart in the Europe Division would telephone, fax, and travel to each other's operations to answer the questions: "How can I reduce my five-item angle-grinder product line, and how can my counterpart reduce his/her eight items, yet still come up with five between us that will produce manufacturing efficiencies but cover even more markets?"

This stream of activity at the operational level was part of the input to the planning documents used at the quarterly managerial and strategy conferences. Once approved, the results of these meetings became the plans and budgets by which each of the divisions were measured. In addition, the data developed in these plans were also useful in the preparation of new-product launches. Therefore, as Mr. Grunewald pointed out, the headquarters staff were not seen as

> . . . information sinks, in which we ask for information—and lots of it—which is never seen again by the field. Our knowledge base, and our use of it, and, more importantly, the actions taken on it by top management are what gives us our credibility. In addition, we have established champions in each of our operating divisions who keep the globalization issues alive at all times. In some cases, these champions happen to be the top managers, which signals the importance of the activity and, of course, makes sure that globalization happens at the local level.

ARCHITECTURAL HARDWARE BUSINESS

The line of door-hardware products that came with the Emhart acquisition included locksets, high-security and electronic locks, door closers and exit devices, and master keying systems. (See Exhibit 2 for basic illustrations of these products.) The eight brands were Kwikset, Russwin, Corbin, Price Pfister, DOM, NEMEF, Lane, and ASTRA. According to Black & Decker executives, Kwikset (California) was the world's largest manufacturer of residential door hardware and the U.S. leader in the retail DIY market. Russwin/Corbin (Connecticut) was another well-known U.S. manufacture of premium-priced commercial and industrial locksets. The following table summarizes the main products of these eight companies:

Black & Decker Architectural Hardware Companies

U.S.-Based

Kwikset	Tubular[2] locks, residential
Russwin/Corbin	Cylindrical, mortise, commercial

Europe

DOM (Germany)	Cylindrical, industrial
NEMEF (Holland)	Commercial (all types)
Corbin (Italy)	Padlocks, commercial locks

Australia

Lane	Residential (Lane), Commercial (ASTRA)

Sales offices for various companies existed in West Germany, France, the U.K., Austria, Italy, Holland, Switzerland, Australia, Hong Kong, and Canada. Each company under Emhart's management had operated as an autonomous unit, with its own design, manufacturing, marketing, and support functions. Manufacturing plants were located in Connecticut, California, West Germany, Australia, the Netherlands, Italy, and Canada. As mentioned earlier, a new president had just been appointed to run the lock companies.

According to Mr. Grunewald, the challenge facing the integration of these various companies was not just internal; an equal task was how to conceptualize the global marketing of their products in the various regions of the world. In his view, the door-hardware-products industry was bound by old traditions and complicated by highly fragmented thinking about market opportunities. For example, the managers of these companies (and the industry in general) tended to view their markets and products along three major but narrowly constructed continuums: (1) technology (from very simple to electronic); (2) security (from minimal to extremely high); and (3) systems (from providing the internal cylinders only to providing the full trim hardware, electronic circuity, switches, etc.). Most companies seemed to position themselves at the extremes in one, or perhaps two, of these dimensions. The old companies also tended to specialize at either the high or low ends of the price continuum, allowing competitors to make inroads into the middle, gray areas. No one manufacturer made or offered products to the total market segments (residential, commercial, decorative, etc.).

With regard to international marketing, any one Emhart company tended to think only in terms of expanding its narrow line abroad, without considering the possibility of integrating and sourcing its global production by center of manufacturing expertise, design expertise, or "feeder/ eater" systems (manufacturing vs. assembly operations). The narrow approach to overseas business made the companies especially thin in Asia, Latin America, the Middle East, and Africa.

This historical "tunnel vision" was, Mr. Grunewald believed, typical for U.S. firms in domestic operations, but it was further exacerbated by the vast differences in distribution, branding preferences, and local-sourcing laws in the various international markets. Some Emhart companies had built a good reputation for service, while others were regarded as "just ok" or "difficult." The companies had developed some strong distributor relationships, however, albeit with low sales volumes and slow growth. The goal of pulling the former Emhart entities into an integrated operation, therefore, would be impeded by the legacies of brand proliferation, marketing inefficiencies, poor market knowledge, and inconsistent merchandising terms and policies.

---

[2]"Tubular" and "cylindrical" refer to internal designs related to the lock's security from break-in (cylindrical locks were more secure).

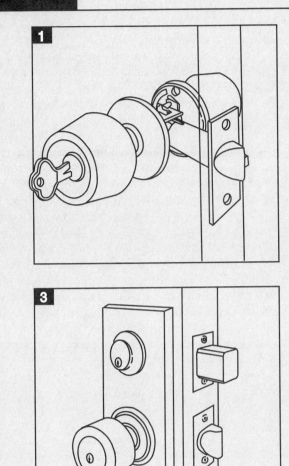

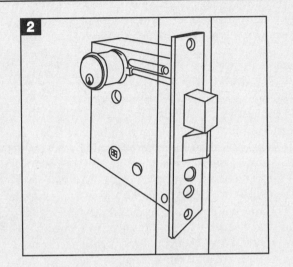

Primary Locks There are three main types. **1** Key-in-knob lock: It's standard in new construction, but always vulnerable because the knob can be ripped off. **2** Mortise lock: Often found in older houses, it looks strong, but it actually weakens the door. Also, the cylinder in this type may be easy to pick. **3** Interconnected lockset: The top lock is a dead bolt, but if the knob below is attacked, both locks may be vulnerable.

SOURCE: *Consumer Reports*, pp. 98–99.

What was attractive to Black & Decker, on the other hand, was the power that one integrated company could bring to an estimated $15 billion world market ($5 billion in locksets alone), an opportunity for power that would more than offset some of the infrastructural differences. Research indicated that about 60 percent of the products were sold through builders and original equipment manufacturers, and 20 percent each through wholesale and retail channels. These fig-ures indicated that a great majority of sales were going into new-construction or building-renovation projects. Unfortunately, Mr. Grunewald believed that the Emhart companies had not built a strong distribution system with regard to the international bid/contract business. The breadth of the various Emhart lock lines would allow a global approach, however, and Black & Decker's current power-tool presence and distribution abroad promised opportunities for synergies.

RECOMMENDATIONS FOR THE GLOBAL LOCK BUSINESS

Essentially, Mr. Grunewald was going to recommend that the International Group establish and take over what he called "on-the-ground" representation in foreign markets while, at the same time, identifying "local champions" in each of the lock factories. "On the ground" referred to setting up marketing managers in Belgium, Brazil, Dubai, Japan, Mexico, New Zealand, and Miami (headquarters of the Latin American Operations). Reporting to these managers would be a product manager for residential hardware and plumbing, a product manager for architectural hardware, and a technical manager for applications and support. The marketing manager, assisted by the product managers, would be responsible for coordinating marketing and sales activities, including the product road, channel determination, servicing, marketing research, business plans, coordination of assembly and repackaging activities, training sessions with local distributors, and other activities.

Mr. Grunewald also saw the need to establish within each lock company a local champion who became for that company the focal point for all activities relating to the business—*as now perceived to be conducted on a global basis.* Among other activities, this person would be the liaison between the company and on-the-ground managers, would serve as project manager for new products (or product modifications required by foreign markets), would represent the international business in establishing product specifications and new-product priorities, and would in general assist the local company in building global opportunities for its business. It would be important that these individuals have senior-level clout and authority, preferably reporting to the top manager in the company.

Mr. Grunewald's recommendation was also to establish at Black & Decker headquarters in Towson, Maryland, a group product manager for hardware products within the International Division. This person would be the central liaison between the global sales and marketing organization and the various hardware businesses. Due to the importance of the Japanese market, the Japanese sales personnel would report directly to this group product manager. All other on-the-ground marketing and sales personnel, however, would report to the general managers of the local businesses. Under the group product manager would be product managers for retail locks, construction/architectural, and bid/contract, as well as the sales manager for hardware in Japan.

In Mr. Grunewald's mind, the establishment of these new jobs would be meaningless unless there were active "avenues of communication" between headquarters, on-the-ground, and local-champion personnel. He drew a chart to explain what he thought were good avenues of communication, and it was his role to see that the avenues were traveled (see Exhibit 3).

What was also yet to be established was an "intercompany organization" (see bottom of Exhibit 3) to facilitate, across all international organizations, such matters as centralized forecasting, order placement, billing, forwarding, expediting, and processing of export documentation. Additionally, a great many details had to be sorted through to ensure the smooth operation and growth of the hardware business. These details included staffing, training, transfer-pricing, and forecasting. Also required was the development of marketing-support documents, such as catalogs, price lists, technical literature, and advertising and sales-support literature.

The advantages of consolidation seemed clear: it would improve market knowledge along the dimensions of competition, consumer segments, product requirements, etc., and it would give Black & Decker the power to winnow out a complacent distribution base, to instill global quality standards throughout the world, to promote product innovation, and in general to bring a unified force and credibility to the now-fragmented effort.

Yet to be resolved, according to Mr. Grunewald's report, were a number of issues that were generally outside of his direct control. How would the new president of the lock business structure the lock companies? Would that business choose to adopt the quarterly planning reviews that characterized the power tools and housewares business? How would the "bashing" of the product roads take place?

What particularly troubled him was the suspicion that Black & Decker was not alone in sensing the global opportunities that existed, and he was hopeful that whatever was decided would not take more than a year to implement.

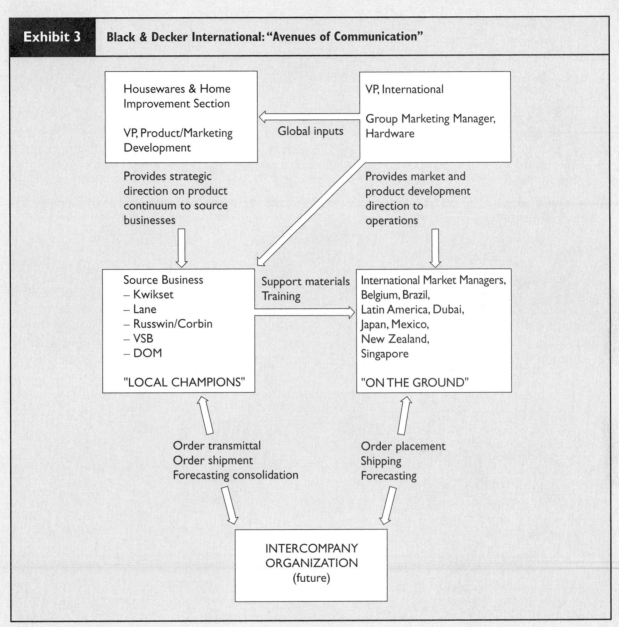

SOURCE: Company documents

Questions

1. What do you think of Grunewald's plan for creating a "global lock business"? What factors favor this action? What factors stand in the way?

2. What are the organizational implications of this strategy? What kind of structure, culture, and systems are necessary to make it work? What would be your action plan for implementation?

3. Assume you were Grunewald's OD consultant. What coaching advice would you have for him in executing this strategic change?

Glossary

This glossary was prepared to help the reader to understand some of the more frequently used terms in OD. Not all the terms in the glossary appear in the text, but they are frequently used in the field. Conversely, the glossary does not attempt to define every term used in the text. Nevertheless, knowledge of the terms in the glossary can be useful in understanding what at times appears to be an overly specialized language.

Accountability Responsibility to produce a promised result within a specific time.

Achievement needs A phrase applied to an individual, referring to the desire to perform work successfully and to advance in one's career.

Achievement orientation In cross-cultural analysis, the extent to which a culture favors the acquisition of power and resources.

Acquisition The purchase of one organization by another. (See *Merger*.)

Action learning A form of action research in which the focus is helping organizations to learn from their actions how to create entirely new structures, processes, and behaviors. Also called *action science, self-design,* or *appreciative inquiry,* this process involves considerable trial-and-error learning as participants try out new ways of operating, assess progress, and make necessary adjustments. (See *Action research.*)

Action research A cyclical process of diagnosis-change-research-diagnosis-change-research. The results of diagnosis produce ideas for changes, the changes are introduced into the same system, and their effects noted through further research and diagnosis. The number of cycles may be infinite.

Active listening Reflecting back to the other person not only what the person has said but also the perceived emotional tone of the message.

Adaptive A term used to describe the behavior of many kinds of systems. Originally used mainly to describe individuals (for example, adaptive behavior), it is now applied to groups and organizations vis-à-vis their environment.

Alliance A partnership between two organizations where their resources and capabilities are combined to pursue mutual goals in developing, manufacturing, or distributing goods and services.

Appreciative inquiry A contemporary approach to planned change. Contrary to typical approaches that assume organizations are like problems to be solved, appreciative inquiry works under the assumption that organizations are like mysteries to be understood. A focus on the "best of what is" in an organization provides the necessary vision for change.

Authenticity A term synonymous with the colloquial phrase "to be straight with another person." It refers to one's openness and honesty.

Balanced scorecard A control and information system that balances traditional financial measures with operational measures relating to an organization's critical success factors.

Behavioral science A phrase for the various disciplines that study human behavior. As such, all of the traditional social sciences are included.

Benchmarking A process where companies find out how other companies do something better than they do and then try to imitate or improve on the activity.

Body language An important part of nonverbal communications that involves the transmittal of thoughts, actions, and feelings through bodily movements and how other people interpret them.

Boundary A term used to describe systems or fields of interacting forces. Boundaries can be physical, such as a wall between two departments in an organization. More subtly, boundaries can be social processes, such as the boundaries between ethnic groups. Boundaries can be temporal: Things done at different times are said to be *bounded* from each other. Any set of forces or factors that tend to differentiate parts of the system can be said to have a boundary effect.

Breakthrough A sudden and significant advance, especially in knowledge, technique, or results.

Career The sequence of behaviors and attitudes associated with past, present, and anticipated future work-related experiences and role activities. A career is work related and lifelong.

Career development Activities directed at helping people to attain career objectives. These may include skill training, performance feedback and coaching, job rotation, mentoring roles, and challenging and visible job assignments.

Career planning Activities aimed at helping people to choose occupations, organizations, and jobs. It involves setting individual career goals.

Change management The tools, techniques, and processes that scope, resource, and direct activities to implement a change. Change management is less concerned about the transfer of knowledge, skill, and capacity to manage change in the future than organization development.

Client system The person, group, or organization that is the object of diagnosis or change efforts. Often shortened to the client. The client may be in the same organization as the consultant, as in the case of a line manager who is the client of a staff group, or the client and consultant may be in different organizations.

Closed system The tendency to disregard relations between a system and its environment. This is often an unwitting simplification and, as such, can lead to error.

Closure, need for A commonly felt need to see something finished or brought to a logical end point. Sometimes it is used to describe a person who is uncomfortable with ambiguity and uncertainty.

Coaching An intervention designed to improve the competencies of individual organization members through committed support, feedback, new views of work, new visions of the organization, and new ways of relating to people.

Collateral organization A parallel, coexisting structure that can be used to supplement the existing formal organization. It is generally used to solve ill-defined problems that do not fit neatly into the formal organizational structure.

Communication, one-way and two-way One-way communication describes an interaction in which one or both parties are paying little attention to what the other is saying or doing. In two-way communication, presumably both parties are engaging and responding to each other.

Competency The skills and knowledge necessary to carry out some specific activity or task.

Conflict management Management's task is to manage conflict by reducing or stimulating it, depending upon the situation, in order to develop the highest level of organizational performance.

Conformance The outputs produced as a part of work and passed on or delivered to the customer that will meet all the requirements to which the producer and the customer have agreed.

Confront The process by which one person attempts to make another person aware of aspects of behavior of which he or she seems unaware. It is used increasingly in the phrase *a confronting style* to describe a person who habitually gives such feedback to others.

Confrontation meeting A structured intervention that helps two (or more) groups resolve interdepartmental misunderstandings or conflict.

Consultant An individual (change agent) who is assisting an organization (client system) to become more effective. An external consultant is not a member of the system. An internal consultant is a member of the organization being assisted but may or may not have a job title that identifies the individual as such.

Content analysis A data analysis technique that derives themes from qualitative data such as interview responses.

Contingency approach This approach suggests that there is no universal best way to design an organization, that the design instead depends upon the situation.

Continuous improvement A philosophy of designing and managing all aspects of an organization in a never-ending quest for quality. The notion is that no matter how well things are going, there are always opportunities to make them better, and hundreds of small improvements can make a big difference in overall functioning. Also known as kaizen.

Contract A formal or informal agreement between the change agent and the client system to perform certain work. The contract typically identifies roles, expectations, resources, and other information required to successfully carry out the consultation process.

Core job dimensions These are the five basic dimensions of work, including skill variety, task identity, task significance, autonomy, and feedback.

Corporate culture This is the pattern of values, beliefs, and expectations shared by organization members. It represents the taken-for-granted and shared assumptions that people make about how work is to be done and evaluated and how employees relate to one another and to significant others, such as suppliers, customers, and government agencies.

Cost of quality The financial impact of poor quality. The cost of quality consists of the cost of conformance, nonconformance, and lost opportunity. The cost of conformance includes expenses associated with prevention measures, inspection, and appraisal. The cost of nonconformance is the dollar impact of not meeting customer expectations. The cost of lost opportunity is the revenue forgone when a customer leaves or does not renew a relationship with the organization.

Customer The person who receives the product of work. A customer may be either internal or external.

Data-based intervention A specific technique in action research. It follows some data collection phase and is an input into the system using the data that have been collected. Alternatively, it can be the act of presenting the data to members of the system, thus initiating a process of system self-analysis.

Defensive A term widely used to describe any kind of resistant behavior.

Development organizations See *Global social change organizations.*

Diagnosis The process of collecting information about a client system and working collaboratively with it to understand the system's current functioning. Diagnosis follows entry and contracting, and precedes action planning and implementation. Diagnosis is expected to point to possible interventions to address system effectiveness.

Differentiation The extent to which individual organizational units are different from each other along a variety of dimensions, such as time, technology, or formality. High uncertainty leads to the need for more differentiation, and low uncertainty leads to the need for less.

Dissonance A term reflecting the behavioral consequences of knowing two or more incompatible things at one time. Dissonance may be used to describe incompatibility in a person's point of view.

Diversity The mix of gender, age, disabilities, cultures, ethnic backgrounds, and lifestyles that characterize the organization's workforce and potential labor pool.

Dominant coalition That minimum group of co-operating employees who control the basic policy-making and oversee the operation of the organization as a whole.

Double-loop learning Organizational behaviors directed at changing existing valued states or goals. This is concerned with radically transforming an organization's structure, culture, and operating procedures. (See *Single-loop learning* and *Organization transformation.*)

Downsizing Interventions aimed at reducing the size of the organization. Although typically associated with layoffs and reductions in force, downsizing also includes attrition, early retirement, selling businesses or divisions, outsourcing, and delayering.

Dyad Two people and their dynamic interrelations; more informally, two people. Its usage has been extended recently to triad, or three people.

Dysfunctional Those aspects of systems that work against the goals. The term is meant to be objective but is often used subjectively to refer to the bad parts of systems. (See *Functional.*)

Empathic From *empathy;* to be able to project oneself into another's feelings and hence to understand the other person. It is used relatively interchangeably with *sensitive* and *understanding.*

Employee involvement Any set of technostructural interventions, such as quality circles, high-involvement organizations, or total quality management, that adjust the power, information flows, rewards, and knowledge and skills in an organization. Also known as quality of work life.

Encounter An entire collection of interventions or techniques that aim to bring people into close and more intimate relations.

Enterprise resource planning (ERP) An information system that collects, processes, and provides data and information about a company, including order processing, product design, purchasing, inventory, manufacturing distribution, human resources, procurement, and forecasting.

Entry The process that describes how an OD practitioner first encounters and establishes a relationship with a client system.

Environment The physical and social context within which any client system (a person, group, or organization) is functioning.

Ethics Standards of acceptable behavior for professional practicing in a particular field, such as law, medicine, or OD. In OD, it concerns how practitioners perform their helping relationship with organization members.

Evaluation feedback Information about the overall effects of a change program. It is generally used for making decisions about whether resources should continue to be allocated to the program.

Expectancy The belief, expressed as a subjective estimate or odds, that a particular act will be successful.

Expectancy model A model of motivation suggesting that people are motivated to choose among different behaviors or intensities of effort if they believe that their efforts will be rewarded in a meaningful fashion.

Experiential A kind of learning process in which the content is experienced as directly as possible, in contrast to being simply read or talked about. The term applies to a wide variety of training techniques. It is often used in the phrase experiential level, in contrast to cognitive level.

Expert power The power and influence that a person has in a situation by virtue of technical or professional expertise. (See *Power.*)

External validity A research term concerned with assessing the general applicability of interventions. This helps to identify contingencies upon which the success of change programs depend. (See *Internal validity.*)

Facilitate A process by which events are "helped to happen." Facilitating is a kind of influence role that is neither authoritarian nor abdicative.

Feedback Information regarding the actual performance or the results of the activities of a system. In communications, it concerns looking for and using helpful responses from others.

Filtering A barrier to communication that occurs when the sender intentionally shifts or modifies the message so that it will be seen more favorably by the receiver.

Fishbowl An experiential training technique in which some members of a group sit in a small inner circle and work the issue while other members sit in an outer circle and observe.

Force-field analysis A qualitative tool that analyzes the forces for and the forces resisting change. It implies two change strategies, increasing the forces for change or decreasing the resistance to change.

Formal (leader, organization, system) A term introduced originally in the Hawthorne studies to designate the set of organizational relationships that were explicitly established in policy and procedure (for example, *the formal organization*). The term has been prefixed to many types of organizational phenomena.

Functional The term describes those parts of a system that promote the attainment of its goals. It comes from a mode of systems analysis that seeks to explain systems by understanding the effects that parts of the system have on one another and the mutual effects between the system and its environment.

Gain sharing This involves paying employees a bonus based upon improvements in the operating results of an organization or department. It generally covers all employees working in a particular department, plant, or company and includes both a bonus scheme and a participative structure for eliciting employees' suggestions and improvements.

Gatekeeping A term from group dynamics that describes a person in a group who regulates interaction patterns by asking people for their ideas or suggesting to others that they should talk less.

Global social change organizations Not-for-profit and nongovernmental organizations whose primary purpose is to bring about change, such as ecological awareness, hunger relief, children's rights, or political stability in a community or society.

Global strategy A worldwide strategy characterized by goals of efficiency and volume; this strategy views the world as one homogenous market.

Goal setting Activities involving managers and subordinates in jointly setting subordinates' goals, monitoring them, and providing counseling and support when necessary.

Group dynamics A set of variables, including power and influence, norms, conflict, communication, decision making, or trust, that individually and collectively describe the functioning of a group

Group maintenance Those behaviors exhibited by members of a group that are functional for holding the group together, increasing members' liking for each other, and differentiating the group from its environment.

Group task activities Activities that are directed at helping the group accomplish its goals. Successful groups are more able to properly combine group maintenance and group task activities than are less successful groups.

Groupthink A form of decision making that occurs when the members' striving for unanimity and closeness overcomes their motivation to realistically appraise alternative courses of action.

Growth A term reflecting theorists' and practitioners' concern for improvement in personal, group, and organizational behavior. Identification of growth stages, rates, and directions is a major focus of contemporary theory and research.

Growth needs The desire for personal accomplishment, learning, and development. An important contingency affecting work design successes; for example, the greater people's growth needs, the more responsive they are to enriched forms of work.

Hawthorne effect When workers' behavior changes and productivity increases because the workers are aware that persons important in their lives are taking an interest in them.

Hidden agenda An undisclosed motive for doing or failing to do something. For example, a plant manager began to use team-building sessions, not because he wanted them but because he knew that his boss was in favor of such sessions.

Human resource systems These comprise mechanisms and procedures for selecting, training, and developing employees. They may include reward systems, goal setting, career planning and development, and stress management.

Ideal future state An articulated vision of the ideal state of the organization; the desired culture, infrastructure, and operation. What does it look like, sound like, feel like? What are people doing, with whom, and how? An ideal future state serves as the direction for present-day change efforts; it serves to bring the future into the present.

Implementation feedback Refers to information about whether an intervention is being implemented as intended. It is generally used to gain a clearer understanding of the behaviors and procedures required to implement a change program and to plan for the next implementation steps. (See *Evaluation feedback*.)

Individualism In cross-cultural analysis, the extent to which a country's culture supports individual growth, development, and achievement.

Industry structure The overall attractiveness of an industry as determined by the power of buyers, power of suppliers, threat of entry, threat of substitute products/services, and rivalry among firms.

Informal (leader, group, organization, system) A term introduced in the Hawthorne studies to designate the set of organizational relationships that emerge over time from the day-to-day experiences that people have with one another. Informal relationships are expressive of the needs that people actually feel in situations, in contrast to needs their leaders think they should feel.

Inputs Human or other resources, such as information, energy, and materials, coming into the system or subsystem. Also, more informally, used to describe people's contributions to a system, particularly their ideas.

Institutionalization Refers to making organizational changes a permanent part of the organization's normal functioning.

Integrated strategic change A model of large-scale organization change that integrates principles of strategic management with processes of planned change. It involves strategic analysis, strategic choice, strategic change plan design, and strategic change plan implementation.

Integration The state of collaboration that exists among departments that are required to achieve unity of effort by the demands of the environment. The term is used primarily for contingency approaches to organizational design. (See *Differentiation*.)

Interaction Almost any behavior resulting from interpersonal relationships. In human relations, it includes all forms of communication, verbal and nonverbal, conscious and unconscious.

Internal validity A research term concerned with assessing whether an intervention is responsible for producing observed results, such as improvements in job satisfaction, productivity, and absenteeism. (See *External validity*.)

Intervention Any action on the part of a change agent. Intervention carries the implication that the action is planned and deliberate and presumably functional. Many suggest that an OD intervention requires valid information, free choice, and a high degree of ownership by the client system of the course of action.

Jargon Overly specialized or technical language.

Job diagnostic survey (JDS) A questionnaire designed to measure job characteristics on such core dimensions as skill variety, task identity, task significance, autonomy, and feedback.

Job enrichment A way of making jobs more satisfying by increasing the skill variety, task identity, significance of the task, autonomy, and feedback from the work itself.

Joint optimization The goal of the sociotechnical system theory approach to work design that states that an organization will function best only if its social and technical systems are designed to fit the needs of one another and the environment.

Joint venture A separate entity for sharing development and production costs and penetrating new markets that is created by two or more firms.

Knowledge management (KM) A process that focuses on how knowledge can be organized and used to improve organization performance. KM tends to focus on the tools and techniques that enable organizations to collect, organize, and translate information into useful knowledge. Organizationally, KM applications are often located in the information systems function and may be under the direction of a chief technology officer. (See *Organization learning*.)

Lab A shorthand term for a wide variety of programs that derive from the laboratory method of training, or T-group, an approach that is primarily experiential.

Large-group interventions Any of several techniques, such as search conferences and open space, designed to work with a whole system, including organization members, suppliers, customers, and other stakeholders.

Leadership A process of influence exercised when institutional, political, psychological, and other resources are used to arouse, engage, and satisfy the motives of followers.

Leadership development A training and education intervention aimed at improving the competencies of managers and executives of an organization.

Learning organization An organization where everyone is involved in identifying and solving problems, enabling the organization to continuously experiment, improve, and increase its capability.

Management by objectives (MBO) A process of periodic manager–subordinate or group meetings designed to accomplish organizational goals by mutual planning of the work, review of accomplishments, and mutual solving of problems that arise in the course of getting the job done.

Management development Training or other processes to increase managers' knowledge and skills in order to improve performance in present jobs or prepare them for promotion. Increasingly tied to career planning and development.

Marginality The degree to which an individual or role must straddle the boundary between two or more groups with differing goals, values systems, and behavioral patterns.

Matrix organization An approach for integrating the activities of different specialists while maintaining specialized organizational units.

Mechanistic organization This type of organization is highly bureaucratic. Tasks are specialized and clearly defined. This is suitable when markets and technology are well established and show little change over time.

Merger The formal and legal integration of two or more organizations into a single entity. (See *Acquisition.*)

Microcosm group A small, representative group selected from the organization at large to address important organizational issues. The key feature of the group is that it is a microcosm or representation of the issue itself.

Mission A statement of the organization's purpose, range of activities, character, and uniqueness.

Model A simplification of some phenomenon for purposes of study and understanding. The concrete embodiment of a theory. To behave in an idealized way so that others might learn or change their behavior by identifying with and adopting those behaviors displayed.

Motivation The conditions responsible for variation in the intensity, quality, and direction of ongoing behavior.

Motivation-hygiene model Originally developed by Frederick Herzberg and associates, the model describes factors in the workplace that dissatisfy people and factors that motivate them.

Multinational strategy A worldwide strategy with goals of local responsiveness and specialization; views the worldwide market as heterogeneous and requiring product and service customization.

Need A central concept in psychology, referring to a biological or psychological requirement for the maintenance and growth of the human animal. It is used among practitioners chiefly to refer to a psychological demand not met in organizational life, with the emphasis on the search for ways in which more such wants can be satisfied.

Need hierarchy A particular theory about the operation of human needs introduced by Abraham Maslow. The model of motivation describes a hierarchy of needs existing within people. The five need levels are physiological, safety, social, ego, and self-actualization. The theory says that higher needs cannot be activated until lower needs are relatively satisfied. This particular theory also was the basis for McGregor's Theory X Theory Y formulation.

Network organization A newly emerging organization structure that involves managing an interrelated set of organizations, each specializing in a particular business function or task. This structure extends beyond the boundaries of any single organization and involves linking different organizations to facilitate interorganizational exchange and task coordination. (See *Transorganizational development.*)

Norms Rules regulating behavior in any social system. They are usually unwritten and are more specific and pointed than values in that deviations from norms are followed by such punishments as kidding, silent disapproval, or in the extreme, banishment.

Off-site Away from the regular place of work, as an off-site lab or conference.

Openness Accepting the communications and confrontations of others and expressing oneself honestly, with authenticity.

Open space meeting See *Large-group interventions.*

Open system The need to take into account relations between a system and its environment. This concept in systems theory is borrowed from the biological sciences. It refers to the nature and functions of transactions that take place between a system and its environment.

Open-systems planning A method for helping organizations or groups to systematically assess their task environment and develop a strategic response to it.

Organic organization This type of organization is relatively flexible and relaxed. The organic style is most appropriate to unstable environmental conditions in which novel problems continually occur. (See *Mechanistic organization.*)

Organization design Involves bringing about a coherence or fit among organizational choices about strategy, organizing mode, and mechanisms for integrating people into the organization. The greater the fit among these organizational dimensions, the greater will be the organizational effectiveness.

Organization development (OD) The systemwide application and transfer of behavioral science knowledge to the planned development, improvement, and reinforcement of the strategies, structures, and processes that lead to organization effectiveness.

Organization development practitioner A generic term for people practicing organization development. These individuals may include managers responsible for developing their organizations or departments, people specializing in OD as a profession, and people specializing in a field currently being integrated with OD (for example, strategy or human resource management) who have gained some familiarity with and competence in OD.

Organization effectiveness An overall term that refers to the outputs of organization strategy and design. Typically includes financial performance, such as profits and costs; stakeholder satisfaction, such as employee and customer satisfaction; and measures of internal productivity, such as cycle times.

Organization learning (OL) A change process that seeks to enhance an organization's capability to acquire and develop new knowledge. It is aimed at helping organizations use knowledge and information to change and improve continually. It involves discovery, invention, production, and generalization. In organizations, OL change processes are typically associated with the human resource function and may be assigned to a special leadership role, such as chief learning officer. (See *Knowledge management*.)

Organization transformation A process of radically altering the organization's strategic direction, including fundamental changes in structures, processes, and behaviors. (See *Double-loop learning*.)

Parallel learning structure See *Collateral organization*.

Participative A term used to describe techniques used by a power figure that aim to involve subordinate, lower-power persons in the decision-making process of an organization (for example, participative management). One aim is to increase the sense of commitment to organizational goals.

Performance appraisal A human resource system designed to provide feedback to an individual or group about its performance and its developmental opportunities. The performance appraisal process may or may not be closely linked to the reward system.

Performance management A constellation of processes that involve goal setting, performance appraisal, and reward systems that guide, develop, reinforce, and control member behavior toward desired organizational outcomes.

Planned change A generic phrase for all systematic efforts to improve the functioning of some human system. It is a change process in which power is usually roughly equal between consultants and clients and in which goals are mutually and deliberately set.

Power The ability to influence others so that one's values are satisfied. It may derive from several sources, including organizational position, expertise, access to important resources, and ability to reward and punish others.

Power distance In cross-cultural analysis, the extent to which people in a country accept large differences in status, income, authority, and equality.

Presenting problem The most salient reason the client system has asked for help from a change agent. For example, a conflict between two people can be a presenting problem or symptom that is caused by structural problems. The presenting problem is often a symptom of the true underlying problem that diagnosis is expected to uncover.

Problem-solving process A systematic, disciplined approach to identifying and solving work-related problems.

Process The way any system is going about doing whatever it is doing. Social process is the way persons are relating to one another as they perform some activity. Organizational process is the way different elements of the organization interact or how different organizational functions are handled.

Process-based organizations A type of organization structure that uses teams focused on the accomplishment of core work processes.

Process consultation A set of activities on the part of the consultant that helps the client to perceive, understand, and act upon the process events that occur in the client's environment.

Process observation A method of helping a group to improve its functioning, usually by having an individual watch the group in action and then feeding back the results. Interviews may also be used. The group (or individuals) then use the data to improve its functioning.

Production group A work group that is separated (by a boundary) from other work groups so that they can operate with relative independence.

Profit An accounting term that measures total revenues minus total costs.

Quality (outcome) Meeting and exceeding customer needs for both internal and external customers.

Quality (process) The continuing commitment by everyone in the organization to understand, meet, and exceed the needs of its customers.

Quality circles Small groups of workers who meet voluntarily to identify and solve productivity problems. These are typically associated with Japanese methods of participative management.

Quality of work life (QWL) A way of thinking about people, work, and organization involving a concern for employee well-being and organizational effectiveness. It generally results in employee participation in important work-related problems and decisions.

Quasi-experimental research designs These designs enable OD evaluators to rule out many rival explanations for OD results other than the intervention itself. They involve choices about what to measure and when to measure; they are most powerful when they include longitudinal measurement, a comparison unit, and statistical analysis.

Re-engineering An intervention that focuses on dramatically redesigning core business processes. Successful re-engineering is often closely related to changes in an organization's information systems.

Refreezing The stabilization of change at a new state of equilibrium.

Return on assets (ROA) An accounting measure formed by the ratio of profits to total assets.

Reward power The present or potential ability to award something for worthy behavior. (See *Power.*)

Rewards, extrinsic Rewards given by the organization, such as pay, promotion, praise, tenure, and status symbols.

Rewards, intrinsic Rewards that must originate and be felt within the person. Intrinsic rewards include feelings of accomplishment, achievement, and self-esteem.

Role A set of systematically interrelated and observable behaviors that belong to an identifiable job or position. Role behavior may be either required or discretionary.

Role ambiguity A result of inadequate information regarding role-related expectation and understanding. This occurs when the individual does not clearly understand all the expectations of a particular role.

Role conflict A result of a conflict between managerial or individual expectations and managerial or individual experiences with regard to performance of the role.

Search conference A 1- to 3-day meeting involving as many organizational stakeholders as possible to reflect on the past, appreciate the present, and envision the future. The search conference specifically avoids a problem-solving approach in an effort to energize the organization toward a new way of working. (See also *Large-group interventions.*)

Selective perception The tendency to perceive only a part of a message, to screen out other information.

Self-awareness A positive goal of most training techniques that aim at behavior changes. Self-awareness means becoming aware of one's existing patterns of behavior in a way that permits a relatively nondefensive comparison of those patterns with potential new ones.

Self-designing organizations A change program aimed at helping organizations to gain the capacity to fundamentally change themselves. It is a highly participative process, involving multiple stakeholders in setting strategic direction, designing appropriate structures and processes, and implementing them. This process helps organizations to learn how to design and implement their own strategic changes.

Self-regulating work group A work group that has a clearly defined series of tasks and a clear boundary so that the group can be generally responsible for its own output, quality, and work space. Also known as a *self-managing team.*

Self-serving activities Activities that satisfy individual needs at the expense of the group.

Sensitivity training A method of helping individuals to develop greater self-awareness and become more sensitive to their effect on others. Individuals learn by interaction with other members of their group.

Single-loop learning Organizational behaviors directed at detecting and correcting deviations from valued states or goals. This is concerned with fine-tuning how an organization currently functions. (See *Double-loop learning.*)

Six sigma A quality standard that specifies a goal of no more than 3.4 defects per million occurrences of an activity or process. Also refers to a management initiative emphasizing the pursuit of higher quality and lower costs.

Skill training Training that is more concerned with improving effectiveness on the job than with abstract learning concepts.

Smoothing Dealing with conflict by denying or avoiding it.

Social construction of reality An approach concerned with the processes by which people, their values, and commonsense and scientific knowledge produce meaning and reality.

Sociotechnical system A term that refers to simultaneously considering both the social system (human) and the technical system in order to best match the technology and the people involved.

Stakeholder A person or group having a vested interest in the organization's functioning and objectives.

Strategic change An approach to bringing about an alignment or congruence among an organization's strategy, structure, and human resource systems, as well as a fit between them and the larger environment. It includes attention to the technical, political, and cultural aspects of organizations.

Strategy A plan of action defining how an organization will use its resources to gain a competitive advantage in the larger environment. It typically includes choices about the functions an organization will perform, the products or services it will provide, and the markets and populations it will serve.

Stress management Activities aimed at coping with the dysfunctional consequences of work-related stress. These generally include diagnosing the causes and symptoms of stress and taking action to alleviate the causes and to improve one's ability to deal with stress.

Structure The structure of a system is the arrangement of its parts. Also, jargon for a change strategy that focuses on the formal organization. This is a particularly important class of interventions when the target for change is an entire organization.

Subsystem A part of a system. A change in any subsystem has an effect on the total system.

Survey feedback A type of data-based intervention that flows from surveys of the members of a system on some subject and reports the results of the surveys to the client system for whatever action appears appropriate.

System A set of interdependent parts that together make up a whole; each contributes something and receives something from the whole, which in turn is interdependent with the larger environment.

T-groups A method of helping individuals to develop greater self-awareness and become more sensitive to their effect on others. Individuals learn by interaction with other members of their group.

Task control The degree to which employees can regulate their own behavior to convert incoming materials into finished (or semifinished) products or other outputs.

Task force A group established to solve a particular problem (it may be disbanded when its work is accomplished).

Team building The process of helping a work group to become more effective in accomplishing its tasks and in satisfying the needs of group members.

Technology Consists of the major techniques (together with their underlying assumptions about cause and effect) that an organization's employees use while engaging in organizational processes or that are programmed into the machines and other equipment.

Theory X Typical Theory X managers believe that people dislike work and will avoid it whenever possible. Such managers feel that they themselves are a small, elite group of individuals who want to lead and take responsibility but that the larger mass of people want to be directed and avoid responsibility.

Theory Y Typical Theory Y managers usually assume that workers will accept responsibility provided they can satisfy personal needs and organizational goals at the same time.

Third-party intervention Activities aimed at helping two or more people within the same organization to resolve interpersonal conflicts.

Total quality management (TQM) A comprehensive and large-scale intervention that aims to focus all organization systems on the continuous improvement of quality.

Training An educational intervention typically focused on supervisors and individual contributors that is intended to increase the skills and knowledge of the workforce.

Transition state A condition that exists when the organization is moving from its current state to a desired future state. During the transition state, the organization learns how to implement the conditions needed to reach the desired future; it typically requires special structures and activities to manage this process.

Transformational change A radical change in how members perceive, think, and behave at work.

Transnational strategy A worldwide strategy with goals of customized products/services and efficient and responsive operations. Attempts to integrate operations on a worldwide basis.

Transorganizational development An intervention concerned with helping organizations to join into partnerships with other organizations to perform tasks or solve problems that are too complex and multifaceted for single organizations to resolve. Includes the following cyclical stages: identification, convention, organization, and evaluation.

Trust level The degree of mutual trust among a set of persons. Raising the trust level is usually a major goal of team building.

Uncertainty avoidance In cross-cultural analysis, the extent to which people in a culture avoid risk taking and prefer routine, knowable situations.

Unfreezing A reduction in the strength of old values, attitudes, or behaviors.

Value judgment Statement or belief based on or reflecting the individual's personal or class values.

Values Relatively permanent ideals (or ideas) that influence and shape the general nature of people's behavior.

Visioning A process typically initiated by key executives to define the mission of the organization and to clarify desired values for the organization, including valued outcomes and valued organizational conditions.

Work design The arrangement of tasks, people, and technology to produce both psychological outcomes and work performance.

Some of the terms used in this glossary were taken or adapted from *Reference Book: Organizational Effectiveness* (Fort Leavenworth, Kan.: U.S. Army Command and General Staff College, 1979).

Name Index

A

Abbott Laboratories, 418
Abitibi-Price, 459
Academy of Management, 13, 351
    Organization Development and
        Change Division, 46
Action Company, 226
        Advanced Micro Devices, 415
AG Communication Systems, 366
Agroforestry Revolving Loan Fund,
    564
Air Emirates, 535
Air New Zealand, 14, 535
Airbus Industrie, 90, 545
Akzo Nobel, 14, 100, 545
Alaska Airlines, 324
Alberto-Culver, 485, 491
Alcoa, 253, 324, 424
Alderfer, C., 246, 248
All-America City Award, 603
Allegheny-Ludlum Steel, 497
Alliance for Redesigning Govern-
    ment, 603
Alston & Bird, 409
Amazon.com, 4, 287, 288–289, 618
American Academy of Nursing, 575
American Airlines, 14, 90, 460
American Association of School
    Administrators, 594
American Crystal Sugar Company,
    405
American Express, 383, 551
American Express Financial
    Advisors, 281
American Healthcare Systems, 164
American Healthways Corporation
    (AMHC), 77, 79–81, 124,
    281, 283, 284, 495, 496–497
American Hospital Association, 575
American Management Association,
    289
American Nursing Association
    (ANA), 573
American Organization Develop-
    ment Institute, 58
American Productivity and Quality
    Center (APQC), 321, 509
American Psychological Association,
    13
American Quality Foundation, 324
American Society for Quality (ASQ),
    321

American Society of Training and
    Development (ASTD), 13, 58
American University, 7, 56
Ameritech, 413
AMEXTRA, 564
AMI Presbyterian St. Luke's
    Hospital, 259
Amnesty International, 559
Analog Devices, 318
Andersen Windows, 298
Anderson, Abram, 554
AOL, 87, 454
Apple Computer, 157, 162, 286,
    415, 556
Argyris, Chris, 13, 61, 501, 509
Arizona State University, 37
Arnotts Ltd., 554
Asea Brown Boveri (ABB), 34, 207,
    283, 347, 348–349, 553, 556
Asian Coalition for Agrarian Reform
    and Rural Development, 558
Assistance Professionals Association,
    426
Association for Quality and Partici-
    pation (AQP), 321–322
AT&T, 259, 289–290, 306, 332, 333,
    368, 374, 381, 408, 424, 426,
    458, 485
Athos, A., 482
Automobile magazine, 320

B

Bain and Company, 506, 507
Baldwin Piano and Organ Company,
    94, 96
Ballmer, Steve, 221, 456
Balt Healthcare Corporation, 231
Bank of America, 14
Banker's Trust, 158
BASF, 551
Baxter Export Corporation, 416, 417
Beckhard, Richard, 1, 2, 7, 12, 13,
    168, 243, 246, 249–250
Beer, Michael, 1, 2, 252
Bekey, George, 37–38
Bell, C. H., Jr., 235, 239, 252
Bell Laboratories, 318
Ben & Jerry's, 415
Benedictine University, 56
Benetton, 286
Bennis, Warren, 13, 252

Bernick, Carol Lavin, 491
Bezos, Jeff, 288–289
BHP Copper, 312
Birmingham, John, 94
Birmingham, Robert, 94
Biscuits Maison, 555
Black & Decker, 372, 650–657
Blake, Robert, 7, 9–10, 252
Block, Peter, 13–14, 78
Blue Cross and Blue Shield of
    Florida, 415
Blue Heron Associates, 571
Blumberg, A., 252
BMW, 451, 545
Boeing, 14, 90, 259, 289–290, 295,
    318, 327, 407–408, 454, 497
Bono, 565
Bordens, 203
Borders Books, 288
Boss, R. W., 239
Boston Orchestra, 94
Bowen, Thella, 31–32
Bowers, D., 140
Bowling Green State University, 13,
    56
BP Amoco, 281, 507, 508, 617
Branch Smith Printing, 326
British Airways, 482
British Petroleum, 172, 366, 416,
    425, 465
Brooks, Pete, 231
Brown, Craig, 13
Browne, John, 508
Brubeck, Dave, 94
Bruno, Jennifer, 427–428
Bryson, John, 597
Buckman Laboratories, 509
Builder's Emporium, 412
Buller, R., 239
Burke, Warner, 1, 2, 13
Burlington Northern Railroad, 426
Business Week, 160, 417, 456, 492

C

Cache Creek, 645
Caesars Tahoe, 236–237, 644–649
Caesars World, 644, 649
Caltech, 37
Calvez, Didier Le, 490–491
Cameron, K., 119
Campbell, Joseph, 554

Campbell Soup Company, 553, 554–555

Canadian Broadcasting Corporation, 497, 508

Capital Services, 281

Cargill, 579

Carlsbad, California, City of, 362–363, 571, 597, 603, 604–605

Carlzon, Jan, 491

Carnegie Foundation, 7

Carroll, S., 372

Cary, Mari Jo, 348

Case, 290–291

Case Western Reserve University, 13, 56

Cathay Pacific Airways, 448

CBS, 94

Cedar-Sinai Hospital, 322–323

Center for Creative Leadership, 45, 218

Center for Effective Organizations, 117, 119, 136, 186, 307, 313

Center for Manufacturing and Automation Research (CMAR), 36–38

Center for Socio-Eco-Nomic Development (CSEND), 544

Center for the Study of Ethics in the Professions, 58

Central Party School (China), 545

Chevron Oil Company, 93, 506, 509

Chicago Orchestra, 94

Chief Executive magazine, 218

China Brief, 562

China Training Centre for Senior Personnel Management Officials (CTCSPMO), 544, 545

Chinese Communist Party (CCP), 544, 545

Chrysler Corporation, 319–320, 454, 485

Ciba-Geigy, 396

CIGNA Property & Casualty, 509

Circuit City, 288, 317

Cisco Systems, 287, 289, 396, 408, 465

Citigroup, 50

Clegg, Frank, 455, 456

Clinton, Bill, 596, 603

Coachville, 217

Coca-Cola, 253, 293, 554, 556

Coch, Lester, 8

Colgate-Palmolive Co., 366, 401, 402–403, 554, 556

Collier, John, 8

Collins, J., 161, 450, 465

Colman, Bob, 293

Columbia University, 56

Committee of Earthquake Victims, 562

Committee on Community Interrelations (American Jewish Congress), 7

Communications Workers of America, 11, 136, 313

Compaq Corporation, 170, 171–172, 197–198, 454

Connecticut Interracial Commission, 7

Container Store, 409

Continental Can, 405

Cooperrider, David, 14

Corky's Pest Control, 298

Corning Glass Works, 336, 337, 383, 405, 465

Council for Excellence in Government, 603

Covisint, 618–619

Craver, Joseph W., 32

Credit Lyonnais, 545

Crosby, Philip, 321

Cummings, Thomas, 13, 464, 467, 493

Cummins Engine, 14

Cyprus Sierrita Corporation, 220

Daimler-Benz, 454, 485

DaimlerChrysler, 295, 318, 618–619

Dana Corporation, 298, 385, 386

Dayton Hudson, 332

Dealogic, 454

Dell Computer, 618

Delphia Corporation, 321

Delta Air Lines, 292, 293–294

Deming, W. Edwards, 318, 321, 593

Denny's, 411

DeSoto, 386

Detroit Edison, 8

DHV Family Business Advisors, 571

Digital Equipment, 413

Disney, 45, 162, 324, 484

Dobbs, Lou, 492

Dominion Foundries and Steel Company, 426

Donnelly Corporation, 386

Dorrance, John, 554

Dow Chemical, 321, 415, 461, 462–463, 505–506

Drucker, P., 370

DuPont, 14, 276, 314

DuPree, Max, 482

Dyer, W., 119, 232, 237–238

Earthlink, 87

Eastman Chemical Company, 323

Eaton, 385

eBay, 4

Edward Jones, 409

Eindhoven University of Technology, 347

Elden, Max, 13

Electrolux, 553

Electromation, Inc., 314

Eli Lilly, 465

Embassy Suites, 645

Emhart Corporation, 650

Equitable Life Assurance Society, 425

Ernst and Young, 324

Eskom, 541

Essential Schools, 596

Esso Standard Oil, 7

ExxonMobil, 7, 276

Family Council, 580

Fandango.com, 618

Federal Express, 418, 465

Federal Mediation and Conciliation Service, 227

Feyerherm, A., 1

Fidelity Investments, 405

Fielding Institute, 56

Fiorina, Carleton (Carly) S., 171, 172, 197–198

Floresta, 563, 564–565

Florida Power and Light, 295, 327

Fluor Corporation, 507

Flynn, Patricia, 427

Forcella, Tom, 169

Ford Foundation, 603

Ford Motor Company, 11, 306, 321, 454, 558, 618–619

Fordyce, J., 250

Fortune, 409, 418, 490, 492

Fortune 1000, 307, 327, 342, 382, 383

Fortune 500, 413, 414, 573, 579

Four Seasons, 490–491

Franco-American SpaghettiOs, 554

Frederickson, H. George, 597

French, John, 8

French, Wendell, 1, 2, 235, 252

Freshbake Foods Group PLC, 554

Frito-Lay, 203

Fuji-Xerox, 465, 466

Fujitsu, 415, 542

G

GAF, 462
Gaines Pet Food, 11, 347, 383
Galbraith, J., 90, 286
Gantman, Dan, 231
Gates, Bill, 450
Gausz-Mandelberg, Carol, 571–579
GE Financial, 324, 325–326
Gellerman, Bill, 66
General Electric, 5, 14, 34, 45, 88, 161, 243, 276, 281, 293, 295, 324, 325–326, 342, 368, 396, 409, 482, 490, 553, 556, 651
General Electric Medical Systems (GEMS), 244, 245
General Foods, 14, 347, 382, 554
General Mills, 7, 306, 340, 342, 382
General Motors, 11, 92, 100, 157, 276, 312, 321, 354, 426, 465, 618–619
George V, 490
George Washington University, 56
Gestalt Institute, 45
Global Trends, 2015 (CIA report), 616
Global Village of Beijing (GVB), 559, 562
Golembiewski, Robert, 252, 597, 600
Gore, Al, 596
Gould, 491
Gould Academy, 7
Greenes, Kent, 508
Greiner, Larry, 13, 166, 452
GTE of California (GTEC), 313
GTE Telephone Operations, 14, 50, 297, 298, 332

H

Habitat for Humanity, 559
Hackman, J., 100, 106, 119, 184, 332, 333–334, 335, 338, 339–340
Hallmark Circuits, 299–300
Hamilton, Edith, 8
Hamot Medical Center, 577–578
Harman, 312
Harrah's Tahoe, 645–646
Harris, R., 168
Hartman, Dale, 36–38
Harvard University, 603
Harvey's, 645, 646
Harwood Manufacturing Company, 8
Hay Group, 396
Heavenly Valley Ski Resort, 647
Herman Miller, 383, 482
Herzberg, F., 106, 332–333

Heskett, J., 482
Heublein, 405
Hewlett-Packard, 14, 34, 45, 170, 171–172, 197–198, 259, 295, 405, 408, 413, 416, 454, 482, 484, 505, 553, 555
H.J. Heinz Co., 554
Hoechst Celanese, 413, 551
Hoffman-LaRoche, 506
Holiday Inn, 465
Honda, 161, 318, 505, 549, 551
Honeywell, 11, 300, 301–302, 424
Horizon, 645, 646
HP-Compaq, 170, 171–172
Hughes Aircraft, 36, 321, 507
Human Systems Development Consortium (HSDC), 66
Hunger Project, 558, 559, 561
Huse, E., 252
Hyundai, 542

I

IBM, 5, 14, 36, 157, 289–290, 337, 381, 406, 408, 450, 455, 465, 484, 551
IBM Credit, 296
ICL, 556
IKEA, 508, 617, 625
Ikebuchi, Kosuke, 473, 474
Illinois Institute of Technology, 58
Imperial Chemical Industries, 14, 333
Indiana Bell Telephone Company, 336–337
Industry Week, 349
Industry–University Cooperative Research Center Program (IUCRCP), 36
Inner Harbor Project (Baltimore), 467
The Innovation Groups, 597, 603
INSEAD, 208
Institute for Manufacturing and Automation Research (IMAR), 36–38, 186
Institute for Social Research (ISR), 117, 119, 312, 422
Institute of Cultural Affairs (ICA), 562–563
Institute of Medicine (IOM), 573
Integra Financial, 173
Intel Corporation, 14, 50, 172, 306, 340, 342, 374, 396, 406, 409, 418, 482
Intercompany Longitudinal Study, 140
Interface, 625

International City/County Management Association, 597
International Coach Federation, 217
International Organization for Standardization (ISO), 322, 348, 624
International Physicians for the Prevention of Nuclear War, 558, 559
International Quality Circle Association, 321
International Society of Six-Sigma Professionals (ISSSP), 321
International Union for the Conservation of Nature and Natural Resources, 558, 559
IRS (Internal Revenue Service), 306
Ishikawa, Masakazu, 474
ITT Corporation, 236, 644, 649

J

Janssen Research Foundation, 251
JCPenney, 484
Jenkins, G., 390
Jenny Craig, 157
JetBlue Airways, 293
Johansson, Leif, 322
John F. Kennedy School of Government, 603
John Hancock Mutual Life Insurance, 14
Johnson & Johnson, 251–252, 281, 366, 405, 418, 424, 426, 427–428, 490
Johnson, David, 554–555
Johnson, Magic, 492
Johnsonville Sausage, 159, 160, 343
Joint Commission on Accreditation of Health Care Organizations, 573
J.P. Morgan, 414
Juran, Joseph M., 318, 320

K

Kanter, R., 45
Kaplan, R., 227
Kawai, 94
Kawamoto, Nobuhiko, 161
Kazanjian, R., 286
Kelman, H., 60
Kikkoman, 579
Killinger, Kerry, 492, 493
Kimberly-Clark, 34
Kinko's, 465
Kizer, Kenneth, 174
Kline, Bill, 294

Knorr, 554
Kobe Steel, Ltd., 324
Kodak, 157, 259
Kotter, J., 90, 482

L

Lake Tahoe Visitors Authority, 646
Lakeside Inn, 645
Lands' End Direct Merchants, 387, 388–389
Lawler, Edward, III, 13, 100, 307–308, 312, 390
Lean Cuisine, 549
Leapfrog Group, 573
Lechmere, 334
Ledford, Gerald, Jr., 14, 100, 312
Lego, 162
Levi Strauss, 50, 374, 482, 579
Levinson, H., 370
Lewin, Kurt, 6–7, 8, 22–24, 25, 28, 125–126, 189, 470
Lewis, Griff, 417
Li and Fung, 283
Likert, Rensis, 7, 8, 9
Lincoln Electric, 385
Linder, John, 417
Linux, 455
Lippitt, Gordon, 61, 74–75
Lippitt, R., 24
Liz Claiborne, 286
L.L. Bean, 497
Lockheed Martin, 321
L'Oreal, 545
Los Angeles Police Department, 423
Loyola University, 56
Luft, J., 224
Lundberg, Craig, 13

M

MacArthur, Douglas, 318
Macy, B., 182
Magma Copper Company, 312
Mandela, Nelson, 541
Mann, Floyd, 8
Marconi Commerce Systems, 158
Marczak, Ann, 38
Margulies, Newton, 13
Marshall, Sir Colin, 482
Martin, J., 483
Matsushita, 542, 549
May Co., 324
McCaskey, M., 100
McDonald's, 87, 92, 406, 411, 425, 465
McDonnell Douglas, 454
McGovern, Gordon, 555

McGraw-Hill, 579
McGregor, Douglas, 7, 370–371
MCI, 286
McKesson, 172, 416
McKinsey, 497, 506
Medtronics, 321
Melkanoff, Michel, 37
Mercer Consulting, 289
Merck, 50, 286, 551
Michelin, 550
Mickelson, Rachel, 571, 579–590
Microsoft Canada, 454, 455–456
Microsoft Corporation, 14, 50, 87, 221, 259, 366, 406, 408, 415, 418, 454, 455–456, 464, 484, 497, 506, 507
Midland-Ross, 386
Millennium Pharmaceuticals, 465
Ministry of Personnel (China), 545
Mirage, 646
Mirvis, P., 182
MIT (Massachusetts Institute of Technology), 207
Mitsubishi, 5
Mobley, Foster W., 571–579
Mohrman, S., 14, 100, 312, 493
Monsanto Company, 372, 373, 374, 409
Morris, C., 100
Morris, Ken, 348
Morton Salt, 318
Motorola, 34, 45, 287, 289, 295, 306, 318, 322, 324, 326–327, 342, 426, 482, 505, 506, 553, 618, 625
Mountain Forum, 558, 559
Mouton, J., 7, 9–10
Murrell, Ken, 14

N

Nabisco, 203
Nadler, D., 90, 482
Nalbandian, John, 597
National & Provincial Building Society, 281
National Academy of Public Administration, 603
National Association of Temporary and Staffing Services, 618
National Civic League, 603
National Education Association, 7
National Performance Review, 321
National Research Council, 292
National Science Foundation (NSF), 36–37, 38
National Survey on Drug Use and Health (2002), 426

National Training Laboratories (NTL), 7, 45, 604–605
Nature Conservancy, 558, 559, 560
NBC, 320–321
NCR, 458, 485
NEC, 542, 549
Neighborhood Housing Services (Pittsburgh), 467
Neon, 318, 319–320
Nescafé, 549
Nestlé, 549
Neusoft Corporation, 14, 535
New Baldwin Corridor Coalition, 467
New United Motor Manufacturing, Inc., 465
New York Police Department, 379
Newberg, Skip, 139
Newman, W., 480
Nike, 283, 470
Nissan, 542, 550
Nixdorf Computer, 205
Nong Shim Company, 549
Nordstrom, 162, 484, 506
Norling, Richard, 164
Northern Telecom, 382
Northrup, 36
Novotel UK, 396
NTI, 56
Nucor Steel, 306

O

Occidental Petroleum, 368
OD Network, 13
Office Depot, 288
Office of Naval Research, 7
Oil, Chemical, and Atomic Workers, 11
Oldham, G., 106, 119, 184, 332, 333–334, 335, 338, 339–340
O'Neill, Paul H., 324, 565
Oracle, 454, 455
Organizational Technologies, 571
Orrefors, 14
Ortiv Glass Corporation, 103–106
Otis Elevator, 553
Ouchi, W., 11, 482
Owen-Jones, Lindsay, 545
Oxy-USA, 368

P

Palmero, Sandra, 455, 456
Park Place Entertainment, 236
Parke-Davis Group, 554
Parker, Mike, 462, 463
Participative Management Program, 9

Pascale, R., 482
Pasmore, William, 13
Patchett, Raymond R., 571, 596–603
Patent Office (Denmark), 543
PeopleSoft, 454, 619
Pepperdine University, 7, 13, 56, 109, 406–407
Pepperidge Farm, 554, 555
PepsiCo, 293, 411, 425, 482
Perkins Cole, 418
Peters, Tom, 160, 482
Philadelphia Orchestra, 94
Philip Morris, 50, 554
Pinellas County Schools, 596
Platt, Lewis, 198
Plenum Publishing, 317
Polaroid, 14, 157
Porras, Jerry, 13, 39, 161
Port of San Diego, 31–32
Porter, Michael, 90, 453
Premier Health Alliance, 164
Price, David, 558
Principal Financial Group, 299
Procter & Gamble, 14, 45, 50, 172, 203, 340, 405, 408, 411, 425, 491, 554
Providian Financial, 321
Prudential Insurance Company of America, 139, 405, 485
Prudential Real Estate Affiliates, Inc. (PREA), 139–140
PSA Peugeot Citroën, 618–619

Q

Quaker Oats, 396, 418
Quality Cup, 321
Quantum, 342
Quinn, R., 119

R

Raia, Anthony, 13
Ralston Purina, 14
Rand Corporation, 595
Raychem, 374
Reconstruction and Development Program (South Africa), 541
Renault-Nissan, 618–619
Reno Air, 460
Research Center for Group Dynamics (MIT), 7, 8
Research Triangle Institute, 419
Reynolds, Richard, 455
Ritz-Carlton Hotel, 158
Robert Wood Johnson Pharmaceutical Research Institute, 251
Robertson, P., 39

Rochester Institute of Technology (RIT), 321
Rockport, 259
Rockwell International, 36, 163, 312
Romanelli, E., 480
Royal College of Psychiatrists (Great Britain), 426
Royal Dutch/Shell, 508–509, 617
Rushton Mines, 312

S

Saab, 14, 347, 543
Sabin, Scott, 564
Sacramento County Office of Education (California), 594
Samick, 94
Samsung, 491
San Diego County Regional Airport Authority (SDCRAA), 31–32
SAP, 296, 619
Savings Development Movement (SDM), 561
SBC Communications, 411
Scandinavian Airlines (SAS), 491, 556
Schein, Edgar, 13, 25, 81, 220, 222, 225, 226
Schein, V., 166, 452
Schon, D., 501, 509
School Development Program, 596
Schulmeyer, Gerhard, 205, 207, 208
Sears, 157, 276, 289–290
Seashore, Edie, 13
Seiki, Aisin, 473–474
Selmer Instruments, 94
Semco S/A, 540–541
Semier, Ricardo, 540–541
Senge, P., 470, 501
Seventh American Forest Congress, 257–258
Shafer-Payne, Angela, 31
Shell Oil Company, 14, 306, 543
Shepard, Herbert, 7
Sherwin-Williams, 342, 424
Shewhart, Walter A., 318
Shingo Prize, 321
Siebel Systems, 465
Siemens AG, 205, 208, 550
Siemens Nixdorf Informationssysteme (SNI), 205–208
Sigmund, Glenn, 139–140
Simon, David, 508
Singapore Airlines, 448
SmithKline Beecham, 545
Snyder, W., 498
Society for Organizational Learning, 508

Society of Industrial and Organizational Psychology, 13
Solar Turbines, 306
Somic Ishikawa, Inc., 474
Sondheim, Stephen, 94
Sony, 484, 549
South Tahoe Gaming Alliance (STGA), 646–647
Southern California Edison, 411
Southwest Airlines, 293, 306, 317, 482
Southwestern Bell Corp. (SBC), 414
Spittler, Paul, 571, 590–596
Spoornet, 541
SSM Health Care, 326
Standard & Poor's, 327, 485, 616
Standard Brands, 203
Standard Oil of New Jersey, 276
Stanford University, 7, 56, 207
Starbucks, 465
Starwood Resorts, 236
State Commission of the Nationalities (China), 545
State Economic and Trade Commission (China), 545
Stayer, Ralph, 159, 160
Steelcase, 413
Steelworkers, 11
Steinway & Son, 93–98
Steinway Musical Instruments Company, 94
Stone Consolidated, 459
Stride Rite Corporation, 416
Suk, Yoo Jong, 549
Sun Microsystems, 5, 286, 324, 455
Sunbeam, 158
The SunHealth Alliance, 164
Survey Research Center, 8
Swanson, 554

T

Tahoe Regional Planning Agency, 646
Taiho Kogyo Co., 474
Tannenbaum, Robert, 7, 13
Target, 289
Tavistock Institute of Human Relations (London), 10, 340, 545
Taylor, Frederick, 331–332
Telkom, 541
Texaco, 411, 413
Texas Instruments, 14, 172, 295, 306, 321, 333, 405, 416, 509
3M, 45, 281, 306, 368, 385, 453, 491, 618
Time-Life, 507
Time/Warner, 454
Timex, 90

Tosi, W., Jr., 372
Toyota, 318, 465, 472, 473–474, 542
Toys "R" Us, 288–289
Travelers Insurance Companies, 338
Tremont Hotel (Chicago), 8
Trist, Eric, 10
TRW Space Systems, 7, 14, 36, 172, 250, 332
Tushman, M., 90, 480, 482
Twain, Mark, 590
Tyson Foods, 317

U

U2, 565
Unilever, 545
Union Carbide, 7, 461, 462–463
Union of Japanese Scientists and Engineers (JUSE), 318
United Auto Workers (UAW), 11, 312, 319
United Furniture Workers' Union, 95
United States Navy, 36
United Technologies, 340, 382, 553
University Associates, 56
University Cooperative Research Center Program (IUCRCP), 38
University of California, Los Angeles (UCLA), 7, 36, 45, 56
University of Michigan, 56, 117, 119, 186, 312, 422
University of Southern California (USC), 36, 37, 117, 119, 136, 186, 307, 313, 406–407, 425
U.S. Army, 497, 508

U.S. Census, 414
U.S. Commerce Department, 327
U.S. Department of Defense, 423, 424
U.S. Department of Labor, 383, 409
U.S. Department of the Treasury, 565
U.S. Federal Trade Commission, 462
U.S. Forest Service, 257
U.S. Post Office, 406
USA Today, 321

V

V-8, 554
Vaill, Peter, 13
Varney, G., 611
Verizon, 40, 306
Viacom, 100
Vitro, 14
Volvo, 322, 347, 355, 454, 508, 543, 550

W

Wal-Mart Stores, 162–163, 317, 415, 505, 579
Walton, R., 229
WarnerLambert Company, 554
Washington Mutual, Inc. (WaMu), 491, 492–493
Washington State Patrol (WSP), 378–379
Waste Management, 158
Waterman, R., 482
Watson, J., 24

Watts, Duncan, 473
Weick, K., 448
Weil, R., 250
Weisbord, M., 89–90, 119
Welch, Jack, 161, 245, 482, 490
Wesley Long Community Hospital, 158
West Paces Ferry Hospital, 323
Westley, B., 24
Weyerhaeuser, 50, 318, 385, 418, 425
Whyte, William, 8
Wiley Series on Organizational Assessment and Change, 182
Woodman, Richard, 13
Woolman, C. E., 293
World Conservation Union, 558
World Vision, 559
World Wildlife Fund, 559
Worley, C., 1
Wurlitzer, 94
Wyndham Hotels, 414
Wynn, Steve, 646

X

Xerox, 36, 281, 289–290, 318, 396, 425, 618
Xiaoyl, Liao, 562

Y

Yahoo!, 4
Yamaha, 94, 96
Young Chang, 94
Young, John, 197–198
Young, Marilyn, 231

Subject Index

A

Absenteeism
  effect of skill-based pay on, 383
  positive effect of EAPs on, 426
Achievement orientation, in global OD, 538
Action learning, 26, 544
Action map, in organization learning, 502
Action planning, 80, 143
  for coaching, 218
Action research, 8, 28, 544
  applied in international settings, 26
  model, 22, 24–26
  process, used by groups in parallel structures, 311–312
  trends in application of, 26
Action science, 26
Active listening, 159
Adaptation and adjustment, 80
Adaptive learning, 501
After-implementation evaluation, 179
Age
  average, of U.S. workforce, 411–412
  in workforce diversity, 411–412
Agency, 470
AIDS, 90, 414
AIDS/HIV, 414
Alignment, in organization system, 88
Alliance interventions, 461, 465–466
Alliances, 152
  defined, 465
  mergers and, among health care providers, 572
  operation and adjustment, 466
  partner selection, 465–466
  strategy formulation for, 465
  structuring and start-up, 466
  types of, 465
Alpha change, 188
Alternative dispute resolution (ADR), 227–228
Americans with Disabilities Act (ADA), 90, 411, 414, 415, 601
Analysis
  of applying individual-level diagnosis to job design, 108, 110–112

content, 123, 125
force-field, 125–126
group-level diagnosis, 103–106
organization-level, Steinway & Sons, 93, 95–98
strategic, involvement of organization members in, 453
Applications
  Amazon.com's network structure, 288–289
  American Healthways' process structure, 284
  approaching employee orientation as a cultural experience, 604–605
  building the executive team at Caesars Tahoe, 235
  Campbell Soup Company moves to a worldwide strategic orientation, 554–555
  changing the appraisal process in the Washington State Patrol (WSP), 378–379
  Chrysler Corporation moves toward high involvement, 319–320
  collecting and analyzing diagnostic data at American Healthways, 124–125
  conflict management at Balt Healthcare Corporation, 231
  contracting at American Healthways Corporation, 79–81
  creating a vision at Premier, 164–165
  embracing employee diversity at Baxter Export Corporation, 417
  employee involvement, 309–312, 314–318, 320–324, 326–327
  entering American Healthways Corporation, 77
  ethics of OD, 61–62
  evaluating change and change management at the World Bank, 190–191
  fragile and robust—network change in Toyota Motor Corporation, 473
  Honeywell IAC's TotalPlant reengineering process, 301–302

improving intergroup relationships in Johnson & Johnson's drug evaluation department, 251–252
institutionalizing structural change at Hewlett-Packard, 197–198
job design at Pepperdine University, 109
job enrichment at the Travelers Insurance Companies, 338
Johnson & Johnson's health and wellness program, 427–428
knowledge management at BP Amoco, 508
leading your business at Microsoft Corporation, 221
lessons learned from the Dow Chemical Company and Union Carbide merger, 462–463
linking career planning, human resources planning, and strategy at Colgate-Palmolive, 402–403
managing strategic change at Microsoft Canada, 455–456
modernizing China's human resource development and training functions, 544–545
motivating change at Johnsonville Sausage, 160
moving to self-managed teams at ABB, 348–349
OD in the Ross family business, 589–590
open-space meeting at a consulting firm, 260–261
operations review and survey feedback at Prudential Real Estate Affiliates (PREA), 139–140
performance enhancement process at Monsanto, 373
personal views of the internal and external consulting positions, 53–54
planned change
  at the San Diego County Regional Airport Authority (SDCRAA), 31–32
  in an underorganized system, 36–38

process consultation at Action Company, 226

revising the reward system at Lands' End, 388–389

self-design at American Health-ways Corporation, 496–497

Seventh American Forest Congress, 257–258

six-sigma success story at GE Financial, 325–326

social and environmental change at Floresta, 564–565

Steinway's strategic orientation, 94–95

strategic downsizing process at Delta Air Lines, 293–294

sustaining transformational change at the Veterans Health Administration (VHA), 174–175

top-management team at Ortiv Glass Corporation, 104

training OD practitioners in data feedback, 136–137

transition management in the HP-Compaq acquisition, 171–172

union–management cooperation at GTE of California, 313–314

using social networks to implement change in a public education institution, 169

Washington Mutual: leveraging culture as competitive advantage, 492–493

a work-out meeting at General Electric Medical Systems (GEMS), 245

work redesign at Hamot Medical Center, 577–578

Application service providers (ASPs), 169

Appreciative inquiry (AI), 27. *See also* Action research

Arctic National Wildlife Refuge, 617

Artifacts, of organization culture, 483–484

The Art of Japanese Management (Pascale and Athos), 482

Assessment, 179. *See also* Evaluation, OD intervention
  in coaching, 217, 218
  performing needs, 219

Assessment centers, 407

Autonomy
  employee, 334
  increase of, in vertical loading, 337
  team, 349

of team members, maintaining sufficient, 344

Aviation & Transportation Security Act, 32

B

Balanced Budget Act, 574

Balkans, 4

Basic assumptions, of organization culture, 484

Behavioral approach, to diagnosing organization culture, 486

Behaviorally anchored rating scale (BARS), 375

Behavioral sciences, 2, 4, 614
  coaching, using principles of applied, 217
  consultation with experts from field of, 24

Behaviors
  changes in, required by OD interventions, 179
  goal setting, to jointly define member work, 366
  network, 470. *See also* Networks
  reinforcing new, 172–173
  strategically driven work, 368
  team, 172
  Type A and B, 421–422

Benchmarks, 324, 349

Benevolent authoritative systems, 9

Berlin Wall, 4, 615

Beta change, 188–189

Bhopal, disaster in, 462

Bifurcation, 622

"Big 5" instrument, 217

Big, Hairy, Audacious Goals (BHAGs), 162–163, 455, 496

Biofeedback, 425–426

Bonus plans, 383, 384, 442. *See also* Gain sharing
  individual, 385

Boundary control, 342, 343

Boundary management, 341

Brainstorming, 206, 256, 323

Bridging organizations, 558

Bridging role, of GSCO change agents, 563, 565

Brokers, 286

Built to Last (Collins and Porras), 482

Burnout, 49, 56–57
  steps to cope with, 57
  use of sabbaticals to avoid, 418

Business strategy, 456

C

California Senate Bill AB93, 32

Canadian Competition Bureau, 462

Career development. *See* Career planning and development

Career planning. *See* Career planning and development

Career planning and development, 152
  career development, 401, 403–410
    individual employee development interventions, 407–408
    performance feedback and coaching interventions, 408–409
    role and structure interventions, 403–407
    work-life balance interventions, 409–410
  career planning process, 398–401
    issues (table 18.1), 399
  career stages, 397–398
    interventions used in various (table 18.2), 404
    table 18.1, 399
  interventions, 396–410
  linking career planning, human resources planning, and strategy at Colgate-Palmolive, 402–403
  needs for effective, 401
  resources included in, 399

Career systems, in HIOs, 315

Carey Award, 321

Cascades, 622

Case studies. *See also* Integrative case studies
  City of Carlsbad, California, restructuring the Public Works Department, 362–363
  employee benefits at HealthCo background, 435
    recent events, 435–437
    three scenarios, 434–435
  evaluating the change agent program at Siemens Nixdorf, 205–208
    change agent program, 207–208
    culture change program, 205–207
  Fourwinds Marina, 522–531
    background data, 523–528
    marina docking area facts, 530–531
    sources of income, 528–530
  Gulf States Metals, Inc., 269–272
    current situation, 269

diagnostic activities and information, 270–272
    an opportunity for OD, 270
    organization structure, 269–270
    plant environment, 270
    production process, 270
initiating change in the manufacturing and distribution division of PolyProd, 209–213
    contributing factors, 212–213
    documentation problem, 210–211
    M&DDIV organization and culture, 209–210
    your plan to initiate change, 213
"It's Your Turn" (management training), 201–202
Metric Division case, 264–268
preliminary diagnosis, in conjunction with OD practitioner, 269–272
Rondell Data Corporation, 514–521
    company history, 515–516
    dismissal, 520–521
    engineering department: research, 516–517
    engineering services department, 517–518
    executive committee, 520
    production department, 519–520
    sales department, 518–519
Sharpe BMW, 438–443
    automotive dealership industry, 438
    background, 438–440
    challenge, 442–443
    customer satisfaction index (CSI), 440–441
    new plan for, 442
    service department repairs, 440
    service technicians' labor market, 442
Sullivan Hospital System (TQM processes), 359–361
Sunflower Incorporated (standardizing operations), 203–204
team building in the Metric Division, 264–268
Cause-and-effect diagrams, 323
Chaebols, 283, 467
Change. *See also* Resistance, to change
    activities
        overview of, 155–157
        practical advice for managing (figure 10.1), 156

capability to, 145
and change management at the World Bank, evaluating, 190–191
consultant-dominated, 26
contingencies related to target of, 145
culture, 153. *See also* Culture change; Culture(s)
guides for facilitating network, 471–472
implementing and evaluating, in family businesses, 588
managing network, 469–472
methods associated with developing and assisting organization members, 152
methods for generating sufficient dissatisfaction to produce, 157–158
motivating, 157–159
programmability and, 193
programs. *See also* Employee involvement (EI)
    goal setting, 151
    performance appraisal, 151
    reward systems, 151
in a public education institution, using social networks to implement, 169
readiness for, 145
situation, contingencies related to, 144–145
target, level of, 193
at the Veterans Health Administration (VHA), 173, 174–175
Change agents
    activities of, 173, 175
    attention to power and political activity by, 163
    building support system for, 170, 172
    capabilities of, 145
    criticism of change program by, 207–208
    employee involvement and, 172. *See also* Employee involvement (EI)
    identification of powerful individuals and groups with interest in changes, by, 166–167
    specification of criteria for network membership by, 467–468
    trade-offs involving, 471–472
    use of power strategy by, 167–168
Change management, 2, 45, 155. *See also* Planned change; Transformational change

distinguishing between organization development and, 3–4
evaluating change and, at the World Bank, 190–191
need for competence in, 144
Change process, 76, 78. *See also* Transformational change
    relation of internal support to, 193–194
    time element of, 173
China, 4, 535, 542–543
    opening of trade with, 615
Clean Water Act, 602
Client
    determining relevant, 73–74
    relationships, in job enrichment, 336–337, 338
Coaching, 149, 216–218
    application stages, 217–218
    goals, 217
    interventions, performance feedback and, 408–409
    results of, 218
Coalition for Environmentally Responsible Economics (CERES)
Codification, in organizing knowledge, 506
Collaborative strategies, 446–447, 461, 463–471
    alliance interventions, 465–466
    rationale for, 463–464
    transactions in, 464
Collateral structures. *See* Parallel structures
Collecting and analyzing diagnostic information, 114–130. *See also* Data gathering
    at American Healthways, 124–125
    data analysis techniques, 123, 125–130
        qualitative tools, 123, 125–126
        quantitative tools, 126–130
    diagnostic relationship/contract, 114–116
    methods for, 116–122
        comparison of different (table 7.1), 117
        interviews, 119–120
        observations, 120–121
        questionnaires, 117, 119
        sampling, 122–123
        unobtrusive measures, 121–122
Commission on the Future of Worker–Management Relations, 314
Commitment, to intervention, 194

Communication, 302
  about reward systems, importance of, 390
  building good, in family businesses, 586
  continued, concerning parallel structure activities, 311
  in different types of organizations, 34
  effective, about changes, 159
  process consultation and, 222–223
Comparison unit, 187, 188
Compatibility, in work design, 346
Compensation specialists, 366–367
Competing values approach, to diagnosing organization culture, 486–488
  figure 20.2, 488
Competition
  strategies for, 446
  stress related to increased global, 409, 480
Competitive advantage
  ability to manage change as key source of, 620–621
  defining, for network, 469
  difficulty of imitation, 451
  diversity as source of, 411
  uniqueness, 450
  value, 450–451
  Washington Mutual: leveraging culture as, 492–493
Competitive strategies, 446, 450–454, 456–461
  identifying knowledge required for, 506
  integrated strategic change, 451–454
  for M&As, 458
  mergers and acquisitions, 454, 456–461
Composition, in group diagnosis, 102
Confidentiality, 78
  issues of, 50
  OD practitioners and, 115
Conflict(s). See also Conflict resolution
  cyclical model of interpersonal (figure 12.2), 228
  episodic model of, 228–229
  informal procedures for resolving intergroup, 249–250
  management at Balt Healthcare Corporation, 231
  ongoing, in OD field, 613–614
  relationship between change orders and (table 7.5), 128

  and rivalry in family businesses, 583–584. See also Family business system
  third-party intervention and, 227–228
  value and goal, 61
Conflict resolution, 146
  process, facilitating, 229–230
Confrontation meeting. See Organization confrontation meeting
Congress, 174, 257, 314, 603
  establishment of Malcolm Baldrige National Quality Award by, 321
Congruence, 192
Connectedness, 622
Connectors, in networks, 471
Consultants, 26, 56–57, 75. See also External consultants; Internal consultants; Organization development practitioners
  assessing need for (table 12.3), 238
  differences between external and internal (table 3.2), 51
  quick solutions and, 40
  resolution of dependency issues by, 61
  third-party, 229. See also Third-party interventions
Consultative roles, in career development, 406
Consultative systems, 9
Content analysis, 123, 125
Content interventions, 225
Content validity, 186
Context orientation, in global OD, 536
Continuous quality improvement (CQI), 61, 542
Control charts, 323
Control system, as job enrichment constraint, 339
Convergent validity, 186
Coordinating mechanisms, in networks, 286
Core purpose, 162
  example of, 165
Core values, 161–162
  example of, 165
Corporate Culture and Performance (Kotter and Heskett), 482
Corporate strategy, 456
Correlation coefficient, 128–129
Cost/benefit trade-off, of alliances, 465
Cost-of-living adjustments (COLA), 382
Creative abrasion, 506

Cross-cultural issues, 230
Cultural diversity, 616–617
Cultural resistance, 159
Culture(s)
  approaching employee orientation as a cultural experience, 604–605
  change, 153. See also Culture change
  creating effective, in health care industry, 575
  effect on intervention of, 145
  features of M&As, 459
  interaction between different, due to globalization, 230
  melding corporate, 171–172
  organization, 50, 92–93, 164. See also Culture change
    inferred, 97
    integration activities for M&As, 460–461
    lack of success in establishing common, 164
  rigid corporate, 205
  and values, in workforce diversity interventions, 415–416
Culture change, 153, 482–491
  application stages, 489–491
  approaches to, 486–489
  program at Siemens Nixdorf, 205–207
  Washington Mutual: leveraging culture as competitive advantage, 492–493
Customer satisfaction, 281
  Sharpe BMW (case study), 438–443

D

Data
  feedback. See Feedback, of diagnostic information
  -gathering role of OD practitioners, 114. See also Organization development practitioners
  misuse of, 60
  unobtrusive, 121–122
Data gathering. See also Collecting and analyzing diagnostic information
  after action, 25
  in conjunction with OD practitioner, 24–25
  and feedback cycle (figure 7.1), 115
  methods, 114
  preliminary, 73

team building and, 235
in third-party intervention, 229
Decision making
authority, of self-managed work teams, 349. *See also* Self-managed work teams
group, 223
improving, 220
including peers and subordinates in process of, 390
in public-sector organizations, 600
Deep assumptions approach, to diagnosing organization culture, 488–489
Defensive behavior, 134
Deforestation, 564–565
Deming Award, 318
Dependency, 60–61, 81
survey feedback and organizational, 138
Deregulation
effect on organizations of, 480
international expansion aided by, 536
Design team selection, 80
Deuterolearning, 501
Developmental training, 408
Development organizations (DOs), 558
Diagnosing organizations, 83–89. *See also* Diagnosis
need for diagnostic models, 84–85
open-systems model, 85–89
organization-level diagnosis, 89–93
Diagnosis, 49. *See also* Diagnosing organizations
components of, 83
of current organization structure, 80
of family-run organizations, 585–586, 588
group-level, 100–106
analysis (Ortiv Glass Corporation), 103–106
groups and jobs, 100–112
individual-level, 106–108, 110–112
joint, 25
linking interventions to, 179
in OD, 83–84
organization, 114
of organizational systems, 88–89
comprehensive model for (figure 6.1), 101
organization-level, 89–93
alignment, 93
analysis, 93, 95–98
design components, 91–93

inputs, 90–91
outputs, 93
in planned change, 29
preliminary, in conjunction with OD practitioner, 24–25
case study–Gulf States Metals, Inc., 269–272
relation of effective change and careful, 40
of state of alliance, 466
of team's design components (Ortiv Glass Corporation), 105–106
of work system, 346
Dialogue approach, in organization learning, 502
Difference tests, 129–130
Diffusion, 195
Disabilities, as workplace diversity factor, 415
DISC profile, 217
Discriminant validity, 186
Disintermediation, 286
Diversity, 410–416
general framework for managing (figure 18.2), 410
little, in health care industry, 573
as source of competitive advantage, 411
Divisional structure, 276–278
advantages and disadvantages of, 277–278
table 14.2, 277
Domestic-partner benefit plans, 415
Double-loop learning, 501, 502, 504, 505, 509
Downsizing, 151, 287, 289–292, 294–295, 480
application stages, 290–292
coaching, used in, 217
increase of EAP use during, 426
process at Delta Air Lines, strategic, 293–294
results of, 292, 294–295
stress related to, 409
tactics (table 14.6), 291
Dual-career employees, 409–410
Dualistic structures. *See* Parallel structures
Due diligence
assessment, performing, 458–459
processes, inadequate, 456
During-implementation assessment, 179

E

Ecological sustainability, 616, 617
E-commerce, 4, 535, 618–619
Economic development, as contingency affecting OD success, 538–540
Economy
cost of stress-related disorders to U.S., 426
globalization of, 615–617
Electronic data interchange, 4
Emergence, 622
Emotional intelligence, 52, 54
Empathy, 159
Employee assistance programs (EAPs), 152, 418, 426
Employee empowerment. *See also* Employee involvement (EI)
relation of culture to, 538
Employee involvement (EI), 11–12, 136, 151, 230, 306–328
applications, 309–312
and change agents, 172. *See also* Change agents
current definition, 306
effects on productivity of, 308–309
figure 15.1, 308
secondary (figure 15.2), 309
generation of ideas for, 313–314
high-involvement organizations, 315–318
key elements that promote, 306–307
parallel structures, 310–312, 314–315
practices, diffusion of, 307–308
programs, 172
total quality management (TQM), 318, 320–324, 326–327
working definition of, 306–307
Employee stock ownership plans (ESOPs), 584
Employee stress and wellness interventions, 152, 418–426
Johnson & Johnson's health and wellness program, 427–428
stress management programs, 419–426
work leaves, 418–419
Empowerment. *See* Employee Involvement (EI)
Enacted environment, 448
Endangered Species Act, 601, 602
Engineering approach, to work design, 331–332, 351

Entering and contracting, 72–81
American Healthways Corporation, 77, 79–81
clarifying the organizational issue,
73
contract development, 76, 78
ground rules, 78
mutual expectations, 76
time and resources, 76, 78
description and scope, 72
determining the relevant client,
73–74
issues involved in family
businesses, 585
personal process issues in, 78, 81
in planned change, 28–29
procurement regulations for
government agencies, 78
selecting an OD practitioner,
74–76
Environment(s)
design of interface between STS
and its, 341
dimensions of, 448–450
information uncertainty, 448
resource dependence, 448–449
external, for piano market, 94
framework of, 447–450
interfaces of organizations and,
446, 480. See also Organizational change
misfits among organization's, 453
organizational adaptation and
creation of, 253
relation of structural design to
organization, 274
relation of, to transformational
change, 485–486
responses to, 450
sharing common view of, 253
stability of organization, 192–193
task, of self-managed work teams,
343, 344
types of, 447–448
Environmental concerns
business models reflecting, 617
effect on OD of, 57, 58
Environmental expectations, 255
Envisioned future, 162–163
bold and valued outcomes, 162–163
desired future state, 163
Equal employment opportunity
(EEO) laws, 414
Equifinality, in organization systems,
87–88
Ethics, 58–63
coercion, 60–61
dilemmas involving, 58–62

role episodic model of (figure
3.2), 59
guidelines for organization
development/human systems
development (OD/HSD) pro-
fessionals, 66–70
misrepresentation, 59–60
misuse of data, 60
need for sensitivity to, in transformational change, 491
of organizational development,
61–62
technical ineptness, 61
value and goal conflict, 61
European Union, 4, 462, 535, 545,
615
Evaluation. See also Evaluation
feedback; Evaluation, OD
intervention
defined, 178
key aspects of effective, 178
processes, 80
Evaluation feedback, 178–181
implementation and (figure 11.1),
179
selecting variables, 181–182
Evaluation, OD intervention,
178–189, 198–199
designing good measures, 182,
184, 186
implementation and evaluation
feedback, 178–181
measurement, 181–182, 184, 186
research design, 186–189
Expectations
mutual, of client and OD practitioner, 76
role of, in generating motivation,
158
Exploitive authoritative systems, 9
External consultants, 50–52, 56–57,
245
differences between internal and
(table 3.2), 51
personal view of, 53–54
External environment, 93
External validity, 187

F

Face validity, 186
Fallback positions, 405
Family business system
business, shareholder, and family
systems, 580
critical issues in, 583–584
defined, 580

key questions for understanding,
586
OD interventions in, 584–588
most common (table 22.2),
587
OD in the Ross family business,
589–590
organization development in,
579–590
values at center of, 580–583
Family Medical Leave Act (FMLA),
418
Family-owned businesses. See
Family business system
Feedback
about progress of OD relationship,
49
channels, in job enrichment, 337,
338
characteristics of effective,
132–134
data
in network creation, 469
ownership of, 134
training OD practitioners in,
136–137
of diagnostic information,
132–141. See also Survey
feedback
employee benefits at HealthCo,
434–437
implementation and evaluation,
178–181. See also Evaluation,
OD intervention
(figure 11.1), 179
performance, and coaching interventions, 408–409
possible effects of (figure 8.1),
133
process
characteristics of, 134–135
in organizations, 87
in performance appraisal,
375
providing, to family business
members, 586
step, in change process, 25
success of data, 132
survey. See Survey feedback
from work itself, 334
FIRO-B profile, 217
First World countries, 560
Focus groups, 119–120
Force-field analysis, 125–126
Forest Congresses, 257
"Four Principles," in open-space
method, 256, 260
Frequency distributions, 126–127

Functional structure, 274–276
  advantages and disadvantages of,
    275–276
    table 14.1, 276
    figure 14.2, 275
Futuring, 253–254

G

Gain sharing, 383, 385–387
  bonus formula, 386
  change management, 386
  frequency of bonus, 386
  importance of design process for,
    385
  participative system, 386
  plans, conditions favoring (table
    17.4), 389
  sharing process, 386
  unit coverage, 386
Gamma change, 189, 481
Gender
  inequity, 413
  in workforce diversity, 412–413
General Accounting Office (GAO),
    387
General consultation skills, needed
    in OD, 49
General environment, 447–448
Generative learning, 501
Genogram, 585
Germany, 4
Global integration, 546, 549,
    556–557
  implementing, 550
Globalization, 4, 5, 13. *See also*
    Global social change organi-
    zations (GSCOs); Organiza-
    tion development, outside the
    United States; Worldwide
    organization development
  of architectural hardware line
    (case study), 650–657
  of the economy, 615–617
  stress related to competition
    caused by, 409, 480
  of work and organizations, 230
Global social change organizations
    (GSCOs), 558–563, 565
  application stages, 560–563
    building the local organization,
      560–561
    creating horizontal linkages, 562
    creating vertical linkages,
      562–563
    change agent roles and skills, 563,
      565

difference between for-profit firms
    and, 559–560
  effects of success on, 561
  increased opportunities for OD in,
    623, 624
  social and environmental change
    at Floresta, 564–565
Goal clarity, in group diagnosis, 101
Goal setting, 151, 366, 368–372
  application stages, 370
  balanced scorecard approach to,
    368, 369
  characteristics, 368
  clarifying goal measurement,
    369–370
  establishing challenging goals, 369
  increased participation in, 375
  joint manager–subordinate, 371
  management by objectives
    (MBO), 370–372
  and MBO, effects of, 372
  principles contributing to success
    of, 391
  processes, performance appraisal
    as link between reward
    systems and, 374
Goal sharing, 387
Grid Organization Development,
    9–10
Group(s). *See also* Team building;
    Teams
  composition, 102
  effectiveness, dimensions of,
    102–103
  functional roles in, 223
  functioning, 102
  goal clarity, 101
  interventions, 225
  interviews, 119–120
  and jobs, diagnosis, 100–112
  -level diagnosis, 100–106
    analysis, 103–106
    design components, 101–102
    fits, 103
    inputs, 100
    outputs, 102
  major components of, 101–102
  norms, 223
  performance norms, 102
  problem solving and decision
    making, 223
  process consultation and, 222–223
  task structure, 102
Group design, 100, 103
  and individual-level diagnosis,
    107
Group functioning, in group
    diagnosis, 102

Group interventions, 225
Group-level diagnosis, 100–106
  analysis, 103–106
  design components, 101–102
  fits, 103
  inputs, 100
  outputs, 102
Growth needs, 353–354
Grupos, 283, 467

H

Hammer Award, 321, 603
Health care industry
  continuing financial challenges,
    574
  environmental trends in, 572–574
  eroding trust in, 574
  imbalanced supply and demand,
    572–573
  increasing calls for patient safety
    and accountability, 573–574
  increasing technology acquisition
    and application, 574
  opportunities for OD practice,
    575–576
  organization development in,
    571–579
  severe workforce shortages and
    little diversity, 573
  success principles for OD in, 576,
    578–579
Health facilities, employee, 425–426
Health Insurance Portability and
    Privacy Act (HIPAA), 426,
    574
Health profiling, 423
High-involvement organizations
    (HIOs), 315–318
  application factors, 317
  Chrysler Corporation moves
    toward becoming, 319–320
  features of, 315–317
  improving selection of employees
    for, 315–316
  management techniques of, used
    in schools, 592–593
  prevalence of teams in, 344
  study results of, 317–318
HIV, 414
Horizontal issues, in MBO process,
    372
Humanism, 57
Human processes, improving, 220. *See
    also* Process consultation (PC)
Human process interventions,
    30, 146, 149–150. *See also*
    Interventions

change programs of
  intergroup relations, 150
  large-group interventions, 150
  organization confrontation
    meeting, 150
coaching, 149. *See also* Coaching
individual, interpersonal, and
  group process approaches,
  216–240
organization process approaches,
  243–261
process consultation, 149
team building, 150. *See also* Team
  building
third-party interventions, 149. *See
  also* Third-party interventions
training and development, 149.
  See also Training and
  development
Human resource interventions, 30
Human resources department, 366
Human resources management
  interventions, 146, 151–152,
  366, 391, 396. *See also* Goal
  setting; Interventions; Performance appraisal; Reward
  systems
  career planning and development,
    152
  employee stress and wellness, 152
  goal setting, 151
  managing workforce diversity, 152
  performance appraisal, 151
  reward systems, 151
Human resources systems, 92
  need for high quality, cost effective,
    in health care industry,
    575–576
Hygiene factors, 332–333

I

"If Japan Can . . . Why Can't We?"
  320–321
Immigrants, entering workforce,
  415–416. *See also* Workforce
  diversity
Implementation feedback, 178–181
  data for, 180
  evaluation and (figure 11.1), 179
  outcome measures of, 180
  selecting variables, 181–182
Implementation, initial, 80
Improshare, 386–387
Income distribution, 616–617
Individual assessment, 219
Individual, interpersonal, and group
  process approaches, 216–240

coaching, 216–218
process consultation, 220, 222–227
team building, 230, 232–235,
  237–239
third-party interventions,
  227–230
training and development,
  218–220
Individual interventions, 223–225
Individual interviews, 119–120
Individualism, in global OD, 538
Individual-level diagnosis, 106–108
  analysis, 108, 110–112
  design components, 107–108
  fits, 108
  inputs, 106–107
Industrial democracy. *See* Employee
  Involvement (EI)
Industrial economies, 539
Industrializing economies, 539
Industrial Revolution, 295
Industry discontinuities, 480
Information
  flows, environments as, 448
  and promotion of EI, 307
  uncertainty, 448
Information management, 209
Information technology, 4–5, 13, 286
  effects on future OD practice, 621
  and use of codification approaches
    for KM, 506
  use of, for reengineering, 296
  use of state-of-the-art, in transna-
    tional strategic orientation,
    555
Innovation
  achieving awareness of, in
    networks, 471
  employee, 45
  managerial, 5, 45
  necessity in OD of constant, 49
  need for, in transformational
    change, 482
  process of, 620
Inputs, 93
  to group design, 100
  individual-level, 106–107
  into strategic orientation, 90–91
In Search of Excellence (Peters and
  Waterman), 482
Instability, 622
Institutionalization, of OD interventions, 189–199
  defined, 178
  framework, 192–198
    (figure 11.2), 192
    indicators of institutionalization,
    195–196

institutionalization processes,
  194–195
intervention characteristics,
  193–194
organization characteristics,
  192–193
indicators to assess level of,
  195–196
Insurance companies, 572
Integrated strategic change (ISC),
  152, 451–454
  application stages, 452–454
  designing and implementing
    strategic change plan, 454
  exercising strategic choice,
    453–454
  key features, 451–452
  managing strategic change at
    Microsoft Canada, 455–456
  performing strategic analysis,
    452–453
Integration, 92
  failed corporate, 485
  problems, 212
Integrative case studies. *See also* Case
  studies
  Black & Decker International:
    globalization of the architec-
    tural hardware line, 650–657
  architectural hardware business,
    654–656
  company background, 650–651
  global product planning and
    review, 653–654
  recommendations for the global
    lock business, 656–657
  vice president, product and
    market development,
    651–653
  B. R. Richardson Timber Products
    Corporation, 629–643
  making a proposal, 629–630
  observations and notes,
    632–643
  preparing the diagnosis, 643
  visiting the plant, 630–632
  managing strategy at Caesars
    Tahoe, 644–649
  customers, 647–648
  executive committee challenge,
    649
  historic perspective, 644–645
  Lake Tahoe—a national
    treasure, 645
  overview of competitive
    environment, 645–647
  resource base, 648–649
Interaction rules, 622

Intergroup relations, 150
  combining survey feedback with, 135
Intergroup relations interventions, 243, 246–250, 252
  at Johnson & Johnson, 251–252
  microcosm groups, 246–248
  purpose of, 248
  resolving intergroup conflict application stages, 248–250
  results of, 252
Intermarket network, 283
Internal company dynamics, 480
Internal consultants, 50–52, 56–57, 245
  clarification of sensitivity issues for, 78
  differences between external and (table 3.2), 51
  personal view of, 53–54
Internal market network, 283
Internal validity, 187
International nongovernmental organizations (INGOs), 558
International private voluntary organizations, 558
Internet, 4, 286, 535. See also World Wide Web
  as backbone of global economy, 618
  -based approaches to training, 219
  diffusion of worm viruses through, 623
  influence on OD of, 615
Internet service providers (ISPs), 87, 169
Interpersonal skills, needed in OD, 48–49, 75
Intervention design. See also Interventions
  capability to change, 145
  consideration of contingencies related to change situation for, 144–145
  cultural context and, 145
  and effect on rate of success of contingencies related to target of change, 145
  need for preliminary training before, 145
  organizational issues of, 146, 148
  process, overview of, 143–153
  readiness for change as condition for, 145
  relation of capabilities of change agent to, 145

Interventions. See also Human process interventions; Human resources management interventions; Intervention design; Strategic interventions; Technostructural interventions
  alliance, 465–466
  attitudinal change, 250
  behavioral, 250
  career planning and development, 396–410
  classroom, 595. See also School systems
  coercion and, 60–61
  conditions for success of, 145
  criteria defining effective, 143–144
  defined, 143
  designing effective, 144–146, 148–149
    contingencies related to change situation, 144–145
  employee stress and wellness, 418–426
  evaluating and institutionalizing organization development. See Evaluation, OD intervention; Institutionalization, OD intervention
  in family business system, 584–588
  features of, that can affect institutionalization processes, 193–194
  goal-setting. See Goal setting
  group, 225
  human process, 30, 146, 149–150
  individual, 223–225
    employee development, 407–408
  institutionalizing, 189–199
  intergroup relations, 246–250, 252
  key targets of OD, 146
  large-group, 150
    combining survey feedback with, 135
  linking, to diagnosis, 179
  major types of, 30
  network, 466–472
  overview of, 149–153
  performance feedback and coaching, 408–409
  performance management, 366
  recent proliferation of OD, 55–56
  role and structure interventions, 403–407
  selecting, 61

shaping competitive and collaborative strategies of organizations, 152–153
skills needed by OD practitioners for design and execution of, 49
specificity of goals in, 193
sponsors of, 194
systemwide process. See Organization process approaches
targets of change as main focus of, 145
third-party. See Third-party interventions
training and development. See Training and development
types of, 58
  and organizational issues (figure 9.1), 147
  and organizational levels (table 9.1), 148
  workforce diversity, 410–416
Interviews, 119–120, 245
Intranets, 621
Intrapersonal skills, needed in OD, 48–49
Involvement, in planning changes, 159

J

Japan, 318, 320–321, 485, 535. See also Total quality management (TQM)
  automobile industry in, 556–557
Job design
  applying individual-level diagnosis to, 108, 110–112
  fits, 108
  in HIOs, 315
  major inputs affecting, 106–107
  at Pepperdine University, 109, 110–112
Job Diagnostic Survey (JDS), 119, 182, 335–336
  modification of, 339
  profile for "good" and "bad" jobs (figure 16.2), 335
Job enlargement, 334
Job enrichment, 331, 332–337, 339–340
  application stages, 335–337
    combining tasks, 336, 338
    establishing client relationships, 336–337, 338
    forming natural work units, 336, 338
    making thorough diagnosis, 335–336

opening feedback channels, 337, 338
vertical loading, 337, 338
barriers to
control system, 339
personnel system, 339
supervisory system, 339
technical system, 337
behavior changes called for in, 179
core dimensions of jobs, 333–334
autonomy, 334
feedback from work itself, 334
skill variety, task identity, and task significance, 334
experiments, 333
implementation concepts for, 338
individual differences affecting reactions to, 334–335
overall measure of, 107–108
results of, 339–340
at the Travelers Insurance Companies, 338
Job expectation technique (JET), 424
Job pathing, 405. See also Job rotation
Job rotation, 334
and challenging assignments, 405–406
Jobs
autonomy, 107
diagnosing groups and, 100–112
feedback, 108
key dimensions of individual, 107–108
skill variety, 107
task identity, 107
task significance, 107
Job sharing, 413
Johari Window, 224–225
diagram (figure 12.1), 224
Joint optimization, 341
Joint ventures, 465, 466
Just-in-time inventory systems, 230, 348, 473

K

Keiretsus, 283, 467, 473
Knowledge. See also Knowledge and experience; Knowledge management (KM)
distributing, 507
generating, 506
organization, 505–507
of organization members regarding behaviors connected to intervention, 195
organizing, 506–507

and skills, contributing to EI success, 307
tacit, 507
Knowledge and experience
use of, by OD practitioners, 55–56
use of consultant's versus client's (figure 3.1), 55
Knowledge management (KM), 153, 479, 505–507. See also Knowledge
at BP Amoco, 508
conceptual framework, 497–499
knowledge services and networks, 507
need for effective leadership in, 500
organization knowledge
facilitated transfer of, 507
as link to performance, 505
outcomes of, 508–509
self-directed methods, 507
stages of, 506–507
Knowledge objects, 506
Kyoto Protocol, 559

L

Ladder of inference, in organization learning, 503–504, 508
Large-group interventions, 150, 243, 252–256
application stages
conducting the meeting, 254–256, 259
following up on meeting outcomes, 259
preparing for the large-group meeting, 254
combining survey feedback with, 135
open-space methods in, 256, 258
open-systems methods in, 254–255, 256
results of, 259
"Law of Two Feet," in open-space method, 256, 260
Leadership development programs, 219
Leading and managing change, 155–175
creating a vision, 155, 161–163
constructing the envisioned future, 162–163
describing core ideology, 161–162
developing political support, 155–156, 163, 165–166
assessing change agent power, 166

identifying key stakeholders, 166–167
influencing stakeholders, 167–168
managing the transition, 156
activity planning, 168
change-management structures, 169–170
commitment planning, 168
motivating change, 155, 157–159
communication, 159
conveying credible positive expectations, 158
creating readiness for change, 157–159
empathy and support, 159
at Johnsonville Sausage, 160
overcoming resistance, 158–159
participation and involvement, 159
revealing discrepancies between current and desired states, 158
overview of change activities, 155–157
sustaining momentum, 156
building support system for change agents, 170, 172
developing new competencies and skills, 172
providing resources for change, 170
reinforcing new behaviors, 172–173
staying the course, 173
Lean manufacturing, 230
Learnings, 80
Learning service providers (LSPs), 169
Left-hand, right-hand technique, in organization learning, 503, 508
Legal sensitivity, in transformational change, 491
Lewin's change model, 22–24, 28, 470
steps in, 23–24
Life stages, 398, 400
Likert Scale, 8
Local responsiveness, 546, 556–557
Longitudinal measurement, 187, 188

M

Malcolm Baldrige National Quality Award, 321, 322, 326, 327, 603

Management by objectives (MBO), 366. *See also* Goal setting
description and purpose, 370–371
effects of goal setting and, 372
establishing action plans for goals, 371
establishing criteria of success, 371
joint manager–subordinate goal setting, 371
origin, 370
process, implementation steps in, 370–371
record maintenance, 372
review process, 371
work group involvement, 371
Management consulting, 45
Managerial Grid, 9–10
Managerial innovation, 5
Managing workforce diversity, 152
Marginality, and professional OD role, 52
Matrix structure, 278–280
advantages and disadvantages of, 278–279
table 14.3, 280
chart (figure 14.4), 279
Mavens, in networks, 471
Means, 126
Measurement, for OD evaluation, 181–186
criterion, 186
definitions and recording categories (table 11.1), 183
designing good measures, 182–186
operational definition, 184
reliability, 184
validity, 186
measures and computational formulae (table 11.2), 185
selecting variables, 181–182
Measurement systems, 92
Medicaid, 572, 574
Medicare, 572, 574
Mentoring, 407–408
Mergers and acquisitions (M&As), 152, 171–172
application stages, 456–461
legal combination phase, 459
operational combination phase, 460–461
precombination phase, 456–457
choosing partner for, 457
coaching, used in, 217
creation of team for, 458
developing integration plans for, 459

due diligence assessment for, 458–459
lessons learned from the Dow Chemical Company and Union Carbide merger, 462–463
major phases and activities in (table 19.1), 457
rationale for, 454, 456
use of, outside the United States, 535
Michigan Organizational Assessment Questionnaire, 119
Microcosm groups
application stages, 247–248
components of, 246
results of, 248
Midlife crisis, 397, 400
Minimal critical specification, in work design, 346
Minimum specification design, 495. *See also* Self-designing organizations
Minnesota Multiphasic Personality Inventory (MMPI), 217
Minorities
career development preferences of, 396
discrimination of, 413–414
at middle- and upper-management levels, 397
underrepresentation of, in health care industry, 573
use of mentoring with, 408
Misrepresentation, 59–60
Mission statements, 91
of effective transnational firms, 556
Mitchell Guide to Car Repairs, 440
Model II learning, 502, 505, 509
values underlying, 504
Model I learning, 501–502
Momentum, sustaining, 156–157
building support system for, 170, 172
developing new competencies and skills, 172
providing resources for change, 170
reinforcing new behaviors, 172–173
staying the course, 173
Motivation, 160. *See also* Reward systems
for change, 155, 157–159
increase of, through employee participation in goal-setting process, 369. *See also* Goal setting
reduction of, due to secrecy, 391

Motivational approach, to work design, 331, 332–337, 339–340, 351. *See also* Job enrichment
Motivators, 332
Moving step, in change process, 24
Multinational organizations. *See* Organization development, outside the United States; Worldwide organization development
Myers-Briggs Type Indicator, 217

N

National Forest System, 257
National Innovations in American Government Awards, 603
National Labor Relations Act (NLRA), 314
National Partnership for Reinventing Government, 603
National Performance Review (NPR), 596, 603
The Natural Step, 624, 625
Natural work units, in job enrichment, 336, 338
Network interventions, 461, 466–472
creating the network, 467–469
fragile and robust—network change in Toyota Motor Corporation, 473–474
managing network change, 469–472
law of the few, 471
power of context, 472
stickiness, 472
Networks, 152, 466–472. *See also* Network structure
convention stage, 468–469
creating, 467–469
creation of instability in, 470–471
creation of interdependence through, 623
evaluation stage, 469
identification stage, 467–468
managing change in, 469–470
multiorganization, 467
organization stage, 469
self-organizing behavior of, 472
Network structure, 283, 285–287, 619–620. *See also* Networks
advantages and disadvantages of, 286–287
table 14.5, 287
Amazon.com's, 288–289
chart (figure 14.7), 285
Normative consensus, 196

Norms
in Model I learning, 502
of organization culture, 484

O

Observations, 120–121
Open information systems, in HIOs, 315
Open-space methods, 256, 258
three-day meeting at consulting firm using, 260–261
Open-systems model, 85–89
alignment, 88
boundaries, 87
diagnosing organizational systems, 88–89
equifinality, 87–88
feedback, 87
inputs, transformations, and outputs, 86
in large-group approaches, 254–255, 256
organizations as open systems, 85–86
Opportunity network, 283
Organizational Culture Assessment Instrument, 119
Organizational Diagnosis Questionnaire, 119
Organization assessment, 219
Organization change, 2
distinguishing between organization development and, 3–4
Organization confrontation meeting, 150, 243–244, 246
application stages, 244
results of, 244, 246
Organization culture. *See also* Organizations, culture of
changing, 482–491
application stages of, 489–491
practical guidelines for, 490–491
concept of, 483–484
diagnosing, 486–489
behavioral approach, 486
competing values approach, 486–488
deep assumptions approach, 488–489
major elements of, 483–484
and organization effectiveness, 484–486
Organization design, 100
and individual-level diagnosis, 106–107

Organization development
action research and survey feedback background, 8
applications. *See* Applications
career opportunities, 5
cycle, final stage of. *See* Evaluation, OD intervention; Institutionalization, of OD interventions
defined, 1–4
diagnosis in, 83–84. *See also* Diagnosing organizations; Diagnosis
effect of cultural context and economic development on, 539–540
evolution in, 12–14
in family-owned businesses, 579–590
general introduction to, 1–17
growth and relevance of, 4–6
in health care industry, 571–579
history of, 6–12
integration of human resources management with, 366
laboratory training background, 7
major types of interventions in, 30. *See also* Interventions
normative background, 9–10
outside the United States, 534–545. *See also* Worldwide organization development
cultural context approach, 536, 539–540
economic development contingency, 538–540
high cultural fit, high industrialization, 543, 545
high cultural fit, moderate industrialization, 541
low cultural fit, high industrialization, 542–543
low cultural fit, moderate industrialization, 540–541
overview, 14–17
process, emergent nature of, 73
productivity and quality-of-life background, 10–12
in public-sector organizations, 596–603
relationship, entering into, 73. *See also* Entering and contracting
role of, in global social change, 534
in school systems, 590–596
theory, needed by OD practitioners, 49–50. *See also* Organization development practitioners

in the United States, cultural values that guide, 35
Organization development evaluation. *See* Evaluation, OD intervention
Organization development interventions. *See* Interventions
Organization development practitioners, 33, 44–63
careers, 56–57
competencies of effective, 46–50
data-gathering role of, 114. *See also* Collecting and analyzing diagnostic information
defining characteristics of term, 44–46
emotional demands on, 52, 54
ethical guidelines for, 145
and human systems development professionals, 66–70
importance of ability to diagnose and understand intergroup relations by, 246
in international settings, 35, 39. *See also* Organization development, outside the United States
knowledge and skill requirements of, 48–50
table 3.1, 47–48
marginality and, 52
need for political skills by, 57–58
positions, 50–52
as process consultant for role clarification, 424
professional, 50–52, 54–57
role of, 50–52, 54–57, 63
in role of salesperson, 471
selecting, 74–76
training, in data feedback, 136–137
types of, 44
use of knowledge and experience, 55–56
use of power strategies by, 163, 165–166
use of "shadow consultants" by, 170, 172
Organization development trends, 611–614
contextual, 614–625
economy, 615–617
organizations, 619–620
technology, 618–619
workforce, 617–618
and implications for future of OD, 613–614, 620–625
application to more diverse organizations, 623–624

cross-cultural aspects, 624
embedding OD in organization operations, 620–621
increased focus on ecological sustainability, 624–625
more technically enabled OD processes, 621
movement toward more inter-disciplinary nature, 622–623
shorter cycle times, 621–622
pragmatic, 612–613
scholarly, 613
traditional, 611–612
Organization learning (OL), 153, 479, 481, 497–509
characteristics, 499–500
conceptual framework, 497–499
outcomes of, 508–509
phases in, 502–505
processes, 500–505
key outcome of, 505
Organization process approaches, 243–261
intergroup relations interventions, 246–250, 252
large-group interventions, 252–256, 259
organization confrontation meeting, 150, 243–244, 246
Organizations, 146, 148
congruence, 192
core values and purpose of, 162
culture of, 50, 92–93, 479. *See also* Culture change
lack of success in establishing common, 164
relative to M&As, 460–461
diagnosing current structure of, 80
effect of environment on. *See* Environment(s)
facing problems, steps for planned change in, 34–35. *See also* Planned change
high-involvement. *See* High-involvement organizations (HIOs)
human process issues in, 146
human resources issues in, 146
increasingly networked and knowledge-based nature of, 619
levels of function in, 148–149
as open systems, 85–86
figure 5.1, 86
physical layouts of, to enhance EI, 317
self-designing. *See* Self-designing organizations

sensitizing, to pressures for change, 157–158
stability of environment and tech-nology, 192–193
strategic issues in, 146, 446
technology and structure issues in, 146
trends shaping change in, 4
unionization, 193
value issues within, 57
Organization transformation, 479. *See also* Culture change; Knowledge management (KM); Organization learning (OL); Self-designing organiza-tions; Transformational change
"Out-of-the-box thinking," 324
Out of the Crisis (Deming), 594
Outputs
of group effectiveness, 102–103
of strategic orientation, 93
Outsourcing, 464

P

Parallel processes, 246
Parallel structures, 310
application stages, 310–312
EI and, 307
results of approaches to, 312, 314–315
Pareto charts, 323
Participative group systems, 9
design features for (table 1.1), 316
Participative management. *See* Employee Involvement (EI)
Participatory action research, 26
Pay
negative effects of misperceptions about, 390
performance-based systems, 383–385
plans, least acceptable, 385
skill-based systems, 382–383
Peer review panels, 32
People's Republic of China (PRC). *See* China
Performance
effect of goal setting on, 368
feedback and coaching interven-tions, 408–409
goals, in process-based structure, 281
of intervention behaviors, 196
issues, 313
job, positive effect of EAPs on, 426

objective and subjective measures of, 375
Performance appraisal, 151, 366, 372, 374–377
application stages, 376–377
criteria for design of system, 376–377
diagnosing current situation, 376
establishing system's purposes and objectives, 376
evaluation and monitoring system, 377
selecting right people, 376
use of pilot tests, 377
changing the appraisal process in the Washington State Patrol (WSP), 378–379
effects of, 377
elements (table 17.1), 374
as link between goal-setting processes and reward sys-tems, 374
process, 374–375
Performance-based pay systems, 383–385
ratings of various (table 17.3), 384
Performance management
components of, 366–367
goal setting, 368–372
model of, 367–368
(figure 17.1), 367
performance appraisal, 372, 374–377
performance enhancement process at Monsanto, 373
reward systems, 377, 379–387, 390–391
Performance management interven-tions, 366
Performance norms, in group-level diagnosis, 102, 105
Personal characteristics, and individ-ual-level diagnosis, 107
Personalization, in organizing knowledge, 507
Personal management interview (PMI), 239
Personnel policies, in HIOs, 316–317
Personnel system, as job enrichment constraint, 339
Phase transitions, 622
Piece-rate quotas, 384
Planned change
action research model, 24–26
comparisons of change models, 23, 28
conceptualization of, 39–40

critique of, 39–41
degree of organization, 34–35
diagnosing, 29
different types of, 30, 33
domestic vs. international settings, 35, 39
entering and contracting, 28–29. *See also* Entering and contracting
evaluating and institutionalizing change, 30
general model of, 28–30
in the global orientation, 550
in GSCOs, 563
interventions, 416
magnitude of change, 30, 33–34
in multinational orientation, 552–553
nature of, 22–41
planing and implementing change, 29–30
positive model, 26–28
practice of, 40–41
at the San Diego County Regional Airport Authority (SDCRAA), 31–32
theories of, 22–28, 41
in the transnational orientation, 555–556
in an underorganized system, 36–38
Plateaued employees, 405–406
Polarization, 248
Political resistance, 158–159
Political support development, 155–156, 157, 163, 165–166
assessing change agent power, 166
identifying key stakeholders, 166–167
influencing stakeholders, 167–168
Positive model of planned change, 22, 26–28, 84–85
five phases of, 27–28
Power distance, in global OD, 537
Power strategies
attention being paid to, 163, 165–166
widely used, 167–168
Predictive validity, 186
Preferences, 196
Privatization, 536
Problem
identification, 24
joint diagnosis of, 25
Problem solving
groups, 223
formation of employee, 311
procedures, 322–323

training, 313
use of organization confrontation meeting for, 246
Process consultation (PC), 149, 220, 222–227
at Action Company, 226
group interventions, 225
group process, 222–223
individual interventions, 223–225
principles to guide actions in, 222
results of, 225–227
Process interventions, 225
in family businesses, 588
Process mapping, 301
Process structure, 280–283
advantages and disadvantages of, 282–283
table 14.4, 282–283
at American Healthways, 284
chart (figure 14.5), 281
Productivity, 7, 10–12
Product life cycle shifts, 480
Profile of Organizational Characteristics, 9
Proposal(s)
elements of an effective (table 4.1), 75
requests for submission of, 74
sample process, 81
Proposition 13 (California), 596
Psychometric tests, 184, 186
Public-sector organizations
comparing private- and, 597–602
intergovernmental relations, 601–602
multiplicity of decision makers, 600
stakeholder access, 601
organization development in, 596–603
recent research and innovations in, 602–603

Q

Qualitative tools, data analysis, 123, 125–126
content analysis, 123, 125
force-field analysis, 125–126
Quality, 209
Fourteen Points and Seven Deadly Sins of, 318 (table 15.2), 320
philosophy, need for managerial commitment to, 172
seven tools of, 322–323
Quality circles, 11
interventions using, 310

Quality control, 160
Quality Control Handbook (Juran), 318
Quality Is Free (Crosby), 321
Quality of work life (QWL), 7, 10–12, 306. *See also* Employee Involvement (EI)
Quantitative tools, data analysis, 126–130
difference tests, 129–130
means, standard deviations, and frequency distributions, 126–128
scattergrams and correlation coefficients, 128–129
Quantum change, 33–34. *See also* Planned change
Questionnaires, 117, 136
sample (table 7.2), 118

R

Random sample, 122–123
Reaction, as evaluation criterion, 220
Realistic job preview, 403–405
Reengineering, 151, 295–300
application stages, 297–300
process, Honeywell IAC's TotalPlant, 301–302
results from, 300
Refreezing step, in change process, 24
Relevant client, determining, 73–74
Research designs, 178, 186–189
alpha change, 188
beta change, 188–189
comparison unit, 187, 188
gamma change, 189, 481
longitudinal measurement, 187, 188
quasi-experimental, 187–189 (table 11.3), 188
statistical analysis, 187, 188
Resistance, to change, 160
strategies for dealing with, 159
types of, 158–159
Resource dependence, 448–449
Restructuring, 230
Carlsbad, California, Public Works Department (case study), 362–363
increase of EAP use during, 426
stress related to, 409
Retirement, phased, 406–407
Reward systems, 151, 366, 377, 379–387
availability, 381
centralized, 380
changes in, global orientation and, 557

design features (table 17.2), 380
durability, 382
focusing on increasing employee flexibility, 416
gain sharing systems, 385–387
hierarchical, 380
in HIOs, 316
internal and external equity, 379–380
job-based vs. performance-based, 379
at Lands' End, revising, 388–389
performance
 appraisal, as link between goal-setting processes and, 374
 -based pay systems, 383–385
 contingency, 381
process issues regarding, 390–391
promotion systems, 387, 390
as reinforcement for new behaviors, 172–173, 194–195
reinforcement of EI with, 307
rewards mix feature, 380–381
security, 381
seniority, 381
skill-based pay systems, 382–383
structural and motivational features of, 379–382
timeliness, 381
value expectancy model, 381
visibility, 382
Robotics, 230
Role analysis technique (RAT), 424
Role clarification, 423–424
Roles, 423–424
 ambiguity, reducing, 424
 of network members, 470, 471
 work, as source of stress, 421
Rucker plan, 386–387
Rumors, 159
Russia, 4

S

Sabbaticals, paid, 418
Salespeople, in networks, 471
Sample selection, 122–123
Sample size, 122
Sampling, 122–123
SARS (severe acute respiratory syndrome), 4, 448, 535
 epidemic, financial and social consequences of, 623
Scanlon plan, 386–387
Scattergrams, 128, 323
 samples (figures 7.3 and 7.4), 129

School-based management (SBM), 593, 594–595
School systems
 classroom interventions, 595
 future directions, 595–596
 high-involvement management in, 592–593
 organization development in, 590–596
 implications for, 592
 total quality management (TQM), 593–594
 unique characteristics of, 591
 use of school-based management (SBM) in, 594–595
Search conferences, 255
Self-design, 26
 at American Healthways Corporation, 496–497
 change strategy, 494–495
Self-designing organizations, 153, 479, 493–497
 application stages of strategy for, 494–495
 designing, 495
 implementing and assessing, 495
 laying foundation, 494–495
Self-managed work teams, 331, 341–345
 application stages, 345–347
 assessment centers and, 407
 model of (figure 1.3), 342
 moving to, at Asea Brown Boveri (ABB), 348–349
 organization support systems, 344–345
 problems between managers and, 344–345
 results of, 347, 350–351
 team process interventions, 343–344
 team task design, 342–343
Self-management competence, needed in OD, 48–49
Self-organization, 622
Sensing and calibration, 195
Sensing meetings, 119–120
September 11, 2001 attacks, 32, 95. *See also* Terrorism
 effect on airline industry of, 293
Service orientation, 139
Service quality concepts, 230
Sexual orientation, and workplace diversity, 414–415
Shadow structures. *See* Parallel structures
Single-loop learning, 501, 502, 505

Site-based management. *See* School-based management (SBM)
Six-sigma programs, 11–12, 324
 success story at GE Financial, 325–326
Skill-based pay systems, 382–383
Skill variety, 107, 334
Small-worlds, 622
Socialization, effect on intervention of, 194
Social movement organizations (SMOs), 558
Social needs, 353–354
Sociotechnical systems (STS)
 approach, 331, 340–347, 350–351
 conceptual background, 340
 environmental relationship premise, 341
 sociotechnical system premise, 340–341
 outcomes of, 341
 self-managed work teams, 341–345
Stakeholders
 access of, in public-sector organizations, 601
 effect of transformational change on organization, 494
 in health care industry, restoring trust in and among, 576
 identifying key, 166–167
 influencing, 166–167
 multiple, with different and conflicting interests, 174
 of problematic issues of forest use, 257–258
Standard deviations, 126
"A Statement of Values and Ethics for Professionals in Organization and Human System Development," 66–70
Statistical analyses, 184, 187, 188
Statistical process control (SPC) techniques, 322–323
Status quo, preserving, 163
Steering committees
 in union–management cooperation, 313–314
 use of, in parallel structures, 310–311
Stewardship, 563, 565
Stock plans, 383, 384
Strange attractors, 622
Strategic alliance, 5
Strategic change, 12, 230
 Carlsbad, California, Public Works Department (case study), 362–363

difference between transformational change and other types of, 481. *See also* Transformational change

interventions. *See also* Collaborative strategies; Competitive strategies; Organization transformation

managing, at Microsoft Canada, 455–456

plan, designing. *See* Integrated strategic change (ISC)

Rondell Data Corporation (case study), 514–521

Strategic interventions, 30, 146, 152–153. *See also* Interventions

alliances, 152

culture change, 153

in family businesses, 586

integrated strategic change, 152

mergers and acquisitions, 152. *See also* Mergers and acquisitions (M&As)

networks, 152

organization learning and knowledge management, 153

self-designing organizations, 153

Strategic management

Fourwinds Marina (case study), 522–531

predominant paradigm in, 451

Strategic orientation

alignment, 93

Campbell Soup Company moves to a worldwide, 554–555

characteristics of, 548

design components, 91–93

global, 549–551

characteristics of, 549–550

transition to, 550–551

implementing, 548–549

inputs, 90–91

in integrated strategic change (ISC), 451–452

international, 548–549

multinational, 551–553

characteristics of, 551–552

implementing, 552–553

outputs of, 93

of Steinway & Sons, 94–95

transnational

characteristics of, 553

implementing, 555–558

transition to, 556–558

worldwide, 546

Strategic plan, 452

Strategies

codification, for organizing knowledge, 506

personalization, 507

Stratified sample, 123

Stress inoculation training, 425

Stress management programs, 419–426

alleviating stressors and coping with stress, 423–426

employee assistance programs (EAPs), 426. *See also* Employee assistance programs (EAPs)

health facilities, 425–426

role clarification, 423–424

stress inoculation training, 425

supportive relationships, 424–425

definition and model, 419–422

individual differences, 421–422

occupational stressors, 421

diagnosis and awareness of stress and its causes, 422–423

charting stressors, 422–423

health profiling, 423

Stretch goals, 369. *See also* Goal setting

Structural change

combining survey feedback with, 135

institutionalizing, at Hewlett-Packard, 197–198

Structural design, 150, 274–287

contingencies influencing (figure 14.1), 275

divisional structure, 276–278

effects of, 148–149

functional structure, 274–276

matrix structure, 278–280

network structure, 283, 285–287

process structure, 280–283

Structural interventions, 225

in family businesses, 588

use of, outside the United States, 535

Structure, 470

Subsistence economies, 538–539

Substance abuse, 427

costs to businesses of, 426

Supervisory system, as job enrichment constraint, 339

Supportive relationships, to alleviate stress, 424–425

Survey feedback, 8, 135–141. *See also* Feedback

data, problem solving with, 136–137

five steps of, 135, 137–138

limitations of, 138, 140

and operations review at Prudential Real Estate Affiliates, 139–140

and organizational dependencies, 138

results of, 140–141

session, planning for, 136

use of, outside the United States, 535

Survey of Organizations, 119

Synchrony, 622

Synergies

"looking for," 458

mergers and, 462, 463

unrealistic expectations of, 456

Systems thinking, 504–505, 508

Systemwide process interventions. *See* Organization process approaches

T

Task control, 342, 343

Task differentiation, 342–343

Task environment, 448

Task identity, 107, 334

Tasks. *See also* Jobs

combining, in job enrichment, 336, 338

differentiation of, in self-managed work teams, 342–343

identity of, in job enrichment, 336

skill variety, 334

Task significance, 107, 334

Task structure, in group-level diagnosis, 102, 105

Team building, 7, 146, 230, 232–235, 237–239

activities, 232

affecting group's relationship with rest of organization, 237

oriented to group's operation and behavior, 235

relevant to one or more individuals, 232, 234–235

applicability of, 232

case study, 264–268

checklist (table 12.1), 233–234

facilitation of other OD interventions by, 230

manager's role in, 237–238

results of, 238–239

Team Development Survey, 119

Team facilitators. *See* Team leaders

Team leaders
    evaluation and reward systems for, 345
    recruitment and selection, 345
    responsibilities of, 344
    support systems for, 345
    training, 345
    use of freed-up time by, 345
Team process interventions, 343–344
Teams, 160. *See also* Self-managed work teams
    behaviors of, 172
    group interviews by self-regulating work, 390
    multidisciplinary, in process structure, 280
    peer consulting, 221
    prevalence of, in high-involvement organizations, 344
    problem-solving, 136
    in process-based structure, 281–282
    top-management (at Ortiv Glass Corporation), 104
Teamwork, 173, 301–302
    cross-functional, 313–314
Teamwork for Employees and Management Act, 314–315
Technical interdependence, 352–353
Technical resistance, 158
Technical system, as job enrichment constraint, 337
Technical uncertainty, 352–353
Technology
    acquisition and application in health care industry, increasing, 574
    effect on workforce of, 618–619
    rapid changes in, 480
    trends influencing OD, 615
Technostructural interventions, 150–151, 274–303. *See also* Work design
    downsizing, 151, 287, 289–292, 294–295
    issues for, 146
    reengineering, 151, 295–300
    structural design, 150, 274–287
Telecommuting, 4, 416, 417
Terrorism, 4, 32, 290, 293
    worldwide, 535
T-groups, 59
Theories in use, 501
Theories of changing. *See* Planned change, theories of
Theory Z (Ouchi), 11, 482
Therapy, confusion of coaching with, 217

Third-party interventions, 149, 227–230
    episodic model of conflict, 228–229
    facilitating conflict resolution process, 229–230
Third World countries, 560
360-degree feedback, 375
Total quality management (TQM), 11–12, 318, 320–324, 473, 542
    application stages, 322–324
    awards for, 321
    evolution of, 324–325
    historical background, 318, 320–321
    implementation
        senior managers' role in, 322
        in state government agencies, 378
    measurement
        of output variations using, 323
        of progress of, 323–324
    popularity in United States of, 320–321
    principles, in schools, 593–594
    processes (case study–Sullivan Hospital System), 359–361
    results of, 326–327
    rewards for accomplishments using, 324
    training requirements for, 322–323
Trade barriers, lowered, 536
Trade-offs
    cost/benefit, of alliances, 465
    involving change agents, 471–472
    in networks, 467
Traditional jobs, 351, 355
    defined, 332
Traditional work groups, 351, 355
    comparison between self-managed teams and, 350
    defined, 332
Training. *See also* Training and development
    in HIOs, 316
    for managers dealing with workplace disability factors, 415
    sensitivity, 414
Training and development, 149, 218–220
    application stages, 219–220
    criteria, 220
    functions, modernizing China's human resource, 544–545
    goals, 219
    results of, 220
Transactions, in collaborative strategies, 464
Transformational change
    characteristics of, 480–482
    demands of, 493–494

    need for continuous learning and change, 482
    need for ethical and legal sensitivity in, 491
    new organizing paradigm demanded by, 481
    role of envisioning, energizing, and enabling in, 482
    role of executives and line management in, 481–482
    Sharpe BMW (case study), 438–443
    sustaining, at the Veterans Health Administration (VHA), 174–175
    systemic and revolutionary, 480–481
    triggered by environmental and internal disruptions, 480
    wide swings in performance experienced during, 485–486
Transition management, 156, 157, 168–170
    activity planning, 168
    change-management structures, 169–170
    commitment planning, 168
    in the HP-Compaq acquisition, 171–172
Transorganizational systems (TSs), 464
Transorganization development, 467
    application stages for (figure 19.3), 468
Triple bottom line, 624
Trust
    alliances and, 466
    establishing, 116
    restoring, in and among stakeholders in health care industry, 576
Turnover rates
    effect of skill-based pay on, 383
    high costs of, 397
    positive effect of EAPs on, 426
    relation of self-managing groups to decreases in, 347
Type A behavior patterns, 421–422, 423
Type B behavior patterns, 421–422

U

Uncertainty avoidance, in global OD, 538
"The Undercover Change Agent," 59
Unfreezing step, in change process, 23–24

UNICEF, 563

Union–management. *See also* Unions
committees, 315
cooperative projects, 306, 310. *See
also* Quality circles
assessment of, 312
at GTE of California, 313–314

Unions, 95, 347. *See also*
Union–management
cooperative projects involving,
306, 310, 313–314
as force for change promotion, 193
organizations with, handling of
salary data at, 391

United Nations
Conference on Environment and
Development, 559
Development Program (UNDP), 545
Food and Agriculture Organiza-
tion, 563

V

Value consensus, 196
Value expectancy model, of reward
systems, 381
Values, 57–58
alignment of cultural and traditional OD, in international
settings, 534
in competitive advantage, 450–451
conference used in change
process, 164
core, 161–162
culture and, in workforce diversity, 415–416
differences of, in public- and
private-sector organizations,
598–600
dilemmas caused by competing,
486–488
emphasizing the right, 485
of family business system model,
580–583
in Model I learning, 501–502
of organization culture, 484
underlying Model II learning, 504
Vertical alignment, in MBO process,
372
Vertical disaggregation, 286
Vertical loading, in job enrichment,
337, 338
Vertical market network, 283
Veterans Eligibility Reform Act of
1996, 174
Vision. *See also* Vision creation
corporate, of effective transnational firms, 556

formulation of clear strategic, for
effective cultural change, 490
Vision creation, 161–163, 174
core ideology, as basis for, 161–162
exercises, 253–254
for issues of forest use, 257–258
for M&As, 458
of preferred future, 27–28
at Premier, 164–165
as purpose and reason for change,
155
Visioning, 80

W

Web sites, 13, 58, 77, 94, 117, 119,
164, 186, 190, 217, 218, 284,
288, 289, 293, 301, 321, 492,
508, 562, 611
with guidelines for establishing
EAPs, 426
Women
career development preferences
of, 396
increase in labor force of,
412–413
at middle- and upper-management levels, 397
in nursing profession, 573
use of mentoring with, 408
Work assessment, 219
Work councils, 315
Work design, 151, 230, 331–356.
See also Employee Involvement (EI)
combining survey feedback with,
135
effort, sanctioning, 345
engineering approach, 331–332,
351
generating appropriate, 346
implementing and evaluating,
346–347
motivational approach, 331,
332–337, 339–340, 351
need for continual change and
improvement, 347
need for effective, in health care
industry, 576
principles, 346
sociotechnical systems (STS)
approach, 331, 340–347,
350–351
specifying support systems, 346
technical and personal factors
affecting, 351–355
meeting both technical and personal needs, 354–355

personal-need factors, 353–354
technical factors, 352–353
that optimizes personal needs
(figure 16.5), 354
that optimizes technology (figure
16.4), 352
work redesign at Hamot Medical
Center, 577–578
Workforce
aging of U.S., 403, 411–412
changes affecting, 617–618
development of, as goal, 219.
See also Training and
development
downsizing, and rise of contingent, 287, 289
effect of technology on, 618–619
flexibility, skill-based pay and, 383
immigrants entering, 415–416
need for committed and involved,
332
need for involvement of, for
change, 160
reduction in airline industry, 290
shortages, in health care industry,
573
Workforce diversity interventions,
410–416
age factors, 411–412
disability factors, 415
embracing employee diversity at
Baxter Export Corporation,
417
gender factors, 412–413
race and ethnicity factors,
413–414
sexual orientation factors,
414–415
Work groups, 100. *See also* Group(s)
Work leaves, 418–419
Work-life balance
desire for, 396
employee benefits at HealthCo
(case study), 434–437
interventions, 409–410
World Bank, 189, 190–191, 535
World Health Organization, 563
World Trade Organization, 562, 617
World War II, 318
use of engineering approach to job
design following, 332
Worldwide organization development, 545–546. *See also*
Organization development,
outside the United States
strategic orientations, 546
World Wide Web, 4, 535. *See also*
Internet